THE **MGMT** SOLU~~TION~~

Print
+
Online

MGMT⁹ delivers all the key terms and core concepts for the **Principles of Management** course.

MGMT Online provides the complete narrative from the printed text with additional interactive media and the unique functionality of **StudyBits**—all available on nearly any device!

What is a StudyBit™? Created through a deep investigation of students' challenges and workflows, the StudyBit™ functionality of **MGMT Online** enables students of different generations and learning styles to study more effectively by allowing them to learn their way. Here's how they work:

COLLECT WHAT'S IMPORTANT
Create StudyBits as you highlight text, images or take notes!

WEAK

FAIR

STRONG

UNASSIGNED

RATE AND ORGANIZE STUDYBITS
Rate your understanding and use the color-coding to quickly organize your study time and personalize your flashcards and quizzes.

StudyBit™

TRACK/MONITOR PROGRESS
Use Concept Tracker to decide how you'll spend study time and study YOUR way!

85%

PERSONALIZE QUIZZES
Filter by your StudyBits to personalize quizzes or just take chapter quizzes off-the-shelf.

CORRECT

INCORRECT

CORRECT

CORRECT

CENGAGE
Learning®

MGMT 9

Chuck Williams

Vice President, General Manager, 4LTR Press:
Neil Marquardt

Product Director, 4LTR Press: Steven E. Joos

Product Manager: Laura Redden

Content/Media Developer: Daniel Celenza

Product Assistant: Lauren Dame

Marketing Manager: Emily Horowitz

Marketing Coordinator: Christopher Walz

Sr. Content Project Manager: Martha Conway

Manufacturing Planner: Ron Montgomery

Production Service: MPS Limited

Sr. Art Director: Bethany Casey

Cover/Internal Designer: Tippy McIntosh

Cover Image: © Veer.com/okea

Title page and back cover images:

Computer and tablet illustration:
©iStockphoto.com/furtaev

Smart Phone illustration:
©iStockphoto.com/dashadima

Intellectual Property Analyst: Diane Garrity

Intellectual Property Project Manager:
Betsy Hathaway

For product information and technology assistance, contact us at
Cengage Learning Customer & Sales Support, 1-800-354-9706

For permission to use material from this text or product,
submit all requests online at **www.cengage.com/permissions**
Further permissions questions can be emailed to
permissionrequest@cengage.com

Unless otherwise noted, all items © Cengage Learning

Library of Congress Control Number: 2015950173

Student Edition ISBN: 978-1-305-66158-5

Student Edition with Online: 978-1-305-66159-2

Cengage Learning
20 Channel Center Street
Boston, MA 02210
USA

Cengage Learning is a leading provider of customized learning solutions with employees residing in nearly 40 different countries and sales in more than 125 countries around the world. Find your local representative at **www.cengage.com**.

Cengage Learning products are represented in Canada by Nelson Education, Ltd.

To learn more about Cengage Learning Solutions, visit **www.cengage.com**

Purchase any of our products at your local college store or at our preferred online store **www.cengagebrain.com**

Printed in the United States of America
Print Number: 01   Printed Year: 2015

CHUCK WILLIAMS
MGMT⁹
Brief Contents

© Veer.com/okea

PART 1   INTRODUCTION TO MANAGEMENT
1 Management 2
2 The History of Management 22
3 Organizational Environments and Cultures 44
4 Ethics and Social Responsibility 66

PART 2   PLANNING
5 Planning and Decision Making 88
6 Organizational Strategy 108
7 Innovation and Change 132
8 Global Management 152

PART 3   ORGANIZING
9 Designing Adaptive Organizations 176
10 Managing Teams 198
11 Managing Human Resource Systems 216
12 Managing Individuals and a Diverse Workforce 246

PART 4   LEADING
13 Motivation 266
14 Leadership 288
15 Managing Communication 310

PART 5   CONTROLLING
16 Control 332
17 Managing Information 350
18 Managing Service and Manufacturing Operations 372

Endnotes 393
Index 423

Contents

Part 1
Introduction to Management

1 Management 2

1-1 Management Is ... 3
1-2 Management Functions 4
1-3 Kinds of Managers 6
1-4 Managerial Roles 10
1-5 What Companies Look for in Managers 13
1-6 Mistakes Managers Make 15
1-7 The Transition to Management: The First Year 17
1-8 Competitive Advantage Through People 19

2 The History of Management 22

2-1 The Origins of Management 23
2-2 Scientific Management 25
2-3 Bureaucratic and Administrative Management 30
2-4 Human Relations Management 33
2-5 Operations, Information, Systems, and Contingency Management 38

3 Organizational Environments and Cultures 44

3-1 Changing Environments 45
3-2 General Environment 48
3-3 Specific Environment 52
3-4 Making Sense of Changing Environments 57
3-5 Organizational Cultures: Creation, Success, and Change 59

4 Ethics and Social Responsibility 66

4-1 Workplace Deviance 67
4-2 U.S. Sentencing Commission Guidelines for Organizations 69
4-3 Influences on Ethical Decision Making 72
4-4 Practical Steps to Ethical Decision Making 76
4-5 To Whom Are Organizations Socially Responsible? 79
4-6 For What Are Organizations Socially Responsible? 82
4-7 Responses to Demands for Social Responsibility 84
4-8 Social Responsibility and Economic Performance 86

Part 2
Planning

5 Planning and Decision Making 88

5-1 Benefits and Pitfalls of Planning   89

5-2 How to Make a Plan That Works   90

5-3 Planning from Top to Bottom   94

5-4 Steps and Limits to Rational
Decision Making   99

5-5 Using Groups to Improve
Decision Making   103

6 Organizational Strategy   108

6-1 Sustainable Competitive Advantage   109

6-2 Strategy-Making Process   111

6-3 Corporate-Level Strategies   117

6-4 Industry-Level Strategies   122

6-5 Firm-Level Strategies   127

7 Innovation and Change   132

7-1 Why Innovation Matters   133

7-2 Managing Innovation   138

7-3 Organizational Decline: The Risk
of Not Changing   143

7-4 Managing Change   145

8 Global Management   152

8-1 Global Business, Trade Rules,
and Trade Agreements   153

8-2 Consistency or Adaptation?   159

8-3 Forms for Global Business   161

8-4 Finding the Best Business Climate   164

8-5 Becoming Aware of Cultural
Differences   169

8-6 Preparing for an International
Assignment   171

Part 3
Organizing

Google

9 Designing Adaptive Organizations   176

9-1 Departmentalization   177

9-2 Organizational Authority   184

9-3 Job Design   187

9-4 Intraorganizational Processes   190

9-5 Interorganizational Processes   193

10 Managing Teams   198

10-1 The Good and Bad of Using Teams   199

10-2 Kinds of Teams   202

10-3 Work Team Characteristics   206

10-4 Enhancing Work Team Effectiveness   211

11 Managing Human Resource Systems   216

11-1 Employment Legislation   217

11-2 Recruiting   221

11-3 Selection   225

11-4 Training   232

11-5 Performance Appraisal   235

11-6 Compensation and Employee Separation   239

12 Managing Individuals and a Diverse Workforce   246

12-1 Diversity: Differences That Matter   247

12-2 Surface-Level Diversity   250

12-3 Deep-Level Diversity   257

12-4 Managing Diversity   259

Part 4
Leading

13 Motivation   266

13-1 Basics of Motivation   267

13-2 Equity Theory   272

13-3 Expectancy Theory   276

13-4 Reinforcement Theory   279

13-5 Goal-Setting Theory   284

13-6 Motivating with the Integrated Model   287

14 Leadership   288

14-1 Leaders versus Managers   289

14-2 Who Leaders Are and What Leaders Do   290

14-3 Putting Leaders in the Right Situation: Fiedler's Contingency Theory   294

14-4 Adapting Leader Behavior: Path-Goal Theory   298

14-5 Adapting Leader Behavior: Normative Decision Theory   301

14-6 Visionary Leadership   305

15 Managing Communication   310

15-1 Perception and Communication Problems   311

15-2 Kinds of Communication   315

15-3 Managing One-on-One Communication   322

15-4 Managing Organization-Wide Communication   327

Part 5
Controlling

16 Control   332

16-1 The Control Process   333

16-2 Control Methods   337

16-3 What to Control?   341

17 Managing Information   350

17-1 Strategic Importance of Information   351

17-2 Characteristics and Costs
of Useful Information   354

17-3 Capturing, Processing, and Protecting
Information   359

17-4 Accessing and Sharing Information
and Knowledge   367

18 Managing Service
and Manufacturing
Operations   372

18-1 Productivity   373

18-2 Quality   376

18-3 Service Operations   381

18-4 Manufacturing Operations   383

18-5 Inventory   386

Endnotes 393
Index 423

1 Management

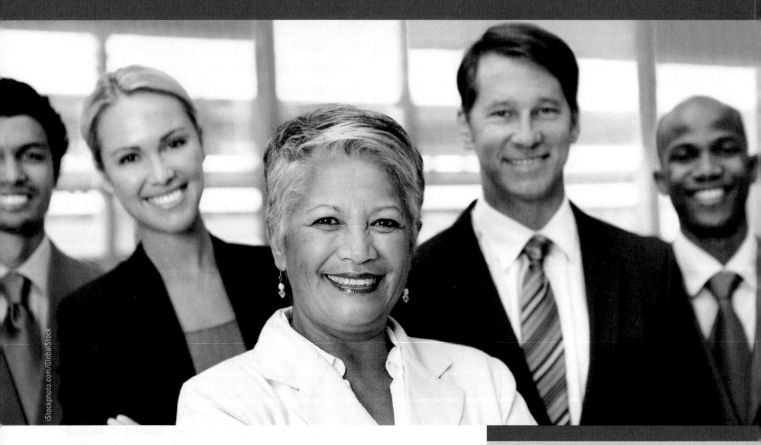

iStockphoto.com/GlobalStock

LEARNING OUTCOMES

1-1 Describe what management is.

1-2 Explain the four functions of management.

1-3 Describe different kinds of managers.

1-4 Explain the major roles and subroles that managers perform in their jobs.

1-5 Explain what companies look for in managers.

1-6 Discuss the top mistakes that managers make in their jobs.

1-7 Describe the transition that employees go through when they are promoted to management.

1-8 Explain how and why companies can create competitive advantage through people.

After you finish this chapter, go to **PAGE 21** for **STUDY TOOLS**

MANAGEMENT IS . . .

Management issues are fundamental to any organization: How do we plan to get things done, organize the company to be efficient and effective, lead and motivate employees, and put controls in place to make sure our plans are followed and our goals met? Good management is basic to starting a business, growing a business, and maintaining a business after it has achieved some measure of success.

To understand how important *good* management is, think about this mistake. Sears, one of the oldest retailers in the United States, has had $7 billion since 2011. Accordingly, it is closing 235 unprofitable stores. And while industry analysts believe that Sears will need to close another 300 to 400 stores, they don't believe that it should be selling off profitable stores, too. However, Sears is so cash-strapped that it has sacrificed future earnings for short-term needs by selling a dozen profitable stores. Robert Futterman, CEO of RKF, a retail leasing and consulting company, said, "Retailers invest in their best stores and refurbish them, they don't sell them."[1]

Ah, bad managers and bad management. Is it any wonder that companies pay management consultants nearly $210 billion a year for advice on basic management issues such as how to outperform competitors to earn customers' business, lead people effectively, organize the company efficiently, and manage large-scale projects and processes?[2] This textbook will help you understand some of the basic issues that management consultants help companies resolve. (And it won't cost you billions of dollars.)

Many of today's managers got their start welding on the factory floor, clearing dishes off tables, helping customers fit a suit, or wiping up a spill in aisle 3. Similarly, lots of you will start at the bottom and work your way up. There's no better way to get to know your competition, your customers, and your business. But whether you begin your career at the entry level or as a supervisor, your job as a manager is not to do the work but to help others do theirs. **Management** is getting work done through others.

Vineet Nayar, CEO of IT services company HCL Technologies, doesn't see himself as the guy who has to do everything or have all the answers. Instead, he sees himself as "the guy who is obsessed with enabling employees to create value." Rather than coming up with solutions himself, Nayar creates opportunities for collaboration, for peer review, and for employees to give feedback on ideas and work processes. Says Nayar, "My job is to make sure everybody is enabled to do what they do well."[3]

Sears is so cash strapped that it has sacrificed future earnings for short-term needs by selling a dozen profitable stores.

Nayar's description of managerial responsibilities suggests that managers also have to be concerned with efficiency and effectiveness in the work process. **Efficiency** is getting work done with a minimum of effort, expense, or waste. Starbucks Coffee measures efficiency, or productivity, in terms of transactions per labor hour, meaning the number of coffee/food transactions each hour relative to the number of Starbucks employees it takes to handle those transactions. At 11.7 transactions per labor hour, Starbucks is 46 percent more efficient today than in 2008 when it averaged 8 transactions per labor hour.[4] Because the company saves an estimated 10 seconds per transaction over credit cards and 20 seconds per transaction compared to cash payments, Starbucks's increased use of mobile payments is a key driver of its ability to process more customers each hour.[5] While Starbucks now handles 5 million mobile transactions per week, or 14 percent of all sales, efficiency is likely to rise even more as mobile transactions have more than doubled in the past year.[6]

Efficiency alone, however, is not enough to ensure success. Managers must also strive for **effectiveness**, which is accomplishing tasks that help fulfill organizational objectives such as customer service and satisfaction. After a 37 percent surge in last-minute holiday shopping (compared to the previous year) overwhelmed UPS and led to tens of thousands of late deliveries, Amazon.com began expanding its

Management getting work done through others

Efficiency getting work done with a minimum of effort, expense, or waste

Effectiveness accomplishing tasks that help fulfill organizational objectives own "last-mile" delivery service to improve customer service and satisfaction, and therefore effectiveness.[7] Although it typically uses UPS, FedEx, and the U.S. Postal Service for deliveries, Amazon hopes that its Amazon Fresh trucks, in use in a limited number of cities, will reduce rising shipping costs, challenge e-tail competitors such as eBay and Walmart, and, if it works, fulfill the "holy grail" of online buying—same-day delivery. Analyst Ajay Agarwal, of Bain Capital Ventures, says, "In the old days, it used to be your milkman coming to your house every week. I think in five years I could imagine . . . some significant fraction of the population having an Amazon truck coming to their house every week."[8]

1-2 MANAGEMENT FUNCTIONS

Henri Fayol, who was a managing director (CEO) of a large steel company in the early 1900s, was one of the founders of the field of management. You'll learn more about Fayol and management's other key contributors when you read about the history of management in Chapter 2. Based on his twenty years of experience as a CEO, Fayol argued that "the success of an enterprise generally depends much more on the administrative ability of its leaders than on their technical ability."[9] A century later, Fayol's arguments still hold true. During a two-year study code-named Project Oxygen, Google analyzed performance reviews and feedback surveys to identify the traits of its best managers. According to Laszlo Bock, Google's vice president for people operations, "We'd always believed that to be a manager, particularly on the engineering side, you need to be as deep or deeper a technical expert than the people who work for you. It turns out that that's absolutely the least important thing." What was most important? "Be a good coach." "Empower; Don't micromanage." "Be product and results-oriented." "Be a good communicator and listen to your team." "Be interested in [your] direct reports' success and well-being." In short, Google found what Fayol observed: administrative ability, or management, is key to an organization's success.[10]

According to Fayol, managers need to perform five managerial functions in order to be successful: planning, organizing, coordinating, commanding, and controlling.[11] Most management textbooks today have updated this list by dropping the coordinating function and referring to Fayol's commanding function as "leading." Fayol's management functions are thus known today in this updated form as planning, organizing, leading, and controlling. Studies indicate that managers who perform these management functions well are more successful, gaining promotions for themselves and profits for their companies. For example, the more time CEOs spend planning, the more profitable their companies are.[12] A twenty-five-year study at AT&T found that employees with better planning and decision-making skills were more likely to be promoted into management jobs, to be successful as managers, and to be promoted into upper levels of management.[13]

The evidence is clear. Managers serve their companies well when they plan, organize, lead, and control. So we've organized this textbook based on these functions of management, as shown in Exhibit 1.1.

Now let's take a closer look at each of the management functions: 1-2a planning, 1-2b organizing, 1-2c leading, and 1-2d controlling.

1-2a Planning

Planning involves determining organizational goals and a means for achieving them. As you'll learn in Chapter 5, planning is one of the best ways to improve performance. It encourages people to work harder, to work for extended periods, to engage in behaviors directly related to goal accomplishment, and to think of better ways to

Planning determining organizational goals and a means for achieving them

Exhibit 1.1
The Four Functions of Management

Planning | Organizing

Leading | Controlling

Harper 3D/Shutterstock.com

© Cengage Learning

do their jobs. But most importantly, companies that plan have larger profits and faster growth than companies that don't plan.

For example, the question "What business are we in?" is at the heart of strategic planning. You'll learn about this in Chapter 6. If you can answer the question "What business are you in?" in two sentences or fewer, chances are you have a very clear plan for your business. But getting a clear plan is not so easy. Sometimes even very successful companies stray from their core business. Alibaba is a China-based e-commerce company whose mission is, "To make it easy to do business anywhere." Like eBay, Alibaba operates online and mobile marketplaces that bring retail and wholesale buyers and sellers together. While Alibaba has 600 million customers in China, it's now expanding to the U.S. market via 11main.com, on which 1,000+ companies will sell everything from clothing to jewelry to arts and crafts. With such a clear mission and focus, it was surprising when Alibaba bought a 50 percent stake in China's Guangzhou Evergrande soccer team. Alibaba's Chairman Jack Ma explained, "I think not understanding soccer doesn't matter. I also didn't understand retail, e-commerce, or the Internet, but that didn't stop me from doing it anyway." Ma's confidence aside, Simon Wong of the London School of Economics warns, "You should focus on what you're good at, and this seems so ancillary to what they're doing today."[14]

You'll learn more about planning in Chapter 5 on planning and decision making, Chapter 6 on organizational strategy, Chapter 7 on innovation and change, and Chapter 8 on global management.

1-2b Organizing

Organizing is deciding where decisions will be made, who will do what jobs and tasks, and who will work for whom in the company. With 1,400 different computer systems; different labor unions representing pilots, flight attendants, and maintenance workers; and different ways of washing planes and boarding and feeding passengers; as well as different classes in the cabins (no first class on Continental), Continental Airlines and United Airlines faced an enormous organizing task to merge their two companies into the world's second-largest airline. Lori Gobillot, vice president of integration management at the time of the reorganization, oversaw thirty-three teams that decided the fastest way to board passengers and which computer systems to use, United's or Continental's, for scheduling

crews, routing planes, handling bags and cargo, and just basic accounting. Said Gobillot, "I tell them to be fact-based, and direct and objective, and keep the emotions out of it—and don't keep score. It's not important how many things come from United and how many come from Continental." Three years after the merger, significant challenges remain. For instance, mechanics continue to use separate information systems (one from United and one from Continental) to track and manage critical airplane maintenance and repair work. Likewise, labor agreements restrict "Continental" flight attendants to working on "Continental" planes and "United" flight attendants to "United" planes.[15] Each decision matters, as reducing costs by as little as a half-cent per mile can result in a $1 billion increase in annual profits for an industry that historically loses billions each year.[16]

You'll learn more about organizing in Chapter 9 on designing adaptive organizations, Chapter 10 on managing teams, Chapter 11 on managing human resources, and Chapter 12 on managing individuals and a diverse workforce.

1-2c Leading

Our third management function, **leading**, involves inspiring and motivating workers to work hard to achieve organizational goals. Eileen Martinson, CEO of software developer Sparta Systems, believes that it is important for leaders to clearly communicate what an organization's goals are. She says, "A boss taught me a long time ago that people are going to remember only two to three things." So at her first company-wide meeting, she communicated just one goal—doubling revenues over the next few years.[17] Martinson says, "The employees completely understand where we are going, and we've built a culture around that. If you have to come in and show me 45 charts and go through a lot of mumbo jumbo that neither of us understands, it's not going to work."[18]

You'll learn more about leading in Chapter 13 on motivation, Chapter 14 on leadership, and Chapter 15 on managing communication.

1-2d Controlling

The last function of management, **controlling**, is

Organizing deciding where decisions will be made, who will do what jobs and tasks, and who will work for whom

Leading inspiring and motivating workers to work hard to achieve organizational goals

Controlling monitoring progress toward goal achievement and taking corrective action when needed

Bravely Changing Course

Video game developer Square Enix has traditionally specialized in making Japanese-style role-playing games (JRPGs). In recent years, Square began focusing on trying to develop global blockbuster titles that would appeal to a global audience. It began to struggle when sales of games such as Tomb Raider, Sleeping Dogs, and Hitman: Absolution did not meet expectations. So it came as some surprise when Square released Bravely Default, a JRPG, and it sold more than 200,000 copies in the U.S. in three weeks. Square president Yosuke Matsuda took this as a cue. "In the past, when we developed console games with a worldwide premise, we lost our focus." Matsuda said. "We weren't able to see this clearly up until now, but fans of JRPGs are really spread around the world." The sales trends of its different games told Square what customers were looking for. In response, Matsuda said that Square would begin to include more JRPGs in its core stable of titles.

Source: Nintendo

While globally appealing video games such as Sleeping Dogs (pictured) have failed to meet sales expectations, Square Enix has had unexpected success with highly targeted titles such as JRPG Bravely Default.

Source: M. Futter, "Square Enix Believes Company Has 'Lost Focus,'" *Game Informer*, March 31, 2014, accessed April 9, 2014. http://www.gameinformer.com/b/news/archive/2014/03/31/square-enix-president-believes-company-has-lost-focus.aspx.

monitoring progress toward goal achievement and taking corrective action when progress isn't being made. The basic control process involves setting standards to achieve goals, comparing actual performance to those standards, and then making changes to return performance to those standards. According to Michael Corbat, CEO of financial services company Citigroup, managerial and company success are contingent on setting goals, measuring performance, and making adjustments and corrections as needed. He recently stated during a meeting of executives, "You are what you measure." Therefore, a central part of his plan to restore Citigroup's financial performance is to measure how well executives perform against the plans they created. The basic idea, said one Citigroup executive, is "You said you would do this. Did you?" Corbat created a scorecard to measure the company's fifty top executives in four categories: capital, clients, culture, and controls. Scores ranging from 100 (the highest) to –40 (the lowest) will show how well each executive is performing. Corbat expects that the control process inherent in the scorecards will help Citigroup develop more accountability and discipline as it tries to recover from years of losses.[19]

Top managers executives responsible for the overall direction of the organization

You'll learn more about the control function in Chapter 16 on control, Chapter 17 on managing information, and Chapter 18 on managing service and manufacturing operations.

1-3 KINDS OF MANAGERS

Not all managerial jobs are the same. The demands and requirements placed on the CEO of Sony are significantly different from those placed on the manager of your local Wendy's restaurant.

*As shown in Exhibit 1.2, there are four kinds of managers, each with different jobs and responsibilities: **1-3a top managers, 1-3b middle managers, 1-3c first-line managers,** and **1-3d team leaders.***

1-3a Top Managers

Top managers hold positions such as chief executive officer (CEO), chief operating officer (COO), chief financial officer (CFO), and chief information officer (CIO) and are responsible for the overall direction of the

Exhibit 1.2
What the Four Kinds of Managers Do

Jobs		Responsibilities
Top Managers		
CEO	CIO	Change
COO	Vice president	Commitment
CFO	Corporate heads	Culture
		Environment
Middle Managers		
General manager		Resources
Plant manager		Objectives
Regional manager		Coordination
Divisional manager		Subunit performance
		Strategy implementation
First-Line Managers		
Office manager		Nonmanagerial worker supervision
Shift supervisor		Teaching and training
Department manager		Scheduling
		Facilitation
Team Leaders		
Team leader		Facilitation
Team contact		External relationships
Group facilitator		Internal relationships

© Cengage Learning

Mmichaeljung/Shutterstock.com / BlueSkyImage/Shutterstock.com / Kzenon/Shutterstock.com / Racorn/Shutterstock.com

organization. Top managers have the following responsibilities.[20] When R. J. Dourney was hired as **Cosi's** CEO, the sandwich chain had struggled for twelve years under nine CEOs who never posted a profit. After just two days on the job, Dourney announced to the company's corporate employees that its Chicago headquarters would close and be relocated in Boston, where Dourney had been a successful franchiser of thirteen Cosi stores before becoming CEO. Dourney immediately closed ten unprofitable stores, updated the menu, and changed Cosi's stock-incentive program to be performance based. He then rolled out a more efficient serving system to serve customers quickly at all locations. In less than a year, those same store sales rose 20 percent while the company's stock price rose 160 percent per share.[21]

Indeed, in both Europe and the United States, 35 percent of all CEOs are eventually fired because of their inability to successfully change their companies.[22] Creating a context for change includes forming a long-range vision or mission for the company. When Satya Nadella was appointed CEO of **Microsoft**, the company was perceived as a shortsighted, lumbering behemoth. Nadella reoriented the company with a series of acquisitions and innovations, including purchasing **Mojang**, maker of the **Minecraft** video game, and a 3D-hologram feature for controlling Windows. After following Microsoft for years, one analyst noted about Nadella's new direction for the company, "Microsoft hasn't really shown any sort of vision like this in a long, long time."[23] As one CEO said, "The CEO has to think about the future more than anyone."[24]

After that vision or mission is set, the second responsibility of top managers is to develop employees' commitment to and ownership of the company's performance. That is, top managers are responsible for creating employee buy-in. Third, top managers must create a positive organizational culture through language and action. Top managers impart company values, strategies, and lessons through what they do and say to others both inside and outside the company. Indeed, no matter what they communicate, it's critical for them to send and reinforce clear, consistent messages.[25] When Phil Martens became CEO of aluminum producer Novelis, he spent his first 100 days visiting plants around the world and discovered that the company, with 11,000 employees, had highly fragmented business practices, operations, and strategies. To clearly communicate, "that we're going to move from a fragmented, regional company to a globally integrated company," Martens had shirts with the slogan, "One Novelis," distributed so that a symbolic picture of the leadership team could be taken. For the picture, said Martens, "We stood in a very defined triangle, very precise, because I wanted to create the image of order, and that we are together."[26] Likewise, it's important to actively manage internal organizational communication. As part of the One Novelis program, Martens created a global safety program, called Together We Are Safe, which monitored health and safety practices across Novelis's global sites, identified best practices, and then adopted and communicated them as a global standard. As a result, from 2009 to 2013, Novelis saw injuries, illnesses, and fatalities drop by over 40 percent.[27]

Finally, top managers are responsible for monitoring their business environments. This means that top managers must closely monitor customer needs, competitors' moves, and long-term business, economic, and social trends.

1-3b Middle Managers

Middle managers hold positions such as plant manager, regional manager, or divisional manager. They are responsible for setting objectives consistent with top management's goals and for planning and implementing subunit strategies for achieving those objectives.[28] Or as one middle manager put it, a middle manager is, "the implementer of the company's strategy" who figures out the "how" to do the "what."[29] Middle manager Michelle Davis, an analytics director at FICO, the company that calculates credit scores, begins her day at 6:30 a.m. "when the hallways are dark" and there are few interruptions. Regular meetings, such as the monthly conference call that she has with the analytics team, start at 7:30 a.m. The rest of her long days are often filled with additional meetings, training sessions that she either leads or participates in, and quick check-ins with her boss and various product management teams across the company, in which she communicates the concerns of her group about the software that banks use when applying credit scores to bank customers.[30]

One specific middle management responsibility is to plan and allocate resources to meet objectives. A second major responsibility is to coordinate and link groups, departments, and divisions within a company. One middle manager described his job as, "A man who can discuss strategy with [the] CXO at breakfast and [then] eat lunch with workers."[31] FICO's Michelle Davis admits that coordinating and linking teams across different groups and departments can be "frustrating," but that it's a significant part of her job. She adds, "It takes time to do management right."[32]

A third responsibility of middle management is to monitor and manage the performance of the subunits and individual managers who report to them. Finally, middle managers are also responsible for implementing the changes or strategies generated by top managers. Why? Because they're closer to the managers and employees who work on a daily basis with suppliers to effectively and efficiently deliver the company's product or service. In short, they're closer to the people who can best solve problems and implement solutions. How important are middle managers to company performance? A study of nearly 400 video game companies conducted at the University of Pennsylvania's Wharton School of Business found

Emerge/Shutterstock.com

Middle managers responsible for setting objectives consistent with top management's goals and for planning and implementing subunit strategies for achieving these objectives that middle managers' effectiveness accounted for 22 percent of the differences in performance across companies. In fact, middle managers were three times as important as the video game designers who develop game characters and story lines. Professor Ethan Mollick, who conducted the study, said that middle managers are the key to "making sure the people at the bottom and the top [of the organization] are getting what they need."[33]

1-3c First-Line Managers

First-line managers hold positions such as office manager, shift supervisor, or department manager. The primary responsibility of first-line managers is to manage the performance of entry-level employees who are directly responsible for producing a company's goods and services. Thus, first-line managers are the only managers who don't supervise other managers. The responsibilities of first-line managers include monitoring, teaching, and short-term planning.

First-line managers encourage, monitor, and reward the performance of their workers. First-line managers are also responsible for teaching entry-level employees how to do their jobs. They also make detailed schedules and operating plans based on middle management's intermediate-range plans. In contrast to the long-term plans of top managers (three to five years out) and the intermediate plans of middle managers (six to eighteen months out), first-line managers engage in plans and actions that typically produce results within two weeks.[34] Consider the typical convenience store manager (e.g., 7-Eleven) who starts the day by driving past competitors' stores to inspect their gasoline prices and then checks the outside of his or her store for anything that might need maintenance, such as burned-out lights or signs, or restocking, such as windshield washer fluid and paper towels. Then comes an inside check, where the manager determines what needs to be done for that day. (Are there enough donuts and coffee for breakfast or enough sandwiches for lunch?) After the day is planned, the manager turns to weekend orders. After accounting for the weather (hot or cold) and the sales trends at the same time last year, the manager makes sure the store will have enough beer, soft drinks, and newspapers on hand. Finally, the manager looks seven to ten days ahead for hiring needs. Because of strict hiring procedures (basic math tests, drug tests, and background checks), it can take that long to hire new employees. Said one convenience store manager, "I have to continually interview, even if I am fully staffed."[35]

1-3d Team Leaders

The fourth kind of manager is a team leader. This relatively new kind of management job developed as companies shifted to self-managing teams, which, by definition, have no formal supervisor. In traditional management hierarchies, first-line managers are responsible for the performance of nonmanagerial employees and have the authority to hire and fire workers, make job assignments, and control resources. In this new structure, the teams themselves perform nearly all of the functions performed by first-line managers under traditional hierarchies.[36]

Team leaders are primarily responsible for facilitating team activities toward accomplishing a goal. This doesn't mean team leaders are responsible for team performance. They aren't. The team is. So how do team leaders help their teams accomplish their goals? Avinoam Nowogrodski, CEO at Clarizen, a software company, says, "Great leaders ask the right questions. They recognize . . . that a team is much better at figuring out the answers."[37] Team leaders help their team members plan and schedule work, learn to solve problems, and work effectively with each other. Management consultant Franklin Jonath says, "The idea is for the team leader to be at the service of the group." It should be clear that the team members own the outcome. The leader is there to bring intellectual, emotional, and spiritual resources to the team. Through his or her actions, the leader should be able to show the others how to think about the work that they're doing in the context of their lives. It's a tall order, but the best teams have such leaders.[38]

Relationships among team members and between different teams are crucial to good team performance and must be well managed by team leaders, who are responsible for fostering good relationships and addressing problematic ones within their teams. Getting along with others is much more important in team structures because team members can't get work done without the help of teammates. Clarizen CEO Avinoam Nowogrodski agrees, saying, "Innovation is created with people who you respect. It will never happen in a group of people who hate each other. If you want to have innovation within your company, you need to have a culture

First-line managers responsible for training and supervising the performance of nonmanagerial employees who are directly responsible for producing the company's products or services

Team leaders managers responsible for facilitating team activities toward goal accomplishment of respect."[39] And, Nowogrodski adds, that starts with the team leader. "If you respect other people, they'll respect you."[40] Tim Clem emerged as a team leader at **GitHub**, a San Francisco–based software company that provides collaborative tools and online work spaces for people who code software. GitHub, itself, also uses team structures and team leaders to decide the software projects on which its 170 employees will work. After only a few months at the company, Clem, who had not previously led a team, convinced his GitHub colleagues to work on a new product he had designed for Microsoft Windows. Without their approval, he would not have gotten the go-ahead and the resources to hire people to do the project. By contrast, a manager, and not the team, would have likely made this decision in a traditional management structure.[41]

Team leaders are also responsible for managing external relationships. Team leaders act as the bridge or liaison between their teams and other teams, departments, and divisions in a company. For example, if a member of Team A complains about the quality of Team B's work, Team A's leader is responsible for solving the problem by initiating a meeting with Team B's leader. Together, these team leaders are responsible for getting members of both teams to work together to solve the problem. If it's done right, the problem is solved without involving company management or blaming members of the other team.[42]

In summary, because of these critical differences, team leaders who don't understand how their roles are different from those of traditional managers often struggle in their jobs.

You will learn more about teams in Chapter 10.

1-4 MANAGERIAL ROLES

Although all four types of managers engage in planning, organizing, leading, and controlling, if you were to follow them around during a typical day on the job, you would probably not use these terms to describe what they actually do. Rather, what you'd see are the various roles managers play. Professor Henry Mintzberg followed five American CEOs, shadowing each for a week and analyzing their mail, their conversations, and their actions. He concluded that managers fulfill three major roles while

Exhibit 1.3
Mintzberg's Managerial Roles

Interpersonal Roles
- Figurehead
- Leader
- Liaison

Informational Roles
- Monitor
- Disseminator
- Spokesperson

Decisional Roles
- Entrepreneur
- Disturbance Handler
- Resource Allocator
- Negotiator

Source: Adapted from "The Manager's Job: Folklore and Fact," by Mintzberg, H. Harvard Business Review, July–August 1975.

performing their jobs—interpersonal, informational, and decisional.[43]

In other words, managers talk to people, gather and give information, and make decisions. Furthermore, as shown in Exhibit 1.3, these three major roles can be subdivided into ten subroles.

*Let's examine each major role—**1-4a interpersonal roles, 1-4b informational roles,** and **1-4c decisional roles**—and their ten subroles.*

1-4a Interpersonal Roles

More than anything else, management jobs are people-intensive. When asked about her experience as a first-time CEO, Kim Bowers, CEO of CST Brands, said, "We have 12,000 employees. [So,] I spend a lot of time out in the field with them."[44] Estimates vary with the level of management, but most managers spend between two-thirds and four-fifths of their time in face-to-face communication with others.[45] If you're a loner, or if you consider dealing with people a pain, then you may not be cut out for management work. In fulfilling the interpersonal role of management, managers perform three subroles: figurehead, leader, and liaison.

Seven Deadlies—Things Great Bosses Avoid

A manager is responsible not only for providing direction and guidance to employees but also for making sure to create a work environment that allows them to be the best. Author and columnist Jeff Haden identifies seven things that managers often do that create an uncomfortable and unproductive work atmosphere:

1. Pressuring employees to attend social events. When your employees are with people from work, even at some party, it might just end up feeling like "work."

2. Pressuring employees to give to charity.

3. Not giving employees time to eat during mealtime hours.

4. Asking employees to do self-evaluations.

5. Asking employees to evaluate their coworkers.

6. Asking employees to do something that you don't want to do.

7. Asking employees to reveal personal information in the spirit of "team building."

Source: J. Haden "7 Things Great Bosses Never Ask Employees to Do" *Inc.com*, March 12, 2015, accessed March 28, 2015. http://www.inc.com/jeff-haden/7-things-the-best-bosses-refuse-to-ask-employees-to-do.html.

In the **figurehead role**, managers perform ceremonial duties such as greeting company visitors, speaking at the opening of a new facility, or representing the company at a community luncheon to support local charities. When **Fendi**, the Italian fashion house, launched a design initiative to raise money for charity, CEO Pietro Beccari hosted a gala at the company's recently opened flagship in New York City.[46]

In the **leader role**, managers motivate and encourage workers to accomplish organizational objectives (see box "Seven Deadlies—Things Great Bosses Avoid"). One way managers can act as leaders is to establish challenging goals. William Xu, the enterprise division chief of Chinese telecom equipment maker Huawei Enterprises, gave his division a 40 percent sales growth target for 2013. Xu said, "The (2013) target was very ambitious to motivate staff."[47]

In the **liaison role**, managers deal with people outside their units. Studies consistently indicate that managers spend as much time with outsiders as they do with their own subordinates and their own bosses. For example, CEOs often sit on other companies' boards. CEO Stephen Zarrilli, of Safeguard Scientifics, which invests in high-growth health care and technology firms, says, "When you sit on another company's board,

you gain perspective—not only about the company and its industry—but, more importantly, about other operating methodologies, governance, and viewpoints that can be very beneficial when you bring them back to your company."[48] Indeed, companies in low-growth, highly competitive industries whose CEOs sit on outside boards earn an average return on assets 15 percent higher than companies with CEOs who don't sit on outside boards![49]

1-4b Informational Roles

Not only do managers spend most of their time in face-to-face contact with others, they spend much of it obtaining and sharing information. Mintzberg found that the managers in his study spent 40 percent of their time giving and getting information from others. In this regard, management

Figurehead role the interpersonal role managers play when they perform ceremonial duties

Leader role the interpersonal role managers play when they motivate and encourage workers to accomplish organizational objectives

Liaison role the interpersonal role managers play when they deal with people outside their units

AP Images/Ted S. Warren

can be viewed as gathering information by scanning the business environment and listening to others in face-to-face conversations, processing that information, and then sharing it with people both inside and outside the company. Mintzberg described three informational subroles: monitor, disseminator, and spokesperson.

In the **monitor role**, managers scan their environment for information, actively contact others for information, and, because of their personal contacts, receive a great deal of unsolicited information. Besides receiving firsthand information, managers monitor their environment by reading local newspapers and the *Wall Street Journal* to keep track of customers, competitors, and technological changes that may affect their businesses. Today's managers can subscribe to electronic monitoring and distribution services that track the news wires (Associated Press, Reuters, and so on) for stories and social media posts related to their businesses. These services deliver customized news that only includes topics the managers specify. Business Wire (http://www.businesswire.com) monitors and distributes daily news headlines from major industries (for example automotive, banking and financial, health, high tech).[50] CyberAlert (http://www.cyberalert.com) keeps round-the-clock track of new stories in categories chosen by each subscriber. It also offers CyberAlert Social, which monitors roughly 25 million individual social media posts daily across 190 million social media sources worldwide. Brandwatch and ViralHeat are additional tools for monitoring social media.[51] Another site, Federal News Service (http://fednews.com), provides subscribers with daily electronic news clips from more than 10,000 online news sites.[52]

Because of their numerous personal contacts and their access to subordinates, managers are often hubs for the distribution of critical information. In the **disseminator role**, managers share the information they have collected with their subordinates and others in the company. At **Qualtrics**, a software company that provides sophisticated online survey research tools, CEO Ryan Smith makes sure that everyone in the company is clear on company goals and plans. Every Monday, employees are asked via email to respond to two questions: "What are you going to get done this week? And what did you get done last week that you said you were going to do?" Smith says, "Then that rolls up into one email that the entire organization gets. So if someone's got a question, they can look at that for an explanation. We share other information, too—every time we have a meeting, we release meeting notes to the organization. When we have a board meeting, we write a letter about it afterward and send it to the organization." Qualtrics also uses an internal database where each quarter employees enter their plans for meeting the company's objectives. Those plans are then made visible to everyone else at Qualtrics.[53]

In contrast to the disseminator role, in which managers distribute information to employees inside the company, managers in the **spokesperson role** share information with people outside their departments or companies. One of the most common ways CEOs serve as spokespeople for their companies is at annual meetings with company shareholders or the board of directors. CEOs also serve as spokespeople to the media when their companies are involved in major news stories. For example, Amazon founder and CEO Jeff Bezos attracted worldwide attention when he announced that Amazon was actively working on ways to use airborne drones to deliver Amazon purchases to its Amazon Prime members who pay $99 a year for the privilege of unlimited two-day delivery. Bezos said, "The Prime Air team is already flight testing our 5th and 6th generation aerial vehicles, and we are in the design phase on generations 7 and 8."[54] As with its Amazon Fresh trucks, drones would be used to speed delivery and reduce costs. While many believe that drone delivery is five years away or more, Bezos says, "It will work, and it will happen, and it's gonna be a lot of fun."[55]

1-4c Decisional Roles

Mintzberg found that obtaining and sharing information is not an end in itself. Obtaining and sharing information with people inside and outside the company is useful to managers because it helps them make good decisions. According to Mintzberg, managers engage in four decisional subroles: entrepreneur, disturbance handler, resource allocator, and negotiator.

Monitor role the informational role managers play when they scan their environment for information

Disseminator role the informational role managers play when they share information with others in their departments or companies

Spokesperson role the informational role managers play when they share information with people outside their departments or companies

In the **entrepreneur role**, managers adapt themselves, their subordinates, and their units to change. For years, **Whole Foods Market**, was the top—and only—organic grocery retailer. When traditional chains, such as Kroger and Walmart, began offering organic produce, meat, and packaged foods for cheaper prices, Whole Foods—sometimes called "Whole Paycheck" due to its high prices—became vulnerable and earnings plummeted. Co-CEO Walter Robb said, "All of a sudden . . . you can get the same stuff in many other places and you could get it cheaper." So the company cut prices, which, "Will tell customers what we are about: values and value," says founder and Co-CEO John Mackey. Whole Foods also launched its first national advertising campaign, started a customer loyalty program, and partnered with **Instacart** to deliver groceries to customers' homes in fifteen cities. Co-CEO Robb says that changes—and lower prices—will continue.[56]

Susan Montgomery/Shutterstock.com

In the **disturbance handler role**, managers respond to pressures and problems so severe that they demand immediate attention and action. In December 2014, Brian Cornell, Target's new CEO, went on a solo tour of the company's Canadian retail stores. Target Canada, the company's first international expansion, had lost $2 billion since starting in 2011. Cornell, CEO for just four months, wanted to see the struggling Canadian stores firsthand. On returning home, he reviewed Target Canada's sales numbers, and just a few weeks later, in January 2015, announced Target would spend $600 million to liquidate all 133 Canadian stores, lay off 17,000 employees, and take a $5.4 billion write down. Cornell said, "Simply put, we were losing money every day," and could not, "find a realistic scenario that got Target Canada to profitability until at least 2021."[57]

In the **resource allocator role**, managers decide who will get what resources and how many resources they will get. Ford's F-series truck, the best selling vehicle in the U.S. for thirty-two consecutive years, generates $22 billion in sales a year and accounts for 12 percent of Ford's global sales and 40 percent of its global profits. In 2009, Ford committed to a multibillion dollar investment to redesign the F-series, whose prices range from $24,000 to $50,000, to be built with a completely aluminum body, something found only in much more expensive cars, such as the the $70,000 Tesla Model S or the $75,000 Audi A8. Ford Chairman Bill Ford, says, "Some people might say, 'Aren't you taking a chance with your best-selling vehicle?'. But that's what you have to do." He said, "I would have had much more anxiety if they had come in with business-as-usual." The 2015 F-series is 700 lbs. lighter, which allowed Ford engineers to replace a 6.2 liter V8 with a 3.5-liter turbocharged V6. While still capable of towing 8,000 pounds, overall gas mileage rose by 16 percent from 19 mpg to 22 mpg, making the F-series the most fuel efficient gas-powered vehicle in its class."[58]

In the **negotiator role**, managers negotiate schedules, projects, goals, outcomes, resources, and employee raises. When **Ryanair**, Europe's low-cost airline, was shopping for 200 new planes in 2014, it pressed Boeing and Airbus to add an extra eight to eleven seats per plane. Doing so cuts costs by 20 percent and earns an extra 1 million euros per plane each year. CEO Michael O'Leary traveled from Ireland to Seattle to personally negotiate the deal and acknowledged pitting Ryanair's longtime supplier Boeing against Airbus, saying, "We were very close to going to Airbus in the spring [of 2014]." O'Leary left Boeing with a deal for 200 planes, each with eight extra seats, and a hefty discount off the $104 million retail price of Boeing's 737-MAX jet (still in development) that brought the total price tag down from $20.8 billion to $11 billion.[59]

1-5 WHAT COMPANIES LOOK FOR IN MANAGERS

I didn't have the slightest idea what my job was. I walked in giggling and laughing because I had been promoted and had no idea what principles or style to be guided by. After the first day, I felt like I had run into a brick wall. (Sales Representative #1)

Suddenly, I found myself saying, boy, I can't be responsible for getting all that revenue. I don't have the time. Suddenly you've got to

Entrepreneur role the decisional role managers play when they adapt themselves, their subordinates, and their units to change

Disturbance handler role the decisional role managers play when they respond to severe pressures and problems that demand immediate action

Resource allocator role the decisional role managers play when they decide who gets what resources and in what amounts

Negotiator role the decisional role managers play when they negotiate schedules, projects, goals, outcomes, resources, and employee raises *go from [taking care of] yourself and say now I'm the manager, and what does a manager do? It takes awhile thinking about it for it to really hit you . . . a manager gets things done through other people. That's a very, very hard transition to make. (Sales Representative #2)*[60]

The preceding statements were made by two star sales representatives who, on the basis of their superior performance, were promoted to the position of sales manager. As their comments indicate, at first they did not feel confident about their ability to do their jobs as managers. Like most new managers, these sales managers suddenly realized that the knowledge, skills, and abilities that led to success early in their careers (and were probably responsible for their promotion into the ranks of management) would not necessarily help them succeed as managers. As sales representatives, they were responsible only for managing their own performance. But as sales managers, they were now directly responsible for supervising all of the sales representatives in their sales territories. Furthermore, they were now directly accountable for whether those sales representatives achieved their sales goals. If performance in nonmanagerial jobs doesn't necessarily prepare you for a managerial job, then what does it take to be a manager?

When companies look for employees who would be good managers, they look for individuals who have technical skills, human skills, conceptual skills, and the motivation to manage.[61] Exhibit 1.4 shows the relative importance of these four skills to the jobs of team leaders, first-line managers, middle managers, and top managers.

Technical skills are the specialized procedures, techniques, and knowledge required to get the job done. For the sales managers described previously, technical skills involve the ability to find new sales prospects, develop accurate sales pitches based on customer needs, and close sales. For a nurse supervisor, technical skills include being able to insert an IV or operate a crash cart if a patient goes into cardiac arrest.

Technical skills are most important for team

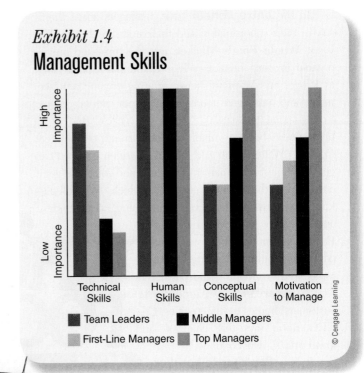

Exhibit 1.4
Management Skills

© Cengage Learning

Viorel Sima/Shutterstock.com

leaders and lower-level managers because they supervise the workers who produce products or serve customers. Team leaders and first-line managers need technical knowledge and skills to train new employees and help employees solve problems. Technical knowledge and skills are also needed to troubleshoot problems that employees can't handle. Technical skills become less important as managers rise through the managerial ranks, but they are still important.

Human skills can be summarized as the ability to work well with others. Managers with human skills work effectively within groups, encourage others to express their thoughts and feelings, are sensitive to others' needs and viewpoints, and are good listeners and communicators. Human skills are equally important at all levels of management, from team leaders to CEOs. However, because lower-level managers spend much of their time solving technical problems, upper-level managers may actually spend more time dealing directly with people. On average, first-line managers spend 57 percent of their time with people, but that percentage increases to 63 percent for middle managers and 78 percent for top managers.[62]

Conceptual skills are the ability to see the organization as a whole, to understand how the different

Technical skills the specialized procedures, techniques, and knowledge required to get the job done

Human skills the ability to work well with others

Conceptual skills the ability to see the organization as a whole, understand how the different parts affect each other, and recognize how the company fits into or is affected by its environment

How to Be an Effective Executive in the Age of Brilliant Machines

In the era of big data, powerful analytics, enterprise software tools, and apps that do just about anything, there's no denying that technology has made many jobs obsolete. Could the same be true for managers? Could technology make management obsolete?

As data science and artificial intelligence begin to permeate business organizations, it will become increasingly critical for managers to have strong human skills. In this era of brilliant machines, managers make the biggest difference by doing the following:

▶ Asking questions—It takes judgment to know who to ask, what questions to ask, and when to ask them.

▶ Attacking exceptions—An algorithm might identify exceptions, but good managers will chase them down to resolve them.

▶ Tolerating ambiguity—The bigger and broader a problem, the better suited it is to a manager who can tolerate ambiguity and has a high level of discernment.

▶ Employing soft skills—Humans have the advantage when it comes to interpersonal skills such as empathy, inspiration, and coaching.

In the era of brilliant machines, the managers who master human skills will be the ones who have the edge.

Source: Irving Wladawksy-Berger, "As Big Data and AI Take Hold, What Will It Take to Be an Effective Executive," *Wall Street Journal*, January 23. 2015. http://blogs.wsj.com/cio/2015/01/23/as-big-data-and-ai-take-hold-what-will-it-take-to-be-an-effective-executive/tab/print/.

parts of the company affect each other, and to recognize how the company fits into or is affected by its external environment such as the local community, social and economic forces, customers, and the competition. Good managers have to be able to recognize, understand, and reconcile multiple complex problems and perspectives. In other words, managers have to be smart! In fact, intelligence makes so much difference for managerial performance that managers with above-average intelligence typically outperform managers of average intelligence by approximately 48 percent.[63] Clearly, companies need to be careful to promote smart workers into management. Conceptual skills increase in importance as managers rise through the management hierarchy.

Good management involves much more than intelligence, however. For example, making the department genius a manager can be disastrous if that genius lacks technical skills, human skills, or one other factor known as the motivation to manage. **Motivation to manage** is an assessment of how motivated employees are to interact with superiors, participate in competitive situations, behave assertively toward others, tell others what to do, reward good behavior and punish poor behavior, perform actions that are highly visible to others, and handle and organize administrative tasks. Managers typically have a stronger motivation to manage than their subordinates, and managers at higher levels usually have a stronger motivation to manage than managers at lower levels. Furthermore, managers with a stronger motivation to manage are promoted faster, are rated as better managers by their employees, and earn more money than managers with a weak motivation to manage.[64]

1-6 MISTAKES MANAGERS MAKE

Another way to understand what it takes to be a manager is to look at the mistakes managers make. In other words, we can learn just as much from what managers shouldn't do as from what they should do. Exhibit 1.5 lists the top ten mistakes managers make.

Several studies of U.S. and British managers have compared "arrivers," or managers who made it all the way to the top of their companies, with "derailers," or managers who were successful early in their careers but were knocked off the fast track by the time they reached the middle to upper levels of management.[65] The researchers found that there were only a few differences between arrivers and

> **Motivation to manage**
> an assessment of how enthusiastic employees are about managing the work of others

Exhibit 1.5
Top Ten Mistakes Managers Make

1. Insensitive to others: abrasive, intimidating, bullying style
2. Cold, aloof, arrogant
3. Betray trust
4. Overly ambitious: thinking of next job, playing politics
5. Specific performance problems with the business
6. Overmanaging: unable to delegate or build a team
7. Unable to staff effectively
8. Unable to think strategically
9. Unable to adapt to boss with different style
10. Overdependent on advocate or mentor

Source: M. W. McCall, Jr., and M. M. Lombardo, "What Makes a Top Executive?" *Psychology Today*, February 1983, 26–31.

derailers. For the most part, both groups were talented, and both groups had weaknesses. But what distinguished derailers from arrivers was that derailers possessed two or more fatal flaws with respect to the way they managed people. Although arrivers were by no means perfect, they usually had no more than one fatal flaw or had found ways to minimize the effects of their flaws on the people with whom they worked.

The top mistake made by derailers was that they were insensitive to others by virtue of their abrasive, intimidating, and bullying management style. The authors of one study described a manager who walked into his subordinate's office and interrupted a meeting by saying, "I need to see you." When the subordinate tried to explain that he was not available because he was in the middle of a meeting, the manager barked, "I don't give a damn. I said I wanted to see you now."[66] Not surprisingly, only 25 percent of derailers were rated by others as being good with people, compared to 75 percent of arrivers.

The second mistake was that derailers were often cold, aloof, or arrogant. Although this sounds like insensitivity to others, it has more to do with derailed

Chrisdorney/Shutterstock.com

managers being so smart, so expert in their areas of knowledge, that they treated others with contempt because they weren't experts, too.[67] For example, AT&T called in an industrial psychologist to counsel its vice president of human resources because she had been blamed for "ruffling too many feathers" at the company.[68] Interviews with the vice president's coworkers and subordinates revealed that they thought she was brilliant, was "smarter and faster than other people," "generates a lot of ideas," and "loves to deal with complex issues." Unfortunately, these smarts were accompanied by a cold, aloof, and arrogant management style. The people she worked with complained that she does "too much too fast," treats coworkers with "disdain," "impairs teamwork," "doesn't always show her warm side," and has "burned too many bridges."[69]

The third mistake made by derailers involved betraying a trust. Betraying a trust doesn't mean being dishonest. Instead, it means making others look bad by not doing what you said you would do when you said you would do it. That mistake, in itself, is not fatal because managers and their workers aren't machines. Tasks go undone in every company every single business day. There's always too much to do and not enough time, people, money, or resources to do it. The fatal betrayal of trust is failing to inform others when things will not be done right or on time. This failure to admit mistakes, failure to quickly inform others of the mistakes, failure to take responsibility for the mistakes, and failure to fix the mistakes without blaming others clearly distinguished the behavior of derailers from arrivers.

The fourth mistake was being overly political and ambitious. Managers who always have their eye on their next job rarely establish more than superficial relationships with peers and coworkers. In their haste to gain credit for successes that would be noticed by upper management, they make the fatal mistake of treating people as though they don't matter. An employee with an overly ambitious boss described him this way: "He treats employees coldly, even cruelly. He assigns blame without regard to responsibility, and takes all the credit for himself. I once had such a boss, and he gave me a new definition of shared risk: If something I did was successful, he took the credit. If it wasn't, I got the blame."[70]

The fatal mistakes of being unable to delegate, build a team, and staff effectively indicate that many derailed managers were unable to make the most basic transition to managerial work: to quit being hands-on doers and get work done through others. Two things go wrong when managers make these mistakes. First, when managers meddle in decisions that their subordinates should be making—when they can't stop being doers—they alienate the people who work for them. Rich Dowd, founder of Dowd Associates, an executive search firm, admits to constantly monitoring and interrupting employees because they weren't doing the job "in the way I saw fit, even when their work was outstanding." According to Richard Kilburg of Johns Hopkins University, when managers interfere with workers' decisions, "You . . . have a tendency to lose your most creative people. They're able to say, 'Screw this. I'm not staying here.'"[71] Indeed, one employee told Dowd that if he was going to do her job for her, she would quit. Second, because they are trying to do their subordinates' jobs in addition to their own, managers who fail to delegate will not have enough time to do much of anything well. An office assistant to a Washington politician came in to work every day to find a long to-do list waiting on her desk, detailing everything she was expected to get done that day, along with how to do it, who to call, and when to give her boss updates on her progress. She said, "Sometimes, this list was 3 or 4 pages long. It must have taken him at least an hour to create."[72]

1-7 THE TRANSITION TO MANAGEMENT: THE FIRST YEAR

In her book *Becoming a Manager: Mastery of a New Identity*, Harvard Business School professor Linda Hill followed the development of nineteen people in their first year as managers. Her study found that becoming a manager produced a profound psychological transition that changed the way these managers viewed themselves and others. As shown in Exhibit 1.6, the evolution of the managers' thoughts, expectations, and realities over the course of their first year in management reveals the magnitude of the changes they experienced.

Initially, the managers in Hill's study believed that their job was to exercise formal authority and to manage tasks—basically being the boss, telling others what to do, making decisions, and getting things done. One of the managers Hill interviewed said, "Being the manager means running my own office, using my ideas and thoughts." Another said, "[The office is] my baby. It's my job to make sure it works."[73] In fact, most

Exhibit 1.6
Stages in the Transition to Management

MANAGERS' INITIAL EXPECTATIONS	AFTER SIX MONTHS AS A MANAGER	AFTER A YEAR AS A MANAGER
JAN FEB MAR	APR MAY JUN	JUL AUG SEP OCT NOV DEC
• Be the boss	• Initial expectations were wrong	• No longer a doer
• Formal authority	• Fast pace	• Communication, listening, and positive reinforcement
• Manage tasks	• Heavy workload	• Learning to adapt to and control stress
• Job is not managing people	• Job is to be problem solver and troubleshooter for subordinates	• Job is people development

Source: L.A. Hill, *Becoming a Manager: Mastery of a New Identity* (Boston: Harvard Business School Press, 1992).

of the new managers were attracted to management positions because they wanted to be in charge. Surprisingly, the new managers did not believe that their job was to manage people. The only aspects of people management mentioned by the new managers were hiring and firing.

After six months, most of the new managers had concluded that their initial expectations about managerial work were wrong. Management wasn't just about being the boss, making decisions, and telling others what to do. The first surprise was the fast pace and heavy workload involved. Said one of Hill's managers, "This job is much harder than you think. It is 40 to 50 percent more work than being a producer! Who would have ever guessed?" The pace of managerial work was startling, too. Another manager said, "You have eight or nine people looking for your time . . . coming into and out of your office all day long." A somewhat frustrated manager declared that management was "a job that never ended . . . a job you couldn't get your hands around."[74]

Informal descriptions like these are consistent with studies indicating that the average first-line manager spends no more than two minutes on a task before being interrupted by a request from a subordinate, a phone call, or an email. The pace is somewhat less hurried for top managers, who spend an average of approximately nine minutes on a task before having to switch to another. In practice, this means that supervisors may perform thirty tasks per hour, while top managers perform seven tasks per hour, with each task typically different from the one that preceded it. A manager described this frenetic level of activity by saying, "The only time you are in control is when you shut your door, and then I feel I am not doing the job I'm supposed to be doing, which is being with the people."[75]

The other major surprise after six months on the job was that the managers' expectations about what they should do as managers were very different from their subordinates' expectations. Initially, the managers defined their jobs as helping their subordinates perform their jobs well. For the managers, who still defined themselves as doers rather than managers, assisting their subordinates meant going out on sales calls or handling customer complaints. One

manager said, "I like going out with the rep, who may need me to lend him my credibility as manager. I like the challenge, the joy in closing. I go out with the reps and we make the call and talk about the customer; it's fun."[76] But when the managers "assisted" in this way, their subordinates were resentful and viewed their help as interference. The subordinates wanted their managers to help them by solving problems that they couldn't solve themselves. After the managers realized this distinction, they embraced their role as problem solver and troubleshooter. Thus, they could help without interfering with their subordinates' jobs.

After a year on the job, most of the managers thought of themselves as managers and no longer as doers. In making the transition, they finally realized that people management was the most important part of their job. One of Hill's interviewees summarized the lesson that had taken him a year to learn by saying, "As many demands as managers have on their time, I think their primary responsibility is people development. Not production, but people development."[77] Another indication of how much their views had changed was that most of the managers now regretted the rather heavy-handed approach they had used in their early attempts to manage their subordinates. "I wasn't good at managing . . . , so I was bossy like a first-grade teacher." "Now I see that I started out as a drill sergeant. I was inflexible, just a lot of how-to's." By the end of the year, most of the managers had abandoned their authoritarian approach for one based on communication, listening, and positive reinforcement.

Finally, after beginning their year as managers in frustration, the managers came to feel comfortable with their subordinates, with the demands of their jobs, and with their emerging managerial styles. While being managers had made them acutely aware of their limitations and their need to develop as people, it also provided them with an unexpected reward of coaching and developing the people who worked for them. One manager said, "It gives me the best feeling to see somebody do something well after I have helped them. I get excited." Another stated, "I realize now that when I accepted the position of branch manager that it is truly an exciting vocation.

It is truly awesome, even at this level; it can be terribly challenging and terribly exciting."[78]

1-8 COMPETITIVE ADVANTAGE THROUGH PEOPLE

If you walk down the aisle of the business section in your local bookstore, you'll find hundreds of books that explain precisely what companies need to do to be successful. Unfortunately, the best-selling business books tend to be faddish, changing dramatically every few years. One thing that hasn't changed, though, is the importance of good people and good management: companies can't succeed for long without them.

In his books *Competitive Advantage through People: Unleashing the Power of the Work Force* and *The Human Equation: Building Profits by Putting People First*, Stanford University business professor Jeffrey Pfeffer contends that what separates top-performing companies from their competitors is the way they treat their workforces—in other words, their management style.[79]

Pfeffer found that managers in top-performing companies used ideas such as employment security, selective hiring, self-managed teams and decentralization, high pay contingent on company performance, extensive training, reduced status distinctions (between managers and employees), and extensive sharing of financial information to achieve financial performance that, on average, was 40 percent higher than that of other companies. These ideas, which are explained in detail in Exhibit 1.7, help organizations develop workforces that are smarter, better trained, more motivated, and more committed than their competitors' workforces. And—as indicated by the phenomenal growth and return on investment earned by these companies—smarter, better trained, more motivated, and more committed workforces provide superior products and service to customers. Such customers keep buying and, by telling others about their positive experiences, bring in new customers.

According to Pfeffer, companies that invest in their people will create long-lasting competitive advantages

Exhibit 1.7
Competitive Advantage Through People: Management Practices

1. Employment Security—Employment security is the ultimate form of commitment companies can make to their workers. Employees can innovate and increase company productivity without fearing the loss of their jobs.

2. Selective Hiring—If employees are the basis for a company's competitive advantage, and those employees have employment security, then the company needs to aggressively recruit and selectively screen applicants in order to hire the most talented employees available.

3. Self-Managed Teams and Decentralization—Self-managed teams are responsible for their own hiring, purchasing, job assignments, and production. Self-managed teams can often produce enormous increases in productivity through increased employee commitment and creativity. Decentralization allows employees who are closest to (and most knowledgeable about) problems, production, and customers to make timely decisions. Decentralization increases employee satisfaction and commitment.

4. High Wages Contingent on Organizational Performance—High wages are needed to attract and retain talented workers and to indicate that the organization values its workers. Employees, like company founders, shareholders, and managers, need to share in the financial rewards when the company is successful. Why? Because employees who have a financial stake in their companies are more likely to take a long-run view of the business and think like business owners.

5. Training and Skill Development—Like a high-tech company that spends millions of dollars to upgrade computers or research and development labs, a company whose competitive advantage is based on its people must invest in the training and skill development of its people.

6. Reduction of Status Differences—A company should treat everyone, no matter what the job, as equal. There are no reserved parking spaces. Everyone eats in the same cafeteria and has similar benefits. The result is improved communication as employees focus on problems and solutions rather than on how they are less valued than managers.

7. Sharing Information—If employees are to make decisions that are good for the long-term health and success of the company, they need to be given information about costs, finances, productivity, development times, and strategies that was previously known only by company managers.

Source: J. Pfeffer, *The Human Equation: Building Profits by Putting People First* (Boston: Harvard Business School Press, 1996).

The CFO: Not Just A Bean Counter

Having served as CFO at ADT Corp., Nalco Holdings Co., UAL Corp., and currently CFO at Xerox Corp., Kathryn Mikells knows a thing or two about the challenges of being a new CFO. Mikells describes several keys that can help new CFOs be successful. One of the most important steps is taking the time to talk to senior management and get a sense of where the company is and what challenges it faces. She also believes that the CFO should involve herself in strategic planning. "Strategy tends to tie directly into resource allocation and capital allocation," she says. "It's really important that [they] all link together." She also stresses the importance of getting a good feel for your team. A new CFO wants to quickly figure out what direction the team is going and what kind of skills the members have.

Source: K. Mikells, "Xerox CFO; An Atmosphere for Transformation," Interview by N. Knox, *The Wall Street* Journal, April 4, 2014, accessed April 9, 2014. http://blogs.wsj.com /cfo/2014/04/04/xerox-cfo-an-atmosphere-for-transformation/?mod=WSJ_business_cfo.

that are difficult for other companies to duplicate. Other studies also clearly demonstrate that sound management practices can produce substantial advantages in four critical areas of organizational performance: sales revenues, profits, stock market returns, and customer satisfaction.

In terms of sales revenues and profits, a study of nearly 1,000 U.S. firms found that companies which use *just some* of the ideas shown in Exhibit 1.7 had $27,044 more sales per employee and $3,814 more profit per employee than companies that didn't. For a 100-person company, these differences amount to $2.7 million more in sales and nearly $400,000 more in annual profit! For a 1,000-person company, the difference grows to $27 million more in sales and $4 million more in annual profit![80]

Another study that considers the effect of investing in people on company sales found that poorly performing companies were able to improve their average return on investment from 5.1 percent to 19.7 percent and increase sales by $94,000 per employee. They did this by adopting management techniques as simple as setting performance expectations (establishing goals, results, and schedules), coaching (informal, ongoing discussions between managers and subordinates about what is being done well and what could be done better), reviewing employee performance (annual, formal discussion about results), and rewarding employee performance (adjusting salaries and bonuses based on employee performance and results).[81] Two decades of research across 92 companies indicates that the average increase in company performance from

using these management practices is typically around 20 percent.[82] So, in addition to significantly improving the profitability of healthy companies, sound management practices can turn around failing companies.

To determine how investing in people affects stock market performance, researchers matched companies on *Fortune* magazine's list of "100 Best Companies to Work for in America" with companies that were similar in industry, size, and—this is key—operating performance. Both sets of companies were equally good performers; the key difference was how well they treated their employees. For both sets of companies, the researchers found that employee attitudes such as job satisfaction changed little from year to year. The people who worked for the "100 Best" companies were consistently much more satisfied with their jobs and employers year after year than were employees in the matched companies. More importantly, those stable differences in employee attitudes were strongly related to differences in stock market performance. Over a three-year period, an investment in the "100 Best" would have resulted in an 82 percent cumulative stock return compared with just 37 percent for the matched companies.[83] This difference is remarkable given that both sets of companies were equally good performers at the beginning of the period.

Finally, research also indicates that managers have an important effect on customer satisfaction. Many people find this surprising. They don't understand how managers, who are largely responsible for what goes on inside the company, can affect what goes on outside the company. They wonder how managers, who often interact with customers under negative conditions (when customers are angry or dissatisfied), can actually improve customer satisfaction. It turns out that managers influence customer satisfaction through employee satisfaction. When employees are satisfied with their jobs, their bosses, and the companies they work for, they provide much better service to customers.[84] In turn, customers are more satisfied, too. In fact, customers of companies on *Fortune*'s list of "100 Best," where employees are much more satisfied with their jobs and their companies, have much higher customer satisfaction scores than do customers of comparable companies that are not on *Fortune*'s list. Over an eight-year period, that difference in customer satisfaction also resulted in a 14 percent annual stock market return for the "100 Best" companies compared to a 6 percent return for the overall stock market.[85]

You will learn more about the service-profit chain in Chapter 18 on managing service and manufacturing operations.

STUDY TOOLS 1

LOCATED IN TEXTBOOK

☐ Rip-out and review chapter review card

LOCATED AT WWW.CENGAGEBRAIN.COM

☐ Review key term flashcards and create your own from StudyBits

☐ Track your knowledge and understanding of key concepts, using the concept tracker

☐ Complete practice and graded quizzes to prepare for tests

☐ Complete interactive content within the exposition

☐ View chapter highlight box content at the beginning of each chapter

2 The History of Management

LEARNING OUTCOMES

2-1 Explain the origins of management.

2-2 Explain the history of scientific management.

2-3 Discuss the history of bureaucratic and administrative management.

2-4 Explain the history of human relations management.

2-5 Discuss the history of operations, information, systems, and contingency management.

After you finish this chapter, go to **PAGE 42** for **STUDY TOOLS**

2-1 THE ORIGINS OF MANAGEMENT

Each day, managers are asked to solve challenging problems with a limited amount of time, people, or resources. Yet it's still their responsibility to get things done on time and within budget. Tell today's managers to "reward workers for improved production or performance," "set specific goals to increase motivation," or "innovate to create and sustain a competitive advantage," and they'll respond, "Duh! Who doesn't know that?" A mere 125 years ago, however, business ideas and practices were so different that today's widely accepted management ideas would have been as self-evident as space travel, smart phones, and flying drones. In fact, management jobs and careers didn't exist 125 years ago, so management was not yet a field of study. Now, of course, managers and management are such an important part of the business world that it's hard to imagine organizations without them. So if there were no managers 125 years ago, but you can't walk down the hall today without bumping into one, where did management come from?

Although we can find the seeds of many of today's management ideas throughout history, not until the past two centuries did systematic changes in the nature of work and organizations create a compelling need for managers.

2-1a Management Ideas and Practices throughout History

Examples of management thought and practice can be found throughout history.[1] For example, the earliest recorded instance of information management dates to ancient Sumer (modern Iraq), *circa* 8000–3000 BCE. Sumerian businessmen used small clay tokens to calculate quantities of grain and livestock—and later, value-added goods such as perfume or pottery—that they owned and traded in temples and at city gates. Different shapes and sizes represented different types and quantities of goods. The tokens were also used to store data. They were kept in small clay envelopes, and the token shapes were impressed on the outside of the envelope to indicate what was inside. Eventually, someone figured out that it was easier to just write these symbols with a stylus on a tablet instead of using the tokens. In the end, the new technology of *writing* led to more efficient management of the business of Sumerian temples.[2]

A task as enormous as building the great pyramids in Egypt was bound to present practical problems that would lead to the development of management ideas. Egyptians recognized the need for planning, organizing, and controlling; for submitting written requests; and for consulting staff for advice before making decisions. The enormity of the task they faced is evident in the pyramid of King Khufu, which contains 2.3 million blocks of stone. Each block had to be quarried, cut to precise size and shape, cured (hardened in the sun), transported by boat for two to three days, moved to the construction site, numbered to identify where it would be placed, and then shaped and smoothed so that it would fit perfectly into place. It took 20,000 workers 23 years to complete this pyramid; more than 8,000 were needed just to quarry and transport the stones. A typical quarry expedition might include 100 army officers, 50 government and religious officials, and 200 members of the king's court to lead; 130 stonemasons to cut the stones; and 5,000 soldiers, 800 barbarians, and 2,000 bond servants to load and unload the stones from the ships.[3]

Exhibit 2.1 shows how other management ideas and practices throughout history relate to the management functions we discuss in this textbook.

2-1b Why We Need Managers Today

Working from 8:00 a.m. to 5:00 p.m., coffee breaks, lunch hours, crushing rush hour traffic, and punching a time clock are things we associate with today's working world. Work hasn't always been this way, however. In fact, the design of jobs and organizations has changed dramatically over the past 500 years. For most of humankind's history, for example, people didn't commute to work.[4] Work usually occurred in homes or on farms. In 1720, almost 80 percent of the 5.5 million people in England lived and worked in the country. And as recently as 1870, two-thirds of Americans earned their living from agriculture. Even most of those who didn't earn their living from agriculture didn't commute to work. Blacksmiths, furniture makers, leather goods makers, and other skilled tradespeople or craftspeople who formed trade guilds (the historical predecessors of labor unions) in England as early as 1093 typically worked out of shops in or next to their homes.[5] Likewise, cottage workers worked with each other out of small homes that were often built in a semicircle. A family in each cottage would complete a different production step, and work passed from one cottage to the next until production was complete. With small, self-organized work groups, no commute, no bosses, and no common building, there wasn't a strong need for management.

Exhibit 2.1
Management Ideas and Practices throughout History

Time	Individual or Group	Planning	Organizing	Leading	Controlling	Contributions to Management Thought and Practice
5000 BCE	Sumerians				√	Written record keeping
4000 BCE to 2000 BCE	Egyptians	√	√		√	Planning, organizing, and controlling to build the pyramids; submitting requests in writing; making decisions after consulting staff for advice
1800 BCE	Hammurabi				√	Controls and using witnesses in legal cases
600 BCE	Nebuchadnezzar		√	√		Wage incentives and production control
500 BCE	Sun Tzu	√		√		Strategy and identifying and attacking opponents' weaknesses
400 BCE	Xenophon	√	√	√	√	Management as separate art
400 BCE	Cyrus		√	√	√	Human relations and motion study
175	Cato		√			Job descriptions
284	Diocletian		√			Delegation of authority
900	al-Farabi			√		Leadership traits
1100	Ghazali			√		Managerial traits
1418	Barbarigo		√			Different organizational forms/structures
1436	Venetians				√	Numbering, standardization, and interchangeability of parts
1500	Sir Thomas More			√		Critique of poor management and leadership
1525	Machiavelli		√	√		Cohesiveness, power, and leadership in organizations

Source: C. S. George, Jr., *The History of Management Thought* (Englewood Cliffs, NJ: Prentice Hall, 1972).

During the Industrial Revolution (1750–1900), however, jobs and organizations changed dramatically.[6] First, unskilled laborers running machines began to replace high-paid, skilled artisans. This change was made possible by the availability of power (steam engines and, later, electricity) as well as numerous related inventions, including Darby's coke-smelting process and Cort's puddling and rolling process (both for making iron), as well as Hargreaves's spinning jenny and Arkwright's water frame (both for spinning cotton). Whereas artisans made entire goods by themselves by hand, this new production system was based on a division of labor: each worker, interacting with machines, performed separate, highly specialized tasks that were but a small part of all the steps required to make manufactured goods. Mass production was born as rope- and chain-driven assembly lines moved work to stationary workers who concentrated on performing one small task over and over again. While workers focused on their singular tasks, managers were needed to coordinate the different parts of the production system and optimize its overall performance. Productivity skyrocketed at companies that understood this. At **Ford Motor Company**, where the assembly line was developed, the time required to assemble a car dropped from 12.5 work hours to just 93 minutes after switching to mass production.[7]

Second, instead of being performed in fields, homes, or small shops, jobs occurred in large, formal organizations where hundreds, if not thousands, of people worked under one roof.[8] In 1849, for example, **Chicago Harvester** (the predecessor of International Harvester) ran the largest factory in the United States with just 123 workers. Yet by 1913, Henry Ford employed 12,000 employees in his Highland Park, Michigan, factory alone. Because the number of people working in manufacturing quintupled from 1860 to 1890, and individual factories employed so many workers under one roof, companies now had a strong need for disciplinary rules to impose order and structure. For the first time, they needed managers who knew how to organize large groups, work with employees, and make good decisions.

2-2 SCIENTIFIC MANAGEMENT

Before 1880, business educators taught only basic book-keeping and secretarial skills, and no one published books or articles about management.[9] Today you can turn to dozens of academic journals (such as the Academy of Management's *Journal* or *Review*, *Administrative Science Quarterly*, the *Strategic Management Journal*, and the *Journal of Applied Psychology*), hundreds of business school and practitioner journals (such as *Harvard Business Review*, *MIT Sloan Management Review*, and the *Academy of Management Perspectives*), and thousands of books and articles if you have a question about management. In the next four sections, you will learn about some important contributors to the field of management and how their ideas shaped our current understanding of management theory and practice.

Bosses, who were hired by the company owner or founder, used to make decisions by the seat of their pants—haphazardly, without any systematic study, thought, or collection of information. If the bosses decided that workers should work twice as fast, little or no thought was given to worker motivation. If workers resisted, the bosses often resorted to physical beatings to get workers to work faster, harder, or longer. With no incentives for bosses and workers to cooperate with one another, both groups played the system by trying to take advantage of each other. Moreover, each worker did the same job in his or her own way with different methods and different tools. In short, there were no procedures to standardize operations, no standards by which to judge whether performance was good or bad, and no follow-up to determine whether productivity or quality actually improved when changes were made.[10]

This all changed, however, with the advent of **scientific management**, which involved thorough study and testing of different work methods to identify the best, most efficient ways to complete a job.

Let's find out more about scientific management by learning about 2-2a Frederick W. Taylor, the father of scientific management; 2-2b Frank and Lillian Gilbreth and motion studies; and 2-2c Henry Gantt and his Gantt charts.

2-2a Father of Scientific Management: Frederick W. Taylor

Frederick W. Taylor (1856–1915), the father of scientific management, began his career as a worker at **Midvale**

Frederick W. Taylor was affected by his three-year struggle to get the men who worked for him to do, as he called it, "a fair day's work."

ullstein bild via Getty Images

Steel Company. He was promoted to patternmaker, supervisor, and then chief engineer. At Midvale, Taylor was deeply affected by his three-year struggle to get the men who worked for him to do, as he called it, "a fair day's work." Taylor, who had worked alongside the men as a coworker before becoming their boss, said, "We who were the workmen of that shop had the quantity output carefully agreed upon for everything that was turned out in the shop. We limited the output to about, I should think, one third of what we could very well have done." Taylor explained that, as soon as he became the boss, "the men who were working under me . . . knew that I was onto the whole game of **soldiering**, or deliberately restricting output."[11] When Taylor told his workers, "I have accepted a job under the management of this company and

> **Scientific management** thoroughly studying and testing different work methods to identify the best, most efficient way to complete a job
>
> **Soldiering** when workers deliberately slow their pace or restrict their work output

Exhibit 2.2
Taylor's Four Principles of Scientific Management

First:	Develop a science for each element of a man's work, which replaces the old rule-of-thumb method.
Second:	Scientifically select and then train, teach, and develop the workman, whereas in the past, he chose his own work and trained himself as best he could.
Third:	Heartily cooperate with the men so as to ensure all of the work being done is in accordance with the principles of the science that has been developed.
Fourth:	There is an almost equal division of the work and the responsibility between the management and the workmen. The management take over all the work for which they are better fitted than the workmen, while in the past, almost all of the work and the greater part of the responsibility were thrown upon the men.

Source: F. W. Taylor, *The Principles of Scientific Management* (New York: Harper, 1911).

I am on the other side of the fence . . . I am going to try to get a bigger output," the workers responded, "We warn you, Fred, if you try to bust any of these rates [a **rate buster** was someone who worked faster than the group] we will have you over the fence in six weeks."[12]

Over the next three years, Taylor tried everything he could think of to improve output. By doing the job himself, he showed workers that it was possible to produce more output. He hired new workers and trained them himself, hoping they would produce more. But "very heavy social pressure" from the other workers kept them from doing so. Pushed by Taylor, the workers began breaking their machines so that they couldn't produce. Taylor responded by fining them every time they broke a machine and for any violation of the rules, no matter how small, such as being late to work. Tensions became so severe that some of the workers threatened to shoot Taylor. Looking back at the situation, Taylor reflected, "It is a horrid life for any man to live, not to be able to look any workman in the face all day long without seeing hostility there and feeling that every man around one is his virtual enemy." He said, "I made up my mind either to get out of the business entirely and go into some other line of work or to find some remedy for this unbearable condition."[13]

The remedy that Taylor eventually developed was scientific management. Taylor, who once described scientific management as "seventy-five percent science and twenty-five percent common sense," emphasized that the goal of scientific management was to use systematic study to find the "one best way" of doing each task. To do that, managers had to follow the four principles shown in Exhibit 2.2. The first principle was to "develop a science" for each element of work. Study it. Analyze it. Determine the "one best way" to do the work. For example, one of Taylor's controversial proposals at the time was to give rest breaks to factory workers doing physical labor. We take morning, lunch, and afternoon breaks for granted, but in Taylor's day, factory workers were expected to work without stopping.[14] When Taylor said that breaks would increase worker productivity, no one believed him. Nonetheless, through systematic experiments, he showed that workers receiving frequent rest breaks were able to greatly increase their daily output.

Second, managers had to scientifically select, train, teach, and develop workers to help them reach their full potential. Before Taylor, supervisors often hired on the basis of favoritism and nepotism. Who you knew was often more important than what you could do. By contrast, Taylor instructed supervisors to hire "first-class" workers on the basis of their aptitude to do a job well. In one of the first applications of this principle, physical reaction times were used to select bicycle ball-bearing inspectors, who had to be able to examine ball bearings as fast as they were produced on a production line. For similar reasons, Taylor also recommended that companies train and develop their workers—a rare practice at the time.

The third principle instructed managers to cooperate with employees to ensure that the scientific principles were actually implemented. Labor unrest was widespread at the time; the number of labor strikes against companies doubled between 1893 and 1904. As Taylor knew from personal experience, workers and management more often than not viewed each other as enemies. Taylor's advice ran contrary to the common wisdom of the day. He said, "The majority of these men believe that the fundamental interests of employees and employers are necessarily antagonistic. Scientific management, on

Rate buster a group member whose work pace is significantly faster than the normal pace in his or her group

MGMT Trends

For modern workers, the principles of scientific management, derived from studying bricklaying or shoveling, seem outdated. While today's workers shovel information instead, they aren't any less concerned about productivity, especially if they get 200+ emails a day! Like Taylor and the Gilbreths, today's researchers are exploring ways to make information workers more productive. What they're finding is that self-control, the ability to concentrate, stay on task, and not get sidetracked by nonwork activities (that is, Facebook), is key. In a year-long study of Indian data entry workers who were paid 2 rupees for every 100 data fields they completed, half the employees established daily targets, say, 5,000 data fields, for which they were then paid the normal rate of 2 rupees per 100 data fields. But if they fell short of the target, they were paid just 1 rupee per 100 data fields. Daily targets helped workers maintain self-control, producing and earning 50 percent more than workers under the regular system! Just as scientific management and time-and-motion studies revolutionized factory productivity a century ago, it just might be that tools which maximize self-control hold the same potential to increase productivity for today's information workers.

Source: S. Mullainathan, "Looking at Productivity as a State of Mind," *International New York Times*, September 28, 2014, BU6.

friendly help from those who are over him, instead of being, at the one extreme, driven or coerced by his bosses, and at the other left, to his own unaided devices."[16]

Above all, Taylor believed these principles could be used to determine a "fair day's work," that is, what an average worker could produce at a reasonable pace, day in and day out. After that was determined, it was management's responsibility to pay workers fairly for that fair day's work. In essence, Taylor was trying to align management and employees so that what was good for employees was also good for management. In this way, he believed, workers and managers could avoid the conflicts he had experienced at Midvale Steel.

Although Taylor remains a controversial figure among some academics who believe that his ideas were bad for workers, his key ideas have stood the test of time.[17] These include using systematic analysis to identify the best methods; scientifically selecting, training, and developing workers; promoting cooperation between management and labor; developing standardized approaches and tools; setting specific tasks or goals and then rewarding workers with financial incentives; and giving workers shorter work hours and frequent breaks. In fact, his ideas are so well accepted and widely used that we take most of them for granted. As eminent management scholar Edwin Locke said, "The point is not, as is often claimed, that he was 'right in the context of his time,' but is now outdated, but that *most of his insights are still valid today*."[18]

2-2b Motion Studies: Frank and Lillian Gilbreth

The husband and wife team of Frank and Lillian Gilbreth are best known for their use of motion studies to simplify work, but they also made significant contributions to the employment of disabled workers and to the field of industrial psychology. Like Taylor, their early experiences significantly shaped their interests and contributions to management.

Though admitted to MIT, Frank Gilbreth (1868–1924) began his career as an apprentice bricklayer. While learning the trade, he noticed the bricklayers using three different sets of motions—one to teach others how to lay bricks, a second to work at a slow pace, and a third to work at a fast pace.[19] Wondering which was best, he studied the various approaches and began eliminating unnecessary motions. For example, by designing a stand that could be raised to waist height, he eliminated the need to bend over to pick up each brick. Turning to grab a brick was faster and easier than bending down. By having lower-paid workers place all the bricks with their most

the contrary, has for its very foundation the firm conviction that the true interests of the two are one and the same; that prosperity for the employer cannot exist through a long term of years unless it is accompanied by prosperity for the employee and vice versa; and that it is possible to give the workman what he most wants—high wages—and the employer what he wants—a low labor cost for his manufactures."[15] (See the MGMT Trends box for more on this point.)

The fourth principle of scientific management was to divide the work and the responsibility equally between management and workers. Prior to Taylor, workers alone were held responsible for productivity and performance. But, said Taylor, "Almost every act of the workman should be preceded by one or more preparatory acts of the management, which enable him to do his work better and quicker than he otherwise could. And each man should daily be taught by and receive the most

Frank and Lillian Gilbreth are best known for their use of motion studies to simplify work.

were hand cranked and thus variable in their film speed, so Frank invented the microchronometer, a large clock that could record time to 1/2,000th of a second. By placing the microchonometer next to the worker in the camera's field of vision and attaching a flashing strobe light to the worker's hands to better identify the direction and sequence of key movements, the Gilbreths could use film to detect and precisely time even the slightest, fastest movements. Motion study typically yielded production increases of 25 to 300 percent.[21]

Taylor also strove to simplify work, but he did so by managing time rather than motion as the Gilbreths did.[22] Taylor developed time study to put an end to soldiering and to determine what could be considered a fair day's work. **Time study** worked by timing how long it took a "first-class man" to complete each part of his job. A standard time was established after allowing for rest periods, and a worker's pay would increase or decrease depending on whether the worker exceeded or fell below that standard.

Lillian Gilbreth (1878–1972) was an important contributor to management in her own right. She was the first woman to receive a PhD in industrial psychology as well as the first woman to become a member of the Society of Industrial Engineers and the American Society of Mechanical Engineers. When Frank died in 1924, she continued the work of their management consulting company (which they had shared for over a dozen years). Lillian, who was concerned with the human side of work, was one of the first contributors to industrial psychology, originating ways to improve office communication, incentive programs, job satisfaction, and management training. Her work also convinced the government to enact laws regarding workplace safety, ergonomics, and child labor.

2-2c Charts: Henry Gantt

Henry Gantt (1861–1919) was first a protégé and then an associate of Frederick W. Taylor. Gantt is best known for the Gantt chart, but he also made significant contributions to management with respect to pay-for-performance plans and the training and development of workers. As shown in Exhibit 2.3, a **Gantt chart** visually indicates what tasks must be completed at which times in order to complete a project. It accomplishes this by showing time in various units on the x-axis and tasks on the y-axis. For example, Exhibit 2.3 shows that the following tasks must be completed by the following dates: in order to start construction on a new company headquarters by the week of November 18, the architectural firm must be selected by October 7, architectural planning done by November 4, permits obtained from the city by

attractive side up, bricklayers didn't waste time turning a brick over to find it. By mixing a more consistent mortar, bricklayers no longer had to tap each brick numerous times to put it in the right position. Together, Gilbreth's improvements raised productivity from 120 to 350 bricks per hour and from 1,000 bricks to 2,700 bricks per day.

As a result of his experience with bricklaying, Gilbreth and his wife, Lillian, developed a long-term interest in using motion study to simplify work, improve productivity, and reduce the level of effort required to safely perform a job. Indeed, Frank Gilbreth said, "The greatest waste in the world comes from needless, ill-directed, and ineffective motions."[20] **Motion study** broke each task or job into separate motions and then eliminated those that were unnecessary or repetitive. Because many motions were completed very quickly, the Gilbreths used motion-picture films, then a relatively new technology, to analyze jobs. Most film cameras at that time

Motion study breaking each task or job into its separate motions and then eliminating those that are unnecessary or repetitive

Time study timing how long it takes good workers to complete each part of their jobs

Gantt chart a graphical chart that shows which tasks must be completed at which times in order to complete a project or task

Exhibit 2.3
Gantt Chart for Starting Construction on a New Headquarters

Tasks	Weeks	23 Sep to 29 Sep	30 Sep to 6 Oct	7 Oct to 13 Oct	14 Oct to 20 Oct	21 Oct to 27 Oct	28 Oct to 3 Nov	4 Nov to 10 Nov	11 Nov to 17 Nov	18 Nov to 25 Nov
Interview and select architectural firm		Architect by October 7								
Hold weekly planning meetings with architects				Planning with architects by November 4						
Obtain permits and approval from city							Permits and approval by November 11			
Begin preparing site for construction								Site preparation done by November 18		
Finalize loans and financing									Financing finalized by November 18	
Begin construction										Start building

© Cengage Learning

iStockphoto.com/Nullplus

November 11, site preparation finished by November 18, and loans and financing finalized by November 18.

Though simple and straightforward, Gantt charts were revolutionary in the era of seat-of-the-pants management because of the detailed planning information they provided. As Gantt wrote, "By using the graphical forms, its [the Gantt chart's] value is very much increased, for the general appearance of the sheet is sufficient to tell how closely the schedule is being lived up to; in other words, whether the plant is being run efficiently or not."[23] Gantt said, "Such sheets show at a glance where the delays occur, and indicate what must have our attention in order to keep up the proper output." The use of Gantt charts is so widespread today that nearly all project management software and computer spreadsheets have the capability to create charts that track and visually display the progress being made on a project.

Finally, Gantt, along with Taylor, was one of the first to strongly recommend that companies train and develop their workers.[24] In his work with companies, he found that workers achieved their best performance levels if they were trained first. At the time, however, supervisors were reluctant to teach workers what they knew for fear that they could lose their jobs to more knowledgeable workers. Gantt overcame the supervisors' resistance by rewarding them with bonuses for properly training all of their workers. Said Gantt, "This is the first recorded attempt to make it in the financial interest of the foreman to teach the individual worker, and the importance of it cannot be overestimated, for it changes the foreman from a driver of men to their friend and helper."[25] Gantt's approach to training was straightforward: "(1) A scientific investigation in detail of each piece of work, and the determination of the best method and the shortest time in which the work can be done. (2) A teacher capable of teaching the best method and the shortest time. (3) Reward for both teacher and pupil when the latter is successful."[26]

2-3 BUREAUCRATIC AND ADMINISTRATIVE MANAGEMENT

Bureaucracy the exercise of control on the basis of knowledge, expertise, or experience

The field of scientific management developed quickly in the United States between 1895 and 1920 and focused on improving the efficiency of manufacturing facilities and their workers. At about the same time, equally important ideas about bureaucratic and administrative management were developing in Europe. German sociologist Max Weber presented a new way to run entire organizations (bureaucratic management) in *The Theory of Social and Economic Organization*, published in 1922. Henri Fayol, an experienced French CEO, published his ideas about how and what managers should do in their jobs (administrative management) in *General and Industrial Management* in 1916.

*Let's find out more about the contributions Weber and Fayol made to management by learning about **2-3a bureaucratic management** and **2-3b administrative management.***

2-3a Bureaucratic Management: Max Weber

Today, when we hear the term *bureaucracy*, we think of inefficiency and red tape, incompetence and ineffectiveness, and rigid administrators blindly enforcing nonsensical rules. When German sociologist Max Weber (1864–1920) first proposed the idea of bureaucratic organizations, however, these problems were associated with monarchies and patriarchies rather than bureaucracies. In monarchies, where kings, queens, sultans, and emperors ruled, and patriarchies, where a council of elders, wise men, or male heads of extended families ruled, the top leaders typically achieved their positions by virtue of birthright. For example, when the queen died, her oldest son became king, regardless of his intelligence, experience, education, or desire. Likewise, promotion to prominent positions of authority in monarchies and patriarchies was based on who you knew (politics), who you were (heredity), or ancient rules and traditions.

It was against this historical background of monarchical and patriarchal rule that Weber proposed the then-new idea of bureaucracy. *Bureaucracy* comes from the French word *bureaucratie*. Because *bureau* means desk or office and *cratie* or *cracy* means to rule, *bureaucracy* literally means to rule from a desk or office. According to Weber, **bureaucracy** is "the exercise of control on the basis of knowledge."[27] Rather than ruling by virtue of favoritism or personal or family connections, people in a bureaucracy would lead by virtue of their rational-legal authority—in other words, their knowledge, expertise, or experience. Furthermore, the aim of bureaucracy is not to protect authority but to achieve an organization's goals in the most efficient way possible.

Exhibit 2.4 shows the seven elements that, according to Weber, characterize bureaucracies. First, instead of hiring people because of their family or political connections or personal loyalty, they should be hired because

Exhibit 2.4
Elements of Bureaucratic Organizations

Qualification-based hiring:	Employees are hired on the basis of their technical training or educational background.
Merit-based promotion:	Promotion is based on experience or achievement. Managers, not organizational owners, decide who is promoted.
Chain of command:	Each job occurs within a hierarchy, the chain of command, in which each position reports and is accountable to a higher position. A grievance procedure and a right to appeal protect people in lower positions.
Division of labor:	Tasks, responsibilities, and authority are clearly divided and defined.
Impartial application of rules and procedures:	Rules and procedures apply to all members of the organization and will be applied in an impartial manner, regardless of one's position or status.
Recorded in writing:	All administrative decisions, acts, rules, and procedures will be recorded in writing.
Managers separate from owners:	The owners of an organization should not manage or supervise the organization.

Source: M. Weber, *The Theory of Social and Economic Organization*, trans. A. Henderson and T. Parsons (New York: The Free Press, 1947), 329–334.

their technical training or education qualifies them to do the job well. Second, along the same lines, promotion within the company should no longer be based on who you know (politics) or who you are (heredity) but on your experience or achievements. And to further limit the influence of personal connections in the promotion process, *managers* rather than organizational owners should decide who gets promoted. Third, each position or job is part of a chain of command that clarifies who reports to whom throughout the organization. Those higher in the chain of command have the right, if they so choose, to give commands, take action, and make decisions concerning activities occurring anywhere below them in the chain. Unlike in many monarchies or patriarchies, however, those lower in the chain of command are protected by a grievance procedure that gives them the right to appeal the decisions of those in higher positions. Fourth, to increase efficiency and effectiveness, tasks and responsibilities should be separated and assigned to those best qualified to complete them. Authority is vested in these task-defined positions rather than in people, and the authority of each position is clearly defined in order to reduce confusion and conflict. If you move to a different job in a bureaucracy, your authority increases or decreases commensurate with the responsibilities of that job. Fifth, because of his strong distaste for favoritism, Weber believed that an organization's rules and procedures should apply to all members regardless of their position or status. Sixth, to ensure consistency and fairness over time and across different leaders and supervisors, all rules, procedures, and decisions should be recorded in writing. Finally, to reduce favoritism, "professional" managers rather than company owners should manage or supervise the organization.

When viewed in historical context, Weber's ideas about bureaucracy represent a tremendous improvement in how organizations should be run. Fairness supplanted favoritism, the goal of efficiency replaced the goal of personal gain, and logical rules and procedures took the place of traditions or arbitrary decision making.

Today, however, after more than a century of experience, we recognize that bureaucracy has limitations as well. Weber called bureaucracy the "iron cage" and said, "Once fully established, bureaucracy is among those social structures which are the hardest to destroy."[28] In bureaucracies, managers are supposed to influence employee behavior by fairly rewarding or punishing employees for compliance or noncompliance with organizational policies, rules, and procedures. In reality, however, most employees would argue that bureaucratic managers emphasize punishment for noncompliance much more than rewards for compliance. Ironically, bureaucratic management was created to prevent just this type of managerial behavior.

2-3b Administrative Management: Henri Fayol

Though his work was not translated and widely recognized in the United States until 1949, Frenchman Henri Fayol (1841–1925) was as important a contributor to the field of management as Taylor. Like Taylor and the Gilbreths, Fayol's work experience significantly shaped his thoughts and ideas about management. But, whereas Taylor's ideas changed companies from the shop floor up, Fayol's ideas were shaped by his experience as a managing director (CEO) and generally changed companies from the board of directors down.[29] Fayol is best known for developing five functions of managers and fourteen principles of management, as well as for his belief that management can and should be taught to others.

The most formative events in Fayol's business career came during his twenty-plus years as the managing director of Compagnie de Commentry-Fourchambault et Décazeville, commonly known as **Comambault**, a vertically integrated steel company that owned several coal and iron ore mines and employed 10,000 to 13,000 workers. Fayol was initially hired by the board of directors to shut down the "hopeless" steel company. The company was facing increased competition from English and German steel companies, which had lower costs, and from new steel mills in northern and eastern France, which were closer to major markets and thus could avoid the high shipping costs incurred by Fayol's company, located in central France.[30] In the five years before Fayol became CEO, production had dropped more than 60 percent, from 38,000 to 15,000 annual metric tons. Comambault had exhausted a key supply of coal needed for steel production, had already shut down one steel mill, and was

DOING THE RIGHT THING

When 1 + 1 = 3

One of the most common reasons for justifying mergers is synergy, namely that 1 + 1 = 3, meaning the merged companies will be more efficient, productive, and profitable together than apart. A study by Bain & Company shows that 70 percent of merger deals don't generate anticipated synergies. Why? Executives, eager to justify the mergers, strongly overestimated what could be achieved and hadn't done the rigorous analysis that would have helped them learn whether the merger would have truly produced synergies. One exception, AB InBev, the global beverage conglomerate, routinely calculates accurate—and high—synergy levels and then meets those forecasts. Every time it acquires a company, AB InBev

Source: Anheuser-Busch InBev

establishes an integration plan, an oversight program, and a change management program. It then sets standards and benchmarks and adopts the best practices of whichever company has the better operation. And when companies approach mergers like that, 1 + 1 = 3.

Source: L. Miles, "How Merging Companies Can Beat the Synergy Odds," *Forbes*, January 9, 2015, accessed April 24, 2015. www.forbes.com/sites/baininsights/2015/01/09 /how-merging-companies-can-beat-the-synergy-odds/.

losing money at another.[31] The company had quit paying dividends to shareholders and had no cash to invest in new technology, such as blast furnaces, that could lower its costs and increase productivity.

So the board hired Fayol as CEO to quickly dissolve and liquidate the business. But, after "four months of reflection and study," he presented the board with a plan, backed by detailed facts and figures, to save the company.[32] With little to lose, the board agreed. Fayol then began the process of turning the company around by obtaining supplies of key resources such as coal and iron ore; using research to develop new steel alloy products; carefully selecting key subordinates in research, purchasing, manufacturing, and sales and then delegating responsibility to them; and cutting costs by moving the company to a better location closer to key markets.[33] Looking back ten years later, Fayol attributed his and the company's success to changes in management practices. He wrote, "When I assumed the responsibility for the restoration of Décazeville, I did not rely on my technical superiority. . . . I relied on my ability as an organizer [and my] skill in handling men."[34]

Based on his experience as a CEO, Fayol argued that "the success of an enterprise generally depends much more on the administrative ability of its leaders than on their technical ability."[35] And, as you learned in Chapter 1, Fayol argued that managers need to perform five managerial functions if they are to be successful: planning, organizing, coordinating, commanding, and controlling.[36] Because most management textbooks have dropped the coordinating function and now refer to Fayol's commanding function as "leading," these functions are widely known as planning (determining organizational goals and a means for achieving them), organizing (deciding where decisions will be made, who will do what jobs and tasks, and who will work for whom), leading (inspiring and motivating workers to work hard to achieve organizational goals), and controlling (monitoring progress toward goal achievement and taking corrective action when needed). In addition, according to Fayol, effective management is based on the fourteen principles in Exhibit 2.5.

2-4 HUMAN RELATIONS MANAGEMENT

As we have seen, scientific management focuses on improving efficiency; bureaucratic management focuses on using knowledge, fairness, and logical rules and procedures; and administrative management focuses on how

and what managers should do in their jobs. The human relations approach to management focuses on *people*, particularly the psychological and social aspects of work. This approach to management sees people not as just extensions of machines but as valuable organizational resources in their own right. Human relations management holds that people's needs are important and that their efforts, motivation, and performance are affected by the work they do and their relationships with their bosses, coworkers, and work groups. In other words, efficiency alone is not enough. Organizational success also depends on treating workers well.

Let's find out more about human relations management by learning about 2-4a Mary Parker Follett's theories of constructive conflict and coordination, 2-4b Elton Mayo's Hawthorne Studies, and 2-4c Chester Barnard's theories of cooperation and acceptance of authority.

2-4a Constructive Conflict and Coordination: Mary Parker Follett

Mary Parker Follett (1868–1933) was a social worker with a degree in political science who, in her fifties, after twenty-five years of working with schools and nonprofit organizations, began lecturing and writing about management and working extensively as a consultant for business and government leaders in the United States and Europe. Although her contributions were overlooked for decades, perhaps because she was a woman or perhaps because they were so different, many of today's "new" management ideas can clearly be traced to her work.

Follett believed that the best way to deal with conflict was not **domination**, where one side wins and the other

Domination an approach to dealing with conflict in which one party satisfies its desires and objectives at the expense of the other party's desires and objectives

Exhibit 2.5
Fayol's Fourteen Principles of Management

1 **Division of work**
Increase production by dividing work so that each worker completes smaller tasks or job elements.

2 **Authority and responsibility**
A manager's authority, which is the "right to give orders," should be commensurate with the manager's responsibility. However, organizations should enact controls to prevent managers from abusing their authority.

3 **Discipline**
Clearly defined rules and procedures are needed at all organizational levels to ensure order and proper behavior.

4 **Unity of command**
To avoid confusion and conflict, each employee should report to and receive orders from just one boss.

5 **Unity of direction**
One person and one plan should be used in deciding the activities to be carried out to accomplish each organizational objective.

6 **Subordination of individual interests to the general interests**
Employees must put the organization's interests and goals before their own.

7 **Remuneration**
Compensation should be fair and satisfactory to both the employees and the organization; that is, don't overpay or underpay employees.

8 **Centralization**
Avoid too much centralization or decentralization. Strike a balance depending on the circumstances and employees involved.

9 **Scalar chain**
From the top to the bottom of an organization, each position is part of a vertical chain of authority in which each worker reports to just one boss. For the sake of simplicity, communication outside normal work groups or departments should follow the vertical chain of authority.

10 **Order**
To avoid confusion and conflict, order can be obtained by having a place for everyone and having everyone in his or her place; in other words, there should be no overlapping responsibilities.

11 **Equity**
Kind, fair, and just treatment for all will develop devotion and loyalty. This does not exclude discipline, if warranted, and consideration of the broader general interests of the organization.

12 **Stability of tenure of personnel**
Low turnover, meaning a stable work force with high tenure, benefits an organization by improving performance, lowering costs, and giving employees, especially managers, time to learn their jobs.

13 **Initiative**
Because it is a "great source of strength for business," managers should encourage the development of initiative, or the ability to develop and implement a plan, in others.

14 **Esprit de corps**
Develop a strong sense of morale and unity among workers that encourages coordination of efforts.

Sources: H. Fayol, *General and Industrial Management* (London: Pittman & Sons, 1949); M. Fells, "Fayol Stands the Test of Time," *Journal of Management History* 6 (2000): 345–360; C. Rodrigues, "Fayol's 14 Principles of Management Then and Now: A Framework for Managing Today's Organizations Effectively," *Management Decision* 39 (2001): 880–889.

loses, or **compromise**, where each side gives up some of what it wants, but integration. Said Follett, "There is a way beginning now to be recognized at least, and even occasionally followed: when two desires are *integrated*, that means that a solution has been found in which both desires have found a place that neither side has had to sacrifice anything."[37] So, rather than one side dominating the other or both sides compromising, the point of **integrative conflict resolution** is to have both parties indicate their preferences and then work together to find an alternative that meets the needs of both. According to Follett, "Integration involves invention, and the clever thing is to recognize this, and not to let one's thinking stay within the boundaries of two alternatives which are mutually exclusive." Indeed, Follett's ideas about the positive use of conflict and an integrative approach to conflict resolution predate accepted thinking in the negotiation and conflict resolution literature by six decades (see the best-selling book *Getting to Yes: Negotiating Agreement without Giving In* by Roger Fisher, William Ury, and Bruce Patton).

Exhibit 2.6 summarizes Follett's contributions to management in her own words. She casts power as "with" rather than "over" others. Giving orders involves discussing instructions and dealing with resentment. Authority flows from job knowledge and experience rather than position. Leadership involves setting the tone for the team rather than being aggressive and dominating, which may be harmful. Coordination and control should be based on facts and information. In the end, Follett's contributions added significantly to our understanding of the human, social, and psychological sides of management. Peter Parker, the former chairman of the London School of Economics, said about Follett: "People often puzzle about who is the father of management. I don't know who the father was, but I have no doubt about who was the mother."[38]

2-4b Hawthorne Studies: Elton Mayo

Australian-born Elton Mayo (1880–1948) is best known for his role in the famous Hawthorne Studies at the **Western Electric Company**. The Hawthorne Studies were conducted in several stages between 1924 and 1932 at a Western Electric plant in Chicago. Although Mayo didn't join the studies until 1928, he played a significant role thereafter, writing about the results in his book, *The Human Problems of an Industrial Civilization*.[39] The first stage of the Hawthorne Studies investigated the effects of lighting levels and incentives on employee productivity in the Relay Test Assembly Room, where workers took approximately a minute to put "together a coil, armature, contact springs, and insulators in a fixture and secure the parts by means of four machine screws."[40]

Two groups of six experienced female workers, five to do the work and one to supply needed parts, were separated from the main part of the factory by a ten-foot partition and placed at a standard work bench with the necessary parts and tools. Over the next five years, the experimenters introduced various levels and combinations of lighting, financial incentives, and rest pauses (work breaks) to study the effect on productivity. Curiously, however, production levels increased whether the experimenters increased or decreased the lighting, paid workers based on individual production or group production, or increased or decreased the number and length of rest pauses. In fact, Mayo and his fellow researchers were surprised that production steadily increased from 2,400 relays per day at the beginning of the study to 3,000 relays per day five years later. The question was: Why?

Mayo and his colleagues eventually concluded that two things accounted for the results. First, substantially more attention was paid to these workers than to workers in the rest of the plant. Mayo wrote, "Before every change of program [in the study], the group is consulted. Their comments are listened to and discussed; sometimes their objections are allowed to negate a suggestion. The group unquestionably develops a sense of participation in the critical determinations and becomes something of a social unit."[41]

For years, the "Hawthorne Effect" has been *incorrectly* defined as increasing productivity by paying more attention to workers.[42] But it is not simply about attention from management. The Hawthorne Effect cannot be understood without giving equal importance to the social units, which became intensely cohesive groups. Mayo said, "What actually happened was that six individuals became a team and the team gave itself wholeheartedly and spontaneously to cooperation in the experiment. The consequence was that they felt themselves to be participating freely and without afterthought, and they were happy in the knowledge that they were working without coercion from above or limits from below."[43]

For the first time, human factors related to work were found to be more important than the physical conditions or design of the work. Together, the increased attention from

Compromise an approach to dealing with conflict in which both parties give up some of what they want in order to reach agreement on a plan to reduce or settle the conflict

Integrative conflict resolution an approach to dealing with conflict in which both parties indicate their preferences and then work together to find an alternative that meets the needs of both

Exhibit 2.6

MARY PARKER FOLLETT SAYS . . .

On constructive conflict...

"As conflict—difference—is here in this world, as we cannot avoid it, we should, I think, use it to work for us. Instead of condemning it, we should set it to work for us."

On power...

"It seems to me that whereas power usually means power-over, the power of some person or group over some other person or group, it is possible to develop the conception of power-with, a jointly developed power, a co-active, not a coercive power."

On the giving of orders...

"An advantage of not exacting blind obedience, of discussing your instructions with your subordinates, is that if there is any resentment, any come-back, you get it out into the open, and when it is in the open, you can deal with it."

On authority...

"Authority should go with knowledge and experience, that is where obedience is due, no matter whether it is up the line or down."

On leadership...

"Of the greatest importance is the ability to grasp a total situation. . . . Out of a welter of facts, experience, desires, aims, the leader must find the unifying thread. He must see a whole, not a mere kaleidoscope of pieces. . . . The higher up you go, the more ability you have to have of this kind."

On coordination...

"The most important thing to remember about unity is—that there is no such thing. There is only unifying. You cannot get unity and expect it to last a day—or five minutes. Every man in a business should be taking part in a certain process and that process is unifying."

On control...

"Central control is coming more and more to mean the co-relation of many controls rather than a superimposed control."

Source: M. Parker Follett, *Mary Parker Follett—Prophet of Management: A Celebration of Writings from the 1920s*, ed. P. Graham (Boston: Harvard Business School Press, 1995).

Ammit Jack/Shutterstock.com

management and the development of a cohesive work group led to significantly higher levels of job satisfaction and productivity. In short, the Hawthorne Studies found that workers' feelings and attitudes affected their work.

The next stage of the Hawthorne Studies was conducted in the Bank Wiring Room, where "the group consisted of nine wiremen, three solderers, and two inspectors. Each of these groups performed a specific task and collaborated with the other two in completion of each unit of equipment. The task consisted of setting up the banks of terminals side-by-side on frames, wiring the corresponding terminals from bank to bank, soldering the connections, and inspecting with a test set for short circuits or breaks in the wire. One solderman serviced the work of the three wiremen."[44] While productivity increased in the Relay Test Assembly Room no matter what the researchers did, productivity dropped in the Bank Wiring Room. Again, the question was: Why?

Mayo and his colleagues found that the differences in performance were due to group dynamics. The workers in the Bank Wiring Room had been an existing work group for some time and had already developed strong negative norms that governed their behavior. For instance, despite a group financial incentive for production, the group members decided that they would wire only 6,000 to 6,600 connections a day (depending on the kind of equipment they were wiring), well below the production goal of 7,300 connections that management had set for them. Individual workers who worked at a faster pace were socially ostracized from the group or

"binged" (hit on the arm) until they slowed their work pace. Thus, the group's behavior was reminiscent of the soldiering that Taylor had observed. Mayo concluded, "Work [was] done in accord with the group's conception of a day's work; this was exceeded by only one individual who was cordially disliked."[45]

In the end, the Hawthorne Studies demonstrated that the workplace was more complex than previously thought, that workers were not just extensions of machines, and that financial incentives weren't necessarily the most important motivator for workers. By highlighting the crucial role, positive or negative, that groups, group norms, and group behavior play at work, Mayo strengthened Follett's point about coordination—make just one change in an organization and others, some expected and some unexpected, will occur. Thanks to Mayo and his colleagues and their work on the Hawthorne Studies, managers better understood the effect that group social interactions, employee satisfaction, and attitudes had on individual and group performance.

2-4c Cooperation and Acceptance of Authority: Chester Barnard

Like Fayol, Chester Barnard (1886–1961) had experiences as a top executive that shaped his views of management. Barnard began his career in 1909 as an engineer and translator for AT&T, becoming a general manager at Pennsylvania Bell Telephone in 1922 and then president of New Jersey Bell Telephone in 1927.[46] Barnard's ideas, published in his classic book, *The Functions of the Executive*, influenced companies from the board of directors down. He is best known for his ideas about cooperation and the acceptance of authority.

Barnard proposed a comprehensive theory of cooperation in formal organizations. In fact, he defines an **organization** as a "system of consciously coordinated activities or forces of two or more persons."[47] In other words, organization occurs whenever two people work together for some purpose, whether it be classmates working together to complete a class project, Habitat for Humanity volunteers donating their time to build a house, or managers working with subordinates to reduce costs, improve quality, or increase sales. Barnard placed so much emphasis on cooperation because cooperation is *not* the normal state of affairs: "Failure to cooperate, failure of cooperation, failure of organization, disorganization, disintegration, destruction of organization—and reorganization—are characteristic facts of human history."[48]

According to Barnard, the extent to which people willingly cooperate in an organization depends on how workers perceive executive authority and whether they're willing to accept it. Many managerial requests or directives fall within a *zone of indifference* in which acceptance of managerial authority is automatic. For example, if your supervisor asks you for a copy of the monthly inventory report, and compiling and writing that report is part of your job, you think nothing of the request and automatically send it. In general, people will be indifferent to managerial directives or orders if they (1) are understood, (2) are consistent with the purpose of the organization, (3) are compatible with the people's personal interests, and (4) can actually be carried out by those people. Acceptance of managerial authority (that is, cooperation) is not automatic, however. Ask people to do things contrary to the organization's purpose or to their own benefit and they'll put up a fight. While many people assume that managers have the authority to do whatever they want, Barnard, referring to the "fiction of superior authority," believed that workers ultimately grant managers their authority.

Organization a system of consciously coordinated activities or forces created by two or more people

2-5 OPERATIONS, INFORMATION, SYSTEMS, AND CONTINGENCY MANAGEMENT

In this last section, we review four other significant historical approaches to management that have influenced how today's managers produce goods and services on a daily basis, gather and manage the information they need to understand their businesses and make good decisions, understand how the different parts of the company work together as a whole, and recognize when and where particular management practices are likely to work.

To better understand these ideas, let's learn about 2-5a operations management, 2-5b information management, 2-5c systems management, and 2-5d contingency management.

2-5a Operations Management

In Chapter 18, you will learn about *operations management*, which involves managing the daily production of goods and services. In general, operations management uses a quantitative or mathematical approach to find ways to increase productivity, improve quality, and manage or reduce costly inventories. The most commonly used operations management tools and methods are quality control, forecasting techniques, capacity planning, productivity measurement and improvement, linear programming, scheduling systems, inventory systems, work measurement techniques (similar to the Gilbreths' motion studies), project management (similar to Gantt's charts), and cost-benefit analysis.[49]

Since the sixteenthth century, skilled craftspeople made the lock, stock, and barrel of a gun by hand. After each part was made, a skilled gun finisher assembled the parts into a complete gun. But the gun finisher did not simply screw the different parts of a gun together, as is done today. Instead, each handmade part required extensive finishing and adjusting so that it would fit together with the other handmade gun parts. Hand-fitting was necessary because, even when made by the same skilled craftspeople, no two parts were alike. In fact, gun finishers played a role similar to that of fine watchmakers who meticulously assembled expensive watches—without them, the product simply wouldn't work. Today, we would say that these parts were low quality because they varied so much from one part to another.

All this changed in 1791 when the U.S. government, worried about a possible war with France, ordered 40,000 muskets from private gun contractors. All but one contractor built handmade muskets assembled by skilled gun finishers who made sure that all the parts fit together. Thus, each musket was unique. If a part broke, a replacement part had to be handcrafted. But one contractor, Eli Whitney of New Haven, Connecticut (who is better known for his invention of the cotton gin), determined that if gun parts were made accurately enough, guns could be made with standardized, interchangeable parts. So he designed machine tools that allowed unskilled workers to make each gun part the same as the next. Said Whitney, "The tools which I contemplate to make are similar to an engraving on copper plate from which may be taken a great number of impressions perceptibly alike."[50] Years passed before Whitney delivered his 10,000 muskets to the U.S. government. But he demonstrated the superiority of interchangeable parts to President-elect Thomas Jefferson in 1801 by quickly and easily assembling complete muskets from randomly picked piles of musket parts. Today, because of Whitney's ideas, most products, from cars to toasters to space shuttles, are manufactured using standardized, interchangeable parts.

But even with this advance, manufacturers still could not produce a part unless they had seen or examined it firsthand. Thanks to Gaspard Monge, a Frenchman of modest beginnings, this soon changed. Monge's greatest achievement was his book *Descriptive Geometry*.[51] In it, he explained techniques for drawing three-dimensional objects on paper. For the first time, precise drawings permitted manufacturers to make standardized, interchangeable parts without first examining a prototype. Today, thanks to Monge, manufacturers rely on CAD (computer-aided design) and CAM (computer-aided manufacturing) to take three-dimensional designs straight from the computer to the factory floor.

Once standardized, interchangeable parts became the norm, and after parts could be made from design drawings alone, manufacturers ran into a costly problem that they had never faced before: too much inventory. *Inventory* is the amount and number of raw materials, parts, and finished products that a company has in its possession. In fact, large factories were accumulating parts inventories sufficient for two to three months, much more than they needed on a daily basis to run their manufacturing operations. A solution to this problem was found in 1905 when the Oldsmobile Motor Works in Detroit burned down.[52] Management rented a new production facility to get production up and running as quickly as possible after the fire. But because the new facility was much smaller, there was no room to store large stockpiles of inventory (which the company couldn't afford anyway as it was short on funds). Therefore, the company made do with what it called "hand-to-mouth inventories," in which each production station had only enough parts on hand to do a short production run. Because all of its parts suppliers were close by, Oldsmobile could place orders in the morning and receive them in the afternoon (even without telephones), just as with today's computerized just-in-time inventory systems. So, contrary to common belief, just-in-time inventory systems were not invented by Japanese manufacturers. Instead, they were invented out of necessity more than a century ago because of a fire.

2-5b Information Management

For most of recorded history, information has been costly, difficult to obtain, and slow to spread. Because of the immense labor and time it took to hand copy information, books, manuscripts, and written documents of any kind were rare and extremely expensive. Word of Joan of Arc's death in 1431 took eighteen months to travel from France across Europe to Constantinople (now Istanbul, Turkey).

Consequently, throughout history, organizations have pushed for and quickly adopted new information technologies that reduce the cost or increase the speed with which they can acquire, store, retrieve, or communicate information. The first technologies to truly revolutionize the business use of information were paper and the printing press. In the fourteenth century, water-powered machines were created to pulverize rags into pulp to make paper. Paper prices, which were already lower than those of animal-skin parchments, dropped dramatically. Less than a half-century later,

Mmaxer/Shutterstock.com

messengers to keep in contact with their more than forty branch managers. The post messengers, who predated the U.S. Postal Service Pony Express by 400 years, could travel 90 miles per day, twice what average riders could cover, because the Medicis were willing to pay for the expense of providing them with fresh horses. This need for timely information also led companies to quickly adopt the telegraph in the 1860s, the telephone in the 1880s, and, of course, Internet technologies in the past three decades.

2-5c Systems Management

Today's companies are much more complex than they used to be. They are larger and employ more people. They most likely manufacture, service, *and* finance what they sell, not only in their home markets but in foreign markets throughout the world, too. They also operate in complex, fast-changing, competitive, global environments that can quickly turn competitive advantages into competitive disadvantages. How, then, can managers make sense of this complexity, both within and outside their organizations?

One way to deal with organizational and environmental complexity is to take a systems view of organizations. The systems approach is derived from theoretical models in biology and social psychology developed in the 1950s and 1960s.[53] A **system** is a set of interrelated elements or parts that function as a whole. Rather than viewing one part of an organization as separate from the other parts, a systems approach encourages managers to complicate their thinking by looking for connections between the different parts of the organization. Indeed, one of the more important ideas in the systems approach to management is that organizational systems are composed of parts or **subsystems**, which are simply smaller systems within larger systems. Subsystems and their connections matter in systems theory because of the possibility for managers to create synergy. **Synergy** occurs when two or more subsystems working together can produce more than they can working apart. In other words, synergy occurs when $1 + 1 = 3$.

Systems can be open or closed. **Closed systems** can function without interacting with their environments. But nearly all organizations should be viewed as **open systems** that interact with their environments and depend on them for survival. Therefore, rather than viewing what goes on within the organization as separate from what goes on outside it, the systems approach encourages managers to look for connections between the different parts of the organization and the different parts of its environment. Exhibit 2.7

Johannes Gutenberg invented the printing press, which greatly reduced the cost and time needed to copy written information. In fifteenth-century Florence, Italy, a scribe would charge one florin (an Italian unit of money) to hand copy one document page. By contrast, a printer would set up and print 1,025 copies of the same document for just three florins. Within fifty years of its invention, Gutenberg's printing press cut the cost of information by 99.8 percent!

What Gutenberg's printing press did for publishing, the manual typewriter did for daily communication. Before 1850, most business correspondence was written by hand and copied using the letterpress. With the ink still wet, the letter would be placed into a tissue-paper book. A hand press would then be used to squeeze the book and copy the still-wet ink onto the tissue paper. By the 1870s, manual typewriters made it cheaper, easier, and faster to produce and copy business correspondence. Of course, in the 1980s, slightly more than a century later, typewriters were replaced by personal computers and word processing software with the same results.

Finally, businesses have always looked for information technologies that would speed access to timely information. The Medici family, which opened banks throughout Europe in the early 1400s, used post

System a set of interrelated elements or parts that function as a whole

Subsystems smaller systems that operate within the context of a larger system

Synergy when two or more subsystems working together can produce more than they can working apart

Closed systems systems that can sustain themselves without interacting with their environments

Open systems systems that can sustain themselves only by interacting with their environments, on which they depend for their survival

Exhibit 2.7
Systems View of Organizations

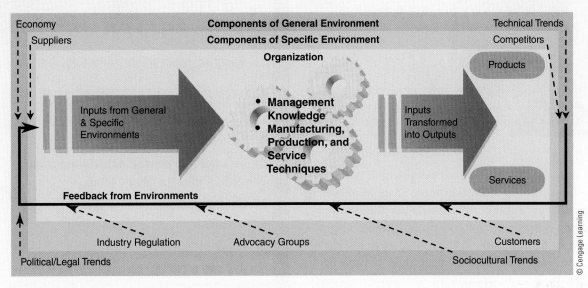

illustrates how the elements of systems management work together.

A systems view of organizations offers several advantages. First, it forces managers to view their organizations as part of and subject to the competitive, economic, social, technological, and legal/regulatory forces in their environments.[54] Second, it forces managers to be aware of how the environment affects specific parts of the organization. Third, because of the complexity and difficulty of trying to achieve synergies among different parts of the organization, the systems view encourages managers to focus on better communication and cooperation within the organization. Finally, it makes managers acutely aware that good internal management of the organization may not be enough to ensure survival. Survival also depends on making sure that the organization continues to satisfy critical environmental stakeholders such as shareholders, employees, customers, suppliers, governments, and local communities.

2-5d Contingency Management

Earlier, you learned that the goal of scientific management was to use systematic study to find the one best way of doing each task and then use that one best way everywhere. The problem, as you may have gathered from reading about the various approaches to management, is that no one in management seems to agree on what that one best way is. Furthermore, more than 100 years of management research has shown that there are clear boundaries or limitations to most management theories and practices. No management ideas or practices are universal. Although any theory or practice may work much of the time, none works all the time. How, then, is a manager to decide what theory to use? Well, it depends on the situation. The **contingency approach** to management clearly states that there are no universal management theories and that the most effective management theory or idea depends on the kinds of problems or situations that managers or organizations are facing at a particular time and place.[55] In short, the best way depends on the situation.

One of the practical implications of the contingency approach to management is that management is much harder than it looks. In fact, because of the clarity and obviousness of management theories (OK, most of them), students and workers often wrongly assume that a company's problems would be quickly and easily solved if management would take just a few simple steps. If this were true, few companies would have problems.

A second implication of the contingency approach is that managers need to look for key

Contingency approach holds that there are no universal management theories and that the most effective management theory or idea depends on the kinds of problems or situations that managers are facing at a particular time and place

Wavebreakmedia/Shutterstock.com

contingencies that differentiate today's situation or problems from yesterday's situation or problems. Moreover, it means that managers need to spend more time analyzing problems, situations, and employees before taking action to fix them. Finally, it means that as you read this text and learn about management ideas and practices, you need to pay particular attention to qualifying phrases such as "usually," "in these situations," "for this to work," and "under these circumstances." Doing so will help you identify the key contingencies that will help you become a better manager.

STUDY TOOLS 2

LOCATED IN TEXTBOOK

☐ Rip-out and review chapter review card

LOCATED AT WWW.CENGAGEBRAIN.COM

☐ Review key term flashcards and create your own from StudyBits

☐ Track your knowledge and understanding of key concepts, using the concept tracker

☐ Complete practice and graded quizzes to prepare for tests

☐ Complete interactive content within the exposition

☐ View chapter highlight box content at the beginning of each chapter

YOUR FEEDBACK MATTERS.

© iStockphoto.com/mustafahacalak | © Cengage Learning 2011

3 Organizational Environments and Cultures

LEARNING OUTCOMES

3-1 Discuss how changing environments affect organizations.

3-2 Describe the four components of the general environment.

3-3 Explain the five components of the specific environment.

3-4 Describe the process that companies use to make sense of their changing environments.

3-5 Explain how organizational cultures are created and how they can help companies be successful.

After you finish this chapter, go to **PAGE 65** for

STUDY TOOLS

3-1 CHANGING ENVIRONMENTS

This chapter examines the internal and external forces that affect business. We begin by explaining how the changes in external organizational environments affect the decisions and performance of a company. Next, we examine the two types of external organizational environment: the general environment that affects all organizations and the specific environment unique to each company. Then, we learn how managers make sense of their changing general and specific environments. The chapter finishes with a discussion of internal organizational environments by focusing on organizational culture. But first, let's see how the changes in external organizational environments affect the decisions and performance of a company.

External environments are the forces and events outside a company that have the potential to influence or affect it. In most cities, taxi prices (what's charged on the meter) and taxi licenses (for drivers and cars) are highly regulated. The taxi industry, however, is threatened by Uber, a five-year old Internet company. After signing up as an Uber customer (name, password, credit card information), customers use the Uber app on their smartphones to order rides. Tap Uber. Enter a destination. Tap a button indicating your location. Then, the Uber app indicates the cost and how long till the car arrives. Afterwards, it sends email receipts and automatically pays the driver. No cash changes hands. Customers love Uber because it's often faster than hailing a cab on the street. Taxi drivers and companies hate it because it represents competition, which is why 30,000 taxi drivers across London, Berlin, Madrid, and Paris parked their taxis in protest. Steve McNamara, a spokesperson for London's Licensed Taxi Driver Association, said, "We have nothing against competition. But Uber is being allowed to 'operate outside the law.'"[1] So far, London's taxi regulation agency has ruled that Uber apps and cars do not have taxi meters, therefore, they can't be regulated as taxi cabs. While London's famous black cab taxi drivers disagree, the goal of these protests is to influence regulatory agencies to prevent Uber from operating, or to force Uber to buy expensive, limited-in-number taxi licenses.

*Let's examine the three basic characteristics of changing external environments: **3-1a environmental change; 3-1b environmental complexity; 3-1c resource scarcity; and 3-1d the uncertainty that environmental change, complexity, and resource scarcity can create for organizational managers.***

Over a six-year span, Apple released eight different iPhone models. This picture shows the difference in size between the iPhone 6 and 6 Plus.

3-1a Environmental Change

Environmental change is the rate at which a company's general and specific environments change. In **stable environments**, the rate of environmental change is slow. The funeral business changes little from year to year. Families arrange for services for their loved ones with a funeral home, which then obtains a casket from one of three U.S. manufacturers, cares for the remains, hosts a visitation or memorial service, and organizes the burial or cremation, perhaps connecting the family with the cemetery or columbarium for purchase of a final resting place—all for an average price of $6,460. Although there have been some changes—such as cremation increasing from 4 percent in 1960 to 43 percent today, advances in embalming that are healthier (for the embalmer and the environment), and a small percentage of imported caskets (less than 10 percent) that have increased profits—the basic business of preparing bodies for burial, internment, or cremation hasn't changed significantly in over a century.[2]

> **External environments** all events outside a company that have the potential to influence or affect it
>
> **Environmental change** the rate at which a company's general and specific environments change
>
> **Stable environment** an environment in which the rate of change is slow

Whereas the funeral industry has a stable environment, BlackBerry competes in an extremely dynamic external environment. In **dynamic environments**, the rate of environmental change is fast. BlackBerry competitors, such as Apple, Samsung, HTC, and Motorola, frequently updated models with innovative features and new technology. Over a six-year span, Apple released eight different iPhone models, the 3G and 3GS, the 4 and 4S, the 5 and 5S, and the 6 and 6 Plus, each having better features and functionality. For instance, the new iPhone 6 Plus has a 64-bit processing chip, a 5.5-inch retina HD display, new slow motion and time lapse video recording capabilities, and a fingerprint scanner on the home button that serves as a secure biometric password for accessing the phone and paying for purchases in stores and within apps with Apple Pay.[3]

Although you might think that a company's external environment would be either stable or dynamic, research suggests that companies often experience both. According to **punctuated equilibrium theory**, companies go through long periods of stability (equilibrium) during which incremental changes occur; followed by short, complex periods of dynamic, fundamental change (revolutionary periods); and finishing with a return to stability (new equilibrium).[4]

The U.S. airline industry is a classic example of punctuated equilibrium, as three times in the past thirty years it has experienced revolutionary periods followed by a temporary return to stability. The first, from mid-1979 to mid-1982, occurred immediately after airline deregulation in 1978. Prior to deregulation, the federal government controlled where airlines could fly, how much they could charge, when they could fly, and the number of flights they could have on a particular route. After deregulation, these choices were left to the airlines. The large financial losses during this period clearly indicate that the airlines had trouble adjusting to the intense competition from new airlines that occurred after deregulation. By mid-1982, however, profits returned to the industry and held steady until mid-1989.

Then, after experiencing record growth and profits, U.S. airlines lost billions of dollars between 1989 and 1993 as the industry went through dramatic changes. Key expenses, including jet fuel and employee salaries, which had held steady for years, suddenly increased. Furthermore, revenues, which had grown steadily year after year, suddenly dropped because of dramatic changes in the airlines' customer base. Business travelers, who had typically paid full-price fares, comprised more than half of all passengers during the 1980s. However, by the late 1980s, the largest customer base had changed to leisure travelers, who wanted the cheapest flights they could get.[5] With expenses suddenly up, and revenues suddenly down, the airlines responded to these changes in their business environment by laying off 5 to 10 percent of their workers, canceling orders for new planes, and eliminating unprofitable routes. Starting in 1993 and lasting till 1998, these changes helped the airline industry achieve profits far in excess of their historical levels. The industry began to stabilize, if not flourish, just as punctuated equilibrium theory predicts.[6]

The third revolutionary period for the U.S. airline industry began with the terrorist attacks of September 11, 2001, in which planes were used as missiles to bring down the World Trade Center towers and damage the Pentagon. The immediate effect was a 20 percent drop in scheduled flights, a 40 percent drop in passengers, and losses so large that the U.S. government approved a $15 billion bailout to keep the airlines in business. Heightened airport security also affected airports, the airlines themselves, and airline customers. Five years after the 9/11 attacks, United Airlines, U.S. Airways, Delta, and American Airlines had reduced staffing by 169,000 full-time jobs to cut costs after losing a combined $42 billion.[7] Due to their financially weaker position, the airlines restructured operations to take advantage of the combined effect of increased passenger travel, a sharply reduced cost structure, and a 23 percent reduction in the fleet to return their businesses to profitability.[8] But, just as the airlines were heading toward a more stable period of equilibrium in 2006 and 2007, the price of oil jumped dramatically, doubling, if not tripling, the price of jet fuel, which prompted the airlines to charge for luggage (to increase revenues and discourage heavy baggage) and cut flights using older, fuel-inefficient jets.

In 2013, however, stability and profitability largely returned. Compared to 2007, the airlines cut total seat capacity 14 percent; filled 83 percent of seats, up from 80 percent; and with stronger demand and fewer flights, saw round-trip fares rise by 4 percent, even after adjusting for inflation. In 2008, U.S. airlines collectively lost $23.7 billion, but by the

Markus Mainka/Shutterstock.com

Dynamic environment an environment in which the rate of change is fast

Punctuated equilibrium theory the theory that companies go through long periods of stability (equilibrium), followed by short periods of dynamic, fundamental change (revolutionary periods), and then a new equilibrium

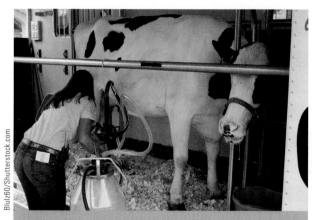

The dairy industry is an excellent example of a simple external environment.

end of 2014, they had logged their fifth consecutive year of profits.[9] Multiple airline mergers—Delta and Northwest, United and Continental, Southwest and AirTran, and U.S. Airways and American Airlines—reduced competition and routes even further, especially at nonhub airports such as Cincinnati, where the number of flights has plummeted by two-thirds since 2007. Bob Cortelyou, Delta's senior vice president for network planning, explained that the airlines are making these moves because, "We want an airline industry that is stable and profitable."[10]

3-1b Environmental Complexity

Environmental complexity refers to the number and the intensity of external factors in the environment that affect organizations. **Simple environments** have few environmental factors, whereas **complex environments** have many environmental factors. The dairy industry is an excellent example of a relatively simple external environment. Even accounting for decades-old advances in processing, automatic milking machines, and breeding techniques, where the latter has increased annual yield from 5,000 pounds of milk per cow in 1942 to 21,000 pounds today, milk is produced the same way today as it was 100 years ago.[11] So while food manufacturers introduce dozens of new dairy-based products each year, U.S. milk production has grown a modest 1.7 percent per year over the past decade. In short, producing milk is a highly competitive industry with a few key environmental factors.[12]

At the other end of the spectrum, few industries find themselves in more complex environments today than the personal computer (PC) business. Since the early 1980s, PC sales have grown spectacularly. But with consumers now spending technology dollars on tablets, e-readers, and smartphones (some as big as tablets and e-readers!), sales of Windows-based PCs dropped 14 percent from 2012 to 2013 and by 1.7 percent from 2013 to 2014. PC manufacturers saw similar trends, with HP, Dell, Acer Group, and Asus all posting double-digit declines. Microsoft's Windows 8 operating system, which brought touchscreen capabilities and design to PCs, Microsoft tablets, and smartphones, was supposed to revive PC sales, but consumers found it confusing and difficult. Reviews of the publicly available Windows 10 Technical Preview, released prior to the official product launch, are broadly positive and seem to indicate that Windows 10 will provide a positive, stable user experience on all device formats—PCs, Windows smartphones and tablets, and the Xbox console. James Phillips, general manager of Microsoft's Power Business Intelligence product, said, "The organization knows it's go-time. There are changes in the market we need to respond to."[13]

3-1c Resource Scarcity

The third characteristic of external environments is resource scarcity. **Resource scarcity** is the abundance or shortage of critical organizational resources in an organization's external environment. Italy-based **Ferrero Group** makes **Nutella**, the popular food spread made with hazelnuts, skim milk, and cocoa. A 13-ounce jar of Nutella contains 50 hazelnuts, so Ferrero buys 100,000 tons of hazelnuts each year, roughly 25 percent of the world supply, to produce 82 million pounds of Nutella. But, with sales growing 6 percent a year and competitors, such as Hershey, Jif, and Kroger, now making their own chocolate-hazelnut spreads, demand for the limited global supply of hazelnuts, grown primarily on a narrow strip of Turkish coastland, is skyrocketing. Hazelnut prices jumped by 60 percent in 2014, thanks to growing demand and a combination of frost and hail damage. With supplies of its key ingredient at risk, Ferrero bought Turkish-based Oltan Group, the world's largest hazelnut procurer and supplier, with five production facilities in Europe.[14]

3-1d Uncertainty

As Exhibit 3.1 shows, environmental change, environmental complexity, and resource scarcity affect environmental **uncertainty**,

---

Environmental complexity the number and the intensity of external factors in the environment that affect organizations

Simple environment an environment with few environmental factors

Complex environment an environment with many environmental factors

Resource scarcity the abundance or shortage of critical organizational resources in an organization's external environment

Uncertainty extent to which managers can understand or predict which environmental changes and trends will affect their businesses

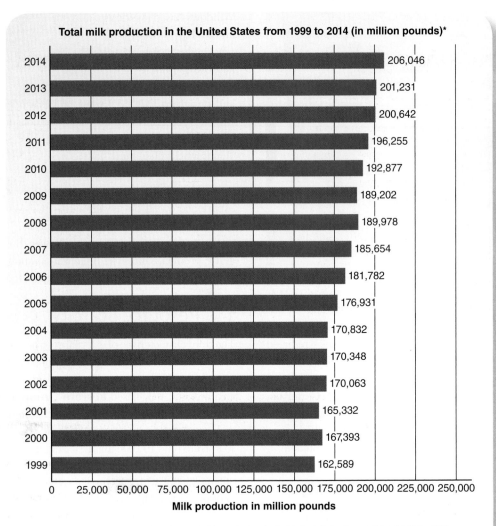

Total milk production in the United States from 1999 to 2014 (in million pounds)*

Year	Milk production
2014	206,046
2013	201,231
2012	200,642
2011	196,255
2010	192,877
2009	189,202
2008	189,978
2007	185,654
2006	181,782
2005	176,931
2004	170,832
2003	170,348
2002	170,063
2001	165,332
2000	167,393
1999	162,589

Milk production in million pounds

Note: This statistic describes the total milk production in the United States from 1999 to 2014. In 1999, approximately 163 billion pounds of milk were produced. This figure excludes milk sucked by calves.

Source: http://www.statista.com/statistics/194937/total-US-milk-production-since-1999/

which is how well managers can understand or predict the external changes and trends affecting their businesses. Starting at the left side of the exhibit, environmental uncertainty is lowest when environmental change and environmental complexity are at low levels, and resource scarcity is low (that is, resources are plentiful). In these environments, managers feel confident that they can understand, predict, and react to the external forces that affect their businesses. By contrast, the right side of the exhibit shows that environmental uncertainty is highest when environmental change and complexity are extensive, and resource scarcity is a problem. In these environments, managers may not be confident that they can understand, predict, and handle the external forces affecting their businesses.

General environment the economic, technological, sociocultural, and political/legal trends that indirectly affect all organizations

GENERAL ENVIRONMENT

As Exhibit 3.2 shows, two kinds of external environments influence organizations: the general environment and the specific environment. The **general environment** consists of the economy and the technological, sociocultural, and political/legal trends that indirectly affect *all*

M. Unal Ozmen/Shutterstock.com

Exhibit 3.1
Environmental Change, Environmental Complexity, and Resource Scarcity

When environmental change and complexity are at high levels, and resource scarcity is high (that is, resources are scarce), uncertainty is high, and managers may not be at all confident that they can understand, predict, and handle the external forces affecting their businesses.

When environmental change and complexity are at low levels, and resource scarcity is low (that is, resources are plentiful), uncertainty is low, and managers feel confident that they can understand, predict, and react to the external forces that affect their businesses.

Environmental Uncertainty

High
Medium
Low

Environmental Characteristics

- Environmental Complexity
- Resource Scarcity
- Environmental Change

© Cengage Learning

Exhibit 3.2
General and Specific Environments

GENERAL ENVIRONMENT

SOCIOCULTURAL TRENDS

TECHNOLOGY

COMPETITION

CUSTOMERS

ADVOCACY GROUPS

ORGANIZATION

SUPPLIERS

INDUSTRY REGULATION

ECONOMY

POLITICAL/LEGAL TRENDS

SPECIFIC ENVIRONMENT

© Cengage Learning

organizations. Changes in any sector of the general environment eventually affect most organizations. For example, when the Federal Reserve lowers its prime lending rate, most businesses benefit because banks and credit card companies often lower the interest rates they charge for loans. Consumers, who can then borrow money more cheaply, might borrow more to buy homes, cars, refrigerators, and large-screen LCD TVs.

Each organization also has a **specific environment** that is unique to that

Specific environment the customers, competitors, suppliers, industry regulations, and advocacy groups that are unique to an industry and directly affect how a company does business firm's industry and directly affects the way it conducts day-to-day business. Yum! Brands first entered China in the late 1980s with its KFC and Pizza Hut restaurants. As the Chinese economy boomed and wealthier Chinese consumers began spending their growing discretionary income on fast food, Yum! Brands sales grew exponentially. By 2012, KFC's and Pizza Hut's Chinese sales accounted for half of Yum's! global revenue. During that time, Yum! relied on Chinese growth to drive overall sales and profits, and therefore made few changes to its restaurants or its menus. In the past few years, however, China's economy has cooled off, and numerous competitors have entered China, building new restaurants and bringing a wider variety of menu options, especially healthier foods. Finally, because of an avian flu outbreak in spring 2013, Chinese consumers began eating much less poultry. Together, these changes have directly affected and reduced Yum! Brands' Chinese sales by 16 percent.[15]

The specific environment, which will be discussed in detail in Section 3-3 of this chapter, includes customers, competitors, suppliers, industry regulation, and advocacy groups.

But first let's take a closer look at the four components of the general environment: 3-2a the economy and 3-2b the technological, 3-2c sociocultural, and 3-2d political/ legal trends that indirectly affect all organizations.

3-2a Economy

The current state of a country's economy affects virtually every organization doing business there. In general, in a growing economy, more people are working, and wages are growing, and therefore consumers have relatively more money to spend. More products are bought and sold in a growing economy than in a static or shrinking economy. Although an individual firm's sales will not necessarily increase, a growing economy does provide an environment favorable to business growth. In contrast, in a shrinking economy, consumers have less money to spend, and relatively fewer products are bought and sold. Thus, a shrinking economy makes growth for individual businesses more difficult.

Because the economy influences basic business decisions, such as whether to hire more employees, expand production, or take out loans to purchase equipment, managers scan their economic environments for signs of significant change. Unfortunately, the economic statistics that managers rely on when making these decisions are notoriously poor predictors of *future* economic activity. The Organization for Economic Cooperation and Development (OECD), an influential, but independent, nonprofit organization that works with governments to improve economic and social well-being, regularly publishes country economic forecasts. Over the past seven years, however, the OECD found that its forecasts were consistently overly optimistic and wrong.[16] So a manager who hired ten more employees because OECD forecasts data suggested future growth, could very well have had to lay off those workers when the forecasted economic growth did not occur.

Because economic statistics can be poor predictors, some managers try to predict future economic activity by keeping track of business confidence. **Business confidence indices** show how confident actual managers are about future business growth. For example, the Conference Board's CEO Confidence Index is a quarterly survey of 100 CEOs in large companies across a variety of different industries that examines attitudes regarding future growth in the economy or particular industries.[17] Another useful index is the *Wall Street Journal* (*WSJ*)/ Vistage Small Business CEO Survey, which surveys small business CEOS about their sentiments regarding their general economy and how optimistic they are about future revenues, profitability, and business spending.[18] Managers often prefer business confidence indices to economic statistics because they know that other managers make business decisions that are in line with their expectations concerning the economy's future. So if the Conference Board or WSJ/Vistage Small Business CEO Survey business confidence indices are dropping, a manager might decide against hiring new employees, increasing production, or taking out additional loans to expand the business.

3-2b Technological Component

Technology is the knowledge, tools, and techniques used to transform inputs (raw materials, information, and so on) into outputs (products and services). For example, the inputs of authors, editors, and artists (knowledge) and the use of equipment such as computers and printing presses (technology) transformed paper, ink, and glue (raw materials) into this book (the finished product). In the case of a service company such as an airline, the technology consists of equipment, including airplanes, repair tools, and computers, as well as the knowledge of mechanics, ticketers, and flight crews. The output is the service of transporting people from one place to another.

Business confidence indices indices that show managers' level of confidence about future business growth

Technology the knowledge, tools, and techniques used to transform inputs into outputs

Changes in technology can help companies provide better products or produce their products more efficiently. Although technological changes can benefit a business, they can also threaten it. Companies must embrace new technology and find effective ways to use it to improve their products and services or decrease costs. If they don't, they will lose out to those companies that do.

3-2c Sociocultural Component

The sociocultural component of the general environment refers to the demographic characteristics, general behavior, attitudes, and beliefs of people in a particular society. Sociocultural changes and trends influence organizations in two important ways.

First, changes in demographic characteristics, such as the number of people with particular skills or the growth of or decline in the number of people with particular population characteristics (marital status, age, gender, ethnicity) affect how companies staff their businesses. With the cruise industry growing just 3–4 percent per year, Carnival Cruise Lines has increased the number of cruises sailing out of China, the industry's fastest growing market, from one in 2011 to four today. While 700,000 Chinese took cruises last year, compared to 10 million Americans, Carnival expects 20–30 percent annual growth in China, which will result in 5 million Chinese taking cruises by 2020.[19]

Second, sociocultural changes in behavior, attitudes, and beliefs also affect the demand for a business's products and services. For example, European car sales are at their lowest point in two decades, 30 percent below

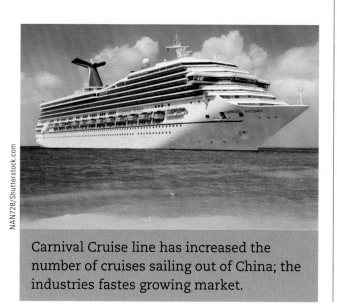

Carnival Cruise line has increased the number of cruises sailing out of China; the industries fastes growing market.

1990 levels. Europe's driving-age population, having peaked in 2011, is shrinking because of declining birthrates. Jean-Marc Gales, who heads an industry lobbying group for European auto suppliers, said, "Demographics . . . are not positive for most European countries."[20] Demographics alone could reduce European auto sales by 400,000 cars a year. European attitudes toward car ownership are also changing. Angus Ross, a Brit who lives in Paris, said, "Owning a car just isn't so important for my generation." With extensive public transportation in Europe, it's easier to get by without a car. Likewise, Europe's economy remains weak, so a larger percentage of Europeans are without jobs, and those with jobs are more cautious with their spending. Indeed, 41-year-old Sergio Felice, a Barcelona bank consultant, says he doesn't plan to buy a car until he's in his 60s. "I prefer to put the money I don't spend on a car in a retirement plan." Instead, he uses a motorcycle and rents cars for weekend trips. That way, he says, "I still get to have a car whenever I want."

3-2d Political/Legal Component

The political/legal component of the general environment includes the legislation, regulations, and court decisions that govern and regulate business behavior. New laws and regulations continue to impose additional responsibilities on companies. Unfortunately, many managers are unaware of these new responsibilities. For example, under the 1991 Civil Rights Act (http://www.eeoc.gov/policy/cra91.html), if an employee is sexually harassed by anyone at work (a supervisor, a coworker, or even a customer), the company—not just the harasser—is potentially liable for damages, attorneys' fees, and back pay.[21] Under the Family and Medical Leave Act (http://www.dol.gov/dol/topic/benefits-leave/fmla.htm), which applies to employers with fifty or more employees, employees who have been on the job one year are guaranteed twelve weeks of unpaid leave per year to tend to their own illnesses or to their elderly parents, a newborn baby, or a newly adopted child. Employees are guaranteed the same job, pay, and benefits when they return to work.[22] The most recent major regulation to affect U.S. businesses is the Patient Protection and Affordable Care Act (http://www.hhs.gov/healthcare/rights/), which requires businesses with more than 100 full-time employees to offer affordable health care insurance to full-time employees and their families. To demonstrate that they are in compliance, companies must file tax forms showing their individual employees' health care costs on a monthly basis. Penalties for not filing proper tax forms can be up to $3,000 per employee.[23]

NAN728/Shutterstock.com

Many managers are also unaware of the potential legal risks associated with traditional managerial decisions about recruiting, hiring, and firing employees. Increasingly, businesses and managers are being sued for negligent hiring and supervision, defamation, invasion of privacy, emotional distress, fraud, and misrepresentation during employee recruitment.[24] More than 14,000 suits for wrongful termination (unfairly firing employees) are filed each year.[25] In fact, wrongful termination lawsuits increased by 77 percent during the 1990s.[26] Likewise, Equal Employment Opportunity Commission filings alleging wrongful discharge average around 20,000 cases per year[27] One in four employers will at some point be sued for wrongful termination. It can cost $300,000 to settle such a case after it goes to court, but employers lose 50 percent to 70 percent of court cases,[28] and the former employee is awarded, on average, $1 million or more.[29] On the other hand, employers who settle before going to court typically pay just $10,000 to $100,000 per case.[30]

Not everyone agrees that companies' legal risks are too severe. Indeed, many believe that the government should do more to regulate and restrict business behavior and that it should be easier for average citizens to sue dishonest or negligent corporations. From a managerial perspective, the best medicine against legal risk is prevention. As a manager, it is your responsibility to educate yourself about the laws, regulations, and potential lawsuits that could affect your business. Failure to do so may put you and your company at risk of sizable penalties, fines, or legal charges.

3-3 SPECIFIC ENVIRONMENT

As you just learned, changes in any sector of the general environment (economic, technological, sociocultural, and political/legal) eventually affect most organizations. Each organization also has a specific environment that is unique to that firm's industry and directly affects the way it conducts day-to-day business. For instance, if your customers decide to use another product, your main competitor cuts prices 10 percent, your best supplier can't deliver raw materials, federal regulators mandate reductions in pollutants in your industry, or environmental groups accuse your company of selling unsafe products, the impact from the specific environment on your business is immediate.

Let's examine how the **3-3a customer, 3-3b competitor, 3-3c supplier, 3-3d industry regulation,** *and* **3-3e advocacy group components of the specific environment affect businesses.**

3-3a Customer Component

Customers purchase products and services. Companies cannot exist without customer support. Monitoring customers' changing wants and needs is critical to business success. There are two basic strategies for monitoring customers: reactive and proactive.

Reactive customer monitoring involves identifying and addressing customer trends and problems after they occur. One reactive strategy is to listen closely to customer complaints and respond to customer concerns. **Listen360** is a company that helps businesses monitor customer satisfaction and complaints by contacting their customers and asking two questions, "How likely are you to recommend this business?" followed by an open-ended question to explain why. Customer responses fall into three categories: "promoters," who would recommend the business to others; "passives," who are neither negative nor positive; and "detractors," unhappy customers who would not recommend the business. When customers are unhappy, the business receives a report detailing what products and services the customer purchased, what it would cost the company if it lost that customer's business, and a "voice of the customer" report that scans the answers to the open-ended question for key words about specific likes, dislikes, and concerns. According to Heather Anderson, director of marketing for The Little Gym, a children's fitness franchise, "Many owners have also chosen to get an immediate notification via text message if they receive a detractor comment, so they can respond within minutes of receiving the feedback."[31]

Companies that respond quickly to customer letters of complaint (that is, reactive customer monitoring) are viewed much more favorably than companies that are slow to respond or never respond.[32] In particular, studies have shown that customers are much more likely to purchase products or services again from a company when that company sends a follow-up letter to thank the customer for writing; offers a sincere, specific response to the complaint (not a form letter, but an explanation of how the problem will be handled); and offers a small gift, coupons, or a refund to make up for the problem.[33]

Proactive monitoring of customers means identifying and addressing customer needs, trends, and issues *before* they occur. Cable TV's *The Weather Channel* forecasts weather worldwide. But it changed its name to *The Weather Co.* to reflect its growing use of seventy-five years of weather data to predict consumer needs and behaviors *before* they occur. CEO David Kenny says, "People generally check the weather because they're planning to do something. We are getting better at knowing the kind of things people will be planning based on where and when they are checking the weather and what the weather is."[34] Michaels, a nationwide arts and crafts chain, planned to advertise on The Weather Co.'s website and TV channel on rainy days, on which it believed customers would be more likely to buy and then do arts and crafts projects. WeatherFX, the Weather Co.'s data analytic unit, examined daily sales for each Michaels store, which it then combined with corresponding weather data. Instead of sales increasing on rainy days, WeatherFX found that sales increased three days before. In other words, people bought arts and crafts at Michaels to have something to do before rainy weather arrived. This kind of proactive monitoring has proven so valuable that WeatherFX now accounts for half of the Weather Co.'s advertising revenue.[35]

3-3b Competitor Component

Competitors are companies in the same industry that sell similar products or services to customers. Ford, Toyota, Honda, Nissan, Hyundai, and Kia all compete for automobile customers. NBC, ABC, CBS, and Fox (along with hundreds of cable channels) compete for TV viewers' attention. McDonald's, Burger King, Wendy's, Hardee's, Chick-fil-A, and a host of others compete for fast-food customers' dollars. Often the difference between business success and failure comes down to whether your company is doing a better job of satisfying customer wants and needs than the competition. Consequently, companies need to keep close track of what their competitors are doing. To do this, managers perform a **competitive analysis**, which involves deciding who your competitors are, anticipating competitors' moves, and determining competitors' strengths and weaknesses.

Surprisingly, managers often do a poor job of identifying potential competitors because they tend to focus on only two or three well-known competitors with similar goals and resources.[36]

Another mistake managers may make when analyzing the competition is to underestimate potential competitors' capabilities. When this happens, managers don't take the steps they should to continue to improve their products or services. The result can be significant decreases in both market share and profits. For decades, TV viewers had two options—watch the four or five channels that could be picked up with an antenna or purchase a package from a local cable supplier, which almost always operated as a local monopoly. Then, a third choice

came along—buy a package from a satellite provider, such as DirecTV or DISH Network. In the past five years, however, the television marketplace has changed dramatically, and cable TV companies now find themselves surrounded by competitors. Netflix started the process by offering an inexpensive DVD-by-mail service, which began eroding cable TV dominance. Over the past five years, however, online content providers and streaming services and devices such as Netflix, Hulu, YouTube, iTunes, Roku, Apple TV, and Amazon Instant Video allow consumers to watch their favorite TV shows and movies at a fraction of the cost of a monthly cable subscription. Cable companies have been slow to respond. From 2010 to 2014, the forty most widely distributed cable channels lost 3.2 million subscribers, as consumers trimmed their cable TV bills by cutting out popular channels such as TNT, USA, ESPN, and Disney. It's also estimated that somewhere between a quarter million and a half million cable/satellite TV customers "cut the cord" in 2014, completely dropping their subscriptions. According to Bryan Rader, CEO of Bandwidth Consulting LLC, a firm that tracks pay-TV trends, "We're at a tipping point of consumers thinking Internet first and TV second."[37]

Competitors companies in the same industry that sell similar products or services to customers

Competitive analysis a process for monitoring the competition that involves identifying competition, anticipating their moves, and determining their strengths and weaknesses

3-3c Supplier Component

Suppliers are companies that provide material, human, financial, and informational resources to other companies. U.S. Steel buys iron ore from suppliers to make steel products. When IBM sells a mainframe computer, it also provides support staff, engineers, and other technical consultants to the company that bought the computer. If you're shopping for desks, chairs, and office supplies, chances are that Staples will be glad to help your business open a revolving charge account to pay for your purchases. When a clothing manufacturer has spent $100,000 to purchase new high-pressure water drills to cut shirt and pant patterns to precise sizes, the water drill manufacturer, as part of the purchase, will usually train the workers to use the machinery.

A key factor influencing the impact and quality of the relationship between companies and their suppliers is how dependent they are on each other.[38] **Supplier dependence** is the degree to which a company relies on that supplier because of the importance of the supplier's product to the company and the difficulty of finding other sources for that product. Even though Apple and Samsung are fierce competitors when it comes to smartphones and tablets, and they have sued and countersued each other over alleged patent infringements, Apple has been highly dependent on Samsung for the computer chips, flash drives, and high resolution touch screens in iPhones and iPads for more than a decade. Stanford University professor Michael Marks said that Apple's choices for alternative suppliers, "aren't good, which is why they keep buying from Samsung."[39] Indeed, Apple awarded Taiwan Semiconductor the contract chips to go in its iPhone 6. Within six months of the release of the newest iPhone, however, Apple announced that, for future iPhone models, it would go back to buying chips from Samsung.[40]

Buyer dependence is the degree to which a supplier relies on a buyer because of the importance of that buyer to the supplier's sales and the difficulty of finding other buyers of its products. While Samsung is one of Apple's key suppliers (that is, supplier dependence), Apple, in turn, is Samsung's key buyer of computer components. Apple's purchase of $10 billion of chips, flash memory drives, and touch screens in 2013 represented 17 percent of Samsung's $59.13 billion components business. Regaining the Apple chip order for future versions of the iPhone helped Samsung turn a $914 million loss in 2013 into a $914 profit.[41]

A high degree of buyer or seller dependence can lead to **opportunistic behavior,** in which one party benefits at the expense of the other. Apple was concerned with the possibility of opportunistic behavior when it stopped buying touch screens from Samsung in 2010. Technology analyst Hiroshi Hayase explained, "If you buy screens from your competitor, you will be sharing some key information on your next product."[42] Consequently, Apple shifted its touch screen orders to Sharp

---

Suppliers companies that provide material, human, financial, and informational resources to other companies

Supplier dependence the degree to which a company relies on a supplier because of the importance of the supplier's product to the company and the difficulty of finding other sources of that product

Buyer dependence the degree to which a supplier relies on a buyer because of the importance of that buyer to the supplier and the difficulty of finding other buyers for its products

Opportunistic behavior a transaction in which one party in the relationship benefits at the expense of the other

---

Staples is a prime example of a supplier.

Federal Regulatory Agencies and Commissions

Consumer Product Safety Commission
Reduces risk of injuries and deaths associated with consumer products, sets product safety standards, enforces product recalls, and provides consumer education **http://www.cpsc.gov**

Department of Labor
Collects employment statistics and administers labor laws concerning safe working conditions, minimum hourly wages and overtime pay, employment discrimination, and unemployment insurance **http://www.dol.gov**

Environmental Protection Agency
Reduces and controls pollution through research, monitoring, standard setting, and enforcement activities **http://www.epa.gov**

Equal Employment Opportunity Commission
Promotes fair hiring and promotion practices **http://www.eeoc.gov**

Federal Communications Commission
Regulates interstate and international communications by radio, television, wire, satellite, and cable **http://www.fcc.gov**

Federal Reserve System
As the nation's central bank, controls interest rates and money supply and monitors the U.S. banking system to produce a growing economy with stable prices **http://www.federalreserve.gov**

Federal Trade Commission
Restricts unfair methods of business competition and misleading advertising and enforces consumer protection laws **http://www.ftc.gov**

Food and Drug Administration
Protects the nation's health by making sure food, drugs, and cosmetics are safe **http://www.fda.gov**

National Labor Relations Board
Monitors union elections and stops companies from engaging in unfair labor practices **http://www.nlrb.gov**

Occupational Safety and Health Administration
Saves lives, prevents injuries, and protects the health of workers **http://www.osha.gov**

Securities and Exchange Commission
Protects investors in the bond and stock markets, guarantees access to information on publicly traded securities, and regulates firms that sell securities or give investment advice **http://www.sec.gov**

and Toshiba. This is also why Apple began working with Toshiba in 2009, to build flash memory for iPads and iPhones, and with TSMC (Taiwan Semiconductor Manufacturing Company) in 2010, to build computer chips.[43] As of June 2014, Apple only purchases 10 percent of its flash memory from Samsung. TSMC started chip production for Apple in 2014, which will allow Apple to significantly reduce its reliance on Samsung over the next few years.[44]

In contrast to opportunistic behavior, **relationship behavior** focuses on establishing a mutually beneficial, long-term relationship between buyers and suppliers.[45] DreamWorks Studios, which makes films and TV shows, has had a long-term strategic relationship with Hewlett-Packard (H-P), which makes computers and software. DreamWorks, the buyer, advises H-P, the supplier, on the advanced servers and data management it needs to produce animated films, or even traditional films, which today contain significant portions of computer-generated images.[46] The average DreamWorks film is created using 300 graphics workstations, 60 million rendering hours (a rendering hour is an hour of computer time used to process an image), the simultaneous use of 17,000 computer core chips, and more than 200 terabytes of storage.[47] In fact, the DreamWorks animation data center in Redwood City, California, is run completely on H-P systems.

3-3d Industry Regulation Component

Whereas the political/legal component of the general environment affects all businesses, the **industry regulation** component consists of regulations and rules that govern the practices and procedures of specific industries, businesses, and professions. To combat rising rates of

Relationship behavior the establishment of mutually beneficial, long-term exchanges between buyers and suppliers

Industry regulation regulations and rules that govern the business practices and procedures of specific industries, businesses, and professions

Walmart's "Three Strikes" Is Out for Safety; Now It's Zero Tolerance

Since Walmart clothing was found in a Bangladesh factory where a fire killed 112 workers, Walmart has adopted a much stricter policy on global sourcing standards. Previously, Walmart had used a three-strikes approach, but after the fire, the retailer warned suppliers that there would be zero-tolerance going forward. It also said it would immediately sever ties with organizations that subcontracted to other factories without Walmart's knowledge. The retailer said it had thought the factory where the fire occurred was no longer making Walmart's clothes. It began posting names of factories that suppliers are not allowed to contract with as well as requiring pre-approval audits for new factories.

Source: S. Banjo, "Wal-Mart Toughens Supplier Policies," *The Wall Street Journal*, January 21, 2013. accessed April 11, 2014. http://online.wsj.com/news/articles/SB10001424127887323301104578256183164905720?KEYWORDS=supplier+relationship&mg=reno64-wsj.

---

obesity, the U.S. Food and Drug Administration (FDA) established menu-labeling regulations requiring restaurants to clearly and conspicuously display calorie information next to the name and price of the menu item.[48]

Regulatory agencies affect businesses by creating and enforcing rules and regulations to protect consumers, workers, or society as a whole. The menu-labeling regulations angered the pizza industry, which serves 41 million Americans a day. Given the number of possible combinations of pizza toppings, crust types, and sauces, the pizza industry argues that posting accurate calorie information is practically impossible. (For a store offering twenty toppings, one type of crust, and one type of sauce, there are more than 24×10^{17} possible pizza combinations.) Ron Berger, CEO of Figaro's Pizza chain in Oregon, says, "Having to post that information on a menu board is a very costly exercise in humoring government bureaucrats." To make matters worse, the proposed regulations require pizzerias to post the calories for a whole pizza, not for individual slices.[49]

The nearly 100 federal agencies and regulatory commissions can affect almost any kind of business. For example, children's toys that contain high-powered magnets, such as Buckyballs, were once marketed as desktop toys for adults. But from 2009 to 2013, nearly 3,000 children visited emergency rooms after swallowing high-powered magnets, which can cause serious injury or death by pinching the intestinal track. So, in 2014, the Consumer Products Safety Commission (CPSC) ruled that high-powered magnets in toys needed to be too large to ingest or too weak to cause internal harm. Within six months, all of the magnet makers, except one, Zen Magnets, which is appealing the ruling in court, had ceased production.[50]

3-3e Advocacy Groups

Advocacy groups are groups of concerned citizens who band together to try to influence the business practices of specific industries, businesses, and professions. The members of a group generally share the same point of view on a particular issue. For example, environmental advocacy groups might try to get manufacturers to reduce smokestack pollution emissions. Unlike the industry regulation component of the specific environment, advocacy groups cannot force organizations to change their practices. Nevertheless, they can use a number of techniques to try to influence companies, including public communications, media advocacy, web pages, blogs, and product boycotts.

The **public communications** approach relies on *voluntary* participation by the news media and the advertising industry to send out an advocacy group's message. Hydraulic fracturing, better known

---

Advocacy groups concerned citizens who band together to try to influence the business practices of specific industries, businesses, and professions

Public communications an advocacy group tactic that relies on voluntary participation by the news media and the advertising industry to get the advocacy group's message out as fracking, is a process by which natural gas or petroleum is extracted from a layer of underground rocks. Proponents argue that fracking dramatically increases oil and gas supplies, lowers costs, and reduces dependence on foreign oil. Anti-fracking advocacy groups, such as **Artists Against Fracking** (**AAF**), however, argue that it contaminates groundwater, causes air pollution, and economically harms people who live near the mines. AAF was started by Sean Lennon and Yoko Ono to persuade New York Governor Andrew Cuomo to ban fracking in New York State. In addition to roadside billboards, petitions, and television ads, AAF released a music video called "Don't Frack My Mother," starring celebrities Susan Sarandon, Joseph Gordon-Levitt, the Black Keys, and Maggie Gyllenhaal.[51]

Media advocacy is much more aggressive than the public communications approach. A **media advocacy** approach typically involves framing the group's concerns as public issues (affecting everyone); exposing questionable, exploitative, or unethical practices; and creating controversy that is likely to receive extensive news coverage.

A **product boycott** is a tactic in which an advocacy group actively tries to persuade consumers not to purchase a company's product or service. Food in many Muslim countries is routinely tested by government agencies to make sure it is *Halal*, or free of traces of pork, alcohol, or other foods not allowed under Islamic law. So when the Malaysian Ministry of Health reported that traces of pork were found in Cadbury Dairy Milk Hazelnut and Cadbury Dairy Milk Roast Almond bars, the Muslim Consumers Association of Malaysia (MCAM) called for a boycott. MCAM's research head, Sheikh Abdul Kareem Khadaied, said, "This is an issue that cuts across religion. It affects the vegetarians as much as it affects the Muslims."[52] Subsequent tests revealed no traces of pork in Cadbury products, but MCAM's Sheikh Abdul Kareem Khadaied still insisted on a boycott until the discrepancy between the tests was resolved.[53]

3-4 MAKING SENSE OF CHANGING ENVIRONMENTS

In Chapter 1, you learned that managers are responsible for making sense of their business environments. As our discussions of the general and specific environments have indicated, however, making sense of business environments is not an easy task.

Because external environments can be dynamic, confusing, and complex, managers use a three-step process to make sense of the changes in their external environments: 3-4a environmental scanning, 3-4b interpreting environmental factors, and 3-4c acting on threats and opportunities.

3-4a Environmental Scanning

Environmental scanning involves searching the environment for important events or issues that might affect an organization. Managers scan the environment to stay up to date on important factors in their industry and to reduce uncertainty. They want to know if demand will increase, prices for key components will rise, and whether competitors sales are rising or falling. This is why Google paid $500 million to buy Skybox, a company that captures high-resolution satellite images. By 2016, Skybox will have six dedicated satellites that take complete images of the earth twice daily. By 2018, it will have twenty-four dedicated satellites that do so three times a day and can provide real-time video of trucks moving down highways. The timeliness and resolution of its images will be so good that when traveling, you'll be able to use Google Maps street view to see if you left the front porch light on at your house. That also means Walmart's sales can be accurately predicted by counting the number of cars in its parking lots. Want to know when the next iPhone will be released? You'll be able to monitor the number of trucks coming and going from Foxconn factories in Taiwan, where they're manufactured. Co-founder Dan Berkenstock says, "We think we are going to fundamentally change humanity's understanding of the economic landscape on a daily basis."[54]

Organizational strategies also affect environmental scanning. In other words, managers pay close attention to trends and events that are directly related to their company's ability to compete in the marketplace.[55] With nearly 70 percent of China's water sources polluted from industry and agriculture, consumers are understandably concerned about drinking tap water. Furthermore, water purified at Chinese treatment plants is often recontaminated by hazardous

Media advocacy an advocacy group tactic that involves framing issues as public issues; exposing questionable, exploitative, or unethical practices; and forcing media coverage by buying media time or creating controversy that is likely to receive extensive news coverage

Product boycott an advocacy group tactic that involves protesting a company's actions by persuading consumers not to purchase its product or service

Environmental scanning searching the environment for important events or issues that might affect an organization

SSL Headquarters

Skybox Headquarters

AP Images/PRNewsFoto/SSL

materials when transported to homes. According to Hope Lee, an analyst with Euromonitor, "You don't dare drink the tap water in China." China's water problem, however, represents a business opportunity for Nestlé's bottled water business, especially with sales flat in North America and Europe. Chinese sales of bottled water, by contrast, are expected to grow significantly from $9 billion in 2012 to $16 billion in 2017. Therefore, Nestlé is rapidly expanding in China, selling water in five-gallon jugs, often through company-owned stores that provide free delivery to consumers' homes. Nestlé's Chinese sales have jumped 27 percent from the previous year.[56]

Finally, environmental scanning is important because it contributes to organizational performance. Environmental scanning helps managers detect environmental changes and problems before they become organizational crises.[57] Furthermore, companies whose CEOs do more environmental scanning have higher profits.[58] CEOs in better-performing firms scan their firms' environments more frequently and scan more key factors in their environments in more depth and detail than do CEOs in poorer-performing firms.[59]

3-4b Interpreting Environmental Factors

After scanning, managers determine what environmental events and issues mean to the organization. Typically, managers view environmental events and issues as either

threats or opportunities. When managers interpret environmental events as threats, they take steps to protect the company from further harm. For more than a century, dry cereal was found on nearly every breakfast table in the United States. At its peak, Kellogg's and its cast of cartoon cereal mascots held a dominating 45 percent share of the market. Today, however, Kellogg's sales are dropping. Instead of having cereal for breakfast, many Americans now prefer a variety of alternatives, such as a piece of fruit, a breakfast sandwich, a granola bar, or a protein shake, all of which they can eat in their car or at their desk. Kellogg's CEO John Bryant acknowledges

Mahathir Mohd Yasin/Shutterstock.com

"Kellogg's saw sales of Fruit Loops rise three percent annually when it started interpreting the marketing environment correctly."

the threat to the company, saying, "The good news is that more people are eating breakfast; the bad news is that there are more alternatives."[60] Kellogg's CEO John Bryant implemented Project K, a cost-cutting program, from which a percentage of the savings would be invested in product innovation. Kellogg's also hired additional sales people to create more attractive in-store product displays. And, the company changed how it markets some of its cereals. For example, sales of Fruit Loops rose 3 percent after they were marketed to adults as a late-night snack.[61]

By contrast, when managers interpret environmental events as opportunities, they consider strategic alternatives for taking advantage of those events to improve company performance. The Panama Canal, open since 1914, handles 5 percent of the world's shipping traffic. Ships traveling from San Francisco to New York City, or from Asia to the U.S. East Coast, sail 8,000 fewer miles compared to rounding Cape Horn at the southern tip of South America. While wide and deep enough to handle today's so-called Panamax ships with 5,000 20-foot TEU (twenty-foot equivalent unit) containers, the Panama Canal is losing business because the shipping industry is changing to larger Post Panamax ships carrying 8,000 to 18,000 TEUs. Post Panamax ships are much more fuel efficient and save on canal charges, too, which can run as much as $450,000 per ship.[62] For example, instead of sending two 4,500 TEU ships through the Panama Canal to transport goods from Asia to the U.S. East Coast, the Maersk Line will send one Post Panamax ship loaded with 9,000 TEUs through the Suez Canal.[63] Faced with the loss of a significant amount of shipping traffic (Post Panamax ships will handle 65 percent of sea transportation by 2030), the Panama Canal Authority District began a $5.25 billion expansion to handle ships—ships with up to 13,000 TEUs. With the 2015 addition of a parallel 50-foot wide canal, the Panama Canal will instantly double its cargo shipping capacity.[64]

3-4c Acting on Threats and Opportunities

After scanning for information on environmental events and issues and interpreting them as threats or opportunities, managers have to decide how to respond to these environmental factors. Deciding what to do under conditions of uncertainty is always difficult. Managers can never be completely confident that they have all the information they need or that they correctly understand the information they have.

Because it is impossible to comprehend all the factors and changes, managers often rely on simplified models of external environments called cognitive maps. **Cognitive maps** summarize the perceived relationships between environmental factors and possible organizational actions. For example, the cognitive map shown in Exhibit 3.3 represents a small clothing-store owner's interpretation of her business environment. The map shows three kinds of variables. The first variables, shown as rectangles, are environmental factors, such as a Walmart or a large mall twenty minutes away. The second variables, shown in ovals, are potential actions that the store owner might take, such as a low-cost strategy; a good-value, good-service strategy; or a "large selection of the latest fashions" strategy. The third variables, shown as trapezoids, are company strengths, such as low employee turnover, and weaknesses, such as small size.

The plus and minus signs on the map indicate whether the manager believes there is a positive or negative relationship between variables. For example, the manager believes that a low-cost strategy won't work because Walmart and Target are nearby. Offering a large selection of the latest fashions would not work either—not with the small size of the store and that large nearby mall. However, the manager believes that a good-value, good-service strategy would lead to success and profits due to the store's low employee turnover, good knowledge of customers, reasonable selection of clothes at reasonable prices, and good location.

 3-5

ORGANIZATIONAL CULTURES: CREATION, SUCCESS, AND CHANGE

We have been looking at trends and events outside of companies that have the potential to affect them. By contrast, the **internal environment** consists of the trends and events *within* an organization that affect the management, employees, and **organizational culture**. Internal environments are important because they affect what people think,

Exhibit 3.3
Cognitive Maps

Good value/good service most likely to produce success and profits.

- Target — Low-cost
- Walmart — Low-cost
- Low rent and taxes + Low-cost
- Low-cost + Reasonable selection and prices
- Good location + Good value Good service
- Large mall twenty minutes away + Good value Good service
- Good value Good service + Reasonable selection and prices
- Good value Good service + Know customers well
- Good value Good service + Low employee turnover
- Large mall twenty minutes away − Large selection of latest fashions
- Large selection of latest fashions − Too small to get volume discounts

Environmental Factors   Potential Strategies   Company Strengths and Weaknesses

© Cengage Learning

feel, and do at work. The key component in internal environments is organizational culture, or the set of key values, beliefs, and attitudes shared by members of the organization.

Under Armour, the sporting apparel and accessories maker, got its start two decades ago when founder and CEO Kevin Plank, a former college football player and special teams captain, sewed shorts and shirts himself in his grandmother's Baltimore, Maryland, basement. Today, Under Armour is a fast-growing—sales increased 27 percent in 2013—$2.3 billion company that competes with Nike, Reebok, and Adidas. One of the keys to its meteoric rise may be its "faster-stronger-better" internal culture. Plank says, "We as a company don't sleep much. We work harder. We have a commitment that I think would be exhausting to someone else." To sustain that hard-driving, competitive culture, Under Armour builds camaraderie and a team orientation among employees. New employees are given big welcome breakfasts. Staff members are treated to outdoor movie nights, tuition reimbursement, and discounted tickets to sporting events, and there is a club for working mothers that offers support and advice. Says Plank, "I manage the company much like a team. Coming out of school and starting the business, sales and marketing were offense, and manufacturing was defense, and finance and operations were like special teams. What I've come to find out is that when the company is the best, it's not that one team is playing and another team is winning on the side, it's that everyone is on the field together."[65]

*Let's take a closer look at **3-5a how organizational cultures are created and maintained, 3-5b the characteristics of successful organizational cultures,** and **3-5c how companies can accomplish the difficult task of changing organizational cultures.***

3-5a Creation and Maintenance of Organizational Cultures

A primary source of organizational culture is the company founder. Founders like Walt Disney (Disney) and Steve Jobs (Apple) created organizations in their own images and imprinted them with their beliefs, attitudes, and values. According to Professor Zeynep Ton, "The founder is in a better position than anyone else to say this is what our business is about, this is what we won't give up. They have to stick to their values 100 percent of the time, not 95 percent of the time." Founder Kip Tindell infused the **Container Store** with his personal philosophy, "Pay employees well and treat them with respect; consider suppliers and customers as family; have fun."[66] Tindell has turned that philosophy into seven Foundational Principles (see http://standfor.containerstore.com /our-foundation-principles/) that drive the Container Store's culture and actions. Not only are full-time employees given a week of training on the principles, the principles have been printed on company shopping bags, t-shirts, and packing tape. One strong sign that the principles have shaped the company culture is the low rate of employee turnover. Whereas the median turnover rate for part-time retail workers is 75 percent, at the Container Store, it is only 10 percent.[67] How are values, attitudes, and beliefs sustained in organizational cultures? Answer: stories and heroes.

People tell **organizational stories** to make sense of organizational events and changes and to emphasize culturally consistent assumptions, decisions, and actions.[68] Andreessen Horowitz (AH) is a venture capital (VC) firm that invests millions in high-potential technology startups. AH's co-founders, Mark Andreessen and Ben Horowitz have significant experience—and success—starting high-tech companies that have sold for nearly $2 billion. Horowitz said, "When we started Andreessen Horowitz, we knew that one of the most frustrating things for entrepreneurs is that VCs do not respect their time. As entrepreneurs, every time we'd visit a VC [trying to secure funding for our companies], we'd wait in the lobby for 30 to 45 minutes. So at the core of the firm, we wanted a cultural tenet to be respect for the entrepreneur and the entrepreneurial process. But how do you get that into people's minds? The mechanism I came up with was to tell VCs that if you are late for a meeting with an entrepreneur, then the fine is $10 a minute. That is a very big fine. It is shocking to people who have to pay it. And that's the point. Because every time somebody pays a fine, *we get to tell the story* of why the person is paying so much money."[69]

A second way in which organizational culture is sustained is by recognizing and celebrating heroes. By

Exhibit 3.4
Keys to an Organizational Culture That Fosters Success

Consistency

Clear Mission

Adaptability

Employee Involvement

iStockphoto.com/Stillfx

definition, **organizational heroes** are organizational people admired for their qualities and achievements within the organization. Francisco D'Souza, CEO of Cognizant, an information technology firm with 170,000 employees, explains that, "Culture gets passed along not by writing it down, but through the rituals you have in the organization, the legends you refer to, and the heroes of the organization. So we institutionalized a set of things to create rituals, heroes, and legends."[70] Cognizant does that by having each regional division name an associate of the year who heroically exemplifies the company's culture. Likewise, to broaden cultural recognition beyond individuals to key teams and groups, Cognizant has each division celebrate a project of the year. D'Souza explains that, "We rent stadiums around the world and bring all the employees and their families for a celebration, with entertainment and awards."[71]

3-5b Successful Organizational Cultures

Preliminary research shows that organizational culture is related to organizational success. As shown in Exhibit 3.4, cultures based on adaptability, involvement, a clear mission, and

Organizational stories stories told by organizational members to make sense of organizational events and changes and to emphasize culturally consistent assumptions, decisions, and actions

Organizational heroes people celebrated for their qualities and achievements within an organization consistency can help companies achieve higher sales growth, return on assets, profits, quality, and employee satisfaction.[72]

Adaptability is the ability to notice and respond to changes in the organization's environment. Cultures need to reinforce important values and behaviors, but a culture becomes dysfunctional if it prevents change. Unfortunately, that was the case at **Mattel**, the toy company, where Barbie sales are down 18 percent this year after dropping 13 percent the year before. Sales of Fisher-Price toys have declined three straight years. With revenues shrinking, Mattel has cut $550 million in expenses just to maintain profits. New CEO Bryan Stockton is trying to turn things around by changing the PowerPoint-presentation, meeting-driven, slow-to-make decisions culture. For example, it took eight meetings and thirty design iterations to approve the school crest for the Monster High toy line. As such, Mattel drifted from its creative roots focused on fun and play toward a conservative culture focused on the bottom line. To jump-start culture change, CEO Stockton has generated new rules for meetings: No more than ten participants (except for training meetings), every meeting must have a specific purpose, and "There should be no more than a TOTAL of three meetings to make any decision."[73] Change is slow, but it took just one meeting to approve the new package designs for the 2016 Hot Wheels toys.

Company mission is the business's purpose or reason for existing. In organizational cultures with a clear company mission, the organization's strategic purpose and direction are apparent to everyone in the company. When managers are uncertain about their business environments, the mission helps guide the discussions, decisions, and behavior of the people in the company. BPV Capital Management is a Knoxville, Tennessee, mutual fund with thirty-eight employees. Alluding to the common dream of owning a retirement home with wonderful weather and a great view, founder Mike West explains that "BPV" stands for "back porch vista"; BPV exists "to help American families retire well." More specifically, its mission is, "To ensure that investors who work hard and save have the opportunity to retire comfortably, regardless of net worth." Says West, "Our values and the promise that we make to every advisor and investor are driven by that core ideology."[74]

Finally, in **consistent organizational cultures**, the company actively defines and teaches organizational values, beliefs, and attitudes (see box "At Eaton, Integration Starts Early"). Consistent

At Eaton, Integration Starts Early

When two companies merge, there is always the risk that the culture of one company will clash with the other, making it miserable for people to work together. As Alexander Cutler, CEO of diversified manufacturer Eaton, says, "Our rule has always been that no acquisition is better than a bad acquisition." Cutler would know, too: since 2000, Eaton has acquired more than sixty-five other companies. According to Cutler, assessment of cultural integration should start before the deal is finalized. Leadership styles and ethical standards should receive close attention. After the deal is closed, Cutler is quick to work toward opening communication channels. The new employees will begin ethics training courses. Eaton representatives will visit sites of the acquired firm and begin discussions with management at the new firm about corporate values and operational processes. Cutler adds, "It's not a situation where the Eaton idea wins. We want to understand the best way to do things."

Source: J. Katz, "The Key to Corporate Cultures? Start Early," *IndustryWeek*, February 14, 2013. accessed April 14, 2014. http://www.industryweek.com /corporate-culture/key-merging-corporate-cultures-start-early?page=1.

with its code of conduct to "Do no harm to people. Protect the environment, and comply with all laws and regulations," when Royal Dutch Shell, the multinational energy company, buys smaller drilling companies, the first thing it does is shut down the drilling rigs for several weeks to retrain the workers in terms of safety and environmental procedures. J. R. Justus, Shell's general manager in Appalachia, says, "I don't think there's any question that the culture around safety has changed considerably since Shell came here. We've got a lot more technical resources to bring to bear than a smaller independent company would." In terms of Shell's improvements to environmental practices, Shell, unlike many smaller drilling companies, lines oil wells with steel pipe surrounded by cement, which fills the gaps between the pipe and surrounding earth, so that gas or fluids can't seep into rock layers or water sources. As a result, Shell is cited for environmental citations just 6.5 percent of the time compared to 14 percent for mid sized drillers and 17 percent for small ones.[75]

Having a consistent or strong organizational culture doesn't guarantee good company performance. When core beliefs are widely shared and strongly held, it is very difficult to bring about needed change. Consequently, companies with strong cultures tend to perform poorly when they need to adapt to dramatic changes in

Exhibit 3.5
Three Levels of Organizational Culture

SEEN
(Surface level)

HEARD
(Expressed values
and beliefs)

BELIEVED
(Unconscious
assumptions and
beliefs)

- Symbolic artifacts such as dress codes
- Workers' and managers' behaviors
- What people say
- How decisions are made and explained
- Widely shared assumptions and beliefs
- Buried deep below surface
- Rarely discussed or thought about

Anton Zabielskyi/Shutterstock.com

their external environments. Their consistency sometimes prevents them from adapting to those changes.[76]

3-5c Changing Organizational Cultures

As shown in Exhibit 3.5, organizational cultures exist on three levels.[77] On the first, or surface, level are the reflections of an organization's culture that can be seen and observed, such as symbolic artifacts (for example, dress codes and office layouts) and workers' and managers' behaviors. Next, just below the surface, are the values and beliefs expressed by people in the company. You can't see these values and beliefs, but they become clear if you carefully listen to what people say and observe how decisions are made or explained. Finally, unconsciously held assumptions and beliefs about the company are buried deep below the surface. These are the unwritten views and rules that are so strongly held and so widely shared that they are rarely discussed or even thought about unless someone attempts to change them

or unknowingly violates them. Changing such assumptions and beliefs can be very difficult. Instead, managers should focus on the parts of the organizational culture they can control. These include observable surface-level items, such as workers' behaviors, symbolic artifacts, and expressed values and beliefs, which can be influenced through employee selection. Let's see how these can be used to change organizational cultures.

One way of changing a corporate culture is to use behavioral addition or behavioral substitution to establish new patterns of behavior among managers and employees. **Behavioral addition** is the process of having managers and employees perform a new behavior, while **behavioral substitution** is having

Behavioral addition the process of having managers and employees perform new behaviors that are central to and symbolic of the new organizational culture that a company wants to create

Behavioral substitution the process of having managers and employees perform new behaviors central to the new organizational culture in place of behaviors that were central to the old organizational culture

Construction as Culture

Visible artifacts are, at their core, about defining corporate identity—especially, it seems, for tech companies, which are often championed as fun, relaxed, productive campuses. Apple, Facebook, and Google have taken the quest for the coolest, most collaborative headquarters to a new level. Each company has enlisted the services of an architectural icon who is reflective of its corporate culture to design its corporate offices. Apple has hired Sir Norman Foster (stoic); Google has hired Bjarke Ingels and Thomas Heatherwick (fun); and Facebook has hired Frank Gehry (expressionist). Through architecture, each company hopes to create a structure that communicates its mission, work, and personality.

Source: K. Campell-Dollaghan, "The Forgotten Offices That Shaped Apple, Google, and Facebook," Gizmodo.com, April 1, 2015. http://gizmodo.com/the-forgotten-offices-that-inspired-apple-facebook-an-1694978864.

managers and employees perform a new behavior in place of another behavior. The key in both instances is to choose behaviors that are central to and symbolic of the old culture you're changing and the new culture that you want to create. When Bob Flexon became CEO of **Dynegy**, which provides wholesale energy to utilities, energy cooperatives, and municipalities, the company was losing hundreds of millions of dollars. So, he not only cut costs, he began changing the company culture by emphasizing new behaviors. The first move was to ditch his expansive corner office—with a $15,000 marble desk and Oriental rugs—for a 64-foot cubicle identical to those used by everyone else at Dynegy's new headquarters, which is now on a single floor in a cheaper building (resulting in annual savings of $5 million). In terms of culture, Flexon and his leadership team created a new set of expectations regarding management and employee behavior. To start, employees received their first performance appraisals in two years (behavioral addition), including judgments regarding how well they were embracing the new cultural norms of safety, accountability, and agility. Next, managers and employees were expected to "Be Here Now," which means no distractions when engaging with others. For example, chief administrative officer Carolyn Burke has told employees who are tapping on their smartphones in meetings,

Visible artifacts visible signs of an organization's culture, such as the office design and layout, company dress code, and company benefits and perks, such as stock options, personal parking spaces, or the private company dining room

"Hey, be here now." Likewise, CEO Flexon has a "Be Here Now" plaque underneath his computer monitor to remind him to not read emails during phone calls (behavioral substitution).[78]

Another way in which managers can begin to change corporate culture is to change the **visible artifacts** of their old culture, such as the office design and layout, company dress code, and recipients (or nonrecipients) of company benefits and perks such as stock options, personal parking spaces, or the private company dining room. In the 1990s, AOL was the dominant force among Internet service and content providers. So many people had AOL accounts that its well-known "You've Got Mail" alert was the title of a Hollywood movie. However, intense competition from high-speed Internet providers, two decades of bad decisions, and a costly merger with and then split from Time Warner reduced it to a Silicon Valley dinosaur. AOL is trying to shed that image and create a new culture that emphasizes creativity, collaboration, and innovation. Brad Garlinghouse, former president of AOL, said, "AOL wasn't building great products, and the brand was reflecting that. We have to expunge the ghosts of AOL and start fresh." A key component of AOL's culture change is the tear down and complete redesign of offices in Palo Alto, California. Whereas its old offices had drab halls, cubicles, and high walls that limited employee interactions, the newly redesigned offices have an open design featuring a central space with glass-walled work rooms for team collaboration; round standalone rooms with opaque glass for quiet work that requires privacy and concentration; and public spaces with pool, ping-pong, and foosball tables; couches and chairs with laptop stands; and a cafeteria that's open 24/7. Consistent with its culture change, AOL also took the unusual move of opening up its redesigned offices to seventy-five employees from twenty-five start-up companies, who work with and share ideas with AOL's staffers. CEO Tim Armstrong said, "We really have tried to make our offices into centers of creativity where we can invite other people to come in and work for us. The opportunity is to take some of the world's best entrepreneurs and technologists and have them work in a deeply engaging place."[79]

Cultures can also be changed by hiring and selecting people with values and beliefs consistent with the company's desired culture. *Selection* is the process of gathering information about job applicants to decide who should be offered a job. As discussed in Chapter 11 on human resources, most selection instruments measure whether job applicants have the knowledge, skills, and abilities needed to succeed in their jobs. But companies are increasingly testing job applicants to determine

Changing corporate culture can go a long way in boosting employee moral.

how they fit with the company's desired culture (that is, values and beliefs). In the past ten years, the Cleveland Browns football team has had only one season in which it won more than six games. During that time, the Browns had seven different head coaches. When Mike Pettine became the head coach in spring 2014, he inherited a team with a culture marked by instability, losing, and inexperience; only four Browns' players had ever been to the playoffs. When he started signing new players for the upcoming season, a key qualification (in addition to talent) was experience on a team with a winning culture. Consistent with his goal of building that winning culture, five of the first seven players he signed had been to the playoffs, while three had played in the Super Bowl.[80]

The second step is to ensure that applicants fit with the culture by using selection tests, instruments, and exercises to measure these values and beliefs in job applicants. (See Chapter 11 for a complete review of applicant and managerial selection.) During the hiring process, Amazon uses a group of employees called "Bar Raisers," who interview job candidates from other areas of the company, asking difficult and unexpected questions. Bar Raisers, who spend two to three hours on each job candidate, conducting phone and face-to-face interviews and participating in evaluation meetings, have the power to veto any applicant they've assessed. Founder Jeff Bezos started the Bar Raiser program to create a

consistent corporate culture by "raising the bar" when it came to hiring talent. Rather than hiring people for particular jobs, Bezos asks Bar Raisers to focus on hiring people who can succeed in Amazon's culture. John Vlastelica, an HR consultant who worked at Amazon in its early days, says, "You want someone who can adapt to new roles in the company, not just someone who can fill the role that's vacant." Susan Harker, Amazon's vice president of global talent acquisition, says, "We want to be as objective and scientific in our hiring as possible. The point is to optimize our chances of having long-term employees." And, unlike many companies, that means hiring talented people who fit Amazon's culture. Human resource consultant Valerie Frederickson says, "There is no company that sticks to its process like Amazon does. They don't just hire the best of what they see; they're willing to keep looking and looking for the right talent."[81]

Corporate cultures are very difficult to change. Consequently, there is no guarantee that any one approach—changing visible cultural artifacts, using behavioral substitution, or hiring people with values consistent with a company's desired culture—will change a company's organizational culture. The best results are obtained by combining these methods. Together, these are some of the best tools managers have for changing culture because they send the clear message to managers and employees that "the accepted way of doing things" has changed.

4 Ethics and Social Responsibility

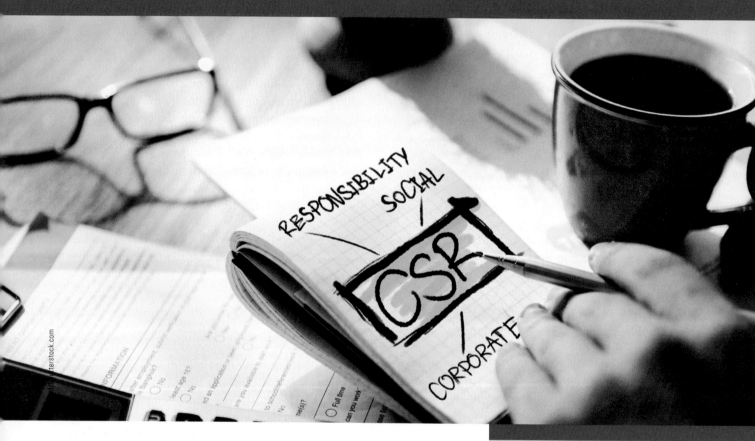

LEARNING OUTCOMES

4-1 Identify common kinds of workplace deviance.

4-2 Describe the U.S. Sentencing Commission Guidelines for Organizations, and explain how they both encourage ethical behavior and punish unethical behavior by businesses.

4-3 Describe what influences ethical decision making.

4-4 Explain what practical steps managers can take to improve ethical decision making.

4-5 Explain to whom organizations are socially responsible.

4-6 Explain for what organizations are socially responsible.

4-7 Explain how organizations can respond to societal demands for social responsibility.

4-8 Explain whether social responsibility hurts or helps an organization's economic performance.

After you finish this chapter, go to **PAGE 87** for

STUDY TOOLS

WORKPLACE DEVIANCE

Today, it's not enough for companies to make a profit. We also expect managers to make a profit by doing the right things. Unfortunately, no matter what managers decide to do, someone or some group will be unhappy with the outcome. Managers don't have the luxury of choosing theoretically optimal, win-win solutions that are obviously desirable to everyone involved. In practice, solutions to ethical and social responsibility problems aren't optimal. Often, managers must be satisfied with a solution that just makes do or does the least harm. Rights and wrongs are rarely crystal clear to managers charged with doing the right thing. The business world is much messier than that.

Ethics is the set of moral principles or values that defines right and wrong for a person or group. Unfortunately, numerous studies have consistently produced distressing results about the state of ethics in today's business world. One global ethics study reported that only 28 percent of respondents believed businesses were ethical. Another study found that just 25 percent trust business leaders to honestly correct mistakes and that less than 20 percent believed that business leaders would be truthful and make ethical decisions.[1] According to the Ethics Recourse Center's National Business Ethics Survey, 41 percent of employees observed unethical behavior at work. Twenty-four percent of unethical behavior was committed by senior managers, while 60 percent was committed by managers (of all kinds). Moreover, 9 percent of employees report being pressured to compromise ethical standards at work.[2] The good news, however, is that 63 percent of employees observing unethical behavior reported it.[3]

Other studies contain additional good news about workplace ethics. When people believe their work environment is ethical, they are six times more likely to stay with that company than if they believe they work in an unethical environment.[4] In fact, a survey by Deloitte reported that employees who were considering leaving their jobs cited "loss of trust" as the greatest factor.[5] One study asked 444 white-collar workers which qualities they considered to be important in company leaders. The results? Honesty (30 percent) and communication (22 percent) ranked by far the highest. Interestingly, these two qualities also ranked highest as areas in which business leaders needed to improve—16 percent of respondents said that leaders need to improve their honesty, and 11 percent cited communication.[6] According to Eduardo Castro-Wright, vice chairman of Walmart Stores Inc., "There's nothing that destroys credibility more than not being

able to look someone in the eye and have them know that they can trust you."[7] In short, much needs to be done to make workplaces more ethical, but—and this is very important—most managers and employees want this to happen.

Ethical behavior follows accepted principles of right and wrong. Depending on which study you look at, one-third to three-quarters of all employees admit that they have stolen from their employers, committed computer fraud, embezzled funds, vandalized company property, sabotaged company projects, faked injuries to receive workers' compensation benefits or insurance, or been "sick" from work when they

Ethics the set of moral principles or values that defines right and wrong for a person or group

Ethical behavior behavior that conforms to a society's accepted principles of right and wrong

Exhibit 4.1
Types of Workplace Deviance

Organizational

Production Deviance
- Leaving early
- Taking excessive breaks
- Intentionally working slowly
- Wasting resources

Property Deviance
- Sabotaging equipment
- Accepting kickbacks
- Lying about hours worked
- Stealing from company

Minor ←→ **Serious**

Political Deviance
- Showing favoritism
- Gossiping about coworkers
- Blaming coworkers
- Competing nonbeneficially

Personal Aggression
- Sexual harassment
- Verbal abuse
- Stealing from coworkers
- Endangering coworkers

Interpersonal

Source: Adapted from "A Typology of Deviant Workplace Behaviors" (Figure), S. L. Robinson and R. J. Bennett. Academy of Management Journal, 1995, Vol. 38.

intentionally working slower, or wasting resources. Every spring, employees fill out their tournament brackets for March Madness in hopes of winning office betting pools (which are technically illegal) for most accurately predicting which teams advance during the NCAA basketball tournament. Employees commonly spend time talking about which teams made or didn't make the tournament, setting up brackets, and managing office pools. In addition, the first two days of tournament play occur on a Thursday and Friday during working hours. Outplacement firm Challenger, Gray, and Christmas estimates that 60 million American office workers participate in March Madness office pools. In 2015, as the University of Kentucky was chasing its first undefeated season in more than thirty years, John Challenger said, "If Kentucky plays their first game during the workday, it wouldn't be shocking if every single working person in the state called in sick for the day or took an extra-long lunch break." Although he was joking, with 56 percent of 60 million U.S. workers spending at least one work hour on the tournament, that lost time costs employers $1.9 billion. And that doesn't even consider how much more time employees will spend not working as they watch the games at work online, or get updates via Twitter or special sports apps on their smartphones.[10]

weren't really sick. Experts estimate that unethical behaviors like these, which researchers call *workplace deviance*, may cost companies as much as $3.7 trillion a year, or roughly 5 percent of their revenues.[8]

Workplace deviance is unethical behavior that violates organizational norms about right and wrong. As Exhibit 4.1 shows, workplace deviance can be categorized by how deviant the behavior is, from minor to serious, and by the target of the deviant behavior, either the organization or particular people in the workplace.[9]

Company-related deviance can affect both tangible and intangible assets. One kind of workplace deviance, called **production deviance**, hurts the quality and quantity of work produced. Examples include leaving early, taking excessively long work breaks,

Property deviance is unethical behavior aimed at company property or products. Examples include sabotaging, stealing, or damaging equipment or products, and overcharging for services and then pocketing the difference. For example, in Nigeria, thieves steal 150,000 barrels a day of oil from oil company pipelines. Jacob Mandi, a diver who has grown rich stealing oil from pipelines, says, "We know which [pipeline] is gas, products, crude. We can sense whether it is hot or cold. We need nobody's help to know what's inside." Eni S.p.A., an Italian oil company, closed its production facilities in Nigeria because it was losing 60 percent of its production to thieves like Mandi.[11]

Organizational employees, however, do a significant amount of property deviance themselves. **Employee shrinkage**, when employees steal company merchandise, accounts for 43 percent of theft from U.S. retailers and costs $18 billion a year. In fact, employee theft costs U.S. retailers more than shoplifters do![12] A survey of twenty-three large retailers employing more than 3 million workers found that one out of forty employees is caught stealing each year and that a dishonest employee steals 5.4 times as much as the typical shoplifter.[13] Likewise, 58 percent of office workers acknowledge taking

Workplace deviance
unethical behavior that violates organizational norms about right and wrong

Production deviance
unethical behavior that hurts the quality and quantity of work produced

Property deviance
unethical behavior aimed at the organization's property or products

Employee shrinkage
employee theft of company merchandise

company property for personal use, according to a survey conducted for lawyers.com. "Sweethearting" occurs when employees discount or don't ring up merchandise their family or friends bring to the cash register. A recent study found that sweethearting costs the retail service industry (that is, restaurants, hotels, hair salons, car washes, and so on) $80 billion annually. Of the employees surveyed, 67 percent indicated that, in the month prior to the survey, they had participated in some form of sweethearting, primarily in hopes of receiving similar deals and discounts from the customers to whom they had extended a sweetheart deal.[14] In "dumpster diving," employees unload trucks, stash merchandise in a dumpster, and then retrieve it after work.[15]

Whereas production and property deviance harm companies, political deviance and personal aggression are unethical behaviors that hurt particular people within companies. **Political deviance** is using one's influence to harm others in the company. Examples include making decisions based on favoritism rather than performance, spreading rumors about coworkers, or blaming others for mistakes they didn't make. **Personal aggression** is hostile or aggressive behavior toward others. Examples include sexual harassment, verbal abuse, stealing from coworkers, or personally threatening coworkers. Another kind of personal aggression is workplace violence. Fortunately, like nearly all kinds of crime, workplace violence has dropped significantly since 1993, when 16 of every 1,000 employees experienced nonfatal workplace violence. Today, the rate has dropped to just 4 of every 1,000 employees. Furthermore, the rate of workplace violence is one-third the level of nonworkplace violence. So, overall, you are less likely to encounter violence at work. Still, 475 people were killed at work in 2012, the most recent year for which data are available. That means 10 percent of workplace deaths are homicides.[16] For more information on workplace violence, see the Bureau of Labor Statistics website, http://www.bls.gov/iif/osh_wpvs.htm.

4-2 U.S. SENTENCING COMMISSION GUIDELINES FOR ORGANIZATIONS

A male supervisor is sexually harassing female coworkers. A sales representative offers a $10,000 kickback to persuade an indecisive customer to do business with his company. A company president secretly meets with the CEO of her biggest competitor, and they agree not to compete in markets where the other has already established customers. Each of these behaviors is clearly unethical (and, in these cases, also illegal). Historically, if management was unaware of such activities, the company could not be held responsible for them. Since 1991, however, when the U.S. Sentencing Commission Guidelines for Organizations were established, companies can be prosecuted and punished *even if management didn't know about the unethical behavior.* Penalties can be substantial, with maximum fines approaching a whopping $300 million.[17] Later changes to the Guidelines resulted in much stricter ethics training requirements and emphasized the importance of creating a legal and ethical company culture.[18]

*Let's examine **4-2a to whom the guidelines apply and what they cover** and **4-2b how, according to the guidelines, an organization can be punished for the unethical behavior of its managers and employees.***

4-2a Who, What, and Why?

Nearly all businesses are covered by the U.S. Sentencing Commission's guidelines. This includes nonprofits, partnerships, labor unions, unincorporated organizations and associations, incorporated organizations, and even pension funds, trusts, and joint stock companies. If your organization can be characterized as a business (remember, nonprofits count, too), then it is subject to the guidelines.[19] For example, World Vision, a nonprofit Christian humanitarian aid organization, has a compliance program based on the U.S. sentencing guidelines. The program includes regular audits, a code of conduct, ethics standards, and anti-bribery and corruption policies (because much of its humanitarian work is carried out in third world countries).[20]

The guidelines cover offenses defined by federal laws such as invasion of privacy, price fixing, fraud, customs violations, antitrust violations, civil rights violations, theft, money laundering, conflicts of interest, embezzlement, dealing in stolen goods, copyright infringements, extortion, and more. But it's not enough merely to stay within the law. The purpose of the guidelines is not just to punish companies *after* they or their employees break the law but also to encourage companies to take proactive steps that will discourage or prevent white-collar crime *before* it happens. The guidelines also give companies an incentive to cooperate with and disclose illegal activities to federal authorities.[21]

Political deviance using one's influence to harm others in the company

Personal aggression hostile or aggressive behavior toward others

Exhibit 4.2

Offense Levels, Base Fines, Culpability Scores, and Possible Total Fines under the U.S. Sentencing Commission Guidelines for Organizations

Offense Level	Base Fine	Culpability Scores					
		0.05	0.5	1.0	2.0	3.0	4.0
6 or less	$ 5,000	$ 250	$ 2,500	$ 5,000	$ 10,000	$ 15,000	$ 20,000
7	7,500	375	3,750	7,500	15,000	22,500	30,000
8	10,000	500	5,000	10,000	20,000	30,000	40,000
9	15,000	750	7,500	15,000	30,000	45,000	60,000
10	20,000	1,000	10,000	20,000	40,000	60,000	80,000
11	30,000	1,500	15,000	30,000	60,000	90,000	120,000
12	40,000	2,000	20,000	40,000	80,000	120,000	160,000
13	60,000	3,000	30,000	60,000	120,000	180,000	240,000
14	85,000	4,250	42,500	85,000	170,000	255,000	340,000
15	125,000	6,250	62,500	125,000	250,000	375,000	500,000
16	175,000	8,750	87,500	175,000	350,000	525,000	700,000
17	250,000	12,500	125,000	250,000	500,000	750,000	1,000,000
18	350,000	17,500	175,000	350,000	700,000	1,050,000	1,400,000
19	500,000	25,000	250,000	500,000	1,000,000	1,500,000	2,000,000
20	650,000	32,500	325,000	650,000	1,300,000	1,950,000	2,600,000
21	910,000	45,500	455,000	910,000	1,820,000	2,730,000	3,640,000
22	1,200,000	60,000	600,000	1,200,000	2,400,000	3,600,000	4,800,000
23	1,600,000	80,000	800,000	1,600,000	3,200,000	4,800,000	6,400,000
24	2,100,000	105,000	1,050,000	2,100,000	4,200,000	6,300,000	8,400,000
25	2,800,000	1,40,000	1,400,000	2,800,000	5,600,000	8,400,000	11,200,000
26	3,700,000	185,000	1,850,000	3,700,000	7,400,000	11,100,000	14,800,000
27	4,800,000	240,000	2,400,000	4,800,000	9,600,000	14,400,000	19,200,000
28	6,300,000	315,000	3,150,000	6,300,000	12,600,000	18,900,000	25,200,000
29	8,100,000	405,000	4,050,000	8,100,000	16,200,000	24,300,000	32,400,000
30	10,500,000	525,000	5,250,000	10,500,000	21,000,000	31,500,000	42,000,000
31	13,500,000	675,000	6,750,000	13,500,000	27,000,000	40,500,000	54,000,000
32	17,500,000	875,000	8,750,000	17,500,000	35,000,000	52,500,000	70,000,000
33	22,000,000	1,100,000	11,000,000	22,000,000	44,000,000	66,000,000	88,000,000
34	28,500,000	1,425,000	14,250,000	28,500,000	57,000,000	85,500,000	114,000,000
35	36,000,000	1,800,000	18,000,000	36,000,000	72,000,000	108,000,000	144,000,000
36	45,500,000	2,275,000	22,750,000	45,500,000	91,000,000	136,500,000	182,000,000
37	57,500,000	2,875,000	28,750,000	57,500,000	115,000,000	172,500,000	230,000,000
38 or more	72,500,000	3,625,000	36,250,000	72,500,000	145,000,000	217,500,000	290,000,000

Source: U.S. Sentencing Commission, *Guidelines Manual*, §3E1.1 (Nov. 2009), 509–531, accessed June 4, 2010. http://www.ussc.gov/guidelines-manual/guidelines-manual.

Terry Hankins/iStockphoto.com

4-2b Determining the Punishment

The guidelines impose smaller fines on companies that take proactive steps to encourage ethical behavior or voluntarily disclose illegal activities to federal authorities. Essentially, the law uses a carrot-and-stick approach. The stick is the threat of heavy fines that can total millions of dollars. The carrot is a greatly reduced fine, but only if the company has started an effective compliance program (discussed next) to encourage ethical behavior *before* the illegal activity occurs.[22] The method used to determine a company's punishment illustrates the importance of establishing a compliance program, as illustrated in Exhibit 4.2.

The first step is to compute the *base fine* by determining what *level of offense* (that is, its seriousness) has occurred. The level of the offense varies depending on the kind of crime, the loss incurred by the victims, and how much planning went into the crime. For example, simple fraud is a level 6 offense (there are thirty-eight levels in all). But if the victims of that fraud lost more than $5 million, that level 6 offense becomes a level 22 offense. Moreover, anything beyond minimal planning to commit the fraud results in an increase of two levels to a level 24 offense. How much difference would this make to a company? As Exhibit 4.2 shows, crimes at or below level 6 incur a base fine of $5,000, whereas the base fine for level 24 is $2.1 million, a difference of $2.095 million! The base fine for level 38, the top-level offense, is a hefty $72.5 million.

After assessing a *base fine*, the judge computes a culpability score, which is a way of assigning blame to the company. The culpability score can range from 0.05 to 4.0. The greater the corporate responsibility in conducting, encouraging, or sanctioning illegal or unethical activity, the higher the culpability score. A company that already has a compliance program and voluntarily reports the offense to authorities will incur a culpability score of 0.05. By contrast, a company whose management secretly plans, approves, and participates in illegal or unethical activity will receive the maximum score of 4.0.

The culpability score is critical because the total fine is computed by multiplying the base fine by the culpability score. Going back to our level 24 fraud offense, the left point of the upper arrow in Exhibit 4.2 shows that a company with a compliance program that turns itself in will be fined only $105,000 ($2,100,000 × 0.05). In contrast, a company that secretly planned, approved, and participated in illegal activity will be fined $8.4 million ($2,100,000 × 4.0), as shown by the right point of the upper arrow. The difference is even greater for level 38 offenses. As shown by the left point of the bottom arrow, a company with a compliance program and a 0.05 culpability score is fined only $3.625 million, whereas a company with the maximum 4.0 culpability score is fined a whopping $290 million, as indicated by the right point of the bottom arrow. These differences clearly show the importance of having a compliance program in place. Over the past decade, 1,494 companies have been charged under the U.S. Sentencing Guidelines. Seventy-six percent of those charged were fined, with the average fine exceeding $2 million. Company fines are on average twenty times larger now than before the implementation of the guidelines in 1991.[23]

Fortunately for companies that want to avoid paying these stiff fines, the U.S. Sentencing Guidelines clearly spell out the seven necessary components of an effective compliance program.[24] Exhibit 4.3 lists those components. Caremark International, a managed-care service provider in Delaware, pleaded guilty to criminal charges related to its physician contracts and improper patient referrals. When shareholders sued the company for negligence and poor management, the Delaware court dismissed the case, ruling that the company's ethics compliance program, built on the components described in Exhibit 4.3, was a good-faith attempt to monitor employees and that the company did not knowingly allow illegal and unethical behavior to occur. The court went on to

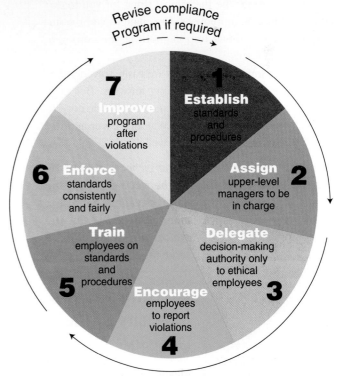

Exhibit 4.3

Compliance Program Steps from the U.S. Sentencing Commission Guidelines for Organizations

Source: D. R. Dalton, M. B. Metzger, and J. W. Hill, "The 'New' U.S. Sentencing Commission Guidelines: A Wake-up Call for Corporate America," *Academy of Management Executive* 8 (1994): 7–16.

rule that a compliance program based on the U.S. Sentencing Guidelines was enough to shield the company from liability.[25]

4-3 INFLUENCES ON ETHICAL DECISION MAKING

As the senior human resources executive at United Parcel Service (UPS), you're facing an ethical dilemma. With health care costs rising 11.25 percent this year, or nearly five times the rate of inflation, plus implementation of the federal Affordable Care Act, which has added significant additional expenses, fees, and rules that must be followed (or you're in violation of the law), it's becoming increasingly difficult for UPS to maintain the affordability of its current health care coverage. The CEO and the executive team have asked you to consider a range of scenarios, from no price changes coupled with reduced coverage to significant price increases but no changes in coverage to something in the middle with moderate price changes and some changes in coverage.[26] As the senior human resources executive at UPS, what would be the ethical thing for you to do? With 322,000 U.S. employees, any changes you recommend will have a huge impact, both at the corporate and individual levels.

Although some ethical issues are easily solved, many do not have clearly right or wrong answers. But even though the answers are rarely clear, managers do need to have a clear sense of *how* to arrive at an answer in order to manage this ethical ambiguity well.

The ethical answers that managers choose depend on **4-3a the ethical intensity of the decision, 4-3b the moral development of the manager,** *and* **4-3c the ethical principles used to solve the problem.**

4-3a Ethical Intensity of the Decision

Managers don't treat all ethical decisions the same. The UPS manager who has to decide how changes in health care prices and coverage might affect 322,000 employees is going to treat that decision much more seriously than the decision of how to deal with an assistant who has been taking paper home for personal use. These decisions differ in their **ethical intensity**, or the degree of concern people have about an ethical issue. When addressing an issue of high ethical intensity, managers are more aware of the impact their decision will have on others. They are more likely to view the decision as an ethical or moral decision than as an economic decision. They are also more likely to worry about doing the right thing.

Six factors must be taken into account when determining the ethical intensity of an action, as shown in Exhibit 4.4. **Magnitude of consequences** is the total harm or benefit derived from an ethical decision. The more people who are harmed or the greater the harm to those people, the larger the consequences. **Social consensus** is agreement on whether behavior is bad or good. **Probability of effect** is the chance that something will happen that results in harm to others. If we combine these factors, we can see the effect they can have on ethical intensity. For example, if there is *clear agreement* (social consensus) that a managerial decision or action is *certain* (probability of effect) to have *large negative consequences* (magnitude of consequences) in some way, then people will be highly concerned about that managerial decision or action, and ethical intensity will be high.

Ethical intensity the degree of concern people have about an ethical issue

Magnitude of consequences the total harm or benefit derived from an ethical decision

Social consensus agreement on whether behavior is bad or good

Probability of effect the chance that something will happen that results in harm to others

Exhibit 4.4

Six Factors That Contribute to Ethical Intensity

Magnitude of consequences

Social consensus

Probability of effect

Temporal immediacy

Proximity of effect

Concentration of effect

Source: Republished with permission of Academy of Management; P.O. Box 3020, Briar Cliff Manor, NY, 10510-8020. T.M. Jones, "Ethical Decision Making by Individuals in Organizations: An Issue Contingent Model," *Academy of Management Review 16* (1991) 366–395; Reproduced by permission of the publisher via Copyright Clearance Center, Inc.

Trevor Hunt/iStockphoto.com

Temporal immediacy is the time between an act and the consequences the act produces. Temporal immediacy is stronger if a manager has to lay off workers next week as opposed to three months from now. **Proximity of effect** is the social, psychological, cultural, or physical distance of a decision maker from those affected by his or her decisions. Thus, proximity of effect is greater when a manager lays off employees he knows than when he lays off employees he doesn't know. Finally, whereas the magnitude of consequences is the total effect across all people, **concentration of effect** is how much an act affects the average person. For instance, eliminating health care coverage for 100 employees has a greater concentration of effect than reducing the health care benefits for 1,000 employees by 10 percent.

Which of these six factors has the most impact on ethical intensity? Studies indicate that managers are much more likely to view decisions as ethical issues when the magnitude of consequences (total harm) is high and there is a social consensus (agreement) that a behavior or action is bad.[27]

4-3b Moral Development

It's Friday. Another long week of classes and studying is over, and all you want to do is sit down and relax. "A movie sounds good," you think to yourself, but you don't want to spend $12 to trek down to the megaplex. And, while it would cost less than a $1.50 to rent a DVD, you're too tired to make the short trip down to the corner drugstore's Redbox machine. Your roommate says he's got the perfect solution and gives you the URL of a website that streams all the latest blockbuster movies and TV shows for free. The writers, actors, and producers won't earn a dime if you watch the pirated copy of the movie. Furthermore, it's illegal to download or watch streamed copies of pirated shows. But how will the movie studios ever find out? Are the cops going to come through your door because you watched a pirated copy of *Insurgence*? Will you watch the movie? What are you going to do?

In part, according to psychologist Lawrence Kohlberg, your decision will be based on your level of moral development. Kohlberg identified three phases of moral development, with two stages in each phase (see Exhibit 4.5).[28] At the **preconventional level of moral development**, people decide based on selfish reasons. For example, if you are in Stage 1, the punishment and obedience stage, your primary concern will be to avoid trouble for yourself.

So you won't watch the pirated movie because you are afraid of being caught and punished. Yet, in Stage 2, the instrumental exchange stage, you worry less about punishment and more about doing things that directly advance your wants and needs. So you will watch the pirated movie.

People at the **conventional level of moral development** make decisions that conform to societal expectations. In other words, they look outside themselves to others for guidance on ethical issues. In Stage 3, the "good boy, nice girl" stage, you normally do what the other "good boys" and "nice girls" are doing. If everyone else is watching the pirated movie, you will, too. But if they aren't, you won't either. In the law and order stage, Stage 4, you again look for external guidance and do whatever the law permits, so you won't watch the movie.

Temporal immediacy the time between an act and the consequences the act produces

Proximity of effect the social, psychological, cultural, or physical distance between a decision maker and those affected by his or her decisions

Concentration of effect the total harm or benefit that an act produces on the average person

Preconventional level of moral development the first level of moral development, in which people make decisions based on selfish reasons

Conventional level of moral development the second level of moral development, in which people make decisions that conform to societal expectation

POSTCONVENTIONAL LEVEL OF MORAL DEVELOPMENT

CONVENTIONAL LEVEL OF MORAL DEVELOPMENT

PRECONVENTIONAL LEVEL OF MORAL DEVELOPMENT

Exhibit 4.5
Kohlberg's Stages of Moral Development

Stage 1	Stage 2	Stage 3	Stage 4	Stage 5	Stage 6
Punishment and Obedience	Instrumental Exchange	Good Boy, Nice Girl	Law and Order	Social Contract	Universal Principle
Preconventional		Conventional		Postconventional	
Self-Interest		Societal Expectations		Internalized Principles	

© Cengage Learning

People at the **postconventional level of moral development** use internalized ethical principles to solve ethical dilemmas. In Stage 5, the social contract stage, you will refuse to watch the pirated movie because, as a whole, society is better off when the rights of others—in this case, the rights of actors, producers, directors, and writers—are not violated. In Stage 6, the universal principle stage, you might or might not watch the pirated movie, depending on your principles of right and wrong. Moreover, you will stick to your principles even if your decision conflicts with the law (Stage 4) or what others believe is best for society (Stage 5). For example, those with socialist or communist beliefs would probably choose to watch the pirated movie because they believe goods and services should be owned by society rather than by individuals and corporations.

Kohlberg believed that people would progress sequentially from earlier stages to later stages as they became more educated and mature. But only 20 percent of adults ever reach the postconventional stage of moral development, where internal principles guide their decisions. Most adults are in the conventional stage of moral development, in which they look outside themselves to others for guidance on ethical issues. This means that most people in the workplace look to and need leadership when it comes to ethical decision making.[29]

4-3c Principles of Ethical Decision Making

Beyond an issue's ethical intensity and a manager's level of moral maturity, the particular ethical principles that managers use will also affect how they solve ethical dilemmas. Unfortunately, there is no one ideal principle to use in making ethical business decisions.

According to professor LaRue Hosmer, a number of different ethical principles can be used to make business decisions: long-term self-interest, religious injunctions, government requirements, individual rights, personal virtue, distributive justice, and utilitarian benefits.[30] All of these ethical principles encourage managers and employees to take others' interests into account when making ethical decisions. At the same time, however, these principles can lead to very different ethical actions, as we can see by using these principles to decide what UPS might do regarding its employees' health care coverage.

According to the **principle of long-term self-interest**, you should never take any action that is not in your or your organization's long-term self-interest. Although this sounds as if the principle promotes selfishness, it doesn't. What we do to maximize our long-term interests (save more, spend less, exercise every day, watch what we eat) is often very different from what we do to maximize short-term interests (max out our credit cards, be couch potatoes, eat whatever we want). Health care costs at UPS have nearly doubled in the past eight years. Furthermore, they are expected to rise 11.25 percent this year, nearly five times faster than the rate of inflation.[31] On one hand, reducing health care costs would be in UPS's long-term self-interest. So, UPS might choose to to significantly reduce or eliminate health care coverage for as many employees as possible. On the other hand, cutting health care benefits might make it much more difficult for UPS to attract and retain good employees, and it would most certainly lead to much more difficult contract negotiations with the labor unions that represent its non-managerial employees. So, based on those concerns, UPS would absorb the cost increases

Postconventional level of moral development the third level of moral development, in which people make decisions based on internalized principles

Principle of long-term self-interest an ethical principle that holds that you should never take any action that is not in your or your organization's long-term self-interest itself, thus maintaining current health care coverage levels for its employees. In this instance, the principle of long-term self-interest doesn't provide clear guidance.

According to the **principle of religious injunctions**, you should never take an action that is unkind or that harms a sense of community, such as the positive feelings that come from working together to accomplish a commonly accepted goal. Using this principle, and knowing how contentious these changes would be, UPS would absorb the 11.25 percent increase and maintain current levels of health benefits.

According to the **principle of government requirements**, the law represents the minimal moral standards of society, so you should never take any action that violates the law. According to the Affordable Care Act, companies with more than fifty employees can be fined for not providing adequate coverage to employees and their children (up to the age of 26). However, the law does not require that spouses be covered. So, based on the law, you could recommend that everyone else but employees' spouses maintain health care benefits.[32]

The **principle of individual rights** holds that you should never take an action that infringes on others' agreed-upon rights. With a large unionized workforce, any changes that UPS makes to its health care coverage must be consistent with existing labor union contracts. Because union contracts covering 250,000 workers specify that spouses are entitled to health care benefits, UPS would only be able to change health care benefits and costs for non-union workers and managers at this time.[33] However, it could attempt to change unionized workers benefits when their contract comes open for renegotiation, typically every three years.

The Affordable Care Act (ACA) has created additional expenses, fees, and rules for companies like UPS. In April 2014, President Barak Obama spoke in Washington about ACA sign-ups crossing the 8-million mark.

The **principle of personal virtue** holds that you should never do anything that is not honest, open, and truthful and that you would not be glad to see reported in the newspapers or on TV. Using the principle of personal virtue, UPS would have quietly absorbed the increased costs of health care coverage and maintained current benefit levels. Had it done so, it could have avoided the publication of a *Wall Street Journal* article on this topic.

Under the **principle of distributive justice**, you should never take any action that harms the least fortunate among us in some way. This principle is designed to protect the poor, the uneducated, and the unemployed. Because UPS cannot change health care benefits for its unionized workers (until the next contract is negotiated), it is limited to changing health care benefits for its managers and office workers. But because health care coverage is mandatory under the Affordable Care Act for companies with more than fifty employees, UPS can only make significant changes to the spouses of managerial employees. Given that UPS pays competitive wages and benefits, is it likely that those spouses can be characterized as poor? Probably not. Might those spouses be uneducated, meaning without a college or high school degree? Perhaps, but probably not in most cases. Unemployed? Certainly, there could be spouses who are out of a job or who have chosen to stay at home to care for children. But would UPS want to be seen as cutting health care benefits of unemployed spouses? The principle of distributive justices says it would not.

Finally, the **principle of utilitarian benefits** states that you should never take an action that does not result in greater good for society. In short, you should do whatever creates the greatest good for the greatest number. At first, this principle seems to

Principle of religious injunctions an ethical principle that holds that you should never take any action that is not kind and that does not build a sense of community

Principle of government requirements an ethical principle that holds that you should never take any action that violates the law, for the law represents the minimal moral standard

Principle of individual rights an ethical principle that holds that you should never take any action that infringes on others' agreed-upon rights

Principle of personal virtue an ethical principle that holds that you should never do anything that is not honest, open, and truthful and that you would not be glad to see reported in the newspapers or on TV

Principle of distributive justice an ethical principle that holds that you should never take any action that harms the least fortunate among us: the poor, the uneducated, the unemployed

Principle of utilitarian benefits an ethical principle that holds that you should never take any action that does not result in greater good for society suggest that UPS should absorb the higher costs and not change health care benefits. After all, it can be argued that maintaining health care benefits for 330,000 employees contributes to the greater good. If UPS did this with any regularity, however, the costs would be enormous (remember that health care costs have doubled in the past eight years and are increasing much faster than the rate of inflation), profits would shrink, and UPS would have to cut its stock dividend, and the price of its stock would drop, harming countless shareholders, many of whom rely on UPS stock price appreciation and dividend growth for retirement income. Likewise, reduced profitability could lead to even more severe cost cutting, such as layoffs, which could produce more harm than reduced benefits. In this case, the principle does not lead to a clear choice.

So, what did UPS decide to do? Management factored in many of the concerns raised by these ethical principles and announced that it would no longer provide health care benefits for employed spouses of non-unionized workers who already had health benefits from their employers. No one else was affected.[34] Do you think UPS's decision was ethical? Some of you might believe that UPS is not fulfilling the commitments it made to its managerial employees and their families and that as a large corporation, it can afford the increase. Others might argue that UPS's decision was legal, that it honored existing contracts, and that ultimately cuts of some kind would be required given the exponential rise in costs. Indeed, a UPS spokesperson explained that this decision was the best way to continue offering health coverage premiums at current levels for the largest number of UPS employees.

4-4 PRACTICAL STEPS TO ETHICAL DECISION MAKING

Overt integrity test a written test that estimates job applicants' honesty by directly asking them what they think or feel about theft or about punishment of unethical behaviors

Personality-based integrity test a written test that indirectly estimates job applicants' honesty by measuring psychological traits, such as dependability and conscientiousness

Companies are putting more emphasis on ethical decision making. Eighty-one percent now provide ethics training. Sixty-seven percent include ethical conduct as a standard part of performance evaluations. And, seventy-four percent communicate internally about disciplinary actions that are taken when unethical behavior occurs.[35]

*Managers can encourage more ethical decision making in their organizations by **4-4a carefully selecting and hiring ethical employees, 4-4b establishing a specific code of ethics, 4-4c training employees to make ethical decisions, and 4-4d creating an ethical climate.***

4-4a Selecting and Hiring Ethical Employees

As an employer, how can you increase your chances of hiring honest employees, the kind who would return a wallet filled with money to its rightful owner? **Overt integrity tests** estimate job applicants' honesty by asking them directly what they think or feel about theft or about punishment of unethical behaviors.[36] For example, an employer might ask an applicant, "Would you ever consider buying something from somebody if you knew the person had stolen the item?" or "Don't most people steal from their companies?" Surprisingly, unethical people will usually answer "yes" to such questions because they believe that the world is basically dishonest and that dishonest behavior is normal.[37]

Personality-based integrity tests indirectly estimate job applicants' honesty by measuring psychological traits such as dependability and conscientiousness. For example, prison inmates serving time for white-collar crimes (counterfeiting, embezzlement, and fraud) scored much lower than a comparison group of middle-level managers on scales measuring reliability, dependability, honesty, conscientiousness, and abiding by rules.[38] These results show that companies can selectively hire and promote people who will be more ethical.

4-4b Codes of Ethics

Today, almost all large corporations have an ethics code in place. Even if a company has a code of ethics, two things must still happen if those codes are to encourage ethical decision making and behavior.[39] First, a company must communicate its code to others both inside and outside the company.

Second, in addition to having an ethics code with general guidelines such as "do unto others as you would have others do unto you," management must also develop practical ethical standards and procedures specific to the company's line of business. Hershey's, the leading producer of chocolate and confectionary goods in North America, also does business in ninety countries. Visitors to Hershey's website can download the company's "Code of Ethical Business Conduct" in eight languages. The code sets specific ethical standards on topics ranging from treatment of coworkers to protecting the environment to maintenance of financial records. For example, the code states specifically, "If management, our auditors or government investigators request information or documentation from us, we must cooperate. This means we may not conceal, alter or destroy such information. Falsifying business records, destroying documents or lying to auditors, investigators or government officials is a serious offense." Likewise, Hershey's code states that information about competitors can only be obtained in legal and ethical ways and that it is wrong to attempt to pry confidential information from others. "If a coworker, customer or business partner has competitive information that they are required to keep confidential, we must not encourage them to disclose it."[40] Specific codes of ethics such as this make it much easier for employees to decide what to do when they want to do the right thing.

4-4c Ethics Training

In addition to establishing ethical standards for the company, managers must sponsor and be involved in ethics and compliance training in order to create an ethical company culture.[41] The first objective of ethics training is to develop employees' awareness of ethics.[42] This means helping employees recognize which issues are ethical issues and then avoiding rationalizing unethical behavior by thinking, "This isn't really illegal or immoral" or "No one will ever find out." Several companies have created board games, produced videos, or invited special speakers to improve awareness of ethical issues.[43] Howard Winkler, project manager for ethics and compliance at Southern Co., an Atlanta-based energy provider, uses a wide range of tools to educate and engage its employees on ethics. Like many companies, Southern's mandatory ethics training requires employees to go online, read the code of ethics, and certify they have done so. Says Winkler, "When its put online, it usually has all the charm and engagement of a software licensing agreement."[44] So Winkler replaced it with a ten-minute video where actors explained the company's policies. He varies delivery methods to keep employees interested, using videos, contests, and internal social media to communicate important ethics issues. Winkler even had a convicted felon come in to talk about how small ethical compromises

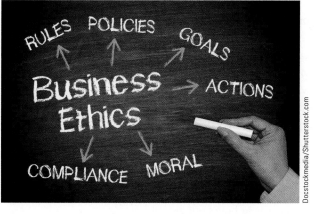

eventually lead to bigger unethical behavior, such as fraud, the charges that sent him to jail for five years. "It created an enormous impression," Winkler says, because, "This person didn't start out his career looking to commit fraud. The main message was that once you make the first ethical compromise, you are embarking on a path that can lead all the way to a prison cell."[45] Winkler also regularly creates opportunities for senior executives to speak with employees about ethics issues. This multifaceted approach appears to be working, as internal surveys indicate that 93 percent of employees recognize that their continued career at Southern "depends on my ethical behavior."

The second objective for ethics training programs is to achieve credibility with employees. Not surprisingly, employees can be highly suspicious of management's reasons for offering ethics training. Some companies have hurt the credibility of their ethics programs by having outside instructors and consultants conduct the classes.[46] Employees often complain that outside instructors and consultants are teaching theory that has nothing to do with their jobs and the practical dilemmas they actually face on a daily basis. CA Technologies made its ethics training practical and relevant by creating a series of comical training videos with a fictional manager, Griffin Peabody, who is shown facing a series of ethics issues, such as conflicts of interest, competitive intelligence, workplace harassment, client expenses, and conduct outside of the workplace (search "Griffin Peabody" at YouTube.com). Chief ethics officer Joel Katz says, "It's easy for it [that is, ethics training] to become a check-the-box exercise. We use Griffin's escapades to teach compliance lessons in a funny way." For instance, since CA Technologies acquires lots of companies—a common practice in technology industries—it's critical, and required by law, that its employees keep potential acquisitions confidential to prevent insider trading. Chief compliance officer Gary Brown says, "They think they can tell a friend, 'Guess what I was working on today.' They have to realize it is a much bigger problem." To reinforce this point, Griffin Peabody is visited by Securities and Exchange Commission investigators after publicly disclosing information about a company that is being acquired.[47]

Ethics training becomes even more credible when top managers teach the initial ethics classes to their subordinates who in turn teach their subordinates.[48] At Intuitive Research and Technology Corp., an engineering services company in Huntsville, Alabama, Howard "Hal" Brewer, the company's co-founder and president, is the company's ethics champion. Every new employee attends a session called "Let's Talk Ethics with Hal," led by Brewer and the director of human resources, Juanita Phillips. Brewer explains how employees' decisions impact the company, situations they will likely encounter with outside organizations they do business with, and then how to respond. What effect does having the co-founder and president talk to every employee about ethics? Philips says about Hal, "He makes it clear that he is the ethics officer. His strength is that he means every word of it, and he shows it in how he lives every day in terms of running the company."[49] Michael Hoffman, executive director for the Center for Business Ethics at Bentley University, says that having managers teach ethics courses greatly reinforces the seriousness with which employees treat ethics in the workplace.[50]

The third objective of ethics training is to teach employees a practical model of ethical decision making. A basic model should help them think about the consequences their choices will have on others and consider how they will choose between different solutions. Exhibit 4.6 presents a basic model of ethical decision making.

4-4d Ethical Climate

Organizational culture is key to fostering ethical decision making. The 2015 National Business Ethics Survey reported that only 33 percent of employees who work at companies with a strong ethical culture (where core beliefs are widely shared and strongly held) have observed others engaging in unethical behavior, whereas 62 percent of those who work in organizations with weak ethical cultures (where core beliefs are not widely shared or strongly held) have observed others engaging in unethical behavior.[51] Employees of companies with strong ethical cultures are also more likely to report misconduct that they observe (87 percent versus 32 percent in weak ethical cultures).[52]

The first step in establishing an ethical climate is for managers, especially top managers, to act ethically themselves. It's no surprise that in study after study, when researchers ask, "What is the most important influence on your ethical behavior at work?" the answer comes back, "My manager."

A second step in establishing an ethical climate is for top management to be active in and committed to the company ethics program.[53] Top managers who consistently talk about the importance of ethics and back up that talk by participating in their companies' ethics programs send the clear message that ethics matter. When management engages and communicates about ethical issues, employees are less likely to break rules and more likely to report ethical violations.[54] Business writer Dayton Fandray says, "You can have ethics offices and officers and training programs and reporting systems, but if the CEO doesn't seem to care, it's all just a sham. It's not surprising to find that the companies that really do care about ethics make a point of including senior management in all of their ethics and compliance programs."[55]

A third step is to put in place a reporting system that encourages managers and employees to report potential ethics violations. **Whistle-blowing**, that is, reporting others' ethics violations, is a difficult step for most people to take.[56] Managers who have been interviewed about whistle-blowing have said, "In every organization, someone's been screwed for standing up. If anything, I figured that by taking a strong stand I might get myself in trouble. People might look at me as a goody two-shoes. Someone might try to force me out."[57] Indeed, in large companies without an effective compliance program, 62 percent of workers have observed unethical behavior, 32 percent of those have reported the misconduct, and 59 percent of those who reported the unethical behavior experienced some kind of retaliation.[58]

An AirTran Airways pilot, for example, was removed from "flight status," meaning he was ineligible to fly, after filing ten safety reports in two days, all concerning an unbalanced tire on one of AirTran's passenger jets. Three weeks later, following a seventeen-minute hearing, he was fired

Whistle-blowing reporting others' ethics violations to management or legal authorities

Exhibit 4.6
A Basic Model of Ethical Decision Making

1. **Identify the problem.** What makes it an ethical problem? Think in terms of rights, obligations, fairness, relationships, and integrity. How would you define the problem if you stood on the other side of the fence?

2. **Identify the constituents.** Who has been hurt? Who could be hurt? Who could be helped? Are they willing players, or are they victims? Can you negotiate with them?

3. **Diagnose the situation.** How did it happen in the first place? What could have prevented it? Is it going to get worse or better? Can the damage now be undone?

4. **Analyze your options.** Imagine the range of possibilities. Limit yourself to the two or three most manageable. What are the likely outcomes of each? What are the likely costs? Look to the company mission statement or code of ethics for guidance.

5. **Make your choice.** What is your intention in making this decision? How does it compare with the probable results? Can you discuss the problem with the affected parties before you act? Could you disclose without qualm your decision to your boss, the CEO, the board of directors, your family, or society as a whole?

6. **Act.** Do what you have to do. Don't be afraid to admit errors. Be as bold in confronting a problem as you were in causing it.

Source: L. A. Berger, "Train All Employees to Solve Ethical Dilemmas," *Best's Review—Life-Health Insurance Edition* 95 (1995): 70–80.

for allegedly not satisfactorily answering questions at the hearing. However, the Occupational Safety and Health Administration (OSHA) ruled that the firing was retaliatory, that AirTran violated whistle-blower protection laws, and that AirTran should reinstate the pilot and pay him more than $1 million in back pay and compensatory damages. OSHA Assistant Secretary of Labor Dr. David Michaels said, "Airline workers must be free to raise safety and security concerns, and companies that diminish those rights through intimidation or retaliation must be held accountable. Airline safety is of vital importance, not only to the workers, but to the millions of Americans who use our airways."[59]

A 2014 ruling by the U.S. Supreme Court greatly expands protections for whistle-blowers. The Court declared that the strong whistle-blowers protections built into the 2002 Sarbanes-Oxley Act, which apply to employees of publicly traded companies, should also apply to the employees of contractors and subcontractors that work with those public companies. This ruling extends whistle-blowers protection laws beyond the 5,000 publicly traded companies covered by Sarbanes-Oxley to an additional 6 million private companies.[60]

To encourage employees to report ethics violations, that is, to act as whistle-blowers, many companies have installed confidential ethics hotlines. The information obtained from the hotline at Paychex, a multibillion dollar payroll services firm in Rochester, New York, is reported directly to the company's board of directors and audit committee, which can then trigger an investigation independent of company management.[61]

The factor that does the most to discourage whistle-blowers from reporting problems is lack of company action on their complaints.[62] Thus, the final step in developing an ethical climate is for management to fairly and consistently punish those who violate the company's code of ethics. The key, says Paychex CEO Martin Mucci, is "to deal with it quickly, severely, and publicize it."[63] Says Mucci, "Our employees know that if they are caught cheating in any way, even if only to make a few dollars or improve their scores, they will most likely be terminated. Then we review that with the entire management team. We have done that with managers of locations, top sales representatives–we don't treat anyone differently."[64] Amazingly, though, not all companies fire ethics violators. In fact, 8 percent of surveyed companies admit that they would promote top performers even if they violated ethical standards.[65]

 4-5

TO WHOM ARE ORGANIZATIONS SOCIALLY RESPONSIBLE?

Social responsibility is a business's obligation to pursue policies, make decisions, and take actions that benefit society.[66] Unfortunately,

> **Social responsibility**
> a business's obligation to pursue policies, make decisions, and take actions that benefit society

because there are strong disagreements over to whom and for what in society organizations are responsible, it can be difficult for managers to know what is or will be perceived as socially responsible corporate behavior. In a recent McKinsey & Company study of 1,144 top global executives, 79 percent predicted that at least some responsibility for dealing with future social and political issues would fall on corporations, but only 3 percent said they themselves do a good job of dealing with these issues.[67] So what should managers and corporations do to be socially responsible?

There are two perspectives regarding to whom organizations are socially responsible: the shareholder model and the stakeholder model. According to the late Nobel Prize–winning economist Milton Friedman, the only social responsibility that organizations have is to satisfy their owners, that is, company shareholders. This view—called the **shareholder model**—holds that the only social responsibility that businesses have is to maximize profits. By maximizing profit, the firm maximizes shareholder wealth and satisfaction. More specifically, as profits rise, the company stock owned by shareholders generally increases in value.

Friedman argued that it is socially irresponsible for companies to divert time, money, and attention from maximizing profits to social causes and charitable organizations. The first problem, he believed, is that organizations cannot act effectively as moral agents for all company shareholders. Although shareholders are likely to agree on investment issues concerning a company, it's highly unlikely that they have common views on what social causes a company should or should not support.

The second major problem, Friedman said, is that the time, money, and attention diverted to social causes undermine market efficiency.[68] In competitive markets, companies compete for raw materials, talented workers, customers, and investment funds. A company that spends money on social causes will have less money to purchase quality materials or to hire talented workers who can produce a valuable product at a good price. If customers find the company's product less desirable, its sales and profits will fall. If profits fall, the company's stock price will decline, and the company will have difficulty attracting investment funds that could be used to fund long-term growth. In the end, Friedman argues, diverting the firm's money, time, and resources to social causes hurts customers, suppliers, employees, and shareholders. Russell Roberts, an economist and research fellow at Stanford University's Hoover Institution, agrees, saying, "Doesn't it make more sense to have companies do what they do best, make good products at fair prices, and then let consumers use the savings for the charity of their choice?"[69]

By contrast, under the **stakeholder model**, management's most important responsibility is the firm's long-term survival (not just maximizing profits), which is achieved by satisfying the interests of multiple corporate stakeholders (not just shareholders).[70] **Stakeholders** are persons or groups with a legitimate interest in a company.[71] Because stakeholders are interested in and affected by the organization's actions, they have a stake in what those actions are. In 2013, an environmental group, As You Sow, along with company shareholders, asked Exxon Mobile via a formal shareholder proposal at Exxon's annual shareholder meeting to provide detailed information about the impact of fracking, a technique in which water is injected at high pressure into oil shale deposits to force lose oil and natural gas. Exxon declined to answer, stating, "the minimal environmental impacts of hydraulic fracturing have been well-documented." But, in the face of increased concerns about fracking, the company agreed in April 2014 to provide a report on fracking's impact on air quality, water, and chemical usage at Exxon sites. A company spokesperson said the agreement was, "a productive evolution of our relationship with some of these shareholder groups." After formally withdrawing its shareholder proposal, As You Sow president Danielle Fugere, commented that, "It does feel like Exxon is changing the way it's doing business. [But if the report doesn't provide much information], "we did reserve the right to bring a [shareholder] resolution next year."[72]

Stakeholder groups may try to influence the firm to advance their interests. Exhibit 4.7 shows the various stakeholder groups that the organization must satisfy to assure its long-term survival. Being responsible to multiple stakeholders raises two basic questions. First, how does a company identify organizational stakeholders? Second, how does a company balance the needs of different stakeholders? Distinguishing between primary and secondary stakeholders can help answer these questions.[73]

Some stakeholders are more important to the firm's survival than others. **Primary stakeholders** are groups on which the organization depends for its

Shareholder model a view of social responsibility that holds that an organization's overriding goal should be profit maximization for the benefit of shareholders

Stakeholder model a theory of corporate responsibility that holds that management's most important responsibility, long-term survival, is achieved by satisfying the interests of multiple corporate stakeholders

Stakeholders persons or groups with a stake, or legitimate interest, in a company's actions

Primary stakeholder any group on which an organization relies for its long-term survival

Exhibit 4.7
Stakeholder Model of Corporate Social Responsibility

Source: Republished with permission of Academy of Management, P.O. Box 3020, Briar Cliff Manor, NY, 10510-8020. "The Stakeholder Theory of the Corporation: Concepts, Evidence and Implications" (Figure), T. Donaldson and L. E. Preston, *Academy of Management Review* 20 (1995). Reproduced by permission of the publisher via Copyright Clearance Center, Inc.

Secondary stakeholders, such as the media and special interest groups, can influence or be influenced by the company. Unlike the primary stakeholders, however, they do not engage in regular transactions with the company and are not critical to its long-term survival. Meeting the needs of primary stakeholders is therefore usually more important than meeting the needs of secondary stakeholders. Nevertheless, secondary stakeholders are still important because they can affect public perceptions and opinions about socially responsible behavior.

The Keystone XL Pipeline, proposed by TransCanada Corporation, would carry 800,000 barrels of crude oil per day from the tar sands in Alberta, Canada, to oil refineries in Texas and Louisiana. Even though the project is approved by 75 percent of Americans and 68 percent of Canadians and would create tens of thousands of jobs, environmental groups are trying to kill or delay the project. The Natural Resources Defense Council, for example, argues that the pipeline will increase oil sands production, which they argue is one of the most energy- and carbon-intensive methods of retrieving oil. Another environmental advocacy group, 350.org, which sponsors grassroots protests against projects that increase carbon production, held a 40,000-person rally in the nation's capital against the Keystone XL Pipeline. It also supported the Do The Math Tour, which traveled to twenty cities, arguing that governments and energy companies should leave the oil sands in the ground.[75]

So, to whom are organizations socially responsible? Many commentators, especially economists and financial analysts, continue to argue that organizations are responsible only to shareholders. Increasingly, however, top managers have come to believe that they and their companies must be socially responsible to their stakeholders. Today, surveys show that as many as 80 percent of top-level managers believe that it is unethical to focus just on shareholders. Twenty-nine states have changed their laws to allow company boards of directors to consider the needs of employees, creditors, suppliers, customers, and

long-term survival; they include shareholders, employees, customers, suppliers, governments, and local communities. When managers are struggling to balance the needs of different stakeholders, the stakeholder model suggests that the needs of primary stakeholders take precedence over the needs of secondary stakeholders. But among primary stakeholders, are some more important than others? According to the life cycle theory of organizations, the answer is yes. In practice, the answer is also yes, as CEOs typically give somewhat higher priority to shareholders, employees, and customers than to suppliers, governments, and local communities, no matter what stage of the life cycle a company is in.[74] Addressing the concerns of primary stakeholders is important because if a stakeholder group becomes dissatisfied and terminates its relationship with the company, the company could be seriously harmed or go out of business.

Secondary stakeholder any group that can influence or be influenced by a company and can affect public perceptions about the company's socially responsible behavior

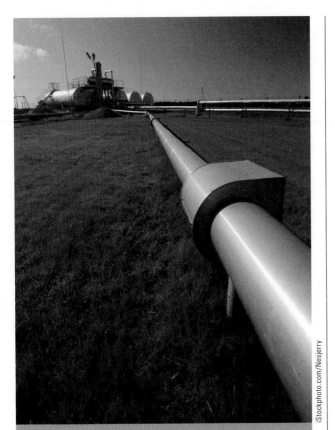

"Even though the Keystone XL pipeline is approved by an overwhelming majority of the public, environmental groups are trying to kill or delay the project."

local communities, as well as those of shareholders.[76] Although there is not complete agreement, a majority of opinion makers would argue that companies must be socially responsible to their stakeholders.

4-6 FOR WHAT ARE ORGANIZATIONS SOCIALLY RESPONSIBLE?

Economic responsibility
a company's social responsibility to make a profit by producing a valued product or service

Legal responsibility
a company's social responsibility to obey society's laws and regulations

If organizations are to be socially responsible to stakeholders, what are they to be socially responsible *for*? Companies can best benefit their stakeholders by fulfilling their economic, legal, ethical, and discretionary responsibilities.[77] Economic and legal responsibilities are at the bottom of the pyramid because they play a larger part in a company's social responsibility than do ethical and discretionary responsibilities. However, the relative importance of these various responsibilities depends on society's expectations of corporate social responsibility at a particular point in time.[78] A century ago, society expected businesses to meet their economic and legal responsibilities and little else. Today, when society judges whether businesses are socially responsible, ethical and discretionary responsibilities are considerably more important than they used to be (see box "Grooveshark Faces the Music").

Historically, **economic responsibility**, or making a profit by producing a product or service valued by society, has been a business's most basic social responsibility. Organizations that don't meet their financial and economic expectations come under tremendous pressure. For example, company boards are quick these days to fire CEOs. Typically, all it takes is two or three bad quarters in a row. Don Mattrick, a former Electronic Arts executive, left Microsoft's Xbox division to become CEO of **Zynga**, maker of popular online games such as Farmville and Words with Friends. When Mattrick was hired, Zynga had $1.28 billion in annual revenue and roughly 3,000 employees. After less than two years as CEO, there were just 2,000 employees, and sales had fallen by roughly 50 percent to $690 million. Rich Greenfield, an analyst with BTIG, said "I'm not surprised by Don Mattrick getting fired," given Zynga's poor performance during his tenure.[79] Likewise, when Symantec, the software virus company fired its second CEO in less than two years, the explanation was, "We weren't making enough progress in product innovation. We were not seeing revenue growth."[80] William Rollnick, who became acting chairman of Mattel after the company fired its previous CEO, says, "There's zero forgiveness. You screw up and you're dead."[81] According to the Conference Board, approximately 25 percent of CEOs of large companies are fired each year.[82]

Legal responsibility is a company's social responsibility to obey society's laws and regulations as it tries to meet its economic responsibilities. After purchasing a controlling interest in **Yoplait**, the world's second-largest maker of fresh dairy products, **General Mills**, the U.S. food giant and maker of Cheerios, uncovered a secret. Yoplait had been part of a secret dairy cartel, the members of which met regularly at cafés around Paris, France, to fix prices, exchange information about commercial strategies, and divide sales territories. The illegal cartel represented over 90 percent of the French dairy market, and a Yoplait executive had documented

Grooveshark Faces the Music

When Grooveshark co-founders Sam Tarantino and Josh Greenberg launched their free streaming music service, they did it backwards. First, they uploaded thousands of songs to their platform—and urged employees to do the same—and then they tried to obtain licenses to stream the songs legally. Over seven years, the streaming site grew to have a collection of roughly 20 million songs and 30 million subscribers, yet the company never secured permissions to stream songs by artists from several major record labels. Vivendi, Sony, and Warner Music sued Grooveshark, which was ultimately found guilty of copyright infringement. Tarantino said he had been in a catch-22—record labels wouldn't license the music unless he could give them financial guarantees, and his investors wouldn't give him money

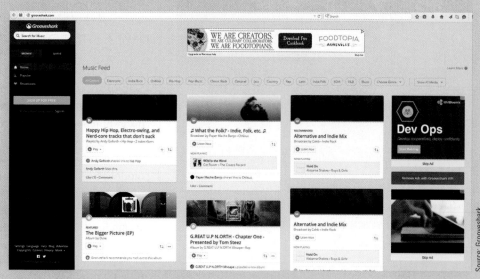

unless he had rights to stream the music. Tarantino said his investors told him, "You have all these lawsuits—we're not going to give you a big check."

Sources: H. Karp, "Grooveshark Tries to Play by the Rules with Online Radio App," *Wall Street Journal*, December 8, 2014, accessed March 28, 2015, http://www.wsj.com/articles/grooveshark-tries-to-play-by-the-rules-with-online-radio-app-1418014861.

the group's proceedings for years in a ruled notebook. General Mills handed over evidence to the authorities, and a company spokesperson said, "General Mills has strict corporate policies for our operations, including antitrust compliance."[83]

Ethical responsibility is a company's social responsibility to not violate accepted principles of right and wrong when conducting its business. Bribery is specifically prohibited in most ethics codes, particularly when conducting global business, and is illegal under the U.S. Foreign Corrupt Practices Act. Walmart executives in Mexico are alleged to have used $24 million in bribes to Mexican authorities to earn quick approval for construction projects as it rapidly expanded the number of Walmart and Sam's Club stores in Mexico.[84] Walmart informed the U.S. Securities and Exchange Commission that it was conducting a formal investigation after a *New York Times* article indicated that Walmart's top leaders in Mexico not only knew about the payments but also facilitated and hid them from Walmart headquarters in Bentonville, Arkansas.[85] In a company statement,

Walmart said, "If these allegations are true, it is not a reflection of who we are or what we stand for. We are deeply concerned by these allegations and are working aggressively to determine what happened."[86] The company then took the step of removing Jose Luis Rodriguezmacedo Rivera, its Mexican general counsel "effective immediately…," and, "… in the interests of the investigation." The company has since directly linked executive pay and bonuses to "overhauling" its ethics compliance program.[87]

Discretionary responsibilities pertain to the social roles that businesses play in society beyond their economic, legal, and ethical responsibilities. Hurricane Sandy, the largest Atlantic hurricane ever recorded, caused approximately $75 billion in damage—with

ethical responsibility a company's social responsibility not to violate accepted principles of right and wrong when conducting its business

Discretionary responsibilities the social roles that a company fulfills beyond its economic, legal, and ethical responsibilities

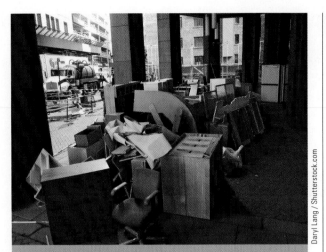

J.P. Morgan allowed businesses and home owners to skip mortgage payments for 90 days and suspended all of its foreclosure activities in storm-damaged areas.

New York State and New Jersey taking the brunt of the 1,100 mile-wide storm. As recovery efforts began, many companies stepped in with donations, contributions, and other forms of valuable assistance. J.P. Morgan, for example, pledged $2 million to the Red Cross, $1 million to local agencies, and $5 billion in special loans to small and mid-sized businesses. The bank also allowed storm-affected customers to skip mortgage payments for ninety days and suspended all of its foreclosure activity in storm-damaged areas. Entertainment companies Time Warner, News Corporation, Walt Disney, and Viacom each pledged to donate $1–$2 million. Meanwhile, Adidas, the sporting goods company, donated $600,000 worth of jackets, while Terramar Sports, which makes outdoor clothing and gear, donated $500,000 worth of long underwear and thermal clothing to people displaced from their homes by the storm.[88]

Carrying out discretionary responsibilities such as these is voluntary. Companies are not considered unethical if they don't perform them. Today, however, corporate stakeholders expect companies to do much more than in the past to meet their discretionary responsibilities.

Social responsiveness
a company's strategy to respond to stakeholders' economic, legal, ethical, or discretionary expectations concerning social responsibility

Reactive strategy a social responsiveness strategy in which a company does less than society expects

Defensive strategy a social responsiveness strategy in which a company admits responsibility for a problem but does the least required to meet societal expectations

RESPONSES TO DEMANDS FOR SOCIAL RESPONSIBILITY

Social responsiveness refers to a company's strategy to respond to stakeholders' economic, legal, ethical, or discretionary expectations concerning social responsibility. A social responsibility problem exists whenever company actions do not meet stakeholder expectations. One model of social responsiveness identifies four strategies for responding to social responsibility problems: reactive, defensive, accommodative, and proactive. These strategies differ in the extent to which the company is willing to act to meet or exceed society's expectations.

A company using a **reactive strategy** will do less than society expects. In Spring 2014, General Motors (GM) publicly acknowledged that since 2001 it had knowingly produced 1.6 million GM cars with faulty ignition switches. The issue, which is linked to twelve auto-related deaths, could happen when turning the ignition key from "off" to "accessory" (used to power accessories, such as radios, without the engine running) and then back "on."[89] The car would start, but the ignition switch, which was only partially engaged, could switch off, causing car engines to unexpectedly stop. Service technicians first documented the issue in 2001. Engineers knew in 2004. GM management found out in 2011.[90] Despite knowing about the problem for so long, GM did not issue a safety recall because engineering managers thought drivers could still maintain control of their cars even if their motors suddenly turned off. The defective switches were not redesigned until 2007, and the first vehicle recall was not issued until February 2013. Ironically, the problem is easily fixed with a $5 replacement part that takes minutes to install. GM is offering to either repair the switches or give customers a $500 allowance toward the purchase or lease of a new GM vehicle. It's estimated that GM will spend $1.3 billion just to fix affected vehicles.[91] The Center for Auto Safety, a nonprofit organization, has called for GM to waive legal immunity from lawsuits, which it obtained via its 2009 bankruptcy, and to set aside an additional $1 billion as a dedicated fund for victims.[92]

By contrast, a company using a **defensive strategy** would admit responsibility for a problem but would do the least required to meet societal expectations. Foxconn is a Taiwanese electronics manufacturing company which

In India, Social Responsibility Is the Law

In India, a new law has changed the landscape for social responsibility; India's largest companies are now required to contribute 2 percent of profits to charity. The law applies to companies worth more than 5 billion rupees ($83 million) with either annual turnover greater than 10 billion rupees or 50 million rupees in profits. Issues that contributions can be directed toward include hunger, poverty, education, women's rights, child mortality, disease, and environmental issues. It has yet to be seen how effective this measure will be, and many companies may simply see the law as another tax burden. According to Dasra, a company from Mumbai that connects corporate donors with nonprofit organizations, many companies favor the opportunity to determine where their money goes, rather than just being taxed by the government. Deval Sanghavi, a partner at Dasra, says, "The government thinks corporations might have a greater impact if they decide how to spend the money themselves." Still, many Indian charities will have to improve their administrative capabilities to be able to handle the volume of donations that are now forthcoming.

Source: S. Seervai, "Indian Companies and Charities Aren't Ready for New Giving Law," *The Wall Street Journal*, April 11, 2014. accessed April 17, 2014. http://blogs.wsj.com/indiarealtime /2014/04/11/indian-companies-and-charities-arent-ready-for-new-giving-law/?KEYWORDS =social+responsibility.

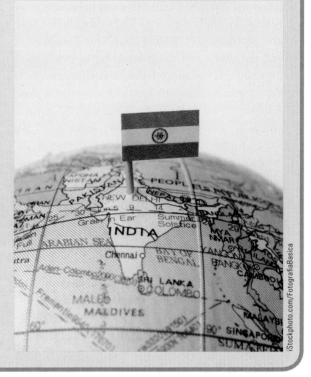

operates Chinese factories that produce 40 percent of the world's consumer electronic products. Over the past four years, at the Foxconn factories that make iPhones and iPads, eighteen employees attempted suicide, most by leaping to their deaths. After the eleventh suicide, the company placed suicide nets that reach twenty feet out around the perimeter of each building. An extensive *New York Times* investigation found that employees often worked seven days a week, were exposed to dangerous chemicals, and lived in crowded, company-supplied dorm rooms, some with as many as twenty people per three-bedroom apartment. However, Apple, which had been conducting audits of its suppliers' manufacturing facilities for many years, was slow to respond. A consultant with Business for Social Responsibility, a company Apple hired for advice on labor issues, said, "We've spent years telling Apple there are serious problems and recommending changes. They don't want to pre-empt problems, they just want to avoid embarrassments." A former Apple executive said, "If you see the same pattern of problems, year after year, that means the company's ignoring the issue rather than solving it. Noncompliance is tolerated, as long as the suppliers

promise to try harder next time. If we meant business, core violations would disappear." After the *New York Times* story, Apple began working with the Fair Labor Association, a nonprofit organization that promotes and monitors safe working conditions. Four years after the problems began, following the Fair Labor Association's report, Apple and Foxconn agreed to increase pay, limit workers to a maximum of forty-nine hours a week, build more dormitories, and hire thousands of additional workers.[93]

A company using an **accommodative strategy** will accept responsibility for a problem and take a progressive approach by doing all that could be expected to solve the problem. Novartis, a Swiss drug maker, experienced a series of scandals in its Japanese clinical research trials, such as data being altered to indicate more positive results for an experimental blood pressure drug, and covering up the severe side effects associated with a potential leukemia treatment. An independent panel commissioned by the company found Japanese sales staff had "ethically

Accommodative strategy a social responsiveness strategy in which a company accepts responsibility for a problem and does all that society expects to solve that problem inappropriate" links to clinical researchers. Novartis's global pharmaceuticals head, David Epstein, apologized to Japanese regulators, saying that the link between sales and research came as a "complete shock" and that, because sales staff had made attempts to influence research results,"We fully expect to find other clinical trials that are problematic." Stating that,"Our company culture and the way we do business in Japan needs to change urgently, he announced the immediate resignation of their Japanese division's top three executives, along with a freeze on all doctor-led clinical trials in Japan until a complete investigation could be conducted."[94] Novartis would furthermore begin training programs in its Japanese division to make clear what was and was not acceptable in the context of sales and clinical research.[95]

Finally, a company using a **proactive strategy** will anticipate responsibility for a problem before it occurs, do more than expected to address the problem, and lead the industry in its approach. McDonald's CEO Steve Easterman announced that at its 14,350 U.S. stores, it will stop selling menu items made from chickens treated with antibiotics. Scientists and doctors have long warned that treating livestock with antibiotics to prevent infections before they occur is accelerating the development of antibiotic-resistant bacteria. Indeed, 2 million Americans a year develop bacterial infections resistant to antibiotics, and, according to the Centers for Disease Control and Prevention, 23,000 of them will die. McDonald's is making these changes even though it will significantly increase its costs (antibiotic-free chickens are two to three times more expensive to raise). McDonald's size is expected to broadly influence the chicken growing industry to stop raising chicken with antibiotics. Gail Hansen of the Pew Charitable Trust, an organization critical of the use of antibiotics in meat, said McDonald's new policy, "Will have a ripple effect probably throughout the entire food industry."[96]

4-8 SOCIAL RESPONSIBILITY AND ECONOMIC PERFORMANCE

Proactive strategy a social responsiveness strategy in which a company anticipates a problem before it occurs and does more than society expects to take responsibility for and address the problem

One question that managers often ask is, "Does it pay to be socially responsible?" In previous editions of this textbook, the answer was no, as early research indicated that there was not an inherent relationship between social responsibility and economic performance.[97] Recent research, however, leads to different conclusions. There is no trade-off between being socially responsible and economic performance.[98] And there is a small, positive relationship between being socially responsible and economic performance that strengthens with corporate reputation.[99] Let's explore what each of these results means.

First, as noted earlier, there is no trade-off between being socially responsible and economic performance.[100] Being socially responsible usually won't make a business less profitable. What this suggests is that the costs of being socially responsible—and those costs can be high, especially early on—can be offset by a better product or corporate reputation, which results in stronger sales or higher profit margins. When businesses enhance their reputations by being socially responsible, they hope to maximize *willingness to pay,* that is, customers paying more for products and services that are socially responsible. In an effort to align its business practices with its core mission, **CVS Caremark** changed its name to **CVS Health** and stopped selling cigarettes at CVS pharmacies. Researchers analyzing eighteen months of data from CVS pharmacies had found that 6 percent of people filling prescriptions for respiratory diseases, such as asthma and chronic obstructive pulmonary disorder (COPD), had bought a pack of cigarettes. Removing cigarettes from CVS stores cost the company $2 billion in annual revenues, resulting in a 4.5-percent drop in front-of-the-store sales (candy, magazines, toiletries). However, sales from pharmacy services rose 16 percent to $22.5 billion during that time. CVS attributed that increase, which offset the loss of cigarette revenue, to acquiring larger corporate and insurance clients to whom CVS now provides pharmacy benefits to their employees and patients. One year after making this change, CVS was still the only pharmacy chain to not sell cigarettes.[101]

Second, it usually *does* pay to be socially responsible, and that relationship becomes stronger particularly when a company or its products have a strong reputation for social responsibility.[102] Finally, even if there is generally a small positive relationship between social responsibility and economic performance that becomes stronger when a company or its products have a positive reputation for social responsibility, and even if there is no trade-off between being socially responsible and economic performance, there is no guarantee that socially responsible companies will be profitable. Simply put, socially responsible companies experience the same ups and downs in economic performance that traditional businesses do. General Motors' Chevy Volt features a plug-in hybrid engine, producing outstanding fuel efficiency of 60 miles per gallon and the ability to drive 800 miles between fill-ups. The Volt is a tremendous technological and environmental product, but it's been a disaster for GM's bottom line. GM's investment in the Volt, so far, is estimated at $1.2 billion. But, because of the technology involved, the Volt is difficult and expensive to assemble, so much so that Reuters estimates that GM loses $50,000 per Volt! Sales have been incredibly disappointing. Priced at $39,995, GM has sold only 58,000 Volts in four years, far short of its goal of 60,000 per year. Sales picked up slightly only after GM offered a 25 percent discount on top of the Volt's already steep price discounts, which are three to four times higher than the rest of the auto industry. At the end of 2014, GM dropped the price of the Volt by another $5,000, hoping to increase sales. But by March 2015, it had a 210-day inventory of unsold Volts (60 days is optimal). GM then announced it would stop production of the Volt for seven months to clear the inventory backlog. GM's attempt at building a highly fuel-efficient, environmentally friendly car may have been good for the planet, but it has been a drag on GM's profits and finances.[103]

Being socially responsible may be the right thing to do, and it is usually associated with increased profits, but it doesn't guarantee business success.

STUDY TOOLS 4

LOCATED IN TEXTBOOK
- [ ] Rip-out and review chapter review card

LOCATED AT WWW.CENGAGEBRAIN.COM
- [ ] Review key term flashcards and create your own from StudyBits
- [ ] Track your knowledge and understanding of key concepts, using the concept tracker
- [ ] Complete practice and graded quizzes to prepare for tests
- [ ] Complete interactive content within the exposition
- [ ] View chapter highlight box content at the beginning of each chapter

PART 2

5 Planning and Decision Making

Priorities

1.
2.
3.
4.

LEARNING OUTCOMES

5-1 Discuss the benefits and pitfalls of planning.

5-2 Describe how to make a plan that works.

5-3 Discuss how companies can use plans at all management levels, from top to bottom.

5-4 Explain the steps and limits to rational decision making.

5-5 Explain how group decisions and group decision-making techniques can improve decision making.

After you finish this chapter, go to **PAGE 107** for **STUDY TOOLS**

5-1 BENEFITS AND PITFALLS OF PLANNING

Even inexperienced managers know that planning and decision making are central parts of their jobs. Figure out what the problem is. Generate potential solutions or plans. Pick the best one. Make it work. Experienced managers, however, know how hard it really is to make good plans and decisions. One seasoned manager says: "I think the biggest surprises are the problems. Maybe I had never seen it before. Maybe I was protected by my management when I was in sales. Maybe I had delusions of grandeur, I don't know. I just know how disillusioning and frustrating it is to be hit with problems and conflicts all day and not be able to solve them very cleanly."[1]

Planning is choosing a goal and developing a method or strategy to achieve that goal. Thanks to strong business and defense industry growth, northern Virginia's population will rise 26 percent by 2040. The **Virginia Railway Express** (VRE), the region's commuter train service, is already feeling the effects. VRE's ridership has grown by 30 percent in the past decade, and its trains are at 90 percent capacity. To meet growing demand, VRE's goals are to add reverse peak and express trains by 2030 and double ridership by 2040. To reach those goals, it will lengthen existing trains by 20 percent, add additional stations and longer rail lines to serve more commuters, and widen a bridge to double the number of trains traveling in both directions. The total budget for the expansion is several billion dollars, and planners have created a comprehensive document, VRE System Plan 2040, to ensure that VRE meets its goals. VRE's CEO, Doug Allen, said, "More people would take VRE if the stations were more convenient, more accessible, and had more parking."[2]

Are you one of those naturally organized people who always makes a daily to-do list, writes everything down so you won't forget, and never misses a deadline because you keep track of everything with your handy time-management notebook, iPhone, or PC? Or are you one of those flexible, creative, go-with-the-flow people who dislikes planning and organizing because it restricts your freedom, energy, and performance? Some people are natural planners. They love it and can see only its benefits. Others dislike planning and can see only its disadvantages. It turns out that *both* views have real value.

Planning has advantages and disadvantages. Let's learn about **5-1a the benefits** *and* **5-1b the pitfalls of planning.**

5-1a Benefits of Planning

Planning offers several important benefits: intensified effort, persistence, direction, and creation of task strategies.[3] First, managers and employees put forth greater effort when following a plan. Take two workers. Instruct one to "do your best" to increase production, and instruct the other to achieve a 2 percent increase in production each month. Research shows that the one with the specific plan will work harder.[4]

Second, planning leads to persistence, that is, working hard for long periods. In fact, planning encourages persistence even when there may be little chance of short-term success.[5] McDonald's founder Ray Kroc, a keen believer in the power of persistence, had this quotation from President Calvin Coolidge hung in all of his executives' offices: "Nothing in the world can take the place of persistence. Talent will not; nothing is more common than unsuccessful men with talent. Genius will not; unrewarded genius is almost a proverb. Education will not; the world is full of educated derelicts. Persistence and determination alone are omnipotent."[6]

The third benefit of planning is direction. Irving Wladawsky-Berger of the Institute for Data Driven Design explains that planning through goal setting is especially important when organizations experience major transitions. "A major way of rallying the organization to embrace the needed transformation is to have a compelling target to shoot for, a kind of promised land everyone can aim for instead of wandering in the desert without a clear path forward," Wladawsky-Berger says.[7]

The fourth benefit of planning is that it encourages the development of task strategies. In other words, planning not only encourages people to work hard for extended periods and to engage in behaviors directly related to goal accomplishment, it also encourages them to think of better ways to do their jobs. Finally, perhaps the most compelling benefit of planning is that it has been proven to work for both companies and individuals. On average, companies with plans have larger profits and grow much faster than companies without plans.[8] The same holds true for individual managers and employees: There is no better way to improve the performance of the people who work in a company than to have them set goals and develop strategies for achieving those goals.

5-1b Pitfalls of Planning

Despite the significant benefits associated with planning, it is not a cure-all. Plans won't fix all

> **Planning** choosing a goal and developing a strategy to achieve that goal

With booming music, heady scents, and windows darkened by shutters, A&F stores became less popular with shoppers

organizational problems. In fact, many management authors and consultants believe that planning can harm companies in several ways.[9]

The first pitfall of planning is that it can impede change and prevent or slow needed adaptation. Sometimes companies become so committed to achieving the goals set forth in their plans or on following the strategies and tactics spelled out in them that they fail to see that their plans aren't working or that their goals need to change. When Mike Jeffries became Abercrombie & Fitch's (A&F) CEO in 1992, he recast the brand as sexy, fit, and exclusive. **Abercrombie** grew into a $4.5 billion company with 1,000 stores in 19 countries. Its preppy jeans, polos, and logo t-shirts became iconic among U.S. teens. Provocative advertising on billboards, posters, and shopping bags included images of shirtless men and scantily clad women. With booming music, heady scents, and windows darkened by shutters, A&F stores were more like a rave than shopping. By 2013, logos were no longer popular, and stores offering unique styles at low prices, such as H&M, thrived. When asked which brands they no longer wore, teen girls ranked A&F and Hollister (an A&F brand) second and third, respectively. Even when profits dropped by half, and A&F closed 220 mall stores (with plans to close 120 more), Jeffries refused to change the brand. Finally, in mid-2014, he allowed stores to remove the shutters and cut the scents they used by 25 percent. But with declining brand equity and flagging financials, it was too late. Jeffries was pushed out by the board.[10]

The second pitfall is that planning can create a false sense of certainty. Planners sometimes feel that they know exactly what the future holds for their competitors, their suppliers, and their companies. However, all plans are based on assumptions: "The price of gasoline will increase by 4 percent per year"; "Exports will continue to rise." For plans to work, the assumptions on which they are based must hold true. If the assumptions turn out to be false, then the plans based on them are likely to fail.

The third potential pitfall of planning is the detachment of planners. In theory, strategic planners and top-level managers are supposed to focus on the big picture and not concern themselves with the details of implementation (that is carrying out the plan). According to management professor Henry Mintzberg, detachment leads planners to plan for things they don't understand.[11] Plans are meant to be guidelines for action, not abstract theories. Consequently, planners need to be familiar with the daily details of their businesses if they are to produce plans that can work.

British-based **Tesco**, the third-largest retailer in the world, spent five years researching and planning before it spent $1.6 billion to enter the U.S. grocery business by building 199 Fresh & Easy stores. Former CEO Terry Leahy said, "Our team went over to live in the U.S. We stayed in people's homes. We went through their fridges. We did all our research, and we're good at research." Unfortunately, because they had never competed in the U.S. grocery business, Tesco's research and planning failed to account for Americans' different tastes. For example, at 10,000 square feet, or 20 percent of the size of a typical American supermarket, Fresh & Easy stores were too small and had too limited a selection, and, at first, didn't have bakeries, which Americans like. Tesco relied heavily on its Fresh & Easy brand of premade meals, popular in England but unknown in the United States, where shoppers prefer brand-name products. According to Natalie Berg, director of Planet Retail, "The main thing is that they underestimated how Americans shop."[12]

5-2 HOW TO MAKE A PLAN THAT WORKS

Planning is a double-edged sword. If done right, planning brings about tremendous increases in individual and organizational performance. If planning is done wrong, however, it can have just the opposite effect and harm individual and organizational performance.

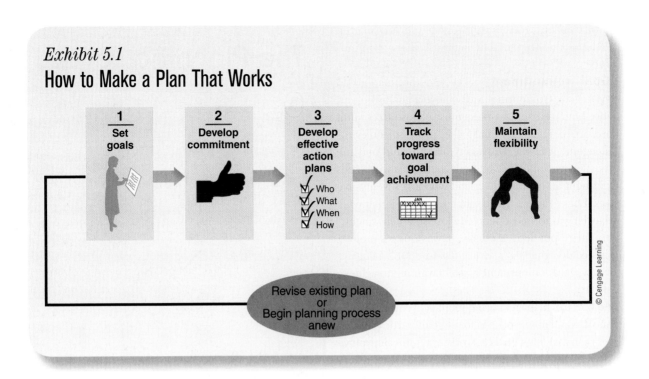

Exhibit 5.1
How to Make a Plan That Works

1	2	3	4	5
Set goals	Develop commitment	Develop effective action plans	Track progress toward goal achievement	Maintain flexibility

☑ Who
☑ What
☑ When
☑ How

Revise existing plan
or
Begin planning process
anew

© Cengage Learning

*In this section, you will learn how to make a plan that works. As depicted in Exhibit 5.1, planning consists of **5-2a setting goals, 5-2b developing commitment to the goals, 5-2c developing effective action plans, 5-2d tracking progress toward goal achievement,** and **5-2e maintaining flexibility in planning.***

5-2a Setting Goals

The first step in planning is to set goals. To direct behavior and increase effort, goals need to be specific and challenging.[13] For example, deciding to "increase sales this year" won't direct and energize workers as much as deciding to "increase North American sales by 4 percent in the next six months." Specific, challenging goals provide a target for which to aim and a standard against which to measure success.

One way of writing effective goals for yourself, your job, or your company is to use the S.M.A.R.T. guidelines. **S.M.A.R.T. goals** are **S**pecific, **M**easurable, **A**ttainable, **R**ealistic, and **T**imely.[14] With annual sales of $83 billion, Cincinnati-based **Procter & Gamble** is a global leader in consumer products in 180 countries. It's size, however, makes managing growth difficult. To combat this difficulty, in 2013, CEO A.G. Lafley established a goal of cutting P&G's massive brand portfolio of roughly 165 brands to 65 core brands, organized into 10 key categories, by 2016.[15] Let's see how P&G's objectives measure up to the S.M.A.R.T. guidelines for goals.

First, is the goal *Specific*? Yes, as opposed to saying that it wants to be smaller, P&G identified exactly

how many brands it wants in its portfolio by 2016—its 65 best-selling brands. Is the goal *Measurable*? Yes, P&G's best-performing brands generate 95 percent of its profits, which are growing faster than the rest of P&G, while its poorer performing brands haves sales and profits that are shrinking 3 percent and 16 percent per year, respectively.[16] Whether the goal is *Attainable* or not depends on many factors. First, P&G needs to find potential buyers for the 100 brands it is selling. After it identifies potential buyers, they must agree on a purchase price (a complex task with billion-dollar businesses). Then, it must clear the financial and legal hurdles involved in transferring ownership of each brand. But, major merger and acquisitions transactions aren't new, certainly for P&G, and it's unlikely these issues will be problematic. Finally, while the goals are ambitious, they are *Timely*. When P&G announced the goal in 2013, it gave itself three years to divest 50 of the 100 brands it has identified for sale. So, far P&G has made good progress. By the end of the first quarter of 2015, it had already divested or had deals to sell 35 of its lowest-performing brands.[17]

5-2b Developing Commitment to Goals

Just because a company sets a goal doesn't mean that people will try to accomplish it. If workers don't care about a goal, that

S.M.A.R.T. goals goals that are specific, measurable, attainable, realistic, and timely goal won't encourage them to work harder or smarter. Thus, the second step in planning is to develop commitment to goals.[18]

Goal commitment is the determination to achieve a goal. Commitment to achieve a goal is not automatic. Managers and workers must choose to commit themselves to a goal. Edwin Locke, professor emeritus of management at the University of Maryland and the foremost expert on how, why, and when goals work, tells a story about an overweight friend who lost seventy-five pounds. Locke says, "I asked him how he did it, knowing how hard it was for most people to lose so much weight." His friend responded, "Actually, it was quite simple. I simply decided that I *really wanted* to do it."[19] Put another way, goal commitment is really wanting to achieve a goal.

So how can managers bring about goal commitment? The most popular approach is to set goals participatively. Rather than assigning goals to workers ("Johnson, you've got till Tuesday of next week to redesign the flux capacitor so it gives us 10 percent more output"), managers and employees choose goals together. The goals are more likely to be realistic and attainable if employees participate in setting them. Another technique for gaining commitment to a goal is to make the goal public. For example, college students who publicly communicated their semester grade goals ("This semester, I'm shooting for a 3.5") to important people in their lives (usually a parent or sibling) were much more committed to achieving their grades than those who did not. Still another way to increase goal commitment is to obtain top management's support. Top management can show support for a plan or program by providing funds, speaking publicly about the plan, or participating in the plan itself.

5-2c Developing Effective Action Plans

The third step in planning is to develop effective action plans. An **action plan** lists the specific steps (how), people (who), resources (what), and time period (when) for accomplishing a goal. For its first eight years in business, Facebook focused on growth, but now its top leadership team, known as the "M team," is developing specific action plans to hold Facebook managers and employees accountable for

Goal commitment the determination to achieve a goal

Action plan a plan that lists the specific steps, people, resources, and time period needed to attain a goal

Proximal goals short-term goals or subgoals

Distal goals long-term or primary goals

The Planning Fallacy

One of the most common mistakes made in the planning process is underestimating the amount of time a task will take. This concept is so prevalent, in fact, that it has a name: the planning fallacy. Roger Buehler, a psychology professor at Ontario's Wilfrid Laurier University, says that the average person underestimates the time necessary to complete a task by 40 percent. Although management plans are often more complex than those involved in a single employee's job, similar tactics may be useful to reduce the effects of planning fallacy in both. A study published in the *Journal of Experimental Social Psychology* found that breaking a task down into very detailed steps can help chronically poor planners more accurately estimate the amount of time required to complete a task. Another strategy, devised from a study published in *Organizational Behavior and Human Decision Processes*, involves forming a mental image of a task from an outside perspective to improve predictions of time allotment.

Source: S. Reddy, "Why Are You Always Late? It Could Be the Planning Fallacy," *Wall Street Journal*, February 3, 2015, D1, D4.

increasing profit and, ultimately, its stock price. For example, software engineers who write code for Facebook's website and mobile apps were challenged to solve revenue-related issues. Andrew Bosworth, heading the new department of advertising engineering, worked with software engineers to write code so that ads could be run for the first time on mobile phones and tablets. However, instead of the ads being on the right side of the screen, the ads appear in the center, where they're impossible to miss. That step, along with nine other action plans that Facebook is pursuing, helped increase revenue to $1.46 billion, up 38 percent from $1.06 billion a year earlier. Twenty-five percent of Facebook's overall revenue now comes from mobile ads.[20]

5-2d Tracking Progress

The fourth step in planning is to track progress toward goal achievement. There are two accepted methods of tracking progress. The first is to set proximal goals and distal goals. **Proximal goals** are short-term goals or subgoals, whereas **distal goals** are long-term or primary goals.[21]

The second method of tracking progress is to gather and provide performance feedback. Regular, frequent performance feedback allows workers and managers to track their progress toward goal achievement and make adjustments in effort, direction, and strateies.[22] Exhibit 5.2 shows the impact of feedback on safety behavior at a large bakery company with a worker safety record that was two-and-a-half times worse than the industry average. During the baseline period, workers in the wrapping department, who measure and mix ingredients, roll the bread dough, and put it into baking pans, performed their jobs safely about 70 percent of the time (see 1 in Exhibit 5.2). The baseline safety record for workers in the makeup department, who bag and seal baked bread and assemble, pack, and tape cardboard cartons for shipping, was somewhat better at 78 percent (see 2). The company then gave workers thirty minutes of safety training, set a goal of 90 percent safe behavior, and then provided daily feedback (such as a chart similar to Exhibit 5.2). Performance improved dramatically. During the intervention period, safely performed behaviors rose to an average of 95.8 percent for wrapping workers (see 3) and 99.3 percent for workers in the makeup department (see 4), and never fell below 83 percent. Thus, the combination of training, a challenging goal, and feedback led to a dramatic increase in performance. The importance of feedback alone can be seen in the reversal stage, when the company quit posting daily feedback on safe behavior. Without daily feedback, the percentage of safely performed behaviors returned to baseline levels—70.8 percent for the wrapping department (see 5) and 72.3 percent for the makeup department (see 6). For planning to be effective, workers need both a specific, challenging goal and regular feedback to track their progress. In fact, additional research indicates that the effectiveness of goal setting can be doubled by the addition of feedback.[23]

5-2e Maintaining Flexibility

Because action plans are sometimes poorly conceived and goals sometimes turn out not to be achievable, the last step in developing an effective plan is to maintain flexibility. One method of maintaining flexibility while planning is to adopt an options-based approach.[24] The goal of **options-based planning** is to keep options open by making small, simultaneous investments in many

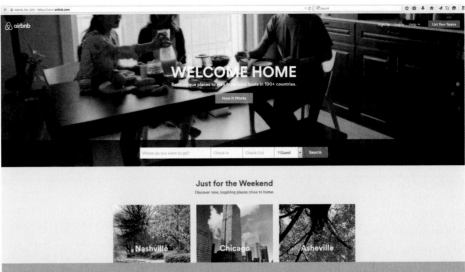

Airbnb made the transition from $200 a week in revenue to being a multibillion dollar global enterprise by maintaining flexibility.

alternative plans. Then, when one or a few of these plans emerge as likely winners, you invest even more in these plans while discontinuing or reducing investment in the others. That's exactly the strategy **Airbnb** used to go from being a company generating a meager $200 per week in revenue to being a multibillion-dollar global enterprise. Airbnb programmers have permission to make small bets on new features and measure the response. After being assigned the task—on his first day—of reevaluating the company's property rating system, a new Airbnb designer wanted to test using a heart instead of a star icon. His rationale was that Airbnb's service was aspirational and people established an emotional connection to the places they stay. The company changed the feature to a heart to test it and discovered that the heart icon increased customer engagement 30 percent over the star icon.[25]

In part, options-based planning is the opposite of traditional planning. Whereas the purpose of an action plan is to commit people and resources to a particular course of action, the purpose of options-based planning is to leave those commitments open by maintaining **slack resources**—that is, a cushion of resources, such as extra time, people, money, or production capacity, that can be used to address and adapt to unanticipated changes, problems, or opportunities.[26] Holding options open gives you choices. And choices, combined with slack

Options-based planning maintaining planning flexibility by making small, simultaneous investments in many alternative plans

Slack resources a cushion of extra resources that can be used with options-based planning to adapt to unanticipated changes, problems, or opportunities

Exhibit 5.2
Effects of Goal Setting, Training, and Feedback on Safe Behavior in a Bread Factory

Baseline
Wrapping Department

Intervention
(safety training, specific goals, and daily feedback)

Reversal
(no daily feedback)

① Safety average 70%

③ Safety average increases to 95.8%

⑤ 70.8%

Baseline
Makeup Department

Intervention   **Reversal**

② Safety average 78%

④ Safety average increases to 99.3%

Without feedback, safety average falls back

⑥ 72.3%

Percentage of Incidents Performed Safely

Observation Sessions

Canadapanda/Shutterstock.com

Source: J. Komaki, K. D. Barwick, and L. R. Scott. "A Behavioral Approach to Occupational Safety: Pinpointing and Reinforcing Safe Performance in a Food Manufacturing Plant," *Journal of Applied Psychology* 63 (1978).

resources, give you flexibility. The winter of 2014, which broke records nationwide for cold and snow, forced railroad companies to run and staff more trains with shorter loads that are easier to start and stop in bad weather. Unlike its competitors, Union Pacific railroad had already created "surge capacity," or slack resources, to handle the situation. Instead of selling or scrapping old locomotives when it bought new ones, Union Pacific "retired" them to long-term storage. So when the severe weather hit, it had 600 extra locomotives ready to go, including 550 extra workers on furlough or standby who were immediately ready to work. That winter, CSX Corp., a competitor, saw its operating ratio, a measure of operational

efficiency, drop more than 4 percent, whereas thanks to slack resources, Union Pacific's rose 2 percent.[27]

5-3 PLANNING FROM TOP TO BOTTOM

Planning works best when the goals and action plans at the bottom and middle of the organization support the goals and action plans at the top of the organization. In other words, planning works best when everybody pulls in the same direction. Exhibit 5.3 illustrates this planning

Exhibit 5.3
Planning from Top to Bottom

© Cengage Learning

continuity, beginning at the top with a clear definition of the company purpose and ending at the bottom with the execution of operational plans.

Let's see how 5-3a top managers create the organization's purpose statement and strategic objective, 5-3b middle managers develop tactical plans and use management by objectives to motivate employee efforts toward the overall purpose and strategic objective, and 5-3c first-level managers use operational, single-use, and standing plans to implement the tactical plans.

5-3a Starting at the Top

Top management is responsible for developing long-term **strategic plans** that make clear how the company will serve customers and position itself against competitors in the next two to five years. During his first term as **Procter & Gamble's** CEO, A.G. Lafley focused on acquisitions and growth. His strategic focus turned P&G into the world's largest consumer-products company. When he returned as CEO, he began purposefully to shrink the giant company, exiting roughly 100 product lines within two years. The reason? The company had grown too large to compete. Lafley sold Camay and

Zest brands to archrival Unilever and exited the battery business by selling Duracell and the pet-food business by selling Iams. He also looked to sell Wella and Clairol, two brands that he acquired during his first term as P&G's CEO. "Decade after decade, we have to find the strategy and the business model that wins with consumers," Lafley said, and trimming P&G's portfolio "strategically resets P&G's where-to-play choices for at least the next five years."[28]

Strategic planning begins with the creation of an organizational purpose. A **purpose statement**, which is often referred to as an organizational mission or vision, is a statement of a company's purpose or reason for existing.[29] Purpose statements should be brief—no more than two sentences. They should also be enduring, inspirational, clear, and consistent with widely shared company beliefs and values. An excellent example of a well-crafted purpose statement is that of

Daniel Acker/AFP/Getty Images

Strategic plans overall company plans that clarify how the company will serve customers and position itself against competitors over the next two to five years

Purpose statement a statement of a company's purpose or reason for existing

Avon, the cosmetics company. It guides everyone in the organization and provides a focal point for the delivery of beauty products and services to the customers, women around the world. The purpose is the same whether Avon is selling lipstick to women in India, shampoo packets to women in the Amazon, or jewelry to women in the United States. Despite these regional differences in specific strategy, the overall goal—understanding the needs of women globally—does not change. Other examples of organizational purpose statements that have been particularly effective include Walt Disney Company's "to make people happy" and Schlage Lock Company's "to make the world more secure."[30]

A clear mission can also help employees prioritize better and work more efficiently. Early in her career, president and COO of Change.org Jennifer Dulski and her team worked past 9:00 p.m. almost every day. A supervisor took notice and told her she was working too hard. His advice: "Write down at the top of a piece of paper the mission you're trying to accomplish. Now take your entire to-do list and check every item against the mission."[31]

The **strategic objective**, which flows from the purpose, is a more specific goal that unifies company-wide efforts, stretches and challenges the organization, and possesses a finish line and a time frame.[32] Collins and Porras define an organization's mission: "A mission is a clear and compelling goal that serves to unify an organization's efforts. An effective mission must stretch and challenge the organization, yet be achievable." However, many others define *mission* as an organization's purpose. In this edition, to be more specific and avoid confusion, we use Collins and Porras's term *purpose statement*, meaning a clear statement of an organization's purpose or reason for existence. Furthermore, we will continue to use Collins and Porras's definition of a mission (that is "a clear and compelling goal . . .") but instead call it "the strategic objective."

For example, in 1961, President John F. Kennedy established a strategic objective for NASA with this simple statement: "Achieving the goal, before this decade is out, of landing a man on the moon and returning him safely to earth."[33] NASA achieved this strategic objective on July 20, 1969, when astronaut Neil Armstrong walked on the moon. Once the strategic objective has been accomplished, a new one should be chosen. However, the new strategic objective

John F. Kennedy made it a strategic objective for the United States to land on the moon by the end of the 1960s.

Print Collector/Hulton Archive/Getty Images

must grow out of the organization's purpose, which does not change significantly over time. Tesla Motors builds completely electric cars—not hybrids—that are faster than most gas-powered cars and can cover more than 300 miles on a full charge. But Teslas are extraordinarily expensive. Its first car, the Tesla Roadster, a high-performance sports car in production from 2008 to 2012, cost $109,000 without add-ons. The four-door Model S, which began production in 2012, starts at $70,000, but a completely loaded version costs $93,400. Based on those prices, it seems that Tesla's mission is building luxury, electric sports cars. But, it's not. Founder Elon Musk explains that, "the strategy at Tesla is to enter at the high end of the market, where customers are prepared to pay a premium, and then drive down market as fast as possible to high volume and lower prices with each successive model."[34] In other words, Musk says, "When someone buys the Tesla Roadster sports car, they are actually helping pay for development of the low cost family car."[35] Tesla's Model X, a smaller sedan with gull-wing rear doors, is estimated to sell for $70,000 when it debuts in 2016. But at a technology conference in 2013, Musk said that Tesla's goal was to release an electric car for under $30,000 in the next five years, thus eventually fulfilling the company's mission.[36]

5-3b Bending in the Middle

Middle management is responsible for developing and carrying out tactical plans to accomplish the organization's strategic objective. **Tactical plans** specify how a company will use resources, budgets, and people to accomplish specific goals related to its strategic objective for the next five years. Whereas strategic plans and objectives are used to focus company efforts over the next two to five years, tactical plans and objectives are used to direct behavior, efforts, and attention over the next six months to two years. After two years of declining same-store revenues and corporate profits, which resulted in the hiring of a new CEO, McDonald's has begun implementing and carrying out a number of tactical plans to restore profitability and accomplish its new strategic objective of becoming a "modern and progressive burger company."[37]

Over the next year it will shut 700 poor-performing restaurants in China, Japan, and the U.S.[38]

Within the next two years, it will roll out its "Create Your Taste" program, which, through an app on an in-store tablet computer, allows customers to build a burger however they want. Create Your Taste started in four Californian restaurants in 2013, was available in thirty restaurants in five states as of April 2015, and it will be in 2,000 McDonalds by 2016.[39]

Also, it has begun testing all-day breakfast in some of its San Diego stores. While customers have been asking for all-day breakfast for years, McDonald's official response was, "Our grills just aren't big enough for breakfast and lunch." New CEO Steve Easterbrook is encouraging new approaches. If successful in San Diego, McDonald's will consider expanding it to all of its U.S. restaurants in 2016.[40]

Management by objectives is a management technique often used to develop and carry out tactical plans. **Management by objectives** is a four-step process in which managers and their employees (1) discuss possible goals; (2) collectively select goals that are challenging, attainable, and consistent with the company's overall goals; (3) jointly develop tactical plans that lead to the accomplishment of tactical goals and objectives; and (4) meet regularly to review progress toward accomplishment of those goals. In Chapter 1, we learned that on Mondays, **Qualtrics**, which sells online survey research tools, sends out a company-wide email describing each employee's goals for the coming week and whether they met their prior week's goals. Those weekly goals, however, are derived from quarterly goals containing detailed, measurable objectives and key results, such as revenue and customer satisfaction. Similar to the weekly email, Qualtrics's internal database, which is open to all who work there, shows each employee's quarterly goals and results, individual weekly goals, performance reviews and bonuses, successes and failures from which others can learn, and full career histories.[41] CEO Adam Bryant says, "When everyone's rowing together toward the same objective, it's extremely powerful. We're trying

to execute at a very high level, and we need to make sure everyone knows where we're going."[42]

5-3c Finishing at the Bottom

Lower-level managers are responsible for developing and carrying out **operational plans**, which are the day-to-day plans for producing or delivering the organization's products and services. Operational plans direct the behavior, efforts, and priorities of operative employees for periods ranging from thirty days to six months. There are three kinds of operational plans: single-use plans, standing plans, and budgets.

Single-use plans deal with unique, one-time-only events. In 1905, **General Electric Co.** set up a banking division to finance the sale of its equipment to utility companies. By the 1930s, it financed appliances sales to consumers. By 2015, GE Capital had $500 billion in assets and was the seventh-largest U.S. bank. To sharpen its strategic focus and return to its industrial roots, GE aims to obtain 90 percent of earnings from industrial businesses in 2016, up from 58 percent in 2014. Accordingly, GE created a single-use plan, called "Project Hubble," to dismantle and sell off GE Capital. Over a two-year period, GE will sell its $74 billion lending unit, including roughly $165 million in loans to companies such as Wendy's, and liquidate $26.5 billion in commercial real estate. GE will use the proceeds from this one-time only event to invest further in its remaining industrial businesses, while also rewarding shareholders with $90 billion in dividends and stock buybacks.[43]

Unlike single-use plans that are created, carried out once, and then never used again, standing plans save managers time because after the plans are created, they can be used repeatedly to handle frequently recurring events. If you encounter a problem that you've seen before, someone in your company has probably written a standing plan that explains how to address it. When a snowstorm hit Atlanta in 2014, **Delta Airlines** transformed a Boeing 767 into sleeping quarters for stranded employees. Instead of going to the airport hotel—or to

Management by objectives a four-step process in which managers and employees discuss and select goals, develop tactical plans, and meet regularly to review progress toward goal accomplishment

Operational plans day-to-day plans, developed and implemented by lower-level managers, for producing or delivering the organization's products and services over a thirty-day to six-month period

Single-use plans plans that cover unique, one-time-only events

Standing plans plans used repeatedly to handle frequently recurring events

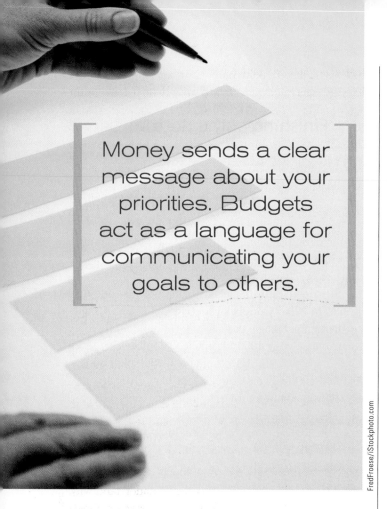

Money sends a clear message about your priorities. Budgets act as a language for communicating your goals to others.

FredFroese/iStockphoto.com

means missing work, while "presenteeism" is coming to work when you're sick.[45] Ann Stevens at ClearRock, a leadership and career consulting company, says, "People get really, really ticked off at co-workers who spread germs in the workplace." But people come to work sick because of policies that reward people for good attendance or because of policies with a limited number of sick days. Use them up and you're stuck if you're sick again. Both reasons are why more companies are using paid-time-off policies that don't distinguish among sick days, personal days, or vacation days. This give employees maximum flexibility and discourages them from coming to work sick. Carol Sladek, at Aon Hewitt, a human resource consulting firm, says, "If you have the flu, stay home. Just stay home . . . .."[46]

Procedures are more specific than policies because they indicate the series of steps that should be taken in response to a particular event. All commercial airplanes require regular cleaning. With no regulatory standards, airlines set their own procedures. At **Singapore Airlines**, which flies longer international flights, a twelve-person team takes roughly forty minutes to clean a Boeing 777-300 jet during a normal stopover. At **United Airlines**, most domestic flights require a quick turn (thirty minutes or less), so the cleaning procedures focus on the following tasks:

▶ Removing visible trash and cleaning out the seat-back pockets

▶ Cleaning and restocking the bathrooms and galleys

▶ Pulling up the armrests

▶ Wiping crumbs off seats

▶ Cleaning large spills

In addition to between flights, United conducts more thorough overnight cleanings (vacuuming and cleaning restrooms and galleys) and "deep cleanings," in which the plane is "scrubbed from nose to tail," every thirty-five to fifty-five days.[47]

Rules and regulations are even more specific than procedures because they specify what must happen or not happen. They describe precisely how a particular action should be performed. For instance, many companies have rules and regulations forbidding managers from writing job reference letters for employees who have worked at their firms because a negative reference may prompt a former employee to sue for defamation of character.[48]

After single-use plans and standing plans, budgets are the third kind of operational plan. **Budgeting** is quantitative planning because it forces managers to decide how to allocate available money to best accomplish

uncomfortable cots in the terminal—employees slept on the plane's business class lie-flat seats and were rested and ready when the runways were clear in the morning. The contingency plan was so successful that Delta added it to its standard storm-response planning in 2015. Using a standing plan rather than reinventing the wheel allows Delta to save time. Delta's senior vice president of operations, Dave Holtz, says, "We don't want to limit our ability to get customers going because employees can't get there."[44] There are three kinds of standing plans: policies, procedures, and rules and regulations.

Policies indicate the general course of action that company managers should take in response to a particular event or situation. A well-written policy will also specify why the policy exists and what outcome the policy is intended to produce. Absenteeism

Policies standing plans that indicate the general course of action that should be taken in response to a particular event or situation

Procedures standing plans that indicate the specific steps that should be taken in response to a particular event

Rules and regulations standing plans that describe how a particular action should be performed or what must happen or not happen in response to a particular event

Budgeting quantitative planning through which managers decide how to allocate available money to best accomplish company goals company goals. According to Jan King, author of *Business Plans to Game Plans*, "Money sends a clear message about your priorities. Budgets act as a language for communicating your goals to others."

5-4 STEPS AND LIMITS TO RATIONAL DECISION MAKING

Decision making is the process of choosing a solution from available alternatives.[49] **Rational decision making** is a systematic process in which managers define problems, evaluate alternatives, and choose optimal solutions that provide maximum benefits to their organizations. Thus, for example, your boss comes to you requesting that you define and evaluate the various options for the company's social media strategy; after all, you tweet and use Facebook, Google+, Instagram, Groupon, and so on and he doesn't even know how to reboot his computer. Furthermore, your solution has to be optimal. Because budgets and expertise are limited, the company gets one, maybe two, tries to make their social media strategy work. If you choose incorrectly, the company's investment will just go to waste, without increasing sales and market share. What would you recommend?

*Let's learn more about each of these: **5-4a define the problem, 5-4b identify decision criteria, 5-4c weigh the criteria, 5-4d generate alternative courses of action, 5-4e evaluate each alternative,** and **5-4f compute the optimal decision.** Then we'll consider **5-4g limits to rational decision making.***

5-4a Define the Problem

The first step in decision making is identifying and defining the problem. A **problem** exists when there is a gap between a desired state (what is wanted) and an existing state (the situation you are actually facing). You're the VP of HR for Guitar Center, a music instrument retailer with 240 U.S. locations. Each store has a combination of full-time and part-time employees, who all want schedules that fits their personal lives and gives them the most hours. Furthermore, daily customer flow is steady on the weekends. But during the workweek, it's inconsistent—light in the morning (stores open at 10:00 a.m. to 11:00 a.m), heavier around lunch, then

lighter till about 3:00 p.m. Customer flow becomes heavier again between 3:00 p.m and 6:00 p.m. (after school and people getting off work), and then heaviest in the evening from 6:00 p.m. till stores close at 8:00 p.m. or 9:00 p.m. Your problem, and it's not easy, is how to match employees' schedules and wishes to lighter and heavier parts of the day throughout the week so that there are enough employees to help customers, but not so many so that stores are overstaffed.[50]

The presence of a gap between an existing state and a desired state is no guarantee that managers will make decisions to solve problems. Three things must occur for this to happen.[51] First, managers have to be aware of the gap. They have to know there is a problem before they can begin solving it. For example, after noticing that people were spending more money on their pets, a new dog food company created an expensive, high-quality dog food. To emphasize its quality, the dog food was sold in cans and bags with gold labels, red letters, and detailed information about its benefits and nutrients. Yet the product did not sell very well, and the company went out of business in less than a year. Its founders didn't understand why. When they asked a manager at a competing dog food company what their biggest mistake had been, the answer was, "Simple. You didn't have a picture of a dog on the package."[52] This problem would have been easy to solve if management had only been aware of it.

Being aware of a problem isn't enough to begin the decision-making process. Managers have to be motivated to reduce the gap between a desired and an existing state. Sales of carbonated soda have declined as public health concerns over obesity and diabetes have grown. In response, **Pepsi Cola** and **Coca-Cola** diversified by adding water, juice, and energy drinks to their product lines. But after missing its growth target (3–4 percent) for two straight years, Coke CEO Muhtar Kent settled on a simple strategy to close Coke's sales gap—sell more soda. The company launched Freestyle self-serve soda machines that allow consumers to custom mix more than 100 drink flavors (there are now 27,000 Freestyle machines in U.S. restaurants) and is working with **Keurig Green Mountain Inc.** to develop an in-home countertop soda machine. Coke also

MekCar/Shutterstock.com

> **Decision making** the process of choosing a solution from available alternatives
>
> **Rational decision making** a systematic process of defining problems, evaluating alternatives, and choosing optimal solutions
>
> **Problem** a gap between a desired state and an existing state

announced a $3 billion cost-cutting program, including some 1,500 layoffs. Soda accounts for 70 percent of Coke's revenue, and Classic Coke and Diet Coke are the top-selling sodas in the United States. With Coke's stalled stock prices making it a potential takeover target, management is highly motivated to address flagging soft drink sales. CEO Kent says, "If we don't do what we need to do quickly, effectively, execute 100 percent, then somebody else will come and do it for us."[53]

Finally, it's not enough to be aware of a problem and be motivated to solve it. Managers must also have the knowledge, skills, abilities, and resources to fix the problem. So how did Guitar Center solve its scheduling problem? The company replaced the Excel spreadsheets that it had been using to manually manage schedules with powerful Dayforce scheduling software from Ceridian Corporation. Guitar Centers' Chris Salles says that, "We load [customer traffic and transactions] in fifteen-minute intervals into Dayforce, and it generates labor-demand curves that let each store know how many people they should staff for every fifteen minutes." Plus, employees can go online to indicate their weekly availability, to see their schedules, and to swap and cover shifts with co-workers.[54]

5-4b Identify Decision Criteria

Decision criteria are the standards used to guide judgments and decisions. Typically, the more criteria a potential solution meets, the better that solution will be. Again, imagine your boss asks you to determine the best options for the company's social media strategy. What general factors would be important when selecting one social media tool over another? Are you trying to increase your search rankings? Provide customer support? Are you trying to reach a particular target market? Is it young single women ages eighteen to 25 or, perhaps, married women ages 25 to 35? Are you reaching out directly to consumers or to businesses (that is business-to-business)? Will your strategy focus on visual content, demonstrations, or detailed, complex knowledge? Answering questions like these will help you identify the criteria that will guide the social media strategy you recommend.

5-4c Weigh the Criteria

After identifying decision criteria, the next step is deciding which criteria are more or less important.

Decision criteria the standards used to guide judgments and decisions

Absolute comparisons a process in which each decision criterion is compared to a standard or ranked on its own merits

Relative comparisons a process in which each decision criterion is compared directly with every other criterion

Exhibit 5.4
Absolute Weighting of Decision Criteria for a Car Purchase

5 critically important
4 important
3 somewhat important
2 not very important
1 completely unimportant

1. Predicted reliability		1	2	3	4	(5)
2. Owner satisfaction		1	(2)	3	4	5
3. Predicted depreciation		(1)	2	3	4	5
4. Avoiding accidents		1	2	3	(4)	5
5. Fuel economy		1	2	3	4	(5)
6. Crash protection		1	2	3	(4)	5
7. Acceleration		(1)	2	3	4	5
8. Ride		1	2	(3)	4	5
9. Front seat comfort		1	2	3	4	(5)

© Cengage Learning

Although there are numerous mathematical models for weighing decision criteria, all require the decision maker to provide an initial ranking of the criteria. Some use **absolute comparisons**, in which each criterion is compared with a standard or is ranked on its own merits. For example, *Consumer Reports* uses nine criteria when it rates and recommends new cars: predicted reliability, current owners' satisfaction, predicted depreciation (the price you could expect if you sold the car), ability to avoid an accident, fuel economy, crash protection, acceleration, ride, and front seat comfort.[55]

Different individuals will rank these criteria differently, depending on what they value or require in a car. Exhibit 5.4 shows the absolute weights that someone buying a car might use. Because these weights are absolute, each criterion is judged on its own importance using a five-point scale, with 5 representing "critically important" and 1 representing "completely unimportant." In this instance, predicted reliability, fuel economy, and front seat comfort were rated most important, and acceleration and predicted depreciation were rated least important.

Another method uses **relative comparisons**, in which each criterion is compared directly with every

Exhibit 5.5
Relative Comparison of Home Characteristics

Home Characteristics	L	SSQ	IP	SR	QS	NBH
Daily commute (L)		+1	−1	−1	−1	0
School system quality (SSQ)	−1		−1	−1	−1	−1
In-ground pool (IP)	+1	+1		0	0	+1
Sun room (SR)	+1	+1	0		0	0
Quiet street (QS)	+1	+1	0	0		0
Newly built house (NBH)	0	+1	−1	0	0	
Total weight	+2	+5	−3	−2	−2	0

© Cengage Learning

other criterion.[56] Exhibit 5.5 shows six criteria that someone might use when buying a house. Moving down the first column of Exhibit 5.5, we see that the time of the daily commute has been rated less important (−1) than school system quality; more important (+1) than having an in-ground pool, a sun room, or a quiet street; and just as important as the house being brand new (0). Total weights, which are obtained by summing the scores in each column, indicate that the school system quality and daily commute are the most important factors to this home buyer, while an in-ground pool, sun room, and a quiet street are the least important. So with relative comparison, criteria are directly compared with each other.

5-4d Generate Alternative Courses of Action

After identifying and weighting the criteria that will guide the decision-making process, the next step is to identify possible courses of action that could solve the problem. In general, at this step, the idea is to generate as many alternatives as possible. Let's assume that you're trying to select a city in Europe to be the location of a major office. After meeting with your staff, you generate a list of possible alternatives: Amsterdam, the Netherlands; Barcelona or Madrid, Spain; Berlin, Dusseldorf, Frankfurt, or Munich, Germany; Brussels, Belgium; London, England; and Paris, France.

5-4e Evaluate Each Alternative

The next step is to systematically evaluate each alternative against each criterion. Because of the amount of information that must be collected, this step can take much longer and be much more expensive than other steps in the decision-making process. When selecting a European city for your office, you could contact economic development offices in each city, systematically interview businesspeople or executives who operate there, retrieve and use published government data on each location, or rely on published studies such as Cushman & Wakefield's *European Cities Monitor*, which conducts an annual survey of more than five hundred senior European executives who rate thirty-four European cities on twelve business-related criteria.[57]

No matter how you gather the information, once you have it, the key is to use that information systematically to evaluate each alternative against each criterion. Exhibit 5.6 shows how each of the ten cities on your staff's list fared with respect to each of the twelve criteria (higher scores are better), from qualified staff to freedom from pollution. Although London has the most qualified staff, the best access to markets and telecommunications, and is the easiest city to travel to and from, it is also one of the most polluted and expensive cities on the list. Paris offers excellent access to markets and clients, but if your staff is multilingual, Brussels may be a better choice.

5-4f Compute the Optimal Decision

The final step in the decision-making process is to compute the optimal decision by determining the optimal value of each alternative. This is done by multiplying the rating for each criterion (Step 5-4e) by the weight for that criterion (Step 5-4c), and then

iStockphoto.com/Jason Walton

Exhibit 5.6
Criteria Ratings Used to Determine the Best Location for a New Office

Criteria Weights:	Access to Markets	Qualified Staff	Telecommunications	Easy to Travel to/from City	Cost & Value of Office Space	Cost of Staff	Available Office Space	Languages Spoken	Business Climate	Travel within City	Quality of Life	Freedom from Pollution	Weighted Average	Ranking
	0.60	0.53	0.52	0.42	0.33	0.32	0.25	0.21	0.20	0.20	0.16	0.16		
Amsterdam	0.42	0.40	0.39	0.68	0.30	0.19	0.30	0.96	0.47	0.34	0.44	0.63	1.72	5
Barcelona	0.23	0.32	0.16	0.29	0.52	0.59	0.52	0.23	0.31	0.47	1.08	0.42	1.45	8
Berlin	0.44	0.39	0.41	0.35	0.78	0.40	0.79	0.50	0.34	0.78	0.38	0.29	1.85	4
Brussels	0.46	0.43	0.37	0.48	0.44	0.17	0.42	0.98	0.37	0.29	0.41	0.27	1.65	7
Dusseldorf	0.30	0.30	0.23	0.21	0.37	0.14	0.28	0.18	0.17	0.22	0.20	0.26	0.97	10
Frankfurt	0.68	0.57	0.70	1.17	0.38	0.11	0.44	0.57	0.38	0.35	0.17	0.18	2.16	3
London	1.50	1.36	1.27	1.79	0.27	0.10	0.42	1.48	0.55	1.26	0.46	0.15	4.03	1
Madrid	0.45	0.46	0.27	0.41	0.52	0.61	0.67	0.22	0.29	0.53	0.67	0.13	1.70	6
Munich	0.34	0.47	0.48	0.37	0.18	0.03	0.18	0.30	0.22	0.47	0.62	0.57	1.36	9
Paris	1.09	0.84	0.89	1.36	0.22	0.10	0.37	0.58	0.30	1.07	0.52	0.12	2.83	2

Source: "European Cities Monitor 2011," Cushion & Wakefield, 2011, accessed 27 May 2013. http://www.berlin-partner.de/fileadmin/user_upload/01_chefredaktion/02_pdf/studien-rankings/2011/Cushman%20&%20Wakefield%20-%20European%20Cities%20Monitor%20%282011%20english%29.pdf

summing those scores for each alternative course of action that you generated (Step 5-4d). For example, the 500 executives participating in Cushman & Wakefield's survey of the best European cities for business rated the twelve decision criteria in terms of importance, as shown in the first row of Exhibit 5.6. Access to markets, qualified staff, telecommunications, and easy travel to and from the city were the four most important factors, while quality of life and freedom from pollution were the least important factors. To calculate the optimal value for Paris, the weight for each category is multiplied by its score in each category (.53 × .84 in the qualified staff category, for example). Then all of these scores are added together to produce the optimal value, as follows:

$$(.60 \times 1.09) + (.53 \times .84) + (.52 \times .89) +$$
$$(.42 \times 1.36) + (.33 \times .22) + (.32 \times .10) +$$
$$(.25 \times .37) + (.21 \times .58) + (.20 \times .30) +$$
$$(.20 \times 1.07) + (.16 \times .52) + (.16 \times .12) = 2.83$$

Because London has a weighted average of 4.03 compared to 2.83 for Paris and 2.16 for Frankfurt (the

cities with the next-best ratings), London clearly ranks as the best location for your company's new European office because of its large number of qualified staff; easy access to markets; outstanding ease of travel to, from, and within the city; excellent telecommunications; and top-notch business climate.

5-4g Limits to Rational Decision Making

In general, managers who diligently complete all six steps of the rational decision-making model will make better decisions than those who don't. So, when they can, managers should try to follow the steps in the rational decision-making model, especially for big decisions with long-range consequences.

To make completely rational decisions, managers would have to operate in a perfect world with no real-world constraints. Of course, it never actually works like that in the real world. Managers face time and money constraints. They often don't have time to make extensive lists of decision criteria. And they often don't have the resources to test all possible solutions against all possible criteria.

In theory, fully rational decision makers **maximize** decisions by choosing the optimal solution. In practice, however, limited resources along with attention, memory, and expertise problems make it nearly impossible for managers to maximize decisions. Consequently, most managers don't maximize—they satisfice. Whereas maximizing is choosing the best alternative, **satisficing** is choosing a "good-enough" alternative.

In the opening to this section, your boss comes to you asking for a recommendation on the best options for the company's social media strategy. With so many options and the fast pace of change, deciding isn't easy. In other words, there's no optimal solution that will satisfy all criteria. For instance, if you're trying to increase your search rankings, you should use Google+ and YouTube, both of which are owned and linked to Google and its search results. If you're interested in providing customer support, then pay close attention to what your customers are saying on Facebook and Twitter, and reach out to them when they're having problems or are dissatisfied. If your target market is young single women ages 18 to 25, use Twitter and Facebook, but if it's married women ages 25 to 35, use Pinterest. If reaching out directly to consumers, use Pinterest and Facebook, but if reaching out to businesses, use LinkedIn and Twitter. Finally, if your strategy focuses on visual content, use Pinterest; if your intent is to demonstrate what your product or service does, use YouTube; and if you've got detailed, complex knowledge, use Twitter and blogs.[58] Your decision will be complete when you find a "good-enough alternative" that does the best job of meeting your decision criteria.

5-5 USING GROUPS TO IMPROVE DECISION MAKING

A survey of 2,044 human resources and organizational leaders found that 84 percent of companies used teams for special projects, while 74 percent used teams to address departmental issues and innovation.[59] In other words, groups were used to solve problems and make decisions. Companies rely so heavily on groups to make decisions because when done properly, group decision making can lead to much better decisions than those typically made by individuals. In fact, numerous studies show that groups consistently outperform individuals on complex tasks.

*Let's explore the **5-5a advantages and pitfalls of group decision making** and see how the following group decision-making methods—**5-5b structured conflict, 5-5c the nominal group technique, 5-5d the Delphi technique,** and **5-5e electronic brainstorming**—can be used to improve decision making.*

5-5a Advantages and Pitfalls of Group Decision Making

Groups can do a much better job than individuals in two important steps of the decision-making process: defining the problem and generating alternative solutions. Still, group decision making is subject to some pitfalls that can quickly erase these gains. One possible pitfall is groupthink. **Groupthink** occurs in highly cohesive groups when group members feel intense pressure to agree with each other so that the group can approve a proposed solution.[60] Because groupthink leads to consideration of a limited number of solutions and restricts discussion of any considered solutions, it usually results in poor decisions. Groupthink is most likely to occur under the following conditions:

▶ The group is insulated from others with different perspectives.

▶ The group leader begins by expressing a strong preference for a particular decision.

▶ The group has no established procedure for systematically defining problems and exploring alternatives.

▶ Group members have similar backgrounds and experiences.[61]

A second potential problem with group decision making is that it takes considerable time. Reconciling schedules so that group members can meet takes time. Furthermore, it's a rare group that consistently holds productive, task-oriented meetings to effectively work through the decision-making process. Some of the most common complaints about meetings (and thus group decision making) are that the meeting's purpose is unclear, participants are unprepared, critical people are absent or late, conversation doesn't stay focused on

Maximize choosing the best alternative

Satisficing choosing a "good-enough" alternative

Groupthink a barrier to good decision making caused by pressure within the group for members to agree with each other the problem, and no one follows up on the decisions that were made.

A third possible pitfall to group decision making is that sometimes one or two people, perhaps the boss or a strong-willed, vocal group member, can dominate group discussions and limit the group's consideration of different problem definitions and alternative solutions. And, unlike individual decisions where people feel personally responsible for making a good choice, another potential problem is that group members may not feel accountable for the decisions made and actions taken by the group. Ironically, a fourth pitfall to group decision making is equality bias, which causes individuals to treat all group members as equally competent. More highly competent people tend to underestimate their abilities, while less competent people overestimate theirs. A recent study showed that even though the more competent person in a pair of study participants was correct over 70 percent of the time, the more competent person would agree to the less competent partner's decision roughly 40 percent of the time. Likewise, the less competent person in the pair would agree with the more competent partner's choice only 50 percent of the time—even though the other person was correct over 70 percent of the time. Study author Dr. Bahudar Bahrami noted, "Even when we showed them exactly how competent they each were, they still gave each other more or less equal say. Incredibly, this still continued when people were rewarded with real money for making correct decisions." Bahrami suggests two key reasons for equality bias. First, individuals do not want to exclude the other group members by asserting their competence. Second, individuals may be reluctant to take responsibility for group decisions.[62]

Although these pitfalls can lead to poor decision making, this doesn't mean that managers should avoid using groups to make decisions. When done properly, group decision making can lead to much better decisions. The pitfalls of group decision making are not inevitable. Managers can overcome most of them by using the various techniques described next.

5-5b Structured Conflict

C-type conflict (cognitive conflict) disagreement that focuses on problem- and issue-related differences of opinion

A-type conflict (affective conflict) disagreement that focuses on individuals or personal issues

Most people view conflict negatively. Yet the right kind of conflict can lead to much better group decision making. **C-type conflict**, or "cognitive conflict," focuses on problem- and issue-related differences of opinion.[63] In c-type conflict, group members disagree because their different experiences and expertise lead them to view the problem and its potential solutions differently. C-type conflict is also characterized by a willingness to examine, compare, and reconcile those differences to produce the best possible solution. Douglas Merrill, CEO of big-data firm ZestFinance, says, "Without conflict of some sort, you can't get to better answers. The challenge is to build a culture that enables conflict without the kind of painful conflict that some companies thrive on."[64] Ray Dalio, founder and CEO of Bridgewater Associates, the world's largest hedge fund, says anyone in the company can say that what the firm is doing doesn't make sense to them. At most investment firms, he says, "people keep that [kind of criticism] to themselves." But at Bridgewater, "you have a right and an obligation to say 'I think this is terrible' and explore whether or not that's true." Ultimately, he believes that, "if you can't have independent thinking, you can't know what your weaknesses are, and sort those things out, you're not going to be successful."[65]

By contrast, **a-type conflict**, meaning "affective conflict," refers to the emotional reactions that can occur when disagreements become personal rather than professional. A-type conflict often results in hostility, anger, resentment, distrust, cynicism, and apathy. Unlike c-type conflict, a-type conflict undermines team effectiveness by preventing teams from engaging in the activities characteristic of c-type conflict that are critical to team effectiveness. Examples of a-type conflict statements are "your idea," "our idea," "my department," "you don't know what you are talking about," or "you don't understand our situation." Rather than focusing on issues and ideas, these statements focus on individuals.[66]

A-type conflict: When disagreements become personal rather than professional

The **devil's advocacy** approach can be used to create c-type conflict by assigning an individual or a subgroup the role of critic. The following five steps establish a devil's advocacy program:

1. Generate a potential solution.
2. Assign a devil's advocate to criticize and question the solution.
3. Present the critique of the potential solution to key decision makers.
4. Gather additional relevant information.
5. Decide whether to use, change, or not use the originally proposed solution.[67]

When properly used, the devil's advocacy approach introduces c-type conflict into the decision-making process. Contrary to the common belief that conflict is bad, studies show that these methods lead not only to less a-type conflict but also to improved decision quality and greater acceptance of decisions after they have been made.[68]

Another method of creating c-type conflict is **dialectical inquiry**, which creates c-type conflict by forcing decision makers to state the assumptions of a proposed solution (a thesis) and then generate a solution that is the opposite (antithesis) of the proposed solution. The following are the five steps of the dialectical inquiry process:

1. Generate a potential solution.
2. Identify the assumptions underlying the potential solution.
3. Generate a conflicting counterproposal based on the opposite assumptions.
4. Have advocates of each position present their arguments and engage in a debate in front of key decision makers.
5. Decide whether to use, change, or not use the originally proposed solution.

5-5c Nominal Group Technique

Nominal means "in name only." Accordingly, the **nominal group technique** (NGT) received its name because it begins with a quiet time in which group members independently write down as many problem definitions and alternative solutions as possible. In other words, the NGT begins by having group members act as individuals. After the quiet time, the group leader asks each member to share one idea at a time with the group. As they are read aloud, ideas are posted on flip charts or wallboards for all to see. This step continues until all ideas have been shared. In the next step, the group discusses the advantages and disadvantages of the ideas. The NGT closes with a second quiet time in which group members independently rank the ideas presented. Group members then read their rankings aloud, and the idea with the highest average rank is selected.[69]

IBM manager Phil Gilbert used the NGT when his team developed a new email tool called IBM Verse. Instead of instructing them to come up with the next big thing in email, Gilbert had them spend ten minutes quietly writing down what they disliked about email on sticky notes—one idea per note, and no talking. As people finished writing, they stuck their notes on a big whiteboard until there weren't any more to post. The team leader then organized the sticky notes into logical groupings for review. Then the team left (Gilbert says sometimes briefly or for days). When they return to the whiteboard, they bring additional ideas. Regarding the NGT process, Gilbert says, "It makes for better teams, and it leads to better outcomes. When you give voice to more people, the best ideas win, not the loudest ones."[70]

The nominal group technique improves group decision making by decreasing a-type conflict. But it also restricts c-type conflict. Consequently, the nominal group technique typically produces poorer decisions than the devil's advocacy and dialectical inquiry approaches. Nonetheless, more than eighty studies have found that nominal groups produce better ideas than those produced by traditional groups.[71]

5-5d Delphi Technique

In the **Delphi technique**, the members of a panel of experts respond to questions and to each other until reaching agreement on an issue. The first step is to assemble a panel of experts. Unlike other approaches to group decision making, however, it isn't necessary to bring the panel members together in one place. Because the Delphi technique does not require the experts to leave their offices or disrupt their schedules, they are more likely to participate.

Devil's advocacy a decision-making method in which an individual or a subgroup is assigned the role of critic

Dialectical inquiry a decision-making method in which decision makers state the assumptions of a proposed solution (a thesis) and generate a solution that is the opposite (antithesis) of that solution

Nominal group technique a decision-making method that begins and ends by having group members quietly write down and evaluate ideas to be shared with the group

Delphi technique a decision-making method in which members of a panel of experts respond to questions and to each other until reaching agreement on an issue

The second step is to create a questionnaire consisting of a series of open-ended questions for the group. In the third step, the group members' written responses are analyzed, summarized, and fed back to the group for reactions until the members reach agreement. Asking group members why they agree or disagree is important because it helps uncover their unstated assumptions and beliefs. Again, this process of summarizing panel feedback and obtaining reactions to that feedback continues until the panel members reach agreement.

5-5e Electronic Brainstorming

Brainstorming, in which group members build on others' ideas, is a technique for generating a large number of alternative solutions. Brainstorming has four rules:

1. The more ideas, the better.
2. All ideas are acceptable, no matter how wild or crazy they might seem.
3. Other group members' ideas should be used to come up with even more ideas.
4. Criticism or evaluation of ideas is not allowed.

Although brainstorming is great fun and can help managers generate a large number of alternative solutions, it does have a number of disadvantages. Fortunately, **electronic brainstorming**, in which group members use computers to communicate and generate alternative solutions, overcomes the disadvantages associated with face-to-face brainstorming.[72]

The first disadvantage that electronic brainstorming overcomes is **production blocking**, which occurs when you have an idea but have to wait to share it because someone else is already presenting an idea to the group. During this short delay, you may forget your idea or decide that it really wasn't worth sharing. Production blocking doesn't happen with electronic brainstorming. All group members are seated at computers, so everyone can type in ideas whenever they occur. There's no waiting your turn to be heard by the group.

The second disadvantage that electronic brainstorming overcomes is **evaluation apprehension**, that is, being afraid of what others will think of your ideas. For example, Robert Murphy, an online marketing representative, had prepared for a meeting with his boss and six coworkers by conducting research and bringing detailed notes to the meeting. Then, when the discussion began, his evaluation apprehension regarding what his boss and colleagues would say about his ideas overwhelmed his preparation. Says Murphy, "I just sat there like a lump, fixated on the fact that I was quiet."[73]

With electronic brainstorming, all ideas are anonymous. When you type in an idea and press the Enter key to share it with the group, group members see only the idea. Furthermore, many brainstorming software programs also protect anonymity by displaying ideas in random order. So if you laugh maniacally when you type "Cut top management's pay by 50 percent!" and then press the Enter key, it won't show up immediately on everyone's screen. This makes it doubly difficult to determine who is responsible for which comments.

In the typical layout for electronic brainstorming, all participants sit in front of computers around a U-shaped table. This configuration allows them to see their computer screens, the other participants, a large main screen, and a meeting leader or facilitator. Step 1 in electronic brainstorming is to anonymously generate as many ideas as possible. Groups commonly generate 100 ideas in a half-hour period. Step 2 is to edit the generated ideas, categorize them, and eliminate redundancies. Step 3 is to rank the categorized ideas in terms of quality. Step 4, the last step, has three parts: generate a series of action steps, decide the best order for accomplishing these steps, and identify who is responsible for each step. All four steps are accomplished with computers and electronic brainstorming software.[74]

Studies show that electronic brainstorming is much more productive than face-to-face brainstorming. Four-person electronic brainstorming groups produce 25 to 50 percent more ideas than four-person regular brainstorming groups, and twelve-person electronic brainstorming groups produce 200 percent more ideas than

Brainstorming a decision-making method in which group members build on each others' ideas to generate as many alternative solutions as possible

Electronic brainstorming a decision-making method in which group members use computers to build on each others' ideas and generate as many alternative solutions as possible

Production blocking a disadvantage of face-to-face brainstorming in which a group member must wait to share an idea because another member is presenting an idea

Evaluation apprehension fear of what others will think of your ideas

Fight or Flight in the Workplace

Conflict is a part of life, and that includes the workplace. Aggravations range from the seemingly small (a messy coworker) to the significant (a teammate who steals credit or clients) and everything in between. How is a person to know which issues are worth fighting for (or over)? Executive coach Lynne Eisaguirre suggests only tackling problems that are truly important and matter to your employer, your colleagues, or your ability to do your job. If you decide to engage, plan ahead for the confrontation and be sure you can control your emotions. Address your concerns to someone who has power to resolve them. And recognize that sometimes retreat is the best option. In general, avoid conflicts that touch on issues outside your area of responsibility or that are unimportant to your employer. Don't pick battles with people more powerful than you or just because you dislike someone.

Source: S. Shellenbarger, "To Fight, or Not to Fight? How to Pick Your Battles in the Workplace," *Wall Street Journal*, December 16, 2014. http://www.wsj.com/articles/picking-your-workplace-battles-1418772621.

regular groups of the same size! In fact, because production blocking (having to wait your turn) is not a problem in electronic brainstorming, the number and quality of ideas generally increase with group size.[75]

Even though it works much better than traditional brainstorming, electronic brainstorming has disadvantages, too. An obvious problem is the expense of computers, networks, software, and other equipment. As these costs continue to drop, however, electronic brainstorming will become cheaper.

Another problem is that the anonymity of ideas may bother people who are used to having their ideas accepted by virtue of their position (that is the boss). On the other hand, one CEO said, "Because the process is anonymous, the sky's the limit in terms of what you can say, and, as a result, it is more thought-provoking. As a CEO, you'll probably discover things you might not want to hear but need to be aware of."[76]

A third disadvantage is that outgoing individuals who are more comfortable expressing themselves verbally may find it difficult to express themselves in writing. Finally, the most obvious problem is that participants have to be able to type. Those who can't type, or who type slowly, may be easily frustrated and find themselves at a disadvantage compared to experienced typists.

STUDY TOOLS 5

LOCATED IN TEXTBOOK
☐ Rip-out and review chapter review card

LOCATED AT WWW.CENGAGEBRAIN.COM
☐ Review key term flashcards and create your own from StudyBits
☐ Track your knowledge and understanding of key concepts, using the concept tracker
☐ Complete practice and graded quizzes to prepare for tests
☐ Complete interactive content within the exposition
☐ View chapter highlight box content at the beginning of each chapter

6 Organizational Strategy

ORGANIZATION CHART INFOGRAPHICS

Vice President
Reports into an executive and is usually responsible for one or two business units.

Mid-Level Manager
Responsible for guiding daily business operations.

Mid-Level Manager
Responsible for guiding daily business operations.

Account Manager
Responsible for managing the daily relationship with a customer or business.

Sales Representative
Responsible for selling new products and services to new clients.

Account Manager
Responsible for managing the daily relationship with a customer or business.

Sales Representative
Responsible for selling new products and services to new clients.

TechnoVectors/Shutterstock.com

LEARNING OUTCOMES

6-1 Specify the components of sustainable competitive advantage, and explain why it is important.

6-2 Describe the steps involved in the strategy-making process.

6-3 Explain the different kinds of corporate-level strategies.

6-4 Describe the different kinds of industry-level strategies.

6-5 Explain the components and kinds of firm-level strategies.

After you finish this chapter, go to **PAGE 130** for **STUDY TOOLS**

6-1 SUSTAINABLE COMPETITIVE ADVANTAGE

Just five years ago, there was no market for tablet computers. A number of computer makers sold touch screen laptops, but other than some programs that allowed users to handwrite notes, there was little to distinguish these machines from traditional laptops. All of that changed when Apple released its iPad tablet computer that is controlled by a multitouch display and can run hundreds of thousands of applications allowing users to read books, watch movies, listen to music, check the weather, or play games. With its innovative product, Apple in effect created a new market for portable, touch-based tablet computers. The iPad is not without its competitors, however. There is, for example, the Amazon Kindle Fire, Barnes & Noble's Nook HD, and Samsung's Android-based Galaxy Tab. The latest competitor is the Microsoft Surface, which comes with a touch screen, a combination cover/detachable keyboard, and two versions of the Windows operating system. The Surface, however, has done little to dim enthusiasm for the iPad. Critics complain about the lack of apps for Surface, just 47,000 compared to more than 300,000 for the iPad, the higher price ($999 for a 256 gb Surface Pro with an Intel i7 chip versus $929 for a 64 gb iPad with an A7 chip and a high-definition screen), and that the Windows 8 touch interface on the Surface is more difficult to learn and use than the iPad's. Despite these competitors, Apple still dominates tablet sales, selling 63.4 million iPads in 2014 compared to just 1 million Surfaces, 40 million Galaxies, and 3.3 million Kindles.[1] Likewise, a report on Web usage, meaning the percentage of tablet Web traffic (that is surfing the Web with your tablet rather than your PC or smartphone), found that Apple generated 79.9 percent of all tablet Web traffic in North America compared to 6.7 percent for Amazon, 6 percent for Samsung, and 1.6 percent for Microsoft.[2]

How can a company like Apple, which dominates a particular industry, maintain its competitive advantage as strong, well-financed competitors enter the market? What steps can Apple and other companies take to better manage their strategy-making process?

Resources are the assets, capabilities, processes, employee time, information, and knowledge that an organization controls. Firms use their resources to improve organizational effectiveness and efficiency. Resources are critical to organizational strategy because they can help companies create and sustain an advantage over competitors.[3]

Organizations can achieve a **competitive advantage** by using their resources to provide greater value for customers than competitors can. For example, the iPad's competitive advantage came partly from its sleek, attractive design and partly from the reputation of Apple's iPod and iPhone as innovative, easy-to-use products.

The goal of most organizational strategies is to create and then sustain a competitive advantage. A competitive advantage becomes a **sustainable competitive advantage** when other companies cannot duplicate the value a firm is providing to customers. Sustainable competitive advantage is *not* the same as a long-lasting competitive advantage, though companies obviously want a competitive advantage to last a long time. Instead, a competitive advantage is *sustained* if competitors have tried unsuccessfully to duplicate the advantage and have, for the moment,

---

Resources the assets, capabilities, processes, employee time, information, and knowledge that an organization uses to improve its effectiveness and efficiency and create and sustain competitive advantage

Competitive advantage providing greater value for customers than competitors can

Sustainable competitive advantage a competitive advantage that other companies have tried unsuccessfully to duplicate and have, for the moment, stopped trying to duplicate

Manaemedia/Shutterstock.com

stopped trying to duplicate it. It's the corporate equivalent of your competitors saying, "We give up. You win. We can't do what you do, and we're not even going to try to do it anymore." Four conditions must be met if a firm's resources are to be used to achieve a sustainable competitive advantage. The resources must be valuable, rare, imperfectly imitable, *and* nonsubstitutable.

Valuable resources allow companies to improve their efficiency and effectiveness. Unfortunately, changes in customer demand and preferences, competitors' actions, and technology can make once-valuable resources much less valuable. Before the iPad was introduced, netbooks appeared to be the next big thing in mobile computing. These laptops were small and light, making them ultra portable; were very affordable, averaging anywhere from $200 to $500; and let users run basic programs such as Web browsing and word processing on the go. At first, sales were brisk—in 2009, 7.5 million netbooks were sold in the United States and more than 34 million worldwide. But all that changed. The iPad had a touch screen, an intuitive operating system, and a large selection of app software, while netbooks were often criticized for having small, hard-to-use keyboards, a slow operating system, and a lack of software options. While it took only twenty-eight days for Apple to sell its first 1 million iPads, netbook sales fell by 40 percent in one year.[4] Only one year after netbook sales peaked, tablet sales passed them, and netbook sales have been steadily declining ever since.[5]

For sustained competitive advantage, valuable resources must also be rare resources. Think about it: How can a company sustain a competitive advantage if all of its competitors have similar resources and capabilities? Consequently, **rare resources**, resources that are not controlled or possessed by many competing firms, are necessary to sustain a competitive advantage. One of Apple's truly rare resources is its ability to reconfigure existing technology into a package that is easy to use, elegantly designed, and therefore highly desired by customers. Apple used its wealth of experience from developing the iPod, iPod touch, and iPhone to create an operating system for the iPad that was easy to use and, more importantly, basically identical to what was found on its other products. In other words, it created a single platform that would give users the same experience across multiple devices. An iPhone user who just purchased an iPad will have little difficulty learning how to use it. This is not the case with the iPad's chief competitors, tablets powered by Google's Android. Because it is open source, meaning that manufacturers can alter the basic operating system in different ways, there is less uniformity across various Android devices. Simply put, one Android tablet might look and work differently than another, and one company might offer an app that will not work on another Android device.[6]

As this example shows, valuable and rare resources can create temporary competitive advantage. For sustained competitive advantage, however, other firms must be unable to imitate or find substitutes for those valuable, rare resources. **Imperfectly imitable resources** are those resources that are impossible or extremely costly or difficult to duplicate. Both Google and Amazon operate online app stores that are in some way similar to Apple's App Store. Users can log on to the sites, browse for programs, and purchase and download them to their devices. There is a big difference, however, in security. Apple's App Store is a closed platform, meaning that if a software developer wants to sell an app on Apple's site, the company first puts it through a review process to check for content and security issues. As noted earlie, however, Android is an open platform, which means that while Google has improved in security prescreening, it is far easier for Android developers with bad intentions to create and sell applications that can harm devices or steal personal information. According to a study conducted in 2015 by Symantec, the technology security company, 17 percent of 6.3 million available Android apps are malware.[7] And Verizon's 2015 Data Breach Investigations report shows that, although there are extremely few malware-infested mobile devices on its network (only 100 per week), 96 percent of those are Android devices. The report states, "Android wins. Not just wins, but Android wins so hard that most of the suspicious activity logged from iOS devices was just failed Android exploits."[8]

Valuable, rare, imperfectly imitable resources can produce sustainable competitive advantage only if they are also **nonsubstitutable resources**, meaning that no other resources can replace them and produce similar value or competitive advantage. This is most evident in the dominance of Apple's iTunes software. The industry has tried to produce equivalent substitutes for iTunes, but competitors have had to experiment with different business models to get customers to accept them. For example, Amazon MP3 not only gives consumers access to 20 million digital songs, it allows consumers to store their files on Amazon's cloud servers. In essence, this means

Valuable resource
a resource that allows companies to improve efficiency and effectiveness

Rare resource a resource that is not controlled or possessed by many competing firms

Imperfectly imitable resource a resource that is impossible or extremely costly or difficult for other firms to duplicate

Nonsubstitutable resource a resource that produces value or competitive advantage and has no equivalent substitutes or replacements that users can buy a song from Amazon and stream it to any device they own, from their desktop computer to their Android tablet. Apple responded by introducing its own cloud-based service called iCloud, which, combined with a service called iTunes Match, provides consumers with an online locker in which they can store music, video, or photo files, as well as apps, to access from multiple devices, whether they bought them from Apple or not. In addition, iCloud lets users synchronize other data, such as appointments, email, and documents, between their iPhone, iPad, and Mac computers.[9] Likewise, iTunes faces growing competition from music streaming services, such as Spotify, that provide basic free services for a limited number of hours per month and sell premium subscriptions for about $10 a month. Spotify has more than 60 million users, a quarter of whom are premium subscribers, providing roughly 1.8 billion a year in revenues. By contrast, iTunes has 800 million users worldwide and earns Apple roughly $20 billion a year in revenue. Apple has responded to Spotify and other music streaming companies by adding 56 new countries to the iTunes store for a total of 155 worldwide. Furthermore, Apple launched iTunes Radio, its own streaming music service, and then paid $3 billion to acquire Beats Music, a music subscription service also known for its high end headphones.[10]

In summary, Apple reaped the rewards of a first-mover advantage when it introduced the iPad. The company's history of developing customer-friendly software, the innovative capabilities of the iPad, the uniformity of experience, and the security of the App Store provide customers with a service that has been valuable, rare, relatively nonsubstitutable, and, in the past, imperfectly imitable. Past success is, however, no guarantee of future success: Apple needs to continue developing and improving its products or risk being unseated by a more nimble competitor whose products are more relevant and have higher perceived value for consumers.

6-2 STRATEGY-MAKING PROCESS

To create a sustainable competitive advantage, a company must have a strategy.[11] Exhibit 6.1 displays the three steps of the strategy-making process:

6-2a assess the need for strategic change, 6-2b conduct a situational analysis, and then **6-2c choose strategic alternatives.** Let's examine each of these steps in more detail.

Exhibit 6.1
Three Steps of the Strategy-Making Process

© Cengage Learning

6-2a Assessing the Need for Strategic Change

The external business environment is much more turbulent than it used to be. With customers' needs constantly growing and changing, and with competitors working harder, faster, and smarter to meet those needs, the first step in creating a strategy is determining the need for strategic change. In other words, the company should determine whether it needs to change its strategy to sustain a competitive advantage.[12]

Determining the need for strategic change might seem easy to do, but it's really not. There's a great deal of uncertainty in strategic business environments. Furthermore, top-level managers are often slow to recognize the need for strategic change, especially at successful companies that have created and sustained competitive advantages. Because they are acutely aware of the strategies that made their companies successful, they continue to rely on those

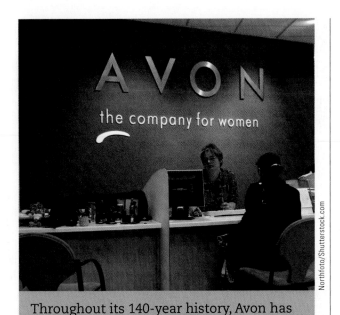

Throughout its 140-year history, Avon has used a direct-selling model.

strategies, even as the competition changes. In other words, success often leads to **competitive inertia**—a reluctance to change strategies or competitive practices that have been successful in the past. Throughout its 140-year history, **Avon** used a direct-selling model in which customers bought beauty products, perfume, and more from their local Avon sales representatives. But since 2011, sales are down 50 percent to $8.9 billion. The company's team of 6 million sales representatives has shrunk nineteen quarters in a row.[13] And, in 2014, Avon lost nearly $400 million when sales dropped by 21 percent, even though the direct sales industry grew globally by 3.2 percent during the same period.[14] In fact, direct selling competitors, such as Mary Kay, and store/Internet competitors, such as Ultra Salon and Sephora, are experiencing strong growth. Despite Avon's steady decline, CEO Sherilyn McCoy is committed to the company's strategy, saying, "We continue to stay the course on our plans to return Avon to sustainable, profitable growth."[15] Why has Avon stuck with a strategy that is clearly not working? Competitive inertia—because it was successful for more than 140 years. CEO Sherilyn McCoy says, "I'm not one to shy away from challenges, and Avon certainly hasn't disappointed me on that front."[16] So is Avon beginning to recognize that it fundamentally needs to change its strategy? Perhaps. In April 2015, it was exploring options to sell its North American division. Critics would contend, however, that selling a problematic part of the company doesn't represent a wholesale change in strategy.

Besides being aware of the dangers of competitive inertia, what can managers do to improve the speed and accuracy with which they determine the need for strategic change? One method is to actively look for signs of strategic dissonance. **Strategic dissonance** is a discrepancy between a company's intended strategy and the strategic actions managers take when actually implementing that strategy.[17] With Japan's shrinking population, little economic growth, stiff competition from Japan's high-speed railways, and airline deregulation leading to new low-cost airlines, **All Nippon Airways (ANA)**, Japan's largest airline, needed to cut costs and move quickly to respond to competitors. However, that intended strategy was at odds (that is strategic dissonance) with its long-standing high-price, high-quality service strategy. So, it started two low-cost airlines, Peach Aviation and AirAsia Japan. While that provided low-cost flights to customers, an unintended benefit for ANA was seeing how Peach and AirAsia made faster decisions to respond to competition and lower costs. For example, AirAsia's top management decided to expand service to Nagoya, Japan, three months faster than planned but got the work done in one-third of the planned time! At ANA, that decision would have taken six months and involved fifty people from across the company in multiple discussions. Yoshinori Odagiri, a long-time ANA executive who became AirAsia's CEO, said, "I was taken aback by the decision-making speed." So, to overcome strategic dissonance and make sure that its new low-cost, speed-to-market strategy is infused through the entire company, ANA has now brought Peach and AirAsia directly into its organizational structure.[18]

Note, however, that strategic dissonance is not the same thing as when a strategy does not produce the results that it's supposed to. When Xhibit, the maker of the SkyMall catalogs found on airplanes (and then at SkyMall.com), filed for bankruptcy, the issue wasn't strategic dissonance. It was that SkyMall's strategy of using catalogs to sell quirky, expensive products such as a $200 pet ramp staircase, a $170 portable icemaker, or a $60 "Tablift Hands-Free Tablet Holder," to bored travelers no longer worked. Why read the SkyMall catalog when you've got books, movies, and music on your smartphone or tablet? Or, when your plane has Wi-Fi, and you can surf the Internet?[19]

Competitive inertia a reluctance to change strategies or competitive practices that have been successful in the past

Strategic dissonance a discrepancy between a company's intended strategy and the strategic actions managers take when implementing that strategy

6-2b Situational Analysis

A situational analysis can also help managers determine the need for strategic change. A **situational analysis**, also called a **SWOT analysis**, for *strengths, weaknesses, opportunities*, and *threats*, is an assessment of the strengths and weaknesses in an organization's internal environment and the opportunities and threats in its external environment.[20] Ideally, as shown in Step 2 of Exhibit 6.1, a SWOT analysis helps a company determine how to increase internal strengths and minimize internal weaknesses while maximizing external opportunities and minimizing external threats.

Aldi's business model focuses on selling a limited number of groceries and household items in a small setting.

An analysis of an organization's internal environment, that is, a company's strengths and weaknesses, often begins with an assessment of its distinctive competencies and core capabilities. A **distinctive competence** is something that a company can make, do, or perform better than its competitors. For example, *Consumer Reports* magazine consistently ranks Honda and Subaru cars as tops in quality and reliability.[21] Similarly, *PC Magazine* readers ranked Apple's desktop and laptop computers best in terms of service and reliability.[22]

Whereas distinctive competencies are tangible—for example, a product or service is faster, cheaper, or better—the core capabilities that produce distinctive competencies are not. **Core capabilities** are the less visible, internal decision-making routines, problem-solving processes, and organizational cultures that determine how efficiently inputs can be turned into outputs. Distinctive competencies cannot be sustained for long without superior core capabilities.

For years, large retail stores such as Walmart and Target have been trying to open stores in New York City only to be met with protests. Aldi, however, recently opened two stores in the city, not only with no protests but even with some politicians in attendance. The reason that Aldi faces little opposition as it opens stores in dense, urban settings is that it is able to make money in small, high-rent stores that are dictated by location. It operates with a business model that focuses on selling a limited number of groceries and household items in a small setting; its typical stores are just 16 percent the size of a typical Walmart store and carry just 1,500 or so items, compared to 100,000 items in a superstore. Furthermore, most of its items are private brands, that is, goods that Aldi buys and packages itself. All of this means that Aldi can offer prices that are 20 percent less than Walmart's, making it an attractive place for city dwellers to shop.[23]

After examining internal strengths and weaknesses, the second part of a situational analysis is to look outside the company and assess the opportunities and threats in the external environment. In Chapter 3, you learned that *environmental scanning* involves searching the environment for important events or issues that might affect the organization, such as pricing trends or new products and technology. In a situational analysis, however, managers use environmental scanning to identify specific opportunities and threats that can either improve or harm the company's ability to sustain its competitive advantage. Identification of strategic groups and formation of shadow-strategy task

Situational (SWOT) analysis an assessment of the strengths and weaknesses in an organization's internal environment and the opportunities and threats in its external environment

Distinctive competence what a company can make, do, or perform better than its competitors

Core capabilities the internal decision-making routines, problem-solving processes, and organizational cultures that determine how efficiently inputs can be turned into outputs forces are two ways to do this (see box "Shadow-Strategy Task Force").

Strategic groups are not groups that actually work together. They are companies—usually competitors—that managers closely follow. More specifically, a **strategic group** is a group of other companies within an industry against which top managers compare, evaluate, and benchmark their company's strategic threats and opportunities.[24] (*Benchmarking* involves identifying outstanding practices, processes, and standards at other companies and adapting them to your own company.) Typically, managers include companies as part of their strategic group if they compete directly with those companies for customers or if those companies use strategies similar to theirs. The U.S. home improvement industry has annual sales in excess of 303 billion. Total home improvement products sales increased 4.0 percent in 2014 to $303 billion. The professional market increased 3.4 percent in 2014 over 2013, and the consumer market will see a sales increase of 4.3 percent.[25] It's likely that the managers at Home Depot, the largest U.S. home improvement and hardware retailer, assess strategic threats and opportunities by comparing their company to a strategic group consisting of the other major home improvement supply companies. Exhibit 6.2 shows the number of stores, the size of the typical new store, and the overall geographic distribution (states, countries) of Home Depot stores compared with Lowe's, Ace Hardware, and 84 Lumber.

In fact, when scanning the environment for strategic threats and opportunities, managers tend to categorize the different companies in their industries as core, secondary, and transient firms.[26] **Core firms** are the central companies in a strategic group. Home Depot operates more than 2,200 stores covering all fifty states, Puerto Rico, the U.S. Virgin Islands, Guam, Mexico, and Canada. The company has more than 350,000 employees and annual revenues of $83.2 billion. By comparison, Lowe's has more than 1,766 stores and 265,000 employees in the United States, Canada, and Mexico; stocks about 36,000 products in each store; and has annual revenues of $56.2 billion.[27] Clearly, Lowe's is the closest competitor to Home Depot and is the core firm in Home Depot's strategic group. Even though Ace Hardware has more stores (4,600) than Home Depot and appears to be a bigger multinational player (seventy different countries), Ace's different franchise structure and small, individualized stores (10,000 to 14,000 square feet, with each store laid out differently with a different mix of products) keep it from being a core firm in Home Depot's strategic group.[28] Likewise, Home Depot's management probably doesn't include Aubuchon Hardware in its core strategic group, because Aubuchon has only 125 stores in New England and upstate New York.[29]

When most managers scan their environments for strategic threats and opportunities, they concentrate on the strategic actions of core firms, not unrelated firms such as Aubuchon. Where does a firm like Ace Hardware fit in? Ace's 20/20 vision employs a customer-focused strategy to grow Ace's brand and improve store performance.[30]

Secondary firms are firms that use strategies related to but somewhat different from those of core firms. 84 Lumber has roughly 250 stores in thirty states, but even though its stores are open to the public, the company focuses on supplying professional contractors, to whom it sells 85 percent of its products. Without the wide variety of products on the shelves or assistance available to the average consumer, people without expertise in building or remodeling probably don't find 84 Lumber stores very accessible. Home Depot would most likely classify 84 Lumber as a secondary firm in its strategic group analysis.[31] Managers need to be aware of

Exhibit 6.2
Core and Secondary Firms in the Home Improvement Industry

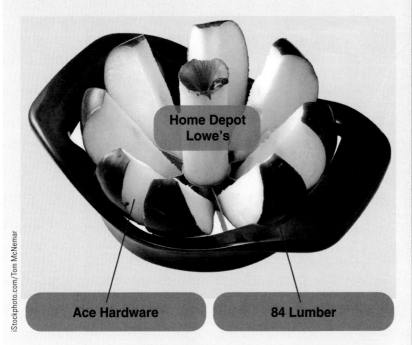

Home Depot
Lowe's

Ace Hardware

84 Lumber

iStockphoto.com/Tom McNemar

	# of Stores	# of States	Countries	Size of Typical Store (sq. feet)
Home Depot	2,269	50	3	104,000
Lowe's	1,766	50	3	112,000
Ace Hardware	4,700	50	70	10,000 to 14,000
84 Lumber	249	30	1	33,000

choose an aggressive, *risk-seeking strategy* that aims to extend or create a sustainable competitive advantage.

The choice to seek risk or avoid risk typically depends on whether top management views the company as falling above or below strategic reference points. **Strategic reference points** are the targets that managers use to measure whether their firm has developed the core competencies that it needs to achieve a sustainable competitive advantage. If a hotel chain decides to compete by providing superior quality and service, then top management will track the success of this strategy through customer surveys or published hotel ratings such as those provided by the prestigious *Mobil Travel Guide*. If a hotel chain decides to compete on price, it will regularly conduct market surveys to check the prices of other hotels. The competitors' prices are the hotel managers' strategic reference points against which to compare their own pricing strategy. If competitors can consistently underprice them, then the managers need to determine whether their staff and resources have the core competencies to compete on price.

As shown in Exhibit 6.3, when a company is performing above or better than its strategic reference points, top management will typically be satisfied with the company's strategy. Ironically, this satisfaction tends to make top management conservative and risk-averse. Because the company already has a sustainable competitive advantage, the worst thing that could happen would be to lose it, so new issues or changes in the company's external environment are viewed as threats. By contrast, when a company is performing below or worse than its strategic reference points, top management will typically be dissatisfied with the company's strategy. In this instance, managers are much more likely to choose a daring, risk-taking strategy. If the current strategy is producing substandard results, the company has nothing to lose by switching to risky new strategies in the hope that it can create a sustainable competitive advantage. Managers of

the potential threats and opportunities posed by secondary firms, but they usually spend more time assessing the threats and opportunities associated with core firms.

6-2c Choosing Strategic Alternatives

After determining the need for strategic change and conducting a situational analysis, the last step in the strategy-making process is to choose strategic alternatives that will help the company create or maintain a sustainable competitive advantage. According to *strategic reference point theory*, managers choose between two basic alternative strategies. They can choose a conservative, *risk-avoiding strategy* that aims to protect an existing competitive advantage. Or they can

Strategic reference points the strategic targets managers use to measure whether a firm has developed the core competencies it needs to achieve a sustainable competitive advantage

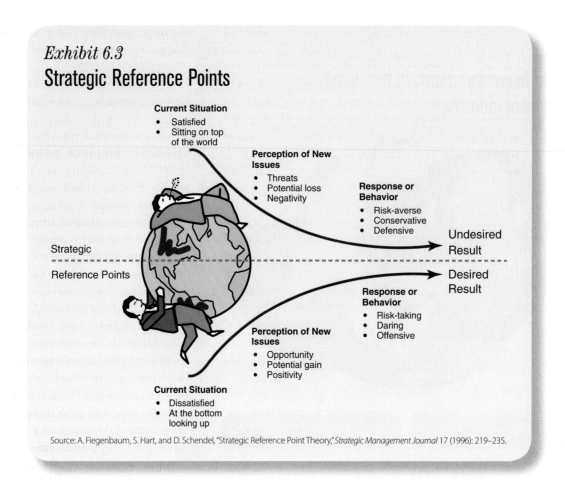

Exhibit 6.3
Strategic Reference Points

Current Situation
- Satisfied
- Sitting on top of the world

Perception of New Issues
- Threats
- Potential loss
- Negativity

Response or Behavior
- Risk-averse
- Conservative
- Defensive

Undesired Result

Strategic Reference Points

Desired Result

Response or Behavior
- Risk-taking
- Daring
- Offensive

Perception of New Issues
- Opportunity
- Potential gain
- Positivity

Current Situation
- Dissatisfied
- At the bottom looking up

Source: A. Fiegenbaum, S. Hart, and D. Schendel, "Strategic Reference Point Theory," *Strategic Management Journal* 17 (1996): 219–235.

companies in this situation view new issues or changes in the external environment as opportunities for potential gain.

Strategic reference point theory is not deterministic, however. Managers are not predestined to choose risk-averse or risk-seeking strategies for their companies. In fact, one of the most important elements of the theory is that managers *can* influence the strategies chosen by their company by *actively changing and adjusting* the strategic reference points they use to judge strategic performance. If a company has become complacent after consistently surpassing its strategic reference points, then top management can change from a risk-averse to a risk-taking orientation by raising or changing the standards of performance (that is the strategic reference points). This is just what happened at eBay.

When John Donahoe first joined eBay, Amazon was growing, Google helped shoppers find what they wanted on other Web sites, and eBay's auction business was shrinking dramatically. But few at eBay saw the problem. According to the *Wall Street Journal*, employees "became so absurdly self-congratulatory that people clapped at the end of meetings, even after discussions over declining customer satisfaction."[32] Founder Pierre Omidyar said, "They didn't seem to see what was going on outside the company

in terms of competition. They had lost their ability to innovate, to create new things."[33] In other words, success had made eBay complacent and risk averse.

When Donahoe later became eBay's CEO, he raised standards, thus changing the strategic reference points eBay had been using to assess its strategic performance. His first week on the job, he told everyone that eBay needed a major turnaround. Said Donahoe, "Our sellers hated that word. Our employees hated it. Investors hated it. But it was the first step ... we had to confront reality."[34] To encourage a daring, offensive-minded strategy, he funded a mobile app team that produced the eBay RedLaser (barcode price scanning that finds products locally and online) and eBay Motors apps, which have been downloaded 120 million times; he told his team to find a way to deliver purchased products in one day (called eBay Now); and he sent a design team offsite to create a fresh graphics-based look to its aging text-based Web site. His ultimate challenges, however, were to double eBay's active users to 225 million, increase revenue from $14 billion to $23.5 billion, and increase customer payments from $145 billion to $300 billion, all within the next three years. Says Donahoe, "The turnaround is behind us, and we are now playing offense."[35]

So even when (perhaps *especially* when) companies have achieved a sustainable competitive advantage, top managers must adjust or change strategic reference points to challenge themselves and their employees to develop new core competencies for the future. In the long run, effective organizations will frequently revise their strategic reference points to better focus managers' attention on the new challenges and opportunities that occur in their ever-changing business environments.

6-3 CORPORATE-LEVEL STRATEGIES

To formulate effective strategies, companies must be able to answer these three basic questions:

▸ What business are we in?

▸ How should we compete in this industry?

▸ Who are our competitors, and how should we respond to them?

These simple but powerful questions are at the heart of corporate-, industry-, and firm-level strategies.

Corporate-level strategy is the overall organizational strategy that addresses the question, "What business or businesses are we in or should we be in?"

*There are two major approaches to corporate-level strategy that companies use to decide which businesses they should be in: **6-3a portfolio strategy** and **6-3b grand strategies.***

6-3a Portfolio Strategy

One of the standard strategies for stock market investors is **diversification**, or owning stocks in a variety of companies in different industries. The purpose of this strategy is to reduce risk in the overall stock portfolio (the entire collection of stocks). The basic idea is simple: if you invest in ten companies in ten different industries, you won't lose your entire investment if one company performs poorly. Furthermore, because they're in different industries, one company's losses are likely to be offset by another company's gains. Portfolio strategy is based on these same ideas. We'll start by taking a look at the theory and ideas behind portfolio strategy and then proceed with a critical review which suggests that some of the key ideas behind portfolio strategy are *not* supported.

Portfolio strategy is a corporate-level strategy that minimizes risk by diversifying investment among

various businesses or product lines.[36] Just as a diversification strategy guides an investor who invests in a variety of stocks, portfolio strategy guides the strategic decisions of corporations that compete in a variety of businesses. For example, portfolio strategy could be used to guide the strategy of a company such as 3M, which makes 55,000 products for five different business groups: Consumer (Post-its, Scotch tape); Electronics and Energy (electronic devices, telecoms equipment, renewable energy solutions); Health Care (medical, surgical, and dental products, health information systems); Industrial (tapes, abrasives, adhesives, specialty materials, filtration systems); and Safety and Graphics (safety and security products, track and trace solutions, graphic solutions).[37]

Just as investors consider the mix of stocks in their stock portfolio when deciding which stocks to buy or sell, managers following portfolio strategy try to acquire companies that fit well with the rest of their corporate portfolio and to sell those that don't. **Procter & Gamble** used to have a diverse portfolio of food, beverage, household, beauty, health care, pharmaceutical, pet food, and battery brands. However, when it decided to focus on its core business of household, beauty, and health care products, it began selling off brands that did not relate to its core business, a process that included the sale of Duracell to Warren Buffett's **Berkshire Hathaway** for $4.7 billion and Iams and Eukanuba pet foods to **Mars** for $2.9 billion.[38]

First, according to portfolio strategy, the more businesses in which a corporation competes, the smaller its overall chances of failing. Think of a corporation as a stool and its businesses as the legs of the stool. The more legs or businesses added to the stool, the less likely it is to tip over. Using this analogy, portfolio strategy reduces 3M's risk of failing because the corporation's survival depends on essentially five different business sectors. Managers employing portfolio strategy can either develop new businesses internally or look for **acquisitions**, that is, other companies to buy. Either way, the goal is to add legs to the stool.

Second, beyond adding new businesses to the corporate portfolio, portfolio strategy predicts that companies can reduce risk even more through

Corporate-level strategy the overall organizational strategy that addresses the question "What business or businesses are we in or should we be in?"

Diversification a strategy for reducing risk by buying a variety of items (stocks or, in the case of a corporation, types of businesses) so that the failure of one stock or one business does not doom the entire portfolio

Portfolio strategy a corporate-level strategy that minimizes risk by diversifying investment among various businesses or product lines

Acquisition the purchase of a company by another company

unrelated diversification— creating or acquiring companies in completely unrelated businesses (more on the accuracy of this prediction later). According to portfolio strategy, when businesses are unrelated, losses in one business or industry should have minimal effect on the performance of other companies in the corporate portfolio. General Electric, which was founded in part by Thomas Edison, is the largest conglomerate in the world and has a presence in a wide range of businesses. Its appliances division produces refrigerators, ovens, and dishwashers for household and business use, and its consumer electronics division makes digital cameras. Its lighting division, of course, sells lightbulbs, as well as traffic signals and specialty lighting. Its aviation division, meanwhile, is one of the world leaders in making jet engines. GE also has divisions in energy distribution, energy, business finance and consulting, health care, oil and gas, rail, software and services, and water.[39]

Exhibit 6.4
Boston Consulting Group Matrix

Because most internally grown businesses tend to be related to existing products or services, portfolio strategy suggests that acquiring new businesses is the preferred method of unrelated diversification.[40]

Third, investing the profits and cash flows from mature, slow-growth businesses into newer, faster-growing businesses can reduce long-term risk. The best-known portfolio strategy for guiding investment in a corporation's businesses is the Boston Consulting Group (BCG) matrix.[41] The **BCG matrix** is a portfolio strategy that managers use to categorize their corporation's businesses by growth rate and relative market share, which helps them decide how to invest corporate funds. The matrix, shown in Exhibit 6.4, separates businesses into four categories based on how fast the market is growing (high growth or low growth) and the size of the business's share of that market (small or large). **Stars** are companies that have a large share of a fast-growing market. To take advantage of a star's fast-growing market and its strength in that market (large share), the corporation must invest substantially in it. The investment is usually worthwhile, however, because many stars produce sizable future profits. **Question marks** are companies that have a small share of a fast-growing market. If the corporation invests in these companies, they may eventually become stars, but their relative weakness in the market (small share) makes investing in question marks riskier than investing in stars. **Cash cows** are companies that have a large share of a slow-growing market. Companies in this situation are often highly profitable, hence the name "cash cow."

Finally, **dogs** are companies that have a small share of a slow-growing market. As the name suggests, having a small share of a slow-growth market is often not profitable.

Because the idea is to redirect investment from slow-growing to fast-growing companies, the BCG matrix starts by recommending that while the substantial cash flows from cash cows last, they should be reinvested in stars (see 1 in Exhibit 6.4) to help them grow even faster and obtain even more market share. Using this strategy, current profits help produce future profits. Over time, as their market growth slows, some stars may turn into cash cows (see 2). Cash flows should also be directed to some question marks (see 3). Though riskier than stars, question marks have great potential because of their fast-growing market. Managers must decide which question marks are most likely to turn into stars (and therefore warrant further investment) and which ones are too risky and should be sold. Over time, managers hope some question marks will become stars as their small markets become large ones (see 4). Finally, because dogs lose money, the corporation should "find them new owners" or "take them to the pound." In other words, dogs should either be sold to other companies or closed down and liquidated for their assets (see 5).

Although the BCG matrix and other forms of portfolio strategy are relatively popular among managers, portfolio strategy has some drawbacks. The most significant drawback is that contrary to the predictions of portfolio strategy, the evidence suggests that acquiring unrelated businesses is *not* useful. As shown in Exhibit 6.5, there is a U-shaped relationship between diversification and risk. The left side of the curve shows that single businesses with no diversification are extremely risky (if the single business fails, the entire business fails). So, in part, the portfolio strategy of diversifying is correct—competing in a variety of different businesses can lower risk. However, portfolio strategy is partly wrong, too—the right side of the curve shows that conglomerates composed of completely unrelated businesses are even riskier than single, undiversified businesses.

A second set of problems with portfolio strategy has to do with the dysfunctional consequences that can occur when companies are categorized as stars, cash cows, question marks, or dogs. Contrary to expectations, the BCG matrix often yields incorrect judgments about a company's potential. In other words, managers using the BCG matrix aren't very good at accurately determining which companies should be categorized as stars, cash cows, questions marks, or dogs. The most common mistake is simply miscategorizing highly profitable

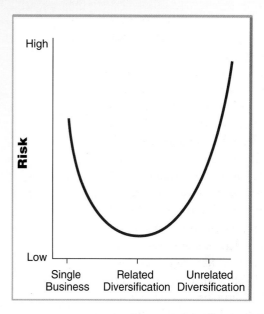

Exhibit 6.5

U-Shaped Relationship between Diversification and Risk

Source: M. Lubatkin & P.J. Lane, "Psst! . . . The Merger Mavens Still Have It Wrong," *Academy of Management* Executive 10 (1996) 21–39.

companies as dogs.[42] In part, this is because the BCG matrix relies on past performance (previous market share and previous market growth), which is a notoriously poor predictor of future company performance. More worrisome, however, is research that indicates the BCG matrix actually makes managers worse at judging the future profitability of a business. A study conducted in six countries over five years gave managers and business students clear information about the current and future profits (that is slow or fast growth) of three companies and asked them to select the one that would be most successful in the future. Although not labeled this way, one company was clearly a star, another was a dog, and the last was a cash cow. Just exposing people to the ideas in the BCG matrix led them to incorrectly categorize less profitable businesses as the most successful businesses 64 percent of the time, while actually *using* the BCG matrix led to making the same mistake 87 percent of the time.[43]

Furthermore, using the BCG matrix can also weaken the strongest performer in the corporate portfolio: the cash cow. As funds are redirected from cash cows to stars, corporate managers essentially take away the

Dog a company with a small share of a slow-growing market

Adidas—Three Stripes Are Out

When looking at the performance of the U.S. division of **Adidas AG**, it is fair to ask if the company has a bad strategy, bad execution, or both. In 2010, Adidas executives launched a strategic plan to generate sales growth of more than 45 percent by 2015. After four years, however, the company had negative sales growth and a 10 percent market share, well below Nike and Under Armour. Despite landing a contract to supply the NBA with jerseys, Adidas failed to sign key NBA players to endorse the brand, allowing Nike, adept at signing top talent, to capture more than 90 percent of the basketball-shoe retail market. Adidas faces additional challenges connecting with fickle U.S. consumers whose primary sports interest is not professional soccer. In response, Adidas is working to shorten its product development cycle from eighteen to six months. President Mark King is optimistic of Adidas's strategy and execution, saying, "We have so many assets that nobody knows about, and if we could tell those stories in a much better, U.S.-centric way, this brand. . . could definitely change its cool factor."

Source: E. E. Jervell and S. Germano, "How Adidas Aims to Get Its Cool Back," *Wall Street Journal*, March 22, 2015. http://www.wsj.com/articles/how-adidas-aims-to-get-its-cool-back-1427072066.

Nike has gained a major advantage over Adidas in the shoe and apparel industry by signing stars like Kevin Durant to large endorsement deals.

resources needed to take advantage of the cash cow's new business opportunities. As a result, the cash cow becomes less aggressive in seeking new business or in defending its present business. While Nokia is best known for its mobile phones, it also has separate companies for Web mapping and location services and software (HERE Drive+, HERE Maps, and HERE Transit), and telecommunications hardware, software, and services (Nokia Siemens Networks).

The Office productivity suite (Word, PowerPoint, Excel) has long been one of Microsoft's two cash cows (the other is its Windows operating system).[44] But with free alternatives, such as Google Docs, Apache's Open Office, and Apple's Pages, Numbers, and Keynote apps (free on every Mac computer purchased since September 25, 2014), and strongly declining sales of PCs worldwide, Office, while still highly profitable, is facing major challenges that threaten its long-time dominance and ability to throw off cash.[45] These threats come at a time when Microsoft needs to divert cash from Office into its cloud-based file storage and Azure (cloud services, big data, servers, virtual machines, and Web site hosting) platforms to turn those questions marks into future stars, as well as its struggling Surface tablets, a business which it hopes to transform from a dog to a question mark (and eventually a star). The risk, however, is that diverting cash from Office may make it less able to defend its current business or to grow by seeking new business.[46]

Finally, labeling a top performer as a cash cow can harm employee morale. Cash-cow employees realize that they have inferior status and that instead of working for themselves, they are now working to fund the growth of stars and question marks.

So, what kind of portfolio strategy does the best job of helping managers decide which companies to buy or sell? The U-shaped curve in Exhibit 6.5 indicates that, contrary to the predictions of portfolio strategy, the best approach is probably **related diversification**, in which the different business units share similar products, manufacturing, marketing, technology, or cultures. The key to related diversification is to acquire or create new companies with core capabilities that complement the core capabilities of businesses already in the corporate portfolio. Hormel Foods is an example of related diversification in the food business. The company both manufactures and markets a variety of foods, from deli meats to salsa to the infamous SPAM.

We began this section with the example of 3M and its 55,000 products sold in five different business groups. While seemingly different, most of 3M's product divisions are based in some fashion on its distinctive competencies in adhesives and tape (for example wet or dry sandpaper, Post-it notes, Scotchgard fabric protector, transdermal skin patches, and reflective material used in traffic signs). Furthermore, all of 3M's divisions share its strong corporate culture that promotes and encourages risk taking and innovation. In sum, in contrast to a single, undiversified business or unrelated diversification, related diversification reduces risk because the different businesses can work as a team, relying on each other for needed experience, expertise, and support.

6-3b Grand Strategies

A **grand strategy** is a broad strategic plan used to help an organization achieve its strategic goals.[47] Grand strategies guide the strategic alternatives that managers of individual businesses or subunits may use in deciding what businesses they should be in. There are three kinds of grand strategies: growth, stability, and retrenchment/recovery.

The purpose of a **growth strategy** is to increase profits, revenues, market share, or the number of places (stores, offices, locations) in which the company does business. Companies can grow in several ways. They can grow externally by merging with or acquiring other companies in the same or different businesses. AT&T is growing slowly at 3 percent per year. DirecTV, a satellite TV service, is growing at less than 1 percent a year. In hopes of accelerating growth for both companies, AT&T agreed to buy DirectTV for $48.5 billion. CBS News business analyst Jill Schlesinger says, "AT&T wants content. DirecTV has content."[48] AT&T is also interested in selling phone services to DirecTV's 18 million customers in Latin America. But the primary benefit that could accelerate growth for both companies is the ability to combine and discount their services for consumers. For example, instead of paying more to buy separate Internet, TV (subscription and pay TV packages), and wireless phone services, DirecTV's 20 million customers and AT&T's 107 million customers would then be able to buy those services together in a discounted bundle.[49]

Another way to grow is internally, directly expanding the company's existing business or creating and growing new businesses. Nestlé, the largest food company in the world, faced a serious challenge—it had to find a way to grow while having to deal with record-high prices for cocoa and sugar, two key ingredients for its chocolate products. To boost growth, Nestlé spent $24 million to promote Aero, a chocolate bar that is filled with bubbles of air. While the bubbles give the chocolate a creamier texture, they also help bulk up the candy bar without adding more ingredients, quite helpful at a time of high commodity costs. Thanks to the company's promotional emphasis, sales of Aero increased by 20 percent from the previous year, which helped the company as a whole earn a profit of $10.3 billion and sales growth of 7.5 percent.[50]

The purpose of a **stability strategy** is to continue doing what the company has been doing, just doing it better. Companies following a stability strategy try to improve the way in which they sell the same products or services to the same customers. Since its inception in 1909 as a window-washing company in San Francisco, **ABM Industries** has focused on providing facility services to businesses. Today, ABM's 100,000 employees in the U.S. and twenty other countries offer facility services management for electrical and lighting solutions, energy management, building maintenance and repair, janitorial services, landscape and ground maintenance, security, and parking services. In short, for more than 100 years, ABM has reduced costs by keeping businesses' facilities safe, clean, comfortable, and energy efficient.[51] Companies often choose a stability strategy when their external environment doesn't change much or after they have struggled with periods of explosive growth.

Related diversification creating or acquiring companies that share similar products, manufacturing, marketing, technology, or cultures

Grand strategy a broad corporate-level strategic plan used to achieve strategic goals and guide the strategic alternatives that managers of individual businesses or subunits may use

Growth strategy a strategy that focuses on increasing profits, revenues, market share, or the number of places in which the company does business

Stability strategy a strategy that focuses on improving the way in which the company sells the same products or services to the same customers

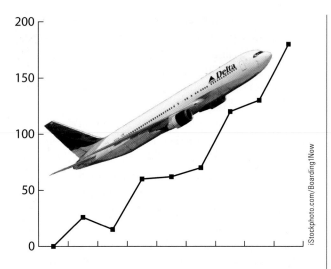

The purpose of a **retrenchment strategy** is to turn around very poor company performance by shrinking the size or scope of the business or, if a company is in multiple businesses, by closing or shutting down different lines of the business. The first step of a typical retrenchment strategy might include making significant cost reductions: laying off employees; closing poorly performing stores, offices, or manufacturing plants; or closing or selling entire lines of products or services.[52] Barclays Plc, a London-based bank for more than 300 years, got its start in 1690 when founders John Freame and Thomas Gould served as goldsmith bankers that, much like today's banks, stored gold and money, made loans, transferred deposits from account to account, and handled foreign exchange currencies.[53] By 2008, Barclays aspired to become a global bank serving customers, businesses, and investors worldwide. In 2014, however, following numerous financial scandals and poor financial performance, Barclays began an aggressive retrenchment strategy. Chairman Michael Rake said, "It's just no longer doable for us to be a global, universal bank."[54] Following a strategy that Rake termed "bold simplification," Barclays will cut 19,000 employees by 2016, exit commodities trading, sell half of its investment bank, and sell its retail banking operations in France, Spain, and Italy. Rake explained that, "In the future, Barclays will be leaner, stronger, much better balanced and well positioned to deliver lower volatility, higher returns and growth. My goal is unchanged: to create a

Barclays that does business in the right way, with the right values, and delivers the returns that our shareholders deserve. However, the way in which we will achieve this is different."[55]

After cutting costs and reducing a business's size or scope, the second step in a retrenchment strategy is recovery. **Recovery** consists of the strategic actions that a company takes to return to a growth strategy. This two-step process of cutting and recovery is analogous to pruning roses. Prior to each growing season, roses should be cut back to two-thirds their normal size. Pruning doesn't damage the roses; it makes them stronger and more likely to produce beautiful, fragrant flowers. The retrenchment-and-recovery process is similar.

Like pruning, the cuts are made as part of a recovery strategy intended to allow companies to eventually return to a successful growth strategy. When company performance drops significantly, a strategy of retrenchment and recovery may help the company return to a successful growth strategy.

6-4 INDUSTRY-LEVEL STRATEGIES

Industry-level strategy addresses the question, "How should we compete in this industry?"

Let's find out more about industry-level strategies by discussing 6-4a the five industry forces that determine overall levels of competition in an industry as well as 6-4b the positioning strategies and 6-4c adaptive strategies that companies can use to achieve sustained competitive advantage and above-average profits.

6-4a Five Industry Forces

According to Harvard professor Michael Porter, five industry forces determine an industry's overall attractiveness and potential for long-term profitability: the character of the rivalry, the threat of new entrants, the threat of substitute products or services, the bargaining power of suppliers, and the bargaining power of buyers. The stronger these forces, the less attractive the industry becomes to corporate investors because it is more difficult for companies to be profitable. Porter's industry forces are illustrated in Exhibit 6.6. Let's examine how these forces are bringing changes to several kinds of industries.

Exhibit 6.6
Porter's Five Industry Forces

Source: Based on the Simon & Schuster, Inc. Porter, M. E. *Competitive Strategy: Techniques for Analyzing Industries and Competitors.* New York: Free Press, 1980.

Character of the rivalry is a measure of the intensity of competitive behavior among companies in an industry. Is the competition among firms aggressive and cutthroat, or do competitors focus more on serving customers than on attacking each other? Both industry attractiveness and profitability decrease when rivalry is cutthroat. For example, selling cars is a highly competitive business. Pick up a local newspaper on Friday, Saturday, or Sunday morning, and you'll find dozens of pages of car advertising ("Anniversary Sale-A-Bration," "Ford March Savings!" and "$99 Down, You Choose!"). In fact, competition in new-car sales

Because of intense competition from existing and new companies, Amazon Web Services" cut prices by 40% to keep corporate customers satisfied.

GongTo/Shutterstock.com

is so intense that if it weren't for used-car sales, repair work, and replacement parts, many auto dealers would actually lose money.

The **threat of new entrants** is a measure of the degree to which barriers to entry make it easy or difficult for new companies to get started in an industry. If new companies can enter the industry easily, then competition will increase, and prices and profits will fall. Altos Research provides real-time statistics and analysis of real estate markets for investors and news services such as Bloomberg Financial. Because its business relies on access to terabytes of market data, it leases computing power and data storage from Amazon Web Services (AWS), the market leader in cloud services. Without any negotiation, AWS cut its costs in half, enough to pay for two new programmers. Altos' CEO Michael Simonsen said, "Nobody ever gives you a 40 percent price break overnight."[56] If so, why did AWS—and Microsoft and Google—all cut their prices by a third or more? The threat of new entrants spurred them.[57] In addition to new competitors over the past few years, such as Box.com, GoDaddy.com, and ZenBox, Oracle, and Salesforce.com, both Hewlett-Packard, which makes personal and network computers, and Cisco Systems, which makes the routers, switches, and systems that drive the Internet and corporate networks, are each investing $1 billion to develop cloud software and data centers.[58] On the other hand, if there are sufficient barriers to entry, such as large capital requirements to buy expensive equipment or plant facilities or the need for specialized knowledge, then competition will be weaker, and prices and profits will generally be higher.

The **threat of substitute products or services** is a measure of the ease with which customers can find substitutes for an industry's products or services. If customers can easily find substitute products or services, the competition will be greater, and profits will be lower. If there are few or no substitutes, competition will be

Character of the rivalry a measure of the intensity of competitive behavior between companies in an industry

Threat of new entrants a measure of the degree to which barriers to entry make it easy or difficult for new companies to get started in an industry

Threat of substitute products or services a measure of the ease with which customers can find substitutes for an industry's products or services

CHAPTER 6: Organizational Strategy 123

weaker, and profits will be higher. In many cities, hailing a cab can be frustrating. Enter **Uber**, a smartphone app that connects people needing rides with drivers who will take them where they want to go. Open Uber, choose your preferred vehicle (taxi, town car, or SUV), position the pin on the map in the app showing where you'd like to be picked up, do the same for your destination, and then Uber's app estimates the cost, charges your credit card, emails the receipt, indicates on the map how far away the car is, and then lets you know when the driver has arrived to pick you up. Average wait time is only three to ten minutes. Uber maintains quality control by using social media to gather feedback on drivers' timeliness, politeness, and service. Drivers with negative feedback lose the chance to drive for Uber. Taxi services, not surprisingly, are not happy about competing with Uber, and its drivers have sued Uber—unsuccessfully—in San Francisco, New York, and Washington, DC, to shield themselves from competition.[59]

Bargaining power of suppliers is a measure of the influence that suppliers of parts, materials, and services to firms in an industry have on the prices of these inputs. When companies can buy parts, materials, and services from numerous suppliers, the companies will be able to bargain with the suppliers to keep prices low. On the other hand, if there are few suppliers, or if a company is dependent on a supplier with specialized skills and knowledge, then the suppliers will have the bargaining power to dictate price levels.

Bargaining power of buyers is a measure of the influence that customers have on the firm's prices. If a company sells a popular product or service to multiple buyers, then the company has more power to set prices. By contrast, if a company is dependent on just a few high-volume buyers, those buyers will typically have enough bargaining power to dictate prices. Most agricultural commodities, such as beef and soybeans, are sold by farmers to commodity traders who then sell them to buyers around the world. Australian farmers, who are generally the world's second-largest growers of wheat, beef, cotton, and sugar, typically sell their agricultural produce to Archer Daniels Midland, Bunge Ltd., Cargill, and Dreyfus, the "ABCD" trading houses, who control 60 percent of the wheat bought and shipped from Australia. Consequently, the trading houses have incredible bargaining power, which means that Australian farmers end up with much smaller prices for their agriculture products. Some Aussie farmers are trying to counter this bargaining power by selling directly to global buyers. Glen Rogan, who farms cotton in Queensland, Australia, says, "To make a reasonable living as a farmer under current prices was becoming untenable." So he sold 6,500 bales of cotton directly to Asian cotton mills, getting 30 percent more than he would have through the trading houses. Says Rogan, selling directly to cotton mills "was the only way I could see to stay relevant and viable."[60]

6-4b Positioning Strategies

After analyzing industry forces, the next step in industry-level strategy is to protect your company from the negative effects of industry-wide competition and to create a sustainable competitive advantage. According to Michael Porter, there are three positioning strategies: cost leadership, differentiation, and focus.

Cost leadership means producing a product or service of acceptable quality at consistently lower production costs than competitors so that the firm can offer the product or service at the lowest price in the industry. Cost leadership protects companies from industry forces by deterring new entrants, who will have to match low costs and prices. Cost leadership also forces down the prices of substitute products and services, attracts bargain-seeking buyers, and increases bargaining power with suppliers, who have to keep their prices low if they want to do business with the cost leader. But Burt Flickinger, a retail consultant with the Strategic Resource Group (SRG), believes that Idaho-based WinCo, which brands itself as "The Supermarket Low Price Leader," "may be the best retailer in the western U.S. WinCo is really unstoppable at this point."[61] Jon Springer, with Super Market News,' says, "While many supermarkets strive to keep within a few percentage points of Walmart Stores' prices, WinCo Foods often undersells the massive discount chain."[62] How? With minimalist stores, having customers bag their groceries, not accepting credit cards (which saves 3 percent per transaction), limiting selection within product categories, and by buying directly from farms and factories, WinCo cuts out food distributors who mark up prices and sell more expensive brands. WinCo's prices are so much better than Walmart's that

Bargaining power of suppliers a measure of the influence that suppliers of parts, materials, and services to firms in an industry have on the prices of these inputs

Bargaining power of buyers a measure of the influence that customers have on a firm's prices

Cost leadership the positioning strategy of producing a product or service of acceptable quality at consistently lower production costs than competitors can, so that the firm can offer the product or service at the lowest price in the industry

SRG's Flickinger says, "They're Walmart's worst nightmare."[63]

Differentiation means making your product or service sufficiently different from competitors' offerings that customers are willing to pay a premium price for the extra value or performance that it provides. Differentiation protects companies from industry forces by reducing the threat of substitute products. It also protects companies by making it easier to retain customers and more difficult for new entrants trying to attract new customers. Would you pay $113 for a mop? Or $26.99 for a polishing cloth? Norway-based Norwex makes premium-priced cleaning products that clean your house with water and no chemicals or cleaning agents. For instance, a Norwex Microfiber cloth contains microfibers that are 1/200th the thickness of a human hair.[64] The microfibers capture and can hold seven times their weight, which means that they capture dirt, grease, and moisture. Does it work? Microbiologist Kristen Gibson says, "A damp microfiber cloth is a really good tool for removing microorganisms, including viruses and bacteria."[65] Her research, funded by the U.S. Department of Agriculture, found that microfibers removed viruses, unlike typical cloth towels that simply spread viruses from one surface to another. Norwex advises using the cloths dry to dust and wet (with water) to clean. And while its products are expensive, with the average family spending $600–800 a year on cleaning supplies and chemicals, Norwex claims that consumers save time and money because its products are reusable.[66]

With a **focus strategy**, a company uses either cost leadership or differentiation to produce a specialized product or service for a limited, specially targeted group of customers in a particular geographic region or market segment. Focus strategies typically work in market niches that competitors have overlooked or have difficulty serving. Once a week, Mike Hallatt drives from Vancouver, B.C., to the nearest **Trader Joe's** in Bellingham, Washington, where he buys $6,000 of Trader Joe's merchandise. Hallatt marks up his purchases by an average of $2 and sells them at **Pirate Joe's**, his Vancouver grocery store that is an unapologetic knockoff of Trader Joe's. Hallett says Pirate Joe's is, "an unaffiliated unauthorized re-seller of Trader Joe's products (we were sued, they lost, now they are appealing)."[67] Because Trader Joe's has no plans to enter Canada, Hallatt is able to focus on Canadians—in Vancouver and afar (www.piratejoes.ca will soon be ready for Internet shopping)—who want to buy Trader Joe's grocery products without crossing the Canadian border. Hallatt says, "We'll ship anywhere in Canada, but if we start getting orders from Japan, why not?"[68]

Pirate Joe's slogan is "Unauthorized, Unaffiliated, Unafriad." This refers to the pressure by North American grocer, Trader Joe's, to change their name.

6-4c Adaptive Strategies

Adaptive strategies are another set of industry-level strategies. Whereas the aim of positioning strategies is to minimize the effects of industry competition and build a sustainable competitive advantage, the purpose of adaptive strategies is to choose an industry-level strategy that is best suited to changes in the organization's external environment. There are four kinds of adaptive strategies: defenders, prospectors, analyzers, and reactors.[69]

Differentiation the positioning strategy of providing a product or service that is sufficiently different from competitors' offerings that customers are willing to pay a premium price for it

Focus strategy the positioning strategy of using cost leadership or differentiation to produce a specialized product or service for a limited, specially targeted group of customers in a particular geographic region or market segment

Defenders seek moderate, steady growth by offering a limited range of products and services to a well-defined set of customers. In other words, defenders aggressively "defend" their current strategic position by doing the best job they can to hold on to customers in a particular market segment.

Not surprisingly, ultra-premium carmakers, such as **Ferrari** and **Aston-Martin**, are not as interested in growth as they are in retaining the luxury brand image. That's because higher sales volume leads to ubiquity, which makes it harder to charge premium pricing. The retail price of a new Ferrari California is roughly $200,000, but a new LaFerrari model has an MSRP of $1.4 million. To retain is exclusivity, Ferrari has a self-imposed production cap of 7,000 vehicles a year. At Aston Martin, the level is much lower, at 4,000 cars per year. "This is not a car company that is ever going to be selling a lot of cars," said Andy Palmer, CEO of Aston Martin. "Part of its mystique is its exclusivity."[70]

Prospectors seek fast growth by searching for new market opportunities, encouraging risk taking, and being the first to bring innovative new products to market. Prospectors are analogous to gold miners who "prospect" for gold nuggets (that is new products) in hope that the nuggets will lead them to a rich deposit of gold (that is fast growth). 3M has long been known for its innovative products, particularly in the area of adhesives. Since 1904, it has invented sandpaper; masking, cellophane, electrical, and Scotch tapes; the first commercially available audiotapes and videotapes; and its most famous invention, Post-it notes. Lately, 3M has invented a film that increases the brightness of LCD displays on laptop computers; developed a digital system for construction companies to detect underground telecommunication, gas, water, sewer, or electrical lines without digging; and created a pheromone spray that, by preventing harmful insects from mating, will protect apple, walnut, tomato, cranberry, and grape crops. For more on 3M's innovative products, see the 3M innovation archive (http://solutions.3m.com/innovation/en_US/).

Analyzers are a blend of the defender and prospector strategies. They seek moderate, steady growth

Defenders companies using an adaptive strategy aimed at defending strategic positions by seeking moderate, steady growth and by offering a limited range of high-quality products and services to a well-defined set of customers

Prospectors companies using an adaptive strategy that seeks fast growth by searching for new market opportunities, encouraging risk taking, and being the first to bring innovative new products to market

Analyzers companies using an adaptive strategy that seeks to minimize risk and maximize profits by following or imitating the proven successes of prospectors

The Postal Service Gets Back in the Game

Having reported losses for the past twenty-one of twenty-three quarters, the **United States Postal Service** (USPS) is looking to attract new business, particularly in the online retail market. So, when FedEx and UPS announced prices increases for ground shipments ahead of the holiday season, the USPS responded by cutting its prices in half for customers who ship more than 50,000 packages a year. It's only one strategy the agency is using to increase its market share. USPS has begun offering Sunday delivery and is testing grocery delivery for Amazon in the San Francisco area. And the agency plans to invest $10 billion on new trucks and sorting equipment to help it become more competitive.

Source: L. Stevens, "U.S. Mail Cuts Prices, Chafing UPS and FedEx," *Wall Street Journal*, September 5, 2014, B1; G. Bensinger and L. Stevens, "Amazon Tries U.S. Mail for Groceries," *Wall Street Journal*, September 5, 2014, B2.

and limited opportunities for fast growth. Analyzers are rarely first to market with new products or services. Instead, they try to simultaneously minimize risk and maximize profits by following or imitating the proven successes of prospectors. Netflix has achieved growth not only through its mail-order DVD service but also through its video streaming service, which allows users to watch a variety of movies and TV shows almost instantly. In fact, the streaming service has been so successful that Netflix has nearly two times more streaming customers than DVD customers. Motivated by Netflix's success, Redbox (with Verizon) and Amazon now offer similar streaming services. Redbox, the DVD rental kiosk operator, and Verizon, the wireless carrier, teamed up to offer Redbox Instant. Nonsubscribers can reserve movies and games at Redbox kiosks or rent or buy individual movies via streaming services. Subscribers, who pay $8 a month, also get four DVD credits to use at Redbox kiosks and access to Redbox's entire streaming library. Amazon Prime members, who pay $99 a year, get free two-day shipping on Amazon Prime products, can borrow one Kindle book free each month, and have access to 41,000 TV shows and movies on Amazon's Instant Video.[71] After Netflix tried to differentiate itself by developing exclusive, original shows like *House of Cards* and *Orange Is the New Black*, Amazon followed suit by offering its own original series, *Alpha House and Betas*.[72]

Finally, unlike defenders, prospectors, or analyzers, **reactors** do not follow a consistent strategy. Rather than anticipating and preparing for external opportunities and threats, reactors tend to react to changes in their external environment after they occur. Not surprisingly, reactors tend to be poorer performers than defenders, prospectors, or analyzers. A reactor approach is inherently unstable, and firms that fall into this mode of operation must change their approach or face almost certain failure.

6-5 FIRM-LEVEL STRATEGIES

Microsoft unveils its Xbox One video-game console; Sony counters with its PlayStation 4. Starbucks Coffee opens a store, and nearby locally run coffeehouses respond by improving service, increasing portions, and holding the line on prices. In the German luxury car industry, **BMW**, **Audi**, and **Mercedes** have an intense three-way rivalry that goes well beyond sales volume to include investments in technology, quality rankings, and profitability. According to one Audi executive, to get approval for a new project, "I just have to say BMW is already doing it, and it goes through." The rivalry is just as heated over at BMW. When it comes to Audi, one BMW executive said, "We like to stick it to them."[73] Attack and respond, respond and attack. **Firm-level strategy** addresses the question, "How should we compete against a particular firm?"

*Let's find out more about the firm-level strategies (direct competition between companies) by reading about **6-5a the basics of direct competition** and **6-5b the strategic moves involved in direct competition between companies.***

Microsoft introduces the next generation of Xbox One at the E3 conference in June 2014.

Barone Firenze/Shutterstock.com

6-5a Direct Competition

Although Porter's five industry forces indicate the overall level of competition in an industry, most companies do not compete directly with all the firms in their industry. For example, McDonald's and Red Lobster are both in the restaurant business, but no one would characterize them as competitors. McDonald's offers low-cost, convenient fast food in a seat-yourself restaurant, while Red Lobster offers mid-priced seafood dinners complete with servers and a bar.

Instead of competing with an entire industry, most firms compete directly with just a few companies within it. **Direct competition** is the rivalry between two companies offering similar products and services that acknowledge each other as rivals and take offensive and defensive positions as they act and react to each other's strategic actions.[74] Two factors determine the extent to which firms will be in direct competition with each other: market commonality and resource similarity. **Market commonality** is the degree to which two companies have overlapping products, services, or customers in multiple markets. The more markets in which there is product, service, or customer overlap, the more intense the direct competition between the two companies. **Resource similarity** is the extent to which a competitor has similar amounts and kinds of resources, that is, similar assets, capabilities, processes, information, and knowledge used to create and sustain an advantage over competitors. From a competitive standpoint, resource similarity means that your direct competitors can probably match the strategic actions that your company takes.

Exhibit 6.7 shows how market commonality and resource similarity interact to determine when and where companies are in direct competition.[75] The overlapping area in each quadrant (between the triangle and the rectangle, or between the differently colored rectangles) depicts market commonality. The larger the overlap, the

Reactors companies that do not follow a consistent adaptive strategy but instead react to changes in the external environment after they occur

Firm-level strategy a corporate strategy that addresses the question, "How should we compete against a particular firm?"

Direct competition the rivalry between two companies that offer similar products and services, acknowledge each other as rivals, and act and react to each other's strategic actions

Market commonality the degree to which two companies have overlapping products, services, or customers in multiple markets

Resource similarity the extent to which a competitor has similar amounts and kinds of resources

Exhibit 6.7
A Framework of Direct Competition

Source: M. Chen, "Competitor Analysis and InterFirm Rivalry: Toward a Theoretical Integration," *Academy of Management Review* 21 (1996): 100–134.

greater the market commonality. Shapes depict resource similarity, with rectangles representing one set of competitive resources and triangles representing another. Quadrant I shows two companies in direct competition because they have similar resources at their disposal and a high degree of market commonality. These companies try to sell similar products and services to similar customers. McDonald's and Burger King would clearly fit here as direct competitors. While we normally think about them competing to sell hamburgers, with wholesale beef prices near record highs, they're also direct competitors when it comes to selling chicken. For example, after McDonald's began selling fifty chicken nuggets for $9.99 (or 20 cents each), Burger King responded by selling ten-packs of chicken nuggets for $1.49.[76]

In Quadrant II, the overlapping parts of the triangle and rectangle show two companies going after similar customers with some similar products or services but doing so with different competitive resources. McDonald's and Wendy's restaurants would fit here. Wendy's is after the same lunchtime and dinner crowds that McDonald's is. Nevertheless, with its more expensive hamburgers, fries, shakes, and salads, Wendy's is less of a direct competitor to McDonald's than Burger King is. For example, Wendy's has recently rebranded itself more like a casual dining restaurant, redesigning its locations with lounge seating, fireplaces, Wi-Fi, and digital menu boards.[77] Wendy's goal is to convert 85 percent of its company-owned locations

and 35 percent of its franchised stores by 2017.[78] Even though Wendy's competes less directly with McDonald's, there are signs that McDonald's may be shifting its strategy to compete more directly with Wendy's by upgrading its menu to include a premium burger priced around $5 and a grilled chicken sandwich with Applewood smoked bacon, caramelized onions, and an artisan roll.[79]

In Quadrant III, the very small overlap shows two companies with different competitive resources and little market commonality. McDonald's and Luby's cafeterias fit here. Although both are in the fast-food business, there's almost no overlap in terms of products and customers. Luby's sells baked chicken, turkey, roasts, meat loaf, and vegetables, none of which are available at McDonald's. Furthermore, Luby's customers aren't likely to eat at McDonald's. In fact, Luby's is not really competing with other fast-food restaurants, but with eating at home. Company surveys show that close to half of its customers would have eaten at home, not at another restaurant, if they hadn't come to Luby's.[80]

Finally, in Quadrant IV, the small overlap between the two rectangles shows that McDonald's and Subway compete with similar resources but with little market commonality. In terms of resources, sales at McDonald's are much larger, but Subway has grown substantially in the past decade and now has 42,227 stores in 110 countries, compared to McDonald's with 36,258 stores in more than 100 countries.[81]

Though Subway and McDonald's compete, they aren't direct competitors in terms of market commonality in the way that McDonald's and Burger King are because Subway, unlike McDonald's, sells itself as a provider of healthy fast food. Thus, the overlap is much smaller in Quadrant IV than in Quadrant I. With detailed nutritional information available in its stores, and its close relationship with the American Heart Association, Subway's goal "is to emphasize that the Subway brand represents all that is good about health and well-being."[82]

6-5b Strategic Moves of Direct Competition

While corporate-level strategies help managers decide what business to be in, and industry-level strategies help them determine how to compete within an industry, firm-level strategies help managers determine when, where, and what strategic actions should be taken against a direct

T-Mobile has launched a strategic initiative aimed at removing key restrictions found in its competitors wireless services.

competitor. Firms in direct competition can make two basic strategic moves: attack and response. These moves occur all the time in virtually every industry, but they are most noticeable in industries where multiple large competitors are pursuing customers in the same market space.

An **attack** is a competitive move designed to reduce a rival's market share or profits. For example, the two leaders in the e-reader market, Amazon and Barnes & Noble, have been engaged in a lengthy battle over prices. The Amazon's Kindle Paperwhite was designed to compete with Barnes & Noble's Nook Touch with Glowlight, a black-and-white e-reader with a built-in light for night reading.[83] When the Paperwhite was released, Barnes & Noble cut the price on the Nook Touch by $20 to match Paperwhite's price.[84]

A **response** is a countermove, prompted by a rival's attack, that is designed to defend or improve a company's market share or profit. There are two kinds of responses.[85] The first is to match or mirror your competitor's move. This is what Barnes & Noble did when it lowered the price of its Nook Simple Touch, which had been selling for $139, to $99.[86]

The second kind of response, however, is to respond along a different dimension from your competitor's move or attack. Wireless carriers, such at AT&T, Verizon, and Sprint, have typically responded to competitors' attacks by cutting prices, expanding coverage, or speeding up their networks. T-Mobile, the smallest of the major wireless carriers, faired poorly on those dimensions and lost 2 million customers as a result two years ago.[87] In the past 18 months, however, T-Mobile has taken 3.3 million customers from its competitors by responding with an "uncarrier" strategy that removes key restrictions found in its competitors' wireless services.[88] Overage charges? Not at T-Mobile, which offers unlimited minutes, texts, and data (go beyond your data "cap," and T-Mobile slows down your data rather than charge you). Exorbitant roaming charges for international plans? T-Mobile charges a meager 20 cents per minute for international calls, while providing unlimited international data and texts at no extra charge in 120 countries. Streaming music on your phone? Thirty minutes a day uses 900 megabytes a month against the typical 1 or 2 gigabyte data plan. At T-Mobile, though, streaming music does NOT count against data usage. Upgrade your phone just once every two years? At T-Mobile, upgrade whenever you want by trading in your old phone and receiving credits for remaining payments (up to half of the original cost). Finally, termination fees to keep you locked into in a two-year contract? Not at T-Mobile, where you can quit at any time. In fact, T-Mobile will pay your termination fee if you leave your current carrier to sign with it.[89]

Market commonality and resource similarity determine the likelihood of an attack or response, that is, whether a company is likely to attack a direct competitor or to strike back with a strong response when attacked. When market commonality is large, and companies have overlapping products, services, or customers in multiple markets, there is less motivation to attack and more motivation to respond to an attack. The reason for this is straightforward: when firms are direct competitors in a large number of markets, they have a great deal at stake. For instance, GE makes 70 percent of the freight locomotive rail cars in the North American market, with the remaining 30 percent sold by Caterpillar, which bought EMD, a locomotive manufacturer, in 2010. To become more competitive with GE, Caterpillar closed EMD's unionized locomotive manufacturing plant in the city of London, Ontario, Canada, replacing it with brand-new non-unionized plants in Muncie, Indiana, and Brazil. Bill Ainsworth, who leads Caterpillar's railroad business, says the new Muncie plant "will be the most efficient locomotive-manufacturing plant in the world."[90]

Attack a competitive move designed to reduce a rival's market share or profits

Response a competitive countermove, prompted by a rival's attack, to defend or improve a company's market share or profit

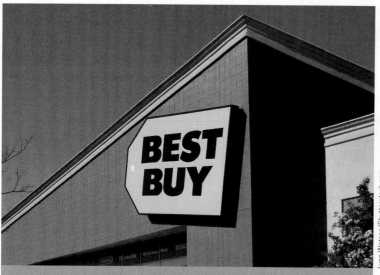

Best Buy has seen profits drop almost 90 percent in its attempt to keep up with Amazon and its pricing tactics.

same product on Amazon.com and provide a coupon for a discount and free shipping. The Firefly app on Amazon's Fire phone, as well as the Amazon App for iPhone and Android phones, can now recognize more than 70 million products just by taking a picture. A mobile industry analyst calls this "showrooming on steroids." According to IDC, a market research firm, one out of five shoppers uses a mobile device to make purchases from online retailers while store shopping at brick-and-mortar retailers.[92]

Best Buy is the world's largest electronics retailer. Today, 60 percent of its consumers "showroom shop," looking at products in Best Buy stores and then checking their smartphones to find prices at online stores like Amazon. Best Buy responded aggressively to Amazon's showrooming app by matching online prices year round in its stores and by offering deep Black Friday discounts the day after Thanksgiving (typically the heaviest shopping day of the year). Best Buy's retaliatory responses, however, have come at a steep cost, with profits dropping over 90 percent and the announcement of more than fifty store closings in 2012. Consequently, when deciding when, where, and what strategic actions to take against a direct competitor, managers should always consider the possibility of retaliation.[93]

In response to Caterpillar's cost-cutting moves, GE eliminated 950 jobs at its unionized plant in Pennsylvania, shifting production work to a new, non-unionized manufacturing plant in Texas. With GE's union wages running $25 to $36 an hour compared to $14.50 an hour at Caterpillar's non-unionized Muncie plant, GE had to respond by finding a way to lower costs.[91]

Whereas market commonality affects the likelihood of an attack or a response to an attack, resource similarity largely affects response capability, that is, how quickly and forcefully a company can respond to an attack. When resource similarity is strong, the responding firm will generally be able to match the strategic moves of the attacking firm. Consequently, a firm is less likely to attack firms with similar levels of resources because it is unlikely to gain any sustained advantage when the responding firms strike back. On the other hand, if one firm is substantially stronger than another (that is there is low resource similarity), then a competitive attack is more likely to produce sustained competitive advantage.

In general, the more moves (that is attacks) a company initiates against direct competitors, and the greater a company's tendency to respond when attacked, the better its performance. More specifically, attackers and early responders (companies that are quick to launch a retaliatory attack) tend to gain market share and profits at the expense of late responders. This is not to suggest that a full-attack strategy always works best. In fact, attacks can provoke harsh retaliatory responses.

When Amazon unveiled its first showrooming app in 2011, brick-and-mortar retailers were outraged. When users scanned a barcode, the app would direct them to the

YOUR FEED-BACK YOUR BOOK

Our research never ends. Continual feedback from you ensures that we keep up with your changing needs.

4LTR PRESS

www.cengage.com/4ltrpress

CENGAGE
Learning®

7 Innovation and Change

Chones/Shutterstock.com

LEARNING OUTCOMES

7-1 Explain why innovation matters to companies.

7-2 Discuss the different methods that managers can use to effectively manage innovation in their organizations.

7-3 Discuss why not changing can lead to organizational decline.

7-4 Discuss the different methods that managers can use to better manage change as it occurs.

After you finish this chapter, go to **PAGE 151** for **STUDY TOOLS**

7-1 WHY INNOVATION MATTERS

At age 57, composer Richard Einhorn lost his hearing and feared he would never hear music again. So when he went to New York's Metropolitan Opera and was given special headphones to amplify the music, he was hopeful, but the sound quality was poor and filled with background noise, static, and interference. However, when he attended a performance of *Wicked* at the Kennedy Center in Washington, DC, he said, "For the first time since I lost most of my hearing, live music was perfectly clear, perfectly clean, and incredibly rich. There I was at 'Wicked' weeping uncontrollably—and I don't even like musicals." The superb sound at the Kennedy Center was due to a device called a hearing loop, in which a copper wire around the edges of a room broadcasts signals to special receivers built directly into most hearing aids. But unlike other such devices, hearing loops filter background noise and only broadcast sounds coming directly from strategically placed microphones. Janice Schacter Lintz, of the Hearing Access Program, which advocates for the installation of hearing loops in public places, says that with 10,000 baby boomers turning 65 every day and with one-third of people over 65 experiencing hearing loss, "This isn't just about disability rights—it's about good customer service. That's a big group of customers who won't go to museums or theaters or restaurants where they can't hear. Put in a loop, and they can hear clearly without any of the bother or embarrassment of wearing a special headset."[1] **Organizational innovation** is the successful implementation of creative ideas, like the hearing loop at the Kennedy Center in Washington, DC.

We can only guess what changes technological innovations will bring in the next twenty years. Will we carry computers in our pockets? Today's smartphones are a step in that direction. Will solar power and wind power get cheap and efficient enough so that your home can have a standalone power source off the main electrical grid? Will fully automated, self-driving cars chauffeur you (working in the back seat on a computing tablet via high-speed Internet) to work in the next decade? Who knows? The only thing we do know about the next twenty years is that innovation will continue to change our lives.

Let's begin our discussion of innovation by learning about 7-1a technology cycles and 7-2b innovation streams.

Exhibit 7.1
S-Curves and Technological Innovation

Source: R. N. Foster, *Innovation: The Attacker's Advantage* (New York: Summitt, 1986).

7-1a Technology Cycles

In Chapter 3, you learned that technology consists of the knowledge, tools, and techniques used to transform inputs (raw materials and information) into outputs (products and services). A **technology cycle** begins with the birth of a new technology and ends when that technology reaches its limits and dies as it is replaced by a newer, substantially better technology.[2] For example, technology cycles occurred when air conditioners supplanted fans, when Henry Ford's Model T replaced horse-drawn carriages, when planes replaced trains as a means of cross-country travel, when vaccines that prevented diseases replaced medicines designed to treat them, and when battery-powered wristwatches replaced mechanically powered, stem-wound wristwatches.

From Gutenberg's invention of the printing press in 1448 to the rapid advance of the Internet, studies of hundreds of technological innovations have shown that nearly all technology cycles follow the typical **S-curve pattern of innovation** shown in Exhibit 7.1.[3] Early in a technology cycle, there is still much to learn, so progress is slow, as depicted by point A on the S-curve. The flat slope indicates that increased effort (in terms of money or

Organizational innovation the successful implementation of creative ideas in organizations

Technology cycle a cycle that begins with the birth of a new technology and ends when that technology reaches its limits and is replaced by a newer, substantially better technology

S-curve pattern of innovation a pattern of technological innovation characterized by slow initial progress, then rapid progress, and then slow progress again as a technology matures and reaches its limits research and development) brings only small improvements in technological performance.

Fortunately, as the new technology matures, researchers figure out how to get better performance from it. This is represented by point B of the S-curve in Exhibit 7.1. The steeper slope indicates that small amounts of effort will result in significant increases in performance. At point C, the flat slope again indicates that further efforts to develop this particular technology will result in only small increases in performance. More importantly, however, point C indicates that the performance limits of that particular technology are being reached. In other words, additional significant improvements in performance are highly unlikely.

Intel's technology cycles have followed this pattern. Intel spends billions to develop new computer chips and to build new facilities to produce them. Intel has found that the technology cycle for its integrated circuits is about three years. In each three-year cycle, Intel spends billions to introduce a new chip, improves the chip by making it a little bit faster each year, and then replaces that chip at the end of the cycle with a brand-new, different chip that is substantially faster than the old chip. At first, though (point A), the billions Intel spends typically produce only small improvements in performance. But after six months to a year with a new chip design, Intel's engineering and production people typically figure out how to make the new chips much faster than they were initially (point B). Yet, despite impressive gains in performance, Intel is unable to make a particular computer chip run any faster because the chip reaches its design limits.

After a technology has reached its limits at the top of the S-curve, significant improvements in performance usually come from radical new designs or new performance-enhancing materials. In Exhibit 7.1, that new technology is represented by the second S-curve. The changeover or discontinuity between the old and new technologies is represented by the dotted line. At first, the old and new technologies will likely coexist. Eventually, however, the new technology will replace the old technology. When that happens, the old technology cycle will be complete, and a new one will have started. The changeover between newer and older computer chip designs typically takes about one year. Over time, improving existing technology (tweaking the performance of the current technology cycle), combined with replacing old technology with new technology cycles (that is new, faster computer chip designs replacing older ones), has increased the speed of Intel's computer processors by a factor of 300. Today's super-powerful Xeon processors, which provide instantaneous processing and results, have 5.5 billion transistors compared to 3.1 million transistors

for 1990s 32-bit processors, 275,000 transistors for the earliest 1980s 32-bit processors, or just 4,500 transistors for the 8-bit processors, which began personal computing in the 1970s.[4]

Though the evolution of Intel's chips has been used to illustrate S-curves and technology cycles, it's important to note that technology cycles and technological innovation don't necessarily involve faster computer chips or cleaner-burning automobile engines. Remember, *technology* is simply the knowledge, tools, and techniques used to transform inputs into outputs. So a technology cycle occurs whenever there are major advances or changes in the *knowledge*, *tools*, and *techniques* of a field or discipline, whatever it may be.

For example, one of the most important technology cycles in the history of civilization occurred in 1859, when 1,300 miles of central sewer line were constructed throughout London to carry human waste to the sea more than eleven miles away. This extensive sewer system replaced the widespread practice of dumping raw sewage directly into streets, where people walked through it and where it drained into public wells that supplied drinking water. Though the relationship between raw sewage and cholera wasn't known at the time, preventing waste runoff from contaminating water supplies stopped the spread of that disease, which had killed millions of people for centuries in cities throughout the world.[5] Safe water supplies immediately translated into better health and longer life expectancies. In fact, the water you drink today is safe thanks to this technological breakthrough. So, when you think about technology cycles, don't automatically think "high tech." Instead, broaden your perspective by considering advances or changes in *any* kind of knowledge, tools, and techniques.

7-1b Innovation Streams

In Chapter 6, you learned that organizations can create *competitive advantage* for themselves if they have a *distinctive competence* that allows them to make, do, or perform something better than their competitors. A competitive advantage becomes sustainable if other companies cannot duplicate the benefits obtained from that distinctive competence. Technological innovation, however, can enable competitors to duplicate the benefits obtained from a company's distinctive advantage. It can also quickly turn a company's competitive advantage into a competitive disadvantage.

Twenty-five years ago, digital cameras replaced film-based technology. But with digital camera sales down 40 percent in four years (and still dropping), digital camera makers are losing their competitive advantage to smartphones with HD photo and video capabilities far better than basic digital cameras. Shigenobu Nagamori, CEO of Nidec, which makes electric motors used in consumer electronics, says that thanks to smartphones, we should, "assume that the inexpensive cameras are dead, just like PCs."[6] Tsugio Tsuchiya, a general manager at Tamron which makes lenses for more advanced DSLRS (digital single-lens reflex cameras), worries that, "Smartphones pose a threat not just to compact cameras but entry-level DSLRS," which start at $400 and use interchangeable lenses, such as telescoping zooms.[7] But even that advantage may soon be lost. HTC's Symon Whitehorn says, "I think we're looking at about 18 months to two years until that [zoom] lens barrier begins breaking down, and it becomes much harder to justify buying a dedicated camera outside of specialist or nostalgia reasons."[8]

Companies that want to sustain a competitive advantage must understand and protect themselves from the strategic threats of innovation. Over the long run, the best way for a company to do that is to create a stream of its own innovative ideas and products year after year. Consequently, we define **innovation streams** as patterns of innovation over time that can create sustainable competitive advantage.[9] Exhibit 7.2 shows a typical innovation consisting of a series of

Exhibit 7.2
Innovation Streams: Technology Cycles over Time

Source: Adapted from M. L. Tushman, P. C. Anderson, and C. O'Reilly, "Technology Cycles, Innovation Streams and Ambidextrous Organizations: Organization Renewal Through Innovation Streams and Strategic Change," *On Managing Strategic Innovation and Change*, eds. M. L. Tushman and P. C. Anderson (New Oxford Press, 1997) 3–23.

technology cycles. Recall that a technology cycle begins with a new technology and ends when that technology is replaced by a newer, substantially better technology. The innovation stream in Exhibit 7.2 shows three such technology cycles.

An innovation stream begins with a **technological discontinuity**, in which a scientific advance or a unique combination of existing technologies creates a significant breakthrough in performance or function. Imagine the inefficiency of just one train running on the train track between two cities. It goes to the first, returns to the second, and so on. That, however, is exactly how elevators work, up to the top, down to the bottom,

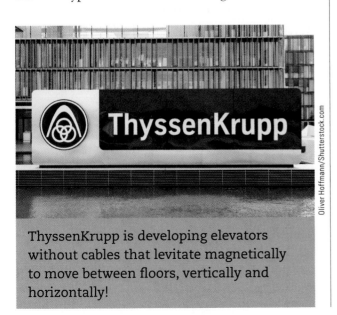

ThyssenKrupp is developing elevators without cables that levitate magnetically to move between floors, vertically and horizontally!

Innovation streams
patterns of innovation over time that can create sustainable competitive advantage

Technological discontinuity the phase of an innovation stream in which a scientific advance or unique combination of existing technologies creates a significant breakthrough in performance or function just one car per elevator shaft. **ThyssenKrupp**, maker of the Multi elevator, hopes to solve that problem by replacing the steel safety cable and pulleys used to move elevators with magnetic levitation (similar to that used on high-speed trains) that allows elevators cars to "float" to their destinations. This not only reduces the space needed for elevators by half, but without cables, multiple cars can use the same shaft, just like a subway line, and they can even move horizontally, from one side of a building to another, all of which will allow the design of wider, uniquely shaped buildings.[10]

Technological discontinuities are followed by a **discontinuous change**, which is characterized by technological substitution and design competition. **Technological substitution** occurs when customers purchase new technologies to replace older technologies. For example, just twenty years ago, nearly all phone calls were made via hardwired landline telephones. But, according to the U.S. National Health Interview Survey, 52.1 percent of U.S. homes don't have landline phones.[11] That's up from 17 percent in 2008.[12] Furthermore, only 3.5 percent of U.S. homes have landlines only.[13] Finally, with AT&T and Verizon replacing their old cable-based phone systems with wireless IP-based networks, landline phones won't even be an option within several years.[14] Ironically, the growing number of free Wi-Fi hotspots may also pose a threat to wireless carriers by making it easy to use a smartphone without a mobile network. Charissa Struble canceled her contract with Verizon and switched to Wi-Fi only, saying, "I just got tired of paying an exorbitant bill."[15] With almost 3,100 hotspots per 100,000 people in the United States, the risk of customer defection is growing. Rick Osterloh, president of Motorola Mobility, said, "The percentage of time that a phone is in Wi-Fi coverage is very high. This is the beginning of a trend."[16]

Discontinuous change is also characterized by **design competition**, in which the old technology and several different new technologies compete to establish a new technological standard or dominant design. Because of large investments in old technology and because the new and old technologies are often incompatible with each other, companies and consumers are reluctant to switch to a different technology during a design competition. For example, the telegraph was so widely used as a means of communication in the late 1800s that at first almost no one understood why telephones would be a better way to communicate. It's hard to envision today, with everyone constantly checking cell phones for email, texts, tweets, and voice mail, but as Edwin Schlossberg explains in his book *Interactive Excellence*, "People could not imagine why they would want or need to talk immediately to someone who was across town or, even more absurdly, in another town. Although people could write letters to one another, and some could send telegraph messages, the idea of sending one's voice to another place and then instantly hearing another voice in return was simply not a model that existed in people's experience. They also did not think it was worth the money to accelerate sending or hearing a message."[17] In addition, during design competition, the older technology usually improves significantly in response to the competitive threat from the new technologies; this response also slows the changeover from older to newer technologies.

Discontinuous change is followed by the emergence of a **dominant design**, which becomes the new accepted market standard for technology.[18] Dominant designs emerge in several ways. One is critical mass, meaning that a particular technology can become the dominant design simply because most people use it, for example, Blu-ray beating out HD-DVD. Critical mass will likely determine the dominant design for wireless device charging, where instead of plugging in your device to recharge, you simply place it on top of a recharging station containing magnetic charging coils. Over the last few years, three different wireless technologies were trying to become the dominant standard: the Power Matters Alliance (PMA) backing Duracell's Powermat, a Duracell and Procter &

Qualcomm CEO, Steve Mollenkopf, agrees that there is a lot of work left to do when it comes to defining standards for 5G smart phones.

David Becker/Getty Images News/Getty Images

Discontinuous change
the phase of a technology cycle characterized by technological substitution and design competition

Technological substitution
the purchase of new technologies to replace older ones

Design competition
competition between old and new technologies to establish a new technological standard or dominant design

Dominant design a new technological design or process that becomes the accepted market standard

Gamble joint venture supported by Google, AT&T, Starbucks, and McDonald's; the Alliance for Wireless Power (A4WP) and its Rezence charging mats, backed by Samsung, Broadcom, Deutsche Telekom, and Texas Instruments; and the Wireless Power Consortium (WPC) and its Qi charging mats, supported by LG Electronics, Energizer, and Nokia. However, PMA and A4WP joined forces to create a new, combined standard for wireless charging devices.[19] Again, why does this matter? It matters because the market for wireless charging, estimated at $785 million, is projected to increase to $8.5 billion by 2018. In other words, becoming the dominant standard is worth billions to the winner.[20]

The best technology doesn't always become the dominant design because a number of other factors come into play. For instance, a design can become dominant if it solves a practical problem. The QWERTY keyboard (named for the top left line of letters) became the dominant design for typewriters because it slowed typists who, by typing too fast, caused mechanical typewriter keys to jam. Though computers can easily be switched to the Dvorak keyboard layout, which doubles typing speed and cuts typing errors in half, QWERTY lives on as the standard keyboard. In this instance, the QWERTY keyboard solved a problem that, with computers, is no longer relevant. Yet it remains the dominant design not because it is the best technology, but because most people learned to type that way and continue to use it.

Dominant designs can also emerge through independent standards bodies. The International Telecommunication Union (ITU) (www.itu.ch) is an independent organization that establishes standards for the communications industry. The ITU was founded in Paris in 1865 because European countries all had different telegraph systems that could not communicate with each other. Messages crossing borders had to be transcribed from one country's system before they could be coded and delivered on another. After three months of negotiations, twenty countries signed the International Telegraph Convention, which standardized equipment and instructions, enabling telegraph messages to flow seamlessly from country to country. Today, as in 1865, various standards are proposed, discussed, negotiated, and changed until agreement is reached on a final set of standards that communication industries (Internet, telephony, satellites, radio) will follow worldwide.

For example, the telecommunications industry has yet to agree on standards for 5G, or fifth-generation, service on mobile devices. Telecom operators are hoping for a 5G standard data-transmission speed of 10 gigabits per second, fast enough to download high-def movies within seconds. Another desired 5G standard is for two

The Patent Trial and Appeal Board

The Patent Trial and Appeal Board was launched in September 2012 as part of a congressional overhaul of the patent system. Created primarily to rule on patent lawsuit findings, the new regulatory body is overseen by 181 judges, all of whom have deep experience in intellectual property and technical fields. Companies in patent infringement lawsuits may appeal to the board to challenge whether a patent should have been issued in the first place. Of its twenty-five rulings issued so far, only a handful have upheld any portion of the challenged patent. Many advocates have cheered the board, saying that it both helps corporations fight back against cases based on vague and flawed patents and defends against groups that collect large patent portfolios to use solely for infringement cases. Opponents have complained, however, that the board makes it difficult for patent holders, especially small inventors, to hold onto patents that they could barely afford to secure in the first place. This could disincentivize work on technological advancement, they argue. The board has proven controversial, but it certainly promises to influence the way innovations are made going forward.

Source: A. Jones, "New Weapon in Corporate Patent Wars," *The Wall Street Journal*, March 10, 2014, accessed April 25, 2014, http://online.wsj.com/news/articles/SB10001424052702304020104579431393308282698?KEYWORDS=new+weapon+in+corporate+patent+wars&mg=reno64-wsj.

5G devices to communicate with each other with a latency (or wait time) of just 1 millisecond, down from 50 milliseconds with 4G. Shorter 5G latencies would allow doctors in remote hospitals to conduct life-saving robotics-based surgeries on patients in other locations. The standards and technology are far from final, however. According to Qualcomm CEO Steve Mollenkopf, "There's still a lot to do."[21]

No matter how it happens, the emergence of a dominant design is a key event in an innovation stream. First, the emergence of a dominant design indicates that there are winners and losers. Technological innovation is both competence enhancing and competence destroying. Companies that bet on the now-dominant design usually prosper. By contrast, when companies bet on the wrong design or the old technology, they may experience **technological lockout**, which occurs when a new dominant design (that is a significantly better technology) prevents a company from competitively

> **Technological lockout** the inability of a company to competitively sell its products because it relies on old technology or a nondominant design

Shopping for Innovations

Not all innovations are developed internally. Sometimes companies in vastly different industries connect to generate true innovations, such as when Intel CEO Brian Krzanich attends fashion week. He says, "When I show up at fashion week, what I'm trying to do is connect with these innovators to partner with them and show them what's possible. I want to know what problems they want solved so that I can go back and work on those problems." Krzanich's networking has produced results. A glove laden with Intel sensors leads the wearer through every step of changing a tire, and a robotic Spider Dress, designed by Anouk Wipprect and using Intel technology, monitors the wearer's stress levels and extends a set of protective legs if it senses someone is getting too close.

Source: R. Feitelberg, "Intel CEO Plugs into FAST A/W 2015," *WWD*, February 14, 2015, p. 2.

selling its products or makes it difficult to do so.[22] For example, while 85 percent of U.S. movie theatres (totaling 34,161 screens) use digital technology, 1,000 small theaters may go out of business because they can't afford the $60,000 cost to buy digital projectors. Patrick Corcoran, spokesman for the National Association of Theatre Owners, says, "When you have a business and technology that has always worked for you, it's hard to imagine it going away. Some [theatres] are looking at the money they have to lay out. Some are scrambling to try to raise funds."[23]

In fact, more companies are likely to go out of business in a time of discontinuous change and changing standards than in an economic recession or slowdown.

Second, the emergence of a dominant design signals a shift from design experimentation and competition to **incremental change,** a phase in which companies innovate by lowering the cost and improving the functioning and performance of the dominant design. For example, manufacturing efficiencies enable Intel to cut the cost of its chips by one-half to two-thirds during a technology cycle, while doubling or tripling their speed. This focus on improving the dominant design continues until the next technological discontinuity occurs.

> **Incremental change** the phase of a technology cycle in which companies innovate by lowering costs and improving the functioning and performance of the dominant technological design

7-2 MANAGING INNOVATION

One consequence of technology cycles and innovation streams is that managers must be equally good at managing innovation in two very different circumstances. First, during discontinuous change, companies must find a way to anticipate and survive the technological changes that can suddenly transform industry leaders into losers and industry unknowns into powerhouses. Companies that can't manage innovation following technological discontinuities risk quick organizational decline and dissolution. Second, after a new dominant design emerges following discontinuous change, companies must manage the very different process of incremental improvement and innovation. Companies that can't manage incremental innovation slowly deteriorate as they fall further behind industry leaders.

Unfortunately, what works well when managing innovation during discontinuous change doesn't work well

Exhibit 7.3
Components of Creative Work Environments

Source: T. M. Amabile, R. Conti, H. Coon, J. Lazenby, and M. Herron, "Assessing the Work Environment for Creativity," *Academy of Management Journal* 39 (1996): 1154–1184.

when managing innovation during periods of incremental change (and vice versa).

Consequently, to successfully manage innovation streams, companies need to be good at three things: 7-2a managing sources of innovation, 7-2b managing innovation during discontinuous change, and 7-2c managing innovation during incremental change.

7-2a Managing Sources of Innovation

Innovation comes from great ideas. So a starting point for managing innovation is to manage the sources of innovation, that is, where new ideas come from. One place where new ideas originate is with brilliant inventors. But only a few companies have the likes of a Thomas Edison or Alexander Graham Bell. Given that great thinkers and inventors are in short supply, what might companies do to ensure a steady flow of good ideas?

Well, when we say that innovation begins with great ideas, we're really saying that innovation begins with creativity. As we defined it at the beginning of this chapter, creativity is the production of novel and useful ideas.[24] Although companies can't command employees to be creative ("You *will* be more creative!"), they can jump-start innovation by building **creative work environments** in which workers perceive that creative thoughts and ideas are welcomed and valued. As Exhibit 7.3 shows, creative work environments have six components that encourage creativity: challenging work, organizational encouragement, supervisory

encouragement, work group encouragement, freedom, and a lack of organizational impediments.[25]

Work is *challenging* when it requires effort, demands attention and focus, and is perceived as important to others in the organization. According to researcher Mihaly Csikszentmihalyi (pronounced ME-high-ee CHICK-sent-me-high-ee), challenging work promotes creativity because it creates a rewarding psychological experience known as "flow." **Flow** is a psychological state of effortlessness, in which you become completely absorbed in what you're doing and time seems to fly. When flow occurs, who you are and what you're doing become one. Csikszentmihalyi first encountered flow when studying artists: "What struck me by looking at artists at work was their tremendous focus on the work, this enormous involvement, this forgetting of time and body. It wasn't justified by expectation of rewards, like, 'Aha, I'm going to sell this painting.'"[26] Csikszentmihalyi has found that chess players, rock climbers, dancers, surgeons, and athletes regularly experience flow, too. Today, achieving flow is increasingly challenging. A recent study by Professor Gloria Mark at the University of California, Irvine, found that workers focus on their computer screen an average of 1 minute 15 seconds before shifting their attention, down from 2 minutes 18 seconds in 2008. Office furniture maker **Steelcase** has designed a workstation that, according to designer Mark McKenna, encourages flow by reducing workers' latent anxiety and distractions from physical surroundings. But Gloria Mark is skeptical, arguing that workers suffer more from digital distractions. In 2015, she found that on a daily basis, workers visited Facebook an average of 21 times and checked email 74 times.[27]

Removing distractions assists in creating an environment conducive to flow. Another key part of creating flow experiences, and thus creative work environments, is to achieve a balance between skills and task challenge. Workers become bored when they can do more than is required of them. Or, they become anxious when their skills aren't sufficient to accomplish a task. When skills and task challenges are balanced, however, flow and creativity can occur.

Creative work environments workplace cultures in which workers perceive that new ideas are welcomed, valued, and encouraged

Flow a psychological state of effortlessness, in which you become completely absorbed in what you're doing, and time seems to pass quickly

A creative work environment requires three kinds of encouragement: organizational, supervisory, and work group. *Organizational encouragement* of creativity occurs when management encourages risk taking and new ideas, supports and fairly evaluates new ideas, rewards and recognizes creativity, and encourages the sharing of new ideas throughout different parts of the company. When David Richter became the VP of information technology at **Kimberly-Clark**, the division had just had a round of layoffs in which nearly everyone was fired. A year later, 200 IT engineers were hired back. He said, "We had very low morale and very low employee engagement. . . . People were in a self-preservation mode." Creativity, innovation, and risk taking were at a standstill because people were afraid they would lose their jobs again. He said, "There was a palpable fear that if you tried something and failed, it would damage your career forever." So Richter encouraged creativity by rewarding creative ideas with "start-up" funding. Anyone with an idea could pitch it to him in thirty minutes or less. They didn't need a PowerPoint presentation. The only requirement before the pitch was a one-page form asking for an explanation regarding the benefit, the resources it would take, and the scope of the idea. Richter said, "It's as simple as that. Make me a pitch. And, if it's good. Let's proceed." If pilot trial of the idea succeeded, then Richter provided significant resources to implement it throughout the division. Finally, to celebrate and encourage risk taking, he shared all employees' ideas, whether they worked or not, on the division's intranet. Says Richter, "Failure is simply the opportunity to begin again, this time more intelligently. It's about what we learn from the failure. Not the failure itself. We celebrate that learning."[28]

Supervisory encouragement of creativity occurs when supervisors provide clear goals, encourage open interaction with subordinates, and actively support development teams' work and ideas. When it comes to clear goals, MIT's Andrew McAfee says be specific. He says goals such as, "We need to figure out why so many people are leaving our site before completing a transaction," or, "How can we increase sales to women in their 30s?" are much better at generating innovations than broad goals such as, "What should our next great idea be?"[29] Burberry, the luxury British brand, on the other hand, has innovated by fostering open interaction across all levels. Former CEO Angela Ahrendts says that Burberry's "Strategic Innovation Council," is "a monthly forum for our next generation of great thinkers, chaired by our chief creative officers. And the remit of the council is simple: to dream."[30] Likewise, Burberry took a social media platform used for working with customers and turned it into "Burberry Chat," which allows everyone in the company to participate in broad and targeted discussions, ensuring, she says, that "everyone has a voice, and every voice is heard."[31]

Work group encouragement occurs when group members have diverse experience, education, and backgrounds, and the group fosters mutual openness to ideas; positive, constructive challenge to ideas; and shared commitment to ideas. *Freedom* means having autonomy over one's day-to-day work and a sense of ownership and control over one's ideas. Numerous studies have indicated that creative ideas thrive under conditions of freedom.

To foster creativity, companies may also have to *remove impediments* to creativity from their work environments. Internal conflict and power struggles, rigid management structures, and a conservative bias toward the status quo can all discourage creativity. They create the perception that others in the organization will decide which ideas are acceptable and deserve support. Like Richter at Kimberly-Clark, when Jim Donald became CEO at **Extended Stay America**, the company had just gotten out of bankruptcy, and managers and employees were worried about losing their jobs and were afraid to make decisions that involved spending money. Said Donald, "They were waiting to be told what to do. They were afraid to do things." So he removed the greatest impediment to creativity, their fear, by handing out "Get Out of Jail, Free," cards. If anyone made a decision or took big risks to try new things or improve performance, they could "play" their "Get Out of Jail, Free" card, just like in the Monopoly board game, without worrying about the consequences. Donald says that hotel managers have been sending in the cards, along with brief notes explaining what they tried. For instance, a New Jersey manager heard that a movie production crew would be filming in the area, so she cold-called them and struck a deal that resulted in a lengthy stay for the crew resulting in $250,000 in revenue for her hotel.[32]

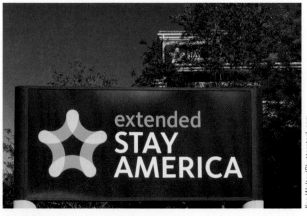

7-2b Experiential Approach: Managing Innovation during Discontinuous Change

A study of seventy-two product-development projects (that is innovation) in thirty-six computer companies across the United States, Europe, and Asia sheds light on how to manage innovation. Companies that succeeded in periods of discontinuous change (characterized by technological substitution and design competition, as described earlier) typically followed an experiential approach to innovation.[33] The **experiential approach to innovation** assumes that innovation is occurring within a highly uncertain environment and that the key to fast product innovation is to use intuition, flexible options, and hands-on experience to reduce uncertainty and accelerate learning and understanding. The experiential approach to innovation has five aspects: design iterations, testing, milestones, multifunctional teams, and powerful leaders.[34]

An *iteration* is a repetition. So a **design iteration** is a cycle of repetition in which a company tests a prototype of a new product or service, improves on the design, and then builds and tests the improved product or service prototype. A **product prototype** is a full-scale working model that is being tested for design, function, and reliability. For example, Facebook-owned Oculus VR designed virtual reality headsets (that is goggles) to be used in simulations and digital games. Oculus shipped 60,000 units of its first product prototype and used the resulting product feedback to develop its second prototype, the DK2, which it pre-sold to game developers who will not only test the DK2 but also how well the digital games they're designing perform using the DK2.[35]

Testing is a systematic comparison of different product designs or design iterations. Companies that want to create a new dominant design following a technological discontinuity quickly build, test, improve, and retest a series of different product prototypes. While many companies are developing driverless cars, prototype testing has occurred in controlled environments (Google's driverless car always has a driver at the wheel when on public roads—just in case) that often lack the authenticity—and chaos—of daily driving. That changed in 2015 with the opening of **M City**, a 23-acre mini-metropolis in Ann Arbor, Michigan, with forty building facades, a bridge, a tunnel, a traffic circle, gravel roads, angled intersections, obstructed views, and even robotic jaywalkers pushing baby carriages. M City allows researchers to test what happens if, say, a red light fails, something they could never do on real city streets. Hideki Hada, an electronics

© HerrBullermann/Shutterstock.com

systems manager at **Toyota**, said, "We would never do any dangerous or risky tests on the open road, so this will be a good place to test some of the next technology."[36]

By trying a number of very different designs or making successive improvements and changes in the same design, frequent design iterations reduce uncertainty and improve understanding. Simply put, the more prototypes you build, the more likely you are to learn what works and what doesn't. Also, when designers and engineers build a number of prototypes, they are less likely to fall in love with a particular prototype. Instead, they'll be more concerned with improving the product or technology as much as they can. Testing speeds up and improves the innovation process, too. When two very different design prototypes are tested against each other, or the new design iteration is tested against the previous iteration, product design strengths and weaknesses

Experiential approach to innovation an approach to innovation that assumes a highly uncertain environment and uses intuition, flexible options, and hands-on experience to reduce uncertainty and accelerate learning and understanding

Design iteration a cycle of repetition in which a company tests a prototype of a new product or service, improves on that design, and then builds and tests the improved prototype

Product prototype a full-scale, working model that is being tested for design, function, and reliability

Testing the systematic comparison of different product designs or design iterations quickly become apparent. Likewise, testing uncovers errors early in the design process when they are easiest to correct. Finally, testing accelerates learning and understanding by forcing engineers and product designers to examine hard data about product performance. When there's hard evidence that prototypes are testing well, the confidence of the design team grows. Also, personal conflict between design team members is less likely when testing focuses on hard measurements and facts rather than on personal hunches and preferences.

Milestones are formal project review points used to assess progress and performance. For example, a company that has put itself on a twelve-month schedule to complete a project might schedule milestones at the three-month, six-month, and nine-month points on the schedule. By making people regularly assess what they're doing, how well they're performing, and whether they need to take corrective action, milestones provide structure to the general chaos that follows technological discontinuities. Regularly meeting milestones gives people a sense of accomplishment and can shorten the innovation process by creating a sense of urgency that keeps people on task. **Google** spends $9.8 billion annually on research and development. But, its growth and size have slowed the pace of innovation. Google Chairman Eric Schmidt says, "All of us believe we could execute faster." To create a sense of urgency, Google's Advanced Technology and Project Lab now puts a strict two-year limit on research projects. After two years, unsuccessful projects are killed, while successful projects are moved inside Google, spun off, or licensed to other companies. The two-year time frame forces project teams to make fast, focused decisions. Google CEO Eric Schmidt says, "We like this model because it puts pressure on people to perform and do relevant things or stop."[37]

Multifunctional teams are work teams composed of people from different departments. Multifunctional teams accelerate learning and understanding by mixing and integrating technical, marketing, and manufacturing activities. By involving all key departments in development from the start, multifunctional teams speed innovation through early identification of new ideas or problems that would typically not have been generated or addressed until much later. **Apple** CEO Tim Cook assigned Steve Zadesky, a former Ford engineer who headed the teams that developed the iPhone and the iPad, to lead a secretive car project, code-named "Titan," to apparently compete with Tesla's electric

cars. Zadesky is building a multifunctional team by drafting employees from different parts of Apple, while also recruiting outsiders with experience developing concept cars at Ford and Mercedes Benz and expertise in electric-car battery technology.[38]

Powerful leaders provide the vision, discipline, and motivation to keep the innovation process focused, on time, and on target. Powerful leaders are able to get resources when they are needed, are typically more experienced, have high status in the company, and are held directly responsible for the products' success or failure. On average, powerful leaders can get innovation-related projects done nine months faster than leaders with little power or influence.

7-2c Compression Approach: Managing Innovation during Incremental Change

Whereas the experiential approach is used to manage innovation in highly uncertain environments during periods of discontinuous change, the compression approach is used to manage innovation in more certain environments during periods of incremental change. Whereas the goals of the experiential approach are significant improvements in performance and the establishment of a *new* dominant design, the goals of the compression approach are lower costs and incremental improvements in the performance and function of the *existing* dominant design.

The general strategies in each approach are different, too. With the experiential approach, the general strategy is to build something new, different, and substantially better. Because there's so much uncertainty—no one knows which technology will become the market leader—companies adopt a winner-take-all approach by trying to create the market-leading, dominant design. With the compression approach, the general strategy is to compress the time and steps needed to bring about small, consistent improvements in performance and functionality. Because a dominant technology design already exists, the general strategy is to continue improving the existing technology as rapidly as possible. For example, after using an experiential approach and investing $50 billion to develop its groundbreaking 787 Dreamliner passenger jet, Boeing is now switching to a compression approach to innovation. Chief Operating Officer Dennis Muilenburg said, "In the past, we may have said our best engineers are working on the new thing. Now we want our best engineers working on innovative reuse."[39] Likewise, Ray Conner, CEO of Boeing's commercial airplane unit said, "It's not to say

Milestones formal project review points used to assess progress and performance

Multifunctional teams work teams composed of people from different departments you don't innovate [but] how do you innovate to make it more producible? How do you innovate to make it more reliable?"[40]

In short, a **compression approach to innovation** assumes that innovation is a predictable process, that incremental innovation can be planned using a series of steps, and that compressing the time it takes to complete those steps can speed up innovation. The compression approach to innovation has five aspects: planning, supplier involvement, shortening the time of individual steps, overlapping steps, and multifunctional teams.[41]

In Chapter 5, *planning* was defined as choosing a goal and a method or strategy to achieve that goal. When *planning for incremental innovation*, the goal is to squeeze or compress development time as much as possible, and the general strategy is to create a series of planned steps to accomplish that goal. Planning for incremental innovation helps avoid unnecessary steps and enables developers to sequence steps in the right order to avoid wasted time and delays between steps. Planning also reduces misunderstandings and improves coordination.

Most planning for incremental innovation is based on the idea of generational change. **Generational change** occurs when incremental improvements are made to a dominant technological design such that the improved version of the technology is fully backward compatible with the older version.[42] Most computers, for instance, have USB (universal serial bus) input slots to connect and power USB thumb drives, monitors, or external hard drives used for backup storage. USB 3.1, the latest USB standard, can transfer more than 10 Gbps (gigabytes per second), compared to USB 3.0 devices, which operate at 5 Gbps, or USB 2.0 devices, which operate at roughly 1/2 Gbps.[43] What happens if you buy a new computer with USB 3.1 slots, but still own a USB 3.0 external hard drive and a USB 2.0 thumb drive? Both will work because they are backward compatible with USB 3.1, but at slower speeds.

Because the compression approach assumes that innovation can follow a series of preplanned steps, one of the ways to shorten development time is *supplier involvement*. Delegating some of the preplanned steps in the innovation process to outside suppliers reduces the amount of work that internal development teams must do. Plus, suppliers provide an alternative source of ideas and expertise that can lead to better designs.

Another way to shorten development time is simply to *shorten the time of individual steps* in the innovation process. A common way to do that is through computer-aided design (CAD). CAD speeds up the design process by allowing designers and engineers to make and test design changes using computer models rather than physically testing expensive prototypes. CAD also speeds innovation by making it easy to see how design changes affect engineering, purchasing, and production. For example, 3-D design software reduces the time and cost involved in creating new products. **Ansys** simulation software shows how products will actually operate in the real world. Created by 600 PhDs, it uses advanced algorithms to mirror the physics of heat, friction, fluids, loads, and stress, allowing users to simulate anything from tennis rackets to passenger jet lift coefficients for takeoffs and landings. Instead of testing dozens of mock-up products, Ansys users save time and money by letting the software do the testing. Jim Shaikh wanted to design a baby bottle that instantly heated milk to the right temperature every time, so he used Ansys to test different designs and plastics. The best design, according to the software, was a bottle with an internal element that heats milk as it passes through the nipple to the baby. Only after finalizing the design via thousands of tests on Ansys did Shaikh spend $1,500 to produce a prototype of the finished product.[44]

In a sequential design process, each step must be completed before the next step begins. But sometimes multiple development steps can be performed at the same time. *Overlapping steps* shorten the development process by reducing delays or waiting time between steps.

iStockphoto.com/Edin

7-3 ORGANIZATIONAL DECLINE: THE RISK OF NOT CHANGING

Founded in 1921 in Boston as a store for ham radio enthusiasts, **RadioShack** grew to more than 7,000 stores by stocking a wide range of components used to build or repair various electronic devices. In fact, before starting **Apple**, co-founders Steve Jobs and Steve Wozniak bought parts at RadioShack to make a "blue box" device that illegally

Compression approach to innovation an approach to innovation which assumes that incremental innovation can be planned using a series of steps and that compressing those steps can speed innovation

Generational change change based on incremental improvements to a dominant technological design such that the improved technology is fully backward compatible with the older technology switched on free long distance calling (which mattered when long distance calls were 40 cents a minute).[45] RadioShack's growth was first propelled by hobbyists (nerds like Jobs and Wozniak), then by battery sales, computers, and cell phones. The TRS-80, introduced in 1977, was one of the first broadly popular PCs. Following computers, which it stopped making in 1993, its next growth cycle came from cell phones. The phone companies at first relied on RadioShack to sign up and service customers, but this changed as they eventually established their own retail stores. RadioShack moved away from its focus on serving technology power users and hobbyists by opening unsuccessful big-box electronics and appliance stores, such as Computer City and Incredible Universe, on which it lost hundreds of millions of dollars in the 1990s. Outmaneuvered by BestBuy in brick-and-mortar retailing, and never really competitive on the Web, RadioShack filed for bankruptcy in spring 2015 after losing $936 million since 2011, the last year it was profitable.[46]

Businesses operate in a constantly changing environment. Recognizing and adapting to internal and external changes can mean the difference between continued success and going out of business. Companies that fail to change run the risk of organizational decline.[47] **Organizational decline** occurs when companies don't anticipate, recognize, neutralize, or adapt to the internal or external pressures that threaten their survival. In other words, decline occurs when organizations don't recognize the need for change. There are five stages of organizational decline: blinded, inaction, faulty action, crisis, and dissolution.

In the *blinded stage*, decline begins because key managers fail to recognize the internal or external changes that will harm their organizations. This blindness may be due to a simple lack of awareness about changes or an inability to understand their significance. It may also come from the overconfidence that can develop when a company has been successful.

In the *inaction stage*, as organizational performance problems become more visible, management may recognize the need to change but still take no action. The managers may be waiting to see if the problems will correct themselves. Or, they may find it difficult to change the practices and policies that previously led to success. Possibly, too, they wrongly assume that they can easily correct the problems, so they don't feel the situation is urgent.

In the *faulty action stage*, faced with rising costs and decreasing profits and market share, management will announce belt-tightening plans designed

"Radioshack filed for bankruptcy in 2015 and was acquired by its largest lender, hedge fund, Standard General."

to cut costs, increase efficiency, and restore profits. In other words, rather than recognizing the need for fundamental changes, managers assume that if they just run a tighter ship, company performance will return to previous levels.

In the *crisis stage*, bankruptcy or dissolution (breaking up the company and selling its parts) is likely to occur unless the company completely reorganizes the way it does business. At this point, however, companies typically lack the resources to fully change how they run their businesses. Cutbacks and layoffs will have reduced the level of talent among employees. Furthermore, talented managers who were savvy enough to see the crisis coming will have found jobs with other companies, often with competitors. At this stage, hoping to generate enough cash to fund a much-needed redesign of its remaining stores, RadioShack took out $835 million in loans and closed 1,100 stores, However, during the 2014 holiday season, its corporate finances amounted to the equivalent of just $15,000 cash per store.[48]

In the *dissolution stage*, after failing to make the changes needed to sustain the organization, the company is dissolved through bankruptcy proceedings or by selling assets to pay suppliers, banks, and creditors. At this point, a new CEO may be brought in to oversee the closing of stores, offices, and manufacturing facilities; the final layoff of managers and employees; and the sale of assets. It is important to note that decline is reversible at each of the first four stages and that not all companies in decline reach final dissolution. RadioShack declared bankruptcy in February 2015, and was acquired by its largest lender, hedge fund Standard General. Seventeen hundred stores will continue operating, but 1,400 will feature Sprint/Radio Shack signage and branding. Sprint and its employees will use roughly one-third of each store to sell and display Sprint mobile phones and related products.[49]

Organizational decline
a large decrease in organizational performance that occurs when companies don't anticipate, recognize, neutralize, or adapt to the internal or external pressures that threaten their survival

7-4 MANAGING CHANGE

According to social psychologist Kurt Lewin, change is a function of the forces that promote change and the opposing forces that slow or resist change.[50] **Change forces** lead to differences in the form, quality, or condition of an organization over time. In contrast to change forces, **resistance forces** support the status quo, that is, the existing conditions in an organization. Change is difficult under any circumstances. Production schedules on movie sets have changed dramatically as a result of directors having switched from film to digital recordings. When shooting with film, a new film reel has to be loaded every ten minutes, creating frequent breaks when stars would return to their trailers to read, rehearse, or rest. Because there are no film reels with digital recording, shooting can occur continuously, significantly reducing film production time and costs. A number of famous actors, however, don't like the change. Actor Robert Downey, Jr. complained, "I can't work like this. I never get to go to my trailer … I'm on my feet fourteen hours a day. I'm shooting all the time."[51]

The Kiss of Yes occurs when some of the strongest resisters support changes in public, but then ignore them in private.

Resistance to change is caused by self-interest, misunderstanding and distrust, and a general intolerance for change.[52] People resist change out of *self-interest* because they fear that change will cost or deprive them of something they value. Resistance might stem from a fear that the changes will result in a loss of pay, power, responsibility, or even perhaps one's job.

People also resist change because of *misunderstanding and distrust*; they don't understand the change or the reasons for it, or they distrust the people—typically management—behind the change. Resistance isn't always visible at first. In fact, some of the strongest resisters may initially support the changes in public, nodding and smiling their agreement, but then ignore the changes in private and do their jobs as they always have. Management consultant Michael Hammer calls this deadly form of resistance the "Kiss of Yes."[53]

Resistance may also come from a generally low tolerance for change. Some people are simply less capable of handling change than others. People with a *low tolerance for change* feel threatened by the uncertainty associated with change and worry that they won't be able to learn the new skills and behaviors needed to successfully negotiate change in their companies.

Because resistance to change is inevitable, successful change efforts require careful management.

*In this section, you will learn about **7-4a managing resistance to change, 7-4b what not to do when leading organizational change,** and **7-4c different change tools and techniques.***

7-4a Managing Resistance to Change

According to psychologist Kurt Lewin, managing organizational change is a basic process of unfreezing, change intervention, and refreezing. **Unfreezing** is getting the people affected by change to believe that change is needed. During the **change intervention** itself, workers and managers change their behavior and work practices. **Refreezing** is supporting and reinforcing the new changes so that they stick.

Resistance to change is an example of frozen behavior. Given the choice between changing and not changing, most people would rather not change. Because resistance to change is natural and inevitable, managers need to unfreeze resistance to change to create successful change programs. The following methods can be used to manage resistance to change: education and communication, participation, negotiation, top-management support, and coercion.[54]

When resistance to change is based on insufficient, incorrect, or misleading information, managers should *educate*

Change forces forces that produce differences in the form, quality, or condition of an organization over time

Resistance forces forces that support the existing conditions in organizations

Resistance to change opposition to change resulting from self-interest, misunderstanding and distrust, and a general intolerance for change

Unfreezing getting the people affected by change to believe that change is needed

Change intervention the process used to get workers and managers to change their behaviors and work practices

Refreezing supporting and reinforcing new changes so that they stick employees about the need for change and *communicate change-related information to them.* Managers must also supply the information and funding, or other support employees need to make changes. For example, resistance to change can be particularly strong when one company buys another company. This is because one company in the merger usually has a higher status due to its size or its higher profitability or the fact that it is the acquiring company. These status differences are important to managers and employees, particularly if they're in the lower-status company, who worry about retaining their jobs or influence after the merger. That fear or concern can greatly increase resistance to change.[55] When PMA Companies, an insurance risk management firm, was acquired by Old Republic International, an insurance company, PMA's CEO Vince Donnelly communicated frequently with PMA's employees about the merger. Four months before the acquisition became official, he traveled to each of the company's twenty offices and gave employees a detailed description of how their day-to-day operations would change and why the acquisition was good for everyone involved. He also held quarterly updates with employees via videoconference. Said Donnelly, "It's not just one and done. Communication needs to be continual. You need to continue to reinforce the messages that you want people to internalize. So you need to understand that communication is a continuous process and not something that you do just once." He went on to say, "What you are asking people to do is trust you, [trust] that you have the best interest of everybody in mind, and [trust that] when there is news to tell, you're going to hear it directly from the CEO—good, bad or indifferent."[56]

Another way to reduce resistance to change is to have those affected by the change *participate in planning and implementing the change process.* Employees who participate have a better understanding of the change and the need for it. Furthermore, employee concerns about change can be addressed as they occur if employees participate in the planning and implementation process. When United Airlines and Continental Airlines merged to form one of the world's largest airlines, there were thousands of decisions to be made to integrate the two companies, such as combining websites, ticketing systems, pay and promotion policies, and so on. They even had to decide which coffee to serve, as Continental served coffee from Fresh Brew, and United served Starbucks. While seemingly a small decision, United and Continental serve a combined 62 million cups of coffee each year. Sandra Pineau-Boddison, the vice president of food services, picked a fourteen-member team consisting of people from flight operations, finance, food service, and marketing to make the decision, even asking them to blindly taste twelve different coffees to identify which tasted best. Then, she took the committee's selection and asked the company's board of directors, as well as 1,100 flight attendants who also tried the new brew, for input.[57]

Employees are also less likely to resist change if they are allowed *to discuss and agree on who will do what* after change occurs. Craig Durosko, founder of **Sun Design Home Remodeling Specialists** in Burke, Virginia, says, "Unfortunately, the way most employees find out when a company isn't doing well is when their paychecks bounce or when they show up and the front doors are locked. When changes go down and they don't know about it, they can't do anything about it." So, when Sun Design's business shrank dramatically during the recession, Durosko explained the problem, sharing detailed financial information, and then asked his employees what could be done to minimize losses. He says, "No less than 20 employees gave line-by-line specific *things they could do* to make a difference."[58]

Resistance to change also decreases when change efforts receive *significant managerial support.* Managers must do more than talk about the importance of change, though. They must provide the training, resources, and autonomy needed to make change happen. Finally, resistance to change can be managed through **coercion,** or the use of formal power and authority to force others to change. Because of the intense negative reactions it can create (for example fear, stress, resentment, sabotage of company products), coercion should be used only when a crisis exists or when all other attempts to reduce resistance to change have failed.

7-4b What Not to Do When Leading Change

So far, you've learned about the basic change process (unfreezing, change intervention, refreezing) and managing resistance to change. Harvard Business School professor John Kotter argues that knowing what *not* to do is just as important as knowing what to do when it comes to achieving successful organizational change.[59]

Managers commonly make certain errors when they lead change. The first two errors occur during the unfreezing phase, when managers try to get the people affected by change to believe that change is really needed. The first and potentially most serious error is *not establishing a great enough sense of urgency.* In fact, Kotter estimates that more than half of all change efforts

Coercion the use of formal power and authority to force others to change fail because the people affected are not convinced that change is necessary. People will feel a greater sense of urgency if a leader in the company makes a public, candid assessment of the company's problems and weaknesses.

Nokia went from being the world's largest cell phone company in 2007 to nearly going out of business and then selling off its handset division to Microsoft in 2013. Frank Nuovo, who designed several of Nokia's most successful mobile phones, notes that Nokia was working on innovations, such as tablet computers and touch-screen devices, long before Apple's iPad or iPhone came to market. Nuovo said, "We realized at Nokia that touch [screen technology] was increasingly important and were working towards doing it, but when a company is really busy holding on to what it has built, it is difficult to put enough of a push towards something so drastically new and engender urgency in it." He further explained that instead of a sense of urgency, "There was a real sense of saying 'we will get to that eventually.'"[60] Nokia sacrificed innovation in favor of supporting existing customers and technology. As a result, companies like Apple began releasing new game-changing products, and Nokia was left behind.[61]

The second mistake that occurs in the unfreezing process is *not creating a powerful enough coalition*. Change often starts with one or two people. But change has to be supported by a critical and growing group of people to build enough momentum to change an entire department, division, or company. Besides top management, Kotter recommends that key employees, managers, board members, customers, and even union leaders be members of a *core change coalition* that guides and supports organizational change. Celestica Inc., located in Toronto, Canada, is an electronics manufacturing services company that produces complex printed circuit assemblies, such as PC motherboards and networking cards, flat-screen TVs, and Xbox video game systems for Microsoft. Celestica's CEO Craig Muhlhauser says, "In a turnaround, there are three kinds of employees, those on your side, those on the fence, and those who will never buy in. The latter have to be let go, and those on the fence should be persuaded to contribute or leave." Says Muhlhauser, "We have to make change, change is difficult and as we make change, it is important to realize that there are people who are going to resist that change. In talking to those people, the objective is to move everybody into the column of supporters. But that is probably unachievable."[62] It's also important to strengthen this core change coalition's resolve by periodically bringing its members together for off-site retreats.

Nokia went from being the world's largest cell phone company in 2007 to selling off its handset division to Microsoft in 2013, due in part to no sense of urgency when it came to innovation.

The next four errors that managers make occur during the change phase, when a change intervention is used to try to get workers and managers to change their behavior and work practices. *Lacking a vision* for change is a significant error at this point. As you learned in Chapter 5, a *vision* (defined as a *purpose statement* in Chapter 5) is a statement of a company's purpose or reason for existing. A vision for change makes clear where a company or department is headed and why the change is occurring. Change efforts that lack vision tend to be confused, chaotic, and contradictory. By contrast, change efforts guided by visions are clear, are easy to understand, and can be effectively explained in five minutes or less.

Undercommunicating the vision by a factor of ten is another mistake in the change phase. According to Kotter, companies mistakenly hold just one meeting to announce the vision. Or, if the new vision receives heavy emphasis in executive speeches or company newsletters, senior management then undercuts the vision by behaving in ways contrary to it. Successful communication of the vision requires that top managers link everything the company does to the new vision and that they "walk the talk" by behaving in ways consistent with the vision. Furthermore, even companies that begin change with a clear vision sometimes make the mistake of *not removing obstacles to the new vision*. They leave formidable barriers to change in place by failing to redesign jobs, pay plans, and technology to support the new way of doing things. One of the biggest obstacles that Nokia CEO Stephen Elop removed soon after joining the company was Symbian, the core operating software on more than 400 million

Nokia phones. Killing Symbian saved Nokia $1.4 billion a year in software maintenance and research and development costs. The software was out of date and buggy, and Nokia's computer software engineers had not delivered a new smartphone on schedule or on budget since 2009. Plus, app developers hated programming for Symbian. Tuomas Artman, who used to work at Nokia, said, "Developing for Symbian could make you want to slice your wrists."[63]

Killing Symbian not only saved billions in costs, it also allowed Nokia to strike an exclusive deal with Microsoft to use Windows Phone 7 software on its phones. Microsoft agreed to allow Nokia to innovate by creating new features for Windows Phone and injected hundreds of millions of dollars of marketing funds to support Nokia's efforts to sell new Windows-based smartphones. The change helped both companies, as Microsoft only had a 4 percent share of the smartphone market by itself, whereas in May 2013, Nokia and Microsoft had a combined 15 percent market share.[64]

Another error in the change phase is *not systematically planning for and creating short-term wins*. Most people don't have the discipline and patience to wait two years to see if the new change effort works. Change is threatening and uncomfortable, so people need to see an immediate payoff if they are to continue to support it. Kotter recommends that managers create short-term wins by actively picking people and projects that are likely to work extremely well early in the change process.

The last two errors that managers make occur during the refreezing phase, when attempts are made to support and reinforce changes so that they stick. *Declaring victory too soon* is a tempting mistake in the refreezing phase. Managers typically declare victory right after the first large-scale success in the change process. Declaring success too early has the same effect as draining the gasoline out of a car: it stops change efforts dead in their tracks. With success declared, supporters of the change process stop pushing to make change happen. After all, why push when success has been achieved? Rather than declaring victory, managers should use the momentum from short-term wins to push for even bigger or faster changes. This maintains urgency and prevents change supporters from slacking off before the changes are frozen into the company's culture.

The last mistake that managers make is *not anchoring changes in the corporation's culture*. An *organization's culture* is the set of key values, beliefs, and attitudes shared by organizational members that determines the accepted way of doing things in a company. As

you learned in Chapter 3, changing cultures is extremely difficult and slow. According to Kotter, two things help anchor changes in a corporation's culture. The first is directly showing people that the changes have actually improved performance. The second is to make sure that the people who get promoted fit the new culture. If they don't, it's a clear sign that the changes were only temporary.

7-4c Change Tools and Techniques

Imagine that your boss came to you and said, "All right, genius, you wanted it. You're in charge of turning around the division." Where would you begin? How would you encourage change-resistant managers to change? What would you do to include others in the change process? How would you get the change process off to a quick start? Finally, what approach would you use to promote long-term effectiveness and performance? Results-driven change, the General Electric workout, and organizational development are different change tools and techniques that can be used to address these issues.

One of the reasons that organizational change efforts fail is that they are activity oriented rather than results oriented. In other words, they focus primarily on changing company procedures, management philosophy, or employee behavior. Typically, there is much buildup and preparation as consultants are brought in, presentations are made, books are read, and employees and managers are trained. There's a tremendous emphasis on doing things the new way. But, with all the focus on "doing,"

Taina Sohlman/Shutterstock.com

Shell's new CEO, Ben van Beurden, split the company into 150 performance units, each to be evaluated on its profitability.

almost no attention is paid to *results*, to seeing if all this activity has actually made a difference.

By contrast, **results-driven change** supplants the emphasis on activity with a laser-like focus on quickly measuring and improving results.[65] When Ben van Beurden became CEO of Royal Dutch Shell, one of the world's largest oil companies, he put everyone in the company on notice by proclaiming that oil refining profits were "simply too low," and that Shell needed, "better operational discipline." Furthermore, he changed managers' focus from "professional excellence," which served Shell well after a serious financial scandal, to specific results-driven goals. So Beurden split Shell into 150 performance units, each to be evaluated on its profitability, with profitable units continuing, and unprofitable units closing or being sold. Likewise, managers now had to compete for additional funds for their units by submitting formal requests to a central committee, which in turn had its spending recommendations reviewed by a "challenge committee."[66]

Another advantage of results-driven change is that managers introduce changes in procedures, philosophy, or behavior only if they are likely to improve measured performance. In other words, managers and workers actually test to see if changes make a difference. A third advantage of results-driven change is that quick, visible improvements motivate employees to continue to make additional changes to improve measured performance. Exhibit 7.4 describes the basic steps of results-driven change.

The **General Electric workout** is a special kind of results-driven change. The "workout" involves a three-day meeting that brings together managers and employees from different levels and parts of an organization to quickly generate and act on solutions to specific business problems.[67] On the first morning, the boss discusses the agenda and targets specific business problems that the group will solve. Then, the boss leaves, and an outside facilitator breaks the group (typically thirty to forty people) into five or six teams and helps them spend the next day and a half discussing and debating solutions.

On day three, in what GE calls a "town meeting," the teams present specific solutions to their boss, who has been gone since day one. As each team's spokesperson makes specific suggestions, the boss has only three options: agree on the spot, say no, or ask for more information so that a decision can be made by a specific, agreed-on date. GE boss Armand Lauzon sweated his way through a town meeting. To encourage him to say yes, his workers set up the meeting room to put pressure on Lauzon. He says, "I was wringing wet within half an hour. They had 108 proposals, I had about a minute to

say yes or no to each one, and I couldn't make eye contact with my boss without turning around, which would show everyone in the room that I was chicken."[68] In the end, Lauzon agreed to all but eight suggestions. Furthermore, after those decisions were made, no one at GE was allowed to overrule them.

Organizational development is a philosophy and collection of planned change interventions designed to improve an organization's long-term health and performance. Organizational development takes a long-range approach to change; assumes that top-management support is necessary for change to succeed; creates change by educating workers and managers to change ideas, beliefs, and behaviors so that problems can be solved in new ways; and emphasizes employee participation in diagnosing, solving, and evaluating problems.[69] As shown in Exhibit 7.5, organizational development interventions begin with the recognition of a problem. Then, the company designates a **change agent** to be formally in charge of guiding

---

Exhibit 7.4

How to Create a Results-Driven Change Program

1. Set measurable, short-term goals to improve performance.
2. Make sure your action steps are likely to improve measured performance.
3. Stress the importance of immediate improvements.
4. Solicit help from consultants and staffers to achieve quick improvements in performance.
5. Test action steps to see if they actually yield improvements. If they don't, discard them and establish new ones.
6. Use resources you have or that can be easily acquired. It doesn't take much.

Source: R. H. Schaffer and H. A. Thomson, "Successful Change Programs Begin with Results," *Harvard Business Review on Change* (Boston: Harvard Business School Press, 1998), 189–213.

Results-driven change change created quickly by focusing on the measurement and improvement of results

General Electric workout a three-day meeting in which managers and employees from different levels and parts of an organization quickly generate and act on solutions to specific business problems

Organizational development a philosophy and collection of planned change interventions designed to improve an organization's long-term health and performance

Change agent the person formally in charge of guiding a change effort

Exhibit 7.5
General Steps for Organizational Development Interventions

1. Entry	A problem is discovered, and the need for change becomes apparent. A search begins for someone to deal with the problem and facilitate change.
2. Startup	A change agent enters the picture and works to clarify the problem and gain commitment to a change effort.
3. Assessment & feedback	The change agent gathers information about the problem and provides feedback about it to decision makers and those affected by it.
4. Action planning	The change agent works with decision makers to develop an action plan.
5. Intervention	The action plan, or organizational development intervention, is carried out.
6. Evaluation	The change agent helps decision makers assess the effectiveness of the intervention.
7. Adoption	Organizational members accept ownership and responsibility for the change, which is then carried out through the entire organization.
8. Separation	The change agent leaves the organization after first ensuring that the change intervention will continue to work.

Source: W. J. Rothwell, R. Sullivan, and G. M. McLean, *Practicing Organizational Development: A Guide for Consultants* (San Diego: Pfeiffer & Co., 1995).

Exhibit 7.6
Different Kinds of Organizational Development Interventions

Large-System Interventions

| Sociotechnical systems | An intervention designed to improve how well employees use and adjust to the work technology used in an organization. |
| Survey feedback | An intervention that uses surveys to collect information from the members of the system, reports the results of that survey to the members, and then uses those results to develop action plans for improvement. |

Small-Group Interventions

| Team building | An intervention designed to increase the cohesion and cooperation of work group members. |
| Unit goal setting | An intervention designed to help a work group establish short- and long-term goals. |

Person-Focused Interventions

| Counseling/coaching | An intervention designed so that a formal helper or coach listens to managers or employees and advises them on how to deal with work or interpersonal problems. |
| Training | An intervention designed to provide individuals with the knowledge, skills, or attitudes they need to become more effective at their jobs. |

Source: W. J. Rothwell, R. Sullivan, and G. M. McLean, *Practicing Organizational Development: A Guide for Consultants* (San Diego: Pfeiffer & Co., 1995).

the change effort. This person can be someone from within the company or a professional consultant. The change agent clarifies the problem, gathers information, works with decision makers to create and implement an action plan, helps to evaluate the plan's effectiveness, implements the plan throughout the company, and then leaves (if from outside the company) after making sure the change intervention will continue to work.

Organizational development interventions are aimed at changing large systems, small groups, or people.[70] More specifically, the purpose of *large-system interventions* is to change the character and performance of an organization, business unit, or department. *Small-group intervention* focuses on assessing how a group functions and helping it work more effectively to accomplish its goals. *Person-focused intervention* is intended to increase interpersonal effectiveness by helping people to become aware of their attitudes and behaviors and to acquire new skills and knowledge. Exhibit 7.6 describes the most frequently used organizational development interventions for large systems, small groups, and people.

STUDY TOOLS 7

LOCATED IN TEXTBOOK
- ☐ Rip-out and review chapter review card

LOCATED AT WWW.CENGAGEBRAIN.COM
- ☐ Review key term flashcards and create your own from StudyBits
- ☐ Track your knowledge and understanding of key concepts, using the concept tracker
- ☐ Complete practice and graded quizzes to prepare for tests
- ☐ Complete interactive content within the exposition
- ☐ View chapter highlight box content at the beginning of each chapter

8 Global Management

My Life Graphic/Shutterstock.com

LEARNING OUTCOMES

8-1 Discuss the impact of global business and the trade rules and agreements that govern it.

8-2 Explain why companies choose to standardize or adapt their business procedures.

8-3 Explain the different ways that companies can organize to do business globally.

8-4 Explain how to find a favorable business climate.

8-5 Discuss the importance of identifying and adapting to cultural differences.

8-6 Explain how to successfully prepare workers for international assignments.

After you finish this chapter, go to **PAGE 175** for **STUDY TOOLS**

8-1 GLOBAL BUSINESS, TRADE RULES, AND TRADE AGREEMENTS

Business is the buying and selling of goods or services. Buying this textbook was a business transaction. So was selling your first car and getting paid for babysitting or for mowing lawns. **Global business** is the buying and selling of goods and services by people from different countries. The Timex watch that I wore while I was writing this chapter was purchased at a Walmart in Texas. But because it was made in the Philippines, I participated in global business when I paid Walmart. Walmart, for its part, had already paid Timex, which had paid the company that employs the Filipino managers and workers who made my watch. Of course, there is more to global business than buying imported products at Walmart.

Global business presents its own set of challenges for managers. How can you be sure that the way you run your business in one country is the right way to run that business in another? This chapter discusses how organizations answer that question. We will start by examining global business in two ways: first exploring its impact on U.S. businesses and then reviewing the basic rules and agreements that govern global trade. Next, we will examine how and when companies go global by examining the trade-off between consistency and adaptation and discussing how to organize a global company. Finally, we will look at how companies decide where to expand globally, including finding the best business climate, adapting to cultural differences, and better preparing employees for international assignments.

If you want a simple demonstration of the impact of global business, look at the tag on your shirt, the inside of your shoes, and the inside of your digital camera (take out your battery). Chances are all of these items were made in different places around the world. As I write this, my shirt, shoes, and digital camera were made in Thailand, China, and Korea. Where were yours made?

*Let's learn more about **8-1a the impact of global business, 8-1b how tariff and nontariff trade barriers have historically restricted global business, 8-1c how today global and regional trade agreements are reducing those trade barriers worldwide, and 8-1d how consumers are responding to those changes in trade rules and agreements.***

8-1a The Impact of Global Business

Multinational corporations are corporations that own businesses in two or more countries. In 1970, more than half of the world's 7,000 multinational corporations were headquartered in just two countries: the United States and the United Kingdom. There are now roughly 103,000 multinational corporations, more than fourteen times as many as in 1970, and 9,692, or 9.4 percent, are based in the United States.[1] Today, 73,144 multinationals, or 71 percent, are based in other developed countries (for example Germany, Italy, Canada, and Japan), while 30,209, or 29.3 percent, are based in developing countries (for example Colombia and South Africa). So, today, multinational companies can be found by the thousands all over the world!

Another way to appreciate the impact of global business is by considering direct foreign investment. **Direct foreign investment** occurs when a company builds a new business or buys an existing business in a foreign country. French information technology company **Cap Gemini** made a direct foreign investment in the U.S. when it purchased its U.S. rival IGATE for $4 billion.[2]

Of course, companies from many other countries also own businesses in the United States. As Exhibit 8.1 shows, companies from the United Kingdom, Japan, the Netherlands, Canada, France, Switzerland, Germany, and Luxembourg have the largest direct foreign investment in the United States. Overall, foreign companies invest more than $2.7 trillion a year to do business in the United States.

But direct foreign investment in the United States is only half the picture. U.S. companies also have made large direct foreign investments in countries throughout the world. **FedEx** is paying $4.8 billion to buy TNT Express, a Dutch package-delivery company. FedEx will gain TNT's door-to-door delivery routes in forty countries, doubling its European market share to over 20 percent, which will now rival the 25 percent share of its key competitor, UPS. FedEx executive Michael Glenn said, "The combination of FedEx's existing network and TNT's broad ground-based network will. . . result [in]. . . enhanced coverage, a broader portfolio, obviously, [and] better pickup and delivery cost."[3]

> **Global business** the buying and selling of goods and services by people from different countries
>
> **Multinational corporation** a corporation that owns businesses in two or more countries
>
> **Direct foreign investment** a method of investment in which a company builds a new business or buys an existing business in a foreign country

Exhibit 8.1
Direct Foreign Investment in the United States

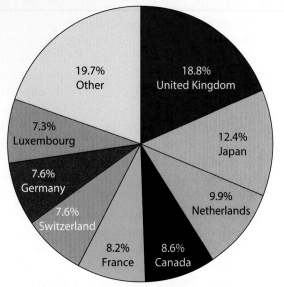

- 19.7% Other
- 18.8% United Kingdom
- 12.4% Japan
- 9.9% Netherlands
- 8.6% Canada
- 8.2% France
- 7.6% Switzerland
- 7.6% Germany
- 7.3% Luxembourg

Source: BEA News, "Direct Investment Positions for 2013 Now Available," *Bureau of Economic Analysis*, June 25, 2014, accessed May 5, 2015. http://bea.gov/international/di1fdibal.htm.

As Exhibit 8.2 shows, U.S. companies have made their largest direct foreign investments in the Netherlands, the United Kingdom, Luxembourg, Canada, and Bermuda. Overall, U.S. companies invest more than $4.6 trillion a year to do business in other countries.

So, whether foreign companies invest in the United States or U.S. companies invest abroad, direct foreign investment is an increasingly important and common method of conducting global business.

Trade barriers government-imposed regulations that increase the cost and restrict the number of imported goods

Protectionism a government's use of trade barriers to shield domestic companies and their workers from foreign competition

Tariff a direct tax on imported goods

Nontariff barriers nontax methods of increasing the cost or reducing the volume of imported goods

8-1b Trade Barriers

Although today's consumers usually don't care where the products they buy come from (more on this in Section 8-1d), national governments have traditionally preferred that consumers buy domestically made products in hopes that such purchases would increase the number of domestic businesses and workers. Infact, governments have done much more than hope that you will buy from domestic companies. Historically, governments have actively used **trade barriers** to make it much more expensive or difficult (or sometimes impossible) for consumers to buy or consume imported goods. For example, the Mexican government adds a 25 percent tariff to clothes, textiles, and footwear imported to Mexico. Stephen Lamar of the American Apparel & Footwear Association explained that the tariffs, ". . .will make it more expensive for our members to export to Mexico from the U.S. and everywhere. It's disappointing."[4] By establishing these restrictions and taxes, the Mexican government is engaging in **protectionism**, which is the use of trade barriers to protect local companies and their workers from foreign competition.

Governments have used two general kinds of trade barriers: tariff and nontariff barriers. A **tariff** is a direct tax on imported goods. Tariffs increase the cost of imported goods relative to that of domestic goods. The Indian import tax on raw and refined sugar is 25 to 40 percent.[5]

Nontariff barriers are nontax methods of increasing the cost or reducing the volume of imported goods. There are five types of nontariff barriers: quotas, voluntary export restraints, government import standards, government subsidies, and customs valuation/classification. Because there are so many different kinds of nontariff

Exhibit 8.2
U.S. Direct Foreign Investment Abroad

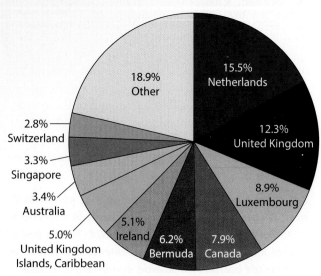

- 18.9% Other
- 15.5% Netherlands
- 12.3% United Kingdom
- 8.9% Luxembourg
- 7.9% Canada
- 6.2% Bermuda
- 5.1% Ireland
- 5.0% United Kingdom Islands, Caribbean
- 3.4% Australia
- 3.3% Singapore
- 2.8% Switzerland

Source: BEA News, "Direct Investment Positions for 2013 Now Available," *Bureau of Economic Analysis*, June 25, 2014, accessed May 5, 2015. http://bea.gov/international/di1usdbal.htm.

barriers, they can be an even more potent method of shielding domestic industries from foreign competition.

Quotas are specific limits on the number or volume of imported products. For example, the Chinese government only allows thirty-four imported movies each year. To get around the quota, films must be at least partially shot in China, co-financed by a Chinese firm, and have some Chinese cultural elements.[6]

Like quotas, **voluntary export restraints** limit the amount of a product that can be imported annually. The difference is that the exporting country rather than the importing country imposes restraints. Usually, however, the "voluntary" offer to limit exports occurs because the importing country has implicitly threatened to impose quotas. For example, to protect Brazilian auto manufacturers from less expensive Mexican-made cars, the Brazilian government convinced Mexico to "voluntarily" restrict auto exports to Brazil to no more than $1.55 billion a year for three years.[7] According to the World Trade Organization (see the discussion in Section 8-1c), however, voluntary export restraints are illegal and should not be used to restrict imports.[8]

In theory, **government import standards** are established to protect the health and safety of citizens. In reality, such standards are often used to restrict or ban imported goods. A 2014 U.S. law established elaborate safety standards for pangasius, a Vietnamese fish similar to the U.S. catfish. Vietnamese pangasius fish farmers must open their facilities to USDA inspectors, submit detailed sanitation plans, build inspection systems comparable to those in the United States, and submit their catfish for inspection before they leave Vietnam *and* again at U.S. ports of entry.[9] Lisa Wedding of the National Fisheries Institute says the new law, "is not about food safety and never has been."[10] She says, "For years there has been an ongoing attempt to block imports and thus stifle competition. The food-safety part of the equation is a charade."[11] Imports of pangasius increased from 7 million pounds in 2014 to 215 million pounds in 2014.

Many nations also use **subsidies**, such as long-term, low-interest loans, cash grants, and tax deferments, to develop and protect companies in special industries. As part of the 1934 Sugar Act and the 2008 Farm Bill, American sugar processors, who employ 142,000 people, receive government guaranteed loans and a government subsidized price of 21 cents per pound, roughly twice the price of sugar outside the United States Furthermore, when U.S. sugar producers aren't able to sell all of their sugar, the U.S. Department of Agriculture buys

it and then sells it at a loss to ethanol producers.[12] The Competitive Enterprise Institute estimates the annual cost of subsidies at $3.5 billion a year.[13] Phillip Hayes of the U.S. Sugar Alliance says, "Other countries subsidize their sugar industries." Indeed, Brazilian sugar processors, which provide half of the world's sugar, receive $2.5 billion a year in subsidies from their government.[14]

The last type of nontariff barrier is **customs classification**. As products are imported into a country, they are examined by customs agents, who must decide which of nearly 9,000 categories they should be classified into (see the Official Harmonized Tariff Schedule of the United States at www.usitc.gov /tata/hts/index.htm for more information). The category assigned by customs agents can greatly affect the size of the tariff and whether the item is subject to import quotas. For example, the U.S. Customs Service has several customs classifications for imported shoes. Tariffs on imported leather or "nonrubber" shoes are about 10 percent, whereas tariffs on imported rubber shoes, such as athletic footwear, range from 20 to 84 percent. The difference is large enough that some importers try to make their rubber shoes look like leather in hopes of receiving the nonrubber customs classification and lower tariff.

8-1c Trade Agreements

Thanks to the trade barriers described previously, buying imported goods has often been much more expensive and difficult than buying domestic goods. During the 1990s, however, the regulations governing global trade were transformed. The most significant change was that 124 countries agreed to adopt the **General Agreement on Tariffs and Trade (GATT)**. GATT, which existed from

Quota a limit on the number or volume of imported products

Voluntary export restraints voluntarily imposed limits on the number or volume of products exported to a particular country

Government import standard a standard ostensibly established to protect the health and safety of citizens but, in reality, is often used to restrict imports

Subsidies government loans, grants, and tax deferments given to domestic companies to protect them from foreign competition

Customs classification a classification assigned to imported products by government officials that affects the size of the tariff and the imposition of import quotas

General Agreement on Tariffs and Trade (GATT) a worldwide trade agreement that reduced and eliminated tariffs, limited government subsidies, and established protections for intellectual property

1947 to 1995, was an agreement to regulate trade among (eventually) more than 120 countries, the purpose of which was "substantial reduction of tariffs and other trade barriers and the elimination of preferences."[15] GATT members engaged in eight rounds of trade negotiations, with the Uruguay Round signed in 1994 and going into effect in 1995. Although GATT itself was replaced by the **World Trade Organization (WTO)** in 1995, the changes that it made continue to encourage international trade. Today, the WTO and its member countries are negotiating what's known as the Doha Round, which seeks to advance trade opportunities for developing countries in areas ranging from agriculture to services to intellectual property rights. The WTO, headquartered in Geneva, Switzerland, administers trade agreements, provides a forum for trade negotiations, handles trade disputes, monitors national trade policies, and offers technical assistance and training for developing countries for its 161 member countries.

Through tremendous decreases in tariff and nontariff barriers, the Uruguay round of GATT made it much easier and cheaper for consumers in all countries to buy foreign products. First, tariffs were cut 40 percent on average worldwide by 2005. Second, tariffs were eliminated in ten specific industries: beer, alcohol, construction equipment, farm machinery, furniture, medical equipment, paper, pharmaceuticals, steel, and toys. Third, stricter limits were put on government subsidies. For example, the Uruguay round of GATT put limits on how much national governments can subsidize private research in electronic and high-tech industries (see the discussion of subsidies in Section 8-1b). Fourth, the Uruguay round of GATT established protections for

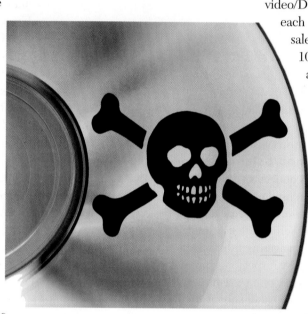

intellectual property, such as trademarks, patents, and copyrights.

Protection of intellectual property has become an increasingly important issue in global trade because of widespread product piracy. For example, the International Federation of the Phonographic Industry estimates that one-third of all Internet users download music from illegal access sites.[16] The Information Technology & Innovation Foundation found that 24 percent of global Internet traffic is used to download pirated music, movies, and other copyrighted content.[17] Likewise, according to BSA | The Software Alliance, 42 percent of all software used in the world is pirated, costing companies $63 billion in lost sales.[18]

Product piracy is also costly to the movie industry, as movie studios, distributors, and theaters, as well as video/DVD distributors, lose $18 billion each year to pirates. In fact, digital sales of movies rose 6 percent to 10 percent for two movie studios after Megaupload, an illegal site for downloading movies, was closed.[19]

Finally, trade disputes between countries now are fully settled by arbitration panels from the WTO. In the past, countries could use their veto power to cancel a panel's decision. For instance, the French government routinely vetoed rulings that its large cash grants to French farmers constituted unfair subsidies. Now, however, countries that are members of the WTO no longer have veto power. Thus, WTO rulings are complete and final. Exhibit 8.3 provides a brief overview of the WTO and its functions.

The second major development that has reduced trade barriers has been the creation of **regional trading zones**, or zones in which tariff and nontariff barriers are reduced or eliminated for countries within the trading zone. The largest and most important trading zones are in Europe (the Maastricht Treaty), North America (the North American Free Trade Agreement, or NAFTA), Central America (Dominican Republic-Central America Free Trade Agreement, or CAFTA-DR), South America (Union of South American Nations, or USAN), and Asia (the Association of Southeast Asian Nations, or ASEAN, and Asia-Pacific

World Trade Organization (WTO) the successor to GATT; the only international organization dealing with the global rules of trade between nations; its main function is to ensure that trade flows as smoothly, predictably, and freely as possible

Regional trading zones areas in which tariff and nontariff barriers on trade between countries are reduced or eliminated

Fabio Alcini/Shutterstock.com

Exhibit 8.3
World Trade Organization

☑ FACT FILE

WORLD TRADE
ORGANIZATION

Location: Geneva, Switzerland
Established: January 1, 1995
Created by: Uruguay Round
negotiations (1986–1994)
Membership: 161 countries
(on April 26, 2015)
Budget: 197 million Swiss
francs for 2013
Secretariat staff: 640
Head: Roberto Azevêdo
(Director-General)

Functions:
- Administering WTO trade agreements
- Forum for trade negotiations
- Handling trade disputes
- Monitoring national trade policies
- Technical assistance and training for developing countries
- Cooperation with other international organizations

Source: "Fact File: What Is the WTO?" *World Trade Organization*. https://www.wto.org/english/thewto_e/whatis_e/whatis_e.htm.

Economic Cooperation, or APEC). The map in Exhibit 8.4 shows the extent to which free-trade agreements govern global trade.

In 1992, Belgium, Denmark, France, Germany, Greece, Ireland, Italy, Luxembourg, the Netherlands, Portugal, Spain, and the United Kingdom adopted the **Maastricht Treaty of Europe**. The purpose of this treaty was to transform their twelve different economies and twelve currencies into one common economic market, called the European Union (EU), with one common currency. On January 1, 2002, a single common currency, the euro, went into circulation in twelve of the EU's members (Austria, Belgium, Finland, France, Germany, Greece, Ireland, Italy, Luxembourg, the Netherlands, Portugal, and Spain). Austria, Finland, and Sweden joined the EU in 1995, followed by Cyprus, the Czech Republic, Estonia, Hungary, Latvia, Lithuania, Malta, Poland, Slovakia, and Slovenia in 2004; Bulgaria and Romania in 2007; and Croatia in 2013, bringing the total membership to twenty-eight countries.[20] Macedonia, Iceland, Montenegro, Serbia, and Turkey have applied and are being considered for membership.

Prior to the treaty, trucks carrying products were stopped and inspected by customs agents at each border. Furthermore, because the required paperwork, tariffs, and government product specifications could be radically different in each country, companies often had to file twelve different sets of paperwork, pay twelve different tariffs, produce twelve different versions of their basic product to meet various government specifications, and exchange money in twelve different currencies. Likewise, open business travel, which we take for granted in the United States, was complicated by inspections at each border crossing. If you lived in Germany but worked in Luxembourg, your car was stopped and your passport was inspected twice every day as you traveled to and from work. Also, every business transaction required a currency exchange, for example, from German deutsche marks to Italian lira, or from French francs to Dutch guilders. Imagine all of this happening to millions of trucks, cars, and workers each day, and you can begin to appreciate the difficulty and cost of conducting business across Europe before the Maastricht Treaty. For more information about the Maastricht Treaty, the EU, and the euro, see http://europa.eu/index_en.htm.

NAFTA, the **North American Free Trade Agreement** among the United States, Canada, and Mexico, went into effect on January 1, 1994. More than any other regional trade agreement, NAFTA has liberalized trade between countries so that businesses can plan for one market (North America) rather than for three separate markets. One of NAFTA's most important achievements was to eliminate most product tariffs *and* prevent the three countries from increasing existing tariffs or introducing new ones. Overall, Mexican and Canadian exports to the United States are up 596 percent and 192 percent, respectively, since NAFTA went into effect. U.S. exports to Mexico and Canada are up 420 percent and 191 percent, growing twice as fast as U.S. exports to any other part of the world. In fact, Mexico and Canada now account for 32 percent of all U.S. exports.[21]

Maastricht Treaty of Europe a regional trade agreement among most European countries

North American Free Trade Agreement (NAFTA) a regional trade agreement among the United States, Canada, and Mexico

Exhibit 8.4
Global Map of Regional Trade Agreements

Maastricht Treaty of Europe Austria, Belgium, Bulgaria, Croatia, Cyprus, the Czech Republic, Denmark, Estonia, Finland, France, Germany, Greece, Hungary, Ireland, Italy, Latvia, Lithuania, Luxembourg, Malta, the Netherlands, Poland, Portugal, Romania, Slovakia, Slovenia, Spain, Sweden, and the United Kingdom.

ASEAN (Association of Southeast Asian Nations) Brunei Darussalam, Cambodia, Indonesia, Lao PDR, Myanmar, the Philippines, Singapore, Thailand, and Vietnam.

APEC (Asia-Pacific Economic Cooperation) Australia, Canada, Chile, the People's Republic of China, Hong Kong (China), Japan, Mexico, New Zealand, Papua New Guinea, Peru, Russia, South Korea, Taiwan, the United States, and all members of ASEAN except Cambodia, Lao PDR, and Myanmar.

NAFTA (North American Free Trade Agreement) Canada, Mexico, and the United States.

CAFTA-DR (Dominican Republic-Central American Free Trade Agreement) Costa Rica, the Dominican Republic, El Salvador, Guatemala, Honduras, Nicaragua, and the United States.

UNASUR (Union of South American Nations) Argentina, Bolivia, Brazil, Chile, Colombia, Ecuador, Guyana, Paraguay, Peru, Suriname, Uruguay, and Venezuela.

© Cengage Learning®

CAFTA-DR, the **Dominican Republic-Central America Free Trade Agreement** among the United States, the Dominican Republic, and the Central American countries of Costa Rica, El Salvador, Guatemala, Honduras, and Nicaragua, went into effect in August 2005. With a combined population of 51.1 million, the CAFTA-DR countries together are the twelfth-largest U.S. goods trading partner in the world and the third-largest U.S. export market in Latin America, after Mexico and Brazil. U.S. companies export nearly $30 billion in goods each year to the CAFTA-DR countries.[22]

On May 23, 2008, twelve South American countries signed the **Union of South American Nations (UNASUR)** Constitutive Treaty, which united the countries of the former Mercosur (Argentina, Brazil, Paraguay, Uruguay, and Venezuela) and the countries of the Andean Community (Bolivia, Colombia, Ecuador, and Peru) with Guyana, Suriname, and Chile. UNASUR aims to create a unified South America by permitting free movement between nations, creating a common infrastructure that includes an interoceanic highway, and establishing the region as a single market by eliminating all tariffs by 2019. UNASUR is one of the largest trading zones in the world, encompassing 361 million people in South America with a combined gross domestic product (GDP) of nearly $973 billion.[23]

Dominican Republic-Central America Free Trade Agreement (CAFTA-DR) a regional trade agreement among Costa Rica, the Dominican Republic, El Salvador, Guatemala, Honduras, Nicaragua, and the United States

Union of South American Nations (UNASUR) a regional trade agreement among Argentina, Brazil, Paraguay, Uruguay, Venezuela, Bolivia, Colombia, Ecuador, Peru, Guyana, Suriname, and Chile

ASEAN, the **Association of Southeast Asian Nations**, and **APEC**, the **Asia-Pacific Economic Cooperation**, are the two largest and most important regional trading groups in Asia. ASEAN is a trade agreement among Brunei Darussalam, Cambodia, Indonesia, Lao PDR, Malaysia, Myanmar, the Philippines, Singapore, Thailand, and Vietnam, which form a market of more than 616 million people with a combined GDP of $2.3 trillion.[24] U.S. trade with ASEAN countries exceeds $200 billion a year.

In fact, the United States is ASEAN's fourth-largest trading partner (China is its largest), and ASEAN's member nations constitute the fifth-largest trading partner of the United States. An ASEAN free-trade area will be established in 2015 for the six original countries (Brunei Darussalam, Indonesia, Malaysia, the Philippines, Singapore, and Thailand) and in 2018 for the newer member countries (Cambodia, Lao PDR, Myanmar, and Vietnam).[25]

APEC is a broad agreement that includes Australia, Canada, Chile, the People's Republic of China, Hong Kong, Japan, Mexico, New Zealand, Papua New Guinea, Peru, Russia, South Korea, Taiwan, the United States, and all the members of ASEAN except Cambodia, Lao PDR, and Myanmar. APEC's twenty-one member countries contain 2.79 billion people, account for 44 percent of all global trade, and have a combined GDP of over $41 trillion.[26]

APEC countries began reducing trade barriers in 2000, though all the reductions will not be completely phased in until 2020.[27]

8-1d Consumers, Trade Barriers, and Trade Agreements

The average worker earns nearly $48,820 in Finland, $61,710 in Sweden, $102,700 in Norway, and $53,470 in the United States.[28] Yet after adjusting these incomes for how much they can buy, the Finnish income is worth just $39,860, the Swedish $46,170, and the Norwegian $65,450.[29] This is the same as saying $1 of income can buy only $0.82 worth of goods in Finland, $0.75 in Sweden, and $0.64 in Norway. In other words, Americans can buy much more with their incomes than those in many other countries can.

One reason that Americans get more for their money is that the U.S. marketplace is the most competitive in the world and has been one of the easiest for foreign companies to enter.[30] Although some U.S. industries, such as textiles, have been heavily protected from foreign competition by trade barriers, for the most part, American consumers (and businesses) have had plentiful choices among American-made and foreign-made products. More important, the high level of competition between foreign and domestic companies that creates these choices helps keep prices low in the United States. Furthermore, it is precisely the lack of choice and the low level of competition that keep prices higher in countries that have not been as open to foreign companies and products. For example, Japanese trade barriers on agricultural products are high. In fact, over 45 percent of the value of Japan's agricultural industry comes from trade barriers or subsidies. The tariffs on rice alone amount to $8.4 billion in additional costs to Japanese consumers and taxpayers.[31]

So why do trade barriers and free-trade agreements matter to consumers? They're important because free-trade agreements increase choices, competition, and purchasing power and thus decrease what people pay for food, clothing, necessities, and luxuries. Accordingly, today's consumers rarely care where their products and services come from. From seafood to diamonds, people don't care where products are from—they just want to know which brand or kind is cheaper. And why do trade barriers and free-trade agreements matter to managers? The reason, as you're about to read, is that while free-trade agreements create new business opportunities, they also intensify competition, and addressing that competition is a manager's job.

8-2 CONSISTENCY OR ADAPTATION?

After a company has decided that it *will* go global, it must decide *how* to go global. For example, if you decide to sell in Singapore, should you try to find a local business partner who speaks the language, knows the laws, and understands the customs and norms of Singapore's culture? Or should you simply export your products from your home country? What do you do if you are also entering Eastern Europe, perhaps starting in Hungary? Should you use the same approach in Hungary that you use in Singapore?

Association of Southeast Asian Nations (ASEAN) a regional trade agreement among Brunei Darussalam, Cambodia, Indonesia, Laos, Malaysia, Myanmar, the Philippines, Singapore, Thailand, and Vietnam

Asia-Pacific Economic Cooperation (APEC) a regional trade agreement among Australia, Canada, Chile, the People's Republic of China, Hong Kong, Japan, Mexico, New Zealand, Papua New Guinea, Peru, Russia, South Korea, Taiwan, the United States, and all the members of ASEAN except Cambodia, Lao PDR, and Myanmar

In this section, we return to a key issue: How can you be sure that the way you run your business in one country is the right way to run that business in another? In other words, how can you strike the right balance between global consistency and local adaptation?

Global consistency means that a multinational company with offices, manufacturing plants, and distribution facilities in different countries uses the same rules, guidelines, policies, and procedures to run all of those offices, plants, and facilities. Managers at company headquarters value global consistency because it simplifies decisions. For example, rather than stock its new São Paulo, Brazil, store with apparel according to South American seasonality, **Ralph Lauren** followed the North American seasons, putting winter apparel on the shelves during the Brazilian summer.[32] By contrast, a company following a policy of **local adaptation** modifies its standard operating procedures to adapt to differences in foreign customers, governments, and regulatory agencies. For example, Netflix changed its production schedule in Europe to accommodate French and German preferences for voice dubbing, rather than subtitles. It also reworked its payment system to accept bank transfers instead of credit cards, which are unpopular in Germany. A Netflix spokesperson said, "Every market around the globe has its nuances. Our challenge is becoming a great global company where we really understand the nuances of each market and do a great job for consumers around the world."[33] Local adaptation is typically preferred by local managers who are charged with making the international business successful in their countries.

If companies lean too much toward global consistency, they run the risk of using management procedures poorly suited to particular countries' markets, cultures, and employees (that is a lack of local adaptation). Home Depot became the biggest hardware and home improvement retailer in the United States thanks to its big-box model featuring huge stores, thousands of suburban locations, a vast range of products, and strong customer service. But, after eight years, Home Depot closed its seven Chinese stores. Unlike Americans, who are do-it-yourselfers when it comes to home improvement because it saves money, the widespread availability of low-cost labor makes China more of a "do-it-for-me culture," says a Home Depot spokesperson. Furthermore, unlike the United States, where completing DIY projects is admired, there's a stigma associated with performing manual labor in China. A Chinese middle-class customer said, "Poor people are the only group in China who would bother taking on a DIY project because they cannot afford to hire others."[34] And, unlike in the United States, where a much higher percentage of people own their homes, most Chinese, especially those with the discretionary income to afford home projects, rent small apartments in cities, which further diminished Home Depot's opportunities in China.[35]

If, however, companies focus too much on local adaptation, they run the risk of losing the cost effectiveness and productivity that result from using standardized rules and procedures throughout the world. Because its French stores are nearly identical to its U.S. stores, Starbucks has never been profitable in France. As a result, says Parisian Marion Bayod, "I never go into Starbucks; it's impersonal, the coffee is mediocre, and it's expensive. For us, it's like another planet." Likewise, Parisian Laurent Pauzié says Starbucks stores, "are only here to comfort tourists when they're lost." Canadian Kate Menzies, who lives in Paris, concedes that while Starbucks may not be popular for its coffee, it "is one of the few places with public toilets and free WiFi in the city."[36] Starbucks, however, is now embracing local adaptation. Rather than offering strong coffee in paper cups as in the United States, its French stores will offer a lighter-tasting "blonde" espresso in glass coffee cups (because the French prefer to sit and drink) in larger redesigned stores with sumptuous wooden bars, bright chandeliers, and velvet couches, similar to traditional Parisian cafés. While Starbucks hopes these changes will attract French customers, spending tens of millions more to adapt its stores to French tastes may also sacrifice the cost effectiveness and productivity that make it profitable in the United States.[37]

Global consistency
when a multinational company has offices, manufacturing plants, and distribution facilities in different countries and runs them all using the same rules, guidelines, policies, and procedures

Local adaptation modifying rules, guidelines, policies, and procedures to adapt to differences in foreign customers, governments, and regulatory agencies

A Company That Exports Companies

Export Now, founded by former U.S. Ambassador to Singapore Frank Lavin, specializes in exports. The Ohio-based company doesn't sell anything, however. Instead, it sets up an infrastructure that other companies can use for exports. For an annual fee and a percentage of sales, Export Now will handle all of the customs and legal issues involved in exporting and provide an online retail space for their customers' products. According to Lavin, his service allows clients to avoid wholesalers, middlemen, or distributors, meaning that they can charge consumers in China the same prices they do in the United States. So far, the items available on Export Now's virtual mall include Osprey backpacks, singing toothbrushes from Brush Buddies, and hearing aid products from McKeon Products.

Source: N. Leiber, "Ex-U.S. Ambassador Helps Companies Break into China," *Bloomberg Businessweek*, September 13, 2012, accessed June 10, 2013. http://www.businessweek.com/articles/2012-08-23/making-it-easier-to-sell-made-in-usa-in-china.

8-3 FORMS FOR GLOBAL BUSINESS

Besides determining whether to adapt organizational policies and procedures, a company must also determine how to organize itself for successful entry into foreign markets.

Historically, companies have generally followed the phase model of globalization, in which a company makes the transition from a domestic company to a global company in the following sequential phases: 8-3a exporting, 8-3b cooperative contracts, 8-3c strategic alliances, and 8-3d wholly owned affiliates. At each step, the company grows much larger, uses those resources to enter more global markets, is less dependent on home-country sales, and is more committed in its orientation to global business. Some companies, however, do not follow the phase model of globalization. Some skip phases on their way to becoming more global and less domestic. Others don't follow the phase model at all. These are known as 8-3e global new ventures. This section reviews these forms of global business.[38]

8-3a Exporting

When companies produce products in their home countries and sell those products to customers in foreign countries, they are **exporting**. Exporting as a form of global business offers many advantages. It makes the company less dependent on sales in its home market and provides a greater degree of control over research, design, and production decisions. **Cayuga Milk Ingredients** built a $100 million factory in New York to serve domestic customers. However, 79 percent of the plant's milk production is exported to Mexico and Saudi Arabia. CEO Kevin Ellis says, "We can't go back from the international market. There aren't enough people to consume [dairy products] in this country."[39] Today, 16 percent of U.S. milk production is exported. Over the past decade, the U.S.share of global dairy exports has risen from 7 to 20 percent.[40] Though advantageous in a number of ways, exporting also has its disadvantages. The primary disadvantage is that many exported goods are subject to tariff and nontariff barriers that can substantially increase their final cost to consumers. A second disadvantage is that transportation costs can significantly increase the price of an exported product. There is a third disadvantage of exporting: companies that export depend on foreign importers for product distribution. If, for example, the foreign importer makes a mistake on the paperwork that accompanies a shipment of imported goods, those goods can be returned to the foreign manufacturer at the manufacturer's expense.

8-3b Cooperative Contracts

When an organization wants to expand its business globally without making a large financial commitment to do so, it may sign a **cooperative contract** with a foreign business owner who pays the company a fee for the right to conduct that business in his or her country. There are two kinds of cooperative contracts: licensing and franchising.

Under a **licensing** agreement, a domestic company, the *licensor*, receives royalty payments for allowing another company, the *licensee*, to produce its product, sell its service, or use its brand name in a particular foreign market. For example, in Turkey, *Desperate Women*, a Turkish adaptation of *Desperate Housewives*, is produced by MBC Group (the licensee)

Exporting selling domestically produced products to customers in foreign countries

Cooperative contract an agreement in which a foreign business owner pays a company a fee for the right to conduct that business in his or her country

Licensing an agreement in which a domestic company, the licensor, receives royalty payments for allowing another company, the licensee, to produce the licensor's product, sell its service, or use its brand name in a specified foreign market

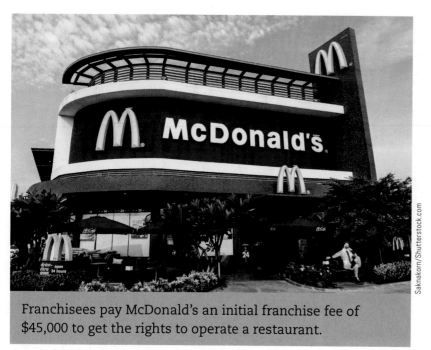

Franchisees pay McDonald's an initial franchise fee of $45,000 to get the rights to operate a restaurant.

under a license from the Walt Disney Company (the licensor), which owns ABC, the network that produced *Desperate Housewives*. Similar licensing agreements are behind *Married with Children* being remade and adapted with local actors in twelve countries and *Glee* being remade and broadcast in China with Chinese actors.[41] Forty percent of the revenue generated by popular television shows comes from foreign broadcast licenses.[42]

One of the most important advantages of licensing is that it allows companies to earn additional profits without investing more money. As foreign sales increase, the royalties paid to the licensor by the foreign licensee increase. Moreover, the licensee, not the licensor, invests in production equipment and facilities to produce the product. Licensing also helps companies avoid tariff and nontariff barriers. Because the licensee manufactures the product within the foreign country, tariff and nontariff barriers don't apply.

The biggest disadvantage associated with licensing is that the licensor gives up control over the quality of the product or service sold by the foreign licensee. Unless the licensing agreement contains specific restrictions, the licensee controls the entire business from production to marketing to final sales. Many licensors include inspection clauses in their

license contracts, but closely monitoring product or service quality from thousands of miles away can be difficult. An additional disadvantage is that licensees can eventually become competitors, especially when a licensing agreement includes access to important technology or proprietary business knowledge.

A **franchise** is a collection of networked firms in which the manufacturer or marketer of a product or service, the *franchisor*, licenses the entire business to another person or organization, the *franchisee*. For the price of an initial franchise fee plus royalties, franchisors provide franchisees with training, assistance with marketing and advertising, and an exclusive right to conduct business in a particular location. Most franchise fees run between $5,000 and $35,000. Franchisees pay McDonald's, one of the largest franchisors in the world, an initial franchise fee of $45,000. Another $1,000,708 to $2,335,146 is needed beyond that to pay for food inventory, kitchen equipment, construction, landscaping, and other expenses (the cost varies by location). While franchisees typically borrow part of this cost from a bank, McDonald's requires applicants to have over $750,000 in nonborrowed assets and requires a 40 percent down payment in cash for the initial investment.[43] Typical royalties are around 8.5 percent of gross sales, but sometimes they go as high as 12 percent.[44] So franchisors are well rewarded for the help they provide to franchisees. More than 400 U.S. companies franchise their businesses to foreign franchise partners.

Despite franchising's many advantages, franchisors face a loss of control when they sell businesses to franchisees who are thousands of miles away. Franchising specialist Cheryl Scott says, "One franchisor I know was wondering why the royalties coming from India were so small when he knew the shop was always packed. It was because the franchisee wasn't putting all of the sales through the cash register."[45]

Although there are exceptions, franchising success may be somewhat culture-bound. Because most global franchisors begin by franchising their businesses in similar countries or regions (Canada is by far the first choice for U.S. companies taking their first step into global franchising), and because 65 percent of franchisors make absolutely no change in their business for overseas franchisees, that success may not generalize to cultures with different lifestyles, values, preferences, and technological infrastructures. Customizing menus to local tastes is one of the primary ways that fast-food companies can succeed in international markets. Dunkin' Donuts struggled at first in India with its traditional coffee and donuts menu because Indians don't eat sweets for breakfast, which they eat at home with their families. Dunkin' adjusted by changing store schedules to afternoon and evening hours and creating a new menu featuring non-beef burgers, sandwiches, and wraps using potatoes, pepper chicken, and spicy vegetables as ingredients. It also customized its donut menu to local tastes, adding donuts with curry, pistachios, and rice pudding. Two new menu items are the Brute Tough Guy Veg burger and the It's a Mistake donut, a white-chocolate donut topped with guava and chili.[46]

8-3c Strategic Alliances

Companies forming **strategic alliances** combine key resources, costs, risks, technology, and people. Hewlett-Packard, the world's largest electronics manufacturer, with a 28 percent share of the computer server market, and Foxconn, the Taiwanese firm that assembles some of the world's most popular electronic devices, such as the iPhone and iPad, have formed a strategic alliance to co-develop large servers that can handle cloud computing and process "big data" for multinational firms.[47] The most common strategic alliance is a **joint venture**, which occurs when two existing companies collaborate to form a third company. The two founding companies remain intact and

In 2014, Kroger purchased Tesco's interest in Dunhumby and launched it's own market research division.

unchanged, except that together they now own the newly created joint venture.

One of the advantages of global joint ventures is that, like licensing and franchising, they help companies avoid tariff and nontariff barriers to entry. Another advantage is that companies participating in a joint venture bear only part of the costs and the risks of that business. Many companies find this attractive because of the expense of entering foreign markets or developing new products.

Global joint ventures can be especially advantageous to smaller local partners who link up with larger, more experienced foreign firms that can bring advanced management, resources, and business skills to the joint venture.

Global joint ventures are not without problems, though. Because companies share costs and risks with their joint venture partners, they must also share profits. Managing global joint ventures can also be difficult because they represent a merging of four cultures: the country and the organizational culture of the first partner, and the country and the organizational culture of the second partner. Often, to be fair to all involved, each partner in the global joint venture will have equal ownership and power. But this can result in power struggles and a lack of leadership. Because of these problems, companies forming global joint ventures should carefully develop detailed contracts that specify the obligations of each party. U.S.-based **Kroger** supermarkets and UK consumer research firm **dunnhumby** (owned by UK supermarket chain **Tesco**) were fifty-fifty partners in dunnhumby USA for twelve years. The joint venture helped Kroger build customized marketing programs that resulted in a huge advantage over its competitors and forty-five straight quarters of growth. When Tesco needed cash after losing $9.52 billion in 2014, Kroger bought Tesco's interest in dunnhumby USA, ending the global joint venture. Kroger then launched 84.51°, which is its own consumer research division.[48]

8-3d Wholly Owned Affiliates (Build or Buy)

Approximately one-third of multinational companies enter foreign markets through wholly owned affiliates. In 2013, Japan-based Lixil, a maker of household kitchen and bathroom products, entered

Strategic alliance an agreement in which companies combine key resources, costs, risks, technology, and people

Joint venture a strategic alliance in which two existing companies collaborate to form a third, independent company the North American and European markets by purchasing two long-established companies, American Standard Brands, a U.S.-based maker of toilets, as well as bathroom and kitchen fixtures, and Germany's GROHE Group, a maker of luxury bathroom and kitchen metal fittings.[49] Unlike licensing arrangements, franchises, or joint ventures, **wholly owned affiliates**, such as American Standard Brands and GROHE, are 100 percent owned by their parent company, in this case, Lixil.

The primary advantage of wholly owned businesses is that the parent company receives all of the profits and has complete control over the foreign facilities. The biggest disadvantage is the expense of building new operations or buying existing businesses. Although the payoff can be enormous if wholly owned affiliates succeed, the losses can be immense if they fail because the parent company assumes all of the risk. London-based Standard Chartered PLC is a banking and financial services company with 87,000 employees who work at branches in seventy countries. Ninety percent of its business comes from its wholly owned affiliates in Africa, the Middle East, and Asia. While still profitable overall, Standard Chartered lost $200 million last year at its South Korean units, which are now being sold at a sizable loss to a Japanese bank.[50]

8-3e Global New Ventures

Companies used to evolve slowly from small operations selling in their home markets to large businesses selling to foreign markets. Furthermore, as companies went global, they usually followed the phase model of globalization. Recently, however, three trends have combined to allow companies to skip the phase model when going global. First, quick, reliable air travel can transport people to nearly any point in the world within one day.

M. Unal Ozmen/Shutterstock.com

Second, low-cost communication technologies such as email, teleconferencing and phone conferencing via the Internet, and cloud computing make it easier to communicate with global customers, suppliers, managers, and employees. Third, there is now a critical mass of businesspeople with extensive personal experience in all aspects of global business.[51] This combination of developments has made it possible to start companies that are global from inception. With sales, employees, and financing in different countries, **global new ventures** are companies that are founded with an active global strategy.[52]

Although there are several different kinds of global new ventures, all share two common factors. First, the company founders successfully develop and communicate the company's global vision from inception. Second, rather than going global one country at a time, new global ventures bring a product or service to market in several foreign markets at the same time. **MakerBot** 3-D printers "print" items made of rigid plastic based on specifications from computer-aided design software such as AutoDesk. NASA's Jet Propulsion Laboratory uses MakerBot's Replicator 2 (hat tip to *Star Trek*) to print prototype parts cheaply and quickly. Cofounder Bre Pettis believes that MakerBot can fundamentally disrupt global manufacturing and replace "two centuries of mass production" by giving anyone with an idea the tools to design his or her own products without a factory. Though just five years old, MakerBot, which has been global since inception, has distributors in fourteen countries, including Australia, Brazil, China, Germany, Japan, and the United Kingdom.[53]

8-4 FINDING THE BEST BUSINESS CLIMATE

When deciding where to go global, companies try to find countries or regions with promising business climates.

An attractive global business climate 8-4a positions the company for easy access to growing markets, 8-4b is an effective but cost-efficient place to build an office or manufacturing facility, and 8-4c minimizes the political risk to the company.

Wholly owned affiliates foreign offices, facilities, and manufacturing plants that are 100 percent owned by the parent company

Global new ventures new companies that are founded with an active global strategy and have sales, employees, and financing in different countries

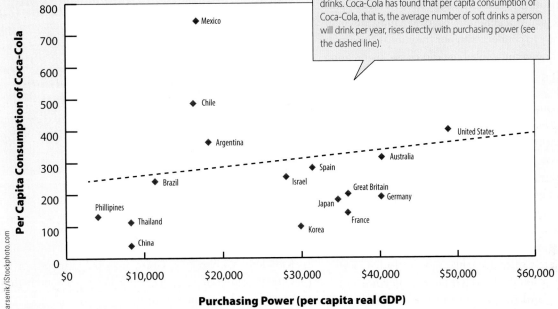

Exhibit 8.5
How Consumption of Coca-Cola Varies with Purchasing Power Around the World

Typically, the higher the purchasing power in a country, the better that country will be for doing business. Why? Because higher purchasing power means that consumers have more money to spend on nonessential products, such as soft drinks. Coca-Cola has found that per capita consumption of Coca-Cola, that is, the average number of soft drinks a person will drink per year, rises directly with purchasing power (see the dashed line).

Per Capita Consumption of Coca-Cola

Purchasing Power (per capita real GDP)

Mexico · Chile · Argentina · United States · Spain · Brazil · Israel · Australia · Great Britain · Japan · Germany · France · Phillipines · Thailand · Korea · China

Sources: "Coca-Cola 2012 Annual Review," *Coca-Cola Company*, accessed June 10, 2013. http://www.coca-colacompany.com/annual-review/2012/year_in_review .html; "GNI Per Capita Ranking, Atlas Method and PPP Based," *The World Bank*, April 15, 2013, accessed June 10, 2013. http://data.worldbank.org/data-catalog /GNI-per-capita-Atlas-and-PPP-table.

arsenik/iStockphoto.com

8-4a Growing Markets

The most important factor in an attractive business climate is access to a growing market. For example, no product is known and purchased by as many people throughout the world as Coca-Cola. Yet even Coke, which is available in more than 200 countries, still has tremendous potential for further global growth. Coca-Cola gets 80 percent of its sales outside of North America, and emerging markets, where it has seen its fastest growth, now account for half of Coke's sales worldwide.[54]

Two factors help companies determine the growth potential of foreign markets: purchasing power and foreign competitors. **Purchasing power** is measured by comparing the relative cost of a standard set of goods and services in different countries. For example, a twenty-ounce Coke costs $5.06 in Oslo, Norway. Because that same twenty-ounce Coke costs only $1.75 in the United States, the average American has more purchasing power than the average Norwegian.[55] Purchasing power is growing in countries such as India and China, which

have low average levels of income. This is because basic living expenses such as food, shelter, and transportation are very inexpensive in those countries, so consumers still have money to spend after paying for necessities, especially as salaries increase thanks to demand from international trade (see box "Paying for a 'Mac Attack'").

Consequently, countries with high and growing levels of purchasing power are good choices for companies looking for attractive global markets. As Exhibit 8.5 shows, Coke has found that the per capita consumption of Coca-Cola, or the number of Cokes a person drinks per year, rises directly with purchasing power. For example, in China, Brazil, and Australia, where the average person earns, respectively, $11,850, $14,750 and $42,110 annually, the number of Coca-Cola soft drinks consumed per year increases, respectively, from 39 to 241 to 315. The more purchasing power people have, the more likely they are to purchase soft drinks. And the Coca-Cola Company expects strong growth

Purchasing power the relative cost of a standard set of goods and services in different countries to continue in these markets, stating in its annual report, "To measure our growth potential, we look to our per capita consumption—the average number of eight-ounce servings of our beverages consumed each year in a given market. It is predicted that by the year 2020, the world will have nearly 1 billion more people whose disposable incomes will afford them choices and opportunities unthinkable a generation ago. We must discover innovative ways to connect with our traditional consumer base and this emerging global middle class—by creating new products and packaging formats for all lifestyles and occasions."[56]

The second part of assessing the growth potential of global markets involves analyzing the degree of global competition, which is determined by the number and quality of companies that already compete in a foreign market. As the Tata-Starbucks joint venture begins opening stores in India, one of its primary competitors is Café Coffee Day, India's most popular coffee chain, which in the past few years has grown from a dozen stores to more than 1,200 locations in 175 cities. Café Coffee Day, like most of India's coffee shops, charges about $1 for a small cappuccino, which is about one-third the cost of the same drink in U.S. stores. By contrast, Starbucks plans to focus on selling premium coffee, tea, and food.[57]

8-4b Choosing an Office/Manufacturing Location

Companies do not have to establish an office or manufacturing location in each country they enter. They can license, franchise, or export to foreign markets, or they can serve a larger region from one country. But there are many reasons why a company might choose to establish a location in a foreign country. Some foreign offices are established through global mergers and acquisitions, and some are established because of a commitment to grow in a new market. Chinese-owned **Volvo Car** is building a $500 million factory in the United States to take advantage of the low cost of labor; avoid exchange rate fluctuations, which affect cars imported into the United States from other countries; and to fulfill its commitment to grow its U.S. sales.[58] CEO Håkan Samuelsson said, "Volvo Cars cannot claim to be a true global carmaker without an industrial presence in the U.S. The U.S. is an absolutely crucial part of our global transformation."[59]

Other companies choose locations by seeking a tax haven (although this is more difficult for U.S. companies due to legal concerns) or as part of creating a global brand. Ireland is a popular location to establish a

Volvo is builing a $500 million factory in the United States, to take advantage of the low cost of labor.

Ed Aldridge/Shutterstock.com

company headquarters because of its corporate tax rate of 12.5 percent, which is much lower than the United Kingdom (25 percent), Germany (30.2 percent), or the United States (35 percent), which has the second highest corporate tax rate in the world.[60]

The criteria for choosing an office/manufacturing location are different from the criteria for entering a foreign market. Rather than focusing on costs alone, companies should consider both qualitative and quantitative factors. Two key qualitative factors are workforce quality and company strategy. Workforce quality is important because it is often difficult to find workers with the specific skills, abilities, and experience that a company needs to run its business. Workforce quality is one reason that many companies doing business in Europe locate their customer call centers in the Netherlands. Workers in the Netherlands are the most linguistically gifted in Europe, with 77 percent trilingual (speaking Dutch, English, and a third language) and 90 percent bilingual (Dutch and English). Comparable numbers across Europe are 25 percent and 54 percent.[61] Furthermore, compared to sixty countries worldwide, the Netherlands ranks fourth in terms of the supply of skilled labor, tenth for workers with financial skills, and second for competent managers (the United States ranks fifteenth, seventh, and fifth).[62]

A company's strategy is also important when choosing a location. For example, a company pursuing a low-cost strategy may need plentiful raw materials, low-cost transportation, and low-cost labor. A company pursuing a differentiation strategy (typically a higher-priced, better product or service) may need access to high-quality materials and a highly skilled and educated workforce.

Paying for a "Mac Attack"

Every year, The Economist magazine produces the Big Mac Index to illustrate differences in purchasing power across countries. By comparing the price of a single item, in this case, a Big Mac from McDonald's, the index shows how much (or how little) consumers in each country get for their money. According to the latest index, a Big Mac costs an average of $4.62 in the United States, $5.01 in Canada, $5.25 in Brazil, and $7.14 in Switzerland, meaning that residents of those countries get far less for their money than U.S. residents do. Conversely, consumers in Russia only have to pay $2.62 for their Big Mac, while consumers in Turkey pay $3.76 and consumers in India pay only $1.54.

Source: "The Big Mac Index," *Economist*, January 23, 2014, accessed April 29, 2014. http://www.economist.com/content/big-mac-index.

Quantitative factors such as the kind of facility being built, tariff and nontariff barriers, exchange rates, and transportation and labor costs should also be considered when choosing an office/manufacturing location. A real estate specialist in company location decisions explains how things change with different types of facility: "If it's an assembly plant, a company might be inclined to look for incentives that would subsidize its hiring. With a distribution facility, an adequate transportation network will likely be critical. A corporate headquarters will need a good communications network, a multilingual labor force, and easy access by air. On the other hand, a research and development operation will require proximity to a high-tech infrastructure and access to good universities."[63] Companies rely on studies such as FM Global's annually published "Resilience Index" to compare business climates throughout the world.[64] Exhibit 8.6 offers a quick overview of the best cities for business based on a variety of criteria. This information is a good starting point if your company is trying to decide where to put an international office or manufacturing plant.

8-4c Minimizing Political Risk

When managers think about political risk in global business, they envision burning factories and riots in the streets. Although political events such as these receive dramatic and extended coverage in the media, the political risks that most companies face usually are not covered as breaking stories on Fox News or CNN. Nonetheless, the negative consequences of ordinary political risk can be just as devastating to companies that fail to identify and minimize that risk.[65]

When conducting global business, companies should attempt to identify two types of political risk: political uncertainty and policy uncertainty.[66] **Political uncertainty** is associated with the risk of major changes in political regimes that can result from war, revolution, death of political leaders, social unrest, or other influential events. **Policy uncertainty** refers to the risk associated with changes in laws and government policies that directly affect the way foreign companies conduct business.

Policy uncertainty is the most common—and perhaps most frustrating—form of political risk in global business, especially when changes in laws and government policies directly undercut sizable investments made by foreign companies. India is the third-largest retail market in the world behind the United States and China. The Indian government has long protected Indian retail stores by preventing foreign retailers from entering India unless they had a joint venture partner. So when India changed that policy, global retailers such as Walmart (United States), Carrefour (France), and Tesco (United Kingdom) began making plans to enter India on their own. The Indian government, however, reversed that decision following large protests

Political uncertainty the risk of major changes in political regimes that can result from war, revolution, death of political leaders, social unrest, or other influential events

Policy uncertainty the risk associated with changes in laws and government policies that directly affect the way foreign companies conduct business

Exhibit 8.6
World's Best Countries for Business

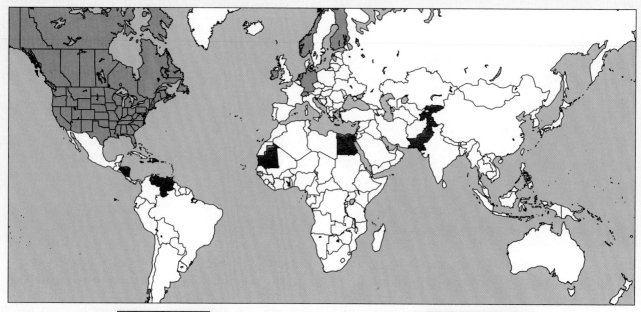

Top 10 Countries				Worst 10 Countries			
1.	Norway	6.	Germany	1.	Tajikistan	6.	Dominican Republic
2.	Switzerland	7.	Qatar	2.	Egypt	7.	Nicaragua
3.	The Netherlands	8.	Canada	3.	Pakistan	8.	Mauritania
4.	Ireland	9.	Finland	4.	Jamaica	9.	Kyrgyz Republic
5.	Luxembourg	10.	United States	5.	Honduras	10.	Venezuela

Sources: S. Adams, "2015's Most and Least Reliable Countries to Do Business In," *Forbes*, March 31, 2015, accessed April 28, 2015. http://www.forbes.com/sites /susanadams/2015/03/31/2015s-most-and-least-reliable-countries-to-do-business-in/; "Table 1: The Top 10 in 2015," Resilience Index 2015, *FM Global*. http://www .fmglobal.com/assets/pdf/Resilience_Methodology.pdf, p. 5; "Table 2: The Bottom 10 in 2015," Resilience Index 2015, *FM Global*. http://www.fmglobal.com/assets/pdf /Resilience_Methodology.pdf, p. 5.

from small-business owners and politicians who feared that huge retail stores would put locally owned mom-and-pop shops out of business. Kamlesh Gupta and her husband own such a shop, the Radha Krisna Store in Central Delhi. She said that if large retailers are allowed into India, "Everything will be over. If they sell goods cheaper than us, who will come here? Already, we have lost 20 percent of our business since Big Bazaar and Reliance [two other Indian retailers] started operating in the last two years." As a result, the only option for foreign retailers such as Walmart, and it's not an attractive one, is to form joint ventures to establish "cash-and-carry" stores that sell to businesses but not consumers.[67]

Several strategies can be used to minimize or adapt to the political risk inherent in global business. An *avoidance strategy* is used when the political risks associated with a foreign country or region are viewed as too great. If firms are already invested in high-risk areas, they may divest or sell their businesses.

If they have not yet invested, they will likely postpone their investment until the risk shrinks. Russia is an attractive market for automakers because it has a growing middle class but ranks fifty-seventh worldwide in terms of the number of cars per 1,000 people (just 300). With the potential of a growing market, General Motors opened a manufacturing facility in St. Petersburg in 2008 to produce 98,000 cars a year. Four years later, GM was hoping to double production capacity. But by 2015, the Russian car market was shrinking and amid increasingly business-unfriendly regulations, GM closed the plant, taking a $600 million writeoff.[68] GM's president, Daniel Ammann, said, "This decision avoids significant investment into a market that has very challenging long-term prospects."[69]

Exhibit 8.7 shows the long-term political stability of various countries in the Middle East (higher scores indicate less political risk). The following factors, which were used to compile these ratings, indicate greater political

Exhibit 8.7
Overview of Political Risk in the Middle East

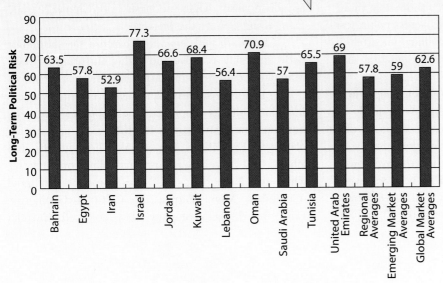

Higher scores indicate less long-term political risk, which is calculated by estimating government instability, socioeconomic conditions, internal or external conflicts, military involvement in politics, religious and ethnic tensions, foreign debt as a percent of gross domestic product, exchange rate instability, and whether there is high inflation.

Bahrain 63.5, Egypt 57.8, Iran 52.9, Israel 77.3, Jordan 66.6, Kuwait 68.4, Lebanon 56.4, Oman 70.9, Saudi Arabia 57, Tunisia 65.5, United Arab Emirates 69, Regional Averages 57.8, Emerging Market Averages 59, Global Market Averages 62.6

Source: "United Arab Emirates Business Forecast Report, 2014 2nd Quarter," *Business Monitor International*, April 1, 2014, 1–50.

risk: government instability, poor socioeconomic conditions, internal or external conflict, military involvement in politics, religious and ethnic tensions, high foreign debt as a percentage of GDP, exchange rate instability, and high inflation.[70] An avoidance strategy would likely be used for the riskiest countries shown in Exhibit 8.7, such as Iran and Saudi Arabia, but might not be needed for the less risky countries, such as Israel or Oman. Risk conditions and factors change, so be sure to make risk decisions with the latest available information from resources such as the PRS Group (www.prsgroup.com), which supplies information about political risk to 80 percent of *Fortune* 500 companies.

Control is an active strategy to prevent or reduce political risks. Firms using a control strategy lobby foreign governments or international trade agencies to change laws, regulations, or trade barriers that hurt their business in that country. Seattle-based Amazon.com, the world's largest Internet retailer, is lobbying the Indian government to change laws that prevent foreign companies from selling directly to Indian consumers. Today, Indian consumers use Amazon's Junglee.com to compare prices, but it only links to Indian retailers. Ankur Bisen

of Technopak, an Indian-based retail consulting firm, says, "Amazon's intent in launching Junglee.com was to have a presence in the Indian market till rules are changed to allow them to do business here." Amazon is eager to expand in India, where retail Internet sales are predicted to increase from $600 million today to $70 billion in 2020.[71]

Another method for dealing with political risk is *cooperation*, which involves using joint ventures and collaborative contracts, such as franchising and licensing. Although cooperation does not eliminate the political risk of doing business in a country, it can limit the risk associated with foreign ownership of a business. For example, a German company forming a joint venture with a Chinese company to do business in China may structure the joint venture contract so that the Chinese company owns 51 percent or more of the joint venture. Doing so qualifies the joint venture as a Chinese company and exempts it from Chinese laws that apply to foreign-owned businesses. However, cooperation cannot always protect against *policy risk* if a foreign government changes its laws and policies to directly affect the way foreign companies conduct business.

 8-5

BECOMING AWARE OF CULTURAL DIFFERENCES

National culture is the set of shared values and beliefs that affects the perceptions, decisions, and behavior of the people from a particular country. The first step in dealing with culture is to recognize that

> **National culture** the set of shared values and beliefs that affects the perceptions, decisions, and behavior of the people from a particular country

there are meaningful differences. In recent years, Indian companies have targeted a group of mid-sized, independent, often family-owned, German companies (called Mittlestand) for acquisition. When Rail.One GmbH was acquired by PCM Group, an Indian conglomerate, the new owners didn't change the Bavarian management because, says PCM Chairman Kamal Mittal, "We didn't want to disturb the business."[72] Professor Geert Hofstede spent twenty years studying cultural differences in fifty-three different countries. His research shows that there are six consistent cultural dimensions across countries: power distance, individualism, masculinity, uncertainty avoidance, short-term versus long-term orientation, and indulgence versus restraint.[73]

Power distance is the extent to which people in a country accept that power is distributed unequally in society and organizations. In countries where power distance is weak, such as Denmark and Sweden, employees don't like their organization or their boss to have power over them or tell them what to do. They want to have a say in decisions that affect them. As Exhibit 8.8 shows, Russia, China and Nigeria, with scores of 93, 80, and 80,

respectively, are much stronger in power distance than Germany (35), the Netherlands (38), and the United States (40).

Individualism is the degree to which societies believe that individuals should be self-sufficient. In individualistic societies, employees put loyalty to themselves first and loyalty to their company and work group second. In Exhibit 8.8, the United States (91), the Netherlands (80), France (71), and Germany (67) are the strongest in individualism, while Indonesia (14), China (20), and Hong Kong (25) are the weakest.

Masculinity and *femininity* capture the difference between highly assertive and highly nurturing cultures. Masculine cultures emphasize assertiveness, competition, material success, and achievement, whereas feminine cultures emphasize the importance of relationships, modesty, caring for the weak, and quality of life. In Exhibit 8.8, Japan (95), Germany (66), and China (66) have the most masculine orientations, while the Netherlands (14) has the most feminine orientation. Manu Parpia, the CEO of Geometric, Ltd., the Indian company that acquired German

Exhibit 8.8
Hofstede's Six Cultural Dimensions

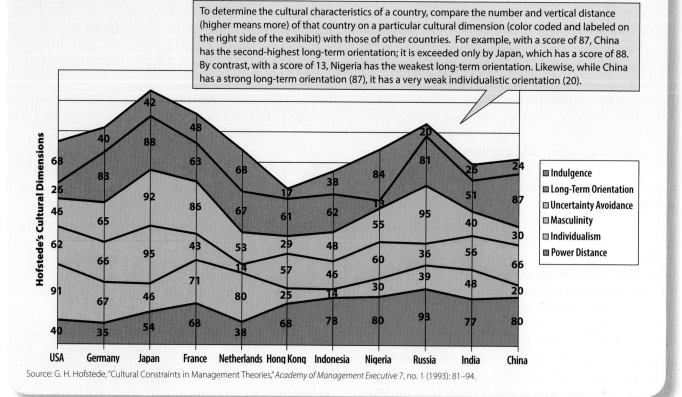

To determine the cultural characteristics of a country, compare the number and vertical distance (higher means more) of that country on a particular cultural dimension (color coded and labeled on the right side of the exihibit) with those of other countries. For example, with a score of 87, China has the second-highest long-term orientation; it is exceeded only by Japan, which has a score of 88. By contrast, with a score of 13, Nigeria has the weakest long-term orientation. Likewise, while China has a strong long-term orientation (87), it has a very weak individualistic orientation (20).

Source: G. H. Hofstede, "Cultural Constraints in Management Theories," *Academy of Management Executive* 7, no. 1 (1993): 81–94.

engineering company 3Cap, noted that, compared to India, "German culture is more precise, very process oriented [and] quite blunt. The emphasis on process in India is much lower, because if you focused on process, nothing would get done."[74]

The cultural difference of *uncertainty avoidance* is the degree to which people in a country are uncomfortable with unstructured, ambiguous, unpredictable situations. In countries with strong uncertainty avoidance, such as Greece and Portugal, people tend to be aggressive and emotional and seek security rather than uncertainty. In Exhibit 8.8, Russia (95), Japan (92), and France (86) are strongest in uncertainty avoidance, while Hong Kong (29) and China (30) are the weakest. Rail.One CEO Jochen Riepl has noticed this dimension playing itself out during meetings with PCM officials. "In India, a 'no' is a kind of invitation to start a discussion. In Germany, a 'no' is a 'no,'" he says.[75]

The cultural dimension of *short-term/long-term orientation* addresses whether cultures are oriented to the present and seek immediate gratification or to the future and defer gratification. Not surprisingly, countries with short-term orientations are consumer-driven, whereas countries with long-term orientations are savings-driven. In Exhibit 8.8, Japan (88) and China (87) have very strong long-term orientations, while Nigeria (13) and the United States (26), have very strong short-term orientations. The cultural dimension of *indulgence versus restraint* addresses the degree to which a society allows relatively free gratification of basic drives related to enjoying life and having fun versus strict social norms that regulate and suppress gratification of needs and wants. Nigeria (81), the United States (68), and the Netherlands (68) are strongest in indulgence, while Hong Kong (17), Russia (20), and China (24) practice the most restraint. Part of what makes Mittelstand companies comfortable with new Indian owners is that Indian bidders usually offer long-term commitments. Attorney Christopher Wright says of Indian investors, "They tend to have a long-term vision and [that] gives German companies some assurance."[76]

To generate a graphical comparison of two different countries' cultures, go to http://geert-hofstede.com/countries.html. Select a "Country" from the drop-down list, and then select a "Comparison Country." A graph comparing the countries on each of Hofstede's six cultural differences will be generated automatically.

Cultural differences affect perceptions, understanding, and behavior. Recognizing cultural differences is critical to succeeding in global business. Nevertheless, as Hofstede pointed out, descriptions of cultural differences are based on averages—the average level of uncertainty avoidance in Portugal, the average level of power distance in Argentina, and so forth. Accordingly, says Hofstede, "If you are going to spend time with a Japanese colleague, you shouldn't assume that overall cultural statements about Japanese society automatically apply to this person."[77] Similarly, cultural beliefs may differ significantly from one part of a country to another.[78]

After becoming aware of cultural differences, the second step is deciding how to adapt your company to those differences. Unfortunately, studies investigating the effects of cultural differences on management practices point more to difficulties than to easy solutions.

Another difficulty is that cultural values are changing, albeit slowly, in many parts of the world. The fall of communism in Eastern Europe and the former Soviet Union and the broad economic reforms in China have produced sweeping changes on two continents in the past four decades. Thanks to increased global trade resulting from free-trade agreements, major economic transformations are also under way in India, China, Central America, and South America. Consequently, when trying to adapt management practices to cultural differences, companies must ensure that they are not basing their adaptations on outdated and incorrect assumptions about a country's culture.

 ## 8-6 PREPARING FOR AN INTERNATIONAL ASSIGNMENT

During the 2014 Winter Olympics in Sochi, Russia, American reporters discovered that Russians on the streets, at their hotels, or in restaurants, would not return their smiles. When one reporter asked why this was, a Russian told him, "In Russia, only two types of people smile: idiots and rich people." In Russia, you only smile if you have a particularly good reason. And if you smile just to be friendly, like Americans, Russians will think you're insincere, or maybe a bit crazy. Also, Russians typically don't smile while working because, well, they're at work. But, at home, with friends and family, Russian smiles and laughter are as big and hearty as anyplace in the world.[79]

If you become an **expatriate**, someone who lives and works outside his or her native country, chances are you'll run into

Expatriate someone who lives and works outside his or her native country cultural surprises just like the American reporters covering the Sochi Olympics. The difficulty of adjusting to language, cultural, and social differences is the primary reason for expatriate failure in overseas assignments. For example, although there have recently been disagreements among researchers about these numbers, it is probably safe to say that 5 to 20 percent of American expatriates sent abroad by their companies will return to the United States before they have successfully completed their assignments.[80] Of those who do complete their international assignments, about one-third are judged by their companies to be no better than marginally effective.[81] Because even well-planned international assignments can cost as much as three to five times an employee's annual salary, failure in those assignments can be extraordinarily expensive.[82] Furthermore, while it is difficult to find reliable indicators, studies typically show that 8 to 25 percent of expatriate managers leave their companies following an international assignment.[83]

The chances for a successful international assignment can be increased through **8-6a language and cross-cultural training** *and* **8-6b consideration of spouse, family, and dual-career issues.**

8-6a Language and Cross-Cultural Training

Predeparture language and cross-cultural training can reduce the uncertainty that expatriates feel, the misunderstandings that take place between expatriates and natives, and the inappropriate behaviors that expatriates unknowingly commit when they travel to a foreign country. In fact, simple things such as using a phone, locating a public toilet, asking for directions, finding out how much things cost, exchanging greetings, or understanding what people want can become tremendously complex when expatriates don't know a foreign language or a country's customs and cultures. For example, Bing, the name of Microsoft's search engine, means "illness" or "pancake" in Mandarin Chinese, so Microsoft had to change the name to "Biying" from the Chinese expression "you qui bi ying," which means, more appropriately, "seek and you shall find." Likewise, in Indonesia, an oil rig supervisor yelled to a worker to take a boat to shore. While the boss thought he was sharing instructions, the Indonesian and his workers thought he was being criticized in public, which is not done in their culture. Outraged at this behavior, they chased the supervisor with axes.[84]

Expatriates are still citizens of their native countries.

Expatriates who receive predeparture language and cross-cultural training make faster adjustments to foreign cultures and perform better on their international assignments.[85] Unfortunately, only a third of the managers who go on international assignments are offered any kind of predeparture training, and only half of those actually participate in the training![86] Suzanne Bernard, director of international mobility at Bombardier Aerospace in Canada, says, "We always offer cross-cultural training, but it's very seldom used by executives leaving in a rush at the last minute."[87] This is somewhat surprising given the failure rates for expatriates and the high cost of those failures. Furthermore, with the exception of some language courses, predeparture training is not particularly expensive or difficult to provide. Three methods can be used to prepare workers for international assignments: documentary training, cultural simulations, and field experiences.

Documentary training focuses on identifying specific critical differences between cultures. For example, when sixty workers at Axcelis Technologies in Beverly, Massachusetts, were preparing to do business in India, they learned that while Americans make eye contact and shake hands firmly when greeting others, Indians, as a sign of respect, do just the opposite, avoiding eye contact and shaking hands limply.[88]

After learning specific critical differences through documentary training, trainees can participate in *cultural simulations*, in which they practice adapting to cultural differences. EMC, a global provider of

After learning specific critical differences through documentary training, trainees can participate in cultural simulations, in which they practice adapting to cultural differences.

information storage solutions, uses cultural simulations to train its people. In its early days, EMC was largely based in the United States, but with research labs, offices, and customers on every continent, cross-cultural interactions are a daily part of business. EMC's cultural simulations use photos and audio and video clips to present real-world situations. EMC employees must decide what to do and then learn what happened as a result of their choices. Whether it's interacting with customers or dealing with EMC employees from other countries, at every step they have the opportunity to learn good and bad methods of responding to cultural differences. EMC requires its worldwide workforce of 40,500 people to regularly use the cultural simulations. Louise Korver-Swanson, EMC's global head of executive development, said, "This is about ensuring that we're truly a global company. We need everyone in the organization to be tuned in."[89]

Finally, *field simulation* training, a technique made popular by the U.S. Peace Corps, places trainees in an ethnic neighborhood for three to four hours to talk to residents about cultural differences. For example, a U.S. electronics manufacturer prepared workers for assignments in South Korea by having trainees explore a nearby South Korean neighborhood and talk to shopkeepers and people on the street about South Korean politics, family orientation, and day-to-day living.

8-6b Spouse, Family, and Dual-Career Issues

Not all international assignments are difficult for expatriates and their families, but the evidence clearly shows that how well an expatriate's spouse and family adjust to the foreign culture is the most important factor in determining the success or failure of an international assignment.[90] In fact, a Harvard Business Review study found that 32 percent of those offered international assignments turned them down because they did not want their families to have to relocate,

Expat Assignment as Career Builder

Among U.S. companies, expatriate assignments are becoming more common and even de rigueur for managers who want to advance their careers. Accepting foreign assignments gives managers the opportunity to test their mettle and gain deeper understandings about global markets. Before becoming CFO of Starwood Hotels, Thomas Mangas oversaw finances for Procter & Gamble in ten countries while working in Turkey and Central Asia. He says, "The experience of being in another country is essential. I don't believe you can get there by being there a week or two and flying back out."

Source: K. Johnson, "Career Builder: A Stint Abroad," *Wall Street Journal*, February 10, 2015, B7.

while 28 percent turned them down "to protect their marriages."[91] Unfortunately, despite its importance, there has been little systematic research on what does and does not help expatriates' families successfully adapt. A number of companies, however, have found that adaptability screening and intercultural training for families can lead to more successful overseas adjustment.

Adaptability screening is used to assess how well managers and their families are likely to adjust to foreign cultures. For example, Prudential Relocation Management's international division has developed an "Overseas Assignment Inventory" (OAI) to assess a spouse and family's open-mindedness, respect for others' beliefs, sense of humor, and marital communication. The OAI was initially used to help the U.S. Peace Corps, the U.S. Navy, and the Canadian International Development Agency select people who could adapt well in foreign cultures. Success there led to its use in helping companies assess whether managers and their spouses were good candidates for international assignments.[92] Likewise, Pennsylvania-based AMP, a worldwide producer of electrical connectors, conducts extensive psychological screening of expatriates and their spouses when making international assignments. But adaptability screening does not just involve a company assessing an employee; it can also involve an employee screening international assignments for desirability. Because more employees are becoming aware of the costs of international assignments (spouses having to give up or change jobs, children having to change schools, everyone having to learn a new language), some companies are willing to pay for a pre-assignment trip so the employee and his or her spouse can investigate the country *before* accepting the international assignment.[93]

Only 40 percent of expatriates' families receive language and cross-cultural training, yet such training is just as important for the families of expatriates as for the expatriates themselves.[94] In fact, it may be more important because, unlike expatriates, whose professional jobs often shield them from the full force of a country's culture, spouses and children are fully immersed in foreign neighborhoods and schools. Households must be run, shopping must be done, and bills must be paid. When Judy Holland's husband was transferred to Shanghai, his company sent the family to a two-day cultural immersion class in the United Kingdom, where the family learned about business etiquette, the cultural importance of the number 8, the Chinese zodiac, and how to eat with chopsticks. The class even prepared the Hollands for differences they might not have anticipated, such as, in China, it's uncommon to find men's shoes in sizes larger than a U.S. 9.5 (Holland's husband wore a U.S. 11.5). Holland was grateful for the instruction, saying, "Nothing can fully prepare you for China, but it certainly took the shock out of arriving." Soon after arriving, however, her sense of confidence eroded. "I remember standing in a house with no furniture, not knowing anyone, and wishing they had buddied me up with someone from my husband's company."[95] In addition to helping families prepare for the cultural differences they will encounter, language and cross-cultural training can help reduce uncertainty about how to act and decrease misunderstandings between expatriates and their families and locals. For example, in the West, people enjoy a fairly large circle of personal space and are only comfortable with family and intimate friends being within inches of their bodies. But in China, where personal space is measured in inches and not feet, the constant jostling by strangers can be perceived as an encroachment and unhinge many Westerners. New Zealander Marita Light, who spent five years in China, found that recalibrating her expectations and being intentionally open helped. "Letting go of my judgments and consciously being more open enabled more creativity in how I dealt with awkward situations. It was a much more rewarding way to live in China."[96]

STUDY TOOLS 8

LOCATED IN TEXTBOOK
☐ Rip-out and review chapter review card

LOCATED AT WWW.CENGAGEBRAIN.COM
☐ Review key term flashcards and create your own from StudyBits

☐ Track your knowledge and understanding of key concepts, using the concept tracker

☐ Complete practice and graded quizzes to prepare for tests

☐ Complete interactive content within the exposition

☐ View chapter highlight box content at the beginning of each chapter

9 Designing Adaptive Organizations

LEARNING OUTCOMES

9-1 Describe the departmentalization approach to organizational structure.

9-2 Explain organizational authority.

9-3 Discuss the different methods for job design.

9-4 Explain the methods that companies are using to redesign internal organizational processes (that is intraorganizational processes).

9-5 Describe the methods that companies are using to redesign external organizational processes (that is interorganizational processes).

After you finish

this chapter, go to

PAGE 196 for

STUDY TOOLS

9-1

DEPARTMENTALI-ZATION

Organizational structure is the vertical and horizontal configuration of departments, authority, and jobs within a company. Organizational structure is concerned with questions such as, "Who reports to whom?" and "Who does what?" and "Where is the work done?" **Thomson Reuters**, which provides critical information for businesses and professionals, is organized into four separate business units: Financial & Risk ($6.5 billion in annual revenues), which provides information to traders, investors, and marketplaces; Legal ($3.4 billion), which provides information to global businesses, law firms, governments, and universities; Tax & Accounting ($1.4 billion), which provides information to tax professionals, companies, and governments; and Intellectual Property & Science ($1 billion), which provides information to life sciences companies, scientific and scholarly researchers, and those in need of intellectual property solutions. The company's former CEO Thomas Glocer said that these changes will "streamline our organization and enable us to work better across business units to achieve growth and capture operating efficiencies from scale. The professional markets in which we operate are marked by increasing collaboration among specialists, and Thomson Reuters must operate with the speed and agility needed to serve these demanding professionals."[1]

You can see Thomson Reuters's organizational structure in Exhibit 9.1. In the first half of the chapter, you will learn about the traditional vertical and horizontal approaches to organizational structure, including departmentalization, organizational authority, and job design.

An **organizational process** is the collection of activities that transform inputs into outputs that customers value.[2] Organizational process asks, "How do things get done?" For example, Microsoft uses basic internal and external processes, shown in Exhibit 9.2, to write computer software. The process starts when Microsoft gets feedback from customers through Internet discussion forums, tweets, emails, and phone calls. This information helps Microsoft understand customers' needs and problems and identify important software issues and needed changes and functions. Microsoft then rewrites the software, testing it internally at the company and then externally through its beta testing process, in which customers who volunteer or are selected by Microsoft give the company extensive feedback. The feedback is then used to make improvements to the software. For example, Microsoft made three versions of Windows 10 available for a public beta test over a year before releasing it for sale. Over 2 million consumers and businesses downloaded and installed the beta, and then posted the bugs or errors they found on Microsoft's forums. Microsoft hoped the beta test for Windows 10 went as well as the beta test for Windows 7, during which users found and reported 2,000 bugs, all of which Microsoft corrected before releasing the software.[3] The beta testing process may take as long as a year and involve thousands of knowledgeable people. After final corrections are

Exhibit 9.1
Organizational Chart at Thomson Retuers

The organizational chart displays the horizontal and vertical dimensions at Thomson Reuters.

Source: "About Us," Thompson Reuters, March 13, 2015, accessed April 30, 2015. http://ir.thomsonreuters.com/phoenix.zhtml?c=76540&p=irol-reportsAnnual

Organizational structure the vertical and horizontal configuration of departments, authority, and jobs within a company

Organizational process the collection of activities that transforms inputs into outputs that customers value

Exhibit 9.2
Process View of Microsoft's Organization

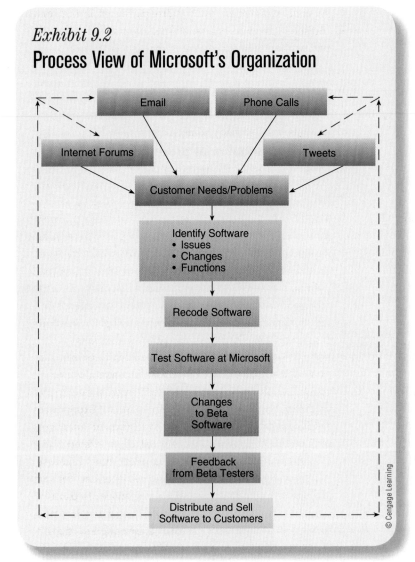

© Cengage Learning

made to the software, the company distributes and sells it to customers. Customers then start the process again by giving Microsoft more feedback.

This process view of Microsoft, which focuses on how things get done, is very different from the hierarchical view of Thomson Reuters, which focuses on accountability, responsibility, and positions within the chain of command. In the second half of the chapter, you will learn how companies use reengineering and empowerment to redesign their internal organizational processes. The chapter ends with a discussion about the ways in which companies are redesigning their external processes, that is, how they are changing to improve their interactions with those outside the company. In that discussion, you will explore the basics of modular and virtual organizations.

Traditionally, organizational structures have been based on some form of departmentalization. **Departmentalization** is a method of subdividing work and workers into separate organizational units that take responsibility for completing particular tasks.[4] EBay has separate departments or divisions for payment systems, warehousing and logistics, and marketplaces and selling.[5]

*Traditionally, organizational structures have been created by departmentalizing work according to five methods: **9-1a functional, 9-1b product, 9-1c customer, 9-1d geographic,** and **9-1e matrix.***

9-1a Functional Departmentalization

The most common organizational structure is functional departmentalization. Companies tend to use this structure when they are small or just starting out. **Functional departmentalization** organizes work and workers into separate units responsible for particular business functions or areas of expertise. A common functional structure might have individuals organized into accounting, sales, marketing, production, and human resources departments.

Not all functionally departmentalized companies have the same functions. The insurance company and the advertising agency shown in Exhibit 9.3 both have sales, accounting, human resources, and information systems departments, as indicated by the pale orange boxes. The purple and green boxes indicate the functions that are different. As would be expected, the insurance company has separate departments for life, auto, home, and health insurance. The advertising agency has departments for artwork, creative work, print advertising, and Internet advertising. So the functional departments in a company that uses functional structure depend, in part, on the business or industry a company is in.

Functional departmentalization has some advantages. First, it allows work to be done by highly qualified specialists. While the accountants in the accounting department take responsibility for producing accurate revenue and expense figures, the engineers in research and development can focus their efforts on designing a

Exhibit 9.3
Functional Departmentalization

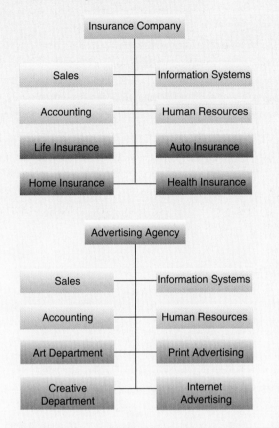

Insurance Company
- Sales
- Information Systems
- Accounting
- Human Resources
- Life Insurance
- Auto Insurance
- Home Insurance
- Health Insurance

Advertising Agency
- Sales
- Information Systems
- Accounting
- Human Resources
- Art Department
- Print Advertising
- Creative Department
- Internet Advertising

© Cengage Learning

product that is reliable and simple to manufacture. Second, it lowers costs by reducing duplication. When the engineers in research and development come up with a fantastic new product, they don't have to worry about creating an aggressive advertising campaign to sell it. That task belongs to the advertising experts and sales representatives in marketing. Third, with everyone in the same department having similar work experience or training, communication and coordination are less problematic for departmental managers.

At the same time, functional departmentalization has a number of disadvantages. To start, cross-department coordination can be difficult. Managers and employees are often more interested in doing what's right for their function than in doing what's right for the entire organization. A good example is the traditional conflict between marketing and manufacturing. Marketing typically pushes for spending more money to make more products with more capabilities to meet customer needs. By contrast, manufacturing pushes for fewer products with simpler designs so that manufacturing facilities can ship finished products on time and keep costs within expense budgets.

As companies grow, functional departmentalization may also lead to slower decision making and produce managers and workers with narrow experience and expertise.

9-1b Product Departmentalization

Product departmentalization organizes work and workers into separate units responsible for producing particular products or services. Exhibit 9.4 shows the product departmentalization structure used by United Technologies Corporation (UTC), which is organized along four different areas each with its own product line: Building & Industrial Systems (Carrier heating, ventilating, and air-conditioning; Kidde fire safety, security products and services; and Otis elevators and escalators), Aircraft Propulsion (Pratt & Whitney jet engines, and Inernational Aero Engines), Aerospace and Defense (wing and cockpit controls, landing systems and sensors, aerostructures, electric power systems and plane interiors) and Sikorsky (military and commercial helicopters).[6]

One of the advantages of product departmentalization is that, like functional departmentalization, it allows managers and workers to specialize in one area of expertise. Unlike the narrow expertise and experiences in functional departmentalization, however, managers and workers develop a broader set of experiences and expertise related to an entire product line. Likewise, product departmentalization makes it easier for top managers to assess work-unit performance. Because of the clear separation of their four different product divisions, UTC's top managers can easily compare the performance of UTC Aerospace & Defense division and the Pratt & Whitney aircraft engines division. In 2014, Pratt & Whitney had a $1.5 billion advantage over UTC Aerospace in net sales ($14.5 billion versus $14.2 billion). However, UTC Aerospace had a profit of $2.4 billion (a 16.9 percent margin) compared to a profit of $2 billion (13.8 percent margin) for Pratt & Whitney.[7]

Finally, decision making should be faster because managers and workers are responsible for the entire product line rather than for separate functional departments; in other words, there are fewer conflicts compared to functional departmentalization.

The primary disadvantage of product departmentalization is duplication. You can see in Exhibit 9.4 that both the Building & Industrial division and the Aircraft Propulsion division have customer service, engineering, human resources, legal, manufacturing, and

Product departmentalization organizing work and workers into separate units responsible for producing particular products or services

Exhibit 9.4
Product Departmentalization: UTC

Building & Industrial Systems			Aircraft Propulsion		Aerospace & Defense	Sikorsky Helicopters
Otis Elevators & Escalators	Carrier HVAC	Kidde Fire Safety and Security	Pratt & Whitney Aircraft Engines	International Aero Engines	Wing and cockpit controls, landing systems and sensors, aerostructures, electric power systems and plane interiors.	Military & Commercial Helicopters
— Customer Service — Engineering — Human Resources — Information Technology — Legal — Maintenance & Field Operations — Manufacturing — Marketing & Sales — Sourcing & Logistics			— Administrative Services — Communication & Public Relations — Customer Service & Support — E-Business — Engineering — Enterprise Resource Planning — Environmental Health & Safety — Facilities & Services — Human Resources — Legal — Manufacturing — Procurement — Quality			

Source: "At a Glance," UTC, accessed April 30, 2015. http://www.utc.com/Our-Businesses/Pages/At-A-Glance.aspx.

procurement (similar to sourcing and logistics) departments. Duplication like this often results in higher costs. If UTC were instead organized by function, one lawyer could handle matters related to both elevators and aircraft engines rather than working on only one or the other.

A second disadvantage is the challenge of coordinating across the different product departments. UTC would probably have difficulty standardizing its policies and procedures in product departments as different as the Carrier (heating, ventilating, and air-conditioning) and Sikorsky (military and commercial helicopters) divisions.

9-1c Customer Departmentalization

Customer departmentalization organizes work and workers into separate units responsible for particular kinds of customers. For example, as Exhibit 9.5 shows, Swisscom AG, Switzerland's leading telecommunications provider, is organized into departments by type of customer:

residential customers (fixed line and voice, mobile and voice, broadband Internet, and digital TV), small- and medium-sized businesses (fixed line and voice, mobile line and voice, Internet and data services, and maintenance and operation of IT infrastructure), enterprise customers (fixed line, voice and data; mobile line and tablets, voice and data; Internet and data services; and maintenance and operation of IT infrastructure), and IT network and innovation (broadband Internet, data services, co-location of data services, and storage to wholesale customers).[8]

The primary advantage of customer departmentalization is that it focuses the organization on customer needs rather than on products or business functions. Furthermore, creating separate departments to serve specific kinds of customers allows companies to specialize and adapt their products and services to customer needs and problems. The primary disadvantage of customer departmentalization is that, like product departmentalization, it leads to duplication of resources. This is why Swisscom AG also has five "group" functions—communication, strategy, security, business steering, and human resources—that support each of its four customer

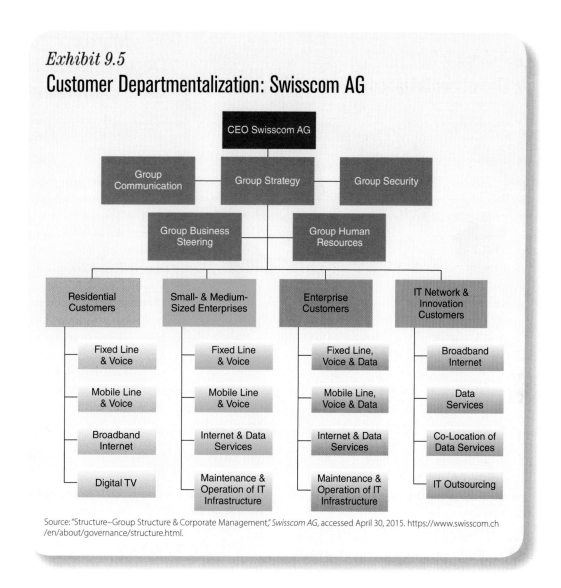

Exhibit 9.5

Customer Departmentalization: Swisscom AG

CEO Swisscom AG

Group Communication — Group Strategy — Group Security

Group Business Steering — Group Human Resources

Residential Customers	Small- & Medium-Sized Enterprises	Enterprise Customers	IT Network & Innovation Customers
Fixed Line & Voice	Fixed Line & Voice	Fixed Line, Voice & Data	Broadband Internet
Mobile Line & Voice	Mobile Line & Voice	Mobile Line, Voice & Data	Data Services
Broadband Internet	Internet & Data Services	Internet & Data Services	Co-Location of Data Services
Digital TV	Maintenance & Operation of IT Infrastructure	Maintenance & Operation of IT Infrastructure	IT Outsourcing

Source: "Structure–Group Structure & Corporate Management," *Swisscom AG*, accessed April 30, 2015. https://www.swisscom.ch /en/about/governance/structure.html.

departments, and avoids the disadvantage of duplication common to customer departmentalization structures. It can be difficult to achieve coordination across different customer departments, as is also the case with product departmentalization. Finally, the emphasis on meeting customers' needs may lead workers to make decisions that please customers but hurt the business.

9-1d Geographic Departmentalization

Geographic departmentalization organizes work and workers into separate units responsible for doing business in particular geographic areas. Exhibit 9.6 shows the geographic departmentalization used by **AB InBev**, the largest beer brewer in the world. AB InBev has 153 beverage plants in twenty-five countries, 155,000 employees, and annual revenue of $47.1 billion.[9] As shown in Exhibit 9.6, AB InBev has six regional groups:

North America, Mexico, Latin America North, Latin America South, Europe, and Asia Pacific. Each of these regions would be a sizable company by itself. The smallest region, Mexico, for instance, sold 38.8 million hectoliters of beverages for annual revenue of $4.6 billion.

The primary advantage of geographic departmentalization is that it helps companies respond to the demands of different markets. This can be especially important when the company sells in different countries. For example, while AB InBev has three brands sold worldwide (Budweiser, Stella Artois, and Corona), and three sold in multiple countries (Beck's, Hoegaarden, and Leffe), most of its brands are local. You'll find the Antarctica and Brahma brands in Brazil, the Belle-Vue and Jupiler brands in Belgium,

Geographic departmentalization organizing work and workers into separate units responsible for doing business in particular geographic areas

Exhibit 9.6
Geographic Departmentalization: AB InBev Company

Source: "Country Information," Anheuser-Busch InBev, accessed June 16, 2014. http://www.ab-inbev.com/go/about_abinbev/country_information.

© Cengage Learning®

9-1e Matrix Departmentalization

Matrix departmentalization is a hybrid structure in which two or more forms of departmentalization are used together. The most common matrix combines the product and functional forms of departmentalization, but other forms may also be used. Exhibit 9.7 shows the matrix structure used by Procter & Gamble, which has 180,000 employees working in seventy different countries.[12] Across the top of Exhibit 9.7, you can see that the company uses a product structure where it groups its twenty-three billion-dollar brands into four global business units: global beauty (beauty care, retail hair color, salon professional, and prestige); global baby, feminine, and family care (baby care, family care, and feminine care); global health and grooming (shave care, Braun, oral care, and health care); and global fabric and home care (fabric care and home care). Global business units are responsible for product initiatives or upgrades, which are typically launched simultaneously with a worldwide marketing campaign. The left side of the figure, however, shows that the company is also using a functional structure based on three functions: selling and marketing operations (SMOs), which makes sure that a product is sold, distributed, shelved, and priced well within a particular region of the world (SMO regions include North America, Asia, Australia, Europe, Latin America, and India/Middle East/Africa (IMEA); global business services, which enable the company to operate efficiently, work effectively with business partners, and increase employee productivity; and lean corporate functions, which provide global business units with the functional business assistance (that is finance, accounting, human resources, and information technology) they need.[13]

The boxes in the figure represent the matrix structure created by the combination of the product and functional structures. For example, P&G's Gillette Group (Gillette is a global brand for men's grooming products

and the Sibirskaya Korona and Klinskoye brands in Russia.[10]

Another advantage is that geographic departmentalization can reduce costs by locating unique organizational resources closer to customers. For instance, it is cheaper in the long run for AB InBev to build bottling plants in each region than to, for example, transport beer to Mexico, where it has seven beverage plants, after it has been brewed and bottled in Brazil, where it has twenty-five beverage plants.[11]

The primary disadvantage of geographic departmentalization is that it can lead to duplication of resources. For example, while it may be necessary to adapt products and marketing to different geographic locations, it's doubtful that AB InBev needs significantly different inventory tracking systems from location to location. Also, even more than with the other forms of departmentalization, it can be difficult to coordinate departments that are literally thousands of miles from each other and whose managers have very limited contact with each other.

Matrix departmentalization a hybrid organizational structure in which two or more forms of departmentalization, most often product and functional, are used together

iStockphoto.com/Micropic

Exhibit 9.7

Matrix Departmentalization: Procter & Gamble

| Global Business Units | | | | | | | | | | | |
| Global Beauty, Hair, & Personal Care | | | Global Baby, Feminine, & Family Care | | | Global Health & Grooming | | | | Global Fabric & Home Care | |
Beauty Care	Retail Hair Care	Salon Professional & Prestige	Baby Care	Family Care	Feminine Care	Braun	Shave Care	Oral Care	Health Care	Fabric Care	Home Care
Selling & Market Operations Olay	Pantene	Wella	Pampers	Bounty	Tampax	Braun	Gillette	Crest	Vicks	Tide	Swiffer
Global Business Services											
Lean Corporate Functions											

Sources: "Strength in Structure," P&G, accessed May 5, 2015. http://www.pg.com/en_US/company/global_structure_operations/corporate_structure.shtml.

within the Shave Care segment of the Global Health & Grooming unit) would work with SMOs to sell, market, and distribute Gillette products worldwide; use global business services to work with suppliers and keep costs down; and then rely on corporate functions for assistance in hiring employees, billing customers, and paying suppliers. Similar matrix combinations are shown for Olay, Pantene Wella, Pampers, Bounty, Tampax, Braun, Crest, Vicks, Tide, and Swiffer within each of the segments of P&G's four global business units.

Several things distinguish matrix departmentalization from the other traditional forms of departmentalization.[14] First, most employees report to two bosses, one from each core part of the matrix. For example, in Exhibit 9.7 a manager on the Pampers team responsible for marketing would report to a boss in the baby care segment of the Global Baby, Feminine, & Family global business unit as well as to a manager in the market development function. Second, by virtue of their hybrid design, matrix structures lead to much more cross-functional interaction than other forms of departmentalization. In fact, while matrix workers are typically members of only one functional department (based on their work experience and expertise), they are also commonly members of several ongoing project, product, or customer groups. Third, because of the high level of cross-functional interaction, matrix departmentalization requires significant coordination between managers in the different parts of the matrix. In particular, managers have the complex job of tracking and managing the multiple demands (project, product, customer, or functional) on employees' time.

The primary advantage of matrix departmentalization is that it allows companies to manage in an efficient manner large, complex tasks such as researching, developing, and marketing pharmaceuticals or carrying out complex global businesses. Efficiency comes from avoiding duplication. For example, rather than having an entire marketing function for each project, the company simply assigns and reassigns workers from the marketing department (or market development at P&G) as they are needed at various stages of product completion. More specifically, an employee may simultaneously be part of five different ongoing projects but may be actively completing work on only a few projects at a time. Another advantage is the pool of resources available to carry out large, complex tasks. Because of the ability to quickly pull in expert help from all the functional areas of the company, matrix project managers have a much more diverse set of expertise and experience at their disposal than managers in the other forms of departmentalization.

Matrix structures are notorious for confusion and conflict between project bosses in different parts of the matrix.

The primary disadvantage of matrix departmentalization is the high level of coordination required to manage the complexity involved in running large, ongoing projects at various levels of completion. Matrix structures are notorious for confusion and conflict between project bosses in different parts of the matrix. Disagreements or misunderstandings about schedules, budgets, available resources, and the availability of employees with particular functional expertise are common in matrix structures. Because of these problems, many matrix structures evolve from a **simple matrix**, in which managers in different parts of the matrix negotiate conflicts and resources directly, to a **complex matrix**, in which specialized matrix managers and departments are added to the organizational structure. In a complex matrix, managers from different parts of the matrix might report to the same matrix manager, who helps them sort out conflicts and problems.

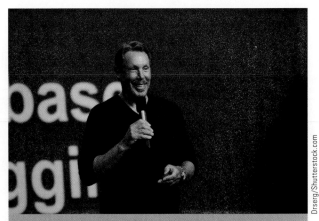

Unity of command was broken in 2014 when Oracle CEO, Larry Ellison, stepped down and appointed his successors, Co-CEOs Mark Hurd and Safra Cruz.

9-2 ORGANIZATIONAL AUTHORITY

The second part of traditional organizational structures is authority. **Authority** is the right to give commands, take action, and make decisions to achieve organizational objectives.[15]

Traditionally, organizational authority has been characterized by the following dimensions: 9-2a chain of command, 9-2b line versus staff authority, 9-2c delegation of authority, and 9-2d degree of centralization.

9-2a Chain of Command

Consider again the United Technologies organizational structure. A manager in any of the corporation's divisions ultimately reports to the head of that division. That division head, in turn, reports to the corporation's CEO Gregory. This line, which vertically connects every job in the company to higher levels of management, represents the chain of command. The **chain of command** is the vertical line of authority that clarifies who reports to whom throughout the organization. People higher in the chain of command have the right, *if they so choose*, to give commands, take action, and make decisions concerning activities occurring anywhere below them in the chain. In the following discussion about delegation and decentralization, you will learn that managers don't always choose to exercise their authority directly.[16]

One of the key assumptions underlying the chain of command is **unity of command**, which means that workers should report to just one boss.[17] In practical terms, this means that only one person can be in charge at a time. Matrix organizations, in which employees have two bosses, automatically violate this principle. This is one of the primary reasons that matrix organizations are difficult to manage. Unity of command serves an important purpose: to prevent the confusion that might arise when an employee receives conflicting commands from two different bosses. When Larry Ellison stepped down in 2014 after thirty-five years as Oracle's CEO, he violated unity of command by appointing Mark Hurd and Safra Catz to succeed him as co-CEOs. Hurd oversees sales and marketing, and Catz focuses on finance, internal operations, and manufacturing. With Ellison now Oracle's chief technology officer, unity of command could be further fragmented. Management professor Lindred Greer doesn't expect this to work, as her research indicates that having co-CEOs "causes conflict," leads to "negative performance by [executive] teams, and may likely result in the development of "hostile mindsets" as the co-CEOs struggle to work together.[18]

Simple matrix a form of matrix departmentalization in which managers in different parts of the matrix negotiate conflicts and resources

Complex matrix a form of matrix departmentalization in which managers in different parts of the matrix report to matrix managers, who help them sort out conflicts and problems

Authority the right to give commands, take action, and make decisions to achieve organizational objectives

Chain of command the vertical line of authority that clarifies who reports to whom throughout the organization

Unity of command a management principle that workers should report to just one boss

9-2b Line versus Staff Authority

A second dimension of authority is the distinction between line and staff authority. **Line authority** is the right to command immediate subordinates in the chain of command. For example, Thomson Reuters CEO James C. Smith has line authority over the president of the company's Financial & Risk Information division. Smith can issue orders to that division president and expect them to be carried out. In turn, the president of the Financial & Risk Information division can issue orders to his subordinates, who run the trading, investors, marketplaces, and governance, risk, and compliance divisions, and expect them to be carried out. By contrast, **staff authority** is the right to advise but not command others who are not subordinates in the chain of command. For example, a manager in human resources at Thomson Reuters might advise the manager in charge of the Thomson Reuters Tax & Accounting group on a hiring decision but cannot order him or her to hire a certain applicant.

The terms *line* and *staff* are also used to describe different functions within the organization. A **line function** is an activity that contributes directly to creating or selling the company's products. So, for example, activities that take place within the manufacturing and marketing departments would be considered line functions. A **staff function**, such as accounting, human resources, or legal services, does not contribute directly to creating or selling the company's products but instead supports line activities. For example, marketing managers might consult with the legal staff to make sure the wording of a particular advertisement is legal.

9-2c Delegation of Authority

Managers can exercise their authority directly by completing tasks themselves, or they can choose to pass on some of their authority to subordinates. **Delegation of authority** is the assignment of direct authority and responsibility to a subordinate to complete tasks for which the manager is normally responsible.

When a manager delegates work, three transfers occur, as illustrated in Exhibit 9.8. First, the manager transfers full responsibility for the assignment to the subordinate. At Apple, when you've been delegated to a certain task, you become the DRI, or the "directly responsible individual." As a former Apple employee explains, "Any effective meeting at Apple will have an action list. Next to each action item will be the DRI," who of course, is responsible for completing that delegated responsibility. Furthermore, when you're trying

Exhibit 9.8
Delegation: Responsibility, Authority, and Accountability

Manager   Subordinate

Responsibility

Authority

Accountability

Fuse/Jupiter Images

Source: C. D. Pringle, D. F. Jennings, and J. G. Longenecker, Managing Organizations: Functions and Behaviors. Merrill Publishing, 1984, Columbus, Ohio.

to figure out who to contact to get something done in Apple's corporate structure, people simply ask, "Who's the DRI on that?"[19]

Many managers, however, find giving up full responsibility somewhat difficult. Helene Gayle, CEO of CARE U.S.A., a nonprofit dedicated to reducing poverty, admits that early in her career, she tried to do too much by herself without delegating. She says, "For me, it wasn't a question of not being willing to delegate, it was switching from being on the technical side as an individual contribuor—where the way you prove yourself is to be smart—to focusing on how you actually make a team work and bring out others' contributions."[20] One reason it is difficult for some managers to delegate is that they often fear that the task won't be done as well as if they did it themselves. However, one CEO says, "If you can delegate a task to somebody who can do it 75 percent to 80 percent as well as you can today, you delegate it immediately." Why? Many tasks don't need to be done perfectly; they just need to be *done*. And delegating tasks that someone else can do frees managers to assume other important

---

Line authority the right to command immediate subordinates in the chain of command

Staff authority the right to advise, but not command, others who are not subordinates in the chain of command

Line function an activity that contributes directly to creating or selling the company's products

Staff function an activity that does not contribute directly to creating or selling the company's products but instead supports line activities

Delegation of authority the assignment of direct authority and responsibility to a subordinate to complete tasks for which the manager is normally responsible responsibilities. Delegating authority can generate a related problem: micromanaging. Sometimes managers delegate only to interfere later with how the employee is performing the task. But delegating full responsibility means that the employee—not the manager—is now completely responsible for task completion. Good managers need to trust their subordinates to do the job.

The second transfer that occurs with delegation is that the manager gives the subordinate full authority over the budget, resources, and personnel needed to do the job. To do the job effectively, subordinates must have the same tools and information at their disposal that managers had when they were responsible for the same task. In other words, for delegation to work, delegated authority must be commensurate with delegated responsibility.

The third transfer that occurs with delegation is the transfer of accountability. The subordinate now has the authority and responsibility to do the job and, in return, is accountable for getting the job done. In other words, managers delegate their managerial authority and responsibility to subordinates in exchange for results.

9-2d Degree of Centralization

If you've ever called a company's toll-free number with a complaint or a special request and been told by the customer-service representative, "I'll have to ask my manager" or "I'm not authorized to do that," you know that centralization of authority exists in that company. **Centralization of authority** is the location of most authority at the upper levels of the organization. In a centralized organization, managers make most decisions, even the relatively small ones. That's why the customer-service representative you called couldn't make a decision without first asking the manager.

If you are lucky, however, you may have talked to a customer-service representative at another company who said, "I can take care of that for you right now." In other words, the person was able to handle your problem without any input from or consultation with company management. **Decentralization** is the location of a significant amount of authority in the lower levels of the organization. An organization is decentralized if it has a high degree of delegation at all levels. In a decentralized organization,

As Toyota became the largest automaker in the world, car quality declined as it increased its use of unstardardized parts across different cars and continents.

workers closest to problems are authorized to make the decisions necessary to solve the problems on their own.

McDonald's is moving away from centralized decision making regarding menu items in its U.S. stores. Whereas it used to offer the same menu items in Louisiana, such as sweet tea (a standard item at southern restaurants), as it did in Minnesota, it will now leave menu and marketing decisions up to managers in twenty-two different regions. McDonald's U.S. President Mike Andres said, "We must evolve our culture and organizational structure to put decision making closer to our customers."[21]

Decentralization has a number of advantages. It develops employee capabilities throughout the company and leads to faster decision making and more satisfied customers and employees. Furthermore, a study of 1,000 large companies found that companies with a high degree of decentralization outperformed those with a low degree of decentralization in terms of return on assets (6.9 percent versus 4.7 percent), return on investment (14.6 percent versus 9.0 percent), return on equity (22.8 percent versus 16.6 percent), and return on sales (10.3 percent versus 6.3 percent). Surprisingly, the same study found that few large companies actually are decentralized. Specifically, only 31 percent of employees in these 1,000 companies were responsible for recommending improvements to management. Overall, just 10 percent of employees received the training and information needed to support a truly decentralized approach to management.[22]

With results like these, the key question is no longer *whether* companies should decentralize, but *where* they should decentralize. One rule of thumb is to stay centralized where standardization is important and to decentralize where standardization is unimportant. **Standardization** is solving problems by consistently

Centralization of authority the location of most authority at the upper levels of the organization

Decentralization the location of a significant amount of authority in the lower levels of the organization

Standardization solving problems by consistently applying the same rules, procedures, and processes applying the same rules, procedures, and processes. Toyota became the largest auto manufacturer in the world by producing highly reliable cars at competitive costs. But as the company grew, it significantly increased the number of kinds of parts used in its cars, for example, using 100 different radiators in the cars it made around the world. Using that many varieties for the same part not only increased costs, it decreased quality, which then reduced Toyota sales. Toyota's leadership addressed this issue by using standardization to significantly reduce the variety of kinds of basic parts. For example, it used just 21 different kinds of radiators in its cars rather than 100, as before. This led to greater volume for each part and lower costs. Standardization has proven so successful that Toyota aims to reduce the variety of parts it uses across all its car models by 75 percent by grouping 100 different model platforms and 800 different engine types into larger, but many fewer, model families.[23]

9-3 JOB DESIGN

Could you stand to do the same simple tasks an average of 50 times per hour, 400 times per day, 2,000 times per week, 8,000 times per month? Few can. Fast-food workers rarely stay on the job more than six months. In fact, McDonald's and other fast-food restaurants have well over 60 percent employee turnover each year.[24] As a drive through employee at McDonald's you would repeatedly perform the following steps:

1. "Welcome to McDonald's. May I have your order please?"

2. Listen to the order. Repeat it for accuracy. State the total cost. "Please drive to the second window."

3. Take the money. Make change.

4. Give customers drinks, straws, and napkins.

5. Give customers food.

6. "Thank you for coming to McDonald's."

In this section, you will learn about **job design**—the number, kind, and variety of tasks that individual workers perform in doing their jobs.

You will learn ***9-3a why companies continue to use specialized jobs such as the McDonald's drive-through job*** *and* ***9-3b how job rotation, job enlargement, job enrichment,*** *and* ***9-3c the job characteristics model are being used to overcome the problems associated with job specialization.***

9-3a Job Specialization

Job specialization occurs when a job is composed of a small part of a larger task or process. Specialized jobs are characterized by simple, easy-to-learn steps; low variety; and high repetition, such as the McDonald's drive-through window job just described. One of the clear disadvantages of specialized jobs is that, being so easy to learn, they quickly become boring. This, in turn, can lead to low job satisfaction and high absenteeism and employee turnover, all of which are very costly to organizations.

Why, then, do companies continue to create and use specialized jobs? The primary reason is that specialized jobs are very economical. As we learned from Frederick W. Taylor and Frank and Lillian Gilbreth in Chapter 2, after a job has been specialized, it takes little time to learn and master. Consequently, when experienced workers quit or are absent, the company can replace them with new employees and lose little productivity. For example, next time you're at McDonald's, notice the pictures of the food on the cash registers. These pictures make it easy for McDonald's trainees to quickly learn to take orders. Likewise, to simplify and speed operations, the drink dispensers behind the counter are set to automatically fill drink cups. Put a medium cup below the dispenser. Punch the medium drink button. The soft-drink machine then fills the cup to within a half-inch of the top, while the worker goes to get your fries. At McDonald's, every task has been simplified in this way. Because the work is designed to be simple, wages can remain low because it isn't necessary to pay high salaries to attract highly experienced, educated, or trained workers.

9-3b Job Rotation, Enlargement, and Enrichment

Because of the efficiency of specialized jobs, companies are often reluctant to eliminate them. Consequently, job redesign efforts have focused on modifying jobs to keep the benefits of specialized jobs while reducing their obvious costs and disadvantages. Three methods—job rotation, job enlargement, and job enrichment—have been used to try to improve specialized jobs.[25]

Job rotation attempts to overcome the disadvantages of job specialization by periodically moving work-ers from one specialized job

> **Job design** the number, kind, and variety of tasks that individual workers perform in doing their jobs
>
> **Job specialization** a job composed of a small part of a larger task or process
>
> **Job rotation** periodically moving workers from one specialized job to another to give them more variety and the opportunity to use different skills

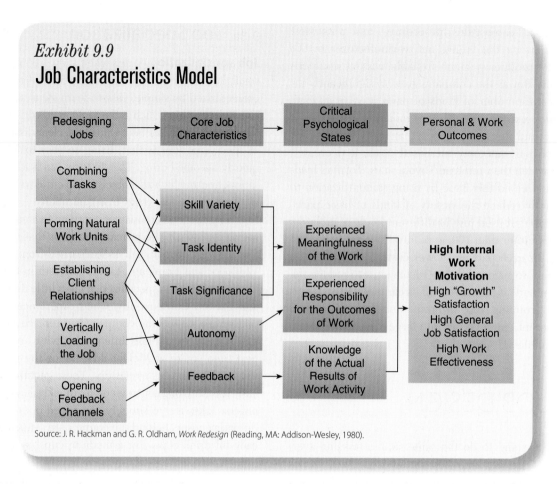

Exhibit 9.9
Job Characteristics Model

Source: J. R. Hackman and G. R. Oldham, *Work Redesign* (Reading, MA: Addison-Wesley, 1980).

to another to give them more variety and the opportunity to use different skills. For example, an office receptionist who does nothing but answer phones could be systematically rotated to a different job, such as typing, filing, or data entry, every day or two. Likewise, the "mirror attacher" in an automobile plant might attach mirrors in the first half of the work shift and then install bumpers during the second half. Because employees simply switch from one specialized job to another, job rotation allows companies to retain the economic benefits of specialized work. At the same time, the greater variety of tasks makes the work less boring and more satisfying for workers.

Another way to counter the disadvantages of specialization is to enlarge the job. **Job enlargement** increases the number of different tasks that a worker performs within

one particular job. Instead of being assigned just one task, workers with enlarged jobs are given several tasks to perform. For example, an enlarged "mirror attacher" job might include attaching the mirror, checking to see that the mirror's power adjustment controls work, and then cleaning the mirror's surface. Though job enlargement increases variety, many workers report feeling more stress when their jobs are enlarged. Consequently, many workers view enlarged jobs as simply more work, especially if they are not given additional time to complete the additional tasks.

Job enrichment attempts to overcome the deficiencies in specialized work by increasing the number of tasks *and* by giving workers the authority and control to make meaningful decisions about their work.[26]

9-3c Job Characteristics Model

In contrast to job rotation, job enlargement, and job enrichment, which focus on providing variety in job tasks, the **job characteristics model (JCM)** is an approach to job redesign that seeks to formulate jobs in ways that motivate workers and lead to positive work outcomes.[27]

As shown in Exhibit 9.9, the primary goal of the model is to create jobs that result in positive personal

Job enlargement increasing the number of different tasks that a worker performs within one particular job

Job enrichment increasing the number of tasks in a particular job and giving workers the authority and control to make meaningful decisions about their work

Job characteristics model (JCM) an approach to job redesign that seeks to formulate jobs in ways that motivate workers and lead to positive work outcomes and work outcomes, such as internal work motivation, satisfaction with one's job, and work effectiveness. Of these, the central concern of the JCM is internal motivation. **Internal motivation** is motivation that comes from the job itself rather than from outside rewards such as a raise or praise from the boss. If workers feel that performing the job well is itself rewarding, then the job has internal motivation. Statements such as "I get a nice sense of accomplishment" or "I feel good about myself and what I'm producing" are examples of internal motivation.

In Exhibit 9.9, you can see that the JCM specifies three critical psychological states that must occur for work to be internally motivating. First, workers must *experience the work as meaningful*; that is, they must view their job as being important. Second, they must *experience responsibility for work outcomes*—they must feel personally responsible for the work being done well. Third, workers must have *knowledge of results*; that is, they must know how well they are performing their jobs. All three critical psychological states must occur for work to be internally motivating.

For example, grocery store cashiers usually have knowledge of results. When you're slow, your checkout line grows long. If you make a mistake, customers point it out: "No, I think that's on sale for $2.99, not $3.99." Likewise, cashiers experience responsibility for work outcomes. At the end of the day, the register is totaled, and the money is counted. Ideally, the money matches the total sales in the register. If the money in the till is less than what's recorded in the register, most stores make the cashier pay the difference. Consequently, most cashiers are very careful to avoid being caught short at the end of the day. Nonetheless, despite knowing the results and experiencing responsibility for work outcomes, most grocery store cashiers (at least where I shop) aren't internally motivated because they don't experience the work as meaningful. With scanners, it takes little skill to learn or do the job. Anyone can do it. In addition, cashiers have few decisions to make, and the job is highly repetitive.

What kinds of jobs produce the three critical psychological states? Moving another step to the left in Exhibit 9.9, you can see that these psychological states arise from jobs that are strong on five core job characteristics: skill variety, task identity, task significance, autonomy, and feedback. **Skill variety** is the number of different activities performed in a job. **Task identity** is the degree to which a job, from beginning to end, requires completion of a whole and identifiable piece of work. **Task significance**

is the degree to which a job is perceived to have a substantial impact on others inside or outside the organization. **Autonomy** is the degree to which a job gives workers the discretion, freedom, and independence to decide how and when to accomplish the work. Finally, **feedback** is the amount of information the job provides to workers about their work performance.

To illustrate how the core job characteristics work together, let's use them to assess more thoroughly why the McDonald's drive-through window job is not particularly satisfying or motivating. To start, skill variety is low. Except for the size of an order or special requests ("no onions"), the process is the same for each customer. At best, task identity is moderate. Although you take the order, handle the money, and deliver the food, others are responsible for a larger part of the process—preparing the food. Task identity will be even lower if the McDonald's has two drive-through windows because each drive-through window worker will have an even more specialized task. The first is limited to taking the order and making change, while the second just delivers the food.

Task significance, the impact you have on others, is probably low. Autonomy is also very low: McDonald's has strict rules about dress, cleanliness, and procedures. But the job does provide immediate feedback such as positive and negative customer comments, car horns honking, the amount of time it takes to process orders, and the number of cars in the drive-through. With the exception of feedback, the low levels of the core job characteristics show why the drive-through window job is not internally motivating for many workers.

What can managers do when jobs aren't internally motivating? The far left column of Exhibit 9.9 lists five job redesign techniques that managers can use to strengthen a job's core characteristics.

Internal motivation motivation that comes from the job itself rather than from outside rewards

Skill variety the number of different activities performed in a job

Task identity the degree to which a job, from beginning to end, requires the completion of a whole and identifiable piece of work

Task significance the degree to which a job is perceived to have a substantial impact on others inside or outside the organization

Autonomy the degree to which a job gives workers the discretion, freedom, and independence to decide how and when to accomplish the job

Feedback the amount of information the job provides to workers about their work performance

Combining tasks increases skill variety and task identity by joining separate, specialized tasks into larger work modules. For example, some trucking firms are now requiring truck drivers to load their rigs as well as drive them. The hope is that involving drivers in loading will ensure that trucks are properly loaded, thus reducing damage claims.

Work can be formed into *natural work units* by arranging tasks according to logical or meaningful groups. Although many trucking companies randomly assign drivers to trucks, some have begun assigning drivers to particular geographic locations (for example, the Northeast or Southwest) or to truckloads that require special driving skill (for example, oversized loads or hazardous chemicals). Forming natural work units increases task identity and task significance.

Establishing client relationships increases skill variety, autonomy, and feedback by giving employees direct contact with clients and customers. In some companies, truck drivers are expected to establish business relationships with their regular customers. When something goes wrong with a shipment, customers are told to call drivers directly.

Vertical loading means pushing some managerial authority down to workers. For truck drivers, this means that they have the same authority as managers to resolve customer problems. In some companies, if a late shipment causes problems for a customer, the driver has the authority to fully refund the cost of that shipment without first obtaining management's approval.

The last job redesign technique offered by the model, *opening feedback channels*, means finding additional ways to give employees direct, frequent feedback about their job performance. For example, with advances in electronics, many truck drivers get instantaneous data as to whether they're on schedule and driving their rigs in a fuel-efficient manner. Likewise, the increased contact with customers

also means that many drivers now receive monthly data on customer satisfaction.

9-4 INTRAORGANIZATIONAL PROCESSES

More than forty years ago, Tom Burns and G. M. Stalker described how two kinds of organizational designs, mechanistic and organic, are appropriate for different kinds of organizational environments.[28] **Mechanistic organizations** are characterized by specialized jobs and responsibilities; precisely defined, unchanging roles; and a rigid chain of command based on centralized authority and vertical communication. This type of organization works best in stable, unchanging business environments. By contrast, **organic organizations** are characterized by broadly defined jobs and responsibilities; loosely defined, frequently changing roles; and decentralized authority and horizontal communication based on task knowledge. This type of organization works best in dynamic, changing business environments.

The organizational design techniques described in the first half of this chapter—departmentalization, authority, and job design—are better suited for mechanistic organizations and the stable business environments that were more prevalent before 1980. By contrast, the organizational design techniques discussed in the second part of the chapter, are more appropriate for organic organizations and the increasingly dynamic environments in which today's businesses compete. The key difference between these approaches is that mechanistic organizational designs focus on organizational structure, whereas organic organizational designs are concerned with **intraorganizational process**, which is the collection of activities that take place within an organization to transform inputs into outputs that customers value.

Let's take a look at how companies are using **9-4a reengineering** *and* **9-4b empowerment** *to redesign intraorganizational processes like these.*

9-4a Reengineering

In their best-selling book *Reengineering the Corporation*, Michael Hammer and James Champy define **reengineering** as "the *fundamental* rethinking and *radical* redesign of business *processes* to achieve *dramatic* improvements in critical, contemporary measures of performance, such as cost, quality, service and

Publishers Turn the Page on Their Office Plans

Despite its creative-intellectual vibe, the book publishing industry could best be described as mechanistic. Editors moved incrementally up the career ladder through well-defined hierarchies as they pursued a private, corner office. These days, however, the genteel, old-fashioned industry is feeling the pressure from competition, prompting many of its members to become more organic. One way they are doing this is by moving from hives of walled offices to completely open floorplans. Before Hachette Book Group moved into its new Manhattan space, CEO Michael Pietsch toured companies with many office configurations and became increasingly attracted to the 100 percent open plan. "As I looked at these places, there was just this energy and buzz and sense of excitement and collaborative human endeavor that really was kind of exhilarating." So, in Hachette's new office, everyone—including Pietsch—has a cube.

Source: J. Mahler, "Cubicles Rise in a Brave New World of Publishing," *New York Times*, November 10, 2014, A1.

Robin Marchant/Getty Images Entertainment/Getty Images

speed."[29] Hammer and Champy further explained the four key words shown in italics in this definition. The first key word is *fundamental*. When reengineering organizational designs, managers must ask themselves, "Why do we do what we do?" and "Why do we do it the way we do?" The usual answer is "Because that's the way we've always done it." The second key word is *radical*. Reengineering is about significant change, about starting over by throwing out the old ways of getting work done. The third key word is *processes*. Hammer and Champy noted that "most business people are not process oriented; they are focused on tasks, on jobs, on people, on structures, but not on processes." The fourth key word is *dramatic*. Reengineering is about achieving quantum improvements in company performance.

An example from IBM Credit's operation illustrates how work can be reengineered.[30] IBM Credit lends businesses money to buy IBM computers. Previously, the loan process began when an IBM salesperson called the home office to obtain credit approval for a customer's purchase. The first department involved in the process took the credit information over the phone from the salesperson and recorded it on the credit form. The credit form was sent to the credit checking department, then to the pricing department (where the interest rate was determined), and on through a total of five departments. In all, it took the five departments six days to approve or deny the customer's loan. Of course, this delay cost IBM business. Some customers got their loans elsewhere. Others, frustrated by the wait, simply canceled their orders.

Finally, two IBM managers decided to walk a loan straight through each of the departments involved in the process. At each step, they asked the workers to stop what they were doing and immediately process their loan application. They were shocked by what they found. From start to finish, the entire process took just ninety minutes! The six-day turnaround time was almost entirely due to delays in handing off the work from one department to another. The solution: IBM redesigned the process so that one person, not five people in five separate departments, now handles the entire loan approval process without any handoffs. The results were indeed dramatic. Reengineering the credit process reduced approval time from six days to four hours and allowed IBM Credit to increase the number of loans it handled by a factor of 100!

Mathias Rosenthal/Shutterstock.com

Reengineering changes an organization's orientation from vertical to horizontal. Instead of taking orders from upper management, lower- and middle-level managers and workers take orders from a customer who is at the beginning and end of each process. Instead of running independent functional departments, managers and workers in different departments take ownership of cross-functional processes. Instead of simplifying work so that it becomes increasingly specialized, reengineering complicates work by giving workers increased autonomy and responsibility for complete processes.

In essence, reengineering changes work by changing **task interdependence**, the extent to which collective action is required to complete an entire piece of work. As shown in Exhibit 9.10, there are three kinds of task interdependence.[31] In **pooled interdependence**, each job or department contributes to the whole independently. In **sequential interdependence**, work must be performed in succession because one group's or job's outputs become the inputs for the next group or job. Finally, in **reciprocal interdependence**, different jobs or groups work together in a back-and-forth manner to complete the process. By reducing the handoffs between different jobs or groups, reengineering decreases sequential interdependence. Likewise, reengineering decreases pooled interdependence by redesigning work so that formerly independent jobs or departments now work together to complete processes. Finally, reengineering increases reciprocal interdependence by making groups or individuals responsible for larger, more complete processes in which several steps may be accomplished at the same time.

As an organizational design tool, reengineering promises big rewards, but it has also come under severe criticism. The most serious complaint is that because it allows a few workers to do the work formerly done by many, reengineering is simply a corporate code word for cost cutting and worker layoffs.[32] For this reason, detractors claim that reengineering hurts morale and performance. Even though ordering times were reduced from three weeks to three days, Levi Strauss ended an $850 million reengineering project because of the fear and turmoil it created in the company's workforce. One low point occurred when Levi management, encouraged by its reengineering consultants, told 4,000 workers that they would have to "reapply for their jobs" as the company shifted from its traditional vertical structure to a process-based form of organizing. Thomas Kasten, Levi Strauss's vice president for reengineering and customer service at that time, says, "We felt the pressure building up [over reengineering efforts], and we were worried about the business."[33] Today, even reengineering gurus Hammer and Champy admit that roughly 70 percent of all reengineering projects fail because of the effects on people in the workplace. Says Hammer, "I wasn't smart enough about that [the people issues]. I was reflecting my engineering background and was insufficiently appreciative of the human dimension. I've [now] learned that's critical."[34]

9-4b Empowerment

Another way of redesigning intraorganizational processes is through empowerment. **Empowering workers** means permanently passing decision-making authority and responsibility from managers to workers. For workers to be fully empowered, companies must give them the information and resources they need to make and carry out good decisions and then reward them for taking individual initiative.[35] In other words, employees won't feel very empowered if they constantly have someone looking over their shoulders. French-based Carrefour, the second largest retailer in the world, has seen its profits and market share consistently shrink over the past decade. New CEO Georges Plassat feels that Carrefour had "excess centralization preventing it from delivering results." The clearest sign of that was Carrefour headquarters determining which products to sell at what prices in each store worldwide. Today, however, Plassat says, "There is a change in culture" to empower local store managers to make these decisions. For example, the store manager, not headquarters, decides how much floor space to use to sell TVs, how many kinds of TVs to sell (a full range or only the best sellers), and how the TVs are priced. Says Plassat, "We have specialists in the store[s] who know what is selling," and top management now listens to them.[36]

Task interdependence the extent to which collective action is required to complete an entire piece of work

Pooled interdependence work completed by having each job or department independently contribute to the whole

Sequential interdependence work completed in succession, with one group's or job's outputs becoming the inputs for the next group or job

Reciprocal interdependence work completed by different jobs or groups working together in a back-and-forth manner

Empowering workers permanently passing decision-making authority and responsibility from managers to workers by giving them the information and resources they need to make and carry out good decisions

Exhibit 9.10
Reengineering and Task Interdependence

Pooled
Interdependence

→ Finished
Product ←

Sequential
Interdependence

→ → → Finished
Product

Reciprocal
Interdependence

Finished
Product

© Cengage Learning

When workers are given the proper information and resources and are allowed to make good decisions, they experience strong feelings of empowerment. **Empowerment** is a feeling of intrinsic motivation in which workers perceive their work to have meaning and perceive themselves to be competent, having an impact, and capable of self-determination.[37] Work has meaning when it is consistent with personal standards and beliefs. Workers feel competent when they believe they can perform an activity with skill. The belief that they are having an impact comes from a feeling that they can affect work outcomes. A feeling of self-determination arises from workers' belief that they have the autonomy to choose how best to do their work.

Empowerment can lead to changes in organizational processes because meaning, competence, impact, and self-determination produce empowered employees who take active rather than passive roles in their work.

At Ritz-Carlton hotels, all employees are empowered to spend up to $2,000 to solve customer service issues. That's not $2,000 per year or $2,000 per day, it's $2,000 per incident. And, employees can spend that $2,000 without asking for managerial approval. Carmine Gallo, president of Gallo Communications Group, and his wife were eating at a particularly busy Ritz-Carlton restaurant, which meant the service was slow. Gallo says, "During one especially busy time at the hotel's restaurant, the waiter apologized for the wait, gave us complimentary appetizers, and paid for our desserts. When I asked him why he did so he said, 'I'm empowered to keep my guests happy.'"[38]

9-5 INTERORGANIZATIONAL PROCESSES

An **interorganizational process** is a collection of activities that occur *among companies* to transform inputs into outputs that customers value. In other words, many companies work together to create a product or service that keeps customers happy. Nutella, the chocolate and hazelnut spread, is headquartered in Italy, has five factories in Europe, two in South America, and one each in Russia, North America, and Australia. Those factories work with suppliers in Turkey (hazelnuts), Malaysia (palm oil), Nigeria (cocoa), Brazil (sugar), and France (vanilla). The 250,000 tons of Nutella produced each year are then sold to grocers by sales offices and sales brokers in seventy-five different countries.[39]

In this section, you'll explore interorganizational processes by learning about 9-5a modular organizations and 9-5b virtual organizations.

9-5a Modular Organizations

Stephen Roach, former chief economist for investment bank Morgan Stanley, says that companies increasingly want to take "functions that aren't central to their core competency" and outsource them.[40] Except for the core business activities that they can perform better, faster, and cheaper than others,

Empowerment feeling of intrinsic motivation in which workers perceive their work to have impact and meaning and perceive themselves to be competent and capable of self-determination

Interorganizational process a collection of activities that take place among companies to transform inputs into outputs that customers value

modular organizations outsource all remaining business activities to outside companies, suppliers, specialists, or consultants. The term *modular* is used because the business activities purchased from outside companies can be added and dropped as needed, much like adding pieces to a three-dimensional puzzle. Exhibit 9.11 depicts a modular organization in which the company has chosen to keep training, human resources, sales, product design, manufacturing, customer service, research and development, and information technology as core business activities but has outsourced the noncore activities of product distribution, web page design, advertising, payroll, accounting, and packaging.

The primary advantage of modular organizations is that they can cost significantly less to run than traditional organizations because they pay for outsourced labor, expertise, or manufacturing capabilities only when needed. Merck, one of the world's leading pharmaceutical companies, is transforming into a modular organization. As little as three years ago, two-thirds of Merck's research budget was spent on in-house scientists and research labs that conducted expensive clinical research trials to test the drugs that Merck had in development. Today, Merck spends only one-third of its research budget on in-house clinical research. It outsources the rest to Quintiles, a company with 29,000 employees in 100 countries, that specializes in conducting large-scale clinical research trials for pharmaceutical companies such as Merck.[41] To obtain cost advantages, however, modular organizations need reliable partners—vendors and suppliers with whom they can work closely and can trust.

Modular organizations have disadvantages, too. The primary disadvantage is the loss of control that occurs when key business activities are outsourced to other companies. Also, companies may reduce their competitive advantage in

two ways if they mistakenly outsource a core business activity. First, as a result of competitive and technological change, the noncore business activities a company has outsourced may suddenly become the basis for competitive advantage. Second, related to that point, suppliers to whom work is outsourced can sometimes become competitors.

9-5b Virtual Organizations

In contrast to modular organizations, in which the interorganizational process revolves around a central company, a **virtual organization** is part of a network in which many companies share skills, costs, capabilities, markets, and customers with each other. Exhibit 9.12 shows a virtual organization in which, for today, the parts of a virtual company consist of product design, purchasing, manufacturing, advertising, and

Exhibit 9.11
Modular Organization

Outsourced Noncore Business Activities

Product Distribution · Website Design · Advertising · Training · Research & Development · Payroll · Human Resources · Information Technology · Customer Service · Accounting · Sales · Product Design · Manufacturing · Packaging

Core Business Activities

© Cengage Learning

Modular organization
an organization that outsources noncore business activities to outside companies, suppliers, specialists, or consultants

Virtual organization
an organization that is part of a network in which many companies share skills, costs, capabilities, markets, and customers to collectively solve customer problems or provide specific products or services

360b/Shutterstock.com

information technology. Unlike modular organizations, in which the outside organizations are tightly linked to one central company, virtual organizations work with some companies in the network alliance, but not with all. So, whereas a puzzle with various pieces is a fitting metaphor for a modular organization, a potluck dinner is an appropriate metaphor for a virtual organization. All participants bring their finest food dish but eat only what they want.

Another difference is that the working relationships between modular organizations and outside companies tend to be more stable and longer lasting than the shorter, often temporary, relationships found among the virtual companies in a network alliance. The composition of a virtual organization is always changing. The combination of network partners that a virtual corporation has at any one time depends on the expertise needed to solve a particular problem or provide a specific product or service. For instance, today the business might need to focus on advertising and product design, as shown in Exhibit 9.12, but tomorrow, the business could want something completely different. In this sense, the term "virtual organization" means the organization that exists "at the moment."

Virtual organizations have a number of advantages. They let companies share costs, and because members can quickly combine their efforts to meet customers' needs, they are fast and flexible. Finally, because each member of the network alliance is the best at what it does, virtual organizations should in theory provide better products and services in all respects.

As with modular organizations, a disadvantage of virtual organizations is that after work has been outsourced, it can be difficult to control the quality of work done by network partners. The greatest disadvantage, however, is that tremendous managerial skills are required to make a network of independent organizations work well together, especially because their relationships tend to be short and based on a single task or project. Virtual organizations are using

Exhibit 9.12

Virtual Organizations

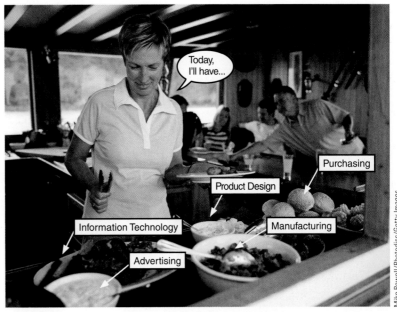

Mike Powell/Photodisc/Getty Images

two methods to solve this problem. The first is to use a *broker*. In traditional, hierarchical organizations, managers plan, organize, and control. But with the horizontal, interorganizational processes that characterize virtual organizations, the job of a broker is to create and assemble the knowledge, skills, and resources from different companies for outside parties, such as customers.[42] The second way to make networks of virtual organizations more manageable is to use a *virtual organization agreement* that, somewhat like a contract, specifies the schedules, responsibilities, costs, payouts, and liabilities for participating organizations.[43]

STUDY TOOLS 9

LOCATED IN TEXTBOOK

☐ Rip-out and review chapter review card

LOCATED AT WWW.CENGAGEBRAIN.COM

☐ Review key term flashcards and create your own from StudyBits

☐ Track your knowledge and understanding of key concepts, using the concept tracker

☐ Complete practice and graded quizzes to prepare for tests

☐ Complete interactive content within the exposition

☐ View chapter highlight box content at the beginning of each chapter

YOUR FEED-BACK YOUR BOOK

Our research never ends. Continual feedback from you ensures
that we keep up with your changing needs.

10 Managing Teams

Jirsak/Shutterstock.com

After you finish this chapter, go to **PAGE 215** for STUDY TOOLS

10-1 THE GOOD AND BAD OF USING TEAMS

Ninety-one percent of organizations are significantly improving their effectiveness by using work teams.[1] Procter & Gamble and Cummins Engine began using teams in 1962 and 1973, respectively. Boeing, Caterpillar, Champion International, Ford Motor Company, 3M, and General Electric established work teams in the mid- to late-1980s. Today, most companies use teams to tackle a variety of issues.[2] "Teams are ubiquitous. Whether we are talking about software development, Olympic hockey, disease outbreak response, or urban warfare, teams represent the critical unit that 'gets things done' in today's world."[3]

Work teams consist of a small number of people with complementary skills who hold themselves mutually accountable for pursuing a common purpose, achieving performance goals, and improving interdependent work processes.[4] By this definition, computer programmers working on separate projects in the same department of a company would not be considered a team. To be a team, the programmers would have to be interdependent and share responsibility and accountability for the quality and amount of computer code they produced.[5] Teams are becoming more important in many industries because they help organizations respond to specific problems and challenges. Though work teams are not the answer for every situation or organization, if the right teams are used properly and in the right settings, teams can dramatically improve company performance over more traditional management approaches while also instilling a sense of vitality in the workplace that is otherwise difficult to achieve.

Let's begin our discussion of teams by learning about 10-1a the advantages of teams, 10-1b the disadvantages of teams, and 10-1c when to use and not use teams.

10-1a The Advantages of Teams

Companies are making greater use of teams because teams have been shown to improve customer satisfaction, product and service quality, speed and efficiency in product development, employee job satisfaction, and decision making.[6] For example, one survey indicated that 80 percent of companies with more than 100 employees use teams, and 90 percent of all U.S. employees work part of their day in a team.[7]

Teams help businesses increase *customer satisfaction* in several ways. One way is to create work teams that are trained to meet the needs of specific customers. After financial scandals tarnished London-based Barclays Bank's reputation, it hired a director of customer experience to lead teams that were directly responsible for making sure, "the voice of the customer is heard."[8] One of those customers is business consultant and blogger Maz Iqbal. When Iqbal moved his business's bank accounts to Barclays from another bank, he blogged that his initial interactions were "frustrating." When he subsequently changed his company's registered name, he expected more paperwork, inefficiency, and frustration. Instead, before he visited his local branch, Barclays mailed him new checks and credit cards already imprinted with his company's new name. Said an obviously satisfied Iqbal, "I feel grateful. Why? Because Barclays Bank helped me out—saved me time, effort, concern—without me even asking them to help me out. They anticipated a need and met it."[9]

Teams also help firms improve *product and service quality* in several ways.[10] In contrast to traditional organizational structures, in which management is responsible for organizational outcomes and performance, teams take direct responsibility for the quality of the products and service they produce and sell. Oriental Trading Company (OTC) sells party supplies, arts and crafts, toys and games, and teaching supplies on the Internet. Like most retail websites, OTC's site allows customers to write comments about the products they buy. When customers complained about its Inflatable Solar System, giving it two stars out of five, members of OTC's intradepartmental teams sprang to action. A team member from the quality department worked directly with the manufacturer to improve quality. Another from copywriting worked with a team member from merchandising to post new photos of the improved product along with a more accurate product description. Other members of the team contacted dissatisfied customers to tell them that OTC had listened and had taken steps to address their concerns. Seven weeks after the first negative comment appeared on OTC's website, the improved product was available for sale. Customers consistently rate the new version at four out of five stars.[11]

Another reason for using teams is that teamwork often leads to increased *job satisfaction*.[12] Teamwork can be more satisfying than traditional work

> **Work team** a small number of people with complementary skills who hold themselves mutually accountable for pursuing a common purpose, achieving performance goals, and improving interdependent work processes

Avoiding Team-Building Fiascos

Regardless of where they fall on the spectrum of too boring or too extreme, corporate team-building activities are a notorious source of dread and eye rolling. According to David Jacobsen, founder of **TrivWorks** team-building company, "The worst possible outcome is having the exact opposite of what you intended happen," Jacobson says. "You've crushed morale and left your employees alienated or disconnected." Team building can be positive and meaningful, however, if overeager managers can stick to a few guidelines:

1. Clearly identify the purpose and goals of the activity and let your staff know up front.

2. Let the purpose and goals dictate the type of activity.

3. Avoid activities that simulate violence, cause harm, or humiliate the participants.

4. Draw clear connections between the activity and how the team performs in the workplace.

5. Incorporate a challenge.

The key is to make the activity relevant. "If the exercise is good, your team will take what they did or learned back to the workplace," says Jacobson. "They're going to collaborate and communicate better."

Source: J. A. Graves, "Corporate Team-Building Activities: The Good, the Bad, and the Really Ugly," *U.S. News*, September 24, 2014, accessed May 2, 2015. http://money.usnews.com/money/careers/articles/2014/09/25/corporate-team-building-activities-the-good-the-bad-and-the-really-ugly/.

because it gives workers a chance to improve their skills. This is often accomplished through **cross-training**, in which team members are taught how to do all or most of the jobs performed by the other team members. The advantage for the organization is that cross-training allows a team to function normally when one member is absent, quits, or is transferred. The advantage for workers is that cross-training broadens their skills and increases their capabilities while also making their work more varied and interesting.

Teamwork is also satisfying because work teams often receive proprietary business information that typically is available only to managers. The **Great Little Box Company (GLBC)**, which makes corrugated boxes, custom product displays, and flexible and protective packaging for manufacturers, has an "open books" philosophy, where team members are given full access to the company's financial information. Founder Robert Meggy says, "It makes people feel more a part of the company. It instills a sense of trust. Regardless of whether the news is good or bad, people want to know and, ultimately, will try harder to make the company more profitable." After all, he says, "We want employees to run the company like their own business." Team member and customer-service representative Sandra Fung says, "If we have been profitable that month, it makes me feel good to learn that I have contributed to that." Finally, to drive home the importance of teams and teamwork, everyone receives equal monthly profit sharing checks. Says Meggy, "When it comes to teamwork, everyone is equal here. The truck drivers, the controller, office staff, plant supervisor—everybody gets the same amount."[13]

Team members also gain job satisfaction from unique leadership responsibilities that are not typically available in traditional organizations. Finally, teams share many of the advantages of group decision making discussed in Chapter 5. For instance, because team members possess different knowledge, skills, abilities, and experiences, a team is able to view problems from multiple perspectives. This diversity of viewpoints increases the odds that team decisions will solve the underlying causes of problems and not just address the symptoms. The increased knowledge and information available to teams also make it easier for them to generate more alternative solutions, a critical part of improving the quality of decisions. Because team members are involved in decision-making

Cross-training training team members to do all or most of the jobs performed by the other team members processes, they are also likely to be more committed to making those decisions work. In short, teams can do a much better job than individuals in two important steps of the decision-making process: defining the problem and generating alternative solutions.

10-1b The Disadvantages of Teams

Although teams can significantly improve customer satisfaction, product and service quality, speed and efficiency in product development, employee job satisfaction, and decision making, using teams does not guarantee these positive outcomes. In fact, if you've ever participated in team projects in your classes, you're probably already aware of some of the problems inherent in work teams. Despite all of their promise, teams and teamwork are also prone to these significant disadvantages: initially high turnover, social loafing, and the problems associated with group decision making.

The first disadvantage of work teams is *initially high turnover*. Teams aren't for everyone, and some workers balk at the responsibility, effort, and learning required in team settings. When Zappos, the online shoe company changed from a traditional to a team-based structure (what it calls Holacracy), where there are no bosses and no titles, and employees manage themselves, it offered everyone in the company three months of severance pay to leave if they decided that it wasn't right for them. Turns out that of its 1,500 employees, 14 percent, decided to leave. Zappos' John Bunch, who is managing the transition to Holacracy, said, "Whatever the number of people who took the offer was the right number as they made the decision that was right for them and right for Zappos."[14]

Social loafing is another disadvantage of work teams. **Social loafing** occurs when workers withhold their efforts and fail to perform their share of the work.[15]

Zappos moved to what it calls "Holacracy." There are no bosses, no titles, and employees manage themselves.

Ethan Miller/Getty Images News/Getty Images

A nineteenth-century French engineer named Maximilian Ringlemann first documented social loafing when he found that one person pulling on a rope alone exerted an average of 139 pounds of force on the rope. In groups of three, the average force dropped to 117 pounds per person. In groups of eight, the average dropped to just 68 pounds per person. Ringlemann concluded that the larger the team, the smaller the individual effort. In fact, social loafing is more likely to occur in larger groups where identifying and monitoring the efforts of individual team members can be difficult.[16] In other words, social loafers count on being able to blend into the background, where their lack of effort isn't easily spotted.

From team-based class projects, most students already know about social loafers or "slackers," who contribute poor, little, or no work whatsoever. Not surprisingly, a study of 250 student teams found that the most talented students are typically the least satisfied with teamwork because of having to carry slackers and do a disproportionate share of their team's work.[17] Perceptions of fairness are negatively related to the extent of social loafing within teams.[18]

Finally, teams share many of the *disadvantages of group decision making* discussed in Chapter 5, such as groupthink. In *groupthink*, members of highly cohesive groups feel intense pressure not to disagree with each other so that the group can approve a proposed solution. Because groupthink restricts discussion and leads to consideration of a limited number of alternative solutions, it usually results in poor decisions. Also, team decision making takes considerable time, and team meetings can often be unproductive and inefficient. Another possible pitfall is *minority domination*, where just one or two people dominate team discussions, restricting consideration of different problem definitions and alternative solutions. Minority domination is especially likely to occur when the team leader talks so much during team discussions, effectively discouraging other team members from speaking up. When that happens, team performance drops significantly.[19] Finally, team members may not feel accountable for the decisions and actions taken by the team.

10-1c When to Use Teams

As the two previous subsections made clear, teams have significant advantages *and* disadvantages. Therefore, the question is not whether to use teams, but *when* and *where* to use teams for maximum benefit and minimum cost. As Doug Johnson, associate director

Social loafing behavior in which team members withhold their efforts and fail to perform their share of the work

Exhibit 10.1

When to Use and When Not to Use Teams

Use Teams When . . .

✓ there is a clear, engaging reason or purpose.

✓ the job can't be done unless people work together.

✓ rewards can be provided for teamwork and team performance.

✓ ample resources are available.

Don't Use Teams When . . .

✗ there isn't a clear, engaging reason or purpose.

✗ the job can be done by people working independently.

✗ rewards are provided for individual effort and performance.

✗ the necessary resources are not available.

Source: R. Wageman, "Critical Success Factors for Creating Superb Self-Managing Teams," *Organizational Dynamics* 26, no. 1 (1997): 49–61.

iStockphoto.com/Tunart

at the Center for Collaborative Organizations at the University of North Texas, puts it, "Teams are a means to an end, not an end in themselves. You have to ask yourself questions first. Does the work require interdependence? Will the team philosophy fit company strategy? Will management make a long-term commitment to this process?"[20] Exhibit 10.1 provides some additional guidelines on when to use or not use teams.[21]

First, teams should be used when there is a clear, engaging reason or purpose for using them. Too many companies use teams because they're popular or because the companies assume that teams can fix all problems. Teams are much more likely to succeed if they know why they exist and what they are supposed to accomplish, and they are more likely to fail if they don't.

Second, teams should be used when the job can't be done unless people work together. This typically means that teams are needed when tasks are complex, require multiple perspectives, or require repeated interaction with others to complete. Because of the enormous complexity of today's cars, you would think that auto companies routinely use interconnected design teams. After all, the typical car has 30,000 parts, eighty different computer modules, indicators sensing how close other cars are when parking or going 70 mph, and the ability to automatically adjust braking, cornering, gas mileage, and acceleration. But auto companies don't routinely use interconnected design teams, as most designers are responsible for separate sections or parts of the car. Achim Badstübner, head of **Audi Group** exterior design, says, "We tend to make the mistake that we have an exterior department, an interior department and a technology

department, and they all know what they're doing but the connection is not so good." Audi, however, takes a team approach. Badstübner says, "I think it's very important to basically lock them in one room, literally speaking. Then there is an interaction: you talk to the guy who does seats and he tells you something about his expertise and you might take something from him that helps you to develop a new wheel, for example." Badstübner says by connecting the teams, "you get a different result because through this method you get the best of every brain. I think you can't survive if you just depend on one brain to do a complex thing like [design] a car."[22]

Third, teams should be used when rewards can be provided for teamwork and team performance. Rewards that depend on team performance rather than individual performance are the key to rewarding team behaviors and efforts. You'll read more about team rewards later in the chapter, but for now it's enough to know that if the type of reward (individual versus team) is not matched to the type of performance (individual versus team), teams won't work.

10-2 KINDS OF TEAMS

*Let's continue our discussion of teams by learning about the different kinds of teams that companies such as Google and Maytag use to make themselves more competitive. We look first at **10-2a how teams differ in terms of autonomy, which is the key dimension that makes one team different from another**, and then at **10-2b some special kinds of teams**.*

Exhibit 10.2
Team Autonomy Continuum

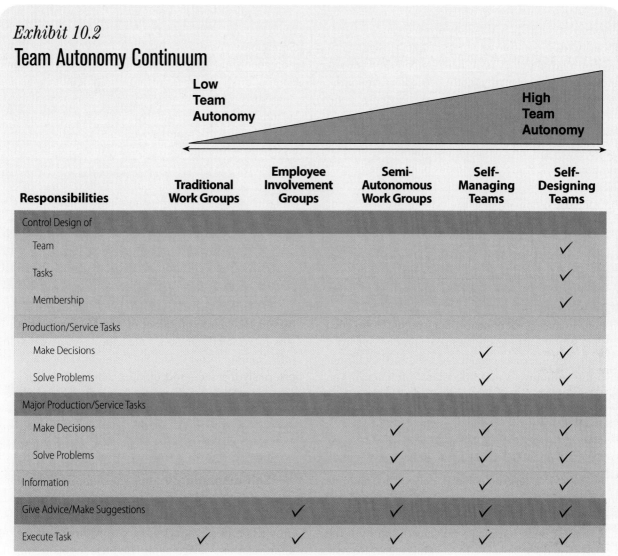

Low Team Autonomy ⟷ High Team Autonomy

Responsibilities	Traditional Work Groups	Employee Involvement Groups	Semi-Autonomous Work Groups	Self-Managing Teams	Self-Designing Teams
Control Design of					
Team					✓
Tasks					✓
Membership					✓
Production/Service Tasks					
Make Decisions				✓	✓
Solve Problems				✓	✓
Major Production/Service Tasks					
Make Decisions			✓	✓	✓
Solve Problems			✓	✓	✓
Information			✓	✓	✓
Give Advice/Make Suggestions		✓	✓	✓	✓
Execute Task	✓	✓	✓	✓	✓

Sources: R. D. Banker, J. M. Field, R. G. Schroeder, and K. K. Sinha, "Impact of Work Teams on Manufacturing Performance: A Longitudinal Field Study," *Academy of Management Journal* 39 (1996): 867–890; J. R. Hackman, "The Psychology of Self-Management in Organizations," in *Psychology and Work: Productivity, Change, and Employment*, ed. M. S. Pallak and R. Perlof (Washington, DC: American Psychological Association), 85–136.

10-2a Autonomy, the Key Dimension

Teams can be classified in a number of ways, such as permanent or temporary, or functional or cross-functional. However, studies indicate that the amount of autonomy possessed by a team is the key difference among teams.[23] *Autonomy* is the degree to which workers have the discretion, freedom, and independence to decide how and when to accomplish their jobs. Exhibit 10.2 shows how five kinds of teams differ in terms of autonomy. Moving left to right across the autonomy continuum at the top of the exhibit, traditional work groups and employee involvement groups have the least autonomy, semi-autonomous work groups have more autonomy, and,

finally, self-managing teams and self-designing teams have the most autonomy. Moving from bottom to top along the left side of the exhibit, note that the number of responsibilities given to each kind of team increases directly with its autonomy. Let's review each of these kinds of teams and their autonomy and responsibilities in more detail.

The smallest amount of autonomy is found in **traditional work groups**, where two or more people work together to achieve a shared goal. In these groups, workers are responsible for doing the work or executing the task, but they do not have direct responsibility

> **Traditional work group** a group composed of two or more people who work together to achieve a shared goal

or control over their work. Workers report to managers, who are responsible for their performance and have the authority to hire and fire them, make job assignments, and control resources. For instance, suppose that an experienced worker blatantly refuses to do his share of the work, saying, "I've done my time. Let the younger employees do the work." In a team with high autonomy, the responsibility of getting this employee to put forth his fair share of effort would belong to his teammates. But, in a traditional work group, that responsibility belongs to the boss or supervisor. The supervisor in this situation calmly confronted the employee and told him, "We need your talent, [and] your knowledge of these machines. But if you won't work, you'll have to go elsewhere." Within days, the employee's behavior improved.[24]

Employee involvement teams, which have somewhat more autonomy, meet on company time on a weekly or monthly basis to provide advice or make suggestions to management concerning specific issues such as plant safety, customer relations, or product quality.[25] Though they offer advice and suggestions, they do not have the authority to make decisions. Membership on these teams is often voluntary, but members may be selected because of their expertise. The idea behind employee involvement teams is that the people closest to the problem or situation are best able to recommend solutions. For more than three years, production of Boeing's 787 Dreamliner was delayed by multiple problems—parts shortages, improper installation, failed test flights, and more. Because of production delays, Boeing must build ten planes per month, up from the typical two and a half planes. To meet this aggressive goal, it established nearly 200 employee involvement teams to analyze the way 787s are assembled and make changes to maximize efficiency. For example, one employee involvement team found that ducts already installed in the plane were being damaged because workers were kicking and stepping on them while doing other work. The damaged ducts then had to be removed and replaced. The team recommended that temporary covers be placed over the ducts, thus eliminating delays and increased costs.[26]

Semi-autonomous work groups not only provide advice and suggestions to management but also have the authority to make decisions and solve problems related to the major tasks required to produce a product or service. Semi-autonomous groups regularly receive information about budgets, work quality and performance, and competitors' products. Furthermore, members of semi-autonomous work groups are typically cross-trained in a number of different skills and tasks. In short, semi-autonomous work groups give employees the authority to make decisions that are typically made by supervisors and managers.

That authority is not complete, however. Managers still play a role, though one that is much reduced compared with traditional work groups, in supporting the work of semi-autonomous work groups. The role a manager plays on a team usually evolves over time. "It may start with helping to transition problem-solving responsibilities to the team, filling miscellaneous requests for the team, and doing ad hoc tasks," says Steven Hitchcock, president of Axis Performance Advisors in Portland, Oregon. Later, the team may develop into a mini-enterprise, and the former manager becomes externally focused—sort of an account manager for the customer. Managers have to adjust what they do based on the sophistication of the team.[27] A lot of what managers of semi-autonomous work groups do is ask good questions, provide resources, and facilitate performance of group goals.

Self-managing teams are different from semi-autonomous work groups in that team members manage and control *all* of the major tasks *directly related* to production of a product or service without first getting approval from management. This includes managing and controlling the acquisition of materials, making a product or providing a service, and ensuring timely delivery. At Connecticut Spring & Stamping, a precision manufacturing firm, self-managing teams determine the master schedule that controls the order in which parts will flow from machines to workers, the location and proximity of machines and work stations, when and who gets overtime work (and how much), and how teams will be rewarded. For example, the teams designed a three-stage program in which constant improvement in on-time delivery is required to receive rewards. All of these decisions are made without management's input or approval.[28]

The use of self-managing teams has significantly increased productivity at a number of other companies, increasing quality by 12 percent at AT&T, reducing errors by 13 percent at FedEx, and helping 3M increase production by 300 percent at one of its manufacturing plants.[29] Seventy-two percent of *Fortune* 1,000 companies have at least one self-managing team, up from 28 percent in 1987.[30]

Employee involvement team team that provides advice or makes suggestions to management concerning specific issues

Semi-autonomous work group a group that has the authority to make decisions and solve problems related to the major tasks of producing a product or service

Self-managing team a team that manages and controls all of the major tasks of producing a product or service

Self-designing teams have all the characteristics of self-managing teams, but they can also control and change the design of the teams themselves, the tasks they do and how and when they do them, and the membership of the teams. Valve a Bellevue, Washington maker of video games, has no managers. In fact, the company defines "manager" in its employee handbook as, "The kind of people we don't have any of. So, if you see one, tell somebody, because it's probably the ghost of whoever was in this building before us."[31] "We do have a founder/president, but even he isn't your manager. This company is yours to steer—toward opportunities and away from risks. You have the power to green-light projects. You have the power to ship projects."[32] But what makes Valve's team self-designing (and not just self-managing), is that they control and change the teams themselves by deciding who gets hired, fired, promoted, and what they get paid (which is determined by peer rankings regarding contributions to team projects).[33]

10-2b Special Kinds of Teams

Companies are also increasingly using several other kinds of teams that can't easily be categorized in terms of autonomy: cross-functional teams, virtual teams, and project teams. Depending on how these teams are designed, they can be either low- or high-autonomy teams.

Cross-functional teams are intentionally composed of employees from different functional areas of the organization.[34] Because their members have different functional backgrounds, education, and experience, cross-functional teams usually attack problems from multiple perspectives and generate more ideas and alternative solutions, all of which are especially important when trying to innovate or solve problems creatively.[35] Cross-functional teams can be used almost anywhere in an organization and are often used in conjunction with matrix and product organizational structures (see Chapter 9). They can also be used either with part-time or temporary team assignments or with full-time, long-term teams.

Virtual teams are groups of geographically and/or organizationally dispersed coworkers who use a combination of telecommunications and information technologies to accomplish an organizational task.[36] Virtual teams are increasingly common, and are used by 28 percent of U.S.-based corporations and 66 percent of multinational firms.[37] Members of virtual teams rarely meet face-to-face; instead, they use email, videoconferencing, and group communication software. Virtual teams can be employee involvement teams, self-managing teams, or nearly any kind of team discussed in this chapter. Virtual

teams are often (but not necessarily) temporary teams that are set up to accomplish a specific task.

Virtual teams are highly flexible because employees can work with each other regardless of physical location or time zones, but they're also much more complex than face-to-face teams when it comes to purpose, communication, and trust. Virtual teams often suffer from a lack of understanding regarding the team's purpose and team member roles. Dave Davis of RedFly Marketing has managed virtual teams for more than a decade and says, "You'd be surprised how many people will wait until halfway through a project to admit they don't understand something."[38] Because of distance and different time zones, 38 percent of virtual team members cite communication as their biggest challenge. Digital communication (email, IM, virtual conferencing) accounts for 63 percent of communication on virtual teams, yet 23 percent of team members find that long email discussion threads threaten (rather than help) effective project communication.[39] So, it's important for members to know when to use different communication media. Mary Ellen Slater, a manager at **Reputation Capital**, says, "At Rep Cap, we IM each other throughout the day, but there are times when a phone call or face-to-face meeting is better. A new project or something that deviates from our usual process may merit a phone call."[40] Finally, trust is critical for virtual teams to be successful. Andrea Rozman, owner of Your Gal Friday, a company that provides virtual personal assistants, says, "You have to take that leap of faith. You have to believe that once you hand them the work, they will do it, and get it done on time."[41] See Exhibit 10.3 for more information on managing virtual teams.

Project teams are created to complete specific, one-time projects or tasks within a limited time.[42] Project teams are often used to develop new products, significantly improve existing products, roll out new information systems, or build new factories or offices. The project team is typically led by a project manager who has the overall responsibility for planning, staffing, and managing the team, which usually includes employees from different functional areas. Effective project teams demand both individual and

Self-designing team
a team that has the characteristics of self-managing teams but also controls team design, work tasks, and team membership

Cross-functional team
a team composed of employees from different functional areas of the organization

Virtual team a team composed of geographically and/or organizationally dispersed coworkers who use telecommunication and information technologies to accomplish an organizational task

Project team a team created to complete specific, one-time projects or tasks within a limited time

Exhibit 10.3
Tips for Managing Virtual Teams

1. Invest in an online resource where members can learn quickly about one another.

2. Choose a few team members who already know each other.

3. Break the team's work up into modules so that progress in one location is not overly dependent on progress in another.

4. Create an online site where a team can collaborate, exchange ideas, and inspire one another.

5. Encourage frequent communication, but don't try to force social gatherings.

6. Assign only tasks that are challenging and interesting.

7. Ensure the task is meaningful to the team and the company.

8. When building a virtual team, solicit volunteers as much as possible.

Source: L. Gratton, "Working Together… When Apart," *Wall Street Journal*, June 19, 2012, accessed May 8, 2015. http://www.wsj.com/articles/SB118165895540732559.

collective responsibility.[43] One advantage of project teams is that drawing employees from different functional areas can reduce or eliminate communication barriers. In turn, as long as team members feel free to express their ideas, thoughts, and concerns, free-flowing communication encourages cooperation among separate departments and typically speeds up the design process.[44] Another advantage of project teams is their flexibility. When projects are finished, project team members either move on to the next project or return to their functional units. For example, publication of this book required designers, editors, page compositors, and web designers, among others. When the task was finished, these people applied their skills to other textbook projects. Because of this flexibility, project teams are often used with the matrix organizational designs discussed in Chapter 9.

10-3 WORK TEAM CHARACTERISTICS

"Why did I ever let you talk me into teams? They're nothing but trouble."[45] Lots of managers have this reaction after making the move to teams. Many don't realize that this reaction is normal, both for them and

Norms informally agreed-on standards that regulate team behavior

for workers. In fact, such a reaction is characteristic of the *storming* stage of team development (discussed in Section 10-3e). Managers who are familiar with these stages and with the other important characteristics of teams will be better prepared to manage the predictable changes that occur when companies make the switch to team-based structures.

*Understanding the characteristics of work teams is essential for making teams an effective part of an organization. Therefore, in this section you'll learn about **10-3a team norms, 10-3b team cohesiveness, 10-3c team size, 10-3d team conflict,** and **10-3e the stages of team development.***

10-3a Team Norms

Over time, teams develop **norms**, which are informally agreed-on standards that regulate team behavior.[46] Norms are valuable because they let team members know what is expected of them. While leading Orbis International, a nonprofit organization in which a DC-10 jet, converted to a "Flying Eye Hospital," transports volunteer doctors and nurses to treat eye disease throughout the world, Jilly Stephens noticed a problem with punctuality. She said, "When I first got to the field, you would have the nurses, engineers, whoever, waiting, and you would maybe have one [person] who just couldn't drag himself out of bed and everybody's waiting." So she simply decided that there would be a new norm for the team: they leave on time. "If they aren't there [on time], the bus leaves. You get to the airport yourself. If we were in Tunisia, that meant finding a bike and cycling across the desert to get to the airport." Says Stephens, "We saw behaviors change fairly rapidly."[47]

Studies indicate that norms are one of the most powerful influences on work behavior because they regulate the everyday actions that allow teams to function effectively. Team norms are often associated with positive outcomes such as stronger organizational commitment, more trust in management, and stronger job and organizational satisfaction.[48] Effective work teams develop norms about the quality and timeliness of job performance, absenteeism, safety, and honest expression of ideas and opinions.

Surgeon Atul Gawande, author of *The Checklist Manifesto*, says that with 6,000 drugs, 4,000 medical procedures, and doctors and nurses specializing in hundreds of medical subfields, "The complexity of what we [in modern medicine] have to deliver on exceeds our abilities as experts partly because the volume of knowledge has exceeded what training can possibly provide."[49] So, in his operating rooms, Gawande and his surgical teams use and review checklists to make sure each small but critical step is completed. Before administering anesthesia, the nurse and anesthetist will determine if the site of the surgery is marked, whether the anesthesia machine and medication check have been completed, and whether the patient has a difficult airway or is at risk of aspiration (vomiting into the airway). Likewise, before the first incision takes place, all team members will be asked to introduce themselves and the roles they'll be performing, and the surgeon will be asked to state where the incision will be made and what kind of critical, nonroutine steps might be taken if things don't go as planned.[50] The review checklists are a powerful way of making sure that all members of the surgical team do what they're supposed to, that is, follow agreed-on standards of behavior or norms.

Norms can also influence team behavior in negative ways. For example, most people would agree that damaging organizational property; saying or doing something to hurt someone at work; intentionally doing one's work badly, incorrectly, or slowly; griping about coworkers; deliberately bending or breaking rules; and doing something to harm the company or boss are negative behaviors. A study of workers from thirty-four teams in twenty different organizations found that teams with negative norms strongly influenced their team members to engage in these negative behaviors. In fact, the longer individuals were members of a team with negative norms and the more frequently they interacted with their teammates, the more likely they were to perform negative behaviors. Because team norms typically develop early in the life of a team, these results indicate how important it is for teams to establish positive norms from the outset.[51]

10-3b Team Cohesiveness

Cohesiveness is another important characteristic of work teams. **Cohesiveness** is the extent to which team members are attracted to a team and motivated to remain in it.[52] What can be done to promote team cohesiveness? First, make sure that all team members are present at team meetings and activities. Team cohesiveness suffers when members are allowed to withdraw from the team and miss team meetings and events.[53] Second, create additional opportunities for teammates to work together by rearranging work schedules and creating common workspaces. Bank of America discovered the value of cohesive teams when it did a study tracking employee behavior. When Bank of America experimented by having call center employees wear sensors monitoring their movements throughout the office, it found that the most productive employees were in cohesive teams that communicated frequently. So, to encourage more interaction, it scheduled team members to all have breaks at the same time, rather than solo breaks. As a result, worker productivity rose 10 percent.[54] When task interdependence is high, and team members have lots of chances to work together, team cohesiveness tends to increase.[55] Third, engaging in nonwork activities as a team can help build cohesion. The NBA's Golden State Warriors do something that most NBA teams don't—they eat together when on the road. Ten-year veteran center Andrew Bogut says, "We go out together and eat together way more than any other team I've been on." Why? They like each other. Center Festus Ezili says, "And you see it on the court." Indeed, when this was written, the Warriors had the number one offense, the number two defense, and the most assists in the league, including secondary assists, "the pass before the pass which created the basket." Forward David Lee says, "Chemistry is not something you can fake. You either have it or you don't."[56] Finally, companies build team cohesiveness by making employees feel that they are part of an organization.

10-3c Team Size

The relationship between team size and performance appears to be curvilinear. Very small or very large teams may not perform as well as moderately sized teams. For most teams, the right size is somewhere between six and nine members.[57] A team of this size is small enough for the team members to get to know each other and for each member to have an opportunity to contribute in a meaningful way to the success of the team. At the same time, the team is large enough to take advantage of team members' diverse skills, knowledge, and perspectives. It is also easier to instill a sense of responsibility and mutual accountability in teams of this size.[58] Team size has a significant impact on the value of a company as well. Among companies with a market capitalization of $10 billion or more, those with smaller boards of directors outperform their peers by 8.5 percent, and those with larger boards underperform their peers by nearly 11 percent. With only seven directors, **Netflix's** board was able to spend nine months discussing a potential price increase. Director Jay Hoag says, "We get in-depth. That's easier with a small group." Netflix outperforms its sector peers by 32 percent.[59] The General Motors board of directors, however, has fourteen members. Its chairman, Tim Solso says, "Often you have people saying the same thing. It's just not as efficient as a smaller board."[60] Like GM, pharmaceutical company **Eli Lilly** also has fourteen members, and someone close to the company said its board "is too big to encourage the kinds of discussions you want. . . . a number of people feel constrained asking a second or third question."[61]

> **Cohesiveness** the extent to which team members are attracted to a team and motivated to remain in it

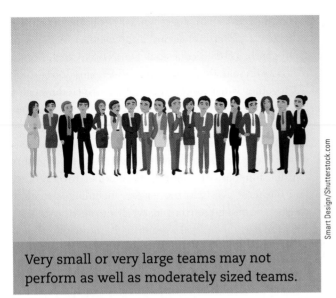

Very small or very large teams may not perform as well as moderately sized teams.

When teams get too large, team members find it difficult to get to know one another, and the team may splinter into smaller subgroups. When this occurs, subgroups sometimes argue and disagree, weakening overall team cohesion. As teams grow, there is also a greater chance of *minority domination*, where just a few team members dominate team discussions. Even if minority domination doesn't occur, larger groups may not have time for all team members to share their input. And when team members feel that their contributions are unimportant or not needed, the result is less involvement, effort, and accountability to the team.[62] Large teams also face logistical problems such as finding an appropriate time

or place to meet. Finally, the incidence of social loafing, discussed earlier in the chapter, is much higher in large teams.

Just as team performance can suffer when a team is too large, it can also be negatively affected when a team is too small. Teams with just a few people may lack the diversity of skills and knowledge found in larger teams. Also, teams that are too small are unlikely to gain the advantages of team decision making (multiple perspectives, generating more ideas and alternative solutions, and stronger commitment) found in larger teams.

What signs indicate that a team's size needs to be changed? If decisions are taking too long, if the team has difficulty making decisions or taking action, if a few members dominate the team, or if the commitment or efforts of

team members are weak, chances are the team is too big. In contrast, if a team is having difficulty coming up with ideas or generating solutions, or if the team does not have the expertise to address a specific problem, chances are the team is too small.

10-3d Team Conflict

Conflict and disagreement are inevitable in most teams. But this shouldn't surprise anyone. From time to time, people who work together are going to disagree about what and how things get done. What causes conflict in teams? Although almost anything can lead to conflict—casual remarks that unintentionally offend a team member or fighting over scarce resources—the primary cause of team conflict is disagreement over team goals and priorities.[63] Other common causes of team conflict include disagreements over task-related issues, interpersonal incompatibilities, and simple fatigue.

Though most people view conflict negatively, the key to dealing with team conflict is not avoiding it, but rather making sure that the team experiences the right kind of conflict. In Chapter 5, you learned about *c-type conflict*, or *cognitive conflict*, which focuses on problem-related differences of opinion, and *a-type conflict*, or *affective conflict*, which refers to the emotional reactions that can occur when disagreements become personal rather than professional.[64]

Cognitive conflict is strongly associated with improvements in team performance, whereas affective conflict is strongly associated with decreases in team performance.[65] Why does this happen? With cognitive conflict, team members disagree because their different experiences and expertise lead them to different views of the problem and solutions. Indeed, managers who participated on teams that emphasized cognitive conflict described their teammates as "smart," "team players," and "best in the business." They described their teams as "open," "fun," and "productive." One manager summed up the positive attitude that team members had about cognitive conflict by saying, "We scream a lot, then laugh, and then resolve the issue."[66] Thus, cognitive conflict is also characterized by a willingness to examine, compare, and reconcile differences to produce the best possible solution.

By contrast, affective conflict often results in hostility, anger, resentment, distrust, cynicism, and apathy. Managers who participated on teams that experienced affective conflict described their teammates as "manipulative," "secretive," "burned out," and "political."[67] Dana Browlee, who runs a corporate training company in Atlanta, gives the example of the naysayer, who, "whatever you bring up, it will never work," and the silent plotter, who she says, "may be the quiet person sitting in the back, but as soon as the [team] meeting is over, they're over by the Coke machine, planning your demise."[68] Surprisingly, affective conflict can make people uncomfortable and cause them to withdraw and decrease their commitment to a team.[69] Affective conflict also lowers the satisfaction of team members, may lead to personal hostility between coworkers, and can decrease team cohesiveness.[70] So, unlike cognitive conflict, affective conflict undermines team performance by preventing teams from engaging in the kinds of activities that are critical to team effectiveness.

So, what can managers do to manage team conflict? First, they need to realize that emphasizing cognitive conflict alone won't be enough. Studies show that cognitive and affective conflicts often occur together in a given team activity! Sincere attempts to reach agreement on a difficult issue can quickly deteriorate from cognitive to affective conflict if the discussion turns personal, and tempers and emotions flare. While cognitive conflict is clearly the better approach to take, efforts to engage in cognitive conflict should be managed well and checked before they deteriorate causing the team to become unproductive.

Can teams disagree and still get along? Fortunately, they can. In an attempt to study this issue, researchers examined team conflict in twelve high-tech companies.

In four of the companies, work teams used cognitive conflict to address work problems but did so in a way that minimized the occurrence of affective conflict.

There are several ways teams can have a good fight.[71] First, work with more, rather than less, information. A senior retail executive said, "Disagreement is great as long as it's fact-based."[72] If data are plentiful, objective, and up-to-date, teams will focus on issues, not personalities. Second, develop multiple alternatives to enrich debate. Focusing on multiple solutions diffuses conflict by getting the team to keep searching for a better solution. Positions and opinions are naturally more flexible with five alternatives than with just two. Third, establish common goals. Remember, most team conflict arises from disagreements over team goals and priorities. Therefore, common goals encourage collaboration and minimize conflict over a team's purpose. The late Steve Jobs, former CEO of Apple, explained it this way: "It's okay to spend a lot of time arguing about which route to take to San Francisco when everyone wants to end up there, but a lot of time gets wasted in such arguments if one person wants to go to San Francisco and another secretly wants to go to San Diego."[73] Fourth, inject humor into the workplace. Humor relieves tension, builds cohesion, and just makes being in teams fun. Fifth, maintain a balance of power by involving as many people as possible in the decision process. And, sixth, resolve issues without forcing a consensus. Consensus means that everyone must agree before decisions are finalized. Effectively, requiring consensus gives everyone on the team veto power. Nothing gets done until everyone agrees, which, of course, is nearly impossible. As a result, insisting on consensus usually promotes affective rather than cognitive conflict. If team members can't agree after constructively discussing their options, it's better to have the team leader make the final choice. Most team members can accept the team leader's choice if they've been thoroughly involved in the decision process.

10-3e Stages of Team Development

As teams develop and grow, they pass through four stages of development. As shown in Exhibit 10.4, those stages are forming, storming, norming, and performing.[74] Although not every team passes through each of these stages, teams that do tend to be better performers.[75] This holds true even for teams composed of seasoned executives. After a period of time, however, if a team is not managed well, its performance may start to deteriorate as the team begins a process of decline and progresses through the stages of de-norming, de-storming, and de-forming.[76]

Exhibit 10.4
Stages of Team Development

Sources: J. F. McGrew, J. G. Bilotta, and J. M. Deeney, "Software Team Formation and Decay: Extending the Standard Model for Small Groups," *Small Group Research* 30, no. 2 (1999): 209–234; B. W. Tuckman, "Development Sequence in Small Groups," *Psychological Bulletin* 63, no. 6 (1965): 384–399.

Forming is the initial stage of team development. This is the getting-acquainted stage in which team members first meet each other, form initial impressions, and try to get a sense of what it will be like to be part of the team. Some of the first team norms will be established during this stage as team members begin to find out what behaviors will and won't be accepted by the team. During this stage, team leaders should allow time for team members to get to know each other, set early ground rules, and begin to set up a preliminary team structure.

Conflicts and disagreements often characterize the second stage of team development, **storming**. As team members begin working together, different personalities and work styles may clash. Team members become more assertive at this stage and more willing to state opinions. This is also the stage when team members jockey for position and try to establish a favorable role for themselves on the team. In addition, team members are likely to disagree about what the group should do and how it should do it. Team performance is still relatively low, given that team cohesion is weak and team members are still reluctant to support each other. Because teams that get stuck in the storming stage are almost always ineffective, it is important for team leaders to focus the team on team goals and on improving team performance. Team members need to be particularly patient and tolerant with each other in this stage.

During **norming**, the third stage of team development, team members begin to settle into their roles as team members. Positive team norms will have developed by this stage, and teammates should know what to expect from each other. Petty differences should have been resolved, friendships will have developed, and group cohesion will be relatively strong. At this point, team members will have accepted team goals, be operating as a unit, and, as indicated by the increase in performance, be working together effectively. This stage can be very short and is often characterized by someone on the team saying, "I think things are finally coming together." Note, however, that teams may also cycle back and forth between storming and norming several times before finally settling into norming.

In the last stage of team development, **performing**, performance improves because the team has finally matured into an effective, fully functioning team. At this point, members should be fully committed to the team and think of themselves as members of a team and not just employees. Team members often become intensely loyal to one another at this stage and feel mutual accountability for team successes and failures. Trivial disagreements, which can take time and energy away from the work of the team, should be rare. At this stage, teams get a lot of work done, and it is fun to be a team member.

The team should not become complacent, however. Without effective management, its performance may begin to decline as the team passes through the stages

Forming the first stage of team development, in which team members meet each other, form initial impressions, and begin to establish team norms

Storming the second stage of development, characterized by conflict and disagreement, in which team members disagree over what the team should do and how it should do it

Norming the third stage of team development, in which team members begin to settle into their roles, group cohesion grows, and positive team norms develop

Performing the fourth and final stage of team development, in which performance improves because the team has matured into an effective, fully functioning team of **de-norming**, **de-storming**, and **de-forming**.[77] John Puckett, manufacturing vice president for circuit-board manufacturer XEL Communications, says, "The books all say you start in this state of chaos and march through these various stages, and you end up in this state of ultimate self-direction, where everything is going just great. They never tell you it can go back in the other direction, sometimes just as quickly."[78]

10-4 ENHANCING WORK TEAM EFFECTIVENESS

Making teams work is a challenging and difficult process. Nonetheless, companies can increase the likelihood that teams will succeed by carefully managing **10-4a the setting of team goals and priorities** *and* **10-4b how work team members are selected,** **10-4c trained,** *and* **10-4d compensated.**[79]

10-4a Setting Team Goals and Priorities

In Chapter 5, you learned that having specific, measurable, attainable, realistic, and timely (S.M.A.R.T.) goals is one of the most effective means for improving individual job performance. Fortunately, team goals also improve team performance. In fact, team goals lead to much higher team performance 93 percent of the time.[80]

Why is setting *specific* team goals so critical to team success? One reason is that increasing a team's performance is inherently more complex than just increasing one individual's job performance. For instance, consider that any team is likely to involve at least four different kinds of goals: each member's goal for the team, each member's goal for himself or herself on the team, the team's goal for each member, and the team's goal for itself.[81] In other words, without a specific goal for the team itself (the last of the four goals listed), team members may head off in all directions at once pursuing these other goals. Consequently, setting a specific goal *for the team* clarifies team priorities by providing a clear focus and purpose.

Challenging team goals affect how hard team members work. In particular, they greatly reduce the incidence of social loafing. When faced with difficult goals, team members necessarily expect everyone to contribute. Consequently, they are much more likely to notice and complain if a teammate isn't doing his or her share. In fact, when teammates know each other well, when

To effectively motivate teams:

1. Teams must have a high degree of autonomy.
2. Teams must be empowered with control of resources.
3. Teams need structural accommodation.
4. Teams need bureaucratic immunity.

iStockphoto.com/RoscoPhoto

team goals are specific, when team communication is good, and when teams are rewarded for team performance (discussed later in this section), there is only a one in sixteen chance that teammates will be social loafers.[82]

What can companies and teams do to ensure that team goals lead to superior team performance? One increasingly popular approach is to give teams stretch goals. *Stretch goals* are extremely ambitious goals that workers don't know how to reach.[83] The world's largest auto company, GM, went bankrupt in 2009. Now, just six years later, GM wants to be "the world's most valuable automotive company." How big a stretch is this goal? Pretty big. GM's value (that is market capitalization) when this was written was $44 billion, sixth among the world's top nine auto companies and well behind market leader Toyota, which has a market cap of $181 billion. So, GM will have to more than triple its stock price relative to

De-norming a reversal of the norming stage, in which team performance begins to decline as the size, scope, goal, or members of the team change

De-storming a reversal of the storming phase, in which the team's comfort level decreases, team cohesion weakens, and angry emotions and conflict may flare

De-forming a reversal of the forming stage, in which team members position themselves to control pieces of the team, avoid each other, and isolate themselves from team leaders

Toyota to achieve this goal. GM spokesman Jim Cain explains, "It's a way to get people focused around a couple of issues. We don't have competitive [profit] margins. If we can get competitive [profit] margins, it'll drive the stock price." And how will GM do that? It's not clear.[84]

Four things must occur for stretch goals to effectively motivate teams.[85] First, teams must have a high degree of autonomy or control over how they achieve their goals. Second, teams must be empowered with control of resources, such as budgets, workspaces, computers, or whatever else they need to do their jobs. Third, teams need structural accommodation. **Structural accommodation** means giving teams the ability to change organizational structures, policies, and practices if doing so helps them meet their stretch goals. Finally, teams need bureaucratic immunity. **Bureaucratic immunity** means that teams no longer have to go through the frustratingly slow process of multilevel reviews and sign-offs to get management approval before making changes. Once granted bureaucratic immunity, teams are immune from the influence of various organizational groups and are accountable only to top management. Research teams at Google X, Google's research lab, work on "moonshots," meaning hard to accomplish projects such as self-driving cars and Google Glass, eyeglasses that display email and can record videos and photos. Google X's teams work in two buildings half a mile from Google's main campus to separate and free them from Google's main business. With bureaucratic immunity, teams can act quickly, and even experiment, with little fear of failure. Richard DeVaul, who heads the Rapid Evaluation and Design Kitchen teams at Google X, says, "Google X is very consciously looking at things that Google in its right mind wouldn't do. They build the rocket pad far away from the widget factory, so if the rocket blows up, it's hopefully not disrupting the core business."[86]

10-4b Selecting People for Teamwork

University of Southern California management professor Edward Lawler says, "People are very naive about how easy it is to create a team. Teams are the Ferrari of work design. They're high performance but high maintenance and expensive."[87] It's almost impossible to have an effective work team without carefully selecting people who are suited for teamwork or for working on a particular team. A focus on teamwork (individualism-collectivism), team level, and team diversity can help companies choose the right team members.[88]

Are you more comfortable working alone or with others? If you strongly prefer to work alone, you may not be well suited for teamwork. Studies show that job satisfaction is higher in teams when team members prefer working with others.[89] An indirect way to measure someone's *preference for teamwork* is to assess the person's degree of individualism or collectivism. **Individualism-collectivism** is the degree to which a person believes that people should be self-sufficient and that loyalty to one's self is more important than loyalty to one's team or company.[90] *Individualists*, who put their own welfare and interests first, generally prefer independent tasks in which they work alone. In contrast, *collectivists*, who put group or team interests ahead of self-interests, generally prefer interdependent tasks in which they work with others. Collectivists would also rather cooperate than compete and are fearful of disappointing team members or of being ostracized from teams. Given these differences, it makes sense to select team members who are collectivists rather than individualists. In fact, many companies use individualism-collectivism as an initial screening device for team members. If team diversity is desired, however, individualists may also be appropriate, as discussed next. To determine your preference for teamwork, take the Team Player Inventory shown in Exhibit 10.5.

Having too many people that want to be stars on your team may result in coordination issues as the team develops and faces performance challenges.

Structural accommodation the ability to change organizational structures, policies, and practices in order to meet stretch goals

Bureaucratic immunity the ability to make changes without first getting approval from managers or other parts of an organization

Individualism-collectivism the degree to which a person believes that people should be self-sufficient and that loyalty to one's self is more important than loyalty to team or company

Exhibit 10.5
The Team Player Inventory

		Strongly Disagree				Strongly Agree
1.	I enjoy working on team/group projects.	1	2	3	4	5
2.	Team/group project work easily allows others to not pull their weight.	1	2	3	4	5
3.	Work that is done as a team/group is better than work done individually.	1	2	3	4	5
4.	I do my best work alone rather than in a team/group.	1	2	3	4	5
5.	Team/group work is overrated in terms of the actual results produced.	1	2	3	4	5
6.	Working in a team/group gets me to think more creatively.	1	2	3	4	5
7.	Teams/groups are used too often when individual work would be more effective.	1	2	3	4	5
8.	My own work is enhanced when I am in a team/group situation.	1	2	3	4	5
9.	My experiences working in team/group situations have been primarily negative.	1	2	3	4	5
10.	More solutions/ideas are generated when working in a team/group situation than when working alone.	1	2	3	4	5

Reverse score items 2, 4, 5, 7, and 9. Then add the scores for items 1 to 10. Higher scores indicate a preference for teamwork, whereas lower total scores indicate a preference for individual work.

Source: T. J. B. Kline, "The Team Player Inventory: Reliability and Validity of a Measure of Predisposition Toward Organizational Team-Working Environments," *Journal for Specialists in Group Work 24*, no. 1 (1999): 102–112.

Team level is the average level of ability, experience, personality, or any other factor on a team. For example, a high level of team experience means that a team has particularly experienced team members. This does not mean that every member of the team has considerable experience, but that enough team members do to significantly raise the average level of experience on the team. Team level is used to guide selection of teammates when teams need a particular set of skills or capabilities to do their jobs well. For example, **SAP**, a German software company, has struggled to deliver cloud-based solutions and hopes to replicate a team approach to innovation pioneered by Xerox Parc in the 1970s. So it hired Alan Kay, a renowned technologist who was a computer scientist at Xerox Parc, to build a similar high-level team. So far, Kay has recruited twenty polymathic technologists, funded their research projects, and then given them the independence to work alone to pursue their research interests.[91] (A polymath is someone who is a genius in more than one field.) Kay understands the risks of having too many "stars." Based on his research on NBA teams, management professor Adam Galinsky says, "If you have too many people [on teams], and they all want to be stars, coordination [on the team] goes down. But if you have a bunch of star programmers all working on their own projects, and they don't need to integrate their programs with each other, then more stars is probably better."[92]

Whereas team level represents the average level or capability on a team, **team diversity** represents the variances or differences in ability, experience, personality, or any other factor on a team.[93] From a practical perspective, why is team diversity important? Andy Zynga, CEO of NineSigma International, an innovation consulting firm, says, "Technologists, engineers, and designers not only have their own expertise, they have their own way of applying their expertise. Ironically, the more success they've had with their approach to a solution, the harder it is to imagine a different one."[94] Team diversity ensures that strong teams not only have talented members (that is, a high team level), but those talented members also have different abilities, experiences, and personalities from which to view and solve problems.

After the right team has been put together in terms of individualism-collectivism, team level, and team diversity, it's important to keep the team together as long as practically possible. Interesting research by the National Transportation Safety Board shows that 73 percent of serious mistakes made by jet cockpit crews are made the very

Team level the average level of ability, experience, personality, or any other factor on a team

Team diversity the variances or differences in ability, experience, personality, or any other factor on a team first day that a crew flies together as a team and that 44 percent of serious mistakes occur on their very first flight together that day (pilot teams fly two to three flights per day). Moreover, research has shown that fatigued pilot crews who have worked together before make significantly fewer errors than rested crews who have never worked together.[95] Their experience working together helps them overcome their fatigue and outperform new teams that have not worked together before. So, after you've created effective teams, keep them together as long as possible.

10-4c Team Training

After selecting the right people for teamwork, you need to train them. To be successful, teams need significant training, particularly in interpersonal skills, decision-making and problem-solving skills, conflict resolution skills, and technical training. Organizations that create work teams *often underestimate the amount of training* required to make teams effective. This mistake occurs frequently in successful organizations where managers assume that if employees can work effectively on their own, they can work effectively in teams. In reality, companies that successfully use teams provide thousands of hours of training to make sure that teams work. Stacy Myers, a consultant who helps companies implement teams, says, "When we help companies move to teams, we also require that employees take basic quality and business knowledge classes as well. Teams must know how their work affects the company, and how their success will be measured."[96]

Most commonly, members of work teams receive training in interpersonal skills. **Interpersonal skills** such as listening, communicating, questioning, and providing feedback enable people to have effective working relationships with others. Consultant Peter Grazier, founder of Teambuilding Inc., says, "Teams have told us that if they had to do it over again, they would have more of the people skills up front. They don't struggle with the technical stuff. They tend to struggle with the people skills."[97] Because of teams' autonomy and responsibility, many companies also give team members training in *decision-making and problem-solving skills* to help them do a better job of cutting costs and improving quality and customer service. Many organizations also teach teams *conflict resolution skills*. Teambuilding Inc.'s Grazier explains that "the diversity of values and personalities makes a team powerful, but it can be the greatest source of conflict. If you're a detail person, and I'm not, and we

> **Interpersonal skills** skills, such as listening, communicating, questioning, and providing feedback, that enable people to have effective working relationships with others

The Rights and Wrongs of Socializing

Looking for a way to bring your team members closer together? There may be nothing better than a team outing. Whether it's dinner on a Friday night or a weekend retreat to Niagara Falls, a group outing is a great way to develop cohesiveness and interpersonal skills within a team. There are, however, certain situations to avoid. For example, you may not want to go to a bar for drinks if a team member is a recovering alcoholic. You may not want to schedule an event too late at night, or too far away, if some team members have young children at home. So do the right thing—make sure you get to know your team members, and their unique circumstances, so that you can plan team activities that everyone can participate in and enjoy.

Source: "7 Ways to Socialize with Your Employees (Without Getting in Trouble)" *Inc.*, August 11, 2010, accessed August 19, 2010. http://www.inc.com/guides/2010/08/7-ways-to-socialize-with-your-employees.html.

get on a team, you might say that we need more analysis on a problem before making a decision, [while I] may want to make a decision [right away]. But, if I've been trained in problem-solving and conflict resolution, then I look at your detail [focus] as something that is needed in a team because it's a shortcoming of mine."[98] Taine Moufarrige, executive director of Servcorp, a global company hosting serviced and virtual offices for about 12,000 clients, agrees. Says Moufarrige, "It's not just about disagreements, it's about working through problems, managing differences of opinion, and that's vital for moving forward."[99]

Firms must also provide team members with the *technical training* they need to do their jobs, particularly if they are being cross-trained to perform all of the different jobs on the team. Before teams were created at Milwaukee Mutual Insurance, separate employees performed the tasks of rating, underwriting, and processing insurance policies. After extensive cross-training, however, each team member can now do all three jobs.[100] Cross-training is less appropriate for teams of highly skilled workers. For instance, it is unlikely that a group of engineers, computer programmers, and systems analysts would be cross-trained for each other's jobs.

Team leaders need training, too, as they often feel unprepared for their new duties. New team leaders face myriad problems ranging from confusion about their new roles as team leaders (compared with their old jobs as managers or employees) to not knowing where to go for help when their teams have problems. The solution is extensive training. Overall, does team training work? One recent study found that across a wide variety of settings, tasks, team types, and 2,650 teams in different organizations, team training was positively related to team performance outcomes.[101]

10-4d Team Compensation and Recognition

Compensating teams correctly is very difficult. For instance, one survey found that only 37 percent of companies were satisfied with their team compensation plans and even fewer, just 10 percent, reported being "very positive."[102] One of the problems, according to Susan Mohrman of the Center for Effective Organizations at the University of Southern California, is that "there is a very strong set of beliefs in most organizations that people should be paid for how well they do. So when people first get put into team-based organizations, they really balk at being paid for how well the team does. It sounds illogical to them. It sounds like their individuality and their sense of self-worth are being threatened."[103] Consequently, companies need to carefully choose a team compensation plan and then fully explain how teams will be rewarded. One basic requirement for team compensation to work is that the level of rewards (individual versus team) must match the level of performance (individual versus team).

Employees can be compensated for team participation and accomplishments in three ways: skill-based pay, gainsharing, and nonfinancial rewards. **Skill-based pay** programs pay employees for learning additional skills or knowledge.[104] These programs encourage employees to acquire the additional skills they will need to perform multiple jobs within a team and to share knowledge with others within their work groups.[105] For example, at the Patience & Nicholson (P&N) drill bit factory in Kaiapoi, New Zealand, workers produce 50,000 drill bits a day for export to Australia, Taiwan, Thailand, and other locations primarily in Asia. P&N uses a skill-based pay system. As employees learn how to run the various machines required to produce drill bits, their pay increases. According to operations manager Rick Smith, workers who are dedicated to learning can increase their pay by $6 an hour over the course of three or four years.[106]

In **gainsharing** programs, companies share the financial value of performance gains, such as productivity increases, cost savings, or quality improvements, with their workers.[107] *Nonfinancial rewards* are another way to reward teams for their performance. These rewards, which can range from vacations to T-shirts, plaques, and coffee mugs, are especially effective when coupled with management recognition, such as awards, certificates, and praise.[108] Nonfinancial awards tend to be most effective when teams or team-based interventions, such as total quality management (see Chapter 18), are first introduced.[109]

Olavs/Shutterstock.com

Which team compensation plan should your company use? In general, skill-based pay is most effective for self-managing and self-directing teams performing complex tasks. In these situations, the more each team member knows and can do, the better the whole team performs. By contrast, gainsharing works best in relatively stable environments where employees can focus on improving productivity, cost savings, or quality.

Skill-based pay compensation system that pays employees for learning additional skills or knowledge

Gainsharing a compensation system in which companies share the financial value of performance gains, such as increased productivity, cost savings, or quality, with their workers

11 Managing Human Resource Systems

PEOPLE

TRAIN

EMPOWER

REWARD

Thinglass/Shutterstock.com

LEARNING OUTCOMES

11-1 Explain how different employment laws affect human resource practice.

11-2 Explain how companies use recruiting to find qualified job applicants.

11-3 Describe the selection techniques and procedures that companies use when deciding which applicants should receive job offers.

11-4 Describe how to determine training needs, and select the appropriate training methods.

11-5 Discuss how to use performance appraisal to give meaningful performance feedback.

11-6 Describe basic compensation strategies, and discuss the four kinds of employee separations.

After you finish this chapter, go to **PAGE 245** for **STUDY TOOLS**

11-1 EMPLOYMENT LEGISLATION

Human resource management (HRM), or the process of finding, developing, and keeping the right people to form a qualified workforce, is one of the most difficult and important of all management tasks. This chapter is organized around the three parts of the human resource management process shown in Exhibit 11.1: attracting, developing, and keeping a qualified workforce.

This chapter will walk you through the steps of the HRM process. We explore how companies use recruiting and selection techniques to attract and hire qualified employees to fulfill human resource needs. The next part of the chapter discusses how training and performance appraisal can develop the knowledge, skills, and abilities of the workforce. The chapter concludes with a review of compensation and employee separation, that is, how companies can keep their best workers through effective compensation practices and how they can manage the separation process when employees leave the organization.

Before we explore how human resource systems work, you need to understand better the complex legal environment in which they exist. So we'll begin the chapter by reviewing the federal laws that govern human resource management decisions.

DSI Security Services, which hires and provides security guards for organizations, spends hundreds of hours each year interviewing applicants with criminal histories who are prevented by laws in twenty-three states from working as security guards. "It defies common sense," says COO and general counsel Eddie Sorrels.[1] So why does DSI interview applicants with criminal histories that it cannot hire? Because the U.S. Equal Employment Opportunity Commission (EEOC) advises that while it is appropriate to conduct background checks later in the hiring process, applicants should not be asked about criminal records on application forms. With African American men six times more likely to be incarcerated than Whites and three times more likely than Hispanics, the EEOC, as well as thirteen states, are concerned that asking about criminal records early in the hiring process could lead to racial discrimination.[2] The NAACP's ReNika Moore says, "People who are trying to work, trying to be productive citizens, are being blocked from jobs."[3] As discussed later in the chapter, however, companies use background checks to provide safe environments for employees and customers and to avoid negligent hiring lawsuits in which they may be liable for an employee's harmful actions. So, what are employers to do? Scott Fallavollita, who owns United Tool & Machine

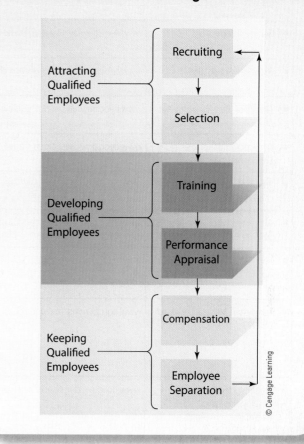

Exhibit 11.1
The Human Resource Management Process

© Cengage Learning

in Wilmington, Massachusetts, said, "I think most people can see both sides and really want to do the right thing."[4]

As the DSI Security Services example illustrates, the human resource planning process occurs in a very complicated legal environment.

*Let's explore employment legislation by reviewing **11-1a the major federal employment laws that affect human resource practice, 11-1b how the concept of adverse impact is related to employment discrimination,** and **11-1c the laws regarding sexual harassment in the workplace.***

11-1a Federal Employment Laws

Exhibit 11.2 lists the major federal employment laws and their websites, where you can find more detailed information. Except for the Family and Medical Leave Act and the Uniformed

> **Human resource management (HRM)** the process of finding, developing, and keeping the right people to form a qualified workforce

Exhibit 11.2
Summary of Major Federal Employment Laws

■ Genetic Information Nondiscrimination Act of 2008	www.eeoc.gov/laws/types/genetic.cfm	Prohibits discrimination on the basis of genetic information.
■ Equal Pay Act of 1963	www.eeoc.gov/laws/statutes/epa.cfm	Prohibits unequal pay for males and females doing substantially similar work.
■ Title VII of the Civil Rights Act of 1964	www.eeoc.gov/laws/statutes/titlevii.cfm	Prohibits employment discrimination on the basis of race, color, religion, gender, or national origin.
■ Age Discrimination in Employment Act of 1967	www.eeoc.gov/laws/statutes/adea.cfm	Prohibits discrimination in employment decisions against persons age 40 and older.
■ Pregnancy Discrimination Act of 1978	www.eeoc.gov/laws/statutes/pregnancy.cfm	Prohibits discrimination in employment against pregnant women.
■ Americans with Disabilities Act of 1990	www.eeoc.gov/laws/statutes/ada.cfm	Prohibits discrimination on the basis of physical or mental disabilities.
■ Civil Rights Act of 1991	www.eeoc.gov/laws/statutes/cra-1991.cfm	Strengthened the provisions of the Civil Rights Act of 1964 by providing for jury trials and punitive damages.
■ Family and Medical Leave Act of 1993	www.dol.gov/whd/fmla/index.htm	Permits workers to take up to twelve weeks of unpaid leave for pregnancy and/or birth of a new child, adoption or foster care of a new child, illness of an immediate family member, or personal medical leave.
■ Uniformed Services Employment and Reemployment Rights Act of 1994	www.dol.gov/compliance/laws/comp-userra.htm	Prohibits discrimination against those serving in the armed forces reserve, the National Guard, or other uniformed services; guarantees that civilian employers will hold and then restore civilian jobs and benefits for those who have completed uniformed service.

© Cengage Learning

Services Employment and Reemployment Rights Act, which are administrated by the Department of Labor (www.dol.gov), all of these laws are administered by the EEOC (www.eeoc.gov). The general effect of this body of law, which is still evolving through court decisions, is that employers may not discriminate in employment decisions on the basis of sex, age, religion, color, national origin, race, disability, or genetic history.[5] The intent is to make these factors irrelevant in employment decisions. Stated another way, employment decisions should be based on factors that are "job related," "reasonably necessary," or a "business necessity" for successful job performance. The only time that sex, age, religion, and the like can be used to make employment decisions is when they are considered a bona fide occupational qualification. Title VII of the 1964 Civil Rights Act says that it is legal to hire and employ someone on the basis of sex, religion, or national origin when there is a **bona fide occupational qualification (BFOQ)** that is "reasonably necessary to the normal operation of that particular business." A Baptist church hiring a new minister can reasonably specify that being a Baptist rather than a Catholic or Presbyterian is a BFOQ for the position. However, it's unlikely that the church could specify race or national origin as a BFOQ. In general, the courts and the EEOC take a hard look when a business claims that sex, age, religion, color, national origin, race, or disability is a BFOQ. For example, citing the risk for sexual abuse and misconduct, the **San Francisco Sheriff's Department**

Bona fide occupational qualification (BFOQ) an exception in employment law that permits sex, age, religion, and the like to be used when making employment decisions, but only if they are "reasonably necessary to the normal operation of that particular business." BFOQs are strictly monitored by the Equal Employment Opportunity Commission prohibited male prison guards from supervising female inmates. Dozens of deputies filed a lawsuit arguing that sex was not a BFOQ for a prison guard, and the courts agreed, ruling that background checks and psychological testing could weed out applicants likely to engage in misconduct.[6]

It is important to understand, however, that these laws apply to the entire HRM process and not just to selection decisions (for example, hiring or promotion). These laws also cover all training and development activities, performance appraisals, terminations, and compensation decisions. Employers who use sex, age, race, or religion to make employment-related decisions when those factors are unrelated to an applicant's or employee's ability to perform a job may face charges of discrimination from employee lawsuits or the EEOC.

In addition to the laws presented in Exhibit 11.2, there are two other important sets of federal laws: labor laws and the laws and regulations governing safety standards. Labor laws regulate the interaction between management and labor unions that represent groups of employees. These laws guarantee employees the right to form and join unions of their own choosing. For more information about labor laws, see the National Labor Relations Board at www.nlrb.gov.

The Occupational Safety and Health Act (OSHA) requires that employers provide employees with a workplace that is "free from recognized hazards that are causing or are likely to cause death or serious physical harm." This law is administered by the Occupational Safety and Health Administration (which, like the act, is referred to as OSHA). OSHA sets safety and health standards for employers and conducts inspections to determine whether those standards are being met. Employers who do not meet OSHA standards may be fined.[7] Even though working with wild animals has inherent risks, OSHA found that **Sea World** did not have adequate procedures in place to protect employees and supervisors properly from killer whales while riding on or swimming with the animals. Building fast-rising pool floors and emergency air systems to protect its trainers did not prevent the death of a trainer at a park in Orlando, so OSHA fined the company $25,770.

For more information about OSHA, see www.osha .gov.

11-1b Adverse Impact and Employment Discrimination

The EEOC has investigatory, enforcement, and informational responsibilities. Therefore, it investigates charges of discrimination, enforces the employment discrimination laws in federal court, and publishes guidelines that organizations can use to ensure they are in compliance with the law. One of the most important guidelines, jointly issued by the EEOC, the U.S. Department of Labor, the U.S. Department of Justice, and the federal Office of Personnel Management, is the *Uniform Guidelines on Employee Selection Procedures*, which can be read in their entirety at www.uniformguidelines.com /uniformguidelines.html. These guidelines define two important criteria, disparate treatment and adverse impact, which are used in determining whether companies have engaged in discriminatory hiring and promotion practices.

Disparate treatment, which is *intentional* discrimination, occurs when people, despite being qualified, are *intentionally* not given the same hiring, promotion, or membership opportunities as other employees because of their race, color, age, sex, ethnic group, national origin, or religious beliefs.[8] Bobby Nickel, a former facilities manager at Staples, the office supply retailer, was awarded $26 million by a jury that found Staples guilty of harassing him by calling him an "old coot" and an "old goat" and firing him because he was an older employee with a higher salary.[9]

Alexmillos/Shutterstock.com

> **Disparate treatment** intentional discrimination that occurs when people are purposely not given the same hiring, promotion, or membership opportunities because of their race, color, sex, age, ethnic group, national origin, or religious beliefs

Legally, a key element of discrimination lawsuits is establishing motive, meaning that the employer intended to discriminate. If no motive can be established, then a claim of disparate treatment may actually be a case of adverse impact. **Adverse impact**, which is *unintentional* discrimination, occurs when members of a particular race, sex, or ethnic group are *unintentionally* harmed or disadvantaged because they are hired, promoted, or trained (or any other employment decision) at substantially lower rates than others. The courts and federal agencies use the **four-fifths (or 80%) rule** to determine if adverse impact has occurred. Adverse impact is determined by calculating the impact ratio, which divides the decision rate for a protected group of people by the decision rate for a nonprotected group (usually white males). If the impact ratio is less than 80%, then adverse impact may have occurred. For example, if twenty out of one hundred black applicants are hired (20/100 = 20%), but sixty white applicants are hired (60/100 = 60%), then adverse impact has occurred because the impact ratio is less than 80% (.20/.60 = 33%).

Violation of the four-fifths rule is not an automatic indication of discrimination, however. If an employer can demonstrate that a selection procedure or test is valid, meaning that the test accurately predicts job performance or that the test is job related because it assesses applicants on specific tasks actually used in the job, then the organization may continue to use the test. If validity cannot be established, however, then a violation of the four-fifths rule may likely result in a lawsuit brought by employees, job applicants, or the EEOC itself.

11-1c Sexual Harassment

According to the EEOC, **sexual harassment** is a form of discrimination in which unwelcome sexual advances, requests for sexual favors, or other verbal or physical conduct of a sexual nature occurs. From a legal perspective, there are two kinds of sexual harassment, quid pro quo and hostile work environment.[10]

Quid pro quo sexual harassment occurs when employment outcomes, such as hiring, promotion, or simply keeping one's job, depend on whether an individual submits to being sexually harassed. For example, in a quid pro quo sexual harassment lawsuit against First Student, a company that provides school bus transportation, four females alleged that a supervisor made explicit comments about their bodies and what he wanted to do to them. He was also alleged to have touched a female worker's breasts, exposed himself, and then rubbed himself against her. When his sexual advances were refused, he punished the women by cutting their work hours, while promising longer hours to the other women if they would do what he asked. This made it a quid pro quo case by linking sexual acts to economic outcomes.[11]

A **hostile work environment** occurs when unwelcome and demeaning sexually related behavior creates an intimidating, hostile, and offensive work environment. In contrast to quid pro quo cases, a hostile work environment may not result in economic injury. However, it can lead to psychological injury when the work environment becomes stressful. A federal court jury found Mercy General Hospital in Sacramento, California, guilty of creating a sexually hostile work environment for Ani Chopourian, a cardiac surgery physician assistant. Chopourian was awarded $125 million in punitive damages, $3.5 million for lost wages and benefits, and $39 million for mental anguish. Chopourian was frequently subjected to touching and sex talk in the operating room. She says, "One harasser told me one

Rommel Canlas/Shutterstock.com

Adverse impact unintentional discrimination that occurs when members of a particular race, sex, or ethnic group are unintentionally harmed or disadvantaged because they are hired, promoted, or trained (or any other employment decision) at substantially lower rates than others

Four-fifths (or 80%) rule a rule of thumb used by the courts and the EEOC to determine whether there is evidence of adverse impact; a violation of this rule occurs when the impact ratio (calculated by dividing the decision ratio for a protected group by the decision ratio for a nonprotected group) is less than 80%, or four-fifths

Sexual harassment a form of discrimination in which unwelcome sexual advances, requests for sexual favors, or other verbal or physical conduct of a sexual nature occurs while performing one's job

Quid pro quo sexual harassment a form of sexual harassment in which employment outcomes, such as hiring, promotion, or simply keeping one's job, depend on whether an individual submits to sexual harassment

Hostile work environment a form of sexual harassment in which unwelcome and demeaning sexually related behavior creates an intimidating and offensive work environment day, 'You'll give in to me.' I'd look at him [and say], 'I'll never give in to you.' I'd look at my supervisor and say, 'Do something.' They'd just laugh."[12] She was fired after filing eighteen complaints in two years. Mercy General is appealing the decision.

Finally, what should companies do to make sure that sexual harassment laws are followed and not violated?[13] First, respond immediately when sexual harassment is reported. A quick response encourages victims of sexual harassment to report problems to management rather than to lawyers or the EEOC. Furthermore, a quick and fair investigation may serve as a deterrent to future harassment. A lawyer for the EEOC says, "Worse than having no sexual harassment policy is a policy that is not followed. It's merely window dressing. You wind up with destroyed morale when people who come forward are ignored, ridiculed, retaliated against, or nothing happens to the harasser."[14]

Then take the time to write a clear, understandable sexual harassment policy that is strongly worded, gives specific examples of what constitutes sexual harassment, spells outs sanctions and punishments, and is widely publicized within the company. This lets potential harassers and victims know what will not be tolerated and how the firm will deal with harassment should it occur.

Next, establish clear reporting procedures that indicate how, where, and to whom incidents of sexual harassment can be reported. The best procedures ensure that a complaint will receive a quick response, that impartial parties will handle the complaint, and that the privacy of the accused and accuser will be protected. At DuPont, Avon, and Texas Industries, employees can call a confidential hotline 24 hours a day, 365 days a year.[15]

Finally, managers should also be aware that most states and many cities or local governments have their own employment-related laws and enforcement agencies. So compliance with federal law is often not enough. In fact, organizations can be in full compliance with federal law and at the same time be in violation of state or local sexual harassment laws.

11-2 RECRUITING

Gail Hyland-Savage, CEO of the real estate and marketing firm Michaelson, Connor & Boul, says, "Staffing is absolutely critical to the success of every company. To be competitive in today's economy, companies need the best people to create ideas and execute them for the organization. Without a competent and talented workforce, organizations will stagnate and eventually perish. The right employees are the most important resources of companies today."[16]

Recruiting is the process of developing a pool of qualified job applicants.

*Let's examine **11-2a what job analysis is and how it is used in recruiting, 11-2b how companies use internal recruiting**, and **11-2c external recruiting to find qualified job applicants.***

11-2a Job Analysis and Recruiting

Job analysis is a "purposeful, systematic process for collecting information on the important work-related aspects of a job."[17] A job analysis typically collects four kinds of information:

▶ Work activities, such as what workers do and how, when, and why they do it

▶ The tools and equipment used to do the job

▶ The context in which the job is performed, such as the actual working conditions or schedule

▶ The personnel requirements for performing the job, meaning the knowledge, skills, and abilities needed to do a job well[18]

Job analysis information can be collected by having job incumbents and/or supervisors complete questionnaires about their jobs, by direct observation, by interviews, or by filming employees as they perform their jobs.

Job descriptions and job specifications are two of the most important results of a job analysis. A **job description** is a written description of the basic tasks, duties, and responsibilities required of an employee holding a particular job. **Job specifications**, which are often included as a separate section of a job description, are a summary of the qualifications needed to successfully perform the job. Exhibit 11.3 shows a job description for a firefighter for the city of Portland, Oregon.

Because a job analysis specifies what a job entails as well as the knowledge, skills, and abilities that are

Recruiting the process of developing a pool of qualified job applicants

Job analysis a purposeful, systematic process for collecting information on the important work-related aspects of a job

Job description a written description of the basic tasks, duties, and responsibilities required of an employee holding a particular job

Job specifications a written summary of the qualifications needed to successfully perform a particular job

Exhibit 11.3
Job Description for a Firefighter for the City of Portland, Oregon

Yes, as a Firefighter you will fight fire and provide emergency medical services to your community. But it doesn't end there: your firefighting career offers you the opportunity to expand your skills to include Hazardous Materials Response, Specialty Response Teams (dive, rope rescue, confined space, etc.), Paramedic Care, Public Education and Information, Fire Investigation, and Fire Code Enforcement.

Teamwork

Professional Firefighters work as a team at emergency scenes. The workday also includes training, fire station and equipment maintenance, fire prevention activities, and public education. As a Firefighter, you must be in excellent physical condition to meet the demands of the job; this means you must work quickly, handling heavy equipment for long periods of time while wearing special protective gear in hot and hazardous environments. If you can meet the challenge of strenuous work and like the idea of helping people, consider applying for the position of Firefighter.

Work Schedule

Portland Fire & Rescue Firefighters work a 24-on/48-off shift. This means that Firefighters report to work at 8:00 a.m. the day of their shift and continue working until 8:00 a.m. the following morning. Our Firefighters then have the following two days (48 hours) off. Firefighters are required to work shifts on holidays and weekends. Portland Fire & Rescue also has 40-hour-a-week firefighters who work in Training, Inspections/Investigations, Public Education, Logistics, and Emergency Management. These positions are usually filled after a Firefighter has met the minimum requirements for these positions.

Source: Portland Fire and Rescue, accessed August 13, 2008. http://www.portlandonline.com/fire/index.cfm?a=haea&c=cgbil.

iStockphoto.com/Kendall Griffin

needed to do the job well, companies must complete a job analysis *before* beginning to recruit job applicants. Job analyses, job descriptions, and job specifications are the foundation on which all critical human resource activities are built. They are used during recruiting and selection to match applicant qualifications with the requirements of the job. Reddit, a news consolidation website where readers vote on which stories and discussions are the most important, wanted to hire a new programmer, but it didn't want to sort through thousands of applications from people who had no coding skills but thought it would be cool to work for the popular website. So it used the job description as a test to make sure the company would only receive applications from highly skilled programmers. Applications for the job were to be sent to S@reddit.com, with "S" representing a real email address that applicants had to figure out by solving a series of problems and equations. If you couldn't figure it out, you couldn't send in your job application. This puzzle helped Reddit match applicant qualifications to the requirements of the job.[19]

Job descriptions are also used throughout the staffing process to ensure that selection devices and the decisions based on these devices are job related. For example, the questions asked in an interview should be based on the most important work activities identified by a job analysis. Likewise, during performance appraisals, employees should be evaluated in areas that a job analysis has identified as the most important in a job.

Job analyses, job descriptions, and job specifications also help companies meet the legal requirement that their human resource decisions be job related. To be judged *job related*, recruitment, selection, training, performance appraisals, and employee separations must be valid and be directly related to the important aspects of the job, as identified by a careful job analysis. In fact, in *Griggs v. Duke Power Co.* and *Albemarle Paper Co. v. Moody*, the U.S. Supreme Court stated that companies should use job analyses to help establish the job relatedness of their human resource procedures.[20] The EEOC's *Uniform Guidelines on*

Employee Selection Procedures also recommend that companies base their human resource procedures on job analysis.

11-2b Internal Recruiting

Internal recruiting is the process of developing a pool of qualified job applicants from people who already work in the company. Internal recruiting, sometimes called "promotion from within," improves employee commitment, morale, and motivation. Recruiting current employees also reduces recruitment start-up time and costs, and because employees are already familiar with the company's culture and procedures, they are more likely to succeed in new jobs. Crédit Suisse was posting less than half of its open jobs internally until it discovered that those taking a new job within the company were more likely to stay long term. So, it now posts 80 percent of its openings internally—even cold-calling employees to let them know when jobs have opened. Doing so has resulted in promotions for 300 of its people. William Wolf, the bank's global head of talent acquisition and development, says, "We believe we've saved a number of them from taking jobs at other banks."[21] Job posting and career paths are two methods of internal recruiting.

Job posting is a procedure for advertising job openings within the company to existing employees. A job description and requirements are typically posted on a bulletin board, in a company newsletter, or in an internal computerized job bank that is accessible only to employees. Job posting helps organizations discover hidden talent, allows employees to take responsibility for career planning, and makes it easier for companies to retain talented workers who are dissatisfied in their current jobs and would otherwise leave the company.[22] In fact, a LinkedIn survey of workers who changed jobs found that 42 percent would have stayed with their former employers if a relevant position had been available.[23] LinkedIn vice president Parker Barrile says it's often the case that, "People quit their job, not the company."[24]

Booz Allen Hamilton, an international consulting firm, uses an internal recruiting platform called Inside First, which lists job openings and current employee profiles indicating skills, experience, languages

Andy Dean Photography/Shutterstock.com

spoken, and willingness to relocate. Thirty percent of its positions are now filled with internal hires thanks to Inside First, compared to 10 percent before.[25]

A study of seventy large global companies found that organizations that formalize internal recruiting and job posting have a lower average rate of turnover (11%) compared to companies that don't (15%).[26] Likewise, a University of Pennsylvania study found external hires generally are more costly, less reliable hires. Specifically, external hires get paid 18 percent to 20 percent more than internal hires, are 61 percent more likely to be fired, and are 21 percent more likely to quit their jobs.[27]

A *career path* is a planned sequence of jobs through which employees may advance within an organization. According to Brian Hoyt of RetailMeNot, an online coupon company in Austin, Texas, "Workers were saying, 'It isn't enough for me to work at a fun Internet company,' . . . they wanted to know where their career was going."[28] So the company revamped its internal recruiting system, adding to each job posting a detailed list of responsibilities, required competencies, and skills needed to get each job. Garrett Bircher, an associate product manager, said that when he when was hired, the company lacked a coherent approach. "Now, I feel more secure," he says. "I know four jobs ahead of me now where I want to go and what it takes to get there."[29]

Career paths help employees focus on long-term goals and development while also helping companies increase employee retention. As you can see in Garrett Bircher's case, career paths can also help employees gain a broad range of experience, which is especially useful at higher levels of management.

11-2c External Recruiting

External recruiting is the process of developing a pool of qualified job applicants from outside the company. Walmart will guarantee a job over the next five years to any veteran who applies for a job within twelve months of being honorably discharged. Walmart estimates it will hire 100,000 veterans during that time. William Simon, CEO and president of Walmart USA, says, "Let's be clear: Hiring a veteran can be one of the best decisions any of us can make. These are leaders with discipline, training, and a passion for service." The focus on veterans—company outsiders—is a critical part of Walmart's recruiting strategy in all parts of the company.[30]

> **Internal recruiting** the process of developing a pool of qualified job applicants from people who already work in the company
>
> **External recruiting** the process of developing a pool of qualified job applicants from outside the company

Walmart estimates it will hire 100,00 veterans during the next five years.

External recruitment methods include advertising (newspapers, magazines, direct mail, radio, or television), employee referrals (asking current employees to recommend possible job applicants), walk-ins (people who apply on their own), outside organizations (universities, technical/trade schools, professional societies), employment services (state or private employment agencies, temporary help agencies, and professional search firms), special events (career conferences or job fairs), Internet job sites (CareerBuilder.com and Monster.com), and social media (LinkedIn and Facebook), as well as career portals on company websites. Which external recruiting method should you use? Historically, studies show that employee referrals, walk-ins, advertisements, and state employment agencies tend to be used most frequently for office/clerical and production/service employees. By contrast, advertisements and college/university recruiting are used most frequently for professional/technical employees. When recruiting managers, organizations tend to rely most heavily on advertisements, employee referrals, and search firms.[31]

Recently, social media sites and industry-specific job boards have been gaining momentum at the expense of generalist job boards and newspapers. **Facebook**'s job search platform is used effectively to recruit lower-skilled workers, and sites such as **LinkedIn** and **Ladders.com** tend to attract more highly-skilled or senior-level job seekers.[32] Even though 76 percent of people seeking jobs using social media found their current jobs through Facebook, LinkedIn continues to be where job hunters do most of their looking.[33] Whereas only 26 percent of recruiters have hired someone through Facebook, 89 percent of recruiters have hired someone through LinkedIn.[34]

One of the biggest trends in recruiting is identifying passive candidates, people who are not actively seeking a job but who might be receptive to a change. Why pursue passive candidates? About half of all workers would be willing to change jobs if recruited by another company.[35] Apps such as **Switch**, **Poacht**, and **Poachable** allow passive candidates to indicate they are open to jobs without letting their bosses know. Then, like online dating sites, they use algorithms and questionnaires to match people with potential jobs, to which they indicate their level of interest. Yahoo!, Walmart, Amazon, eBay—and, yes, even Facebook—have used these apps to post openings. Poachable CEO Tom Leung says, "Going on some job board feels so 1990. Now we can say we know a lot about you, [but] we don't contact you unless we have a match."[36]

Some companies are even hosting virtual job fairs, where job applicants click on recruiting booths to learn about the company, see the kinds of available jobs, and speak with company representatives via video chat or instant message. Because they don't need to send HR representatives on long trips and can interact with potential hires from all over the world, Boeing, Progressive, Citibank, and Amazon have found virtual job fairs to be an efficient, cost-effective way to find qualified candidates. Still an important part of external recruiting, job fairs are being repositioned as branding events. With nearly half of its U.S. workforce expected to retire by 2025, the insurance and risk management industry is aggressively recruiting younger workers. **Allstate** bolsters its campus recruiting and job fairs with trivia nights, free food, and hackathons to attract computer science majors. And instead of wearing business suits, its campus recruiters wear t-shirts emblazoned with "Jobhunting is Mayhem," a reference to the star character in its popular ad campaign.[37]

11-3 SELECTION

After the recruitment process has produced a pool of qualified applicants, the selection process is used to determine which applicants have the best chance of performing well on the job. When hiring programmers, Jocelyn Golden, Facebook's engineering director, says, "I'd rather have the top student out of U.T. or University of Central Florida than the 30th best from Stanford." Anyone who successfully completes a timed online coding challenge gets a phone interview. Phone interviews involve discussion of applicants' résumés but finish with programming exercises. Applicants invited to Facebook's campus for onsite interviews must solve more difficult coding problems, including a take-home "hack." Facebook engineer Carlos Bueno says, "If it says 'expert in X' [on your résumé], we will try to schedule you with a proven expert in X, so be prepared. If you are not, leave it off."[38]

As this example illustrates, **selection** is the process of gathering information about job applicants to decide who should be offered a job. To make sure that selection decisions are accurate and legally defensible, the EEOC's *Uniform Guidelines on Employee Selection Procedures* recommend that all selection procedures be validated. **Validation** is the process of determining how well a selection test or procedure predicts future job performance. The better or more accurate the prediction of future job performance, the more valid a test is said to be.

*Let's examine common selection procedures such as **11-3a application forms and résumés, 11-3b references and background checks, 11-3c selection tests**, and **11-3d interviews**.*

11-3a Application Forms and Résumés

The first selection devices that most job applicants encounter when they seek a job are application forms and résumés. Both contain similar information about an applicant, such as name, address, job and educational history, and so forth. Though an organization's application form often asks for information already provided by the applicant's résumé, most organizations prefer to collect this information in their own format for entry into a **human resource information system (HRIS)**.

Employment laws apply to application forms just as they do to all selection devices. Application forms may ask applicants only for valid, job-related information. Nonetheless, application forms commonly ask applicants for non-job-related information such as marital status, maiden name, age, or date of high school graduation. One study found that 73 percent of organizations had application forms that violated at least one federal or state law.[39] Likewise, interviewers may not ask about medical histories or genetics, religious beliefs, or citizenship. Exhibit 11.4 provides a more detailed explanation and list of the kinds of information that companies may *not* request in application forms, during job interviews, or in any other part of the selection process.

Courts will assume that you consider all of the information you request of applicants even if you actually don't. Be sure to ask only those questions that relate directly to the candidate's ability and motivation to perform the job. Furthermore, using social media such as Facebook and LinkedIn at the initial stage of the hiring process can give employers access to information they're not allowed to obtain directly from applicants. Attorney James McDonald says, "I advise employers that it's not a good idea to use social media as a screening tool. You need to control the information you receive so you're only

---

Selection the process of gathering information about job applicants to decide who should be offered a job

Validation the process of determining how well a selection test or procedure predicts future job performance; the better or more accurate the prediction of future job performance, the more valid a test is said to be

Human resource information system (HRIS) a computerized system for gathering, analyzing, storing, and disseminating information related to the HRM process

Courts assume that companies consider all of the information they request from applicants when they are applying.

getting information that is legal for you to take into accounting."[40]

Résumés also pose problems for companies, but in a different way. A CareerBuilder survey of hiring managers found that 58 percent had found a lie on a résumé, with the most common being embellished skills, employment dates, job titles, academic degrees, and the companies one for which one has supposedly worked. Applicants in financial services (73%), leisure and hospitality (71%), and IT and health care (both 63%) were the most likely to have lies caught on resumes.[41] Therefore, managers should verify the information collected via résumés and application forms by comparing it with additional information collected during interviews and other stages of the selection process, such as references and background checks, which are discussed next.

11-3b References and Background Checks

In the United States, drivers for **Uber**'s ride-sharing service undergo an independent screening by Hirease, a company that runs each applicant's name through seven years of federal and county background checks, sex offender registries, and motor vehicle records. Despite those checks, Uber still cleared an applicant, who had spent fourteen years in federal prison on drug charges, to be a driver on its network in the Houston area. While giving a ride to a drunken female passenger, the driver allegedly took her to his home and raped her. Lara Cottingham, an administrator for the city of Houston says, "Not all background checks are created equal. It's easy to lie about your name . . . Social Security number . . . where

Exhibit 11.4
Don't Ask! Topics to Avoid in an Interview

1. **Children.** Don't ask applicants if they have children, plan to have them, or have or need child care. Questions about children can unintentionally single out women.

2. **Age.** Because of the Age Discrimination in Employment Act, employers cannot ask job applicants their age during the hiring process. Because most people graduate high school at the age of eighteen, even asking for high school graduation dates could violate the law.

3. **Disabilities.** Don't ask if applicants have physical or mental disabilities. According to the Americans with Disabilities Act, disabilities (and reasonable accommodations for them) cannot be discussed until a job offer has been made.

4. **Physical characteristics.** Don't ask for information about height, weight, or other physical characteristics. Questions about weight could be construed as leading to discrimination toward overweight people, and studies show that they are less likely to be hired in general.

5. **Name.** Yes, you can ask an applicant's name, but you cannot ask a female applicant for her maiden name because it indicates marital status. Asking for a maiden name could also lead to charges that the organization was trying to establish a candidate's ethnic background.

6. **Citizenship.** Asking applicants about citizenship could lead to claims of discrimination on the basis of national origin. However, according to the Immigration Reform and Control Act, companies may ask applicants if they have a legal right to work in the United States.

7. **Lawsuits.** Applicants may not be asked if they have ever filed a lawsuit against an employer. Federal and state laws prevent this to protect whistle-blowers from retaliation by future employers.

8. **Arrest records.** Applicants cannot be asked about their arrest records. Arrests don't have legal standing. However, applicants can be asked whether they have been convicted of a crime.

9. **Smoking.** Applicants cannot be asked if they smoke. Smokers might be able to claim that they weren't hired because of fears of higher absenteeism and medical costs. However, they can be asked if they are aware of company policies that restrict smoking at work.

10. **AIDS/HIV.** Applicants can't be asked about AIDS, HIV, or any other medical condition, including genetics. Questions of this nature would violate the Americans with Disabilities Act, as well as federal and state civil rights laws.

11. **Religion.** Applicants can't be asked about religious beliefs. Questions of this nature would violate federal and state civil rights laws.

12. **Genetic information.** Employers should avoid asking about genetic test results or family medical history. This would violate the Genetic Information Nondiscrimination Act, or GINA, which was designed to help encourage people to get more genetic screening done without the fear of employers or insurers using that information to deny employment or coverage.

Sources: J. S. Pouliot, "Topics to Avoid with Applicants," *Nation's Business* 80, no. 7 (1992): 57; M. Trottman, "Employers Beware When Asking about Workers' Health," *Wall Street Journal*, July 22, 2013, accessed July 9, 2014. http://blogs .wsj.com/atwork/2013/07/22/employers-beware-when-asking-about-workers -health/; L. Weber, "Hiring Process Just Got Dicier," *Wall Street Journal*, July 3, 2014, accessed July 9, 2014. http://www.wsj.com/articles/hiring-process -just-got-dicier-1404255998.

you've lived."[42] Houston requires all drivers to undergo an FBI background check, including fingerprinting. Nearly all companies ask an applicant to provide **employment references**, such as the names of previous employers or coworkers, whom they can contact to learn more about the candidate. **Background checks** are used to verify the truthfulness and accuracy of information that applicants provide about themselves and to uncover negative, job-related background information not provided by applicants. Background checks are conducted by contacting "educational institutions, prior employers, court records, police and governmental agencies, and other informational sources, either by telephone, mail, remote computer access, or through in-person investigations."[43]

Unfortunately, previous employers are increasingly reluctant to provide references or background check information for fear of being sued by previous employees for defamation.[44] If former employers provide potential employers with unsubstantiated information that damages applicants' chances of being hired, applicants can (and do) sue for defamation. As a result, 54 percent of employers will not provide information about previous employees.[45] Many provide only dates of employment, positions held, and date of separation.

When previous employers decline to provide meaningful references or background information, they put other employers at risk of *negligent hiring* lawsuits, in which an employer is held liable for the actions of an employee who would not have been hired if the employer had conducted a thorough reference search and background check.[46] Heyl Logistics hired Washington Transportation, a trucking firm, to deliver bottled water, but its driver took drugs, fell asleep, hit a truck, and killed another driver. The killed driver's family sued Heyl Logistics for negligent hiring, alleging it should have known that Washington Transportation operated without a license, did not test its drivers for drug use, and carried no insurance. Heyl was found guilty, Washington Transportation's driver was sent to prison for negligent homicide and driving under the influence, and the family was awarded $5.2 million in punitive damages.[47]

With previous employers generally unwilling to give full, candid references and with negligent hiring lawsuits awaiting companies that don't get such references and background information, what can companies do? They can conduct criminal record checks, especially if the job for which the person is applying involves money, drugs, control over valuable goods, or access to the elderly, people with disabilities, or people's homes.[48] According to the Society for Human Resource Management, 69 percent of organizations conduct criminal record checks, and 47 percent conduct credit checks.[49]

Now that companies provide criminal record checks for $10 an applicant, pulling data from 3,100 court systems nationwide, there's no excuse to not check. Louis DeFalco, corporate director of safety, security, and investigations at ABC Fine Wine & Spirits, which has 175 stores in Florida, makes the case for criminal record checks: "If I have a guy with four arrests and bad credit versus someone who has never been in trouble in his life, who am I going to hire? It's not rocket science."[50] While companies are legally entitled to use criminal background checks at some point in the hiring process, they should, as was discussed at the beginning of the chapter, follow state laws and EEOC guidelines that restrict asking applicants about criminal records on initial application forms.[51]

Another option is to use public networking sites such as LinkedIn to identify and contact the colleagues, customers, and suppliers who are linked or connected to job applicants. LinkedIn's former CEO Dan Nye says that the company called twenty-three of his LinkedIn connections without his knowledge before offering him a face-to-face interview. With the growing use and popularity of social networking websites, Nye says such practices are "fair game." One downside to this approach is that it could unintentionally alert an applicant's current employer that the person is seeking another job. As a result, says Chuck Wardell, managing director at Korn/Ferry International, an executive recruitment firm, "You have to be careful referencing people who have jobs because you might blow them out of their jobs."[52]

After doing a background check, dig deeper for more information. Ask references to provide additional references. Next, ask applicants to sign a waiver that permits you to check references, run a background check, or contact anyone else with knowledge of their work performance or history. Likewise, ask applicants if there is anything they would like the company to know or if they expect you to hear anything unusual when contacting references.[53] This in itself is often enough to get applicants to share information they typically withhold. When you've finished checking, keep the findings confidential to minimize the chances of a defamation charge. Always document all reference and background checks, noting who was called and what information was obtained. Document everything, not just information you received.

Employment references sources such as previous employers or coworkers who can provide job-related information about job candidates

Background checks procedures used to verify the truthfulness and accuracy of information that applicants provide about themselves and to uncover negative, job-related background information not provided by applicants

To reduce the likelihood that negligent hiring lawsuits will succeed, it's particularly important to document even which companies and people refused to share reference checks and background information.

Finally, consider hiring private investigators to conduct background checks, which can often uncover information missed by traditional background checks. For example, while traditional background checks should be able to verify applicants' academic credentials, a private investigator hired by the *Wall Street Journal* found that 7 out of 358 senior executives at publicly traded firms had falsified claims regarding the college degrees they had earned.[54] Likewise, private investigators can potentially identify when applicants hire companies that provide fake references from fake bosses (to avoid negative references from previous employers). Indeed, one such business claims, "We can replace a supervisor with a fictitious one, alter your work history, provide you with a positive employment reputation, and give you the glowing reference you need."[55]

11-3c Selection Tests

Selection tests give organizational decision makers a chance to know who will likely do well in a job and who won't. Pre-hiring assessments are growing in popularity, with 57 percent of large U.S. employers using some sort of pre-hiring test to ensure a better fit. "The incentives to screen before hiring have increased over time, while costs have declined," says economist Steve Davis. "Both those things are encouraging employers to move away what was essentially a trial employment situation to just screening out people in advance."[56] The basic idea behind selection testing is to have applicants take a test that measures something directly or indirectly related to doing well on the job. The selection tests discussed here are specific ability tests, cognitive ability tests, biographical data, personality tests, work sample tests, and assessment centers.

Specific ability tests measure the extent to which an applicant possesses the particular kind of ability needed to do a job well. Specific ability tests are also called **aptitude tests** because they measure aptitude for doing a particular task well. For example, if you took the SAT to get into college, then you've taken the aptly named Scholastic Aptitude Test, which is one of the best predictors of how well students will do in college (that is scholastic performances).[57] Specific ability tests also exist for mechanical, clerical, sales, and physical work. For example, clerical workers have to be good at accurately reading and scanning numbers as they type or enter data. Exhibit 11.5 shows items similar to the Minnesota Clerical Test, in which applicants have only a short time to determine if the two columns of numbers and letters are identical. Applicants who are good at this are likely to do well as clerical or data entry workers.

Cognitive ability tests measure the extent to which applicants have abilities in perceptual speed, verbal comprehension, numerical aptitude, general reasoning, and spatial aptitude. In other words, these tests indicate how quickly and how well people understand words, numbers, logic, and spatial dimensions. Whereas specific ability tests predict job performance in only particular types of jobs, cognitive ability tests accurately predict job performance in almost all kinds of jobs.[58] Why is this so? The reason is that people with strong cognitive or mental abilities are usually good at learning new things, processing complex information, solving problems, and making decisions, and these abilities are important in almost all jobs.[59] In fact, cognitive

Specific ability tests (aptitude tests) tests that measure the extent to which an applicant possesses the particular kind of ability needed to do a job well

Cognitive ability tests tests that measure the extent to which applicants have abilities in perceptual speed, verbal comprehension, numerical aptitude, general reasoning, and spatial aptitude

Exhibit 11.5
Clerical Test Items Similar to Those Found on the Minnesota Clerical Test

	Numbers/Letters		Same	
1.	3468251	3467251	Yes	No
			O	O
2.	4681371	4681371	Yes	No
			O	O
3.	7218510	7218520	Yes	No
			O	O
4.	ZXYAZAB	ZXYAZAB	Yes	No
			O	O
5.	ALZYXMN	ALZYXNM	Yes	No
			O	O
6.	PRQZYMN	PRQZYMN	Yes	No
			O	O

Source: N. W. Schmitt and R. J. Klimoski, *Research Methods in Human Resource Management* (Mason, OH: South-Western, 1991).

ability tests are almost always the best predictors of job performance. Consequently, if you were allowed to use just one selection test, a cognitive ability test would be the one to use.[60] (In practice, though, companies use a battery of different tests because doing so leads to much more accurate selection decisions.)

Biographical data, or **biodata**, are extensive surveys that ask applicants questions about their personal backgrounds and life experiences. The basic idea behind biodata is that past behavior (personal background and life experience) is the best predictor of future behavior. For example, during World War II, the U.S. Air Force had to test tens of thousands of men without flying experience to determine who was likely to be a good pilot. Because flight training took several months and was very expensive, quickly selecting the right people for training was important. After examining extensive biodata, the Air Force found that one of the best predictors of success in flight school was whether students had ever built model airplanes that actually flew. This one biodata item was almost as good a predictor as the entire set of selection tests that the air force was using at the time.[61]

Most biodata questionnaires have more than 100 items that gather information about habits and attitudes, health, interpersonal relations, money, what it was like growing up in your family (parents, siblings, childhood years, teen years), personal habits, current home (spouse, children), hobbies, education and training, values, preferences, and work.[62] In general, biodata are very good predictors of future job performance, especially in entry-level jobs.

You may have noticed that some of the information requested in biodata surveys is related to those topics employers should avoid in applications, interviews, or other parts of the selection process. This information can be requested in biodata questionnaires provided that the company can demonstrate that the information is job related (that is valid) and does not result in adverse impact against protected groups of job applicants. Biodata surveys should be validated and tested for adverse impact before they are used to make selection decisions.[63]

Work sample tests, also called *performance tests*, require applicants to perform tasks that are actually done on the job. So, unlike specific ability tests, cognitive ability tests, biographical data surveys, and personality tests, which are indirect predictors of job performance, work sample tests directly measure job applicants' capability to do the job. For example, a candidate applying to be a pharmacist might be asked to consult medical databases and accurately fill prescriptions. An applicant for a sales position might have to role-play a sales pitch. **Hire Results**, which designs work sample tests, has doubled the number of work sample tests it conducts for employers over the past five years. At **Coupons.com**, only candidates who successfully complete a series of business challenges are offered an interview. Business consultant Brian Stern, who has designed application tryouts for companies such as Starbucks, Walmart, and Sherwin-Williams, says tryouts (that is, work sample tests) are gaining in popularity because, "A job tryout says 'show me your stuff.'"[64] Work sample tests are generally very good at predicting future job performance; however, they can be expensive to administer and can be used for only one kind of job. For example, an auto dealership could not use a work sample test for mechanics as a selection test for sales representatives.

Assessment centers use a series of job-specific simulations that are graded by multiple trained observers to determine applicants' ability to perform managerial work. Unlike the previously described selection tests that are commonly used for specific jobs or entry-level jobs, assessment centers are most often used to select applicants who have high potential to be good managers. Assessment centers often last two to five days and require participants to complete a number of tests and exercises that simulate managerial work.

Some of the more common assessment center exercises are in-basket exercises, role-plays, small-group presentations, and leaderless group discussions. An *in-basket exercise* is a paper-and-pencil test in which an applicant is given a manager's in-basket containing memos, phone messages, organizational policies, and other communications normally received by and available to managers. Applicants have a limited time to read through the in-basket, prioritize the items, and decide how to deal with each item. Experienced managers then score the applicants' decisions and recommendations. Exhibit 11.6 shows an item that could be used in an assessment center for evaluating applicants for a job as a store manager.

In a *leaderless group discussion*, another common assessment center exercise, a group of six applicants is given approximately two hours to solve a problem, but no one is put in charge (hence the name *leaderless* group discussion). Trained observers watch and score each participant on the extent to which he or she facilitates discussion, listens, leads, persuades, and works well with others.

Biographical data (biodata) extensive surveys that ask applicants questions about their personal backgrounds and life experiences

Work sample tests tests that require applicants to perform tasks that are actually done on the job

Assessment centers a series of managerial simulations, graded by trained observers, that are used to determine applicants' capability for managerial work

Exhibit 11.6
In-Basket Item for an Assessment Center for Store Managers

```
February 28
Sam & Dave's Discount Warehouse
Orange, California

Dear Store Manager,

Last week, my children and I were shopping in your store.
After doing our grocery shopping, we stopped in the
electronics department and asked the clerk, whose name
is Donald Block, to help us find a copy of the latest
version of the Madden NFL video game. Mr. Block was rude,
unhelpful, and told us to find it for ourselves as he
was busy.

I've been a loyal customer for over six years and expect
you to immediately do something about Mr. Block's
behavior. If you don't, I'll start doing my shopping
somewhere else.

Sincerely,
Margaret Quinlan
```

Source: Adapted from N. W. Schmitt and R. J. Klimoski, *Research Methods in Human Resource Management* (Mason, OH: South-Western 1991).

Are tests perfect predictors of job performance? No, they aren't. Some people who do well on selection tests will do poorly in their jobs. Likewise, some people who do poorly on selection tests (and therefore weren't hired) would have been very good performers. Nonetheless, valid tests will minimize selection errors (hiring people who should not have been hired and not hiring people who should have been hired) while maximizing correct selection decisions (hiring people who should have been hired and not hiring people who should not have been hired). Charles Handler, president of Rocket-Hire, a consulting firm on selection tests, says, "Predicting what humans will do is really . . . hard. Tests are a predictor and better than a coin toss, but you have to be realistic about them."[65] In short, tests increase the chances that you'll hire the right person for the job, that is, someone who turns out to be a good performer. So, although tests

aren't perfect, almost nothing predicts future job performance as well as the selection tests discussed here.

11-3d Interviews

In **interviews**, company representatives ask job applicants job-related questions to determine whether they are qualified for the job. Interviews are probably the most frequently used and relied on selection device. There are several basic kinds of interviews: unstructured, structured, and semistructured.

In **unstructured interviews**, interviewers are free to ask applicants anything they want, and studies show that they do. Because interviewers often disagree about which questions should be asked during interviews, different interviewers tend to ask applicants very different questions.[66] Furthermore, individual interviewers even seem to have a tough time asking the same questions from one interview to the next. This high level of variety can make things difficult. As a result, while unstructured interviews do predict job performance with some success, they are about half as accurate as structured interviews at predicting which job applicants should be hired.[67]

By contrast, with **structured interviews**, standardized interview questions are prepared ahead of time so that all applicants are asked the same job-related questions.[68] Structuring interviews also ensures that interviewers ask only for important, job-related information. Not only are the accuracy, usefulness, and validity of the interview improved, but the chances that interviewers will ask questions about topics that violate employment laws (see Exhibit 11.4) are reduced.

The primary advantage of structured interviews is that comparing applicants is much easier because they are all asked the same questions. **Google** uses structured interviews by having different interviewers ask the candidate the same question. Because Google hires by committee, each member of the hiring committee will ask an identical set of questions, allowing committee members to compare how an individual candidate answered the questions each time. Laszlo Bock, head of human resources at Google, says that the practice enables easy comparisons between interviews and identification of interviewer bias.[69] Four kinds of questions are typically asked in structured interviews. Situational questions ask applicants how they would respond in a hypothetical situation ("What would you do if . . .?"). These questions

Interview a selection tool in which company representatives ask job applicants job-related questions to determine whether they are qualified for the job

Unstructured interviews interviews in which interviewers are free to ask the applicants anything they want

Structured interviews interviews in which all applicants are asked the same set of standardized questions, usually including situational, behavioral, background, and job-knowledge questions are more appropriate for hiring new graduates, who are unlikely to have encountered real-work situations because of their limited work experience. Behavioral questions ask applicants what they did in previous jobs that were similar to the job for which they are applying ("In your previous jobs, tell me about . . ."). These questions are more appropriate for hiring experienced individuals. Background questions ask applicants about their work experience, education, and other qualifications ("Tell me about the training you received at . . ."). Job-knowledge questions ask applicants to demonstrate their job knowledge (for example, nurses might be asked, "Give me an example of a time when one of your patients had a severe reaction to a medication. How did you handle it?").[70]

Semistructured interviews lie between structured and unstructured interviews. A major part of the semistructured interview (perhaps as much as 80%) is based on structured questions, but some time is set aside for unstructured interviewing to allow the interviewer to probe into ambiguous or missing information uncovered during the structured portion of the interview.

How well do interviews predict future job performance? Contrary to what you've probably heard, recent evidence indicates that even unstructured interviews do a fairly good job.[71] When conducted properly, however, structured interviews can lead to much more accurate hiring decisions than unstructured interviews. In some cases, the validity of structured interviews can rival that of cognitive ability tests.

But even more important, because interviews are especially good at assessing applicants' interpersonal skills, they work particularly well with cognitive ability tests. Combining the two—using structured interviews together with cognitive ability tests to identify smart people who work well with others—leads to even better selection decisions than using either alone.[72] Exhibit 11.7 provides a set of guidelines for conducting effective structured employment interviews.

Exhibit 11.7
Guidelines for Conducting Effective Structured Interviews

Interview Stage	What to Do
Planning the Interview	• Identify and define the knowledge, skills, abilities, and other (KSAO) characteristics needed for successful job performance. • For each essential KSAO, develop key behavioral questions that will elicit examples of past accomplishments, activities, and performance. • For each KSAO, develop a list of things to look for in the applicant's responses to key questions.
Conducting the Interview	• Create a relaxed, nonstressful interview atmosphere. • Review the applicant's application form, résumé, and other information. • Allocate enough time to complete the interview without interruption. • Put the applicant at ease; don't jump right into heavy questioning. • Tell the applicant what to expect. Explain the interview process. • Obtain job-related information from the applicant by asking those questions prepared for each KSAO. • Describe the job and the organization to the applicant. Applicants need adequate information to make a selection decision about the organization.
After the Interview	• Immediately after the interview, review your notes and make sure they are complete. • Evaluate the applicant on each essential KSAO. • Determine each applicant's probability of success, and make a hiring decision.

Source: B. M. Farrell, "The Art and Science of Employment Interviews," *Personnel Journal* 65 (1986): 91–94.

11-4 TRAINING

According to the American Society for Training and Development, a typical investment in training increases productivity by an average of 17 percent, reduces employee turnover, and makes companies more profitable.[73] Giving employees the knowledge and skills they need to improve their performance is just the first step in developing employees, however. The second step—and not enough companies do this—is giving employees formal feedback about their actual job performance.

Training means providing opportunities for employees to develop the job-specific skills, experience, and knowledge they need to do their jobs or improve their performance. American companies spend an estimated $164 billion a year on training.[74]

To make sure those training dollars are well spent, companies need to **11-4a determine specific training needs, 11-4b select appropriate training methods, and 11-4c evaluate training**.

11-4a Determining Training Needs

Needs assessment is the process of identifying and prioritizing the learning needs of employees. Needs assessments can be conducted by identifying performance deficiencies, listening to customer complaints, surveying employees and managers, or formally testing employees' skills and knowledge.

Note that training should never be conducted without first performing a needs assessment. Sometimes, training isn't needed at all or isn't needed for all employees. Unfortunately, however, many organizations simply require all employees to attend training whether they need to or not. As a result, employees who are not interested or don't need the training may react negatively during or after training. Likewise, employees who should be sent for training but aren't may also react negatively. Consequently, a needs assessment is an important tool for deciding who should or should not attend training. In fact, employment law restricts employers from discriminating on the basis of age, sex, race, color, religion, national origin, or disability when selecting training participants. Just like hiring decisions, the selection of training participants should be based on job-related information.

Training developing the skills, experience, and knowledge employees need to perform their jobs or improve their performance

Needs assessment the process of identifying and prioritizing the learning needs of employees

Mind the Gap! Companies Take Training to the Schools

Roughly 2 million U.S. jobs go unfilled because of shortfalls in working training, education, or skills, and by 2020, roughly one third of U.S. jobs will require more than a high-school diploma but less than a bachelor's degree. To fill that gap, companies across the country are investing in technical training at the high school and community college levels, but few initiatives compare to the vocational programs developed by German robotics company Festo, which has been building and delivering industrial training programs and growing at a rate of 8 percent per year since the 1970s. The training division, called Festo Didactic, arrived in the United States in 2015, and its managers are passionate about its ability to help fill the U.S. skills gap. Festo Didactic's strategy is to target companies, governments, colleges, and even high schools and younger, all in a quest to elevate the skill levels of U.S. workers. CEO Nader Imani says, "We feel almost like missionaries at times, but there's a hard-headed business case as well."

Source: C. Gummer, "German Robots School U.S. Workers," *Wall Street Journal*, September 10, 2014, accessed May 7, 2015. http://www.wsj.com/articles/german-style-training-for-american-factory-workers-1410296094; A. Campoy, "Training Programs Target Skills Gap," *Wall Street Journal*, April 24, 2015, A3.

11-4b Training Methods

Assume that you're a training director for a hospital system and that you're in charge of making sure all employees in the biocontaminant unit can safely treat patients with Ebola.[75] Exhibit 11.8 lists a number of training methods you could use: films and videos, lectures, planned readings, case studies, coaching and mentoring, group discussions, on-the-job training, role-playing, simulations and games, vestibule training, and computer-based learning. Which method would be best?

To choose the best method, you should consider a number of factors, such as the number of people to be trained, the cost of training, and the objectives of the training. For instance, if the training objective is to impart information or knowledge to trainees, then you

Exhibit 11.8
Training Objectives and Methods

Training Objective	Training Methods
Impart Information and Knowledge	■ *Films and videos.* Films and videos present information, illustrate problems and solutions, and effectively hold trainees' attention.
	■ *Lectures.* Trainees listen to instructors' oral presentations.
	■ *Planned readings.* Trainees read about concepts or ideas before attending training.
Develop Analytical and Problem-Solving Skills	■ *Case studies.* Cases are analyzed and discussed in small groups. The cases present a specific problem or decision, and trainees develop methods for solving the problem or making the decision.
	■ *Coaching and mentoring.* Coaching and mentoring of trainees by managers involves informal advice, suggestions, and guidance. This method is helpful for reinforcing other kinds of training and for trainees who benefit from support and personal encouragement.
	■ *Group discussions.* Small groups of trainees actively discuss specific topics. The instructor may perform the role of discussion leader.
Practice, Learn, or Change Job Behaviors	■ *On-the-job training.* New employees are assigned to experienced employees. The trainee learns by watching the experienced employee perform the job and eventually by working alongside the experienced employee. Gradually, the trainee is left on his or her own to perform the job.
	■ *Role-playing.* Trainees assume job-related roles and practice new behaviors by acting out what they would do in job-related situations.
	■ *Simulations and games.* Experiential exercises place trainees in realistic job-related situations and give them the opportunity to experience a job-related condition in a relatively low-cost setting. The trainee benefits from hands-on experience before actually performing the job, where mistakes may be more costly.
	■ *Vestibule training.* Procedures and equipment similar to those used in the actual job are set up in a special area called a "vestibule." The trainee is then taught how to perform the job at his or her own pace without disrupting the actual flow of work, making costly mistakes, or exposing the trainee and others to dangerous conditions.
Impart Information and Knowledge; Develop Analytical and Problem-Solving Skills; and Practice, Learn, or Change Job Behaviors	■ *Computer-based learning.* Interactive videos, software, CD-ROMs, PCs, teleconferencing, and the Internet may be combined to present multimedia-based training.

Source: A. Fowler, "How to Decide on Training Methods," *People Management* 25, no. 1 (1995): 36.

should use films and videos, lectures, and planned readings. In our example, trainees might read a manual or attend a lecture about how to put on and remove personal protective gear.

If developing analytical and problem-solving skills is the objective, then use case studies, coaching and mentoring, and group discussions. In our example, trainees might view a video documenting how a team handled exposure to the disease, talk with first responders who have worked in West Africa, and discuss what they would do in a similar situation.

If practicing, learning, or changing job behaviors is the objective, then use on-the-job training, role-playing, simulations and games, and vestibule training. Employees at the biocontainment unit of the University of Texas Southwestern Medical Center (UTSMC) role-play putting on and taking off their protective gear. Because of the number of steps involved, this is done in teams to ensure compliance so as to prevent the spread of the deadly disease. UTSMC sprays the fake Ebola patients used during the training with spicy, peppery Tabasco sauce. Dr. Bruce Myer says that if doctors and nurses get Tabasco on their skin, "it gives immediate feedback," to let them know a potentially deadly mistake has just been made.[76]

If training is supposed to meet more than one of these objectives, then your best choice may be to combine one of the previous methods with computer-based training. Siemens, which makes everything from power plants to electronic scanners, developed an online video game called Plantville, in which users take on the role of Pete, the plant manager. The goal is to revitalize three old factories by hiring new workers, redesigning factory layouts, and replacing old machines with new ones from Siemens. Raj Batra, president of the Industry Automation division at Siemens, says, "The virtual activity in Plantville mimics the real-world environment where plant managers continually watch key performance indicators and strive to maximize productivity and efficiency." Plantville's "hands-on" experience helps employees and outsiders better understand the intricacies of running a factory and serves not only as a training tool for employees but also as a recruiting tool for outsiders. Sign up to play and join 21,000 gamers from 160 countries at Plantville.com.[77]

These days, many companies are adopting Internet training, or "computer-based learning." E-learning can offer several advantages. Because employees don't need to leave their jobs, travel costs are greatly reduced. Also, because employees can take training modules when it is convenient (that is they don't have to fall behind at their jobs to attend week-long training courses), workplace productivity should increase, and employee stress should

decrease. And, if a company's technology infrastructure can support it, e-learning can be much faster than traditional training methods. Westinghouse Electric, which provides technology, services, and equipment for the nuclear electric power industry, had difficulty hiring managers and workers with prior nuclear experience. Former director of talent management Jim Ice says, "We were bringing in first-line employees and even managers that hadn't been in the nuclear industry before." So it invested "tens of millions" of dollars to create Westinghouse University, which has 100 percent of its classes online and is organized into seven "colleges": project management, nuclear, technical, leadership, business, behavioral, and manufacturing. For example, employees take Westinghouse University courses where they learn to analyze air samples and conduct radiation surveys.[78]

There are, however, several disadvantages to e-learning. First, despite its increasing popularity, it's not always the appropriate training method. E-learning can be a good way to impart information, but it isn't always as effective for changing job behaviors or developing problem-solving and analytical skills. Second, e-learning requires a significant investment in computers and high-speed Internet and network connections for all employees. Finally, though e-learning can be faster, many employees find it so boring and unengaging that they may choose to do their jobs rather than complete e-learning courses when sitting alone at their desks. E-learning may become more interesting, however, as more companies incorporate game-like features such as avatars and competition into their e-learning courses.

11-4c Evaluating Training

After selecting a training method and conducting the training, the last step is to evaluate the training. Training can be evaluated in four ways: on *reactions* (how satisfied trainees were with the program), on *learning* (how much employees improved their knowledge or skills), on *behavior* (how much employees actually changed their on-the-job behavior because of training), or on *results* (how much training improved job performance, such as increased sales or quality, or decreased costs).[79]

In general, training provides meaningful benefits for most companies if it is done well. For example, a study by the American Society for Training and Development shows that a training budget as small as $680 per employee can increase a company's total return on investment by 6 percent.[80] Chuck Runyon, CEO of Anytime Fitness, which has 2,500 locations, says, "The only thing worse than training people and having them leave is not training people and having them stay."[81]

11-5 PERFORMANCE APPRAISAL

Performance appraisal is the process of assessing how well employees are doing their jobs. Most employees and managers intensely dislike the performance appraisal process. Samuel Culbert, professor of management at UCLA, says there is nothing constructive about performance appraisals and calls them a "dysfunctional pretense." Culbert says, "It's a negative to corporate performance, an obstacle to straight-talk relationships, and a prime cause of low morale at work."[82]

Many people share this view. In fact, 70 percent of employees are dissatisfied with the performance appraisal process in their companies. Likewise, according to the Society for Human Resource Management, 90 percent of human resource managers are dissatisfied with the performance appraisal systems used by their companies.[83]

Performance appraisals are used for four broad purposes: making administrative decisions (for example, pay increase, promotion, retention), providing feedback for employee development (for example, performance, developing career plans), evaluating human resource programs (for example, validating selection systems), and for documentation purposes (for example, documenting performance ratings and decisions based on those ratings).[84]

Let's explore how companies can avoid some of these problems with performance appraisals by **11-5a accurately measuring job performance** *and* **11-5b effectively sharing performance feedback with employees**.

11-5a Accurately Measuring Job Performance

Workers often have strong doubts about the accuracy of their performance appraisals—and they may be right. For example, it's widely known that assessors are prone to errors when rating worker performance. Three of the most common rating errors are central tendency, halo, and leniency. *Central tendency error* occurs when assessors rate all workers as average or in the middle of the scale. *Halo error* occurs when assessors rate all workers as performing at the same level (good, bad, or average) in all parts of their jobs. *Leniency error* occurs when assessors rate all workers as performing particularly well. One of the reasons managers make these errors is that they often don't spend enough time gathering or reviewing performance data. Mark Farrugia, vice president of human resources at **Sun Communities**, a maker of manufactured housing, is concerned that managers are giving high scores on performance appraisals to make their lives easier (and employees happier) or to maximize bonuses for employees they are worried are thinking of leaving. He says, "I'm more and more convinced that [performance appraisal] ratings are doing more harm than good," he says.[85] What can be done to minimize rating errors and improve the accuracy with which job performance is measured? In general, two approaches have been used: improving performance appraisal measures themselves and training performance raters to be more accurate.

One of the ways companies try to improve performance appraisal measures is to use as many objective performance measures as possible. **Objective performance measures** are measures of performance that are easily and directly counted or quantified. Common objective performance measures include output, scrap, waste, sales, customer complaints, and rejection rates.

But when objective performance measures aren't available (and frequently they aren't), subjective performance measures have to be used instead. **Subjective performance measures** require that someone judge or assess a worker's performance. The most common kind of subjective performance measure is the graphic rating scale (GRS) shown in Exhibit 11.9. Graphic rating scales are most widely used because they are easy to construct, but they are very susceptible to rating errors.

A popular alternative to graphic rating scales is the **behavior observation scale (BOS)**. BOSs requires raters to rate the frequency with which workers perform specific behaviors representative of the job dimensions that are critical

Performance appraisal the process of assessing how well employees are doing their jobs

Objective performance measures measures of job performance that are easily and directly counted or quantified

Subjective performance measures measures of job performance that require someone to judge or assess a worker's performance

Behavior observation scales (BOSs) rating scales that indicate the frequency with which workers perform specific behaviors that are representative of the job dimensions critical to successful job performance

Exhibit 11.9
Subjective Performance Appraisal Scales

	Very poor	Poor	Average	Good	Very good
Graphic Rating Scale					
Example 1: Quality of work performed is	1	2	3	4	5

	Very poor (20% errors)	Poor (15% errors)	Average (10% errors)	Good (5% errors)	Very good (less than 5% errors)
Example 2: Quality of work performed is	1	2	3	4	5

Behavioral Observation Scale	Almost Never				Almost Always
Dimension: Customer Service					
1. Greets customers with a smile and a "hello."	1	2	3	4	5
2. Calls other stores to help customers find merchandise that is not in stock.	1	2	3	4	5
3. Promptly handles customer concerns and complaints.	1	2	3	4	5

	Almost Never				Almost Always
Dimension: Money Handling					
1. Accurately makes change from customer transactions.	1	2	3	4	5
2. Accounts balance at the end of the day, no shortages or surpluses.	1	2	3	4	5
3. Accurately records transactions in computer system.	1	2	3	4	5

© Cengage Learning

to successful job performance. Exhibit 11.9 shows a BOS for two important job dimensions for a retail salesperson: customer service and money handling. Notice that each dimension lists several specific behaviors characteristic of a worker who excels in that dimension of job performance. (Normally, the scale would list seven to twelve items per dimension, not three, as in the exhibit.) Notice also that the behaviors are good behaviors, meaning they indicate good performance, and the rater is asked to judge how frequently an employee engaged in those good behaviors. The logic behind the BOS is that better performers engage in good behaviors more often.

Rater training training performance appraisal raters in how to avoid rating errors and increase rating accuracy

Not only do BOSs work well for rating critical dimensions of performance, but studies also show that managers strongly prefer BOSs for giving performance feedback; accurately differentiating between poor, average, and good workers; identifying training needs; and accurately measuring performance. And in response to the statement, "If I were defending a company, this rating format would be an asset to my case," attorneys strongly preferred BOSs over other kinds of subjective performance appraisal scales.[86]

The second approach to improving the measurement of workers' job performance is **rater training**. The most effective is frame-of-reference training, in which a group of trainees learn how to do performance appraisals by watching a videotape of an employee at work. Next, they evaluate the performance of the person in the videotape. A trainer (an expert in the subject matter) then shares his or her evaluations, and trainees' evaluations are compared with the expert's. The expert then explains the rationales behind his or her evaluations. This process is repeated until the differences in evaluations given by trainees and evaluations by the expert are minimized. The underlying logic behind the frame-of-reference training is that by adopting the frame of reference used by an expert, trainees will be able to accurately observe, judge, and use relevant appraisal scales to evaluate the performance of others.[87]

11-5b Sharing Performance Feedback

After gathering accurate performance data, the next step is to share performance feedback with employees. Unfortunately, even when performance appraisal ratings are accurate, the appraisal process often breaks down at the feedback stage. Employees become defensive and dislike hearing any negative assessments of their work, no matter how small. Managers become defensive, too, and dislike giving appraisal feedback as much as employees dislike receiving it. In response, many companies are asking managers to ease up on harsh feedback and instead accentuate the positive by focusing on employee strengths. In the past, Michelle Russell of **Boston Consulting Group** says, "We would bring them in and beat them down a bit."[88] Some employees would suffer a crisis of confidence and performance and then quit. At **Intel**, telling employees they "need improvement" deflates morale, says HR manager Devra Johnson, "We call them the walking wounded."[89]

What can be done to overcome the inherent difficulties in performance appraisal feedback? First, be mindful of being overly critical and making employees so defensive that they quit listening. The top half of Exhibit 11.10 offers some suggestion for being less negative and more positive in feedback sessions. Also, because performance appraisal ratings have traditionally been

the judgments of just one person, the boss, another possibility is to use **360-degree feedback**. In this approach, feedback comes from four sources: the boss, subordinates, peers and coworkers, and the employees themselves. The data, which are obtained anonymously (except for the boss's), are compiled into a feedback report comparing the employee's self-ratings with those of the boss, subordinates, and peers and coworkers. Usually, a consultant or human resource specialist discusses the results with the employee. The advantage of 360-degree programs is that negative feedback ("You don't listen") is often more credible when it comes from several people.

Herbert Meyer, who has been studying performance appraisal feedback for more than thirty years, recommends a list of topics to discuss in performance appraisal feedback sessions (see the bottom half of Exhibit 11.10).[90] Furthermore, managers can do three different things to make performance reviews more comfortable and productive. First, they should separate developmental feedback, which is designed to improve future performance, from administrative feedback, which is used as a reward for past performance, such as for raises. When managers give developmental feedback, they're acting as coaches, but when they give administrative feedback, they're acting as judges. These roles, coaches and judges, are clearly incompatible. As coaches, managers encourage, pointing out opportunities for growth and improvement, and employees are typically open and receptive to feedback. But as judges, managers are evaluative, and employees are typically defensive and closed to feedback.

Second, Meyer suggests that performance appraisal feedback sessions be based on self-appraisals, in which employees carefully assess their own strengths, weaknesses, successes, and failures in writing. Because employees play an active role in the review of their performance, managers can

360-degree feedback a performance appraisal process in which feedback is obtained from the boss, subordinates, peers and coworkers, and the employees themselves

PlusONE/Shutterstock.com

How and What to Discuss in a Performance Appraisal Feedback Session

How to Discuss Performance Feedback

	A	B
1	**Don't say...**	**Instead say...**
2	"What are we stuck on?"	"What are we doing really well?"
3	"Nice work."	"You show great promise with...."
4	"You need to get better at...."	"This is another way that's been successful."
5	"We can't do this."	"We haven't done this yet."

✔ Overall progress—an analysis of accomplishments and shortcomings

✔ Problems encountered in meeting job requirements

✔ Opportunities to improve performance

✔ Long-range plans and opportunities— for the job and for the individual's career

✔ General discussion of possible plans and goals for the coming year

Source: H. H. Meyer, "A Solution to the Performance Appraisal Feedback Enigma," *Academy of Management Executive* 5, no. 1 (1991): 68–76; R. Feintzeig, "Everything Is Awesome! Why You Can't Tell Employees They're Doing a Bad Job." *Wall Street Journal*, February 10, 2015, accessed May 7, 2015. http://www.wsj.com/articles/everything-is-awesome-why-you-cant-tell-employees-theyre-doing-a-bad-job-1423613936.

be coaches rather than judges. Also, because the focus is on future goals and development, both employees and managers are likely to be more satisfied with the process and more committed to future plans and changes. And, because the focus is on development and not administrative assessment, studies show that self-appraisals lead to more candid self-assessments than traditional supervisory reviews.[91]

Finally, what people do with the performance feedback they receive really matters. A study of 1,361 senior managers found that managers who reviewed their 360-degree feedback with an executive coach (hired by the company) were more likely to set specific goals for improvement, ask their bosses for ways to improve, and subsequently improve their performance.[92]

A five-year study of 252 managers found that their performance improved dramatically if they met with their subordinates to discuss their 360-degree feedback ("You don't listen") and how they were going to address it ("I'll restate what others have said before stating my opinion"). Performance was dramatically lower for managers who never discussed their 360-degree feedback with subordinates and for managers who did not routinely do so. Why is discussing 360-degree feedback with subordinates so effective? These discussions help managers understand their weaknesses better, force them to develop a plan to improve, and demonstrate to the

A New Way of Onboarding

For many, the first day of work is often the worst. Many companies are trying to change this by mixing up the typical onboarding process of stacks of paperwork and orientation meetings. According to Harvard Business School associate professor Francesca Gino, people find greater satisfaction and perform better when they're able to bring more of themselves to the job. Studies indicate that activities emphasizing autonomy and learning contribute to greater employee satisfaction and retention. Dog-boarding site Rover.com tries to help employees experience this from day one, allowing them to jump into projects immediately. Business process outsourcer Wipro experimented with an employee-centric onboarding program whereby new hires discussed their strengths and were given personalized sweatshirts. After six months, they discovered that those who went through the employee-centric program were 32 percent more likely to stay with the company.

Source: R.E. Silverman, "Companies Try to Make the First Day for New Hires More Fun," *Wall Street Journal*, May 28, 2013, accessed May 8, 2014. http://www.wsj.com/news/articles/SB10001424127887323336104578501631475934850?KEYWORDS=companies+try+to+make+the+first+day&mg=reno64-wsj.

subordinates the managers' public commitment to improving.[93] In short, it helps to have people discuss their performance feedback with others, but it particularly helps to have them discuss their feedback with the people who provided it.

11-6 COMPENSATION AND EMPLOYEE SEPARATION

While China has more than a billion people, 80 percent of its manufacturers are having difficulty finding and keeping workers. Employers are responding by hiking wages, which have increased 74 percent in four years. **Pacific Resources International**, which has ten Chinese factories, pays its workers 20 percent more than minimum wage, provides insurance and free meals, and only asks employees to work forty to forty-five hours a week, which is low in China. Still, it loses employees to the insurance industry, where salaries are 40 percent larger.[94] Factories, which have already raised pay, are now addressing nonfinancial issues in hopes of becoming more attractive places to work. **Flextronics International** sponsors company picnics, talent shows (karaoke), speed-dating for unmarried workers, sports facilities for soccer and basketball, and hair salons. Chief procurement officer Tom Linton says, "If you are able to get employees connected socially, they're more likely to stay."[95]

Compensation includes both the financial and the nonfinancial rewards that organizations give employees in exchange for their work. **Employee separation** is a broad term covering the loss of an employee for any reason. *Involuntary separation* occurs when employers terminate or lay off employees. *Voluntary separation* occurs when employees quit or retire. Because employee separations affect recruiting, selection, training, and

compensation, organizations should forecast the number of employees they expect to lose through terminations, layoffs, turnover, or retirements when doing human resource planning.

Let's learn more about compensation by examining the 11-6a compensation decisions that managers must make as well as 11-6b termination, 11-6c downsizing, 11-6d retirement, and 11-6e turnover.

11-6a Compensation Decisions

There are three basic kinds of compensation decisions: pay level, pay variability, and pay structure.[96] *Pay-level decisions* regard whether to pay workers at a level that is below, above, or at current market wages. Companies use job evaluation to set their pay structures. **Job evaluation** determines the worth of each job by determining the market value of the knowledge, skills, and requirements needed to perform it. After conducting a job evaluation, most companies try to pay the going rate, meaning the current market wage. There are always companies, however, whose financial situation causes them to pay considerably less than current market wages.

Some companies choose to pay above-average wages to attract and keep employees. *Above-market wages* can attract a larger, more qualified pool of job applicants, increase the rate of job acceptance, decrease the time it takes to fill positions, and increase the time that employees stay.[97] While the average U.S. grocery store cashier makes $20,000 per year, entry-level cashiers at **QuikTrip**, a chain of convenience stores and gas stations, make $40,000 per year. Despite paying employees twice as much as its competitors, QuikTrip is profitable and growing. Compared to other convenience stores, its sales per square foot are 50 percent higher, and its sales per labor hour are 66 percent larger. Furthermore, QuikTrip trains new workers for two weeks before putting them in stores, teaching them everything from the right way to clean bathrooms to ordering merchandise and tracking inventory. Finally, because the company pays well and invests in its workers, most of its managers work their way up from entry-level cashier jobs. QuikTrip's Mike Thornbrugh says, "They can see that if you work hard, if you're smart, the opportunity to grow within the company is very, very good."[98]

Compensation the financial and nonfinancial rewards that organizations give employees in exchange for their work

Employee separation the voluntary or involuntary loss of an employee

Job evaluation a process that determines the worth of each job in a company by evaluating the market value of the knowledge, skills, and requirements needed to perform it

iStockphoto.com/samxmeg

Prominent companies like United Airlines, Avis and Polaroid, offer their employees a chance to "own" part of the company through ESOPs.

Pay-variability decisions concern the extent to which employees' pay varies with individual and organizational performance. Linking pay to performance is intended to increase employee motivation, effort, and job performance. Piecework, sales commissions, profit sharing, employee stock ownership plans, and stock options are common pay-variability options. For instance, under **piecework** pay plans, employees are paid a set rate for each item produced up to some standard (for example, thirty-five cents per item produced for output up to 100 units per day). After productivity exceeds the standard, employees are paid a set amount for each unit of output over the standard (for example, forty-five cents for each unit above 100 units). Under a sales **commission** plan, salespeople are paid a percentage of the purchase price of items they sell. The more they sell, the more they earn. At Installation & Services Technologies, which sells point-of-sales systems (high-tech cash registers), a salesperson's pay is determined in large part by how much he or she sells. All members of the sales staff receive a small base salary (about 35 percent of total pay) and a commission based on how much gross profit they make on sales—17 percent for $1 to $50,000, 24 percent for $50,001 to $100,000, and 30 percent over $100,000. Plus, every time a salesperson reaches a new profit level, he or she receives an extra $1,000.[99]

Because pay plans such as piecework and commissions are based on individual performance, they can reduce the incentive that people have to work together. Therefore, companies also use group rewards (discussed in Chapter 10) and organizational incentives, such as profit sharing, employee stock ownership plans, and stock options, to encourage teamwork and cooperation.

With **profit sharing**, employees receive a portion of the organization's profits over and above their regular compensation. Southwest Airlines posted a profit of $754 million in 2013. Thirty percent of those profits, $228 million, will go to its employees as a result of the company's profit-sharing plan.[100]

Employee stock ownership plans (ESOPs) compensate employees by awarding them shares of the company stock in addition to their regular compensation. Central States Manufacturing, a steel cutting firm in Lowell, Arkansas, is 100 percent owned by its 517 employees. Six and a half percent of each employee's annual pay goes into a tax-deferred ESOP account. Aaron King, a 60-year old truck driver with the company for twenty-three years, has accumulated $1.25 million in his ESOP account. Because of the ESOP, he says, "We hold one another accountable. Somebody leaving a bundle of metal where it could be run over—a $3,000 bundle—we go and get that guy and talk to him. [Because] It's going to come out of all of our paychecks."[101]

Stock options give employees the right to purchase shares of stock at a set price. Options work like this. Let's say you are awarded the right (or option) to buy 100 shares of stock from the company for $5 a share. If the company's stock price rises to $15 a share, you can exercise your options, sell the stock for $15 a share, come out with $1,000. When you exercise your options, you pay the company $500 (100 shares at $5 a share), but because the stock is selling for $15 in the stock market, you can sell your 100 shares for $1,500 and make $1,000. Of course, as the company's profits and share values increase, stock options become even more valuable to employees. Stock options have no value, however, if the company's stock falls below the option "grant price," the price at which the options have been issued to you. The options you have on 100 shares

Piecework a compensation system in which employees are paid a set rate for each item they produce

Commission a compensation system in which employees earn a percentage of each sale they make

Profit sharing a compensation system in which a company pays a percentage of its profits to employees in addition to their regular compensation

Employee stock ownership plan (ESOP) a compensation system that awards employees shares of company stock in addition to their regular compensation

Stock options a compensation system that gives employees the right to purchase shares of stock at a set price, even if the value of the stock increases above that price of stock with a grant price of $5 aren't going to do you a lot of good if the company's stock is worth $2.50. Proponents of stock options argue that this gives employees and managers a strong incentive to work hard to make the company successful. If they do, the company's profits and stock price increase, and their stock options increase in value. If they don't, profits stagnate or turn into losses, and their stock options decrease in value or become worthless. To learn more about ESOPs and stock options, see the National Center for Employee Ownership (www.nceo.org).

The incentive has to be more than just a piece of paper, however. It has to motivate employees with the real opportunity to grow the value of the company and their wealth. **Adworkshop**, a digital marketing agency that does website design and development, search marketing, media buying, and creative work, became an employee-owned company in 2007. Account supervisor Kelly Frady says the ESOP has energized employee commitment. She says, "Everyone knows that you do well, and your stock will rise. It's a driving factor in making the company succeed in the long term." In the United States, 10,900 employee-owned businesses, worth $860 billion, are owned by 10 million employees.[102]

Pay-structure decisions are concerned with internal pay distributions, meaning the extent to which people in the company receive very different levels of pay.[103] With *hierarchical pay structures,* there are big differences from one pay level to another. The highest pay levels are for people near the top of the pay distribution. The basic idea behind hierarchical pay structures is that large differences in pay between jobs or organizational levels should motivate people to work harder to obtain those higher-paying jobs. Many publicly owned companies have hierarchical pay structures, paying huge salaries to their top managers and CEOs. For example, CEOs of *Fortune* 500 companies, the 500 largest U.S. firms, now make an average of $15.2 million per year, which is 296 times the average employee salary of $52,100.[104]

By contrast, *compressed pay structures* typically have fewer pay levels and smaller differences in pay between levels. Pay is less dispersed and more similar across jobs in the company. The basic idea behind compressed pay structures is that similar pay levels should lead to higher levels of cooperation, feelings of fairness and a common purpose, and better group and team performance.

So should companies choose hierarchical or compressed pay structures? The evidence isn't straightforward, but studies seem to indicate that there are significant problems with the hierarchical approach. The most damaging finding is that there appears to be little link between organizational performance and the pay of top managers.[105] Furthermore, studies of professional athletes indicate that hierarchical pay structures (for example, paying superstars forty to fifty times as much as the lowest-paid athlete on the team) hurt the performance of teams and individual players.[106] Likewise, managers are twice as likely to quit their jobs when their companies have very strong hierarchical pay structures (that is when they're paid dramatically less than the people above them).[107] For now, it seems that hierarchical pay structures work best for independent work, where it's easy to determine the contributions of individual performers, and little coordination with others is needed to get the job done. In other words, hierarchical pay structures work best when clear links can be drawn between individual performance and individual rewards. By contrast, compressed pay structures, in which everyone receives similar pay, seem to work best for interdependent work, which requires employees to work together. Some companies are pursuing a middle ground: combining hierarchical and compressed pay structures by giving ordinary workers the chance to earn more through ESOPs, stock options, and profit sharing.

11-6b Terminating Employees

The words "You're fired!" may have never been directed at you, but lots of people hear them, as more than 400,000 people a year get fired from their jobs. Getting fired is a terrible thing, but many managers make it even worse by bungling the firing process, needlessly provoking the person who was fired and unintentionally inviting lawsuits. Manager Craig Silverman had to fire the head of a company whom his organization had just acquired. He was specifically instructed to invite her to a meeting, which would require her to travel halfway across the country, and then fire her immediately on arrival. He said, "I literally had to tell the car service to wait. I don't think it ever entered [her] mind that [she] would be terminated."[108] When Zynga terminated almost all of the employees from OMGPOP, a startup company it had acquired a year before, one of the employees tweeted, "I learned via Facebook I was laid off today and @omgpop office is closed. Thanks @zynga for again reminding me how not to operate a business."[109] A computer systems engineer was fired on "Take Your Daughter to Work Day," with his eight-year-old daughter sitting next to him in the human resource manager's office. He and his daughter were both escorted from the building.[110] How would you feel if you had been fired in one of these ways? Though firing is never pleasant (and managers hate firings nearly as much as employees do), managers can do several things to minimize the problems inherent in firing employees.

To start, in most situations, firing should not be the first option. Instead, employees should be given a chance to change their behavior. When problems arise, employees should have ample warning and must be specifically informed as to the nature and seriousness of the trouble they're in. After being notified, they should be given sufficient time to change their behavior. Ron Cohen is CEO and founder of **Acorda Therapeutics**, a company that develops therapies to restore neurological function for people with multiple sclerosis and spinal cord injuries. Cohen first fired an employee when he was 31 years old. He says it was painful, and "I wound up hugging the employee, and she was crying on my shoulder." Since then, however, when he fires someone, they've had plenty of opportunities to address performance issues. Says Cohen, "I've learned over the years that if the employee doesn't expect it and know it's coming, you're not doing your job as a manager."[111]

If problems continue, the employees should again be counseled about their job performance, what could be done to improve it, and the possible consequences if things don't change (such as a written reprimand, suspension without pay, or firing). Sometimes this is enough to solve the problem. If the problem isn't corrected after several rounds of warnings and discussions, however, the employee may be terminated.[112]

Second, employees should be fired only for a good reason. Employers used to hire and fire employees under the legal principle of employment at will, which allowed them to fire employees for a good reason, a bad reason, or no reason at all. (Employees could also quit for a good reason, a bad reason, or no reason whenever they desired.) As employees began contesting their firings in court, however, the principle of wrongful discharge emerged. **Wrongful discharge** is a legal doctrine that requires employers to have a job-related reason to terminate employees. In other words, like other major human resource decisions, termination decisions should be made on the basis of job-related factors such as violating company rules or consistently poor performance. And with former employees winning 68 percent of wrongful discharge cases and the average wrongful termination award at $532,000 and climbing, managers should record the job-related reasons for the termination, document specific instances of rule violations or continued poor performance, and keep notes and documents from the counseling sessions held with employees.[113]

11-6c Downsizing

Downsizing is the planned elimination of jobs in a company (see box "How to Conduct Layoffs"). Whether it's because of cost cutting, declining market share, previous overaggressive hiring and growth, or outsourcing, companies typically eliminate 1 million to 1.26 million jobs a year.[114] Two-thirds of companies that downsize will downsize a second time within a year.[115] In 2012, Cisco cut 8,000 employees—about 9 percent of its workforce—in an effort to cut costs. In March 2013, it cut another 500 workers. Then, just five months later, Cisco cut 4,000 more employees—around 5 percent of its workforce—despite meeting earnings expectations.[116]

Oleg Golovnev/Shutterstock.com

Does down-sizing work? In theory, downsizing is supposed to lead to higher productivity and profits, better stock performance, and increased organizational flexibility. However, numerous studies demonstrate that it doesn't. For instance, a fifteen-year study of downsizing found that downsizing 10 percent of a company's workforce produced only a 1.5 percent decrease in costs; that downsizing firms increased their stock price by only 4.7 percent over three years, compared with 34.3 percent for firms that didn't; and that profitability and productivity were generally not improved by downsizing. Downsizing can also result

Wrongful discharge a legal doctrine that requires employers to have a job-related reason to terminate employees

Downsizing the planned elimination of jobs in a company

How to Conduct Layoffs

1. Provide clear reasons and explanations for the layoffs.

2. To avoid laying off employees with critical or irreplaceable skills, knowledge, and expertise, get input from human resources, the legal department, and several levels of management.

3. Train managers in how to tell employees that they are being laid off (that is stay calm; make the meeting short; explain why but don't be personal; and provide information about immediate concerns such as benefits, finding a new job, and collecting personal goods).

4. Give employees the bad news early in the day, and try to avoid laying off employees before holidays.

5. Provide outplacement services and counseling to help laid-off employees find new jobs.

6. Communicate with employees who have not been laid off to explain how the company and their jobs will change.

Source: M. Boyle, "The Not-So-Fine Art of the Layoff," *Fortune*, March 19, 2001, 209.

iStockphoto.com/WillSelarep

in the loss of skilled workers who would be expensive to replace when the company grows again. These results make it clear that the best strategy is to conduct effective human resource planning and avoid downsizing altogether. Downsizing should always be a last resort.[117]

If companies do find themselves in financial or strategic situations where downsizing is required for survival, however, they should train managers in how to break the news to downsized employees, have senior managers explain in detail why downsizing is necessary, and time the announcement so that employees hear it from the company and not from other sources, such as TV or online reports.[118] Finally, companies should do everything they can to help downsized employees find other jobs. One of the best ways to do this is to use **outplacement services** that provide employment counseling for employees faced with downsizing. Outplacement services often include advice and training in preparing résumés, getting ready for job interviews, and even identifying job opportunities in other companies. Sixty-nine percent of companies provide outplacement services for laid-off employees, 61 percent provide extended health coverage, and most offer up to 26 weeks of severance payments.[119] Offering this kind of assistance can soften the blow from being laid off, preserve goodwill, and lower the risk of future lawsuits.[120]

Companies also need to pay attention to the survivors, the employees remaining after layoffs have occurred. University of Pennsylvania management professor Peter Cappelli says that survivors "may feel like they could just as easily be the next person laid off."[121] Lori Stewart Coletti, director of client services at Elaine Construction, a Newton, Massachusetts–based firm, said, "The general feeling is, 'Could I be next?' That's the level of uncertainty that you really have to combat."[122] The key to working with layoff survivors, according to Barry Nickerson, president of Dallas-based Marlow Industries, which downsized from 800 to 200 employees, is "Communicate. Communicate. Communicate." Nickerson says, "Every time we had a change we had a meeting to explain exactly what we were doing. We were very open with our employees about where we were financially. We would explain exactly the current status and where we were."[123]

11-6d Retirement

Early retirement incentive programs (ERIPs) offer financial benefits to employees to encourage them to retire early. Companies use ERIPs to reduce the

Outplacement services employment-counseling services offered to employees who are losing their jobs because of downsizing

Early retirement incentive programs (ERIPs) programs that offer financial benefits to employees to encourage them to retire early number of employees in the organization, to lower costs by eliminating positions after employees retire, to lower costs by replacing high-paid retirees with lower-paid, less-experienced employees, or to create openings and job opportunities for people inside the company. For example, the state of Wyoming offered its employees a lump-sum bonus, additional insurance benefits, and increased monthly retirement payments to encourage early retirement. Its ERIP must have been fairly attractive, because 56 percent of the state employees eligible for early retirement accepted. Thirty percent of the 437 positions vacated by the early retirees remained empty, saving the state $23.2 million over the first forty-six months of the program and a projected $65 million over eight years. After accounting for the costs of the increased early retirement benefits, the predicted savings came to more than $148,000 per retiree.[124]

Although ERIPs can save companies money, they can pose a big problem for managers if they fail to accurately predict which employees—the good performers or the poor performers—and how many will retire early. Consultant Ron Nicol says, "The thing that doesn't work is just asking for volunteers. You get the wrong volunteers. Some of your best people will feel they can get a job anywhere. Or you have people who are close to retirement and are a real asset to the company."[125] When Progress Energy, in Raleigh, North Carolina, identified 450 jobs it wanted to eliminate with an ERIP, it carefully shared the list of jobs with employees, indicated that layoffs would follow if not enough people took early retirement, and then held eighty meetings with employees to answer questions. Despite this care, an extra 1,000 employees, for a total of 1,450, took the ERIP offer and applied for early retirement![126]

Because of the problems associated with ERIPs, many companies are now offering **phased retirement**, in which employees transition to retirement by working reduced hours over a period of time before completely retiring. The advantage for employees is that they have more free time but continue to earn salaries and benefits without changing companies or careers. The advantage for

companies is that it allows them to reduce salaries and hiring and training costs and retain experienced, valuable workers.[127]

11-6e Employee Turnover

In 2015, 51 percent of workers with a job were either actively seeking or open to a new job.[128] **Employee turnover** is the loss of employees who voluntarily choose to leave the company. In general, most companies try to keep the rate of employee turnover low to reduce recruiting, hiring, training, and replacement costs. Not all kinds of employee turnover are bad for organizations, however. In fact, some turnover can actually be good. **Functional turnover** is the loss of poor-performing employees who choose to leave the organization.[129] Functional turnover gives the organization a chance to replace poor performers with better workers. In fact, one study found that simply replacing poor-performing workers with average workers would increase the revenues produced by retail salespeople in an upscale department store by $112,000 per person per year.[130] By contrast, **dysfunctional turnover**, the loss of high performers who choose to leave, is a costly loss to the organization. To minimize dysfunctional turnover, **VoloMetrix, Inc.** uses algorithms to identify so-called flight risks—employees who are gearing up to quit. Software examines anonymized data from employee emails and calendars to identify patterns of communication that indicate the employee is spending less time interacting with colleagues and attending only required meetings. The analysis helps the company predict a departure up to a year in advance, which is important, as the median cost of turnover for most jobs is 21 percent of the employee's annual salary.[131]

Employee turnover should be carefully analyzed to determine whether good or poor performers are choosing to leave the organization. If the company is losing too many high performers, managers should determine the reasons and find ways to reduce the loss of valuable employees. The company may have to raise salary levels, offer enhanced benefits, or improve working conditions to retain skilled workers. One of the best ways to influence functional and dysfunctional turnover is to link pay directly to performance. A study of four sales forces found that when pay was strongly linked to performance via sales commissions and bonuses, poor performers were much more likely to leave (that is, functional turnover). By contrast, poor performers were much more likely to stay when paid large, guaranteed monthly salaries and small sales commissions and bonuses.[132]

Phased retirement employees transition to retirement by working reduced hours over a period of time before completely retiring

Employee turnover loss of employees who voluntarily choose to leave the company

Functional turnover loss of poor-performing employees who voluntarily choose to leave a company

Dysfunctional turnover loss of high-performing employees who voluntarily choose to leave a company

STUDY TOOLS 11

LOCATED IN TEXTBOOK
☐ Rip-out and review chapter review card

LOCATED AT WWW.CENGAGEBRAIN.COM
☐ Review key term flashcards and create your own from StudyBits
☐ Track your knowledge and understanding of key concepts, using the concept tracker
☐ Complete practice and graded quizzes to prepare for tests
☐ Complete interactive content within the exposition
☐ View chapter highlight box content at the beginning of each chapter

12 Managing Individuals and a Diverse Workforce

Wavebreakmedia/Shutterstock.com

LEARNING OUTCOMES

12-1 Describe diversity and explain why it matters.

12-2 Understand the special challenges that the dimensions of surface-level diversity pose for managers.

12-3 Explain how the dimensions of deep-level diversity affect individual behavior and interactions in the workplace.

12-4 Explain the basic principles and practices that can be used to manage diversity.

After you finish this chapter, go to **PAGE 264** for **STUDY TOOLS**

12-1 DIVERSITY: DIFFERENCES THAT MATTER

Workplace diversity as we know it is changing. Exhibit 12.1 shows predictions from the U.S. Census Bureau of how the U.S. population will change over the next forty years. The percentage of white, non-Hispanic Americans in the general population is expected to decline from 61.8 percent in 2015 to 42.6 percent by 2060. By contrast, the percentage of black Americans will increase (from 12.4% to 13.2%), as will the percentage of Asian Americans (from 5.1% to 7.9%). Meanwhile, the proportion of Native Americans will hold steady at 0.7 percent. The fastest-growing group by far, though, will be Hispanics, who are expected to increase from 17.8 percent of the total population in 2015 to 30.6 percent by 2060. Other significant changes have already occurred. For example, today women hold 46.8 percent of the jobs in the United States, up from 38.2 percent in 1970.[1] Furthermore, white males, who composed 63.9 percent of the workforce in 1950, hold just 35.8 percent of today's jobs.[2]

These rather dramatic changes have taken place in a relatively short time. And, as these trends clearly show, the workforce of the near future will be increasingly Hispanic, Asian American, and female. It will also be older, as the average baby boomer approaches the age of 70 around 2020. Because many boomers are likely to postpone retirement and work well into their 70s to offset predicted reductions in Social Security and Medicare benefits, the workforce may become even older than expected. For instance, between 1992 and 2022, 16- to 24-year olds (16.9% to 11.3%), 25- to 34-year olds (27.6% to 22.5%), and 35- to 44-year-olds (26.5% to 21.3%) will have become a smaller part of the U.S. labor force. By contrast, those 45- to 54-year-olds (17.3% to 19.3%), 55- to 64-year-olds (9.0% to 17.3%), and 65 years and older (2.7% to 6.7%) will all have become larger parts of the U.S. labor force.[3]

Diversity means variety. Therefore, **diversity** exists in organizations when there is a variety of demographic, cultural, and personal differences among the people who work there and the customers who do business there. With 36,000 locations in 120 countries, few businesses have the diversity of locations and customers that McDonald's has.[4] Thanks to its global footprint, McDonald's has 160 global menu items, ranging from a Rice Burger (chicken or beef between two rice cakes) in Taiwan, to a Paneer Salsa Wrap (flatbread stuffed with fried

> **Diversity** a variety of demographic, cultural, and personal differences among an organization's employees and customers

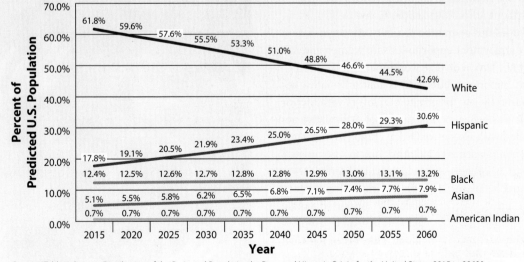

Exhibit 12.1

Percent of the Projected Population by Race and Hispanic Origin for the United States: 2015 to 2060

Source: "Table 6. Percent Distribution of the Projected Population by Race, and Hispanic Origin for the United States: 2015 to 2060," U.S. Census Bureau, accessed July 10, 2014. http://www.census.gov/population/projections/data/national/2012/summarytables.html.

paneer cheese, lettuce, red cabbage, celery, mayo, cheddar cheese, and salsa) in India, to McMollettes (English muffins covered with refried beans, cheese, and pico de gallo) in Mexico.[5] Former McDonald's former CEO Don Thompson said that diversity is not about "chasing the number, but chasing the insight, the experience, the background. Diversity fuels innovation, and innovation fuels success. You don't get products like what we've done, you don't create some of the newer products without having the insight." Thompson recognized, however, that progress still needed to be made, saying, "We still have a long way to go, especially as we become a more global company."[6]

*You'll begin your exploration of diversity by learning **12-1a** that diversity is not affirmative action and **12-1b** that diversity makes good business sense.*

12-1a Diversity Is Not Affirmative Action

A common misconception is that workplace diversity and affirmative action are the same, yet these concepts differ in several critical ways, including their purpose, how they are practiced, and the reactions they produce. To start, **affirmative action** refers to purposeful steps taken by an organization to create employment opportunities for minorities and women.[7] By contrast, diversity has a broader focus that includes demographic, cultural, and personal differences.

A second difference is that affirmative action is a policy for actively creating diversity, but diversity can exist even if organizations don't take purposeful steps to create it. A local restaurant located near a university in a major city is likely to have a more diverse group of employees than one located in a small town. So, organizations can achieve diversity without affirmative action. Conversely, affirmative action does not guarantee diversity. An organization can create employment opportunities for women and minorities yet not have a diverse workforce.

A third important difference is that affirmative action is required by law for private employers with fifty or more employees, whereas diversity is not. Affirmative action originated with Executive Order 11246 (www.dol.gov/ofccp/regs/compliance/fs11246.htm) but is also related to the 1964 Civil Rights Act, which bans discrimination in voting, public places, federal government programs, federally supported public education, and employment. Title VII of the Civil Rights Act (www.eeoc.gov/laws/statutes/titlevii.cfm) requires that workers have equal employment opportunities when being hired or promoted. More specifically, Title VII prohibits companies from discriminating on the basis of race, color, religion, sex, or national origin. Title VII also created the Equal Employment Opportunity Commission, or EEOC (www.eeoc.gov), to administer these laws. By contrast, there is no federal law or agency to oversee diversity. Organizations that pursue diversity goals and programs do so voluntarily.

Fourth, affirmative action programs and diversity programs have different purposes. The purpose of affirmative action programs is to compensate for past discrimination, which was widespread when legislation was introduced in the 1960s; to prevent ongoing discrimination; and to provide equal opportunities to all, regardless of race, color, religion, sex, or national origin. Organizations that fail to uphold affirmative action laws may be required to

- hire, promote, or give back pay to those not hired or promoted;
- reinstate those who were wrongly terminated;
- pay attorneys' fees and court costs for those who bring charges against them; or
- take other actions that make individuals whole by returning them to the condition or place they would have been had it not been for discrimination.[8]

Affirmative action
purposeful steps taken by an organization to create employment opportunities for minorities and women

Consequently, affirmative action is basically a punitive approach.[9] By contrast, the general purpose of diversity programs is to create a positive work environment where no one is advantaged or disadvantaged, where "we" is everyone, where everyone can do his or her best work, where differences are respected and not ignored, and where everyone feels comfortable.[10] So, unlike affirmative action, which punishes companies for not achieving specific sex and race ratios in their workforces, diversity programs seek to benefit both organizations and their employees by encouraging organizations to value all kinds of differences.

Despite the overall success of affirmative action in making workplaces much fairer than they used to be, many people argue that some affirmative action programs unconstitutionally offer preferential treatment to females and minorities at the expense of other employees, a view accepted by some courts.[11] The American Civil Rights institute successfully campaigned via state ballot initiatives to ban race- and sex-based affirmative action in college admissions, government hiring, and government contracting programs in California (1996), Washington (1998), and Michigan (2006). Led by Ward Connerly, the institute backed similar efforts in Arizona, Colorado, Missouri, Nebraska, and Oklahoma in 2008. In an April 2014 decision, the U.S. Supreme Court ruled 6-2 that state ballot initiatives banning race- and sex-based action are constitutional.[12] Opponents of affirmative action, like Connerly, believe that affirmative action policies establish only surface-level diversity and, ironically, promote preferential treatment.[13]

Research shows that people who have gotten a job or promotion as a result of affirmative action are commonly viewed as unqualified, even when clear evidence of their qualifications exists.[14] This effect is so robust that those benefitting from affirmative action experience doubts about their competence.[15] So, while affirmative action programs have created opportunities for minorities and women, they unintentionally produce persistent doubts and self-doubts regarding the qualifications of those who are believed to have obtained their jobs as a result of affirmative action.

12-1b Diversity Makes Good Business Sense

Those who support the idea of diversity in organizations often ignore its business aspects altogether, claiming instead that diversity is simply the right thing to do. Yet diversity actually makes good business sense in several ways: cost savings, attracting and retaining talent, and driving business growth.[16]

Diversity helps companies with *cost savings* by reducing turnover, decreasing absenteeism, and avoiding expensive lawsuits.[17] Because of lost productivity and the cost of recruiting and selecting new workers, companies lose substantial amounts of money when employees quit their jobs. In fact, turnover costs typically amount to more than 90 percent of employees' salaries. By this estimate, if an executive who makes $200,000 leaves, the organization will have to spend approximately $180,000 to find a replacement; even the lowest-paid hourly workers can cost the company as much as $10,000 when they quit. Because turnover rates for African Americans average 40 percent higher than for whites, and since women quit their jobs at twice the rate men do, companies that manage diverse workforces well can cut costs by reducing the turnover rates of these employees.[18] And, with women absent from work 60 percent more often than men, primarily because of family responsibilities, diversity programs that address the needs of female workers can also reduce the substantial costs of absenteeism.

Diversity programs also save companies money by helping them avoid discrimination lawsuits, which have increased by a factor of twenty since 1970 and quadrupled just since 1995. In one survey conducted by the Society for Human Resource Management, 78 percent of respondents reported that diversity efforts helped them

Bikeriderlondon/Shutterstock.com

avoid lawsuits and litigation costs.[19] In fact, because companies lose two-thirds of all discrimination cases that go to trial, the best strategy from a business perspective is not to be sued for discrimination at all. When companies lose, the average individual settlement amounts to more than $600,000.[20] And settlement costs can be substantially higher in class-action lawsuits, in which individuals join together to sue a company as a group. Investment brokerage firm Merrill Lynch faced a class-action lawsuit alleging it denied 1,400 African American stock brokers promotions, bonus-based compensation, and fair access to client accounts and resources. Merrill Lynch settled the case for $160 million and agreed to changes that "will enhance opportunities for financial advisors in the future," which will be monitored by a committee of African American brokers who work at the firm.[21]

Diversity also makes business sense by helping companies *attract and retain talented workers*.[22] Diversity-friendly companies tend to attract better *and* more diverse job applicants. Very simply, diversity begets more diversity. Companies that make *Fortune* magazine's list of the fifty best companies for minorities or are recognized by *Working Women* and *Diversity Inc.* magazine have already attracted a diverse and talented pool of job applicants. But, after being recognized for their efforts, they subsequently experience big increases in both the quality and the diversity of people who apply for jobs. Research shows that companies with acclaimed diversity programs not only attract more talented workers but also have higher performance in the stock market.[23]

The third way that diversity makes business sense is by *driving business growth*. In the United States today, there are 45 million African Americans, 55.8 million Hispanic Americans, and 19.4 million Asian Americans with, respectively, $1 trillion, $1.2 trillion, and $713 billion in purchasing power. Given the size of those markets, it shouldn't be surprising that a survey conducted by the Society for Human Resource Management found that tapping into "diverse customers and markets" was the number-one reason managers gave for implementing diversity programs.[24] Kimberly-Clark, maker of well-known household brands such as Kotex, Depend, Kleenex, Huggies, and Scott paper products, has a customer base that is 83 percent female. But, from first-level managers to the boardroom, women are strongly in the minority. So, from China to the U.S. to Latin America, Kimberly-Clark is implementing more generous maternity leave and flexible working schedules in hopes of growing and

retaining promising female leaders who understand the company's customers.[25] Likewise, with an increasingly large share of global sales outside of their home countries, multinational firms are putting key leaders or divisions closer to global customers. Procter & Gamble moved its global cosmetics and personal-care division to Singapore from Cincinnati. GE relocated its X-ray unit to Beijing from Wisconsin. And German-based Daimler-Benz is now requiring that young managers tapped for its "high potential" training and development program must be from outside of Germany.[26] When companies have diverse workforces, they are better able to understand the needs of their increasingly diverse customer bases.

Diversity also helps companies grow through higher-quality problem solving. Though diverse groups initially have more difficulty working together than homogeneous groups, diverse groups eventually establish a rapport and do a better job of identifying problems and generating alternative solutions, the two most important steps in problem solving.[27] When Novartis CEO David Epstein ran Novartis Oncology earlier in his career, he was given the opportunity to build his leadership team from scratch. The division at that time was heavily staffed with Americans and Europeans. But because the team was responsible for products and customers in seventy different countries, he picked his leaders based on career successes and diverse experiences. Says Epstein, "I ended up with a team that came from all over the world. We had phenomenally productive discussions. At the beginning, it was very difficult because we had different cultural backgrounds and the norms within which we communicated were different, but after a while I saw the power of people with different backgrounds and what they could contribute to business ideas. Once we got that group working as a high-performing team, we were able to accomplish feats that nobody thought were possible."[28]

12-2 SURFACE-LEVEL DIVERSITY

A survey that asked managers "What is meant by diversity to decision makers in your organization?" found that they most frequently mentioned race, culture, sex, national origin, age, religion, and regional origin.[29] When managers describe workers this way, they are focusing on surface-level diversity. **Surface-level diversity** consists of differences that are immediately observable, typically unchangeable, and easy to measure.[30] In other words,

Surface-level diversity differences such as age, sex, race/ethnicity, and physical disabilities that are observable, typically unchangeable, and easy to measure independent observers can usually agree on dimensions of surface-level diversity, such as another person's age, sex, race/ethnicity, or physical capabilities.

Most people start by using surface-level diversity to categorize or stereotype other people. But those initial categorizations typically give way to deeper impressions formed from knowledge of others' behaviors and psychological characteristics such as personality and attitudes.[31] When you think of others this way, you are focusing on deep-level diversity. **Deep-level diversity** consists of differences that are communicated through verbal and nonverbal behaviors and are learned only through extended interaction with others.[32] Examples of deep-level diversity include personality differences, attitudes, beliefs, and values. In other words, as people in diverse workplaces get to know each other, the initial focus on surface-level differences such as age, race/ethnicity, sex, and physical capabilities is replaced by deeper, more complex knowledge of coworkers.

If managed properly, the shift from surface- to deep-level diversity can accomplish two things.[33] First, coming to know and understand each other better can result in reduced prejudice and conflict. Second, it can lead to stronger social integration. **Social integration** is the degree to which group members are psychologically attracted to working with each other to accomplish a common objective, or, as one manager put it, "working together to get the job done."

Because age, sex, race/ethnicity, and disabilities are usually immediately observable, many managers and workers use these dimensions of surface-level diversity to form initial impressions and categorizations of coworkers, bosses, customers, or job applicants. Whether intentionally or not, sometimes those initial categorizations and impressions lead to decisions or behaviors that discriminate. Consequently, these dimensions of surface-level diversity pose special challenges for managers who are trying to create positive work environments where everyone feels comfortable, and no one is advantaged or disadvantaged.

Let's learn more about those challenges and the ways that **12-2a age, 12-2b sex, 12-2c race/ethnicity, and 12-2d mental or physical disabilities can affect decisions and behaviors in organizations.**

12-2a Age

Age discrimination is treating people differently (for example, in hiring and firing, promotion, and compensation decisions) because of their age. The victims of age discrimination are almost always older workers, and the discrimination is based on the assumption that "you can't teach an old dog new tricks." It's commonly believed that older

Alex74/Shutterstock.com

It's commonly – and wrongly – believed that older workers are less motivated, less productive, more prone to illness and accidents.

workers are less motivated, less productive, more prone to illness and accidents, not interested in learning new things, cost more, and make greater—more expensive—use of health care benefits.[34] Facebook founder and CEO Mark Zuckerberg once said, "I want to stress the importance of being young and technical... Young people are just smarter."[35] Consistent with that stereotype, Apple, Yahoo!, and Dropbox are among the companies that have specified preferences for "new grads" in job openings. Because that clearly violates the Age Discrimination in Employment Act, companies such as Zipcar, Panasonic, and, yes, Facebook, now list being a "digital native" as a job requirement.[36] Ingrid Fredeen of **NAVEX Global**, a supplier of ethics and compliance programs, says the term makes her cringe because it implies that "only young applicants need apply."[37]

The increase in age discrimination claims filed with the EEOC, 20,588 in 2014, up from 15,785 in 1997[38], suggests that discriminatory attitudes like this still exist.

So, what's reality and what's myth? Do older employees actually cost more? In some ways, they do. The older people are and the longer they stay with a company, the more the company pays for salaries, pension plans, and vacation time. But older workers cost companies less, too,

Deep-level diversity differences such as personality and attitudes that are communicated through verbal and nonverbal behaviors and are learned only through extended interaction with others

Social integration the degree to which group members are psychologically attracted to working with each other to accomplish a common objective

Age discrimination treating people differently (for example in hiring and firing, promotion, and compensation decisions) because of their age

One Is the Loneliest Number

Even as the number of women in the managerial ranks of U.S. companies is growing, in many companies, it seems there is an upper limit. Researchers have found that, if there is a woman on an executive team, then the chances of another woman joining the team drops by 51 percent. Among the 1,500 Standard & Poor's companies, 8.7 percent have a top female manager, but when one of the top five executive positions in the company is held by a woman, she is usually the only one on the team. Researcher Cristian Dezso speculates that top male managers may just want to fill a quota and "check a box. They are one and done."

Source: R. Feintzeig, "One Often Appears to Be the Limit for Women at the Top," *Wall Street Journal*, April 8, 2015, B6.

Rafael Croonen/Shutterstock.com

because they show better judgment, care more about the quality of their work, and are less likely to quit, show up late, or be absent, the cost of which can be substantial.[39] A meta-analysis combining the results of 118 individual studies also found that older workers are more likely to help others at work and are much less likely to use drugs or alcohol at work, engage in workplace aggression, or be involved in accidents. The authors of this study concluded, "The stereotype of older workers as difficult colleagues, then, seems largely unfounded."[40]

As for the widespread belief that job performance declines with age, the scientific evidence clearly refutes this stereotype. Performance does not decline with age, regardless of the type of job.[41]

What can companies do to reduce age discrimination?[42] To start, managers need to recognize that age discrimination is much more pervasive than they probably think. Whereas "old" used to mean mid-50s, in today's workplace "old" is closer to 40. When 773 CEOs were asked, "At what age does a worker's productivity peak?" the average age they gave was 43. Thus, age discrimination may be affecting more workers because perceptions about age have changed. In addition, with the aging of the baby boomers, age discrimination is more likely to occur simply because there are millions more older workers than there used to be. And, because studies show that interviewers rate younger job candidates as more qualified (even when they aren't), companies need to train managers and recruiters to make hiring and promotion decisions on the basis of qualifications, not age.

Companies also need to monitor the extent to which older workers receive training. The U.S. Bureau of Labor Statistics found that the number of training courses and number of hours spent in training drop dramatically after employees reach the age of 44.[43] Finally, companies need to ensure that younger and older workers interact with each other. One study found that younger workers generally hold positive views of older workers and that the more time they spent working with older coworkers, the more positive their attitudes became.[44]

12-2b Sex

Sex discrimination occurs when people are treated differently because of their sex. Sex discrimination and racial/ethnic discrimination (discussed in the next section) are often associated with the so-called **glass ceiling**, the invisible barrier that prevents women and minorities from advancing to the top jobs in organizations.

To what extent do women face sex discrimination in the workplace? Almost every year, the EEOC receives between 23,000 and 30,000 charges of sex-based discrimination.[45] In some ways, there is much less sex discrimination than there used to be. For example, whereas women held only 17 percent of managerial jobs in 1972, today they hold 51.4 percent of managerial and professional jobs, and they hold 47 percent of all jobs in the workplace.[46] Likewise, women own 40 percent of all U.S. businesses. Whereas women owned 2.8 million businesses in

Sex discrimination treating people differently because of their sex

Glass ceiling the invisible barrier that prevents women and minorities from advancing to the top jobs in organizations

Exhibit 12.2
Women's Earnings as a Percentage of Men's, 1979–2013

Source: "Women's Earnings, 1979–2012 : The Editor's Desk," U.S. Bureau of Labor Statistics, November 4, 2013, accessed July 12, 2014. http://www.bls.gov/opub /ted/2013/ted_20131104.htm; BLS Reports, "Highlights of Women's Earnings in 2013," U.S. Bureau of Labor Statistics, December 2014, accessed May 9, 2015. http://www .bls.gov/opub/reports/cps/highlights-of-womens-earnings-in-2013.pdf.

1982 and 5.4 million businesses in 1997, today they own 9.1 million businesses, generating $1.4 trillion in sales and employing 7.9 million people![47] Finally, though women still earn less than men on average, the differential is narrowing, as Exhibit 12.2 shows. Women earned 82 percent of what men did in 2013, up from 63 percent in 1979.[48]

Although progress is being made, sex discrimination continues to operate via the glass ceiling at higher levels in organizations, as shown in Exhibit 12.3. For instance, while the trends are going upward, women were the top earners in just 8.1 percent of companies in 2014.[49]

The Mommy-Daddy Track

Research has long shown that women who take time off from work for the birth of a child or for family obligations tend to have lower lifetime earnings. A recent survey conducted by *The Atlantic* aimed to find out if the same was true for men. In processing survey data from 12,000 respondents, researchers controlled multiple variables as a way to isolate the impact of taking time off to care for family. Their results show that, for men and women alike, taking time off for family carries a financial risk. Still, women were ten times more like to report that they actually *had* modified their work commitments for family than men.

Source: S. Coltrane, "The Risky Business of Paternity Leave," *The Atlantic*, December 28, 2014, accessed May 7, 2015. http://www.theatlantic.com/business/archive/2013 /12/the-risky-business-of-paternity-leave/282688/.

Likewise, only 14.6 percent of corporate officers (that is top management) were women, and the numbers were even lower for women of color. Indra K. Nooyi, PepsiCo's CEO, and Ursula Burns, Xerox's CEO, are the only women of color heading *Fortune* 500 companies.[50] In fact, only 24 of the 500 largest companies in the United States have women CEOs.[51] Similarly, only 16.9 percent of the members of U.S. corporate boards of directors are women.[52]

Is sex discrimination the sole reason for the slow rate at which women have been promoted to middle and upper levels of management and corporate boards? Some studies indicate that it's not.[53] In some instances, the slow progress appears to be due to career and job choices. Whereas men's career and job choices are often driven by the search for higher pay and advancement, women are more likely to choose jobs or careers that also give them a greater sense of accomplishment, more control over their work schedules, and easier movement in and out of the workplace.[54] For instance, 82 percent of women without children are interested in being promoted to the next level compared to 73 percent of women with two or more children.[55] As those numbers suggest, women are historically much more likely than men to prioritize family over work at some time in their careers. For example, 96 percent of 600 female Harvard MBAs held jobs while they were in their 20s. That dropped to 71 percent in their late 30s when they had children but then increased to 82.5 percent in their late 40s as their children became older.[56] Even Indra Nooyi, PepsiCo's CEO, says, "My observation . . . is that the

Exhibit 12.3
Women at *Fortune* 500 and 1000 Companies

Legend: 2014, 2008, 2000, 1995

Fortune 500 Companies

Top Earners:
- 8.10% (2014)
- 6.20% (2008)
- 4.10% (2000)
- 1.20% (1995)

Corporate Officers:
- 14.60% (2014)
- 15.70% (2008)
- 12.50% (2000)
- 8.70% (1995)

Boards of Directors:
- 16.90% (2014)
- 15.20% (2008)
- 11.70% (2000)
- 9.50% (1995)

(Scale: 0.0%, 4.0%, 8.0%, 12.0%, 16.0%, 20.0%)

Source: "U.S. Women in Business," Catalyst, June 10, 2014, accessed July 11, 2014. http://www.catalyst.org/knowledge/us-women-business-0.

biological clock and the career clock are in total conflict with each other. Total, complete conflict. When you have to have kids you have to build your career. Just as you're rising to middle management your kids need you because they're teenagers, they need you for the teenage years . . . And as you grow even more, your parents need you because they're aging. So . . . we cannot have it all."[57]

Beyond these reasons, however, it's likely that sex discrimination does play a role in women's slow progress into the higher levels of management. And even if you don't think so, many of the women you work with probably do. In fact, studies indicate that 90 percent of women believe the glass ceiling hurts their careers, and 80 percent said they left their last job because of the glass ceiling and that starting a business allows them to avoid the career limitations of the glass ceiling.[58] Discrimination is believed to be the most significant factor behind the lack of women at top levels of management.[59]

So, what can companies do to make sure that women have the same opportunities for development and advancement as men? One strategy is mentoring, or pairing promising female executives with senior executives from whom they can seek advice and support.[60] **Salesforce**, a leading customer relationship management software company, has a mentoring program for women. So, co-founder Parker Harris, who encourages Salesforce managers to speak up about their

Racial and ethnic discrimination treating people differently because of their race or ethnicity

ambitions, was surprised when he discovered that Leyla Seka, who ran their mobile apps unit, was preparing to leave. Seka wanted to lead a larger division but thought her bosses didn't think she was capable, so she didn't share her aspirations. In fact, her bosses found her so capable, they hired her to run Desk.com, a company recently acquired by Salesforce, and coached her as she developed her leadership skills. "I've never had more fun at work, and I've never felt more challenged," she says. "I almost missed this opportunity by shutting the doors on myself."[61] In fact, 91 percent of female executives had a mentor at some point and felt their mentor was critical to their advancement.

Another strategy is to make sure that male-dominated social activities don't unintentionally exclude women. Nearly half (47%) of women in the workforce believe that "exclusion from informal networks" makes it more difficult to advance their careers (by contrast, just 18% of male CEOs thought this was a problem). For instance, at company conferences, **Rockwell Automation** has replaced cocktail receptions (that is, hanging out at the bar), which are a traditional social function at conferences, with alternative activities, such as chili cook-offs.[62] Another is to designate a go-to person other than their supervisors that women can talk to if they believe that they are being held back or discriminated against because of their sex. Make sure this person has the knowledge and authority to conduct a fair, confidential internal investigation.

12-2c Race/Ethnicity

Racial and ethnic discrimination occurs when people are treated differently because of their race or ethnicity. To what extent is racial and ethnic discrimination a factor in the workplace? Every year, the EEOC receives between 26,000 and 36,000 charges of racial discrimination, which is more than any other type of charge of discrimination.[63] However, it is true that since the passage of the 1964 Civil Rights Act and Title VII, there is much less racial and ethnic discrimination than there used to be. For example, twenty-five *Fortune* 500 firms had an African American (6), Hispanic (10), or Asian (9)

Syda Productions/Shutterstock.com

CEO in 2014, whereas none did in 1988.[64] Nonetheless, strong racial and ethnic disparities still exist. For instance, whereas 11.2 percent of employed Americans are black, only 6.5 percent of managers and 2.9 percent of CEOs are black. Similarly, 15.6 percent of employed Americans are Hispanic, but only 8.5 percent are managers and 4.3 percent are CEOs. By contrast, Asians, who constitute 5.7 percent of employed workers, are better represented, holding 5.4 percent of management jobs and 4.8 percent of CEO jobs.[65]

What accounts for the disparities between the percentages of minority groups in the general population and their smaller representation in management positions? Some studies have found that the disparities are due to preexisting differences in training, education, and skills. When African Americans, Hispanics, Asian Americans, and whites have similar skills, training, and education, they are much more likely to have similar jobs and salaries.[66]

Other studies, however, provide increasingly strong direct evidence of racial or ethnic discrimination in the workplace. For example, one study directly tested hiring discrimination by sending pairs of black and white males and pairs of Hispanic and non-Hispanic males to apply for the same jobs. Each pair had résumés with identical qualifications, and all were trained to present themselves in similar ways to minimize differences during interviews. The researchers found that the white males got three times as many job offers as the black males, and that the non-Hispanic males got three times as many offers as the Hispanic males.[67] Another study, which used similar methods to test hiring procedures at 149 different companies, found that whites received 10 percent more interviews than blacks. Half of the whites interviewed then received job offers, but only 11 percent of the blacks. And when job offers were made, blacks were much more likely to be offered lower-level positions, while whites were more likely to be offered jobs at higher levels than the jobs they had applied for.[68]

Critics of these studies point out that it's nearly impossible to train different applicants to give identical responses in job interviews and that differences in interviewing skills may have somehow accounted for the results. However, researchers at the University of Chicago mailed thousands of résumés to employers that were identical except for the candidate's name, which was either stereotypically black, such as "Jamal," or stereotypically white, such as "Brendan." Applicants with the "white" name were called back for interviews 50 percent more often those with "black" names.[69] Comparable studies in the United Kingdom with Indian and Pakistani applicants and in Australia with Greek and Vietnamese applicants produced similar results.[70] In short, the evidence indicates that there is strong and persistent racial and ethnic discrimination in the hiring processes of many organizations.

What can companies do to make sure that people of all racial and ethnic backgrounds have the same opportunities?[71] Start by looking at the numbers. Compare the hiring rates of whites with the hiring rates for racial and ethnic applicants. Do the same thing for promotions within the company. See if nonwhite workers quit the company at higher rates than white workers. Also, survey employees to compare white and nonwhite employees' satisfaction with jobs, bosses, and the company as well as their perceptions concerning equal treatment. Next, if the numbers indicate racial or ethnic disparities, consider employing a private firm to test your hiring system by having applicants of different races with identical qualifications apply for jobs in your company.[72] Although disparities aren't proof of discrimination, it's much better to investigate hiring and promotion disparities yourself than to have the EEOC or a plaintiff's lawyer do it for you.

Another step companies can take is to eliminate unclear selection and promotion criteria. Vague criteria allow decision makers to focus on nonjob-related characteristics that may unintentionally lead to employment discrimination. Instead, selection and promotion criteria should spell out the specific knowledge, skills, abilities, education, and experience needed to perform a job well. Finally, as explained in Chapter 11, "Managing Human Resource Systems," it is also important to train managers and others who make hiring and promotion decisions.

12-2d Mental or Physical Disabilities

According to the Americans with Disabilities Act (www.ada.gov), a **disability** is a mental or physical impairment that substantially limits one or more major life activities.[73] Approximately 38 million Americans—12.1 percent of the population—are disabled.[74] **Disability discrimination** occurs when people are treated differently because of their disabilities. To what

Disability a mental or physical impairment that substantially limits one or more major life activities

Disability discrimination treating people differently because of their disabilities

A recent summit in Michigan gave speakers from companies like Walgreens, Meijer and Trijicon a chance to discuss the benefits of hiring employees with disabilities.

Tupungato/Shutterstock.com

extent is disability discrimination a factor in the workplace? While 76.3 percent of the U.S. population was employed in 2012, only 33.5 percent of disabled people had jobs. Individuals with sensory disabilities, such as blindness (37.7%) or deafness (50.2%), had the highest employment rates; those with self-care disabilities (16.2%), who can't dress or bathe themselves, or with independent living disabilities (15.7%), who can't do basic errands such as shopping or go to the doctor without assistance, were the least likely to work.[75] Likewise, 28.4 percent of disabled people are in poverty, compared to 11.9 percent of those without disabilities.[76] Numerous studies also indicate that managers and the general public believe that discrimination against people with disabilities is common and widespread.[77]

What accounts for the disparities between those with and without disabilities? Contrary to popular opinion, it has nothing to do with how well people with disabilities can do their jobs. Studies show that as long as companies make reasonable accommodations for disabilities (for example, changing procedures or equipment), people with disabilities perform their jobs just as well as people without disabilities. Furthermore, they have better safety records and are not any more likely to be absent or quit their jobs.[78] At a recent disability summit sponsored by the state of Michigan, speakers from Walgreens, Meijer, and Trijicon said that, compared to employees without disabilities, disabled employees were more dependable, took less time off, and had better safety records.[79]

What can companies do to make sure that people with disabilities have the same opportunities as everyone else? Beyond educational efforts to address incorrect

stereotypes and expectations, a good place to start is to commit to reasonable workplace accommodations such as changing work schedules, reassigning jobs, acquiring or modifying equipment, or providing assistance when needed. Accommodations for disabilities needn't be expensive. According to the Job Accommodation Network, 58 percent of accommodations don't cost anything at all, while those with costs are typically just $500.[80]

At Laser Soft Info Systems, an India-based software developer, 15 percent of the staff has some disability, with causes ranging from hearing, speech, and sight impairment to cerebral palsy, polio, or accidents, and work throughout the company. "We don't have any rule that teams must take a minimum or maximum number of people with disabilities in their roles. They are recruited like any other associate," says Suresh Kamath, Laser Soft's founder and president. Laser Soft's accommodations include wheelchair ramps, wider office aisles, elevators with audio controls for the blind, and facilitators to provide physical assistance when an employee asks for it. The company also allows employees to work from home should it become difficult to make it into the office.[81]

Some of the accommodations just described involve *assistive technology* that gives workers with disabilities the tools they need to overcome their disabilities. Providing workers with assistive technology is also an effective strategy to recruit, retain, and enhance the productivity of people with disabilities. According to the National Council on Disability, 92 percent of workers with disabilities who use assistive technology report that it helps them work faster and better, 81 percent indicate that it helps them work longer hours, and 67 percent say that it is critical to getting a job.[82] To learn about assistive technologies that can help workers with disabilities, see AbleData (www.abledata.com), which lists 40,000 products, or the National Rehabilitation Information Center (www.naric.com), which provides information for specific disabilities.

Finally, companies should actively recruit qualified workers with disabilities. Numerous organizations, such as Mainstream, Kidder Resources, the American Council of the Blind (www.acb.org), the National Federation of the Blind (http://nfb.org), the National Association of the Deaf (www.nad.org), the Epilepsy Foundation (www.epilepsy.com), and the National Amputation Foundation (www.nationalamputation.org), actively work with employers to find jobs for qualified people with disabilities. Companies can also place advertisements in publications, such as *Careers and the disABLED*, or on online job boards, such as Recruit AbilityJobs.com or RecruitDisability.org, that specifically target workers with disabilities.

12-3 DEEP-LEVEL DIVERSITY

As you learned in Section 12-2, people often use the dimensions of surface-level diversity to form initial impressions about others. Over time, however, as people have a chance to get to know each other, initial impressions based on age, sex, race/ethnicity, and mental or physical disabilities give way to deeper impressions based on behavior and psychological characteristics. When we think of others this way, we are focusing on deep-level diversity. *Deep-level diversity* represents differences that can be learned only through extended interaction with others. Examples of deep-level diversity include differences in personality, attitudes, beliefs, and values. In short, recognizing deep-level diversity requires getting to know and understand one another better. And that matters, because it can result in less prejudice, discrimination, and conflict in the workplace. These changes can then lead to better *social integration*, the degree to which organizational or group members are psychologically attracted to working with each other to accomplish a common objective.

Stop for a second and think about your boss (or the boss you had in your last job). What words would you use to describe him or her? Is your boss introverted or extraverted? Emotionally stable or unstable? Agreeable or disagreeable? Organized or disorganized? Open or closed to new experiences? When you describe your boss or others in this way, what you're really doing is describing dispositions and personality.

A **disposition** is the tendency to respond to situations and events in a predetermined manner. **Personality** is the relatively stable set of behaviors, attitudes, and emotions displayed over time that makes people different from each other.[83] For example, which of your aunts or uncles is a little offbeat, a little out of the ordinary? What were they like when you were small? What are they like now? Chances are that she or he is pretty much the same wacky person. In other words, the person's core personality hasn't changed. For example, as a child, Kip Tindell, CEO of the Container Store, would reorganize the pantry or closets when his parents were out of the house. "If your house is unbelievably messy, I probably won't come back to visit. I'll meet you at a restaurant. I'm just not comfortable around mess. You don't have to be obsessive-compulsive about it. Well, OK, maybe just a tiny bit."[84] Research conducted in different cultures, different settings, and different languages has shown that five basic dimensions of personality account for most of the differences in peoples' behaviors, attitudes, and emotions (or why your boss is the way he or she is!). The *Big Five Personality Dimensions* are extraversion, emotional stability, agreeableness, conscientiousness, and openness to experience.[85]

Extraversion is the degree to which someone is active, assertive, gregarious, sociable, talkative, and energized by others. In contrast to extraverts, introverts are less active, prefer to be alone, and are shy, quiet, and reserved. For the best results in the workplace, introverts and extraverts should be correctly matched to their jobs.

Emotional stability is the degree to which someone is not angry, depressed, anxious, emotional, insecure, or excitable. People who are emotionally stable respond well to stress. In other words, they can maintain a calm, problem-solving attitude in even the toughest situations (for example, conflict, hostility, dangerous conditions, or extreme time pressures). By contrast, emotionally unstable people find it difficult to handle the most basic demands of their jobs under only moderately stressful situations and become distraught, tearful, self-doubting, and anxious. Emotional stability is particularly important for high-stress jobs such as police work, firefighting, emergency medical treatment, piloting planes, or commanding Tragically, Investigators found emotional stability was a factor in the deliberate crash of a Germanwings flight that killed 150 people. The co-pilot, who had struggled with depression before, used Google, just days before to search for ways to commit suicide.[86] When the pilot left the cabin for a bathroom break, the co-pilot locked the cabin door and set the plane's auto pilot to descend to a lower altitude where it slammed into a mountain. While most Asian airlines conduct regular psychological assessments of their pilots, U.S. and European airlines only screen for emotional stability issues during initial pilot recruitment and training, or if staff members report unusual behavior.[87]

Agreeableness is the degree to which someone is cooperative, polite, flexible, forgiving, good-natured, tolerant, and trusting. Basically, agreeable people are easy to work with and be around, whereas disagreeable people are distrusting and difficult to work with and be around. A number of companies have made general attitude or agreeableness

Disposition the tendency to respond to situations and events in a predetermined manner

Personality the relatively stable set of behaviors, attitudes, and emotions displayed over time that makes people different from each other

Extraversion the degree to which someone is active, assertive, gregarious, sociable, talkative, and energized by others

Emotional stability the degree to which someone is not angry, depressed, anxious, emotional, insecure, and excitable

Agreeableness the degree to which someone is cooperative, polite, flexible, forgiving, good-natured, tolerant, and trusting

What a Jerk!

Most people have worked with (and been frustrated by or begrudgingly admiring of) an overly ambitious colleague who seems to accomplish a lot but is, at the same time, manipulative, narcissistic, and inconsiderate. Toby Bishop, formerly with the Association of Certified Fraud Examiners, says, "It's hard to go anywhere and not find such people." People who exhibit those traits might advance in their careers, but over time, they also tend to derail because their focus is on short-term benefits for themselves rather than longer-term results for the organization. According to management professor Seth Spain, managers can benefit from understanding this "dark triad" of personality traits so that they can rein in any extreme cases before they become problematic. How to spot dark traits among co-workers? Be on the lookout for bullying, overly ingratiating behavior, and extreme or continuous flattery."

Source: S. Shellenbarger, "What Corporate Climbers Can Tell Us," *Wall Street Journal*, July 14, 2014, accessed May 7, 2015. http://www.wsj.com/articles/what-corporate-climbers-can-teach-us-1404862389.

the most important factor in their hiring decisions. Small-business owner Roger Cook says, "Hire nice people. I'm looking for personal—not professional—traits. I want a good or nice person. I can teach the skills. I call their references and ask, 'Is he or she a nice person?' I take a close look at how applicants answer questions and carry themselves. Why nice people? Because they're trustworthy; they get along with other crew members: they are good with customers, and they are usually hard workers."[88]

Conscientiousness is the degree to which someone is organized, hardworking, responsible, persevering, thorough, and achievement oriented. One management consultant wrote about his experiences with a conscientious employee: "He arrived at our first meeting with a typed copy of his daily schedule, a sheet bearing his home and office phone numbers, addresses, and his email address. At his request, we established a timetable for meetings for the next four months. He showed up on time every time, day planner in hand, and carefully listed tasks and due dates. He questioned me exhaustively if he didn't understand an assignment and returned on schedule with the completed work or with a clear explanation as to why it wasn't done."[89] Conscientious employees are also more likely to engage in positive behaviors, such as helping new employees, coworkers, and supervisors, and are less likely to engage in negative behaviors, such as verbally or physically abusing coworkers or stealing.[90]

Openness to experience is the degree to which someone is curious, broadminded, and open to new ideas, things, and experiences; is spontaneous; and has a high tolerance for ambiguity. Most companies need people who are strong in terms of openness to experience to fill certain positions, but for other positions, this dimension is less important. People in marketing, advertising, research, or other creative jobs need to be curious, open to new ideas, and spontaneous. By contrast, openness to experience is not particularly important to accountants, who need to apply stringent rules and formulas consistently to make sense out of complex financial information.

Which of the Big Five Personality Dimensions has the largest impact on behavior in organizations? The cumulative results of multiple studies indicate that conscientiousness is related to job performance across five different occupational groups (professionals, police, managers, salespeople, and skilled or semiskilled workers).[91] In short, people "who are dependable, persistent, goal directed, and organized tend to be higher performers on

Conscientiousness
the degree to which someone is organized, hardworking, responsible, persevering, thorough, and achievement oriented

Openness to experience
the degree to which someone is curious, broad-minded, and open to new ideas, things, and experiences; is spontaneous; and has a high tolerance for ambiguity

virtually any job; viewed negatively, those who are careless, irresponsible, low achievement striving, and impulsive tend to be lower performers on virtually any job."[92] The results also indicate that extraversion is related to performance in jobs, such as sales and management, that involve significant interaction with others. In people-intensive jobs like these, it helps to be sociable, assertive, and talkative and to have energy and be able to energize others. Finally, people who are extraverted and open to experience seem to do much better in training. Being curious and open to new experiences as well as sociable, assertive, talkative, and full of energy helps people perform better in learning situations.[93] Hyper Island CEO Johanna Frelin sums up the importance of personality by saying, "There is a growing desire for talent with a unique combination of skill and flexibility—people who can collaborate, adapt quickly, and are enjoyable company, but also have the drive to get things done. All those traits boil down to a personality that is essential for businesses operating in an ever-changing digital landscape."[94]

12-4 MANAGING DIVERSITY

How much should companies change their standard business practices to accommodate the diversity of their workers? What do you do when a talented top executive has a drinking problem that seems to affect his behavior only at company business parties (for entertaining clients), where he has made inappropriate advances toward female employees? What do you do when, despite aggressive company policies against racial discrimination, employees continue to tell racist jokes and publicly post cartoons displaying racist humor? And, because many people confuse diversity with affirmative action, what do you do to make sure that your company's diversity practices and policies are viewed as benefiting all workers and not just some workers?

No doubt about it, questions like these make managing diversity one of the toughest challenges that managers face.[95] Nonetheless, there are steps companies can take to begin to address these issues.

As discussed earlier, diversity programs try to create a positive work environment where no one is advantaged or disadvantaged, where "we" is everyone, where everyone can do his or her best work, where differences are respected and not ignored, and where everyone feels comfortable.

Let's begin to address those goals by learning about 12-4a different diversity paradigms, 12-4b diversity principles, and 12-4c diversity training and practices.

12-4a Diversity Paradigms

There are several different methods or paradigms for managing diversity: the discrimination and fairness paradigm, the access and legitimacy paradigm, and the learning and effectiveness paradigm.[96]

The *discrimination and fairness paradigm*, which is the most common method of approaching diversity, focuses on equal opportunity, fair treatment, recruitment of minorities, and strict compliance with the equal employment opportunity laws. Under this approach, success is usually measured by how well companies achieve recruitment, promotion, and retention goals for women, people of different racial/ethnic backgrounds, or other underrepresented groups. According to a recent workplace diversity practices survey conducted by the Society for Human Resource Management, 66 percent to 91 percent of companies use specialized strategies to recruit, retain, and promote talented women and minorities. The percentages increase with company size, and companies of more than 500 employees are the most likely to use these strategies. Of companies with more than 500 employees, 77 percent systematically collect measurements on diversity-related practices.[97] One manager says, "If you don't measure something, it doesn't count. You measure your market share. You measure your profitability. The same should be true for diversity. There has to be some way of measuring whether you did, in fact, cast your net widely and whether the company is better off today in terms of the experience of people of color than it was a few years ago. I measure my market share and my profitability. Why not this?"[98] The primary benefit of the discrimination and fairness paradigm is that it generally brings about fairer treatment of employees and increases demographic diversity. The primary limitation is that the focus of diversity remains on the surface-level diversity dimensions of sex, race, and ethnicity.[99]

The *access and legitimacy paradigm* focuses on the acceptance and celebration of differences to ensure that the diversity within the company matches the diversity found among primary stakeholders, such as customers, suppliers, and local communities. This is similar to the *business growth* advantage of diversity discussed earlier in the chapter. The basic idea behind this approach is to create a demographically diverse workforce that attracts a broader customer base. For example, the diversity strategy at Oshkosh, a maker of specialty trucks and truck bodies, states, "We operate and sell our products and services in over 100 countries on six continents, each with its own culture, customs, and business practices. We seek employees who are passionate about serving customers and who reflect our diverse customer base so that we can truly understand our customers to better serve and delight them."[100]

The primary benefit of this approach is that it establishes a clear business reason for diversity. Like the discrimination and fairness paradigm, however, it focuses only on the surface-level diversity dimensions of sex, race, and ethnicity. Furthermore, employees who are assigned responsibility for customers and stakeholders on the basis of their sex, race, or ethnicity may eventually feel frustrated and exploited.

Whereas the discrimination and fairness paradigm focuses on assimilation (having a demographically representative workforce), and the access and legitimacy paradigm focuses on differentiation (having demographic differences inside the company match those of key customers and stakeholders), the *learning and effectiveness paradigm* focuses on integrating deep-level diversity differences, such as personality, attitudes, beliefs, and values, into the actual work of the organization. One sign that a company hasn't yet created a learning and effectiveness paradigm is that people withhold their opinions for fear of being seen as different. For example, while Helena Morrissey is the CEO of Newton Investment Management, a London firm that invests $71 billion for its clients, she admits to sometimes keeping her business opinions to herself for fear of being seen as "the annoying" woman at the table. She says, "At a recent meeting, I wasn't comfortable with a controversial point and I spoke up, but I also had a different view on the next item on the agenda but instead of speaking up I held back." Says Morrissey, "I have been conscious of feeling that where I did have different views from the rest of the [all-male] group, I may be being perceived as the 'difficult woman' rather than being listened to for what I was saying." She felt this way despite there being "no evidence that the men were actually feeling that."[101]

The learning and effectiveness paradigm is consistent with achieving organizational plurality. **Organizational plurality** is a work environment where (1) all members are empowered to contribute in a way that maximizes the benefits to the organization, customers, and themselves, and (2) the individuality of each member is respected by not segmenting or polarizing people on the basis of their membership in a particular group.[102]

The learning and effectiveness diversity paradigm offers four benefits.[103] First, it values common ground. David Thomas of the Harvard Business School explains, "Like the fairness paradigm, it promotes equal opportunity for all individuals. And like the access paradigm, it acknowledges cultural differences among people and recognizes the value in those differences. Yet this new model for managing diversity lets the organization internalize differences among employees so that it learns and grows because of them. Indeed, with the model fully in place, members of the organization can say, 'We are all on the same team, with our differences—not despite them.'"[104]

Second, this paradigm makes a distinction between individual and group differences. When diversity focuses

Organizational plurality
a work environment where (1) all members are empowered to contribute in a way that maximizes the benefits to the organization, customers, and themselves, and (2) the individuality of each member is respected by not segmenting or polarizing people on the basis of their membership in a particular group

"We are all on the same team...

only on differences between groups, such as females versus males, large differences within groups are ignored.[105] For example, think of the women you know at work. Now, think for a second about what they have in common. After that, think about how they're different. If your situation is typical, the list of differences should be just as long as the list of commonalties, if not longer. In short, managers can achieve a greater understanding of diversity and their employees by treating them as individuals and by realizing that not all African Americans, Hispanics, women, or white males want the same things at work.[106]

Third, because the focus is on individual differences, the learning and effectiveness paradigm is less likely to encounter the conflict, backlash, and divisiveness sometimes associated with diversity programs that focus only on group differences. Taylor Cox, one of the leading management writers on diversity, says, "We are concerned here with these more destructive forms of conflict which may be present with diverse workforces due to language barriers, cultural clash, or resentment by majority-group members of what they may perceive as preferential and unwarranted treatment of minority-group members."[107] And Ray Haines, a consultant who has helped companies deal with the aftermath of diversity programs that became divisive, says, "There's a large amount of backlash related to diversity training. It stirs up a lot of hostility, anguish, and resentment but doesn't give people tools to deal with [the backlash]. You have people come in and talk about their specific ax to grind."[108] Not all diversity programs are divisive or lead to conflict. But by focusing on individual

rather than group differences, the learning and effectiveness paradigm helps to minimize these potential problems.

Finally, unlike the other diversity paradigms that simply focus on surface-level diversity, the learning and effectiveness paradigm focuses on bringing different talents and perspectives (that is deep-level diversity) *together* to make the best organizational decisions and to produce innovative, competitive products and services.

12-4b Diversity Principles

Diversity paradigms are general approaches or strategies for managing diversity. Whatever diversity paradigm a manager chooses, diversity principles will help managers do a better job of *managing company diversity programs*.[109]

Swift Punishment

When two Asian men ordered meals at their local Chick-Fil-A, the cashier did not ask for their names, which are usually printed on the receipts. Instead, she typed in two derogatory words about the customers' Asian heritage, which then showed up on the receipts. When the restaurant manager found out what happened, he acted quickly by firing the employee. What's more, the company rushed to issue a detailed apology in which it fully admitted to what the employee had done and pledged to serve all customers with respect.

Source: "Chick-fil-A Cashier Fired for Racist Receipts Mocking Asians" *MSNBC.com*, December 14, 2011, accessed March 15, 2012. http://usnews.nbcnews.com/_newsz /2011/12/14/9444087-chick-fil-a-cashier-fired-for-racist-receipts-mocking-asians?lite

with our differences—not despite them."

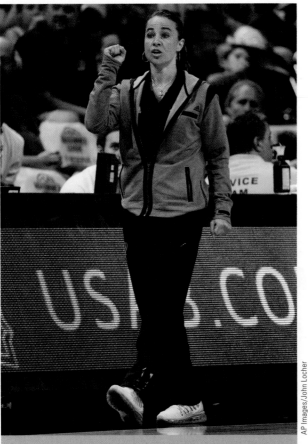

After her playing days in the WNBA, Becky Hammon has gone on to become the first female assistant in the NBA; due to her capabilities as a coach and not because she is a woman.

AP Images/John Locher

Begin by *carefully and faithfully following and enforcing federal and state laws regarding equal opportunity employment*. Diversity programs can't and won't succeed if the company is being sued for discriminatory actions and behavior. Faithfully following the law will also reduce the time and expense associated with EEOC investigations or lawsuits. Start by learning more at the EEOC website (www.eeoc.gov). Following the law also means strictly and fairly enforcing company policies.

Treat group differences as important but not special. Surface-level diversity dimensions such as age, sex, and race/ethnicity should be respected but should not be treated as more important than other kinds of differences (that is deep-level diversity). Remember, the shift in focus from surface- to deep-level diversity helps people know and understand each other better, reduces prejudice and conflict, and leads to stronger social integration with people wanting to work together and get the job done. Also, *find the common ground*. Although respecting differences is important, it's just as important, especially with diverse workforces, to actively find ways for employees to see and share commonalties.

Tailor opportunities to individuals, not groups. Special programs for training, development, mentoring, or promotion should be based on individual strengths and weaknesses, not on group status. Instead of making mentoring available for just one group of workers, create mentoring opportunities for everyone who wants to be mentored. DuPont Corporation's mentoring program, for example, is voluntary and open to all employees. Through candid and confidential conversations, DuPont's mentors help younger workers and managers with problem solving and career and leadership development.[110]

Maintain high standards. Companies have a legal and moral obligation to make sure that their hiring and promotion procedures and standards are fair to all. At the same time, in today's competitive markets, companies should not lower standards to promote diversity. This not only hurts the organizations but also feeds the stereotype that applicants who are hired or promoted in the name of affirmative action or diversity are less qualified. After a knee injury ended the career of WNBA player and Olympic medalist Becky Hammon, she became a coaching intern for the NBA's San Antonio Spurs. While rehabing her knee, Hammon attended coaches' meetings, gave instructions during practices, and, when asked, willingly shared her opinions with head coach Gregg Popovich, who has led the Spurs to five NBA championships. Popovich told her, "As cool as it would be to hire you [as a full-time assistant coach], you'd have to be qualified, and I'd have to make sure you're qualified." She agreed. When Popovich hired her after the completion of her internship, Hammon said, "Honestly, I don't think he gives two cents that I'm a woman. And, I don't want to be hired because I'm a woman . . . I'm getting hired because I'm capable."[111]

Solicit negative as well as positive feedback. Diversity is one of the most difficult management issues. No company or manager gets it right from the start. Consequently, companies should aggressively seek positive and negative feedback about their diversity programs. One way to do that is to use a series of measurements to see if progress is being made. Jaya Bohlmann, a former vice president at Sodexo, a food services and facilities management company, said, "We measure our progress systematically, using an objective scorecard that ties 15 percent of managers' compensation and 25 percent of our executives' compensation to their success [to ensure that] we continue to attract, develop, and retain a diverse and highly skilled workforce. We report on our diversity progress annually, posting the reports on our website."[112]

Set high but realistic goals. Just because diversity is difficult doesn't mean that organizations shouldn't try to accomplish as much as possible. The general purpose of diversity programs is to try to create a positive work environment where no one is advantaged or disadvantaged, where "we" is everyone, where everyone can do his or her best work, where differences are respected and not ignored, and where everyone feels comfortable. Even if progress is slow, companies should not shrink from these goals.

12-4c Diversity Training and Practices

Organizations use diversity training and several common diversity practices to manage diversity. There are two basic types of diversity training programs, skills-based and awareness. **Skills-based diversity training** teaches employees the practical skills they need for managing a diverse workforce, skills such as flexibility and adaptability, negotiation, problem solving, and conflict resolution.[113] By contrast, **awareness training** is designed to raise employees' awareness of diversity issues and to challenge underlying assumptions or stereotypes we may have about others. **Dell Inc.** enrolled several male executives in a six-month program run by Catalyst, a nonprofit group that tracks and advocates for women's advancement. The program teaches managers to recognize the hurdles facing women in the workplace. As a result of the training, Doug Hillary, a Dell vice president, checked in with a female staff member with two young children and asked her if he was adequately accommodating her family needs. She told him that, actually, he was regularly scheduling staff conference calls at an hour when she was dropping her children off at school. He changed the meeting times, saying that, previously, "He didn't pay as much attention."[114]

Some companies use the Implicit Association Test (IAT) for awareness training.[115] The IAT measures the extent to which people associate positive or negative thoughts (that is underlying assumptions or stereotypes) with blacks or whites, men or women, homosexuals or heterosexuals, young or old, or other groups. For the race IAT (versions also exist for weight, age, sexuality, and other ethnic groups), test takers are shown black or white faces that they must instantly pair with various words. Response times (shorter responses generally indicate stronger associations) and the pattern of associations indicate the extent to which people are biased. Most people are, and strongly so. For example, 88 percent of whites have a more positive mental association toward whites than toward blacks but, surprisingly, 48 percent of blacks show the same bias. Do the strong biases measured by the IAT mean we're likely to discriminate against others? Thankfully, no.[116] But they indicate the importance of becoming aware of our potential biases and then monitoring our workplace behavior and decision making. So, taking the IAT is a good way to increase awareness of diversity issues. To take the IAT and to learn more about the decade of research behind it, go to https://implicit.harvard.edu/implicit/demo.

Companies also use diversity audits, diversity pairing, and minority experiences for top executives to better manage diversity. **Diversity audits** are formal assessments that measure employee and management attitudes, investigate the extent to which people are advantaged or disadvantaged with respect to hiring and promotions, and review companies' diversity-related policies and procedures. At Intel, the world's leading computer chip manufacturer, diversity is a key part of its competitive strategy and vision. Accordingly, Intel's managers develop annual diversity action plans with specific measures and indicators that are reviewed every three months. For example, since the creation of Intel's Women's Initiative in 2004, the percentage of women in technical middle-level to senior-level jobs has increased by 24 percent.[117]

Intel also assesses its diversity practices through an annual survey about the company's policies and their effectiveness at creating a supportive environment. The survey results are shared with all employees and used to create or revise action plans consistent with its annual diversity action plans.[118]

Earlier in the chapter, you learned that *mentoring*, pairing a junior employee with a senior employee, is a common strategy for creating learning and promotional opportunities for women. Diversity pairing is a special kind of mentoring. In **diversity pairing**, people of different cultural backgrounds, sexes, or races/ethnicities are paired for mentoring. The hope is that stereotypical beliefs and attitudes will change as people get to know each other as individuals.[119] Consultant Tom McGee, who has set up mentoring programs for

Skills-based diversity training training that teaches employees the practical skills they need for managing a diverse workforce, such as flexibility and adaptability, negotiation, problem solving, and conflict resolution

Awareness training training that is designed to raise employees' awareness of diversity issues and to challenge the underlying assumptions or stereotypes they may have about others

Diversity audits formal assessments that measure employee and management attitudes, investigate the extent to which people are advantaged or disadvantaged with respect to hiring and promotions, and review companies' diversity-related policies and procedures

Diversity pairing a mentoring program in which people of different cultural backgrounds, sexes, or races/ethnicities are paired together to get to know each other and change stereotypical beliefs and attitudes numerous companies, supports diversity pairing, saying, "The assumption that people participating in diversity mentoring programs are looking for someone of the same race or gender has been proved wrong in many cases."[120]

For more than twenty years, Xerox has been fostering a culture where women and minorities are prepared and considered for top positions. CEO Ursula Burns, the first African American woman to lead a major U.S. company, worked as special assistant to Xerox's president of marketing and customer operations, Wayland Hicks. Reginald Brown, Jr., CEO of Brown Technology Group, who worked with Burns at Xerox, said, "These [appointments as special assistants] were jobs in the company that division presidents put their best people in. Most of them were white males, so to have an African American female in such a position of power, you knew early on she had great potential." Burns was then given a similar role with former Xerox CEO Paul A. Allaire. When Anne Mulcahy became CEO in 2001, Burns was gradually given control of day-to-day operations while Mulcahy repaired Xerox's financial position and customer service. David Thomas, a Harvard Business School professor, says that because of steps (such as diversity pairing) to promote diversity at Xerox, "you have a culture where having women and people of color as candidates for powerful jobs has been going on for two decades."[121]

Finally, because top managers are still overwhelmingly white and male, a number of companies believe that it is worthwhile to *have top executives experience what it is like to be in the minority.* This can be done by having top managers go to places or events where nearly everyone else is of a different sex or racial/ethnic background. For example, managers at Raytheon are required to spend an entire day in the office in a wheelchair so that they have a better understanding of the challenges faced by their disabled colleagues. Managers and executives at Sodexho Alliance are asked to spend time working with organizations that represent minorities. One male manager became the sponsor of a women employees group at Sodexho and accompanied a female colleague to a meeting of the Women's Food Service Forum. The manager called the experience, in which he was at a conference with 1,500 women, "profound" and said that it taught him what it feels like to be different. He also describes how his experiences working with women made him more sensitive to women's feelings and even led him to change the social activities that he plans with coworkers from golf to dinner cruises. Rohini Anand, Sodexho's chief diversity officer, endorses this experiential approach, saying, "To really engage people, you have to create a series of epiphanies and take leaders through those epiphanies."[122]

STUDY TOOLS 12

LOCATED IN TEXTBOOK

☐ Rip-out and review chapter review card

LOCATED AT WWW.CENGAGEBRAIN.COM

☐ Review key term flashcards and create your own from StudyBits

☐ Track your knowledge and understanding of key concepts, using the concept tracker

☐ Complete practice and graded quizzes to prepare for tests

☐ Complete interactive content within the exposition

☐ View chapter highlight box content at the beginning of each chapter

ONE APPROACH.
70 UNIQUE SOLUTIONS.

13 Motivation

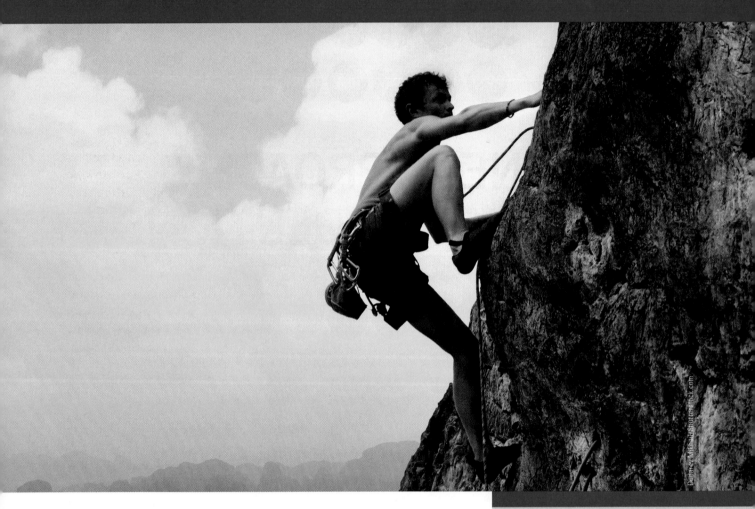

Dudarev Mikhail/Shutterstock.com

LEARNING OUTCOMES

13-1 Explain the basics of motivation.

13-2 Use equity theory to explain how employees' perceptions of fairness affect motivation.

13-3 Use expectancy theory to describe how workers' expectations about rewards, effort, and the link between rewards and performance influence motivation.

13-4 Explain how reinforcement theory works and how it can be used to motivate.

13-5 Describe the components of goal-setting theory and how managers can use them to motivate workers.

13-6 Discuss how the entire motivation model can be used to motivate workers.

After you finish
this chapter, go to
PAGE 287 for
STUDY TOOLS

13-1 BASICS OF MOTIVATION

What makes people happiest and most productive at work? Is it money, benefits, opportunities for growth, interesting work, or something else altogether? And if people desire different things, how can a company keep everyone motivated? It takes insight and hard work to motivate workers to join the company, perform well, and then stay with the company. In fact, a 2013 worldwide study by Gallup found that only 13 percent of employees are "engaged" or motivated at work, whereas 63 percent are "not engaged," meaning they are unmotivated and not interested in organizational goals or outcomes. Even worse, 24 percent of employees are "actively disengaged" and are "unhappy, unproductive, and liable to spread negativity."[1]

So what is motivation? **Motivation** is the set of forces that initiates, directs, and makes people persist in their efforts to accomplish a goal.[2] *Initiation of effort* is concerned with the choices that people make about how much effort to put forth in their jobs. ("Do I really knock myself out or just do a decent job?") *Direction of effort* is concerned with the choices that people make in deciding where to put forth effort in their jobs. ("I should be spending time with my high-dollar accounts instead of learning this new computer system!") *Persistence of effort* is concerned with the choices that people make about how long they will put forth effort in their jobs before reducing or eliminating those efforts. ("I'm only halfway through the project, and I'm exhausted. Do I plow through to the end, or just call it quits?") Initiation, direction, and persistence are at the heart of motivation.

At 37signals, a Chicago software company, co-founder Jason Fried has avoided using promotions to reward his thirty employees. Says Fried, "We revere 'horizontal' ambition—in which employees who love what they do are encouraged to dig deeper, expand their knowledge, and become better at it. We always try to hire people who yearn to be master craftspeople, that is, designers who want to be great designers, not managers of designers; developers who want to master the art of programming, not management."[3]

Which would motivate you more, the chance to become a master craftsperson or the opportunity for promotion and management responsibilities? Or, in Gallup's terms, are you engaged at work? Are your co-workers? If you and your co-workers are "disengaged" or "actively disengaged," why? Are there parts of the job that interest and energize you? If so, what are they

Exhibit 13.1
A Basic Model of Work Motivation and Performance

© Cengage Learning

and why? Answering questions like these is at the heart of figuring out how best to motivate people at work.

Let's learn more about motivation by building a basic model of motivation out of **13-1a effort and performance, 13-1b need satisfaction,** *and* **13-1c extrinsic and intrinsic rewards** *and then discussing* **13-1d how to motivate people with this basic model of motivation.**

13-1a Effort and Performance

When most people think of work motivation, they think that working hard (effort) should lead to a good job (performance). Exhibit 13.1 shows a basic model of work motivation and performance, displaying this process. The first thing to notice about Exhibit 13.1 is that this is a basic model of work motivation *and* performance. In practice, it's almost impossible to talk about one without mentioning the other. Not surprisingly, managers often assume motivation to be the only determinant of performance, saying things such as "Your performance was really terrible last quarter. What's the matter? Aren't you as motivated as you used to be?" In fact, motivation is just one of three primary determinants of job performance. In industrial psychology, job performance is frequently represented by this equation:

$$\text{Job Performance} = \text{Motivation} \times \text{Ability} \times \text{Situational Constraints}$$

In this formula, *job performance* is how well someone performs the requirements of the job. *Motivation,* as defined previously, is effort, the degree to which someone works hard to do the job well. *Ability* is the degree to which workers possess the knowledge, skills, and talent

> **Motivation** the set of forces that initiates, directs, and makes people persist in their efforts to accomplish a goal

Exhibit 13.2
A Basic Model of Work Motivation and Performance

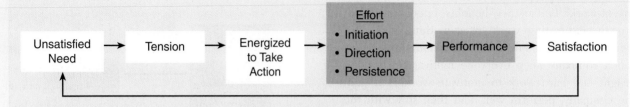

As shown on the left side of this exhibit, a person's unsatisfied need creates an uncomfortable internal state of tension that must be resolved. So, according to needs theories, people are motivated by unmet needs. But after a need is met, it no longer motivates. When this occurs, people become satisfied, as shown on the right side of the exhibit.

© Cengage Learning

needed to do a job well. And *situational constraints* are factors beyond the control of individual employees, such as tools, policies, and resources that have an effect on job performance.

Because job performance is a multiplicative function of motivation times ability times situational constraints, job performance will suffer if any one of these components is weak. This doesn't mean that motivation doesn't matter. It just means that all the motivation in the world won't translate into high performance when an employee has little ability and high situational constraints. So, even though we will spend this chapter developing a model of work motivation, it is important to remember that ability and situational constraints affect job performance as well.

13-1b Need Satisfaction

In Exhibit 13.1 we started with a very basic model of motivation in which effort leads to job performance. But managers want to know, "What leads to effort?" Determining employee needs is the first step to answering that question.

Needs are the physical or psychological requirements that must be met to ensure survival and well-being.[4] As shown on the left side of Exhibit 13.2, a person's unmet need creates an uncomfortable, internal state of tension that must be resolved. For example, if you normally skip breakfast but then have to work through lunch, chances are you'll be so hungry by late afternoon that the only thing you'll be motivated to do is find something to eat. So, according to needs theories,

> **Needs** the physical or psychological requirements that must be met to ensure survival and well-being

people are motivated by unmet needs. But a need no longer motivates once it is met. For example, when the author of the Mr. Everyday Dollar financial strategies website learned that he had become a millionaire at 35, he described it as a, "huge letdown," saying, "You might think when your account rolls over to seven digits that fireworks light up the sky, confetti falls, and champagne starts flowing. I can tell you that doesn't happen, in fact, it's pretty anticlimactic; I was like, 'Oh, cool,' and then went back to work." In other words, once obtained, his need for financial independence, no longer motivated him as much.[5] When this occurs, people become satisfied, as shown on the right side of Exhibit 13.2.

Note: Throughout the chapter, as we build on this basic model, the parts of the model that we've already discussed will appear shaded in color. For example, because we've already discussed the effort → performance part of the model, those components are shown with a colored background. When we add new parts to the model, they will have a white background. We're adding need satisfaction to the model at this step, so the need-satisfaction components of unsatisfied need, tension, energized to take action, and satisfaction are shown with a white background. This shading convention should make it easier to understand the work motivation model as we add to it in each section of the chapter.

Because people are motivated by unmet needs, managers must learn what those unmet needs are and address them. This is not always a straightforward task, however, because different needs theories suggest different needs categories. Consider three well-known

Featured in: CNNMoney msn YAHOO!

MR. EVERYDAY DOLLAR $$$
Financial freedom. Early retirement.

ABOUT   CONTACT   HOW TO

ERYDAY DOLLAR
IARIES

The Everyday Dollar Diaries – Part 1
Today is the first post in the new Everyday Dollar Diaries series. In this series, I collect personal journals from real people who have tracked their normal spending habits over seven [...]

LATEST POSTS

The American Dream Is a Financial Nightmare
Posted on May 26, 2015 | 12 Comments
The year was 2001, I was 21-years-old, with one semester of college left. I wasn't taking school very serious anymore, so me and my roommate we were going through cases of Natural [...]

Continue Reading...

The Everyday Dollar Diaries – Part 1
Posted on May 11, 2015 | 4 Comments
Today is the first post in the new Everyday Dollar Diaries series. In this series, I collect personal journals from real people who have tracked their normal spending habits over seven [...]

Continue Reading...

"The Only 2 Funds You Need To Invest In (Hint: Even Warren Buffett Recommends Them)"

LAZY & UNCOMPLICATED INVESTING
An Effortless & Simple Investment Guide $$$

Name:

Email:

Free Download!

Your email is safe with me, I promise

Source: Mr. Everyday Dollar

Consistent with needs theories, which state that satisfied needs no longer motivate, the owner of the website "Mr. Everyday Dollar" found out that becoming a millionaire was "anticlimactic."

needs theories. Maslow's Hierarchy of Needs suggests that people are motivated by *physiological* (food and water), *safety* (physical and economic), *belongingness* (friendship, love, social interaction), *esteem* (achievement and recognition), and *self-actualization* (realizing your full potential) needs.[6] Alderfer's ERG Theory collapses Maslow's five needs into three: *existence* (safety and physiological needs), *relatedness* (belongingness), and *growth* (esteem and self-actualization).[7] McClelland's Learned Needs Theory suggests that people are motivated by the need for *affiliation* (to be liked and accepted), the need for *achievement* (to accomplish challenging goals), or the need for *power* (to influence others).[8]

Things become even more complicated when we consider the different predictions made by these theories. According to Maslow, needs are arranged in a hierarchy from low (physiological) to high (self-actualization). Within this hierarchy, people are motivated by their lowest unsatisfied need. As each need is met, they work their way up the hierarchy from physiological to self-actualization needs. By contrast, Alderfer says that people can be motivated by more than one need at a time. Furthermore, he suggests that people are just as likely to move down the needs hierarchy

as up, particularly when they are unable to achieve satisfaction at the next higher need level. McClelland argues that the degree to which particular needs motivate varies tremendously from person to person, with some people being motivated primarily by achievement and others by power or affiliation. Moreover, McClelland says that needs are learned, not innate. For instance, studies show that children whose parents own a small business or hold a managerial position are much more likely to have a high need for achievement.[9]

So, with three different sets of needs and three very different ideas about how needs motivate, how do we provide a practical answer to managers who just want to know what leads to effort? Fortunately, the research evidence simplifies things a bit. To start, studies indicate that there are two basic kinds of needs categories.[10] *Lower-order needs* are concerned with safety and with physiological and existence requirements, whereas *higher-order needs* are concerned with relationships (belongingness, relatedness, and affiliation), challenges and accomplishments (esteem, self-actualization, growth, and achievement), and influence (power). Studies generally show that higher-order needs will not motivate people as long as lower-order needs remain unsatisfied.[11]

For example, imagine that you graduated from college six months ago and are still looking for your first job. With money running short (you're probably living on your credit cards), and the possibility of having to move back in with your parents looming (if this doesn't motivate you, what will?), your basic needs for food, shelter, and security drive your thoughts, behavior, and choices at this point. But after you land that job, find a great place (of your own!) to live, and put some money in the bank, these basic needs should decrease in importance as you begin to think about making new friends and taking on challenging work assignments. In fact, after lower-order needs are satisfied, it's difficult for managers to predict which higher-order needs will motivate behavior.[12] Some people will be motivated by affiliation, while others will be motivated by growth or esteem. Also, the relative importance of the various needs may change over time but not necessarily in any predictable pattern. So, what leads to effort? In part, needs do. After we discuss rewards in Subsection 13-1c, in Subsection 13-1d, we

Exhibit 13.3
Adding Rewards to the Model

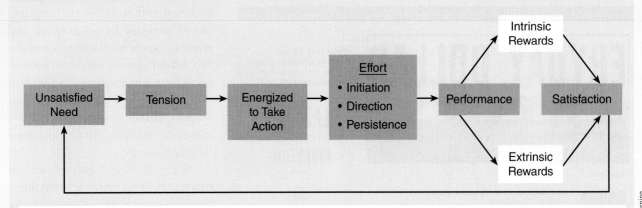

Performing a job well can be rewarding intrinsically (the job itself is fun, challenging, or interesting) or extrinsically (as you receive better pay, promotions, and so on). Intrinsic and extrinsic rewards lead to satisfaction of various needs.

© Cengage Learning

discuss how managers can use what we know from need-satisfaction theories to motivate workers.

13-1c Extrinsic and Intrinsic Rewards

No discussion of motivation would be complete without considering rewards. Let's add two kinds of rewards, extrinsic and intrinsic, to the model in Exhibit 13.3.[13]

Extrinsic rewards are tangible and visible to others and are given to employees contingent on the performance of specific tasks or behaviors.[14] External agents (managers, for example) determine and control the distribution, frequency, and amount of extrinsic rewards, such as pay, company stock, benefits, and promotions. For example, eighty percent of 1,000 large- and medium-sized U.S. companies surveyed by Hewitt Associates, a consulting company based in Lincolnshire, Illinois, offer incentives or bonuses to reward employees.[15]

Lincoln Electric, a manufacturer of arc welding tools and technology, has paid annual profit sharing bonuses to its factory workers for eighty straight years. In 2013, Lincoln paid out one-third of its pre-tax profits, $100.7 million, to employees who received bonuses of $33,029 each, worth 62 percent of total wages. In the eighty years in which Lincoln has paid profit-sharing bonuses, the percentage has never dropped below 25 percent of total wages and has been as high as 120 percent. Over the past decade, bonuses have averaged 40 percent of total salary.[16]

Why do companies need to offer extrinsic rewards? To get people to do things they wouldn't otherwise do. Companies use extrinsic rewards to motivate people to perform four basic behaviors: join the organization, regularly attend their jobs, perform their jobs well, and stay with the organization.[17] Think about it. Would you show up at work every day to do the best possible job that you could just out of the goodness of your heart? Very few people would.

Intrinsic rewards are the natural rewards associated with performing a task or activity for its own sake. For example, aside from the external rewards management offers for doing something well, employees often find the activities or tasks they perform interesting and enjoyable. Examples of intrinsic rewards include a sense of accomplishment or achievement, a feeling of responsibility, the chance to learn something new or interact with others, or simply the fun that comes from performing an interesting, challenging, and engaging task.

Each year, 1,300 students enter the **U.S. Military Academy at West Point**. About 1,000 will graduate , and roughly 40 percent of graduates stay beyond the Army's five years of required service. To better understand why some cadets graduate and serve longer than others, a team of researchers analyzed fourteen years of data on 10,000 cadets. Regardless of race, sex, religion, scholastic achievement, or economic background, cadets who were motivated by

Extrinsic reward a reward that is tangible, visible to others, and given to employees contingent on the performance of specific tasks or behaviors

Intrinsic reward a natural reward associated with performing a task or activity for its own sake

Cadets motivated by intrinsic rewards, such as wanting to be an Army officer, were 20 percent more likely to make it through West Point's rigorous program than those motivated by extrinsic factors.

intrinsic rewards, such as wanting to be an Army officer, were 20 percent more likely to make it through West Point's rigorous program than those motivated by extrinsic factors, such as attending West Point because their parents wanted them to. Compared to those with weak internal motivation, internally motivated cadets were also more likely to be considered for early promotion (35% vs. 16%).[18]

Which types of rewards are most important to workers in general? A number of surveys suggest that both extrinsic and intrinsic rewards are important and that employee preferences for either intrinsic or extrinsic rewards are relatively stable.[19] A 2014 Society for Human Resource Management national survey found that over the past six years, three extrinsic factors—pay, benefits, and job security/organizational financial stability—and two intrinsic factors, the work itself and opportunities to use one's skills and abilities, have consistently been among the top five factors rated as "very important" by employees.[20]

13-1d Motivating with the Basics

So, given the basic model of work motivation in Exhibit 13.3, what practical steps can managers take to motivate employees to increase their effort?

The first step is to *start by asking people what their needs are.* Jonathan Robinson, the CEO of **Freetextbooks .com**, an online college textbook seller (sorry, the textbooks aren't really free), says the key to motivating employees is finding out what they like and then giving them the rewards they want. To do that, Robinson gives each new hire a brief survey asking them about their favorite candy, restaurant, hobby, or music. Says Robinson, "You just have to know your team. We're pretty small so I have to stay in tune with the preferences and pulse of our employees. The perks are in the details." As a result, he recently gave one employee a free round of golf, another $100 to be used at a great restaurant, and another IMAX theater tickets. Because he asked, all got what they wanted.[21] So, if you want to meet employees' needs, just ask.

Next, *satisfy lower-order needs first.* Because higher-order needs will not motivate people as long as lower-order needs remain unsatisfied, companies should satisfy lower-order needs first. In practice, this means providing the equipment, training, and knowledge to create a safe workplace free of physical risks; paying employees well enough to provide financial security; and offering a benefits package that will protect employees and their families through good medical coverage and health and disability insurance. Indeed, the Society for Human Resource Management study mentioned previously found that three of the five most important factors in 2013—compensation/pay (60%), job security (59%), and benefits (53%)—were all lower-order needs.[22] Consistent with the idea of satisfying lower-order needs first, a survey of 12,000 employees found that inadequate compensation is the number-one reason employees leave organizations. This is why The Container Store CEO Kip Tindell pays his employees an average salary of $48,000 per year, twice the average retail salary. As a result, says Tindell, "My employees advance on Maslow's hierarchy [from lower- to higher-order needs]." He says, "I didn't think about this when we started out. But it's the most powerful thing you can do."[23]

Third, managers should *expect people's needs to change.* As some needs are satisfied or situations change, what motivated people before may not motivate them now. Likewise, what motivates people to accept a job may not necessarily motivate them after they have the job. For instance, David Stum, president of the Loyalty Institute, says, "The [attractive] power of pay and benefits is only [strong] during the recruitment stage. After employees take the job, pay and benefits become entitlements to them. They think: 'Now that I work here, you owe me that.'"[24] Managers should also expect needs to change as people mature. For older employees, benefits are as important as pay, which is always ranked as more important by younger employees. Older employees also rank job security as more important than personal and family time, which is more important to younger employees.[25]

Finally, *as needs change and lower-order needs are satisfied, create opportunities for employees to satisfy higher-order needs.* Recall that intrinsic rewards such as accomplishment, achievement, learning something new, and interacting with others are the natural rewards associated with performing a task or activity for its own sake. And, with the exception of influence (power),

What's Better than Cash? Try Something Unconventional

Perks like flex time and working from home that used to be uncommon are increasingly standard, and companies are digging to find unconventional, noncash incentives that inspire and reward workers. Software company 2HB gives employees a $50 grooming perk each month to go toward manicures, pedicures, and haircuts. Freeborn & Peters law firm holds an annual luggage party—employees show up with a packed bag, and four are chosen for an all-expenses-paid weekend in Las Vegas. Apple's pregnancy benefits and Facebook's surrogacy benefits pay up to $20,000 toward expenses incurred by female employees who want to freeze their eggs.

Source: B. Helmrich, "Think Freezing Eggs Is Odd? Check Out These Strange Employee Benefits," *Business News Daily*, October 14, 2014, accessed May 8, 2015. http://www .businessnewsdaily.com/7321-strange-job-benefits.html.

Valua Vitaly/Shutterstock.com

intrinsic rewards correspond very closely to higher-order needs that are concerned with relationships (belongingness, relatedness, and affiliation) and challenges and accomplishments (esteem, self-actualization, growth, and achievement). Therefore, one way for managers to meet employees' higher-order needs is to create opportunities for employees to experience intrinsic rewards by providing challenging work, encouraging employees to take greater responsibility for their work, and giving employees the freedom to pursue tasks and projects they find naturally interesting.

13-2 EQUITY THEORY

We've seen that people are motivated to achieve intrinsic and extrinsic rewards. However, if employees don't believe that rewards are fairly awarded or don't believe that they can achieve the performance goals the company has set for them, they won't be very motivated.

Fairness, or what people perceive to be fair, is also a critical issue in organizations. **Equity theory** says that people will be motivated at work when they *perceive* that they are being treated fairly.

> **Equity theory** a theory that states that people will be motivated when they perceive that they are being treated fairly

In particular, equity theory stresses the importance of perceptions. So, regardless of the actual level of rewards people receive, they must also perceive that, relative to others, they are being treated fairly. For example, you learned in Chapter 11 that the CEOs of the largest U.S. firms now make $15.2 million per year, which is 296 times their average employee salary of $52,100.[26] The ten highest paid CEOs averaged earnings of $61.6 million per year, led by John H. Hammergren, the CEO of Discovery Communications, who made $156.1 million.[27] By contrast, in most companies with less than $1 billion a year in revenues, CEOs typically make 2.3 to 12.5 times what the average employee makes.[28]

Many people believe that CEO pay is obscenely high and unfair. Others believe that CEO pay is fair because the supply and demand for executive talent largely determine what CEOs are paid. They argue that if it were easier to find good CEOs, then CEOs would be paid much less. Equity theory doesn't focus on objective equity (that is, that CEOs make 296 times more than blue-collar workers). Instead, equity theory says that equity, like beauty, is in the eye of the beholder.

*Let's learn more about equity theory by examining **13-2a the components of equity theory, 13-2b how people react to perceived inequity**, and **13-2c how to motivate people using equity theory**.*

Kroster/Shutterstock.com

13-2a Components of Equity Theory

The basic components of equity theory are inputs, outcomes, and referents. **Inputs** are the contributions employees make to the organization. They include education and training, intelligence, experience, effort, number of hours worked, and ability. **Outcomes** are what employees receive in exchange for their contributions to the organization. They include pay, fringe benefits, status symbols, and job titles and assignments. And, because perceptions of equity depend on comparisons, **referents** are other people with whom people compare themselves to determine if they have been treated fairly. The referent can be a single person (comparing yourself with a coworker), a generalized other (comparing yourself with "students in general," for example), or even yourself over time ("I was better off last year than I am this year"). Usually, people choose to compare themselves with referents who hold the same or similar jobs or who are otherwise similar in gender, race, age, tenure, or other characteristics.[29] For example, 1,300 employees at Amazon's eight German distribution centers have gone on strike in pursuit of higher pay. The workers want to be paid 12 euros an hour, similar to employees (that is, their referents) at German retail and catalog-order companies. Amazon, however, argues that the employees, who are paid 9.30 euros an hour plus bonuses and shares of Amazon stock (after two years), are paid at the top end of the range for logistical employees who work in distribution warehouses. So, with clearly different referents, it's no surprise they disagree on what constitutes fair pay.[30]

According to equity theory, employees compare their outcomes (the rewards they receive from the organization) with their inputs (their contributions to the organization). This comparison of outcomes with inputs is called the **outcome/input (O/I) ratio**. After an internal comparison in which they compare their outcomes with their inputs, employees then make an external comparison in which they compare their O/I ratio with the O/I ratio of a referent.[31]

When people perceive that their O/I ratio is equal to the referent's O/I ratio, they conclude that they are being treated fairly. But when people perceive that their O/I ratio is different from their referent's O/I ratio, they conclude that they have been treated inequitably or unfairly.

Inequity can take two forms, underreward and overreward. **Underreward** occurs when a referent's O/I ratio is better than your O/I ratio. In other words, you are getting fewer outcomes relative to your inputs than the referent you compare yourself with is getting. When people perceive that they have been underrewarded, they tend to experience anger or frustration. Auto assembly workers at Toyota's two Indian facilities went on strike out of frustration that they were being paid unfairly. Toyota is offering 3,050 rupees ($51) a month, but workers want to be paid 4,000 rupees a month ($67) and have more holidays and company-provided housing. Satish Rangaswamy, the general secretary of the union representing the workers, said, "Whenever it makes a good profit in a year, it [Toyota] shifts all the profit to the headquarters, that is [in] Japan. Why can't they share it with our employees?"[32]

By contrast, **overreward** occurs when a referent's O/I ratio is worse than your O/I ratio. In this case, you are getting more outcomes relative to your inputs than your referent is. In theory, when people perceive that they have been overrewarded, they experience guilt. But, not surprisingly, people have a very high tolerance for overreward. It takes a tremendous amount of overpayment before people decide that their pay or benefits are more than they deserve.

13-2b How People React to Perceived Inequity

So what happens when people perceive that they have been treated inequitably at work? Exhibit 13.4 shows that perceived inequity

Inputs in equity theory, the contributions employees make to the organization

Outcomes in equity theory, the rewards employees receive for their contributions to the organization

Referents in equity theory, others with whom people compare themselves to determine if they have been treated fairly

Outcome/input (O/I) ratio in equity theory, an employee's perception of how the rewards received from an organization compare with the employee's contributions to that organization

Underreward a form of inequity in which you are getting fewer outcomes relative to inputs than your referent is getting

Overreward a form of inequity in which you are getting more outcomes relative to inputs than your referent

Magnifiko/Shutterstock.com

Exhibit 13.4
Adding Equity Theory to the Model

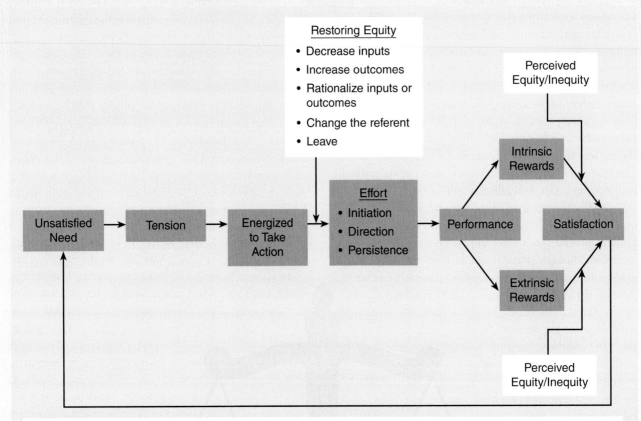

Restoring Equity
- Decrease inputs
- Increase outcomes
- Rationalize inputs or outcomes
- Change the referent
- Leave

When people perceive that they have been treated inequitably at work because of the intrinsic or extrinsic rewards they receive relative to their efforts, they are dissatisfied (or frustrated or angry), their needs aren't met, and those reactions lead to tension and a strong need to take action to restore equity in some way.

© Cengage Learning

affects satisfaction. In the case of underreward, this usually translates into frustration or anger; with overreward, the reaction is guilt. These reactions lead to tension and a strong need to take action to restore equity in some way. At first, a slight inequity may not be strong enough to motivate an employee to take immediate action. If the inequity continues, or there are multiple inequities, however, tension may build over time until a point of intolerance is reached and the person is energized to take action.

Revenues at **Plum Creek Timber** had been flat for two years and net income was dropping when CEO Rick Holley informed the company's board of directors that he was returning 44,445 restricted stock options valued at $1.85 million that the board's compensation committee had awarded him ten months earlier. Holley said, "I didn't feel comfortable taking them . . . This has been a

year where total shareholder returns are down 10 percent or more. It just wasn't the right thing to do."[33]

When people perceive that they have been treated unfairly, they may try to restore equity by reducing inputs, increasing outcomes, rationalizing inputs or outcomes, changing the referent, or simply leaving. We will discuss these possible responses in terms of the inequity associated with underreward, which is much more common than the inequity associated with overreward.

People who perceive that they have been underrewarded may try to restore equity by *decreasing or withholding their inputs (that is, effort)*. After filing for bankruptcy and seeking sizable pay and benefits cuts, American Airlines pilots engaged in a sick-out that cancelled hundreds of flights. Furthermore, pilots who showed for work allegedly delayed flights by filing maintenance requests that required mechanics to inspect planes before departure. While the pilots' union denied the slowdown, its president said, "The pilots of American Airlines are angry. While AMR management continues paying lip service to needing a consensual agreement with us, their punitive approach of extracting far more value than they need is hardly conducive to reaching a consensual agreement."[34]

Increasing outcomes is another way people try to restore equity. This might include asking for a raise or pointing out the inequity to the boss and hoping that he or she takes care of it. Sometimes, however, employees may go to external organizations such as labor unions, federal agencies, or the courts for help in increasing outcomes to restore equity. For instance, the U.S. Department of Labor estimates that 10 percent of workers are not getting the extra overtime pay they deserve when they work more than forty hours a week. These are known as Fair Labor Standards Act (FLSA) violations.[35] After a U.S. Department of Labor ruling, Walmart paid $5.26 million in back wages to 4,500 security guards who were at first denied overtime pay after incorrectly being classified as exempt employees (who are ineligible for overtime).[36] Somewhere between 25,000 and 30,000 FLSA cases are brought each year, and employees win two-thirds of them.[37] From 2001 to 2011, the number of FLSA filings in federal court rose by nearly 500 percent.[38]

Another method of restoring equity is to *rationalize or distort inputs or outcomes*. Instead of decreasing inputs or increasing outcomes, employees restore equity by making mental or emotional adjustments in their O/I ratios or the O/I ratios of their referents. For example, suppose that a company downsizes 10 percent of its workforce. It's likely that the people who still have jobs will be angry or frustrated with company management because of the layoffs. If alternative jobs are difficult to find, however, these survivors may rationalize or distort their O/I ratios and conclude, "Well, things could be worse. At least I still have my job." Rationalizing or distorting outcomes may be used when other ways to restore equity aren't available.

Changing the referent is another way of restoring equity. In this case, people compare themselves with someone other than the referent they had been using for previous O/I ratio comparisons. Because people usually choose to compare themselves with others who hold the same or similar jobs or who are otherwise similar (that is, friends, family members, neighbors who work at other companies), they may change referents to restore equity when their personal situations change, such as a decrease in job status or pay.[39]

13-2c Motivating with Equity Theory

What practical steps can managers take to use equity theory to motivate employees? They can *start by looking*

People who perceive that they have been underrewarded at the office, may withhold their efforts until they feel they are fairly compensated.

for and correcting major inequities. Among other things, equity theory makes us aware that an employee's sense of fairness is based on subjective perceptions. What one employee considers grossly unfair may not affect another employee's perceptions of equity at all. Although these different perceptions make it difficult for managers to create conditions that satisfy all employees, it's critical that they do their best to take care of major inequities that can energize employees to take disruptive, costly, or harmful actions such as decreasing inputs or leaving. So, whenever possible, managers should look for and correct major inequities.

For example, with Chinese wages rising between 10 and 15 percent per year on average and 30 percent a year where demand is high, the average factory worker in China, who makes between $317 and $350 a month, is generally underpaid.[40] So for two consecutive years, Lenovo CEO Yang Yuanqing has given his annual bonus to Lenovo's 10,000 employees. Approximately 90 percent of his 2013 $3.25 million bonus will go to factory employees in China, each of whom will receive about $325 dollars, roughly a month's salary. Lenovo spokeswoman Angela Lee said, "As you can imagine, an extra $300 [or more] in a manufacturing environment in China does make an impact, especially to employees supporting families."[41] Lenovo's communication to employees stated, "This payment is personally funded by Yuanqing. He believes that he has the responsibility as an owner of the company, and the opportunity as our leader, to ensure all of our employees understand the impact they have on building Lenovo."[42]

Second, managers can *reduce employees' inputs*. Increasing outcomes is often the first and only strategy that companies use to restore equity, yet reducing employee inputs is just as viable a strategy. In fact, with dual-career

Transparent Pay—Not a Big Deal

Dane Atkison has run almost a dozen companies during his career, often paying different employees vastly different salaries for the same skill set, only because some negotiated better than others. Tired of employee outrage when significant differences are discovered, he adopted a transparent salary system at his new tech company **SumAll**. During the hiring process, he lets candidates know what the job pays—no negotiating allowed—and that everyone knows everyone else's salary. Sometimes seasoned job candidates balk. Atkison remembers one candidate who told him, "This is unfair because I can't actually negotiate." And although tensions sometimes surface, Atkison says talking to employees about their perceptions of inequity gives him the chance to explain why some people make more money than others.

Source: L. Pollak, "The Company Where Everyone Knows Everyone Else's Salary," *Planet Money* on National Public Radio, July 2, 2014, accessed May 8, 2015. http://www.npr.org/blogs/money/2014/07/02/327758712/the-company-where-everyone-knows-everyone-elses-salary.

---

couples working fifty-hour weeks, more and more employees are looking for ways to reduce stress and restore a balance between work and family. Consequently, it may make sense to ask employees to do less, not more; to have them identify and eliminate the 20 percent of their jobs that doesn't increase productivity or add value for customers; and to eliminate company-imposed requirements that really aren't critical to the performance of managers, employees, or the company (for example, unnecessary meetings and reports). According to Chinese labor laws, employees may not work more than thirty-six hours of overtime per month, or no more than nine overtime hours per week. However, after a catastrophic plant explosion and a series of employee suicides disrupted production at a Foxconn factory in China, factory workers, who assemble everything from iPads to laptop computers, worked 80 to 100 overtime hours each month on top of their 174 regular hours to make up for the production shortfalls. During this time, employees regularly worked twelve-hour shifts, six days a week, or sixty hours a month over the legal limit. As a result of pressure from Apple and from international workers' rights groups, Foxconn has agreed to immediately increase pay as much as 25 percent and limit the number of hours an employee works to forty-nine per week.[43]

Finally, managers should *make sure decision-making processes are fair*. Equity theory focuses on **distributive justice**, the perceived degree to which outcomes and rewards are fairly distributed or allocated. However, **procedural justice**, the perceived fairness of the procedures used to make reward allocation decisions, is just as important.[44] Procedural justice matters because even when employees are unhappy with their outcomes (that is, low pay), they're much less likely to be unhappy with company management if they believe that the procedures used to allocate outcomes were fair. For example, employees who are laid off tend to be hostile toward their employer when they perceive that the procedures leading to the layoffs were unfair. By contrast, employees who perceive layoff procedures to be fair tend to continue to support and trust their employers.[45] Also, if employees perceive that their outcomes are unfair (that is, distributive injustice) but that the decisions and procedures leading to those outcomes were fair (that is, procedural justice), they are much more likely to seek constructive ways of restoring equity, such as discussing these matters with their manager. By contrast, if employees perceive both distributive and procedural injustice, they may resort to more destructive tactics, such as withholding effort, absenteeism, tardiness, or even sabotage and theft.[46]

13-3 EXPECTANCY THEORY

One of the hardest things about motivating people is that not everyone is attracted to the same rewards. **Expectancy theory** says that people will be motivated to the extent to

Fair—or foolish?

Dan Price's announcement that he was going to cut his salary from $1 million to $70,000 per year so that he could increase the salary of his employees to $70,000 per year was met with a combination of cheers and jeers. Price is the CEO of Gravity Payments, a credit-card processing company, where his employees' average annual salary had been $48,000. And although his decision enjoyed a positive response from labor activists, others were skeptical that Price's method of creating equity would be successful. Management professor Patrick Rogers says, "Mr. Price probably thinks happy workers are productive workers. However, there's just no evidence that this is true. So he'll improve happiness, only in the short term, and will not improve productivity. Which doesn't bode well for his long-term viability as a firm."

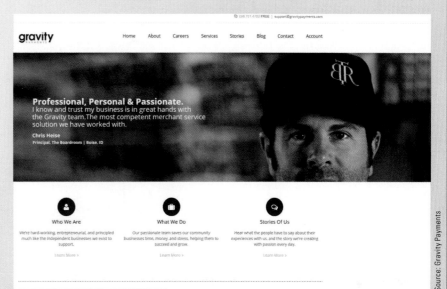

Source: Gravity Payments

Sources: P. Cohen, "Praise and Skepticism as One Executive Sets Minimum Wage to $70,000 a Year," *New York Times*, April 19, 2015, B1; A. Kaufman, "CEO Slashes $1 Million Salary to Give Lowest-Paid Workers a Raise," *Huffington Post*, April 14, 2015, accessed May 8, 2015. http://www.huffingtonpost.com/2015/04/14/gravity-payments-raise_n_7061676.html.

which they believe that their efforts will lead to good performance, that good performance will be rewarded, and that they will be offered attractive rewards.[47]

*Let's learn more about expectancy theory by examining **13-3a the components of expectancy theory** and **13-3b how to use expectancy theory as a motivational tool.***

13-3a Components of Expectancy Theory

Expectancy theory holds that people make conscious choices about their motivation. The three factors that affect those choices are valence, expectancy, and instrumentality.

Valence is simply the attractiveness or desirability of various rewards or outcomes. Expectancy theory recognizes that the same reward or outcome—say, a promotion—will be highly attractive to some people, will be highly disliked by others, and will not make much difference one way or the other to still others. Accordingly, when people are deciding how much effort to put forth, expectancy theory says that they will consider the valence of all possible rewards and outcomes that they can receive from their jobs.

The greater the sum of those valences, each of which can be positive, negative, or neutral, the more effort people will choose to put forth on the job. Consultant Carol Schultz spent nine years working for a company where the boss rewarded top-performing employees with five-day trips to expensive resorts, with the company paying for the flight, the hotel, and one dinner, leaving employees to pay for the rest of their food and all of their drinks and resort activities. Said Schultz, "It always irked me that they'd fly us to some expensive resort and expect us to pay for everything outside of our flight and hotel room. To me, this was no 'reward.'" In other words, when Schultz added up all of the valences, the positive valence of rewarding her with an expensive resort trip could not overcome the negative valence of getting stuck with large food, drink, and resort expenses.[48]

Expectancy is the perceived relationship between effort and performance. When expectancies are strong, employees believe that their hard work and efforts will result in good performance, so they work harder. By contrast, when

Valence the attractiveness or desirability of a reward or outcome

Expectancy the perceived relationship between effort and performance

Exhibit 13.5
Adding Expectancy Theory to the Model

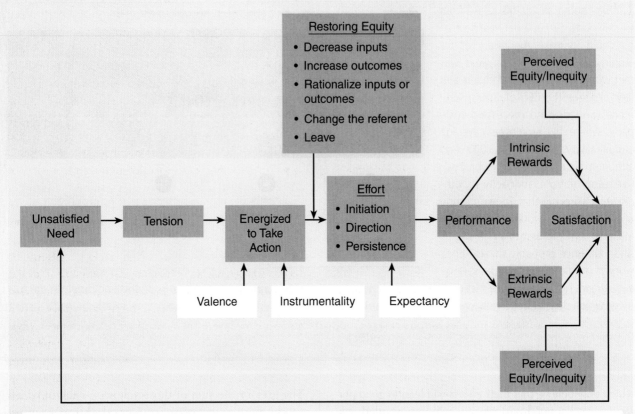

If rewards are attractive (valence) and linked to performance (instrumentality), then people are energized to take action. In other words, good performance gets them rewards that they want. Intended effort (that is, becoming energized to take action) turns into actual effort when people expect that their hard work and efforts will result in good performance. After all, why work hard if that hard work is wasted?

© Cengage Learning

expectancies are weak, employees figure that no matter what they do or how hard they work, they won't be able to perform their jobs successfully, so they don't work as hard.

Instrumentality is the perceived relationship between performance and rewards. When instrumentality is strong, employees believe that improved performance will lead to better and more rewards, so they choose to work harder. When instrumentality is weak, employees don't believe that better performance will result in more or better rewards, so they choose not to work as hard.

Expectancy theory holds that for people to be highly motivated, all three variables—valence,

Instrumentality the perceived relationship between performance and rewards

expectancy, and instrumentality—must be high. Thus, expectancy theory can be represented by the following simple equation:

**Motivation =
Valence × Expectancy × Instrumentality**

If any one of these variables (valence, expectancy, or instrumentality) declines, overall motivation will decline, too.

Exhibit 13.5 incorporates the expectancy theory variables into our motivation model. Valence and instrumentality combine to affect employees' willingness to put forth effort (that is, the degree to which they are energized to take action), while expectancy transforms intended effort ("I'm really going to work hard in this job") into actual effort. If you're offered rewards that you desire and you believe that you will in fact receive these rewards for good performance, you're highly likely to be energized to take action. However, you're not likely to actually exert effort unless you also believe that you can do the job (that is, that your efforts will lead to successful performance).

13-3b Motivating with Expectancy Theory

What practical steps can managers take to use expectancy theory to motivate employees? First, they can *systematically gather information to find out what employees want from their jobs*. In addition to individual managers directly asking employees what they want from their jobs (see Subsection 13-1d, "Motivating with the Basics"), companies need to survey their employees regularly to determine their wants, needs, and dissatisfactions. Because people consider the valence of all the possible rewards and outcomes that they can receive from their jobs, regular identification of wants, needs, and dissatisfactions gives companies the chance to turn negatively valent rewards and outcomes into positively valent rewards and outcomes, thus raising overall motivation and effort. Mark Peterman, vice president of client solutions at Maritz Incentives, says that individual employees are motivated in vastly different ways: "For some, being honored in front of one's peers is a great award, but for others, the thought of being put on display in front of peers embarrasses them." And companies have a long way to go to ensure that their employees feel valued, Peterman says. A Maritz survey found that only 27 percent of employees who want to be recognized by nonmonetary incentives are recognized that way.[49] Such findings suggest that employers should routinely survey employees to identify not only the range of rewards that are valued by most employees but also to understand the preferences of specific employees.

Second, managers can *take specific steps to link rewards to individual performance in a way that is clear and understandable to employees*. Unfortunately, most employees are extremely dissatisfied with the link between pay and performance in their organizations, and their companies are, too. Mercer's 2013 Pay for Performance Survey found that while 55 percent of firms say they link rewards to performance, only 42 percent measure to make sure that happens, and 48 percent say that programs linking performance to rewards need improvement.[50]

One way to establish a clear connection between pay and performance (see Chapter 11 for a discussion of compensation strategies) is for managers to publicize the way in which pay decisions are made. This is especially important given that only 52 percent of employees know how their pay increases are determined.[51] Inspired by fantasy sports leagues, **Clayton Homes** director of inside sales, David Schwall, had his sales managers become team "owners" who drafted sales representatives onto their sales teams, which competed against each other in a rotating schedule, with the best four teams moving on to the "championships." Sales reps (players) scored points by making more calls to sales leads, by increasing the percentage of leads who made appointments at Clayton Homes retail stores, and upping the percentage of leads whose phone calls were successfully transferred to a local store. Scores were tallied in real time, and the best scores were posted on TVs for everyone to see (poor scores were only visible within teams), with an individual's theme music played when sales milestones were reached. The connection between efforts and results was clear, prompting one sales rep to say, "When I saw one of my colleagues leaving, I thought—'Yes, now I can catch up and climb above him in the ranks.'" Calls rose by 18 percent, appointments jumped by 200 percent, as did visits to stores. And, after the "season" was over, employees were eager for the next season to begin, saying they missed the immediate feedback, recognition, and energy.[52]

Finally, managers should *empower employees to make decisions if management really wants them to believe that their hard work and effort will lead to good performance*. If valent rewards are linked to good performance, people should be energized to take action. However, this works only if they also believe that their efforts will lead to good performance. One of the ways that managers destroy the expectancy that hard work and effort will lead to good performance is by restricting what employees can do or by ignoring employees' ideas. In Chapter 9, you learned that *empowerment* is a feeling of intrinsic motivation in which workers perceive their work to have meaning and perceive themselves to be competent, to have an impact, and to be capable of self-determination.[53] So, if managers want workers to have strong expectancies, they should empower them to make decisions. Doing so will motivate employees to take active rather than passive roles in their work.

13-4 REINFORCEMENT THEORY

When used properly, rewards motivate and energize employees. But when used incorrectly, they can demotivate, baffle, and even anger them. Goals are supposed to motivate employees. But leaders who focus blindly on meeting goals at all costs often find that they destroy motivation.

Reinforcement theory says that behavior is a function of its consequences, that behaviors followed by positive consequences (that is, reinforced) will occur more frequently, and that behaviors either followed by negative consequences or not followed by positive consequences will occur less frequently.[54] United Airlines employees get a $50 monthly bonus if 80 percent of domestic or international flights arrive on time. The bonus increases to $100 when both domestic and international flights arrive on time 80 percent of the time. Motivated by the bonuses, United employees achieved on-time rates of 85.5 percent for domestic flights and 81.2 percent for international flights in November 2012, the second-best performance in five years. And during the Thanksgiving holiday, arguably the busiest travel season, United averaged 88.3 percent on-time arrivals.[55] More specifically, **reinforcement** is the process of changing behavior by changing the consequences that follow behavior.[56]

Reinforcement has two parts: reinforcement contingencies and schedules of reinforcement. **Reinforcement contingencies** are the cause-and-effect relationships between the performance of specific behaviors and specific consequences. For example, if you get docked an hour's pay for being late to work, then a reinforcement contingency exists between a behavior (being late to work) and a consequence (losing an hour's pay). A **schedule of reinforcement** is the set of rules regarding reinforcement contingencies such as which behaviors will be reinforced, which consequences will follow those behaviors, and the schedule by which those consequences will be delivered.[57]

Exhibit 13.6 incorporates reinforcement contingencies and reinforcement schedules into our motivation model. First, notice that extrinsic rewards and the schedules of reinforcement used to deliver them are the primary methods for creating reinforcement contingencies in organizations. In turn, those reinforcement contingencies directly affect valences (the attractiveness of rewards), instrumentality (the perceived link between rewards and performance), and effort (how hard employees will work).

Let's learn more about reinforcement theory by examining **13-4a the components of reinforcement theory, 13-4b the different schedules for delivering reinforcement, and 13-4c how to motivate with reinforcement theory.**

13-4a Components of Reinforcement Theory

As just described, *reinforcement contingencies* are the cause-and-effect relationships between the performance of specific behaviors and specific consequences. There are four kinds of reinforcement contingencies: positive reinforcement, negative reinforcement, punishment, and extinction.

Positive reinforcement strengthens behavior (that is, increases its frequency) by following behaviors with desirable consequences. While some companies are penalizing unhealthy behaviors, others have chosen to reward employees who practice healthy behaviors. For each of its full-time employees, **JetBlue** puts up to $400 a year into a wellness account that the employee can use to pay for a variety of healthy activities, ranging from smoking-cessation programs to Ironman triathlons. Similarly, at **Johnson & Johnson**, employees who participate in a health assessment and health coaching receive a $500 credit toward their annual medical insurance premium. Seventy-four percent (up from 57 percent in 2009) of employers now offer similar incentives with their wellness programs.[58]

Negative reinforcement strengthens behavior by withholding an unpleasant consequence when employees perform a specific behavior. Negative reinforcement is also called *avoidance learning* because workers perform a behavior to *avoid* a negative consequence. With the cost of health care averaging $12,136 annually per employee, companies are linking positive health actions and outcomes to the avoidance of negative consequences. At Honeywell, an automation and aerospace company, employees participating in voluntary health screenings to check their cholesterol, body mass

Reinforcement theory the theory that behavior is a function of its consequences, that behaviors followed by positive consequences will occur more frequently, and that behaviors followed by negative consequences, or not followed by positive consequences, will occur less frequently

Reinforcement the process of changing behavior by changing the consequences that follow behavior

Reinforcement contingencies cause-and-effect relationships between the performance of specific behaviors and specific consequences

Schedule of reinforcement rules that specify which behaviors will be reinforced, which consequences will follow those behaviors, and the schedule by which those consequences will be delivered

Positive reinforcement reinforcement that strengthens behavior by following behaviors with desirable consequences

Negative reinforcement reinforcement that strengthens behavior by withholding an unpleasant consequence when employees perform a specific behavior

Exhibit 13.6
Adding Reinforcement Theory to the Model

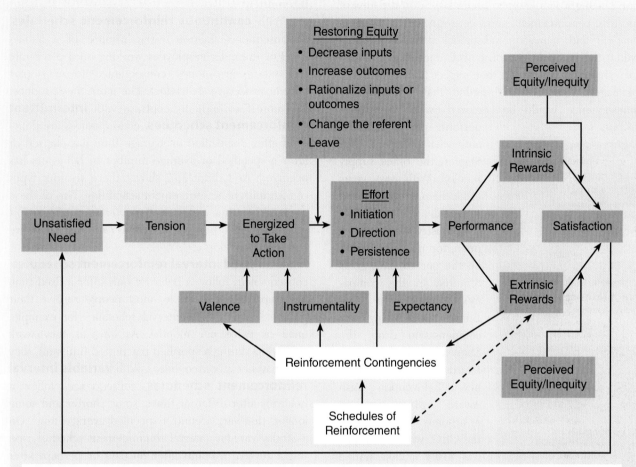

Extrinsic rewards and the schedules of reinforcement used to deliver them are the primary methods for creating reinforcement contingencies in organizations. In turn, those reinforcement contingencies directly affect valence (the attractiveness of rewards), instrumentality (the perceived link between rewards and performance), and effort (how hard employees will work).

© Cengage Learning

index, and more will avoid a $4,000 increase in the cost of their medical insurance. Even though the company was threatened with discrimination lawsuits, it stood by the program, saying, "Honeywell wants its employees to be well-informed about their health status. We don't believe that those employees who do work to lead healthier lifestyles should subsidize health care premiums for those who don't."[59] The company claims that 60 percent of those screened have found and addressed at least one health risk so far.

By contrast, **punishment** weakens behavior (that is, decreases its frequency) by following behaviors with undesirable consequences. For example, the standard

disciplinary or punishment process in most companies is an oral warning ("Don't ever do that again"), followed by a written warning ("This letter is to discuss the serious problem you're having with . . ."), followed by three days off without pay ("While you're at home not being paid, we want you to think hard about . . ."), followed by being fired ("That was your last chance"). Though punishment can weaken behavior, managers have to be careful to avoid the backlash that sometimes occurs when employees are punished at work.

Punishment reinforcement that weakens behavior by following behaviors with undesirable consequences

Extinction is a reinforcement strategy in which a positive consequence is no longer allowed to follow a previously reinforced behavior. By removing the positive consequence, extinction weakens the behavior, making it less likely to occur. Based on the idea of positive reinforcement, most companies give company leaders and managers substantial financial rewards when the company performs well. Based on the idea of extinction, you would then expect that leaders and managers would not be rewarded (that is, the positive consequence would be removed) when companies perform poorly. This is *not* what happened at Staples, the office supply retailer. With two years of declining revenue and store sales and a below-the-industry average stock price, top managers didn't hit the performance goals required in the company's compensation plan. But instead of seeing their compensation drop, the Staples board of directors awarded top managers a new "Reinvention Cash Award," which resulted in a bonus of $300,000 to the CEO, whose total pay was $10.8 million, and a bonus of $49,000 to the CFO, whose total pay was $2.2 million.[60] If companies really want pay to reinforce the right kinds of behaviors then, unlike at Staples, rewards have to be removed when company management doesn't produce successful performance.

13-4b Schedules for Delivering Reinforcement

As mentioned earlier, a *schedule of reinforcement* is the set of rules regarding reinforcement contingencies, such as which behaviors will be reinforced, which consequences will follow those behaviors, and the schedule by which those consequences will be delivered. There are two categories of reinforcement schedules: continuous and intermittent.

With **continuous reinforcement schedules**, a consequence follows every instance of a behavior. For example, employees working on a piece-rate pay system earn money (consequence) for every part they manufacture (behavior). The more they produce, the more they earn. By contrast, with **intermittent reinforcement schedules**, consequences are delivered after a specified or average time has elapsed or after a specified or average number of behaviors has occurred. As Exhibit 13.7 shows, there are four types of intermittent reinforcement schedules. Two of these are based on time and are called *interval reinforcement schedules*; the other two, known as *ratio schedules*, are based on behaviors.

With **fixed interval reinforcement schedules**, consequences follow a behavior only after a fixed time has elapsed. For example, most people receive their paychecks on a fixed interval schedule (for example, once or twice per month). As long as they work (behavior) during a specified pay period (interval), they get a paycheck (consequence). With **variable interval reinforcement schedules**, consequences follow a behavior after different times, some shorter and some longer, that vary around a specified average time. On a 90-day variable interval reinforcement schedule, you might receive a bonus after 80 days or perhaps after 100 days, but the average interval between performing your job well (behavior) and receiving your bonus (consequence) would be 90 days.

With **fixed ratio reinforcement schedules**, consequences are delivered following a specific number of behaviors. For example, a car salesperson might receive a $1,000 bonus after every ten sales. Therefore, a salesperson with only nine sales would not receive the bonus until he or she finally sold a tenth car.

With **variable ratio reinforcement schedules**, consequences are delivered following a different number of behaviors, sometimes more and sometimes less, that vary around a specified average number of behaviors. With a ten-car variable ratio reinforcement schedule, a salesperson might receive the bonus after seven car sales, or after twelve, eleven, or nine sales, but the average number of cars sold before receiving the bonus would be ten cars.

Which reinforcement schedules work best? In the past, the standard advice was to use continuous reinforcement when employees were learning new

---

Extinction reinforcement in which a positive consequence is no longer allowed to follow a previously reinforced behavior, thus weakening the behavior

Continuous reinforcement schedule a schedule that requires a consequence to be administered following every instance of a behavior

Intermittent reinforcement schedule a schedule in which consequences are delivered after a specified or average time has elapsed or after a specified or average number of behaviors has occurred

Fixed interval reinforcement schedule an intermittent schedule in which consequences follow a behavior only after a fixed time has elapsed

Variable interval reinforcement schedule an intermittent schedule in which the time between a behavior and the following consequences varies around a specified average

Fixed ratio reinforcement schedule an intermittent schedule in which consequences are delivered following a specific number of behaviors

Variable ratio reinforcement schedule an intermittent schedule in which consequences are delivered following a different number of behaviors, sometimes more and sometimes less, that vary around a specified average number of behaviors

Exhibit 13.7
Intermittent Reinforcement Schedules

	Fixed	Variable
INTERVAL (TIME)	Consequences follow behavior after a fixed time has elapsed.	Consequences follow behavior after different times, some shorter and some longer, that vary around a specific average time.
RATIO (BEHAVIOR)	Consequences follow a specific number of behaviors.	Consequences follow a different number of behaviors, sometimes more and sometimes less, that vary around a specified average number of behaviors.

© Cengage Learning

behaviors because reinforcement after each success leads to faster learning. Likewise, the standard advice was to use intermittent reinforcement schedules to maintain behavior after it is learned because intermittent rewards are supposed to make behavior much less subject to extinction.[61] Research shows, however, that except for interval-based systems, which usually produce weak results, the effectiveness of continuous reinforcement, fixed ratio, and variable ratio schedules differs very little.[62] In organizational settings, all three consistently produce large increases over noncontingent reward schedules. So managers should choose whichever of these three is easiest to use in their companies.

13-4c Motivating with Reinforcement Theory

What practical steps can managers take to use reinforcement theory to motivate employees? University of Nebraska business professor Fred Luthans, who has been studying the effects of reinforcement theory in organizations for more than a quarter of a century, says that there are five steps to motivating workers with reinforcement theory: *identify*, *measure*, *analyze*, *intervene*, and *evaluate* critical performance-related behaviors.[63]

Identify means singling out critical, observable, performance-related behaviors. These are the behaviors that are most important to successful job performance. In addition, they must also be easily observed so that they can be accurately measured. *Measure* means determining the baseline frequencies of these behaviors. In other words, find out how often workers perform them. *Analyze* means studying the causes and consequences of these behaviors. Analyzing the causes helps managers create the conditions

that produce these critical behaviors, and analyzing the consequences helps them determine if these behaviors produce the results that they want. *Intervene* means changing the organization by using positive and negative reinforcement to increase the frequency of these critical behaviors. *Evaluate* means assessing the extent to which the intervention actually changed workers' behavior. This is done by comparing behavior after the intervention to the original baseline of behavior before the intervention.

In addition to these five steps, managers should remember three other key things when motivating with reinforcement theory. First, *Don't reinforce the wrong behaviors*. Although reinforcement theory sounds simple, it's actually very difficult to put into practice. One of the most common mistakes is accidentally reinforcing the wrong behaviors. Sometimes managers reinforce behaviors that they don't want! If you want to become a merit-based company, stop rewarding behavior that is not exceptional, says Dave Anderson, a management consultant. According to him, "the average car salesperson in the United States sells ten cars per month, but many pay plans begin to pay bonuses at

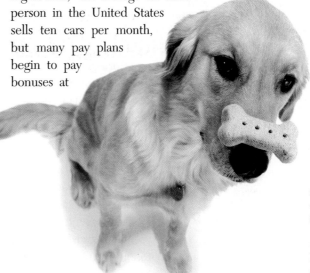

iStockphoto.com/Charles Mann

seven, eight, nine, or ten cars. Under a typical plan, an employee who sells eight cars gets a $200 bonus, another $250 for selling two additional cars, and $300 for selling two more cars. The total bonus for selling twelve cars in a month is $750." Anderson notes, "Based on national averages, such a pay plan financially rewards average and below-average results." Many of his clients have revised their system and only pay an $800 bonus to an employee *after* he or she has sold twelve cars, thus ending bonus payments for employees who sell fewer than the target amount of cars.[64] In this system, you pay more for better performance but don't fall into the trap of rewarding and endorsing the wrong things—that is, rewarding below-average performance.

Managers should also *correctly administer punishment at the appropriate time*. Many managers believe that punishment can change workers' behavior and help them improve their job performance. Furthermore, managers believe that fairly punishing workers also lets other workers know what is or isn't acceptable.[65] A danger of using punishment is that it can produce a backlash against managers and companies. But, if administered properly, punishment can weaken the frequency of undesirable behaviors without creating a backlash.[66] To be effective, the punishment must be strong enough to stop the undesired behavior and must be administered objectively (same rules applied to everyone), impersonally (without emotion or anger), consistently and contingently (each time improper behavior occurs), and quickly (as soon as possible following the undesirable behavior). In addition, managers should clearly explain what the appropriate behavior is and why the employee is being punished. Employees typically respond well when punishment is administered this way.[67]

Finally, managers should *choose the simplest and most effective schedule of reinforcement*. When choosing a schedule of reinforcement, managers need to balance effectiveness against simplicity. In fact, the more complex the schedule of reinforcement, the more likely it is to be misunderstood and resisted by managers and employees. For example, a forestry and logging company experimented with a unique variable ratio schedule. When tree-planters finished planting a bag of seedlings (about 1,000 seedlings per bag), they got to flip a coin. If they called the coin flip correctly

(heads or tails), they were paid $4, double the regular rate of $2 per bag. If they called the coin flip incorrectly, they got nothing. The company began having problems when several workers and a manager, who was a part-time minister, claimed that the coin flip was a form of gambling. Then another worker found that the company was taking out too much money for taxes from workers' paychecks. Because the workers didn't really understand the reinforcement schedule, they blamed the payment plan associated with it and accused the company of trying to cheat them out of their money. After all of these problems, the researchers who implemented the variable ratio schedule concluded that "the results of this study may not be so much an indication of the relative effectiveness of different schedules of reinforcement as they are an indication of the types of problems that one encounters when applying these concepts in an industrial setting."[68] In short, choose the simplest, most effective schedule of reinforcement. Because continuous reinforcement, fixed ratio, and variable ratio schedules are about equally effective, continuous reinforcement schedules may be the best choice in many instances by virtue of their simplicity.

13-5 GOAL-SETTING THEORY

The basic model of motivation with which we began this chapter showed that individuals feel tension after becoming aware of an unfulfilled need. When they experience tension, they search for and select courses of action that they believe will eliminate this tension. In other words, they direct their behavior toward something. This something is a goal. A **goal** is a target, objective, or result that someone tries to accomplish. **Goal-setting theory** says that people will be motivated to the extent to which they accept specific, challenging goals and receive feedback that indicates their progress toward goal achievement.

Let's learn more about goal setting by examining **13-5a the components of goal-setting theory** *and* **13-5b how to motivate with goal-setting theory**.

13-5a Components of Goal-Setting Theory

The basic components of goal-setting theory are goal specificity, goal difficulty, goal acceptance, and performance feedback.[69] **Goal specificity** is the extent to

Goal a target, objective, or result that someone tries to accomplish

Goal-setting theory the theory that people will be motivated to the extent to which they accept specific, challenging goals and receive feedback that indicates their progress toward goal achievement

Goal specificity the extent to which goals are detailed, exact, and unambiguous

Performance feedback is key to attaining goals. To improve employee awareness when it came to health, Accenture provided their employees with pedometers, to track the amount of steps they took daily.

which goals are detailed, exact, and unambiguous. Specific goals, such as "I'm going to have a 3.0 average this semester," are more motivating than general goals, such as "I'm going to get better grades this semester."

Goal difficulty is the extent to which a goal is hard or challenging to accomplish. Difficult goals, such as "I'm going to have a 3.5 average and make the dean's list this semester," are more motivating than easy goals, such as "I'm going to have a 2.0 average this semester."

Goal acceptance, which is similar to the idea of goal commitment discussed in Chapter 5, is the extent to which people consciously understand and agree to goals. Accepted goals, such as "I really want to get a 3.5 average this semester to show my parents how much I've improved," are more motivating than unaccepted goals, such as "My parents really want me to get a 3.5 average this semester, but there's so much more I'd rather do on campus than study!"

Performance feedback is information about the quality or quantity of past performance and indicates whether progress is being made toward the accomplishment of a goal. To improve employees' health and lower health care costs, Accenture, a global consulting company, gave 3,000 employees pedometers to record how many steps they took per day. More steps earned employees more points toward an electronic game from which they could earn cash awards. Linking awards to the feedback from pedometers led to employees

walking 500 more steps per day. But employees walked an additional 664 steps per day on average after a Facebook-like "friends" feature allowed them to compare their daily steps to their friends'. In short, in this case, performance feedback led to larger improvements than rewards. Stanford researcher Balaji Prabhakar said, "Money gets the ball rolling, but we know from the data that having friends has a big effect."[70]

How does goal setting work? To start, challenging goals focus employees' attention (that is, direction of effort) on the critical aspects of their jobs and away from unimportant areas. Goals also energize behavior. When faced with unaccomplished goals, employees typically develop plans and strategies to reach those goals. Goals also create tension between the goal, which is the desired future state of affairs, and where the employee or company is now, meaning the current state of affairs. This tension can be satisfied only by achieving or abandoning the goal. Finally, goals influence persistence. Because goals only go away when they are accomplished, employees are more likely to persist in their efforts in the presence of goals, especially with performance feedback. Exhibit 13.8 incorporates goals into the motivation model by showing how goals directly affect tension, effort, and the extent to which employees are energized to take action.

13-5b Motivating with Goal-Setting Theory

What practical steps can managers take to use goal-setting theory to motivate employees? Managers can do three things, beginning with *assign specific, challenging goals*. One of the simplest, most effective ways to motivate workers is to give them specific, challenging goals. At **The Container Store**, every morning begins with a huddle during which sales managers announce the sales goals for the day. Because 12 percent of sales go toward their higher-than-industry-average salaries, everyone understands that sales volume is critical. Minute-by-minute status reports are posted for all stores in a particular region so that staff can see not only if they are keeping up, but how they are performing compared to other stores. And staff members who are struggling are coached by managers so that they can better contribute to meeting the goal.[71]

Goal difficulty the extent to which a goal is hard or challenging to accomplish

Goal acceptance the extent to which people consciously understand and agree to goals

Performance feedback information about the quality or quantity of past performance that indicates whether progress is being made toward the accomplishment of a goal

Exhibit 13.8
Adding Goal-Setting Theory to the Model

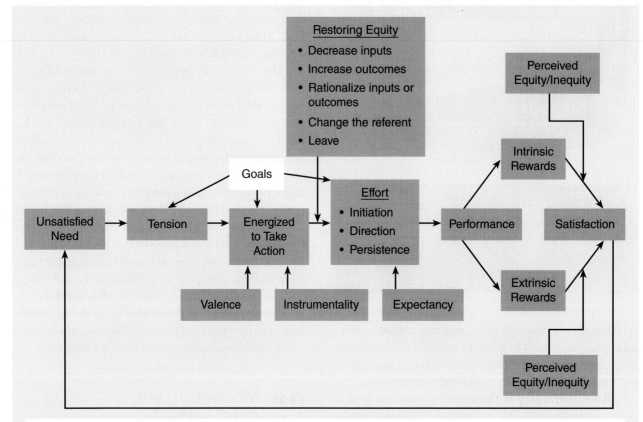

Goals create tension between the goal, which is the desired future state of affairs, and where the employee or company is now, meaning the current state of affairs. This tension can be satisfied only by achieving or abandoning the goal. Goals also energize behavior. When faced with unaccomplished goals, employees typically develop plans and strategies to reach those goals. Finally, goals influence persistence.

© Cengage Learning

Second, managers should *make sure workers truly accept organizational goals*. Specific, challenging goals won't motivate workers unless they really accept, understand, and agree to the organization's goals. For this to occur, people must see the goals as fair and reasonable. Employees must also trust management and believe that managers are using goals to clarify what is expected from them rather than to exploit or threaten them ("If you don't achieve these goals . . ."). Participative goal setting, in which managers and employees generate goals together, can help increase trust and understanding and thus acceptance of goals. Furthermore, providing workers with training can help increase goal acceptance, particularly when workers don't believe they are capable of reaching the organization's goals.[72]

Finally, managers should *provide frequent, specific, performance-related feedback*. After employees have accepted specific, challenging goals, they should receive frequent performance-related feedback so that they can track their progress toward goal completion. Feedback leads to stronger motivation and effort in three ways.[73] Receiving specific feedback about the quality of their performance can encourage employees who don't have specific, challenging goals to set goals to improve their performance. After people meet goals, performance feedback often encourages them to set higher, more difficult goals. And feedback lets people know whether they need to increase their efforts or change strategies in order to accomplish their goals.

13-6 MOTIVATING WITH THE INTEGRATED MODEL

We began this chapter by defining motivation as the set of forces that initiates, directs, and makes people persist in their efforts to accomplish a goal. We also asked the basic question that managers ask when they try to figure out how to motivate their workers: What leads to effort? The answer to that question is likely to be somewhat different for each employee. So, if you're having difficulty figuring out why people aren't motivated where you work, check your Review Card for a useful, theory-based starting point.

STUDY TOOLS 13

LOCATED IN TEXTBOOK
☐ Rip-out and review chapter review card

LOCATED AT WWW.CENGAGEBRAIN.COM
☐ Review key term flashcards and create your own from StudyBits
☐ Track your knowledge and understanding of key concepts, using the concept tracker
☐ Complete practice and graded quizzes to prepare for tests
☐ Complete interactive content within the exposition
☐ View chapter highlight box content at the beginning of each chapter

14 Leadership

Alan Jeffery/Shutterstock.com

LEARNING OUTCOMES

14-1 Explain what leadership is.

14-2 Describe who leaders are and what effective leaders do.

14-3 Explain Fiedler's contingency theory.

14-4 Describe how path-goal theory works.

14-5 Explain the normative decision theory.

14-6 Explain how visionary leadership (that is, charismatic or transformational) helps leaders achieve strategic leadership.

After you finish this chapter, go to **PAGE 309** for **STUDY TOOLS**

LEADERS VERSUS MANAGERS

If you've ever been in charge, or even just thought about it, chances are you've considered questions such as these: Do I have what it takes to lead? What are the most important things leaders do? How can I transform a poorly performing department, division, or company? Do I need to adjust my leadership depending on the situation and the employee? Why doesn't my leadership inspire people? If you feel overwhelmed at the prospect of being a leader, you're not alone—millions of leaders in organizations across the world struggle with these fundamental leadership issues on a daily basis.

The most common view of leaders is that they are "in charge." But leadership is about more than just making decisions and giving orders. Bill Flemming, president of **Skanska USA Building**, a division of one of the world's largest construction companies, notes, "When people [I lead] ask me a question [about solving a problem], I don't always answer it with, 'Yes, this is what I want you to do,' or, 'This is what I'd do.'" He goes on, "I've seen organizations where the boss makes all the decisions. That's not leadership; that's a boss. I don't want to be the boss, I want to be the leader. So I want to get you to help me figure out what we've got to do here. Because if you're deeply immersed in the problem or the issue, you probably know a lot more about it than I'm going to know. So what do you think is going to work?"[1]

Whether you construct buildings, create and innovate to bring new products to markets, or simply help a company gain competitive advantage and thereby increase profits, **leadership** is the process of influencing others to achieve group or organizational goals. The knowledge and skills you'll learn in this chapter won't make the task of leadership less daunting, but they will help you navigate your journey as a leader.

According to late business professor Warren Bennis, the primary difference between leaders and managers is that leaders are concerned with doing the right thing, while managers are concerned with doing things right.[2] In other words, leaders begin with the question "What should we be doing?" while managers start with "How can we do what we're already doing better?" Etsy.com is an online marketplace where creative entrepreneurs sell items, such as arts and crafts for homes, gifts, jewelry, and clothes, to customers. When Chad Dickerson inherited the difficult task of replacing Etsy's founder and CEO, he focused on the leadership issue of what Etsy should be doing. He said, "We were losing our minds; the site was blowing up every day. I started a small group of the best engineers, and I called it the Breakfast Club." He told them, "I know you don't like to get up early, but I want you to come here for breakfast three days a week, and we're going to talk about the future only, nothing about what's going on [today]. We're going to build the Etsy future."[3]

Leaders focus on vision, mission, goals, and objectives, while managers focus on productivity and efficiency. Managers see themselves as preservers of the status quo, while leaders see themselves as promoters of change and challengers of the status quo in that they encourage creativity and risk taking. Virginia Rometty, IBM's CEO, plans to keep her $100 billion company growing and innovating by doing one thing—pressing managers and employees to take risks and embrace change. Rometty recently visited a team of IBM software developers, and when the team leader assured her they would meet their year-end roll-out target, Rometty whipped around and replied, "No, no, no! Too slow. What can I do you help you move faster?" For this year's planning retreat, she told her top executives, "Your assignment: one paragraph on what is IBM 10 years from now—no constraints, no sacred cows." When IBM leaders asked for more time and money to roll out IBM's SmartCloud services, she told them, "The market is moving too fast. I can't give you more time." Finally, on a Saturday morning at Starbucks near his home, IBM VP Jeff Smith saw Rometty out of the corner of his eye and pulled his baseball cap down to avoid being seen. Rometty saw him nonetheless, walked straight over to him, lifted his cap, and asked, "What are we doing to change the company?"[4]

Another difference is that managers have a relatively short-term perspective, while leaders take a long-term view. Managers are concerned with control and limiting the choices of others, while leaders are more concerned with expanding people's choices and options.[5] Managers also solve problems so that others can do their work, while leaders inspire and motivate others to find their own solutions. Finally, managers are also more concerned with *means*, how to get things done, while leaders are more concerned with *ends*, what gets done.

Although leaders are different from managers, organizations need them both. Managers are critical to getting out the day-to-day work, and leaders are critical to inspiring employees and setting the organization's long-term direction. The key issue for any organization is the extent to which

> **Leadership** the process of influencing others to achieve group or organizational goals

it is properly led and properly managed. As Bennis said in summing up the difference between leaders and managers, "American organizations (and probably those in much of the rest of the industrialized world) are underled and overmanaged. They do not pay enough attention to doing the right thing, while they pay too much attention to doing things right."[6]

14-2 WHO LEADERS ARE AND WHAT LEADERS DO

Chuck Robbins, CEO of **Cisco**, has a strong background in sales and is known as a relationship builder who is responsive and has a warm personal style.[7] By contrast, Tony Rothman, CEO of **Sony Pictures**, is known for being a hard-nosed businessman, focused more on tasks than people, who is not afraid to cut costs or ruffle the feathers of the studio's talent to bring a movie in on or under budget.[8]

> **Trait theory** a leadership theory that holds that effective leaders possess a similar set of traits or characteristics
>
> **Traits** relatively stable characteristics, such as abilities, psychological motives, or consistent patterns of behavior

Which one is likely to be successful as a CEO? According to a survey of 1,542 senior managers, it's the extrovert. Of those 1,542 senior managers, 47 percent felt that extroverts make better CEOs, while 65 percent said that

Sony CEO, Tony Rothman, is known for being a hard-nosed businessman, focused more on tasks than people.

being an introvert hurts a CEO's chances of success.[9] So clearly, senior managers believe that extroverted CEOs are better leaders. But are they? Not necessarily. In fact, a relatively high percentage of CEOs, 40 percent, are introverts. Yahoo! CEO Marissa Mayer admits she is an introvert who suffers from shyness, so much so that she even wants to leave parties at her home. She says, "I will literally look at my watch and say, 'You can't leave until time X. And if you're still having a terrible time at time X, you can leave.'" She's learned, though, that if she stays till "time X," she relaxes and begins to enjoy herself.[10]

So, what makes a good leader? Does leadership success depend on who leaders are, such as introverts or extroverts, or on what leaders do and how they behave?

Let's learn more about who leaders are by investigating 14-2a leadership traits and 14-2b leadership behaviors.

14-2a Leadership Traits

Trait theory is one way to describe who leaders are. **Trait theory** says that effective leaders possess a similar set of traits or characteristics. **Traits** are relatively stable characteristics such as abilities, psychological motives, or consistent patterns of behavior. For example, trait theory holds that leaders are taller and more confident and have greater physical stamina (that is, higher energy levels) than nonleaders. In fact, studies show we perceive those in authority as being taller than they actually are, and that taller people see themselves as more qualified to lead.[11] Indeed, while just 14.5 percent of men are six feet tall, 58 percent of *Fortune* 500 CEOs are six feet or taller. Author Malcolm Gladwell says, "We have a sense, in our minds, of what a leader is supposed to look like, and that stereotype is so powerful that when someone fits it, we simply become blind to other considerations."[12] Likewise, in terms of physical stamina, companies whose CEOs have run and finished a marathon have a stock valuation that is 5 percent larger than those whose CEO had not.[13] Trait theory is also known as the "great person" theory because early versions of the theory stated that leaders are born, not made. In other words, you either have the right stuff to be a leader, or you don't. And if you don't, there is no way to get it.

For some time, it was thought that trait theory was wrong and that there are no consistent trait differences between leaders and nonleaders, or between effective and ineffective leaders. However, more recent evidence shows that "successful leaders are not like other people," that successful leaders are indeed different from the rest of us.[14] More specifically, leaders are different from nonleaders in the following traits: drive, the desire to lead, honesty/integrity, self-confidence, emotional stability, cognitive ability, and knowledge of the business.[15]

Drive refers to high levels of effort and is characterized by achievement, motivation, initiative, energy, and tenacity. In terms of achievement and ambition, leaders always try to make improvements or achieve success in what they're doing. Because of their initiative, they have strong desires to promote change or solve problems. Leaders typically have more energy—they have to, given the long hours they put in and followers' expectations that they be positive and upbeat. Thus, leaders must have physical, mental, and emotional vitality. Leaders are also more tenacious than nonleaders and are better at overcoming obstacles and problems that would deter most of us. In an interview of Jack Ma, founder and board chair of China-based e-commerce giant **Alibaba**, veteran journalist Charlie Rose mentioned that Ma had faced a lot of rejection. Ma replied, "There's an examination for young people [in China] to go to university. I failed it three times. I failed a lot. So, I applied to thirty different jobs and got rejected. I went for a job with the police; they said, 'You're no good.' I even went to KFC when it came to my city. Twenty-four people went for the job. Twenty-three were accepted. I was the only guy. . . ."[16]

Successful leaders also have a stronger *desire to lead*. They want to be in charge and think about ways to influence or convince others about what should or shouldn't be done. *Honesty/integrity* is also important to leaders. *Honesty*, being truthful with others, is a cornerstone of leadership. Without it, leaders won't be trusted. When leaders are honest, subordinates are willing to overlook other flaws. Mike Lazzo, the executive vice president and creative director of **Comedy Central's Adult Swim**, is known for giving honest feedback directly—even when it's negative. Robert Smigel, creator of "The Jack and Triumph Show," says, "He can be humorously blunt, which is refreshing compared to other network people who think you can't take criticism without hearing five compliments first."[17] *Integrity* is the extent to which leaders do what they say they will do. Leaders may be honest and have good intentions, but if they don't consistently deliver on what they promise, they won't be trusted.

Self-confidence, or believing in one's abilities, also distinguishes leaders from nonleaders. Self-confident leaders are more decisive and assertive and are more likely to gain others' confidence. Moreover, self-confident leaders will admit mistakes because they view them as learning opportunities rather than as refutations of their leadership capabilities. LinkedIn CEO Jeff Weiner admits how challenging it can be for managers to recognize their mistakes. One of the most difficult mistakes, he says, can be accepting when new hires don't work out.

Does Coke's CEO Lack Sparkle?

For a company whose current motto "Open Happiness" is only one in a history of upbeat, feel-good slogans, Coke's CEO Muhtar Kent can be decidedly gruff. Critics complain that he surrounds himself with "yes people" and may not realize when he's shutting down discussion. Coke veteran Sandy Douglas says, "It's a full-contact sport to argue strategy with Mr. Kent." Despite an abrupt, and perhaps autocratic, leadership style, Kent is devoted to Coke and its operations. He even carries a paint chip with the exact color of Coke red in his pocket so that, wherever he is in the world, he can compare it to delivery trucks, bottles, cans, and vending machines. And he understands the challenges facing the soft drink industry. "If we don't do what we need to do quickly, effectively, execute 100%," he says, "then somebody else will come and do it for us."

Source: M. Esterl, "Coke's Chief's Solution for Lost Fizz: More Soda," *Wall Street Journal*, A1, A12.

Muhtar Kent, CEO of Coca-Cola

Simon Dawson/Bloomberg/Getty Images

"It's not easy to admit this to yourself. After all, as the CEO or owner, you're largely responsible for the fact that the employee is now in over his or her head," Weiner says. "Plus, admitting the mistake means that you'll have to overcome your internal wiring to 'finish the job' and 'not give up.' Persistence is often an admirable trait, but not when it prevents you from making a necessary midcourse adjustment."[18]

Leaders also have *emotional stability*. Even when things go wrong, they remain even-tempered and consistent in their outlook and in the way they treat others. Leaders who can't control their emotions, who anger quickly or attack and blame others for mistakes, are unlikely to be trusted.

Leaders are also smart—they typically have strong *cognitive abilities*. This doesn't mean that leaders are necessarily geniuses—far from it. But it does mean that leaders have the capacity to analyze large amounts of seemingly unrelated, complex information and see patterns, opportunities, or threats where others might not see them. Finally, leaders also know their stuff, which means they have superior technical knowledge about the businesses they run. Leaders who have a good *knowledge of the business* understand the key technological decisions and concerns facing their companies. More often than not, studies indicate that effective leaders have long, extensive experience in their industries. Tom Staggs has been with **Walt Disney Co.** nearly forty years, starting as a strategic planner. As CFO, he was involved in digital strategy and acquiring Pixar and Marvel. He ran Disney's parks and resorts division, rolling out the My Magic Plus wireless wristband technology to help park guests make purchases and better plan their trips, and oversaw the $5.5 billion construction of Disney Shanghai. In 2015, he was promoted to Chief Operating Officer and is a leading candidate to be the next CEO.[19]

14-2b Leadership Behaviors

Thus far, you've read about who leaders *are*. But traits alone are not enough to make a successful leader. They are, however, a precondition for success. After all, it's hard to imagine a truly successful leader who lacks most of these qualities. Leaders who have these traits (or many of them) must then take actions that encourage people to achieve group or organizational goals.[20] Accordingly, we now examine what leaders *do*, meaning the behaviors they perform or the actions they take to influence others to achieve group or organizational goals.

Researchers at the University of Michigan, Ohio State University, and the University of Texas examined the specific behaviors that leaders use to improve subordinate satisfaction and performance. Hundreds of studies were conducted, and hundreds of leader behaviors were examined. At all three universities, two basic leader behaviors emerged as central to successful leadership: initiating structure (called *job-centered leadership* at the University of Michigan and *concern for production* at the University of Texas) and considerate leader behavior (called *employee-centered leadership* at the University of Michigan and *concern for people* at the University of Texas).[21] These two leader behaviors form the basis for many of the leadership theories discussed in this chapter.

Tom Staggs has had extremely successful career at Walt Disney Co. His accomplishments include the acquisition of Pixar and the construction and completion of Disney Shanghai.

Initiating structure is the degree to which a leader structures the roles of followers by setting goals, giving directions, setting deadlines, and assigning tasks. A leader's ability to initiate structure primarily affects subordinates' job performance. CEO Carlos Ghosn has decreed that by 2016 Nissan will obtain an 8 percent global market share and an 8 percent profit. This unusually specific strategic plan, called "Nissan Power 88," has clear deadlines, direction, and tasks. It specifies that by 2016 Nissan will deliver an all-new car "every six weeks for six years," for a total of sixty-six different models worldwide, it will launch ninety new technologies (fifteen per year) for its cars, sell 1.56 million electric cars, and its Infiniti brand will sell 10 percent of all luxury cars worldwide. Said Ghosn, "Nissan Power 88 is a demanding business plan, but our company has a proven track record of achieving challenging objectives."[22]

Consideration is the extent to which a leader is friendly, approachable, and supportive and shows concern for employees. Consideration primarily affects subordinates' job satisfaction. Specific leader consideration behaviors include listening to employees' problems and concerns, consulting with employees before making decisions, and treating employees as equals. Cheryl Bachelder, CEO of Popeye's, spends a lot of time listening to franchisees who own and run Popeye's restaurants. Before her arrival, Popeye's had suffered several years of management turnover, strained relationships with franchisees, and weak sales. To turn the chain around, Bachelder outlined a very specific plan and then consulted franchisees every step of the way. She listened when they asked to delay plans to remodel restaurants until they got their sales up and could afford the construction. Determining a national beverage supplier (that is, Coke or Pepsi) is a contentious issue in fast food, but Popeye's needed to consolidate for cost savings. So, she convened a team, with equal numbers of franchisees who sold Coke and Pepsi, and then had them listen to supplier presentations and pick the winner.[23] Asked about her leadership style, Bachelder responded, "We give dignity to human beings, and we attempt to be humble. People perform better under those conditions."[24]

Although researchers at all three universities generally agreed that initiating structure and consideration were basic leader behaviors, their interpretation differed on how these two behaviors are related to one another and which are necessary for effective leadership. The University of Michigan studies indicated that initiating structure and consideration were mutually exclusive behaviors on opposite ends of the same continuum. In other words, leaders who wanted to be more considerate would have to do less initiating of structure (and vice versa). The University of Michigan studies also indicated that only considerate leader behaviors (that is, employee-centered behaviors) were associated with successful leadership. By contrast, researchers at Ohio State University and the University of Texas found that initiating structure and consideration were independent behaviors, meaning that leaders can be considerate and initiate structure at the same time. Additional evidence confirms this finding.[25] The same researchers also concluded that the most effective leaders were strong on both initiating structure and considerate leader behaviors.

This "high-high" approach can be seen in the upper-right corner of the Blake/Mouton leadership grid, shown in Exhibit 14.1. Blake and Mouton used two leadership behaviors, concern for people (that is, consideration) and concern for production (that is, initiating structure), to categorize five different leadership styles. Both behaviors are rated on a nine-point scale, with 1 representing "low" and 9 representing "high." Blake and Mouton suggest that a "high-high," or 9,9, leadership style is the best. They call this style *team management* because leaders who use it display a high concern for people (9) and a high concern for production (9).

By contrast, leaders use a 9,1 *authority-compliance* leadership style when they have a high concern for production and a low concern for people. A 1,9 *country club* style occurs when leaders care about having a friendly, enjoyable work environment but don't really pay much attention to production or performance. The worst leadership style, according to the grid, is the 1,1 *impoverished* leader, who shows little concern for people or production and does the bare minimum needed to keep his or her job. Finally, the 5,5 *middle-of-the-road* style occurs when leaders show a moderate amount of concern for both people and production.

Is the team management style, with a high concern for production and a high concern for people, the best leadership style? Logically, it would seem so. Why wouldn't you want to show high concern for both people and production? Nonetheless, nearly fifty years of research indicates that there isn't one best leadership style. The best leadership style depends on the situation. In other words, no one leadership behavior by itself and no one combination of leadership behaviors works well across all situations and employees.

Initiating structure the degree to which a leader structures the roles of followers by setting goals, giving directions, setting deadlines, and assigning tasks

Consideration the extent to which a leader is friendly, approachable, and supportive and shows concern for employees

Exhibit 14.1
Blake/Mouton Leadership Grid

High 9

1,9 Country Club Management
Thoughtful attention to needs of people for satisfying relationships leads to a comfortable, friendly organizational atmosphere and work tempo.

9,9 Team Management
Work accomplished is from committed people. Interdependence through a common stake in organizational purpose leads to relationships of trust and respect.

5,5 Middle-of-the-Road Management
Adequate organization performance is possible through balancing the need to get work done with maintaining morale of people at a satisfactory level.

1,1 Impoverished Management
Exertion of minimum effort to get required work done is appropriate to sustain organization membership.

9,1 Authority-Compliance
Efficiency in operations results from arranging conditions of work in such a way that human elements interfere to a minimum degree.

Low 1

Concern for people (vertical axis: High 9, 8, 7, 6, 5, 4, 3, 2, Low 1)

Concern for production (horizontal axis: 1 Low, 2, 3, 4, 5, 6, 7, 8, 9 High)

Source: R. R. Blake and A. A. McCanse, "The Leadership Grid®," Leadership Dilemmas—Grid Solutions (Houston: Gulf Publishing Company), 21.

14-3 PUTTING LEADERS IN THE RIGHT SITUATION: FIEDLER'S CONTINGENCY THEORY

After leader traits and behaviors, the situational approach to leadership is the third major method used in the study of leadership. We'll review three major situational approaches to leadership—Fiedler's contingency theory, path-goal theory,

Leadership style the way a leader generally behaves toward followers

and Vroom, Yetton, and Jago's normative decision model. All assume that the effectiveness of any **leadership style**, the way a leader generally behaves toward followers, depends on the situation.[26] A study of 130 restaurants in a pizza franchise examined the interaction between how extroverted store managers were and how involved employees were in trying "to bring about improved procedures [in the store.]" Profits were 16 percent *above* average in stores with extroverted managers and less involved employees. In those instances, the strengths of the more outgoing boss fit well with the less involved employees. By contrast, profits were 14 percent *below* average in stores with extroverted leaders and highly involved employees. Why? Because the extroverted leaders were less comfortable with employees who wanted a say in making improvements. Again, leadership success depends on the situation.[27]

According to situational leadership theories, there is no one best leadership style. But one of these situational theories differs from the other three in one significant way. Fiedler's contingency theory assumes that leadership styles are consistent and difficult to change. Therefore, leaders must be placed in or matched to a situation that fits their leadership style. By contrast, the other three situational theories all assume that leaders are capable of adapting and adjusting their leadership styles to fit the demands of different situations.

Fiedler's **contingency theory** states that in order to maximize work group performance, leaders must be matched to the right leadership situation.[28] More specifically, the first basic assumption of Fiedler's theory is that leaders are effective when the work groups they lead perform well. So, instead of judging leaders' effectiveness by what they do (that is, initiating structure and consideration) or who they are (that is, trait theory), Fiedler assesses leaders by the conduct and performance of the people they supervise. Second, Fiedler assumes that leaders are generally unable to change their leadership styles and that they will be more effective when their styles are matched to the proper situation. "There are some things that each of us are naturally good at, and there are some things that we probably are going to struggle with," says Angus Davis, CEO of Swipely, which makes customer-management software. "It's better to find a way to just work around your flaws rather than focusing too much on just trying to correct them. If you're a great guitar player, it's silly to focus too much on your piano skills."[29]

Third, Fiedler assumes that the favorableness of a situation for a leader depends on the degree to which the situation permits the leader to influence the behavior of group members. Fiedler's third assumption is consistent with our definition of leadership as the process of influencing others to achieve group or organizational goals. In other words, in addition to traits, behaviors, and a favorable situation to match, leaders have to be allowed to lead.

*Let's learn more about Fiedler's contingency theory by examining **14-3a the least preferred coworker and leadership styles, 14-3b situational favorableness,** and **14-3c how to match leadership styles to situations**.*

14-3a Leadership Style: Least Preferred Coworker

When Fiedler refers to *leadership style*, he means the way that leaders generally behave toward their followers. Do the leaders yell and scream and blame others when things go wrong? Or do they correct mistakes by listening and then quietly but directly make their point? Do they take credit for others' work when things go right? Or do they make sure that those who did the work receive the credit they rightfully deserve? Do they let others make their own decisions and hold them accountable for the results? Or do they micromanage, insisting that all decisions be approved first by them? Fiedler also assumes that leadership styles are tied to leaders' underlying needs and personalities. Because personalities and needs are relatively stable, he assumes that leaders are generally incapable of changing their leadership styles. In other words, the way that leaders treat people now is probably the way they've always treated others. So, according to Fiedler, if your boss's first instinct is to yell and scream and blame others, chances are he or she has always done that.

Fiedler uses a questionnaire called the Least Preferred Coworker (LPC) scale to measure leadership style. When completing the LPC scale, people are instructed to consider all of the people with whom they have ever worked and then to choose the one person with whom they have worked *least* well. Fiedler explains, "This does not have to be the person you liked least well, but should be the one person with whom you have the most trouble getting the job done."[30]

Would you describe your LPC as pleasant, friendly, supportive, interesting, cheerful, and sincere? Or would you describe the person as unpleasant, unfriendly, hostile, boring, gloomy, and insincere? People who describe their LPC in a positive way (scoring 64 and above) have *relationship-oriented* leadership styles. After all, if they can still be positive about their least preferred coworker, they must be people-oriented. By contrast, people who describe their LPC in a negative way (scoring 57 or below) have *task-oriented* leadership styles. Given a choice,

> **Contingency theory** a leadership theory states that to maximize work group performance, leaders must be matched to the situation that best fits their leadership style

they'll focus first on getting the job done and second on making sure everyone gets along. Finally, those with moderate scores (from 58 to 63) have a more *flexible* leadership style and can be somewhat relationship-oriented or somewhat task-oriented.

14-3b Situational Favorableness

Fiedler assumes that leaders will be more effective when their leadership styles are matched to the proper situation. More specifically, Fiedler defines **situational favorableness** as the degree to which a particular situation either permits or denies a leader the chance to influence the behavior of group members.[31] In highly favorable situations, leaders find that their actions influence followers. But in highly unfavorable situations, leaders have little or no success influencing the people they are trying to lead.

Three situational factors determine the favorability of a situation: leader-member relations, task structure, and position power. The most important situational factor is **leader-member relations**, which refers to how well followers respect, trust, and like their leaders. When leader-member relations are good, followers trust the leader, and

there is a friendly work atmosphere. **Task structure** is the degree to which the requirements of a subordinate's tasks are clearly specified. With highly structured tasks, employees have clear job responsibilities, goals, and procedures. **Position power** is the degree to which leaders are able to hire, fire, reward, and punish workers. The more influence leaders have over hiring, firing, rewards, and punishments, the greater their power.

Exhibit 14.2 shows how leader-member relations, task structure, and position power can be combined into eight situations that differ in their favorability to leaders. In general, Situation I, on the left side of Exhibit 14.2, is the most favorable leader situation. Followers like and trust their leaders and know what to do because their tasks are highly structured. Also, the leaders have the formal power to influence workers through hiring, firing, rewarding, and punishing them. Therefore, it's relatively easy for a leader to influence followers in Situation I. By contrast, Situation VIII, on the right side of Exhibit 14.2, is the least favorable situation for leaders. Followers don't like or trust their leaders. Plus, followers are not sure what they're supposed to be doing, given that their tasks or jobs are highly unstructured. Finally, leaders find it difficult to influence followers because they don't have the ability to hire, fire, reward, or punish the people who work for them. In short, it's very difficult to influence followers given the conditions found in Situation VIII.

14-3c Matching Leadership Styles to Situations

After studying thousands of leaders and followers in hundreds of different situations, Fiedler found that the

Situational favorableness the degree to which a particular situation either permits or denies a leader the chance to influence the behavior of group members

Leader-member relations the degree to which followers respect, trust, and like their leaders

Task structure the degree to which the requirements of a subordinate's tasks are clearly specified

Position power the degree to which leaders are able to hire, fire, reward, and punish workers

How LPC is described	Leadership style
positively	relationship-oriented
negatively	task-oriented
moderately	flexible

Exhibit 14.2
Situational Favorableness

Leader-Member Relations	Good	Good	Good	Good	Poor	Poor	Poor	Poor
Task Structure	High	High	Low	Low	High	High	Low	Low
Position Power	Strong	Weak	Strong	Weak	Strong	Weak	Strong	Weak
Situation	I	II	III	IV	V	VI	VII	VIII
	Favorable		**Moderately Favorable**				**Unfavorable**	

© Cengage Learning

performance of relationship- and task-oriented leaders followed the pattern displayed in Exhibit 14.3.

Relationship-oriented leaders with high LPC scores were better leaders (that is, their groups performed more effectively) under moderately favorable situations. In moderately favorable situations, the leader may be liked somewhat, tasks may be somewhat structured, and the leader may have some position power. In this situation, a relationship-oriented leader improves leader-member relations, which is the most important of the three situational factors. In turn, morale and performance improve.

By contrast, as Exhibit 14.3 shows, task-oriented leaders with low LPC scores are better leaders in highly favorable and unfavorable situations. Task-oriented leaders do well in favorable situations where leaders are liked, tasks are structured, and the leader has the power to hire, fire, reward, and punish. In these favorable situations, task-oriented leaders effectively step on the gas of a well-tuned car. Their focus on performance sets the

goal for the group, which then charges forward to meet it. But task-oriented leaders also do well in unfavorable situations where leaders are disliked, tasks are unstructured, and the leader doesn't have the power to hire, fire, reward, and punish. In these unfavorable situations, the task-oriented leader sets goals, which focus attention on performance and clarify what needs to be done, thus overcoming low task structure. This is enough to jump-start performance even if workers don't like or trust the leader.

Finally, though not shown in Exhibit 14.3, people with moderate LPC scores, who can be somewhat relationship-oriented or somewhat task-oriented, tend to do fairly well in all situations because they can adapt their behavior. Typically, though, they don't perform quite as well as relationship-oriented or task-oriented leaders whose leadership styles are well matched to the situation.

Recall, however, that Fiedler assumes leaders to be incapable of changing their leadership styles.

Exhibit 14.3
Matching Leadership Styles to Situations

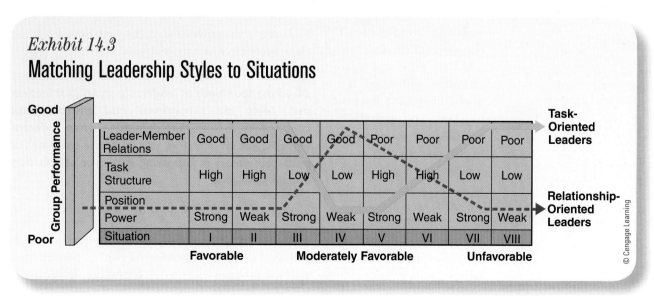

© Cengage Learning

Accordingly, the key to applying Fiedler's contingency theory in the workplace is to accurately measure and match leaders to situations or to teach leaders how to change situational favorableness by changing leader-member relations, task structure, or position power. Although matching or placing leaders in appropriate situations works particularly well, practicing managers have had little luck reengineering situations to fit their leadership styles. The primary problem, as you've no doubt realized, is the complexity of the theory.

In a study designed to teach leaders how to reengineer their situations to fit their leadership styles, Fiedler found that most of the leaders simply did not understand what they were supposed to do to change their situations. Furthermore, if they didn't like their LPC profile (perhaps they felt they were more relationship-oriented than their scores indicated), they arbitrarily changed it to better suit their view of themselves. Of course, the theory won't work as well if leaders are attempting to change situational factors to fit their perceived leadership style rather than their real leadership style.[32]

14-4 ADAPTING LEADER BEHAVIOR: PATH-GOAL THEORY

Just as its name suggests, **path-goal theory** states that leaders can increase subordinate satisfaction and performance by clarifying and clearing the paths to goals and by increasing the number and kinds of rewards available for goal attainment. Said another way, leaders need to clarify how followers can achieve organizational goals, take care of problems that prevent followers from achieving goals, and then find more and varied rewards to motivate followers to achieve those goals.[33]

Leaders must meet two conditions for path clarification, path clearing, and rewards to increase followers' motivation and effort. First, leader behavior must be a source of immediate or future satisfaction for followers.

The things you do as a leader must either please your followers today or lead to activities or rewards that will satisfy them in the future. One of the key cultural principles followed by Charlie Kim, CEO of New York-based Next Jump, which runs web-based reward programs for 90,000 companies, is "Better Me + Better You = Better Us." Kim says, "The culture we're building is predicated on the concept of long-term, sustained happiness."[34] This is why Next Jump's leadership frequently asks its people what *would* make them happier. Because of the long hours they put in, employees were spending half a day per weekend in a NYC laundromat doing their laundry. So they asked if washers and dryers could be installed at work to be used (and which they would pay for) when working late hours. Recognizing the problem (not laundry, but the secondary effect of long hours resulting in lost weekend time), Next Jump now pays for laundry service. Employees bring in laundry on Fridays and it returns done on Mondays in a bag with Next Jump's logo and this phrase: "My company gets my laundry. I get my weekends back."[35] Next Jump's culture is so positive, rewarding, and satisfying that 18,000 people applied for thirty-five openings last year. Furthermore, while the quit rate in the tech industry is 22 percent per year, Next Jump has an incredibly low 1 percent quit rate.

Second, while providing the coaching, guidance, support, and rewards necessary for effective work performance, leader behaviors must complement and not duplicate the characteristics of followers' work environments. Thus, leader behaviors must offer something unique and valuable to followers beyond what they're already experiencing as they do their jobs or what they can already do for themselves.

In contrast to Fiedler's contingency theory, path-goal theory assumes that leaders *can* change and adapt their leadership styles. Exhibit 14.4 illustrates this process, showing that leaders change and adapt their leadership styles contingent on their subordinates or the environment in which those subordinates work.

Let's learn more about path-goal theory by examining **14-4a the four kinds of leadership styles that leaders use,** **14-4b the subordinate and environmental contingency factors that determine when different leader styles are effective,** *and* **14-4c the outcomes of path-goal theory in improving employee satisfaction and performance.**

14-4a Leadership Styles

As illustrated in Exhibit 14.4, the four leadership styles in path-goal theory are directive, supportive, participative, and achievement oriented.[36] **Directive leadership**

Path-goal theory a leadership theory states that leaders can increase subordinate satisfaction and performance by clarifying and clearing the paths to goals and by increasing the number and kinds of rewards available for goal attainment

Directive leadership a leadership style in which the leader lets employees know precisely what is expected of them, gives them specific guidelines for performing tasks, schedules work, sets standards of performance, and makes sure that people follow standard rules and regulations

Exhibit 14.4
Path-Goal Theory

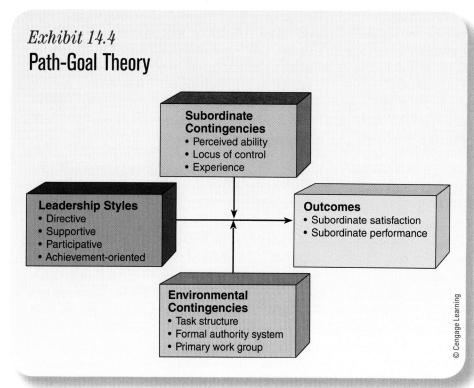

Subordinate Contingencies
• Perceived ability
• Locus of control
• Experience

Leadership Styles
• Directive
• Supportive
• Participative
• Achievement-oriented

Outcomes
• Subordinate satisfaction
• Subordinate performance

Environmental Contingencies
• Task structure
• Formal authority system
• Primary work group

© Cengage Learning

involves letting employees know precisely what is expected of them, giving them specific guidelines for performing tasks, scheduling work, setting standards of performance, and making sure that people follow standard rules and regulations. Directive leadership is very similar to initiating structure.

Supportive leadership involves being approachable and friendly to employees, showing concern for them and their welfare, treating them as equals, and creating a friendly climate. Supportive leadership is very similar to considerate leader behavior. Supportive leadership often results in employee satisfaction with the job

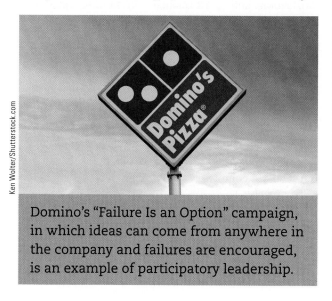

Ken Wolter/Shutterstock.com

Domino's "Failure Is an Option" campaign, in which ideas can come from anywhere in the company and failures are encouraged, is an example of participatory leadership.

and with leaders. This leadership style may also result in improved performance when it increases employee confidence, lowers employee job stress, or improves relations and trust between employees and leaders.[37]

Participative leadership involves consulting employees for their suggestions and input before making decisions. Participation in decision making should help followers understand which goals are most important and clarify the paths to accomplishing them. Furthermore, when people participate in decisions, they become more committed to making them work. In Domino's Pizza's "Failure Is an Option" advertising campaign, Scott Hinshaw, Domino's EVP of operations, says, "In order to get better, in order to move ahead, you're going to make mistakes."[38] Domino's President Russell Weiner explains, "Not every risk we have taken has turned out to be successful, but as a brand we have learned that sometimes you have to fail in order to be great."[39] Andy Wetzel, Director of Product and Brand Innovation, uses the cookie pizza—an idea that never made it out of the test kitchens—as an example. Participative leadership is at the heart of Domino's innovation culture because everyone in the company, down to franchisees and entry-level employees, is encouraged to test new ideas. Patrick Doyle, Domino's CEO, says, "At a big company, new ideas don't typically come from the local store level. But a great idea can come from anywhere."[40] Indeed, some of Domino's best ideas, such as Parmesan Bread Bites, which were created by a franchise manager in Findlay, Ohio, come straight from Domino's stores.[41]

Achievement-oriented leadership means setting challenging goals, having high

Supportive leadership a leadership style in which the leader is friendly and approachable to employees, shows concern for employees and their welfare, treats them as equals, and creates a friendly climate

Participative leadership a leadership style in which the leader consults employees for their suggestions and input before making decisions

Achievement-oriented leadership a leadership style in which the leader sets challenging goals, has high expectations of employees, and displays confidence that employees will assume responsibility and put forth extraordinary effort

CHAPTER 14: Leadership 299

expectations of employees, and displaying confidence that employees will assume responsibility and put forth extraordinary effort. **Asustek**, a Taiwanese computer and phone maker, is the world's largest producer of computer motherboards and the fifth-largest producer of laptop computers (sold under the Asus brand). CEO Jerry Shen has challenged his managers and employees to make Asustek the world's largest supplier of touchscreen notebooks and the world's second-largest seller of tablets, just behind Apple. Chen believes its Nexus 7, a $199 Android tablet with a 7-inch screen, and its VivoBook, a $500 Android tablet with an 11.6-inch screen, combined with its plans to offer an inexpensive 7-inch Windows 8 tablet will help Asustek achieve this challenging goal. One year after announcing the goal, Asustek had moved ahead of Amazon's Kindle tablets to third place behind Samsung and Apple.[42]

14-4b Subordinate and Environmental Contingencies

As shown in Exhibit 14.4, path-goal theory specifies that leader behaviors should be adapted to subordinate characteristics. The theory identifies three kinds of subordinate contingencies: perceived ability, experience, and locus of control. *Perceived ability* is simply how much ability subordinates believe they have for doing their jobs well. Subordinates who perceive that they have a great deal of ability will be dissatisfied with directive leader behaviors. Experienced employees are likely to react in a similar way. Because they already know how to do their jobs (or perceive that they do), they don't need or want close supervision. By contrast, subordinates with little experience or little perceived ability will welcome directive leadership.

Locus of control is a personality measure that indicates the extent to which people believe that they have control over what happens to them in life. *Internals* believe that what happens to them, good or bad, is largely a result of their choices and actions. *Externals*, on the other hand, believe that what happens to them is caused by external forces beyond their control. Accordingly, externals are much more comfortable with a directive leadership style, whereas internals greatly prefer a participative leadership style because they like to have a say in what goes on at work.

Path-goal theory specifies that leader behaviors should complement rather than duplicate the characteristics of followers' work environments. There are three kinds of environmental contingencies: task structure, the

formal authority system, and the primary work group. As in Fiedler's contingency theory, *task structure* is the degree to which the requirements of a subordinate's tasks are clearly specified. When task structure is low, and tasks are unclear, directive leadership should be used because it complements the work environment. When task structure is high and tasks are clear, however, directive leadership is not needed because it duplicates what task structure provides. Alternatively, when tasks are stressful, frustrating, or dissatisfying, leaders should respond with supportive leadership.

The *formal authority system* is an organization's set of procedures, rules, and policies. When the formal authority system is unclear, directive leadership complements the situation by reducing uncertainty and increasing clarity. But when the formal authority system is clear, directive leadership is redundant and should not be used.

Primary work group refers to the amount of work-oriented participation or emotional support that is provided by an employee's immediate work group. Participative leadership should be used when tasks are complex, and there is little existing work-oriented participation in the primary work group. When tasks are stressful, frustrating, or repetitive, supportive leadership is called for.

Finally, because keeping track of all of these subordinate and environmental contingencies can get a bit confusing, Exhibit 14.5 provides a summary of when directive, supportive, participative, and achievement-oriented leadership styles should be used.

14-4c Outcomes

Does following path-goal theory improve subordinate satisfaction and performance? Preliminary evidence suggests that it does.[43] In particular, people who work for supportive leaders are much more satisfied with their jobs and their bosses. Likewise, people who work for directive leaders are more satisfied with their jobs and bosses (but not quite as much as when their bosses are supportive) and perform their jobs better, too. Does adapting one's leadership style to subordinate and environmental characteristics improve subordinate satisfaction and performance? At this point, because it is difficult to completely test this complex theory, it's too early to tell.[44] However, because the data clearly show that it makes sense for leaders to be both supportive *and* directive, it also makes sense that leaders could improve subordinate satisfaction and performance by adding participative and achievement-oriented leadership styles to their capabilities as leaders.

Exhibit 14.5
Path-Goal Theory: When to Use Directive, Supportive, Participative, or Achievement-Oriented Leadership

Directive Leadership	Supportive Leadership	Participative Leadership	Achievement-Oriented Leadership
Unstructured tasks	Structured, simple, repetitive tasks Stressful, frustrating tasks	Complex tasks	Unchallenging tasks
Workers with external locus of control	Workers lack confidence	Workers with internal locus of control	
Unclear formal authority system	Clear formal authority system	Workers not satisfied with rewards	
Inexperienced workers		Experienced workers	
Workers with low perceived ability		Workers with high perceived ability	

© Cengage Learning

14-5 ADAPTING LEADER BEHAVIOR: NORMATIVE DECISION THEORY

Many people believe that making tough decisions is at the heart of leadership. Yet experienced leaders will tell you that deciding *how* to make decisions is just as important. The **normative decision theory** (also known as the *Vroom-Yetton-Jago model*) helps leaders decide how much employee participation (from none to letting employees make the entire decision) should be used when making decisions.[45]

Let's learn more about normative decision theory by investigating 14-5a decision styles and 14-5b decision quality and acceptance.

14-5a Decision Styles

Unlike nearly all of the other leadership theories discussed in this chapter, which have specified *leadership* styles, that is, the way a leader generally behaves toward followers, the normative decision theory specifies five different *decision* styles, or ways of making decisions. (See Chapter 5 for a more complete review of decision making in organizations.) As shown in Exhibit 14.6, those styles vary from *autocratic decisions* (AI or AII) on the left, in which leaders make the decisions by themselves, to *consultative decisions* (CI or CII), in which leaders share problems with subordinates but still make the decisions themselves, to *group decisions* (GII) on the right, in which leaders share the problems with subordinates and then have the group make the decisions.

GE Aircraft Engines in Durham, North Carolina, uses a similar approach when making decisions. According to *Fast Company* magazine, "At GE/Durham, every decision is either an 'A' decision, a 'B' decision, or a 'C' decision. An 'A' decision is one that the plant manager makes herself, without consulting anyone."[46] One plant manager said, "I don't make very many of those, and when I do make one, everyone at the plant knows it. I make maybe ten or twelve a year."[47] "B" decisions are also made by the plant manager but with input from the people affected. "C" decisions, the most common type, are made by consensus, by the people directly involved, with plenty of discussion. With "C" decisions, the view of the plant manager doesn't necessarily carry more weight than the views of those affected.[48]

14-5b Decision Quality and Acceptance

Management consultant John Canfield says, "Leaders are responsible for improving the performance

> **Normative decision theory** a theory that suggests how leaders can determine an appropriate amount of employee participation when making decisions

Determining Your Priorities

Leaders are often asked to participate in a flood of strategic initiatives, both internal and external. According to Sandy Ogg, the former chief human resources officer at Unilever, executives often have more than 100 invitations to participate in corporate initiatives at any one time, so he devised a three-step decision tree to help busy executives identify where to invest their time and effort. First, make a list of every initiative asking for your participation. Second, rank each initiative according to the stature of its sponsor, the quality of the team, the time frame, and the budget. Finally, put less effort into low-ranking initiatives to free up time for higher-ranking initiatives.

Source: H. Ibarra, "The Way to Become a 'Strategic' Executive," *Wall Street Journal*, February 23, 2015, R7.

of organizations. Two significant components of [a leader's] decisions are the quality of the decision and the level of buy-in associated with it. Effective leaders want them both."[49] According to the normative decision theory, using the right degree of employee participation improves the quality of decisions and the extent to which employees accept and are committed to decisions (that is, buy-in). Exhibit 14.7 lists the decision rules that normative decision theory uses to increase the quality of a decision and the degree to which employees accept and commit to it.

The quality, leader information, subordinate information, goal congruence, and problem structure rules are used to increase decision quality. For example, the

---

Exhibit 14.6
Normative Theory, Decision Styles, and Levels of Employee Participation

Leader solves the problem or makes the decision ———————————————————→ **Leader is willing to accept any decision supported by the entire group**

AI	AII	CI	CII	GII
Using information available at the time, the leader solves the problem or makes the decision.	The leader obtains necessary information from employees and then selects a solution to the problem. When asked to share information, employees may or may not be told what the problem is.	The leader shares the problem and gets ideas and suggestions from relevant employees on an individual basis. Individuals are not brought together as a group. Then the leader makes the decision, which may or may not reflect their input.	The leader shares the problem with employees as a group, obtains their ideas and suggestions, and then makes the decision, which may or may not reflect their input.	The leader shares the problem with employees as a group. Together, the leader and employees generate and evaluate alternatives and try to reach an agreement on a solution. The leader acts as a facilitator and does not try to influence the group. The leader is willing to accept and implement any solution that has the support of the entire group.

Source: Table 2.1, Decision Methods for Group and Individual Problems, from *Leadership and Decision-Making* (Pittsburgh: University of Pittsburgh Press, 1973), by V. H. Vroom and P. W. Yetton.

Exhibit 14.7
Normative Theory Decision Rules

Decision Rules to Increase Decision Quality
Quality Rule. If the quality of the decision is important, then don't use an autocratic decision style.
Leader Information Rule. If the quality of the decision is important, and if the leader doesn't have enough information to make the decision on his or her own, then don't use an autocratic decision style.
Subordinate Information Rule. If the quality of the decision is important, and if the subordinates don't have enough information to make the decision themselves, then don't use a group decision style.
Goal Congruence Rule. If the quality of the decision is important, and subordinates' goals are different from the organization's goals, then don't use a group decision style.
Problem Structure Rule. If the quality of the decision is important, the leader doesn't have enough information to make the decision on his or her own, and the problem is unstructured, then don't use an autocratic decision style.

Decision Rules to Increase Decision Acceptance
Commitment Probability Rule. If having subordinates accept and commit to the decision is important, then don't use an autocratic decision style.
Subordinate Conflict Rule. If having subordinates accept the decision is important and critical to successful implementation, and subordinates are likely to disagree or end up in conflict over the decision, then don't use an autocratic or consultative decision style.
Commitment Requirement Rule. If having subordinates accept the decision is absolutely required for successful implementation, and subordinates share the organization's goals, then don't use an autocratic or consultative style.

Sources: Adapted from V. H. Vroom, "Leadership," in *Handbook of Industrial and Organizational Psychology*, ed. M. D. Dunnette (Chicago: Rand McNally, 1976); V. H. Vroom and A. G. Jago, *The New Leadership: Managing Participation in Organizations* (Englewood Cliffs, NJ: Prentice Hall, 1988).

leader information rule states that if a leader doesn't have enough information to make a decision on his or her own, then the leader should not use an autocratic decision style. The commitment probability, subordinate conflict, and commitment requirement rules shown in Exhibit 14.7 are used to increase employee acceptance and commitment to decisions. For example, the commitment requirement rule says that if decision acceptance and commitment are important, and the subordinates share the organization's goals, then you shouldn't use an autocratic or consultative style. In other words, if followers want to do what's best for the company, and you need their acceptance and commitment to make a decision work, then use a group decision style and let them make the decision. As you can see, these decision rules help leaders improve decision quality and follower acceptance and commitment by eliminating decision styles that don't fit the particular decision or situation they're facing. Normative decision theory, like path-goal theory, is situational in nature. The abstract decision rules in Exhibit 14.7 are framed as yes/no questions, which makes the process of applying these rules more concrete. These questions are shown in the decision tree displayed in Exhibit 14.8. You start at the left side of the tree and answer the first question,

"How important is the technical quality of this decision?" by choosing "high" or "low." Then you continue by answering each question as you proceed along the decision tree until you get to a recommended decision style.

Let's use the model to make the decision of whether to change from private offices to open offices and cubicles. The problem sounds simple, but it is actually more complex than you might think. Follow the yellow line in Exhibit 14.8 as we work through the decision in the following discussion.

PROBLEM: CHANGE TO OPEN OFFICES AND CUBICLES?

1. *Quality requirement: How important is the technical quality of this decision?* High. This question has to do with whether there are quality differences in the alternatives and whether those quality differences matter. In other words: Is there a lot at stake in this decision? People have incredibly strong reactions to giving up private offices for cubicles. While companies use open offices to increase communication, workers will see this as a loss of privacy and status. Yes, there is a lot at stake.

Exhibit 14.8

Normative Decision Theory Tree for Determining the Level of Participation in Decision Making

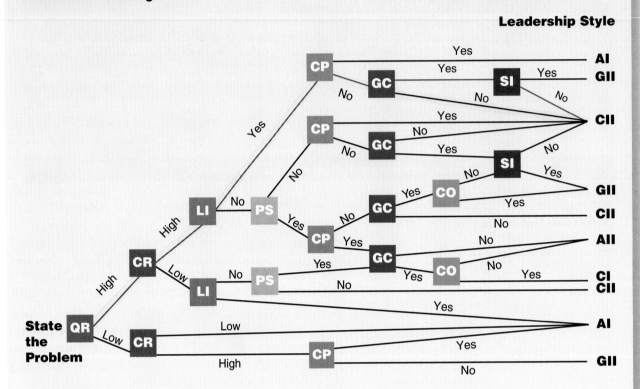

Leadership Style

State the Problem

Problem Attributes

QR   Quality requirement: How important is the technical quality of this decision?

CR   Commitment requirement: How important is subordinate commitment to the decision?

LI   Leader's information: Do you have sufficient information to make a high-quality decision?

PS   Problem structure: Is the problem well structured?

CP   Commitment probability: If you were to make the decision by yourself, are you reasonably certain that your subordinate(s) would be committed to the decision?

GC   Goal congruence: Do subordinates share the organizational goals to be attained in solving this problem?

CO   Subordinate conflict: Is conflict among subordinates over preferred solutions likely?

SI   Subordinate information: Do subordinates have sufficient information to make a high-quality decision?

Source: Figure 9.3, Decision-Process Flow Chart for Both Individual and Group Problems, from *Leadership and Decision-Making* (Pittsburgh: University of Pittsburgh Press, 1973), by V. H. Vroom and P. W. Yetton.

2. *Commitment requirement: How important is subordinate commitment to the decision?* High. Changes in offices, from private to open settings, require subordinate commitment or they fail. In fact, it's not uncommon for companies to abandon open offices after trying them.

3. *Leader's information: Do you have sufficient information to make a high-quality decision?* Yes. Let's assume that you've done your homework. Much has been written about open offices and cubicles, from how to make the change to the effects it has in companies (which are mixed, sometimes positive, and sometimes negative.).

4. *Commitment probability: If you were to make the decision by yourself, is it reasonably certain that your subordinate(s) would be committed to the decision?* No. Studies of companies that change from private offices to open offices find that employees' initial reactions are almost uniformly negative. Employees are likely to be angry if you change something as personal as their offices without consulting them.

5. *Goal congruence: Do subordinates share the organizational goals to be attained in solving this problem?* Probably not. The goals that usually accompany a change to open offices are a more informal culture, better communication, and less money spent on renting or buying office space (because open offices and cubicles take less square footage than private offices), none of which will matter much to employees who are losing their private offices.

6. *CII is the answer:* With a CII, or consultative decision process, the leader shares the problem with employees as a group, obtains their ideas and suggestions, and then makes the decision, which may or may not reflect their input. So, given the answers to these questions (remember, different managers won't necessarily answer these questions the same way), the normative decision theory recommends that leaders consult with their subordinates before deciding whether to change from private offices to open offices and cubicles.

How well does the normative decision theory work? A prominent leadership scholar has described it as the best supported of all leadership theories.[50] In general, the more managers violate the decision rules in Exhibit 14.7, the less effective their decisions are, especially with respect to subordinate acceptance and commitment.[51]

14-6 VISIONARY LEADERSHIP

Strategic leadership is the ability to anticipate, envision, maintain flexibility, think strategically, and work with others to initiate changes that will create a positive future for an organization.[52] When he first became CEO at Ryder System, Robert Sanchez gave an ineffective one-hour speech trying to lay out his strategic priorities in truck rental and leasing, logistics and supply chain, and truck fleet management. The speech, he says, was overly complex with too many financial terms and numbers, so, "People weren't paying attention. Several front-line employees gave blank stares when I asked if they understood what we were trying to accomplish." When strategic change didn't take hold as fast as he liked, he reshaped his message into a fifteen-minute focused presentation at the company's management summit. There, he had much more success creating urgency to change when he displayed a slide with 100 trucks representing their markets. Only two were yellow, which is Ryder's color. That, he says, finally, "Clicked with a lot of people."[53] Thus, strategic leadership captures how leaders inspire their companies to change and their followers to give extraordinary effort to accomplish organizational goals.

In Chapter 5, we defined a purpose statement, which is often referred to as an organizational mission or vision, as a statement of a company's purpose or reason for existing. Similarly, **visionary leadership** creates a positive image of the future that motivates organizational members and provides direction for future planning and goal setting.[54]

*Two kinds of visionary leadership are **14-6a charismatic leadership** and **14-6b transformational leadership**.*

14-6a Charismatic Leadership

Charisma is a Greek word meaning "divine gift." The ancient Greeks saw people with charisma as inspired by the gods and capable of incredible accomplishments. German sociologist Max Weber viewed charisma as a special bond between leaders and followers.[55] Weber wrote that the special qualities

Strategic leadership the ability to anticipate, envision, maintain flexibility, think strategically, and work with others to initiate changes that will create a positive future for an organization

Visionary leadership leadership that creates a positive image of the future that motivates organizational members and provides direction for future planning and goal setting of charismatic leaders enable them to strongly influence followers. Weber also noted that charismatic leaders tend to emerge in times of crisis and that the radical solutions they propose enhance the admiration that followers feel for them. In fact, charismatic leaders tend to have incredible influence over followers who may be inspired by their leaders and become fanatically devoted to them. From this perspective, charismatic leaders are often seen as larger-than-life or more special than other employees of the company.

Charismatic leaders have strong, confident, dynamic personalities that attract followers and enable the leaders to create strong bonds with their followers. Followers trust charismatic leaders, are loyal to them, and are inspired to work toward the accomplishment of the leader's vision. Followers who become devoted to charismatic leaders may go to extraordinary lengths to please them. Therefore, we can define **charismatic leadership** as the behavioral tendencies and personal characteristics of leaders that create an exceptionally strong relationship between them and their followers. Charismatic leaders also

> articulate a clear vision for the future that is based on strongly held values or morals;

> model those values by acting in a way consistent with the vision;

> communicate high performance expectations to followers; and

> display confidence in followers' abilities to achieve the vision.[56]

Does charismatic leadership work? Studies indicate that it often does. In general, the followers of charismatic leaders are more committed and satisfied, are better performers, are more likely to trust their leaders, and simply work harder.[57] Nonetheless, charismatic leadership also has risks that are at least as large as its benefits. The problems are likely to occur with ego-driven charismatic leaders who take advantage of fanatical followers.

In general, there are two kinds of charismatic leaders, ethical charismatics and unethical charismatics.[58] **Ethical charismatics** provide developmental opportunities for followers, are open to positive and negative feedback, recognize others' contributions, share information, and have moral standards that emphasize the larger interests of the group, organization, or society. Twenty years ago, J. J. Irani, then CEO of Tata Steel, had to close down a money-losing steel plan in Jamshedpur, India. Given that Tata not only guaranteed all employees' jobs but also jobs for their children (after you had worked at Tata twenty-five years), this was the first time that any Tata employees would lose their jobs.

Charismatic leadership
the behavioral tendencies and personal characteristics of leaders that create an exceptionally strong relationship between them and their followers

Ethical charismatics
charismatic leaders who provide developmental opportunities for followers, are open to positive and negative feedback, recognize others' contributions, share information, and have moral standards that emphasize the larger interests of the group, organization, or society

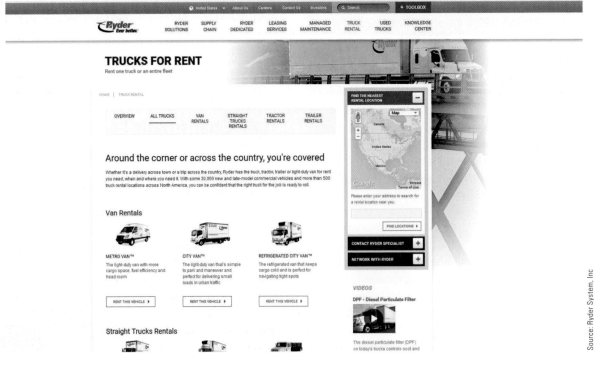

Source: Ryder System, Inc

Rather than doing only what was best for Tata, Irani decided that laid-off employees, age 40 or under, would receive full salaries for the remainder of their working lives. Laid-off employees over 40 would get salaries plus a 20 percent to 50 percent bonus, depending on how close they were to retirement. Moreover, workers' families would receive the payments even if the workers died prior to retiring. Tata benefitted, too, because it no longer had to pay payroll taxes, and part of the deal was that workers' payments would not increase over time. Over time, its labor costs shrunk, but its reputation as a caring employer among Indian managers and workers persisted.[59] As you would expect, ethical charismatics like Irani produce stronger commitment, higher satisfaction, more effort, better performance, and greater trust.

By contrast, **unethical charismatics** control and manipulate followers, do what is best for themselves instead of their organizations, want to hear only positive feedback, share information that is only beneficial to themselves, and have moral standards that put their interests before everyone else's. Russell Wasendorf, Sr., former CEO and founder of Peregrine Financial Group, a commodities trading firm, stole $215 million over the course of twenty years from his clients and the company. Wasendorf printed false bank statements to hide his theft, used some of the stolen money to falsely boost Peregrine's financial performance, and used the money to live well above his means, "hiring a 'four-star chef' to run Peregrine's cafeteria, building an expansive house with a swimming pool, and sinking investor money into ventures like an Italian restaurant—the staff of which he once flew to Italy for a vacation." The 65-year-old Wasendorf was sentenced to fifty years in prison.[60]

Because followers can become just as committed to unethical charismatics as to ethical charismatics, unethical characteristics pose a tremendous risk for companies. Professor Diane Chandler explains, "By being greatly influenced by charismatic leaders, followers are apt to agree with, feel affection for, and obey them. With charismatic leaders fostering a sense of strong identification with followers, they may likewise curry followers' inordinate allegiance to them in the face of unethical or moral leadership indiscretion."[61]

Exhibit 14.9 shows the stark differences between ethical and unethical charismatics on several leader behaviors: exercising power, creating the vision, communicating with followers, accepting feedback, stimulating followers intellectually, developing followers, and living by moral standards. For example, ethical charismatics account for the concerns and wishes of their followers when creating a vision by having followers participate in the development of the company vision. By contrast, unethical charismatics develop a vision by themselves solely to meet their personal agendas. One unethical charismatic said, "The key thing is that it is my idea; and I am going to win with it at all costs."[62]

14-6b Transformational Leadership

While charismatic leadership involves articulating a clear vision, modeling values consistent with that vision, communicating high performance expectations, and establishing very strong relationships with followers, **transformational leadership** goes further by generating awareness and acceptance of a group's purpose and mission and by getting employees to see beyond their own needs and self-interest for the good of the group.[63] Like charismatic leaders, transformational leaders are visionary, but they transform their organizations by getting their followers to accomplish more than they intended and even more than they thought possible.

Transformational leaders are able to make their followers feel that they are a vital part of the organization and help them see how their jobs fit with the organization's vision. By linking individual and organizational interests, transformational leaders encourage followers to make sacrifices for the organization because they know that they will prosper when the organization prospers. Transformational leadership has four components: charismatic leadership or idealized influence, inspirational motivation, intellectual stimulation, and individualized consideration.[64]

Charismatic leadership or idealized influence means that transformational leaders act as role models for their followers. Because transformational leaders put others' needs ahead of their own and share risks with their followers, they are admired, respected, and trusted, and followers want to emulate them. When Whole Foods' profit dropped 10 percent and the company needed to trim costs, co-CEO John Mackey voluntarily cut his pay by 67 percent. Likewise, Jay Leno, who hosted the Tonight Show for twenty-two years, voluntarily took a $15 million cut in pay when NBC announced that it needed to cut $20 million in costs for the show. While twenty employees were let go,

Unethical charismatics charismatic leaders who control and manipulate followers, do what is best for themselves instead of their organizations, want to hear only positive feedback, share only information that is beneficial to themselves, and have moral standards that put their interests before everyone else's

Transformational leadership leadership that generates awareness and acceptance of a group's purpose and mission and gets employees to see beyond their own needs and self-interests for the good of the group

Exhibit 14.9
Ethical and Unethical Charismatics

Charismatic Leader Behaviors	Ethical Charismatics . . .	Unethical Charismatics . . .
Exercising power	. . . use power to serve others.	. . . use power to dominate or manipulate others for personal gain.
Creating the vision	. . . allow followers to help develop the vision.	. . . are the sole source of vision, which they use to serve their personal agendas.
Communicating with followers	. . . engage in two-way communication and seek out viewpoints on critical issues.	. . . engage in one-way communication and are not open to suggestions from others.
Accepting feedback	. . . are open to feedback and willing to learn from criticism.	. . . have inflated egos, thrive on attention and admiration of sycophants, and avoid candid feedback.
Stimulating followers intellectually	. . . want followers to think and question status quo as well as leader's views.	. . . don't want followers to think but instead want uncritical acceptance of leader's ideas.
Developing followers	. . . focus on developing people with whom they interact, express confidence in them, and share recognition with others.	. . . are insensitive and unresponsive to followers' needs and aspirations.
Living by moral standards	. . . follow self-guided principles that may go against popular opinion and have three virtues: courage, a sense of fairness or justice, and integrity.	. . . follow standards only if they satisfy immediate self-interests, manipulate impressions so that others think they are doing the right thing, and use communication skills to manipulate others to support their personal agendas.

Source: J. M. Howell and B. J. Avolio, "The Ethics of Charismatic Leadership: Submission or Liberation?" *Academy of Management Executive 6*, no. 2 (1992): 43–54.

Leno's voluntary pay cut absorbed 75 percent of the needed cost reduction so that many other long-time staffers on the show could keep their jobs.[65] Thus, in contrast to purely charismatic leaders (especially unethical charismatics), transformational leaders can be counted on to do the right thing and maintain high standards for ethical and personal conduct.

Inspirational motivation means that transformational leaders motivate and inspire followers by providing meaning and challenge to their work. By clearly communicating expectations and demonstrating commitment to goals, transformational leaders help followers envision future states, such as the organizational vision or mission. In turn, this leads to greater enthusiasm and optimism about the future.

Intellectual stimulation means that transformational leaders encourage followers to be creative and innovative, to question assumptions, and to look at problems and situations in new ways even if their ideas are different from those of leaders. Intolerant of mediocrity and the status quo, Sir James **Dyson**, is a unique combination of inventor, engineer, businessman, and artist. From its launch of the dual cyclone vacuum, his company has grown from a few people all using one phone to 6,000 employees in the United Kingdom, Singapore, and Malaysia booking nearly $2 billion in annual revenue

Verbaska/Shutterstock.com

from vacuums, lighting, robotics, and even agriculture. Dyson's top-secret laboratory is staffed by more than 1,000 engineers, and even though Sir James is no longer involved in the daily operation of the company, he still holds monthly "James Reviews" of new initiatives. Engineer Annmarie Nicolson says, "It can be nerve-wracking because he's so inquisitive. He'll always ask you a question you don't have an answer to. We'll sit for hours brainstorming, and we'll filter it down to what we think works best and build a prototype. James will say, 'Have you thought about this?' and we'll say, 'Well no, we haven't.'"[66]

Individualized consideration means that transformational leaders pay special attention to followers' individual needs by creating learning opportunities, accepting and tolerating individual differences, encouraging two-way communication, and being good listeners.

Finally, a distinction needs to be drawn between transformational leadership and transactional leadership. While transformational leaders use visionary and inspirational appeals to influence followers, **transactional leadership** is based on an exchange process in which followers are rewarded for good performance and punished for poor performance. When leaders administer rewards fairly and offer followers the rewards that they want, followers will often reciprocate with effort. A problem, however, is that transactional leaders often rely too heavily on discipline or threats to bring performance up to standards. This may work in the short run, but it's much less effective in the long run. Also, as discussed in Chapters 11 and 13, many leaders and organizations have difficulty successfully linking pay practices to individual performance. As a result, studies consistently show that transformational leadership is much more effective on average than transactional leadership. In the United States, Canada, Japan, and India at all organizational levels, from first-level supervisors to upper-level executives, followers view transformational leaders as much better leaders and are much more satisfied when working for them. Furthermore, companies with transformational leaders have significantly better financial performance.[67]

Transactional leadership leadership based on an exchange process in which followers are rewarded for good performance and punished for poor performance

STUDY TOOLS 14

LOCATED IN TEXTBOOK
☐ Rip-out and review chapter review card

LOCATED AT WWW.CENGAGEBRAIN.COM
☐ Review key term flashcards and create your own from StudyBits
☐ Track your knowledge and understanding of key concepts, using the concept tracker
☐ Complete practice and graded quizzes to prepare for tests
☐ Complete interactive content within the exposition
☐ View chapter highlight box content at the beginning of each chapter

15 Managing Communication

LEARNING OUTCOMES

15-1 Explain the role that perception plays in communication and communication problems.

15-2 Describe the communication process and the various kinds of communication in organizations.

15-3 Explain how managers can manage effective one-on-one communication.

15-4 Describe how managers can manage effective organization-wide communication.

After you finish this chapter, go to **PAGE 331** for **STUDY TOOLS**

15-1 PERCEPTION AND COMMUNICATION PROBLEMS

It's estimated that managers spend over 80 percent of their day communicating with others.[1] Indeed, much of the basic management process—planning, organizing, leading, and controlling—cannot be performed without effective communication. If this weren't reason enough to study communication, consider that effective oral communication—achieved by listening, following instructions, conversing, and giving feedback—is the most important skill for college graduates who are entering the workforce.[2] **Communication** is the process of transmitting information from one person or place to another. While some bosses sugarcoat bad news, smart managers understand that effective, straightforward communication between managers and employees is essential for success.

One study found that when *employees* were asked whether their supervisor gave recognition for good work, only 13 percent said their supervisor gave a pat on the back, and a mere 14 percent said their supervisor gave sincere and thorough praise. But when the *supervisors* of these employees were asked if they gave recognition for good work, 82 percent said they gave pats on the back, while 80 percent said that they gave sincere and thorough praise.[3] Given that these managers and employees worked closely together, how could they have had such different perceptions of something as simple as praise?

Let's learn more about perception and communication problems by examining 15-1a the basic perception process, 15-1b perception problems, 15-1c how we perceive others, and 15-1d how we perceive ourselves. We'll also consider how all of these factors make it difficult for managers to communicate effectively.

15-1a Basic Perception Process

As shown in Exhibit 15.1, **perception** is the process by which individuals attend to, organize, interpret, and retain information from their environments. And because communication is the process of transmitting information from one person or place to another, perception is obviously a key part of communication. Yet perception can also be a key obstacle to communication.

As people perform their jobs, they are exposed to a wide variety of informational stimuli such as emails, direct conversations with the boss or coworkers, rumors

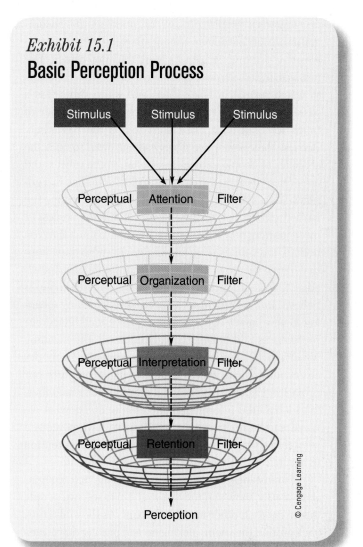

Exhibit 15.1
Basic Perception Process

heard over lunch, stories about the company in the press, or a video broadcast of a speech from the CEO to all employees. Just being exposed to an informational stimulus, however, is no guarantee that an individual will pay attention or attend to that stimulus. People experience stimuli through their own **perceptual filters**—the personality-, psychology-, or experience-based differences that influence them to ignore or pay attention to particular stimuli. Because of filtering, people exposed to the same information will often disagree about what they saw or heard. As shown in Exhibit 15.1, perceptual filters affect each part of the *perception process*: attention, organization, interpretation, and retention.

Communication the process of transmitting information from one person or place to another

Perception the process by which individuals attend to, organize, interpret, and retain information from their environments

Perceptual filters the personality-, psychology-, or experience-based differences that influence people to ignore or pay attention to particular stimuli

Attention is the process of noticing, or becoming aware of, particular stimuli. Because of perceptual filters, we attend to some stimuli and not others. For instance, a study at the University of Illinois asked viewers to watch people in black shirts and white shirts toss a basketball back and forth and to count the number of times someone in a black shirt tossed the basketball. Because their perceptual filters had narrowed to track the activities of people in black shirts, half of the viewers did not notice when the experimenters had someone in a gorilla suit walk through the midst of the people tossing the basketball back and forth.[4] *Organization* is the process of incorporating new information (from the stimuli that you notice) into your existing knowledge. Because of perceptual filters, we are more likely to incorporate new knowledge that is consistent with what we already know or believe. *Interpretation* is the process of attaching meaning to new knowledge. Because of perceptual filters, our preferences and beliefs strongly influence the meaning we attach to new information (for example, "This decision must mean that top management supports our project"). Finally, *retention* is the process of remembering interpreted information. Retention affects what we recall and commit to memory after we have perceived something. Of course, perceptual filters affect retention as much as they do organization and interpretation.

For instance, imagine that you miss the first ten minutes of a TV show and turn on your TV to see two people talking to each other in a living room. As they talk, they walk around the room, picking up and putting down various items. Some items, such as a ring, watch, and credit card, appear to be valuable, while others appear to be drug-related, such as a water pipe for smoking marijuana. In fact, this situation was depicted on videotape in a well-known study that manipulated people's perceptual filters.[5] Before watching the video, one-third of the study participants were told that the people were there to rob the apartment. Another third were told that police were on their way to conduct a drug raid and that the people in the apartment were getting rid of incriminating evidence. The remaining third of the participants were told that the people were simply waiting for a friend.

After watching the video, participants were asked to list all of the objects from the video that they could remember. Not surprisingly, the different perceptual filters (theft, drug raid, and waiting for a friend) affected what the participants attended to, how they organized the information, how they interpreted it, and ultimately which objects they remembered. Participants who thought a theft was in progress were more likely to remember the valuable objects in the video. Those who thought a drug raid was imminent were more likely to remember the drug-related objects. There was no discernible pattern to the items remembered by those who thought that the people in the video were simply waiting for a friend.

In short, because of perception and perceptual filters, people are likely to pay attention to different things, organize and interpret what they pay attention to differently, and, finally, remember things differently. Consequently, even when people are exposed to the same communications (for example, organizational memos, discussions with managers or customers), they can end up with very different perceptions and understandings. This is why communication can be so difficult and frustrating for managers. Let's review some of the communication problems created by perception and perceptual filters.

15-1b Perception Problems

Perception creates communication problems for organizations because people exposed to the same communication and information can end up with completely different ideas and understandings. Two of the most common perception problems in organizations are selective perception and closure.

At work, we are constantly bombarded with sensory stimuli: phones ringing, people talking in the background, computers dinging as new email arrives, people calling our names, and so forth. As limited processors of information, we cannot possibly notice, receive, and interpret all of this information. As a result, we attend to and accept some stimuli but screen out and reject others. This isn't a random process.

Selective perception is the tendency to notice and accept objects and information consistent with our values, beliefs, and expectations, while ignoring or screening out inconsistent information. For example, in a research study, pedestrians are stopped on a sidewalk by a man who asks for directions. Ten seconds into giving directions, two people carrying a door walk between the man who asked for directions, on the left, and the pedestrian, on the right. When the door goes by, the man who asked for directions quickly switches places with one of the young men carrying the door. The pedestrian, however, doesn't see this switch because the door blocks the view. Like the invisible gorilla example above, 50 percent of the time people don't even notice that they're talking

Selective perception the tendency to notice and accept objects and information consistent with our values, beliefs, and expectations, while ignoring or screening inconsistent information to a different man and go right back to giving directions. Selective perception, is one of the biggest contributors to misunderstandings and miscommunication, because it strongly influences what people see, hear, read, and understand at work.[6]

After we have initial information about a person, event, or process, **closure** is the tendency to fill in the gaps where information is missing, that is, to assume that what we don't know is consistent with what we already do know. If employees are told that budgets must be cut by 10 percent, they may automatically assume that 10 percent of employees will lose their jobs, too, even if that isn't the case. Not surprisingly, when closure occurs, people sometimes fill in the gaps with inaccurate information, which can create problems for organizations.

15-1c Perceptions of Others

Attribution theory says that we all have a basic need to understand and explain the causes of other people's behavior.[7] In other words, we need to know why people do what they do. According to attribution theory, we use two general reasons or attributions to explain people's behavior: an *internal attribution*, in which behavior is thought to be voluntary or under the control of the individual, and an *external attribution*, in which behavior is thought to be involuntary and outside of the control of the individual.

IDoncept/Shutterstock.com

If you've ever seen someone changing a flat tire on the side of the road and thought to yourself, "What rotten luck—somebody's having a bad day," you perceived the person through an external attribution known as the defensive bias. The **defensive bias** is the tendency for people to perceive themselves as personally and situationally similar to someone who is having difficulty or trouble.[8] When we identify with the person in a situation, we tend to use external attributions (that is, features related to the situation) to explain the person's behavior. For instance, because flat tires are common, it's easy to perceive ourselves in that same situation and put the blame on external causes such as running over a nail.

Now, let's assume a different situation, this time in the workplace:

A utility company worker puts a ladder on a utility pole and then climbs up to do his work. As he's doing his work, he falls from the ladder and seriously injures himself.[9]

Answer this question: Who or what caused the accident? If you thought, "It's not the worker's fault. Anybody could fall from a tall ladder," then you interpreted the incident with a defensive bias in which you saw yourself as personally and situationally similar to someone who is having difficulty or trouble. In other words, you made an external attribution by attributing the accident to an external cause or some feature of the situation.

Most accident investigations, however, initially blame the worker (that is, an internal attribution) and not the situation (that is, an external attribution). Typically, 60 to 80 percent of workplace accidents each year are blamed on "operator error," that is, on the employees themselves. In reality, more complete investigations usually show that workers are responsible for only 30 to 40 percent of all workplace accidents.[10] Why are accident investigators so quick to blame workers? The reason is that they are committing the **fundamental attribution error**, which is the tendency to ignore external causes of behavior and to attribute other people's actions to internal causes.[11] In other words, when investigators examine the possible causes of an accident, they're much more likely to assume that the accident is a function of the person and not the situation.

Which attribution—the defensive bias or the fundamental attribution error—are workers likely to make when something goes wrong? In general,

Closure the tendency to fill in gaps of missing information by assuming that what we don't know is consistent with what we already know

Attribution theory the theory that we all have a basic need to understand and explain the causes of other people's behavior

Defensive bias the tendency for people to perceive themselves as personally and situationally similar to someone who is having difficulty or trouble

Fundamental attribution error the tendency to ignore external causes of behavior and to attribute other people's actions to internal causes

Exhibit 15.2
Defensive Bias and Fundamental Attribution Error

The Coworker	The Employee	The Boss

How can they expect us to make sales if they don't have hot-selling inventory in stock? We can't sell what's not there.

That's the third sale I've lost this week because company management doesn't keep enough inventory in stock. I can't sell it if we don't have it.

That new employee isn't very good. I may have to get rid of him if his sales don't improve.

Defensive Bias—
the tendency for people to perceive themselves as personally and situationally similar to someone who is having difficulty or trouble

Defensive Bias—
the tendency for people to perceive themselves as personally and situationally similar to someone who is having difficulty or trouble

Fundamental Attribution Error—
the tendency to ignore external causes of behavior and to attribute other people's actions to internal causes

© Cengage Learning

as shown in Exhibit 15.2, employees and coworkers are more likely to perceive events and explain behavior from a defensive bias. Because they do the work themselves and see themselves as similar to others who make mistakes, have accidents, or are otherwise held responsible for things that go wrong at work, employees and coworkers are likely to attribute problems to external causes such as failed machinery, poor support, or inadequate training. By contrast, because they are typically observers (who don't do the work themselves) and see themselves as situationally and personally different from workers, managers tend to commit the fundamental attribution error and blame mistakes, accidents, and other things that go wrong on workers (that is, an internal attribution).

Consequently, workers and managers in most workplaces can be expected to take opposite views when things go wrong. Therefore, the defensive bias, which is typically used by workers, and the fundamental attribution error, which is typically made by managers, together present a significant challenge to effective communication and understanding in organizations.

15-1d Self-Perception

The **self-serving bias** is the tendency to overestimate our value by attributing successes to ourselves (internal causes) and attributing failures to others or the environment (external causes).[12] The self-serving bias can make it especially difficult for managers to talk to employees about performance problems. In general, people have a need to maintain a positive self-image. This need is so strong that when people seek feedback at work, they typically want verification of their worth (rather than information about performance deficiencies) or assurance that mistakes or problems weren't their fault.[13] People can become defensive and emotional when managerial communication threatens their positive self-image. They quit listening, and communication becomes ineffective. In the second half of the chapter, which focuses on improving communication, we'll explain ways in which managers can minimize this self-serving bias and improve effective one-on-one communication with employees.

Self-serving bias the tendency to overestimate our value by attributing successes to ourselves (internal causes) and attributing failures to others or the environment (external causes)

15-2 KINDS OF COMMUNICATION

There are many kinds of communication—formal, informal, coaching/counseling, and nonverbal—but they all follow the same fundamental process.

Let's learn more about the different kinds of communication by examining 15-2a the communication process, 15-2b formal communication channels, 15-2c informal communication channels, 15-2d coaching and counseling, or one-on-one communication, and 15-2e nonverbal communication.

15-2a The Communication Process

At the beginning of this chapter, we defined *communication* as the process of transmitting information from one person or place to another. Exhibit 15.3 displays a model of the communication process and its major components: the sender (message to be conveyed, encoding the message, transmitting the message); the receiver (receiving message, decoding the message, and the message that was understood); and noise, which interferes with the communication process.

The communication process begins when a *sender* thinks of a message he or she wants to convey to another person. For example, you had a flu shot and a pneumonia shot, and yet you've had an unexplainable fever for nine days, so you visit the doctor. The doctor asks a series of questions regarding your appetite, fatigue, tenderness in your abdomen, and whether your fever comes and goes during the day. The doctor, the sender, runs some tests and then has you, the receiver, come back the next day to provide a diagnosis and recommend a treatment.

The next step is to encode the message. **Encoding** means putting a message into a written, verbal, or symbolic form that can be recognized and understood by the receiver. In our example, this means the doctor has to take the technical language of medicine and lab test results and communicate it

in a way that patients can understand. This is not easy to do. And the difficulty of doing this well is compounded by the average doctor's visit lasting less than fifteen minutes. And, while your visit might be fifteen minutes, you're not getting a full fifteen minutes to talk to the doctor. Not surprisingly, 60 percent of patients feel as if their doctor is rushing through their exam. Despite this, 58 percent of surveyed patients say their doctors do a good job of explaining things to them. But, as we'll see in a few steps, that doesn't mean communication has been effective.[14]

The sender then *transmits the message* via *communication channels*. The traditional communication channel for doctors and patients is face-to-face discussion in the doctor's office. Ironically, though, the introduction of electronic health records may be interfering with that. Dr. Rita Redberg, at the University of California San Francisco Medical Center, says, "The recent introduction of electronic health records in the office, for example, requires many doctors to spend much of a patient exam looking at a computer screen instead of the patient in order to record information." Studies show that one-third of the time, doctors forget to give patients critical information. Another critical study found that across thirty different medical conditions, patients only received all

> **Encoding** putting a message into a written, verbal, or symbolic form that can be recognized and understood by the receiver

Exhibit 15.3
The Interpersonal Communication Process

Sender   **Receiver**

Message to be conveyed — - - → **Feedback to Sender** - - - → Message that was understood

Encode message   NOISE   NOISE   NOISE   Decode message

Transmit message   **Communication Channel**   Receive message

© Cengage Learning

the information they needed from their doctors about 55 percent of the time.[15] Why? In an average fifteen-minute doctor's visit, the doctor will spend just 1.3 minutes telling the patient about his or her condition, prognosis, and treatment. Furthermore, as we will see, that 1.3 minutes is filled with information that is too complex and technical for the typical patient to understand.[16]

With some communication channels such as the telephone and face-to-face communication, the sender receives immediate feedback, whereas with others such as email (or text messages and file attachments), fax, beepers, voice mail, memos, and letters, the sender must wait for the receiver to respond. Unfortunately, because of technical difficulties (for example, fax down, dead battery in the cell phone, inability to read email attachments) or people-based transmission problems (for example, forgetting to pass on the message), messages aren't always transmitted.

If the message is transmitted and received, however, the next step is for the receiver to decode it. **Decoding** is the process by which the receiver translates the verbal or symbolic form of the message into an understood message. Surveys indicate that many patients clearly do not understand what their doctors are telling them. Up to 85 percent of hospitalized patients don't even know the name of the doctor in charge of their treatment. As many as 58 percent don't know why they were admitted to the hospital. Likewise, in a typical fifteen-minute doctor's appointment, half of patients will leave without understanding what their doctor has told to them to do to get better.[17] Unfortunately, even when patients seem to understand what their doctors are telling them in that fifteen-minute visit, it turns out that they immediately forget 80 percent of that medical information, and then half of what they remember is wrong![18]

The last step of the communication process occurs when the receiver gives the sender feedback. **Feedback to sender** is a return message to the sender that indicates the receiver's understanding of the message (of what the receiver was supposed to know, to do, or not to do). Feedback makes senders aware of possible miscommunications and enables them to continue communicating until the receiver understands the intended message. Because of the difficulties of communicating complex medical information in too little time, many doctors now employ the "teach-back" method at the end of a patient visit, where they ask patients to explain in their own words what they've heard the doctor say regarding their problem (diagnosis), whether they'll get better (prognosis), and what the patient is supposed to do after they leave the doctor's office (that is, treatment plan and managing medications).[19] Even so, much progress needs to be made as about half of patients are not even asked if they have questions.[20]

Unfortunately, feedback doesn't always occur in the communication process. Complacency and overconfidence about the ease and simplicity of communication can lead senders and receivers to simply assume that they share a common understanding of the message and, consequently, to not use feedback to improve the effectiveness of their communication. This is a serious mistake, especially as messages and feedback are always transmitted with and against a background of noise. Part of the background noise in medicine is how well medical information is communicated between medical professionals. After all, medicine is a "team sport" involving various doctors, physician assistants, nurses, and other care professionals for each patient. Medical mistakes kill 500 people per day, and 80 percent of those deaths are caused by miscommunication that occurs when patients are transferred from one set of caregivers to another, for instance, the night-shift nurses not communicating key information to the day-shift nurses, or one doctor not being aware of the diagnosis and treatment plan of another doctor on a case.[21]

Noise is anything that interferes with the transmission of the intended message. Noise can occur in any of the following situations:

▶ The sender isn't sure what message to communicate.

▶ The message is not clearly encoded.

▶ The wrong communication channel is chosen.

▶ The message is not received or decoded properly.

Decoding the process by which the receiver translates the written, verbal, or symbolic form of a message into an understood message

Feedback to sender in the communication process, a return message to the sender that indicates the receiver's understanding of the message

Noise anything that interferes with the transmission of the intended message

Olly/Shutterstock.com

An App for Sender's Remorse

Most everyone has experienced sender's remorse—that sinking feeling you get when you send an email to the wrong person, or divulge one opinion too many about a coworker in an interoffice memo. Gmail and Outlook have features for recalling emails, but they rarely work as desired. UnSend.it is an app that aims to solve sender's remorse by converting messages to JPEG images and embedding the JPEG into the email body. Until the recipient opens the message, the sender can edit or replace the JPEG. The app does have a few practical limitations. Most Outlook and Gmail inboxes block images by default, and users of any service might find a business email containing an image with no text a little suspect. Additionally, without a CC function, UnSend.it is only suitable for direct communications to one or more recipients. But for those with overzealous sending habits, it might just provide the extra time for an email do-over.

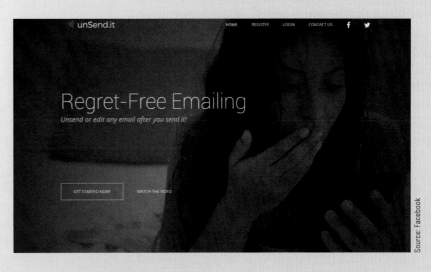

Source: Facebook

Source: K. Wiggers, "Sent an Email to the Wrong Person? UnSend.it Lets You Remove It from Their Inbox," Digital Trends, April 7, 2015, accessed April 23, 2015. http://www.digitaltrends.com/computing/unsend-it-email-app/.

▶ The receiver doesn't have the experience or time to understand the message. Emotional outbursts are an often unrecognized type of noise. Whether yelling, crying, sulking, or table pounding, strong emotions interfere with the transmission of intended messages. The outburst itself, however, is a signal that what's being discussed touches strongly held beliefs or values. The first step in addressing noise related to strong emotions is spotting early indicators, such as body language not matching words. Acknowledge the difficulty of the issue, and then ask them to share their views. Next, listen to the response, and ask follow-up questions. Finally, work toward resolution by helping them articulate their core issues.[22] We'll cover listening and asking questions in greater detail in the "Coaching and Counseling: One-on-One Communication" section later in this chapter.

Jargon, which is vocabulary particular to a profession or group, is another form of noise that interferes with communication in the workplace. Any idea what "rightsizing," "unsiloing," "pain points," "drilling down," and "sync up" mean? Rightsizing means laying off workers. Unsiloing means getting workers in different parts of the company (that is, different vertical silos) to work with others outside their own areas. Pain points are customer

problems that represent opportunities for businesses to fix. Drilling down is moving from a general analysis to a more specific, in-depth focus with greater detail. Finally, sync up means making sure everyone knows what is happening.[23] Unfortunately, the business world is rife with jargon. Carol Hymowitz of the *Wall Street Journal* points out, "A new crop of buzzwords usually sprouts every three to five years, or about the same length of time many top executives have to prove themselves. Some can be useful in swiftly communicating, and spreading, new business concepts. Others are less useful, even devious."[24]

15-2b Formal Communication Channels

An organization's **formal communication channel**, is the system of official channels that carry organizationally approved messages and information. Organizational objectives, rules, policies, procedures,

Jargon vocabulary particular to a profession or group that interferes with communication in the workplace

Formal communication channel the system of official channels that carry organizationally approved messages and information instructions, commands, and requests for information are all transmitted via the formal communication system or channel. There are three formal communication channels: downward communication, upward communication, and horizontal communication.[25]

Downward communication flows from higher to lower levels in an organization. Downward communication is used to issue orders down the organizational hierarchy, to give organizational members job-related information, to give managers and workers performance reviews from upper managers, and to clarify organizational objectives and goals.[26] Michael Beer, professor emeritus at Harvard Business School, says, "You can never overcommunicate. When you think you've communicated well, go out three or four more times and communicate again." Beer's consulting firm, TruePoint, studied forty CEOs whose companies have been above-average performers for more than a decade. He found that those remarkable leaders spend an enormous amount of time in communicating downward. They have a simple story, and that story gets out every place they go."[27]

Upward communication flows from lower levels to higher levels in an organization. Upward communication is used to give higher-level managers feedback about operations, issues, and problems; to help higher-level managers assess organizational performance and effectiveness; to encourage lower-level managers and employees to participate in organizational decision making; and to give those at lower levels the chance to share their concerns with higher-level authorities. At restaurants, tables with big groups bring big tips, so competition among servers can get fierce—and unfriendly—to wait on them. The "system" of assigning tables where waitress Michelle Burke worked as a waitress involved servers racing to the table, and whoever got there first got the table. Burke says this made her, "angry at work, and after work," and that she, "finally decided to take a stand." So she discussed the problem with her manager. First, she explained the situation and that most of the staff were upset. Then she proposed rotating the big tables among servers, which she said would be fairer, but also give customers better service. He boss agreed and adopted her suggestion.[28]

Shut It Down—How to Handle Gossip (About You)

There can be a fine line between news and gossip, and, at some point, you might find yourself a target of the rumor mill. How should you handle it? Groundless gossip can often be extinguished with simple denial. Sometimes, however, a direct denial only attracts more attention. In those cases, consider asking the person spreading the rumors to be an advocate for you to help shut down the gossip. And as a proactive measure, maintain strong alliances with colleagues above, below, and at your own level of the organization. That way, you'll know who to enlist on your behalf to diffuse gossip about you.

Source: S. Shellenbarger, "What to Do When You Are the Subject of Office Gossip," *Wall Street Journal*, October 7, 2014, accessed May 12, 2015. http://www.wsj.com/articles/what-to-do-when-you-are-the-subject-of-office-gossip-1412701581.

Horizontal communication flows among managers and workers who are at the same organizational level, such as when a day shift nurse comes in at 7:30 a.m. for a half-hour discussion with the midnight nurse supervisor who leaves at 8:00 a.m. Horizontal communication helps facilitate coordination and cooperation between different parts of a company and allows coworkers to share relevant information. It also helps people at the same level resolve conflicts and solve problems without involving high levels of management. Two executives at **Business Value Group** regularly undermined each other wherever their responsibilities overlapped. Rather than complain to their boss, one of the managers, Patrick Hehir, went directly to his colleague, Paul Humphries, and said, "I'm playing games with you and you're playing games with me, yet you and I both talk with others on our team about collaborating more."[29] Humphries described his relief at finally addressing the problem as, "liberating." They discussed their concerns, agreeing to handle all future issues face-to-face.[30]

In general, what can managers do to improve formal communication? First, decrease reliance on downward communication. Second, increase chances for upward communication by increasing personal contact with lower-level managers and workers. Third, encourage much better use of horizontal communication.

15-2c Informal Communication Channels

An organization's **informal communication channel**, sometimes called the **grapevine**, is the transmission of messages from employee to employee outside of formal communication channels. The grapevine arises out of curiosity, that is, the need to know what is going on in an organization and how it might affect you or others. To satisfy this curiosity, employees need a consistent supply of relevant, accurate, in-depth information about what is going on in the company and why. At **Net Optics**, a manufacturer of computer networking equipment, CEO Bob Shaw understands the importance of the grapevine to better communication. He says, "If there's something out there that the organization's not clear on, my role and responsibility is to make sure I fill it in with the right information." So Net Optics has a rumor jar in which employees can insert anonymous notes about the rumors they've heard. Then, at the monthly company meeting, Shaw pulls out the notes, reads them to the employees, and addresses each one. Shaw says, "I never know what's going to be in there, so it's as much a surprise for me as it is for the audience." After two employees lost their jobs (for performance reasons), notes asked if the rumor that the company was going to have layoffs was true. Shaw explained that not only was Net Optics not downsizing, it was quite successful and growing.[31]

> "THE MAIN FOCUS OF RUMOR IS TO FIGURE OUT THE TRUTH. IT'S THE GROUP TRYING TO MAKE SENSE OF SOMETHING THAT'S IMPORTANT TO THEM."

Exhibit 15.4
Grapevine Communication Networks

Gossip Chain   Cluster Chain

Source: K. Davis and J. W. Newstrom, *Human Behavior at Work: Organizational Behavior*, 8th ed. (New York: McGraw-Hill, 1989).

Grapevines arise out of informal communication networks such as the gossip or cluster chains shown in Exhibit 15.4. In a *gossip chain*, one highly connected individual shares information with many other managers and workers. By contrast, in a *cluster chain*, numerous people simply tell a few of their friends. The result in both cases is that information flows freely and quickly through the organization. Some believe that grapevines are a waste of employees' time, that they promote gossip and rumors that fuel political speculation, and that they are sources of highly unreliable, inaccurate information. Yet studies clearly show that grapevines are highly accurate sources of information for a number of reasons.[32] First, because grapevines typically carry "juicy" information that is interesting and timely, information spreads rapidly. During Allstate's annual Leaders Forum, a gathering of 2,000 agents and employees, CEO Thomas Wilson announced plans for reducing the company's sales force and changing sales commission rates. Later that evening, a group of employees were at the hotel bar, complaining about the changes and about Wilson, when Joseph Lacher, the president of Allstate's home and auto insurance division, was allegedly overheard using two expletives in reference to Wilson. By the next day, nearly all conference attendees had heard

There is a fine line between news and gossip. At some point, you might find yourself a target of the rumor mill.

Informal communication channel (grapevine) the transmission of messages from employee to employee outside of formal communication channels about Lacher's critical remarks. Lacher was abruptly let go just a few weeks later.[33]

Second, because information is typically spread by face-to-face conversation, receivers can send feedback to make sure they understand the message that is being communicated. This reduces misunderstandings and increases accuracy. Third, because most of the information in a company moves along the grapevine rather than through formal communication channels, people can usually verify the accuracy of information by checking it out with others.

What can managers do to manage organizational grapevines? The very worst thing they can do is withhold information or try to punish those who share information with others. The grapevine abhors a vacuum, so rumors and anxiety will flourish in the absence of information from company management. Why does this occur? According to workplace psychologist Nicholas DiFonzo, "The main focus of rumor is to figure out the truth. It's the group trying to make sense of something that's important to them."[34] A better strategy is to embrace the grapevine and keep employees informed about possible changes and strategies. Failure to do so will just make things worse. And, in addition to using the grapevine to communicate with others, managers should not overlook the grapevine as a tremendous source of valuable information and feedback. In fact, research shows that, contrary to popular belief, grapevines are fast, accurate, and focused on information more than gossip.[35]

15-2d Coaching and Counseling: One-on-One Communication

When the Wyatt Company surveyed 531 U.S. companies undergoing major changes and restructuring, it asked the CEOs, "If you could go back and change one thing, what would it be?" The answer: "The way we communicated with our employees." The CEOs said that instead of flashy videos, printed materials, or formal meetings, they would make greater use of one-on-one communication, especially with employees' immediate supervisors instead of with higher-level executives whom employees didn't know.[36]

Coaching and counseling are two kinds of one-on-one communication. **Coaching** is communicating with someone for the direct purpose of improving the person's on-the-job performance or behavior.[37] Managers tend to make several mistakes when coaching employees. First, they wait for a problem to arise before coaching.

Coaching communicating with someone for the direct purpose of improving the person's on-the-job performance or behavior

Counseling communicating with someone about non-job-related issues that may be affecting or interfering with the person's performance

Jim Concelman, manager for leadership development at Development Dimensions International, says, "Of course, a boss has to coach an employee if a mistake has been made, but they shouldn't be waiting for the error. While it is a lot easier to see a mistake and correct it, people learn more through success than through failure, so bosses should ensure that employees are experiencing as many successes as possible. Successful employees lead to a more successful organization."[38] Second, when mistakes *are* made, managers wait much too long before talking to the employee about the problem. The late management professor Ray Hilgert said, "A manager must respond as soon as possible after an incident of poor performance. Don't bury your head. . . . When employees are told nothing, they assume everything is okay."[39] Jack Welch, who was CEO at GE for two decades, says, "I've spoken to more than 500,000 people around the world, and I always ask audiences, 'How many of you know where you stand in your organization?'" He says, "Typically no more than 10 percent raise their hands. That's criminal! As a manager, you owe candor to your people. They must not be guessing about what the organization thinks of them. My experience is that most employees appreciate this reality check, and today's 'Millenials' practically demand it."[40] In short, says Welch, "You have no right to be a leader if someone who works for you doesn't know where they stand."[41] So coach your employees about their job performance.

In contrast to coaching, **counseling** is communicating with someone about nonjob-related issues such as stress, child care, health issues, retirement planning, or legal issues that may be affecting or interfering with the person's performance. But counseling does not mean that managers should try to be clinicians, even though an estimated 20 percent of employees are dealing with personal problems at any one time. Dana Kiel, regional director in Account Management at Magellan Health, says, "We call it the quicksand. If you're a good supervisor, you do care about your employees, but it's not your job to be a therapist."[42] Instead, managers should discuss specific performance problems, listen if the employee chooses to share personal issues, and then recommend that the employee call the company's *Employee Assistance Program (EAP)*. EAPs are typically free when provided as part of a company's benefit package. In emergencies or times of crisis, EAPs can offer immediate counseling and support; they can also provide referrals to organizations and professionals that can help employees and their family members address personal issues. Apparel maker Levi Strauss, for example, established an EAP called HIV Connect, which aims to improve employees' access to HIV/AIDS education, testing, treatment, and care. Paurvi

Bhatt, senior director of strategic health initiatives and the employee HIV/AIDS program at Levi Strauss, says, "How we make [HIV] relevant is [by] understanding the importance of prevention and how it affects people at work. Addressing HIV isn't just addressing the health side, but learning how to manage the issue at work. This, like a lot of issues, can affect teamwork and collaboration." HIV Connect is a part of Levi Strauss's larger EAP program.[43]

15-2e Nonverbal Communication

Nonverbal communication is any communication that doesn't involve words. Nonverbal communication almost always accompanies verbal communication and may either support and reinforce the verbal message or contradict it. The importance of nonverbal communication is well established. Researchers have estimated that as much as 93 percent of any message is transmitted nonverbally, with 55 percent coming from body language and facial expressions, and 38 percent coming from the tone and pitch of the voice.[44] Because many nonverbal cues are unintentional, receivers often consider nonverbal communication to be a more accurate representation of what senders are thinking and feeling than the words they use. If you have ever asked someone out on a date and been told "yes," but realized that the real answer was "no," then you understand the importance of paying attention to nonverbal communication.

Kinesics and paralanguage are two kinds of nonverbal communication.[45] **Kinesics** (from the Greek word *kinesis*, meaning "movement") are movements of the body and face.[46] These movements include arm and hand gestures, facial expressions, eye contact, folding arms, crossing legs, and leaning toward or away from another person. For example, people tend to avoid eye contact when they are embarrassed or unsure of the message they are sending. Crossed arms or legs usually indicate defensiveness or that the person is not receptive

Consultant, Suzanne Bales, says that some of her CEO clients check their phones so much during meetings, "it's the equivalent of not showing up for half of the meeting."

Source: Bates Communications Inc

to the message or the sender. Also, people tend to smile frequently when they are seeking someone's approval.

It turns out that kinesics play an incredibly important role in communication. Studies of married couples' kinesic interactions can predict whether they will stay married with 93 percent accuracy.[47] The key is the ratio of positive to negative kinesic interactions between husbands and wives as they communicate. Negative kinesic expressions such as eye rolling suggest contempt, whereas positive kinesic expressions such as maintaining eye contact and nodding suggest listening and caring. When the ratio of positive to negative interactions drops below 5 to 1, the chances for divorce quickly increase. Kinesics operate similarly in the workplace, providing clues about people's true feelings, over and above what they say (or don't say).

Unfortunately, not making or maintaining eye contact is an increasingly frequent occurrence in today's workplace. Consultant Suzanne Bates, author of *Speak Like a CEO*, says that some

Nonverbal communication any communication that doesn't involve words

Kinesics movements of the body and face

What If Your Emotions Were an Open Book?

Over the course of his career, 80-year-old psychologist Dr. Paul Ekman built a catalog of more than 5,000 facial muscle movements that communicate one of six base emotions: anger, disgust, fear, happiness, sadness, or surprise. What started out for Ekman as an anthropological study has recently been transformed by big data, as a host of software start-ups are building programs to uncover people's hidden emotions. One software company, Emotient, has video recorded encounters with hundreds of thousands of people and extracted 90,000 data points from each frame. Rival company Affectiva has measured billions of emotional reactions from 2.4 million face videos taken in eighty countries. Enthusiastic organizations such as Procter & Gamble, Coca-Cola, and others have used the software to gauge consumers' emotional reactions to products and advertisements; law-enforcement agencies have used the software in criminal interrogations; and retailers have used it to determine how people are feeling as they exit their stores. But despite their foundation on big data, emotional software programs run the risk of misinterpreting emotions or incorrectly labeling people as liars. Critics are wary, however, because people are not always aware they are being recorded. Privacy advocate Ginger McCall says, "I can see few things more invasive than trying to record someone's emotions in a database."

LanKS/Shutterstock.com

Source: E. Dwoskin and E. M. Rusli, "The Technology That Unmasks Your Hidden Emotions," *Wall Street Journal*, January 28, 2015, accessed May 12, 2015. http://www.wsj.com/articles/startups-see-your-face-unmask-your-emotions-1422472398.

of her CEO clients check their phones so much during appointments that, "it's the equivalent of not showing up for half of the meeting." And that, she says, breeds resentment in others who think, "I'm just as busy as the CEO. I just have different things to juggle."[48] In fact, a survey of business professionals found that strong majorities think it is inappropriate to answer phone calls (86%) or write texts or emails (84%) in meetings or at business lunches (66%). The kinesics related to checking smartphones in these situations communicate a lack of respect, attention, listening, and self-control.[49] TalentSmart's Travis Bradberry says, "Take a page out of the Old West and put a basket by the conference room door with an image of a smartphone and the message, 'Leave your guns at the door.'"[50]

Paralanguage includes the pitch, rate, tone, volume, and speaking pattern (use of silences, pauses, or hesitations) of one's voice. When people are unsure of what to say, for example, they tend to decrease their communication effectiveness by speaking softly. When people are nervous, they tend to speak faster and louder. How much does paralanguage matter? A study in which 1,000 people listened to 120 different speeches found that the tone of the speaker's voice accounted for 23 percent of the difference in listener's evaluations of the speech, compared to speech content, which accounted for only 11 percent.[51]

> **Paralanguage** the pitch, rate, tone, volume, and speaking pattern (that is, use of silences, pauses, or hesitations) of one's voice

So paralanguage was twice as important as what was actually said.

In short, because nonverbal communication is so informative, especially when it contradicts verbal communication, managers need to learn how to monitor and control their nonverbal behaviors.

15-3 MANAGING ONE-ON-ONE COMMUNICATION

When it comes to improving communication, managers face two primary tasks, managing one-on-one communication and managing organization-wide communication.

On average, first-line managers spend 57 percent of their time with people, middle managers spend 63 percent of their time directly with people, and top managers spend as much as 78 percent of their time dealing with people.[52] These numbers make it clear that managers spend a great deal of time in one-on-one communication with others.

*Let's learn more about managing one-on-one communication by reading how to **15-3a choose the right communication medium, 15-3b be a good listener,** and **15-3c give effective feedback.***

15-3a Choosing the Right Communication Medium

Sometimes messages are poorly communicated simply because they are delivered using the wrong **communication medium**, which is the method used to deliver a message. For example, the wrong communication medium is being used when an employee returns from lunch, picks up the note left on her office chair, and learns she has been fired. The wrong communication medium is also being used when an employee pops into your office every ten minutes with a simple request. (An email would be better.)

There are two general kinds of communication media: oral and written communication. *Oral communication* includes face-to-face interactions and group meetings through telephone calls, videoconferencing, or any other means of sending and receiving spoken messages. Studies show that managers generally prefer oral communication over written because it provides the opportunity to ask questions about parts of the message that they don't understand. Oral communication is also a rich communication medium because it allows managers to receive and assess the nonverbal communication that accompanies spoken messages (that is, body language, facial expressions, and the voice characteristics associated with paralanguage). Furthermore, you don't need a PC and an Internet connection to conduct oral communication. Simply schedule an appointment, track someone down in the hall, or catch someone on the phone. **A&E Network** executive Mel Berning travels two weeks a month, and when he is at headquarters, he forgoes what he calls "antiseptic" formal meetings and instead prefers impromptu informal meetings in which he breezes into the offices of direct reports in the morning. "You have a conversation that is less hurried and less guarded," he says. "Face-to-face encounters are so much more revealing than a text or an email."[53]

In fact, former *Wall Street Journal* columnist Jason Fry worries that voice mail and email have made managers less willing to engage in meaningful, face-to-face oral communication than before. In fact, 67 percent of managers admit to using email as a substitute for face-to-face conversations. While there are advantages to email (for example, it creates a record of what's been said), it's often better to talk to people instead of just emailing them. Fry writes, "If you're close enough that the person you're emailing uses the plonk of your return key as a cue to look for the little Outlook envelope, [it's] best [to] think carefully about whether you should be typing instead of talking."[54] But the oral medium should not be used for *all* communication. In general, when the message is simple, such as a quick request or a presentation of straightforward information, a memo or email is often the better communication medium.

Written communication includes letters, email, and memos. Although most managers still like and use oral communication, email in particular is changing how they communicate with workers, customers, and each other. Email is the dominant form of communication in organizations primarily because of its convenience and speed. For instance, because people read six times faster than they can listen, they usually can read thirty email messages in ten to fifteen minutes.[55] By contrast, dealing with voice messages can take a considerable amount of time.

Written communication such as email is well suited for delivering straightforward messages and information. Furthermore, with email accessible at the office, at home, and on the road (by laptop computer, cell phone, or web-based email), managers can use email to stay in touch from anywhere at almost any time. And, because email and other written communications don't have to be sent and received simultaneously, messages can be sent and stored for reading at any time. Consequently, managers can send and receive many more messages using email than by using oral communication, which requires people to get together in person or by phone or videoconference.

Email has its own drawbacks, however. One is that it lacks the formality of paper memos and letters. It is easy to fire off a rushed email that is not well written or fully thought through. The opportunity to lash out with an angry email reply is incredibly tempting. To avoid that temptation and the damage it does to your work relationships, Pamela Rutledge of the Media Psychology Research Center recommends asking yourself, "Do I want an outcome where someone throws a cup of coffee at me? Or do I want an outcome where we work toward a solution?"[56] Another drawback to email is that it lacks nonverbal cues, making emails very easy to misinterpret.

Although written communication is well suited for delivering straightforward messages and information, it is not well suited to complex, ambiguous, or emotionally laden messages, which are better delivered through oral communication.

15-3b Listening

Are you a good listener? You probably think so. In fact, most people, including managers, are terrible

Communication medium the method used to deliver an oral or written message listeners. A recent study from Stanford Graduate School of Business showed that listening was among the least mentioned strengths in CEO performance evaluations.[57] You qualify as a poor listener if you frequently interrupt others, jump to conclusions about what people will say before they've said it, hurry the speaker to finish his or her point, are a passive listener (not actively working at your listening), or simply don't pay attention to what people are saying.[58] On this last point—attentiveness— college students were periodically asked to record their thoughts during a psychology course. On average, 20 percent of the students were paying attention (only 12% were actively working at being good listeners), 20 percent were thinking about sex, 20 percent were thinking about things they had done before, and the remaining 40 percent were thinking about other things unrelated to the class (for example, worries, religion, lunch, daydreaming).[59]

How important is it to be a good listener? In general, about 45 percent of the total time you spend communicating with others is spent listening. Furthermore, listening is important for managerial and business success, even for those at the top of an organization. T-Mobile CEO John Legere says that when he took the top job at the telecommunications company, he needed *Wireless for Dummies*. His response to his lack of familiarity with the industry was simple—listen. He listened to customer service calls, visited stores to listen to customers and employees, and even interacted with users over social media. Legere says, "My business philosophy is to listen to your employees, listen to your customers. Shut up and do what they tell you. And each of our uncarrier moves and the way I run my company is completely aligned with that."[60]

Listening is a more important skill for managers than ever because Generation X and Millennial employees tend to expect a high level of interaction with their supervisors. They want feedback on their performance, but they also want to offer feedback and know that it is heard. In fact, managers with better listening skills are rated more highly by their employees and are much more likely to be promoted.[61]

So, what can you do to improve your listening ability? First, understand the difference between hearing and listening. According to *Webster's New World Dictionary*, **hearing** is the "act or process of perceiving sounds," whereas **listening** is "making a conscious effort to hear." In other words, we react to sounds, such as bottles breaking or music being played too loud, because hearing is an involuntary physiological process. By contrast, listening is a voluntary behavior. So, if you want to be a good listener, you have to choose to be a good listener. Typically, that means choosing to be an active, empathetic listener.[62]

Active listening means assuming half the responsibility for successful communication by actively giving the speaker nonjudgmental feedback that shows you've accurately heard what he or she said. Active listeners make it clear from their behavior that they are listening carefully to what the speaker has to say. Active listeners put the speaker at ease, maintain eye contact, and show the speaker that they are attentively listening by nodding and making short statements.

Several specific strategies can help you be a better active listener. First, engage in *immediacy behaviors,* such as putting your phone away, turning off the TV, leaning forward and making eye contact, and using short words such as "yes," "uh-huh," "okay," to encourage the speaker to continue and to demonstrate that you're listening.[63] Second, clarify responses by asking the speaker to explain confusing or ambiguous statements. Third, when there are natural breaks in the speaker's delivery, use this time to paraphrase or summarize what has been said. *Paraphrasing* is restating what has been said in your own words. *Summarizing* is reviewing the speaker's main points or emotions. Paraphrasing and summarizing give the speaker the chance to correct the message if the active listener has attached the wrong meaning to it. Paraphrasing and summarizing also show the speaker that the active listener is interested in the speaker's message.

Exhibit 15.5 reviews immediacy behaviors and lists specific statements that listeners can use to clarify responses, paraphrase, or summarize what has been said. Active listeners also avoid evaluating the message or being critical until the message is complete. They recognize that their only responsibility during the transmission of a message is to receive it accurately and derive the intended meaning from it. Evaluation and criticism can take place after the message is accurately received. Finally, active listeners recognize that a large portion of any message is transmitted nonverbally and thus pay very careful attention to nonverbal cues (that is, immediacy behaviors) transmitted by the speaker.

Hearing the act or process of perceiving sounds

Listening making a conscious effort to hear

Active listening assuming half the responsibility for successful communication by actively giving the speaker nonjudgmental feedback that shows you've accurately heard what he or she said

Exhibit 15.5

Immediacy Behaviors, and Paraphrasing and Summarizing Responses for Active Listeners

Immediacy Behaviors	Clarifying Responses	Paraphrasing Responses	Summarizing Responses
Put your phone away.	Could you explain that again?	What you're really saying is	Let me summarize . . . .
Turn off the TV.	I don't understand what you mean.	If I understand you correctly	Okay, your main concerns are . . . .
Sit close and lean forward.	I'm not sure how	In other words	To recap, what you've said . . . .
Make eye contact.	I'm confused. Would you run through that again?	So your perspective is that	Thus far, you've discussed . . . .
Use "yes," "uh-huh," "okay," and other short words to encourage the speaker to continue.		Tell me if I'm wrong, but what you seem to be saying is	

Source: E. Atwater, *I Hear You*, rev. ed. (New York: Walker, 1992); E. Bernstein, "How 'Active Listening' Makes Both Participants in a Conversation Feel Better," *Wall Street Journal*, January 12, 2015, accessed May 13, 2015. http://www.wsj.com/articles/how-active-listening-makes-both-sides-of-a-conversation-feel-better-1421082684.

Empathetic listening means understanding the speaker's perspective and personal frame of reference and giving feedback that conveys that understanding to the speaker. Empathetic listening goes beyond active listening because it depends on our ability to set aside our own attitudes or relationships to be able to see and understand things through someone else's eyes. Empathetic listening is just as important as active listening, especially for managers, because it helps build rapport and trust with others. When Cheryl Bachelder became CEO of Popeyes Louisiana Kitchen, a fast-food franchise famous for its fried chicken, trust between headquarters and its 1,600 franchised restaurants was low. She says, "During the first meeting I had with franchisees, they wanted a palace coup—they wanted everyone replaced, and they didn't trust anyone. You only trust people you know, and that was the problem."[64] Bachelder improved things by listening. She says, "We started listening to them. I know that sounds simplistic, but we were at a stage where, in our quarterly meetings with franchisees, the company told them stuff and didn't listen. When we told them we wanted to remodel the restaurants, the first thing they said was, 'No, we need to get our sales up so we have cash to invest.' We were disappointed, but we waited. We showed them our first design, and they hated it and thought it cost too much. We came back with a new store design that was more cost-effective, and we built twelve new stores in New Orleans that they could go and see and touch, and we laid out all the costs. We got our sales up . . . and had a new design they loved, and they started getting excited about remodeling."[65] Indeed, after listening to franchisees' concerns, Popeye's remodeled 80 percent of its restaurants.

The key to being a more empathetic listener is to show your desire to understand and to reflect people's feelings. You can *show your desire to understand* by listening, that is, asking people to talk about what's most important to them and then by giving them sufficient time to talk before responding or interrupting.

Reflecting feelings is also an important part of empathetic listening because it demonstrates that you understand the speaker's emotions. Unlike active listening, in which you restate or summarize the informational content of what has been said, the focus is on the affective part of the message. As an empathetic listener, you can use the following statements to *reflect the speaker's emotions*:

▶ So, right now it sounds like you're feeling . . . .

▶ You seem as if you're . . . .

▶ Do you feel a bit . . . ?

▶ I could be wrong, but I'm sensing that you're feeling . . . .

In the end, says management consultant Terry Pearce, empathetic listening can be boiled down to these three steps. First, wait ten seconds before you respond. It will seem an eternity, but waiting prevents you from interrupting others and rushing your response. Second, to be sure you understand what the speaker wants, ask questions to clarify the speaker's intent. Third, only then should you respond first with feelings and then facts (notice that facts *follow* feelings).[66]

Empathetic listening understanding the speaker's perspective and personal frame of reference and giving feedback that conveys that understanding to the speaker

A word of caution, however: not everyone appreciates having what they said repeated back to them. Manager Candy Friesen says that whenever she did that, "I seemed to engender animosity or hostility. . . . the person to whom you're speaking may not appreciate having his thoughts paraphrased one little bit."[67] So, when applying these listening techniques, pay attention to the body language and tone of voice of the person you're communicating with to make sure they appreciate your attempts to be a better listener.

15-3c Giving Feedback

In Chapter 11, you learned that performance appraisal feedback (that is, judging) should be separated from developmental feedback (that is, coaching).[68] We can now focus on the steps needed to communicate feedback one-on-one to employees.

To start, managers need to recognize that feedback can be constructive or destructive. **Destructive feedback** is disapproving without any intention of being helpful and almost always causes a negative or defensive reaction in the recipient. By contrast, **constructive feedback** is intended to be helpful, corrective, and/or encouraging. It is aimed at correcting performance deficiencies and motivating employees. Business author Tim Harford says the problem with constructive feedback is that it's given like a sandwich—something nice to start with, some constructive feedback in the middle, and then something positive at the end. Harford says, "We say [to the people we're managing], 'That was a great piece of work, there was just a small problem.'" "What we tend to hear," he says, is, "That was a great piece of work."[69]

For feedback to be constructive rather than destructive, it must be immediate, focused on specific behaviors, and problem-oriented. *Immediate feedback* is much more effective than delayed feedback because manager and worker can recall the mistake or incident more accurately and discuss it in detail. For example, if a worker is rude to a customer, and the customer immediately reports the incident to management, and if the manager, in turn, immediately discusses the incident with the employee, there should be little disagreement over what was said or done. By contrast, it's unlikely that either the manager or the worker will be able to accurately

For feedback to be constructive rather than desctructive, it must be immediate and focused on specific behaviors and problems.

remember the specifics of what occurred if the manager waits several weeks to discuss the incident. When that happens, it's usually too late to have a meaningful conversation.

Specific feedback focuses on particular acts or incidents that are clearly under the control of the employee. For instance, instead of telling an employee that he or she is "always late for work," it's much more constructive to say, "In the last three weeks, you have been thirty minutes late on four occasions and more than an hour late on two others." Furthermore, specific feedback isn't very helpful unless employees have control over the problems that the feedback addresses. Giving negative feedback about behaviors beyond someone's control is likely to be seen as unfair. Similarly, giving positive feedback about behaviors beyond someone's control may be viewed as insincere.

Last, *problem-oriented feedback* focuses on the problems or incidents associated with the poor performance rather than on the worker or the worker's personality. Giving feedback does not give managers the right to personally attack workers. Although managers may be frustrated by a worker's poor performance, the point of problem-oriented feedback is to draw attention to the problem in a nonjudgmental way so that the employee has enough information to correct it. For example, if an employee has body odor, a surprisingly common workplace problem, don't leave deodorant, soap, or shampoo on the person's desk (for all to see) or say, "You stink." *HR Magazine* advises handling the problem this way: "Because this is a sensitive issue and the employee will

Destructive feedback feedback that disapproves without any intention of being helpful and almost always causes a negative or defensive reaction in the recipient

Constructive feedback feedback intended to be helpful, corrective, and/or encouraging likely be uncomfortable and embarrassed in discussing it, keep the meeting private and confidential. Be compassionate but direct. Treat it as you would handle any other job-related performance issue. Explain the problem and the need to correct it. Be specific about expectations. . . . If the employer has a dress and grooming policy, refer to the policy and provide the employee with a copy."[70]

15-4 MANAGING ORGANIZATION-WIDE COMMUNICATION

Although managing one-on-one communication is important, managers must also know how to communicate effectively with a larger number of people throughout an organization.

*Learn more about organization-wide communication by reading the following sections about **15-4a improving transmission by getting the message out** and **15-4b improving reception by finding ways to hear what others feel and think.***

15-4a Improving Transmission: Getting the Message Out

Several methods of electronic communication—email, collaborative discussion sites, televised/videotaped speeches and conferences, and broadcast voice mail—now make it easier for managers to communicate with people throughout the organization and get the message out.

Although we normally think of email, the transmission of messages via computers, as a means of one-on-one communication, it also plays an important role in organization-wide communication. With the click of a button, managers can send an email to everyone in the company via distribution lists. When Microsoft announced it would be laying off 18,000 employees, 14 percent of its workforce, CEO Satya Nadella announced the news in a speech to Microsoft employees, accompanied by a long, detailed email, in which he said, "Nothing is off the table in how we think about shifting our culture to deliver on this core strategy [to become a mobile-first, cloud-first company]. Organizations will change. Mergers and acquisitions will occur. Job responsibilities will evolve. New partnerships will be formed. Tired traditions will be questioned. Our priorities will be adjusted. New skills will be built. New ideas will be heard. New

hires will be made. Processes will be simplified. And if you want to thrive at Microsoft and make a world impact, you and your team must add numerous more changes to this list that you will be enthusiastic about driving."[71] He finished by saying, "Culture change means we will do things differently. Often people think that means everyone other than them. In reality, it means all of us taking a new approach and working together to make Microsoft better."[72]

Collaborative websites are another means of electronically promoting organization-wide communication. **Online discussion forums** use web- or software-based discussion tools to allow employees across the company to easily ask questions and share knowledge with each other. The point is to share expertise and not duplicate solutions already discovered by others in the company. Furthermore, because collaborative discussion sites remain online, they provide a historical database for people who are dealing with particular problems for the first time.

Collaborative discussion sites are typically organized by topic, project, or person and can take the shape of blogs that allow readers to post comments, wikis to allow collaborative discussions, document sharing and editing, or traditional discussion forums (see Chapter 17, Managing Information, for further explanation). **Slack** is a robust group communication platform (on computers, smartphones, and tablets) that includes automatic archiving, a powerful search engine, and more informal and accessible online collaboration. Slack's "open channels" increase communication transparency by making messages, files, comments, images, and video visible to everyone else in the team (or company). And with everything searchable, anyone can quickly catch up to find out where projects or discussions stand. Walmart, Comcast, Blue Bottle Coffee Company, the *New York Times*, and many other companies have adopted Slack primarily because it increases communication effectiveness so much that email usage within teams or companies often drops by 70 or 80 percent. *New York Times* reporter Farhad Manjoo is based in California and has found that Slack helps him stay connected to "the mother ship in New York. Using Slack, I can peer into discussions that would never have been accessible to me. I can see how the producers and editors who are handling my column are discussing how to present it, and how the team overseeing the home page is thinking about my work."[73]

> **Online discussion forums** the in-house equivalent of Internet newsgroups. By using web- or software-based discussion tools that are available across the company, employees can easily ask questions and share knowledge with each other

Exhibit 15.6
Establishing Collaborative Discussion Sites

Step 1 → Step 2 → Step 3 → Step 4

Knowledge Audit | Online Directory | Discussion Groups on Intranet | Reward Information Sharing

© Cengage Learning

Exhibit 15.6 lists the steps companies need to take to establish successful collaborative discussion sites. First, pinpoint your company's top intellectual assets through a knowledge audit and spread that knowledge throughout the organization. Second, create an online directory detailing the expertise of individual workers and make it available to all employees. Third, set up collaborative discussion sites on the intranet so that managers and workers can collaborate on problem solving. Finally, reward information sharing by making the online sharing of knowledge a key part of performance ratings.

Televised/videotaped speeches and meetings are a third electronic method of organization-wide communication. **Televised/videotaped speeches and meetings** are simply speeches and meetings originally made to a small audience that are either simultaneously broadcast to other locations in the company or videotaped for subsequent distribution and viewing by a broader audience.

Voice messaging, or voice mail, is a telephone answering system that records audio messages. In one survey, 89 percent of respondents said that voice messaging is critical to business communication, 78 percent said that it improves productivity, and 58 percent said they would rather leave a message on a voice messaging system than with a receptionist.[74] Nonetheless, most people are unfamiliar with the ability to *broadcast voice mail* by sending a recorded message to everyone in the company. Broadcast voice mail gives top managers a quick, convenient way to address their workforces via oral communication—but only if people actually listen to the message, and that turns out to be

a challenge with today's workers, who are much more likely to use their smartphones for social media rather than phone calls. Consequently, company leaders are increasingly using tools like Yammer, a Facebook-like social media platform for companies, or Lync, a version of Skype for companies, to broadcast text or video-based messages to their workforces. Ryan Holmes, CEO of Hootsuite, a social media measurement and monitoring system for companies, says, "I believe that social media is the new water cooler, in the sense that more and more people are talking, sharing stories, and generally bonding through social channels like Facebook and Twitter. In this way, social media is like an ongoing team building exercise. When C-Suite members join that conversation, they become more in touch with their employees and only then can they use those channels to drive internal engagement."[75]

15-4b Improving Reception: Hearing What Others Feel and Think

When people think of "organization-wide" communication, they think of the CEO and top managers getting their message out to people in the company. But organization-wide communication also means finding ways to hear what people throughout the organization are thinking and feeling. This is important because most employees and managers are reluctant to share their thoughts and feelings with top managers. Surveys indicate that only 29 percent of first-level managers feel that their companies encourage employees to express their opinions openly. Another study of twenty-two companies found that 70 percent of the people surveyed were afraid to speak up about problems they knew existed at work.

Withholding information about organizational problems or issues is called **organizational silence**. Organizational silence occurs when employees believe that telling management about problems won't make a difference or that they'll be punished or hurt in some way for sharing such information.[76] A survey of executives found that 85 percent had at some point kept quiet when they saw a serious problem at work.[77] At Jetstar Airways, an Australia-based airline, pilots were afraid to speak up about fatigue from flying too many hours. Captain Richard Woodward, then vice president of the Australian and International Pilots Association, said that his organization had received dozens of complaints from Jetstar pilots, but that the pilots were afraid to complain to Jetstar management because "there was a culture of

Televised/videotaped speeches and meetings speeches and meetings originally made to a smaller audience that are either simultaneously broadcast to other locations in the company or videotaped for subsequent distribution and viewing

Organizational silence when employees withhold information about organizational problems or issues

Google™ | Official Blog

Insights from Googlers into our products, technology and the Google culture

Search

Introducing the Knowledge Graph: things, not strings

May 16, 2012 at 1:00 PM   +1   695

Cross-posted on the Inside Search Blog

Search is a lot about discovery—the basic human need to learn and broaden your horizons. But searching still requires a lot of hard work by you, the user. So today I'm really excited to launch the Knowledge Graph, which will help you discover new information quickly and easily.

Take a query like [taj mahal]. For more than four decades, search has essentially been about matching keywords to queries. To a search engine the words [taj mahal] have been just that—two words.

But we all know that [taj mahal] has a much richer meaning. You might think of one of the world's most beautiful monuments, or a Grammy Award-winning musician, or possibly even a casino in Atlantic City, NJ. Or, depending on when you last ate, the nearest Indian restaurant. It's why we've been working on an intelligent model—in geek-speak, a "graph"—that understands real-world entities and their relationships to one another: things, not strings.

The Knowledge Graph enables you to search for things, people or places that Google knows about—landmarks, celebrities, cities, sports teams, buildings, geographical features, movies, celestial objects, works of art and more—and instantly get information that's relevant to your query. This is a critical first step towards building the next generation of search, which taps into the collective intelligence of the web and understands the world a bit more like people do.

Google's Knowledge Graph isn't just rooted in public sources such as Freebase, Wikipedia and the CIA World Factbook. It's also augmented at a much larger scale—because we're focused on comprehensive breadth and depth. It currently contains more than 500 million objects, as well as more than 3.5 billion facts about and relationships between these different objects. And it's tuned based on what people search for, and what we find out on the web.

The Knowledge Graph enhances Google Search in three main ways to start:

1. Find the right thing

Language can be ambiguous—do you mean Taj Mahal the monument, or Taj Mahal

More blogs from Google   © Google

Connect with us
Subscribe to this blog:

FeedBurner

RSS Feed

Browse all of Google's blogs for specific interests & topics:

Blog Directory

Follow Google alerts and news on Twitter:

@Google

We'd love to hear your feedback — discuss Google's products with others:

Product Forums

g+   Follow

A corporate blog is an effective way for leaders to communicate to broad groups throughout a company.

---

fear and intimidation at that airline."[78] One pilot scheduler told his pilots, "Toughen up princesses! You aren't fatigued, you are tired and can't be bothered to go into work." A report from Australia's Civil Aviation Safety Authority concluded, "There remains reluctance from a number of flight crew to report fatigue risk and/or to say no to an extension of duty based on the perceived punitive nature of taking such actions."[79]

Company hotlines, survey feedback, frequent informal meetings, surprise visits, and blogs are additional ways of overcoming organizational silence. **Company hotlines** are phone numbers that anyone in the company can call anonymously to leave information for upper management. Company hotlines are incredibly useful, as 47 percent of the calls placed to them result in an investigation and some form of corrective action

Company hotlines phone numbers that anyone in the company can call anonymously to leave information for upper management

Take a Memo: The Rise in Anonymous Venting

A new app called Memo allows employees to vent about their employers by posting anonymous "memos" (vents). Users of the app can post new memos, comment on existing memos, and even upload photos and documents to support their memos. Employees at companies such as Delta Airline, Ernst & Young, and Hasbro are using Memo to vent about compensation, managerial inefficiency, and working from home. After a user is verified, Memo removes all identifiable data about the person's activity, making that person's posts completely anonymous. Memos (posts) are organized onto public message boards that can be seen by all users and private boards organized by company. Not all companies are thrilled at the availability of Memo. Visa, Boeing, and Hewlett-Packard have all circulated internal corporate memos (the traditional kind) discouraging employees from using the app and reminding them of the risk of proprietary information being released to the public.

Source: L. Gellman, "App Lets Workers Vent Anonymously," *Wall Street Journal*, January 20, 2015, accessed May 12, 2015. http://www.wsj.com/articles/memo-app-lets-workers-vent-anonymously-1421805377.

Leremy/Shutterstock.com

within the organization. Anonymity is critical, too, because as those investigations proceeded, 54 percent of the callers did not want their identities revealed.[80]

Survey feedback is information that is collected by survey from organization members and then compiled, disseminated, and used to develop action plans for improvement. Many organizations make use of survey feedback by surveying their managers and employees several times a year. **Sunovian Pharmaceuticals**, a small drug maker in Massachusetts, which had a divided office, with employees on the second floor and executives two floors up, discovered through its annual survey that employees felt walled off from their leaders. So, chief commercial officer Rick Russell, who managed 1,100 people, put a desk in a glass-walled office in the middle of the second floor, which employees quickly dubbed "the fish bowl," where he worked every Friday without an assistant. Soon, the company's chief medical officer joined him, and the following year, survey feedback showed that employee trust in senior leadership improved. Russell says, "You have to rally the troops. You can't do it from a memo."[81]

Frequent *informal meetings* between top managers and lower-level employees are one of the best ways for top managers to hear what others think and feel. Many people assume that top managers are at the center of everything that goes on in organizations, but top managers commonly feel isolated from most of their lower-level managers and employees.[82] Consequently, more and more top managers are scheduling frequent informal meetings with people throughout their companies.

Mazor Robotics, an Israeli-based medical technology company, has facilities in the United States, Asia, and Europe. With employees scattered worldwide, maintaining good communication is critical. CEO Ori Hadomi says, "I think that the most constructive and the most productive way to communicate is informal communication." So once a week he has a joint one-hour phone call with people in all of the offices. With no set agenda, employees take turns explaining what is going on in their division, what was accomplished in the past few days, and what kind of issues are coming up in the near future. Says Hadomi, "So in one hour, everyone is synchronized. And when I talk with many of the employees I hear that it's a very important meeting for them because it gives them the opportunity to hear about the business."

Have you ever been around when a supervisor learns that upper management is going to be paying a visit? First, there's shock. Next, there's anxiety. And then there's panic, as everyone is told to drop what he or she is doing to polish, shine, and spruce up the workplace so

Survey feedback
information that is collected by surveys from organizational members and then compiled, disseminated, and used to develop action plans for improvement

that it looks perfect for the visit. Of course, when visits are conducted under these conditions, top managers don't get a realistic look at what's going on in the company. Consequently, one of the ways to get an accurate picture is to pay *surprise visits* to various parts of the organization. These visits should not just be surprise inspections but should also be used as opportunities to encourage meaningful upward communication from those who normally don't get a chance to communicate with upper management.

Blogs are another way to hear what people are thinking and saying, both inside and outside the organization. A **blog** is a personal website that provides personal opinions or recommendations, news summaries, and reader comments. When the recession hit, **GTE Financial**, a Florida-based credit union with twenty-one locations, saw its assets shrink from $2.2 billion to $1.5 billion and had to lay off 245 of its 690 employees. When new CEO Joe Brancucci came on board, he reduced check and ATM fees that were frustrating customers, reduced bad loans from 4.06 percent to 3.58 percent, and, after cutting employees' pay, created pay incentives linked to growth in loans and new members. But, from a communication standpoint, the most important thing he did was start an internal blog to which he posted updates to all of GTE's employees. Brancucci says he never "sugarcoated anything. I talked about what we were going through, the situations we faced, why we faced them, and why we were making changes." Now quarterly financial statements are posted on the blog. "Our membership knows exactly what's going on. We don't hide anything," adds Brancucci.[84]

Monitoring social media, such as blogs, Twitter, and Facebook, written by people outside the company can be a good way to find out what others are saying or thinking about your organization or its products or actions. But keeping up with these communication media requires someone in the firm to actively monitor what is being said on social media. At its Texas headquarters, Dell operates a Social Media Listening Command Center, where staff members track what is being said about Dell on a variety of social media sites such as Facebook, Twitter, and YouTube, as well as blogs. When they see that a Dell customer posts a problem with a Dell product, they quickly contact the customer and take steps to address the issue. Nearly two-thirds of Dell consumers contacted through the Social Media Listening Command Center report positive service experiences. Manish Mehta, Dell's then–vice president for social media and community, says, "Customers were thrilled and elated that Dell

was reaching out to them. It changed their perception of the company."[85]

Finally, in addition to being a way to deliver organizational communication, so-called *town hall meetings* can be an effective way for companies to hear feedback from employees. In 2014, Dubai-based **Emirates Airline** carried 44.5 million passengers, and by 2020, it expects that number to rise to 70 million. To meet growing demand, Emirates Airline will hire 5,000 additional cabin staff, but in the meantime, the 20,000 current cabin crew employees are working more hours on shorter layovers. Crew members who had worked their way to first-class assignments, a prestigious posting, are having to return to economy class to cover staff shortages. Many staff members have had annual leave allocations deferred. To better understand crew member complaints, the airline held three town hall meetings—the first of which lasted four hours—during which staff aired grievances to senior management. Terry Daly, Emirates' senior vice president of service delivery announced the meetings in an email, writing that he was "aware that there are a number of subjects that are causing concern at the moment" and that the meetings would be "an opportunity to talk about these directly with me."[86]

Blog a personal website that provides personal opinions or recommendations, news summaries, and reader comments

STUDY TOOLS 15

LOCATED IN TEXTBOOK

☐ Rip-out and review chapter review card

LOCATED AT WWW.CENGAGEBRAIN.COM

☐ Review key term flashcards and create your own from StudyBits

☐ Track your knowledge and understanding of key concepts, using the concept tracker

☐ Complete practice and graded quizzes to prepare for tests

☐ Complete interactive content within the exposition

☐ View chapter highlight box content at the beginning of each chapter

16 Control

Anopix/Shutterstock.com

LEARNING OUTCOMES

16-1 Describe the basic control process.

16-2 Discuss the various methods that managers can use to maintain control.

16-3 Describe the behaviors, processes, and outcomes that today's managers are choosing to control in their organizations.

After you finish this chapter, go to **PAGE 349** for **STUDY TOOLS**

16-1 THE CONTROL PROCESS

For all companies, past success is no guarantee of future success. Even successful companies fall short or face challenges and thus have to make changes. **Control** is a regulatory process of establishing standards to achieve organizational goals, comparing actual performance to the standards, and taking corrective action when necessary to restore performance to those standards. Control is achieved when behavior and work procedures conform to standards and when company goals are accomplished.[1] Control is not just an after-the-fact process, however. Preventive measures are also a form of control.

The French Open grand slam tennis tournament at Roland Garros Stadium in Paris uses birds of prey, specifically raptors, to prevent—and thus control—pigeon problems, such as pigeon droppings and play interrupted by pigeons landing on the courts. With nearly 430,000 people in attendance during the two-week tournament, Roland Garros is the equivalent of a Parisian corner cafe for pigeons thanks to all the food served and thrown away. But with raptors circling the skies, "It creates a sense of danger for the pigeons and they won't dare to land," says Raptor trainer Ludwig Verschatse.[2] While the raptors can't be airborne when crowds are in attendance during the day, they circle high over Roland Garros each morning before play starts and in the evening as play ends for the day. To avoid protests from animal rights groups, the raptors are fed 10 percent of their body weight each day so they aren't tempted to catch and eat the pigeons. Similar prevention or control strategies are used at the Australian Open, which uses eagles, and at Wimbledon, which uses a hawk named Rufus.

The basic control process **16-1a begins with the establishment of clear standards of performance; 16-1b involves a comparison of performance to those standards; 16-1c takes corrective action, if needed, to repair performance deficiencies; 16-1d is a dynamic, cybernetic process;** *and* **16-1e consists of three basic methods: feedback control, concurrent control, and feedforward control.** *However, as much as managers would like,* **16-1f control isn't always worthwhile or possible.**

16-1a Standards

The control process begins when managers set goals such as satisfying 90 percent of customers or increasing sales by 5 percent. Companies then specify the performance standards that must be met to accomplish those goals. **Standards** are a basis of comparison for measuring the extent to which organizational performance is satisfactory or unsatisfactory. For example, many pizzerias use thirty to forty minutes as the standard for delivery time. Because anything longer is viewed as unsatisfactory, they'll typically reduce the price if they can't deliver a hot pizza to you within that time period.

So how do managers set standards? How do they decide which levels of performance are satisfactory and which are unsatisfactory? The first criterion for a good standard is that it must enable goal achievement. If you're meeting the standard but still not achieving company goals, then the standard may have to be changed. When introduced, Apple's iPhone 5 had an aluminum body crafted to be stronger, lighter, thinner, and more stylish than previous models. However, after only a few days of light use, the back and sides of the phone could end up scratched or dented. Even worse, early customers reported finding scratches on brand-new phones right out of the box. Apple responded by asking its iPhone manufacturer, Foxconn, to implement stricter quality-control standards in the manufacture and handling of iPhone 5s in its factories, as well as more rigorous inspections so that iPhones with scratches do not get shipped to customers.[3]

Companies also determine standards by listening to customers' comments, complaints, and suggestions or by observing competitors. Sarah Beatty started Green Depot, which sells environmentally responsible construction materials, because "greenwashing"—representing products as green when they're not—was widespread among competitors. Beatty hired engineers to help Green Depot develop CLEAR standards, for **C**onservation (recycled, reclaimed, reused, or rapidly renewable resources), **L**ocal (low-carbon footprint), **E**nergy (energy-conserving or renewable resources), **A**ir quality (nontoxic, nonallergenic, or no gases or particulates), and **R**esponsibility (green jobs, worker protection, and truthful marketing). When the standards were developed, Beatty and her team sent out ten-page questionnaires to manufacturers, asking for detailed explanations regarding product production and materials. Each product is measured on each of the five standards. If a standard has been met, Green Depot displays an icon for that standard on the product's page on GreenDepot.com. As Green Depot's website

> **Control** a regulatory process of establishing standards to achieve organizational goals, comparing actual performance against the standards, and taking corrective action when necessary
>
> **Standards** a basis of comparison for measuring the extent to which various kinds of organizational performance are satisfactory or unsatisfactory

Kering Sets the Standard for Sustainability in Fashion

Of the dozens of brands owned by fashion conglomerate Kering, several are implementing large-scale sustainability initiatives. Stella McCartney, a longtime animal-rights activist, has developed a technique for producing real leather in a laboratory using DNA from cows. Gucci, which still uses actual hides for its leather, has developed a tanning process that uses far less pollutants, and it is sharing that technology and methodology with anyone who wants it. Across all its companies, Kering is testing a technique developed by a British firm that allows color, chemicals, and fibers to be separated so that the fiber can be recycled. The conglomerate also has a fifty-person team dedicated to sustainability that works with an associate committee of fifteen experts from the energy and transportation sectors. For CEO François-Henri Pinault, sustainability extends beyond cost-savings and brand building. Of the tanning technology, he says, "If you find a solution like this and you use it as a competitive advantage, you miss completely the point."

Source: R. Feitelberg, "Pinault Delves into Sustainability," *WWD*, April 6, 2015, 2.

explains, "Our Green Depot Icon System is designed to show at a glance why we call a particular item green."[4]

Standards can also be determined by benchmarking other companies. **Benchmarking** is the process of determining how well other companies (not just competitors) perform business functions or tasks. In other words, benchmarking is the process of determining other companies' standards. When setting standards by benchmarking, the first step is to determine what to benchmark. Organizations can benchmark anything from cycle time (how fast) to quality (how well) to price (how much). For example, based on national benchmarking studies of thousands of fire departments, many firefighters are expected to respond to an alarm within fifteen seconds 95 percent of the time. Additionally, 90 percent of the time, it should take no more than sixty seconds to leave the firehouse, and then no more than four minutes to arrive at the scene.[5]

After setting standards, the next step is to identify the companies

> **Benchmarking** the process of identifying outstanding practices, processes, and standards in other companies and adapting them to your company

against which to benchmark those standards. The last step is to collect data to determine other companies' performance standards. Intuit, maker of financial software and websites such as QuickBooks, Intuit Payroll, and TurboTax, gets nearly 40 percent of its revenues by selling its products and services to tens of thousands of small- to medium-sized businesses in different industries. Fred Shilmover, CEO of InsightSquared, which sells data-analytic tools to those businesses, says, "Intuit figured out how to leverage its internal data team for their customers, when those companies couldn't gather enough data on their own to understand the bigger [industry and business] trends."[6] And because Intuit also sells add-on products and services to help manage payroll, inventory, financing, customers, point of sale trends, and online/social media marketing, he says those businesses "can now benchmark their costs [and organizational performance in all of those areas] against each other." This benchmarking shows them whether they perform at, above, or below thousands of other companies on a number of critical dimensions.

16-1b Comparison to Standards

The next step in the control process is to compare actual performance to performance standards. Although this sounds straightforward, the quality of the comparison depends largely on the measurement and information systems a company uses to keep track of performance. The better the system, the easier it is for companies to track their progress and identify problems that need to be fixed.

On average, 5 percent of hospital patients catch an infection at the hospital. It costs an average of $15,000 per incident to treat such infections, and 100,000 patients will die each year from them. Why? Because in most hospitals, health care workers wash their hands only 50 percent of the time before examining or touching a patient. Because of the risks, the Center for Disease Control created a video, "Hand Hygiene Saves Lives," to be shown to patients admitted to hospitals. In the video, a patient's wife asks her husband's doctor, on entering the hospital room, to wash his hands before beginning the medical exam.[7]

So, how can a hospital measure the rate at which its employees wash their hands so it can compare the actual rate of handwashing to its goal for handwashing? At the University Health Network in Toronto, researchers electronically monitored the hand-hygiene system. Pushing the lever on a soap dispenser sent a signal time-stamping the handwashing event and logging it into a central database. Even though the hospital was able to measure the rate of handwashing digitally, it found that with the presence of an auditor—a person in a white lab coat (who did not know the purpose of the study)—the rate of handwashing nearly tripled to 3.75 washes per hour versus 1.07 washes per hour when no auditor was present.[8]

16-1c Corrective Action

The next step in the control process is to identify performance deviations, analyze those deviations, and then develop and implement programs to correct them. This is similar to the planning process discussed in Chapter 5. Regular, frequent performance feedback allows workers and managers to track their performance and make adjustments in effort, direction, and strategies.

After discovering that its ICU staff were washing their hands only 6.5 percent of the time, North Shore University Hospital decided that frequent feedback was the best way to change its health care workers' handwashing behavior. So, it provided feedback in two ways. First, an LED display by the nurses' station shows that shift's handwashing percentage and an evaluation, such as "Great Shift!" Second, the nursing shift manager receives an email with the shift's handwashing rates three hours into the shift and then again at the shift's conclusion. Since this system was installed, handwashing rates at North Shore's ICU have risen from 6.5 percent to 81 percent.[9]

16-1d Dynamic, Cybernetic Process

As shown in Exhibit 16.1, control is a continuous, dynamic, cybernetic process. Control begins by setting standards, measuring performance, and then comparing performance to the standards. If the performance deviates from the standards, then managers and employees analyze the deviations and develop and implement corrective programs that (they hope) achieve the desired performance by meeting the standards. Managers must repeat the entire process again and again in an endless feedback loop (a continuous process). Thus, control is not a one-time achievement or result. It continues over time (that is, it is dynamic) and requires daily, weekly, and monthly attention from managers to maintain performance levels at the standard (that is, it is cybernetic). **Cybernetic** derives from the Greek word *kubernetes*, meaning "steersman," that is, one who steers or keeps on course.[10] The control process shown in Exhibit 16.1 is cybernetic because constant attention to the feedback loop is necessary to keep the company's activity on course.

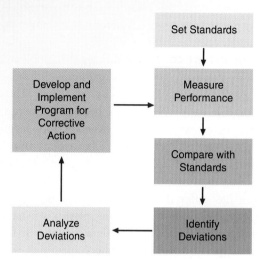

Exhibit 16.1
Cybernetic Control Process

Source: From *Business Horizons*, June 1972, H. Koontz and R. W. Bradspies, "Managing through Feedforward Control: A Future Directed View," pp. 25–36.

16-1e Feedback, Concurrent, and Feedforward Control

The three basic control methods are feedback control, concurrent control, and feedforward control. **Feedback control** is a mechanism for gathering information about performance deficiencies *after* they occur. This information is then used to correct or prevent performance deficiencies. Study after study has clearly shown that feedback improves both individual and organizational performance. In most instances, any feedback is better than no feedback.

If feedback has a downside, it's that feedback always comes after the fact. For example, when an electrical transformer malfunctions on a neighborhood utility pole, 90 percent of the time the cause of the problem is a squirrel. Brian Manthey, manager of media relations for We Energies, says, "If they are on a wire and touch a piece of equipment that's grounded, the current flows through them. They're killed and sometimes the power to homes and businesses goes out."[11] And, there's never any warning until after the fact and usually nothing left of the squirrel because of the electrical surge or because predators have taken the remains. Utility companies have experimented with a wide range

Cybernetic the process of steering or keeping on course

Feedback control a mechanism for gathering information about performance deficiencies after they occur of solutions, such as arrester caps and brushing covers to protect the wires, and free-spinning baffles that make squirrels fall off the wires. But a foolproof method has yet to be invented.[12] The city of Austin, Texas, estimates that squirrels cause 300 power outages a year. Squirrel-related power outages cost California's economy up to $317 million per year.[13]

Concurrent control addresses the problems inherent in feedback control by gathering information about performance deficiencies *as* they occur. Thus, it is an improvement over feedback because it attempts to eliminate or shorten the delay between performance and feedback about the performance. Concussions represent one of the biggest health concerns for football players. Sometimes, however, it can be difficult to tell whether a player has suffered a concussion. And, because they don't want to come out of the game, players won't always be honest with doctors about their symptoms. Other times, teams, especially high school and small college teams, don't have staff who have been properly trained to diagnose concussions. To address this problem, Battle Sports Science created the Impact Indicator, a helmet chin strap equipped with an accelerometer that instantly measures the force that a player experiences when hit. When sensors detect a hit so hard that there is a 50 percent chance or better of injury, an indicator light flashes, letting sideline medical personnel know that they should further examine the player for possible signs of a concussion.[14]

Feedforward control is a mechanism for gathering information about performance deficiencies *before* they occur. In contrast to feedback and concurrent control, which provide feedback on the basis of outcomes and results, feedforward control provides information about performance deficiencies by monitoring inputs rather than outputs. Thus, feedforward control seeks to prevent or minimize performance deficiencies before they happen. Power companies have traditionally relied on consumers to call in power outages. Then, when repair crews arrive, fault detectors displaying a flag or a light can tell them which line is out, but the crews still have to visually inspect

miles of power lines, often in weather with poor visibility, to find the precise cause of the outage. Tollgrade, however, is making sensors the size of a loaf of bread, which sit on and are powered by the electricity flowing through the wires, that can notify power companies about problems before they happen (that is, feedforward). With GPS (location) and wireless (communication) capabilities, the sensors monitor the fluctuations in the flow of electricity—from outages to drops to normal transmissions to surge overloads—and instantaneously send text alerts to power company engineers when there are problems.[15] Pennsylvania's Orange & Rockland Utilities were alerted to an electrical line problem over a Fourth of July weekend, and the advanced notice of the outage offered ample time for repair crews to fix the issue before a single customer could complain. Haukur Asgeirsson, technology manager at DTE Energy says, "You can actually go out there and do some preemptive work before a permanent outage occurs. It looks actually very promising."[16]

16-1f Control Isn't Always Worthwhile or Possible

Control is achieved when behavior and work procedures conform to standards, and goals are accomplished. By contrast, **control loss** occurs when behavior and work procedures do not conform to standards.[17] For the first time in its 108-year history, Blue Bell Creameries experienced an outbreak of listeria, a bacterium that thrives in refrigerated conditions, which can cause fever, muscle aches, nausea, abdominal pain, and sometimes death. As a result, Blue Bell announced a voluntary, complete recall of 8 million gallons of ice cream and frozen yogurt products across twenty-three states.[18]

Maintaining control is important because control loss prevents organizations from achieving their goals. When control loss occurs, managers need to find out what, if anything, they could have done to prevent it. Usually, that means identifying deviations from standard performance, analyzing the causes of those deviations, and taking corrective action. Even so, implementing controls isn't always worthwhile or possible. Let's look at regulation costs and cybernetic feasibility to see why this is so.

To determine whether control is worthwhile, managers need to carefully assess **regulation costs**, that is, whether the costs and unintended consequences of control exceed its benefits. If a control process costs more than it benefits, it may not be worthwhile. Because glass can be recycled over and over again, and because it was

Concurrent control
a mechanism for gathering information about performance deficiencies as they occur, thereby eliminating or shortening the delay between performance and feedback

Feedforward control
a mechanism for monitoring performance inputs rather than outputs to prevent or minimize performance deficiencies before they occur

Control loss the situation in which behavior and work procedures do not conform to standards

Regulation costs the costs associated with implementing or maintaining control profitable to recycle, waste companies paid cities for the glass they collected. In fact, to increase the amount of glass collected for recycling, the waste industry encouraged cities to allow households to mix glass, plastic, and cans together in one recycling bin. The unintended consequence of that decision, according to Curt Bucey of Strategic Materials, the largest U.S. glass recycler, is that half of the "glass" loads headed to recycling aren't glass. Bucey says, "Now what comes with the glass are rocks, shredded paper, chicken bones people left in their take-out containers, and hypodermic needles."[19] Because very expensive equipment is needed to separate glass from other materials, Strategic Materials now charges cities from $10 to $40 per ton, depending on how "dirty" their glass recycling loads are. And for cities used to being paid for recycling glass, having to pay waste companies to take their glass comes as a high regulation cost. James Young, director of solid waste programs around Charleston, South Carolina, says, "When you're losing money and time processing glass for not much revenue, it is just a losing battle, and not sustainable."[20]

Another factor to consider is **cybernetic feasibility**, the extent to which it is possible to implement each of the three steps in the control process. If one or more steps cannot be implemented, then maintaining effective control may be difficult or impossible.

16-2 CONTROL METHODS

In January 2010, a gallon of diesel fuel cost $2.95. By May 2014, the price had climbed 34 percent to $3.95.[21] Consequently, companies with truck fleets became much more aggressive in exploring ways to reduce fuel costs and increase gas mileage. For example, in May 2014, Kroger bought forty natural gas-powered trucks that use a state-of-the-art cold natural gas tank (for increased driving range). Natural gas costs $1.50 less per gallon than diesel fuel.[22] UPS, on the other hand, is controlling fuel costs by using composite materials in trucks that are 1,000 pounds lighter than its standard steel and aluminum trucks. Combined with 13 percent better

Tupungato/Shutterstock.com

aerodynamics, UPS's composite trucks use 40 percent less diesel fuel. Dale Spencer, director of engineering for UPS, says, "This technology is available to us today. We don't have to worry about plugging it in or getting propane or CNG (compressed natural gas)."[23]

Managers can use five different methods to achieve control in their organizations: 16-2a bureaucratic, 16-2b objective, 16-2c normative, 16-2d concertive, and 16-2e self-control.

16-2a Bureaucratic Control

When most people think of managerial control, what they have in mind is bureaucratic control. **Bureaucratic control** is top-down control, in which managers try to influence employee behavior by rewarding or punishing employees for compliance or noncompliance with organizational policies, rules, and procedures. Most employees, however, would argue that bureaucratic managers emphasize punishment for noncompliance much more than rewards for compliance.

As you learned in Chapter 2, bureaucratic management and control were created to prevent just this type of managerial behavior. By encouraging managers to apply well-thought-out rules, policies, and procedures in an impartial, consistent manner to everyone in the organization, bureaucratic control is supposed to make companies more efficient, effective, and fair. Ironically, it frequently has just the opposite effect. Managers who use bureaucratic control often emphasize following the rules above all else.

Another characteristic of bureaucratically controlled companies is that, due to their rule- and policy-driven decision making, they are highly resistant to change and slow to respond to customers and competitors. Recall from Chapter 2 that even Max Weber, the German philosopher who is largely credited with popularizing bureaucratic ideals in the late nineteenth century, referred to bureaucracy as the "iron cage." He said, "Once fully established, bureaucracy is among those social structures which are the hardest to destroy."[24] Of course, the national government, with hundreds of bureaus, agencies, and departments, is typically the largest bureaucracy in most countries. Under new U.S. Department of Transportation rules for long-haul truckers, drivers can now drive

Cybernetic feasibility the extent to which it is possible to implement each step in the control process

Bureaucratic control the use of hierarchical authority to influence employee behavior by rewarding or punishing employees for compliance or noncompliance with organizational policies, rules, and procedures only seventy hours per week, down from eighty-two. And, they must take a thirty-four hour break over two nights between work weeks. Intended to increase safety by preventing tired truck drivers from getting behind the wheel, the changes are instead increasing driver turnover (ironically putting less experienced drivers on the road), putting more trucks on the road during rush hour, and forcing drivers to try to sleep when they're not tired and to drive when they are. Manny Hernandez, who has driven trucks for three decades, says the new rules prevent him from getting home to see his family. Wherever he is when the seventy hour limit kicks in, he has to stop for thirty-four hours over two nights. Says Hernandez, "It can be a nightmare of having to sit for forty-eight hours, tired, when all you want to do is get home. . . . Who made up these rules?" he asks. "Did they have any experience in driving truck[s], and traffic and dealing with customers and [the time lost from] your [truck] breakdowns? Sometimes I think they're trying to choke out the trucking industry."[25]

16-2b Objective Control

In many companies, bureaucratic control has evolved into **objective control**, which is the use of observable measures of employee behavior or output to assess performance and influence behavior. Whereas bureaucratic control focuses on whether policies and rules are followed, objective control focuses on observing and measuring worker behavior or output. The Angus Barn, a steakhouse in Raleigh, North Carolina, has a strict privacy policy because it is visited by numerous celebrities—employees and managers are to keep all guests' dining experiences private. A waiter was fired for violating the policy after uploading a copy of NFL quarterback Peyton Manning's dinner receipt, following Manning's dinner at the restaurant. The picture, which quickly went viral, showed that Manning had left a generous tip of $200, on top of an 18 percent gratuity that the restaurant had already added to the bill. Speaking about the incident and the firing, Van Eure, the owner of the Angus Barn, said, "This goes against every policy we have. It's just horrible."[26]

There are two kinds of objective control: behavior control and output control. **Behavior control** is regulating behaviors and actions that workers perform on the job. The basic assumption of behavior control is that if you do the right things (that is, the right behaviors) every day, then those things should lead to goal achievement. Behavior control is still management-based, however, which means that managers are responsible for monitoring and then rewarding or punishing workers for exhibiting desired or undesired behaviors.

Instead of measuring what managers and workers do, **output control** measures the results of their efforts. Whereas behavior control regulates, guides, and measures how workers behave on the job, output control gives managers and workers the freedom to behave as they see fit as long as they accomplish prespecified, measurable results. Output control is often coupled with rewards and incentives.

Three things must occur for output control to lead to improved business results. First, output control measures must be reliable, fair, and accurate. Second, employees and managers must believe that they can produce the desired results. If they don't, then the output controls won't affect their behavior. Third, the rewards or incentives tied to output control measures must truly be dependent on achieving established standards of performance. The "Drive Safe & Save" program at State Farm Insurance is based on output control. Using a device that plugs into your car's diagnostic port, State Farm tracks when you drive, and your braking, acceleration, left and right turns, and whether you exceed 80 mph. Drivers who participate are eligible for discounts up to 50 percent, with their driving scores determining the size of the discount. Ed Scharlau of Austin, Texas, says, "How I drive should affect my insurance premium." Moreover, he says the program's daily feedback has him and his wife talking, "about our own driving and what we see around us: 'Oops, did we just lose points?'"[27]

16-2c Normative Control

Rather than monitoring rules, behavior, or output, another way to control what goes on in organizations is to use normative control to shape the beliefs and values of the people who work there. With **normative controls**, a company's widely shared values and beliefs guide workers' behavior and decisions.

JPMorgan Chase realizes that culture has as much to do with control as algorithms, so it has designated more than 300 executives as "cultural ambassadors" who focus on standards. The company published a memo that encouraged employees to flag any compliance concerns and emphasized that poor compliance and scandals

---

Objective control the use of observable measures of worker behavior or outputs to assess performance and influence behavior

Behavior control the regulation of the behaviors and actions that workers perform on the job

Output control the regulation of workers' results or outputs through rewards and incentives

Normative control the regulation of workers' behavior and decisions through widely shared organizational values and beliefs

JPMorgan Chase realizes that culture has as much to do with control as algorithms, so it has added and designated more than 300 executives as "cultural ambassadors."

damage the bank's reputation and affect everyone, both professionally and financially. The goal of the program is to reshape the beliefs and values of the bank's employees so that compliance and ethical financial stewardship are part of the company culture.[28]

Normative controls are created in two ways. First, companies that use normative controls are very careful about who they hire. While many companies screen potential applicants on the basis of their abilities, normatively controlled companies are just as likely to screen potential applicants based on their attitudes and values. Four Seasons hotels, a luxury five-star brand, are renowned for their exceptional guest service. Founder Isadore Sharp says, "Competence we can teach. Attitude is ingrained."[29] Former executive vice-president of HR, Nick Mutton agrees, saying, "Job skills can be taught later. The quality of our people—their attitude, professionalism, personal growth—is actually what we are as a business. Our focus

on attitude is paramount because engaged employees who care about our customers create our product, and that clearly contributes directly to our bottom line."[30]

Second, with normative controls, managers and employees learn what they should and should not do by observing experienced employees and by listening to the stories they tell about the company. We learned the importance of storytelling and organizational culture in Chapter 3. For normative controls to work, however, managers must not only select the right people, they must reward employees who honor those attitudes and values, and deal with those who don't. Elite SEM is a New York City-based search engine marketing firm that helps *Fortune* 500 companies increase their profile when potential customers do web searches. Elite SEM values hiring people with advanced technical skills and cooperative attitudes. More specifically, the company prides itself on being a "jerk-free workplace." So, there are consequences for employees and managers who, as CEO Ben Kirshner says, "don't embrace our core values." When a new employee refused to work late his first week on the job, he was let go. Kirshner says, "He was a bad seed!" And, because of the long hours people put in to meet client needs, Elite SEM has a free meal policy. So when another new employee ordered himself groceries and $30 breakfasts, Kirshner says, "Everyone jumped on him."[31]

16-2d Concertive Control

Whereas normative controls are based on beliefs that are strongly held and widely shared throughout a company, **concertive controls** are based on beliefs that are shaped and negotiated by work groups.[32] Whereas normative controls are driven by strong organizational cultures, concertive controls usually arise when companies give work groups complete autonomy and responsibility for task completion (see Chapter 10, "Managing Teams," for a complete discussion of the role of autonomy in teams and groups). The most autonomous groups operate without managers and are completely responsible for controlling work group processes, outputs, and behavior. Such groups do their own hiring, firing, worker discipline, scheduling, materials ordering, budget making and meeting, and decision making.

Concertive control is not established overnight. Highly autonomous work groups evolve through two phases as they develop concertive control. In phase one, group members learn to work with each other, supervise each other's work, and develop the

Concertive control the regulation of workers' behavior and decisions through work group values and beliefs values and beliefs that will guide and control their behavior. And because they develop these values and beliefs themselves, work group members feel strongly about following them.

In the steel industry, Nucor was long considered an upstart compared with the "biggies," U.S. Steel and Bethlehem Steel. Today, however, not only has Nucor managed to outlast many other mills, the company has bought out thirteen other mills in the past five years. Nucor has a unique culture that gives real power to employees on the line and fosters teamwork throughout the organization. This type of teamwork can be a difficult thing for a newly acquired group of employees to get used to. For example, at Nucor's first big acquisition in Auburn, New York, David Hutchins is a frontline supervisor or "lead man" in the rolling mill, where steel from the furnace is spread thin enough to be cut into sheets. When the plant was under the previous ownership, if the guys doing the cutting got backed up, the guys doing the rolling—including Hutchins—would just take a break. He says, "We'd sit back, have a cup of coffee, and complain: 'Those guys stink.'" It took six months to convince the employees at the Auburn plant that the Nucor teamwork way was better than the old way. Now, Hutchins says: "At Nucor, we're not 'you guys' and 'us guys.' It's all of us guys. Wherever the bottleneck is, we go there, and everyone works on it."[33]

The second phase in the development of concertive control is the emergence and formalization of objective rules to guide and control behavior. The beliefs and values developed in phase one usually develop into more objective rules as new members join teams. The clearer those rules, the easier it becomes for new members to figure out how and how not to behave.

Ironically, concertive control may lead to even more stress for workers to conform to expectations than bureaucratic control. Under bureaucratic control, most workers only have to worry about pleasing the boss. But with concertive control, their behavior has to satisfy the rest of their team members. For example, one team member says,

YOU ARE IN CONTROL!

Alexmillos/Shutterstock.com

"I don't have to sit there and look for the boss to be around; and if the boss is not around, I can sit there and talk to my neighbor or do what I want. Now the whole team is around me and the whole team is observing what I'm doing."[34] Plus, with concertive control, team members have a second, much more stressful role to perform: that of making sure that their team members adhere to team values and rules.

16-2e Self-Control

Self-control, also known as **self-management**, is a control system in which managers and workers control their own behavior.[35] Self-control does not result in anarchy, in which everyone gets to do whatever he or she wants. In self-control, or self-management, leaders and managers provide workers with clear boundaries within which they may guide and control their own goals and behaviors.[36] Leaders and managers also contribute to self-control by teaching others the skills they need to maximize and monitor their own work effectiveness. In turn, individuals who manage and lead themselves establish self-control

Self-control (self-management) a control system in which managers and workers control their own behavior by setting their own goals, monitoring their own progress, and rewarding themselves for goal achievement

Resistance Is Futile! (Or Is It?)

The easiest way to resist temptation may be to avoid it altogether. A study by researchers at Florida State gave participants the option of taking an online test in one of two formats. The standard format was static, but the stylized format included art on both sides of the screen that would change periodically. Of participants with high self-control, 67 percent selected the standard black-and-white test. By contrast, only 43 percent of the participants with low self-control chose the standard test; the majority chose the stylized test, even though they had been warned ahead of time of the potential distraction. The secret of highly disciplined people is proactive avoidance, or simply avoiding situations in which their self-control might fail.

Source: A. Lukits, "The Secret to Resisting Temptation," *Wall Street Journal*, November 24, 2014, accessed May 13, 2015. http://www.wsj.com/articles/the-secret-to-resisting-temptation-1416852990.

by setting their own goals, monitoring their own progress, rewarding or punishing themselves for achieving or for not achieving their self-set goals, and constructing positive thought patterns that remind them of the importance of their goals and their ability to accomplish them.[37]

For example, let's assume you need to do a better job of praising and recognizing the good work that your staff does for you. You can use goal setting, self-observation, and self-reward to manage this behavior on your own. For self-observation, write "praise/recognition" on a three-by-five-inch card. Put the card in your pocket. Put a check on the card each time you praise or recognize someone. (Wait until the person has left before you do this.) Keep track for a week. This serves as your baseline, or starting point. Simply keeping track will probably increase how often you do this. After a week, assess your baseline, or starting point, and then set a specific goal. For instance, if your baseline was twice a day, you might set a specific goal to praise or recognize others' work five times a day. Continue monitoring your performance with your cards. After you've achieved your goal every day for a week, give yourself a reward (perhaps a movie or lunch with a friend at a new restaurant) for achieving your goal.[38]

As you can see, the components of self-management, self-set goals, self-observation, and self-reward have their roots in the motivation theories you read about in Chapter 13. The key difference, though, is that the goals, feedback, and rewards originate from employees themselves and not from their managers or organizations.

16-3 WHAT TO CONTROL?

In the first section of this chapter, we discussed the basics of the control process and the fact that control isn't always worthwhile or possible. In the second section, we looked at the various ways in which control can be achieved. In this third and final section, we address an equally important issue: What should managers control? Costs? Quality? Customer satisfaction? The way managers answer this question has critical implications for most businesses.

If you control for just one thing, such as costs, as many grocers have done in their meat departments, then other dimensions such as marketing, customer service, and quality are likely to suffer. But if you try to control for too many things, then managers and employees become confused about what's really important. In the end, successful companies find a balance that comes from doing three or four things right, such as managing costs, providing value, and keeping customers and employees satisfied.

After reading this section, you should be able to explain **16-3a the balanced scorecard approach to control** and how companies can achieve balanced control of company performance by choosing to control **16-3b budgets, cash flows, and economic value added; 16-3c customer defections; 16-3d quality;** and **16-3e waste and pollution.**

16-3a The Balanced Scorecard

Most companies measure performance using standard financial and accounting measures such as return on capital, return on assets, return on investments, cash flow, net income, and net margins. The **balanced scorecard** encourages managers to look beyond such traditional financial measures to four different perspectives on company performance. How do customers see us (the customer perspective)? At what must we excel (the internal perspective)? Can we continue to improve and create value (the innovation and learning perspective)? How do we look to shareholders (the financial perspective)?[39]

The balanced scorecard has several advantages over traditional control processes that rely solely on financial measures. First, it forces managers at each level of the company to set specific goals and measure performance in each of the four areas. For example, Exhibit 16.2 shows that Southwest Airlines uses nine different measures in its balanced scorecard to determine whether it is meeting the standards it has set for itself in the control process. Of those, only three—market value, seat revenue, and plane lease costs (at various compounded annual growth rates, or CAGR)—are standard financial measures of performance. In addition, Southwest measures its Federal Aviation Administration (FAA) on-time arrival rating and the cost of its airfares compared with those of competitors (customer perspective); how much time each plane spends on the ground after landing and the percentage of planes that depart on time (internal business perspective); and the percentage of its ground crew workers, such as mechanics and luggage handlers, who own company stock and have received job training (learning perspective).

The second major advantage of the balanced scorecard approach to control is that it minimizes the chances of **suboptimization**, which occurs when performance improves in one area at the expense of decreased performance in others. Jon Meliones, medical director of pediatric cardio ICU at Duke Children's Hospital,

> **Balanced scorecard** measurement of organizational performance in four equally important areas: finances, customers, internal operations, and innovation and learning
>
> **Suboptimization** performance improvement in one part of an organization but only at the expense of decreased performance in another part

Exhibit 16.2
Southwest Airlines—Balanced Scorecard

	Goals	Standards	Measures	Initiatives
Financial	Profitability	30% CAGR	Market Value	
	Increased Revenue	20% CAGR	Seat Revenue	
	Lower Costs	5% CAGR	Plane Lease Cost	
Customer	On-Time Flights	#1	FAA On-Time Arrival Rating	Quality Management, Customer Loyalty Program
	Lowest Prices	#1	Customer Ranking (Market Survey)	
Internal	Fast Ground Turnaround	30 Minutes	Time on Ground	Cycle Time Optimization Program
		90%	On-Time Departure	
Innovation and Learning	Ground Crew Alignment with Company Goals	Year 1: 70% Year 3: 90% Year 5: 100%	% Ground Crew Shareholders	Employee Stock Option Plan, Ground Crew Training
			% Ground Crew Trained	

Source: G. Anthes, "ROI Guide: Balanced Scorecard," *Computer World*, February 17, 2003, accessed September 5, 2008. http://www.computerworld.com/article/2579980/it-management/roi-guide--balanced-scorecard.html.

Kao/Shutterstock.com

says, "We explained the [balanced scorecard] theory to clinicians and administrators like this: if you sacrifice too much in one quadrant to satisfy another, your organization as a whole is thrown out of balance. We could, for example, cut costs to improve the financial quadrant by firing half the staff, but that would hurt quality of service, and the customer quadrant would fall out of balance. Or we could increase productivity in the internal business quadrant by assigning more patients to a nurse, but doing so would raise the likelihood of errors—an unacceptable trade-off."[40]

Let's examine some of the ways in which companies are controlling the four basic parts of the balanced scorecard:

the financial perspective (budgets, cash flows, and economic value added), the customer perspective (customer defections), the internal perspective (total quality management), and the innovation and learning perspective (sustainability).

16-3b The Financial Perspective: Controlling Budgets, Cash Flows, and Economic Value Added

The traditional approach to controlling financial performance focuses on accounting tools such as cash flow analysis, balance sheets, income statements, financial ratios, and budgets. **Cash flow analysis** predicts how changes in a business will affect its ability to take in more cash than

> **Cash flow analysis** a type of analysis that predicts how changes in a business will affect its ability to take in more cash than it pays out

it pays out. **Balance sheets** provide a snapshot of a company's financial position at a particular time (but not the future). **Income statements**, also called profit and loss statements, show what has happened to an organization's income, expenses, and net profit (income less expenses) over a period of time. **Financial ratios** are typically used to track a business's liquidity (cash), efficiency, and profitability over time compared with other businesses in its industry. Finally, **budgets** are used to project costs and revenues, prioritize and control spending, and ensure that expenses don't exceed available funds and revenues. In a typical budgeting process, a manager uses the previous year's budget and adjusts it to reflect the current situation, but **zero-based budgeting** requires managers to outline a budget from scratch each year. In doing so, they must justify every expenditure—down to the number of color photocopies and garbage bags used—every year. Heinz, Kraft, and Anheuser-Busch all use zero-based budgeting, as does chicken-processor Pilgrim's Pride, which zealously monitors the amount of paper used to print documents, soap employees use in washrooms, and Gatorade workers drink each shift. According to one plant manager, the budgeting process has transformed the culture. When one worker said to him, "Hey, I need a flashlight," he responded, "Do you really need a flashlight?"[41]

By themselves, none of these tools—cash flow analyses, balance sheets, income statements, financial ratios, or budgets—tell the whole financial story of a business. They must be used together when assessing a company's financial performance. Because these tools are reviewed in detail in your accounting and finance classes, only a brief overview is provided here. Still, these are necessary tools for controlling organizational finances and expenses, and they should be part of your business toolbox. Unfortunately, most managers don't have a good understanding of these accounting tools even though they should.[42]

Though no one would dispute the importance of cash flow analyses, balance sheets, income statements, financial ratios, or budgets for determining the financial health of a business, accounting research also indicates that the complexity and sheer amount of information contained in these accounting tools can shut down the brain and glaze over the eyes of even the most experienced manager.[43] Sometimes there's simply too much information to make sense of. The balanced scorecard simplifies things by focusing on one simple question when it comes to finances: How do we look to shareholders? One way to answer that question is through something called economic value added.

Conceptually, **economic value added (EVA)** is not the same thing as profits. It is the amount by which profits exceed the cost of capital in a given year. It is based on the simple idea that capital is necessary to run a business and that capital comes at a cost. Although most people think of capital as cash, after it is invested (that is, spent), capital is more likely to be found in a business in the form of computers, manufacturing plants, employees, raw materials, and so forth. And just like the interest that a homeowner pays on a mortgage or that a college student pays on a student loan, there is a cost to that capital.

The most common costs of capital are the interest paid on long-term bank loans used to buy all those resources, the interest paid to bondholders (who lend organizations their money), and the dividends (cash payments) and growth in stock value that accrue to shareholders. EVA is positive when company profits (revenues minus expenses minus taxes) exceed the cost of capital in a given year. In other words, if a business is to truly grow, its revenues must be large enough to cover both short-term costs (annual expenses and taxes) and long-term costs (the cost of borrowing capital from bondholders and shareholders). If you're a bit confused, the late Roberto Goizueta, the former CEO of Coca-Cola, explained it this way: "You borrow money at a certain rate and invest it at a higher rate and pocket the difference. It is simple. It is the essence of banking."[44]

Exhibit 16.3 shows how to calculate EVA. First, starting with a company's income statement, you calculate the net operating profit after taxes (NOPAT) by subtracting taxes owed from income from operations. (Remember, a quick review of an income statement is on the Financial Review Card found at the back of your book.) The NOPAT shown in Exhibit 16.3 is $3,500,000. Second, identify how much capital the company has invested (that is, spent). Total liabilities (what the company owes) less accounts payable and less accrued expenses, neither of which you pay interest on, provides a rough approximation of this amount. In Exhibit 16.3, total capital invested is $16,800,000. Third, calculate the cost (that is, rate) paid for capital by determining the interest paid to bondholders (who lend organizations their money), which is usually somewhere between

Exhibit 16.3
Calculating Economic Value Added (EVA)

1. Calculate net operating profit after taxes (NOPAT).	$ 3,500,000
2. Identify how much capital the company has invested (that is, spent).	$16,800,000
3. Determine the cost (that is, rate) paid for capital (usually between 5 percent and 8 percent).	10%
4. Multiply capital used (Step 2) times cost of capital (Step 3).	(10% × $16,800,000) = $1,680,000
5. Subtract the total dollar cost of capital from net profit after taxes.	$3,500,000 NOPAT − $1,680,000 Total cost of capital $1,820,000 EVA

© Cengage Learning

5 and 8 percent, and the return that stockholders want in terms of dividends and stock price appreciation, which is historically about 13 percent. Take a weighted average of the two to determine the overall cost of capital. In Exhibit 16.3, the cost of capital is 10 percent. Fourth, multiply the total capital ($16,800,000) from Step 2 by the cost of capital (10 percent) from Step 3. In Exhibit 16.3, this amount is $1,680,000. Fifth, subtract the total dollar cost of capital in Step 4 from the NOPAT in Step 1. In Exhibit 16.3, this value is $1,820,000, which means that our example company has created economic value or wealth this year. If our EVA number had been negative, meaning that the company didn't make enough profit to cover the cost of capital from bondholders and shareholders, then the company would have destroyed economic value or wealth by taking in more money than it returned.[45]

Why is EVA so important? First and most importantly, because it includes the cost of capital, it shows whether a business, division, department, profit center, or product is really paying for itself. The key is to make sure that managers and employees can see how their choices and behaviors affect the company's EVA. For example, because of EVA training and information systems, factory workers at Herman Miller, a leading office furniture manufacturer, understand that using more efficient materials, such as less expensive wood-dust board instead of real wood sheeting, contributes an extra dollar of EVA from each desk the company makes. On its website, Herman Miller explains, "Under the terms of the EVA plan, we shifted our focus from budget performance to long-term continuous improvements and the creation of economic

value. When we make plans for improvements around here, we include an EVA analysis. When we make decisions to add or cut programs, we look at the impact on EVA. Every month, we study our performance in terms of EVA, and this measurement system is one of the first things new recruits to the company learn."[46] "The result is a highly motivated and business-literate workforce that challenges convention and strives to create increasingly greater value for both customers and owners. Every month the company and all employees review performance in terms of EVA, which has proven to be a strong corollary to shareholder value."[47]

Second, because EVA can easily be determined for subsets of a company such as divisions, regional offices, manufacturing plants, and sometimes even departments, it makes managers and workers at all levels pay much closer attention to their segment of the business. In other words, EVA motivates managers and workers to think like small-business owners who must scramble to contain costs and generate enough business to meet their bills each month. And, unlike many kinds of financial controls, EVA doesn't specify what should or should not be done to improve performance. Thus, it encourages managers and workers to be creative in looking for ways to improve EVA performance.

Remember that EVA is the amount by which profits exceed the cost of capital in a given year. So the more that EVA exceeds the total dollar cost of capital, the better a company has used investors' money that year. For example, Apple had an EVA of $28 billion in 2012, by far the largest EVA in the

Rose Carson/Shutterstock.com

world. The next-closest company was Google at $5.28 billion. To put Apple's 2012 EVA performance in perspective, note that its EVA grew by an astronomical 74 percent per year between 2010 and 2012 and that 2012's EVA of $28 billion is 16.5 times Apple's average EVA of "just" $1.7 billion a year from 2005 to 2009. Apple's EVA financial performance in 2012 was truly extraordinary and the largest ever achieved by any company.[48]

16-3c The Customer Perspective: Controlling Customer Defections

The second aspect of organizational performance that the balanced scorecard helps managers monitor is customers. It does so by forcing managers to address the question, "How do customers see us?" Unfortunately, most companies try to answer this question through customer satisfaction surveys, but these are often misleadingly positive. Most customers are reluctant to talk about their problems because they don't know who to complain to or think that complaining will not do any good. In fact, a study by the Australian federal Office of Consumer Affairs found that 96 percent of unhappy customers never complain to anyone in the company.[49]

One reason that customer satisfaction surveys can be misleading is that sometimes even very satisfied customers will leave to do business with competitors. Rather than poring over customer satisfaction surveys from current customers, studies indicate that companies may do a better job of answering the question, "How do customers see us?" by closely monitoring **customer defections**, that is, by identifying which customers are leaving the company and measuring the rate at which they are leaving. Unlike the results of customer satisfaction surveys, customer defections and retention have a great effect on profits.

Because most accounting systems measure the financial impact of a customer's current activity (sales), rather than the lifetime value of each customer, few managers realize the financial impact that even a low rate of customer defection can have on a business. Businesses frequently lose 15 to 20 percent of their customers each year, so even a small improvement in retention can have a significant impact on profits. In fact, retaining just 5 percent more customers per year can increase annual profits 25 to 100 percent. Managers, therefore, should pay closer attention to customer defections. John Tschohl, an author and business consultant, worked with a network of seventeen blood plasma donation

Focus on the Best Customers by Firing the Worst

Ironically, serving the best customers requires differentiating the best from the worst. Uber and Lyft want their drivers to be able to focus on their best customers, so their robust ranking systems allow drivers to rate each passenger on a scale of one to five stars after each ride. Drivers' ratings can identify customers who have vomited in their car or whose driving requests appear to make the driver a chauffeur for criminal activity. (Airbnb and OpenTable use similar customer-rating systems.) Identifying bad customers actually allows companies (and drivers and property owners) to cultivate a great clientele by avoiding bad customers and focusing on serving the needs of the best.

Source: J. Weed, "For Uber, Airbnb and Other Companies, Customer Ratings Go Both Ways," *New York Times*, December 1, 2014, B7.

centers to determine the financial impact of defections. With 40,600 donors each year, analysis of the network showed that the "lifetime" of a typical donor—the time when the donor was active—was 3.4 years. During that time, each lifetime donor contributed roughly $6,000 in profits to the company. Each year, however, a cohort of 2,340 donors defected, making the network's annual customer defection rate 6 percent. While the defection rate was modest, the financial impact was considerable, resulting in more than $100 million in lost revenue and $60 million less in profits each year, or $200 million in profits over the lifetime (3.4 years) of a single cohort (2,430 people) of defectors.[50]

Beyond the clear benefits to the bottom line, the second reason to study customer defections is that customers who have left are much more likely than current customers to tell you what you are doing wrong. Perhaps the best way to tap into this source of good feedback is to have top-level managers from various departments talk directly to customers who have left. It's also worthwhile to have top managers talk to dissatisfied customers who are still with the company. Finally, companies that understand why customers leave not only can take steps to fix ongoing problems but also can identify which customers are likely to leave and can make changes to prevent them from leaving.

Customer defections a performance assessment in which companies identify which customers are leaving and measure the rate at which they are leaving

16-3d The Internal Perspective: Controlling Quality

The third part of the balanced scorecard, the internal perspective, consists of the processes, decisions, and actions that managers and workers make within the organization. In contrast to the financial perspective of EVA and the outward-looking customer perspective, the internal perspective focuses on internal processes and systems that add value to the organization. For McDonald's, it could be processes and systems that enable the company to provide consistent, quick, low-cost food. For Toyota, it could be reliability—when you turn on your car, it starts, no matter whether the car has 20,000 or 200,000 miles on it. Yet, no matter what area a company chooses, the key is to excel in that area. Consequently, the internal perspective of the balanced scorecard usually leads managers to a focus on quality.

Quality is typically defined and measured in three ways: excellence, value, and conformance to expectations.[51] When the company defines its quality goal as *excellence*, managers must try to produce a product or service of unsurpassed performance and features. *Condé Nast Traveler* magazine has been ranking global airlines for twenty-six years. For twenty-five of those years, Singapore Airlines was named the best airline in the world.[52] Whereas many airlines try to cram passengers into every available inch on a plane, Singapore Airlines delivers creature comforts to encourage repeat business and lure customers willing to pay premium prices. On its newer planes, the first-class cabin is divided into eight private mini-rooms, each with an unusually wide leather seat that folds down flat for sleeping, a twenty-three-inch LCD TV that doubles as a computer monitor, and an adjustable table.

These amenities and services are common for private jets but truly unique in the commercial airline industry.[53] Singapore Airlines was the first airline, in the 1970s, to introduce a choice of meals, complimentary drinks, and earphones in coach class. It was the first to introduce worldwide video, news, telephone, and fax services, and it was the first to feature personal video monitors for movies, news, documentaries, and games. Singapore Airlines has had AC power for laptop computers for some time, and recently it became the first airline to introduce on-board high-speed Internet access.

Value is the customer perception that the product quality is excellent for the price offered. At a higher price, for example, customers may perceive the product to be less of a value. When a company emphasizes value as its quality goal,

> **Value** customer perception that the product quality is excellent for the price offered

managers must simultaneously control excellence, price, durability, and any other features of a product or service that customers strongly associate with value. The Kia Optima was recently recognized by *Kiplinger's Personal Finance* as a Best New Car Value. It has a turbocharged engine with not only the highest horsepower in its class but also the highest fuel efficiency as well. Standard equipment includes Bluetooth connectivity, power seats, satellite radio, a cooled glove box, and a voice-controlled entertainment system. The car is also backed by a five-year warranty, as well as a five-year roadside assistance program. With all these features and a $25,000 to $30,000 price that is several thousand dollars cheaper than the Toyota Camry and Honda Accord, sales have jumped 131 percent.[54]

When a company defines its quality goal as conformance to specifications, employees must base decisions and actions on whether services and products measure up to the standard. In contrast to excellence and value-based definitions of quality that can be somewhat ambiguous, measuring whether products and services are "in spec" is relatively easy. Furthermore, while conformance to specifications (for example, precise tolerances for a part's weight or thickness) is usually associated with manufacturing, it can be used equally well to control quality in nonmanufacturing jobs. Exhibit 16.4 shows a checklist that a cook or restaurant owner would use to ensure quality when buying fresh fish.

The way in which a company defines quality affects the methods and measures that workers use to control quality. Accordingly, Exhibit 16.5 shows the advantages and disadvantages associated with the excellence, value, and conformance to specification definitions of quality.

16-3e The Innovation and Learning Perspective: Sustainability

The last part of the balanced scorecard, the innovation and learning perspective, addresses the question, "Can we continue to improve and create value?" Thus, the innovation and learning perspective involves continuous improvement in ongoing products and services (discussed in Chapter 18), as well as relearning and redesigning the processes by which products and services are created (discussed in Chapter 7). Because these are discussed in more detail elsewhere in the text, this section reviews an increasingly important topic, sustainability. Exhibit 16.6 shows the four levels of sustainability, ranging from waste disposal, which produces the smallest minimization of waste, to waste prevention and reduction, which produces the greatest minimization.[55]

Exhibit 16.4
Conformance to Specifications Checklist for Buying Fresh Fish

Fresh Whole Fish	Acceptable	Not Acceptable
Gills	✓ bright red, free of slime, clear mucus	✗ brown to grayish, thick, yellow mucus
Eyes	✓ clear, bright, bulging, black pupils	✗ dull, sunken, cloudy, gray pupils
Smell	✓ inoffensive, slight ocean smell	✗ ammonia, putrid smell
Skin	✓ opalescent sheen, scales adhere tightly to skin	✗ dull or faded color, scales missing or easily removed
Flesh	✓ firm and elastic to touch, tight to the bone	✗ soft and flabby, separating from the bone
Belly cavity	✓ no viscera or blood visible, lining intact, no bone protruding	✗ incomplete evisceration, cuts or protruding bones, off-odor

Sources: "A Closer Look: Buy It Fresh, Keep It Fresh," *Consumer Reports Online*, accessed June 20, 2005. http://www.seagrant.sunysb.edu/SeafoodTechnology/SeafoodMedia/CR02-2001/CR-SeafoodII020101.htm; "How to Purchase: Buying Fish," *AboutSeaFood*, accessed June 20, 2005. http://www.aboutseafood.com/faqs/purchase1.html.

Exhibit 16.5
Advantages and Disadvantages of Different Measures of Quality

Quality Measure	Advantages	Disadvantages
Excellence	Promotes clear organizational vision.	Provides little practical guidance for managers.
	Being/providing the "best" motivates and inspires managers and employees.	Excellence is ambiguous. What is it? Who defines it?
Value	Appeals to customers who know excellence "when they see it."	Difficult to measure and control.
	Customers recognize differences in value.	Can be difficult to determine what factors influence whether a product/service is seen as having value.
	Easier to measure and compare whether products/services differ in value.	Controlling the balance between excellence and cost (that is, affordable excellence) can be difficult.
Conformance to Specifications	If specifications can be written, conformance to specifications is usually measurable.	Many products/services cannot be easily evaluated in terms of conformance to specifications.
	Should lead to increased efficiency.	Promotes standardization, so may hurt performance when adapting to changes is more important.
	Promotes consistency in quality.	May be less appropriate for services, which are dependent on a high degree of human contact.

Source: Briar Cliff Manor, NY, 10510-8020; C. A. Reeves and D. A. Bednar, "Defining Quality: Alternatives and Implications," *Academy of Management Review* 19 (1994): 419–445.

The goals of the top level, *waste prevention and reduction*, are to prevent waste and pollution before they occur or to reduce them when they do occur. In its new $1.2 billion stadium in Santa Clara, California, the National Football League's San Francisco 49ers installed Bander Bermuda Grass on the field because it uses half the water of regular sports turf. The stadium has an 18,000 square-foot garden on top of the luxury box suites to provide insulation and reduce energy use, 1,000 solar panels to generate energy, and a rainwater collection system for cooling and irrigation. In all, the stadium is energy neutral, meaning it generates all of its own energy for home games. 49ers President Paraag Marathe says, "Where we are in Silicon Valley it's sort of our mandate. If it wasn't environmentally responsible, we wouldn't be as successful."[56]

There are three strategies for waste prevention and reduction:

1. *Good housekeeping*—performing regularly scheduled preventive maintenance for offices, plants, and equipment. Examples of good housekeeping include fixing leaky valves quickly to prevent wasted water and making sure machines are running properly so that they don't use more fuel than necessary. Likewise, companies are also beginning to apply good housekeeping practices to their cloud computing services. Companies tend to overestimate their capacity needs, but because cloud computing charges work similarly to a taxicab (the meter is always running), companies can end up spending a lot of money on unused computing power. To remedy this problem, engineers at **Netflix** wrote software that automatically shuts down service during off-peak hours and resumes it when activity picks back up. **ThermoFisher**, a biotechnology company, did likewise and also downgraded to less powerful cloud computing servers that better matched its needs—and cost a lot less to use.[57]

2. *Material/product substitution*—replacing toxic or hazardous materials with less harmful materials.

In the new Levi's Stadium, there are 1,000 solar panels that are used to generate energy, and a rainwater collection system for cooling and irrigation.

3. *Process modification*—changing steps or procedures to eliminate or reduce waste.

At the second level of sustainability, *recycle and reuse*, wastes are reduced by reusing materials as long as possible or by collecting materials for on- or off-site recycling. H&M, a worldwide clothing retailer, uses recycled polyester from more than 9.5 million PET water bottles in its products and has an in-store recycling program through which it has collected more than 5,000 metric tons of used clothing that it either donates to charities, recycles into rags, or uses to make new jeans. H&M sells five new kinds of denim clothing made with at least 20 percent recycled cotton and 28 percent recycled polyester. Henrik Lampa, H&M's sustainability manager, says, "We don't want clothes to become waste; we want them to become a resource instead."[58]

A growing trend in recycling is *design for disassembly*, where products are designed from the start for easy disassembly, recycling, and reuse after they are no longer usable. Japan-based Kyocera used design for disassembly principles to create laser printers that are cartridge-free (because of their complexity, printer cartridges are difficult to recycle). To make its printers easy to take apart at the end of their life cycle, Kyocera designed them with just five parts, down from seventy, used plastic clips instead of metal

Exhibit 16.6 **Four Levels of Sustainability**

- Waste Prevention & Reduction
- Recycle & Reuse
- Waste Treatment
- Waste Disposal

Source: Business Horizons, September-October 1995, D. R. May and B. L. Flannery, "Cutting Waste with Employee Involvement Teams," pp. 28–38.

fasteners, and marked each part with codes explaining how they should be recycled. Kyocera's careful designs have reduced carbon footprints by 55 percent, waste by 85 percent, and costs by 54 percent.[59]

At the third level of sustainability, waste treatment, companies use biological, chemical, or other processes to turn potentially harmful waste into harmless compounds or useful by-products. Usually, supermarkets throw away the food they don't sell, but in the United Kingdom, several supermarket chains are using warm water and bacteria to convert food waste to a methane-rich biogas that powers electricity plants. Because the supermarkets are taxed $98 for every ton of trash that goes into landfills, Marks & Spencer now sends 89 percent of its food waste for biogas conversion, saving the company $163 million a year.[60]

The fourth and lowest level of sustainability is *waste disposal*. Wastes that cannot be prevented, reduced, recycled, reused, or treated should be safely disposed of in processing plants or in environmentally secure landfills that prevent leakage and contamination of soil and underground water supplies. Contrary to common belief, all businesses, not just manufacturing firms, have waste disposal problems. For example, with the average computer lasting just three years, approximately 60 million computers come out of service each year, creating disposal problems for offices all over the world. But organizations can't just throw old computers away because they have lead-containing cathode ray tubes in the monitors, toxic metals in the circuit boards, paint-coated plastic, and metal coatings that can contaminate groundwater.[61] Many companies give old computers and computer equipment to local computer recycling centers that distribute usable computers to nonprofit organizations or safely dispose of lead and other toxic materials. A number of retailers and electronics manufacturers operate recycling programs to keep electronics out of landfills.

For example, customers can drop off computers, TVs, DVD players, batteries, and other items at Best Buy stores. There is a $10 recycling fee for anything with a screen, but Best Buy offsets that with a $10 gift card. Best Buy will recycle 80 million pounds of electronics this year. But for those items that still function, Costco and Newegg.com work with Gazelle.com, which buys, refurbishes, and resells 250,000 items overseas and on eBay. College student Bobby Lozano sold his used iPod Nano and LG EnV Touch phone to Gazelle, because he says, "I got an iPhone, so I no longer needed the other two." Gazelle wiped the devices of personal information and put $70 into his PayPal account.[62]

17 Managing Information

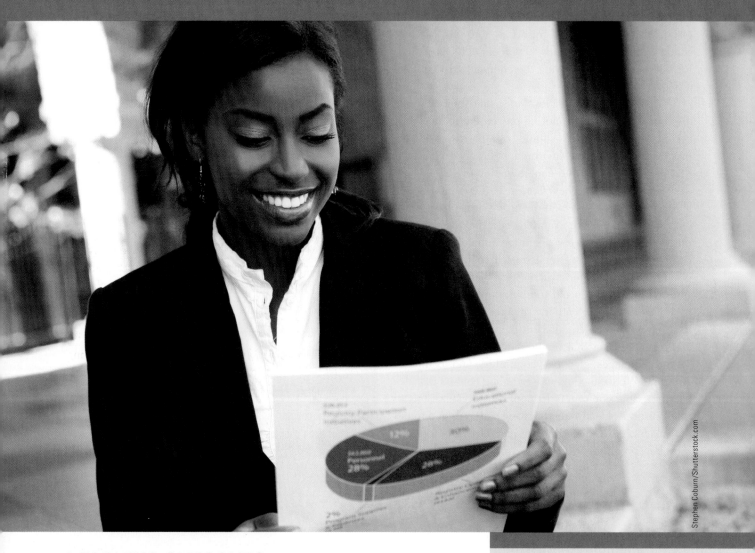

Stephen Coburn/Shutterstock.com

LEARNING OUTCOMES

17-1 Explain the strategic importance of information.

17-2 Describe the characteristics of useful information (that is, its value and costs).

17-3 Explain the basics of capturing, processing, and protecting information.

17-4 Describe how companies can access and share information and knowledge.

After you finish

this chapter, go to

PAGE 371 for

STUDY TOOLS

17-1 STRATEGIC IMPORTANCE OF INFORMATION

A generation ago, computer hardware and software had little to do with managing business information. Rather than storing information on hard drives, managers stored it in filing cabinets. Instead of uploading daily sales and inventory levels by satellite to corporate headquarters, they mailed hard-copy summaries to headquarters at the end of each month. Instead of word processors, reports were typed on electric typewriters. Instead of spreadsheets, calculations were made on adding machines. Managers communicated by sticky notes, not email. Phone messages were written down by assistants and coworkers, not forwarded in your email as a sound file with the message converted to text. Workers did not use desktop, laptop, or tablet computers or smartphones as daily tools to get work done. Instead, they scheduled limited access time to run batch jobs on the mainframe computer (and prayed that the batch job computer code they wrote would work).

Today, a generation later, computer hardware and software are an integral part of managing business information. This is due mainly to something called **Moore's law**. Gordon Moore is one of the founders of Intel Corporation, which makes 75 percent of the integrated processors used in PCs. In 1965, Moore predicted that computer-processing power would double and that its cost would drop by 50 percent every two years.[1] As Exhibit 17.1 shows, Moore was right. Computer power, as measured by the number of transistors per computer chip, *has* more than doubled every few years, as have hard drive sizes and pixel density (that is, screen resolution). Consequently, the computer sitting in your lap or on your desk (or in your hand!) is not only smaller but also much cheaper and more powerful than the large mainframe computers used by *Fortune* 500 companies thirty years ago. For instance, your iPhone replaces thirteen of the fifteen items, such as a desktop computer, mobile phone, CD player, camcorder, and so on, commonly sold by Radio Shack in 1991, items that would have cost you $3,071.21 then, or, after adjusting for inflation, $5,374.46 today. So your $600 iPhone not only replaces a trunkful of 1991 electronics gear, it does so for only 11 percent of the cost.[2] That's Moore's law in action. Will Moore's law eventually fail and technological progress eventually slow? Perhaps, as the physics and costs of developing faster, more powerful chips (today's

Frits van Paasschen, CEO of Starwood Hotels & Resorts, values information much more than data. If employees send him a bulky spreadsheet, he sends it back, asking them to summarize the key points instead.

chips are already based on circuitry 1 billionth of a meter thin) may eventually slow the rate of development. But chip makers are already addressing the challenges of smaller circuitry with practical solutions such as stacking circuits on top of each other. Instead of one layer of circuity, so-called 3-D NAND chips will have thirty-two to forty-eight layers on each chip that already can hold 384 gigabytes, three times as much as one-layer chips.[3]

Raw data are facts and figures. For example, 11, $762, 32, and 26,100 are some data that I used the day I wrote this section of the chapter. However, facts and figures aren't particularly useful unless they have meaning. For example, you probably can't guess what these four pieces of raw data represent, can you? If you can't, these data are useless. That's why researchers make the distinction between raw data and information. Whereas raw data consist of facts and figures, **information** is useful data that can influence someone's choices and behavior. One way to think about the difference between data and information is that information has context. Frits van Paasschen, CEO of **Starwood Hotels & Resorts**, values information much more than data. If employees send him a bulky spreadsheet, he won't even open it. "When I get the massive file, the first thing I'll do is send it back and say tell me the key points that I actually need to understand."[4]

Moore's law the prediction that about every two years, computer processing power would double and its cost would drop by 50 percent

Raw data facts and figures

Information useful data that can influence people's choices and behavior

Exhibit 17.1

Moore's Law

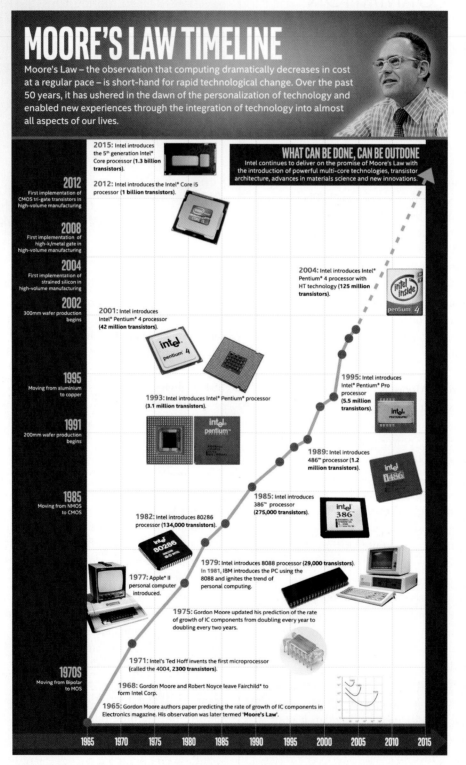

MOORE'S LAW TIMELINE

Moore's Law – the observation that computing dramatically decreases in cost at a regular pace – is short-hand for rapid technological change. Over the past 50 years, it has ushered in the dawn of the personalization of technology and enabled new experiences through the integration of technology into almost all aspects of our lives.

2015: Intel introduces the 5th generation Intel® Core processor (**1.3 billion transistors**).

2012: Intel introduces the Intel® Core i5 processor (**1 billion transistors**).

WHAT CAN BE DONE, CAN BE OUTDONE
Intel continues to deliver on the promise of Moore's Law with the introduction of powerful multi-core technologies, transistor architecture, advances in materials science and new innovations.

2012
First implementation of CMOS tri-gate transistors in high-volume manufacturing

2008
First implementation of high-k/metal gate in high-volume manufacturing

2004
First implementation of strained silicon in high-volume manufacturing

2004: Intel introduces Intel® Pentium® 4 processor with HT technology (**125 million transistors**).

2002
300mm wafer production begins

2001: Intel introduces Intel® Pentium® 4 processor (**42 million transistors**).

1995
Moving from aluminium to copper

1995: Intel introduces Intel® Pentium® Pro processor (**5.5 million transistors**).

1993: Intel introduces Intel® Pentium® processor (**3.1 million transistors**).

1991
200mm wafer production begins

1989: Intel introduces 486™ processor (**1.2 million transistors**).

1985
Moving from NMOS to CMOS

1985: Intel introduces 386™ processor (**275,000 transistors**).

1982: Intel introduces 80286 processor (**134,000 transistors**).

1979: Intel introduces 8088 processor (**29,000 transistors**). In 1981, IBM introduces the PC using the 8088 and ignites the trend of personal computing.

1977: Apple® II personal computer introduced.

1975: Gordon Moore updated his prediction of the rate of growth of IC components from doubling every year to doubling every two years.

1971: Intel's Ted Hoff invents the first microprocessor (called the 4004, **2300 transistors**).

1970S
Moving from Bipolar to MOS

1968: Gordon Moore and Robert Noyce leave Fairchild® to form Intel Corp.

1965: Gordon Moore authors paper predicting the rate of growth of IC components in Electronics magazine. His observation was later termed '**Moore's Law**'.

1965 1970 1975 1980 1985 1990 1995 2000 2005 2010 2015

"Moore's Law Timeline," Intel, http://download.intel.com, accessed September 27, 2015.

So what did those four pieces of data mean to me? Well, 11 stands for Channel 11, the local CBS affiliate on which I watched part of the men's PGA golf tournament; $762 is how much it would cost me to rent a minivan for a week if I go skiing over spring break; 32 is for the 32-gigabyte storage card that I want to add to my digital camera (prices are low, so I'll probably buy it); and 26,100 means that it's time to get the oil changed in my car.

In today's hyper competitive business environments, information is as important as capital (that is, money) for business success, whether it's about product inventory, pricing, or costs. It takes money to get businesses started, but businesses can't survive and grow without the right information.

Information has strategic importance for organizations because it can be used to 17-1a obtain first-mover advantage and 17-1b sustain competitive advantage after it has been created.

17-1a First-Mover Advantage

First-mover advantage is the strategic advantage that companies earn by being the first in an industry to use new information technology to substantially lower costs or to differentiate a product or service from that of competitors. Pandora, for example, pioneered music streaming and leads this highly competitive market with a 9.13 percent share of the total U.S. radio listening market (which includes all radio stations and streaming services), up from 7.29 percent a year earlier. Pandora, which is free to listeners because it makes money via advertising, has 79.2 million active listeners, up from 75.3 million a year ago.[5]

While first-mover advantage typically leads to above average profits and market share, it doesn't immunize a company from competition. Pandora already faces three primary competitors: Spotify (60 million listeners, 15 million subscribers), Deezer (16 million listeners, 6 million subscribers), and Apple's iTunes Radio (free/ad-based, 40 million listeners). Two brand-new entrants to music streaming, Amazon's Prime Music, which is free for Amazon's estimated 40 million Prime members (who pay $99 a year for Prime membership which includes two-day

shipping and a number of other benefits), and Apple's Beats Music (300,000 subscribers), acquired for $3 billion from Beats Electronics for its Beats Music subscription service, represent new, serious threats to Pandora.[6]

Many first-movers have failed to capitalize on their strategic advantages. Netscape lost first-mover advantage in web browsers, as did MySpace in social media, and Yahoo! in search engines.[7] A study of thirty first-movers found two key factors mattered in terms of sustaining first-mover advantage: the pace at which product technology is changing and how fast the market is growing.[8] As these examples show, if better technology is quickly being introduced by new market entrants, and the market is quickly growing (which attracts new competitors who want a share of that growing market), it can be difficult to sustain first-mover advantage.

> The key to sustaining a competitive advantage is using information technology to continuously improve and support the core functions of a business.

17-1b Sustaining Competitive Advantage

As described, companies that use information technology to establish first-mover advantage usually have higher market shares and profits. According to the resource-based view of information technology shown in Exhibit 17.2, companies need to address three critical questions to sustain a competitive advantage through information technology. First, does the information technology create value for the firm by lowering costs or providing a better product or service? If an information technology doesn't add value, then investing in it would put the firm at a competitive disadvantage relative to companies that choose information technologies that do add value.

Second, is the information technology the same or different across competing firms? If all the firms have access to the same information technology and use it in the same way, then no firm has an advantage over another (that is, there is competitive parity).

iStockphoto.com/ManuelBurgos

First-mover advantage
the strategic advantage that companies earn by being the first to use new information technology to substantially lower costs or to make a product or service different from that of competitors

Exhibit 17.2
Using Information Technology to Sustain a Competitive Advantage

Source: Adapted from F. J. Mata, W. L. Fuerst, and J. B. Barney, "Information Technology and Sustained Competitive Advantage: A Resource-Based Analysis," *MIS Quarterly* 19, no. 4 (December 1995): 487–505.

hard drives. The key is using information technology to continuously improve and support the core functions of a business. While American Airlines was the first airline to issue tablet computers to pilots to replace manuals and navigation charts (previously held in binders in forty-pound carry-on bags), British Airways is using iPads to improve a core part of its business—the level of customer service flight attendants deliver to high-value business- and first-class travelers. Previously, prior to each departure, flight attendants read through stacks of printouts to memorize key passengers' preferences. Now, however, with iPads automatically updated hours before flights depart and available discreetly in the cabin throughout the flight, attendants have immediate access to passengers' likes and dislikes, special meal requests, and even medical needs. Furthermore, the iPads contain seating charts showing where loyalty club members are seated, so attendants can greet them personally when they board. Flight attendant Daljit Kaur says, "I'm ahead of myself in knowing where our corporate and high-value customers are sitting, and who needs help." Because flight attendants can attend to them so well, "They look at you and say 'have you been on a special course?'" Finally, flight attendants use the iPads to submit customer complaints. Pippa Grech, who manages British Airways' iPad program, says, "The crew does it so that passengers don't have to run around on holiday trying to do it themselves. Otherwise, by the time they get off the plane, they think 'oh, I won't bother about it.'"[9]

17-2 CHARACTERISTICS AND COSTS OF USEFUL INFORMATION

Last year, NFL players swapped thick three-ring binders for PlayerLync, an electronic platform for viewing playbooks on tablet computers. Denver Broncos tight end Jacob Tamme says, "It changes the way you prepare. You can come off the practice field, get in the cold tub, and watch film . . . on your iPad."[10] The next wave of useful information is coming via devices that players wear in practice or games. Cameras on quarterbacks' helmets show where the quarterback was looking during play check downs (that is, "My first receiver is covered. Look at the 2nd receiver. He's covered. Look at the running back in the backfield. He's open. Throw to him.").

Third, is it difficult for another company to create or buy the information technology used by the firm? If so, then the firm has established a sustainable competitive advantage over competitors through information technology. If not, then the competitive advantage is just temporary, and competitors should eventually be able to duplicate the advantages the leading firm has gained from information technology.

In short, the key to sustaining a competitive advantage is not faster computers, more memory, or larger

Greg Menard, Co-Founder and CTO of PlayerLync, shows how players and coaching staff for The Denver Broncos review game tape on tablet computers.

RJ Sangosti/Denver Post/Getty Images

Likewise, radio frequency identification tags (discussed in Section 17-3a) in shoulder pads indicate how fast players run, whether they consistently work hard in practice, or how many calories they burn. Pittsburgh Steelers general manager Kevin Colbert is excited about the possibilities, saying, "To be able to tell a quarterback where he should be, to be able to show a defense what an offense looks like at ground level would be great. That would be more realistic."[11]

*As the NFL's use of cameras and RFID chips demonstrates, information is useful when it is **17-2a accurate, 17-2b complete, 17-2c relevant,** and **17-2d timely.** However, there can be significant **17-2e acquisition, 17-2f processing, 17-2g storage, 17-2h retrieval,** and **17-2i communication costs** associated with useful information.*

17-2a Accurate Information

Information is useful when it is accurate. Before relying on information to make decisions, you must know that the information is correct. But what if it isn't? Many retailers use customer satisfaction surveys to determine what they need to improve, and checkout wait times are always near the top of the list. But asking customers about checkout wait times can produce inaccurate data. Shoppers accurately estimate wait times of three minutes or less but overestimate four-minute waits, which they report as five or six minutes, and completely misestimate five-minute waits, which they report as ten minutes. Typically, retailers relying on these data overestimate checkout wait time and can end up hiring too many cashiers to solve the problem.[12]

Controlling the Risks of BYOD (Bring Your Own Device) Programs

At work, millions of employees use their own devices to conduct business. Bring-your-own-device programs are convenient and economical for both employees and employers. Employees no longer have to juggle devices and are often reimbursed for a portion of their wireless bills. Employers don't have to buy everyone at the office the latest smartphone. But BYOD programs are not without drawbacks, particularly in the event of a security breach. Using software developed by Fiberlink, employers can remotely wipe every device in their network completely clean—without differentiating between professional and personal information. That means personal photos, music, and apps are erased along with company emails, contacts, and documents. Fiberlink wipes clean nearly 100,000 devices a year, and although the erasures can be inconvenient for employees, the BYOD trend shows no sign of slowing. According to Gartner Research, by 2017, half of all U.S. employers will stop providing hardware to employees for work purposes and will expect them to use their own.

Source: L. Weber, "Workers' Devices Get a Remote Cleaning," *Wall Street Journal*, September 10, 2014, B7.

Kroger, instead, gets more accurate data from infrared cameras that count the number of customers in the store and waiting at checkout registers. These data showed Kroger that its stores had many customers at lunch and in the morning buying just a few items, who would be better served by express lanes, so Kroger added 2,000 more to its stores. As a result of these changes, made on the basis of more accurate information, the average wait at Kroger has dropped from four minutes to twenty-six seconds.[13]

17-2b Complete Information

Information is useful when it is complete. Incomplete or missing information makes it difficult to recognize problems and identify potential solutions. Following an airplane crash, investigators recover critical information from the plane's black box recordings. If the black box is lost or damaged, then investigators may never understand what happened. "Everyone talks about the black box on an airplane," says Vic Charlebois, vice president of flight operations at Canadian airline First Air, "but it is permanently installed on an airplane, and if the airplane goes missing so does the black box."[14] Indeed, when Malaysia Airlines Flight 370 disappeared en route from Kuala Lumpur to Beijing in March 2014, investigators were left guessing as to the cause because the plane and its black box were still missing after a four-month search.[15]

Regulators have long suggested putting live data systems on planes to transmit real time in-flight data, but airlines have hesitated because of costs estimated at $100,000 per plane.[16] Canadian-based First Air is installing a live data streaming service that can provide much more complete and useful information. Made by Canadian-based Flyht, First Air's FLYHTStream system can be preprogrammed to automatically transmit live data under certain conditions, or it can be manually activated by the pilot or ground-based flight controllers. First Air's Vic Charlebois says, "Let's take the case of the Malaysian aircraft. If it was being monitored through satellites and a dispatcher did see it wander off course somewhere, the procedure would be to activate the FLYHTStream and then contact the crew to see what was going on."[17]

17-2c Relevant Information

You can have complete, accurate information, but it's not very useful if it doesn't pertain to the problems you're facing. For instance, if you're unlucky enough to contract bullous pemphigoid, a rare skin condition resulting in large, watery blisters on your inner thighs and upper arms, chances are the dermatologist you visit won't have any relevant experience with this condition to be able to recognize and treat it. And that's exactly what happened to Dr. Kavita Mariwalla, who was stumped when a patient came in with these problems. So she turned to Modernizing Medicine, an iPad-based medical records system to obtain the relevant information needed to determine what was wrong. Modernizing Medicine is a web-based database, containing information from more than 14 million patient visits compiled by 3,700 doctors, that uses the same kind of data mining and artificial intelligence used by websites such as Amazon.com. Dr. Eric Horvitz, Microsoft's managing director of research, says, "Electronic health records [are] like large quarries where there's lots of gold, and we're just beginning to mine them."[18] Dr. Mariwalla was able to quickly access similar cases on Modernizing Medicine's database and find other drugs that had been effective in those cases. Mariwalla said that Modernizing Medicine, "Gives you access to data, and data is king. It's been very helpful, especially in clinically challenging situations."[19]

17-2d Timely Information

Finally, information is useful when it is timely. To be timely, the information must be available when needed to define a problem or to begin to identify possible solutions. If you've ever thought, "I wish I had known that earlier," then you understand the importance of

All natural, organic Vermont Maple Syrup from Meadowbrook Maple, a family-owned and operated farm located in Milton, Vermont.

To reduce the time spent looking for leaks, Meadowbrook Maple Syrup installed a Tap Track system that uses solar power to track line pressure for each tree.

Source: Meadowbrook Acres, Inc.

timely information and the opportunity cost of not having it.

Maple syrup used to come from buckets hanging from taps bored into trees to extrude maple sap. Instead of buckets, modern maple syrup production uses long flexible plastic tubes to transport the sap miles away to sugar-storage houses. When the sap stops flowing because of leaks, it can take workers days to walk the lines to locate them. And with a short 4–6 week season, fixing leaks quickly is critical. Meadowbrook Maple Syrup, in Vermont, has 5,000 taps and 18 miles of tubes spread out over 100 acres. To reduce the time spent looking for leaks, Meadowbrook installed a Tap Track system that uses solar-powered sensors to monitor line pressure at each tree. When the system detects a drop in pressure (indicating a leak), it sends an alert to company computers and smartphones. Eric Sorkin of Thunder Basin Maple Works, described how the Tap Track system directed his workers to a porcupine-caused leak. Just as they fixed that leak, the system alerted them to one nearby. Sorkin said, "You could follow the porcupine right to the next line where he'd cut it. Otherwise, it would have been a few more days before we found those two lines."[20]

17-2e Acquisition Costs

Acquisition cost is the cost of obtaining data that you don't have. Acxiom, a billion-dollar company, gathers and processes data for direct-mail marketing companies. If you've received an unsolicited, "preapproved" credit card application recently (and who hasn't?), chances are Acxiom helped the credit card company gather information about you. Where does Acxiom get that information? The first place it turns is to companies that sell consumer credit reports at a wholesale cost of $1 each. Acxiom also obtains information from retailers. Each time you use your credit card, websites and retailers' checkout scanners gather information about your spending habits and product preferences. Acxiom also uses publicly available information such as motor vehicle and real estate records, as well as website traffic.

So why pay for this information? Acquiring it can help credit card companies better identify who will mail back a signed credit card application and who will rip the credit card application in half and toss it in the trash. Likewise, Acxiom's information helps retailers by categorizing consumers into seventy demographic groups. For example, Nordstrom, an upscale department store, would find it worthwhile to advertise to "Apple Pie Families," married homeowners between the ages of 46 and 65 who live in urban areas, earn $100,000 to $500,000, and have school-age children. Likewise,

Walmart is better off advertising to "Trucks and Trailers," people between the ages of 30 and 45 who earn less than $100,000 and live in rural areas. Paying Acxiom to acquire this kind of data significantly increases the return that retailers and credit card companies get from advertising and direct marketing.

17-2f Processing Costs

Companies often have massive amounts of data but not in the form or combination they need. **Processing cost** is the cost of turning raw data into usable information. While Google offers a wide range of online services, most of its revenues come from search-related ads. But those ads are effective only when Google serves up accurate searches that help people find what they're looking for. While Google already operates ten extraordinarily expensive data centers around the world, it's processing needs keep growing, so it has committed to building a new $1 billion data center in Council Bluffs, Iowa (after already building a $1.5 billion data center there in 2007).[21] Likewise in Europe, it will spend $772 million to build a data center in Eemshaven, Holland, where there is low-cost renewable energy, a landing station for underwater international data cables, and a mild climate.[22] The payback from these multibillion dollar investments? They allow Google to process 40,000 searches per second (3.5 billion per day, 1.2 trillion per year), handle email for 500 million+ Gmail accounts, and serve up YouTube videos to 1 billion users, all with the aim of more accurately targeting ads to the people who use its services.[23]

17-2g Storage Costs

Storage cost is the cost of physically or electronically archiving information for later retrieval and use. While your Facebook account is free, Facebook spends billions so that its more than 1 billion users worldwide can connect with their friends, play online games, and share photos. In addition to existing data centers in Oregon, North Carolina, and Sweden, Facebook is building a 476,000 sq. ft. $300 million data center in Altoona, Iowa. Jay Parikh, Facebook's vice president of Infrastructure Engineering, says, "When complete, Altoona will be among the most advanced and energy-efficient facilities of its kind." Tom Furlong, Facebook's vice president

Acquisition cost the cost of obtaining data that you don't have

Processing cost the cost of turning raw data into usable information

Storage cost the cost of physically or electronically archiving information for later retrieval and use

Treasure Trove of Data

If there are costs associated with information, there is value associated with data. At least that's what the creditors of Caesars Entertainment think of the Caesars's Total Rewards loyalty program, which is 45 million members strong and even has a dedicated ebsite. Fans of the program are obsessed with the upgrades and the ability to redeem points. The company's creditors became equally obsessed with the program when Caesars filed bankruptcy, owing them $18.4 billion. With an estimated valuation of $1 billion, the program was one of Caesars's significant assets and soon part of a legal dispute for who would control the program (and its data). Another company to declare bankruptcy but have a huge data treasure trove is Radio Shack, whose database includes names, addresses, and transaction data gathered over decades on roughly 65 million people. In the case of Radio Shack, its original—and

strict—privacy agreements may be the only thing keeping its data out of its creditors hands.

Sources: K. O'Keefe, "Real Prize in Caesars Fight: Data on Players," *Wall Street Journal*, March 20, 2015, B1; P. Brickley and D. FitzGerald, "RadioShack Is Dead, Long Live RadioShack," *Wall Street Journal*, April 2, 2015, B1.

of Site Operations, says, "This location had fiber, power, and a shovel-ready site." Facebook has plans to triple its initial investment in Iowa to more than a billion.[24]

17-2h Retrieval Costs

Retrieval cost is the cost of accessing already-stored and processed information. One of the most common misunderstandings about information is that it is easy and cheap to retrieve after the company has it. Not so. First, you have to find the information. Then, you've got to convince whoever has it to share it with you. Then the information has to be processed into a form that is useful for you. By the time you get the information you need, it may not be timely anymore.

For example, as companies move toward paperless office systems, how will employees quickly and easily retrieve archived emails, file records, website information, word processing documents, or images? Likewise, how will managers and employees quickly and easily retrieve information about costs, inventory, and sales?

One solution is broadly known as *business intelligence software* (BIS), which transforms stored, unstructured data in real time into meaningful information for business analysis and decision making. For example, retailers now commonly use sensors, video, and bluetooth cell phone tracking to count and monitor the flow of shoppers throughout their stores. These sensors track which entrances and exits are most commonly used, where customers spend most of their time in the store, how long they stay in a particular location, and so on. During the holiday season when stores were crowded, Sunhee Moon, a San Francisco retailer, was surprised to learn that customers spent more time at tables near the back of the store, and not the entrance. So holiday scarves were moved to the back where more customers would see them.[25] Likewise, through bluetooth tracking of your phone, retailers could, for instance, see that you've been to the store four times without buying. The tracking system could then be programmed to send your phone a mobile coupon on entering the store. Because mobile coupons are used ten times more than paper coupons, and smartphone users are 14 percent more likely than those without smartphones to use those mobile coupons while in the store, BIS monitoring gives retailers powerful new tools to track store performance and increase sales.[26]

17-2i Communication Costs

Communication cost is the cost of transmitting information from one place to another. For example, a small business with twenty people needing phone lines, a hosted website, and high-speed Internet access pays Comcast about $1,300 a month for that access. Google, Microsoft, and Facebook do the same for their employees. But because of the size of the data flowing

Retrieval cost the cost of accessing already-stored and processed information

Communication cost the cost of transmitting information from one place to another from their websites to customers, they pay millions more in access fees to Comcast and Time Warner Cable, which provide the backbone through which Internet data run. While such payments are rare, it makes sense that generators of heavy Internet traffic pay more, especially because Comcast's Internet traffic is growing at 55 percent per year. Netflix, which accounts for 35 percent of evening traffic on the Internet due to video streaming, has also begun paying Comcast and other Internet providers so that its streaming services are prioritized in network traffic to customers' homes.[27]

17-3 CAPTURING, PROCESSING, AND PROTECTING INFORMATION

In 1907, Metropolitan Life Insurance built a huge office building in New York City for its brand-new, state-of-the-art information technology system. What was this great breakthrough in information management? Card files. That's right, the same card file system that every library in America used before computers. Metropolitan Life's information technology consisted of 20,000 separate file drawers that sat in hundreds of file cabinets more than fifteen feet tall. This filing system held 20 million insurance applications, 700,000 accounting books, and 500,000 death certificates. Metropolitan Life employed sixty-one workers who did nothing but sort, file, and climb ladders to pull files as needed.[28]

How we get and share information has clearly changed. The cost, inefficiency, and ineffectiveness of using this formerly state-of-the-art system would put an insurance company out of business within months. Today, if storms, fire, or accidents damage policyholders' property, insurance companies write checks on the spot to cover the losses. When policyholders buy a car, they call their insurance agent from the dealership to activate their insurance before driving off in their new cars. And now, insurance companies are marketing their products and services to customers directly from the Internet. From card files to Internet files in just under a century, the rate of change in information technology is spectacular.

*In this section, you will learn about the information technologies that companies use to **17-3a capture, 17-3b process,** and **17-3c protect information.***

17-3a Capturing Information

There are two basic methods of capturing information: manual and electronic. Manual capture of information is a slow, costly, labor-intensive, and often inaccurate process, which entails recording and entering data by hand into a data storage device. For example, when you applied for a driver's license, you probably recorded personal information about yourself by filling out a form. Then, after you passed your driver's test, someone typed your handwritten information into the department of motor vehicles' computer database so that local and state police could access it from their patrol cars in the event they pulled you over for speeding. (Isn't information great?) To avoid the problems inherent in such a system, companies are relying more on electronic capture. They use electronic storage devices such as bar codes, radio frequency identification (RFID) tags, and document scanners to capture and record data electronically.

Bar codes represent numerical data by varying the thickness and pattern of vertical bars. The primary advantage of bar codes is that the data they represent can be read and recorded in an instant with a handheld or pen-type scanner. One pass of the scanner (okay, sometimes several) and "beep!" the information has been captured. Bar codes cut checkout times in half, reduce data entry errors by 75 percent, and save stores money because stockers don't have to go through the labor-intensive process of putting a price tag on each item in the store.[29] And, with mobile phone apps, bar codes are becoming ubiquitous in travel (mobile boarding passes), for customer loyalty and payment programs (Starbucks), and in entertainment, such as movies (Fandango) and live events (LiveNation or TicketMaster). QR (quick response) codes are bar codes with black and white patterns scanned with your smartphone. While they've been used in Japan for a decade, QR codes are being used in a variety of different ways. At Dick's Sporting Goods stores, scanning a QR code for a 12 lb. medicine ball shows a video demonstrating how to perform a lunge, pushups, and a squat toss, all while incorporating the medicine ball in the exercise.[30] Chinese consumers can quickly pay for taxi rides by scanning the taxi driver's QR code using Alipay Wallet (China-based Alibaba's PayPal equivalent).[31] Replicon's CloudClock system works by having employees scan a QR code that prompts a camera to take and time-stamp their picture, indicating when they started and stopped work.[32] Finally, BMO Harris Bank is launching cardless ATM machines where customers

> **Bar code** a visual pattern that represents numerical data by varying the thickness and pattern of vertical bars

With mobile phone apps, bar codes are becoming ubiquitous in travel (mobile boarding passes), for customer loyalty, payment programs and in entertainment, such as movies (Fandango), and live events (TicketMaster).

use their bank app to indicate how much money they want to withdraw. The app generates a QR code that the ATM machine scans and authorizes before dispensing cash in just fifteen seconds, or just one-third of the time of a card-based transaction. Also, QR codes eliminate the risk of card skimming in which hackers tap into the card-reading device in the ATM machine.[33]

Radio frequency identification (RFID) tags contain minuscule microchips and antennas that transmit information via radio waves.[34] Unlike bar codes, which require direct line-of-sight scanning, RFID tags are read by turning on an RFID reader that, like a radio, tunes into a specific frequency to determine the number *and* location of products, parts, or anything else to which the RFID tags are attached. Turn on an RFID reader, and every RFID tag within the reader's range (from several hundred to several thousand feet) is accounted for.

Because they are now so inexpensive, RFID tags and readers are being put to thousands of uses in all kinds of businesses. Disney World is using RFID sensors to offer guests an efficient, personalized vacation experience through RFID-equipped wristbands. MagicBands, as Disney calls them, allow customers to enter the park with a quick wrist swipe instead of using paper tickets, and can be linked to visitors' payment information, which means not having to carry cash or credit cards to pay for a third plate of Mickey waffles. MagicBands also facilitate a personalized experience by sharing names, birthdays and preferences with park employees (at the parents' discretion, of course) so that a birthday girl meeting Cinderella, her favorite princess, is greeted by name and with special wishes for a happy birthday. None of this could happen without RFID.[35]

Electronic scanners, which convert printed text and pictures into digital images, have become an increasingly popular method of capturing data electronically because they are inexpensive and easy to use. The first requirement for a good scanner is a document feeder that automatically feeds document pages into the scanner or turns the pages (often with a puff of air) when scanning books or bound documents. Text that has been digitized cannot be searched or edited like the regular text in your word processing software, however; so the second requirement for a good scanner is **optical character recognition** software to scan and convert original or digitized documents into ASCII (American Standard Code for Information Interchange) text or Adobe PDF documents. ASCII text can be searched, read, and edited with standard word processing, email, desktop publishing, database management, and spreadsheet software, and PDF documents can be searched and edited with Adobe's Acrobat software.

17-3b Processing Information

Processing information means transforming raw data into meaningful information that can be applied to business decision making. Evaluating sales data to determine the best- and worst-selling products, examining repair records to determine product reliability, and monitoring the cost of long-distance phone calls are all examples of processing raw data into meaningful information. And with automated, electronic capture of data, increased processing power, and cheaper and more plentiful ways to store data, managers no longer worry about getting data. Instead, they scratch their heads about how to use the overwhelming amount of data that pours into their businesses every day. Furthermore, most managers

Radio frequency identification (RFID) tags tags containing minuscule microchips that transmit information via radio waves and can be used to track the number and location of the objects into which the tags have been inserted

Electronic scanner an electronic device that converts printed text and pictures into digital images

Optical character recognition the ability of software to convert digitized documents into ASCII (American Standard Code for Information Interchange) text that can be searched, read, and edited by word processing and other kinds of software

Processing information transforming raw data into meaningful information know little about statistics and have neither the time nor the inclination to learn how to use them to analyze data.

One promising tool to help managers dig out from under the avalanche of data is data mining. **Data mining** is the process of discovering patterns and relationships in large amounts of data.[36] Data mining is carried out using complex algorithms such as neural networks, rule induction, and decision trees. If you don't know what those are, that's okay. With data mining, you don't have to. Most managers only need to know that data mining looks for patterns that are already in the data but are too complex for them to spot on their own. Netflix is a subscription-based service for streaming movies and TV shows and renting DVDs, so many felt it was taking a risk by producing its first series, *House of Cards*, a political drama featuring Kevin Spacey. However, with 33 million subscribers hitting "play" 30 million times a day, adding 4 million ratings each day to what they watch, and searching its website 3 million times per day, Netflix had data to mine that most entertainment businesses don't have. Those data showed that customers liked actor Kevin Spacey, the original British version of *House of Cards*, and films by director David Fincher. Chief communications officer Jonathan Friedland says, "Because we have a direct relationship with consumers, we know what people like to watch and that helps us understand how big the interest is going to be for a given show. It gave us some confidence that we could find an audience for a show like 'House of Cards.'"[37]

Data mining typically splits a data set in half, finds patterns in one half, and then tests the validity of those patterns by trying to find them again in the second half of the data set. The data typically come from a **data warehouse**, which stores huge amounts of data that have been prepared for data mining analysis by being cleaned of errors and redundancy. The data in a data warehouse can then be analyzed using two kinds of data mining. **Supervised data mining** usually begins with the user telling the data mining software to look and test for specific patterns and relationships in a data set. Typically, this is done through a series of "what-if?" questions or statements. For instance, a grocery store manager might instruct the data mining software to determine if coupons placed in the Sunday paper increase or decrease sales. By contrast, with **unsupervised data mining**, the user simply tells the data mining software to uncover whatever patterns and relationships it can find in a data set. For example, because New York City (NYC) experiences about 3,000 major fires a year, analysts at the NYC Fire Department use data mining to predict which of the 330,000 buildings in New York are at most risk of catching fire. The data mining program checks for sixty different risk factors commonly correlated with fires, such as the building's age, elevators (which allow smoke and super heated air to move from floor to floor), and whether the building is vacant, abandoned, or has had electrical problems, and then generates a risk score for each building, allowing fire inspectors to prioritize high-risk buildings for on-site inspections.[38] Unsupervised data mining is particularly good at identifying association or affinity patterns, sequence patterns, and predictive patterns. It can also identify what data mining technicians call data clusters.[39]

Association or affinity patterns occur when two or more database elements tend to occur together in a significant way. Most retailers send flyers and coupons about baby products after a woman has given birth (after the birth announcement is made public), but Target wanted to act earlier, sometime around the first twenty weeks of pregnancy, when mothers-to-be start buying items to get ready for their new baby. So it turned to association and affinity patterns to see if there was a way to identify through purchasing patterns when a woman was pregnant. Target's Guest Marketing Analytics department analyzed consumer data from Target's baby registry and found that around the beginning of their second trimester, pregnant women often bought lotion, mineral and vitamin supplements, unscented soap, hand sanitizer, and washcloths. Target found a pattern of twenty-five products that identified pregnant customers with such accuracy that the company could even estimate a due date. For example, if you're female, are 23 years old, and have bought cocoa-butter lotion, a large purse that doubles as a diaper bag, zinc and magnesium supplements (taken by pregnant women), and a blue or pink throw rug, there's an 87 percent chance that you are pregnant. Why? Because those purchases are almost always associated with being pregnant.[40]

Sequence patterns appear when two or more database elements occur together in a significant pattern in which one of the elements precedes

Data mining the process of discovering unknown patterns and relationships in large amounts of data

Data warehouse a database that stores huge amounts of data that have been prepared for data mining analysis by being cleaned of errors and redundancy

Supervised data mining the process when the user tells the data mining software to look and test for specific patterns and relationships in a data set

Unsupervised data mining the process when the user simply tells the data mining software to uncover whatever patterns and relationships it can find in a data set

Association or affinity patterns when two or more database elements tend to occur together in a significant way

Sequence patterns when two or more database elements occur together in a significant pattern in which one of the elements precedes the other the other. Sequence patterns appear when two or more database elements occur together in a significant pattern in which one of the elements precedes the other. Hospitals employ the Modified Early Warning Score (MEWS), which uses commonly measured vital signs, such as blood pressure, temperature, and heart rate, to predict the likelihood of a patient going Code Blue, that is, respiratory or cardiac arrest. Patients with higher MEWS scores are monitored more closely. Doctors at Chicago's NorthShore University HealthSystem used data mining to see how well seventy-two medical variables predicted the likelihood of a patient going Code Blue. On a data set of 133,000 patients, data mining correctly predicted Code Blues 72 percent of the time—four hours before they happened. By contrast, MEWS scores accurately predicted Code Blues just 30 percent of the time.[41]

Predictive patterns are just the opposite of association or affinity patterns. Whereas association or affinity patterns look for database elements that seem to go together, **predictive patterns** help identify database elements that are different. Banks and credit card companies use data mining to find predictive patterns that distinguish customers who are good credit risks from those who are poor credit risks and less likely to pay their loans and monthly bills. Likewise, InterContinental Hotels Group uses data mining to customize marketing messages for different kinds of customers. A typical marketing campaign will have seven to fifteen marketing messages aimed at the typical InterContinental customer. But thanks to data mining, InterContinental's marketing campaigns now have 1,500 marketing messages for twelve different customer groups, each defined thanks to clear differences across 4,000 variables or attributes. For instance, one customer group looking for bargains uses reward points and tends to stay on weekends. So they only get marketing messages about weekend packages and events, in contrast to business travelers who are less price sensitive, pay with corporate credit cards, and stay during the week.[42]

Data clusters are the last kind of pattern found by data mining. **Data clusters** occur when three or more database elements occur together (that is, cluster) in a significant way. For example, after analyzing several years' worth of repair and warranty claims, Ford Motor Company might find that, compared with cars built in its Chicago plant, the cars it builds in Kansas City (first element) are more likely to have problems with over-tightened fan belts (second element) that break

Predictive patterns
patterns that help identify database elements that are different

Data clusters when three or more database elements occur together (that is, cluster) in a significant way (third element) and result in overheated engines (fourth element), ruined radiators (fifth element), and payments for tow trucks (sixth element), which are paid for by Ford's five-year, 60,000-mile power train warranty.

Traditionally, data mining has been very expensive and very complex. Today, however, data mining services and analyses are much more affordable and within reach of most companies' budgets. And, if it follows the path of most technologies, data mining will become even easier and cheaper to use in the future.

17-3c Protecting Information

Protecting information is the process of ensuring that data are reliably and consistently retrievable in a usable format for authorized users but no one else. Unfortunately, that didn't happen when North Korean hackers broke into Sony Pictures corporate computers, releasing malware that completely destroyed key databases, and then revealing embarrassing emails in retribution for a movie comedy, *The Interview*, in which two journalists are recruited by the CIA to assassinate North Korean leader Kim Jong Un.[43] The hackers also released copies of five Sony movies on the Internet, as well as sensitive personal information, including Social Security numbers of 47,000 people. The amount of data destroyed made it difficult at first for investigators to identify the hackers. Sony Entertainment CEO Michael Lynton said, "It took me twenty-four or thirty-six hours to fully understand this was not something we were going to be able to recover from in the next week or two."[44]

People inside and outside companies can steal or destroy company data in various ways, including denial-of-service web server attacks that can bring down some of the busiest and best-run sites on the Internet; viruses and malware, spyware, or adware that spread quickly and can result in data loss and business disruption; keystroke monitoring, in which every mouse click and keystroke you make is monitored, stored, and sent to unauthorized users; password-cracking software that steals supposedly secure passwords; and phishing, where fake but real-looking emails and websites trick users into sharing personal information (user names, passwords, account numbers) leading to unauthorized account access. On average, 30 percent of computers are infected with malware. Of those, 57 percent are infected with viruses, and 21 percent are infected with Trojans, which is malware disguised to look like a normal file or program.[45] Studies show that the threats listed in Exhibit 17.3 are so widespread that automatic attacks will begin on an unprotected computer just fifteen seconds after it connects to the Internet.[46]

As shown in the right-hand column of Exhibit 17.3, numerous steps can be taken to secure data and data networks. Some of the most important are authentication and authorization, firewalls, antivirus software for PCs and email servers, data encryption, and virtual private networks.[47] We will review those steps and then finish this section with a brief review of the dangers of wireless networks.

Two critical steps are required to make sure that data can be accessed by authorized users and no one else. One is **authentication**, that is, making sure users are who they claim to be.[48] The other is **authorization**, that is, granting authenticated users approved access to data, software, and systems.[49] When an ATM prompts you to enter your personal identification number (PIN), the bank is authenticating that you are you. After you've been authenticated, you are authorized to access your funds and no one else's. Of course, as anyone who has lost a PIN or password or had one stolen knows, user authentication systems are not foolproof. In particular, users create security risks by not changing their default account passwords (such as birth dates) or by using weak passwords such as names ("Larry") or complete words ("football") that are quickly guessed by password-cracking software.[50]

This is why many companies are now turning to **two-factor authentication**, which is based on what users know, such as a password, and what they have, in their possession, such as a secure ID card, their phones, or unique information that only they would know.[51] When logging in, users are first asked for their passwords. But then they must provide a second authentication factor, such as an answer to a security question (that is, unique information) or a validation code that has been sent to their mobile phone. Google, for example, requires two-factor authentication for its Google Apps (Gmail, Calendar, Drive, Docs, and so on). After entering their passwords, users can either use the code sent via text to their phone, or a code generated by Google's Authenticator app. Google Authenticator works via your mobile phone connection or Wi-Fi, gives you the ability to generate authentication codes for multiple accounts

---

Protecting information the process of ensuring that data are reliably and consistently retrievable in a usable format for authorized users but no one else

Authentication making sure potential users are who they claim to be

Authorization granting authenticated users approved access to data, software, and systems

Two-factor authentication authentication based on what users know, such as a password and what they have in their possession, such as a secure ID card or key (including non-Google accounts), and generates codes that are only good for sixty seconds.[52]

Unfortunately, stolen or cracked passwords are not the only way for hackers and electronic thieves to gain access to an organization's computer resources. Unless special safeguards are put in place, every time corporate users are online, there's literally nothing between their PCs and the Internet (home users with high-speed DSL or cable Internet access face the same risks). Hackers can access files, run programs, and control key parts of computers if precautions aren't taken. To reduce these risks, companies use **firewalls**, hardware or software devices that sit between the computers in an internal organizational network and outside networks such as the Internet. Firewalls filter and check incoming and outgoing data. They prevent company insiders from accessing unauthorized sites or from sending confidential company information to people outside the company. Firewalls also prevent outsiders from identifying and gaining access to company computers and data. If a firewall is working properly, the computers behind the company firewall literally cannot be seen or accessed by outsiders.

A **virus** is a program or piece of code that, without your knowledge, attaches itself to other programs on your computer and can trigger anything from a harmless flashing message to the reformatting of your hard drive to a system-wide network shutdown. You used to have to do something or run something to get a virus, such as double-clicking an infected email attachment. Today's viruses are much more threatening. In fact, with some viruses, just being connected to a network can infect your computer. *Antivirus software for PCs* scans email, downloaded files, and computer hard drives, disk drives, and memory to detect and stop computer viruses from doing damage. However, this software is effective only to the extent that users of individual computers have and use up-to-date versions. With new viruses appearing all the time, users should update their antivirus software weekly or, even better,

Firewall a protective hardware or software device that sits between the computers in an internal organizational network and outside networks, such as the Internet

Virus a program or piece of code that, without your knowledge, attaches itself to other programs on your computer and can trigger anything from a harmless flashing message to the reformatting of your hard drive to a system-wide network shutdown

Can Your Typing Pattern Replace Your Passwords?

While passwords have long been a staple of digital security, their shortcomings are apparent: simple passwords can be hacked, and complicated passwords can be difficult to remember. A new keyboard that identifies users by their unique typing styles could spur progress toward a "post-password" era, and improve corporate security. The keyboard picks up electrical charges from human skin and uses software to find patterns in users' typing. The scientists behind the keyboard say human typing patterns, comprising rhythm and time between keystrokes, are comparable in uniqueness to fingerprints. The technology does little to advance corporate network security, but it could still be a significant deterrent to hackers targeting individual machines.

Source: C. Boulton, "Keyboard Identifies Computer Users by Their Typing Patterns," *Wall Street Journal*, February 13, 2015, accessed May 13, 2015. http://blogs.wsj.com/cio/2015/02/13/keyboard-identifies-computer-users-by-their-typing-patterns/.

iStockphoto.com/GraphicHead

Exhibit 17.3

Security Threats to Data and Data Networks

Security Problem	Source	Affects	Severity	The Threat	The Solution
Denial of service; web server attacks and corporate network attacks	Internet hackers	All servers	High	Loss of data, disruption of service, and theft of service.	Implement firewall, password control, server-side review, threat monitoring, and bug fixes; turn PCs off when not in use.
Password cracking software and unauthorized access to PCs	Local area network, Internet	All users, especially digital subscriber line and cable Internet users	High	Hackers take over PCs. Privacy can be invaded. Corporate users' systems are exposed to other machines on the network.	Close ports and firewalls, disable file and print sharing, and use strong passwords.
Viruses, worms, Trojan horses, and rootkits	Email, downloaded and distributed software	All users	Moderate to high	Monitor activities and cause data loss and file deletion; compromise security by sometimes concealing their presence.	Use antivirus software and firewalls; control Internet access.
Malware, spyware, adware, malicious scripts, and applets	Rogue web pages	All users	Moderate to high	Invade privacy, intercept passwords, and damage files or file system.	Disable browser script support; use security, blocking, and spyware/adware software.
Email snooping	Hackers on your network and the Internet	All users	Moderate to high	People read your email from intermediate servers or packets, or they physically access your machine.	Encrypt messages, ensure strong password protection, and limit physical access to machines.
Keystroke monitoring	Trojan horses, people with direct access to PCs	All users	High	Records everything typed at the keyboard and intercepts keystrokes before password masking or encryption occurs.	Use antivirus software to catch Trojan horses, control Internet access to transmission, and implement system monitoring and physical access control.
Phishing	Hackers on your network and the Internet	All users, including customers	High	Fake but real-looking emails and websites that trick users into sharing personal information on what they wrongly think is a company's website. This leads to unauthorized account access.	Educate and warn users and customers about the dangers. Encourage both not to click on potentially fake URLs, which might take them to phishing websites. Instead, have them type your company's URL into the web browser.
Spam	Email	All users and corporations	Mild to high	Clogs and overloads email servers and inboxes with junk mail. HTML-based spam may be used for profiling and identifying users.	Filter known spam sources and senders on email servers; have users create further lists of approved and unapproved senders on their PCs.
Cookies	Websites you visit	Individual users	Mild to moderate	Trace web usage and permit the creation of personalized web pages that track behavior and interest profiles.	Use cookie managers to control and edit cookies, and use ad blockers.

Sources: "The 11 Most Common Computer Security Threats . . . And What You Can Do to Protect Yourself from Them," Symantec-Norton, accessed May 12, 2015. http://www.symantec-norton.com/11-most-common-computer-security-threats_k13.aspx; K. Bannan, "Look Out: Watching You, Watching Me," *PC Magazine*, July 2002, 99; A. Dragoon, "Fighting Phish, Fakes, and Frauds," *CIO*, September 1, 2004, 33; B. Glass, "Are You Being Watched?" *PC Magazine*, April 23, 2002, 54; K. Karagiannis, "DDoS: Are You Next?" *PC Magazine*, January 2003, 79; B. Machrone, "Protect & Defend," *PC Magazine*, June 27, 2000, 168–181; "Top 10 Security Threats," *PC Magazine*, April 10, 2007, 66; M. Sarrel, "Master End-User Security," *PC Magazine*, May 2008, 101.

configure their virus software to automatically check for, download, and install updates. By contrast, *corporate antivirus software* automatically scans email attachments such as Microsoft Word documents, graphics, or text files as they come across the company email server. It also monitors and scans all file downloads across company databases and network servers. So, while antivirus software for PCs prevents individual computers from being infected, corporate antivirus software for email servers, databases, and network servers adds another layer of protection by preventing infected files from multiplying and being sent to others.

Another way of protecting information is to encrypt sensitive data. **Data encryption** transforms data into complex, scrambled digital codes that can be decrypted only by authorized users who possess unique decryption keys. One method of data encryption is to use products by Symantec (http://buy.symantec.com/estore/clp/home) to encrypt the files stored on PCs or network servers and databases. This is especially important with laptop computers, which are easily stolen. With people increasingly gaining unauthorized access to email messages—email snooping—it's also important to encrypt sensitive email messages and file attachments. You can use a system called "public key encryption" to do so. First, give copies of your "public key" to anyone who sends you files or email. Have the sender use the public key, which is actually a piece of software, to encrypt files before sending them to you. The only way to decrypt the files is with a companion "private key" that you keep to yourself.

Although firewalls can protect PCs and network servers connected to the corporate network, people away from their offices (for example, salespeople, business travelers, telecommuters) who interact with their company networks via the Internet face a security risk. Because Internet data are not encrypted, "packet sniffer" software easily allows hackers to read everything sent or received except files that have been encrypted before sending. Previously, the only practical solution was to have employees dial in to secure company phone lines for direct access to the company network. Of course, with international and long-distance phone calls, the costs quickly added up. Now, **virtual private networks (VPNs)** have solved this problem by using software to encrypt all Internet data at both ends of the transmission process. Instead of making long-distance calls, employees connect to the Internet. But, unlike typical Internet connections in which data packets are decrypted, the VPN encrypts the data sent by employees outside the company computer network, decrypts the data when they arrive within the company network, and does the same when data are sent back to the computer outside the network. VPN connections provide secure access to everything on a company's network. If your employer or university doesn't provide a VPN, you can purchase VPN services for personal use and protection from well-known providers, such as AnchorFree Hotspot Shield (www.anchorfree.com) or Cloak VPN (www.getcloak.com), for about $3 a month. VPN services should be used when connected to public Wi-Fi systems, such as in hotels, airports, or coffee shops, where anyone on the public network can monitor or spy on what you're doing.

Alternatively, many companies are now adopting web-based **secure sockets layer (SSL) encryption** to provide secure off-site access to data and programs. If you've ever entered your credit card in a web browser to make an online purchase, you've used SSL technology to encrypt and protect that information.

You can tell if SSL encryption is being used on a website if you see a padlock icon (gold in Internet Explorer or Firefox, green in Google Chrome, silver in Safari) or if the URL begins with "https." SSL encryption works the same way in the workplace. Managers and employees who aren't at the office simply connect to the Internet, open a web browser, and then enter a user name and password to gain access to SSL-encrypted data and programs.

Finally, many companies now have wireless networks, which make it possible for anybody with a laptop and a wireless card to access the company network from anywhere in the office. Though wireless networks come equipped with security and encryption capabilities that, in theory, permit only authorized users to access the wireless network, those capabilities are easily bypassed with the right tools. Compounding the problem, many wireless networks are shipped with their security and encryption capabilities turned off for ease of installation.[53] Caution is important even when encryption is turned on, because the WEP (Wired Equivalent Privacy) security protocol is easily compromised. If you work at home or are working on the go, extra care is critical because Wi-Fi networks in homes and public places such as hotel lobbies are among the most targeted by hackers.[54] See the Wi-Fi Alliance site at www.wi-fi.org for the latest

Hiding from Big Data

In the chapter, you read that Target was able to determine that a woman was pregnant—even before she knew it herself—using data collections. Assistant professor of sociology at Princeton University Janet Vertesi decided to try an experiment: she endeavored to keep her own pregnancy secret from big data for as long as possible. Vertesi censored what she did and said on social media, and asked her friends to do the same. She conducted all baby-related web browsing using a traceless browser and made all baby-related purchases with cash or Amazon gift cards bought with cash. She even had orders mailed to an anonymous drop box so that they wouldn't be linked to her home address. "I didn't expect it to be as hard as it was," Vertesi says. "It was extremely impractical and inconvenient." She discovered it was much more expensive, too; avoiding loyalty cards meant missing out on a lot of deals. Vertesi noted that many of the things she had to do, taken together at face value, made it appear like she was doing something illegal. Her final verdict: "I wouldn't recommend [opting out]." Spreading activity over different servers is more effective and less inconvenient.

Source: J. Goldstein, "Meet the Woman Who Did Everything in Her Power to Hide Her Pregnancy from Big Data," *ThinkProgress*, April 29, 2014, accessed June 2, 2014. http://thinkprogress.org/culture/2014/04/29/3432050/can -you-hide-from-big-data/.

information on wireless security and encryption protocols that provide much stronger protection for your company's wireless network.

Finally, companies are combating security threats by hiring *white hat hackers*, so-called good guys, who test security weak points in information systems so that they can be fixed. While this is typically done using traditional hacking tools, as discussed in Exhibit 17.3, white hat hackers also test security via *social engineering*, in which they trick people into giving up passwords and authentication protocols or unknowingly providing unauthorized access to company computers. One test involves emailing a picture of a cat with a purple mohawk and this subject line, "Check out these kitties!" to employees with a link to more cute kitty photos. When you click an embedded link to "more cute kitty photos," you're taken to a company website warning about the dangers of phishing scams. Think that you wouldn't fall for this? Forty-eight percent of employees receiving this email click the link.[55] Another test involves "lost or left-behind" USB thumb drives, ostensibly belonging to competitors. When the person who picked up the thumb drive inserts it into a computer, it installs software that uses the webcam to snap a picture of the employee, who then receives a visit from the IT security team.[56]

17-4 ACCESSING AND SHARING INFORMATION AND KNOWLEDGE

Today, information technologies are letting companies communicate data, share data, and provide data access to workers, managers, suppliers, and customers in ways that were unthinkable just a few years ago.

After reading this section, you should be able to explain how companies use information technology to improve **17-4a internal access and sharing of information, 17-4b external access and sharing of information,** *and* **17-4c the sharing of knowledge and expertise.**

17-4a Internal Access and Sharing

Executives, managers, and workers inside the company use three kinds of information technology to access and share information: executive information systems, intranets, and portals. An **executive information system (EIS)** uses internal and external sources of data to provide managers and executives the information they need to monitor and analyze organizational performance.[57] The goal of an EIS is to provide accurate, complete, relevant, and timely information to managers. With just a few mouse clicks and basic commands such as *find*, *compare*, and *show*, the EIS displays costs, sales revenues, and other kinds of data in color-coded charts and graphs. Managers can drill down to view and compare data by global region, country, state, time period, and product. Managers at Colgate-Palmolive, which makes dental (Colgate toothpastes), personal (Irish Spring soap and Speed Stick antiperspirants), and home care (Palmolive dish soaps) products, as well as pet nutrition (Hill's Science Diet), use their EIS, which they call their "dashboard," to see how well the company is running. Ruben Panizza, Colgate's global IT director of business intelligence, says,

Executive information system (EIS) a data processing system that uses internal and external data sources to provide the information needed to monitor and analyze organizational performance

"These real-time dashboards are a change for people who are used to seeing a lot of numbers with their data. But they quickly realize they can use the information as it's presented in the dashboards to make faster decisions. In the past, executives relied on other people to get custom reports and data. Now, they can look at the information themselves. They see the real data as it is in the system much more easily and quickly. For the first time, many of the company's business leaders are running BI [business intelligence] tools—in this case, dashboards—to monitor the business to see what's going on at a high level."[58]

Intranets are private company networks that allow employees to easily access, share, and publish information using Internet software. Intranet websites are just like external websites, but the firewall separating the internal company network from the Internet permits only authorized internal access.[59] Companies typically use intranets to share information (e.g., about benefits) and to replace paper forms with online forms. Many company intranets are built on the web model as it existed a decade ago. Intranets are evolving to include:

▶ collaboration tools, such as wikis, where team members can post all relevant information for a project they're working on together

▶ customizable email accounts

▶ presence awareness (information on whether someone you are looking for on the network is in the office, in a meeting, working from home, and so on)

▶ instant messaging

▶ simultaneous access to files for virtual team members

Acorda Therapeutics, which develops drugs for neurological conditions, operates a company intranet called Synapse that was recognized as one of the world's ten best intranet sites. Acorda, which doubled in size over the past five years, "needed to develop a tool that would help our associates remain connected to the Company's culture and values, and keep pace with the growing business needs of our organization," says CEO Ron Cohen, MD. One section of Synapse hosts documents that employees might need, from human resources policies and forms to research and development projects and updates. Another feature, called Chatter, functions like Twitter, allowing employees to share photos, documents, and news. Chatter also shows a live feed, where employees respond to Chatter comments, news, and documents, which has the effect of collaboratively shaping ideas. Synapse also has a company-wide seating chart showing where everyone's office is and enabling communication by automatically dialing a person's office phone when you click on his or her profile on Synapse.[60]

Finally, **corporate portals** are a hybrid of executive information systems and intranets. While an EIS provides managers and executives with the information they need to monitor and analyze organizational performance, and intranets help companies distribute and publish information and forms within the company, corporate portals allow company managers and employees to access customized information *and* complete specialized transactions using a web browser.

17-4b External Access and Sharing

Historically, companies have been unable or reluctant to let outside groups have access to corporate information. Now, however, a number of information technologies—electronic data interchange, extranets, web services, and the Internet—are making it easier to share company data with external groups such as suppliers and customers. They're also reducing costs, increasing productivity by eliminating manual information processing (70% of the data output from one company, such as a purchase order, ends up as data input at another company, such as a sales invoice or shipping order), reducing data entry errors, improving customer service, and speeding communications. As a result, managers are scrambling to adopt these technologies.

With **electronic data interchange, or EDI,** two companies convert purchase and ordering information to a standardized format to enable direct electronic transmission of that information from one company's computer system to the other company's system. For example, when a Walmart checkout clerk drags an Apple iPod across the checkout scanner, Walmart's computerized inventory system automatically reorders another iPod through the direct EDI connection that its computer has with Apple's manufacturing and shipping computer. No one at Walmart or Apple fills out paperwork. No one makes phone calls. There are no delays to wait to find out whether Apple has the iPod

Intranets private company networks that allow employees to easily access, share, and publish information using Internet software

Corporate portal a hybrid of executive information systems and intranets that allows managers and employees to use a web browser to gain access to customized company information and to complete specialized transactions

Electronic data interchange (EDI) when two companies convert their purchase and ordering information to a standardized format to enable the direct electronic transmission of that information from one company's computer system to the other company's computer system in stock. The transaction takes place instantly and automatically because the data from both companies were translated into a standardized, shareable, compatible format.

Web services are another way for companies to directly and automatically transmit purchase and ordering data from one company's computer system to another company's computer system. **Web services** use standardized protocols to describe and transfer data from one company in such a way that those data can automatically be read, understood, transcribed, and processed by different computer systems in another company.[61] Route One, which helps automobile dealers process loans for car buyers, was started by the financing companies of DaimlerChrysler, Ford, General Motors, and Toyota. Not surprisingly, each auto company had a different computer system with different operating systems, different programs, and different data structures. RouteOne relies on web services to connect these different computer systems to the wide variety of different databases and software used by various auto dealers, credit bureaus, banks, and other auto financing companies. Without web services, there's no way these different companies and systems could share information.[62]

Now, what's the difference between web services and EDI? For EDI to work, the data in different companies' computer, database, and network systems must adhere to a particular set of standards for data structure and processing. For example, company X, which has a seven-digit parts numbering system, and company Y, which has an eight-digit parts numbering system, would agree to convert their internal parts numbering systems to identical ten-digit parts numbers when their computer systems talk to each other. By contrast, the tools underlying web services such as extensible markup language (or XML) automatically do the describing and transcribing so that data with different structures can be shared across very different computer systems in different companies. (Don't worry if you don't understand how this works, just appreciate what it does.) As a result, by automatically handling those differences, web services allow organizations to communicate data without special knowledge of each other's computer information systems.

In EDI and web services, the different purchasing and ordering applications in each company interact automatically without any human input. No one has to lift a finger to click a mouse, enter data, or hit the Enter key. An **extranet**, by contrast, allows companies to exchange information and conduct transactions by purposely providing outsiders with direct, password-protected, web

browser–based access to authorized parts of a company's intranet or information system.[63]

In an attempt to improve the marketing efforts of the contractors that it works with, Mitsubishi Electric Cooling & Heating developed its Creative Center extranet. The site provides a host of tools that contractors can use to grow their business. These include a range of company-approved marketing tools such as newspaper ads, posters, and banners that each contractor can customize to his or her preference and use to promote both the contractor's business and the Mitsubishi Electric Cooling & Heating brand.[64]

Finally, companies are reducing paperwork and manual information processing by using the Internet to electronically automate transactions with customers; this is similar to the way in which extranets are used to handle transactions with suppliers and distributors. For example, most airlines have automated the ticketing process by eliminating paper tickets altogether. Simply buy an e-ticket via the Internet, and then check yourself in online via an app on your smart phone, or by printing your boarding pass from your PC or an airport kiosk. Internet purchases, ticketless travel, and automated check-ins have together fully automated the purchase of airline tickets. Use of self-service kiosks is expanding, too.

At Hertz Rent-a-Car locations, self-service kiosks come equipped with two monitors. Customers can use one monitor to go through the entire rental process, from verifying identity and insurance to making a payment with a credit card. Customers who need help with the process, especially the first time, can use the other monitor to video chat with a customer service agent who guides them through the process. When done, the kiosk distributes a card with an RFID chip to unlock the customer's rental car. The kiosks allow Hertz to offer 24-hour rentals in nontraditional locations, such as car repair shops or centrally located parking lots, without hiring agents for each location.[65]

In the long run, the goal is to link customer Internet sites with company intranets (or EDI) and extranets so that everyone—all the employees and managers within a company as well as the suppliers and distributors outside the company—involved in

Web services software that uses standardized protocols to describe data from one company in such a way that those data can automatically be read, understood, transcribed, and processed by different computer systems in another company

Extranets networks that allow companies to exchange information and conduct transactions with outsiders by providing them direct, web-based access to authorized parts of a company's intranet or information system

Customers can use video monitors at Hertz to verify their identities and car insurance and pay for their car with a credit card.

providing a service or making a product for a customer is automatically notified when a purchase is made. Companies that use EDI, web services, extranets, and the Internet to share data with customers and suppliers achieve increases in productivity 2.7 times larger than those that don't.[66]

17-4c Sharing Knowledge and Expertise

At the beginning of the chapter, we distinguished between raw data, which consist of facts and figures, and information, which consists of useful data that influence someone's choices and behavior. One more important distinction needs to be made, namely, that data and information are not the same as knowledge.

Knowledge is the understanding that one gains from information. Importantly, knowledge does not reside in information. Knowledge resides in people. That's why companies hire consultants and why family doctors refer patients to specialists. Unfortunately, it can be quite expensive to employ consultants, specialists, and experts. So companies have begun using two information technologies to

capture and share the knowledge of consultants, specialists, and experts with other managers and workers: decision support systems and expert systems.

Whereas an executive information system speeds up and simplifies the acquisition of information, a **decision support system (DSS)** helps managers understand problems and potential solutions by acquiring and analyzing information with sophisticated models and tools.[67] Furthermore, whereas EIS programs are broad in scope and permit managers to retrieve all kinds of information about a company, DSS programs are usually narrow in scope and targeted toward helping managers solve specific kinds of problems. DSS programs have been developed to help managers pick the shortest and most efficient routes for delivery trucks, select the best combination of stocks for investors, and schedule the flow of inventory through complex manufacturing facilities.

It's important to understand that DSS programs don't replace managerial decision making; they *improve* it by furthering managers' and workers' understanding of the problems they face and the solutions that might work. Though used by just 2 percent of physicians, medical DSS programs hold the promise of helping doctors make more accurate patient diagnoses. A British study of eighty-eight cases misdiagnosed or initially misdiagnosed (to be correctly diagnosed much later) found that a medical DSS made the right diagnosis 69 percent of the time.[68] With a medical DSS, doctors enter patient data such as age, gender, weight, and medical symptoms. The medical DSS then produces a list of diseases and conditions, ranked by probability, low or high, or by medical specialty, such as cardiology or oncology. For instance, when emergency room physician Dr. Harold Cross treated a 10-year-old boy who had been ill with nausea and dizziness for two weeks, he wasn't sure what was wrong because the boy had a healthy appetite, no abdominal pain, and just one brief headache. However, when the medical DSS that Dr. Cross used suggested a possible problem in the back of the boy's brain, Cross ordered an MRI scan that revealed a tumor, which was successfully removed two days later. Says Dr. Cross, "My personal knowledge of the literature and physical findings would not have prompted me to suspect a brain tumor."[69]

Expert systems are created by capturing the specialized knowledge and decision rules used by experts and experienced decision makers. They permit nonexpert employees to draw on this expert knowledge base to make decisions. Most expert systems work by using a collection of "if–then" rules to sort through information and recommend a course of action. For example, let's say that you're using your American Express card to help your spouse celebrate a promotion. After dinner and a movie, the two of you stroll by

Knowledge the understanding that one gains from information

Decision support system (DSS) an information system that helps managers understand specific kinds of problems and potential solutions

Expert system an information system that contains the specialized knowledge and decision rules used by experts and experienced decision makers so that nonexperts can draw on this knowledge base to make decisions

Got Your Data! What Are You Going to Do About It?

Security through obscurity used to be a mantra of small businesses. Often operating in limited geographic areas, small businesses were too, well, *small* for cybercriminals to notice, let alone care—until recently. Small businesses are increasingly falling victim to "ransomware," a type of malicious code introduced into their servers that locks up their data. The only way to regain access to the data is by paying a ransom. And even though the ransoms are generally low—$500 or so—the downtime associated with the attack, paying the ransom, and getting back online can seem an eternity for small businesses, 80 percent of which don't use data protection. If your company falls victim to a ransomware attack, disconnect the computer from the network, scrub it, and check other computers on the network for contamination. Then upgrade your Internet security protection.

Source: R. Simon, "'Ransomware' Becomes Bigger Company Threat," *Wall Street Journal*, April 16, 2015, B1.

a travel office with a Las Vegas poster in its window. Thirty minutes later, caught up in the moment, you find yourselves at the airport ticket counter trying to purchase last-minute tickets to Vegas. But there's just one problem. American Express didn't approve your purchase. In fact, the ticket counter agent is now on the phone with an American Express customer service agent. So what put a temporary halt to your weekend escape to Vegas? An expert system that American Express calls Authorizer's Assistant.[70]

The first "if–then" rule that prevented your purchase was the rule "*if* a purchase is much larger than the cardholder's regular spending habits, *then* deny approval of the purchase." This if–then rule, just one of 3,000, is built into American Express's transaction-processing system that handles thousands of purchase requests per second. Now that the American Express customer service agent is on the line, he or she is prompted by the Authorizer's Assistant to ask the ticket counter agent to examine your identification. You hand over your driver's license and another credit card to prove you're you. Then the ticket agent asks for your address, phone number, Social Security number, and your mother's maiden name and relays the information to American Express. Finally, your ticket purchase is approved. Why? Because you met the last series of "if–then" rules. *If* the purchaser can provide proof of identity and *if* the purchaser can provide personal information that isn't common knowledge, *then* approve the purchase.

STUDY TOOLS 17

LOCATED IN TEXTBOOK
- ☐ Rip-out and review chapter review card

LOCATED AT WWW.CENGAGEBRAIN.COM
- ☐ Review key term flashcards and create your own from StudyBits
- ☐ Track your knowledge and understanding of key concepts, using the concept tracker
- ☐ Complete practice and graded quizzes to prepare for tests
- ☐ Complete interactive content within the exposition
- ☐ View chapter highlight box content at the beginning of each chapter

18 Managing Service and Manufacturing Operations

Nattanan726/Shutterstock.com

LEARNING OUTCOMES

18-1 Discuss the kinds of productivity and their importance in managing operations.

18-2 Explain the role that quality plays in managing operations.

18-3 Explain the essentials of managing a service business.

18-4 Describe the different kinds of manufacturing operations.

18-5 Explain why and how companies should manage inventory levels.

After you finish this chapter, go to **PAGE 392** for **STUDY TOOLS**

18-1 PRODUCTIVITY

Furniture manufacturers, hospitals, restaurants, automakers, airlines, and many other kinds of businesses struggle to find ways to produce quality products and services efficiently and then deliver them in a timely manner. Managing the daily production of goods and services, or **operations management**, is a key part of a manager's job. But an organization depends on the quality of its products and services as well as its productivity.

On turnaround day, Royal Caribbean's Oasis of the Seas cruise ship sails into port at 6:00 a.m., dropping off 6,000 passengers, restocking supplies, taking on 6,000 new passengers, and departing by 4:30 p.m. Provision master Rodolfo Corrales says, "Embarkation day is frantic. It's not just busy, it's crazy busy."[1] Corrales and other crewmembers will load 12,000 bags, 24,000 beer bottles, 1,400 champagne bottles, 15,000 pounds of potatoes, 9,000 pounds of tomatoes, and 9,000 cans of soft drinks onto the ship. In 2,700 rooms, attendants will strip the beds and towels, which go into green and red bags (for easier handling of 93,000 pounds of laundry). One hundred eighty-nine housekeepers clean 2,700 cabins and bathrooms. Precisely choreographed jobs and tasks, as well as a service corridor (which passengers never see), nicknamed I-95 because it runs the length of the ship making it easy to quickly get anything anywhere, make all of this happen. None of it is accidental. In fact, Royal Caribbean brought in productivity experts from Porsche, the German carmaker, and DHL, the delivery logistics firm to learn how to best manage the flow of goods, people, and luggage. The ship's hotel director, Martin Rissley, says, "The minute efficiencies you can create in the process make a big difference in the end."[2]

At their core, organizations are production systems. Companies combine inputs such as labor, raw materials, capital, and knowledge to produce outputs in the form of finished products or services. **Productivity** is a measure of performance that indicates how many inputs it takes to produce or create an output.

$$\text{Productivity} = \frac{\text{Outputs}}{\text{Inputs}}$$

The fewer inputs it takes to create an output (or the greater the output from one input), the higher the productivity. For example, ArcellorMittal, which owns steel factories all over the world, measures productivity in terms of man-hours per ton of steel. The fewer man-hours it takes to produce a ton of steel, the higher the productivity. In the United States, average productivity in steel mills is two man-hours per ton of steel. Arcellor-Mittal's best plant, in Gent, Belgium, is 35 percent more efficient than that as it makes a ton of steel using only 1.3 man-hours.[3]

*Let's examine **18-1a why productivity matters** and **18-1b the different kinds of productivity**.*

18-1a Why Productivity Matters

Why does productivity matter? For companies, higher productivity—that is, doing more with less—results in lower costs for the company, lower prices, faster service, higher market share, and higher profits. In 1989, 85 percent of the items on a UPS delivery truck were shipped to businesses. Today, 60 percent of those items are delivered to consumers, with one-third shipping from Amazon.com. Although UPS earns $11 billion a year from e-commerce deliveries, revenues per package are dropping, while per-package delivery costs are rising, all thanks to rising home deliveries. Consequently, UPS is intensifying its already strong focus on productivity by spending $500 million in preparation for the holiday season where, at its peak, it will deliver 34 million packages in one day (double an average day). It is getting large productivity increases, however, from its "Next Generation Sort Aisle," where sorters scan a package barcode (just like in stores), hear a beep (indicating a successful scan), and then read the name of a color-coded chute to which the packages needs to go. Before the scanning system, employees trained for two weeks on computers to memorize 120 ZIP codes. Now, new employees can be trained in two or three days. Rosemary Etheredge, who has worked at UPS for ten years, says, "For new employees, it is much better."[4] In fact, with the Next Generation scanning system, sorters can process 15 percent more packages per day, which means that UPS can hire the same number of temporary holiday season workers as it did two years ago, even though product volumes are rising more than 10 percent per year.[5]

Productivity matters because it results in a higher standard of living in terms of higher wages, charitable giving, and making products more affordable. When companies can do more with less, they can raise employee wages without

> **Operations management** managing the daily production of goods and services
>
> **Productivity** a measure of performance that indicates how many inputs it takes to produce or create an output

caring, conscientious, and giving? Probably not. Yet, because of increases in productivity during this time, the average American's income increased by 50 percent, from $36,433 in 2000 to $54,597 in 2014.[12] Because people earned more money, they were able to share their good fortune with others by giving more to charity.[13]

increasing prices or sacrificing normal profits. For instance, recent government economic data indicated that U.S. companies were paying workers 2.6 percent more than in the previous year. But because workers were producing 1.5 percent more than they had the year before, real labor costs actually increased.[6]

The average American family earned approximately $63,815 in 2013. If productivity grows 1 percent per year, that family's income will increase to $81,838 in 2038. But if productivity grows 2 percent per year, their income in 2038 will be $104,695, an increase of $22,857, and that's without working longer hours.[7]

Thanks to long-term increases in business productivity, the average American family today earns 12.7 percent more than the average family in 1980 and 31.9 percent more than the average family in 1967—and that's after accounting for inflation.[8] Productivity increased an average of 2.2 percent between 1997 and 2006, and then slowed to an average of 1.2 percent from 2007 to 2012.[9] And, from 2002 to 2012, the U.S. economy created nearly 10.1 million new jobs.[10]

And when more people have jobs that pay more, they give more to charity. For example, 2013 Americans donated more than $335 billion to charities, compared to 230 billion in 2000 and $261 billion in 2009.[11] Did Americans become more thoughtful,

Another benefit of productivity is that it makes products more affordable or better. One way to demonstrate this is by comparing how many work hours it would take to earn enough money to buy a product now versus in the past. For instance, in 1958 when the average U.S. wage was $1.98 an hour, a toaster cost $12.95. But in 2012, when the average hourly wage was $19.19, a toaster cost $25.99. The 2012 toaster is not only better (it is, take my word for it), it's cheaper because it took only 1.35 hours of work to pay for it compared to 6.54 hours in 1958. Likewise, a 1958 24-inch black-and-white TV (prime time TV shows weren't broadcast in color until 1965) cost $270 and 136.3 work hours compared to a 2012 26-inch LCD HDTV which cost $250 and 13.03 work hours. Finally, a 1958 stereo phonograph that played vinyl records (look in the attic, your grandparents might still have some) cost $84.95 and 43 work hours, while a 2012 iPod Classic cost $235 and just 12.25 work hours.[14] People like to reminisce about the "good 'ol days," when things were "cheaper." But, mostly, they really weren't. Thanks to steady increases in productivity, most goods become more affordable over time.

Aging U.S. Machinery Ready for Replacement

Many U.S. manufacturers are forsaking capital investments for acquisitions and stock buybacks, putting domestic manufacturing capabilities at risk of falling even further behind foreign competitors in the future. American manufacturers are replacing aging equipment at historically low rates. As of 2014, the average age of industrial equipment in the country was more than ten years, a figure not seen since 1938. Instead, U.S. manufacturers are putting their money toward acquiring other companies, spending more than $80 billion on acquisitions in the first half of 2014, up from $69.5 billion in 2013. Although in the short-term acquisitions can seem like a safer investment than capital equipment, old equipment can only last so long—continued postponement will eventually result in a breakdown that could damage productivity or even endanger workers. Moreover, as the types of manufacturing evolve to meet new product innovations, older machinery may simply not be capable of producing the new products buyers are looking for. Daniel Meckstroth, chief economist for the Manufacturers Alliance for Productivity and Innovation, expects to see a rise in spending on capital equipment, saying, "We've postponed investment so long that it almost has to occur."

Source: J. R. Hagerty, "U.S. Manufacturing Is Rolling on Aged Wheels," *Wall Street Journal*, September 3, 2014, accessed 5 June 2015. http://www.wsj.com/articles/u-s-manufacturing -is-rolling-on-aged-wheels-1409677342.

18-1b Kinds of Productivity

Two common measures of productivity are partial productivity and multifactor productivity. **Partial productivity** indicates how much of a particular kind of input it takes to produce an output.

$$\text{Partial Productivity} = \frac{\text{Outputs}}{\text{Single Kind of Input}}$$

Labor is one kind of input that is frequently used when determining partial productivity. *Labor productivity* typically indicates the cost or number of hours of labor it takes to produce an output. In other words, the lower the cost of the labor to produce a unit of output, or the less time it takes to produce a unit of output, the higher the labor productivity. Labor cost as a percentage of revenue is a basic measure of labor productivity used in the airline industry. The lower the percentage of revenue attributable to labor costs, the more productively an airline uses labor to generate a unit of revenue (that is, dollars, euros, and so on). In Europe, for example, Wizz Air (6.5%), Ryanair (9.5%), and easyJet (12.4%) have some of the lowest labor costs per unit of revenue, especially when compared to major carriers such as British Airways (21.7%), Lufthansa (23.4%), Air France (29.9%), and Scandinavian Airlines (32.1%).[15]

Partial productivity assesses how efficiently companies use only one input, such as labor, when creating outputs. Multifactor productivity is an overall measure of productivity that assesses how efficiently companies use all the inputs it takes to make outputs. More specifically, **multifactor productivity** indicates how much labor, capital, materials, and energy it takes to produce an output.[16]

$$\frac{\text{Multifactor}}{\text{Productivity}} = \frac{\text{Outputs}}{(\text{Labor} + \text{Capital} + \text{Materials} + \text{Energy})}$$

Exhibit 18.1 shows the trends in multifactor productivity across a number of U.S. industries since 1987.

With a 15.7 percent increase between 2009 (scaled at 100) and 2012 and a 7.5 fold increase since 1987, the growth in multifactor productivity in the computer and

Partial productivity
a measure of performance that indicates how much of a particular kind of input it takes to produce an output

Multifactor productivity
an overall measure of performance that indicates how much labor, capital, materials, and energy it takes to produce an output

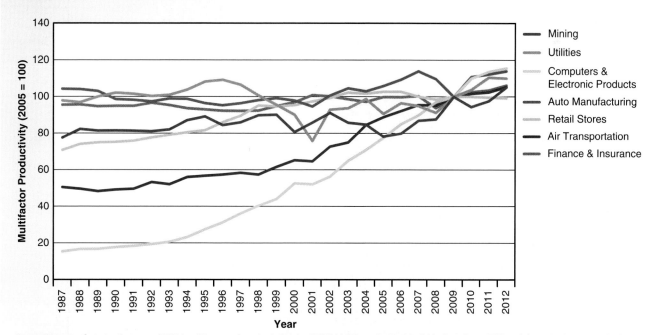

Exhibit 18.1
Multifactor Productivity Growth Across Industries

Source: "Nonmanufacturing Sectors and NIPA-level Nonmanufacturing Industries KLEMS Multifactor Productivity Tables by Industry: Table Multifactor Productivity and Related KLEMS Measures from the NIPA Industry Database, 1987 to 2012," Bureau of Labor Statistics, Division of Industry Productivity Studies, September 18, 2014, accessed May 11, 2015. http://www.bls.gov/mfp/special_requests/klemsmfpxg.zip; "Manufacturing Sector and NIPA-level Manufacturing Industries KLEMS Multifactor Productivity Tables by Industry: Table Multifactor Productivity and Related KLEMS Measures from the NIPA Industry Database, 1987 to 2012," Bureau of Labor Statistics, Division of Industry Productivity Studies, August 21, 2014, accessed May 11, 2015. http://www.bls.gov/mfp/special_requests/prod3.klemsmfp.zip.

electronic products industry far exceeded the productivity growth in mining, utilities, auto manufacturing, retail stores, air transportation, and financial and insurance services, as well as most other industries tracked by the U.S. government.

Should managers use multiple or partial productivity measures? In general, they should use both. Multifactor productivity indicates a company's overall level of productivity relative to its competitors. In the end, that's what counts most. However, multifactor productivity measures don't indicate the specific contributions that labor, capital, materials, or energy make to overall productivity. To analyze the contributions of these individual components, managers need to use partial productivity measures. Doing so can help them determine what factors need to be adjusted or in what areas adjustment can make the most difference in overall productivity.

18-2 QUALITY

With the average car costing $33,560, car buyers want to make sure that they're getting good quality for their money.[17] Fortunately, as indicated by the number of problems per 100 cars (PP100), today's cars are of much higher quality than earlier models. In 1981, Japanese cars averaged 240 PP100. GM's cars averaged 670, Ford's averaged 740, and Chrysler's averaged 870 PP100! In other words, as measured by PP100, the quality of American cars was two to three times worse than that of Japanese cars. By 1992, however, U.S. carmakers had made great strides, significantly reducing the number of problems to an average of 155 PP100. Japanese vehicles had improved, too, averaging just 125 PP100. According to the 2014 J. D. Power and Associates survey of initial car quality, as shown in Exhibit 18.2,

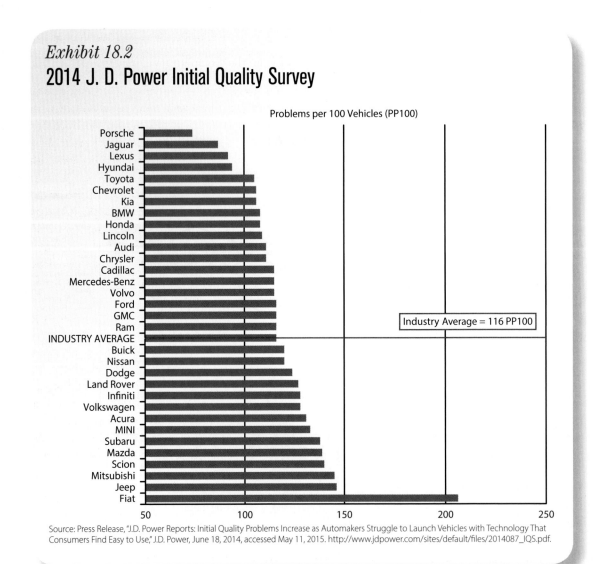

Exhibit 18.2
2014 J. D. Power Initial Quality Survey

Problems per 100 Vehicles (PP100)

Industry Average = 116 PP100

Source: Press Release, "J.D. Power Reports: Initial Quality Problems Increase as Automakers Struggle to Launch Vehicles with Technology That Consumers Find Easy to Use," J.D. Power, June 18, 2014, accessed May 11, 2015. http://www.jdpower.com/sites/default/files/2014087_IQS.pdf.

however, overall quality improved to 116 problems per 100 vehicles, and even the worst rated cars beat the scores of the Japanese cars of decades ago. Category leaders such as Porsche, Jaguar, Lexus, and Hyundai came in with scores under 100. That means less than one problem per car![18]

The American Society for Quality gives two meanings for **quality**. It can mean a product or service free of deficiencies, such as the number of problems per 100 cars, or it can mean the characteristics of a product or service that satisfy customer needs.[19] Today's cars are of higher quality than those produced twenty years ago in both senses. Not only do they have fewer problems per 100 cars, they also have a number of additional standard features (power brakes and steering, stereo/CD/MP3 player, power windows and locks, air bags, cruise control).

In this part of the chapter, you will learn about **18-2a quality-related characteristics for products and services, 18-2b ISO 9000 and 14000, 18-2c the Baldrige National Quality Award,** *and* **18-2d total quality management.**

18-2a Quality-Related Characteristics for Products and Services

Quality products usually possess three characteristics: reliability, serviceability, and durability.[20] A breakdown occurs when a product quits working or doesn't do what it was designed to do. The longer it takes for a product to break down, or the longer the time between breakdowns, the more reliable the product. Consequently, many companies define *product reliability* in terms of the average time between breakdowns. *Serviceability* refers to how easy or difficult it is to fix a product. The easier it is to maintain a working product or fix a broken product, the more serviceable that product is.

A product breakdown assumes that a product can be repaired. However, some products don't break down; they fail. *Product failure* means products can't be repaired. They can only be replaced. *Durability* is defined as the mean time to failure. A typical incandescent lightbulb, for example, has a mean time of failure of 1,000 hours. By contrast, LED bulbs, which use the same technology that lights up HDTVs and cell phone screens, have a mean time to failure of between twenty and twenty-five years. Furthermore, the energy savings from one $10 LED bulb means it will pay for itself within two years and then provide twenty more years of lighting while saving $149 in energy costs over the longer lifetime of the bulb.[21]

While high-quality products are characterized by reliability, serviceability, and durability, services are different. There's no point in assessing the durability of a service because services don't last but are consumed the minute they're performed. For example, after a lawn service has mowed your lawn, the job is done until the mowers come back next week to do it again. Services also don't have serviceability. You can't maintain or fix a service. If a service wasn't performed correctly, all you can do is perform it again. Rather than serviceability and durability, the quality of service interactions often depends on how the service provider interacts with the customer. Was the service provider friendly, rude, or helpful? Five characteristics typically distinguish a quality service: reliability, tangibles, responsiveness, assurance, and empathy.[22]

Service reliability is the ability to consistently perform a service well. Studies clearly show that reliability matters more to customers than anything else when buying services. When you take your clothes to the dry cleaner, you don't want them returned with cracked buttons or wrinkles down the front. If your dry cleaner gives you perfectly clean and pressed clothes every time, it's providing a reliable service.

Also, although services themselves are not tangible (you can't see or touch them), services are provided in tangible places. Thus, *tangibles* refer to the appearance of the offices, equipment, and personnel involved with the delivery of a service. One of the best examples of the effect of tangibles on the perception of quality is the restroom. When you eat at a fancy restaurant, you expect clean, upscale restrooms. How different is your perception of a business, say a gas station, if it has clean restrooms rather than filthy ones?

Responsiveness is the promptness and willingness with which service providers give good service. *Assurance* is the confidence that service providers are knowledgeable, courteous, and trustworthy. *Empathy*

Maxstockphoto/Shutterstock.com

> **Quality** a product or service free of deficiencies, or the characteristics of a product or service that satisfy customer needs

is the extent to which service providers give individual attention and care to customers' concerns and problems.

When Apple first launched its retail stores, they were widely predicted to fail given all of the locations already available where consumers could buy computer and electronics equipment. Those predictions were wrong, however, as 395 million people visited Apple's 416 stores in 2013.[23] Why? Because the stores are great at delivering responsiveness, assurance, and empathy.

At Apple stores, responsiveness manifests itself in a sales philosophy of not selling. Instead, Apple store employees are trained to help customers solve problems. An Apple training manual says, "Your job is to understand all of your customers' needs—some of which they may not even realize they have." David Ambrose, a former Apple store employee, says, "You were never trying to close a sale. It was about finding solutions for a customer and finding their pain points."

Apple store employees demonstrate assurance through the high level of training that they receive. Apple "geniuses," who staff the Genius Bar in each Apple store, are trained at Apple headquarters and, according to Apple's website, "can take care of everything from troubleshooting your problems to actual repairs." Geniuses are regularly tested on their knowledge and problem-solving skills to maintain their certification. Other Apple store employees are highly trained, too, and are not allowed to help customers until they've spent two to four weeks shadowing experienced store employees.

The acronym APPLE instructs employees on how to empathetically engage with customers: "Approach customers with a personalized warm welcome," "Probe politely to understand all the customer's needs," "Present a solution for the customer to take home today," "Listen for and resolve any issues or concerns," and "End with a fond farewell and an invitation to return."

And when customers are frustrated and become emotional, the advice is to "listen and limit your responses to simple reassurances that you are doing so. 'Uh-huh,' 'I understand,' etc."

The results from Apple's retail approach speak for themselves, as Apple retail sales average $4,551 per square foot, higher than Tiffany & Co.

jewelry stores ($3,043), Coach luxury retail ($1,532), or Deckers Outdoor ($1,246), a function-oriented footwear company.[24]

18-2b ISO 9000 and 14000

ISO, pronounced *eye-so*, comes from the Greek word *isos*, meaning "equal, similar, alike, or identical" and is also an acronym for the International Organization for Standardization, which helps set standards for 163 countries. The purpose of this agency is to develop and publish standards that facilitate the international exchange of goods and services.[25] **ISO 9000** is a series of five international standards, from ISO 9000 to ISO 9004, for achieving consistency in quality management and quality assurance in companies throughout the world. **ISO 14000** is a series of international standards for managing, monitoring, and minimizing an organization's harmful effects on the environment.[26] (For more on environmental quality and issues, see subsection 16-3e of Chapter 16 on sustainability.)

The ISO 9000 and 14000 standards publications, which are available from the American National Standards Institute (see the end of this section), are general and can be used for manufacturing any kind of product or delivering any kind of service. Importantly, the ISO 9000 standards don't describe how to make a better-quality car, computer, or widget. Instead, they describe how companies can extensively document (and thus standardize) the steps they take to create and improve the quality of their products. Why should companies go to the trouble to achieve ISO 9000 certification? Because their customers increasingly want them to. In fact, studies show that customers clearly prefer to buy from companies that are ISO 9000 certified. Companies, in turn, believe that being ISO 9000 certified helps them keep customers who might otherwise switch to an ISO 9000–certified competitor.[27]

To become ISO certified, a process that can take months, a company must show that it is following its own procedures for improving production, updating design plans and specifications, keeping machinery in top condition, educating and training workers, and satisfactorily dealing with customer complaints.[28] An accredited third party oversees the ISO certification process, just as a certified public accountant verifies that a company's financial accounts are up to date and accurate. After a company has been certified as ISO 9000 compliant, the accredited third party will issue an ISO 9000 certificate that the company can

ISO 9000 a series of five international standards, from ISO 9000 to ISO 9004, for achieving consistency in quality management and quality assurance in companies throughout the world

ISO 14000 a series of international standards for managing, monitoring, and minimizing an organization's harmful effects on the environment use in its advertising and publications. This is the quality equivalent of the *Good Housekeeping* Seal of Approval. But continued ISO 9000 certification is not guaranteed. Accredited third parties typically conduct periodic audits to make sure the company is still following quality procedures. If it is not, its certification is suspended or canceled.

To get additional information on ISO 9000 guidelines and procedures, see the American National Standards Institute (www.webstore.ansi.org; the ISO 9000 and ISO 14000 standards publications are available here for about $550 and $599, respectively), the American Society for Quality (www.asq.org), and the IOS (www.iso.org).

18-2c Baldrige Performance Excellence Program

The Baldrige Performance Excellence Awards, which are administered by the U.S. government's National Institute for Standards and Technology, is given "to recognize U.S. companies for their achievements in quality and business performance and to raise awareness about the importance of quality and performance excellence as a competitive edge."[29] Each year, up to three awards may be given in the categories of manufacturing, education, health care, service, small business, and nonprofit.

The cost of applying for the Baldrige Award includes a $360 eligibility fee, an application fee of $18,000 for manufacturing firms and $9,600 for small businesses, and a site visitation fee of $50,000 to $60,000 for manufacturing firms and $30,000 to $35,000 for small businesses.[30] Why does it cost so much? Because you get a great deal of useful information about your business even if you don't win. At a minimum, each company that applies receives an extensive report based on 300 hours of assessment from at least eight business and quality experts. At $10 an hour for small businesses and about $20 an hour for manufacturing and service businesses, the *Journal for Quality and Participation* called the Baldrige feedback report "the best bargain in consulting in America."[31] Arnold Weimerskirch, former chair of the Baldrige Award panel of judges and former vice president of quality at Honeywell, says, "The application and review process for the Baldrige Award is the best, most cost-effective and comprehensive business health audit you can get."[32]

Businesses that apply for the Baldrige Award are judged on the seven criteria shown in Exhibit 18.3:

Robotic Bellhop

The next time you order a spare toothbrush or towel from a hotel's front desk, you may find that the delivering bellhop is a little shorter—and more mechanical—than expected. The aloft Hotel in Cupertino, California, employed a three-foot-tall robot named Botlr to complement its human customer service staff. The automated bellhop might be an obvious addition to aloft's service staff, considering the hotel sits across the street from Apple's corporate campus. Both aloft Hotels and the robot's designer, Savioke, insist Botlr isn't going to replace human talent. Instead, the robot is intended to help deliver small items, such as razors, smartphone chargers, and snacks. Traveling up to four miles per hour, Botlr can reach any of the aloft's 150 rooms in less than three minutes. Botlr works for reviews—which can be input on a frontal display—rather than tips. Best of all, the friendly robot will perform a small dance for guests upon receiving a positive review.

Source: J. Markoff, "'Beep' Says the Bellhop," *New York Times*, August 12, 2014, B1.

leadership; strategic planning; customers; measurement, analysis, and knowledge management; workforce; operations; and results.[33] Results are typically the most important category. In other words, in addition to the six other criteria, companies must show that they have achieved superior quality when it comes to products and process, its customers, workforce, leadership, governance (social responsibility), and financial and market results. This emphasis on results is what differentiates the Baldrige Award from the ISO 9000 standards. The Baldrige Award indicates the extent to which companies have actually achieved world-class quality. The ISO 9000 standards simply indicate whether a company is following the management system it put into place to improve quality. In fact, ISO 9000 certification covers less than 10 percent of the requirements for the Baldrige Award.[34]

Why should companies go to the trouble of applying for the Baldrige Award? Baldrige program examiner Betsy Beam explains that it's not just about winning the award; it's about the opportunity to improve. "Ritz-Carlton has won the Baldrige Award twice," Beam says. "Even in ... the years they won, there were 35 opportunities for improvement identified. This is a very difficult journey for any organization, but it's well worth it as changes [that are needed] become obvious."[35]

18-2d Total Quality Management

Total quality management (TQM) is an integrated, organization-wide strategy for improving product and service quality.[36] TQM is not a specific tool or technique. Rather, TQM is a philosophy or overall approach to management that is characterized by three principles: customer focus and satisfaction, continuous improvement, and teamwork.[37]

Although most economists, accountants, and financiers argue that companies exist to earn profits for shareholders, TQM suggests that customer focus and customer satisfaction should be a company's primary goals. **Customer focus** means that the entire organization, from top to bottom, should be focused on meeting customers' needs. The result of that customer focus should be **customer satisfaction**, which occurs when the company's products or services meet or exceed customers' expectations.

At companies where customer satisfaction is taken seriously, such as **Alaska Airlines**, paychecks depend on keeping customers satisfied. Everyone at Alaska Airlines, from the CEO to pilots to people who handle baggage, gets a monthly bonus, 70 percent of which is based on earnings, with the remaining 30 percent split among costs, safety, and customer satisfaction. J.D. Power and Associates rates Alaska Airlines as the highest in customer satisfaction among traditional U.S. airlines from 2008 to 2013. Likewise, according to FlightStats, Alaska Airlines was the best North American airline in terms of on-time arrivals, a key issue in terms of customer satisfaction, from 2010 to 2014.[38]

Continuous improvement is an ongoing commitment to increase product and service quality by constantly assessing and improving the processes and procedures used to create those products and services. How do companies know whether they're achieving continuous improvement? Besides higher customer satisfaction, continuous improvement is usually associated with a reduction in variation. **Variation** is a deviation in the form, condition, or appearance of a product from the quality standard for that product. The less a product varies from the quality standard, or the more consistently a company's products meet a quality standard, the higher the quality. Beyond safety, the quality standard for an airline is on-time departure and arrival. Variation from that standard means delays, and even worse, cancellations. On average, 1.7 percent of flights are cancelled each year, sometimes because of weather, but often because of poor management decisions. Delta Airlines, however, cancels only 0.3 percent of its flights because it stocks extra parts

Total quality management (TQM) an integrated, principle-based, organization-wide strategy for improving product and service quality

Customer focus an organizational goal to concentrate on meeting customers' needs at all levels of the organization

Customer satisfaction an organizational goal to provide products or services that meet or exceed customers' expectations

Continuous improvement an organization's ongoing commitment to constantly assess and improve the processes and procedures used to create products and services

Variation a deviation in the form, condition, or appearance of a product from the quality standard for that product

Exhibit 18.3
Criteria for the Baldrige National Quality Award

2015–2016 Categories/Items

1 Leadership
1.1 Senior Leadership
1.2 Governance and Social Responsibilities

2 Strategic Planning
2.1 Strategy Development
2.2 Strategy Implementation

3 Customers
3.1 Voice of the Customer
3.2 Customer Engagement

4 Measurement, Analysis, and Knowledge Management
4.1 Measurement, Analysis, and Improvement of Organizational Performance
4.2 Knowledge Management, Information, and Information Technology

5 Workforce
5.1 Workforce Environment
5.2 Workforce Engagement

6 Operations
6.1 Work Processes
6.2 Operational Effectiveness

7 Results
7.1 Product and Process Results
7.2 Customer-Focused Results
7.3 Workforce-Focused Results
7.4 Leadership and Governance Results
7.5 Financial and Market Results

Source: "2015–2016 Baldrige Performance Excellence Framework" *Baldrige Performance Excellence Program*, accessed May 11, 2015. http://www.nist.gov/baldrige/publications/upload/2015_2016_Category_and_Item_Commentary_BNP.pdf.

Everyone at Alaska Airlines, from the CEO to the pilots to the people who handle baggage, gets a monthly bonus based, in part, on customer satisfaction.

(engine starters) that often cause delays, maintains twenty extra planes that are brought into service when a jet encounters mechanical problems, and gets around flight hour limitations for flight crews (typically eight hours within twenty-four hours) by having planes make interim stops (meaning less than eight hours) with new crews taking over. With 15,000 daily flights, Delta cancels just forty-five flights per day. But if Delta had an average cancellation rate, it would cancel 255 flights per day, or more than five times as many.[39]

The third principle of TQM is teamwork. **Teamwork** means collaboration between managers and non-managers, across business functions, and between the company and its customers and suppliers. In short, quality improves when everyone in the company is given the incentive to work together and the responsibility and authority to make improvements and solve problems. At the beginning of the chapter, you learned that ArcellorMittal's Gent, Belgium, plant needs only needs 1.3 man-hours to make a ton of steel, or one-third less than average. One of ArcellorMittal's practices is to "twin" its best plants, such as Gent, with its poor performing plants, such as its Burns Harbor, Indiana, plant. Then, it uses teamwork—and competition—to improve both. So it flew 100 Burns Harbor engineers and managers to Gent and told them, "Do as the Belgians do," whereas the Belgians were told to maintain their advantage. Founder Lakshmi Mittal says, "The process doesn't change: melt iron, cast, roll [steel]. But there are always incremental improvements you can make. We wanted Burns Harbor to be more like Gent."[40] Teamwork comes into play as teams from both plants meet regularly to discuss plant performance and share the steps they're taking to improve it. Following practices at Gent, Burns

Harbor began using a different high pressure water nozzle to remove flakes (that is, imperfections) from super-heated steel. Not only did steel quality improve, the nozzle used less water and power, saving $1.4 million in annual energy costs. Likewise, Burns Harbor workers began trimming less steel off the sides of steel coils, saving 725 coils of steel per year, the equivalent of 17,000 cars. Today, thanks to twinning and teamwork, Burns Harbor now produces 900 tons of steel per employee each year, close to Gent's 950.

Customer focus and satisfaction, continuous improvement, and teamwork mutually reinforce each other to improve quality throughout a company. Customer-focused, continuous improvement is necessary to increase customer satisfaction. At the same time, continuous improvement depends on teamwork from different functional and hierarchical parts of the company.

18-3 SERVICE OPERATIONS

At the start of this chapter, you learned that operations management means managing the daily production of goods and services. Then you learned that to manage production, you must oversee the factors that affect productivity and quality. In this half of the chapter, you will learn about managing operations in service and manufacturing businesses. The chapter ends with a discussion of inventory management, a key factor in a company's profitability.

Imagine that your trusty TiVo digital video recorder (DVR) breaks down as you try to record your favorite TV show. You've got two choices. You can run to Walmart and spend $250 to purchase a new DVR, or you can spend less (you hope) to have it fixed at a repair shop. Either way, you end up with the same thing, a working DVR. However, the first choice, getting a new DVR, involves buying a physical product (a good), while the second, dealing with a repair shop, involves buying a service.

Services differ from goods in several ways. First, goods are produced or made, but services are performed. In other words, services are almost always labor-intensive in that someone typically has to perform the service for you. A repair shop could give you the parts needed to repair your old DVR, but you're still going to have a broken DVR without the technician to perform the repairs. Second, goods are tangible, but services are intangible. You can touch and see that new DVR, but you can't touch or see the service provided by the technician who fixed your old DVR. All you can "see" is that the DVR works. Third, services

Teamwork collaboration between managers and nonmanagers, across business functions, and between companies, customers, and suppliers are perishable and unstorable. If you don't use them when they're available, they're wasted. For example, if your DVR repair shop is backlogged on repair jobs, then you'll just have to wait until next week to get your DVR repaired. You can't store an unused service and use it when you like. By contrast, you can purchase a good, such as motor oil, and store it until you're ready to use it.

Because services are different from goods, managing a service operation is different from managing a manufacturing or production operation.

*Let's look at **18-3a the service-profit chain** and **18-3b service recovery and empowerment**.*

18-3a The Service-Profit Chain

One of the key assumptions in the service business is that success depends on how well employees—that is, service providers—deliver their services to customers. But success actually begins with how well management treats service employees, as the service-profit chain, depicted in Exhibit 18.4, demonstrates.[41]

Internal service quality the quality of treatment employees receive from management and other divisions of a company

The key concept behind the service-profit chain is **internal service quality**, meaning the quality of treatment that employees receive from a company's internal service providers, such as management, payroll and benefits, human resources, and so forth. For example, employees at Clif Bar, a maker of organic energy bars and drinks, get 2.5 hours a week to work out at the company's fitness center, which is equipped with a climbing wall and everything from yoga to spin classes to free sessions with trainers and nutritionists; have a concierge that provides car washes, laundry, dry cleaning, and other services; are eligible for incentives for car pools (up to $960 a year), buying a biodiesel car ($6,500) or a commuter bike ($500), or making eco-improvements in their homes ($1,000); and are enrolled in the employee stock ownership plan, which vests after three years, at which point the employee receives full ownership shares of the company. These extraordinary benefits are clearly a sign of a company with an internal service quality orientation.[42]

As depicted in Exhibit 18.4, good internal service leads to employee satisfaction and service capability. *Employee satisfaction* occurs when companies treat employees in a way that meets or exceeds their expectations. In other words, the better employees are treated, the more satisfied they are, and the more likely they are to give high-value service that satisfies customers. How employers treat employees is important because it affects service capability. *Service capability* is an employee's perception of his or her ability to serve customers well. When an organization serves its employees in ways that help them to do their jobs well, employees, in turn, are more likely to believe that they can and ought to provide high-value service to customers.

Finally, according to the service-profit chain shown in Exhibit 18.4, *high-value service* leads to *customer satisfaction* and *customer loyalty*, which, in turn, lead to *long-term profits and growth*.[43] What's the link between customer satisfaction and loyalty and profits? To start, the average business keeps only 70 to 90 percent of its existing

Exhibit 18.4
Service-Profit Chain

Internal Service Quality

Employee Satisfaction

Service · Capability · High Value · Service

= ✔ Customer Satisfaction ✔ Customer Loyalty lead to

Upper Management · Employees · Customers

Profit and Growth

Sources: R. Hallowell, L. A. Schlesinger, and J. Zornitsky, "Internal Service Quality, Customer and Job Satisfaction: Linkages and Implications for Management," *Human Resource Planning* 19 (1996): 20–31; J. L. Heskett, T. O. Jones, G. W. Loveman, W. E. Sasser Jr., and L. A. Schlesinger, "Putting the Service-Profit Chain to Work," *Harvard Business Review* (March–April 1994): 164–174.

customers each year. No big deal, you say? Just replace leaving customers with new customers. Well, there's one significant problem with that solution. It costs ten times as much to find a new customer as it does to keep an existing customer. Also, new customers typically buy only 20 percent as much as established customers. In fact, keeping existing customers is so cost-effective that most businesses could double their profits by simply keeping 5 percent more customers per year![44] How does this work? Imagine that keeping more of your customers turns some of those customers into customers for life. How much of a difference would that make to company profits? Consider that just one lifetime customer spends $8,000 on pizza and over $330,000 on luxury cars![45]

18-3b Service Recovery and Empowerment

When mistakes are made, when problems occur, and when customers become dissatisfied with the service they've received, service businesses must switch from the process of service delivery to the process of **service recovery**, or restoring customer satisfaction to strongly dissatisfied customers.[46] Or as business consultant Barry Moltz explains, "When a customer says they are dissatisfied, the company gets a chance to fix it and turn them into a more loyal customer."[47] Service recovery sometimes requires service employees to not only fix whatever mistake was made but also perform heroic service acts that delight highly dissatisfied customers by far surpassing their expectations of fair treatment. Jason Friend, co-founder of 37signals.com, which provides web-based collaboration software such as Basecamp and Campfire, bought a custom bike via the Web from Mission Bicycle Company in San Francisco. When the bike arrived, he found a large gash on the side of the bike's frame. He described what happened when he contacted Mission: "They said sending the whole bike back would be overkill since the only thing that was damaged was the frame. Further, the bike was rideable—it was just a paint problem—so sending the bike back would mean I didn't have a bike for a week or so. They didn't feel good about that. So here's what they did: They called up a local shop (On The Route) and arranged to ship a new frame to them. Then one of their bike techs would drive down to my office and swap the frames and reassemble the bike for me while I waited. All of this at Mission's expense." He concluded by saying, "That's incredible customer service. I'm a happy customer for life. If you're in the market for a great custom bike, check out the good people and products at Mission Bicycle Company."[48]

Unfortunately, when mistakes occur, service employees often don't have the discretion to resolve customer complaints. Customers who want service employees to correct or make up for poor service are frequently told, "I'm not allowed to do that," "I'm just following company rules," or "I'm sorry, only managers are allowed to make changes of any kind." In other words, company rules prevent them from engaging in acts of service recovery meant to turn dissatisfied customers back into satisfied customers. The result is frustration for customers and service employees and lost customers for the company.

Now, however, many companies are empowering their service employees.[49] In Chapter 9, you learned that *empowering workers* means permanently passing decision-making authority and responsibility from managers to workers. With respect to service recovery, empowering workers means giving service employees the authority and responsibility to make decisions that immediately solve customer problems.[50] For example, when customers call into Nicor National, an energy utility, to ask for credits to their accounts, they are not transferred to a billing department. They are not put on hold while the operator looks for a supervisor or manager. Instead, the operator, who is empowered to make this decision, simply awards the credit without having to check with anyone. According to Barbara Porter, the company's vice president of business development and customer service, empowering the call centers in this way is a quick, easy resolution. "They're professionals and we trust them to make the right decisions," says Porter.[51]

When things go wrong for customers, how well does service recovery work? Sixty-nine percent of customers see quick resolution of their problems as central to good customer service. Furthermore, about half of customers will stop buying from a company when bad customer service is not resolved. Either way, roughly nine out of ten customers will tell others about their poor customer service or how you fixed their problem.[52]

18-4 MANUFACTURING OPERATIONS

Ford makes cars, and Dell does computers. BP produces gasoline, whereas Sherwin-Williams makes paint. Boeing makes jet planes, but Budweiser makes beer. Maxtor makes hard drives, and Maytag makes appliances. The *manufacturing*

> **Service recovery** restoring customer satisfaction to strongly dissatisfied customers

operations of these companies all produce physical goods. But not all manufacturing operations, especially these, are the same.

Let's learn how various manufacturing operations differ in terms of 18-4a the amount of processing that is done to produce and assemble a product and 18-4b the flexibility to change the number, kind, and characteristics of products that are produced.

18-4a Amount of Processing in Manufacturing Operations

Manufacturing operations can be classified according to the amount of processing or assembly that occurs after a customer order is received. The highest degree of processing occurs in **make-to-order operations**. A make-to-order operation does not start processing or assembling products until it receives a customer order. In fact, some make-to-order operations may not even order parts until a customer order is received. Not surprisingly, make-to-order operations produce or assemble highly specialized or customized products for customers. The John Deere 8R tractor, for example, comes with thousands of options that can be customized to the needs of a corn farmer in Kansas or a rice farmer in India. Buyers choose from six types of axles, five transmissions, thirteen types of rear hitches, and fifty-four different wheel and tire configurations. There are 354 option bundles for the basic tractor and 114 option bundles for attachments. Thanks to so many option combinations, Deere produced 7,800 unique 8R tractors in the past year. On average, each tractor configuration was built just 1.5 times, and over half of the configurations were built just once—truly a make-to-order operation.[53]

A moderate degree of processing occurs in **assemble-to-order**

operations. A company using an assemble-to-order operation divides its manufacturing or assembly process into separate parts or modules. The company orders parts and assembles modules ahead of customer orders. Then, based on actual customer orders or on research forecasting what customers will want, those modules are combined to create semicustomized products. For example, when a customer orders a new car, GM may have already ordered the basic parts or modules it needs from suppliers. In other words, based on sales forecasts, GM may already have ordered enough tires, air-conditioning compressors, brake systems, and seats from suppliers to accommodate nearly all customer orders on a particular day. Special orders from customers and car dealers are then used to determine the final assembly checklist for particular cars as they move down the assembly line.

The lowest degree of processing occurs in **make-to-stock operations** (also called build-to-stock). Because the products are standardized, meaning each product is exactly the same as the next, a company using a make-to-stock operation starts ordering parts and assembling finished products before receiving customer orders. Customers then purchase these standardized products—such as Rubbermaid storage containers, microwave ovens, and vacuum cleaners—at retail stores or directly from the manufacturer. Because parts are ordered and products are assembled before customers order the products, make-to-stock operations are highly dependent on the accuracy of sales forecasts. If sales forecasts are incorrect, make-to-stock operations may end up building too many or too few products, or they may make products with the wrong features or without the features that customers want.

18-4b Flexibility of Manufacturing Operations

A second way to categorize manufacturing operations is by **manufacturing flexibility**, meaning the degree to which manufacturing operations can easily and quickly change the number, kind, and characteristics of products they produce. Flexibility allows companies to respond quickly to changes in the marketplace (that is, respond to competitors and customers) and to reduce the lead time between ordering and final delivery of products. There is often a trade-off between flexibility

Make-to-order operation a manufacturing operation that does not start processing or assembling products until a customer order is received

Assemble-to-order operation a manufacturing operation that divides manufacturing processes into separate parts or modules that are combined to create semicustomized products

Make-to-stock operation a manufacturing operation that orders parts and assembles standardized products before receiving customer orders

Manufacturing flexibility the degree to which manufacturing operations can easily and quickly change the number, kind, and characteristics of products they produce

JuliusKielaitis/Shutterstock.com

The Hunt for U.S. Contract Manufacturers

A quick search for contract manufacturers on Chinese website Alibaba.com produces thousands of listings. It used to be just as easy to find a contract manufacturer in the United States, but not anymore. When K'Nex Brands LP, a family-owned toy maker, wanted to bring production of the iconic toy Lincoln Logs back to the United States from China, it encountered problems finding a domestic factory that could produce the small wooden blocks. The remaining wood factories in the United States were set up to make large items, such as furniture and cabinetry. Likewise, when Marshmallow Fun Co., which designs toy guns that shoot marshmallows, wanted to repatriate its toy manufacturing, CEO Beaver Raymond searched for months to find a U.S. factory. The specialty manufacturer he found in Wisconsin required a minimum order quantity of 60,000 units to justify the $80,000 it would need to spend on tooling and plastic molds. (Raymond wanted to order only 10,000.) Managers at K'Nex had better luck. After reading an article about their search in the *Wall Street Journal*, a golf-tee manufacturer in Maine contacted them to let them know their equipment could make Lincoln Logs, the first batch of which hit the shelves in 2015.

Sources: J. R. Hagerty, "It's No Fun Making Toys or Toasters in the USA," *Wall Street Journal*, February 10, 2015, B1, B2; J. R. Hagerty, and M. Magnier, "Companies Tiptoe Back toward `Made in the USA," *Wall Street Journal*, January 14, 2015, A1, A12.

and cost, however, with the most flexible manufacturing operations frequently having higher costs per unit, and the least flexible operations having lower costs per unit. Some common manufacturing operations, arranged in order from the least flexible to the most flexible, are continuous-flow production, line-flow production, batch production, and job shops.

Most production processes generate finished products at a discrete rate. A product is completed, and then—perhaps a few seconds, minutes, or hours later—another is completed, and so on. For instance, if you stood at the end of an automobile assembly line, nothing much would seem to be happening for fifty-five seconds of every minute. In that last five seconds, however, a new car would be started and driven off the assembly line, ready for its new owner. By contrast, in **continuous-flow production**, products are produced continuously rather than at a discrete rate. Like a water hose that is never turned off and just keeps on flowing, production of the final product never stops. Until recently, drug companies used discrete production operations to make drugs, mixing ingredients in huge vats at separate factories. But to cut costs and increase quality, many are switching to continuous-flow production where the raw materials used to make drugs are "fed into a single, continuously running process."[54] Johnson & Johnson, GlaxoSmithKline, and Novartis are building continuous-flow factories, which should reduce operating costs by 30 percent and increase quality because corrections can be made immediately and not after large batches have been produced. Furthermore, continuous-flow pharmaceutical factories are much smaller at 4,000 square feet compared to the typical 100,000 square foot drug making facility, and thus, much less costly to build. Finally, production speeds and output can be dramatically higher.

For instance, while it takes four to six weeks to make 100,000 tablets of Vertex's new cystic-fibrosis drug, its new continuous-flow factory will be able to make that many tablets in an hour![55] Despite their many advantages, continuous-flow production processes are the most standardized and least flexible manufacturing operations. In other words, a continuous-flow factory dedicated to making cystic-fibrosis drugs could not be used to make another kind of drug.

Line-flow production processes are preestablished, occur in a serial or linear manner, and are dedicated to making one type of product. In this way, the ten different steps required to make product X can be completed in a separate manufacturing process (with separate machines, parts, treatments, locations, and workers) from the twelve different steps required to make product Y. Line-flow production processes are inflexible because they are typically dedicated to manufacturing one kind of product. For example, the production process for Tesla Motors' Model S car starts with large rolls of aluminum, which are flattened, cut, and then stamped into the shapes of the car's body panels (that is, roof, trunk, left front, and so on). Stamped panels are then moved to the body shop, where the car's underbody, sides, and front are joined via robotic welding machines. After the shell of the car is formed, it is primed, painted, and moved to the assembly line. There, 3,000 workers and 160 robots install the battery, motor, wiring, interior, seats, and the rest of the car's 30,000-plus parts. The assembly process for a car

Continuous-flow production a manufacturing operation that produces goods at a continuous, rather than a discrete, rate

Line-flow production manufacturing processes that are preestablished, occur in a serial or linear manner, and are dedicated to making one type of product

The Tesla Model S starts with large rolls of aluminum, but is stamped out into the shape of the car.

that handle special manufacturing processes or jobs. In contrast to batch production, which handles large batches of different products, job shops typically handle very small batches, some as small as one product or process per batch. Basically, each job in a job shop is different, and after a job is done, the job shop moves on to a completely different job or manufacturing process for, most likely, a different customer. For example, **Grauch Enterprises** in Philipsburg, Pennsylvania, is a job shop that mills, turns, drills, paints, and finishes everything from plastics, such as nylon, polycarbonates, and laminates, to metals, such as brass, aluminum, stainless and alloy steels, titanium, and cast iron. It made 650 different parts for one customer alone and received one order to make 5,000 units out of 20,000 individual parts. When it comes to making different parts for different customers, owner Fred Grauch says, "There's very little we won't try."[57]

takes three to five days. In total, Tesla's Model S factory produces about 400 cars per week.[56]

The next most flexible manufacturing operation is **batch production**, which involves the manufacture of large batches of different products in standard lot sizes. A worker in a batch production operation will perform the same manufacturing process on 100 copies of product X, followed by 200 copies of product Y, and then 50 copies of product Z. Furthermore, these batches move through each manufacturing department or process in identical order. So, if the paint department follows chemical treatment, and chemical treatment is now processing a batch of 50 copies of product Z, then the paint department's next task will be to paint 50 copies of product Z. Batch production is finding increasing use among restaurant chains. To ensure consistency in the taste and quality of their products, many restaurant chains have central kitchens, or commissaries, that produce batches of food such as mashed potatoes, stuffing, macaroni and cheese, rice, quiche filling, and chili, in volumes ranging from 10 to 200 gallons. These batches are then delivered to the individual restaurant locations, which in turn serve the food to customers.

Next in terms of flexibility is the job shop. **Job shops** are typically small manufacturing operations

18-5) INVENTORY

Inventory is the amount and number of raw materials, parts, and finished products that a company has in its possession. When Ebola killed 5,000 people in West Africa in the fall of 2014, at the time, only a few suppliers made the protective suits (PS) that shield caregivers from direct contact with the deadly bodily fluids of Ebola patients. Manufacturers, such as DuPont, were forced to triage buyers, selling first to those treating Ebola patients, and then to those who were preparing for that possibility, such as the U.S. Centers for Disease Control and Prevention that bought $2.7 million worth of PSs to create a Strategic National Stockpile in the event that Ebola became widespread in the U.S. Still, there were critical shortages. Finally, it took six months to accomplish, but PS maker Lakeland Industries doubled production capacity by buying new manufacturing machines and hiring new workers.[58]

*In this section, you will learn about **18-5a the different types of inventory, 18-5b how to measure inventory levels, 18-5c the costs of maintaining an inventory,** and **18-5d the different systems for managing inventory.***

18-5a Types of Inventory

Exhibit 18.5 shows the four kinds of inventory a manufacturer stores: raw materials, component parts, work-in-process, and finished goods. The flow of inventory through a manufacturing plant begins when the purchasing department buys raw materials from vendors. **Raw material inventories** are the basic inputs in the

Exhibit 18.5
Types of Inventory

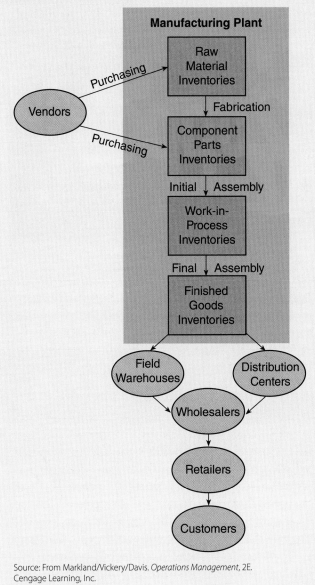

Manufacturing Plant

Vendors → *Purchasing* → Raw Material Inventories

↓ Fabrication

Component Parts Inventories

Initial ↓ Assembly

Work-in-Process Inventories

Final ↓ Assembly

Finished Goods Inventories

→ Field Warehouses / Distribution Centers → Wholesalers → Retailers → Customers

Source: From Markland/Vickery/Davis. *Operations Management*, 2E. Cengage Learning, Inc.

manufacturing process. For example, to begin making a car, automobile manufacturers purchase raw materials such as steel, iron, aluminum, copper, rubber, and unprocessed plastic.

Next, raw materials are fabricated or processed into **component parts inventories**, meaning the basic parts used in manufacturing a product. For example, in an automobile plant, steel is fabricated or processed into a car's body panels, and steel and iron are melted and shaped into engine parts such as pistons or engine blocks. Some component parts are purchased from vendors rather than fabricated in-house.

The component parts are then assembled to make unfinished **work-in-process inventories**, which are also known as partially finished goods. This process is also called *initial assembly*. For example, steel body panels are welded to each other and to the frame of the car to make a "unibody," which comprises the unpainted interior frame and exterior structure of the car. Likewise, pistons, camshafts, and other engine parts are inserted into the engine block to create a working engine.

Next, all the work-in-process inventories are assembled to create **finished goods inventories**, which are the final outputs of the manufacturing process. This process is also called *final assembly*. For a car, the engine, wheels, brake system, suspension, interior, and electrical system are assembled into a car's painted unibody to make the working automobile, which is the factory's finished product. In the last step in the process, the finished goods are sent to field warehouses, distribution centers, or wholesalers, and then to retailers for final sale to customers.

18-5b Measuring Inventory

As you'll learn next, uncontrolled inventory can lead to huge costs for a manufacturing operation. Consequently, managers need good measures of inventory to prevent inventory costs from becoming too large. Three basic measures of inventory are average aggregate inventory, weeks of supply, and inventory turnover.

If you've ever worked in a retail store and had to take inventory, you probably weren't too excited about the process of counting every item in the store and storeroom. It's an extensive task that's a bit easier today because of bar codes that mark items and computers that can count and track them. Nonetheless, inventories still differ from day to day. An inventory count taken at the beginning of the month will likely be different from a count taken at the end of the month. Similarly, an inventory count taken on a Friday will differ from a count taken on a Monday. Because of such differences, companies often measure **average aggregate inventory**, which is the average overall inventory during a particular time period. Average aggregate inventory for a month

Component parts inventories the basic parts used in manufacturing that are fabricated from raw materials

Work-in-process inventories partially finished goods consisting of assembled component parts

Finished goods inventories the final outputs of manufacturing operations

Average aggregate inventory average overall inventory during a particular time period

Americans' Addiction to Free Shipping Gives Rise to Reverse Logistics

It is hard to beat e-commerce for convenience. Not sure what size shoe will fit best? Buy two (or three) different sizes from Zappos.com; when they arrive the next day, try them all on, and simply return the ones that are too tight or too loose. Or return them all if you don't like the color. Regardless, all you need to do is pack them up, affix the return shipping label, and let UPS do the rest.

Over the past twenty years, retailers have developed sophisticated logistics operations designed to deliver products ordered over the Internet to the doorsteps of U.S. consumers in a matter of days or, in some places, even hours. In today's retail environment, however, it is no longer the low price and fast delivery of the product that give a company a competitive edge; low-cost shipping and easy customer returns are also part of escalating competition among retailers. According to Gailen Vick of the Reverse Logistics Association, returns come at a hefty price, particularly for companies that don't have a solid program in place. "If they're doing nothing today, they're losing about 5 percent to 7 percent of their bottom line." That figure is much higher at electronics retailer Best Buy, which in 2014 lost 10 percent of its revenue, or $400 million, because of returned products. Companies without an efficient system for processing customer returns and getting returned product back on the shelves

Ethan Miller/Getty Images News/Getty Images

risk customer dissatisfaction as well as losing money from stockouts or product obsolescence. Gary Shapiro of the Consumer Electronics Association says that the challenges of reverse logistics are here to stay for one simple reason, "Americans think they have a constitutional right to have their products returned."

Source: E. Phillips, "Do Customers Have a Constitutional Right to Return Stuff Ordered Online?" Wall Street Journal, May 1, 2015. http://www.wsj.com/articles/do-customers-have-a-constitutional-right-to-return-stuff-ordered-online-1430490642.

can be determined by simply averaging the inventory counts at the end of each business day for that month. One way companies know whether they're carrying too much or too little inventory is to compare their average aggregate inventory with the industry average for aggregate inventory. For example, seventy-two days of inventory is the average for the automobile industry.

The automobile industry records inventory in terms of days of supply, but most other industries measure inventory in terms of *weeks of supply*, meaning the number of weeks it would take for a company to run out of its current supply of inventory. In general, there is an acceptable number of weeks of inventory for a particular kind of business. Too few weeks of inventory on hand, and a company risks a **stockout**—running out of inventory. When a West Coast dockworkers' contract dispute slowed shipments of U.S. frozen potatoes by

86 percent, 100 McDonald's in Venezuela found themselves unable to sell french fries to customers. So they substituted fried arepa flatbreads or fried yuca (a starchy vegetable used in South American cooking). Maria Guerreiro left a Caracas McDonald's unhappy because she had wanted to buy a Happy Meal (with fries) as a treat for her 2-year old. Said Guerreiro, whose daughter won't eat yuca, "It's a total débâcle."[59]

Another common inventory measure, **inventory turnover**, is the number of times per year that a company sells, or "turns over," its average inventory. For example, if a company keeps an average of 100 finished widgets in inventory each month, and it sold 1,000 widgets this year, then it turned its inventory ten times this year.

In general, the higher the number of inventory turns, the better. In practice, a high turnover means that a company can continue its daily operations with just a small amount of inventory on hand. For example, let's take two companies, A and B, which have identical inventory levels (520,000 widget parts and raw materials) over the

Stockout the point when a company runs out of finished product

Inventory turnover the number of times per year that a company sells, or "turns over," its average inventory

> "IN THEORY, MAKE-TO-ORDER COMPANIES HAVE NO INVENTORY. IN FACT, THEY'VE GOT INVENTORY, BUT YOU HAVE TO MEASURE IT IN HOURS."

course of a year. If company A turns its inventories twenty-six times a year, it will completely replenish its inventory every two weeks and have an average inventory of 20,000 widget parts and raw materials. By contrast, if company B turns its inventories only two times a year, it will completely replenish its inventory every twenty-six weeks and have an average inventory of 260,000 widget parts and raw materials. So, by turning its inventory more often, company A has 92 percent less inventory on hand at any one time than company B.

The average number of inventory turns across all kinds of manufacturing plants is approximately eight per year, although the average can be higher or lower for different industries.[60] For example, whereas the average auto company turns its entire inventory thirteen times per year, some of the best auto companies more than double that rate, turning their inventory 27.8 times per year, or once every two weeks.[61] Turning inventory more frequently than the industry average can cut an auto company's costs by several hundred million dollars per year. Finally, it should be pointed out that even make-to-order companies such as Dell turn their inventory. In theory, make-to-order companies have no inventory. In fact, they've got inventory, but you have to measure it in hours. For example, Dell turns the inventory in its facilities 35.6 times a year, which means that on average it has ten days of inventory on hand in its factories.[62]

18-5c Costs of Maintaining an Inventory

Maintaining an inventory incurs four kinds of costs: ordering, setup, holding, and stockout. **Ordering cost** is not the cost of the inventory itself but the costs associated with ordering the inventory. It includes the costs of completing paperwork, manually entering data into a computer, making phone calls, getting competing bids,

correcting mistakes, and simply determining when and how much new inventory should be reordered. For example, ordering costs are relatively high in the restaurant business because 80 percent of foodservice orders (in which restaurants reorder food supplies) are processed manually. A report, *Enabling Profitable Growth in the Food-Prepared-Away-From-Home Industries*, estimated that the food industry could save $14.3 billion if all restaurants converted to electronic data interchange (see Chapter 17), in which purchase and ordering information from one company's computer system is automatically relayed to another company's computer system. Toward that end, an industry-wide effort, Efficient Foodservice Response (EFR), is underway to improve efficiencies in the foodservice supply chain.[63]

Setup cost is the cost of changing or adjusting a machine so that it can produce a different kind of inventory.[64] For example, 3M uses the same production machinery to make several kinds of industrial tape, but it must adjust the machines whenever it switches from one kind of tape to another. There are two kinds of setup costs: downtime and lost efficiency. *Downtime* occurs whenever a machine is not being used to process inventory. If it takes five hours to switch a machine from processing one kind of inventory to another, then five hours of downtime have occurred. Downtime is costly because companies earn an economic return only when machines are actively turning raw materials into parts or parts into finished products. The second setup cost is *lost efficiency*. Recalibrating a machine to its optimal settings after a switchover typically takes some time. It may take several days of fine-tuning before a machine finally produces the number of high-quality parts that it is supposed to. So, each time a machine has to be changed to handle a different kind of inventory, setup costs (downtime and lost efficiency) rise.

Holding cost, also known as *carrying* or *storage cost*, is the cost of keeping inventory until it is used or sold. Holding cost includes the cost of storage facilities,

Ordering cost the costs associated with ordering inventory, including the cost of data entry, phone calls, obtaining bids, correcting mistakes, and determining when and how much inventory to order

Setup cost the costs of downtime and lost efficiency that occur when a machine is changed or adjusted to produce a different kind of inventory

Holding cost the cost of keeping inventory until it is used or sold, including storage, insurance, taxes, obsolescence, and opportunity costs

B Calkins/Shutterstock.com

insurance to protect inventory from damage or theft, inventory taxes, the cost of obsolescence (holding inventory that is no longer useful to the company), and the opportunity cost of spending money on inventory that could have been spent elsewhere in the company. For example, it's estimated that U.S. airlines have a total of $48 billion worth of airplane parts in stock at any one time for maintenance, repair, and overhauling of their planes. The holding cost for managing, storing, and purchasing these parts is nearly $12 billion—or roughly one-fourth of the cost of the parts themselves.[65]

Stockout cost is the cost incurred when a company runs out of a product. There are two basic kinds of stockout costs. First, the company incurs the transaction costs of overtime work, shipping, and the like in trying to quickly replace out-of-stock inventories with new inventories. The second and perhaps more damaging cost is the loss of customers' goodwill when a company cannot deliver the products it promised. Stockouts occur more often than you might think. In the United States, the supermarket industry's average out-of-stock rate (the percentage of items that are unavailable at a given time) is 7.9 percent, according to research firm Market6. Highly promoted items have, as would be expected, a higher average out-of-stock rate of 13.1 percent. How costly is it for stores to run out of stock? Market6 estimates that running out of stock on the twenty-five best-selling product categories reduces a grocery store's revenue by an average of $200,000 per year, per store.[66] In general, retailers can increase sales 4 percent if they never run out of stock.

18-5d Managing Inventory

Inventory management has two basic goals. The first is to avoid running out of stock and thus angering and dissatisfying customers. This goal seeks to increase inventory to a safe level that won't risk stockouts. The second is to efficiently reduce inventory levels and costs as much as possible without impairing daily operations. This goal seeks a minimum level of inventory. The following inventory management techniques—economic order quantity (EOQ), just-in-time inventory (JIT), and materials requirement planning (MRP)—are different ways of balancing these competing goals.

Economic order quantity (EOQ) is a system of formulas that helps determine how much and how often inventory should be ordered. EOQ takes into account the overall demand (D) for a product while trying to minimize ordering costs (O) and holding costs (H). The formula for EOQ is

$$EOQ = \sqrt{\frac{2DO}{H}}$$

For example, if a factory uses 40,000 gallons of paint a year (D), ordering costs (O) are $75 per order, and holding costs (H) are $4 per gallon, then the optimal quantity to order is 1,225 gallons:

$$EOQ = \sqrt{\frac{2(40,000)(75)}{4}} = 1,225$$

With 40,000 gallons of paint being used per year, the factory uses approximately 110 gallons per day:

$$\frac{4,000 \text{ gallons}}{365 \text{ days}} = 110$$

Consequently, the factory would order 1,225 new gallons of paint approximately every eleven days:

$$\frac{1,225 \text{ gallons}}{110 \text{ gallons per day}} = 11.1 \text{ days}$$

In general, EOQ formulas do a good job of letting managers know what size or amount of inventory they should reorder to minimize ordering and holding costs. Mark Lore, former founder of Diapers.com, explains how it used EOQ formulas to decide precisely how much inventory to keep on hand. He says, "We built software with computational algorithms to determine what the optimal number of boxes to have in the warehouse is and what the sizes of those boxes should be. Should we stock five different kinds of boxes to ship product in? Twenty kinds? Fifty kinds? And what size should those boxes be? Right now, it's twenty-three box sizes, given what we sell, in order to minimize the cost of dunnage (those little plastic air-filled bags or peanuts), the cost of corrugated boxes, and the cost of shipping. We rerun the simulation every quarter."[67] As this example makes clear, EOQ formulas and models can become much more complex as adjustments are made for price changes, quantity discounts, setup costs, and many other factors.[68]

While EOQ formulas try to minimize holding and ordering costs, the just-in-time (JIT) approach to inventory management attempts to eliminate holding costs by reducing inventory levels to near zero. With a

GM Takes the Long View on EOQ

General Motors is taking the long view with its inventory management program and asking its vendors to sign long-term contracts, maybe even lasting decades, for automotive parts. Establishing an economic order quantity minimizes costs, but GM is hoping that locking in longer parts contracts—for higher quantities and higher overall dollar values—will produce a host of other benefits. Longer contracts signal greater commitment to vendors, which GM hopes will improve its vendor relationships. (Parts suppliers rank the quality of GM's relationships with its vendors as poor, behind Toyota, Nissan, and Honda.) In turn, GM hopes better relationships will produce greater collaboration with suppliers and give GM access to more advanced technologies earlier in their development cycle. GM Purchasing Chief Steve Keifer justified the change to longer contracts by saying, "We want [our suppliers] to double down on us." By 2017, GM expects to sign billions of dollars in these contracts with its 30 biggest suppliers.

Linda Parton/Shutterstock.com

Source: J. Bennett, "GM Wants Long-Term Parts Contracts," *Wall Street Journal*, April 15, 2015, B3.

---

just-in-time (JIT) inventory system, component parts arrive from suppliers just as they are needed at each stage of production. By having parts arrive just in time, the manufacturer has little inventory on hand and thus avoids the costs associated with holding inventory. Thanks to its strict JIT inventory system, Apple carries the smallest amount of inventory among technology companies, averaging just 5.2 days of inventory of iPhones, iPads, and MacBook Pros waiting to be shipped. That five days of inventory is equivalent to an inventory turn of 69.2 times a year (remember, more turns is better). Samsung Electronics was next with 18.1 turns a year, followed by Cisco Systems with 12.3 turns a year and Amazon with 8.9.[69]

To have just the right amount of inventory arrive at just the right time requires a tremendous amount of coordination between manufacturing operations and suppliers. One way to promote tight coordination under JIT is close proximity. Most parts suppliers for Toyota's JIT system at its Georgetown, Kentucky, plant are located within 200 miles of the plant. Furthermore, parts are picked up from suppliers and delivered to Toyota as often as sixteen times a day.[70] A second way to promote close coordination under JIT is to have a shared information system that allows a manufacturer and its suppliers to know the quantity and kinds of parts inventory the other has in stock. Generally, factories and suppliers facilitate information sharing by using the same part numbers and names. Ford's seat supplier accomplishes this by sticking a bar code on each seat, and Ford then uses the sticker to route the seat through its factory.

Manufacturing operations and their parts suppliers can also facilitate close coordination by using the system of kanban. **Kanban**, which is Japanese for "sign," is a simple ticket-based system that indicates when it is time to reorder inventory. Suppliers attach kanban cards to batches of parts. Then, when an assembly-line worker uses the first part out of a batch, the kanban card is removed. The cards are then collected, sorted, and quickly returned to the supplier, who begins resupplying the factory with parts that match the order information on the kanban cards. Glenn Uminger, former manager of production control and logistics at Toyota's Georgetown, Kentucky, plant, said they would place, "orders for new parts as the first part is used out of a box." Because prices and batch sizes are typically agreed to ahead of time, kanban tickets greatly reduce paperwork and ordering costs.[71]

A third method for managing inventory is **materials requirement planning (MRP)**.

> **Just-in-time (JIT) inventory system** an inventory system in which component parts arrive from suppliers just as they are needed at each stage of production
>
> **Kanban** a ticket-based JIT system that indicates when to reorder inventory
>
> **Materials requirement planning (MRP)** a production and inventory system that determines the production schedule, production batch sizes, and inventory needed to complete final products

MRP is a production and inventory system that, from beginning to end, precisely determines the production schedule, production batch sizes, and inventories needed to complete final products. The three key parts of MRP systems are the master production schedule, the bill of materials, and the inventory records. The *master production schedule* is a detailed schedule that indicates the quantity of each item to be produced, the planned delivery dates for those items, and the time by which each step of the production process must be completed to meet those delivery dates. Based on the quantity and kind of products set forth in the master production schedule, the *bill of materials* identifies all the necessary parts and inventory, the quantity or volume of inventory to be ordered, and the order in which the parts and inventory should be assembled. *Inventory records* indicate the kind, quantity, and location of inventory that is on hand or that has been ordered. When inventory records are combined with the bill of materials, the resulting report indicates what to buy, when to buy it, and what it will cost to order. Today, nearly all MRP systems are available in the form of powerful, flexible computer software.[72]

Which inventory management system should you use? Economic order quantity (EOQ) formulas are intended for use with **independent demand systems**, in which the level of one kind of inventory does not depend on another. For example, because inventory levels for automobile tires are unrelated to the inventory levels of women's dresses, Sears could use EOQ formulas to calculate separate optimal order quantities for dresses and tires. By contrast, JIT and MRP are used with **dependent demand systems**, in which the level of inventory depends on the number of finished units to be produced. For example, if Yamaha makes 1,000 motorcycles a day, then it will need 1,000 seats, 1,000 gas tanks, and 2,000 wheels and tires each day. So, when optimal inventory levels depend on the number of products to be produced, use a JIT or MRP management system.

Independent demand system an inventory system in which the level of one kind of inventory does not depend on another

Dependent demand system an inventory system in which the level of inventory depends on the number of finished units to be produced

STUDY TOOLS 18

LOCATED IN TEXTBOOK

☐ Rip-out and review chapter review card

LOCATED AT WWW.CENGAGEBRAIN.COM

☐ Review key term flashcards and create your own from StudyBits

☐ Track your knowledge and understanding of key concepts, using the concept tracker

☐ Complete practice and graded quizzes to prepare for tests

☐ Complete interactive content within the exposition

☐ View chapter highlight box content at the beginning of each chapter

Endnotes

1

1. S. Kapner, "Sears Cashes Out of Prime Stores," *Wall Street Journal*, October 8, 2013, accessed April 24, 2015, http://www.wsj.com/articles/SB100014240 5270230364330457910902320738550; S. Kapner, "Sears Bets Big on Technology, but at the Expense of Its Stores," *Wall Street Journal*, December 16, 2014, accessed April 24, 2015, http://www.wsj.com /articles/sears-bets-big-on-technology-but-at-the -expense-of-its-stores-1418787001; K. Gustafson, "Sears to Accelerate Closings, Shutter 235 Stores," CNBC, December 4, 2014, accessed April 24, 2015, http://www.cnbc.com/id/102237069.

2. "Industry Snapshot: Management, Scientific, and Technical Consulting Services (NAICS 5416)," US Census Bureau, accessed April 24, 2015, http:// thedataweb.rm.census.gov/TheDataWeb_HotReport2 /econsnapshot/2012/snapshot.hrml?NAICS=5416.

3. "What Do Managers Do?" Adapted from "The Wall Street Journal Guide to Management" by Alan Murray. *Wall Street Journal*, accessed June 3, 2014, http://guides.wsj.com/management/developing -a-leadership-style/what-do-managers-do/.

4. M. Phillips, "Starbucks Is Now Selling 46% More Things an Hour Than It Was Five Years Ago," Quartz, November 22, 2013, accessed June 11, 2014, http://qz.com/149995/starbucks-is-now-selling-46 -more-things-an-hour-than-it-was-five-years-ago/.

5. Admin, "How Mobile Payments and IoT Can Save Starbucks $1 Million Per Day," Journal of Things, July 16, 2013, accessed June 11, 2014, http://journalofthings.com/how-mobile-payments -and-internet-of-things-saves-starbucks-mone/.

6. T. Soper, "More Than 14% of Starbucks Transactions Are Now Made with a Mobile Device," GeekWire, March 19, 2014, accessed June 11, 2014, http://www .geekwire.com/2014/starbucks-annual-meeting/.

7. S. Banzo, S. Kapner, S. Ng, and L. Stevens, "Late Surge in Web Buying Blindsides UPS, Retailers," *Wall Street Journal*, December 25, 2013, accessed June 11, 2014, http://www.wsj.com/articles/SB10001424052702 3047535045792801942887430208.

8. G. Bensinger and L. Stevens, "Amazon, in Threat to UPS, Tries Its Own Deliveries," *Wall Street Journal*, April 24, 2014, accessed June 11, 2014, http://www.wsj.com/articles/SB10001424052 7023047858404579521522792859590; M. Wohlsen, "Amazon's Drones are Useless. But Its Trucks Could Crush UPS," *Wired*, December 11, 2013, accessed June 12, 2014, http://www.wired.com /2013/12/amazon-fresh-trucks/.

9. D. A. Wren, A. G. Bedeian, and J. D. Breeze, "The Foundations of Henri Fayol's Administrative Theory," *Management Decision* 40 (2002): 906–918.

10. A. Bryant, "Google's Quest to Build a Better Boss," *New York Times*, March 12, 2011, accessed February 23, 2012, http://www.nytimes.com /2011/03/13/business/13hire.html?_r=0; B. Hall, "Google's Project Oxygen Pumps Fresh Air into Management," The Street, February 11, 2014, accessed June 11, 2014, http://www.thestreet.com /story/12328981/1/googles-project-oxygen-pumps -fresh-air-into-management.html.

11. H. Fayol, *General and Industrial Management* (London: Pittman & Sons, 1949).

12. R. Stagner, "Corporate Decision Making," *Journal of Applied Psychology* 53 (1969): 1–13.

13. D. W. Bray, R. J. Campbell, and D. L. Grant, *Formative Years in Business: A Long-Term AT&T Study of Managerial Lives* (New York: Wiley, 1993).

14. P. Mozur, "Deal-Hungry Alibaba Enters New Field: The Soccer Pitch," *Wall Street Journal*, June 6, 2014, accessed June 12, 2014, http://www.wsj.com /articles/alibaba-buys-stake-in-chinese-soccer-team -guangzhou-evergrande-1401940574

15. S. Carey, "United Continental: One Sick Bird," *Wall Street Journal*, June 8, 2014, accessed June 12, 2014, http://www.wsj.com/articles/united-continental -struggles-to-stabilize-1402263534

16. M. J. Credeur, "Making United and Continental Fly in Formation," *Bloomberg Businessweek*, June 30, 2011, accessed February 23, 2012, http://www .bloomberg.com/bw/magazine/making-united -and-continental-fly-in-formation-07012011.html.

17. E. Martinson, "Corner Office: Eileen Martinson of Sparta Systems on Clarity of Leadership," interview by A. Bryant, *New York Times*, January 9, 2014, accessed June 3, 2014, http://www.nytimes.com/2014 /01/10/business/eileen-martinson-of-sparta-systems -on-clarity-of-leadership.html.

18. Ibid.

19. S. Kapner, "Citi's CEO Is Keeping Score— New Chief Plans Broad Benchmarks for Executives," *Wall Street Journal*, March 5, 2013, C1.

20. H. S. Jonas III, R. E. Fry, and S. Srivastva, "The Office of the CEO: Understanding the Executive Experience," *Academy of Management Executive* 4 (1990): 36–47.

21. J. Chesto, "Moving to Boston Is Così's Recipe for Success," *Boston Globe*, March 18, 2015, accessed April 24, 2015, http://www.bostonglobe .com/business/2015/03/17/cosi-recipe-for-success -the-boston-way/3dFx7EaJKv10uGKW4FTIWJ /story.html; J. Lublin, "Rookie CEOs Face a Steep Learning Curve," Wall Street Journal, June 24, 2014, accessed April 24, 2015, http://www.wsj.com/articles /rookie-ceos-face-a-steep-learning-curve-1403656894.

22. Jonas et al., "The Office of the CEO."

23. Dina Bass, "Beyond Windows," *Bloomberg Businessweek*, February 2–8, 2015, pp. 30–31.

24. Jonas et al., "The Office of the CEO."

25. M. Porter, J. Lorsch, and N. Nohria, "Seven Surprises for New CEOs," *Harvard Business Review* (October 2004): 62.

26. P. Martens, "Corner Office: Phil Martens of Novelis, on Consistent Leadership," interview by A. Bryant, *New York Times*, October 26, 2013, accessed June 3, 2014, http://www.nytimes.com/2013/10/27 /business/phil-martens-of-novelis-on-consistent -leadership.html.

27. Novelis, "Sustainability Through Disruptive Innovation: Sustainability Report 2013," 2013, p. 44, accessed June 3, 2014, http://www.novelis .com/Documents/Sustainability/2013_Novelis _Sustainability_Report_En.pdf.

28. Q. Huy, "In Praise of Middle Managers," *Harvard Business Review* (September 2001): 72–79.

29. "Using Their Own Words, Middle Managers Describe the Nature of Their Jobs," *Wall Street Journal*, August 6, 2013, accessed June 12, 2014, www.wsj.com/articles/SB100014241278873234206 04578652110485397972.

30. M. Korn, "What It's Like Being a Middle Manager Today," *Wall Street Journal*, August 5, 2013, accessed June 3, 2014, http://www.wsj.com/articles /SB10001424127887323420604578650074170664066.

31. "Using Their Own Words, Middle Managers Describe the Nature of Their Jobs."

32. Ibid.

33. R. Silverman, "Some Tech Firms Ask: Who Needs Managers?" *Wall Street Journal*, August 6, 2013, accessed June 12, 2014, http://www.wsj.com /articles/SB10001424127887323420604578652051466314748

34. S. Tully, "What Team Leaders Need to Know," *Fortune*, February 20, 1995, 93.

35. B. Francella, "In a Day's Work," *Convenience Store News*, September 25, 2001, 7.

36. L. Liu and A. McMurray, "Frontline Leaders: The Entry Point for Leadership Development in the Manufacturing Industry," *Journal of European Industrial Training* 28, no. 2–4 (2004): 339–352.

37. A. Nowogrodski, "Corner Office: Avinoam Nowogrodski of Clarizen, on the Rewards of Listening," interview by A. Bryant, *New York Times*, March 13, 2014, accessed June 3, 2014, http://www .nytimes.com/2014/03/14/business/avinoam -nowogrodski-of-clarizen-on-the-rewards-of -listening.html.

38. K. Hultman, "The 10 Commandments of Team Leadership," *Training & Development*, February 1, 1998, 12–13.

39. A. Nowogrodski, "Corner Office: Avinoam Nowogrodski of Clarizen, on the Rewards of Listening.

40. Ibid.

41. R. Silverman, "Who's the Boss? There Isn't One," *Wall Street Journal*, June 20, 2012, B1.

42. N. Steckler and N. Fondas, "Building Team Leader Effectiveness: A Diagnostic Tool," *Organizational Dynamics* (Winter 1995): 20–34.

43. H. Mintzberg, *The Nature of Managerial Work* (New York: Harper & Row, 1973).

44. K. Bowers, "Corner Office: Kim Bowers of CST Brands, on Managing Up vs. Managing Down," interview by A. Bryant, *New York Times*, April 5, 2014, accessed June 3, 2014, http://www.nytimes .com/2014/04/06/business/kim-bowers-of-cst-brands -on-managing-up-vs-managing-down.html.

45. C. P. Hales, "What Do Managers Do? A Critical Review of the Evidence," *Journal of Management Studies* 23, no. 1 (1986): 88–115.

46. B. Kilkha, "FENDI Celebrates the Opening of the New York Flagship Store," *Forbes*, 14 February 2015, accessed April 24, 2015, http://www.forbes .com/sites/bettinazilkha/2015/02/14/fendi-celebrates -the-opening-of-the-new-york-flagship-store/.

47. A. Preuschat, "Huawei Enterprise Business Grew More in Europe Than Home Last Year," *Wall Street Journal*, March 10, 2014, accessed June 3, 2014, http://www.wsj.com/articles/SB1000142405270230470 4504579431302282650692.

48. M. Murphy and E. Chasan, "A Boardroom with a View—Outside Directorships Can Offer CFOs

Fresh Perspective, Add to Financial Toolbox," *Wall Street Journal*, May 7, 2013, B7.

49. J. Light, "Study Points to Benefits of Outside Board Seats," *Wall Street Journal*, May 23, 2011, B6.

50. "News by Industry," *Business Wire*, accessed March 11, 2009, http://www.businesswire.com /portal/site/home/news/industries/.

51. "Media Monitoring," *CyberAlert*, accessed March 11, 2009, http://www.cyberalert.com.

52. "What Is FNS News Clips Online?" *FNS NewsClips*, accessed March 11, 2009, http://www .fednews.com/.

53. A. Bryant, "Transparency Is Much More Than a Buzzword," *New York Times*, March 2, 2013, accessed May 14, 2013, http://www.nytimes.com /2013/03/03/business/ryan-smith-of-qualtrics -on-building-a-transparent-culture.html.

54. M. Wohlsen, "Jeff Bezos Says Amazon Is Seriously Serious about Drone Deliveries," Wired, April 11, 2014, accessed June 13, 2014, http://www .wired.com/2014/04/amazon-delivery-drones/.

55. "Amazon Tests Drones for Same-Day Parcel Delivery, Bezos Says," *Bloomberg News*, December 2, 2013, accessed June 13, 2014, http:// www.bloomberg.com/news/articles/2013-12-02 /amazon-testing-octocopters-for-delivery-ceo-tells -60-minutes-.

56. B. Stone, "Half Off Whole Foods: Following a Very Bad Year, The Elite Grocer Says It's Ready to Compete Like a Big-Box Chain," *Bloomberg Businessweek*, February 2–8, 2015, pp. 45–49.

57. M. Townsend, "Why Target Is Raking Up Its Maple Leaves," *Bloomberg Businessweek*, January 26– February 1, 2015, pp.24–25; I. Austen and H. Tabuchi, "Target's Red Ink Runs Out in Canada," The New York Times, January 15, 2015, , accessed April 24, 2015, http://www.nytimes.com/2015/01/16 /business/target-to-close-stores-in-canada.html.

58. M. Ramsey, "Fuel Goal Tests Ford's Mettle," *Wall Street Journal*, January 13, 2014, B1.

59. G. Farley, "Colorful Airline CEO Negotiates Multi-Billion Dollar Deal," KING 5 News, September 9, 2014, accessed April 24, 2015, http://www.king5.com /story/tech/science/aerospace/2014/09/09/michael -oleary-cuts-deal-with-boeing/15364151/; A. Scott, "Ryanair Buys 100 Boeing 737 MAX Jets, Sees Fare Price War," Reuters, September 8, 2014, accessed April 24, 2015, http://uk.reuters.com/article/2014/09/08/uk -boeing-ryanairhldgs-idUKKBN0H31E220140908.

60. L. A. Hill, *Becoming a Manager: Mastery of a New Identity* (Boston: Harvard Business School Press, 1992).

61. R. L. Katz, "Skills of an Effective Administrator," *Harvard Business Review* (September–October 1974): 90–102.

62. C. A. Bartlett and S. Ghoshal, "Changing the Role of Top Management: Beyond Systems to People," *Harvard Business Review* (May–June 1995): 132–142.

63. F. L. Schmidt and J. E. Hunter, "Development of a Causal Model of Process Determining Job Performance," *Current Directions in Psychological Science* 1 (1992): 89–92.

64. J. B. Miner, "Sentence Completion Measures in Personnel Research: The Development and Validation of the Miner Sentence Completion Scales," in *Personality Assessment in Organizations*, ed. H. J. Bernardin and D. A. Bownas (New York: Praeger, 1986), 145–176.

65. M. W. McCall, Jr., and M. M. Lombardo, "What Makes a Top Executive?" *Psychology Today*, February 1983, 26–31; E. van Velsor and J. Brittain, "Why Executives Derail: Perspectives Across Time and Cultures," *Academy of Management Executive* (November 1995): 62–72.

66. Ibid.

67. J. Lublin, "How to Delegate the Right Way," *Wall Street Journal*, March 13, 2014, accessed June 3, 2014, http://www.wsj.com/articles/SB1000142405270 23041851045794354080334598.

68. A. K. Naj, "Corporate Therapy: The Latest Addition to Executive Suite Is Psychologist's Couch," *Wall Street Journal*, August 29, 1994, A1.

69. Ibid.

70. P. Wallington, "Leadership: How to Spot a Toxic Boss," CIO, April 26, 2006, accessed June 13, 2014, http://www.cio.com/article/20139/Leadership _How_to_Spot_a_Toxic_Boss; P. Wallington, "Management2 Toxic!" *Financial Mail*, July 28, 2006, 48.

71. J. Sandberg, "Overcontrolling Bosses Aren't Just Annoying; They're Also Inefficient," *Wall Street Journal*, March 30, 2005, B1.

72. P. Drexler, "Managing Up: When Your Boss Is an Obsessive Micromanager," *Forbes*, June 13, 2013, accessed June 3, 2014, http://www.forbes .com/sites/peggydrexler/2013/06/13/managing-up -when-your-boss-is-an-obsessive-micromanager/.

73. Hill, *Becoming a Manager*, p. 17.

74. Ibid., p. 55.

75. Ibid., p. 57.

76. Ibid., p. 64.

77. Ibid., p. 67.

78. Ibid., p. 161.

79. J. Pfeffer, *The Human Equation: Building Profits by Putting People First* (Boston: Harvard Business School Press, 1996); *Competitive Advantage Through People: Unleashing the Power of the Work Force* (Boston: Harvard Business School Press, 1994).

80. M. A. Huselid, "The Impact of Human Resource Management Practices on Turnover, Productivity, and Corporate Financial Performance," *Academy of Management Journal* 38 (1995): 635–672.

81. D. McDonald and A. Smith, "A Proven Connection: Performance Management and Business Results," *Compensation & Benefits Review* 27, no. 6 (January 1, 1995): 59.

82. J. Combs, Y. Liu, A. Hall, and D. Ketchen, "How Much Do High-Performance Work Practices Matter? A Meta-Analyis of Their Effects on Organizational Performance," *Personnel Psychology*, 2006, 59, 501–528.

83. I. Fulmer, B. Gerhart, and K. Scott, "Are the 100 Best Better? An Empirical Investigation of the Relationship between Being a 'Great Place to Work' and Firm Performance," *Personnel Psychology* (Winter 2003): 965–993.

84. B. Schneider and D. E. Bowen, "Employee and Customer Perceptions of Service in Banks: Replication and Extension," *Journal of Applied Psychology* 70 (1985): 423–433; B. Schneider, J. J. Parkington, and V. M. Buxton, "Employee and Customer Perceptions of Service in Banks," *Administrative Science Quarterly* 25 (1980): 252–267.

85. "How Investing in Intangibles—Like Employee Satisfaction—Translates into Financial Returns," *Knowledge@Wharton*, January 9, 2008, accessed January 24, 2010, http://knowledge .wharton.upenn.edu/article.cfm ?articleid=1873.

2

1. C. S. George, Jr., *The History of Management Thought* (Englewood Cliffs, NJ: Prentice-Hall, 1972).

2. D. Schmandt-Besserat, *How Writing Came About* (Austin: University of Texas Press, 1997).

3. A. Erman, *Life in Ancient Egypt* (London: Macmillan & Co., 1984).

4. J. Burke, *The Day the Universe Changed* (Boston: Little, Brown, 1985).

5. S. A. Epstein, *Wage Labor and Guilds in Medieval Europe* (Chapel Hill: University of North Carolina Press, 1991).

6. R. Braun, *Industrialization and Everyday Life*, trans. S. Hanbury-Tenison (Cambridge: Cambridge University Press, 1990).

7. J. B. White, "The Line Starts Here: Mass-Production Techniques Changed the Way People Work and Live Throughout the World," *Wall Street Journal*, January 11, 1999, R25.

8. R. B. Reich, *The Next American Frontier* (New York: Time Books, 1983).

9. J. Mickelwait and A. Wooldridge, *The Company: A Short History of a Revolutionary Idea* (New York: Modern Library, 2003).

10. H. Kendall, "Unsystematized, Systematized, and Scientific Management," in *Scientific Management: A Collection of the More Significant Articles Describing the Taylor System of Management*, ed. C. Thompson (Easton, PA: Hive Publishing, 1972), 103–131.

11. United States Congress, House, Special Committee, *Hearings to Investigate the Taylor and Other Systems of Shop Management*, vol. 3 (Washington, DC: Government Printing Office, 1912).

12. Ibid.

13. Ibid.

14. A. Derickson, "Physiological Science and Scientific Management in the Progressive Era: Frederic S. Lee and the Committee on Industrial Fatigue," *Business History Review* 68 (1994): 483–514.

15. U.S. Congress, House, Special Committee, 1912.

16. F. W. Taylor, *The Principles of Scientific Management* (New York: Harper, 1911).

17. C. D. Wrege and R. M. Hodgetts, "Frederick W. Taylor's 1899 Pig Iron Observations: Examining Fact, Fiction, and Lessons for the New Millennium," *Academy of Management Journal*, 43 (December 2000): 1283; J. R. Hough and M. A. White, "Using Stories to Create Change: The Object Lesson of Frederick Taylor's 'Pig-tale,'" *Journal of Management*, 27, no. 5 (October 2001): 585–601; E. A. Locke, "The Ideas of Frederick W. Taylor: An Evaluation," *Academy of Management Review* 7, no. 1(1982) 14–24.

18. Locke, "The Ideas of Frederick W. Taylor."

19. George, *The History of Management Thought*.

20. F. Gilbreth and L. Gilbreth, "Applied Motion Study," in *The Writings of the Gilbreths*, ed. W. R. Spriegel and C. E. Myers (1917; reprint, Homewood, IL: Irwin, 1953), 207–274.

21. Ibid.

22. D. Ferguson, "Don't Call It 'Time and Motion Study,'" *IIE Solutions* 29, no. 5 (1997): 22–23.

23. H. Gantt, "A Graphical Daily Balance in Manufacture," *Transactions of the American Society of Mechanical Engineers* 24 (1903): 1325.

24. P. Peterson, "Training and Development: The View of Henry L. Gantt (1861–1919)," *SAM Advanced Management Journal* (Winter 1987): 20–23.

25. H. Gantt, "Industrial Efficiency," *National Civic Federation Report of the 11th Annual Meeting*, New York, January 12, 1991, 103.

26. Ibid.

27. M. Weber, *The Theory of Social and Economic Organization*, trans. A. Henderson and T. Parsons (New York: Free Press, 1947).

28. M. Weber, *The Protestant Ethic and the Spirit of Capitalism* (New York: Scribner's, 1958).

29. George, *The History of Management Thought*.

30. D. A. Wren, "Henri Fayol as Strategist: A Nineteenth Century Corporate Turnaround," *Management Decision*, 39, no. 6 (2001): 475–487; D. Reid, "Fayol: From Experience to Theory," *Journal of Management History* (Archive) 1, no. 3 (1995): 21–36.

31. Ibid.

32. Ibid.

33. Ibid.

34. F. Blancpain, "Les cahiers inédits d'Henri Fayol," trans. D. Wren, *Extrait du bulletin de l'institut international d'administration publique* 28–29 (1974): 1–48.

35. D. A. Wren, A. G. Bedeian, and J. D. Breeze, "The Foundations of Henri Fayol's Administrative Theory," *Management Decision* 40 (2002): 906–918.

36. H. Fayol, *General and Industrial Management* (London: Pittman & Sons, 1949); Wren, Bedeian, and Breeze, "Foundations."

37. P. Graham, ed., *Mary Parker Follett—Prophet of Management: A Celebration of Writings from the 1920s* (Boston: Harvard Business School Press, 1995).

38. D. Linden, "The Mother of Them All," *Forbes*, January 16, 1995, 75.

39. J. H. Smith, "The Enduring Legacy of Elton Mayo," *Human Relations* 51, no. 3 (1998): 221–249.

40. E. Mayo, *The Human Problems of an Industrial Civilization* (New York: Macmillan, 1933).

41. Ibid.

42. "Hawthorne Revisited: The Legend and the Legacy," *Organizational Dynamics* (Winter 1975): 66–80.

43. E. Mayo, *The Social Problems of an Industrial Civilization* (Boston: Harvard Graduate School of Business Administration, 1945).

44. "Hawthorne Revisited: The Legend and the Legacy."

45. Mayo, *The Social Problems of an Industrial Civilization*, 45.

46. George, *The History of Management Thought*.

47. C. I. Barnard, *The Functions of the Executive* (Cambridge, MA: Harvard University Press, 1938), 4.

48. C. I. Barnard, *The Functions of the Executive: 30th Anniversary Edition* (Cambridge, MA: Harvard University Press, 1968), 5.

49. J. Fuller and A. Mansour, "Operations Management and Operations Research: A Historical and Relational Perspective," *Management Decision* 41 (2003): 422–426.

50. D. Wren and R. Greenwood, "Business Leaders: A Historical Sketch of Eli Whitney," *Journal of Leadership & Organizational Studies* 6 (1999): 131.

51. "Monge, Gaspard, comte de Péluse," *Britannica Online*, accessed January 9, 2005, http://www.britannica.com/biography/Gaspard-Monge-comte-de-Peluse.

52. M. Schwartz and A. Fish, "Just-in-Time Inventories in Old Detroit," *Business History* 40, no. 3 (July 1998): 48.

53. D. Ashmos and G. Huber, "The Systems Paradigm in Organization Theory: Correcting the Record and Suggesting the Future," *Academy of Management Review* 12 (1987): 607–621; F. Kast and J. Rosenzweig, "General Systems Theory: Applications for Organizations and Management," *Academy of Management Journal* 15 (1972): 447–465; D. Katz and R. Kahn, *The Social Psychology of Organizations* (New York: Wiley, 1966).

54. R. Mockler, "The Systems Approach to Business Organization and Decision Making," *California Management Review* 11, no. 2 (1968): 53–58.

55. F. Luthans and T. Stewart, "A General Contingency Theory of Management," *Academy of Management Review* 2, no. 2 (1977): 181–195.

3

1. L. Fleisher, "Thousands of Taxi Drivers Protest Uber Across Europe," *Wall Street Journal*, June 12, 2014, B2; C. Matlack, "Europe's Cabbies, Fed Up with Uber, Plan a Day of Traffic Chaos," *Bloomberg Businessweek*, June 10, 2014, accessed June 15, 2014, http://www.businessweek.com/articles/2014-06-10/europes-cabbies-fed-up-with-uber-plan-a-day-of-traffic-chaos.

2. D. Herbert, "Rest in Peace for Less with Caskets Made in China," *Bloomberg Businessweek*, February 20, 2015, accessed April 24, 2015, http://www.bloomberg.com/news/features/2015-02-20/casket-industry-fends-off-chinese-imports-favored-by-vegas-entrepreneur; P. Cain, "The Living Dead: New Embalming Method Aids Surgical Training," *BBC News*, June 15, 2013, accessed April 24, 2015, http://www.bbc.com/news/health-22908661.

3. Tim Stevens, "Apple iPhone 6 Plus Review—The Most Serious Apple Phone Yet," CNET.com, September 16, 2014, accessed March 28, http://www.cnet.com/products/apple-iphone-6-plus/; https://www.apple.com/iphone-6/.

4. E. Romanelli and M. L. Tushman, "Organizational Transformation as Punctuated Equilibrium: An Empirical Test," *Academy of Management Journal* 37 (1994): 1141–1166.

5. H. Banks, "A Sixties Industry in a Nineties Economy," *Forbes*, May 9, 1994, 107–112.

6. L. Cowan, "Cheap Fuel Should Carry Many Airlines to More Record Profits for 1st Quarter," *Wall Street Journal*, April 4, 1998, B17A.

7. "Annual Revenues and Earnings: US Airlines—All Services," Air Transport Association, accessed January 15, 2005, http://www.airlines.org; S. Carey, "Carrier Makes Deeper Cuts as It Seeks Federal Backing Needed to Exit Chapter 11," *Wall Street Journal*, November 27, 2002, A3; S. Carey, "UAL Will Lay Off 1,500 Workers as Part of Cost-Cutting Strategy," *Wall Street Journal*, January 6, 2003, A3; D. Carty, "Oral Testimony of Mr. Donald J. Carty, Chairman and CEO, American Airlines: United States Senate, Committee on Commerce, Science, and Transportation," accessed January 9, 2003, http://www.amrcorp.com; S. McCartney, M. Trottman, and S. Carey, "Northwest, Continental, America West Post Losses as Delta Cuts Jobs," *Wall Street Journal*, November 18, 2002, B4.

8. "Airlines Still in Upheaval, 5 Years after 9/11," CNNMoney.com, September 8, 2006, accessed July 25, 2008, http://money.cnn.com/2006/09/08/news/companies/airlines_sept11/?postversion=2006090813&eref=yahoo.

9. R. Schifter, "Why Airlines Are Flying High," *Wall Street Journal*, February 4, 2015, A15.

10. S. Carey and J. Nicas, "Leaner Airlines, Meaner Routes," *Wall Street Journal*, May 8, 2013, B1.

11. A. Madrigal, "The Perfect Milk Machine: How Big Data Transformed the Dairy Industry," *The Atlantic*, May 1, 2012, accessed April 25, 2015, http://www.theatlantic.com/technology/archive/2012/05/the-perfect-milk-machine-how-big-data-transformed-the-dairy-industry/256423/.

12. "US Dairy: Total Milk Production 2014," Statista, accessed April 25, 2015, http://www.statista.com/statistics/194937/total-us-milk-production-since-1999/.

13. Press Release, "PC Shipments Post the Steepest Decline Ever in a Single Quarter, According to IDC," International Data Corporation, April 10, 2013, accessed May 14, 2013, http://www.idc.com/getdoc.jsp?containerId=prUS24065413; K. Bora, "Worldwide PC Shipments Showed Signs of Improvement Despite 1.7% Annual Decline in Q1 2014," *International Business Times*, April 15, 2014, accessed April 25, 2015, http://www.ibtimes.com/worldwide-pc-shipments-showed-signs-improvement-despite-17-annual-decline-q1-2014-1571663; S. Ovide, "Microsoft to Show Off Windows 10—CEO Nadella, Others to Give Most Detailed Glimpse So Far," *Wall Street Journal*, January, 19, 2015, accessed April 25, 2015, http://www.wsj.com/articles/microsoft-to-show-off-latest-windows-launching-this-year-1421695264; D. Bass, "Beyond Windows," *Bloomberg Businessweek*, February 23–March 1, 2015, pp. 30–31; N. Ralph, "Microsoft Windows 10 Preview," CNET.com, April 2, 2015, accessed April 25, 2015, http://www.cnet.com/products/microsoft-windows-10/.

14. D. Charles, "Thanks to Nutella, The World Needs More Hazelnuts," *All Things Considered*, NPR, September 16, 2014, accessed April 25, 2015, www.npr.org/blogs/thesalt/2014/09/16/347749070/thanks-to-nutella-the-world-needs-more-hazelnuts; V. Wong, "Nutella Hogs Hazelnuts to Meet the World's Insatiable Craving for Chocolaty Goodness," *Bloomberg Businessweek*, August 14, 2014, accessed April 25, 2015, www.businessweek.com/articles/2014-08-14/nutella-buys-hazelnut-supplier-to-protect-against-worldwide-shortage.

15. T. Stynes, "Yum's Sales in China Still Struggling," *Wall Street Journal*, January 13, 2014, accessed June 4, 2014, http://online.wsj.com/news/articles/SB10001424052702304049704579319020232064980?KEYWORDS=yum+brands&mg=reno64-wsj.

16. OECD (2014), "OECD Forecasts During and After the Financial Crisis: A Post Mortem," OECD Economics Department Policy Notes, No. 23, February 2014.

17. "CEO Confidence Improves Slightly," The Conference Board, January 8, 2015, accessed April 25, 2015, https://www.conference-board.org/data/ceoconfidence.cfm.

18. "Unflinching Small Business Optimism," WSJ/Vistage Small Business CEO Survey, February–March 28, 2015, accessed April 25, 2015, http://www.vistage.com/wp-content/uploads/2015/03/WSJ-CEO-Survey-0215.pdf; http://www.vistage.com/press-center/wallsjvistage-ceo-survey/.

19. C. Paris, "Carnival Sails Toward China Growth," *Wall Street Journal*, January 22, 2015, B7.

20. V. Fuhrmans, "Europe's Car Makers Spin Their Wheels," *Wall Street Journal*, September 30, 2013, accessed June 4, 2014, http://online.wsj.com/news/articles/SB10001424127887323623304579052220451906010?KEYWORDS=europe%27s+car+makers+spin&mg=reno64-wsj.

21. "The Civil Rights Act of 1991," US Equal Employment Opportunity Commission, accessed July 25, 2008, http://www.eeoc.gov/policy/cra91.html.

22. "Compliance Assistance—Family and Medical Leave Act (FMLA)," US Department of Labor: Employment Standards Administration, Wage and Hour Division, accessed July 25, 2005, http://www.dol.gov/.

23. A. Loten, "Small Business Owners Scramble to Prepare for New Tax Form," *Wall Street Journal*, March 4, 2015, B5.

24. R. J. Bies and T. R. Tyler, "The Litigation Mentality in Organizations: A Test of Alternative Psychological Explanations," *Organization Science* 4 (1993): 352–366.

25. M. Orey, "Fear of Firing," *BusinessWeek*, April 23, 2007, 52–62.

26. S. Gardner, G. Gomes, and J. Morgan, "Wrongful Termination and the Expanding Public Policy Exception: Implications and Advice," *SAM Advanced Management Journal* 65 (2000): 38.

27. "Bases by Issue: FY 2010 - FY 2014," U.S. Equal Employment Opportunity Commission, accessed April 25, 2015, http://www1.eeoc.gov

//eeoc/statistics/enforcement/bases_by_issue
.cfm?renderforprint=1.

28. J. Mundy, "Wrongful Termination Lawsuits on the Rise," *LawyersandSettlements.com*, January 5, 2011, accessed June 4, 2014, http://www .lawyersandsettlements.com/articles/wrongful -termination/wrongful-termination-law-11-15747 .html#.U48_GvldWSp.

29. Orey, "Fear of Firing."

30. Ibid.

31. "Little Gym Case Study," Listen360, April 2014, accessed April 4, 2015, http://listen360.com /assets/case_studies/LittleGym_4-2014.pdf.

32. R. Johnston and S. Mehra, "Best-Practice Complaint Management," *Academy of Management Experience* 16 (November 2002): 145–154.

33. D. Smart and C. Martin, "Manufacturer Responsiveness to Consumer Correspondence: An Empirical Investigation of Consumer Perceptions," *Journal of Consumer Affairs* 26 (1992): 104.

34. K. Rosman, "Weather Channel Now Also Forecasts What You'll Buy," *Wall Street Journal*, August 14, 2013, accessed June 16, 2014, http://online.wsj .com/news/articles/SB1000142412788732363970457 9012674092402660.

35. Ibid.

36. S. A. Zahra and S. S. Chaples, "Blind Spots in Competitive Analysis," *Academy of Management Executive* 7 (1993): 7–28.

37. K. Hagey and S. Ramachandran, "Pay TV's New Worry: 'Shaving' the Cord," *Wall Street Journal*, October 9, 2014, accessed April 25, 2015, http://www.wsj.com/articles/pay-tvs-new-worry -shaving-the-cord-1412899121; D. Beres, "150,000 Cable Subscribers Cut the Cord Last Quarter," Huffington Post, November 14, 2014, accessed April 25, 2015, http://www.huffingtonpost. com/2014/11/14/cord-cutting_n_6159502.html; E. Deggans, "Evaluating Whether It's Time to Cut the Cord," *Morning Edition* on NPR, March 27, 2015, accessed April 25, 2015, http://www.npr.org/2015 /03/27/395698509/how-to-evaluate-whether-its -time-for-you-to-cut-the-cord; E. Lee, "TV Subscriptions Fall for First Time as Viewers Cut the Cord," *BloombergBusiness*.com, March 19, 2014, accessed April 25, 2015, http://www.bloomberg .com/news/articles/2014-03-19/u-s-pay-tv -subscriptions-fall-for-first-time-as-streaming-gains.

38. K. G. Provan, "Embeddedness, Interdependence, and Opportunism in Organizational Supplier-Buyer Networks," *Journal of Management* 19 (1993): 841–856.

39. J. Lessin, L. Luk, and J. Osawa, "Apple Finds It Difficult to Divorce Samsung," *Wall Street Journal*, June 29, 2013, A1.

40. D. Clark, "Samsung's Chip Choice Is a Mixed Verdict for Qualcomm," *Wall Street Journal*, April 3, 2015, accessed April 25, 2015, http://blogs.wsj .com/digits/2015/04/03/samsungs-chip-choice-is-a -mixed-verdict-for-qualcomm/.

41. J. Lee and I. King, "Samsung Said to Win Apple A9 Chip Orders for Next iPhone," *BloombergBusiness*, April 2, 2015, accessed April 25, 2015, http://www.bloomberg.com/news/articles /2015-04-03/samsung-said-to-win-apple-a9-chip -orders-for-next-iphone.

42. Ibid.

43. Ibid.

44. Ibid.

45. S. Parker and C. Axtell, "Seeing Another Viewpoint: Antecedents and Outcomes of Employee Perspective Taking," *Academy of Management Journal* 44 (2001): 1085–1100; B. K. Pilling, L. A. Crosby, and D. W. Jackson, "Relational Bonds in Industrial Exchange: An Experimental Test

of the Transaction Cost Economic Framework," *Journal of Business Research* 30 (1994): 237–251.

46. M. Hickins, "CIO Journal: H-P Reinvents Itself," *Wall Street Journal*, April 25, 2013, B5.

47. K. O'Brien, "DreamWorks Animation Data Center On-Site," Storage Review, October 24, 2012, accessed June 16, 2014, http://www.storagereview .com/dreamworks_animation_data_center_onsite.

48. "FDA Finalizes Menu and Vending Machine Calorie Labeling Rules," US Food and Drug Administration, November 25, 2014, accessed April 25, 2015, http://www.fda.gov/NewsEvents/Newsroom /PressAnnouncements/ucm423952.htm.

49. A. Martin, "Inside the Powerful Lobby Fighting for Your Right to Eat Pizza," *Chicago Tribune*, March 9, 2015, accessed April 25, 2015, http://www .chicagotribune.com/news/sns-wp-blm-news-bc -pizza-lobby09-20150309-story.html#page=2.

50. "CPSC Approves Strong Federal Safety Standard for High-Powered Magnet Sets to Protect Children and Teenagers," United States Consumer Product Safety Commission, September 25, 2014, Release number 14-283, accessed April 25, 2015, http://www.cpsc.gov/en/Newsroom/News-Releases /2014/CPSC-Approves-Strong-Federal-Safety -Standard-for-High-Powered-Magnet-Sets-to -Protect-Children-and-Teenagers/; M. Lipka, "After Death and Recalls, Feds Ban High-Powered Magnets," *CBS Moneywatch*, September 25, 2014, accessed April 25, 2015, http://www.cbsnews.com /news/after-deaths-and-recalls-feds-ban-high -powered-magnets/; R. Abrams, "High-Power Magnets Get Temporary Reprieve from Safety Rules," *Boston Globe*, April 4, 2015, accessed April 25, 2015, https://www.bostonglobe.com/business /2015/04/03/high-power-magnets-get-temporary -reprieve-from-safety-rules/TK26SoOCz82d3XSu 2655LK/story.html.

51. "Sean Lennon, Yoko Ono Recruit Famous Friends for Anti-Fracking Clip," *Rolling Stone*, March 11, 2013, accessed May 15, 2013, http:// www.rollingstone.com/music/videos/sean-lennon -yoko-ono-recruit-celebrity-friends-for-anti-fracking -clip-20130311.

52. D. Kline, "Cadbury Recall Threatens Its Business in the Muslim World," Motley Fool, May 30, 2014, accessed June 17, 2014, http://www.fool .com/investing/general/2014/05/30/cadbury-recall -threatens-its-business-in-the-musli.aspx.

53. "Cadbury Chocolate Pork Free, Says Malaysian Islamic Body," BBC News, June 2, 2014, accessed June 17, 2014, http://www.bbc.com/news/business -27663857.

54. C. Mims, "Amid Stratospheric Valuations, Google Unearths a Deal with Skybox," *Wall Street Journal*, June 15, 2014, http://online.wsj.com /articles/amid-stratospheric-valuations-google -unearths-a-deal-with-skybox-1402864823 ?KEYWORDS=google+acquisition+satellite.

55. D. F. Jennings and J. R. Lumpkin, "Insights Between Environmental Scanning Activities and Porter's Generic Strategies: An Empirical Analysis," *Journal of Management* 4 (1992): 791–803.

56. "China's Unsafe Water Is Nestlé's Opportunity," *Bloomberg Businessweek*, January 28–February 3, 2013, 19–20.

57. E. Jackson and J. E. Dutton, "Discerning Threats and Opportunities," *Administrative Science Quarterly* 33 (1988): 370–387.

58. B. Thomas, S. M. Clark, and D. A. Gioia, "Strategic Sensemaking and Organizational Performance: Linkages Among Scanning, Interpretation, Action, and Outcomes," *Academy of Management Journal* 36 (1993): 239–270.

59. R. Daft, J. Sormunen, and D. Parks, "Chief Executive Scanning, Environmental Characteristics,

and Company Performance: An Empirical Study," *Strategic Management Journal* 9 (1988): 123–139; V. Garg, B. Walters, and R. Priem, "Chief Executive Scanning Emphases, Environmental Dynamism, and Manufacturing Firm Performance," *Strategic Management Journal* 24 (2003): 725–744; D. Miller and P. H. Friesen, "Strategy-Making and Environment: The Third Link," *Strategic Management Journal* 4 (1983): 221–235.

60. A. Gasparro and A. Prior, "Kellogg's Profit Falls 16% as Cereal Sales Drop," *Wall Street Journal*, July 31, 2014, accessed April 25, 2015, http://www .wsj.com/articles/kelloggs-profit-pressured-by-cereal -sales-1406809902.

61. D. Leonard, "Bad News in Cereal City—Will Kellogg Ever Catch a Break?" *Bloomberg Businessweek*, March 2–8, 2015, pp. 42–47.

62. "Modernization of the Panama Canal," *The Washington Post*, accessed June 17, 2014, http:// www.washingtonpost.com/wp-srv/special/world /modernization-of-panama-canal/index.html.

63. K. Park, "Maersk Line to Dump Panama Canal for Suez as Ships Get Bigger," Bloomberg, March 11, 2013, accessed June 17, 2014, http://www.bloomberg .com/news/2013-03-11/maersk-line-to-dump-panama -canal-for-suez-as-ships-get-bigger.html.

64. "Frequently Asked Questions," Official Website for the Panama Canal Expansion, accessed June 17, 2014, http://micanaldepanama.com/expansion/faq /#prettyPhoto.

65. R. Feitelberg, "Building a Winning Culture," WWD, December 1, 2011, SR12; Under Armour, Inc., "2013 Under Armour Annual Report," February 21, 2014 p. 4.

66. S. Berfield, "Container Store: Conscious Capitalism and the Perils of Going Public," Bloomberg Business, February 19, 2015, accessed April 25, 2015, http://www.bloomberg.com/news/articles /2015-02-19/container-store-conscious-capitalism -and-the-perils-of-going-public.

67. Ibid.; K. Gustafson, "Retail's Turnover a Plus for Economy But Challenge for Stores," CNBC, September 23, 2014, accessed April 25, 2015, http://www.cnbc.com/id/102021496.

68. D. M. Boje, "The Storytelling Organization: A Study of Story Performance in an Office-Supply Firm," *Administrative Science Quarterly* 36 (1991): 106–126.

69. B. Horowitz, "6 Questions for: Nobody Said Startups Would Be Easy," *Inc.*, April 2014, 39–40.

70. F. D'Souza, "Corner Office: Francisco D'Souza of Cognizant, on Finding Company Heroes," interview by A. Bryant, *New York Times*, August 31, 2013, accessed June 4, 2014, http://www.nytimes .com/2013/09/01/business/francisco-dsouza-of -cognizant-on-finding-company-heroes.html.

71. F. D'Souza, "Corner Office: Francisco D'Souza of Cognizant, on Finding Company Heroes."

72. D. R. Denison and A. K. Mishra, "Toward a Theory of Organizational Culture and Effectiveness," *Organization Science* 6 (1995): 204–223.

73. P. Ziobro, "Floundering Mattel Tries to Make Things Fun Again," *Wall Street Journal*, December 22, 2014, accessed April 26, 2015, http://www.wsj.com /articles/floundering-mattel-tries-to-make-things -fun-again-1419305830.

74. "Our Philosophy," BPV Capital Management, June 18, 2014, accessed June 18, 2014, http://www .backporchvista.com/about-bpv/our-philosophy/.

75. D. Gilbert and R. Gold, "As Big Drillers Move In, Safety Goes Up," *Wall Street Journal*, April 2, 2013, A1; "Shell Code of Conduct: How to Live by the Shell General Business Principles," Shell, accessed May 16, 2013, http://s06.static-shell.com /content/dam/shell/static/public/downloads /corporate-pkg/code-of-conduct-english.pdf.

76. A. Zuckerman, "Strong Corporate Cultures and Firm Performance: Are There Tradeoffs?" *Academy of Management Executive*, November 2002, 158–160.

77. E. Schein, *Organizational Culture and Leadership*, 2nd ed. (San Francisco: Jossey-Bass, 1992).

78. J. Lublin, "This CEO Used to Have an Office—At Dynegy, Boss's Drive for a 'Winning' Culture Means More Cubicles and Fewer Emails," *Wall Street Journal*, March 13, 2013.

79. D. MacMillan, "AOL Tries for Some Silicon Valley Cred," *Bloomberg Businessweek*, March 24, 2011, accessed February 26, 2012, http://www.businessweek.com/magazine/content/11_14/b4222043205512.htm.

80. T. Pluto, "Terry's Talkin' about Cleveland Browns Free Agency and Quarterbacks, Tribe's Pitching, Cavs Guards," March 29, 2014, accessed June 17, 2014, http://www.cleveland.com/pluto/index.ssf/2014/03/terrys_talkin_about_the_clevel_5.html.

81. G. Bensinger, "Amazon Recruits Face 'Bar Raisers,'" *Wall Street Journal*, January 8, 2014, B1.

4

1. "2014 Edelman Trust Barometer Annual Global Study," Edelman Berland, accessed June 19, 2014, http://www.edelman.com/insights/intellectual-property/2014-edelman-trust-barometer/; D. Meinhert, "Creating an Ethical Workplace," *HR Magazine* 59 (April 2014): 4, https://www.shrm.org/Publications/hrmagazine/EditorialContent/2014/0414/Pages/0414-ethical-workplace-culture.aspx (accessed June 4, 2014).

2. "2013 National Business Ethics Survey of the U.S. Workforce," Ethics Resource Center, 2014, accessed June 4, 2014, http://www.ethics.org/downloads/2013NBESFinalWeb.pdf.

3. "2013 National Business Ethics Survey of the U.S. Workforce," Ethics Resource Center.

4. C. Smith, "The Ethical Workplace," *Association Management* 52 (2000): 70–73.

5. "Trust in the Workplace: 2010 Ethics & Workplace Survey," Deloitte LLP, 2010, accessed June 4, 2014, http://www.deloitte.com/assets/Dcom-United-States/Local%20Assets/Documents/us_2010_Ethics_and_Workplace_Survey_report_071910.pdf.

6. "Communication, Honesty among Traits Most Desired and Lacking in Corporate Leaders, ASQ Survey Says," Reuters.com, February 11, 2014, accessed April 11, 2015, http://www.reuters.com/article/2014/02/11/idUSnGNX91ymYv+1c2+GNW20140211.

7. A. Bryant, "In a Word, He Wants Simplicity," *New York Times*, May 23, 2009, accessed August 15, 2010, http://www.nytimes.com/2009/05/24/business/24corner.html?_r=2&pagewanted=1.

8. Association of Certified Fraud Examiners, "Report to the Nation on Occupational Fraud and Abuse: 2014 Global Fraud Study," accessed April 11, 2015, http://www.acfe.com/rttn-summary.aspx. K. Gibson, "Excuses, Excuses: Moral Slippage in the Workplace," *Business Horizons* 43, no. 6 (2000): 65; S. L. Robinson and R. J. Bennett, "A Typology of Deviant Workplace Behaviors: A Multidimensional Scaling Study," *Academy of Management Journal* 38 (1995): 555–572.

9. Harvard Management Update, "Learn by 'Failing Forward,'" *Globe & Mail*, October 31, 2000, B17.

10. "Challenger March Madness Report," Challenger, Gray & Christmas, Inc., March 11, 2015, accessed April 11, 2015, http://www.challengergray.com/download/file/fid/215.

11. B. Falcon, "Oil Thieves Plague Shell in Nigeria," *Wall Street Journal*, April 12, 2013, B1.

12. M. Korolov, "Overall Jump Linked to Increase in Employee Theft and Higher Security Spending," CSO Online, November 7, 2014, accessed April 11, 2015, http://www.csoonline.com/article/2845058/loss-prevention/cost-of-retail-crime-skyrockets-nearly-30-percent.html; Global Retail Theft Barometer 2014, accessed April 11, 2015, http://globalretailtheftbarometer.com/.

13. J.L. Hayes, "26th Annual Retail Theft Survey," Hayes International press release, June 25, 2014, accessed April 11, 2015, http://jacklhayes.com/26th-annual-retail-theft-survey/.

14. A. Wren, "Sweethearting: A Bottom Line Drain for Retailers," Chain Store Age, June 21, 2012, accessed April 11, 2015, http://www.chainstoreage.com/article/sweethearting-bottom-line-drain-retailers; M. K. Brady, C. M. Voorhees, M. J. Brusco, "Service Sweethearting: Its Antecedents and Customer Consequences," *Journal of Marketing* 76 (2012): 81–98.

15. J. Norman, "Cultivating a Culture of Honesty," The Orange County [California] Register, October 23, 2006.

16. Workplace death stats: "Revisions to the 2012 Census of Fatal Occupational Injuries (CFOI) Counts," US Bureau of Labor Statistics, April 2014, accessed April 11, 2015, http://www.bls.gov/iif/oshwc/cfoi/cfoi_revised12.pdf.

17. D. Palmer and A. Zakhem, "Bridging the Gap Between Theory and Practice: Using the 1991 Federal Sentencing Guidelines as a Paradigm for Ethics Training," *Journal of Business Ethics* 29, no. 1/2 (2001): 77–84.

18. K. Tyler, "Do the Right Thing: Ethics Training Programs Help Employees Deal with Ethical Dilemmas," *HR Magazine*, February 2005, accessed March 13, 2009, http://www.shrm.org/publications/hrmagazine/editorialcontent/pages/0205tyler.aspx.

19. D. R. Dalton, M. B. Metzger, and J. W. Hill, "The 'New' US Sentencing Commission Guidelines: A Wake-up Call for Corporate America," *Academy of Management Executive* 8 (1994): 7–16.

20. G. Marcias, "Q&A: Gayle Macias, World Vision," interview by B. DiPietro, *Wall Street Journal*, June 12, 2013, accessed June 4, 2014, http://blogs.wsj.com/riskandcompliance/2013/06/12/qa-gayle-macias-world-vision/.

21. B. Ettore, "Crime and Punishment: A Hard Look at White-Collar Crime," *Management Review* 83 (1994): 10–16.

22. F. Robinson and C. C. Pauze, "What Is a Board's Liability for Not Adopting a Compliance Program?" *Healthcare Financial Management* 51, no. 9 (1997): 64.

23. D. Murphy, "The Federal Sentencing Guidelines for Organizations: A Decade of Promoting Compliance and Ethics," *Iowa Law Review* 87 (2002): 697–719.

24. Robinson and Pauze, "What Is a Board's Liability?"

25. B. Schwartz, "The Nuts and Bolts of an Effective Compliance Program," *HR Focus* 74, no. 8 (1997): 13–15.

26. T. Martin, B. Morris, and S. Thurm, "UPS to End Health Benefits for Some Working Spouses of Employees," *Wall Street Journal*, August 21, 2013, accessed June 4, 2014, http://online.wsj.com/news/articles/SB10001424127887323980604579027082775945544?KEYWORDS=UPS+to+end+health&mg=reno64-wsj.

27. S. Morris and R. McDonald, "The Role of Moral Intensity in Moral Judgments: An Empirical Investigation," *Journal of Business Ethics* 14 (1995): 715–726; B. Flannery and D. May, "Environmental Ethical Decision Making in the US Metal-Finishing Industry," *Academy of Management Journal* 43 (2000): 642–662.

28. L. Kohlberg, "Stage and Sequence: The Cognitive-Developmental Approach to Socialization," in *Handbook of Socialization Theory and Research*, ed. D. A. Goslin (Chicago: Rand McNally, 1969); L. Trevino, "Moral Reasoning and Business Ethics: Implications for Research, Education, and Management," *Journal of Business Ethics* 11 (1992): 445–459.

29. L. Trevino and M. Brown, "Managing to Be Ethical: Debunking Five Business Ethics Myths," *Academy of Management Executive* 18 (May 2004): 69–81.

30. L. T. Hosmer, "Trust: The Connecting Link Between Organizational Theory and Philosophical Ethics," *Academy of Management Review* 20 (1995): 379–403.

31. T. Martin, et.al., "UPS to End Health Benefits for Some Working Spouses of Employees."

32. Ibid.

33. Ibid.

34. Ibid.

35. "2013 National Business Ethics Survey of the U.S. Workforce," Ethics Resource Center.

36. H. J. Bernardin, "Validity of an Honesty Test in Predicting Theft Among Convenience Store Employees," *Academy of Management Journal* 36 (1993): 1097–1108.

37. J. M. Collins and F. L. Schmidt, "Personality, Integrity, and White Collar Crime: A Construct Validity Study," *Personnel Psychology* (1993): 295–311.

38. W. C. Borman, M. A. Hanson, and J. W. Hedge, "Personnel Selection," *Annual Review of Psychology* 48 (1997).

39. P. E. Murphy, "Corporate Ethics Statements: Current Status and Future Prospects," *Journal of Business Ethics* 14 (1995): 727–740.

40. "Code of Ethical Business Conduct," The Hershey Company, no date, accessed February 26, 2012, http://www.thehersheycompany.com/investors/corporate-governance/code-of-conduct.aspx.

41. "More Corporate Boards Involved in Ethics Programs; Ethics Training Becoming Standard Practice," *PR Newswire*, October 16, 2006.

42. S. J. Harrington, "What Corporate America Is Teaching about Ethics," *Academy of Management Executive* 5 (1991): 21–30.

43. L. A. Berger, "Train All Employees to Solve Ethical Dilemmas," *Best's Review–Life-Health Insurance Edition* 95 (1995): 70–80.

44. D. Meinhert, "Creating an Ethical Workplace."

45. Ibid.

46. L. Trevino, G. Weaver, D. Gibson, and B. Toffler, "Managing Ethics and Legal Compliance: What Works and What Hurts," *California Management Review* 41, no. 2 (1999): 131–151.

47. M. Swanton, "Compliance Comedy," *Inside Counsel* 22 (2011): 56.

48. "Leader's Guide: A Culture of Trust 2008," Lockheed Martin, accessed July 17, 2008, http://www.lockheedmartin.com/data/assets/corporate/documents/ethics/2008_EAT_Leaders_Guide.pdf.

49. D. Meinhert, "Creating an Ethical Workplace."

50. E. White, "Theory & Practice: What Would You Do? Ethics Courses Get Context; Beyond Checking Boxes, Some Firms Start Talking about Handling Gray Areas," *Wall Street Journal*, June 12, 2006, B3.

51. "The State of Ethics in Large Companies: A Research Report from the National Business Ethics Survey (NBES)," Ethics Research Center, 2015, accessed April 11, 2015, http://www.ethics.org/nbes/wp-content/uploads/2015/03/LargeCompaniesExecSummary.pdf.

52. Ibid.

53. G. Weaver and L. Trevino, "Integrated and Decoupled Corporate Social Performance: Management Commitments, External Pressures, and Corporate Ethics Practices," *Academy of Management Journal* 42 (1999): 539–552; Trevino, Weaver, Gibson, and Toffler, "Managing Ethics and Legal Compliance."

54. "2013 National Business Ethics Survey of the U.S. Workforce," Ethics Resource Center.

55. J. Salopek, "Do the Right Thing," *Training & Development* 55 (July 2001): 38–44.

56. M. Gundlach, S. Douglas, and M. Martinko, "The Decision to Blow the Whistle: A Social Information Processing Framework," *Academy of Management Executive* 17 (2003): 107–123.

57. "Retaliation: When Whistleblowers Become Victims: A Supplemental Report of the 2011 National Business Ethics Survey," Ethics Resource Center, 2012, accessed May 21, 2013, http://www.ethics.org/files/u5/RetaliationFinal.pdf.

58. "2013 National Business Ethics Survey of the U.S. Workforce," Ethics Resource Center; "The State of Ethics in Large Companies: A Research Report from the National Business Ethics Survey (NBES)."

59. "OSHA Found Airline Violated Whistleblower Protection Provision of AIR21," OSHA News Release: 11-1814-ATL, January 17, 2012, accessed May 22, 2013, http://www.osha.gov/pls/oshaweb/owadisp .show_document?p_id=21651&p_table =NEWS_RELEASES; J. Incas, "Ex-AirTran Pilot Ordered Reinstated," *Wall Street Journal*, January 18, 2012, B2.

60. J. Deschenaux, "High Court Extends Employee Whistle-blower Protections," *Society for Human Resource Management*, March 5, 2014, accessed June 4, 2014, http://www.shrm.org/LegalIssues /FederalResources/Pages/High-Court-Extends -Employee-Whistle-blower-Protections.aspx.

61. M. Mucci, "Compliance Without Compliance Officer: Q&A with Martin Mucci of Paychex," interview by G. Millman, *Wall Street Journal*, February 6, 2014, accessed June 4, 2014, http://blogs.wsj.com /riskandcompliance/2014/02/06/compliance-without -a-chief-compliance-officer-qa-with-martin-mucci-of -paychex/?KEYWORDS=ethics+training.

62. M. P. Miceli and J. P. Near, "Whistleblowing: Reaping the Benefits," *Academy of Management Executive* 8 (1994): 65–72.

63. M. Mucci, "Compliance Without Compliance Officer: Q&A with Martin Mucci of Paychex."

64. Ibid.

65. M. Master and E. Heresniak, "The Disconnect in Ethics Training," *Across the Board* 39 (September 2002): 51–52.

66. H. R. Bower, *Social Responsibilities of the Businessman* (New York: Harper & Row, 1953).

67. "Beyond the Green Corporation," *Business-Week*, January 29, 2007.

68. S. L. Wartick and P. L. Cochran, "The Evolution of the Corporate Social Performance Model," *Academy of Management Review* 10 (1985): 758–769.

69. J. Nocera, "The Paradox of Businesses as Do-Gooders," *New York Times*, November 11, 2006, C1.

70. S. Waddock, C. Bodwell, and S. Graves, "Responsibility: The New Business Imperative," *Academy of Management Executive* 16 (2002): 132–148.

71. T. Donaldson and L. E. Preston, "The Stakeholder Theory of the Corporation: Concepts, Evidence, and Implications," *Academy of Management Review* 20 (1995): 65–91.

72. D. Gilbert, "Exxon Agrees to Disclose Fracking Risks," *Wall Street Journal*, April 3, 2014, accessed, http://online.wsj.com/news/articles/SB10001424 052702303847804579479640318263438?mod =WSJ_hps_sections_management&mg=reno64-wsj.

73. M. B. E. Clarkson, "A Stakeholder Framework for Analyzing and Evaluating Corporate Social Performance," *Academy of Management Review* 20 (1995): 92–117.

74. B. Agle, R. Mitchell, and J. Sonnenfeld, "Who Matters to CEOs? An Investigation of Stakeholder Attributes and Salience, Corporate Performance, and CEO Values," *Academy of Management Journal* 42 (1999): 507–525.

75. M. Handley, "Keystone Still Faces Delays, Fierce Opposition from Green Groups," *US News & World Report*, March 7, 2013, accessed May 22, 2013, http://www.usnews.com/news /articles/2013/03/07/keystone-still-faces-delays -fierce-opposition-from-green-groups; P. Vieira, "Survey Finds Majority Backs Keystone Pipeline," *Wall Street Journal*, April 22, 2013, accessed May 22, 2013, http://online.wsj.com/article/SB10001424127 887323735604578438471635120616.html.

76. E. W. Orts, "Beyond Shareholders: Interpreting Corporate Constituency Statutes," *George Washington Law Review* 61 (1992): 14–135.

77. A. B. Carroll, "A Three-Dimensional Conceptual Model of Corporate Performance," *Academy of Management Review* 4 (1979): 497–505.

78. Ibid.

79. J. Owens, "Biz Break: CEO Con Mattrick Leaves Zynga in 'Clear Firing,' Founder Mark Pincus Returns to Helm," Paradise Post, April 8, 2015, accessed April 11, 2015, http://www.paradisepost .com/general-news/20150408/biz-break-ceo-don -mattrick-leaves-zynga-in-clear-firing-founder -mark-pincus-returns-to-helm; R. Greenfield, "Zynga Reminds Us to Be Careful What We Wish For," *Fortune*, April 10, 2015, accessed April 26, 2015, http://fortune.com/2015/04/10/zynga-mark -pincus-gaming/; S. Dredge, "Zynga Founder Mark Pincus Back in Charge as CEO Don Mattrick Steps Down," *The Guardian*, April 9, 2015, accessed April 26, 2015, http://www.theguardian.com /technology/2015/apr/09/zynga-mark-pincus-don -mattrick-social-games.

80. D. Yadron and J. Lublin, "Symantec Fires Another CEO—Struggling Antivirus Software Maker Boots Second Chief in Less than Two Years," *Wall Street Journal*, March 21, 2014, B1.

81. J. Lublin and M. Murrary, "CEOs Leave Faster Than Ever Before as Boards, Investors Lose Patience," *Wall Street Journal Interactive*, October 27, 2000.

82. "Fewer CEOs of Large U.S. Companies Lost Their Job in 2013, Contributing to Record Tenure," The Conference Board, April 9, 2014, accessed June 22, 2014, https://www.conference-board.org /press/pressdetail.cfm?pressid=5152.

83. R. Bender, "Secret Dairy Cartel Ends in $204 Million of Fines," Wall Street Journal, March 13, 2015, B1.

84. S. Banjo, "Wal-Mart will Tie Executive Pay to Compliance Overhaul," *Wall Street Journal*, April 23, 2014, B8.

85. D. Barstow, "Wal-Mart Hushed Up a Vast Mexican Bribery Case," *The New York Times*, April 21, 2012, accessed June 22, 2014, http://www.nytimes .com/2012/04/22/business/at-wal-mart-in-mexico -a-bribe-inquiry-silenced.html?pagewanted=all.

86. M. Bustillo, "Wal-Mart Faces Risk in Mexican Bribe Probe," *Wall Street Journal*, April 23, 2012, B1.

87. S. Banjo, "Wal-Mart will Tie Executive Pay to Compliance Overhaul," *Wall Street Journal*, April 23, 2014, B8.

88. "JPMorgan Chase Offers Relief Following Hurricane Sandy," *Business Wire*, November 1, 2012, accessed May 22, 2013, http://www.businesswire .com/news/home/20121101006246/en/JPMorgan -Chase-Offers-Relief-Hurricane-Sandy; G. Szalai, "Time Warner to Donate $1 Million for Hurricane Sandy Relief Efforts," *The Hollywood Reporter*, November 2, 2012, accessed May 22, 2013, http:// www.hollywoodreporter.com/news/hurricane-sandy -time-warner-donates-million-401982; A. Stonich, "How Outdoor Gear Companies Helped Hurricane Sandy Relief Efforts," *Beyond the Edge-National Geographic Adventure Blog*, December 13, 2012, accessed May 22, 2013, http://adventureblog .nationalgeographic.com/2012/12/13/how-outdoor -gear-companies-helped-hurricane-sandy-relief -efforts/.

89. J. Bennett, "GM Now Says It Detected Ignition Switch Problem Back in 2001," *Wall Street Journal*, March 12, 2014, accessed June 4, 2014, http://online.wsj.com/news/articles/SB10001424052 702304914904579435171004763740?KEYWORDS.

90. Ibid.

91. J. Bennett and S. Hughes, "New Details Emerge in GM Cobalt Recall," *Wall Street Journal*, March 24, 2014, accessed June 4, 2014, http:// online.wsj.com/news/articles/SB1000142405270230 3949704579459783108376974?KEYWORDS=jeff +bennett&mg=reno64-wsj.

92. J. Bennett, "GM Now Says It Detected Ignition Switch Problem Back in 2001. J. White and J. Bennett, "Some at GM Brass Told of Cobalt Woe," *Wall Street Journal*, April 11, 2014, accessed June 4, 2014, http://online.wsj.com/news/articles/SB100014 24052702303873604579495592901143598?KEYW ORDS=jeff+bennett&mg=reno64-wsj.

93. C. Duhigg, "In China, Human Costs Are Built into an iPad," *New York Times*, January 25, 2012, accessed February 28, 2012, http://www.nytimes .com/2012/01/26/business/ieconomy-apples-ipad -and-the-human-costs-for-workers-in-china.html? pagewanted=all; H. Perlberg and T. Culpan, "Apple Says Fair Labor Association Began Foxconn Inspection," *Bloomberg Businessweek*, February 14, 2012, accessed February 28, 2012, http://www.bloomberg .com/news/2012-02-13/apple-says-fair-labor -association-will-inspect-suppliers-including-foxconn .html; J. Stern, "Foxconn, Apple, and the Fair Labor Association Respond to ABC News' Exclusive Report," *ABCNews*, February 22, 2012, accessed February 28, 2012, http://abcnews.go.com/blogs /technology/2012/02/foxconn-apple-and-the-fair-labor -association-respond-to-abc-news-exclusive-report/.

94. M. Negishi and M. Falconi, "Novartis Replaces Top Management in Japan," *Wall Street Journal*, April 3, 2014, accessed June 4, 2014, http://online .wsj.com/news/articles/SB10001424052702303035327 04579478620558665270?mod=WSJ_hps_sections _management&mg=reno64-wsj.

95. Ibid.

96. D. Kesmodel, J. Bunge, and A. Gasparro, "McDonald's to Curb Antibiotics Use," *Wall Street Journal*, March 5, 2015, B1, B2.

97. A. McWilliams and D. Siegel, "Corporate Social Responsibility: A Theory of the Firm Perspective," *Academy of Management Review* 26, no.1 (2001): 117–127; H. Haines, "Noah Joins Ranks of Socially Responsible Funds," *Dow Jones News Service*, October 13, 1995. A meta-analysis of 41 different studies also found no relationship between corporate social responsibility and profitability. Though not reported in the meta-analysis, when confidence intervals are placed around its average sample-weighted correlation of .06, the lower confidence interval includes zero, leading to the conclusion that there is no relationship between

corporate social responsibility and profitability. See M. Orlitzky, "Does Firm Size Confound the Relationship Between Corporate Social Responsibility and Firm Performance?" *Journal of Business Ethics* 33 (2001): 167–180; S. Ambec and P. Lanoie, "Does It Pay to Be Green? A Systematic Overview," *Academy of Management Perspectives*, 22 (2008): 45–62.

98. M. Orlitzky, "Payoffs to Social and Environmental Performance," *Journal of Investing* 14 (2005): 48–51.

99. M. Orlitzky, F. Schmidt, and S. Rynes, "Corporate Social and Financial Performance: A Meta-analysis," *Organization Studies* 24 (2003): 403–441.

100. Orlitzky, "Payoffs to Social and Environmental Performance."

101. J. Millman, "After Cutting Cigarettes, CVS Is Encouraging Other Pharmacies to Do the Same," *Washington Post*, October 20, 2014, accessed April 13, 2015, http://www.washingtonpost.com/blogs/wonkblog/wp/2014/10/20/after-cutting-tobacco-sales-cvs-is-pressuring-other-pharmacies-to-do-the-same/; T. Martin and M. Esterl, "CVS to Stop Selling Cigarettes," *Wall Street Journal*, February 4, 2014, accessed April 13, 2015, http://www.wsj.com/articles/SB10001424052702304851104579363520905849600; H. Stuart, "CVS's Cigarette Ban Appears to Have Boosted Sales," *Huffington Post*, November 4, 2014, accessed April 13, 2015, http://www.huffingtonpost.com/2014/11/04/cvs-cigarettes-sales_n_6101086.html.

102. Orlitzky, Schmidt, and Rynes, "Corporate Social and Financial Performance."

103. "GM Offers Big Discounts to Boost Volt Sales," Fox News, September 24, 2012, accessed May 24, 2013, http://www.foxnews.com/leisure/2012/09/24/gm-offers-big-discounts-to-boost-volt-sales; P. Lienert & B. Woodall, "GM Planning Lower-Priced Version of 2016 Chevy Volt," *Reuters*, April 8, 2014, accessed June 22, 2014, http://www.reuters.com/article/2014/04/08/us-autos-gm-volt-idUSBREA371XW20140408; M. Maynard, "Stunner: GM May Be Losing $50,000 on Each Chevrolet Volt," *Forbes*, September 10, 2012, accessed May 24, 2013, http://www.forbes.com/sites/michelinemaynard/2012/09/10/stunner-gm-may-be-losing-50000-on-each-chevrolet-volt/; B. Woodall, P. Lienert, and B. Klayman, "Insight: GM's Volt: The Ugly Math of Low Sales, High Costs," *Reuters*, September 10, 2012, accessed May 24, 2013, http://www.reuters.com/article/2012/09/10/us-generalmotors-autos-volt-idUSBRE88904320120910. "GM to Suspend Volt Production for 4 Weeks This Summer," *Petoskey News*, April 13, 2015, accessed April 13, 2015, http://www.petoskeynews.com/news/business/gm-to-suspend-volt-production-for-weeks-this-summer/article_6429471f-8537-5722-9d89-09fc17881ca8.html; D. Shepardson, "Chevy Volt Sales Fall 30% in November," *Detroit News*, December 2, 2014, accessed April 13, 2015, http://www.detroitnews.com/story/business/autos/general-motors/2014/12/02/gm-chevrolet-volt-sales/19776623/.

5

1. L. A. Hill, *Becoming a Manager: Master a New Identity* (Boston: Harvard Business School Press, 1992).

2. L. Lazo, "VRE Kicks Off Major Expansion Plan with New Spotsylvania Station," *Washington Post*, April 18, 2015, accessed April 26, 2015, http://www.washingtonpost.com/local/trafficandcommuting/vre-kicks-off-major-expansion-plan-with-a-new-spotsylvania-county-stop/2015/04/18/63576394-e1f8-11e4-b510-962fcfabc310_story.html.

3. E. A. Locke and G. P. Latham, *A Theory of Goal Setting & Task Performance* (Englewood Cliffs, NJ: Prentice Hall, 1990).

4. M. E. Tubbs, "Goal-Setting: A Meta-Analytic Examination of the Empirical Evidence," *Journal of Applied Psychology* 71 (1986): 474–483.

5. J. Bavelas and E. S. Lee, "Effect of Goal Level on Performance: A Trade-Off of Quantity and Quality," *Canadian Journal of Psychology* 32 (1978): 219–240.

6. D. Turner, "Ability, Aspirations Fine, But Persistence Is What Gets Results," *Seattle Times*, February 13, 2005, http://community.seattletimes.nwsource.com/archive/?date=20030215&slug=dale15m.

7. I. Wladawsky-Berger, "Managing Innovation Requires Unique Leaders and Goals," *Wall Street Journal*, August 25, 2013, accessed June 5, 2014, http://blogs.wsj.com/cio/2013/08/25/managing-innovation-requires-unique-leaders-and-goals/?KEYWORDS=achieving+goals.

8. C. C. Miller, "Strategic Planning and Firm Performance: A Synthesis of More Than Two Decades of Research," *Academy of Management Performance* 37 (1994): 1649–1665.

9. H. Mintzberg, "Rethinking Strategic Planning: Part I: Pitfalls and Fallacies," *Long Range Planning* 27 (1994): 12–21, and "Part II: New Roles for Planners," 22–30; H. Mintzberg, "The Pitfalls of Strategic Planning," *California Management Review* 36 (1993): 32–47.

10. S. Berfield and L. Rupp, "The Aging of Abercrombie & Fitch: Behind the Decline of Abercrombie & Fitch and the Fall of Its Mastermind, Michael Jeffries," *BloombergBusiness*, January 22, 2015, accessed April 26, 2015, http://www.bloomberg.com/news/features/2015-01-22/the-aging-of-abercrombie-fitch-i58ltcqx; L. Rupp, "Abercrombie's Next CEO Needs to Revamp Outdated Brand, Again," *Bloomberg Business*, December 9, 2014, accessed April 26, 2015, http://www.bloomberg.com/news/articles/2014-12-10/abercrombies-next-ceo-will-have-to-revamp-outdated-brand-again.

11. Mintzberg, "The Pitfalls of Strategic Planning."

12. P. Sonne and P. Evans, "The $1.6 Billion Grocery Flop: Tesco Poised to Quit US," *Wall Street Journal*, December 6, 2012, accessed May 24, 2013, http://www.wsj.com/articles/SB10001424127887324640104578160514192695162.

13. Locke and Latham, *A Theory of Goal Setting & Task Performance*.

14. A. King, B. Oliver, B. Sloop, and K. Vaverek, *Planning & Goal Setting for Improved Performance: Participant's Guide* (Cincinnati, OH: Thomson Executive Press, 1995).

15. M. Prior, "Lafly: P&G Getting into Shape," *WWD*, February 20, 2015, p. 9, *P&G 2014 Annual Report*, accessed April 26, 2015, http://www.pginvestor.com/interactive/lookandfeel/4004124/PG_Annual_Report_2014.pdf; J. Hawkins, "Procter & Gamble Looking to Trim Its Brand Portfolio by Exiting over 100 Brands," *Mainenewsonline*, February 23, 2015, accessed April 26, 2015, http://mainenewsonline.com/content/15022993-procter-gamble-looking-trim-its-brand-portfolio-exiting-over.

16. Ibid.

17. Ibid.

18. C. Loomis, J. Schlosser, J. Sung, M. Boyle, and P. Neering, "The 15% Delusion: Brash Predictions about Earnings Growth Often Lead to Missed Targets, Battered Stock, and Creative Accounting—and That's When Times Are Good," *Fortune*, February 5, 2001, 102; H. Paster, "Manager's Journal: Be Prepared," *Wall Street Journal*, September 24,

2001, A24; P. Sellers, "The New Breed: The Latest Crop of CEOs Is Disciplined, Deferential, Even a Bit Dull," *Fortune*, November 18, 2002, 66; H. Klein and M. Wesson, "Goal and Commitment and the Goal-Setting Process: Conceptual Clarification and Empirical Synthesis," *Journal of Applied Psychology* 84 (1999): 885–896.

19. Locke and Latham, *A Theory of Goal Setting & Task Performance*.

20. J. Light, "Facebook's Early Buyers Burned, Too," *Wall Street Journal*, June 7, 2012, accessed May 24, 2013, http://online.wsj.com/article/SB10001424052702303506404577448651877204794.html; E. Rustle, "The Facebook IPO, One Year Later," *Wall Street Journal*, May 17, 2013, B1.

21. A. Bandura and D. H. Schunk, "Cultivating Competence, Self-Efficacy, and Intrinsic Interest Through Proximal Self-Motivation," *Journal of Personality & Social Psychology* 41 (1981): 586–598.

22. Locke and Latham, *A Theory of Goal Setting & Task Performance*.

23. M. J. Neubert, "The Value of Feedback and Goal Setting over Goal Setting Alone and Potential Moderators of This Effect: A Meta-Analysis," *Human Performance* 11 (1998): 321–335.

24. E. H. Bowman and D. Hurry, "Strategy Through the Option Lens: An Integrated View of Resource Investments and the Incremental-Choice Process," *Academy of Management Review* 18 (1993): 760–782.

25. "How Design Thinking Transformed Airbnb from a Failing Startup to a Billion Dollar Business," *Design Magazine*, 2014, http://firstround.com/review/How-design-thinking-transformed-Airbnb-from-failing-startup-to-billion-dollar-business/.

26. M. Lawson, "In Praise of Slack: Time Is of the Essence," *Academy of Management Executive* 15 (2000): 125–135.

27. B. Morris, "Union Pacific's Full Steam Ahead," *Wall Street Journal*, April 18, 2014, accessed June 5, 2014, http://blogs.wsj.com/corporate-intelligence/2014/04/18/union-pacifics-full-steam-ahead/?mod=WSJBlog&mod=WSJ_corp_intel.

28. M. Prior, "Lafley: P&G Getting into Shape," *WWD*, February 20, 2015, p. 9; C. Hymowitz and L. Coleman-Lochner, "Lafley Pivots from Builder to Demolition Man as He Shrinks P&G," *Bloomberg News*, April 14, 2015, accessed April 27, 2015, http://www.bloomberg.com/news/articles/2015-04-14/lafley-pivots-from-builder-to-demolition-man-as-he-shrinks-p-g.

29. J. C. Collins and J. I. Porras, "Organizational Vision and Visionary Organizations," *California Management Review* (Fall 1991): 30–52.

30. Ibid.

31. J. Dulski, "Jennifer Dulski of Change.org, on Problem-Solving," interview by A. Bryant, *New York Times*, November 30, 2013, accessed June 5, 2014, http://www.nytimes.com/2013/12/01/business/jennifer-dulski-of-changeorg-on-problem-solving.html?ref=business.

32. Collins and Porras, "Organizational Vision and Visionary Organizations"; J. A. Pearce II, "The Company Mission as a Strategic Goal," *Sloan Management Review* (Spring 1982): 15–24.

33. "President Bush Announces New Vision for Space Exploration Program," The White House, accessed April 17, 2005, http://www.whitehouse.gov/news/releases/2004/01/20040114-1.html.

34. E. Musk, "The Secret Tesla Motors Master Plan (just between you and me)," *Tesla Motors* (blog), August 2, 2006, accessed June 5, 2014, http://www.teslamotors.com/blog/secret-tesla-motors-master-plan-just-between-you-and-me.

35. J. Boudreau, "Tesla Motors begins delivering Model S electric cars in a Silicon Valley milestone,"

San Jose Mercury News, June 22, 2012, accessed June 5, 2014, http://www.mercurynews.com/business/ci_20919722/silicon-valley-milestone-tesla-motors-begins-delivering-model?refresh=no.

36. D. Choy, "Tesla Model X Release Date Early 2015: Price Estimated Just Under $70,000," *LA Times*, June 17, 2014, accessed June 23, 2014, http://www.latintimes.com/tesla-model-x-release-date-early-2015-price-estimated-just-under-70000-report-182247; N. Bilton, "Disruptions: The Echo Chamber of Silicon Valley," *New York Times*, June 2, 2013, accessed June 5, 2014, http://bits.blogs.nytimes.com/2013/06/02/disruptions-the-echo-chamber-of-silicon-valley/.

37. A. Gasparro, "McDonald's to Ax More Under-performing Stores," *Wall Street Journal*, April 22, 2015, accessed April 27, 2015, http://www.wsj.com/articles/mcdonalds-reports-steeper-profit-drop-1429704778.

38. Ibid.

39. M. Sparkes, "McDonald's Will Allow Customers to Build Their Own Burgers," *The Telegraph*, December 10, 2014, accessed April 27, 2015, http://www.telegraph.co.uk/technology/news/11284762/McDonalds-will-allow-customers-to-customise-burgers.html.

40. I. Brat, "McDonald's to Test Expanded Breakfast Hours," *Wall Street Journal*, March 30, 2015, accessed April 27, 2015, http://www.wsj.com/articles/mcdonalds-to-test-expanded-breakfast-hours-1427757395.

41. R. Smith and G. Tabbing, "Why Radical Transparency Is Good Business," *HBR Blog Network*, October 11, 2012, accessed May 25, 2013, https://hbr.org/2012/10/why-radical-transparency-is-good-business.

42. A. Bryant, "Transparency Is Much More Than a Buzzword," *New York Times*, March 2, 2013, accessed May 14, 2013, http://www.nytimes.com/2013/03/03/business/ryan-smith-of-qualtrics-on-building-a-transparent-culture.html?_r=0.

43. T. Mann, and V. McGrane, "GE to Cash Out of Banking Business," *Wall Street Journal*, April 11, 2015, A1.

44. S. McCartney, "Inside an Airline's Winter War Room," *Wall Street Journal*, February 5, 2015, D1.

45. J. Paterson, "Presenteeism on the Rise Among UK Workforce," *Employee Benefits*, May 2013, 3.

46. S. Shellenbarger, "The Art of Calling in Sick—Or Not," *Wall Street Journal*, October 12, 2012, D1.

47. S. McCartney, "The Trouble with Keeping Commercial Flights Clean," *Wall Street Journal*, September 18, 2014, D1.

48. N. Humphrey, "References a Tricky Issue for Both Sides," *Nashville Business Journal* 11 (May 8, 1995): 1A.

49. K. R. MacCrimmon, R. N. Taylor, and E. A. Locke, "Decision Making and Problem Solving," in *Handbook of Industrial & Organizational Psychology*, ed. M. D. Dunnette (Chicago: Rand McNally, 1976), 1397–1453.

50. L. Weber, "Businesses Use New Apps for Workplace Scheduling," *Wall Street Journal*, September 15, 2013, accessed June 23, 2014, http://online.wsj.com/news/articles/SB10001424127887324139404579017193724502688?mg=reno64-wsj.

51. MacCrimmon, Taylor, and Locke, "Decision Making and Problem Solving."

52. G. Kress, "The Role of Interpretation in the Decision Process," *Industrial Management* 37 (1995): 10–14.

53. M. Esterl, "Coke Chief's Solution for Lost Fizz: More Soda," *Wall Street Journal*, March 19, 2015, A1, A12.

54. L. Weber, "Businesses Use New Apps for Workplace Scheduling," *Wall Street Journal*,

September 15, 2013, accessed June 23, 2014, http://online.wsj.com/news/articles/SB10001424127887324139404579017193724502688?mg=reno64-wsj.

55. "New-Vehicle Ratings Comparison by Car Category," *ConsumerReports.org*, February 19, 2005, http://www.consumerreports.org/cro/cars/index.htm.

56. P. Djang, "Selecting Personal Computers," *Journal of Research on Computing in Education* 25 (1993): 327.

57. "European Cities Monitor," *Cushman & Wakefield*, 2010, http://www.europeancitiesmonitor.eu/wp-content/uploads/2010/10/ECM-2010-Full-Version.pdf.

58. J. Stiff, "6 Tips to Build Your Social Media Strategy," *CIO*, May 8, 2013, accessed May 26, 2013, http://www.cio.com/article/732975/6_Tips_to_Build_Your_Social_Media_Strategy.

59. "The Critical Role of Teams," *The Ken Blanchard Companies*, March 23, 2006, accessed June 5, 2014, http://www.kenblanchard.com/img/pub/pdf_critical_role_teams.pdf.

60. I. L. Janis, *Groupthink* (Boston: Houghton Mifflin, 1983).

61. C. P. Neck and C. C. Manz, "From Groupthink to Teamthink: Toward the Creation of Constructive Thought Patterns in Self-Managing Work Teams," *Human Relations* 47 (1994): 929–952; J. Schwartz and M. L. Wald, "'Groupthink' Is 30 Years Old, and Still Going Strong," *New York Times*, March 9, 2003, 5.

62. J. McIntosh, "Assumptions of Quality Could Hinder Group Decision-Making Ability," *Medical News Today*, March 10, 2015, accessed April 27, 2015, http://www.medicalnewstoday.com/articles/290618.php.

63. A. Mason, W.A. Hochwarter, K.R. Thompson, "Conflict: An Important Dimension in Successful Management Teams," *Organizational Dynamics* 24 (1995): 20.

64. D. Merrill, "Corner Office: Douglas Merrill of ZestFinance: Steer Clear of What You Can't Measure," interview by A. Bryant, March 20, 2014, accessed June 5, 2014, http://www.nytimes.com/2014/03/21/business/douglas-merrill-of-zestfinance-steer-clear-of-what-you-cant-measure.html.

65. J. Freeman, "The Soul of a Hedge Fund 'Machine,'" *Wall Street Journal*, June 6, 2014, accessed June 24, 2014, http://online.wsj.com/articles/james-freeman-the-soul-of-a-hedge-fund-machine-1402094722.

66. A. Mason, W. A. Hochwarter, and K. R. Thompson, "Conflict: An Important Dimension in Successful Management Teams," *Organizational Dynamics* 24 (1995): 20.

67. R. Cosier and C. R. Schwenk, "Agreement and Thinking Alike: Ingredients for Poor Decisions," *Academy of Management Executive* 4 (1990): 69–74.

68. K. Jenn and E. Mannix, "The Dynamic Nature of Conflict: A Longitudinal Study of Intragroup Conflict and Group Performance," *Academy of Management Journal* 44, no. 2 (2001): 238–251; R. L. Priem, D. A. Harrison, and N. K. Muir, "Structured Conflict and Consensus Outcomes in Group Decision Making," *Journal of Management* 21 (1995): 691–710.

69. A. Van De Ven and A. L. Delbecq, "Nominal versus Interacting Group Processes for Committee Decision Making Effectiveness," *Academy of Management Journal* 14 (1971): 203–212.

70. P. Gilbert, "Hearing Every Voice in the Room: How IBM Brings Ideas Forward from Its Teams," *New York Times*, December 6, 2014, BU8.

71. A. R. Dennis and J. S. Valicich, "Group, Sub-Group, and Nominal Group Idea Generation: New

Rules for a New Media?" *Journal of Management* 20 (1994): 723–736.

72. R. B. Gallupe, W. H. Cooper, M. L. Grise, and L. M. Bastianutti, "Blocking Electronic Brainstorms," *Journal of Applied Psychology* 79 (1994): 77–86.

73. E. Bernstein, "Speaking Up Is Hard to Do: Researchers Explain Why," *Wall Street Journal*, February 7, 2012, accessed May 27, 2013, http://online.wsj.com/article/SB10001424052970204136404577207020525853492.html.

74. R. B. Gallupe and W. H. Cooper, "Brainstorming Electronically," *Sloan Management Review*, Fall 1993, 27–36.

75. Ibid.

76. G. Kay, "Effective Meetings through Electronic Brainstorming," *Management Quarterly* 35 (1995): 15.

6

1. "Microsoft Surface Usage Share Takes Slight Dip in Early 2014," Chitika, May 20, 2014, accessed June 24, 2014, http://chitika.com/insights/2014/surface-over-time D. Resinger, "What Caused the Tablet Sales Slowdown of Q4 2014," eWeek, February 3, 2015, 11.

2. iPad Usage Share Rises Since July, Drops Slightly Year-over-Year," Chitika, November 6, 2014, accessed April 27, 2015, https://chitika.com/insights/2014/q4-tablet-update.

3. J. Barney, "Firm Resources and Sustained Competitive Advantage," *Journal of Management* 17 (1991): 99–120; J. Barney, "Looking Inside for Competitive Advantage," *Academy of Management Executive* 9 (1995): 49–61.

4. D. Bailey, "Is It Time to Say Goodbye to Netbooks?" *The Motley Fool*, April 30, 2011, accessed March 1, 2012, http://www.fool.com/investing/general/2011/04/30/is-it-time-to-say-goodbye-to-netbooks.aspx; S. Lohr, "Netbooks Lose Status as Tablets Like the iPad Rise," *New York Times*, February 13, 2011, accessed March 1, 2012, http://www.nytimes.com/2011/02/14/technology/14netbook.html?pagewanted=all.

5. C. Arther, "Netbooks Plummet While Tablets and Smartphones Soar, Says Canalys," *The Guardian* (technology blog), February 3, 2012 (5:38), accessed June 5, 2014, http://www.theguardian.com/technology/blog/2012/feb/03/netbooks-pc-canalys-tablet.

6. D. Pogue, "Just How Many Android Tablet Apps Are There?" *New York Times*, July 1, 2011, accessed March 2, 2012, http://pogue.blogs.nytimes.com/2011/07/01/mystery-how-many-android-tablet-apps/.

7. B. Snyder, "Tech's Bottom Line," InfoWorld, April 17, 2015, http://www.infoworld.com/article/2910323/mobile-security/for-android-adware-is-the-threat-not-malware.html; "One in Six Android Apps Is a Malware, Says Study," The Times of India, April 23, 2015, http://timesofindia.indiatimes.com/tech/tech-news/One-in-six-Android-apps-is-a-malware-says-study/articleshow/47021326.cms.

8. 2015 Data Breach Investigations Report, Verizon Enterprise Solutions, p. 18, accessed April 27, 2015, http://www.verizonenterprises.com/DBIR/2015/.

9. J. Newman, "In Defense of Google Music," *Time*, February 24, 2012, accessed March 1, 2012, http://techland.time.com/2012/02/24/in-defense-of-google-music/; D. Pogue, "A Look at Apple's iCloud," *New York Times*, October 13, 2011, accessed March 1, 2012, http://pogue.blogs.nytimes.com/2011/10/13/a-look-at-icloud/; B. Stone, "Will Amazon's Cloud Music Service Fly?" *Bloomberg Businessweek*, March 31, 2011, accessed March 1,

2012, http://www.businessweek.com/magazine/content/11_15/b4223043644684.htm.

10. D. MacMillan and T. Demos, "Spotify Nears Deal to Raise $400 Million at $8.4 Billion Valuation," *Wall Street Journal*, April 10, 2015, accessed April 27, 2015, http://www.wsj.com/articles/spotify-nears-deal-to-raise-400-million-at-8-4-billion-valuation-1428700668; E. Blattberg, "Apple Has Nearly 800 Million iTunes Accounts," *Venture Beat*, April 23, 2014, accessed April 27, 2015, http://venturebeat.com/2014/04/23/apple-has-nearly-800-million-itunes-accounts/.

11. S. Hart and C. Banbury, "How Strategy-Making Processes Can Make a Difference," *Strategic Management Journal* 15 (1994): 251–269.

12. R. A. Burgelman, "Fading Memories: A Process Theory of Strategic Business Exit in Dynamic Environments," *Administrative Science Quarterly* 39 (1994): 24–56; R. A. Burgelman and A. S. Grove, "Strategic Dissonance," *California Management Review* 38 (Winter 1996): 8–28.

13. E. Byron and J. Lublin, "Lackluster Avon Explores Makeover," *Wall Street Journal*, April 27, 2015, accessed April 28, 2015, http://www.wsj.com/articles/lackluster-avon-explores-makeover-1430188201?KEYWORDS=avon.

14. Ibid.

15. J. Lublin and E. Byron, "Avon Explores Strategic Alternatives: Options Include Possible Sale of Struggling North America Business," Wall Street Journal, April 14, 2015, accessed April 27, 2015, http://www.wsj.com/articles/avon-explores-strategic-alternatives-1429030371; S. Mitchell, "Sephora to Open Stores in Australia," *Financial Review*, April 8, 2014, accessed April 27, 2015, http://www.afr.com/business/sephora-to-open-stores-in-australia-20140408-ix7ac; R. Duprey, "Why Procter & Gamble Company Is Shedding Its Cosmetics Business," The Motley Fool.com, April 23, 2015, accessed April 27, 2015, http://www.fool.com/investing/general/2015/04/23/putting-lipstick-on-a-pig-ma-heats-up-in-beauty-ca.aspx.

16. E. Byron and J. Lublin, "Lackluster Avon Explores Makeover."

17. R. A. Burgelman and A. S. Grove, "Strategic Dissonance," *California Management Review* 38 (Winter 1996): 8–28.

18. Y. Koh, "Airline Learns to Be Nimble—Starting Up Budget Carriers Helped All Nippon Restructure Its Own Operations," *Wall Street Journal*, May 23, 2013, B8.

19. J. Mahler, "For SkyMall, It All Seemed So Cool at Six Miles High," *The New York Times*, January 23, 2015, accessed April 28, 2015, http://www.nytimes.com/2015/01/24/business/it-all-seemed-so-cool-at-six-miles-high.html?_r=0.

20. A. Fiegenbaum, S. Hart, and D. Schendel, "Strategic Reference Point Theory," *Strategic Management Journal* 17 (1996): 219–235.

21. "Consumer Reports Automaker Report Cards 2012: Subaru Drives into Top Spot as Honda Slips," *Sacramento Bee*, March 1, 2012, accessed March 1, 2012, http://www.sacbee.com/2012/02/28/4297509/consumer-reports-automaker-report.html.

22. B. Gottesman, "The Tech Brands You Trust Most," *PC Magazine*, October 2011, 30–43.

23. S. Clifford, "Where Wal-Mart Failed, Aldi Succeeds," *New York Times*, March 29, 2011, accessed March 1, 2012, http://www.nytimes.com/2011/03/30/business/30aldi.html?pagewanted=all.

24. A. Fiegenbaum and H. Thomas, "Strategic Groups as Reference Groups: Theory, Modeling and Empirical Examination of Industry and Competitive Strategy," *Strategic Management Journal* 16 (1995): 461–476.

25. "HIRI/IHS Global Insight for 2014 up 4.0%, Expecting 5.7% Sales Growth in 2015," Home Improvement Research Institute, March 2, 2015, accessed April 23, 2015, http://www.hiri.org/.

26. R. K. Reger and A. S. Huff, "Strategic Groups: A Cognitive Perspective," *Strategic Management Journal* 14 (1993): 103–124.

27. "Interconnecting—Delivering a Seamless Customer Experience," 2014 Home Depot Annual Report, accessed April 23, 2015, http://www.homedepotar.com/; "Never Stop Improving," 2014 Lowe's Annual Report, accessed April 23, 2015, http://phx.corporate-ir.net/phoenix.zhtml?c=95223&p=irol-IRHome.

28. "Frequently Asked Questions," Ace Hardware, accessed May 31, 2013, http://www.acehardware.com/corp/index.jsp?page=faq.

29. "About Aubuchon Hardware," accessed April 23, 2015, http://www.hardwarestore.com/corporate.aspx.

30. "Frequently Asked Questions," Ace Hardware, accessed July 29, 2008, http://www.acehardware.com/corp/index.jsp?page=faq; "Company History: 2010s," Ace Hardware, accessed June 5, 2014, http://www.acehardware.com/category/index.jsp?categoryId=34641526.

31. "History of 84 Lumber," accessed April 23, 2015, http://www.84lumber.com/About/History.aspx.

32. J. Mangalindan, "eBay's Back!" *Fortune*, February 5, 2013, 58–65.

33. Ibid.

34. Ibid.

35. G. Bensinger, "eBay's New Goal: Double Its Users," *Wall Street Journal*, March 29, 2013, B5.

36. M. Lubatkin, "Value-Creating Mergers: Fact or Folklore?" *Academy of Management Executive* 2 (1988): 295–302; M. Lubatkin and S. Chatterjee, "Extending Modern Portfolio Theory into the Domain of Corporate Diversification: Does It Apply?" *Academy of Management Journal* 37 (1994): 109–136; M. H. Lubatkin and P. J. Lane, "Psst… The Merger Mavens Still Have It Wrong!" *Academy of Management Executive* 10 (1996): 21–39.

37. "Science Applied to Life, Annual Report 2014," 3M, accessed April 28, 2015, http://investors.3m.com/files/doc_financials/2014/ar/2014_3M_Annual_Report.pdf.

38. P. Morris, "Why Warren Buffett Just Bought Duracell," Money, November 14, 2014, , accessed April 28, 2015, http://time.com/money/3585592/warren-buffett-duracell/; P. Ziobro and E. Byron, "P7G to Unload Duracell as CEO Lafley Focuses on Best Sellers," Wall Street Journal, October 14, 2014, accessed April 28, 2015, http://online.wsj.com/articles/p-g-to-exit-duracell-battery-ops-1414149781; "Mars to Buy Most of P&G's Pet Food Business for $2.9 Billion," Reuters.com, April 9, 2014, accessed April 28, 2015, http://uk.reuters.com/article/2014/04/09/uk-mars-pgpetcare-acquisition-idUKBREA3813B20140409.

39. All Products, GE, accessed April 22, 2015, http://www.ge.com/products.

40. "Affiliated Companies," Samsung, accessed April 7, 2011, http://www.samsung.com/levant/aboutsamsung/samsung/affiliatedcompanies.html.

41. http://www.bcg.com/about/heritage/default.aspx.

42. D. Hambrick, I. MacMillan, and D. Day, "Strategic Attributes and Performance in the BCG Matrix—A PIMS-based Analysis of Industrial Product Businesses," *Academy of Management Journal* 25 (1982): 510–531.

43. J. Armstrong and R. Brodie, "Effects of Portfolio Planning Methods on Decision Making: Experimental Results," *International Journal of Research in Marketing* 11 (1994): 73–84.

44. M. Rogowsky, "Microsoft Office: Could the Cash Cow's Long-Awaited Death Finally Be Imminent," *Forbes*, May 5, 2014, accessed April 28, 2015, http://www.forbes.com/sites/markrogowsky/2014/05/05/microsoft-office-could-the-cash-cows-long-awaited-death-finally-be-imminent/.

45. "Up-to-Date Program for Pages, Numbers, and Keynote," Apple, accessed April 28, 2015, https://www.apple.com/creativity-apps/mac/up-to-date/; T. Green, "What did Microsoft's Earnings Reveal about Its Biggest Cash Cow?" *The Motley Fool*, April 30, 2014, accessed April 28, 2015, http://www.fool.com/investing/general/2014/04/30/microsofts-stellar-quarter-was-driven-by-office.aspx.

46. S. Ovide, "Microsoft Outperforms Its Low Growth Expectations," *Wall Street Journal*, April 24, 2015, B4.

47. J. A. Pearce II, "Selecting among Alternative Grand Strategies," *California Management Review* (Spring 1982): 23–31.

48. "AT&T to Buy DirecTV for $48.5 Billion," CBS News, May 18, 2014, accessed June 24, 2014, http://www.cbsnews.com/news/at-t-to-buy-directv-for-49-billion/.

49. M. Reardon, "AT&T Defends Benefits of Proposed DirecTV Merger," cNet, June 24, 2014, accessed June 24, 2014, http://www.cnet.com/news/at-t-defends-benefits-of-proposed-directv-merger/.

50. M. Laycock, "Aero Sales Help York Nestle Factory in Tough Year," *The Press*, December 31, 2011, accessed March 2, 2012, http://www.yorkpress.co.uk/news/9446032.Aero_sales_help_York_factory_in_tough_year/; T. Mulier, "Breathing More Profit into Chocolate Bars," *Bloomberg Businessweek*, February 24, 2011, accessed March 2, 2012, http://www.businessweek.com/magazine/content/11_10/b4218021563564.htm; "Nestle Reports £6.5bn Annual Profit," *The Independent*, February 16, 2012, accessed March 2, 2012, http://www.independent.co.uk/news/business/news/nestle-reports-65bn-annual-profit-6977817.html.

51. "ABM Launches New Brand," ABM Industries, accessed May 31, 2013, http://www.abm.com/about-abm/pages/our-new-brand.aspx.

52. J. A. Pearce II, "Retrenchment Remains the Foundation of Business Turnaround," *Strategic Management Journal* 15 (1994): 407–417.

53. "Goldsmith Bankers," *Encyclopedia of Money*, accessed June 25, 2014, http://encyclopedia-of-money.blogspot.com/2010/03/goldsmith-bankers.html; "Timeline | 1690: The Start of Barclays," Barclays Plc, accessed June 25, 2014, http://www.barclays.com/about-barclays/history.html.

54. M. Colchester and D. Enrich, "Barclays Dashes Its Global Dreams—U.K. Lender to Cut Investment Bank Nearly in Half as Expansion Efforts Falter; 'Bold Simplification,'" *Wall Street Journal*, May 9, 2014, C1.

55. M. Berry, "Barclays to Axe 14,000 Jobs and Create 'Bad Bank,'" FundWeb, May 8, 2014, accessed June 25, 2014, http://www.fundweb.co.uk/news-and-analysis/uk/barclays-to-axe-14000-jobs-and-create-bad-bank/2009986.article.

56. S. Ovide, "A Price War Erupts in Cloud Services," *Wall Street Journal*, April 15, 2014, accessed June 25, 2014, http://online.wsj.com/news/articles/SB10001424052702303887804579503713914245756.

57. D. Gallagher, "Cloud Investing Beyond Amazon, Google and Microsoft," *Wall Street Journal*, April 15, 2014, accessed June 25, 2014, http://online.wsj.com/news/articles/SB100014240527023038878045795039035972657 52#printMode.

58. S. Ovide, "Cisco Set to Take on Amazon in the Cloud," *Wall Street Journal*, March 24, 2014, B1; A. Spencer, "H-P Sets $1 Billion for 'Cloud' Investment," *Wall Street Journal*, May 7, 2014, B6.

59. A. Kessler, "The Weekend Interview with Travis Kalanick: The Transportation Trustbuster," *Wall Street Journal*, January 26, 2013, A13.

60. C. Henshaw, "Australia Farmers Look to Bypass Trading Companies," *Wall Street Journal*, May 30, 2013, accessed June 1, 2013, http://online .wsj.com/article/SB1000142412788732441260457585 14740822671524.html.

61. B. Tuttle, "Meet the Low-Key, Low-Cost Grocery Chain Being Called 'Walmart's Worst Nightmare,'" *Time*, August 7, 2013, accessed June 25, 2014, http://business.time.com/2013/08/07 /meet-the-low-key-low-cost-grocery-chain-being -called-wal-marts-worst-nightmare/.

62. J. Springer, "Pricing: WinCo Keeps Costs Down and Velocity High," *Super Market News*, April 29, 2013, accessed June 25, 2014, http:// supermarketnews.com/retail-amp-financial/pricing -winco-keeps-costs-down-and-velocity-high.

63. B. Tuttle, "Meet the Low-Key, Low-Cost Grocery Chain Being Called 'Walmart's Worst Nightmare,'" *Time*, August 7, 2013, accessed June 25, 2014, http://business.time.com/2013/08/07 /meet-the-low-key-low-cost-grocery-chain-being -called-wal-marts-worst-nightmare/.

64. "Norweb Microfiber," Norwex, accessed June 26, 2014, http://www.norwex.biz/pws/home 2999999/tabs/microfiber.aspx.

65. E. Byron, "It Cleans, Polishes and Scrubs: It's a $27 Cloth and Water," *Wall Street Journal*, June 25, 2014, D1.

66. "'Our Purpose' Can One Person Change the World? At Norwex—We Think We Can," Norwex, accessed June 26, 2014, http://www.norwex.biz/pws /home2999999/tabs/our-purpose.aspx.

67. Pirate Joe's, , accessed April 28, 2015, http:// www.piratejoes.ca/.

68. C. Dawson, "This Pirate Sells Treasures from Trader Joe's to Canadians: Retailer Drives to US to Stock Up on Grocer's Goodies, Nuts, Coffee, Maple Syrup," *Wall Street Journal*, March 7, 2015, accessed April 28, 2015, http://www.wsj.com/articles /pirate-joes-sells-treasures-from-trader-joes-to -canadians-1425660654.

69. R. E. Miles and C. C. Snow, *Organizational Strategy, Structure, & Process* (New York: McGraw-Hill, 1978); S. Zahra and J. A. Pearce, "Research Evidence on the Miles-Snow Typology," *Journal of Management* 16 (1990): 751–768; W. L. James and K. J. Hatten, "Further Evidence on the Validity of the Self Typing Paragraph Approach: Miles and Snow Strategic Archetypes in Banking," *Strategic Management Journal* 16 (1995): 161–168.

70. W. Boston, "Porsche Tries to Remain Exclusive as Luxury Demand Surges," *Wall Street Journal*, March 17, 2015, http://www.wsj.com/articles /porsche-tries-to-keep-itself-exclusive-as-luxury -demand-surges-1426591087.

71. L. Carlozo, "How Does Walmart's VUDU Movie Streaming Service Stack Up?" *Deal News*, August 3, 2012, accessed June 1, 2013, http://dealnews.com /features/How-Does-Walmarts-VUDU-Movie -Streaming-Service-Stack-Up-/598146.html; D. Kerr, "Redbox Instant Launches Video Streaming to the Public," *cNet*, March 14, 2013, accessed June 1, 2013, http://news.cnet.com/8301-1023_3-57574480 -93/redbox-instant-launches-video-streaming-to-the -public; D. Pogue, "Potluck for the Eyeballs: Amazon's Streaming Service," *New York Times*, August 29, 2012, accessed June 1, 2013, http://www.nytimes .com/2012/08/30/technology/personaltech/amazons -streaming-movie-service-offers-its-own-potluck -state-of-the-art.html?pagewanted=all.

72. C. Katje, "Amazon vs. Netflix: Battle to Become Streaming King Heats Up," *Variety*, August 2, 2013, accessed June 5, 2014. http://

variety.com/2013/biz/news/amazon-turning-svod -space-into-a-two-company-race-1200571585/; M. Shields and D. MacMillan, "Yahoo Makes New Push into Video Content," *Wall Street Journal*, April 6, 2014, accessed June 5, 2014, http://online .wsj.com/news/articles/SB10001424052702304819 00457948582061082406?mg=reno64-wsj.

73. W. Boston, "In Luxury Race, Profits Get Dented," *Wall Street Journal*, March 13, 2015, B1.

74. M. Chen, "Competitor Analysis and Interfirm Rivalry: Toward a Theoretical Integration," *Academy of Management Review* 21 (1996): 100–134; J. C. Baum and H. J. Korn, "Competitive Dynamics of Interfirm Rivalry," *Academy of Management Journal* 39 (1996): 255–291.

75. M. Chen, "Competitor Analysis and Interfirm Rivalry: Toward a Theoretical Integration," Academy of Management Review 21 (1996): 100–124.

76. C. Giammona and L. Patton, "Playing Chicken in the Burger Wars," *BloombergBusiness*, January 19–25, 2015, pp. 28–29.

77. J. White, "Wendy's Wendy Gets a Makeover," *Wall Street Journal*, October 11, 2012, accessed June 5, 2014. http://blogs.wsj.com/corporate -intelligence/2012/10/11/wendy/?KEYWORDS =wendy%27s+strategy.

78. "Wendy's Plans to Double Pace of Image Activation Reimages in 2014," *Yahoo! Finance*, February 27, 2014, accessed June 5, 2014, http:// finance.yahoo.com/news/wendys-plans-double -pace-image-123613973.html.

79. A. Gasparro, "McDonald's New Chief Plots Counter Attack," *Wall Street Journal*, March 2, 2015, B1.

80. L. Lavelle, "The Chickens Come Home to Roost, and Boston Market Is Prepared to Expand," *The Record*, October 6, 1996.

81. "2015 Franchise 500—Subway," *Entrepreneur*, accessed April 28, 2015, http://www.entrepreneur .com/franchises/subway/282839-0.html; accessed April 28, 2015, http://www.subway.com/subwayroot /ExploreOurWorld.aspx; I. Brat, "Jamba Plans to Sell 100 Stores," *Wall Street Journal*, April 2, 2015, B2; "Company Profile—McDonald's Is Global— And in Your Hometown," accessed April 23, 2015, http://www.aboutmcdonalds.com/mcd/investors /company_profile.html.

82. "Frequently Asked Questions," Subway Restaurants, accessed March 18, 2009, http://www .subway.com/ContactUs/CustServFAQs.aspx.

83. B. Heater, "Amazon Kindle Paperwhite Hands-on (Update: video)," *Engadget*, September 6, 2012, accessed June 5, 2014, http://www.engadget.com /2012/09/06/amazon-kindle-paperwhite-hands-on/.

84. S. Buckley, "Nook Simple Touch with GlowLight gets another $20 price drop, undercuts competition," *Engadget*, August 18, 2013, accessed June 5, 2014, http://www.engadget.com/2013/08/18/nook-simple -touch-with-glowlight-gets-another-20-price-drop/.

85. J. Volpe, "E Ink's New Higher Contrast Carta Display Is the Secret behind Amazon's Refreshed Kindle Paperwhite," *Engadget*, September 4, 2013, accessed June 5, 2014, http://www.engadget.com /2013/09/04/e-ink-new-higher-contrast-carta -display-amazon-kindle-paperwhite/.

86. D. Ketchen, Jr., C. Snow, and V. Street, "Improving Firm Performance by Matching Strategic Decision-Making Processes to Competitive Dynamics," *Academy of Management Executive* 18 (2004): 29–43.

87. M. Gottfried, "T-Mobile's Shine Dims Sprint's Deal Hopes," *Wall Street Journal*, March 1, 2014, B14.

88. M. Gottfried, "T-Mobile Takes Toll on Verizon," *Wall Street Journal*, April 25, 2014, C8; E. Mason, "T-Mobile's Loss Widens as Costs Press Higher," *Wall Street Journal*, February 26, 2014, B4; T Gryta & B.

Rubin, "T-Mobile Posts Big Gain in Subscribers," *Wall Street Journal*, May 1, 2014, accessed June 26, 2014, http://online.wsj.com/news/articles/SB1000142 4052702304677904579535291254065308.

89. Z. Epstein, "The Most Important Wireless Carrier in America," *BGR*, October 10, 2013, accessed June 26, 2014, http://bgr.com/2013/10/10/t -mobile-free-international-roaming-analysis/; T. Gryta, "T-Mobile will Waive Data Fees for Music Services," *Wall Street Journal*, June 18, 2014, accessed June 26, 2014, http://online.wsj.com/articles/t-mobile-will -waive-data-fees-for-music-service-1403142678.

90. J. Hagerty and K. Linebaugh, "GE, Caterpillar Face Off in Hot Locomotive Market," *Wall Street Journal*, April 11, 2012, accessed June 1, 2013, http://www.wsj.com/articles/SB10001424052702304 17710457730766329291178

91. K. Linebaugh, "GE to Cut Back Trains," *Wall Street Journal*, April 9, 2013, accessed June 1, 2013, http://www.wsj.com/articles/SB10001424127887324 50470457841303413639849

92. C. Boulton, "Amazon's Fire Phone Aims For 'Showrooming on Steroids' - The CIO Report," Wall Street Journal, June 19, 2014, accessed April 28, 2015, http://blogs.wsj.com/cio/2014/06/19/amazons -fire-phone-aims-for-showrooming-on-steroids/.

93. Associate Press, "Best Buy's Store Closing List: Is Yours on It?" *CBS News*, April 16, 2012, accessed June 1, 2013, http://www.cbsnews.com/8301 -505144_162-57414517/best-buys-store-closing-list -is-yours-on-it/; G. Bensinger, "When Apps Attack: Industries Under Pressure," *Wall Street Journal*, March 27, 2013, accessed June 1, 2013, http:// online.wsj.com/article/SB1000142412788732439280 457835879340982629.html; M. Bustle, "Best Buy Pays Price to Rival Amazon," *Wall Street Journal*, December 14, 2011, accessed June 1, 2013, http:// online.wsj.com/article/SB1000142405297020351 840457709616025252732.html; A. Zimmerman, "Can Electronics Stores Survive?" *Wall Street Journal*, August 20, 2012, accessed June 1, 2013, http://www.wsj.com/articles/SB1000087239639044 77280457762158173940190.6.

7

1. J. Tierney, "A Hearing Aid That Cuts Out All the Clatter," *New York Times*, October 23, 2011, accessed May 2, 2012, http://www.nytimes.com /2011/10/24/science/24loops.html.

2. P. Anderson and M. L. Tushman, "Managing Through Cycles of Technological Change," *Research/Technology Management*, May–June 1991, 26–31.

3. R. N. Foster, *Innovation: The Attacker's Advantage* (New York: Summit, 1986).

4. "The Silicon Engine: A Timeline of Semiconductors in Computers," Computer History Museum, accessed April 22, 2001, http://www.computer history .org/semiconductor/; "The Evolution of a Revolution," Intel, accessed June 2, 2013, http://download. intel.com/pressroom/kits/IntelProcessorHistory .pdf; T. Smith, "Inside Intel's Haswell: What do 1.4 BEELION transistors get you?" *The Register*, June 3, 2013, accessed June 13, 2014, http://www .theregister.co.uk/2013/06/03/feature_inside _haswell_intel_4g_core/; "Intel Xeon E5-2600 v3 Processor Overview," *PC Perspective*, September 8, 2014, accessed April 25, 2015, http://www.pcper .com/reviews/Processors/Intel-Xeon-E5-2600-v3 -Processor-Overview-Haswell-EP-18-Cores.

5. J. Burke, *The Day the Universe Changed* (Boston: Little, Brown, 1985).

6. D. Wakabayashi, "The Point-and-Shoot Camera Faces Its Existential Moment," *Wall Street Journal*,

July 30, 2013, accessed June 30, 2014, http://online .wsj.com/news/articles/SB10001424127887324251504578580263719432252.

7. J. Osawa, "Phones Imperil Fancy Cameras," *Wall Street Journal*, November 7, 2013, accessed June 13, 2014, http://online.wsj.com/news/articles/SB10001424052702304672404579186436962368 68?KEYWORDS=high-end+camera&mg=reno64 -wsj.

8. "HTC Talks Camera Tech: DSLR-Destroying Optical Zooming '18 Months' Away," *Official Vodafone UK blog* (blog), April 18, 2014, accessed June 13, 2014, http://blog.vodafone.co.uk/2014 /04/18/htc-talks-camera-tech-optical-zooming/; J. Osawa, "Are Camera Apps Enough for Photo Enthusiasts?" *Wall Street Journal*, November 8, 2013, accessed June 13, 2014, http://blogs.wsj.com /digits/2013/11/08/are-camera-apps-enough-for -photo-enthusiasts/?KEYWORDS=dslr+camera.

9. M. L. Tushman, P. C. Anderson, and C. O'Reilly, "Technology Cycles, Innovation Streams, and Ambidextrous Organizations: Organization Renewal Through Innovation Streams and Strategic Change," in *Managing Strategic Innovation and Change*, ed. M. L. Tushman and P. Anderson (New York: Oxford Press, 1997), 3–23.

10. L. Grush, "Magnetically Levitating Elevators Could Reshape Skylines—They Go Up, Down, and All Around," *Popular Science*, April 14, 2015, accessed April 26, 2015, http://www.popsci.com /elevator-will-reshape-skylines; "ThyssenKrupp Develops the World's First Rope-Free Elevator System to Enable the Building Industry to Face the Challenges of Global Urbanization," ThyssenKrupp, November 27, 2014, accessed May 4, 2015, http:// www.thyssenkrupp-elevator.com/Show-article.104.0 .html?&L=1&cHash=08b38cb686f00ec874ad82c44 c737427&tx_ttnews%5Btt_news%5D=546.

11. S. J. Blumberg and J. V. Luke, "Wireless Substitution: Early Release of Estimates from the National Health Interview Survey, January–June 2014," US Department of Health and Human Services, Centers for Disease Control and Prevention, December 2014, accessed April 25, 2015, http://www.cdc.gov/nchs/data/nhis/earlyrelease /wireless201412.pdf.

12. Staff, "Landline Phone Penetration Dwindles as Cell-Only Households Grow," Marketing Charts, June 6, 2012, accessed June 2, 2013, http://www .marketingcharts.com/direct/landline-phone -penetration-dwindles-as-cell-only-households -grow-22577/.

13. S. J. Blumberg and J. V. Luke, "Wireless Substitution: Earl Release of Estimates from the National Health Interview Survey, January–June 2014."

14. "AT&T, Verizon Are Leaving Landlines Behind," *Wall Street Journal News Hub*, online video, 17:27, April 8, 2014, accessed June 13, 2014, http://live.wsj.com/video/att-verizon-are-leaving -landlines-behind/7874152B-A635-4092-9B7B -69EB86AE3787.html?KEYWORDS=milestones #!7874152B-A635-4092-9B7B-69EB86AE3787.

15. R. Knutson, "Who Needs a Wireless Carrier? Go Wi-Fi Only," Wall Street Journal, March 2, 2015, B1.

16. Ibid.

17. E. Schlossberg, *Interactive Excellence: Defining and Developing New Standards for the Twenty-First Century* (New York: Ballantine, 1998).

18. W. Abernathy and J. Utterback, "Patterns of Industrial Innovation," *Technology Review* 2 (1978): 40–47.

19. D. Howley, "Wireless Charging Standard Gets One Step Closer," *Laptop Magazine*, February 1, 2014, accessed July 1, 2014, as reported at http://

www.techhive.com/article/2096802/wireless-charging -alliances-teaming-up-to-work-toward-a-cable -free-world.html.

20. "Wireless Charging Surge Seen," *Investor's Business Daily*, March 24, 2014, A02.

21. R. Jones, "Wireless Races to Define 5G," *Wall Street Journal*, March 10, 2015, B7.

22. M. Schilling, "Technological Lockout: An Integrative Model of the Economic and Strategic Factors Driving Technology Success and Failure," *Academy of Management Review* 23 (1998): 267–284; M. Schilling, "Technology Success and Failure in Winner-Take-All Markets: The Impact of Learning Orientation, Timing, and Network Externalities," *Academy of Management Journal* 45 (2002): 387–398.

23. R. Verrier, "Small-town Movie Theaters Threatened by Shift to Digital Cinema," *Los Angeles Times*, May 4, 2013, accessed June 2, 2013, http://articles .latimes.com/print/2013/may/04/entertainment/la-et -ct-last-picture-show-20130504.

24. T. M. Amabile, R. Conti, H. Coon, J. Lazenby, and M. Herron, "Assessing the Work Environment for Creativity," *Academy of Management Journal* 39 (1996): 1154–1184.

25. Ibid.

26. M. Csikszentmihalyi, *Flow: The Psychology of Optimal Experience* (New York: Harper & Row, 1990).

27. R. Feintzeig, "Can Furniture Help Workers Stay Focused?" *Wall Street Journal*, April 22, 2015, B7.

28. L. Emarian, "Creating Culture of IT Innovation Includes Rewarding Failure," *Computer World*, April 6, 2012, accessed June 2, 2013, http://www .computerworld.com/s/article/9225870/Creating _culture_of_IT_innovation_includes_rewarding_failure.

29. A. Ahrendts, "The Experts: How Should Leaders Spur Innovation?" interview by C. Wiens, March 12, 2013, accessed June 13, 2014, http:// online.wsj.com/news/articles/SB10001424127887323826704578352921473825316?mg=reno64-wsj&url =http%3A%2F%2Fonline.wsj.com%2Farticle %2FSB10001424127887323826704578352921473825316.html.

30. Ibid.

31. Ibid.

32. L. Kwoh, "Memo to Staff: Take More Risks," *Wall Street Journal*, March 20, 2013, accessed June 2, 2013, http://online.wsj.com/article/SB10001424127887323636904578370383939044780.html.

33. K. M. Eisenhardt, "Accelerating Adaptive Processes: Product Innovation in the Global Computer Industry," *Administrative Science Quarterly* 40 (1995): 84–110.

34. Ibid.

35. R. Fleming, "Oculus Rift Has Sold Over 85,000 Prototypes," *Digital Trends*, April 16, 2014, accessed June 13, 2014, http://www.digitaltrends.com/gaming /oculus-rift-sold-85000-prototypes/#!YqqBJ.

36. K. Naughton and J. Green, "Crash Test City," *Bloomberg Businessweek*, April 6–12, 2015, pp. 19–20.

37. A. Barr, "Google Lab Puts a Time Limit on Innovation," Wall Street Journal, April 1, 2015, B6.

38. D. Wakabayashi and M. Ramsey, "Apple Gears Up to Challenge Tesla in Electric Cars," *Wall Street Journal*, February 13, 2015, B1; T. Bradshaw, "Batteries Suit Offers Clues to Apple's Car Ambitions," *Financial Times*, February 19, 2015, accessed April 26, 2015, http://www.ft.com/intl/cms/s/0/b061736c-b874 -11e4-a2fb-00144feab7de.html#axzz3YRCCbjHx.

39. D. Gates, "McNerney: No More 'Moonshots' as Boeing Develops New Jets," *The Seattle Times*, May 22, 2014, accessed May 4, 2015, http://www.seattletimes.com/business/mcnerney -no-more-lsquomoonshotsrsquo-as-boeing -develops-new-jets/.

40. D. Gates, "McNerney: No More 'Moonshots' as Boeing Develops New Jets."; J. Ostrower, "At Boeing, Innovation Means Small Steps, Not Giant Leap," *Wall Street Journal*, April 3, 2015, B1.

41. L. Kraar, "25 Who Help the US Win: Innovators Everywhere Are Generating Ideas to Make America a Stronger Competitor. They Range from a Boss Who Demands the Impossible to a Mathematician with a Mop," *Fortune*, March 22, 1991.

42. M. W. Lawless and P. C. Anderson, "Generational Technological Change: Effects of Innovation and Local Rivalry on Performance," *Academy of Management Journal* 39 (1996): 1185–1217.

43. "USB.org—Hi-Speed FAQ," USB Implementers Forum, accessed July 1, 2014, http://www.usb .org/developers/usb20/faq20/; "USB.org—SuperSpeed USB," USB Implementers Forum, accessed July 1, 2014, http://www.usb.org/developers/ssusb/.

44. A. Vance, "Ansys Aids Innovation with Its Simulation Software," *Bloomberg Businessweek*, March 7, 2013, accessed June 2, 2013, http://www .businessweek.com/articles/2013-03-07/ansys-aids -innovation-with-its-simulation-software.

45. J. Brustein, "Inside RadioShack's Collapse— How Did the Electronics Retailer Go Broke? Gradually, Then All at Once," *Bloomberg Businessweek*, February 9–15, 2015, p. 56. "Table 13–AT&T Interstate Residential Tariff Rates for 10-Minute Calls," *The Industry Analysis Division's Reference Book of Rates, Price Indices, and Household Expenditures for Telephone Service*, March 1997, Federal Trade Commission, p. 69, accessed April 25, 2015, http://transition.fcc.gov/Bureaus/Common_Carrier /Reports/FCC-State_Link/IAD/ref97.pdf.

46. J. Brustein, "Inside RadioShack's Collapse— How Did the Electronics Retailer Go Broke? Gradually, Then All at Once."

47. P. Strebel, "Choosing the Right Change Path," *California Management Review* (Winter 1994): 29–51.

48. D. Fitzgeral and M. Jarzemsky, "Besieged RadioShack Spirals Into Bankruptcy," *Wall Street Journal*, February 6, 2015, accessed May 4, 2015, http://www.wsj.com/articles/SB218109728774777646947045804418141397517730.

49. P. Brickley and D. FitzGerald, "RadioShack Is Dead, Long Live RadioShack," *Wall Street Journal*, April 2, 2015, B1.

50. K. Lewin, *Field Theory in Social Science: Selected Theoretical Papers* (New York: Harper & Brothers, 1951).

51. J. Owen, "Film is finished - this could be its last Oscars," *The Independent*, February 24, 2013, accessed June 13, 2014, http://www.independent .co.uk/arts-entertainment/films/news/film-is -finished---this-could-be-its-last-oscars-8508257 .html?printService=print.

52. Lewin, *Field Theory in Social Science*.

53. A. B. Fisher, "Making Change Stick," *Fortune*, April 17, 1995, 121.

54. J. P. Kotter and L. A. Schlesinger, "Choosing Strategies for Change," *Harvard Business Review* (March–April 1979): 106–114.

55. S. Giessner, G. Viki, T. Otten, S. Terry, and D. Tauber, "The Challenge of Merging: Merger Patterns, Premerger Status, and Merger Support," *Personality and Social Psychology Bulletin* 32, no. 3 (2006): 339–352.

56. E. Cassano, "How Vince Donnelly Led PMA Companies Through an Acquisition by Involving Everyone," *Smart Business*, February 1, 2012, accessed March 7, 2012, http://www.sbnonline.com /article/how-vince-donnelly-led-pma-companies -through-an-acquisition-by-involving-everyone/.

57. D. Bennett, "Marriage at 30,000 Feet," *Bloomberg Businessweek*, February 6–12, 2012, 58–63.

58. D. Meinert, "An Open Book," *HR Magazine*, April 2013, 42–46.

59. J. P. Kotter, "Leading Change: Why Transformation Efforts Fail," *Harvard Business Review* 73, no. 2 (March–April 1995): 59.

60. P. Smith, "The Nokia Insider Who Knows Why It Failed Warns Apple It Could Be Next," *Financial Review*, September 6, 2013, accessed June 13, 2014, http://www.afr.com/p/technology/next_nokia_insider_who_knows_why_Z8at1lqZLp3mAutUO0ye0H.

61. Ibid.

62. G. Pitts, "A Classic Turnaround—With Some Twists," *The Globe and Mail*, July 7, 2008, B1.

63. P. Burrows, "Stephen Elop's Nokia Adventure," *Bloomberg Businessweek*, June 2, 2011, accessed June 3, 2013, http://www.businessweek.com/magazine/content/11_24/b4232056703101.htm.

64. J. Rossi, "Nokia Releases New Lumia Phone," *Wall Street Journal*, May 14, 2013, accessed June 5, 2013, http://online.wsj.com/article/SB100014241278873237163045784824822912916580.html.

65. S. Cramm, "A Change of Hearts," *CIO*, April 1, 2003, May 20, 2003, http://www.cio.com/archive/040103/hsleadership.html.

66. J. Scheck, "New Shell CEO Van Beurden Lays Out Turnaround Plan," *Wall Street Journal*, April 27, 2014, accessed July 1, 2014, http://online.wsj.com/news/articles/SB10001424052702304163604579527901868370442?KEYWORDS=Ben+van+Beurden+CEO+Royal+Dutch+Shell&mg=reno64-wsj.

67. R. N. Ashkenas and T. D. Jick, "From Dialogue to Action in GE WorkOut: Developmental Learning in a Change Process," in *Research in Organizational Change and Development*, vol. 6, ed. W. A. Pasmore and R. W. Woodman (Greenwich, CT: JAI Press, 1992), 267–287.

68. T. Stewart, "GE Keeps Those Ideas Coming," *Fortune*, August 12, 1991, 40.

69. W. J. Rothwell, R. Sullivan, and G. M. McLean, *Practicing Organizational Development: A Guide for Consultants* (San Diego, CA: Pfeiffer & Co., 1995).

70. Ibid.

8

1. "Web Table 34. Number of Parent Corporations and Foreign Affiliates, by Region and Economy," *World Investment Report 2011*, United Nations Conference on Trade and Development, accessed June 10, 2013, http://unctad.org/Sections/dite_dir/docs/WIR11_web%20tab%2034.pdf.

2. M. Scott, "Cap Gemini Agrees to Buy IGATE, Merging Rivals Focused on Tech and Outsourcing," New York Times, April 27, 2015, accessed May 5, 2015, http://www.nytimes.com/2015/04/28/business/dealbook/capgemini-agrees-to-buy-igate-for-4-billion.html.

3. L. Stevens, M. van Tartwijk, and T. Fairless, "FedEx's Priority: Bulk Up in Europe," *Wall Street Journal*, April 8, 2015, B1.

4. K. Ellis, "Mexican Import Rules Hit US Fashion Firms," *WWD*, March 3, 2015, pp. 1, 8.

5. "Govt May Hike Sugar Import Duty to 40% to Check Price Fall," *Times of India*, April 21, 2015, accessed May 5, 2015, http://timesofindia.indiatimes.com/business/india-business/Govt-may-hike-sugar-import-duty-to-40-to-check-price-fall/articleshow/47002065.cms.

6. B. Fritz and L. Burkitt, "Chinese Film Company Takes Role in Hollywood," *Wall Street Journal*, April 20, 2015, B1.

7. Reuters, "Mexico Bows to Brazilian Pressure on Auto Exports," *Reuters*, March 15, 2012, accessed June 8, 2013, http://www.reuters.com/article/2012/03/16/mexico-brazil-autos-idUSL2E5EF3G420120316.

8. "Understanding the WTO," *World Trade Organization*, accessed August 5, 2008, http://www.wto.org/english/thewto_e/whatis_e/tif_e/agrm9_e.htm.

9. "Pangasius June 2014," *Globefish*, June 2014, http://www.globefish.org/pangasius-june-2014.html; T. Tracy, "U.S. Catfish Farmers Go After Asian Rival," *Wall Street Journal*, March 24, 2015, B6.

10. T. Tracy, "U.S. Catfish Farmers Go After Asian Rival."

11. Ibid.

12. J. Wehrman, "Farm Bill's Subsidy for Sugar Under Pressure," *The Columbus Dispatch*, June 20, 2013, accessed July 2, 2014, http://www.dispatch.com/content/stories/local/2013/06/20/farm-bills-subsidy-for-sugar-under-pressure.html.

13. A. Wexler, "Big Sugar Is Set for a Sweet Bailout," *Wall Street Journal*, March 13, 2013, accessed July 2, 2014, http://online.wsj.com/news/articles/SB10001424127887324096404578356740206766164.

14. J. Wehrman, "Farm Bill's Subsidy for Sugar Under Pressure," The Columbus Dispatch, June 20, 2013, https://duckduckgo.com/?q=Farm%20Bill's%20Subsidy%20for%20Sugar%20Under%20Pressure, accessed August 25, 2015.

15. "GATT/WTO," *Duke Law: Library & Technology*, accessed June 12, 2009, https://law.duke.edu/lib/researchguides/gatt/.

16. "IFPI Publishes Digital Music Report 2013," *International Federation of the Phonographic Industry*, February 26, 2013, accessed June 8, 2013, http://www.ifpi.org/content/section_resources/dmr2013.html; P. Sonne and M. Colchester, "France, the UK Take Aim at Digital Pirates," *Wall Street Journal*, April 15, 2010, accessed June 9, 2010, http://online.wsj.com/article/SB10001424052702304604024575181820755061494.html.

17. D. Price, "Sizing the Piracy University," *Netnames*, September 2013, accessed July 2, 2014, http://www.netnames.com/sites/default/files/netnames-sizing_piracy_universe-FULLreport-sept2013.pdf.

18. "Shadow Market: 2011 BSA Global Software Piracy Study, Ninth Edition," *BSA | The Software Alliance*, May 15, 2012, accessed June 8, 2013, http://globalstudy.bsa.org/2011/downloads/study_pdf/2011_BSA_Piracy_Study-Standard.pdf.

19. C. Bialik, "Putting a Price Tag on Film Piracy," *Wall Street Journal*, April 5, 2013, accessed June 8, 2013, http://blogs.wsj.com/numbersguy/putting-a-price-tag-on-film-piracy-1228/.

20. "Countries: On the Road to EU Membership," *European Union*, accessed August 11, 2013, http://europa.eu/about-eu/countries/index_en.htm.

21. M. Villarreal and I. Ferguson, "NAFTA at 20: Overview and Trade Effects," *Congressional Research Service*, February 21, 2013, accessed June 10, 2013, http://www.fas.org/sgp/crs/row/R42965.pdf.

22. "Dominican Republic-Central America-United States Free Trade Agreement," US Department of Commerce, April 29, 2014, accessed May 5, 2015, http://export.gov/%5C/FTA/cafta-dr/index.asp.

23. "UNASUR: Union of South American Nations," *Communidad Andina*, accessed July 2, 2014, http://www.communidadandina.org/ingles/sudamerican.htm.

24. "Selected Basic ASEAN Indicators," *Association of Southeast Asian Nations*, April 30, 2014, accessed June 13, 2014, http://www.asean.org/images/resources/Statistics/2014/SelectedKeyIndicatorAsOfApril/table1_as%20of%20Apr14_upload.pdf; "Overview of ASEAN-US Dialogue Relations," *Association of Southeast Asian Nations*, accessed July 2, 2014, http://www.asean.org/news/item/overview-of-asean-us-dialogue-relations.

25. "Selected Basic ASEAN Indicators, 2005," *Association of Southeast Asian Nations*, accessed August 6, 2008, http://www.aseansec.org/stat/Table1.pdf; "Top Ten ASEAN Trade Partner Countries/Regions, 2005," *Association of Southeast Asian Nations*, accessed August 6, 2008, http://www.aseansec.org/Stat/Table20.pdf; "ASEAN Free Trade Area (AFTA)," *Association of Southeast Asian Nations*, accessed August 6, 2008, http://www.aseansec.org/12021.htm.

26. "Frequently Asked Questions," *Asia-Pacific Economic Cooperation*, accessed July 2, 2014, http://www.apec.org/FAQ.aspx/; "StatsAPEC—Data for the Asia-Pacific Region—Economic and Social Statistics & Bilateral Trade and Investment Flows," StatsAPEC, accessed July 2, 2014, http://statistics.apec.org/.

27. "Member Economies," *Asia Pacific Economic Cooperation*, accessed August 6, 2008, http://www.apec.org/About-Us/About-APEC/Member-Economies.aspx; "Frequently Asked Questions (FAQs)," *Asia-Pacific Economic Cooperation*, accessed August 6, 2008, http://www.apec.org/FAQ.aspx.

28. "Gross National Income (GNI) per Capita 2013, Atlas Method and PPP," The World Bank, April 14, 2015, accessed May 5, 2015, http://databank.worldbank.org/data/download/GNIPC.pdf.

29. Ibid.

30. "The Global Competitiveness Report: 2008–2009," *World Economic Forum*, accessed June 14, 2009, http://www.weforum.org/reports/global-competitiveness-report-2008-2009.

31. M. Yamaguchi, "Japan-US Talks on Pacific Trade Accord Get Push from 'Fast-Track' Proposal in US Congress," *US News & World Report*, April 17, 2015, accessed April 28, 2015, http://www.usnews.com/news/business/articles/2015/04/17/trade-talks-in-tokyo-get-push-from-fast-track-deal-in-us; "Commodity Policies," US Department of Agriculture, Economic Research Service, August 7, 2014, accessed April 28, 2015, http://www.ers.usda.gov/topics/international-markets-trade/countries-regions/japan/policy.aspx.

32. L. Lockwood, "Ralph's Brazilian Vibe," *WWD*, April 13, 2015, p. 2.

33. S. Schechner, "Netflix Launches in France in First Phase of Expansion," *Wall Street Journal*, September 16, 2014, B1.

34. M. Gao, "Culture Determines Business Models: Analyzing Home Depot's Failure Case in China for International Retailers from a Communication Perspective," *Thunderbird International Business Review*, March/April 2013: 173-191.

35. L. Burkitt, "Home Depot Learns Chinese Prefer 'Do-It-for-Me,'" *Wall Street Journal*, September 14, 2012, accessed June 8, 2013, http://online.wsj.com/article/SB10000872396390444433504577651072911154602.html.

36. Katie Englehart, "Starbucks Go Home," *Macleans*, January 25, 2013, accessed July 2, 2014, http://online.wsj.com/news/articles/SB10001424052702304607104579209971318755960.

37. A. Sundaram and J. S. Black, "The Environment and Internal Organization of Multinational Enterprises," *Academy of Management Review* 17 (1992): 729–757.

38. H. S. James, Jr., and M. Weidenbaum, *When Businesses Cross International Borders: Strategic Alliances & Their Alternatives* (Westport, CT: Praeger Publishers, 1993).

39. I. Brat and K. Gee, "U.S. Dairies Get Crash Course in Exporting," *Wall Street Journal*, January 9, 2015,

accessed May 5, 2015, http://www.wsj.com/articles /dairy-factory-gears-up-for-production-1420765811

40. Ibid.

41. K. Schweizer, "'Desperate Housewives' Gets Turkish Twist as Disney Looks Abroad," *Bloomberg Businessweek*, September 18, 2012, accessed June 9, 2013, http://www.bloomberg.com/news/articles /2012-09-18/-desperate-housewives-gets-turkish -twist-as-disney-looks-abroad.

42. M. Willens, "NBCUniversal to Produce American TV Shows for European Broadcasters," International Business Times, April 14, 2015, accessed April 28, 2015, http://www.ibtimes.com/nbcuniversal-produce -american-tv-shows-european-broadcasters-1881835.

43. "2015 Franchise 500—McDonald's at a Glance," Entrepreneur.com, accessed April 28, 2015, http://www.entrepreneur.com/franchises /mcdonalds/282570-0.html; "New Restaurants," McDonald's.com, accessed April 28, 2015, http:// www.aboutmcdonalds.com/mcd/franchising /us_franchising/acquiring_a_franchise.html.

44. A. Lutz, "McDonald's Franchisees Are Furious about How Much It Costs to Operate a Restaurant," *Business Insider*, August 6, 2013, accessed June 13, 2014, http://www.businessinsider.com /mcdonalds-franchise-owners-hold-meeting-2013-8.

45. K. Le Mesurier, "Overseas and Overwhelmed," *BRW*, January 25, 2007, 51.

46. P. Rana, "Dipping into India, Dunkin' Donuts Changes Menu," *Wall Street Journal*, November 28, 2014, http://online.wsj.com/articles/dipping-into -india-dunkin-donuts-changes-menu-1417211158.

47. E. Dou, "Hewlett-Packard, Foxconn Launch Joint Server Venture," *Wall Street Journal*, April 30, 2014, accessed June 13, 2014, http://online.wsj.com /news/articles/SB10001424052702303949810457953 3080961860334?mod=WSJ_hp_LEFTWhatsNews Collection&mg=reno64-wsj.

48. S. Chaudhuri, "Tesco Caps Tumultuous Year with Huge Loss," Wall Street Journal, April 22, 2015, http:// www.wsj.com/articles/tesco-reports-full-year-loss -1429683249; "Supermarket Operator Kroger Ends Joint Venture with Dunnhumby, Starts Customer Data Subsidiary," *Associated Press*, April 27, 2015, accessed May 5, 2015, http://www.foxbusiness.com /markets/2015/04/27/supermarket-operator-kroger -ends-joint-venture-with-dunnhumby-starts-customer/; S. Watkins, "Kroger Executive: Dunnhumby Sale Won't Keep Us from Data," *Cincinnati Business Courier*, March 27, 2015, accessed May 5, 2015, http:// www.bizjournals.com/cincinnati/news/2015/03/27 /kroger-executive-nothing-would-preclude-us-from .html?page=all.

49. J. R. Hagerty, "Japanese Toilet Maker Lixil Buys American Standard," June 28, 2013, accessed June 13, 2014, http://online.wsj.com/news/articles /SB10001424127887323419604578573121801745426?KEYWORDS=japanese+toilet+maker&mg =reno64-wsj.

50. P. Margot, "Standard Chartered Looks to Get Slimmer," *Wall Street Journal*, March 4, 2014, C3; P. Margot, "Standard Chartered to Sell 2 Korean Units," *Market Watch*, June 16, 2014, accessed July 2, 2014, https://secure.marketwatch.com/story/standard -chartered-to-sell-2-korean-units-2014-06-16.

51. W. Hordes, J. A. Clancy, and J. Baddaley, "A Primer for Global Start-Ups," *Academy of Management Executive*, May 1995, 7–11.

52. P. Dimitratos, J. Johnson, J. Slow, and S. Young, "Micromultinationals: New Types of Firms for the Global Competitive Landscape," *European Management Journal* 21, no. 2 (April 2003): 164; B. M. Oviatt and P. P. McDougall, "Toward a Theory of International New Ventures," *Journal of International Business Studies* (Spring 1994): 45–64; S. Zahra, "A Theory of International New Ventures:

A Decade of Research," *Journal of International Business Studies* (January 2005): 20–28.

53. B. Keplesky, "MakerBot's Bre Pettis on the Next Industrial Revolution," *Entrepreneur*, March 9, 2013, accessed June 10, 2013, http://www .entrepreneur.com/article/226044; M. Wolf, "How 3D Printing Is Now Helping NASA Get to Space," *Forbes*, January 12, 2013, accessed June 10, 2013, http://www.forbes.com/sites/michaelwolf /2013/01/12/how-3d-printing-is-now-helping-nasa -get-to-space/; "Official International MakerBot Distributors," *MakerBot*, accessed June 10, 2013, http://www.makerbot.com/distributors/.

54. "Shaping Our Future: 2014 Annual Review," Coca-Cola, accessed May 5, 2015,, http://assets. coca-colacompany.com/6c/70/b23ba5fe42bb868467 26cf4779c4/2014-year-in-review-pdf.pdf.

55. "Coca-Cola Bottle (500ml) Prices," Humuch .com, accessed May 5, 2015, http://www.humuch .com/prices/CocaCola-Bottle-20oz500ml/_____/40# .VT_FdiFVhBc.

56. "2010 Annual Report," *The Coca-Cola Company*.

57. "After a Year of Delays."

58. J. Stoll, "Volvo to Open Plant in the US," *Wall Street Journal*, March 30, 2015, accessed May 5, 2015, http://www.wsj.com/articles/volvo-to-open -plant-in-the-u-s-1427688301.

59. D. Shepardson, "Volvo Plans $500M Factory in US to Revive Sales," *The Detroit News*, March 30, 2015, accessed May 5, 2015, http://www.detroitnews .com/story/business/autos/foreign/2015/03/30/volvo -us-plant/70657920/.

60. "Tax Environment," *NFIA*, accessed June 13, 2014, http://www.nfia.com/tax.html; D. Dzombak, "The Highest Corporate Tax Rates in the World," *The Motley Fool*, March 1, 2014, accessed July 2, 2014, http://www.fool.com/investing/general/2014/03/01 /the-highest-corporate-tax-rates-in-the-world.aspx.

61. "Special Eurobarometer 386: Europeans and Their Languages," European Commission, June 2012, accessed May 5, 2015, http://ec.europa.eu/public _opinion/archives/ebs/ebs_386_en.pdf.

62. "IMD World Talent Report 2014," IMD World Competitiveness Center, November 2014, accessed May 5, 2015, http://www.imd.org/uupload/imd .website/wcc/NewTalentReport/IMD_World _Talent_Report_2014bis.pdf.

63. "Foreign Corrupt Business Practices Act," *US Department of Justice*, May 10, 2003, http://www .usdoj.gov/criminal/fraud/.

64. S. Adams, "2015's Most and Least Reliable Countries to Do Business In," *Forbes*, March 31, 2015, accessed April 28, 2015, http://www.forbes. com/sites/susanadams/2015/03/31/2015s-most-and -least-reliable-countries-to-do-business-in/; "Resilience Index," FM Global, http://www.fmglobal.com /assets/pdf/Resilience_Methodology.pdf.

65. J. Oetzel, R. Bettis, and M. Zenner, "How Risky Are They?" *Journal of World Business* 36, no. 2 (Summer 2001): 128–145.

66. K. D. Miller, "A Framework for Integrated Risk Management in International Business," *Journal of International Business Studies*, 2nd Quarter 1992, 311.

67. M. Bahree, "Foreign Retailers Regroup in India," *Wall Street Journal*, December 12, 2011, B3.

68. J. Bennett and J. Stoll, "GM's Hopes for Russia Go in Reverse," *Wall Street Journal*, March 19, 2015, pp. B1, B2; D. Levin, "GM Exits Russia," Fortune, March 27, 2015, accessed May 5, 2015, http://fortune.com/2015/03/27/gm-exits-russia/.

69. D. Levin, "GM Exits Russia."

70. "Chapter 1: Political Outlook," *UAE Business Forecast Report*, 2007, 1st Quarter, 5–10.

71. R. Roy, "Foreign Online Retailers Ask India to Allow Direct Sales," *Wall Street Journal*, February 12, 2013, accessed June 10, 2013, http://www.wsj.com /articles/SB1000142412788732488050457829945425 1603948.

72. C. Alessi, "India Invests in Germany's Family Firms," *Wall Street Journal*, April 11–12, 2015, B4.

73. G. Hofstede, "The Cultural Relativity of the Quality of Life Concept," *Academy of Management Review* 9 (1984): 389–398; G. Hofstede, "The Cultural Relativity of Organizational Practices and Theories," *Journal of International Business Studies*, Fall 1983, 75–89; G. Hofstede, "The Interaction Between National and Organizational Value Systems," *Journal of Management Studies*, July 1985, 347–357; M. Hoppe, "An Interview with Geert Hofstede," *Academy of Management Executive*, February 2004, 75–79.

74. C. Alessi, "India Invests in Germany's Family Firms."

75. Ibid.

76. Ibid.

77. R. Hodgetts, "A Conversation with Geert Hofstede," *Organizational Dynamics*, Spring 1993, 53–61.

78. T. Lenartowicz and K. Roth, "Does Subculture within a Country Matter? A Cross-Cultural Study of Motivational Domains and Business Performance in Brazil," *Journal of International Business Studies* 32 (2001): 305–325.

79. M. Koren, "Why Russians Aren't Smiling at You in Sochi," *National Journal*, February 7, 2014, accessed June 13, 2014, http://www.nationaljournal .com/politics/why-russians-aren-t-smiling-at-you-in -sochi-20140207.

80. J. S. Black, M. Mendenhall, and G. Oddou, "Toward a Comprehensive Model of International Adjustment: An Integration of Multiple Theoretical Perspectives," *Academy of Management Review* 16 (1991): 291–317; R. L. Tung, "American Expatriates Abroad: From Neophytes to Cosmopolitans," *Columbia Journal of World Business*, June 22, 1998, 125; A. Harzing, "The Persistent Myth of High Expatriate Failure Rates," *International Journal of Human Resource Management* 6 (1995): 457–475; A. Harzing, "Are Our Referencing Errors Undermining Our Scholarship and Credibility? The Case of Expatriate Failure Rates," *Journal of Organizational Behavior* 23 (2002): 127–148; N. Forster, "The Persistent Myth of High Expatriate Failure Rates: A Reappraisal," *International Journal of Human Resource Management* 8 (1997): 414–433.

81. J. Black, "The Right Way to Manage Expats," *Harvard Business Review* 77 (March–April 1999): 52; C. Joinson, "No Returns," *HR Magazine*, November 1, 2002, 70.

82. "International assignment perspectives: Critical issues facing the globally mobile workforce," *PricewaterhouseCoopers*, Vol. 5, November 2011, accessed June 13, 2014, http://www.pwc.com /en_US/us/hr-international-assignment-services /publications/assets/ny-12-0258_ias_journal_volume _5_new_images.pdf.

83. R. Feintzeig, "After Stints Abroad, Re-Entry Can Be Hard," *Wall Street Journal*, September 17, 2013, accessed June 14, 2014, http://online.wsj.com /news/articles/SB10001424127887323342404579081382781895274?KEYWORDS=after+stints+abroad &mg=reno64-wsj.

84. "Ten Examples of Cross-Cultural Blunders," *UKProEdits*, June 7, 2012, accessed June 10, 2013, http://ukproedits.com/uncategorized/ten-examples -of-cross-cultural-mistakes.

85. J. S. Black and M. Mendenhall, "Cross-Cultural Training Effectiveness: A Review and Theoretical Framework for Future Research," *Academy of Management Review* 15 (1990): 113–136.

86. K. Essick, "Executive Education: Transferees Prep for Life, Work in Far-Flung Lands," *Wall Street Journal*, November 12, 2004, A6.

87. Ibid.

88. P. W. Tam, "Culture Course—'Awareness Training' Helps US Workers Better Know Their Counterparts in India," *Wall Street Journal*, May 25, 2004, B1.

89. S. Hamm, "Aperian: Helping Companies Bridge Cultures," *BusinessWeek*, September 8, 2008, 16.

90. W. Arthur, Jr., and W. Bennett, Jr., "The International Assignee: The Relative Importance of Factors Perceived to Contribute to Success," *Personnel Psychology* 48 (1995): 99–114; B. Cheng, "Home Truths about Foreign Postings; To Make an Overseas Assignment Work, Employers Need More Than an Eager Exec with a Suitcase. They Must Also Motivate the Staffer's Spouse," *BusinessWeek Online*, accessed March 20, 2009, http://www.businessweek.com/careers/content/jul2002/ca20020715_9110.htm.

91. B. Groysberg and R. Abrahams, "A Successful International Assignment Depends on These Factors," *Harvard Business Review* (blog), February 13, 2014, 10:00, accessed June 15, 2014, http://blogs.hbr.org/2014/02/a-successful-international-assignment-depends-on-these-factors/.

92. "OAI: Overseas Assignment Inventory," *Prudential Real Estate and Relocation Services Intercultural Group*, May 11, 2011, http://www.performanceprograms.com/self-assessments/work-across-cultures/overseas-assignment-inventory/.

93. S. P. Deshpande and C. Viswesvaran, "Is Cross-Cultural Training of Expatriate Managers Effective? A Meta-Analysis," *International Journal of Intercultural Relations* 16, no. 3 (1992): 295–310.

94. D. M. Eschbach, G. Parker, and P. Stoeberl, "American Repatriate Employees' Retrospective Assessments of the Effects of Cross-Cultural Training on Their Adaptation to International Assignments," *International Journal of Human Resource Management* 12 (2001): 270–287; "Culture Training: How to Prepare Your Expatriate Employees for Cross-Cultural Work Environments," *Managing Training & Development*, February 1, 2005.

95. I. Driscoll, "You Love Going Abroad for Work. Your Spouse Hates It." BBC, November 11, 2014, accessed May 5, 2015, http://www.bbc.com/capital/story/20141110-the-reluctant-expat-spouse.

96. Ibid.

9

1. M. Lia, "Thomson Reuters Restructures," *Wall Street Journal*, September 28, 2011, accessed June 12, 2013, http://www.wsj.com/articles/SB10001424052970204138204576598671601828928; "Annual Review 2013," *Thomson Reuters*, accessed June 16, 2013, https://ar.thomsonreuters.com/financial-performance; "Know–Annual Report 2014," Thomson Reuters, March 13, 2015, accessed May 5, 2015, http://ir.thomsonreuters.com/phoenix.zhtml?c=76540&p=irol-irhome.

2. M. Hammer and J. Champy, *Reengineering the Corporation: A Manifesto for Business Revolution* (New York: Harper & Row, 1993).

3. J. Mick, "Windows 8 Public 'Consumer Preview' Beta Is Live," *Daily Tech*, February 29, 2012, accessed March 11, 2012, http://www.dailytech.com/Windows+8+Public+Consumer+Preview+Beta+is+Live/article24123.htm; J. Mick, "Microsoft's Windows 10 Now Has Over 2 Million Public Testers," Daily Tech, January 28, 2015, accessed May 1, 2015, http://www.dailytech.com/Microsofts+Windows+10+Now+Has+Over+2+Million+Public+Testers/article37113.htm.

4. J. G. March and H. A. Simon, *Organizations* (New York: John Wiley & Sons, 1958).

5. M. Isaac, "EBay to Cut 2,400 Jobs, and Weighs 2nd Spinoff," *New York Times*, January 22, 2015, B4.

6. "At a Glance," UTC, accessed July 7, 2014, http://www.utc.com/Our-Businesses/Pages/At-A-Glance.aspx#bis.

7. *United Technologies 2014 Annual Report*, accessed April 30, 2015, http://2014ar.utc.com/assets/pdfs/UTCAR2014_FullReport.pdf.

8. "Structure—Group Structure & Corporate Management," *Swisscom AG*, accessed June 16, 2014, http://www.swisscom.ch/en/about/company/structure.html.

9. *Anheuser-Busch InBev Annual Report 2014*, accessed April 30, 2015, http://www.ab-inbev.com/content/dam/universaltemplate/abinbev/pdf/investors/annual-and-hy-reports/2014/AB_InBev_AR14_EN_full.pdf.

10. Ibid.

11. Ibid.

12. Business Wire, "Procter & Gamble Announces Organization Changes," *Motley Fool*, June 5, 2013, accessed July 7, 2014, http://www.fool.com/investing/businesswire/2013/06/05/procter-gamble-announces-organization-changes.aspx; "P&G Annual Report 2014, accessed April 30, 2015, http://www.pginvestor.com/interactive/lookandfeel/4004124/PG_Annual_Report_2014.pdf; "Strength in Structure," P&G, accessed May 5, 2015, http://www.pg.com/en_US/company/global_structure_operations/corporate_structure.shtml.

13. Ibid.

14. L. R. Burns, "Adoption and Abandonment of Matrix Management Programs: Effects of Organizational Characteristics and Interorganizational Networks," *Academy of Management Journal* 36 (1993): 106–138.

15. H. Fayol, *General and Industrial Management*, trans. C. Storrs (London: Pitman Publishing, 1949).

16. M. Weber, *The Theory of Social and Economic Organization*, trans. and ed. A. M. Henderson and T. Parsons (New York: Free Press, 1947).

17. Fayol, *General and Industrial Management*.

18. C. Zillman, "With Co-CEOs, Companies Flirt with Disaster," *Fortune*, September 20, 2014, accessed May 1, 2015, http://fortune.com/2014/09/20/oracle-two-ceos-disaster/; M. Chan, "Ellison Was the Longest-Tenured Tech CEO. Who Is Now?" *BloombergBusinessweek*, September 9, 2014, accessed May 1, 2015, http://www.bloomberg.com/news/2014-09-19/ellison-was-the-longest-tenured-tech-ceo-who-is-it-now-.html.

19. A. Lashinsky, "Inside Apple, from Steve Jobs Down to the Janitor: How America's Most Successful—and Most Secretive—Big Company Really Works," *Fortune*, May 23, 2011, 125–134.

20. H. Gayle, "Corner Office: Helene Gayle of CARE, on Managers as Dual citizens," interview by A. Bryant, *New York Times*, June 22, 2013, accessed June 16, 2014, http://www.nytimes.com/2013/06/23/business/helene-gayle-of-care-on-managers-as-dual-citizens.html?_r=1&.

21. J. Jargon, "McDonald's Plans to Change U.S. Structure," *Wall Street Journal*, October 20, 2014, accessed May 5, 2015, http://www.wsj.com/articles/mcdonalds-to-change-u-s-structure-1414695278.

22. E. E. Lawler, S. A. Mohrman, and G. E. Ledford, *Creating High Performance Organizations: Practices and Results of Employee Involvement and Quality Management in Fortune 1000 Companies* (San Francisco: Jossey-Bass, 1995).

23. Y. Kubota, "Toyota Unveils Revamped Manufacturing Process," *Wall Street Journal*, March 26, 2015, accessed May 1, 2015, http://www.wsj.com/articles/toyota-unveils-revamped-manufacturing-process-1427371432.

24. "Economists Notebook: Hospitality Employee Turnover Rose in 2014," National Restaurant Association, March 11, 2015, accessed May 1, 2015, http://www.restaurant.org/News-Research/News/Hospitality-employee-turnover-rose-in-2014.

25. R. W. Griffin, *Task Design* (Glenview, IL: Scott, Foresman, 1982).

26. F. Herzberg, *Work and the Nature of Man* (Cleveland, OH: World Press, 1966).

27. R. Hackman and G. R. Oldham, *Work Redesign* (Reading, MA: Addison-Wesley, 1980).

28. T. Burns and G. M. Stalker, *The Management of Innovation* (London: Tavistock, 1961).

29. Hammer and Champy, *Reengineering the Corporation*.

30. Ibid.

31. J. D. Thompson, *Organizations in Action* (New York: McGraw-Hill, 1967).

32. G. James, "World's Worst Management Fads," *Inc.*, May 10, 2013, accessed May 1, 2015 http://www.inc.com/geoffrey-james/worlds-worst-management-fads.html.

33. J. B. White, "'Next Big Thing': Re-Engineering Gurus Take Steps to Remodel Their Stalling Vehicles," *Wall Street Journal Interactive*, November 26, 1996.

34. C. Tuna, "Remembrances: Champion of 'Re-Engineering' Saved Companies, Challenged Thinking," *Wall Street Journal*, September 6, 2008, A12.

35. G. M. Spreitzer, "Individual Empowerment in the Workplace: Dimensions, Measurement, and Validation," *Academy of Management Journal* 38 (1995): 1442–1465.

36. D. Vidalon and P. Denis, "Carrefour Bets on Store Bosses in French Revamp," cNBC, March 12, 2013, accessed July 8, 2014, http://article.wn.com/view/2013/03/12/Carrefour_bets_on_store_bosses_in_French_revamp/.

37. K. W. Thomas and B. A. Velthouse, "Cognitive Elements of Empowerment," *Academy of Management Review* 15 (1990): 666–681.

38. C. Gallo, "How Wegmans, Apple Store and Ritz-Carlton Empower Employees to Offer Best-in-Class Service," *Retail Customer Experience*, December 27, 2012, accessed June 12, 2013, http://www.retailcustomerexperience.com/article/205849/How-Wegmans-Apple-Store-and-Ritz-Carlton-empower-employees-to-offer-best-in-class-service.

39. K. D. Backer and S. Miroudot (2013), "Mapping Global Value Chains," *OECD Trade Policy Papers*, No. 159, OECD Publishing, December 19, 2013, accessed July 8, 2014, http://dx.doi.org/10.1787/5k3v1trgnbr4-en.

40. W. Bulkeley, "New IBM Jobs Can Mean Fewer Jobs Elsewhere," *Wall Street Journal*, March 8, 2004, B1.

41. H. Thomas, "Pharma Companies' Cost Cuts Could Be a Tonic for Quintiles," *Wall Street Journal*, December 21, 2013, B14.

42. C. C. Snow, R. E. Miles, and H. J. Coleman, Jr., "Managing 21st Century Network Organizations," *Organizational Dynamics*, Winter 1992, 5–20.

43. J. H. Sheridan, "The Agile Web: A Model for the Future?" *Industry Week*, March 4, 1996, 31.

10

1. B. Dumaine, "The Trouble with Teams," *Fortune*, September 5, 1994, 86–92.

2. K. C. Stag, E. Salas, and S. M. Fiore, "Best Practices in Cross Training Teams," in *Workforce Cross Training Handbook*, ed. D. A. Nembhard (Boca Raton, FL: CRC Press), 156–175.

3. M. Marks, "The Science of Team Effectiveness," *Psychological Science in the Public Interest* (December 2006): pi–i.

4. J. R. Katzenbach and D. K. Smith, *The Wisdom of Teams* (Boston: Harvard Business School Press, 1993).

5. S. G. Cohen and D. E. Bailey, "What Makes Teams Work: Group Effectiveness Research from the Shop Floor to the Executive Suite," *Journal of Management* 23, no. 3 (1997): 239–290.

6. S. E. Gross, *Compensation for Teams* (New York: American Management Association, 1995); B. L. Kirkman and B. Rosen, "Beyond Self-Management: Antecedents and Consequences of Team Empowerment," *Academy of Management Journal* 42 (1999): 58–74; G. Stalk and T. M. Hout, *Competing Against Time: How Time-Based Competition Is Reshaping Global Markets* (New York: Free Press, 1990); S. C. Wheelwright and K. B. Clark, *Revolutionizing New Product Development* (New York: Free Press, 1992).

7. D. A. Harrison, S. Mohamed, J. E. McGrath, A. T. Florey, and S. W. Vanderstoep, "Time Matters in Team Performance: Effects of Member Familiarity, Entrainment, and Task Discontinuity on Speed and Quality," *Personnel Psychology* 56, no. 3 (August 2003): 633–669.

8. R. Parsons, "Barclays Seeks 'Voice of Customer' for Rebuilding Efforts," *Marketing Week*, September 20, 2013, 12.

9. M. Iqbal, "Blog Archives: Barclays Bank," The Customer & Leadership Blog, May 9, 2014, accessed July 8, 2014, http://thecustomerblog.co.uk/tag/barclays-bank/.

10. R. D. Banker, J. M. Field, R. G. Schroeder, and K. K. Sinha, "Impact of Work Teams on Manufacturing Performance: A Longitudinal Field Study," *Academy of Management Journal* 39 (1996): 867–890.

11. "Entire Organization Rallies to Improve Product Ratings, Sales," *Bazaarvoice*, accessed May 21, 2011, http://www.bazaarvoice.com/resources/case-studies/entire-organization-rallies-improve-product-ratings-sales.

12. J. L. Cordery, W. S. Mueller, and L. M. Smith, "Attitudinal and Behavioral Effects of Autonomous Group Working: A Longitudinal Field Study," *Academy of Management Journal* 34 (1991): 464–476; T. D. Wall, N. J. Kemp, P. R. Jackson, and C. W. Clegg, "Outcomes of Autonomous Workgroups: A Long-Term Field Experiment," *Academy of Management Journal* 29 (1986): 280–304.

13. "Great Little Box Company: A Team Approach to Success," *Industry Canada*, May 7, 2012, accessed June 13, 2013, http://www.ic.gc.ca/eic/site/061.nsf/eng/rd02456.html.

14. R. Silverman, "At Zappos, Some Employees Find Offer to Leave Too Good to Refuse," *Wall Street Journal*, May 7, 2015, accessed May 8, 2015, http://www.wsj.com/articles/at-zappos-some-employees-find-offer-to-leave-too-good-to-refuse-1431047917?KEYWORDS=zappos.

15. R. Liden, S. Wayne, R. Jaworski, and N. Bennett, "Social Loafing: A Field Investigation," *Journal of Management* 30 (2004): 285–304.

16. J. George, "Extrinsic and Intrinsic Origins of Perceived Social Loafing in Organizations," *Academy of Management Journal* 35 (1992): 191–202.

17. T. T. Baldwin, M. D. Bedell, and J. L. Johnson, "The Social Fabric of a Team-Based M.B.A. Program: Network Effects on Student Satisfaction and Performance," *Academy of Management Journal* 40 (1997): 1369–1397.

18. K. H. Price, D. A. Harrison, and J. H. Gavin, "Withholding Inputs in Team Contexts: Member Composition, Interaction Processes, Evaluation Structure and Social Loafing," *Journal of Applied Psychology* 91(6) (2006): 1375–1384.

19. L. P. Tost, F. Gino, and R. P. Larrick, "When Power Makes Others Speechless: The Negative Impact of Leader Power on Team Performance," *Academy of Management Journal* 35, no. 5, October 1, 2013, 1465–1486, accessed June 16, 2014, http://amj.aom.org/content/56/5/1465.

20. C. Joinson, "Teams at Work," *HR Magazine*, May 1, 1999, 30.

21. R. Wageman, "Critical Success Factors for Creating Superb Self-Managing Teams," *Organizational Dynamics* 26, no. 1 (1997): 49–61.

22. R. Etherington, "Audi Announces New Design Strategy," *Dezeen*, December 19, 2012, accessed June 13, 2013, http://www.dezeen.com/2012/12/19/audi-announces-new-car-design-strategy/.

23. Kirkman and Rosen, "Beyond Self-Management: Antecedents and Consequences of Team Empowerment."

24. K. Kelly, "Managing Workers Is Tough Enough in Theory. When Human Nature Enters the Picture, It's Worse," *BusinessWeek*, October 21, 1996, 32.

25. S. Easton and G. Porter, "Selecting the Right Team Structure to Work in Your Organization," in *Handbook of Best Practices for Teams*, vol. 1, ed. G. M. Parker (Amherst, MA: Irwin, 1996).

26. S. Wilhelm, "Quadrupling 787 Production Won't Be Easy for Boeing, Just Necessary," *Puget Sound Business Journal*, February 10, 2012, accessed March 12, 2012, http://www.bizjournals.com/seattle/print-edition/2012/02/10/quadrupling-787-production-wont-be.html?page=all.

27. R. M. Yandrick, "A Team Effort: The Promise of Teams Isn't Achieved without Attention to Skills and Training," *HR Magazine*, June 2001, 46(6), 136–144.

28. "Self-Directed Teams Improve On-Time Delivery and Quality," *Manufacturing.net*, June 29, 2012, accessed June 13, 2013, http://www.manufacturing.net/articles/2012/06/self-directed-teams-improve-on-time-delivery-and-quality.

29. R. Williams, "Self-Directed Work Teams: A Competitive Advantage," *Quality Digest*, accessed November 18, 2009, http://www.qualitydigest.com.

30. Yandrick, "A Team Effort."

31. "Valve: Handbook for New Employees," Valve, accessed May 8, 2015, http://media.steampowered.com/apps/valve/Valve_Handbook_LowRes.pdf.

32. Ibid.

33. R. Silverman, "Who's the Boss? There Isn't One," Wall Street Journal, June 19, 2012, accessed May 8, 2015, http://www.wsj.com/articles/SB10001424052702303379204577474953586383604.

34. R. J. Recardo, D. Wade, C. A. Mention, and J. Jolly, *Teams* (Houston: Gulf Publishing Co., 1996).

35. D. R. Denison, S. L. Hart, and J. A. Kahn, "From Chimneys to Cross-Functional Teams: Developing and Validating a Diagnostic Model," *Academy of Management Journal* 39, no. 4 (1996): 1005–1023.

36. A. M. Townsend, S. M. DeMarie, and A. R. Hendrickson, "Virtual Teams: Technology and the Workplace of the Future," *Academy of Management Executive* 13, no. 3 (1998): 17–29.

37. F. Rendón, "Understanding the Proliferation of Virtual Teams in the Global Economy," *Huffington Post*, April 28, 2014, accessed June 16, 2014, http://www.huffingtonpost.com/frankie-rendon/understanding-the-prolife_b_5212366.html.

38. M.E. Slater, "How to Effectively Delegate to Your Remote Team," *Startup Collective*, accessed May 8, 2015, http://startupcollective.com/effectively-delegate-remote-team/.

39. N. Radley, "Survey: How Team Members Prefer to Communicate on Virtual Projects," Software Advice, July 17, 2014, accessed May 8, 2015, http://blog.softwareadvice.com/articles/project-management/survey-communication-virtual-projects-0714/.

40. Slater, "How to Effective Delegate to Your Remote Team."

41. Ibid.

42. D. Mankin, S. G. Cohen, and T. K. Bikson, *Teams and Technology: Fulfilling the Promise of the New Organization* (Boston: Harvard Business School Press, 1996).

43. A. P. Ammeter and J. M. Dukerich, "Leadership, Team Building, and Team Member Characteristics in High Performance Project Teams," *Engineering Management* 14, no. 4 (2002, December): 3–11.

44. K. Lovelace, D. Shapiro, and L. Weingart, "Maximizing Cross-Functional New Product Teams' Innovativeness and Constraint Adherence: A Conflict Communications Perspective," *Academy of Management Journal* 44 (2001): 779–793.

45. L. Holpp and H. P. Phillips, "When Is a Team Its Own Worst Enemy?" *Training*, September 1, 1995, 71.

46. S. Asche, "Opinions and Social Pressure," *Scientific American* 193 (1995): 31–35.

47. J. Stephens, "Corner Office: Rah-Rah Isn't for Everyone," interview by A. Bryant, *New York Times*, April 9, 2010, accessed June 11, 2010, http://www.nytimes.com/2010/04/11/business/11corner.html?pagewanted=.

48. S. G. Cohen, G. E. Ledford, and G. M. Spreitzer, "A Predictive Model of Self-Managing Work Team Effectiveness," *Human Relations* 49, no. 5 (1996): 643–676.

49. R. Collett, "How to Improve Product Development Productivity—Lessons from the Checklist Manifesto," *The EE Compendium: The Home of Electronic Engineering and Embedded Systems Programming*, accessed May 22, 2011, http://ee.cleversoul.com/news/lessons-from-the-checklist-manifesto.html.

50. "Institute for Healthcare Improvement: World Health Organization (WHO) Surgical Safety Checklist and Getting Started Kit," World Health Organization, accessed July 9, 2014, http://www.ihi.org/resources/Pages/Tools/WHOSurgicalSafetyChecklistGettingStartedKit.aspx; M. Semel, S. Resch, A. Haynes, L. Funk, A. Bader, W. Berry, T. Weiser, and A. Gawande, "Adopting a Surgical Safety Checklist Could Save Money and Improve the Quality of Care in US Hospitals," *Health Affairs* 29, no. 9 (2010): 1593–1599.

51. K. Bettenhausen and J. K. Murnighan, "The Emergence of Norms in Competitive Decision-Making Groups," *Administrative Science Quarterly* 30 (1985): 350–372.

52. M. E. Shaw, *Group Dynamics* (New York: McGraw Hill, 1981).

53. E. Levenson, "The Power of an Idea," *Fortune*, June 12, 2006, 131.

54. R. E. Silverman, "Tracking Sensors Invade the Workplace," *Wall Street Journal*, March 7, 2013, accessed June 16, 2014, http://online.wsj.com/news/articles/SB10001424127887324034804578344303429080678.

55. S. M. Gully, D. S. Devine, and D. J. Whitney, "A Meta-Analysis of Cohesion and Performance: Effects of Level of Analysis and Task Interdependence," *Small Group Research* 26, no. 4 (1995): 497–520.

56. B. Cohen, "Golden State: The Team That Eats Together," *Wall Street Journal*, February 11, 2015, accessed May 8, 2015, http://www.wsj.com/articles/golden-state-the-team-that-eats-together-1423682960.

57. Gully, Devine, and Whitney, "A Meta-Analysis of Cohesion and Performance."

58. F. Tschan and M. V. Cranach, "Group Task Structure, Processes and Outcomes," in *Handbook of Work Group Psychology*, ed. M. A. West (Chichester, UK: Wiley, 1966); J. Lublin, "Smaller Boards Get Bigger Returns," *Wall Street Journal*, August 26, 2014, accessed May 3, 2015, http://www.wsj.com/articles/smaller-boards-get-bigger-returns-1409078628.

59. J. Lublin, "Smaller Boards Get Bigger Returns," *Wall Street Journal*, August 26, 2014, accessed May 8, 2015, http://www.wsj.com/articles/smaller-boards-get-bigger-returns-1409078628.

60. Ibid.

61. Ibid.

62. D. E. Yeatts and C. Hyten, *High-Performing Self-Managed Work Teams* (Thousand Oaks, CA: Sage Publications, 1998); H. M. Guttman and R. S. Hawkes, "New Rules for Strategic Development," *Journal of Business Strategy* 25, no. 1 (2004): 34–39.

63. Yeatts and Hyten, *High-Performing Self-Managed Work Teams*; J. Colquitt, R. Noe, and C. Jackson, "Justice in Teams: Antecedents and Consequences of Procedural Justice Climate," *Personnel Psychology*, April 1, 2002, 83.

64. D. S. Kezsbom, "Re-Opening Pandora's Box: Sources of Project Team Conflict in the '90s," *Industrial Engineering* 24, no. 5 (1992): 54–59.

65. A. C. Amason, W. A. Hochwarter, and K. R. Thompson, "Conflict: An Important Dimension in Successful Management Teams," *Organizational Dynamics* 24 (1995): 20.

66. A. C. Amason, "Distinguishing the Effects of Functional and Dysfunctional Conflict on Strategic Decision Making: Resolving a Paradox for Top Management Teams," *Academy of Management Journal* 39, no. 1 (1996): 123–148.

67. K. M. Eisenhardt, J. L. Kahwajy, and L. J. Bourgeois III, "How Management Teams Can Have a Good Fight," *Harvard Business Review* 75, no. 4 (July–August 1997): 77–85.

68. S. Shellenbarger, "Meet the Meeting Killers," *Wall Street Journal*, May 15, 2012, accessed May 8, 2015, http://www.wsj.com/articles/SB10001424052702304192704577404434001058726.

69. Eisenhardt, Kahwajy, and Bourgeois III, "How Management Teams Can Have a Good Fight."

70. C. Nemeth and P. Owens, "Making Work Groups More Effective: The Value of Minority Dissent," in *Handbook of Work Group Psychology*, ed. M. A. West (Chichester, UK: Wiley, 1996).

71. J. M. Levin and R. L. Moreland, "Progress in Small Group Research," *Annual Review of Psychology* 9 (1990): 72–78; S. E. Jackson, "Team Composition in Organizational Settings: Issues in Managing a Diverse Work Force," in *Group Processes and Productivity*, ed. S. Worchel, W. Wood, and J. Simpson (Beverly Hills, CA: Sage, 1992).

72. J. Lublin, "Arguing with the Boss: A Winning Career Strategy," *Wall Street Journal*, August 9, 2012, accessed May 8, 2015, http://www.wsj.com/articles/SB10000872396390443991704577579201122821724.

73. Eisenhardt, Kahwajy, and Bourgeois, "How Management Teams Can Have a Good Fight."

74. Ibid.

75. B. W. Tuckman, "Development Sequence in Small Groups," *Psychological Bulletin* 63, no. 6 (1965): 384–399.

76. Gross, *Compensation for Teams*.

77. J. F. McGrew, J. G. Bilotta, and J. M. Deeney, "Software Team Formation and Decay: Extending the Standard Model for Small Groups," *Small Group Research* 30, no. 2 (1999): 209–234.

78. J. Case, "What the Experts Forgot to Mention: Management Teams Create New Difficulties, But Succeed for XEL Communication," *Inc.*, September 1, 1993, 66.

79. J. R. Hackman, "The Psychology of Self-Management in Organizations," in *Psychology and Work: Productivity, Change, and Employment*, ed. M. S. Pallak and R. Perloff (Washington, DC: American Psychological Association, 1986), 85–136.

80. A. O'Leary-Kelly, J. J. Martocchio, and D. D. Frink, "A Review of the Influence of Group Goals on Group Performance," *Academy of Management Journal* 37, no. 5 (1994): 1285–1301.

81. A. Zander, "The Origins and Consequences of Group Goals," in *Retrospections on Social Psychology*, ed. L. Festinger (New York: Oxford University Press, 1980), 205–235.

82. M. Erez and A. Somech, "Is Group Productivity Loss the Rule or the Exception? Effects of Culture and Group-Based Motivation," *Academy of Management Journal* 39, no. 6 (1996): 1513–1537.

83. S. Sherman, "Stretch Goals: The Dark Side of Asking for Miracles," *Fortune*, November 13, 1995.

84. J. Muller, "GM's New Goal Is a Stretch: Auto Industry's MVP," *Forbes*, January 31, 2013, accessed June 13, 2013, http://www.forbes.com/sites/joannmuller/2013/01/31/gms-new-goal-seems-a-bit-of-a-stretch-auto-industrys-mvp/.

85. K. R. Thompson, W. A. Hochwarter, and N. J. Mathys, "Stretch Targets: What Makes Them Effective?" *Academy of Management Executive* 11, no. 3 (1997): 48–60.

86. B. Stone, "Inside Google's Secret Lab—Businessweek," May 22, 2013, accessed July 9, 2014, http://www.businessweek.com/articles/2013-05-22/inside-googles-secret-lab.

87. Dumaine, "The Trouble with Teams."

88. G. A. Neuman, S. H. Wagner, and N. D. Christiansen, "The Relationship Between Work-Team Personality Composition and the Job Performance of Teams," *Group & Organization Management* 24, no. 1 (1999): 28–45.

89. M. A. Campion, G. J. Medsker, and A. C. Higgs, "Relations Between Work Group Characteristics and Effectiveness: Implications for Designing Effective Work Groups," *Personnel Psychology* 46, no. 4 (1993): 823–850.

90. B. L. Kirkman and D. L. Shapiro, "The Impact of Cultural Values on Employee Resistance to Teams: Toward a Model of Globalized Self-Managing Work Team Effectiveness," *Academy of Management Review* 22, no. 3 (1997): 730–757.

91. J. Pavlus, "SAP Looks to XRX for R&D Inspiration," *Bloomberg Businessweek*, February 2–8, 2015, p. 32.

92. A. Galinsky, "Is Your Team Too Talented," Columbia Ideas at Work, October 30, 2014, accessed May 8, 2015, http://www8.gsb.columbia.edu/ideas-at-work/publication/1700.

93. J. Bunderson and K. Sutcliffe, "Comparing Alternative Conceptualizations of Functional Diversity in Management Teams: Process and Performance Effects," *Academy of Management Journal* 45 (2002): 875–893.

94. A. Zynga, "The Cognitive Bias Keeping Us from Innovating," *Harvard Business Review* (HBR Blog Network), June 13, 2013, accessed June 16, 2014, http://blogs.hbr.org/2013/06/the-cognitive-bias-keeping-us-from/#disqus_thread.

95. J. Hackman, "New Rules for Team Building—The Times Are Changing—And So Are the Guidelines for Maximizing Team Performance," *Optimize*, July 1, 2002, 50.

96. Joinson, "Teams at Work."

97. Strozniak, "Teams at Work."

98. Ibid.

99. P. Nicholas, "It's All About Flight or Fight," *Weekend Australian*, March 14, 2009, 1.

100. Wellins, Byham, and Dixon, *Inside Teams*.

101. E. Salas, D. DiazGranados, C. Klein, C. Burke, K. Stagl, G. Goodwin, and S. Halpin, "Does Team Training Improve Team Performance? A Meta-Analysis," *Human Factors* 50, no. 6 (2008): 903–933.

102. S. Caudron, "Tie Individual Pay to Team Success," *Personnel Journal* 73, no. 10 (October 1994): 40.

103. Ibid.

104. Gross, *Compensation for Teams*.

105. G. Ledford, "Three Case Studies on Skill-Based Pay: An Overview," *Compensation & Benefits Review* 23, no. 2 (1991): 11–24.

106. T. Law, "Where Loyalty Is Rewarded," *The Press*, September 29, 2008, Business Day 4.

107. J. R. Schuster and P. K. Zingheim, *The New Pay: Linking Employee and Organizational Performance* (New York: Lexington Books, 1992).

108. Cohen and Bailey, "What Makes Teams Work."

109. R. Allen and R. Kilmann, "Aligning Reward Practices in Support of Total Quality Management," *Business Horizons* 44 (May 2001): 77–85.

11

1. J. Emshwiller and G. Fields, "Decadeslong Arrest Wave Vexes Employers," *Wall Street Journal*, December 12, 2014, accessed May 7, 2015, http://www.wsj.com/articles/decadeslong-arrest-wave-vexes-employers-1418438092.

2. S. Thurm, "Background Checks Fuel Jobs Debate," *Wall Street Journal*, June 11, 2013, accessed May 7, 2015, http://www.wsj.com/articles/SB10001424127887323495604578539283518855020.

3. Ibid.

4. Emshwiller and Fields, "Decadeslong Arrest Wave Vexes Employers."

5. "Genetic Information Discrimination," U.S. Equal Employment Opportunity Commission, accessed July 9, 2014, http://www.eeoc.gov/laws/types/genetic.cfm.

6. K. McGowan, "Barring Male Guards for Female Inmates Might Violate Title VII, Ninth Circuit Rules," *Bloomberg BNA*, July 8, 2014, accessed May 7, 2015, http://www.bna.com/barring-male-guards-n17179891923/.

7. P. S. Greenlaw and J. P. Kohl, "Employer 'Business' and 'Job' Defenses in Civil Rights Actions," *Public Personnel Management* 23, no. 4 (1994): 573.

8. Greenlaw and Kohl, "Employer 'Business' and 'Job' Defenses in Civil Rights Actions."

9. City News Service, "66-Year-Old Man Awarded $26 Million in Age Discrimination Lawsuit," *Los Angeles Daily News*, February 27, 2014, accessed July 9, 2014, http://www.dailynews.com/general-news/20140227/66-year-old-man-awarded-26-million-in-age-discrimination-lawsuit-against-staples.

10. W. Peirce, C. A. Smolinski, and B. Rosen, "Why Sexual Harassment Complaints Fall on Deaf Ears," *Academy of Management Executive* 12, no. 3 (1998): 41–54.

11. R. Gray, "First Student to Pay $150K to Settle Sexual Harassment, Retaliation Suit," *School Transportation News*, February 4, 2011, accessed May 23, 2011, http://stnonline.com/index.php/news/blogs

/item/3104-first-student-to-pay-$150k-to-settle-sexual-harassment-retaliation-suit.

12. E. Francis, "$168 Million Awarded to Woman Harassed in 'Raunchy' Cardiac Surgery Unit," ABC News, March 2, 2012, accessed July 9, 2014, http://abcnews.go.com/US/LegalCenter/168-million-awarded-woman-harassed-raunchy-cardiac-surgery/story?id=15835342&singlePage=true.

13. Peirce, Smolinski, and Rosen, "Why Sexual Harassment Complaints Fall on Deaf Ears."

14. Ibid.

15. E. Larson, "The Economic Costs of Sexual Harassment," The Freeman 46, August 1996, accessed August 13, 2008, http://fee.org/freeman/the-economic-costs-of-sexual-harassment.

16. G. Hyland-Savage, "General Management Perspective on Staffing: The Staffing Commandments," in On Staffing, eds. N. C. Bukholder, P. J. Edwards, Jr., and L. Sartain (Hoboken, NJ: Wiley, 2004), 280.

17. R. D. Gatewood and H. S. Field, Human Resource Selection (Fort Worth, TX: Dryden Press, 1998).

18. Ibid.

19. E. Gaydos, "Three Awesome Examples of Great Job Descriptions," TLNT, August 2, 2012, accessed June 14, 2013, http://www.tlnt.com/2012/08/02/three-awesome-examples-of-great-job-descriptions/.

20. Griggs v. Duke Power Co., 401 US 424, 436 (1971); Albemarle Paper Co. v. Moody, 422 US 405 (1975).

21. R. E. Silverman and N. Waller, "The Algorithm That Tells the Boss Who Might Quit," Wall Street Journal, March 13, 2015, accessed May 5, 2015, http://www.wsj.com/articles/the-algorithm-that-tells-the-boss-who-might-quit-1426287935.

22. J. A. Breaugh, Recruitment: Science and Practice (Boston: PWSKent, 1992).

23. R. Albergotti, "LinkedIn Wants to Help You Stay at Your Company," Wall Street Journal (blog), April 10, 2014, accessed June 17, 2014, http://blogs.wsj.com/atwork/2014/04/10/linkedin-wants-to-help-you-stay-at-your-company/.

24. Ibid.

25. R. Silverman and L. Weber, "An Inside Job: More Firms Opt to Recruit from Within," Wall Street Journal, May 29, 2012, accessed June 14, 2013, http://online.wsj.com/article/SB10001424052702303395604577434563715828218.html.

26. L. Klaff, "New Internal Hiring Systems Reduce Cost and Boost Morale," Workforce Management 83 (March 2004): 76–79.

27. R. Silverman and L. Weber, "An Inside Job: More Firms Opt to Recruit from Within," Wall Street Journal, May 29, 2012, accessed June 14, 2013, http://online.wsj.com/article/SB10001424052702303395604577434563715828218.html.

28. R. E. Silverman, "Climbing the Career Ladder with Help," Wall Street Journal, January 14, 2015, B6.

29. Ibid.

30. J. Dao, "Wal-Mart Plans to Hire Any Veteran Who Wants a Job," The New York Times, January 14, 2013, accessed June 14, 2013, http://www.nytimes.com/2013/01/15/us/wal-mart-to-announce-extensive-plan-to-hire-veterans.html?_r=1.

31. J. Breaugh and M. Starke, "Research on Employee Recruitment: So Many Studies, So Many Remaining Questions," Journal of Management 26 (2000): 405–434.

32. J. J. Colao, "The Facebook Job Board Is Here: Recruiting Will Never Look the Same," Forbes, November 14, 2012, accessed May 5, 2015, http://www.forbes.com/sites/jjcolao/2012/11/14/the-facebook-job-board-is-here-recruiting-will-never-look-the-same/; J. Zappe, "Now Almost Gone: The Decline of Print-Based Help-Wanted Ads," Source Con, March 20, 2012, accessed May 5, 2015, http://www.sourcecon.com/news/2012/03/20/now-almost-gone-the-decline-of-print-based-help-wanted-ads/.

33. 2014 Jobvite Job Seeker Nation Study, Jobvite, accessed May 5, 2015, http://web.jobvite.com/rs/jobvite/images/2014%20Job%20Seeker%20Survey.pdf.

34. S. Akiode, "The Social Recruiting Pocket Guide," Herd Wisdom, June 9, 2013, accessed May 5, 2015, http://socialmeep.com/infographic-the-social-recruiting-pocket-guide/.

35. R. E. Silverman, "New Year, New Job? Read This First," Wall Street Journal, January 2, 2015, B1, B4.

36. Ibid.

37. N. Buhayar, "Be a Grand Pooh-Bah of Probability," Bloomberg Businessweek, March 16–22, 2015, pp. 34–35.

38. C. Gordon, "Getting a Job at Facebook: Inside the 'Meritocratic' Hiring Process," AOL Jobs, October 5, 2012, accessed June 14, 2013, http://jobs.aol.com/articles/2012/10/05/want-to-get-a-job-at-facebook-weve-demystified-the-hiring-proc/.

39. C. Camden and B. Wallace, "Job Application Forms: A Hazardous Employment Practice," Personnel Administrator 28 (1983): 31–32.

40. J. Valentino-Devries, "Bosses May Use Social Media to Discriminate Against Job Seekers," Wall Street Journal, November 20, 2013, accessed July 10, 2014, http://online.wsj.com/news/articles/SB10001424052702303755504579208304255139392.

41. "Fifty-Eight Percent of Employers Have Caught a Lie on a Résumé, According to a New Career-Builder Survey," CareerBuilder.com, August 7, 2014, accessed May 7, 2015, http://www.careerbuilder.com/share/aboutus/pressreleasesdetail.aspx?sd=8%2F7%2F2014&id=pr837&ed=12%2F31%2F2014.

42. D. Kerr, "Uber's Background Checks Don't Catch Criminals," Cnet.com, April 17, 2015, accessed May 5, 2015, http://www.cnet.com/news/ubers-background-checks-dont-catch-criminals-says-houston/.

43. S. Adler, "Verifying a Job Candidate's Background: The State of Practice in a Vital Human Resources Activity," Review of Business 15, no. 2 (1993/1994): 3–8.

44. W. Woska, "Legal Issues for HR Professionals: Reference Checking/Background Investigations," Public Personnel Management 36 (Spring 2007): 79–89.

45. "More Than 70 Percent of HR Professionals Say Reference Checking Is Effective in Identifying Poor Performers," Society for Human Resource Management, accessed February 3, 2005, http://www.shrm.org/press_published/CMS_011240.asp.

46. P. Babcock, "Spotting Lies: The High Cost of Careless Hiring," HR Magazine 48, no. 10 (October 2003).

47. E. Leizerman, "Oregon Jury Renders $5.2M Verdict Against Trucking Broker and Driver in Negligent Hiring Case," PRWeb, March 6, 2012, accessed June 14, 2013, http://www.prweb.com/releases/2012/3/prweb9258166.htm.

48. M. Le, T. Nguyen, and B. Kleiner, "Legal Counsel: Don't Be Sued for Negligent Hiring," Nonprofit World, May 1, 2003, 14–15.

49. "SHRM FInds Fewer Employers Using Background Checks in Hiring," July 19, 2012, accessed May 5, 2015, http://www.shrm.org/about/pressroom/pressreleases/pages/backgroundchecks.aspx.

50. D. Belkin, "More Job Seekers Scramble to Erase Their Criminal Past," Wall Street Journal, November 11, 2009, A1.

51. J. Emshwiller and G. Fields, "Decadeslong Arrest Wave Vexes Employers."; S. Thurm, "Background Checks Fuel Jobs Debate," Wall Street Journal, June 11, 2013, accessed May 7, 2015, http://www.wsj.com/articles/SB10001424127887323495604578539283518855020.

52. A. Athavaley, "Job References You Can't Control," Wall Street Journal, September 27, 2007, D1.

53. C. Cohen, "Reference Checks," CA Magazine, November 2004, 41.

54. Keith J. Winstein, "Inflated Credentials Surface in Executive Suite," Wall Street Journal, November 13, 2008, accessed May 30, 2011, http://online.wsj.com/article/SB122652836844922165.html.

55. B. Ellis, "For Hire: Professional Liars for Job Seekers," CNN Money, July 17, 2013, accessed July 10, 2014, http://money.cnn.com/2013/07/17/pf/professional-liars/.

56. L. Weber, "To Get a Job, New Hires Are Put to the Test," Wall Street Journal, April 15, 2015, A1, A10.

57. D. Hambrick and C. Chabris, "Yes, IQ Really Matters," Slate, April 14, 2014, accessed July 10, 2014, http://www.slate.com/articles/health_and_science/science/2014/04/what_do_sat_and_iq_tests_measure_general_intelligence_predicts_school_and.html.

58. J. Hunter, "Cognitive Ability, Cognitive Aptitudes, Job Knowledge, and Job Performance," Journal of Vocational Behavior 29 (1986): 340–362.

59. F. L. Schmidt, "The Role of General Cognitive Ability and Job Performance: Why There Cannot Be a Debate," Human Performance 15 (2002): 187–210.

60. D. Hambrick and C. Chabris, "Yes, IQ Really Matters."

61. E. E. Cureton, "Comment," in Research Conference on the Use of Autobiographical Data as Psychological Predictors, ed. E. R. Henry (Greensboro, NC: The Richardson Foundation, 1965), 13.

62. J. R. Glennon, L. E. Albright, and W. A. Owens, A Catalog of Life History Items (Greensboro, NC: The Richardson Foundation, 1966).

63. Gatewood and Field, Human Resource Selection.

64. R. E. Silverman, "New Year, New Job? Read This First," Wall Street Journal, January 2, 2015, B1, B4.

65. L. Weber, "To Get a Job, New Hires Are Put to the Test," Wall Street Journal, April 15, 2015, A1, A10.

66. M. S. Taylor and J. A. Sniezek, "The College Recruitment Interview: Topical Content and Applicant Reactions," Journal of Occupational Psychology 57 (1984): 157–168.

67. M. Harris, "Reconsidering the Employment Interview: A Review of Recent Literature and Suggestions for Future Research," Personnel Psychology (Winter 1989): 691–726.

68. Taylor and Sniezek, "The College Recruitment Interview."

69. C. Mims, "At Google, The Science of Working Better," Wall Street Journal, March 29, 2015, B1.

70. R. Burnett, C. Fan, S. J. Motowidlo, and T. DeGroot, "Interview Notes and Validity," Personnel Psychology 51, (1998): 375–396; M. A. Campion, D. K. Palmer, and J. E. Campion, "A Review of Structure in the Selection Interview," Personnel Psychology 50, no. 3 (1997): 655–702.

71. T. Judge, "The Employment Interview: A Review of Recent Research and Recommendations

for Future Research," *Human Resource Management Review* 10, no. 4 (2000): 383–406.

72. J. Cortina, N. Goldstein, S. Payne, K. Davison, and S. Gilliland, "The Incremental Validity of Interview Scores Over and Above Cognitive Ability and Conscientiousness Scores," *Personnel Psychology* 53, no. 2 (2000): 325–351; F. L. Schmidt and J. E. Hunter, "The Validity and Utility of Selection Methods in Personnel Psychology: Practical and Theoretical Implications of 85 Years of Research Findings," *Psychological Bulletin* 124, no. 2 (1998): 262–274.

73. K. Tyler, "Training Revs Up," *HR Magazine* (April 2005), *Society for Human Resource Management*, accessed March 23, 2009, http://www.shrm.org.

74. "2013 State of the Industry," *ASTD Research*, 2013, accessed June 17, 2014, https://www.td.org/Publications/Research-Reports/2013/2013-State-of-the-Industry

75. S. Lupkin, "Texas Health Workers Use Tabasco to Help Train for Ebola," Good Morning America, October 23, 2014, , accessed May 7, 2015, http://abcnews.go.com/Health/texas-health-workers-tabasco-train-ebola/story?id=26385702.

76. Lupkin, "Texas Health Workers Use Tabasco to Help Train for Ebola."

77. R. King, "The Games Companies Play," *Bloomberg Businessweek*, April 4, 2011, accessed March 14, 2012, http://www.bloomberg.com/bw/stories/2011-04-05/the-games-companies-playbusinessweek-business-news-stock-market-and-financial-advice; "Siemens' Plantville Celebrates One Year, Announces New Site Features," *Siemens*, March 30, 2012, http://news.usa.siemens.biz/press-release/industry/siemens-plantville-celebrates-one-year-announces-new-site-features

78. "Westinghouse University Case Study: Aligning a Corporate University to Meet the Needs of the Business," *CORP/U*, May 1, 2012, accessed June 14, 2013, http://www.corpu.com/research/westinghouse-university-aligning-corporate-university-meet-needs-business/; L. Weber, "Fine-Tuning the Perfect Employee—Companies Take to Training Staff, New Hires to Make Up for Low-Skilled Workers," *Wall Street Journal*, December 5, 2011, B9.

79. D. L. Kirkpatrick, "Four Steps to Measuring Training Effectiveness," *Personnel Administrator* 28 (1983): 19–25.

80. L. Bassi, J. Ludwig, D. McMurrer, and M. Van Buren, "Profiting from Learning: Do Firms' Investments in Education and Training Pay Off?" *American Society for Training and Development*, accessed August 14, 2008, https://www.td.org/Publications/Research-Reports/2000/Profiting-from-Learning

81. Daley, "It's Shaping Up to Be a Good Year," *Entrepreneur*, January 2014, 92.

82. S. Culbert, "Get Rid of the Performance Review!" *Wall Street Journal*, June 21, 2012, accessed June 14, 2013, http://www.wsj.com/articles/SB122426318874844933.

83. D. Murphy, "Are Performance Appraisals Worse Than a Waste of Time? Book Derides Unintended Consequences," *San Francisco Chronicle*, September 9, 2001, W1.

84. K. R. Murphy and J. N. Cleveland, *Understanding Performance Appraisal: Social, Organizational and Goal-Based Perspectives* (Thousand Oaks, CA: Sage, 1995).

85. R. Feintzeig, "The Trouble with Grading Employees," *Wall Street Journal*, April 22, 2015, B1, B7.

86. U. J. Wiersma and G. P. Latham, "The Practicality of Behavioral Observation Scales, Behavioral Expectation, and Trait Scales," *Personnel Psychology* 39 (1986): 619–628; U. J. Wiersma, P. T. Van Den Berg, and G. P. Latham, "Dutch

Reactions to Behavioral Observation, Behavioral Expectation, and Trait Scales," *Group & Organization Management* 20 (1995): 297–309.

87. D. J. Schleicher, D. V. Day, B. T. Mayes, and R. E. Riggio, "A New Frame for Frame-of-Reference Training: Enhancing the Construct Validity of Assessment Centers," *Journal of Applied Psychology* (August 2002): 735–746.

88. R. Feintzeig, "Everything Is Awesome! Why You Can't Tell Employees They're Doing a Bad Job," Wall Street Journal, February 10, 2015, accessed May 7, 2015, http://www.wsj.com/articles/everything-is-awesome-why-you-cant-tell-employees-theyre-doing-a-bad-job-1423613936.

89. R. Feintzeig, "The Trouble with Grading Employees," *Wall Street Journal*, April 22, 2015, B1, B7.

90. H. H. Meyer, "A Solution to the Performance Appraisal Feedback Enigma," *Academy of Management Executive* 5, no. 1 (1991): 68–76; G. C. Thornton, "Psychometric Properties of Self-Appraisals of Job Performance," *Personnel Psychology* 33 (1980): 263–271.

91. Thornton, "Psychometric Properties of Self-Appraisals of Job Performance."

92. J. Smither, M. London, R. Flautt, Y. Vargas, and I. Kucine, "Can Working with an Executive Coach Improve Multisource Feedback Ratings Over Time? A Quasi-Experimental Field Study," *Personnel Psychology* (Spring 2003): 21–43.

93. A. Walker and J. Smither, "A Five-Year Study of Upward Feedback: What Managers Do with Their Results Matters," *Personnel Psychology* (Summer 1999): 393–422.

94. K. Chu, "China: A Billion Strong But Short on Workers," *Wall Street Journal*, May 1, 2013, accessed June 14, 2013, http://www.wsj.com/articles/SB10001424127887323798104578455153999658318

95. K. Chu, "China Factories Try Karaoke, Speed Dating to Keep Workers," *Wall Street Journal*, May 2, 2013, accessed September 11, 2013, http://www.wsj.com/articles/SB10001424127887323798104578452634075519230

96. G. T. Milkovich and J. M. Newman, *Compensation*, 4th ed. (Homewood, IL: Irwin, 1993).

97. M. L. Williams and G. F. Dreher, "Compensation System Attributes and Applicant Pool Characteristics," *Academy of Management Journal* 35, no. 3 (1992): 571–595.

98. S. Quinton, "The Trader Joe's Lesson: How to Pay a Living Wage and Still Make Money in Retail," *The Atlantic*, March 25, 2013, accessed June 14, 2013, http://www.theatlantic.com/business/archive/2013/03/the-trader-joes-lesson-how-to-pay-a-living-wage-and-still-make-money-in-retail/274322/.

99. S. Cooper and C. Debaise, "Best Ways to Pay Your Sales Staff," *Bloomberg Businessweek*, June 5, 2009, accessed September 6, 2010, http://www.businessweek.com/magazine/content/09_66/s0906028668952.htm.

100. J. Blasi, "Southwest Airlines' Profit-Sharing Payout: What Capitalism Should Be," *Fortune*, April 17, 2014, accessed June 17, 2014, http://fortune.com/2014/04/17/southwest-airlines-profit-sharing-payout-what-capitalism-should-be/.

101. M. Josephs, "The Millionaire Truck Driver and Other ESOP Miracles," *Forbes*, April 30, 2014, accessed June 17, 2014, http://www.forbes.com/sites/maryjosephs/2014/04/30/the-millionaire-truck-driver-and-other-esop-miracles/.

102. A. Loten, "Founders Cash Out, But Do Workers Gain?—US Employee-Owned Firms Top 10,000, with More Expected as Owners Retire; Critics Point to Potential Drawbacks," *Wall Street Journal*, April 18, 2013, B4.

103. M. Bloom, "The Performance Effects of Pay Dispersion on Individuals and Organizations," *Academy of Management Journal* 42, no. 1 (1999): 25–40.

104. "CEOs Make 296 Times More Than Workers, CNN Money, June 12, 2014, accessed May 7, 2015, http://money.cnn.com/2014/06/12/news/economy/ceo-pay/.

105. W. Grossman and R. E. Hoskisson, "CEO Pay at the Crossroads of Wall Street and Main: Toward the Strategic Design of Executive Compensation," *Academy of Management Executive* 12, no. 1 (1998): 43–57.

106. Bloom, "The Performance Effects of Pay Dispersion."

107. M. Bloom and J. Michel, "The Relationships Among Organizational Context, Pay Dispersion, and Managerial Turnover," *Academy of Management Journal* 45 (2002): 33–42.

108. S. Needleman, "Bad Firings Can Hurt Firm's Reputation," *Wall Street Journal*, July 8, 2008, D4.

109. J. Strickland, "Zynga Layoffs: The Aftermath," *Inc*, June 3, 2013, accessed June 17, 2014, http://www.inc.com/julie-strickland/zynga-lay-off-eighteen-percent-staff-close-three-offices.html.

110. A. Rupe, "Horrors from the Bad-Firing File," *Workforce Management*, November 2003, 16.

111. D. Mattel, J. Lublin, and R. Silverman, "Bad Call: How Not to Fire a Worker," *Wall Street Journal*, September 9, 2011, B2.

112. P. Michal-Johnson, *Saying Good-Bye: A Manager's Guide to Employee Dismissal* (Glenview, IL: Scott, Foresman & Co., 1985).

113. M. Bordwin, "Employment Law: Beware of Time Bombs and Shark-Infested Waters," *HR Focus*, April 1, 1995, 19; D. Jones, "Fired Workers Fight Back... and Win; Laws, Juries Shift Protection to Terminated Employees," *USA Today*, April 2, 1998, 01B.

114. Table 3. Industry Distribution: Extended Mass Layoff Separations, Private Nonfarm Sector, 50 Highest Six-Digit NAICS Industries, 2010–2012," Bureau of Labor Statistics, Mass Layoff Statistics, 2010-2012, accessed May 6, 2015, http://www.bls.gov/mls/mlsreport1043.pdf.

115. "Mass Layoffs in December 2007 and Annual Totals for 2007," Bureau of Labor Statistics News, January 24, 2008, accessed August 15, 2008, http://www.bls.gov/news.release/archives/mmls_01242008.pdf.

116. J. Bort, "By Firing 4,000 More People, Cisco Will Have Cut 12,000 Jobs in Two Years," *Business Insider*, August 15, 2013, accessed June 17, 2014, http://www.businessinsider.com/cisco-has-fired-12000-in-last-two-years-2013-8#!KmyxQ.

117. W. F. Cascio, "Employment Downsizing and Its Alternatives: Strategies for Long-Term Success," SHRM Foundation's Effective Practice Guideline Series, Society for Human Resource Management Foundation, accessed July 10, 2014, http://www.shrm.org/about/foundation/products/Documents/Downsizing%20EPG-%20Final.pdf.

118. K. E. Mishra, G. M. Spreitzer, and A. K. Mishra, "Preserving Employee Morale During Downsizing," *Sloan Management Review* 39, no. 2 (1998): 83–95.

119. K. Frieswick, "Until We Meet Again?" *CFO*, October 1, 2001, 41; W. F. Cascio, "Employment Downsizing and Its Alternatives: Strategies for Long-Term Success"; L. Weber and R. Feintzeig, "Assistance for Laid-Off Workers Gets Downsized," *Wall Street Journal*, February 18, 2013, accessed July 10, 2014, http://www.wsj.com/news/articles/SB10001424052702304899704579391254047535652

120. Cascio, "Employment Downsizing and Its Alternatives: Strategies for Long-Term Success."

121. J. Hilsenrath, "Adventures in Cost Cutting," *Wall Street Journal*, May 10, 2004, R1.

122. M. Jackson, "Downsized, But Still in the Game: Keeping Up Morale Crucial After Job Cuts," *Boston Globe*, January 11, 2009, G1.

123. J. Ackerman, "Helping Layoff Survivors Cope: Companies Strive to Keep Morale High," *Boston Globe*, December 30, 2001, H1.

124. D. Ferrari, "Designing and Evaluating Early Retirement Programs: The State of Wyoming Experience," *Government Finance Review* 15, no. 1 (1999): 29–31.

125. Hilsenrath, "Adventures in Cost Cutting."

126. J. Lublin and S. Thurm, "How Companies Calculate Odds in Buyout Offers," *Wall Street Journal*, March 27, 2009, B1.

127. M. Willett, "Early Retirement and Phased Retirement Programs for the Public Sector," *Benefits & Compensation Digest*, April 2005, 31.

128. "2014 Jobvite Job Seeker Nation Study," Jobvite, accessed May 7, 2015, http://web.jobvite.com/rs/jobvite/images/2014%20Job%20Seeker%20Survey.pdf.

129. D. R. Dalton, W. D. Todor, and D. M. Krackhardt, "Turnover Overstated: The Functional Taxonomy," *Academy of Management Review* 7 (1982): 117–123.

130. J. R. Hollenbeck and C. R. Williams, "Turnover Functionality versus Turnover Frequency: A Note on Work Attitudes and Organizational Effectiveness," *Journal of Applied Psychology* 71 (1986): 606–611.

131. R. E. Silverman and N. Waller, "The Algorithm That Tells the Boss Who Might Quit."

132. C. R. Williams, "Reward Contingency, Unemployment, and Functional Turnover," *Human Resource Management Review* 9 (1999): 549–576.

12

1. "Table 6. Percent Distribution of the Projected Population by Race and Hispanic Origin for the United States: 2015 to 2060," U.S. Census Bureau, accessed July 10, 2014, http://www.census.gov/population/projections/data/national/2012/summarytables.html.

2. M. Toosi, "Table 4. Continued- Civilian Labor Force, by Age, Gender, Race, and Ethnicity, 1990, 2000, 2010, and Projected 2020," in "Labor Force Projections to 2020: A More Slowly Growing Workforce," *Monthly Labor Review*, January 2012, 43–64.

3. "Table 3.4. Civilian Labor Force by Age, Sex, Race, and Ethnicity, 1992, 2002, 2012, and Projected 2022 [Numbers in Thousands]," from "Employment Projections: Civilian Labor Force by Age, Sex, Race, and Ethnicity," *Bureau of Labor Statistics*, December 19, 2013, accessed June 17, 2014, http://www.bls.gov/emp/ep_table_304.htm.

4. "Discover McDonald's Around the Globe," *McDonald's*, accessed June 15, 2013, http://www.aboutmcdonalds.com/mcd/country/map.html.

5. O. Putnal, "11 Global McDonald's Menu Items," *Women's Day*, accessed June 15, 2013, http://www.womansday.com/food-recipes/11-global-mcdonalds-menu-items-104999.

6. E. York, "In Speech, McDonald's Thompson Puts Focus on Diversity," *Chicago Tribune*, May 2, 2012, accessed June 15, 2013, http://articles.chicagotribune.com/2012-05-02/business/chi-in-speech-mcdonalds-thompson-puts-focus-on-diversity-20120502_1_diversity-women-and-minority-owned-businesses-mcbites.

7. Equal Employment Opportunity Commission, "Affirmative Action Appropriate Under Title VII of the Civil Rights Act of 1964, as Amended. Chapter XIV—Equal Employment Opportunity Commission, Part 1608," accessed November 5, 2009, http://www.access.gpo.gov/nara/cfr/waisidx_04/29cfr1608_04.html.

8. Equal Employment Opportunity Commission, "Federal Laws Prohibiting Job Discrimination: Questions and Answers," accessed August 21, 2008, http://www.eeoc.gov/facts/qanda.html.

9. A. P. Carnevale and S. C. Stone, *The American Mosaic: An In-Depth Report on the Future of Diversity at Work* (New York: McGraw-Hill, 1995).

10. T. Roosevelt, "From Affirmative Action to Affirming Diversity," *Harvard Business Review* 68, no. 2 (1990): 107–117.

11. A. M. Konrad and F. Linnehan, "Formalized HRM Structures: Coordinating Equal Employment Opportunity or Concealing Organizational Practices?" *Academy of Management Journal* 38, no. 3 (1995): 787–820; see, for example, *Hopwood v. Texas*, 78 F.3d 932 (5th Cir., March 18, 1996). The U.S. Supreme Court has upheld the principle of affirmative action but has struck down some specific programs.

12. J. Bravin, "Court Backs Affirmative Action Ban—Justices Uphold State Initiative to End Race-Based Admissions, But Are Divided on Broader Issue," *Wall Street Journal*, April 23, 2014, A1.

13. P. Schmidt, "5 More States May Curtail Affirmative Action," *The Chronicle of Higher Education*, October 19, 2007, A1.

14. M. E. Heilman, C. J. Block, and P. Stathatos, "The Affirmative Action Stigma of Incompetence: Effects of Performance Information Ambiguity," *Academy of Management Journal* 40, no. 3 (1997): 603–625; D. Evans, "A Comparison of the Other-Directed Stigmatization Produced by Legal and Illegal Forms of Affirmative Action," *Journal of Applied Psychology* 88, no. 1 (2003): 121–130.

15. L. Leslie, D. Mayer, and D. Kravitz, "The Stigma of Affirmative Action: A Stereotyping-Based Theory and Meta-Analytic Test of the Consequences for Performance." *Academy of Management Journal* 57, no. 4 (2014): 964-989.

16. E. Orenstein, "The Business Case for Diversity," *Financial Executive*, May 2005, 22–25; G. Robinson and K. Dechant, "Building a Business Case for Diversity," *Academy of Management Executive* 11, no. 3 (1997): 21–31.

17. E. Esen, "2005 Workplace Diversity Practices: Survey Report," *Society for Human Resource Management*, accessed March 24, 2009, http://www.shrm.org/research.

18. Orenstein, "Business Case for Diversity."

19. Esen, "2005 Workplace Diversity Practices: Survey Report."

20. Orenstein, "Business Case for Diversity."

21. K. Wiese, "Judge Approves Merrill Lynch's $160 Million Racial Bias Settlement," *Bloomberg Businessweek*, December 6, 2013, accessed July 11, 2014, http://www.businessweek.com/articles/2013-12-06/judge-approves-merrill-lynchs-160-million-racial-bias-settlement.

22. P. Wright and S. P. Ferris, "Competitiveness Through Management of Diversity: Effects on Stock Price Valuation," *Academy of Management Journal* 38 (1995): 272–285.

23. Ibid.

24. "State & Country QuickFacts," *US Census Bureau*, June 6, 2013, accessed June 15, 2013, http://quickfacts.census.gov/qfd/states/00000.html; J. Humphreys, "The Multicultural Economy 2012,"

Selig Center for Economic Growth, Terry College of Business, University of Georgia, 2012.

25. S. Murray, "How One Company Put Women in Charge," *Wall Street Journal*, April 1, 2014, accessed July 11, 2014, http://blogs.wsj.com/atwork/2014/04/01/how-one-company-put-women-in-charge/.

26. Anonymous, "Bumpkin Bosses; Schumpeter," *The Economist*, May 10, 2014, 70.

27. W. W. Watson, K. Kumar, and L. K. Michaelsen, "Cultural Diversity's Impact on Interaction Process and Performance: Comparing Homogeneous and Diverse Task Groups," *Academy of Management Journal* 36 (1993): 590–602; K. A. Jehn, G. B. Northcraft, and M. A. Neale, "Why Differences Make a Difference: A Field Study of Diversity, Conflict, and Performance in Workgroups," *Administrative Science Quarterly* 44 (1999): 741–763; E. Kearney, D. Gebert, and S. Voelpel, "When and How Diversity Benefits Teams: The Importance of Team Members' Need for Cognition," *Academy of Management Journal* 52 (2009): 581–598.

28. L. Visconti, "Novartis' David Epstein: A Diverse Team Can 'Accomplish Feats Nobody Thought Possible,'" *DiverstyInc*, February 2, 2013, accessed June 15, 2013, http://www.diversityinc.com/leadership/novartis-david-epstein-a-diverse-team-can-accomplish-feats-nobody-thought-possible/.

29. M. R. Carrell and E. E. Mann, "Defining Workplace Diversity Programs and Practices in Organizations," *Labor Law Journal* 44 (1993): 743–764.

30. D. A. Harrison, K. H. Price, and M. P. Bell, "Beyond Relational Demography: Time and the Effects of Surface- and Deep-Level Diversity on Work Group Cohesion," *Academy of Management Journal* 41 (1998): 96–107.

31. D. Harrison, K. Price, J. Gavin, and A. Florey, "Time, Teams, and Task Performance: Changing Effects of Surface- and Deep-Level Diversity on Group Functioning," *Academy of Management Journal* 45 (2002): 1029–1045.

32. Harrison, Price, and Bell, "Beyond Relational Demography."

33. Ibid.

34. R. Alsop, "Why your grandfather might land a job before you do," *BBC*, October 25, 2013, accessed June 17, 2014, http://www.bbc.com/capital/story/20131024-older-workers-fogey-or-find; E. White, "The New Recruits: Older Workers," *Wall Street Journal*, January 14, 2008, B3.

35. M. Kane, "Say What? 'Young People are Just Smarter,'" CNET, March 28, 2007, accessed May 9, 2015, http://www.cnet.com/news/say-what-young-people-are-just-smarter/.

36. V. Giang, "This Is the Latest Way Employers Mask Age Bias, Lawyers Say," *Fortune*, May 4, 2015, http://fortune.com/2015/05/04/digital-native-employers-bias/, accessed May 9, 2015;

37. Ibid.

38. "Age Discrimination in Employment Act (includes Concurrent Charges with Title VII, ADA and EPA) FY 1997–FY 2014," US Equal Employment Opportunity Commission, accessed May 9, 2015, http://www.eeoc.gov/eeoc/statistics/enforcement/adea.cfm.

39. S. R. Rhodes, "Age-Related Differences in Work Attitudes and Behavior," *Psychological Bulletin* 92 (1983): 328–367.

40. T. Ng and D. Feldman, "The Relationship of Age to Ten Dimensions of Job Performance," *Journal of Applied Psychology* 93, no. 2 (2008): 392–423.

41. G. M. McEvoy and W. F. Cascio, "Cumulative Evidence of the Relationship Between Employee

Age and Job Performance," *Journal of Applied Psychology* 74 (1989): 11–17; T. Ng and D. Feldman, "The Relationship of Age to Ten Dimensions of Job Performance," *Journal of Applied Psychology* 93, no. 2 (2008): 392–423; A. Tergesen, "Why Everything You Think about Aging May Be Wrong," *Wall Street Journal*, November 30, 2014, , accessed May 9, 2015, http://www.wsj.com/articles/why-everything -you-think-about-aging-may-be-wrong-1417408057.

42. S. E. Sullivan and E. A. Duplaga, "Recruiting and Retaining Older Workers for the Millennium," *Business Horizons* 40 (November 12, 1997): 65; E. Townsend, "To Keep Older Workers, Consider New Responsibilities and Guard Against Discrimination," SHRM Foundation, accessed June 17, 2014, http://www.shrm.org/about /foundation/pages/researchthatmatters.aspx.

43. T. Maurer and N. Rafuse, "Learning, Not Litigating: Managing Employee Development and Avoiding Claims of Age Discrimination," *Academy of Management Executive* 15, no. 4 (2001): 110–121.

44. D. Brady, "The Bottom-Line Reasons for Mixing the Young and Old at Work," *Bloomberg Businessweek*, April 10, 2014, accessed July 11, 2014, http://www.businessweek.com/articles/2014 -02-10/workplaces-boost-profits-when-young-and -old-workers-mentor-each-other; B. L. Hassell and P. L. Perrewe, "An Examination of Beliefs About Older Workers: Do Stereotypes Still Exist?" *Journal of Organizational Behavior* 16 (1995): 457–468.

45. "Charge Statistics: FY 1997 Through FY 2012," *US Equal Employment Opportunity Commission*, accessed June 15, 2013, http://eeoc.gov/eeoc /statistics/enforcement/charges.cfm.

46. Women in the Labor Force: A Databook, US Bureau of Labor Statistics, December 2014, accessed May 9, 2015, http://www.bls.gov/opub /reports/cps/women-in-the-labor-force-a-databook -2014.pdf.

47. Update to The 2014 State of Women-Owned Businesses Report: A Summary of Important Trends 1997–2014, Commissioned by American Express OPEN, with the assistance of the Economic Census Branch of the Company Statistics Division of the US Census Bureau, March 2014, accessed May 9, 2015, http://www.womenable.com/content/userfiles/2014 _State_of_Women-owned_Businesses_public.pdf.

48. "Chart 1. Women's Earnings as a Percent of Men's, by Age, Full-Time Wage and Salary Workers, 1979-2012 Annual Averages," in "Highlights of Women's Earnings 2012," US Department of Labor, US Bureau of Labor Statistics, October 2013, accessed May 8, 2014, http://www.bls.gov/cps /cpswom2012.pdf; BLS Reports, "Highlights of Women's Earnings in 2013," US Bureau of Labor Statistics, December 2014, accessed May 9, 2015, http://www.bls.gov/opub/reports/cps/highlights-of -womens-earnings-in-2013.pdf.

49. "US Women in Business," *Catalyst*, June 10, 2014, accessed July 11, 2014, http://www.catalyst .org/knowledge/us-women-business-0.

50. R. Molla, "Meet the Women CEOs of the Fortune 500," *Wall Street Journal*, March 7, 2014, accessed July 12, 2014, http://blogs.wsj.com /atwork/2014/03/07/meet-the-women-ceos-of-the -fortune-500/; "Statistical Overview of Women in the Workplace," *Catalyst*, March 3, 2014, accessed June 17, 2014, http://www.catalyst.org/knowledge /statistical-overview-women-workplace.

51. "Women CEOs of the *Fortune* 1000," *Catalyst*, June 10, 2014, accessed June 17, 2014, http://www .catalyst.org/knowledge/women-ceos-fortune-1000.

52. "Statistical Overview of Women in the Workplace."

53. M. Bertrand and K. Hallock, "The Gender Gap in Top Corporate Jobs," *Industrial & Labor Relations Review* 55 (2001): 3–21.

54. J. R. Hollenbeck, D. R. Ilgen, C. Ostroff, and J. B. Vancouver, "Sex Differences in Occupational Choice, Pay, and Worth: A Supply-Side Approach to Understanding the Male-Female Wage Gap," *Personnel Psychology* 40 (1987): 715–744.

55. S. Shellenbarger, "Does Having Kids Dull Career Opportunities?" *WSJ Blogs: The Juggle*, Wall Street Journal, April 6, 2011, accessed May 28, 2011, http://blogs.wsj.com/juggle/2011/04/06/does -having-kids-dull-job-ambition/.

56. A. Chaker and H. Stout, "Second Chances: After Years Off, Women Struggle to Revive Careers," *Wall Street Journal*, May 6, 2004, A1.

57. C. Friedersdorf, "Why PepsiCo CEO Indra K. Nooyi Can't Have It All," *The Atlantic*, July 1, 2014, accessed July 12, 2014, http://www.theatlantic .com/business/archive/2014/07/why-pepsico-ceo -indra-k-nooyi-cant-have-it-all/373750/.

58. Department of Industry, Labor and Human Relations, Report of the Governor's Task Force on the Glass Ceiling Commission (Madison, WI: State of Wisconsin, 1993); S. Devillard, S. Sancier, C. Werner, I. Maller, and C. Kossoff, "Women Matter 2013, Gender Diversity in Top Management: Moving Corporate Culture, Moving Boundaries," *McKinsey & Company*, November 2013, 10–11; E. O. Wright and J. Baxter, "The Glass Ceiling Hypothesis: A Reply to Critics," *Gender & Society* 14 (2000): 814–821.

59. M. Fix, G. C. Galster, and R. J. Struyk, "An Overview of Auditing for Discrimination," in *Clear and Convincing Evidence: Measurement of Discrimination in America*, ed. M. Fix and R. Struyk (Washington, DC: Urban Institute Press, 1993), 1–68.

60. S. Devillard, S. Sancier, C. Werner, I. Maller, C. Kossoff, "Women Matter 2013, Gender Diversity in Top Management: Moving Corporate Culture, Moving Boundaries," *McKinsey & Company*, November 2013, 13–14.

61. S. Shellenbarger, "One Way to Get Unstuck and Move Up? All You Have to Do Is Ask" *Wall Street Journal*, April 15, 2015, D3.

62. J. Lublin, "Men Enlist in Fight for Gender Equality," Wall Street Journal, March 11, 2015, B7.

63. J. Hoobler, G. Lemmon and S. Wayne, "Women's Managerial Aspirations: An Organizational Development Perspective" *Journal of Management* 40 (2014): 703–730.

64. "Charge Statistics: FY 1997 Through FY 2013," *US Equal Employment Opportunity Commission*, accessed July 12, 2014, http://eeoc.gov/eeoc /statistics/enforcement/charges.cfm.

65. "Ask DiversityInc: Where's the Diversity in Fortune 500 CEOs?" *DiversityInc*, accessed June 17, 2014, http://www.diversityinc.com/diversity-facts /wheres-the-diversity-in-fortune-500-ceos/.

66. "Household Data Annual Averages: Table 11. Employed Persons by Detailed Occupation, Sex, Race, and Hispanic or Latino Ethnicity," in "Labor Force Statistics from the Current Population Survey," *Bureau of Labor Statistics, US Department of Labor*, February 26, 2014, accessed June 17, 2014, http://www.bls.gov/cps/cpsaat11.pdf.

67. D. A. Neal and W. R. Johnson, "The Role of Premarket Factors in Black-White Wage Differences," *Journal of Political Economy* 104, no. 5 (1996): 869–895.

68. Fix, Galster, and Struyk, "An Overview of Auditing for Discrimination."

69. S. Mullainathan, "Racial Bias Even When We Have Good Intentions," New York Times, January 3, 2015, BU6.

70. M. Bendick, Jr., C. W. Jackson, and V. A. Reinoso, "Measuring Employment Discrimination through Controlled Experiments," in *African- Americans and Post-Industrial Labor Markets, ed. James B. Stewart*

(New Brunswick, NJ: Transaction Publishers, 1997), 77–100.

71. P. B. Riach and J. Rich, "Measuring Discrimination by Direct Experimental Methods: Seeking Gunsmoke," *Journal of Post Keynesian Economics* 14, no. 2 (Winter 1991–1992): 143–150.

72. A. P. Brief, R. T. Buttram, R. M. Reizenstein, and S. D. Pugh, "Beyond Good Intentions: The Next Steps Toward Racial Equality in the American Workplace," *Academy of Management Executive* 11 (1997): 59–72.

73. L. E. Wynter, "Business & Race: Federal Agencies, Spurred on by Nonprofit Groups, Are Increasingly Embracing the Use of Undercover Investigators to Identify Discrimination in the Marketplace," *Wall Street Journal*, July 1, 1998, B1.

74. "Americans with Disabilities Act Questions and Answers," *US Department of Justice*, accessed July 12, 2014, http://www.ada.gov/qandaeng.htm.

75. M. Brault, "Americans with Disabilities: 2010, Household Economic Studies," in "Current Population Reports," *US Census Bureau*, issued July 2012, 70–131.

76. M. Brault, "Americans with Disabilities: 2010, Household Economic Studies," in "Current Population Reports," US Census Bureau, issued July 2012, 70–131.

77. Louis Harris & Associates, Inc., *Public Attitudes Toward People with Disabilities* (Washington, DC: National Organization on Disability, 1991); Louis Harris & Associates, Inc., *The ICD Survey II: Employing Disabled Americans* (New York: Louis Harris & Associates, Inc., 1987).

78. R. Greenwood and V. A. Johnson, "Employer Perspectives on Workers with Disabilities," *Journal of Rehabilitation* 53 (1987): 37–45.

79. M. Zelley and R. Keys, "Give Michigan's Disabled a Chance to Work," *Detroit News*, November 14, 2014, accessed May 9, 2015, http://www.detroitnews .com/story/opinion/2014/11/06/give-disabled-workers -chance/18553557/. http://www.washingtonpost.com /blogs/on-leadership/wp/2015/04/06/microsoft -launches-a-pilot-program-for-hiring-autistic-workers/

80. B. Loy, "Accommodation and Compliance Series Workplace Accommodations: Low Cost, High Impact," *Job Accommodation Network*, September 1, 2013, accessed June 17, 2014, https:// askjan.org/media/lowcosthighimpact.html.

81. T. E. Narashimhan and G. Babu, "The Chosen Ones," *Business Standard*, March 11, 2012, accessed March 16, 2012, http://www.business -standard.com/india/news/the-chosen-ones/467290/.

82. "Study on the Financing of Assistive Technology Devices and Services for Individuals with Disabilities: A Report to the President and the Congress of the United States," *National Council on Disability*, accessed August 21, 2008, http://www.ncd.gov /newsroom/publications/assistive.html.

83. R. B. Cattell, "Personality Pinned Down," *Psychology Today* 7 (1973): 40–46; C. S. Carver and M. F. Scheier, *Perspectives on Personality* (Boston: Allyn & Bacon, 1992).

84. S. Berfield, "Will Investors Put the Lid on the Container Store's Generous Wages," Bloomberg Businessweek, February 19,2015, accessed May 8, 2015, http://www.bloomberg.com/news/articles /2015-02-19/container-store-conscious-capitalism -and-the-perils-of-going-public.

85. J. M. Digman, "Personality Structure: Emergence of the Five-Factor Model," *Annual Review of Psychology* 41 (1990): 417–440; M. R. Barrick and M. K. Mount, "The Big Five Personality Dimensions and Job Performance: A Meta-Analysis," *Personnel Psychology* 44 (1991): 1–26.

86. R. Wall, "Germanwings Co-Pilot Andreas Lubitz Appeared to Rehearse Crash, Investigators Say,"

Wall Street Journal, May 6, 2015, accessed May 9, 2015, http://www.wsj.com/articles/germanwings-co -pilot-andreas-lubitz-altered-settings-of-earlier-flight -investigators-say-1430908536.

87. A. George, "How Airlines Screen Their Pilots and Watch Out for Warning Signs," *Popular Mechanics*, April 10, 2015, accessed May 7, 2015, http://www .popularmechanics.com/flight/a14776/how-airlines -screen-pilots-germanwings-9525/.

88. R. Cook, "The Changing 'Face' of Your Business: Finding Good People…and Keeping Them Motivated," *PRO Magazine*, March 2005, 43.

89. O. Behling, "Employee Selection: Will Intelligence and Conscientiousness Do the Job?" *Academy of Management Executive* 12 (1998): 77–86.

90. R. S. Dalal, "A Meta-Analysis of the Relationship Between Organizational Citizenship Behavior and Counterproductive Work Behavior," *Journal of Applied Psychology* 90 (2005): 1241–1255.

91. Barrick and Mount, "The Big Five Personality Dimensions and Job Performance"; M. K. Mount and M. R. Barrick, "The Big Five Personality Dimensions: Implications for Research and Practice in Human Resource Management," *Research in Personnel & Human Resources Management* 13 (1995): 153–200; M. K. Mount and M. R. Barrick, "Five Reasons Why the 'Big Five' Article Has Been Frequently Cited," *Personnel Psychology* 51 (1998): 849–857; D. S. Ones, M. K. Mount, M. R. Barrick, and J. E. Hunter, "Personality and Job Performance: A Critique of the Tett, Jackson, and Rothstein (1991) Meta-Analysis," *Personnel Psychology* 47 (1994): 147–156.

92. Mount and Barrick, "Five Reasons Why the 'Big Five' Article Has Been Frequently Cited."

93. J. A. Lopez, "Talking Desks: Personality Types Revealed in State Workstations," *Arizona Republic*, January 7, 1996, D1.

94. "The Diverse Work Force," *Inc.*, January 1993, 33.

95. J. Stillman, "Hiring? Personality Trumps Skills," *Inc.*, April 7, 2014, accessed May 9, 2015, http://www.inc.com/jessica-stillman/hiring -personality-trumps-skills.html.

96. D. A. Thomas and R. J. Ely, "Making Differences Matter: A New Paradigm for Managing Diversity," *Harvard Business Review* 74 (September-October 1996): 79–90.

97. Esen, "2005 Workplace Diversity Practices: Survey Report."

98. D. A. Thomas and S. Wetlaufer, "A Question of Color: A Debate on Race in the US Workplace," *Harvard Business Review* 75 (September–October 1997): 118–132.

99. E. Esen, "2007 State of Workplace Diversity Management. A Survey Report by the Society for Human Resource Management," 2008.

100. "Oshkosh Corporation—Diversity & Inclusion," Oshkosh, accessed July 12, 2014, http://www .oshkoshcorporation.com/about/diversity.html.

101. J. Espinoza, "Working to Prove Benefits of More Women at the Top," *Wall Street Journal*, February 27, 2011, accessed March 15, 2011, http:// www.wsj.com/articles/SB10001424052748704150604576166483012821352.

102. J. R. Norton and R. E. Fox, *The Change Equation: Capitalizing on Diversity for Effective Organizational Change* (Washington, DC: American Psychological Association, 1997).

103. Ibid.

104. Thomas and Ely, "Making Differences Matter."

105. R. R. Thomas, Jr., *Beyond Race and Gender: Unleashing the Power of Your Total Workforce by Managing Diversity* (New York: AMACOM, 1991).

106. Ibid.

107. T. Cox, Jr., "The Multicultural Organization," *Academy of Management Executive* 5 (1991): 34–47.

108. S. Lubove, "Damned If You Do, Damned If You Don't: Preference Programs Are on the Defensive in the Public Sector, but Plaintiffs' Attorneys and Bureaucrats Keep Diversity Inc. Thriving in Corporate America," *Forbes*, December 15, 1997, 122.

109. L. S. Gottfredson, "Dilemmas in Developing Diversity Programs," in *Diversity in the Workplace*, ed. S. E. Jackson & Associates (New York: Guilford Press, 1992).

110. J. Graham and S. Kerr, "Mentoring," in *Diversity in Engineering: Managing the Workforce of the Future* (Washington, DC: National Academies Press, 2002), accessed June 16, 2013, http:// www.nap.edu/openbook.php?record _id=10377&page=99.

111. J. Longman, "Pioneer of a Crossover Move: How Becky Hammon Became NBA's First Full-Time Female Assistant Coach," *New York Times*, August 12, 2014, B8.

112. "Diversity at Work: Public Relations Makes a Difference for Global Giants."

113. Carnevale and Stone, *The American Mosaic*.

114. J. Lublin, "Men Enlist in Fight for Gender Equality," *Wall Street Journal*, March 11, 2015, B7.

115. A. Greenwald, B. Nosek, and M. Banaji, "Understanding and Using the Implicit Association Test: I. An Improved Scoring Algorithm," *Journal of Personality & Social Psychology* (August 2003): 197–206; J. S. Lublin, "Bringing Hidden Biases into the Light," *Wall Street Journal*, January 9, 2014, accessed June 17, 2014, http://online.wsj.com /news/articles/SB1000142405270230375440457930 8562690896896; "The IAT | The Blind Spot," *The Blind Spot*, accessed July 13, 2014, http:// spottheblindspot.com/the-iat/.

116. F. Oswald, G. Mitchell, H. Blanton, J. Jaccard, and P. Tetlock, "Predicting Ethnic and Racial Discrimination: A Meta-Analysis of IAT Criterion Studies," *Journal of Personality and Social Psychology* 105 (2013): 171–192.

117. "2010 Corporate Responsibility Report," *Intel*, accessed May 5, 2012, http://csrreportbuilder .intel.com/PDFFiles/CSR_2010_Full-Report.pdf.

118. "Intel Corp.—2012 50 Out Front #16," *Diversity MBA Magazine*, September 16, 2011, accessed March 16, 2012, http://diversitymbamagazine .com/tag/intel.

119. R. Joplin and C. S. Daus, "Challenges of Leading a Diverse Workforce," *Academy of Management Executive* 11 (1997): 32–47.

120. A. Fisher, "Should People Choose Their Own Mentors?" *Fortune*, November 29, 2004, 72.

121. N. Byrnes and R. O. Crockett, "An Historic Succession at Xerox," *Business Week*, June 8, 2009, 18–22.

122. P. Dvorak, "How Executives Are Pushed to Foster Diversity," *Wall Street Journal*, December 18, 2006, accessed March 16, 2012, http://online .wsj.com/article/SB116640764543853102.html ?mod=rss_build.

13

1. "State of the Global Workplace: Employee Engagement Insights for Business Leaders Worldwide," Gallup, October 8, 2013, accessed July 13, 2014, http://www.gallup.com/services/178517/state -global-workplace.aspx

2. P. Campbell and R. D. Pritchard, "Motivation Theory in Industrial and Organizational Psychology," in *Handbook of Industrial and Organizational*

Psychology, ed. M. D. Dunnette (Chicago: Rand McNally, 1976).

3. J. Fried, "When the Only Way Up Is Out," *Inc.*, April 2011, 35–36.

4. A. Locke, "The Nature and Causes of Job Satisfaction," in *Handbook of Industrial and Organizational Psychology*, ed. M. D. Dunnette (Chicago: Rand McNally, 1976).

5. Mr. Everyday Dollar, "I Just Became a Millionaire at Age 35, and It's a Huge Letdown," *Business Insider*, March 27, 2015, accessed May 10, 2015, http://www.businessinsider.com/i-just-became-a -millionaire-at-age-35-and-its-a-huge-letdown -2015-3.

6. H. Maslow, "A Theory of Human Motivation," *Psychological Review* 50 (1943): 370–396.

7. P. Alderfer, *Existence, Relatedness, and Growth: Human Needs in Organizational Settings* (New York: Free Press, 1972).

8. C. McClelland, "Toward a Theory of Motive Acquisition," *American Psychologist* 20 (1965): 321–333; D. C. McClelland and D. H. Burnham, "Power Is the Great Motivator," *Harvard Business Review* 54, no. 2 (1976): 100–110.

9. J. H. Turner, "Entrepreneurial Environments and the Emergence of Achievement Motivation in Adolescent Males," *Sociometry* 33 (1970): 147–165.

10. L. W. Porter, E. E. Lawler III, and J. R. Hackman, *Behavior in Organizations* (New York: McGraw-Hill, 1975).

11. C. Ajila, "Maslow's Hierarchy of Needs Theory: Applicability to the Nigerian Industrial Setting," *IFE Psychology* (1997): 162–174.

12. M. A. Wahba and L. B. Birdwell, "Maslow Reconsidered: A Review of Research on the Need Hierarchy Theory," *Organizational Behavior & Human Performance* 15 (1976): 212–240; J. Rauschenberger, N. Schmitt, and J. E. Hunter, "A Test of the Need Hierarchy Concept by a Markov Model of Change in Need Strength," *Administrative Science Quarterly* 25 (1980): 654–670.

13. E. E. Lawler III and L. W. Porter, "The Effect of Performance on Job Satisfaction," *Industrial Relations* 7 (1967): 20–28.

14. Porter, Lawler, and Hackman, *Behavior in Organizations*.

15. E. White, "Employers Increasingly Favor Bonuses to Raises," *Wall Street Journal*, August 28, 2006, B3.

16. F. Koller, "American Factory Workers Getting $33,029 Yearly Bonuses May Sound Insane, But It's True," *The Motley Fool*, February 1, 2014, accessed July 14, 2014, http://www.fool.com/investing/general /2014/02/01/american-factory-workers-getting -33029-yearly-bonu.aspx.

17. Porter, Lawler, and Hackman, *Behavior in Organizations*.

18. J. Bohannon, "One Type of Motivation May Be Key to Success," *Science*, July 1, 2014, accessed May 8, 2015, http://news.sciencemag.org/brain -behavior/2014/07/one-type-motivation-may-be -key-success; A. Wrzesniewski, B. Schwartz, X. Cong, M. Kane, A. Omar, and T. Kolditz, "Multiple Types of Motives Don't Multiply the Motivation of West Point Cadets," Proceedings of the National Academy of Sciences of the United States of America, 111 no. 30 (2014): 10990–10995.

19. C. Caggiano, "What Do Workers Want?" *Inc.*, November 1992, 101–104; "National Study of the Changing Workforce," *Families & Work Institute*, accessed May 31, 2005, http://www.familiesandwork .org/summary/nscw.pdf.

20. C. Lee, A. Alonso, E. Esen, J. Coombs, and Y. Dong, "Employee Job Satisfaction and Engagement: The Road to Economic Recovery," *Society*

for Human Resource Management, May 7, 2014, accessed June 18, 2014, http://www.shrm.org /Research/SurveyFindings/Documents/14-0028%20 JobSatEngage_Report_FULL_FNL.pdf.

21. N. Jackson, "5 Ways to Reward Employees When Raises Aren't an Option," *Entrepreneur*, August 24, 2012, accessed June 16, 2013, http:// www.entrepreneur.com/article/224249.

22. C. Lee, et. al., "Employee Job Satisfaction and Engagement: The Road to Economic Recovery."

23. S. Berfield, "Will Investors Put the Lid on the Container Store's Generous Wages," *Bloomberg Businessweek*, February 19,2015, accessed May 9, 2015, http://www.bloomberg.com/news/articles /2015-02-19/container-store-conscious-capitalism -and-the-perils-of-going-public.

24. J. Laabs, "Satisfy Them with More Than Money," *Personnel Journal* 77, no. 11 (1998): 40.

25. R. Kanfer and P. Ackerman, "Aging, Adult Development, and Work Motivation," *Academy of Management Review* (2004): 440–458.

26. "CEOs Make 296 Times More Than Workers," *CNNMoney*, June 12, 2014, accessed May 10, 2015, http://money.cnn.com/2014/06/12/news /economy/ceo-pay/index.html.

27. V. Giang, "The 15 Highest-Paid CEOs in America," *Business Insider*, October 26, 2013, accessed June 18, 2014, http://www.businessinsider .com/15-highest-paid-ceos-in-america-2013-10?op=1: K. Hagey, "Discovery Communications CEO Gets 2014 Compensation of $156.1 Million," *Wall Street Journal*, April 4, 2015, accessed May 10, 2015, http:// www.wsj.com/articles/discovery-communications -ceo-gets-2014-compensation-of-156-1-million -1428164100..

28. L. Culpepper and E. Hurst, "Reporting CEO- to-Employee Pay Ratios: Navigating the Minefield," *Society for Human Resource Management*, November 1, 2010, accessed June 16, 2013, http:// www.shrm.org/hrdisciplines/compensation/articles /pages/payratios.aspx.

29. C. T. Kulik and M. L. Ambrose, "Personal and Situational Determinants of Referent Choice," *Academy of Management Review* 17 (1992): 212–237.

30. L. Stevens, "Amazon Vexed by Strikes in Germany," *Wall Street Journal*, June 19, 2013, B1.

31. J. S. Adams, "Toward an Understanding of Inequity," *Journal of Abnormal Social Psychology* 67 (1963): 422–436.

32. S. Choudhury and D. Thoppil, "Toyota Sput- ters in India—Workers Remain on Strike, Refuse to Sign Code of Conduct," *Wall Street Journal*, March 28, 2014, B4.

33. D. Primack, "CEO Gives Back Bonus, Says He Doesn't Deserve It," *Fortune*, December 18, 2014, accessed May 8, 2015, http://fortune.com/2014/12/18 /ceo-gives-back-bonus-says-he-doesnt-deserve-it/.

34. C. Elliott, "When Labor Woes Cause Turbu- lence for Fliers," *Washington Post*, September 30, 2012, F2; G. Karp, "American Airlines Cancels Flights on Alleged Pilots' 'Sickout,'" *Chicago Tribune*, September 18, 2012, accessed June 16, 2013, http://articles.chicagotribune.com/2012-09-18 /business/chi-american-airlines-cancels-flights-on -pilots-sickout-20120918_1_dennis-tajer-sickout -american-airlines.

35. "Overtime Pay—Wage and Hour Division (WHD)," U.S. Department of Labor, accessed July 15, 2014, http://www.dol.gov/whd/overtime _pay.htm.

36. S. Banjo, "Wal-Mart to Pay $4.8 Million in Back Wages, Damages," *Wall Street Journal*, May 2, 2013, B3.

37. Wage and Hour Division, "2008 Statistical Fact Sheet," *United States Department of Labor*, December, 2008, accessed June 18, 2014, http:// www.dol.gov/whd/statistics/2008FiscalYear.htm.

38. L. Badoux, "Trends in Wage and Hour Litiga- tion Over Unpaid Work Time and the Precautions Employers Should Take," *ADP*, Roseland, NJ, 2012, accessed June 18, 2014, https://www.adp.com /workforce-management/docs/whitepaper /trendsinwageandhourlitigation_05292012.pdf.

39. C. Chen, J. Choi, and S. Chi, "Making Justice Sense of Local-Expatriate Compensation Disparity: Mitigation by Local Referents, Ideological Explana- tions, and Interpersonal Sensitivity in China- Foreign Joint Ventures," *Academy of Management Journal* (2002): 807–817.

40. K. Bradsher, "Even as Wages Rise, China Exports Grow," *The New York Times*, January 9, 2014, accessed July 15, 2014, http://www.nytimes .com/2014/01/10/business/international/chinese -exports-withstand-rising-labor-costs.html?_r=0; M. Gimein, "If US Wages Rose as Fast as China's, Factories Would Now Pay $50 an Hour," *Bloom- berg*, March 27, 2013, accessed July 15, 2014, http://go.bloomberg.com/market-now/2013/03/27 /if-u-s-wages-rose-as-fast-as-chinas-factories-would -pay-50-an-hour/.

41. J. Quiqley, "Lenovo CEO to Share $3 Million Bonus with 10,000 Employees," *The Diplomat*, September 3, 2013, accessed July 15, 2014, http:// thediplomat.com/2013/09/lenovo-ceo-to-share -3-million-bonus-with-10000-employees/.

42. Bloomberg News, "Lenovo Chief Yang Shares Bonus with Workers a Second Year," *Bloomberg- Businessweek*, September 2, 2013, accessed July 15, 2014, http://www.bloomberg.com/news/articles /2013-09-01/lenovo-chief-yang-shares-bonus-with -workers-for-second-year.

43. "Apple Supplier Foxconn Cuts Working Hours, Workers Ask Why," *Reuters*, March 30, 2012, accessed May 8, 2012, http://www.reuters .com/article/2012/03/30/us-apple-foxconn-workers -idUSBRE82T0FC20120330; D. Barboza, "Foxconn Plant to Lift Pay Sharply at Factories in China," *New York Times*, February 18, 2012, accessed March 21, 2012, http://www.nytimes.com/2012/02/19 /technology/foxconn-to-raise-salaries-for-workers -by-up-to-25.html; M. Brown, "New Report Details Onerous, Illegal Working Conditions at Foxconn," *Wired.com*, May 6, 2011, accessed March 21, 2012, http://www.wired.com/epicenter/2011/05/foxconn -no-suicide-pledge/; H. Koch, "We Were Not a Very Open Company Before," *Spiegel Online*, May 11, 2011, accessed March 21, 2012, http://www.spiegel .de/international/world/0,1518,761934,00.html.

44. R. Folger and M. A. Konovsky, "Effects of Procedural and Distributive Justice on Reactions to Pay Raise Decisions," *Academy of Management Journal* 32 (1989): 115–130; M. A. Konovsky, "Understanding Procedural Justice and Its Impact on Business Organizations," *Journal of Management* 26 (2000): 489–512.

45. E. Barret-Howard and T. R. Tyler, "Procedural Justice as a Criterion in Allocation Decisions," *Journal of Personality & Social Psychology* 50 (1986): 296–305; Folger and Konovsky, "Effects of Procedural and Distributive Justice on Reactions to Pay Raise Decisions."

46. R. Folger and J. Greenberg, "Procedural Justice: An Interpretive Analysis of Personnel Systems," in *Research in Personnel and Human Resources Management*, vol. 3, ed. K. Rowland and G. Ferris (Greenwich, CT: JAI, 1985); R. Folger, D. Rosenfield, J. Grove, and L. Corkran, "Effects of 'Voice' and Peer Opinions on Responses to Inequity," *Journal of Personality & Social Psychology* 37 (1979): 2253–2261; E. A. Lind and T. R. Tyler, *The Social Psychology of Procedural Justice* (New York: Plenum, 1988); Konovsky,

"Understanding Procedural Justice and Its Impact on Business Organizations."

47. V. H. Vroom, *Work and Motivation* (New York: John Wiley & Sons, 1964); L. W. Porter and E. E. Lawler III, *Managerial Attitudes and Per- formance* (Homewood, IL: Dorsey & Richard D. Irwin, 1968).

48. C. Schultz, "When You Reward, Make It About the Employee—Not the Employer," *TLNT*, May 16, 2012, accessed June 16, 2013, http://www.tlnt.com /2012/05/16/when-you-reward-make-it-about-the -employee-not-the-employer/.

49. S. Miller, "Countering the Employee Recogni- tion Gap," SHRM Library, *Society for Human Resource Management*, February 2006, accessed March 25, 2009, http://www.shrm.org.

50. G. Douglas, "Survey Finds Many Employers Not Satisfied with Their Pay-for-Performance Programs," Bloomberg BNA, December 30, 2013, accessed July 15, 2014, http://www.bna.com/survey -finds-employers-n17179881003/.

51. E. Bernstein and H. Blunden, "The Sales Director Who Turned Work into a Fantasy Sports Competition," Harvard Business Review, March 27, 2015, accessed May 10, 2015, https://hbr.org/2015 /03/the-sales-director-who-turned-work-into-a -fantasy-sports-competition.

52. E. Bernstein and H. Blunden, "The Sales Director Who Turned Work into a Fantasy Sports Competition," *Harvard Business Review*, March 27, 2015, accessed May 10, 2015, https://hbr.org/2015 /03/the-sales-director-who-turned-work-into-a -fantasy-sports-competition.

53. K. W. Thomas and B. A. Velthouse, "Cognitive Elements of Empowerment," *Academy of Manage- ment Review* 15 (1990): 666–681.

54. E. L. Thorndike, *Animal Intelligence* (New York: Macmillan, 1911).

55. G. Karp, "United Posts Best On-Time Month of 2012 in November," *Chicago Tribune*, December 3, 2012, accessed June 16, 2013, http://articles .chicagotribune.com/2012-12-03/business/chi-united -posts-best-monthly-ontime-performance-in -november-20121203_1_dispatch-system-software -international-flights-regional-flights.

56. B. F. Skinner, *Science and Human Behavior* (New York: Macmillan, 1954); B. F. Skinner, *Beyond Freedom and Dignity* (New York: Bantam, 1971); B. F. Skinner, *A Matter of Consequences* (New York: New York University Press, 1984).

57. A. M. Dickinson and A. D. Poling, "Schedules of Monetary Reinforcement in Organizational Behavior Management: Latham and Huber Revisited," *Journal of Organizational Behavior Management* 16, no. 1 (1992): 71–91.

58. L. Weber, "Wellness Programs Get a Health Check," *Wall Street Journal*, October 10, 2014, accessed May 10, 2015, http://www.wsj.com /articles/wellness-programs-get-a-health-check -1412725776.

59. L. Weber, "Wellness Program at Honeywell Faces Test," *Wall Street Journal*, October 29, 2014, accessed May 10, 2015, http://www.wsj.com/articles /wellness-program-at-honeywell-faces-test -1414626180.

60. D. Fitzgerald, "Staples Defends Executive Bonuses," *Wall Street Journal*, May 26, 2014, accessed July 15, 2014, http://online.wsj.com/news /articles/SB10001424052702304811904579586173 092378940.

61. J. B. Miner, *Theories of Organizational Behavior* (Hinsdale, IL: Dryden, 1980).

62. Dickinson and Poling, "Schedules of Monetary Reinforcement in Organizational Behavior Management."

63. F. Luthans and A. D. Stajkovic, "Reinforce for Performance: The Need to Go Beyond Pay and Even Rewards," *Academy of Management Executive* 13, no. 2 (1999): 49–57.

64. D. Anderson, *Up Your Business! 7 Steps to Fix, Build or Stretch Your Organization* (New York: Wiley, 2003).

65. K. D. Butterfield, L. K. Trevino, and G. A. Ball, "Punishment from the Manager's Perspective: A Grounded Investigation and Inductive Model," *Academy of Management Journal* 39 (1996): 1479–1512.

66. R. D. Arvey and J. M. Ivancevich, "Punishment in Organizations: A Review, Propositions, and Research Suggestions," *Academy of Management Review* 5 (1980): 123–132.

67. R. D. Arvey, G. A. Davis, and S. M. Nelson, "Use of Discipline in an Organization: A Field Study," *Journal of Applied Psychology* 69 (1984): 448–460; M. E. Schnake, "Vicarious Punishment in a Work Setting," *Journal of Applied Psychology* 71 (1986): 343–345.

68. G. A. Yukl and G. P. Latham, "Consequences of Reinforcement Schedules and Incentive Magnitudes for Employee Performance: Problems Encountered in a Field Setting," *Journal of Applied Psychology* 60 (1975): 294–298.

69. E. A. Locke and G. P. Latham, *Goal Setting: A Motivational Technique That Works* (Englewood Cliffs, NJ: Prentice-Hall, 1984); E. A. Locke and G. P. Latham, *A Theory of Goal Setting and Task Performance* (Englewood Cliffs, NJ: Prentice-Hall, 1990).

70. D. Wessel, "Gaming the System to Beat Rush-Hour Traffic," *Wall Street Journal,* July 31, 2013, accessed July 15, 2014, http://online.wsj.com/news/articles/SB10001424127887323997004578639802367960498.

71. S. Berfield, "Will Investors Put the Lid on the Container Store's Generous Wages," *Bloomberg Businessweek*, February 19,2015, accessed May 10, 2015, http://www.bloomberg.com/news/articles/2015-02-19/container-store-conscious-capitalism-and-the-perils-of-going-public.

72. G. P. Latham and E. A. Locke, "Goal Setting—A Motivational Technique That Works," *Organizational Dynamics* 8, no. 2 (1979): 68.

73. Ibid.

14

1. A. Bryant, "Before the Meeting Adjourns, Tell Me What You'll Do Next," *New York Times*, August 11, 2012, accessed June 17, 2013, http://www.nytimes.com/2012/08/12/business/bill-flemming-of-skanska-usa-building-on-leadership.html?_r=0.

2. W. Bennis, "Why Leaders Can't Lead," *Training & Development Journal* 43, no. 4 (1989).

3. T. Foster, "How Etsy CEO Chad Dickerson Walks the Talk," Inc., December 2013/January 2014, accessed May 10, 2015, http://www.inc.com/magazine/201312/tom-foster/etsy-chad-dickerson-walks-the-talk.html.

4. M. Langley, "IBM Chief Searches for Big Blue's Next Act," *Wall Street Journal*, April 21, 2015, A1, A16.

5. A. Zaleznik, "Managers and Leaders: Are They Different?" *Harvard Business Review* 55 (1977): 76–78; A. Zaleznik, "The Leadership Gap," *Washington Quarterly* 6 (1983): 32–39.

6. Bennis, "Why Leaders Can't Lead."

7. D. Clark, "New CEO Is Insider, Sales Pro," *Wall Street Journal*, May 5, 2015, B1, B5.

8. B. Fritz, "Sony Names New Movie Chief," *Wall Street Journal*, February 24, 2015, accessed May 10,

2015, http://www.wsj.com/articles/sony-pictures-names-tom-rothman-new-movie-chief-1424802775.

9. D. Jones, "Not All Successful CEOs Are Extroverts," *USA Today*, June 7, 2006, B.1.

10. S. Cole, "7 Famous Leaders Who Prove Introverts Can Be Wildly Successful," *Fast Company*, June 18, 2014, accessed May 10, 2015, http://www.fastcompany.com/3032028/the-future-of-work/7-famous-leaders-who-prove-introverts-can-be-wildly-successful.

11. G. Murray, "Caveman Politics," *Psychology Today*, December 15, 2011, accessed June 19, 2014, http://www.psychologytoday.com/blog/caveman-politics/201112/are-you-sure-we-prefer-taller-leaders; G. Murray and J. Schmitz, "Caveman Politics: Evolutionary Leadership Preferences and Physical Stature," *Social Science Quarterly* 92 (2011): 1215-1235.

12. M. Gladwell, "Why Do We Love Tall Men?" Gladwell.com, accessed July 16, 2014, http://gladwell.com/blink/why-do-we-love-tall-men/.

13. Schumpeter, "The Look of a Leader," *The Economist*, September 27, 2014, accessed May 10, 2015, http://www.economist.com/news/business/21620197-getting-top-much-do-how-you-look-what-you-achieve-look-leader.

14. R. J. House and R. M Aditya, "The Social Scientific Study of Leadership: Quo Vadis?" *Journal of Management* 23 (1997): 409–473; T. Judge, R. Illies, J. Bono, and M. Gerhardt, "Personality and Leadership: A Qualitative and Quantitative Review," *Journal of Applied Psychology* (August 2002): 765–782; S. A. Kirkpatrick and E. A. Locke, "Leadership: Do Traits Matter?" *Academy of Management Executive* 5, no. 2 (1991): 48–60.

15. House and Aditya, "The Social Scientific Study of Leadership"; Kirkpatrick and Locke, "Leadership: Do Traits Matter?"

16. C. Rose, "Charlie Rose Talks to . . . Jack Ma," *BloombergBusinessweek*, January 29, 2015, 36.

17. J. Jurgensen, "How to Run a Creative Hothouse," *Wall Street Journal*, March 13, 2015, D1, D2.

18. I. Mochari, "The Most Valuable Lesson Jeff Weiner Learned as LinkedIn's CEO," *Inc*, February 7, 2014, accessed June 19, 2014, http://www.inc.com/ilan-mochari/3-tips-fire-fast.html.

19. B. Fritz and E. Schwartzel, "Iger 'Clone' Rises in Disney's Ranks," *Wall Street Journal*, February 14–15, 2015, B1, B3.

20. Kirkpatrick and Locke, "Leadership: Do Traits Matter?"

21. E. A. Fleishman, "The Description of Supervisory Behavior," *Journal of Applied Psychology* 37 (1953): 1–6; L. R. Katz, *New Patterns of Management* (New York: McGraw-Hill, 1961).

22. C. Dawson, "Nissan Drives to Close Gap," *Wall Street Journal*, June 27, 2011, accessed June 17, 2013, http://www.wsj.com/articles/SB10001424052702304478045764094720712372288; J. Ramsey, "Nissan Announces 'Power 88' Business Plan, All-New Vehicles Every Six Weeks for Six Years," *AutoBlog*, June 27, 2011, accessed June 17, 2013, http://www.autoblog.com/2011/06/27/nissan-announces-power-88-business-plan-all-new-vehicles-ever/.

23. J. Jargon, "At Popeye's, Recipe for a Turnaround," *Wall Street Journal*, March 9, 2014, accessed May 10, 2015, http://www.wsj.com/articles/SB10001424052702304181204579368983741915774.

24. J. Goudreau, "The CEO of Popeyes Says Becoming a 'Servant Leader' Helped Her Turn Around the Struggling Restaurant Chain," *Business Insider*, March 24, 2015, accessed May 10, 2015, http://www.businessinsider.com/popeyes-ceo-servant-leadership-traits-2015-3.

25. P. Weissenberg and M. H. Kavanagh, "The Independence of Initiating Structure and

Consideration: A Review of the Evidence," *Personnel Psychology* 25 (1972): 119–130.

26. R. J. House and T. R. Mitchell, "Path-Goal Theory of Leadership," *Journal of Contemporary Business* 3 (1974): 81–97; F. E. Fiedler, "A Contingency Model of Leadership Effectiveness," in *Advances in Experimental Social Psychology*, ed. L. Berkowitz (New York: Academic Press, 1964); V. H. Vroom and P. W. Yetton, *Leadership and Decision Making* (Pittsburgh: University of Pittsburgh Press, 1973); P. Hersey and K. H. Blanchard, The *Management of Organizational Behavior*, 4th ed. (Englewood Cliffs, NJ: Prentice Hall, 1984); S. Kerr and J. M. Jermier, "Substitutes for Leadership: Their Meaning and Measurement," *Organizational Behavior & Human Performance* 22 (1978): 375–403.

27. A. Grant, F. Gino, and D. Hofmann, "The Hidden Advantage of Quiet Bosses," *Harvard Business Review* 88, no. 12 (2010): 28.

28. F. E. Fiedler and M. M. Chemers, *Leadership and Effective Management* (Glenview, IL: Scott, Foresman, 1974); F. E. Fiedler and M. M. Chemers, *Improving Leadership Effectiveness: The Leader Match Concept*, 2nd ed. (New York: Wiley, 1984).

29. A. Davis, "Corner Office: Angus Davis of Swipely, on Working Around Flaws," interview by A. Bryant, *New York Times*, April 24, 2014, accessed June 19, 2014, http://www.nytimes.com/2014/04/25/business/angus-davis-of-swipely-on-working-around-flaws.html.

30. Fiedler and Chemers, *Improving Leadership Effectiveness*.

31. F. E. Fiedler, "The Effects of Leadership Training and Experience: A Contingency Model Interpretation," *Administrative Science Quarterly* 17, no. 4 (1972): 455; F. E. Fiedler, *A Theory of Leadership Effectiveness* (New York: McGraw-Hill, 1967).

32. L. S. Csoka and F. E. Fiedler, "The Effect of Military Leadership Training: A Test of the Contingency Model," *Organizational Behavior & Human Performance* 8 (1972): 395–407.

33. House and Mitchell, "Path-Goal Theory of Leadership."

34. "Up and Coming Leaders," *Entrepreneur*, March 26, 2014, accessed July 17, 2014, http://www.entrepreneur.com/article/231531.

35. M. Tenney, "More Than Money," *Collector*, October 2013, 26-28.

36. House and Mitchell, "Path-Goal Theory of Leadership."

37. B. M. Fisher and J. E. Edwards, "Consideration and Initiating Structure and Their Relationships with Leader Effectiveness: A Meta-Analysis," *Proceedings of the Academy of Management*, August 1988, 201–205.

38. Kotter International, "Leadership Lessons from Domino's Pizza: NFL Draft Edition," *Forbes*, May 12, 2014, accessed June 19, 2014, http://www.forbes.com/sites/johnkotter/2014/05/12/leadership-lessons-from-dominos-pizza-nfl-draft-edition/.

39. L. Faw, "For Domino's, 'Failure Is an Option,'" *Mediapost Agency Daily*, April 14, 2014, accessed July 17, 2014, http://www.mediapost.com/publications/article/223604/for-dominos-failure-is-an-option.html.

40. Domino's TV Commercial, "Failure Is an Option," YouTube.com, 2014, April 15, 2014, accessed July 17, 2014, https://www.youtube.com/watch?v=wRaM3x78FEw

41. Kotter International, "Innovation Secrets from Domino's Pizza," *Forbes*, March 27, 2012, accessed June 19, 2014, http://www.forbes.com/sites/johnkotter/2012/03/27/innovation-secrets-from-dominos-pizza/.

42. E. Dou, "Asustek Seeks to Challenge Apple in Tablets," *Wall Street Journal*, December 3, 2013, accessed June 18, 2013, http://blogs.wsj.com /digits/2012/12/03/asustek-seeks-to-challenge -apple-in-tablets/; E. Dou, "Asustek to Make Small Windows 8 Tablets," *Wall Street Journal*, May 6, 2013, accessed June 18, 2013, http://online.wsj.com /article/SB100014241278873243265045784661223 67669576.html?mod=WSJ_qtoverview_wsjlatest.

43. J. C. Wofford and L. Z. Liska, "Path-Goal Theories of Leadership: A Meta-Analysis," *Journal of Management* 19 (1993): 857–876.

44. House and Aditya, "The Social Scientific Study of Leadership."

45. V. H. Vroom and A. G. Jago, *The New Leadership: Managing Participation in Organizations* (Englewood Cliffs, NJ: Prentice Hall, 1988).

46. C. Fishman, "How Teamwork Took Flight: This Team Built a Commercial Engine—and Self-Managing GE Plant—from Scratch," *Fast Company*, October 1, 1999, 188.

47. Ibid.

48. Ibid.

49. N. Fallon, "Is Your Management Style Hurting Your Team?" *Business News Daily*, May 14, 2014, accessed June 19, 2014, http://www.businessnewsdaily .com/6409-management-styles-strategies.html.

50. G. A. Yukl, *Leadership in Organizations*, 3rd ed. (Englewood Cliffs, NJ: Prentice Hall, 1995).

51. B. M. Bass, *Bass & Stogdill's Handbook of Leadership: Theory, Research, and Managerial Applications* (New York: Free Press, 1990).

52. R. D. Ireland and M. A. Hitt, "Achieving and Maintaining Strategic Competitiveness in the 21st Century: The Role of Strategic Leadership," *Academy of Management Executive* 13, no. 1 (1999): 43–57.

53. J. Lublin, "Rookie CEOs Face a Steep Learning Curve," June 24, 2014, accessed May 10, 2015, http://www.wsj.com/articles/rookie-ceos-face-a -steep-learning-curve-1403656894.

54. P. Thoms and D. B. Greenberger, "Training Business Leaders to Create Positive Organizational Visions of the Future: Is It Successful?" *Academy of Management Journal* (Best Papers & Proceedings 1995): 212–216.

55. M. Weber, *The Theory of Social and Economic Organizations*, trans. R. A. Henderson and T. Parsons (New York: Free Press, 1947).

56. D. A. Waldman and F. J. Yammarino, "CEO Charismatic Leadership: Levels-of-Management and Levels-of-Analysis Effects," *Academy of Management Review* 24, no. 2 (1999): 266–285.

57. K. B. Lowe, K. G. Kroeck, and N. Sivasubramaniam, "Effectiveness Correlates of Transformational and Transactional Leadership: A Meta -Analytic Review of the MLQ Literature," *Leadership Quarterly* 7 (1996): 385–425.

58. J. M. Howell and B. J. Avolio, "The Ethics of Charismatic Leadership: Submission or Liberation?" *Academy of Management Executive* 6, no. 2 (1992): 43–54.

59. G. Colvin, "The Greatest Business Decisions of All Time: Tata Steel," *Fortune*, October 1, 2012, accessed June 18, 2013, http://money.cnn.com /gallery/news/companies/2012/10/01/greatest -business-decisions.fortune/4.html.

60. J. Bunge, "Peregrine Founder Hit with 50 Years," *Wall Street Journal*, February 1, 2013, C1; T. Polansek and R. Schlader, "Peregrine CEO Pleads Guilty to Fraud; To Stay in Jail," *Reuters*, September 17, 2012, accessed June 19, 2013, http:// www.reuters.com/article/2012/09/17/us-peregrine -wasendorf-idUSBRE88G16U2 0120917.

61. D. J. Chandler, "The Perfect Storm of Leaders' Unethical Behavior: A Conceptual Framework,"
International Journal of Leadership Studies 5, no.1 (2009): 69-93.

62. Howell and Avolio, "The Ethics of Charismatic Leadership."

63. B. M. Bass, "From Transactional to Transformational Leadership: Learning to Share the Vision," *Organizational Dynamics* 18 (1990): 19–36.

64. B. M. Bass, *A New Paradigm of Leadership: An Inquiry into Transformational Leadership* (Alexandra, VA: US Army Research Institute for the Behavioral and Social Sciences, 1996).

65. CNN Wire Staff, "Network: Leno Took 50% Pay Cut to Reduce 'Tonight Show' Layoffs," CNN, September 8, 2012, accessed July 17, 2014, http:// www.cnn.com/2012/09/07/showbiz/jay-leno-tonight -show/; A. Farnham, "Bosses Who Volunteer for Pay Cuts," ABC News, September 11, 2012, accessed July 17, 2014, http://abcnews.go.com /Business/bosses-pay-cuts/story?id=17209062.

66. J. Gapper and T. Powley, "Inside the Dyson Dynasty," *Financial Times*, April 10, 2015, accessed May 10, 2015, http://www.ft.com/intl /cms/s/2/528c518c-de2e-11e4-8d14-00144feab7de .html.

67. Bass, "From Transactional to Transformational Leadership."

15

1. E. E. Lawler III, L. W. Porter, and A. Tannenbaum, "Manager's Attitudes Toward Interaction Episodes," *Journal of Applied Psychology* 52 (1968): 423–439; H. Mintzberg, *The Nature of Managerial Work* (New York: Harper & Row, 1973).

2. J. D. Maes, T. G. Weldy, and M. L. Icenogle, "A Managerial Perspective: Oral Communication Competency Is Most Important for Business Students in the Workplace," *Journal of Business Communication* 34 (1997): 67–80.

3. E. E. Jones and K. E. Davis, "From Acts to Dispositions: The Attribution Process in Person Perception," in *Advances in Experimental and Social Psychology*, vol. 2, ed. L. Berkowitz (New York: Academic Press, 1965), 219–266; R. G. Lord and J. E. Smith, "Theoretical, Information-Processing, and Situational Factors Affecting Attribution Theory Models of Organizational Behavior," *Academy of Management Review* 8 (1983): 50–60.

4. D. Simons and C. Chabris, "Gorillas in Our Midst: Sustained Inattentional Blindness for Dynamic Events," *Perception* 28 (1999): 1059–1074.

5. J. Zadney and H. B. Gerard, "Attributed Intentions and Informational Selectivity," *Journal of Experimental Social Psychology* 10 (1974): 34–52.

6. M. Beck, "What Cocktail Parties Teach Us," *Wall Street Journal*, April 23, 2012, D1.

7. H. H. Kelly, *Attribution in Social Interaction* (Morristown, NJ: General Learning Press, 1971).

8. J. M. Burger, "Motivational Biases in the Attribution of Responsibility for an Accident: A Meta-Analysis of the Defensive-Attribution Hypothesis," *Psychological Bulletin* 90 (1981): 496–512.

9. D. A. Hofmann and A. Stetzer, "The Role of Safety Climate and Communication in Accident Interpretation: Implications for Learning from Negative Events," *Academy of Management Journal* 41, no. 6 (1998): 644–657.

10. C. Perrow, *Normal Accidents: Living with High-Risk Technologies* (New York: Basic Books, 1984).

11. A. G. Miller and T. Lawson, "The Effect of an Informational Opinion on the Fundamental Attribution Error," *Journal of Personality & Social Psychology* 47 (1989): 873–896; J. M. Burger,
"Changes in Attribution Errors Over Time: The Ephemeral Fundamental Attribution Error," *Social Cognition* 9 (1991): 182–193.

12. F. Heider, *The Psychology of Interpersonal Relations* (New York: Wiley, 1958); D. T. Miller and M. Ross, "Self-Serving Biases in Attribution of Causality: Fact or Fiction?" *Psychological Bulletin* 82 (1975): 213–225.

13. J. R. Larson, Jr., "The Dynamic Interplay Between Employees' Feedback-Seeking Strategies and Supervisors' Delivery of Performance Feedback," *Academy of Management Review* 14, no. 3 (1989): 408–422.

14. R. C. Rabin, "15-Minute Visits Take a Toll on the Doctor-Patient Relationship," *Kaiser Health News*, April 21, 2014, accessed June 20, 2014, http:// www.kaiserhealthnews.org/Stories/2014/April/21/15 -minute-doctor-visits.aspx; S. Wilkins, "The Truth About Those High Patient Satisfaction Scores for Doctor-Patient Communication," *Center For Advancing Health* (Prepared Patient Blog), April 11, 2013, accessed June 20, 2014, http://www.cfah.org/blog /2013/the-truth-about-those-high-patient-satisfaction -scores-for-doctor-patient-communication.

15. Ibid.

16. S. Brownlee, "The Doctor Will See You—If You're Quick," *The Daily Beast*, April 16, 2012, accessed July 19, 2014, http://www.thedailybeast .com/newsweek/2012/04/15/why-your-doctor-has -no-time-to-see-you.html.

17. S. Wilkins, "The Truth About Those High Patient Satisfaction Scores for Doctor-Patient Communication."

18. "The Experts: How to Improve Doctor-Patient Communication," *Wall Street Journal*, April 12, 2013, accessed June 20, 2013, http://www.wsj.com /articles/SB1000142412788732405030457841125 1805908228.

19. Ibid.

20. S. Wilkins, "The Truth About Those High Patient Satisfaction Scores for Doctor-Patient Communication," Center for Advancing Health (Prepared Patient Blog), April 11, 2013, accessed June 20, 2014, http://www.cfah.org/blog/2013/the -truth-about-those-high-patient-satisfaction-scores -for-doctor-patient-communication.

21. "The Experts: How to Improve Doctor-Patient Communication."

22. L. Davey, "Managing Emotional Outbursts on Your Team," *Harvard Business Review*, April 30, 2015, accessed May 13, 2015, https://hbr.org/2015/04 /handling-emotional-outbursts-on-your-team.

23. Early. Green, "The Origins of Office Speak," *The Atlantic*, April 24, 2014, accessed June 20, 2014, http://www.theatlantic.com/business/archive/2014 /04/business-speak/361135/.

24. C. Hymowitz, "Mind Your Language: To Do Business Today, Consider Delayering," *Wall Street Journal*, March 27, 2006, B1.

25. G. L. Kreps, *Organizational Communication: Theory and Practice* (New York: Longman, 1990).

26. Ibid.

27. J. Jusko, "A Little More Communication," *Industry Week*, March 1, 2010, 19.

28. "S. Shellenbarger, "To Fight or Not to Fight? How to Pick Your Battles in the Workplace," *Wall Street Journal*, December 14, 2014, B1.

29. Ibid.

30. Ibid.

31. E. Swallow, "How Rumors Could Actually Strengthen Your Company Culture," *Forbes*, March 1, 2013, accessed June 19, 2013, http:// www.forbes.com/sites/ericaswallow/2013/03/01 /rumor-jar/.

32. J. Sandberg, "Ruthless Rumors and the Managers Who Enable Them," *Wall Street Journal*, October 29, 2003, B1.

33. E. Holm and J. S. Lublin, "Loose Lips Trip Up a Good Hands Executive," *Wall Street Journal*, August 1, 2011, C1.

34. K. Voight, "Office Intelligence," *Asian Wall Street Journal*, January 21, 2005, P1.

35. A. Aschale, "Review of the Grapevine Communication," June 2013, http://www.academia.edu/4362950/Review_of_the_Grapevine_Communication.

36. W. C. Redding, *Communication within the Organization: An Interpretive View of Theory and Research* (New York: Industrial Communication Council, 1972).

37. D. T. Hall, K. L. Otazo, and G. P. Hollenbeck, "Behind Closed Doors: What Really Happens in Executive Coaching," *Organizational Dynamics* 27, no. 3 (1999): 39–53.

38. J. Kelly, "Blowing the Whistle on the Boss," *PR Newswire*, November 15, 2004, accessed August 2015, http://www.prnewswire.com/news-releases/blowing-the-whistle-on-the-boss-75393797.html?\$G1Ref.

39. R. McGarvey, "Lords of Discipline," *Entrepreneur Magazine*, January 1, 2000, page number not available.

40. Jack Welch, "'Rank-and-Yank'? That's Not How It's Done," *Wall Street Journal*, November 15, 2013, A.15.

41. N. Goodman, "Jack Welch on How to Manage Employees," *Entrepreneur*, October 5, 2012, accessed July 19, 2014, http://www.entrepreneur.com/blog/224604.

42. C. Hirschman, "Firm Ground: EAP Training for HR and Managers Improves Supervisor-Employee Communication and Helps Organizations Avoid Legal Quagmires," *Employee Benefit News*, June 13, 2005, available athttp://www.highbeam.com/doc/1G1-121455684.html.

43. L. V. Gillespie, "Raising A-Wear-Ness," *Employee Benefit News*, December 1, 2011, accessed March 27, 2012, http://ebn.benefitnews.com/news/hiv-aids-levi-strauss-eap-disease-management-2720149-1.html.

44. A. Mehrabian, "Communication without Words," *Psychology Today* 3 (1968): 53; A. Mehrabian, *Silent Messages* (Belmont, CA: Wadsworth, 1971); R. Harrison, *Beyond Words: An Introduction to Nonverbal Communication* (Upper Saddle River, NJ: Prentice Hall, 1974); A. Mehrabian, *Non-Verbal Communication* (Chicago: Aldine, 1972).

45. M. L. Knapp, *Nonverbal Communication in Human Interaction*, 2nd ed. (New York: Holt, Rinehart & Winston, 1978).

46. H. M. Rosenfeld, "Instrumental Affiliative Functions of Facial and Gestural Expressions," *Journal of Personality & Social Psychology* 24 (1966): 65–72; P. Ekman, "Differential Communication of Affect by Head and Body Cues," *Journal of Personality & Social Psychology* 23 (1965): 726–735; A. Mehrabian, "Significance of Posture and Position in the Communication of Attitude and Status Relationships," *Psychological Bulletin* 71 (1969): 359–372.

47. J. Gottman and R. Levenson, "The Timing of Divorce: Predicting When a Couple Will Divorce over a 14-Year Period," *Journal of Marriage & the Family* 62 (August 2000): 737–745; J. Gottman, R. Levenson, and E. Woodin, "Facial Expressions During Marital Conflict," *Journal of Family Communication* 1, no. 1 (2001): 37–57.

48. T. Bradberry and K. Kruse, "Why Successful People Never Bring Smartphones into Meetings," LinkedIn, September 22, 2014, accessed May 12, 2015, https://www.linkedin.com/pulse/20140922000612-50578967-why-successful-people-never-bring-smartphones-into-meetings.

49. Ibid.

50. Ibid.

51. S. Shellenbarger, "Is This How You Really Talk?" *Wall Street Journal*, April 23, 2013, accessed June 20, 2014, http://www.wsj.com/news/articles/SB10001424127887323735604578440851083674898.

52. C. A. Bartlett and S. Ghoshal, "Changing the Role of Top Management: Beyond Systems to People," *Harvard Business Review*, May–June 1995, 132–142.

53. J. Lublin, "Managers Need to Make Time for Face Time," *Wall Street Journal*, March 18, 2015, B6.

54. J. Fry, "When Talk Isn't Cheap: Is Emailing Colleagues Who Sit Feet Away a Sign of Office Dysfunction, or a Wise Move?" *Wall Street Journal*, November 28, 2009, http://www.wsj.com/articles/SB113293718044406629.

55. "The Joys of Voice Mail," *Inc.*, November 1995, 102.

56. E. Bernstein, "Thou Shalt Not Send in Anger: Recovering from a Snippy Email to Friends, Even the Boss, Is Possible If You Grovel," *Wall Street Journal*, October 14, 2014, D1, D4.

57. D. F. Larcker, S. Miles, B. Tayan, and M. E. Gutman, "2013 CEO Performance Evaluation Survey," *Stanford Graduate School of Business*, accessed June 20, 2014, http://www.gsb.stanford.edu/cldr/research/surveys/performance.html.

58. E. Atwater, *I Hear You*, revised ed. (New York: Walker, 1992).

59. R. G. Nichols, "Do We Know How to Listen? Practical Helps in a Modern Age," in *Communication Concepts and Processes*, ed. J. DeVitor (Englewood Cliffs, NJ: Prentice Hall, 1971); P. V. Lewis, *Organizational Communication: The Essence of Effective Management* (Columbus, OH: Grid Publishing Company, 1975); S. Khan, "Why Long Lectures Are Ineffective," *Time*, October 2, 2012, accessed May 13, 2015, http://ideas.time.com/2012/10/02/why-lectures-are-ineffective/.

60. A. Stevenson, "T-Mobile CEO to Cramer: 'Shut Up and Listen,'"*CNBC*, April 28, 2015, accessed May 13, 2015, http://www.cnbc.com/id/102628529.

61. D. A. Kaplan, "Undercover Employee: A Day on the Job at Three Best Companies," *CNNMoney*, January 20, 2011, accessed March 27, 2012, http://features.blogs.fortune.cnn.com/2011/01/20/undercover-employee-a-day-on-the-job-at-three-best-companies/.

62. L. Gurkow, "The Art of Active Listening," *Jerusalem Post*, May 11, 2014, accessed June 20, 2014, http://www.jpost.com/Jewish-World/Judaism/Active-listening-351878.

63. E. Bernstein, "How 'Active Listening ' Makes Both Participants in a Conversation Feel Better," *Wall Street Journal*, January 12, 2015, accessed May 13, 2015, http://www.wsj.com/articles/how-active-listening-makes-both-sides-of-a-conversation-feel-better-1421082684.

64. J. Jargon, "Fast-Food Turnaround: Popeyes Louisiana Kitchen CEO Cheryl Bachelder Talks About Her Secret for Repairing Relationships with Angry Franchisees," *Wall Street Journal*, March 10, 2014, R3.

65. Ibid.

66. Atwater, *I Hear You*.

67. C. Edwards, "Death of a Pushy Salesman," *BusinessWeek*, July 3, 2006, 108.

68. J. Sandberg, "Not Communicating with Your Boss? Count Your Blessings," *Wall Street Journal*, May 22, 2007, B1.

69. A. Tugend, "You've Been Doing a Fantastic Job. Just One Thing …," *The New York Times*, April 6, 2013, B5.

70. M. Flatt, "How to Give Feedback That Works," *Inc.*, December 21, 2011, accessed March 27, 2012, http://www.inc.com/michael-flatt/how-to-give-feedback-that-works.html.

71. "Satya Nadella's Email to Employees: Bold Ambition and Our Core," Microsoft, July 18, 2014, accessed July 20, 2014, http://www.microsoft.com/en-us/news/ceo/index.html.

72. Ibid.

73. F. Manjoo, "Slack, the Office Messaging App That May Finally Sink Email," *New York Times*, March 22, 2015, B1.

74. A. Bryant, "The Memo List: Where Everyone Has an Opinion," *New York Times*, March 10, 2012, accessed March 27, 2012, http://www.nytimes.com/2012/03/11/business/jim-whitehurst-of-red-hat-on-merits-of-an-open-culture.html.

75. D. Pontefract, "The Social C-Suite," *Chief Learning Officer Magazine*, March 13, 2013, accessed July 20, 2014, http://www.clomedia.com/articles/the-social-c-suite.

76. E. W. Morrison, "Organizational Silence: A Barrier to Change and Development in a Pluralistic World," *Academy of Management Review* 25 (2000): 706–725.

77. M. Heffernan, "Encourage Employees to Speak Up," *Inc*, April 9, 2014, accessed July 21, 2014, http://www.inc.com/margaret-heffernan/encourage-employees-to-speak-up.html.

78. R. Willingham, "Jetstar Pilots 'Afraid to Report Risks,'" *The Age*, March 19, 2011, accessed June 17, 2011, http://www.theage.com.au/travel/travel-news/jetstar-pilots-afraid-to-report-risks-20110318-1c0mi.html.

79. Ibid.

80. "An Inside Look at Corporate Hotlines," Security Director's Report, February 2007, 8.

81. Lublin, "Managers Need to Make Time for Face Time."

82. C. Hymowitz, "Sometimes, Moving Up Makes It Harder to See What Goes on Below," *Wall Street Journal*, October 15, 2007, B1.

83. A. Bryant, "Every Team Should Have a Devil's Advocate," *New York Times*, December 24, 2011, accessed June 21, 2013, http://www.nytimes.com/2011/12/25/business/ori-hadomi-of-mazor-robotics-on-choosing-devils-advocates.html?pagewanted=all.

84. R. Birch, "How GTE FCU Turned Itself Around After 'Closing Down the Shop,'" *Credit Union Journal*, June 18, 2012, 40.

85. D. Kirkpatrick and D. Roth, "Why There's No Escaping the Blog," *Fortune* (Europe), January 24, 2005, 64.

86. R. Jones, "Labor Strife at Emirates Air," *Wall Street Journal*, March 23, 2015, B3.

16

1. R. Leifer and P. K. Mills, "An Information Processing Approach for Deciding Upon Control Strategies and Reducing Control Loss in Emerging Organizations," *Journal of Management* 22 (1996): 113–137.

2. C. Passariello, "Fiercest Match of French Open Tennis Tournament? Raptor vs. Pigeon," *Wall Street Journal*, June 6, 2014, http://wsj.com/articles/fiercest-match-of-french-open-tennis-tournament-raptor-vs-pigeon-1402101392.

3. J. Bookwalter, "Report: Apple Slows iPhone 5 Production to Address Aluminum Scratches," *TechRadar*, October 10, 2012, accessed June 21, 2013, http://www.techradar.com/us/news/phone -and-communications/mobile-phones/report-apple -slows-iphone-5-production-to-address-aluminum -scratches-1103440.

4. "Our Green Filter," *Green Depot*, accessed June 21, 2013, http://www.greendepot.com/greendepot /dept.asp?dept_id=12; N. Leiber, "With Eco-Friendly Building Supplies, Green Depot Thrives in the Construction Rebound," *Bloomberg Businessweek*, April 11, 2013, accessed June 21, 2013, http:// www.businessweek.com/articles/2013-04-11/with -eco-friendly-building-supplies-green-depot-thrives -in-the-construction-rebound.

5. R. Upson and K. Notarianni, "Quantitative Evaluaton of Fire and EMS Mobilization Times," The Fire Protection Research Foundation, May 2010, p. 1.

6. D. Robb, "Is Big Data Right for Small Business?" *Tech Page One*, June 26, 2014, accessed July 21, 2014, http://techpageone.dell.com/technology /is-big-data-right-for-small-business/.

7. L. Landro, "Why Hospitals Want Patients to Ask Doctors, 'Have You Washed Your Hands?'" *Wall Street Journal*, September 30, 2013, accessed July 21, 2014, http://wsj.com/news/articles/SB1000142405270 23039188045791072023605656342.

8. University Health Network, "HealthCare Worker Hand Hygiene Rates Increase Three-Fold When Auditors Visible," *Science Daily*, July 8, 2014, accessed May 14, 2015, http://www.sciencedaily .com/releases/2014/07/140708165727.htm.

9. T. Rosenberg, "An Electronic Eye on Hospital Hand-Washing," *New York Times*, November 24, 2011, http://opinionator.blogs.nytimes.com/2011 /11/24/an-electronic-eye-on-hospital-hand-washing.

10. N. Wiener, *Cybernetics; Or Control and Communication in the Animal and the Machine* (New York: Wiley, 1948).

11. Most. Rohde, "Squirrelly Behavior: Critters Shock the System," *Daily Reporter*, January 4, 2011, accessed June 20, 2011, http://dailyreporter.com/2011/01/04 /squirrely-behavior-critters-shock-the-system/.

12. J. Mooallem, "Squirrel Power!" *New York Times*, August 31, 2013, accessed June 23, 2014, http://www.nytimes.com/2013/09/01/opinion /sunday/squirrel-power.html?pagewanted=all.

13. Ibid.

14. K. Stack, "Concussion-Sensing Chin Strap Raises Questions," *Wired.com*, March 26, 2012, accessed March 28, 2012, http://www.wired.com /playbook/2012/03/battle-sports-science-impact -indicator/.

15. M. Griggs, "In Nasty Weather, High-Tech Sensors Get the Lights Back on Faster," *Popular Science*, December 23, 2014, accessed May 14, 2015, http:// www.popsci.com/high-tech-power-line-sensors -get-lights-turned-faster.

16. D. Cardwell, "Grid Sensors Could Ease Disruptions of Power," *New York Times*, February 3, 2015, B4.

17. Leifer and Mills, "An Information Processing Approach."

18. A Gasparro and J. Newman, "Blue Bell Recall Shows Difficulty of Controlling Listeria," *Wall Street Journal*, April 21, 2015, accessed May 14, 2015, http://www.wsj.com/articles/blue-bell-recall-shows -difficulty-of-controlling-listeria-1429653383.

19. S. Ng, "Big Cracks Spread in Glass Recycling," *Wall Street Journal*, April 23, 2015, B8.

20. Ibid.

21. "Average Diesel Cost Falls for Second Straight Week," *HDT Truckinginfo*, May 12, 2014, accessed June 23, 2014, http://www.truckinginfo.com/channel /fuel-smarts/news/story/2014/05/average-diesel -cost-falls-for-second-straight-week.aspx.

22. "Kroger Co. Adopts Westport iCEPACKTM LNG Tank System for Sustainability and Savings," *PRNewswire*, May 6, 2014, accessed June 23, 2014, http://www.prnewswire.com/news-releases/kroger -co-adopts-westport-ice-pack-lng-tank-system-for -sustainability-and-savings-258148831.html.

23. C. Woodyard, "UPS Tries to Save Fuel by Cutting Weight," *USA Today*, June 9, 2011, accessed March 28, 2012, http://www.usatoday.com/money /autos/environment/2011-06-09-ups-vans-save -energy_n.htm.

24. M. Weber, *The Protestant Ethic and the Spirit of Capitalism* (New York: Scribner's, 1958).

25. B. Morris, "Truckers Tire of Government Sleep Rules," *Wall Street Journal*, accessed July 22, 2014, http://wsj.com/news/articles/SB10001424052702304 672404579182522881942740.

26. D. Gibson, "Angus Barn's Eure: Peyton Manning Check Posting 'Horrible,'" *Triangle Business Journal*, March 7, 2012, accessed March 29, 2012, http://www.bizjournals.com/triangle /blog/2012/03/peyton-leaves-whopper-tip-at -angus-barn.html.

27. L. Scism, "State Farm Is There: As You Drive," *Wall Street Journal*, August 4, 2013, accessed July 22, 2014, http://wsj.com/news/articles/SB100014241278 87323420604578647950497541958.

28. H. Son, "'Bob in Accounting Is Going to Fix Currency Rates.'—'I'll tell Jamie Dimon,'" *BloombergBusinessweek*, April 13–19, 2015, pp. 34–35.

29. Rajul, "Four Seasons Park Lane Shares Hiring Secrets," London Hotel Insight, January 24, 2011, accessed July 23, 2014, http://londonhotelsinsight .com/2011/01/24/four-seasons-park-lane-shares -hiring-secrets/.

30. "About Four Seasons: Nick Mutton," Four Seasons, accessed July 23, 2014, http://www .fourseasons.com/about_four_seasons/nick-mutton/.

31. A. Kadet, "City News—Metro Money/Jerks Need Not Apply," *Wall Street Journal*, January 18, 2014, accessed July 23, 2014, A16.

32. J. R. Barker, "Tightening the Iron Cage: Concertive Control in Self-Managing Teams," *Administrative Science Quarterly* 38 (1993): 408–437.

33. N. Byrnes, "The Art of Motivation," *BusinessWeek*, May 1, 2006, 56–62.

34. Barker, "Tightening the Iron Cage."

35. C. Manz and H. Sims, "Leading Workers to Lead Themselves: The External Leadership of Self -Managed Work Teams," *Administrative Science Quarterly* 32 (1987): 106–128.

36. J. Slocum and H. A. Sims, "Typology for Integrating Technology, Organization and Job Design," *Human Relations* 33 (1980): 193–212.

37. C. C. Manz and H. P. Sims, Jr., "Self -Management as a Substitute for Leadership: A Social Learning Perspective," *Academy of Management Review* 5 (1980): 361–367.

38. C. Manz and C. Neck, *Mastering Self-Leadership*, 3rd ed. (Upper Saddle River, NJ: Pearson, Prentice Hall, 2004).

39. R. S. Kaplan and D. P. Norton, "Using the Balanced Scorecard as a Strategic Management System," *Harvard Business Review* (January– February 1996): 75–85; R. S. Kaplan and D. P. Norton, "The Balanced Scorecard: Measures That Drive Performance," *Harvard Business Review* (January–February 1992): 71–79.

40. J. Meliones, "Saving Money, Saving Lives," *Harvard Business Review* (November–December 2000): 57–65.

41. D. Kesmodel and A. Gasparro, "Lean Recipe Fuels Food Deals," *Wall Street Journal*, March 26, 2015, A1, A6.

42. S. L. Fawcett, "Fear of Accounts: Improving Managers' Competence and Confidence Through Simulation Exercises," *Journal of European Industrial Training* (February 1996): 17.

43. M. H. Stocks and A. Harrell, "The Impact of an Increase in Accounting Information Level on the Judgment Quality of Individuals and Groups," *Accounting, Organizations & Society* (October– November 1995): 685–700.

44. B. Morris, "Roberto Goizueta and Jack Welch: The Wealth Builders," *Fortune*, December 11, 1995, 80–94.

45. G. Colvin, "America's Best & Worst Wealth Creators: The Real Champions Aren't Always Who You Think. Here's an Eye-Opening Look at Which Companies Produce and Destroy the Most Money for Investors—Plus a New Tool for Spotting Future Winners," *Fortune*, December 18, 2000, 207.

46. "About Herman Miller: Operational Excellence," *Herman Miller*, accessed June 20, 2011, http://www.hermanmiller.com/About-Us/About -Herman-Miller/Operational-Excellence.

47. M. Schurman, "A Herman Miller Primer," *Herman Miller*, accessed June 20, 2011, http:// www.hermanmiller.com/MarketFacingTech/hmc /about_us/News_Events_Media/Corporate _Backgrounder.pdf.

48. B. Stewart, *Best-Practice EVA: The Definitive Guide to Measuring and Maximizing Shareholder Value* (New York: Wiley Finance, 2013).

49. "Welcome Complaints," *Office of Consumer and Business Affairs*, Government of South Australia, accessed June 20, 2005, http://www.ocba.sa.gov.au /businessadvice/complaints/03_welcome.html.

50. J. Tschohl, "Cultivate Loyal Customers: The Value of Defection Management," Desk.com, May 23, 2013, accessed May 13, 2015, http://www.desk .com/blog/loyal-customers/.

51. C. A. Reeves and D. A. Bednar, "Defining Quality: Alternatives and Implications," *Academy of Management Review* 19 (1994): 419–445.

52. "The Best Airlines in the World: Readers' Choice Awards 2014," *Condé Nast Traveler*, October 29, 2014, accessed September 8, 2015, http://www.cntraveler.com/stories/2014-10-29/ the-best-airlines-in-the-world-readers-choice-2014; "About Us: Singapore Airlines—Our Awards," *Singapore Airlines*, accessed June 23, 2014, http:// www.singaporeair.com/en_UK/about-us/sia-history /sia-awards/.

53. S. Holmes, "Creature Comforts at 30,000 Feet," *BusinessWeek*, December 18, 2006, 138.

54. C. Krome, "Kia Optima Earns 'Best Value' Award, Debuts SX Limited," *Autobytel*, February 13, 2012, accessed March 29, 2012, http://www .autobytel.com/kia/optima/2012/news/kia-optima -earns-best-value-award-debuts-sx-limited-109911/.

55. D. R. May and B. L. Flannery, "Cutting Waste with Employee Involvement Teams," *Business Horizons*, September–October 1995, 28–38.

56. J. Carlton, "Some NFL Teams Are Going Green," *Wall Street Journal*, May 18, 2014, accessed June 23, 2014, http://wsj.com/news/articles/SB1000 14240527023046779045795378826915504940.

57. C. Boulton, "Exposing the Hidden Waste and Expense of Cloud Computing," *Wall Street Journal*, February 17, 2015, B4.

58. A. K. Streeter, "H&M Collects Your Old Clothes to Make New Jeans," *treehugger*, May 30, 2014, accessed June 23, 2014, http://www.treehugger .com/corporate-responsibility/hm-collecting-your -old-clothes-make-new-jeans.html.

59. M. Perella, "How HP and Kyocera Are Applying Circular Economy to Printing," *The Guardian*, May 28, 2014, accessed June 23, 2014, http://www.theguardian.com/sustainable-business /hp-kyocera-circular-economy-printing.

60. L. Downing, "British Retailers Turn Waste into Power," *Bloomberg Businessweek*, June 14, 2012, accessed June 21, 2013, http://www.businessweek .com/articles/2012-06-14/british-retailers-turn -waste-into-power.

61. "The End of the Road: Schools and Computer Recycling," *Intel*, accessed September 5, 2008, http:// www.intel.com/education/recycling_computers /recycling.htm.

62. M. Meece, "Giving Those Old Gadgets a Proper Green Burial," *New York Times*, January 6, 2011, accessed March 5, 2011, http://www.nytimes .com/2011/01/06/technology/personaltech/06basics .html?ref=recyclingofwastematerials.

17

1. R. Lenzner, "The Reluctant Entrepreneur," *Forbes*, September 11, 1995, 162–166.

2. "Inflation Calculator | Find US Dollar's Value from 1913-2014," US Inflation Calculator, accessed July 24, 2014, http://www.usinflationcalculator .com/; T. Lee, "Today's iPhone Is More Useful Than $3,000 Worth of Gadgets from a 1991 Radio Shack," *The Washington Post*, January 31, 2014, accessed July 24, 2014, http://www.washingtonpost .com/blogs/the-switch/wp/2014/01/31/todays -iphone-is-more-useful-than-3000-worth-of -gadgets-from-a-1991-radio-shack/.

3. D. Clark, "Moore's Law Shows Its Age," *Wall Street Journal*, April 17, 2005, accessed May 12, 2015, http://www.wsj.com/articles/moores-law-runs -out-of-gas-1429282819.

4. S. Norton, "A Post-PC CEO: No Desk, No Desktop," *Wall Street Journal*, November 20, 2014, B5.

5. Zacks, "Pandora Listener Hours Up in May— Analyst Blog," *nasdaq.com*, June 5, 2014, accessed June 24, 2014, http://www.nasdaq.com/article /pandora-listener-hours-up-in-may-analyst-blog -cm359420; "Pandora Dropped 2.3 Million Listeners in Last 3 Months, Stock Falls as Net Loss Widens," Hypebot.com, April 24, 2015, accessed May 12, 2015, http://www.hypebot.com/hypebot /2015/04/pandora-stock-falls-as-net-losses-widen .html.

6. H. Michael, "Updated Numbers: Beats Music Now Has 250,000 Subscribers," PhoneArena, May 29, 2014, accessed July 24, 2014, http://www. phonearena.com /news/Updated-numbers-Beats-Music-now-has -250000-subscribers_id56644; H. Karp and A. Barr, "Apple Taps Tastemakers to Regain Music Mojo," *Wall Street Journal*, May 29, 2014, A1; "Information: What Is Spotify," Spotify, accessed May 12, 2015, https://press.spotify.com/us/informa- tion/; "Hans-Holger Albrecht to Give Midem 2015 Keynote," Deezer, April 21, 2015, accessed May 12, 2015, http://blog.deezer.com/press/tag/gb/; T. Risen, "Consumers Want Free Music from Apple Beats," *US News*, May 6, 2015, accessed May 12, 2015, http://www.usnews.com/news/articles/2015/05/06/ consumers-want-free-music-from-apple-beats; E. Weise, "Amazon Prime Is Big, But How Big?" *USA Today*, February 3, 2015, accessed May 12, 2015, http://www.usatoday.com/story/tech/2015/02/03/ amazon-prime-10-years-old-anniversary/22755509/.

7. D. A. Fields, "The Myth of First-Mover Advantage," *Industry Week*, June 12, 2013, accessed June 24, 2014, http://www.industryweek .com/innovation/myth-first-mover-advantage.

8. F. Suarez and G. Lanzolla, "The Half-Truth of First Mover Advantage," *Harvard Business Review*, April 2005, accessed June 24, 2014, http://hbr.org /2005/04/the-half-truth-of-first-mover-advantage /ar/1.

9. S. Rothwell, "British Airways Crews Read Up on VIPs on iPads," *Bloomberg Businessweek*, February 15, 2012, accessed April 2, 2012, http:// www.bloomberg.com/news/2012-02-16/british -airways-crews-tap-into-ipads-for-lowdown-on -vip-flyers.html.

10. K. Linendoll, "NFL Playbooks: There's an App for That," *ESPN*, November 6, 2012, accessed June 22, 2013, http://espn.go.com/blog/playbook/tech /post/_/id/2808/nfl-teams-prefer-ipads-over -playbooks.

11. K. Clark, "NFL Practices: Getting Geeky," *Wall Street Journal*, August 19, 2014, accessed May 12, 2015, http://www.wsj.com/articles/nfl-practices -getting-geeky-1408488632.

12. R. Smith, "Find the Best Checkout Line— Retailers Try to Speed Up; What Works, What Adds to Shopper Aggravation," *Wall Street Journal*, December 8, 2011, D1.

13. J. Jargon, "Kroger's New Weapon: Infrared Cameras—Technology Helps Kroger Reduce Wait Times to 26 Seconds," *Wall Street Journal*, May 2, 2013, B4.

14. N. Bogart, "Canadian Airline First Air to Live Stream Black Box Data," *Global News*, May 6, 2014, accessed June 24, 2014, http://globalnews .ca/news/1314398/canadian-airline-first-air-to-live -stream-black-box-data/.

15. D. Stacey and G. Raghuvanshi, "Malaysia Airlines Flight 370: Contractor Will Get 300 Days to Complete Search," *Wall Street Journal*, June 4, 2014, accessed July 24, 2014, http:// online.wsj.com/articles/contractor-will-get -300-days-to-complete-malaysia-airlines-flight -370-search-1401849756.

16. A. Pasztor and J. Ostrower, "Missing Malaysia Jet Adds Fuel to 'Live Black Box' Debate," *Wall Street Journal*, March 9, 2014, accessed June 24, 2014, http://online.wsj.com/news/articles/SB100014 24052702304020104579429233516692014 ?KEYWORDS=missing+malaysia+jet+adds +fuel&mg=reno64-wsj.

17. Bogart, "Canadian Airline First Air to Live Stream Black Box Data."

18. D. Hernandez, "Artificial Intelligence Is Now Telling Doctors How to Treat You," *Wired*, June 2, 2014, accessed June 24, 2014, http://www.wired .com/2014/06/ai-healthcare/.

19. Ibid.

20. Associated Press, "Syrup-makers Go High-Tech with Wireless Monitoring," *Wall Street Journal*, April 1, 2014, accessed June 24, 2014, http://online .wsj.com/article/APe9ecdb54499c4294840e59e 763ef3e38.html?KEYWORDS=monitoring.

21. D. Chernicoff, "Another Billion Dollar Data Center Investment for Google," ZDNet, April, 21, 2015, accessed May 12, 2015, http://www.zdnet. com/article/another-billion-dollar-data-center -investment-for-google/.

22. D. Meyer, "Google to Build Gigantic "120-megawatt" Data Center in the Netherlands," Gigaom, September 23, 2014, accessed May 12, 2015, https://gigaom.com/2014/09/23/google-to -build-gigantic-120-megawatt-data-center-in-the -netherlands/.

23. "Google Search Statistics - Internet Live Stats," Google, accessed May 12, 2015, http://www .internetlivestats.com/google-search-statistics/#trend; "Statistics - YouTube," YouTube, accessed May 12, 2015, http://www.youtube.com/yt/press/statistics.html.

24. R. Miller, "Facebook Decloaks, Confirms Plans for Iowa Server Farm," *Data Center Knowledge*, April 23, 2013, accessed June 22, 2013, http://www .datacenterknowledge.com/archives/2013/04/23 /facebook-decloaks-confirms-plans-for-iowa-server -farm/.

25. E. Dwoskin and G. Bensinger, "Hot New Thing at the Mall: Heat Maps Track Shoppers," *Wall Street Journal*, December 9, 2013, B1.

26. K. Kamenec, "How Apples iBeacon Could Upend Retail Shopping," *PC Magazine*, October 24, 2013, accessed July 25, 2014, http://www.pcmag .com/article2/0,2817,2425052,00.asp.

27. S. Ramachandran, "Netflix Will Pay Comcast for Speed," *Wall Street Journal*, February 24, 2014, A1; S. Ramachandran and D. Fitzgerald, "For Web Firms, Faster Access Comes at a Price," *Wall Street Journal*, June 19, 2013, B1; "Netflix Still Dominates Internet Traffic," Advanced Television, November 20, 2014, accessed May 12, 2015, http://advanced -television.com/2014/11/20/netflix-still-dominates -internet-traffic/.

28. S. Lubar, *Infoculture: The Smithsonian Book of Information Age Inventions* (Boston: Houghton Mifflin, 1993).

29. Ibid.

30. G.M., "They've Got Sklz," *Entrepreneur*, January 2012, 43.

31. P. Mozur and J. Osawa, "Can Alibab's Taxi App Be New Growth Driver," *Wall Street Journal*, March 17, 2014, B4.

32. Anonymous, "Home & Digital: #ASKWSJD," *Wall Street Journal*, March 5, 2014, D3.

33. R. Trichur, "Global Finance: No Cards Neces- sary with New ATM Grid," *Wall Street Journal*, March 16, 2015, C3.

34. B. Worthen, "Bar Codes on Steroids," *CIO*, December 15, 2002, 53.

35. B. Barnes, "At Disney Parks, a Bracelet Meant to Build Loyalty (and Sales)," *New York Times*, January 7, 2013, accessed June 22, 2013, http://www.nytimes.com/2013/01/07/business /media/at-disney-parks-a-bracelet-meant-to -build-loyalty-and-sales.html?pagewanted=all& _r=0; M. Wilson, "A $1 Billion Project to Remake the Disney World Experience, Using RFID," *FastCoDesign*, accessed June 22, 2013, http:// www.fastcodesign.com/1671616/a-1-billion -project-to-remake-the-disney-world-experience -using-rfid#1.

36. N. Rubenking, "Hidden Messages," *PC Magazine*, May 22, 2001, 86.

37. D. Carr, "Giving Viewers What They Want," *New York Times*, February 24, 2013, accessed June 22, 2013, http:// www.nytimes. com/2013/02/25/business/media/for-house-of -cards-using-big-data-to-guarantee-its-popularity. html?pagewanted=all.

38. E. Dwoskin, "How New York's Fire Department Uses Data Mining," *Wall Street Journal* (Digits blog), January 24, 2014, 2:12 p.m., accessed June 24, 2014, http://blogs.wsj.com/digits/2014/01/24/how-new -yorks-fire-department-uses-data-mining/.

39. Rubenking, "Hidden Messages."

40. C. Duhigg, "How Companies Learn Your Secrets," *New York Times*, February 16, 2012, accessed April 3, 2012, http://www.nytimes .com/2012/02/19/magazine/shopping-habits .html?pagewanted=all.

41. A. Rutkin, "Machine Predicts Heart Attacks 4 Hours before Doctors," *NewScientist*, August 11, 2014, accessed May 12, 2015, http://www.newscientist .com/article/mg22329814.400-machine-predicts -heart-attacks-4-hours-before-doctors.html# .VVKi5mBtEkE.

42. S. Rosebush and M. Totty, "How Big Data Is Changing the Whole Equation for Business," *Wall Street Journal*, March 11, 2013, R1.

43. K. Johnson, O. Dorell, and E. Weise, "Official: North Korea behind Sony Hack," *USA Today*, December 18, 2014, accessed May 12, 2015, http://www.usatoday.com/story/news/world/2014/12/17/north-korea-sony-hack/20558135/.

44. B. Fritz, D. Yadron, and E. Schwartzel, "Behind the Scenes at Sony as Hacking Crisis Unfolded," *Wall Street Journal*, December 30, 2014, accessed May 12, 2015, http://www.wsj.com/articles/behind-the-scenes-at-sony-as-hacking-crisis-unfolded-1419985719.

45. "Cloud Infographic: Computer Virus Facts and Stats, CloudTweaks, April 11, 2014, accessed May 12, 2015, http://cloudtweaks.com/2014/04/cloud-infographic-computer-virus-facts-stats/.

46. B. Gottesman and K. Karagiannis, "A False Sense of Security," *PC Magazine*, February 22, 2005, 72.

47. F. J. Derfler, Jr., "Secure Your Network," *PC Magazine*, June 27, 2000, 183–200.

48. "Authentication," *PC Magazine*, accessed June 24, 2014, http://www.pcmag.com/encyclopedia/term/38192/authentication.

49. "Authorization," *PC Magazine*, accessed June 24, 2014, http://www.pcmag.com/encyclopedia/term/38202/authorization.

50. L. Seltzer, "Password Crackers," *PC Magazine*, February 12, 2002, 68.

51. "Two-Factor Authentication," *Information Security Glossary*, accessed June 28, 2009, http://www.rsa.kz/node/glossary/default4b75.html?id=1056.

52. W. Gordon, "Here's Everywhere You Should Enable Two-Factor Authentication Right Now," *LifeHacker*, December 10, 2013, accessed July 26, 2014, http://lifehacker.com/5938565/heres-everywhere-you-should-enable-two-factor-authentication-right-now; L. Tung, "Google to Slap Two-Factor Across Apps via Suspicious Logins Trigger," *ZD Net*, May 15, 2014, accessed June 24, 2014, http://www.zdnet.com/google-to-slap-two-factor-across-apps-via-suspicious-logins-trigger-7000029476/.

53. C. Metz "Total Security," *PC Magazine*, October 1, 2003, B3.

54. J. DeAvila, "Wi-Fi Users, Beware: Hot Spots Are Weak Spots," *Wall Street Journal,* January 16, 2008, D1; J. Vijayan, "Hotel Router Vulnerability a Reminder of Untrusted WiFi Risks," March 27, 2015, Information Week Dark Reading, accessed May 12, 2015, http://www.darkreading.com/perimeter/hotel-router-vulnerability-a-reminder-of-untrusted-wifi-risks/d/d-id/1319668.

55. G. A. Fowler, "You Won't Believe How Adorable This Kitty Is! Click For More!" *Wall Street Journal*, March 26, 2013, accessed June 24, 2014, http://online.wsj.com/news/articles/SB10001424127887324373204578373011392662962?mg=reno64-wsj.

56. Ibid.

57. J. van den Hoven, "Executive Support Systems & Decision Making," *Journal of Systems Management* 47, no. 8 (March–April 1996): 48.

58. D. Hannon, "Colgate-Palmolive Empowers Senior Leaders with Executive Dashboards," *InsiderProfiles*, April 1, 2011, accessed June 26, 2011, http://insiderprofiles.wispubs.com/article.aspx?iArticleId=5720.

59. "Intranet," *PC Magazine*, accessed June 24, 2014, http://www.pcmag.com/encyclopedia/term/45310/intranet.

60. "Accorda Therapeutics Announces Company Intranet Named One of Ten Best in the World," *Yahoo! Finance*, February 14, 2013, accessed

June 24, 2013, http://finance.yahoo.com/news/acorda-therapeutics-announces-company-intranet-120000651.html; K. Kass, "It's Not Always the Size That Counts in Internal Communication," *Simply-communicate.com*, http://www.simply-communicate.com/case-studies/company-profile/it%E2%80%99s-not-always-size-counts-internal-communication.

61. "Web Services," *PC Magazine*, accessed June 24, 2014, http://www.pcmag.com/encyclopedia/term/54345/web-services.

62. S. Overby, "This Could Be the Start of Something Small," *CIO*, February 15, 2003, 54.

63. "Extranet," *PC Magazine*, accessed June 24, 2014, http://www.pcmag.com/encyclopedia/term/42945/extranet.

64. "Mitsubishi Opens Sales/Training Center; Establishes Online Creative Centers," *Contracting Business.com*, March 27, 2012, accessed April 3, 2012, http://contractingbusiness.com/news/Mitsubishi-training-creative-centers-0328/.

65. M. Hickins, "Hertz Counts on Self-Service Kiosks to Spur Growth," *Wall Street Journal*, May 8, 2012, accessed June 22, 2013, http://blogs.wsj.com/drivers-seat/2012/05/08/hertz-counts-on-self-service-kiosks-to-spur-growth/.

66. S. Hamm, D. Welch, W. Zellner, F. Keenan, and F. Engardio, "Down But Hardly Out: Downturn Be Damned, Companies Are Still Anxious to Expand Online," *BusinessWeek*, March 26, 2001, 126.

67. K. C. Laudon and J. P. Laudon, *Management Information Systems: Organization and Technology* (Upper Saddle River, NJ: Prentice Hall, 1996).

68. J. Borzo, "Software for Symptoms," *Wall Street Journal*, May 23, 2005, R10.

69. Ibid.

70. R. Hernandez, "American Express Authorizer's Assistant," *Business Rules Journal*, August 2001, accessed June 26, 2011, http://bizrules.info/page/art_amexaa.htm.

18

1. J. Mouawad, "A Luxury Liner Docks, and the Countdown's On," *The New York Times*, March 22, 2015, BU1.

2. Ibid.

3. J. Miller, "Remade in the USA: Indiana Steel Mill Revived with Lessons from Abroad," *Wall Street Journal*, May 21, 2012, A1.

4. L. Stevens, "For UPS, E-Commerce Brings Big Business and Big Problems," *Wall Street Journal*, September 11, 2014, accessed May 11, 2015, http://www.wsj.com/articles/for-ups-e-commerce-brings-big-business-and-big-problems-1410489642.

5. Ibid.

6. "Employment Cost Index News Release Text," Bureau of Labor Statistics, April 30, 2015, accessed May 11, 2015, http://www.bls.gov/news.release/eci.nr0.htm; "Productivity and Costs: First Quarter 2015, Preliminary," Bureau of Labor Statistics, May 6, 2015, accessed May 11, 2015, http://www.bls.gov/news.release/prod2.nr0.htm.

7. "Historical Income Tables—Families: Table F-23—Families by Total Money Income, Race, and Hispanic Origin of Householder: 1967 to 2013," U.S. Census Bureau, Current Population Survey, Annual Social and Economic Supplements, accessed May 11, 2015, http://www.census.gov/hhes/www/income/data/historical/families/2013/f23.xls.

8. Ibid.

9. The Conference Board Total Economy Data Base, Summary Statistics 1997–2014, "Table 3: Growth of Labor Productivity, Real GDP and Total

Hours Worked by Region for Advanced Countries, 1997–2014," *The Conference Board*, accessed May 11, 2015, http://www.conference-board.org/retrievefile.cfm?filename=SummaryTables_Jan20141.pdf&type=subsite.

10. "Employment Projections, Table 1: Civilian Labor Force by Sex, Age, Race, and Ethnicity, 1992, 2002, 2012, and projected 2022," Bureau of Labor Statistics, December 19, 2013, accessed May 11, 2015, http://www.bls.gov/emp/ep_table_301.htm.

11. "Charitable Giving Statistics," *National Philanthropic Trust*, accessed accessed May 11, 2015, http://www.nptrust.org/philanthropic-resources/charitable-giving-statistics/; C. Lourosa-Ricardo, "How America Gives to Charity," Wall Street Journal, December 14, 2014, http://www.wsj.com/articles/how-america-gives-to-charity-1418619046, accessed May 11, 2015.

12. "GDP per Capita by Country 1980-2014: United States," Knoema, accessed May 11, 2015, http://knoema.com/pjeqzh/gdp-per-capita-by-country-1980-2014.

13. "Philanthropy in the American Economy," *Council of Economic Advisers*, February 19, 2002, accessed April 13, 2009, http://clinton4.nara.gov/media/pdf/philanthropy.pdf.

14. M. Perry, "Christmas Shopping 1958 vs. 2012 Illustrates the 'Miracle of the Marketplace' Which Delivers Better and Cheaper Goods," *American Enterprise Institute*, December 28, 2013, accessed July 27, 2014, http://www.aei-ideas.org/2013/12/christmas-shopping-1958-vs-2012-illustrates-the-miracle-of-the-marketplace-which-delivers-better-and-cheaper-goods/.

15. "European Airline Labor Productivity: CAPA Rankings," *CAPA Centre for Aviation*, April 9, 2013, accessed May 11, 2015, http://centreforaviation.com/analysis/european-airline-labour-productivity-capa-rankings-104204.

16. "Productivity (MFP): Frequently Asked Questions," Bureau of Labor Statistics, accessed July 28, 2014, http://www.bls.gov/mfp/mprfaq.htm#1.

17. J. Healey, "Average New Car Price Zips 2.5% to $33,560," *USA Today*, May 4, 2015, accessed May 11, 2015, http://www.usatoday.com/story/money/cars/2015/05/04/new-car-transaction-price-3-kbb-kelley-blue-book/26690191/.

18. C. Woodyard and F. Meier, "GM Makes Big Move Up in J.D. Power Quality Survey," *USA Today*, June 19, 2012, accessed June 23, 2013, http://www.usatoday.com/story/money/cars/2013/06/19/jd-power-initial-quality-survey-gm-ford/2437115/.

19. "Basic Quality Concepts," *American Society for Quality*, accessed August 2, 2009, http://www.asq.org/learn-about-quality/basic-concepts.html.

20. R. E. Markland, S. K. Vickery, and R. A. Davis, "Managing Quality" (Chapter 7), in *Operations Management: Concepts in Manufacturing and Services* (Cincinnati, OH: South-Western College Publishing, 1998).

21. J. Ewoldt, "A Brighter Day for LED Bulbs," *StarTribune*, April 3, 2013, accessed June 23, 2013, http://www.startribune.com/business/201357281.html?prefer=y; M. White, "Light Switch: Why You'll Start Using LED Bulbs This Year," *Time*, April 25, 2013, accessed June 23, 2013, http://business.time.com/2013/04/25/light-switch-why-youll-start-using-led-bulbs-this-year/.

22. L. L. Berry and A. Parasuraman, *Marketing Services* (New York: Free Press, 1991).

23. asymco-admin, "The Quantum Leap in Retail," *Asymco*, October 31, 2013, accessed June 25, 2014, http://www.asymco.com/2013/10/31/the-quantum-leap-in-retail/; R. Devine, "Apple Retail Store Numbers Are Up, 30 New Stores for Fiscal 2014," iMore, October 28, 2013, accessed July 28, 2014,

http://www.imore.com/apple-retail-store-numbers-are-30-new-stores-fiscal-2014.

24. "Apple, Murphy USA, Tiffany & Co. Top New eMarketer Store Productivity Rankings," *eMarketer Retail*, May 26, 2014, accessed July 28, 2014, http://retail.emarketer.com/apple-murphy-usa-tiffany-co-top-new-emarketer-store-productivity-rankings/.

25. "About ISO," *International Organization for Standardization*, accessed June 25, 2014, http://www.iso.org/iso/home/about.htm.

26. "ISO 9000 Essentials," and "ISO 14000 Essentials," *International Organization for Standardization*, accessed September 12, 2009, http://www.iso.org/iso/iso_catalogue/management_standards/iso_9000_iso_14000.htm.

27. J. Briscoe, S. Fawcett, and R. Todd, "The Implementation and Impact of ISO 9000 Among Small Manufacturing Enterprises," *Journal of Small Business Management* 43 (July 1, 2005): 309.

28. R. Henkoff, "The Hot New Seal of Quality (ISO 9000 Standard of Quality Management)," *Fortune*, June 28, 1993, 116.

29. "Baldrige Frequently Asked Questions: Baldrige Performance Excellence Program," *National Institute of Standards and Technology*, accessed September 12, 2009, http://www.nist.gov/baldrige/about/baldrige_faqs.cfm.

30. "Baldrige Award Process Fees," *National Institute of Standards and Technology*, accessed May 11, 2015, http://www.nist.gov/baldrige/enter/award_fees.cfm.

31. "Frequently Asked Questions About the Malcolm Baldrige National Quality Award."

32. Ibid.

33. "Criteria for Performance Excellence," *Baldrige National Quality Program 2008*, accessed September 15, 2008, http://www.quality.nist.gov/PDF_files/2008_Business_Criteria.pdf.

34. Ibid.

35. D. C. Moody, "Beam Integral Part of Prestigious Baldridge Program," *theeasleyprogress.com*, June 4, 2014, accessed June 25, 2014, http://www.theeasleyprogress.com/news/home_top-news/4915403/Beam-integral-part-of-prestigious-Baldridge-Program.

36. J. W. Dean, Jr., and J. Evans, *Total Quality: Management, Organization, and Strategy* (St. Paul, MN: West, 1994).

37. J. W. Dean, Jr., and D. E. Bowen, "Management Theory and Total Quality: Improving Research and Practice Through Theory Development," *Academy of Management Review* 19 (1994): 392–418.

38. "Alaska Airlines Awards and Recognition," Alaska Airlines, accessed May 11, 2015, http://www.alaskaair.com/content/about-us/newsroom/alaska-awards.aspx; M. Kaminsky, "The Weekend Interview with Bill Ayer: An Airline That Makes Money—Really," *Wall Street Journal*, February 4, 2012, A13; T. Maxon, "JetBlue Leads American Customer Satisfaction Index for Second Year," *Dallas Morning News*, June 18, 2012, accessed June 23, 2013, http://aviationblog.dallasnews.com/2013/06/jetblue-leads-american-consumer-satisfaction-index-for-second-year.html/.

39. S. McCartney, "A World Where Flights Aren't Canceled," *Wall Street Journal*, April 2, 2014, accessed July 28, 2014, http://wsj.com/news/articles/SB10001424052702303987004579477412359027986.

40. J. Miller, "Remade in the USA: Indiana Steel Mill Revived with Lessons from Abroad," *Wall Street Journal*, May 21, 2012, A1.

41. R. Hallowell, L. A. Schlesinger, and J. Zornitsky, "Internal Service Quality, Customer and Job Satisfaction: Linkages and Implications for Management," *Human Resource Planning* 19 (1996): 20–31; J. L. Heskett, T. O. Jones, G. W. Loveman, W. E. Sasser, Jr., and L. A. Schlesinger, "Putting the Service-Profit Chain to Work," *Harvard Business Review* (March–April 1994): 164–174.

42. L. Drell, "6 Companies with Awesome Employee Perks," *Mashable Business*, August 7, 2011, accessed April 9, 2012, http://mashable.com/2011/08/07/startup-employee-perks/.

43. J. Paravantis, N. Bouranta, and L. Chitiris, "The Relationship Between Internal and External Service Quality," *International Journal of Contemporary Hospital Management* 21 (2009): 275–293.

44. G. Brewer, "The Ultimate Guide to Winning Customers: The Customer Stops Here," *Sales & Marketing Management* 150 (March 1998): 30; F. F. Reichheld, *The Loyalty Effect: The Hidden Force Behind Growth, Profits, and Lasting Value* (Cambridge, MA: Harvard Business School Press, 2001).

45. J. Heskett, T. Jones, G. Loveman, E. Sasser, and L. Schlesinger, "Putting the Service-Profit Chain to Work," *Harvard Business Review* 86 (July–August 2008): 118–129.

46. L. L. Berry and A. Parasuraman, "Listening to the Customer—The Concept of a Service-Quality Information System," *Sloan Management Review* 38, no. 3 (Spring 1997): 65; C. W. L. Hart, J. L. Heskett, and W. E. Sasser, Jr., "The Profitable Art of Service Recovery," *Harvard Business Review* (July–August 1990): 148–156.

47. A. L. Rodgers, "A 5-Point Plan for Making the Most of Customer Complaints," *Inc.*, January 14, 2014, accessed June 25, 2014, http://www.inc.com/the-build-network/a-5-point-plan-for-making-the-most-of-customer-complaints.html.

48. "Great Customer Service from the Mission Bicycle Company," *37signals.com*, August 16, 2011, accessed April 9, 2012, http://37signals.com/svn/posts/2989-great-customer-service-from-the-mission-bicycle-company.

49. D. E. Bowen and E. E. Lawler III, "The Empowerment of Service Workers: What, Why, How, and When," *Sloan Management Review* 33 (Spring 1992): 31–39; D. E. Bowen and E. E. Lawler III, "Empowering Service Employees," *Sloan Management Review* 36 (Summer 1995): 73–84.

50. Bowen and Lawler, "The Empowerment of Service Workers: What, Why, How, and When."

51. J. Shelly, "Empowering Employees," *Human Resource Executive*, October 2, 2011, accessed April 9, 2012, http://www.hreonline.com/HRE/view/story.jhtml?id=533341639.

52. "Customer Service and Business Results: A Survey of Customer Service from Mid-Size Companies," *ZenDesk*, April 2013, accessed July 28, 2014, http://cdn.zendesk.com/resources/whitepapers/Zendesk_WP_Customer_Service_and_Business_Results.pdf.

53. B. Gruel and S. Singh, "Deere's Big Green Profit Machine," *Bloomberg Businessweek*, July 5, 2012, accessed June 23, 2013, http://www.businessweek.com/articles/2012-07-05/deeres-big-green-profit-machine.

54. J. Rockoff, "Drug Making Breaks Away from Its Old Ways," *Wall Street Journal*, February 8, 2015, , accessed May 11, 2015, http://www.wsj.com/articles/drug-making-breaks-away-from-its-old-ways-1423444049.

55. Ibid.

56. D. Lavrinc, "Peek Inside Tesla's Robotic Factory," *Wired*, July 16, 2013, accessed June 25, 2014, http://www.wired.com/2013/07/tesla-plant-video/.

57. "Job Shop Hits Bull's Eye with Multitasking," *Manufacturing Engineering* (November 2008): 43–105.

58. D. Hinshaw, "U.S. Buys Up Ebola Gear, Leaving Little for Africa," *Wall Street Journal*, November 25, 2014, accessed May 11, 2015, http://www.wsj.com/articles/u-s-buys-up-ebola-gear-leaving-little-for-africa-1416875059.

59. H. Dreier, "McDonald's Runs Out of French Fries in Venezuela," Yahoo News (Associated Press), January 6, 2015, accessed May 11, 2015, http://news.yahoo.com/mcdonalds-runs-french-fries-venezuela-172701168.html.

60. D. Drickhamer, "Reality Check," *Industry Week*, November 2001, 29.

61. D. Drickhamer, "Zeroing In on World-Class," *Industry Week*, November 2001, 36.

62. "Gartner Announces Rankings of Its 2012 Supply Chain Top 25," *Gartner*, May 22, 2012, accessed June 12, 2013, http://www.gartner.com/newsroom/id/2023116; S. Sage, "Apple Boasts Strongest Manufacturing Supply Chain in the World, Turns Over Inventory in Five Days," *iMore*, June 1, 2012, accessed June 23, 2013, http://www.imore.com/apple-boasts-strongest-supply-chain-world-turns-inventory-days.

63. "Efficient Foodservice Response (EFR)," accessed August 3, 2009, http://www.ifdaonline.org/webarticles.

64. J. R. Henry, "Minimized Setup Will Make Your Packaging Line S.M.I.L.E.," *Packaging Technology & Engineering*, February 1, 1998, 24.

65. M. McFadden, "Global Outsourcing of Aircraft Maintenance," *Journal of Aviation Technology and Engineering*, 1 no 2 (2012): 63–73.

66. K. Clark, "An Eagle Eye for Inventory," *Chain Store Age*, May 2005, Supplement, 8A.

67. "The Way I Work: Marc Lore of Diapers.com," *Inc.*, September 1, 2009, accessed March 15, 2010, http://www.inc.com/magazine/20090901/the-way-i-work-marc-lore-of-diaperscom.html.

68. E. Powell, Jr., and F. Sahin, "Economic Production Lot Sizing with Periodic Costs and Overtime," *Decision Sciences* 32 (2001): 423–452.

69. "Gartner Announces Rankings of Its 2014 Supply Chain Top 25," *Gartner*, May 22, 2014, accessed May 11, 2015, http://www.gartner.com/newsroom/id/2747417.

70. N. Shirouzu, "Why Toyota Wins Such High Marks on Quality Surveys," *Wall Street Journal*, March 15, 2001, A1.

71. Ibid.

72. G. Gruman, "Supply on Demand; Manufacturers Need to Know What's Selling Before They Can Produce and Deliver Their Wares in the Right Quantities," *InfoWorld*, April 18, 2005, accessed April 15, 2009, http://www.infoworld.com/article/2669692/database/supply-on-demand.html.

ONE APPROACH.
70 UNIQUE SOLUTIONS.

Index

A

AB InBev, 32, 181–182
ABC Fine Wine & Spirits, 227
ABCD trading houses, 124
Abercrombie & Fitch (A&F), 90
Ability, job performance and, 267–268
AbleData, 256
ABM Industries, 121
Above-market wages, 239
Abrasiveness, in managers, 16
Absenteeism, 98
Absolute comparison, 100
Academic journals, 25
Academy of Management, 25
Academy of Management Perspectives, 25
Accenture, 53
Access and legitimacy paradigm, 259–260
Accommodative strategy, 85–86
Accounting tools, 342–345
Accuracy of job performance, 235–237
Accurate information, 355
Ace Hardware, 115
Acer Group, 48
Achievement-oriented leadership, 301
Achievement-oriented leadership, 299–300
Acorda Therapeutics, 242, 368
Acquisition cost, 357
Acquisitions, 117
Action plans, 92
Active listening, 324
Acxiom, 357
Adaptability, 62
Adaptability screening, 174
Adaptive strategies, 125–127
Adidas, 60
Adidas AG, 120
Administrative ability, 4
Administrative management, 32–33, 34
Administrative Science Quarterly, 25
Adverse impact, 220
Advocacy groups, 56–57
Adworkshop, 241
A&E Network, 323
Affective conflict, 104, 208, 209
Affirmative action, 248–249
Affordable Care Act, 72, 75
African Americans
    as CEOs, 254–255
    Merrill Lynch lawsuit and, 250

population, 247, 250
turnover rates for, 249
Agarwal, Ajay, 4
Age, changing demographics in, 247
Age discrimination, 251–252
Age Discrimination in Employment Act (1967), 218, 251
Aggressive behavior, 69
Agreeableness, 257–258
Agricultural work, 23
Ainsworth, Bill, 129
AirAsia Japan, 112
Airbnb, 93
Airline industry, 46–47, 112, 346, 380–381
AirTran Airways, 47, 78–79
Alaska Airlines, 380, 381
Albermarle Paper Co. v. Moody, 222
Alderfer's ERG Theory, 269
Aldi, 113
Alibaba, 5, 291
All Nippon Airways (ANA), 112
Allaire, Paul A., 264
Allen, Doug, 89
Alliance for Wireless Power (A4WP), 137
Allstate, 225, 319–320
Aloof personality, 16
Altos Research, 123
Amazon, 3–4, 12, 65, 110, 126, 130, 169, 224, 225, 273
Amazon Firefly app, 130
Amazon Fresh trucks, 4
Amazon Instant Video, 53, 126
Amazon Kindle Fire, 109
Amazon Kindle Paperwhite, 129
Amazon MP3, 110–111
Amazon Web Services (AWS), 123
Amazon's Prime Music, 353
Ambitious, managers being overly, 16–17
Ambrose, David, 378
American Airlines, 46, 47, 274–275, 354
American Civil Rights, 249
American Express, 371
American Heart Association, 128
American National Standards Institute, 378, 379
American Society for Quality, 379
American Society of Mechanical Engineers, 28
Americans with Disabilities Act (1990), 218

Ammann, Daniel, 168
AMP, 174
Analyze, 283
Analyzers, 126
AnchorFree Hotspot Shield, 366
Ancient Egypt, 23
Ancient Sumer, 23
Anderson, Dave, 283–284
Anderson, Heather, 52
Andreessen Horowitz (AH), 61
Andreessen, Mark, 61
Andres, Mike, 186
Android devices, 110
Angus Barn, 338
Anheuser-Busch, 343
Ansys, 143
Anthes, G., 342
Antibiotic-free livestock, 86
Anti-fracking advocacy groups, 57
Antivirus software, 364, 365
AOL, 64
Aon Hewitt, 98
APEC (Asia-Pacific Economic Cooperation), 158, 159
Apple, 46, 54–55, 85, 109, 110, 142, 143–144, 185, 251, 272
Apple App Store, 110
Apple iTunes, 53, 110–111
Apple stores, 378
Apple TV, 53
Apple's Beats Music, 353
Applicant selection, changing company culture and, 64–65
Application forms, 225
Aptitude tests, 228
ArcellorMittal, 381
Archer Daniels Midland, 124
Armstrong, Neil, 96
Armstrong, Tim, 64
Arrivers, 15–16
Arrogance, in managers, 16
Artists Against Fracking (AAF), 57
ASCII (American Standard Code for Information Interchange) text, 360
ASEAN (Association of Southeast Asian Nations), 158, 159
Ashton-Martin, 126
Asian American population, 247, 250
Asian Americans, as CEOs, 255
Asia-Pacific Economic Cooperation (APEC), 156–157
Assemble-to-order operations, 384
Assessment centers, 229

Assistive technology, 256
Association of Southeast Asian Nations (ASEAN), 156
Association or affinity patterns, 361
Assurance, 377
Asus, 47
Asustek, 300
AT&T, 16, 121, 129, 136, 137, 204
Attack, 129–130
Attention (perception process), 312
Attribution theory, 313–314
A-type conflict, 104, 208, 209
Audi, 127
Audi Group, 202
Australian farmers, 124
Authentication, 363–364
Authority
    acceptance of, 37–38
    in Fayol's fourteen principles of management, 34
Authority, 184–187
Authority-compliance leadership style, 293, 294
Authorization, 363
Auto advertisements, 123
Auto sales, 51, 126
Autocratic decisions, 301
Autonomy, 203–205
Autonomy, 189
Autonomy, team, 203–205
Average aggregate inventory, 387–388
Avis, 240
Avoidance strategy, 168
Avolio, B.J., 308
Avon, 112, 221
Awareness training, 263
Axis Performance Advisors, 204

B

Bachelder, Cheryl, 293, 325
Background checks, 226–227
Background questions, in interviews, 231
Badstüber, Achim, 202
Bain & Company, 32
Bain Capital Ventures, 4
Balance sheets, 343
Balanced scorecard, 341–342
Baldrige feedback report, 379
Baldrige Performance Excellence Awards, 379, 380
Ballard, David, 37
Bandwidth Consulting, 53
Banjo, S., 56
Bank of America, 207
Bank Wiring Room, 37
Bar codes, 359–360
Bar Raisers, 65
Barbarigo, 24

Barclays Plc, 122
Bargaining power of buyers, 124
Bargaining power of suppliers, 124
Barnard, Chester, 37–38
Barnes & Noble's Nook, 109, 129
Barney, J.B., 354
Base fines, 71
Batch production, 386
Bates, Suzanne, 321–322
Batra, Raj, 234
Battle Sports Science, 336
Bayod, Marion, 160
BCG matrix, 118–120
Beam, Betsy, 379
Beats Music, 111, 353
Beatty, Sarah, 333
Beccari, Pietro, 11
Becoming a Manager: Mastery of a New Identity (Hill), 17
Bednar, D.A., 347
Beer, Michael, 318
Behavior control, 338
Behavior, establishing new patterns of, 63–64
Behavior observation scale (BOS), 235–236
Behavioral addition, 63
Behavioral questions, in interviews, 231
Behavioral substitution, 63–64
Bell, Alexander Graham, 139
Benchmarking, 114, 334
Bennett, J., 391
Bennis, Warren, 289
Berg, Natalie, 90
Berger, Ron, 56
Berkenstock, Dan, 57
Berkshire Hathaway, 117
Bernard, Suzanne, 172
Berning, Mel, 323
Best Buy, 130, 144, 349, 388
Betraying a trust, 16
Bezos, Jeff, 12, 65
Bhatt, Paurvi, 320–321
Big Bazaar, 168
Big Mac Index, 167
Bill of materials, 392
Bing, 172
Biographical data (biodata), 229
Bircher, Garrett, 223
Bisen, Ankur, 169
Bishop, Toby, 258
Biyin, 172
Black Keys, the, 57
BlackBerry, 46
Blake/Mouton leadership grid, 293
Blinded stage of organizational decline, 144
Blogs, 327, 329, 331
Bloomberg Financial, 123
Blue Bell Creameries, 336
Blue Bottle Coffee Company, 327

BMO Harris Bank, 359–360
BMW, 127
Bock, Laszlo, 4, 230
Boeing, 13, 142–143, 204, 225
Bogut, Andrew, 207
Bohlmann, Jaya, 262
Bona fide occupational qualification (BFOQ), 218–219
Bonuses, motivation through, 270, 275, 280, 282, 283–284
Book publishing industry, 191
Booz Allen Hamilton, 223
Boston Consulting Group, 237
Boston Consulting Group (BCG) Matrix, 118–120
Boulton, C., 364
Bowers, Kim, 10
Box.com, 123
Boycotts, 57
BPV Capital Management, 62
Bradspies, R.W., 335
Brainstorming, 106
Brancucci, Joe, 331
Brandwatch, 12
Bravely Default (JRPG), 6
Brewer, Howard "Hal," 78
Bridgewater Associates, 104
British Airways, 354
Broadcast voice mail, 328
Broadcom, 137
Brokers, 196
Browlee, Dana, 209
Brown, Gary, 77
Brown Technology Group, 264
Bryant, Adam, 97
Bryant, John, 58–59
Bucey, Curt, 337
Budgeting, 98–99
Budgets, 343
Buehler, Roer, 92
Bueno, Carlos, 225
Buffett, Warren, 117
Building & Industrial Systems, 179
Build-to-stock operations, 384
Bullying style of management, 16
Bunch, John, 201
Bunge Ltd., 124
Burberry, 140
Bureaucracies, 30–32
Bureaucratic control, 337–338
Bureaucratic immunity, 212
Burger King, 53, 128
Burke, Carolyn, 64
Burke, Michelle, 318
Burns, Ursula, 253, 264
Business confidence indices, 50
Business intelligence software (BIS), 358
Business Plans to Game Plans (King), 99
Business Value Group, 318
Business Wire, 12

Buyer dependence, 54
Buzzwords, 317

C

CA Technologies, 77
Cable companies, 53
CAD (computer-aided design), 39
Cadbury bars, pork found in, 57
Caesars Entertainment, 358
Café Coffee Day, 166
CAFTA-DR (Dominican Republic-Central American Free Trade Agreement), 158
Cain, Jim, 212
CAM (computer-aided manufacturing), 39
Cameras, 134–135
Canfield, John, 301–302
Cap Gemini, 153
Cappelli, Peter, 243
Capturing information, 359–360
CARE U.S.A., 185
Career path, 223
CareerBuilder survey, 226
CareerBuilder.com, 224
Careers and the disABLED, 256
Caremark International, 71–72
Cargill, 124
Carnival Cruise Lines, 51
Carrefour, 167, 192
Case studies, 233
Cash cows, 118, 119, 120
Cash flow analysis, 342–343
Catalyst, 263
Caterpillar, 129, 130
Cato, 24
Catz, Safra, 184
Cayuga Milk Ingredients, 161
Celestica Inc., 147
Census data, 247
Center for Auto Safety, 84
Center for Business Ethics, Bently University, 78
Center for Collaborative Organizations, 201–202
Center for Disease Control, 334
Centers for Disease Control and Prevention, 86
Central States Manufacturing, 240
Central tendency error, 235
Centralization, in Fayol's fourteen principles of management, 34
Centralization of authority, 186–187
CEO Confidence Index, 50
CEOs (chief executive officers), 6–7
    earnings, 241, 272
    firing, 82
    height of, 290
    racial/ethnic disparities in number of, 255

serving as spokespeople, 12
sitting on outside boards, 11
women, 253
Ceridian Corporation, 100
Chain of command, 31, 184
Challenger, John, 68
Challenging team goals, 211
Champy, James, 190–191, 192
Chandler, Diane, 307
Change agent, 149–150
Change forces, 145
Change intervention, 145
Change management, 143–151, 145–151
    anchored in corporation's culture, 148
    coalition for, 147
    communicating vision for, 147–148
    declaring success too soon, 148
    General Electric workout, 149
    organizational development, 149–151
    planning for and creating short-term wins, 148
    planning impeding, 90
    removing obstacles to, 147–148
    resistance to change, 145–146
    results-driven change, 149
    sense of urgency, 146–147
    short-term wins, 148
    vision for change, 147
Change.org, 96
Changing external environments, 45–48
Character of rivalry, 123
Charismatic leadership, 305–307, 308
Charlebois, Vic, 355–356
Chatter, 368
Checklist Manifesto, The, 206
Chevy Volt, 86–87
Chicago Harvester, 24
Chick-Fil-A, 53, 261
Chief executive officers (CEOs). *See* CEOs (chief executive officers)
Chief financial officers (CFOs), 6, 20
Chief information officer (CIO), 6
Chief operating officer (COO), 7
China
    expats in, 174–175
    overtime hours in, 276
    wages in, 275
    water sold in, 57–58
Chocolate-hazelnut spreads, 47
Chopourian, Ani, 220–221
Cigarettes, CVS selling, 86
Cisco Systems, 123, 242, 290, 391
Citibank, 225
Citigroup, 6
Civil Rights Act (1964), 248
Civil Rights Act (1991), 51, 218
Civil Rights Act (1964) Title VII, 218, 248
Clarifying (listening), 324, 325
Clarizen, 9

Clayton Homes, 279
ClearRock, 98
Clem, Tim, 10
Cleveland Browns, 65
Client relationships, establishing, 190
Clif Bar, 382
Cloak VPN, 366
Closed systems, 40
Closure, 313
Cloud-based services, 110–111
Cluster chain, 319
Coach luxury retail, 378
Coaching, 150, 233, 320
Coca-Cola, 99–100, 165–166, 291
Codes of ethics, 76–77
Coercion, 146
Cognitive abilities, in leaders, 292
Cognitive ability tests, 228–229
Cognitive conflict, 104, 208
Cognitive maps, 59, 60
Cognizant, 61
Cohen, P., 277
Cohen, Ron, 242, 368
Cohesiveness, 207
Coletti, Lori Stewart, 243
Colgate-Palmolive, 367–368
Collaborative discussion sites, 327–328
Collectivism-individualism, 212, 213
Collins, Jim, 96
Comambault, 32–33
Combining tasks, 190
Comcast, 327
Comedy Central's Adult Swim, 291
Commission, 240
Commitment probability rule, 303, 304, 305
Commitment requirement rule, 303, 304, 305
Communication, 311–331
    attribution theory, 313–314
    basic perception process, 311–312
    choosing right medium for, 323
    coaching/counseling, 320–321
    defined, 311
    electronic, 327–328
    feedback, 326–327
    formal communication channels, 317–318
    gossip, 318, 319
    grapevines, 319–320
    horizontal, 318
    informal communication channels, 319–320
    listening, 323–326
    nonverbal, 321–322
    one-on-one, 322–326
    oral, 323
    organizational silence, 328–330
    organization-wide, 327–331
    perception of others, 313–314
    perception problems, 312–313

Communication (*Continued*)
    process of, 315–317
    self-perception, 314
    upward, 318
    withholding information, 328–329
    written, 323
Communication channels, 315–316,
    317–320
Communication costs, 358–359
Communication medium, 323
Communication process, 315–317
Company founders, organizational
    culture and, 61
Company hotlines, 329–330
Company mission, 62
Company strategy, overseas location
    and, 166
Company-related deviance, 68
Comparison to standards, 334
Compensating teams, 215
Compensation, 239–241. *See also*
    Salaries
Competitive advantage, 109
    technological innovation and, 134–135
    through people, 19–21
*Competitive Advantage through People:
    Unleashing the Power of the Work
    Force* (Pfeffer), 19
Competitive analysis, 53
Competitive Enterprise Institute, 155
Competitive inertia, 112
Competitors, 53–54
Complete information, 355–356
Complex environments, 47
Complex matrix, 184
Compliance programs, ethics, 71
Component parts inventories, 387
Comprehension approach to innovation,
    142–143
Compressed pay structure, 241
**Compression approach to
    innovation,** 143
Compromise, 33, 35
Computer City, 144
Computer components, 54
Computer-aided design (CAD), 143
Computer-based learning, 233, 234
Computers, 351
Concelman, Jim, 320
Concentration of effect, 73
Conceptual skills, 14–15
Concern for production, 292
Concertive control, 339–340
Concurrent control, 336
Conflict resolution skills, 214
Conflict, workplace, 104–105, 107
Connecticut Spring & Stamping, 204
Conner, Ray, 142–143
Connerly, Ward, 249
Conscientiousness, 258
Consensus, 209

Consideration, 293
Consistent organizational cultures,
    62
Constructive conflict and coordination,
    33, 35, 36
Constructive feedback, 326
Consultative decisions, 301
Consumer Product Safety Commission
    (CPSC), 55, 56
Consumer Reports, 100, 113
Container Store, 61, 257, 271, 285
Continental Airlines, 5, 47, 146
Contingency approach, 41–42
Contingency management, 41–42
Contingency theory, 294–298
Continuous improvement, 380
**Continuous reinforcement
    schedules,** 282–284
Continuous-flow production, 385
Contract manufacturers, 385
Control, 333–349
    accounting tools, 342–345
    balanced scorecard approach to,
        341–342
    benchmarking, 334
    bureaucratic, 337–338
    concertive, 339–340
    concurrent, 336
    corrective action, 335
    customer defections, 345
    cybernetic feasibility, 337
    as cybernetic process, 335
    defined, 333
    economic value added (EVA), 343–345
    feedback, 335–336
    feedforward, 336
    financial performance, 342–345
    methods of, 337–341
    normative, 338–339
    objective, 338
    political risk and, 169
    quality, 346
    regulation costs, 336–337
    self-control, 340–341
    standards, 333–335
    sustainability, 346–349
Control loss, 36
Control methods, 337–341
Control process, 333–337
Controlling, 5–6
**Conventional level of moral
    development,** 73
Cook, Roger, 258
Cook, Tim, 142
Cookies, 365
Coolidge, Calvin, 89
Cooperation
    Barnard's theory of, 37–38
    between managers and employees,
        26–27
    political risk and, 169

Cooperation and acceptance of
    authority, 37–38
Cooperative contracts, 161–163
Corbat, Michael, 6
Core capabilities, 115
Core change coalition, 147
Core firms, 114, 115
Cornell, Brian, 13
Corporate antivirus software, 366
Corporate blogs, 329
Corporate portals, 368
Corporate team-building, 37
Corporate-level strategy, 117–122
Corrales, Rodolfo, 373
Corrective action, in control process,
    335
Cortelyou, Bob, 47
Cosí, 7
Cost leadership, 124–125
Cost savings, 249
Costco, 349
Cottage workers, 23
Cottingham, Lara, 226–227
Counseling, 150, 320–321
Country club leadership style, 293, 294
Coupons.com, 229
Cox, Taylor, 261
Creative work environments,
    139–140
Crédit Suisse, 223
Crisis stage of organizational decline,
    144
Cross, David, 370
Cross-cultural training, 172–173
Cross-functional teams, 205
Cross-training, 200
Csikszentmihalyi, Mihaly, 139
CST Brands, 10
C-Suite, 328
C-type conflict, 104, 105, 208
Culbert, Samuel, 235
Culpability score, in U.S. Sentencing
    Guidelines, 71
Cultural dimensions (Hofstede),
    170–171
Cultural simulations, 172–173
Cuomo, Andrew, 57
Cushman & Wakefield's *European
    Cities Monitor*, 101, 102
Customer defections, 345
Customer departmentalization,
    180–181
Customer focus, 380
Customer loyalty, 382
Customer satisfaction, 20–21
Customer satisfaction, 380, 382
Customer satisfaction surveys, 345
Customers, monitoring, 52–53
Customs classification, 154, 155
Cutler, Alexander, 62
CVS Caremark, 86

CVS Health, 86
CyberAlert, 12
Cybernetic, 335
Cybernetic feasibility, 337
Cyrus, 24

D

Daimler-Benz, 350
Dalio, Ray, 104
Daly, Terry, 331
Dasra, 85
Data Breach Investigations (2015), 110
Data clusters, 362–363
Data encryption, 366
Data mining, 361–363
Data warehouse, 361
Davis, Angus, 295
Davis, Dave, 205
Davis, Michelle, 8
Davis, Steve, 228
Dayforce scheduling software, 100
Decentralization, 186
Decision acceptance, 301–303
Decision criteria, 100
Decision making, 99–107
   computing the optimal decision,
     101–102
   decision criteria, identifying, 100
   decision criteria, weighing, 100–101
   defined, 99
   Delphi technique, 105–106
   electronic brainstorming, 106–107
   ethical, 72–79
   evaluation of each alternative, 101
   generating alternative courses of
     action, 101
   group, 103–107, 201
   groupthink, 103
   limits to rational, 102–103
   nominal group technique (NGT), 105
   problem, defining, 99–100
   structured conflict, 14–105
   team training in, 214
Decision rules, 302–303
Decision styles, 301
Decision support system (DSS), 370
Decisional roles, 12–13
Deckers Outdoors, 378
Decoding, 316
Deep-level diversity, 257–259, 262, 351
Deezer, 353
DeFalco, Louis, 227
Defamation, 227
Defenders, 126
Defensive bias, 313–314
Defensive strategy, 84–85
De-forming, 210–211
Degree of centralization, 186–187
Delegation of authority, 185–186
Dell Inc., 48, 263, 331

Delphi technique, 105–106
Delta Airlines, 46, 47, 97–98, 380–381
Demographics, 51
De-norming, 210–211
Department manager, 9
Department of Justice, 219
Department of Labor, 55, 218, 219
Departmentalization, 177–184
   customer, 180–181
   defined, 178
   functional, 178–179
   geographic, 181–182
   matrix, 182–184
   product, 179–180
Dependent demand systems, 392
Derailers, 15–16
Descriptive Geometry (Monge), 39
Design competition, 136
Design for disassembly, 348–349
Design iteration, 141–142
Desk.com, 254
De-storming, 210–211
Destructive feedback, 326
Deutsche Telekom, 137
DeVaul, Richard, 212
Development time, shortening, 143
Developmental Dimensions
   International, 320
Devil's advocacy, 105
Dezso, Cristian, 252
DHL, 373
Dialectical inquiry, 105
Dickerson, Chad, 289
Dick's Sporting Goods, 359
Differentiation, 125
DiFonzo, Nicholas, 320
Digital cameras, 134–135
Diocletian, 24
Direct competition, 127–130
Direct foreign investment, 153–154
Direct sales industry, 112
Direction of effort, 267
Directive leadership, 301
Directive leadership, 298–299
DirecTV, 53, 121
Disabilities, 225
Disability, 255
Disability discrimination, 255–256
Discipline, in Fayol's fourteen principles
   of management, 34
Discontinuous change, 136, 138–139
Discretionary responsibilities, 83–84
Discretionary responsibility, 83–84
Discrimination
   age, 251–252
   disability, 255–256
   employment, 219–221
   racial and ethnic, 254–255
   sex, 252–254
Discrimination and fairness paradigm,
   259

Discrimination lawsuits, 219–220,
   249–250
DISH Network, 53
Disney Corporation. *See* Walt Disney
   Company
Disney Shanghai, 292
Disney, Walt, 61
Disney World, 360
Disparate treatment, 219–220
Disposition, 257
Disseminator role, 12
Dissolution stage of organizational
   decline, 144
Distal goals, 92
Distinctive competence, 113
Distributive justice, 276
Disturbance handler role, 13
Diversification, 117
Diversity, 247. *See also* Workplace
   diversity
Diversity audits, 263
Diversity Inc., 240
Diversity pairing, 263–264
Diversity principles, 261–263
Diversity training, 263
Division of labor, 31
Division of work, in Fayol's fourteen
   principles of management, 34
Do The Math Tour, 81
Documentary training, 172
Documenting references, 227–228
Dogs, 119
Doha Round, 156
Dominant design, 136–137
Domination, 33–34
Dominican Republic-Central
   America Free Trade Agreement
   (CAFTA-DR), 156
Domino's, 299
Donahoe, John, 116
Donald, Jim, 140
Donnelly, Vince, 146
"Dont' Frack My Mother" (video), 57
Douglas, Sandy, 291
Dourney, R.J., 7
Dowd, Rich, 17
Downsizing, 242–243
Downtime, 389
Downward communication, 318
Doyle, Patrick, 299
DreamWorks Studios, 55
Dreyfus, 124
"Drilling down," 317
Drive, in leaders, 291
Drone delivery, 12
Dropbox, 251
DSI Security Services, 217
D'Souza, Francisco, 61
Dulski, Jennifer, 96
Dumpster diving, 69
Dunkin' Donuts, 163

Dunnhumby, 163
DuPont Corporation, 221, 262, 386
Durability, 377
Duracell, 117, 136–137
Duracell's Powermat, 136–137
Durant, Kevin, 120
Durosko, Craig, 146
DVD-by-mail services, 53
Dvorak keyboard layout, 137
Dwoskin, E., 322
Dynamic environments, 46
Dynegy, 64
Dysfunctional turnover, 244
Dyson, Sir James, 308–309

E

EAPs (employee assistance programs), 320
Early responders, 130
Early retirement incentive programs (ERIPs), 243–244
Easterbrook, Steve, 97
Easterman, Steve, 86
EasyJet, 375
Eaton, 62
EBay, 4, 116, 178, 224
EBay Motors apps, 116
EBay Now, 116
EBay RedLaser, 116
Ebola, 386
Economic order quantity (EOQ), 390
Economic performance, social responsibility and, 86–87
Economic responsibility, 82
Economic value added (EVA), 343–345
Economist, 167
Economy, 50
Edison, Thomas, 118, 139
Edman, Paul, 322
EEOC. *See* Equal Employment Opportunity Commission (EEOC)
Effectiveness, 3–4
Efficiency, 3
Efficient Foodservice Response (EFR), 389
Effort, motivation and, 267–268
Egyptians, 23, 24
80% rule, 220
84 Lumber, 114, 115
Einhorn, Richard, 133
Eisaguirre, Lynne, 107
Elaine Construction, 243
E-learning, 234
Electronic brainstorming, 106–107
Electronic communication, 327–328
Electronic data interchange (EDI), 368–369
Electronic health records, 315

Electronic monitoring and distribution services, 12
Electronic scanners, 360
11main.com, 5
Eli Lilly, 207
Elite SEM, 339
Ellis, Kevin, 161
Ellison, Larry, 184
Elop, Stephen, 1147
Email, 323, 327
Email snooping, 365
EMC, 172–173
EMD, 129
Emirates Airline, 331
Emotional software programs, 322
Emotional stability, 257, 292
Empathy, 377–378
Emphatic listening, 325–326
Employee Assistance Programs (EAPs), 320
Employee compensation, 239–241. *See also* Salaries
Employee involvement teams, 204
Employee referrals, 224
Employee satisfaction, 20, 382
Employee separation, 239
Employee shrinkage, 68–69
Employee stock ownership plans (ESOPs), 240–241
Employee termination, 241–242
Employee turnover, 187, 201, 244
Employee-centered leadership, 292
Employment issues. *See* Human resource management (HRM)
Employment laws, 217–219, 225
Employment references, 227–228
Employment security, 19
Empowering workers, 192–193, 383
Empowerment, 193, 279
Enabling Profitable Growth in the Food-Prepared-Away-From-Home Industries, 389
Encoding, 315
Energizer, 137
Eni S.p.A., 68
Ensign, R.L., 78
Entrepreneur role, 13
Environmental change, 45–47, 49
Environmental complexity, 47, 49
Environmental factors, interpreting, 58–59
Environmental Protection Agency, 55
Environmental scanning, 57–58, 113
Epilepsy Foundation, 256
Epstein, David, 86, 250
Equal division of work, 27
Equal Employment Opportunity Commission (EEOC), 52, 55, 217, 219, 220, 262
Uniform Guidelines on Employee Selection Procedures, 222–223, 225

Equal Pay Act (1963), 218
Equity, in Fayol's fourteen principles of management, 34
Equity theory, 272–276
E-readers, 129
ERG Theory, 269
ERIPs (early retirement incentive programs), 243–244
ESOPs (employee stock ownership plans), 240–241
Esprit de corps, 34
Establishing client relationships, 190
Esterl, M., 291
Ethical behavior, 67–68
Ethical charismatics, 306, 308
Ethical climate, 78–79
Ethical decision making, 72–79
Ethical intensity, 72–73
Ethical responsibility, 83
Ethics
    charismatic leadership, 305–307
    codes of ethics, 76–77
    defined, 67
    ethical climate, 78–79
    ethical intensity, 72–73
    ethics training, 77–78
    hiring ethical employees, 76
    intensity of ethical decisions, 72–73
    model of ethical decision making, 79
    moral development, stages of, 73–74
    principles in ethical decision making, 74–76
    U.S. Sentencing Commission guidelines, 69–72
    whistleblowing, 78–79
    workplace deviance, types of, 68–69
Ethics compliance programs, 71
Ethics training, 77–78
Ethnic discrimination, 254–255
Etsy.com, 289
Eukanuba, 117
Euro, 157
Euromonitor, 58
European Cities Monitor (Cushman & Wakefield), 101, 102
European Union (EU), 157
Evaluate, 283
Evaluation apprehension, 106
Executive information system (EIS), 367–368
Executive Order 11246, 248
Expatriates, 171–175
Expectancy, 277–278
Expectancy theory, 276–279
Experiential approach to innovation, 141–142
Experiential exercises, 233
Expert systems, 370–371
Export Now, 161
Exporting, 161
Extended Stay America, 140

External attribution, 313
External environments, 45
External recruiting, 223–225
Externals, 300
Extinction, 282
Extranets, 369–370
Extraversion, 257
Extrinsic rewards, 270–271
Extroverts, 290
Exxon Mobile, 80
Eye contact, 321

F

Facebook, 103, 224, 225, 251, 272, 328, 357–358
"Failure is an Option" advertising campaign (Domino's), 299
Fair Labor Association, 85
Fair Labor Standards Act (FLSA), 275
Fallavollita, Scott, 217–218
Families, relocating overseas, 173–174
Family and Medical Leave Act (1993), 51, 217–218
Fandray, Dayton, 78
Al-Farabi, 24
Farm Bill (2008), 155
Farming, 23
Farrugia, Mark, 235
Fast Company, 301
Fast-food industry jobs, 187
Faulty action stage of organizational decline, 144
Fayol, Henri, 4, 32–33, 34
Fayol's fourteen principles of management, 34
Federal Communications Commission (FCC), 55
Federal employment laws, 217–219
Federal News Service, 12
Federal regulatory agencies and commissions, 55
Federal Reserve System, 55
Federal Trade Commission, 55
FedEx, 153, 204
Feedback, 189
Feedback channels, 190
Feedback control, 335–336
Feedback to sender, 316
Feedforward control, 336
Feintzeig, R., 252
Feitelberg, R., 138, 334
Felice, Sergio, 51
Feminine cultures, 170–171
Fendi, 11
Ferrari, 126
Ferrero Group, 47
FICO, 8
"Fiction of superior authority," 38
Fiedler's contingency theory, 294–298
Field simulation training, 173

Figaro's Pizza, 56
Figurehead role, 11
Films and videos, training through, 233
Final assembly, 387
Financial ratios, 343
Financial Review Card, 343
Finished good inventories, 387
Firefighter job description, 222
Firefighters, benchmarking, 334
Firewalls, 364, 366
Firing employees, 241–242, 261
Firm-level strategy, 127–130
First Air, 356
First Student, 220
First-line managers, 7, 9
First-mover advantage, 353
Fisher, Roger, 35
Fisher-Price toys, 62
5G devices, 137
Fixed interval reinforcement schedules, 282, 283
Fixed ratio reinforcement schedules, 282
Flemming, Bill, 289
Flexibility, of manufacturing operations, 384–385
Flexible leadership style, 296
Flexon, Bob, 64
Flextronics International, 239
Flickinger, Burt, 124–125
FlightStats, 380
Flow, 139
FM Global, "Resilience Index," 167
Focus strategy, 125
Follett, Mary Parker, 33, 35, 36
Food and Drug Administration (FDA), 55
Ford, Bill, 13
Ford, Henry, 24, 133
Ford Motor Company, 13, 24, 53, 362–363, 391
Foreign Corrupt Practices Act, 83
Foreign direct investment, 153–154
Formal authority system, 300
Formal communication channels, 317–318
Forming, 210
Fortune "100 Best Companies to Work for in America," 20, 21
Fortune 500 Companies, 169, 254, 353
Four-fifths (or 80%) rule, 220
Fowler, A., 233
Foxconn, 84–85, 163, 276, 333
Foxconn factories, Taiwan, 57
Fracking, 56–57
Frady, Kelly, 241
Franchise, 162–163
Franchisee, 162
Franchisor, 162
Freame, John, 122
Fredeen, Ingrid, 251

Frederickson, Valerie, 65
Free shipping, 388
Free trade, 157–159
Freeborn & Peters law firm, 272
Freedom, 140
Freestyle self-serve soda machines, 99
Freetextbooks.com, 271
Frelin, Johanna, 259
French Open grand slam tennis tournament, 333
Fresh & Easy stores, 90
Fresh Brew, 146
Fried, Jason, 267
Friedlander, Jonathan, 361
Friedman, Milton, 80
Friend, Jason, 383
Friesen, Candy, 326
Fry, Jason, 323
Fuerst, W.L., 354
Fugere, Danielle, 80
Functional departmentalization, 178–179
Functional turnover, 244
Functions of the Executive, The (Barnard), 38
Fundamental attribution error, 313–314
Funeral businesses, 45
Fung, Sandra, 200
Furlong, Tom, 357–358
Futter, M., 6
Futterman, Robert, 3

G

Gainsharing, 215
Galaxy Tab, 109
Galdwell, Malcolm, 290
Gales, Jean-Marc, 51
Galinsky, Adam, 213
Gallo, Carmine, 193
Gallo Communications Group, 193
Gantt charts, 28–30
Gantt, Henry, 28–29, 30
GATT (General Agreement on Tariffs and Trade), 155–156
Gawande, Atul, 206–207
Gayle, Helene, 185
Gazelle.com, 349
GE Aircraft Engines, 301
General Agreement on Tariffs and Trade (GATT), 155–156
General and Industrial Management (Fayol), 30, 34
General Electric (GE), 97, 118, 129–130, 250
General Electric workout, 149
General environment, 48–52
defined, 48–49
economy, 50
political/legal component to, 51–52

General environment (*Continued*)
sociocultural component to, 51
technological component to, 50–51
General Mills, 82, 83
General Motors (GM), 84, 86–87, 168, 207, 391
Generational change, 143
Genetic Information Nondiscrimination Act (2008), 218
Geographic departmentalization, 181–182
Geometric Ltd., 170–171
George, C.S. Jr., 24
Germano, S., 120
Getting to Yes: Negotiating Agreement without Giving In (Fisher, Ury, and Patton), 35
Ghazali, 24
Ghosn, Carlos, 293
Gibson, Kristen, 125
Gilbert, Phil, 105
Gilbreth, Frank, 27–28
Gilbreth, Lillian, 27–28
Gilbreth's motion studies, 27, 28
Gino, Francesca, 238
GitHub, 10
Gladwell, Malcolm, 290
Glass ceiling, 252–253
GlaxoSmithKline, 385
Global business, 153. *See also* Global management
Global competition, analyzing degree of, 166
Global consistency, 160
Global management, 153–175
business climate, finding best, 164–169
cooperative contracts, 161–163
cultural differences, 169–171
direct foreign investment, 153–154
exporting, 161
franchises, 162–163
GATT, 155–156
global consistency, 160
growth potential of foreign markets, 165–166
local adaptation, 160
office/manufacturing location, 166–167
overseas assignment preparation, 171–175
political risk, 167–169
regional trading zones, 156–157, 158
strategic alliances, 163
trade agreements, 155–159
trade barriers, 154–155
wholly owned affiliates, 163–164
World Trade Organization (WTO), 156, 157
world's best and worst countries for business, 168
Global new ventures, 163

Global sourcing standards, 56
Glocer, Thomas, 177
GM. *See* General Motors (GM)
Goal, 284
Goal acceptance, 285
Goal commitment, 91–92
Goal congruence, 302–303, 304, 305
Goal congruence rule, 303
Goal difficulty, 285
Goal setting
developing commitment to, 91–92
diversity, 263
teams, 209, 211–212
tracking progress toward achieving, 92–93
Goal specificity, 284–285
Goal-setting theory, 284–286
Gobillot, Lori, 5
Go-Daddy.com, 123
Goizueta, Roberto, 343
Golden, Jocelyn, 225
Goldstein, J., 367
Good boy, nice girl stage (Kohlberg), 73, 74
Good housekeeping, 348
Google, 4, 57, 110, 137, 142, 357, 363–364
Google Advanced Technology and Project Lab, 142
Google Maps, 57
Google X, 212
Gordon-Levitt, Joseph, 57
Gossip, 318, 319
Gossip chain, 319
Gould, Thomas, 122
Government import standards, 154, 155
Government subsidies, 154, 155
Grand strategies, 121–122
Grapevines, 319–320
Graphic rating scale (GRS), 235, 236
Grauch Enterprises, 386
Grauch, Fred, 386
Gravity Payments, 277
Grazier, Peter, 214
Great Little Box Company (GLBC), 200
"Great person" theory (trait theory), 290–292
Grech, Pippa, 354
Green Depot, 333–334
Greenberg, Josh, 83
Greenfield, Rich, 82
Greer, Lindred, 184
Griggs v. Duke Power Co., 222
GROHE Group, 164
Grooveshark, 83
Group decisions, 301
Group discussion training, 233
Group dynamics and cohesion, 35, 37
Groupthink, 103
Growth strategy, 121

GTE Financial, 331
Gucci, 334
Guerreiro, Maria, 388
Guitar Center, 99, 100
Gun finishers, 38–39
Gupta, Kamlesh, 168
Gutenberg, Johannes, 39–40
Gyllenhaal, Maggie, 57

H

Habitat for Humanity, 38
Hachette Book Group, 191
Haden, Jeff, 11, 37
Hadomi, Ori, 330
Hagerty, J.R., 374, 385
Haines, Ray, 261
Hallatt, Mike, 125
Halo error, 235
Hammer, Michael, 145, 190–191, 192
Hammon, Becky, 262
Hammurabi, 24
Handler, Charles, 230
Hansen, Gail, 86
Hardee's, 53
Harker, Susan, 65
Harris, Parker, 254
Harvard Business Review, 25, 173–174
Hawthorne Effect, 35
Hawthorne Studies, 35, 37
Hayase, Hiroshi, 54
Hayes, Phillip, 155
HCL Technologies, 3
Hearing, 324
Hearing loops, 133
Hehir, Patrick, 318
Heinz, 343
Helmrich, B., 272
Hendricks, D., 195
Hernandez, Manny, 338
Hershey's code of ethics, 76–77
Hertz Rent-a-Car, 369
Hewitt Associates, 270
Hewlett Packard (HP), 48, 123, 163
Hewlett-Packard (HP), 55
Heyl Logistics, 227
Hideki Hada, 141
Hierarchical pay structures, 241
Higher-order needs, 269, 271
High-value service, 382
Hilgert, Ray, 320
Hill, Linda, 17
Hillary, Doug, 263
Hinshaw, Scott, 299
Hire Results, 229
Hirease, 226
Hiring employees
in bureaucratic organizations, 30–31
changing company culture and, 64–65
competitive advantage and selective, 19

hiring ethical employees, 76
normative control and, 339
scientific management and, 26
selection process, 225–231
Hispanic population, 247
Historical overview, 23–42
  administrative management, 32–33
  ancient Sumer and Egypt, 23
  bureaucratic management, 30–32
  constructive conflict and coordination,
    33, 35, 36
  contributors to management ideas and
    practices, 24
  cooperation and acceptance of
    authority, 37–38
  cottage industry/farming and, 23
  Gantt charts, 28–30
  Hawthorne studies, 35, 37
  Industrial Revolution, 24
  information management, 39–40
  motion studies, 27–28
  operations management, 38–39
  time study, 28
Hitchcock, Steven, 204
HIV Connect, 320–321
H&M, 348
Hoag, Jay, 207
Hoffman, Michael, 78
Hofstede, Geert, 170
Hofstede's six cultural dimensions,
  170–171
Holding cost, 389–390
Holland, Judy, 174
Holley, Rick, 274
Holmes, Ryan, 328
Holtz, Dave, 98
Home Depot, 114, 115, 160
Honda, 53
Honesty, in leaders, 291
Honeywell, 280–281
Hootsuite, 328
Horizontal communication, 318
Hormel Foods, 121
Horowitz, Ben, 61
Horvitz, Eric, 356
Hosmer, LaRue, 74
Hostile work environment, 220–221
Howell, J.M., 308
Hoyt, Brian, 223
HTC, 46
Huawei Enterprises, 11
Hulu, 53
*Human Equation: Building Profits
  by Putting People First, The*
  (Pfeffer), 19
*Human Problems of an Industrial
  Civilization, The* (Mayo), 35
Human relations management (HRM),
  33, 35–38, 217
**Human resource information
  system (HRIS),** 225

**Human resource management
  (HRM),** 217–244. *See also* Hiring
  employees
  adverse impact, 220
  background checks, 226–228
  compensation decisions, 239–241
  defined, 217
  discrimination, 219–221
  disparate treatment, 219–220
  downsizing, 242–243
  employee separation, 239, 241–244
  employee turnover, 244
  external recruiting, 223–225
  federal employment laws, 217–219
  four-fifths (or 80%) rule, 220
  internal recruiting, 223
  interviews, 226, 230–231
  job analysis, 221–223
  onboarding, 238
  performance appraisal, 235–239
  process, 217
  recruiting, 221–225
  references, 227–228
  retirement, 243–244
  safety standards, 219
  selection, 225–231
  selection tests, 228–230
  sexual harassment, 220–221
  terminating employees, 241–242
  training, 232–235
Human skills, 14
Humor, 209
Humphries, Paul, 318
Hurd, Mark, 184
Hurricane Sandy, 83–84
Hutchins, David, 340
Hydraulic fracturing (fracking), 56–57
Hyland-Savage, Gail, 221
Hymowitz, Carol, 317
Hyundai, 53

I

Iams, 117
IAT (Implicit Association Test), 263
IBM, 54, 105, 289
IBM Credit, 191
Ice, Jim, 234
ICloud, 110–111
Identify, 283
"If-then" rules, 370–371
IGATE, 153
Immediacy behaviors, 324, 325
Immediate feedback, 326
Imperfectly imitable resources, 110
Implicit Association Test (IAT), 263
Impoverished leader, 293, 294
Inaction stage of organizational decline,
  144
In-basket exercise, 229, 230
Income statements, 343

Incredible Universe, 144
Incremental change, 138–139
Independent demand systems, 392
India
  Amazon/Junglee.com, 169
  coffee shops, 166
  Dunkin' Donuts in, 163
  retail market in, 167–168
  social responsibility in, 85
Individualism-collectivism, 212
Individualistic cultures, 170
Individualized consideration, 309
Indulgence *versus* restraint, cultural
  dimension of, 171
Industrial psychology, 28
Industrial Revolution (1750-1900), 24
Industry regulation, 55–56
Industry-level strategies, 122–127
Industry-level strategy, 122–124
Informal communication channels,
  319–320
Informal meetings, 330
Information, 351. *See also* Managing
  information
Information management, 23, 39–40.
  See also Managing information
Information sharing, 19
Information Technology & Innovation
  Foundation, 156
Informational roles, 11–12
Initial assembly, 387
Initiating structure, 293
Initiation of effort, 267
Initiative, in Fayol's fourteen principles
  of management, 34
Innovation. *See* **Organizational
  innovation**
Innovation streams, 134–138
Inputs, 273, 274, 275–276
InsightSquared, 334
Inspirational motivation, 308
Instacart, 13
Installation & Services Technologies,
  240
Institute for Data Driven Design, 89
Instrumental exchange stage
  (Kohlberg), 73, 74
Instrumentality, 278
Integrated model for motivation, 287
Integration, 35
Integrative conflict resolution, 35
Integrity, in leaders, 291
Intel, 134, 138, 263, 351
Intellectual stimulation, 308–309
Intentional discrimination, 219
Interactive Excellence (Schlossberg),
  136
Interchangeable parts, 39
InterContinental Hotels Group, 362
**Intermittent reinforcement
  schedules,** 282, 283

Internal attribution, 313
Internal environment, 59–60. *See also* Organizational culture
Internal motivation, 189
Internal recruiting, 223
Internal service quality, 382–383
Internals, 300
International assignments, preparing for, 171–175
International Federation of the Phonographic Industry, 156
International Telecommunication Union (ITU), 137
International Telegraph Convention, 137
Interorganizational processes, 193–196
Interorganizational processes, 193–196
Interpersonal roles, 10–11
Interpersonal skills, 214
Interpretation (perception process), 311, 312
Interpretation of environmental factors, 58–59
Interval reinforcement schedules, 282, 283
Intervene, 283
Interviews, 226, 230–231
Intranets, 368
Intraorganizational process, 190–193
Intrinsic rewards, 270–272
Introverts, 290
Intuit, 334
Intuitive research and Technology Corp., 78
Inventory, 39
Inventory, 386–392
Inventory records, 392
Inventory turnover, 388–389
Involuntary separation, 239
IPads, 54, 55, 109, 110, 111, 354
IPhone, 46, 54, 55, 110, 333
IPod, 110
Irani, J.J., 306–307
Iraq, ancient, 23
ISO 9000, 378–379
ISO 14000, 378–379
Iteration, 141
ITunes, 53, 110–111
ITunes Match, 111
ITunes Radio, 111, 353

J

Japan, Novartis scandal in, 85–86
Japanese-style role-playing games (JRPGs), 6
Jargon, 317
J.D. Power Initial Quality Survey, 376–377
Jefferson, Thomas, 39

Jeffried, Mike, 90
Jervell, E.E., 120
JetBlue, 280
Jetstar Airways, 328–329
JIT (Just-in-time) inventory, 390–391
Job Accommodation Network, 256
Job analysis, 221–223
Job characteristics model (JCM), 188–190
Job description, 221, 222
Job design, 187–190
Job enrichment, 188
Job evaluation, 239
Job interviews, 225, 226, 230–231
Job performance
  accurately measuring, 235–237
  motivation and, 267–268
Job postings, 223
Job rotation, 187–188
Job satisfaction, teamwork and, 199–200
Job shops, 386
Job specialization, 187
Job specifications, 221, 222
Job-centered leadership, 292
Job-knowledge questions, in interviews, 231
Jobs, Steve, 61, 143, 209
John Deere, 384
Johnson & Johnson, 280, 385
Johnson, Devra, 237
Johnson, Doug, 201–202
Johnson, K., 174
Joint ventures, 163
Jonath, Franklin, 9
Jones, A., 137
Journal for Quality and Participation, 379
Journal of Applied Psychology, 25
J.P. Morgan, 84
JPMorgan Chase, 338–339
Junglee.com, 169
Just-in-time inventory (JIT), 39, 390–391
Justus, J.R., 62

K

Kamath, Suresh, 256
Kanban, 391
Karp, H., 83
Katz, J., 62
Katz, Joel, 77
Kaur, Daljit, 354
Kay, Alan, 213
Keifer, Steve, 391
Kellogg's, 58–59
Kennedy Center, Washington D.C., 133
Kennedy, John F., 96
Kenny, David, 52–53
Kent, Muhtar, 99, 100, 291
Kering, 334

Keurig Green Mountain Inc., 99
Keystone XL Pipeline, 81, 82
Keystroke monitoring, 365
Khadaied, Abdul Kareem, 57
Khufu, King, 23
Kia Optima, 53, 346
Kidder Resources, 256
Kiel, Dana, 320
Kilburg, Richard, 17
Kim, Charlie, 298
Kimberly-Clark, 140, 250
Kindle, 126
Kindle Fire, 109
Kindle Paperwhite, 129
Kinesics, 321–322
King, Aaron, 240
King, Jan, 99
King, Mark, 120
Kirshner, Ben, 339
Kiss of Yes, 145
K'Nex Brands, 385
Knowledge, 370
Knowledge, sharing, 370–371
Kohlberg, Lawrence, 73
Kohlberg's stages of moral development, 73
Koontz, H., 335
Korn/Ferry International, 227
Kotter, John, 146, 148
Kraft, 343
Kroc, Ray, 89
Kroger, 163, 337, 355
Krzanich, Brian, 138
Kyocera, 348–349

L

Labor laws, 219
Labor productivity, 375
Lacher, Joseph, 319–320
Ladders.com, 224
Lafley, A.G., 91, 95
Lakeland Industries, 386
Lampa, Henrik, 348
Landline phones, 136
Language training, 1172
Large-system interventions, 150–151
Laser Soft Info Systems, 256
Late responders, 130
Lauzon, Armand, 149
Lavin, Frank, 161
Lawler, Edward, 212
Layoffs, 242–243
Lazzo, Mike, 291
Leader information rule, 302–303, 304
Leader role, 11
Leaderless group discussion, 229
Leader-member relations, 296
Leadership, 289–309
  Blake/Mouton leadership grid, 293, 294

charismatic, 305–307
defined, 289
Fiedler's contingency theory, 294–298
leaders/managers comparison, 289–290
normative decision theory, 301–305
path-goal theory, 298–301
trait theory, 290–292
transactional, 309
transformational, 307–309
visionary, 305–309
Leadership behaviors, 292–293
Leadership style, 294–298
contingency theory, 295–298
defined, 294
Least Preferred Coworker (LPC) scale, 295–296
matched to situations, 296–298
path-goal theory, 298–300
Leadership traits, 290–292
LeadGenius, 195
Leading, 5
Leahy, Terry, 90
Learning and effectiveness paradigm, 260–261
Least Preferred Coworker (LPC) scale, 295–296
Lectures, training through, 233
Lee, Angela, 275
Lee, David, 207
Lee, Hope, 58
Legal influences, 51–52
Legal responsibility, 82–83
Legere, John, 324
Leniency error, 235
Lennon, Sean, 57
Leno, Jay, 307–308
Lenovo, 275
"Let's Talk Ethical with Hal" program, 78
Leung, Tom, 224–225
Level of offense, U.S. Sentencing Guidelines, 71
Levi Strauss, 192, 320–321
Lewin, Kurt, 145
LG Electronics, 137
Liason role, 11
Licensed Taxi Driver Association, London, 45
Licensee, 161–162
Licensing, 161–162
Licensor, 161–162
Life cycle theory of organizations, 81
Light, Marita, 174–175
Lincoln Electric, 270
Line authority, 185
Line function, 185
Line-flow production, 385–386
LinkedIn, 103, 224, 225, 227
Linton, Tom, 239
Lintz, Janice Schacter, 133

Listen360, 52
Listening, 323–326
Little Gym, 52
Lixil, 164
Local adaptation, 160
Locke, Edwin, 27, 92
Locomotive manufacturing, 129
Locus of control, 300
Long-term orientation, 171
Long-term profits and growth, 382
Lore, Mark, 390
Lost efficiency, 389
Low tolerance for change, 145
Low-cost strategy, 166
Lower-order needs, 269, 271
Lowe's, 115
Loyalty Institute, 271
Lozano, Bobby, 349
Luby's Cafeterias, 128
Lukits, A., 340
Luthans, Fred, 283
Lyft, 345
Lync, 328
Lynton, Michael, 363

M

M City, 141
Ma, Jack, 5, 291
Maastricht Treaty of Europe, 156, 157, 158
Machiavelli, 24
Machinery, aging, 374
Mackey, John, 13, 307
Magellan Health, 320
Magnet makers, 56
Magnitude of consequences, 73
Mahler, J., 191
Mainstream, 256
Make-to-order operations, 384
Make-to-stock operations, 384
Malaysian Ministry of Health, 57
Malware, 363, 365
Management
academic journals, 25
contingency, 41–42
defined, 3
functions, 4–6
history of. *See* Historical overview
information. *See* Managing information
operations. *See* Operations management
systems, 40–41
transition to, 17–19
Management by objectives, 97
Management functions, 4–6
Management skills, 13–15
Managerial roles, 10–13
Managers. *See also* CEOs (chief executive officers)

influencing ethical behavior in others, 78
leaders *vs.*, 289–290
managerial functions performed by, 4–6
mistakes made by, 15–17
starting at the bottom, 3
top managers, 6–8
what companies look for in, 13–15
Managing change. *See* Change management
Managing information, 351–371
accurate information, 355
acquisition costs, 357–358
capturing information, 359–360
communication costs, 358–359
competitive advantage, 353–354
complete information, 355–356
external access and sharing, 368–370
first-mover advantage, 353
internal access and sharing, 367–368
Moore's law, 351, 352
overview, 29–30
processing costs, 357
processing information, 360–363
protecting information, 363–367
raw data-information distinction, 351, 353
relevant information, 356
retrieval costs, 358
security threats, types of, 365
sharing knowledge and expertise, 370–371
storage costs, 357–358
timely information, 356–357
useful information, 354–357
Mandi, Jacob, 68
Mangas, Thomas, 174
Manjoo, Farhad, 327
Manning, Peyton, 338
Manthey, Brian, 335
Manual typewriter, 40
Manufacturers Alliance for Productivity, 374
Manufacturing flexibility, 384–385
Manufacturing, history of, 24
Manufacturing location, choosing, 166–167
Manufacturing operations, 383–386
Marathe, Paraag, 347–348
March Madness, 68
Maritz Incentives, 279
Mariwalla, Kavita, 356
Mark, Gloria, 139
MarkerBot, 164
Market commonality, 127–128, 129
Market6, 390
Markoff, J., 379
Marks & Spencer, 349
Marks, Michael, 54
Marlow Industries, 243

Marshmallow Fun Co., 385
Martens, Phil, 8
Martinson, Eileen, 5
Marvel, 292
Mary Kay, 112
Masculine cultures, 170–171
Maslow's Hierarchy of Needs, 269, 271
Mass production, 24
Master production schedule, 392
Mata, F.J., 354
Material/product substitution, 348
Materials requirement planning (MRP), 390, 391–392
Matrix departmentalization, 182–184
Matrix organizations, 184
Matsuda, Yosuke, 6
Mattel, 62, 82
Mattrick, Don, 82
Maximize (decisions), 103
Mayer, Marissa, 290
Mayo, Elton, 35, 37
Mazor Robotics, 330
MBC Group, 161–162
McAfee, Andrew, 140
McCall, Ginger, 322
McCartney, Stella, 334
McClelland's Learned Needs Theory, 269
McCoy, Sherilyn, 112
McDonald, James, 225
McDonald's, 86, 97, 128, 137, 162, 186, 187, 189, 247–248
McGee, Tom, 263–264
McKenna, Mark, 139
McKinsey & Company, 80
McNamara, Steve, 45
Meadowbrook Maple Syrup, 356, 357
Measure, 283
Mechanistic organizations, 190
Media advocacy, 57
Medici family, 40
Meggy, Robert, 200
Mehta, Manish, 331
Meliones, Jon, 341–342
Menard, Greg, 355
Mentoring, 233, 254, 263–264
Menu-labeling regulations, 56
Menzies, Kate, 160
Mercedes, 127
Merck, 194
Mercy General Hospital, Sacramento, 220–221
Mergers and acquisitions, 32, 166
Merit-based promotions, 31
Merrill, Douglas, 104
Merrill Lynch, 250
Metropolitan Life Insurance, 359
Meyer, Herbert, 237
Michaels, David, 79
Michaels stores, 53
Michaelson, Connor & Boul, 221

Microsoft, 7, 48, 120, 148, 172, 177–178, 327
Microsoft Surface, 109
Microsoft Xbox division, 127
Middle East, political risk in, 168–169
Middle management, planning and, 96–97
Middle managers, 7, 8–9
Middle-of-the road leadership style, 293, 294
Midvale Steel Company, 25
Mikells, Kathryn, 20
Milestones, 142
Miller, Herman, 344
Milwaukee Mutual Insurance, 214
Minecraft, 7
Minnesota Clerical Test, 228
Minority domination, 201, 208
Mintzberg, Henry, 10, 11, 12
Mission Bicycle Company, 383
Mission, organizational (purpose statement), 95–96
Mistakes, by managers, 15–17
Misunderstanding and distrust, resistance to change and, 145
MIT Sloan Management Review, 25
Mitsubishi Electric Cooling & Heating, 369
Mittal, Kamal, 170
Mittal, Lakshmi, 381
Mobile Travel Guide, 115
Modernizing Medicine database, 356
Modified Early Warning Score (MEWS), 362
Modular organizations, 193–194
Mohrman, Susan, 215
Mojang, 7
Mollenkopf, Steve, 136, 137
Mollick, Ethan, 9
Moltz, Barry, 383
Monarchies, 30
Monge, Gaspard, 39
Monitor role, 12
Monster High toy line, 62
Monster.com, 224
Moore, Gordon, 351
Moore, ReNika, 217
Moore's law, 351, 352
Moral development, stages of, 73–74
More, Sir Thomas, 24
Morgan Stanley, 193
Morrissey, Helena, 260
Motion studies, 27–28
Motivation, 267–287
    basic model of, 268, 269
    defined, 267
    effort and performance, 267–268
    equity theory, 272–276
    expectancy theory, 276–279
    goal-setting theory, 284–286
    inspirational leaders and, 308

    integrated model, 287
    manager's role in, 271–272
    need satisfaction, 268–270
    reinforcement theory, 279–284
    rewards, 270–271
    teams, 211
Motivation to manage, 15
Motorola, 46
Moufarrige, Taine, 214
Mr. Everyday Dollar, 268, 269
Mucci, Martin, 79
Muhlhauser, Craig, 147
Muilenburg, Dennis, 142
Mulcahy, Anne, 264
Mullainathan, S., 27
Multifactor productivity, 375–376
Multifunctional teams, 142
Multinational corporations, 153
Murphy, Robert, 106
Muslim Consumers Association of Malaysia (MCAM), 57
Mutton, Nick, 339
Myer, Bruce, 233–234
Myers, Stacy, 214

N

Nadella, Satya, 7, 327
NAFTA (North American Free Trade Agreement), 156, 157, 158
Nagamori, Shigenobu, 135
NASA, 96, 164
National Amputation Foundation, 256
National Association of the Deaf, 256
National Association of Theatre Owners, 138
National Business Ethics Survey, 2015, 78
National Council on Disability, 256
National culture, 169–170
National Federation of the Blind, 256
National Institute for Standards and Technology, 379
National Labor Relations Board, 55, 219
National Transportation Safety Board, 212–214
Native American population, 247
Natural Resources Defense Council, 81
Natural work units, 190
NAVEX Global, 251
Nayer, Vineet, 3
NBA, 207
NCAA basketball tournament, 68
Nebuchadnezzar, 24
Need satisfaction, motivation and, 268–270, 271
Needs, 268
Negative reinforcement, 280–281
Negligent hiring lawsuits, 227, 228
Negotiator role, 13

Nestlé, 58, 121
Net operating profit after taxes (NOPAT), 343
Net Optics, 319
Netbooks, 110
Netflix, 53, 126, 160, 207, 348, 361
Netherlands, 166
New York City (NYC) Fire Department, 361
New York Times, 83, 85, 327
Newegg.com, 349
News Corporation, 84
Newton Investment Management, 260
Next Jump, 298
Nickel, Bobby, 219
Nickerson, Barry, 243
Nicol, Ron, 244
Nicolson, Annmarie, 309
Nicor National, 383
Nigeria, 68
Nike, 60, 120
NineSigma International, 213
Nissan, 53, 293
Noise, 316–317
Nokia, 120, 137, 147–148
Nokia Siemens, 120
Nominal group technique (NGT), 105
Nonfinancial awards, 215
Nonsubstitutable resources, 110–111
Nontariff barriers, 154–155
Nonverbal communication, 321–322
Nook HD, 109
Nook Simple Touch, 129
Nook Touch with Glowlight, 129
Nooyi, Indra, 253–254
Nordstrom, 357
Normative control, 338–339
Normative decision theory, 301–305
Norming, 210
Norms, 206–207
North American Free Trade Agreement (NAFTA), 156, 157, 158
NorthShore University HealthSystem, 361
Northwest Airlines, 47
Norwex, 125
Novartis, 85–86, 250, 385
Novelis, 8
Nowogrodski, Avinoam, 9–10
Nucor, 340
Nuovo, Frank, 147
Nutella, 47
Nye, Dan, 227

O

Obama, Barak, 75
Objective control, 338
Objective performance measures, 235

Occupational Safety and Health Act (OSHA), 219
Occupational Safety and Health Administration (OSHA), 55, 79, 219
Oculus VR, 141
Odagiri, Yoshinori, 112
Office location, choosing overseas, 166–167
Office manager, 9
Official Harmonized Tariff Schedule, 155
Ohio State University, 292, 293
O/I ratio, 273
O'Keefe, K., 358
Older workers, 219, 251–252
Oldsmobile Motor Works, 39
O'Leary, Michael, 13
Oltan Group, 47
OMGPOP, 241
Omidyar, Pierre, 116
Onboarding, 238
"100 Best Companies to Work for in America," 20, 21
One Novelis program, 8
Online discussion forums, 327–328
Ono, Yoko, 57
On-the-job training, 233
Open systems, 40
Opening feedback channels, 190
Openness to experience, 258–259
Operational plans, 97–99
Operations management, 373–392
    Balridge Performance Excellence Award, 379, 380
    defined, 373
    inventory, 386–392
    manufacturing operations, 383–386
    overview, 38–40
    productivity, 373–376
    service operations, 381–383
    total quality management (TQM), 380–381
Opportunistic behavior, 54–55
Optical character recognition, 360
Options-based planning, 93–94
Oracle, 123, 184
Oral communication, 323
Orbis International, 206
Order, in Fayol's fourteen principles of management, 34
Ordering cost, 389
Organic organizations, 190
Organization, 38
Organization (perception process), 311, 312
Organization for Economic Cooperation and Development (OECD), 50
Organizational authority, 184–187
Organizational change. *See* Change management
Organizational culture, 59–65

anchoring change in, 148
changing the culture, 63–65
company founders and, 61
creating the culture, 61
defined, 59–65
keys to success, 61–63
levels of, 63
maintaining the culture, 61
successful, 61–63
Organizational decline, 143–144
Organizational design, 179–196
    authority, 184–187
    chain of command, 181
    customer departmentalization, 180–181
    degree of centralization, 186–187
    empowerment, 192–193
    functional departmentalization, 178–179
    geographic departmentalization, 181–182
    interorganizational processes, 193–196
    intraorganizational processes, 190–193
    job design, 187–190
    matrix departmentalization, 182–184
    modular organizations, 193–194
    process view, 177–178
    reengineering, 190–192
    at Thomson Reuters, 177
    virtual organizations, 194–196
Organizational development, 149–151
Organizational encouragement of creativity, 140
Organizational environment, 45–59
    acting on threats and opportunities, 59
    changing external environments, 45–48
    environmental scanning, 57–58
    general environment, 48–52
    interpreting environmental factors, 58–59
    resource scarcity, 47
    simple/complex environments, 47
    specific environment, 52–57
    uncertainty, 47–48
Organizational innovation, 133–143
    compression approach, 142–143
    creative work environments, 139–140
    defined, 133
    discontinuous change, 136, 141–142
    dominant design, 136–137
    experiential approach, 141–142
    generational change, 143
    innovation streams, 134–138
    managing, 138–143
    technological discontinuity, 135–136
    technological lockout, 137–138
    technological substitution, 136
    technology cycle, 133–134
Organizational mission (purpose statement), 95–96

Organizational plurality, 260
Organizational process, 179–180
Organizational silence, 328–329
Organizational stakeholders, 80–82
Organizational stories, 61
Organizational strategy, 109–130
    adaptive strategies, 125–127
    assessing need for strategic change, 111–112
    corporate-level strategies, 117–122
    direct competition, 127–130
    firm-level strategies, 127–130
    grand strategies, 121–122
    industry-level strategies, 122–127
    Porter's five industry forces, 122–124
    portfolio strategy, 117–121
    positioning strategies, 124–125
    situational analysis, 113–115
    strategic alternatives, choosing, 115–117
    strategy-making process, steps in, 111–117
    sustainable competitive advantage, 109–111
    three steps of, 111
Organizational structure, 179. *See also* Organizational design
Organizations, systems view of. *See* Systems management
Organizing, 5
Oriental Trading Company (OTC), 199
OSHA. *See* Occupational Safety and Health Administration (OSHA)
Oshkosh, 259
Osterloh, Rick, 136
Outcome/input (O/I) ratio, 273
Outcomes, 273, 274, 275, 276
Outplacement services, 243
Output control, 338
Overlapping steps, 143
Overly political and ambitious managers, 16–17
Overreward, 273
Overseas Assignment Inventory (OAI), 174
Overseas assignments, 171–175
Overt integrity tests, 76

P

Paasschen, Frits van, 351
Pacific Resources International, 239
"Packet sniffer" software, 366
"Pain points," 317
Palmer, Andy, 126
Panama Canal, 59
Panama Canal Authority District, 59
Panamax ships, 59
Panasonic, 251
Pandora, 353
Panizza, Ruben, 367–368

Paralanguage, 322
Paraphrasing, 324, 325
Parikh, Jay, 357
Parker, Peter, 35
Parpia, Manu, 170–171
Partial productivity, 375
Participative leadership, 299, 301
Passwords, 363–364
Patent Trial and Appeal Board, 137
Path-goal theory, 298–301
Path-goal theory, 298–301
Patience & Nicholson (P&N), 215
Patient Protection and Affordable Care Act, 51
Patriarchal rule, 30
Patton, Bruce, 35
Pauzié, Laurent, 160
Pay for Performance Survey (2013), 279
Paychex, 79
Pay-level decisions, 239
Pay-structure decisions, 241
Pay-variability decisions, 240
PC Magazine, 113
PCM Group, 170
Peabody, Griffin, 77
Peach Aviation, 112
Pepsi Cola, 99
Perceived ability, 300
Perception, 311
Perception problems, 312–313
Perception process, 311–312
Perceptual filters, 311–312
Peregrine Financial Group, 307
Performance appraisal, 235–239
Performance feedback, 92–93, 94, 285
    sharing, 237–239
Performance tests, 229
Performing, 210
Persistence of effort, 267
Personal aggression, 69
Personal computer (PC) business, 47
Personal computers (PCs), 143–144
Personality, 257
Personality-based integrity tests, 76
Person-focused interventions, 150–151
Peterman, Mark, 279
Pettine, Mike, 65
Pettis, Bre, 164
Pfeffer, Jeffrey, 19–20
Phased retirement, 244
Phillips, James, 48
Phillips, Juanita, 78
Phishing, 365
Piecework, 240
Pietsch, Michael, 191
Pilgrim's Pride, 343
Pinault, François, 334
Pinneau-Boddison, Sandra, 146
Pinterest, 103
Pirate Joe's, 125

Pirated television shows, 73
Pixar, 292
Plank, Kevin, 60
Planned readings, 233
Planning, 4–5, 89–99
    action plan, 92
    advantages of, 89
    budgeting, 98–99
    defined, 4, 89
    disadvantages of, 89–90
    as a double-edge sword, 90
    goal commitment, 91–92
    for incremental innovation, 143
    maintaining flexibility, 93–94
    operational plans, 97–99
    purpose statement, 95–96
    setting goals, 91
    single-use plans, 97
    standing plans, 97–98
    strategic plans, 85
    tactical plans, 96–97
    from top to bottom, 94–99
Planning fallacy, 92
Plantville, 234
Plassat, Georges, 192
PlayerLync, 354–355
Plug-n-play software, 195
Plum Creek Timber, 274
PMA Companies, 146
Poachable, 224
Poacht, 224
Polaroid, 240
Policies, 98
Policy risk, 169
Policy uncertainty, 167–168
Political, being overly, 16–17
Political deviance, 69
Political influences, 51–52
Political risk, 167–169
Political uncertainty, 167
Pony Express, 40
Pooled interdependence, 192
Popeye's, 293
Popeyes Louisiana Kitchen, 325
Popovich, Gregg, 262
Porras, Jerry, 96
Porsche, 373
Porter, Barbara, 383
Porter, Michael, 122
Porter's five industry forces, 122–124
Portfolio strategy, 117–121
Position power, 296
Positioning strategies, 124–125
Positive reinforcement, 280
Post messengers, 40
Postconventional level of moral development, 74
Power distance, 170
Power Matters Alliance (PMA), 136–137
Powerful leaders, 142

Prabhakar, Balaji, 285
Pratt & Whitney, 179
Predictive patterns, 362
Preference for teamwork, 212
Pregnancy Discrimination Act (1978), 218
Presenteeism, 98
Price, Dan, 277
Primary stakeholders, 80–81
Primary work group, 300
Prime lending rate, 49
Principle of distributive justice, 75
Principle of government requirements, 75
Principle of individual rights, 75
Principle of long-term self-interest, 74–75
Principle of personal virtue, 75
Principle of religious injunctions, 75
Principle of utilitarian benefits, 75–76
Principles of scientific management, 26–27
Printing press, 39–40
Proactive customer monitoring, 52–53
Proactive strategy, 82, 86
Probability of effect, 72
Problem, 99
Problem structure rule, 302–303, 304
Problem-oriented feedback, 326–327
Problem-solving skills, training in, 214
Procedural justice, 276
Procedures, 98
Process modification, 348
Processing costs, 357
Processing information, 360–363
Procter & Gamble, 91, 95, 117, 136–137, 174, 182–183, 250
Product and Brand Innovation, 299
Product boycott, 57
Product breakdown, 377
Product departmentalization, 179–180
Product failure, 377
Product piracy, 156
Product prototype, 141–142
Product reliability, 377
Production blocking, 106
Production deviance, 68
Productivity, 373–376
Products, quality, 377–378
Profit and loss statements, 343
Profit sharing, 240
Progress Energy, 244
Progressive, 225
"Project Hubble," 97
Project K, 59
Project Oxygen study, 4
Project teams, 205–206
Promotions, 31
Property deviance, 68

Prospectors, 126
Protecting information, 363–367
Protectionism, 154
Proximal goals, 92
Proximity of effect, 73
PRS Group, 169
Prudential Relocation Management, 174
Public communications, 56–57
Puckett, John, 211
Punctuated equilibrium theory, 46–47
Punishment, 281, 284
Punishment and obedience stage (Kohlberg), 73, 74
Purchasing power, 165–166
Purpose statement, 95–96
Pyramid of King Khufu, 23

Q

Q software, 195
QR (quick response) codes, 359–360
Qualcomm, 137
Qualification-based hiring, 31
Quality, 376–378
  Baldrige Performance Excellence Awards, 379
  controlling, 346, 347
  defined, 377
  ISO 9000 and 14000, 378–379
  J.D. Power Initial Quality Survey, 376–377
  quality-related characteristics for products and services, 377–378
  total quality management, 380–381
Quality of the decision, 301–305
Quality requirement, 303, 304
Quality rule, 302–303, 304
Qualtrics, 12, 97
Question marks, 118, 119, 120
Quid pro quo sexual harassment, 220
QuikTrip, 239
Quotas, 154, 155
QWERTY keyboard, 137

R

Race IAT (Implicit Association Test), 263
Racial and ethnic discrimination, 254–255
Rader, Bryan, 53
Radha Krisna Store, 168
Radio frequency identification (RFID) tags, 360
RadioShack, 143–144
Rail.One GmbH, 170
Rake, Michael, 122
Ralph Lauren, 160

Rapid Evaluation and Design Kitchen teams, 212
Rare resources, 110
Rate buster, 26
Rater training, 236–237
Ratio schedules, 282, 283
Rational decision making, 99
Raw data, 351
Raw material inventories, 386–387
Raymond, Beaver, 385
Raytheon, 264
Reactive customer monitoring, 52
Reactive strategy, 84
Reactors, 127
Recharging stations, 136–137
Reciprocal interdependence, 192
Recovery, 122
RecruitAbilityJobs.com, 256
RecruitDisability.org, 256
Recruiting, 221–225
Recruiting employees, 221–225
Recycle and reuse, 348
Red Lobster, 127
Redberg, Rita, 315
Redbox, 73, 126
Reddit, 222
RedFly Marketing, 205
Reebok, 60
Reengineering, 190–192, 193
Reengineering the Corporation (Hammer and Champy), 190
Reeves, C.A., 347
Referents, 273
Referrals, employee, 224
Refreezing, 145, 148
Regional trading zones, 156–157, 158
Regulation costs, 336–337
Regulations, industry, 55–56
Reinforcement, 280
Reinforcement contingencies, 280
Reinforcement theory, 279–284
Related diversification, 120–121
Relationship behavior, 55
Relationship-oriented leadership styles, 295
Relative comparisons, 100–101
Relay Test Assembly Room, 35, 37
Relevant information, 356
Reliance, 168
Remuneration, 34
Reputation Capital, 205
"Resilience Index" (FM Global), 167
Resistance forces, 145
Resistance to change, 145
Resource allocator role, 13
Resource scarcity, 47, 49
Resource similarity, 127–128, 129
Resources, 109
  defined, 109
  imperfectly imitable, 110
  nonsubstitutable, 110–111

Resources (*Continued*)
  rare, 110
  sustainable competitive advantage
      and, 109–111
  valuable, 110
Response, 129–130
Responsiveness, 377
Restraint *versus* indulgence, 171
Results-driven change, 149
Résumés, 226
RetailMeNot, 223
Retention (perception process), 311, 312
Retirement, 243–244
Retrenchment strategy, 122
Retrieval costs, 358
Reverse logistics, 388
Rewards, motivation and, 270–271
RFID tags, 360
Richter, David, 140
Riepl, Jochen, 171
"Rightsizing," 317
Ringlemann, Maximilian, 201
Risk management, 53
Risk-avoiding strategy, 115, 116
Risk-seeking strategy, 115, 116
Rissley, Martin, 373
Ritz-Carlton hotels, 193
Roach, Stephen, 193
Robb, Walter, 13
Roberts, Russell, 80
Robinson, Jonathan, 271
Rocket-Hire, 230
Rockwell Automation, 254
Rodriguezmacedo Rivera, Jose Luis, 83
Rogers, Patrick, 277
Roku, 53
Role-playing, 233
Rollnick, William, 82
Rometty, Virginia, 289
Rootkits, 365
Rose, Charlie, 291
Ross, Angus, 51
Rotating jobs, 187–188
Rothman, Tony, 290
Route One, 369
Rover.com, 238
Royal Caribbean, 373
Royal Dutch Shell, 62, 148, 149
Rules and procedures, in bureaucratic
      organizations, 31–32
Rules and regulations, 98
Rusli, E.M., 322
Russell, Rick, 330
Rutledge, Pamela, 323
Ryanair, 13, 375
Ryder System, 305

S

Safeguard Scientifics, 11
Safety standards, laws governing, 219

Salaries
  CEOs, 272
  in China, 275
  dependence on organizational
      performance, 19
  link between performance and, 277,
      279
  motivation and, 271
  productivity and, 374
  for women, 253
Salesforce, 254
Salesforce.com, 123
Salles, Chris, 100
Samsung, 46, 54, 109, 137
Samsung Electronics, 391
Samuelsson, Håkan, 166
San Francisco Sheriff's Department,
      218–219
Sanchez, Robert, 305
Sanghavi, Deval, 85
SAP, 213
Sarandon, Susan, 57
Sarbanes-Oxley Act (2002), 79
Satisficing (decisions), 103
Scalar chain, 34
Scandinavian Airlines, 375
Scharlau, Ed, 338
Schedule of reinforcement, 280,
      282–283
Schlage Lock Company, 96
Schlossberg, Edwin, 136
Schmidt, Eric, 142
Scholastic Aptitude Test (SAT), 228
Schultz, Carol, 277
Schwall, David, 279
Scientific management, 25–27
Scott, Cheryl, 162
S-curve pattern of innovation,
      133–134
Sea World, 219
Sears, 3
Secondary firms, 114–115
Secondary stakeholders, 81–82
**Secure sockets layer (SSL)
      encryption,** 366
Securities and Exchange Commission
      (SEC), 55, 78
Seervai, S., 85
Seka, Leyla, 254
Selection (employee), 225–231
Selection instruments, 64
Selection tests, 228–230
Selective hiring, 19
Selective perception, 312–313
Self-confidence, in leaders, 291–292
Self-control (self-management),
      340–341
Self-designing teams, 205
Self-managed teams, 19
Self-managing teams, 204
Self-perception, 314–315

Self-service kiosks, 369
Self-serving bias, 314
Semi-autonomous work groups, 204
Semistructured interviews, 231
Sense of urgency, organizational change
      and, 146–147
Sephora, 112
September 11th terrorist attacks, 46
Sequence patterns, 361–362
Sequential design process, 143
Sequential interdependence, 192
Servcorp, 214
Service capability, 382
Service operations, 381–383
Service recovery, 383
Service reliability, 377
Serviceability, 377
Service-profit chain, 382–383
Setup cost, 389
Sex discrimination, 252–254
Sexual harassment, 220
Sexual harassment policy, 221
Shadow-strategy task force, 114
Shaikh, Jim, 143
Shanska USA Building, 289
Shapiro, Gary, 388
Shareholder model, 80
Sharing information, 19
Sharing performance feedback, 237–239
Sharp, 54–55
Sharp, Isadore, 339
Shaw, Bob, 319
Shellenbarger, S., 107, 258, 318
Shen, Jerry, 300
Shift supervisor, 9
Shilmover, Fred, 334
Short-term orientation, 171
Short-term wins, 148
Short-term/long-term orientation,
      cultural dimension of, 171
Siemens, 234
Silverman, Craig, 241
Silverman, R.E., 238
Simon, R., 371
Simon, William, 223
Simonsen, Michael, 123
Simple environments, 47
Simple matrix, 184
Simulations and games, training
      through, 233
Singapore Airlines, 98, 346
Single-use plans, 97
Situational (SWOT) analysis, 113–115
Situational constraints, 268
Situational favorableness, 296
Situational questions, in interviews,
      230–231
Skill variety, 189
Skill-based pay, 215
Skilled craftspeople, 38–39
Skills-based diversity training, 263

Skybox, 57
SkyMall, 112
Skype, 328
Slack, 327
Slack resources, 93–94
Sladek, Carol, 98
Slater, Mary Ellen, 205
SLL encryption, 366
Small-group interventions, 150–151
S.M.A.R.T. goals, 91, 211
Smartphones, 54, 322
Smith, James C., 185
Smith, Rick, 215
Smith, Ryan, 12
Sochi, Russia, 171
Social consensus, 73
Social contract stage (Kohlberg), 74
Social engineering, 367
Social integration, 257
Social integration, 251
Social loafing, 201
Social media
  managers monitoring, 12
  recruiting employees through, 224
  used during hiring process, 225–226
Social Media Listening Command
  Center, 331
Social responsibility, 79–87
  defined, 79
  discretionary responsibilities, 83–84
  economic performance and, 86–87
  economic responsibility, 82
  ethical responsibility, 83
  in India, 85
  legal responsibility, 82–83
  shareholder model, 80
  social responsiveness strategies, 84–86
  stakeholder model, 80–82
Social responsiveness, 84
Socializing, rights and wrongs of, 214
Society for Human Resource Manage-
  ment, 227, 235, 249–250, 259, 271
Society of Industrial Engineers, 28
Sociocultural influences, 51
Sociotechnical systems, 150
Sodexho Alliance, 264
Soldiering, 25–26
Solso, Tim, 207
Sony, 83, 127
Sony Pictures, 290, 363
Sorkin, Eric, 357
Sorrels, Eddie, 217
Southern Co., 77
Southwest Airlines, 47, 240, 341, 342
Spain, Seth, 258
Spam, 365
Sparta Systems, 5
Speak Like a CEO (Bates), 321
Specialized jobs, 187
Specific ability tests (aptitude tests),
  228

Specific environment
  advocacy groups, 56–57
  competitor component to, 53
  customer component to, 52–53
  defined, 49–50
  industry regulations component to,
    55–56
  supplier component to, 54–55
Specific feedback, 326
Specific team goals, 211
Spokesperson role, 12
Spotify, 111, 353
Springer, Jon, 124
Sprint, 129, 144
Spyware, 365
Square Enix, 6
Squirrel-related power outages,
  335–336
Stability of tenure and personnel, 34
Stability strategy, 121
Stable environments, 45
Staff authority, 185
Staff function, 185
Staggs, Tom, 292
Stakeholder model, 80
Stakeholders, 80–82
Standard Brands, 164
Standard Chartered PLC, 164
Standard General, 144
Standardization, 186–187
Standards (control), 333–335
Standing plans, 97–98
Stanford Graduate School of Business,
  324
Staples, 54, 219, 282
Starbucks, 137, 160, 166
Starbucks Coffee, 3, 127
Stars, 118, 119, 120
Starwood Hotels & Resorts, 351
State Farm Insurance, 338
Status differences, reduction of, 19
Stealing, 68–69
Steelcase, 139
Stephens, Jilly, 206
Stern, Brian, 229
Stevens, Ann, 98
Stevens, L., 126
Stock market diversification, 117
Stock options, 240–241
Stockout, 388
Stockout cost, 389
Stockton, Bryan, 62
Storage costs, 357–358, 389
Stories, organizational, 61, 339
Storming stage of team development,
  206
Strategic alliances, 163
Strategic alternatives, choosing,
  115–117
Strategic change, determining need for,
  111–112

Strategic dissonance, 112
Strategic group, 114
Strategic leadership, 305
Strategic Management Journal, 25
Strategic Materials, 337
Strategic objective, 96
Strategic planning, 5
Strategic plans, 95
Strategic reference point theory,
  115–116, 115–117
Strategic reference points, 115, 116
Strategic Resource Group (SRG), 124
Strategy. *See* Organizational strategy
Streaming movies, 73
Stretch goals, 211
Struble, Charissa, 136
Structural accommodation, 212
Structured conflict, 104–105
Structured interviews, 230–231
Stum, David, 271
Subjective performance measures,
  235
Suboptimization, 341–342
Subordinate conflict, 304, 305
Subordinate conflict rule, 303
Subordinate information rule, 302–303
Subordination of individual interests to
  general interests, 34
Subsidies, 155, 156
Subsystems, 40
Subway, 128
Sugar Act (1934), 155
Sugar industry, 155
Suicide, 85
SumAll, 276
Sumerians, 23, 24
Summarizing (listening), 324, 325
Sun Communities, 235
Sun Design Home Remodeling
  Specialists, 146
Sun Tzu, 24
Sunovian Pharmaceuticals, 330
Supermarket industry, 390
Supervised data mining, 361
Supervisory encouragement of
  creativity, 140
Supplier dependence, 54
Supplier involvement, 143
Suppliers, 54–55
Supported leadership, 299
Supportive leadership, 301
Surface, 109
Surface-level diversity, 250–256, 262
Surprise visits, 330–331
Survey feedback, 150
Surveyer feedback, 330–331
Surveying employees, motivation and,
  271, 279
Sustainability, 346–349
Sustainable competitive advantage,
  109

Sweethearting, 69
Swisscom AG, 180–181
Switch, 224
SWOT analysis, 113–115
Symantec, 82, 110, 366
Symbian, 147–148
Synapse, 368
"Sync up," 317
Synergy, 32, 40
System, 40
Systems management, 40–41
Systems view of organizations, 41

T

Tablet computers, 109
Tablets, 54
Tactical plans, 96–97
Taiwan Semiconductor, 54
Tamme, Jacob, 354
Tamron, 135
Tangibles, 377
Tarantino, Sam, 83
Target, 59, 113, 361
Target Canada, 13
Tariffs, 154
Task identity, 189
Task interdependence, 192, 193
Task significance, 189
Task structure, 296
Task structures, 300
Task-defined positions, in bureaucratic
    organizations, 31
Task-oriented leadership style, 295–296
Tata Steel, 306–307
Tata-Starbucks, 166
Tax rate, overseas location and, 166
Taxi industry, 45
Taylor, Frederick W., 25–27, 28
Team building, 37, 150
Team diversity, 213
Team leaders, 7, 9–10
Team level, 213
Team management leadership style,
    293, 294
Team Player Inventory, 212, 213
Team training, 214–215
Teambuilding Inc., 214
Teams and teamwork, 199–215
    advantages of, 199–201
    autonomy and, 203–205
    characteristics of teams, 206–211
    compensating, 215
    cross-functional teams, 05
    determining your preference for, 212,
        213
    disadvantages of, 201
    enhancing effectiveness of, 211–215
    goal setting, 211–212
    indivisualism-collectivism, 212
    minority domination, 201, 208

motivating, 211
project teams, 205–206
rights and wrongs of socializing, 214
social loafing within, 201
stages of team development, 209–211
team cohesiveness, 207
team conflict, 208–209
team diversity, 213–214
team level, 213
team norms, 206–207
team size, 207–208
team training, 214–215
virtual teams, 205
where and where to use, 201–202
Teamwork, 381
Technical skills, 14
Technical training, 214
Technological discontinuity, 135–136
Technological lockout, 137–138
Technological substitution, 136
Technology, 50–51
Technology cycle, 133–134, 135
Technology, innovation streams,
    134–138
Telecom, 137
**Televised/videotaped speeches and
    meetings,** 328
Television, 53
Temporal immediacy, 73
Termination of employees, 241–242
Terramar Sports, 84
Tesco, 90, 163, 167
Tesla Motors, 96, 385–386
Tesla Roadster, 96
Testing, 141
Texas Industries, 221
Texas Instruments, 137
The Weather Channel, 52–53
*Theory of Social and Economic
    Organization, The* (Fayol), 30, 31
ThermoFisher, 348
37signals.com, 267, 383
Thomas, David, 260, 264
Thomson Reuters, 177, 178, 185
Thornbrugh, Mike, 239
Threat of new entrants, 123
**Threat of substitute products or
    services,** 123–124
Threats, 58–59
3M, 117, 121, 126, 204, 389
350.org, 81
360-degree feedback, 237, 238
Thunder Basin Maple Works, 357
ThyssenKrupp, 135, 136
Tiffany & Co., 378
Time study, 28
Time Warner, 84
Timely information, 356–357
Tindell, Kip, 61, 257, 271
Title VII, Civil Rights Act of 1964, 218,
    248

T-Mobile, 129
TNT Express, 153
Together We Are Safe safety program, 8
Ton, Zeynep, 61
Top management, planning and, 95–96
Top managers, 6–8
Toshiba, 54–55
Total quality management (TQM),
    380–381
Town hall meetings, 331
Toyota, 53, 141, 186, 273, 391
Tracking progress of goals, 92–93
Trade agreements, 155–159
Trade barriers, 154–155, 159
Trade guilds, 23
Trader Joe's, 125
Traditional work groups, 203–204
Training
    competitive advantage and, 19
    cross-training, 200
    defined, 232
    determining needs for, 232
    diversity training, 263
    ethics, 77–78
    evaluation, 234–235
    Gantt's approach to, 30
    language and cross-cultural, 172–173,
        174
    methods, 232–233
    objectives, 233
    of older employees, 252
    organizational development
        intervention, 150
    in problem-solving skills, 214
    rater, 236–237
    team-215, 214
Trait theory, 290–292
Traits, 290
Transactional leadership, 309
TransCanada Corporation, 81
Transfer of accountability, 186
Transformational leadership,
    307–309
Transition to management, 17–19
Trojan horses, 365
TruePoint, 318
Tschohl, John, 345
Tsuchiya, Tsugio, 135
Twitter, 103, 328
2HB, 272
Two-factor authentication, 363–364
Typewriter, 40
Typing patterns, replacing patterns, 364

U

Uber, 45, 124, 226, 345
Ultra Salon, 112
**UNASUR (Union of South American
    Nations),** 158
Uncertainty, 47–48

Uncertainty avoidance, 171
Under Armour, 60, 120
Underreward, 273, 274
Unethical charismatics, 307, 308
Unfreezing, 145, 146, 147
*Uniform Guidelines on Employee
    Selection Procedures* (EEOC),
    222–223, 225
Uniformed Services Employment
    and Reemployment Rights Act,
    217–218
**Union of South American Nations
    (USAN),** 156
Union Pacific, 94
Unit goal setting, 150
United Airlines, 5, 46, 47, 98, 146, 280
United States Postal Service (USPS),
    126
United Technologies Corporation
    (UTC), 179–180
United Tool & Machine, 217
Unity of command, 34
Unity of command, 184
Unity of direction, 34
Universal principle stage (Kohlberg), 74
University Health Network, 334–335
University of Illinois, 312
University of Michigan, 292, 293
University of Texas, 292, 293
University of Texas Southwestern
    Medical Center (UTSMC),
    233–234
Unrelated diversification, 117–118
UnSend.it (app), 317
"Unsiloing," 317
Unstructured interviews, 230
Unsupervised data mining, 361
UPS, 3
UPS (United Parcel Service), 72, 74–76,
    337, 373
Upward communication, 318
Uruguay Round of GATT, 156
Ury, William, 35
U.S. Airways, 46, 47
U.S. Bureau of Labor Statistics, 252
U.S. Customs Service, 155
U.S. Department of Agriculture, 125,
    155
U.S. Department of Labor, 275
U.S. Food and Drug Administration
    (FDA), 55–56
U.S. Military Academy at West point,
    270–271
U.S. National Health Interview Survey,
    136
U.S. Peace Corps, 173
U.S. Postal Service Pony Express, 40
U.S. Sentencing Commission Guidelines
    for Organizations, 69–72
U.S. Steel, 54
USB (universal serial bus) slots, 143

U-shaped relationship between
    diversification and risk, 119
UTC Aerospace, 179

V

Valence, 277, 278
Validation, 225
Valuable resources, 110
Value, 346
Valve a Bellevue, 205
Van Beurden, Ben, 148, 149
**Variable interval reinforcement
    schedules,** 282, 283
**Variable ratio reinforcement
    schedules,** 282
Variation, 380–381
Venting, 209
Verizon, 110, 126, 129, 136
Verschatse, Ludwig, 333
Vertesi, Janet, 367
Vertical loading, 190
Vestibule training, 233
Viacom, 84
Vick, Gailen, 388
Vietnamese fish farmers, 155
Violence, workplace, 69
ViralHeat, 12
Virginia Railway Express (VRE), 89
Virtual job fairs, 225
Virtual organization agreement, 196
Virtual organizations, 194–196
Virtual private networks (VPNs),
    366
Virtual teams, 205, 206
Viruses, 364, 365
Visible artifacts, 64
Vision (purpose statement), 95, 147
Visionary leadership, 305–309
Vivendi, 83
Vlastelica, John, 65
Voice messaging (voice mail), 328
VoloMetrix, Inc., 244
Voluntary export restraints, 154, 155
Voluntary participation, public
    communications and, 56–57
Voluntary separation, 239
Volvo Car, 166
VRE System Plan 2040, 89
Vroom, V.H., 302, 303, 304
Vroom-Yetton-Jago model (normative
    decision theory), 301–304

W

Wageman, R., 202
Wages. *See* Salaries
Walk-ins (external recruitment), 224
Wall Street Journal, 12, 116
*Wall Street Journal (WSJ)/Vistage Small
    Business CEO Survey,* 50

Walmart, 4, 57, 59, 83, 113, 124–125,
    167, 223, 224, 275, 327, 357
Walt Disney Company, 84, 96, 161–162,
    292
Wardell, Chuck, 227
Warner Music, 83
Wasendorf, Russell Sr., 307
Waste disposal, 349
Waste prevention and reduction,
    347–348
Waste treatment, 349
We Energies, 335
WeatherFX, 53
Web services, 369
Weber, L., 355
Weber, M., 31
Weber, Max, 30, 31–32, 305–306, 337
Wedding, Lisa, 155
Weed, J., 345
Weeks of supply, 388
Weimerskirch, Arnold, 379
Weiner, Jeff, 291–292
Welch, Jack, 320
Wendy's, 53, 128
West, Mike, 62
West Point Academy, 270–271
Western Electric Company, 35
Westinghouse Electric, 234
Wetzel, Andy, 299
Whistle-blowing, 78–79
White hat hackers, 367
Whitehorn, Symon, 135
Whitney, Eli, 39
Whole Foods Market, 13, 307
Wholly owned affiliates, 163–164
Wi-Fi Alliance, 366–367
Wiggers, K., 317
Wilson, Thomas, 319–320
WinCo, 124
WinCo Foods, 124–125
Windows 8 operating system, 47
Winkler, Howard, 77
Winter Olympics (2014), 171
Wipprect, Anouk, 138
Wireless device charging stations,
    136–137
Wireless Power Consortium (WPC),
    137
Wizz Air, 375
Wladawsky-Berger, Irving, 15, 89
Wolf, William, 223
Women
    attracting and retaining in the
        workplace, 250
    diversity pairing, 263–264
    on executive teams, limit to, 252
    glass ceiling, 252–253
    sex discrimination, 252–254
    taking time off for family, 253
Women's Food Service Forum, 264
Wong, Simon, 5

Woodward, Richard, 328–329
Work group encouragement of creativity, 140
Work sample tests, 229
Work teams, 199. *See also* Teams and teamwork
Workforce quality, overseas location and, 166
Working Women, 250
Work-in-process inventories, 387
Workplace deviance, 68
Workplace diversity, 247–264
    affirmative action, 248–249
    age discrimination, 251–252
    attracting/retaining talented workers, 250
    business growth driven by, 250
    census data, 247
    cost savings, 249–250
    deep-level diversity, 257–259
    diversity paradigms, 259–261
    diversity principles, 261–263
    diversity training and practices, 263–264
    gender, 252–254
    as making good business sense, 249–250
    managing, 259–264
    mental or physical disabilities, 255–256
    personality, attitudes, beliefs, and values, 257–259
    projected population by race, 2015-2060, 247
    racial and ethnic, 254–255
    surface-level diversity, 250–256
Workplace violence, 69
World Trade Organization (WTO), 155, 156, 157
World Vision, 69
Wozniak, Steve, 143
Wright, Christopher, 171
Written communication, 323
Wrongful discharge, 242
Wrongful termination lawsuits, 52

X

XEL Communications, 211
Xenophon, 24
Xerox, 264
Xerox Parc, 213
Xhibit, 112
Xu, William, 11

Y

Yahoo!, 224, 251
Yammer, 328
Yetton, P.W., 302, 304
Yoplait, 82–83
You Sow, 80
YouTube, 53
Yuanqing, Yang, 275
Yum! Brands, 50

Z

Zadesky, Steve, 142
Zappos, 201, 388
Zarrilli, Stephen, 11
Zen Magnets, 56
ZenBox, 123
ZenPayroll software, 195
Zero-based budgeting, 343
ZestFinance, 104
Zipcar, 251
Zone of indifference, 38
Zuckerberg, Mark, 251
Zynga, 82, 241
Zynga, Andy, 213

A GUIDE FOR NEW MANAGERS: SIX STEPS TO BECOME A SUCCESSFUL MANAGER

—ED MUZIO

If you've recently been hired as a manager, you know the dirty secret: Management positions come with surprisingly little guidance. Whether you were promoted internally or brought in from outside, you were probably expected to hit the ground running, toward only the vaguest of goals.

Many of the problems new managers experience stem from that secret. They are faced with an ill-defined job and equally intense pressure from above and below. Plus, as the pivot points in the information revolution, they are barraged with queries about the work of their groups.

It's easy to see why capable, well-meaning managers resort to micromanagement, detachment, grandstanding, or sheer blockheadedness in an effort to find some sort of stability for themselves and their employees.

How can you avoid these pitfalls? The following six steps will help you define your purpose as manager:

1. DEFINE YOUR OWN JOB CLEARLY.

If you're a new manager, this is your first and most important step. You need a memorable, meaningful definition, something that you can figuratively (or literally) write across your bathroom mirror so that you see it every morning.

I suggest "engender useful output." Your primary responsibility as a manager is to maximize the likelihood that your employees will be productive; your task is to create an environment in which employee output is clearly defined and realistically achievable. If you're not doing that, then it doesn't matter what data you're gathering, which employees you're monitoring, or whose ear you're bending. You may be busy, you may be stressed, and you may look managerial, but you're not doing your job.

2. DEFINE YOUR GROUP'S OUTPUT.

To engender output you must first define it. This task is easier said than done. Today's workplace changes quickly, and managers at all levels are expected to turn the work of their groups on a dime. Your own manager may not be terribly clear on long range company plans, so neither of you may fully understand how the work of your group will change in the next quarter, month, or even week.

Uncertainty about the future is not an excuse for lack of productivity in the present. If your plan is to wait around until everything is known before doing anything, you might as well lock the doors and go home for good! Things will change again and again, and only by delivering on current plans will you and your company learn what works, and what changes to make next. Besides, the definition of your group's required output is the definition of YOUR required output as manager. Defining it is one part good management practice and one part career survival.

3. SEEK MOMENTARY CLARITY RATHER THAN PERMANENT ANSWERS.

Speak with your leaders about what your group can reasonably produce right now and then agree to task your group with producing it right now. Make it clear that unless you hear otherwise, until the next scheduled check-in you will follow the current plan. Then, verbally summarize the output you are committing to engender in about 90 seconds. During follow-up discussions with your management, use that mini-commercial as a way to gently remind them what you are working on so that they can edit your understanding if needed.

When changes, do come, don't fight them. Welcome the new information, openly revise your understanding of what you need to produce, and clearly explain the time and resources you need to accomplish the change. If you can't turn the boat in an hour, say so. It's far better to be up front when something isn't possible than to agree to it under duress but fail to deliver.

4. BECOME AN EXPERT IN DEFINING AND COMMUNICATING EXPECTATIONS.

Of course, your definition is only half the story. To engender output from your group, you need to convert from the commitment you made as manager into what each of your employees must do individually.

Contrary to popular opinion, this doesn't mean telling your employees what to do. It means teaching them to discuss what they are doing themselves—to create their own 90-second mini-commercials—and then working with them on a shared understanding of what's needed. You haven't successfully taught an employee his or her expected output until you hear that person say it to you spontaneously, in a way that matches your own understanding. Then you know it's happening.

This also means your employees must be in the habit of speaking openly about what they are doing. To get honesty, avoid using discussions about current objectives as pop quizzes! When you need to adjust an employee's understanding of his or her work, frame your conversation as being about expectations for the future and defining how to succeed. Don't let it degrade into how the employee should already know these things. Remember: When your employees don't know what they're supposed to be doing, it's at least as likely to be your fault as theirs.

5. KEEP TALKING ABOUT OUTPUT.

A VSO, or *verbalized summary objective statement*, is a kind of mini-commercial in which you state the output you're trying to deliver at the moment. It should take about 90 seconds and should list about 5–7 output goals that together cover about 80% of what you are working on. It's yours to change, adjust, and modify whenever you see fit. It's also yours to use as your introduction whenever you're talking to people in or about your workplace. Use VSOs with your management and teach your employees to use them with you.

Why? Your VSO trains people as to what to expect—and not expect—from you. It provides an avenue for a manager to edit an employee's understanding of the job, and a basis for you to accept or decline requests for additional work. As time goes by, and you deliver on your VSO, you also increase your credibility within the organization as people see that you are following through on your commitments.

6. KEEP AT IT.

Management is like exercise: it's often difficult, you're never done, and it requires self-discipline.

Get in the habit of having conversations with superiors about the output needed from your group and discussions with your employees about their individual contributions to that output. Then remind yourself that your job is to maximize the chances that your employees will produce. This won't make management easy, but it's the first step in making you better at it.

AUTHOR BIO

Edward G. Muzio, CEO of Group Harmonics, is the author of the award winning books *Make Work Great: Supercharge Your Team, Reinvent the Culture, and Gain Influence One Person at a Time* and *Four Secrets to Liking Your Work: You May Not Need to Quit to Get the Job You Want*. An expert in workplace improvement and its relationship to individual enjoyment, Muzio has been featured on Fox Business Network, CBS, and other national media. For more information visit *Make Work Great* and follow the author on Facebook.

LEARNING OUTCOMES

1-1 (P. 3)
Describe what management is. Good management is working through others to accomplish tasks that help fulfill organizational objectives as efficiently as possible.

1-2 (P. 4)
Explain the four functions of management. Henri Fayol's classic management functions are known today as planning, organizing, leading, and controlling. Planning is determining organizational goals and a means for achieving them. Organizing is deciding where decisions will be made, who will do what jobs and tasks, and who will work for whom. Leading is inspiring and motivating workers to work hard to achieve organizational goals. Controlling is monitoring progress toward goal achievement and taking corrective action when needed. Studies show that performing the management functions well leads to better managerial performance.

1-3 (P. 6)
Describe different kinds of managers. There are four different kinds of managers. Top managers are responsible for creating a context for change, developing attitudes of commitment and ownership, creating a positive organizational culture through words and actions, and monitoring their companies' business environments. Middle managers are responsible for planning and allocating resources, coordinating and linking groups and departments, monitoring and managing the performance of subunits and managers, and implementing the changes or strategies generated by top managers. First-line managers are responsible for managing the performance of nonmanagerial employees, teaching entry-level employees how to do their jobs, and making detailed schedules and operating plans based on middle management's intermediate-range plans. Team leaders are

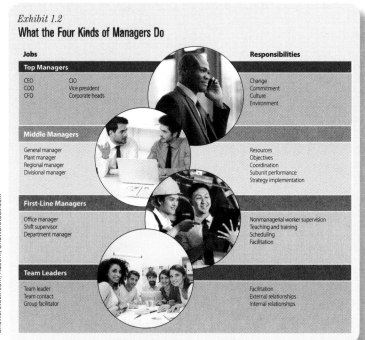

Exhibit 1.2
What the Four Kinds of Managers Do

Jobs		Responsibilities
Top Managers		
CEO	CIO	Change
COO	Vice president	Commitment
CFO	Corporate heads	Culture
		Environment
Middle Managers		
General manager		Resources
Plant manager		Objectives
Regional manager		Coordination
Divisional manager		Subunit performance
		Strategy implementation
First-Line Managers		
Office manager		Nonmanagerial worker supervision
Shift supervisor		Teaching and training
Department manager		Scheduling
		Facilitation
Team Leaders		
Team leader		Facilitation
Team contact		External relationships
Group facilitator		Internal relationships

© Cengage Learning; Mmichaeljung/Shutterstock.com; BlueSkyImage/Shutterstock.com; Kzenon/Shutterstock.com; Racorn/Shutterstock.com

KEY TERMS

1-1
Management getting work done through others

Efficiency getting work done with a minimum of effort, expense, or waste

Effectiveness accomplishing tasks that help fulfill organizational objectives

1-2
Planning determining organizational goals and a means for achieving them

Organizing deciding where decisions will be made, who will do what jobs and tasks, and who will work for whom

Leading inspiring and motivating workers to work hard to achieve organizational goals

Controlling monitoring progress toward goal achievement and taking corrective action when needed

1-3
Top managers executives responsible for the overall direction of the organization

Middle managers responsible for setting objectives consistent with top management's goals and for planning and implementing subunit strategies for achieving these objectives

First-line managers responsible for training and supervising the performance of nonmanagerial employees who are directly responsible for producing the company's products or services

Team leaders managers responsible for facilitating team activities toward goal accomplishment

1-4
Figurehead role the interpersonal role managers play when they perform ceremonial duties

Leader role the interpersonal role managers play when they motivate and encourage workers to accomplish organizational objectives

Liaison role the interpersonal role managers play when they deal with people outside their units

Monitor role the informational role managers play when they scan their environment for information

Disseminator role the informational role managers play when they share information with others in their departments or companies

CHAPTER REVIEW 1

Spokesperson role the informational role managers play when they share information with people outside their departments or companies

Entrepreneur role the decisional role managers play when they adapt themselves, their subordinates, and their units to change

Disturbance handler role the decisional role managers play when they respond to severe pressures and problems that demand immediate action

Resource allocator role the decisional role managers play when they decide who gets what resources and in what amounts

Negotiator role the decisional role managers play when they negotiate schedules, projects, goals, outcomes, resources, and employee raises

1-5

Technical skills the specialized procedures, techniques, and knowledge required to get the job done

Human skills the ability to work well with others

Conceptual skills the ability to see the organization as a whole, understand how the different parts affect each other, and recognize how the company fits into or is affected by its environment

Motivation to manage an assessment of how enthusiastic employees are about managing the work of others

responsible for facilitating team performance, fostering good relationships among team members, and managing external relationships.

1-4 (P. 10)

Explain the major roles and subroles that managers perform in their jobs. Managers perform interpersonal, informational, and decisional roles in their jobs. In fulfilling interpersonal roles, managers act as figureheads by performing ceremonial duties, as leaders by motivating and encouraging workers, and as liaisons by dealing with people outside their units. In performing informational roles, managers act as monitors by scanning their environment for information, as disseminators by sharing information with others in their companies, and as spokespeople by sharing information with people outside their departments or companies. In fulfilling decisional roles, managers act as entrepreneurs by adapting their units to change, as disturbance handlers by responding to larger problems that demand immediate action, as resource allocators by deciding resource recipients and amounts, and as negotiators by bargaining with others about schedules, projects, goals, outcomes, and resources.

1-5 (P. 13)

Explain what companies look for in managers. Companies do not want one-dimensional managers. They want managers with a balance of skills. Managers need to have the knowledge and abilities to get the job done (technical skills), must be able to work effectively in groups and be good listeners and communicators (human skills), must be able to assess the relationships between the different parts of their companies and the external environment and position their companies for success (conceptual skills), and should want to assume positions of leadership and power (motivation to manage).

Exhibit 1.4
Management Skills

Technical skills are most important for team leaders and lower-level managers, human skills are equally important at all levels of management, and conceptual skills and motivation to manage both increase in importance as managers rise through the managerial ranks.

1-6 (P. 15)

Discuss the top mistakes that managers make in their jobs. Another way to understand what it takes to be a manager is to look at the top mistakes managers make. Five of the most important mistakes made by managers are being abrasive and intimidating; being cold, aloof, or arrogant; betraying trust; being overly ambitious; and being unable to delegate, build a team, and staff effectively.

1-7 (P. 17)

Describe the transition that employees go through when they are promoted to management. Managers often begin their jobs by using more formal authority and less people management skills. However, most managers find that being a manager has little to do with "bossing" their subordinates. According to a study of managers in their first year, after six months on the job, the managers were surprised by the fast pace and heavy workload and by the fact that "helping" their subordinates was viewed as interference. After a year on the job, most of the managers had come to think of themselves not as doers but as managers who get things done through others. And, because they finally realized that people management was the most important part of their job, most of them had abandoned their authoritarian approach for one based on communication, listening, and positive reinforcement.

1-8 (P. 19)

Explain how and why companies can create competitive advantage through people. Why does management matter? Well-managed companies are competitive because their workforces are smarter, better trained, more motivated, and more committed. Furthermore, companies that practice good management consistently have greater sales revenues, profits, and stock market performance than companies that don't. Finally, good management matters because it leads to satisfied employees who, in turn, provide better service to customers. Because employees tend to treat customers the same way that their managers treat them, good management can improve customer satisfaction.

LEARNING OUTCOMES

2-1 (P. 23)

Explain the origins of management. Management as a field of study is just 125 years old, but management ideas and practices have actually been used since 5000 BCE. From ancient Sumer to sixteenth-century Europe, there are historical antecedents for each of the functions of management discussed in this textbook: planning, organizing, leading, and controlling. However, there was no compelling need for managers until systematic changes in the nature of work and organizations occurred during the past two centuries. As work shifted from families to factories; from skilled laborers to specialized, unskilled laborers; from small, self-organized groups to large factories employing thousands under one roof; and from unique, small batches of production to standardized mass production; managers were needed to impose order and structure, to motivate and direct large groups of workers, and to plan and make decisions that optimized overall performance by effectively coordinating the different parts of an organizational system.

2-2 (P. 25)

Explain the history of scientific management. Scientific management involves studying and testing different work methods to identify the best, most efficient way to complete a job. According to Frederick W. Taylor, the father of scientific management, managers should follow four scientific management principles. First, study each element of work to determine the one best way to do it. Second, scientifically select, train, teach, and develop workers to reach their full potential. Third, cooperate with employees to ensure that the scientific principles are implemented. Fourth, divide the work and the responsibility equally between management and workers. Above all, Taylor believed these principles could be used to align managers and employees by determining a fair day's work (what an average worker could produce at a reasonable pace) and a fair day's pay (what management should pay workers for that effort). Taylor believed that incentives were one of the best ways to align management and employees.

Frank and Lillian Gilbreth are best known for their use of motion studies to simplify work. Whereas Taylor used time study to determine a fair day's work based on how long it took a "first-class man" to complete each part of his job, Frank Gilbreth used motion-picture films and microchronometers to conduct motion studies to improve efficiency by eliminating unnecessary or repetitive motions. Henry Gantt is best known for the Gantt chart, which graphically indicates when a series of tasks must be completed in order to complete a job or project, but he also developed ideas regarding worker training, specifically, that all workers should be trained and their managers should be rewarded for training them.

2-3 (P. 30)

Discuss the history of bureaucratic and administrative management. Today, we associate bureaucracy with inefficiency and red tape. Yet German sociologist Max Weber thought that bureaucracy—that is, running organizations on the basis of knowledge, fairness, and logical rules and procedures—would accomplish organizational goals much more efficiently than monarchies and patriarchies, where decisions were based on personal or family connections, personal gain, and arbitrary decision making. Bureaucracies are characterized by seven elements: qualification-based hiring; merit-based promotion; chain of command; division of labor; impartial application of rules and procedures; recording rules, procedures, and decisions in writing; and separating managers from owners. Nonetheless, bureaucracies are often inefficient and can be highly resistant to change.

KEY TERMS

2-2

Scientific management thoroughly studying and testing different work methods to identify the best, most efficient way to complete a job

Soldiering when workers deliberately slow their pace or restrict their work output

Rate buster a group member whose work pace is significantly faster than the normal pace in his or her group

Motion study breaking each task or job into its separate motions and then eliminating those that are unnecessary or repetitive

Time study timing how long it takes good workers to complete each part of their jobs

Gantt chart a graphical chart that shows which tasks must be completed at which times in order to complete a project or task

2-3

Bureaucracy the exercise of control on the basis of knowledge, expertise, or experience

2-4

Domination an approach to dealing with conflict in which one party satisfies its desires and objectives at the expense of the other party's desires and objectives

Compromise an approach to dealing with conflict in which both parties give up some of what they want in order to reach agreement on a plan to reduce or settle the conflict

Integrative conflict resolution an approach to dealing with conflict in which both parties indicate their preferences and then work together to find an alternative that meets the needs of both

Organization a system of consciously coordinated activities or forces created by two or more people

2-5

System a set of interrelated elements or parts that function as a whole

Subsystems smaller systems that operate within the context of a larger system

Synergy when two or more subsystems working together can produce more than they can working apart

CHAPTER REVIEW 2

Closed systems systems that can sustain themselves without interacting with their environments

Open systems systems that can sustain themselves only by interacting with their environments, on which they depend for their survival

Contingency approach holds that there are no universal management theories and that the most effective management theory or idea depends on the kinds of problems or situations that managers are facing at a particular time and place

The Frenchman Henri Fayol, whose ideas were shaped by his more than twenty years of experience as a CEO, is best known for developing five management functions (planning, organizing, coordinating, commanding, and controlling) and fourteen principles of management (division of work, authority and responsibility, discipline, unity of command, unity of direction, subordination of individual interests to the general interest, remuneration, centralization, scalar chain, order, equity, stability of tenure of personnel, initiative, and *esprit de corps*).

2-4 (P. 33)

Explain the history of human relations management. Unlike most people who view conflict as bad, Mary Parker Follett believed that it should be embraced rather than avoided. Of the three ways of dealing with conflict—domination, compromise, and integration—she argued that the latter was the best because it focuses on developing creative methods for meeting conflicting parties' needs.

Elton Mayo is best known for his role in the Hawthorne Studies at the Western Electric Company. In the first stage of the Hawthorne Studies, production went up because both the increased attention paid to the workers in the study and their development into a cohesive work group led to significantly higher levels of job satisfaction and productivity. In the second stage, productivity dropped because the workers had already developed strong negative norms. The Hawthorne Studies demonstrated that workers' feelings and attitudes affect their work, that financial incentives aren't necessarily the most important motivator for workers, and that group norms and behavior play a critical role in behavior at work.

Chester Barnard, president of New Jersey Bell Telephone, emphasized the critical importance of willing cooperation in organizations. In general, Barnard argued that people will be indifferent to managerial directives or orders if they (1) are understood, (2) are consistent with the purpose of the organization, (3) are compatible with the people's personal interests, and (4) can actually be carried out by those people. Acceptance of managerial authority (that is, cooperation) is not automatic, however.

2-5 (P. 38)

Discuss the history of operations, information, systems, and contingency management. Operations management uses a quantitative or mathematical approach to find ways to increase productivity, improve quality, and manage or reduce costly inventories. The manufacture of standardized, interchangeable parts; the graphical and computerized design of parts; and the accidental discovery of just-in-time inventory systems were some of the most important historical events in operations management.

Throughout history, organizations have pushed for and quickly adopted new information technologies that reduce the cost or increase the speed with which they can acquire, store, retrieve, or communicate information. Historically, some of the most important technologies that have revolutionized information management were the invention of machines to produce pulp for paper and the printing press in the fourteenth and fifteenth centuries, the manual typewriter in 1850, the telephone in the 1880s, the personal computer in the 1980s, and the Internet in the 1990s.

A system is a set of interrelated elements or parts (subsystems) that function as a whole. Organizational systems obtain inputs from both general and specific environments. Managers and workers then use their management knowledge and manufacturing techniques to transform those inputs into outputs that, in turn, provide feedback to the organization. Organizational systems must also address the issues of synergy and open versus closed systems.

Finally, the contingency approach to management clearly states that there are no universal management theories. The most effective management theory or idea depends on the kinds of problems or situations that managers or organizations are facing at a particular time. This means that management is much harder than it looks.

Exhibit 2.7
Systems View of Organizations

LEARNING OUTCOMES

3-1 (P. 45)
Discuss how changing environments affect organizations. Environmental change, environmental complexity, and resource scarcity are the basic components of external environments. Environmental change is the rate of variation in a company's general and specific environments. Environmental complexity is the number and intensity of factors in the external environment. Resource scarcity is the abundance or shortage of critical resources in the external environment. As the rate of environmental change increases, as the environment becomes more complex, and as resources become more scarce, managers become less confident that they can understand, predict, and effectively react to the trends affecting their businesses. According to punctuated equilibrium theory, companies experience long periods of stability followed by short periods of dynamic, fundamental change, followed by a return to stability.

3-2 (P. 48)
Describe the four components of the general environment. The general environment consists of trends that affect all organizations. Because the economy influences basic business decisions, managers often use economic statistics and business confidence indices to predict future economic activity. Changes in technology, which transforms inputs into outputs, can be a benefit or a threat to a business. Sociocultural trends, such as changing demographic characteristics, affect how companies staff their businesses. Similarly, sociocultural changes in behavior, attitudes, and beliefs affect the demand for businesses' products and services. Court decisions and new federal and state laws have imposed much greater political/legal responsibility on companies. The best way to manage legal responsibilities is to educate managers and employees about laws and regulations as well as potential lawsuits that could affect a business.

Exhibit 3.2
General and Specific Environments

3-3 (P. 52)
Explain the five components of the specific environment. The specific environment is made up of five components: customers, competitors, suppliers, industry regulations, and advocacy groups. Companies can monitor customers' needs by identifying customer problems after they occur or by anticipating problems before they occur. Because they tend to focus on well-known competitors, managers often underestimate their competition or do a poor job of identifying future competitors.

KEY TERMS

3-1
External environments all events outside a company that have the potential to influence or affect it

Environmental change the rate at which a company's general and specific environments change

Stable environment an environment in which the rate of change is slow

Dynamic environment an environment in which the rate of change is fast

Punctuated equilibrium theory the theory that companies go through long periods of stability (equilibrium), followed by short periods of dynamic, fundamental change (revolutionary periods), and then a new equilibrium

Environmental complexity the number and the intensity of external factors in the environment that affect organizations

Simple environment an environment with few environmental factors

Complex environment an environment with many environmental factors

Resource scarcity the abundance or shortage of critical organizational resources in an organization's external environment

Uncertainty extent to which managers can understand or predict which environmental changes and trends will affect their businesses

3-2
General environment the economic, technological, sociocultural, and political/legal trends that indirectly affect all organizations

Specific environment the customers, competitors, suppliers, industry regulations, and advocacy groups that are unique to an industry and directly affect how a company does business

Business confidence indices indices that show managers' level of confidence about future business growth

Technology the knowledge, tools, and techniques used to transform inputs into outputs

3-3
Competitors companies in the same industry that sell similar products or services to customers

CHAPTER REVIEW 3

Competitive analysis a process for monitoring the competition that involves identifying competition, anticipating their moves, and determining their strengths and weaknesses

Suppliers companies that provide material, human, financial, and informational resources to other companies

Supplier dependence the degree to which a company relies on a supplier because of the importance of the supplier's product to the company and the difficulty of finding other sources of that product

Buyer dependence the degree to which a supplier relies on a buyer because of the importance of that buyer to the supplier and the difficulty of finding other buyers for its products

Opportunistic behavior a transaction in which one party in the relationship benefits at the expense of the other

Relationship behavior the establishment of mutually beneficial, long-term exchanges between buyers and suppliers

Industry regulation regulations and rules that govern the business practices and procedures of specific industries, businesses, and professions

Advocacy groups concerned citizens who band together to try to influence the business practices of specific industries, businesses, and professions

Public communications an advocacy group tactic that relies on voluntary participation by the news media and the advertising industry to get the advocacy group's message out

Media advocacy an advocacy group tactic that involves framing issues as public issues; exposing questionable, exploitative, or unethical practices; and forcing media coverage by buying media time or creating controversy that is likely to receive extensive news coverage

Product boycott an advocacy group tactic that involves protesting a company's actions by persuading consumers not to purchase its product or service

3-4

Environmental scanning searching the environment for important events or issues that might affect an organization

Cognitive maps graphic depictions of how managers believe environmental factors relate to possible organizational actions

3-5

Internal environment the events and trends inside an organization that affect management, employees, and organizational culture

Suppliers and buyers are very dependent on each other, and that dependence sometimes leads to opportunistic behavior in which one party benefits at the expense of the other. Regulatory agencies affect businesses by creating rules and then enforcing them. Advocacy groups cannot regulate organizations' practices. Nevertheless, through public communications, media advocacy, and product boycotts, they try to convince companies to change their practices.

3-4 (P. 57)

Describe the process that companies use to make sense of their changing environments. Managers use a three-step process to make sense of external environments: environmental scanning, interpreting information, and acting on threats and opportunities. Managers scan their environments in order to keep up to date on factors influencing their industries, to reduce uncertainty, and to detect potential problems. When managers identify environmental events as threats, they take steps to protect their companies from harm. When managers identify environmental events as opportunities, they formulate alternatives for taking advantage of them to improve company performance. Using cognitive maps can help managers visually summarize the relationships between environmental factors and the actions they might take to deal with them.

3-5 (P. 59)

Explain how organizational cultures are created and how they can help companies be successful. Organizational culture is the set of key values, beliefs, and attitudes shared by members of an organization. Organizational cultures are often created by company founders and then sustained through repetition of organizational stories and recognition of organizational heroes. Companies with adaptable cultures that promote employee involvement, make clear the organization's strategic purpose and direction, and actively define and teach organizational values and beliefs can achieve higher sales growth, return on assets, profits, quality, and employee satisfaction. Organizational cultures exist on three levels: the surface level, where visible artifacts and behaviors can be observed; just below the surface, where values and beliefs are expressed; and deep below the surface, where unconsciously held assumptions and beliefs exist. Managers can begin to change company cultures by focusing on the top two levels. Techniques for changing organizational cultures include using behavioral substitution and behavioral addition, changing visible artifacts, and selecting job applicants who have values and beliefs consistent with the desired company culture.

Organizational culture the values, beliefs, and attitudes shared by organizational members

Organizational stories stories told by organizational members to make sense of organizational events and changes and to emphasize culturally consistent assumptions, decisions, and actions

Organizational heroes people celebrated for their qualities and achievements within an organization

Company mission a company's purpose or reason for existing

Consistent organizational culture a company culture in which the company actively defines and teaches organizational values, beliefs, and attitudes

Behavioral addition the process of having managers and employees perform new behaviors that are central to and symbolic of the new organizational culture that a company wants to create

Behavioral substitution the process of having managers and employees perform new behaviors central to the new organizational culture in place of behaviors that were central to the old organizational culture

Visible artifacts visible signs of an organization's culture, such as the office design and layout, company dress code, and company benefits and perks, such as stock options, personal parking spaces, or the private company dining room

LEARNING OUTCOMES

4-1 (P. 67)

Identify common kinds of workplace deviance. Ethics is the set of moral principles or values that define right and wrong. Workplace deviance is behavior that violates organizational norms about right and wrong and harms the organization or its workers. There are four different types of workplace deviance. Production deviance and property deviance harm the company, whereas political deviance and personal aggression harm individuals within the company.

4-2 (P. 69)

Describe the U.S. Sentencing Commission Guidelines for Organizations, and explain how they both encourage ethical behavior and punish unethical behavior by businesses. Under the U.S. Sentencing Commission guidelines, companies can be prosecuted and fined up to $300 million for employees' illegal actions. Fines are computed by multiplying the base fine by a culpability score. Companies that establish compliance programs to encourage ethical behavior can reduce their culpability scores and their fines.

4-3 (P. 72)

Describe what influences ethical decision making. Three factors influence ethical decisions: the ethical intensity of the decision, the moral development of the manager, and the ethical principles used to solve the problem. Ethical intensity is high when decisions have large, certain, immediate consequences and when the decision maker is physically or psychologically close to those affected by the decision. There are three levels of moral development. At the preconventional level, decisions are made for selfish reasons. At the conventional level, decisions conform to societal expectations. At the postconventional level, internalized principles are used to make ethical decisions. Each of these levels has two stages. Managers can use a number of different principles when making ethical decisions: long-term self-interest, religious injunctions, government requirements, individual rights, personal virtue, distributive justice, and utilitarian benefits.

4-4 (P. 76)

Explain what practical steps managers can take to improve ethical decision making. Employers can increase their chances of hiring ethical employees by testing all job applicants. Most large companies now have corporate codes of ethics. In addition to offering general rules, ethics codes must also provide specific, practical advice. Ethics training seeks to increase employees' awareness of ethical issues; make ethics a serious, credible factor in organizational decisions; and teach employees a practical model of ethical decision making. The most important factors in creating an ethical business climate are the personal examples set by company managers, the involvement of management in the company ethics program, a reporting system that encourages whistle-blowers to report potential ethics violations, and fair but consistent punishment of violators.

4-5 (P. 79)

Explain to whom organizations are socially responsible. Social responsibility is a business's obligation to benefit society. According to the shareholder model, a company's only social responsibility is to maximize shareholder wealth by maximizing company profits. According to the stakeholder model, companies must satisfy the needs and interests of multiple corporate stakeholders, not just shareholders. The needs of primary

KEY TERMS

4-1

Ethics the set of moral principles or values that defines right and wrong for a person or group

Ethical behavior behavior that conforms to a society's accepted principles of right and wrong

Workplace deviance unethical behavior that violates organizational norms about right and wrong

Production deviance unethical behavior that hurts the quality and quantity of work produced

Property deviance unethical behavior aimed at the organization's property or products

Employee shrinkage employee theft of company merchandise

Political deviance using one's influence to harm others in the company

Personal aggression hostile or aggressive behavior toward others

4-3

Ethical intensity the degree of concern people have about an ethical issue

Magnitude of consequences the total harm or benefit derived from an ethical decision

Social consensus agreement on whether behavior is bad or good

Probability of effect the chance that something will happen that results in harm to others

Temporal immediacy the time between an act and the consequences the act produces

Proximity of effect the social, psychological, cultural, or physical distance between a decision maker and those affected by his or her decisions

Concentration of effect the total harm or benefit that an act produces on the average person

Preconventional level of moral development the first level of moral development, in which people make decisions based on selfish reasons

Conventional level of moral development the second level of moral development, in which people make decisions that conform to societal expectations

CHAPTER REVIEW 4

Postconventional level of moral development the third level of moral development, in which people make decisions based on internalized principles

Principle of long-term self-interest an ethical principle that holds that you should never take any action that is not in your or your organization's long-term self-interest

Principle of religious injunctions an ethical principle that holds that you should never take any action that is not kind and that does not build a sense of community

Principle of government requirements an ethical principle that holds that you should never take any action that violates the law, for the law represents the minimal moral standard

Principle of individual rights an ethical principle that holds that you should never take any action that infringes on others' agreed-upon rights

Principle of personal virtue an ethical principle that holds that you should never do anything that is not honest, open, and truthful and that you would not be glad to see reported in the newspapers or on TV

Principle of distributive justice an ethical principle that holds that you should never take any action that harms the least fortunate among us: the poor, the uneducated, the unemployed

Principle of utilitarian benefits an ethical principle that holds that you should never take any action that does not result in greater good for society

4-4

Overt integrity test a written test that estimates job applicants' honesty by directly asking them what they think or feel about theft or about punishment of unethical behaviors

Personality-based integrity test a written test that indirectly estimates job applicants' honesty by measuring psychological traits, such as dependability and conscientiousness

Whistle-blowing reporting others' ethics violations to management or legal authorities

4-5

Social responsibility a business's obligation to pursue policies, make decisions, and take actions that benefit society

Shareholder model a view of social responsibility that holds that an organization's overriding goal should be profit maximization for the benefit of shareholders

Stakeholder model a theory of corporate responsibility that holds that management's most important responsibility, long-term survival, is achieved by satisfying the interests of multiple corporate stakeholders

stakeholders, on which the organization relies for its existence, take precedence over those of secondary stakeholders.

4-6 (P. 82)

Explain for what organizations are socially responsible. Companies can best benefit their stakeholders by fulfilling their economic, legal, ethical, and discretionary responsibilities. Being profitable, or meeting its economic responsibility, is a business's most basic social responsibility. Legal responsibility consists of following a society's laws and regulations. Ethical responsibility means not violating accepted principles of right and wrong when doing business. Discretionary responsibilities are social responsibilities beyond basic economic, legal, and ethical responsibilities.

4-7 (P. 84)

Explain how organizations can respond to societal demands for social responsibility. Social responsiveness is a company's response to stakeholders' expectations concerning socially responsible behavior. There are four social responsiveness strategies. When a company uses a reactive strategy, it denies responsibility for a problem. When it uses a defensive strategy, a company takes responsibility for a problem but does the minimum required to solve it. When a company uses an accommodative strategy, it accepts responsibility for problems and does all that society expects to solve them. Finally, when a company uses a proactive strategy, it does much more than expected to solve social responsibility problems.

4-8 (P. 86)

Explain whether social responsibility hurts or helps an organization's economic performance. Does it pay to be socially responsible? Studies show that there is generally no trade-off between social responsibility and economic performance. In most circumstances, there is generally a small positive relationship between social responsibility and economic performance that becomes stronger when a company or its products have a positive reputation. Social responsibility, however, does not guarantee profitability, as socially responsible companies experience the same ups and downs as other companies.

Stakeholders persons or groups with a stake, or legitimate interest, in a company's actions

Primary stakeholder any group on which an organization relies for its long-term survival

Secondary stakeholder any group that can influence or be influenced by a company and can affect public perceptions about the company's socially responsible behavior

4-6

Economic responsibility a company's social responsibility to make a profit by producing a valued product or service

Legal responsibility a company's social responsibility to obey society's laws and regulations

Ethical responsibility a company's social responsibility not to violate accepted principles of right and wrong when conducting its business

Discretionary responsibilities the social roles that a company fulfills beyond its economic, legal, and ethical responsibilities

4-7

Social responsiveness refers to a company's strategy to respond to stakeholders' economic, legal, ethical, or discretionary expectations concerning social responsibility

Reactive strategy a social responsiveness strategy in which a company does less than society expects

Defensive strategy a social responsiveness strategy in which a company admits responsibility for a problem but does the least required to meet societal expectations

Accommodative strategy a social responsiveness strategy in which a company accepts responsibility for a problem and does all that society expects to solve that problem

Proactive strategy a social responsiveness strategy in which a company anticipates a problem before it occurs and does more than society expects to take responsibility for and address the problem

CHAPTER REVIEW 5
Planning and Decision Making

LEARNING OUTCOMES

5-1 (P. 89)
Discuss the benefits and pitfalls of planning. Planning is choosing a goal and developing a method or strategy for achieving it. Planning is one of the best ways to improve organizational and individual performance. It encourages people to work harder (intensified effort), to work hard for extended periods (persistence), to engage in behaviors directly related to goal accomplishment (directed behavior), and to think of better ways to do their jobs (task strategies). However, planning also has three potential pitfalls. Companies that are overly committed to their plans may be slow to adapt to environmental changes. Planning can create a false sense of security: planning is based on assumptions about the future, and when those assumptions are wrong, plans can fail. Finally, planning can fail when planners are detached from the implementation of their plans.

5-2 (P. 90)
Describe how to make a plan that works. There are five steps to making a plan that works: (1) Set S.M.A.R.T. goals—goals that are **S**pecific, **M**easurable, **A**ttainable, **R**ealistic, and **T**imely. (2) Develop commitment to the goals. Managers can increase workers' goal commitment by encouraging their participation in goal setting, making goals public, and getting top management to show support for goals. (3) Develop action plans for goal accomplishment. (4) Track progress toward goal achievement by setting both proximal and distal goals and by providing workers with regular performance feedback. (5) Maintain flexibility by keeping options open.

Exhibit 5.1
How to Make a Plan That Works

| 1 Set goals | 2 Develop commitment | 3 Develop effective action plans | 4 Track progress toward goal achievement | 5 Maintain flexibility |

✓ Who ✓ What ✓ When ✓ How

Revise existing plan or Begin planning process anew

5-3 (P. 94)
Discuss how companies can use plans at all management levels, from top to bottom. Proper planning requires that the goals at the bottom and middle of the organization support the objectives at the top of the organization. The goals at the top will be longer range than those at the bottom. Top management develops strategic plans, which start with the creation of an organizational purpose statement and strategic objectives. Middle managers use techniques such as management by objectives to develop tactical plans that direct behavior, efforts, and priorities. Finally, lower-level

KEY TERMS

5-1
Planning choosing a goal and developing a strategy to achieve that goal

5-2
S.M.A.R.T. goals goals that are specific, measurable, attainable, realistic, and timely

Goal commitment the determination to achieve a goal

Action plan a plan that lists the specific steps, people, resources, and time period needed to attain a goal

Proximal goals short-term goals or subgoals

Distal goals long-term or primary goals

Options-based planning maintaining planning flexibility by making small, simultaneous investments in many alternative plans

Slack resources a cushion of extra resources that can be used with options-based planning to adapt to unanticipated changes, problems, or opportunities

5-3
Strategic plans overall company plans that clarify how the company will serve customers and position itself against competitors over the next two to five years

Purpose statement a statement of a company's purpose or reason for existing

Strategic objective a more specific goal that unifies company-wide efforts, stretches and challenges the organization, and possesses a finish line and a time frame

Tactical plans plans created and implemented by middle managers that direct behavior, efforts, and attention over the next six months to two years

Management by objectives a four-step process in which managers and employees discuss and select goals, develop tactical plans, and meet regularly to review progress toward goal accomplishment

Operational plans day-to-day plans, developed and implemented by lower-level managers, for producing or delivering the organization's products and services over a thirty-day to six-month period

Single-use plans plans that cover unique, one-time-only events

CHAPTER REVIEW 5

Standing plans plans used repeatedly to handle frequently recurring events

Policies standing plans that indicate the general course of action that should be taken in response to a particular event or situation

Procedures standing plans that indicate the specific steps that should be taken in response to a particular event

Rules and regulations standing plans that describe how a particular action should be performed or what must happen or not happen in response to a particular event

Budgeting quantitative planning through which managers decide how to allocate available money to best accomplish company goals

5-4

Decision making the process of choosing a solution from available alternatives

Rational decision making a systematic process of defining problems, evaluating alternatives, and choosing optimal solutions

Problem a gap between a desired state and an existing state

Decision criteria the standards used to guide judgments and decisions

Absolute comparisons a process in which each decision criterion is compared to a standard or ranked on its own merits

Relative comparisons a process in which each decision criterion is compared directly with every other criterion

Maximize choosing the best alternative

Satisficing choosing a "good-enough" alternative

5-5

Groupthink a barrier to good decision making caused by pressure within the group for members to agree with each other

C-type conflict (cognitive conflict) disagreement that focuses on problem- and issue-related differences of opinion

A-type conflict (affective conflict) disagreement that focuses on individuals or personal issues

Devil's advocacy a decision-making method in which an individual or a subgroup is assigned the role of critic

Dialectical inquiry a decision-making method in which decision makers state the assumptions of a proposed solution (a thesis) and generate a solution that is the opposite (antithesis) of that solution

Nominal group technique a decision-making method that begins and ends by having group members quietly write down and evaluate ideas to be shared with the group

managers develop operational plans that guide daily activities in producing or delivering an organization's products and services. There are three kinds of operational plans: single-use plans, standing plans (policies, procedures, and rules and regulations), and budgets.

5-4 (P. 99)

Explain the steps and limits to rational decision making. Rational decision making is a six-step process in which managers define problems, evaluate alternatives, and compute optimal solutions. Step 1 is identifying and defining the problem. Problems are gaps between desired and existing states. Managers won't begin the decision-making process unless they are aware of a gap, are motivated to reduce it, and possess the necessary resources to fix it. Step 2 is defining the decision criteria used to judge alternatives. In Step 3, an absolute or relative comparison process is used to rate the importance of the decision criteria. Step 4 involves generating many alternative courses of action (that is, solutions). Potential solutions are assessed in Step 5 by systematically gathering information and evaluating each alternative against each criterion. In Step 6, criterion ratings and weights are used to compute the weighted average for each alternative course of action. Rational managers then choose the alternative with the highest value.

The rational decision-making model describes how decisions should be made in an ideal world without constraints. However, managers' limited resources, incomplete and imperfect information, and limited decision-making capabilities restrict their decision-making processes in the real world.

5-5 (P. 103)

Explain how group decisions and group decision-making techniques can improve decision making. When groups view problems from multiple perspectives, use more information, have a diversity of knowledge and experience, and become committed to solutions they help choose, they can produce better solutions than do individual decision makers. However, group decisions can suffer from several disadvantages: groupthink, slowness, discussions dominated by just a few individuals, and unfelt responsibility for decisions. Group decision making works best when group members encourage c-type (cognitive) conflict. Group decision making doesn't work as well when groups become mired in a-type (affective) conflict. The devil's advocacy approach improves group decisions because it brings structured c-type conflict into the decision-making process. By contrast, the nominal group technique improves decision making by reducing a-type conflict. Because it overcomes the problems of production blocking and evaluation apprehension, electronic brainstorming is more effective than face-to-face brainstorming.

Delphi technique a decision-making method in which members of a panel of experts respond to questions and to each other until reaching agreement on an issue

Brainstorming a decision-making method in which group members build on each others' ideas to generate as many alternative solutions as possible

Electronic brainstorming a decision-making method in which group members use computers to build on each others' ideas and generate as many alternative solutions as possible

Production blocking a disadvantage of face-to-face brainstorming in which a group member must wait to share an idea because another member is presenting an idea

Evaluation apprehension fear of what others will think of your ideas

LEARNING OUTCOMES

6-1 (P. 109)

Specify the components of sustainable competitive advantage, and explain why it is important. Firms can use their resources to create and sustain a competitive advantage, that is, to provide greater value for customers than competitors can. A competitive advantage becomes sustainable when other companies cannot duplicate the benefits it provides and have, for now, stopped trying. Four conditions must be met if a firm's resources are to be used to achieve a sustainable competitive advantage. The resources must be valuable, rare, imperfectly imitable, and nonsubstitutable.

6-2 (P. 111)

Describe the steps involved in the strategy-making process. The first step in strategy making is determining whether a strategy needs to be changed to sustain a competitive advantage. The second step is to conduct a situational (SWOT) analysis that examines internal strengths and weaknesses as well as external opportunities and threats. The third step involves choosing a strategy. Strategic reference point theory suggests that when companies are performing better than their strategic reference points, top management will typically choose a risk-averse strategy. When performance is below strategic reference points, risk-seeking strategies are more likely to be chosen.

6-3 (P. 117)

Explain the different kinds of corporate-level strategies. Corporate-level strategies, consisting of portfolio strategies and grand strategies, help managers determine what businesses they should be in. Portfolio strategy focuses on lowering business risk by being in multiple, unrelated businesses and by investing the cash flows from slow-growing businesses into faster-growing businesses. One portfolio strategy is based on the BCG matrix. The most successful way to use the portfolio approach to corporate strategy is to reduce risk through related diversification.

The three kinds of grand strategies are growth, stability, and retrenchment/recovery. Companies can grow externally by merging with or acquiring other companies, or they can grow internally through direct expansion or creating new businesses. Companies choose a stability strategy when their external environment changes very little or after they have dealt with periods of explosive growth. Retrenchment strategy, shrinking the size or scope of a business, is used to turn around poor performance. If retrenchment works, it is often followed by a recovery strategy that focuses on growing the business again.

6-4 (P. 122)

Describe the different kinds of industry-level strategies. The five industry forces determine an industry's overall attractiveness to corporate investors and its potential for long-term profitability. Together, a high level of these elements combine to increase competition and decrease profits. Industry-level strategies focus on how companies choose to compete in their industries. The three positioning strategies can help companies protect themselves from the negative effects of industry-wide competition. The four adaptive strategies help companies adapt to changes in the external environment. Defenders want to defend their current strategic positions. Prospectors look for new market opportunities to bring innovative new products to market. Analyzers minimize risk by following the proven successes of prospectors. Reactors do not follow a consistent adaptive strategy but instead react to changes in the external environment after they occur.

KEY TERMS

6-1

Resources the assets, capabilities, processes, employee time, information, and knowledge that an organization uses to improve its effectiveness and efficiency and create and sustain competitive advantage

Competitive advantage providing greater value for customers than competitors can

Sustainable competitive advantage a competitive advantage that other companies have tried unsuccessfully to duplicate and have, for the moment, stopped trying to duplicate

Valuable resource a resource that allows companies to improve efficiency and effectiveness

Rare resource a resource that is not controlled or possessed by many competing firms

Imperfectly imitable resource a resource that is impossible or extremely costly or difficult for other firms to duplicate

Nonsubstitutable resource a resource that produces value or competitive advantage and has no equivalent substitutes or replacements

6-2

Competitive inertia a reluctance to change strategies or competitive practices that have been successful in the past

Strategic dissonance a discrepancy between a company's intended strategy and the strategic actions managers take when implementing that strategy

Situational (SWOT) analysis an assessment of the strengths and weaknesses in an organization's internal environment and the opportunities and threats in its external environment

Distinctive competence what a company can make, do, or perform better than its competitors

Core capabilities the internal decision-making routines, problem-solving processes, and organizational cultures that determine how efficiently inputs can be turned into outputs

Shadow-strategy task force a committee within a company that analyzes the company's own weaknesses to determine how competitors could exploit them for competitive advantage

CHAPTER REVIEW 6

Strategic group a group of companies within an industry against which top managers compare, evaluate, and benchmark strategic threats and opportunities

Core firms the central companies in a strategic group

Secondary firms the firms in a strategic group that follow strategies related to but somewhat different from those of the core firms

Strategic reference points the strategic targets managers use to measure whether a firm has developed the core competencies it needs to achieve a sustainable competitive advantage

6-3

Corporate-level strategy the overall organizational strategy that addresses the question, "What business or businesses are we in or should we be in?"

Diversification a strategy for reducing risk by buying a variety of items (stocks or, in the case of a corporation, types of businesses) so that the failure of one stock or one business does not doom the entire portfolio

Portfolio strategy a corporate-level strategy that minimizes risk by diversifying investment among various businesses or product lines

Acquisition the purchase of a company by another company

Unrelated diversification creating or acquiring companies in completely unrelated businesses

BCG matrix a portfolio strategy developed by the Boston Consulting Group that categorizes a corporation's businesses by growth rate and relative market share and helps managers decide how to invest corporate funds

Star a company with a large share of a fast-growing market

Question mark a company with a small share of a fast-growing market

Cash cow a company with a large share of a slow-growing market

Dog a company with a small share of a slow-growing market

Related diversification creating or acquiring companies that share similar products, manufacturing, marketing, technology, or cultures

Grand strategy a broad corporate-level strategic plan used to achieve strategic goals and guide the strategic alternatives that managers of individual businesses or subunits may use

Growth strategy a strategy that focuses on increasing profits, revenues, market share, or the number of places in which the company does business

6-5 (P. 127)

Explain the components and kinds of firm-level strategies. Firm-level strategies are concerned with direct competition between firms. Market commonality and resource similarity determine whether firms are in direct competition and thus likely to attack each other and respond to each other's attacks. In general, the more markets in which there is product, service, or customer overlap and the greater the resource similarity between two firms, the more intense the direct competition between them will be.

Stability strategy a strategy that focuses on improving the way in which the company sells the same products or services to the same customers

Retrenchment strategy a strategy that focuses on turning around very poor company performance by shrinking the size or scope of the business

Recovery the strategic actions taken after retrenchment to return to a growth strategy

6-4

Industry-level strategy a corporate strategy that addresses the question, "How should we compete in this industry?"

Character of the rivalry a measure of the intensity of competitive behavior between companies in an industry

Threat of new entrants a measure of the degree to which barriers to entry make it easy or difficult for new companies to get started in an industry

Threat of substitute products or services a measure of the ease with which customers can find substitutes for an industry's products or services

Bargaining power of suppliers a measure of the influence that suppliers of parts, materials, and services to firms in an industry have on the prices of these inputs

Bargaining power of buyers a measure of the influence that customers have on a firm's prices

Cost leadership the positioning strategy of producing a product or service of acceptable quality at consistently lower production costs than competitors can, so that the firm can offer the product or service at the lowest price in the industry

Differentiation the positioning strategy of providing a product or service that is sufficiently different from competitors' offerings that customers are willing to pay a premium price for it

Focus strategy the positioning strategy of using cost leadership or differentiation to produce a specialized product or service for a limited, specially targeted group of customers in a particular geographic region or market segment

Defenders companies using an adaptive strategy aimed at defending strategic positions by seeking moderate, steady growth and by offering a limited range of high-quality products and services to a well-defined set of customers

Prospectors companies using an adaptive strategy that seeks fast growth by searching for new market opportunities, encouraging risk taking, and being the first to bring innovative new products to market

Analyzers companies using an adaptive strategy that seeks to minimize risk and maximize profits by following or imitating the proven successes of prospectors

Reactors companies that do not follow a consistent adaptive strategy but instead react to changes in the external environment after they occur

6-5

Firm-level strategy a corporate strategy that addresses the question "How should we compete against a particular firm?"

Direct competition the rivalry between two companies that offer similar products and services, acknowledge each other as rivals, and act and react to each other's strategic actions

Market commonality the degree to which two companies have overlapping products, services, or customers in multiple markets

Resource similarity the extent to which a competitor has similar amounts and kinds of resources

Attack a competitive move designed to reduce a rival's market share or profits

Response a competitive countermove, prompted by a rival's attack, to defend or improve a company's market share or profit

LEARNING OUTCOMES

7-1 (P. 133)

Explain why innovation matters to companies. Technology cycles typically follow an S-curve pattern of innovation. Early in the cycle, technological progress is slow, and improvements in technological performance are small. As a technology matures, however, performance improves quickly. Finally, as the limits of a technology are reached, only small improvements occur. At this point, significant improvements in performance must come from new technologies. The best way to protect a competitive advantage is to create a stream of innovative ideas and products. Innovation streams begin with technological discontinuities that create significant breakthroughs in performance or function. Technological discontinuities are followed by discontinuous change, in which customers purchase new technologies, and companies compete to establish the new dominant design. Dominant designs emerge because of critical mass, because they solve a practical problem, or because of the negotiations of independent standards bodies. Because technological innovation both enhances and destroys competence, companies that bet on the wrong design often struggle, while companies that bet on the eventual dominant design usually prosper. When a dominant design emerges, companies focus on incremental change, lowering costs, and making small but steady improvements in the dominant design. This focus continues until the next technological discontinuity occurs.

7-2 (P. 138)

Discuss the different methods that managers can use to effectively manage innovation in their organizations. To successfully manage innovation streams, companies must manage the sources of innovation and learn to manage innovation during both discontinuous and incremental change. Because innovation begins with creativity, companies can manage the sources of innovation by supporting a work environment in which creative thoughts and ideas are welcomed, valued, and encouraged. Creative work environments provide challenging work; offer organizational, supervisory, and work group encouragement; allow significant freedom; and remove organizational impediments to creativity.

Discontinuous and incremental change require different strategies. Companies that succeed in periods of discontinuous change typically follow an experiential approach to innovation. The experiential approach assumes that intuition, flexible options, and hands-on experience can reduce uncertainty and accelerate learning and understanding. A compression approach to innovation works best during periods of incremental change. This approach assumes that innovation can be planned using a series of steps and that compressing the time it takes to complete those steps can speed up innovation.

7-3 (P. 143)

Discuss why not changing can lead to organizational decline. The five-stage process of organizational decline begins when organizations don't recognize the need for change. In the blinded stage, managers fail to recognize the changes that threaten their organization's survival. In the inaction stage, management recognizes the need to change but doesn't act, hoping that the problems will correct themselves. In the faulty action stage, management focuses on cost cutting and efficiency rather than facing up to the fundamental changes needed to ensure survival. In the crisis stage, failure is likely unless fundamental reorganization occurs. Finally, in the dissolution stage, the company is dissolved through bankruptcy proceedings; by selling assets to pay creditors; or through

KEY TERMS

7-1

Organizational innovation the successful implementation of creative ideas in organizations

Technology cycle a cycle that begins with the birth of a new technology and ends when that technology reaches its limits and is replaced by a newer, substantially better technology

S-curve pattern of innovation a pattern of technological innovation characterized by slow initial progress, then rapid progress, and then slow progress again as a technology matures and reaches its limits

Innovation streams patterns of innovation over time that can create sustainable competitive advantage

Technological discontinuity the phase of an innovation stream in which a scientific advance or unique combination of existing technologies creates a significant breakthrough in performance or function

Discontinuous change the phase of a technology cycle characterized by technological substitution and design competition

Technological substitution the purchase of new technologies to replace older ones

Design competition competition between old and new technologies to establish a new technological standard or dominant design

Dominant design a new technological design or process that becomes the accepted market standard

Technological lockout the inability of a company to competitively sell its products because it relies on old technology or a nondominant design

Incremental change the phase of a technology cycle in which companies innovate by lowering costs and improving the functioning and performance of the dominant technological design

7-2

Creative work environments workplace cultures in which workers perceive that new ideas are welcomed, valued, and encouraged

Flow a psychological state of effortlessness, in which you become completely absorbed in what you're doing, and time seems to pass quickly

CHAPTER REVIEW 7

Experiential approach to innovation an approach to innovation that assumes a highly uncertain environment and uses intuition, flexible options, and hands-on experience to reduce uncertainty and accelerate learning and understanding

Design iteration a cycle of repetition in which a company tests a prototype of a new product or service, improves on that design, and then builds and tests the improved prototype

Product prototype a full-scale, working model that is being tested for design, function, and reliability

Testing the systematic comparison of different product designs or design iterations

Milestones formal project review points used to assess progress and performance

Multifunctional teams work teams composed of people from different departments

Compression approach to innovation an approach to innovation which assumes that incremental innovation can be planned using a series of steps and that compressing those steps can speed innovation

Generational change change based on incremental improvements to a dominant technological design such that the improved technology is fully backward compatible with the older technology

7-3

Organizational decline a large decrease in organizational performance that occurs when companies don't anticipate, recognize, neutralize, or adapt to the internal or external pressures that threaten their survival

7-4

Change forces forces that produce differences in the form, quality, or condition of an organization over time

Resistance forces forces that support the existing conditions in organizations

Resistance to change opposition to change resulting from self-interest, misunderstanding and distrust, and a general intolerance for change

Unfreezing getting the people affected by change to believe that change is needed

Change intervention the process used to get workers and managers to change their behaviors and work practices

Refreezing supporting and reinforcing new changes so that they stick

Coercion the use of formal power and authority to force others to change

Results-driven change change created quickly by focusing on the measurement and improvement of results

the closing of stores, offices, and facilities. If companies recognize the need to change early enough, however, dissolution may be avoided.

7-4 (P. 145)

Discuss the different methods that managers can use to better manage change as it occurs. The basic change process involves unfreezing, change intervention, and refreezing. Resistance to change stems from self-interest, misunderstanding, and distrust as well as a general intolerance for change. Resistance can be managed through education and communication, participation, negotiation, top management support, and coercion. Knowing what *not* to do is as important as knowing what to do to achieve successful change. Managers should avoid these errors when leading change: not establishing a sense of urgency, not creating a guiding coalition, lacking a vision, undercommunicating the vision, not removing obstacles to the vision, not creating short-term wins, declaring victory too soon, and not anchoring changes in the corporation's culture. Finally, managers can use a number of change techniques. Results-driven change and the General Electric workout reduce resistance to change by getting change efforts off to a fast start. Organizational development is a collection of planned change interventions (large-system, small-group, person-focused), guided by a change agent, that are designed to improve an organization's long-term health and performance.

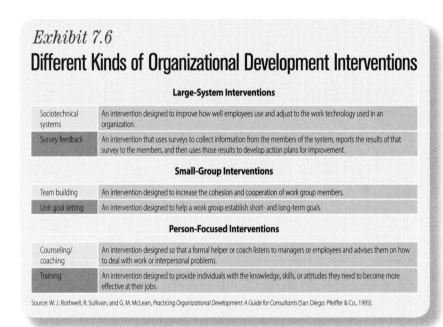

Exhibit 7.6
Different Kinds of Organizational Development Interventions

Large-System Interventions	
Sociotechnical systems	An intervention designed to improve how well employees use and adjust to the work technology used in an organization.
Survey feedback	An intervention that uses surveys to collect information from the members of the system, reports the results of that survey to the members, and then uses those results to develop action plans for improvement.

Small-Group Interventions	
Team building	An intervention designed to increase the cohesion and cooperation of work group members.
Unit goal setting	An intervention designed to help a work group establish short- and long-term goals.

Person-Focused Interventions	
Counseling/ coaching	An intervention designed so that a formal helper or coach listens to managers or employees and advises them on how to deal with work or interpersonal problems.
Training	An intervention designed to provide individuals with the knowledge, skills, or attitudes they need to become more effective at their jobs.

Source: W. J. Rothwell, R. Sullivan, and G. M. McLean, *Practicing Organizational Development: A Guide for Consultants* (San Diego: Pfeiffer & Co., 1995).

General Electric workout a three-day meeting in which managers and employees from different levels and parts of an organization quickly generate and act on solutions to specific business problems

Organizational development a philosophy and collection of planned change interventions designed to improve an organization's long-term health and performance

Change agent the person formally in charge of guiding a change effort

LEARNING OUTCOMES

8-1 (P. 153)

Discuss the impact of global business and the trade rules and agreements that govern it. Today, there are 103,000 multinational corporations worldwide; just 9.4 percent are based in the United States. Global business affects the United States in two ways: through direct foreign investment in the United States by foreign companies and through U.S. companies' investment in businesses in other countries. U.S. direct foreign investment throughout the world amounts to more than $4.2 trillion per year, whereas direct foreign investment by foreign companies in the United States amounts to more than $2.5 trillion per year. Historically, tariffs and nontariff trade barriers such as quotas, voluntary export restraints, government import standards, government subsidies, and customs classifications have made buying foreign goods much harder or more expensive than buying domestically produced products. In recent years, however, worldwide trade agreements such as GATT and the WTO, along with regional trading agreements such as the Maastricht Treaty of Europe, NAFTA, CAFTA-DR, UNASUR, ASEAN, and APEC have substantially reduced tariffs and nontariff barriers to international trade. Companies have responded by investing in growing markets in Asia, Eastern Europe, and Latin America. Consumers have responded by purchasing products based on value rather than geography.

8-2 (P. 159)

Explain why companies choose to standardize or adapt their business procedures. Global business requires a balance between global consistency and local adaptation. Global consistency means using the same rules, guidelines, policies, and procedures in each location. Managers at company headquarters like global consistency because it simplifies decisions. Local adaptation means adapting standard procedures to differences in markets. Local managers prefer a policy of local adaptation because it gives them more control. Not all businesses need the same combination of global consistency and local adaptation. Some thrive by emphasizing global consistency and ignoring local adaptation. Others succeed by ignoring global consistency and emphasizing local adaptation.

8-3 (P. 161)

Explain the different ways that companies can organize to do business globally. The phase model of globalization says that, as companies move from a domestic to a global orientation, they use these organizational forms in sequence: exporting, cooperative contracts (licensing and franchising), strategic alliances, and wholly owned affiliates. Yet, not all companies follow the phase model. For example, global new ventures are global from their inception.

8-4 (P. 164)

Explain how to find a favorable business climate. The first step in deciding where to take your company global is finding an attractive business climate. Be sure to look for a growing market where consumers have strong purchasing power, and foreign competitors are weak. When locating an office or manufacturing facility, consider both qualitative and quantitative factors. In assessing political risk, be sure to examine both political uncertainty and policy uncertainty. If the location you choose has considerable political risk, you can avoid it, try to control the risk, or use a cooperation strategy.

KEY TERMS

8-1

Global business the buying and selling of goods and services by people from different countries

Multinational corporation a corporation that owns businesses in two or more countries

Direct foreign investment a method of investment in which a company builds a new business or buys an existing business in a foreign country

Trade barriers government-imposed regulations that increase the cost and restrict the number of imported goods

Protectionism a government's use of trade barriers to shield domestic companies and their workers from foreign competition

Tariff a direct tax on imported goods

Nontariff barriers nontax methods of increasing the cost or reducing the volume of imported goods

Quota a limit on the number or volume of imported products

Voluntary export restraints voluntarily imposed limits on the number or volume of products exported to a particular country

Government import standard a standard ostensibly established to protect the health and safety of citizens but, in reality, is often used to restrict imports

Subsidies government loans, grants, and tax deferments given to domestic companies to protect them from foreign competition

Customs classification a classification assigned to imported products by government officials that affects the size of the tariff and the imposition of import quotas

General Agreement on Tariffs and Trade (GATT) a worldwide trade agreement that reduced and eliminated tariffs, limited government subsidies, and established protections for intellectual property

World Trade Organization (WTO) the successor to GATT; the only international organization dealing with the global rules of trade between nations; its main function is to ensure that trade flows as smoothly, predictably, and freely as possible

Regional trading zones areas in which tariff and nontariff barriers on trade between countries are reduced or eliminated

CHAPTER REVIEW 8

Maastricht Treaty of Europe a regional trade agreement among most European countries

North American Free Trade Agreement (NAFTA) a regional trade agreement among the United States, Canada, and Mexico

Dominican Republic-Central America Free Trade Agreement (CAFTA-DR) a regional trade agreement among Costa Rica, the Dominican Republic, El Salvador, Guatemala, Honduras, Nicaragua, and the United States

Union of South American Nations (UNASUR) a regional trade agreement among Argentina, Brazil, Paraguay, Uruguay, Venezuela, Bolivia, Colombia, Ecuador, Peru, Guyana, Suriname, and Chile

Association of Southeast Asian Nations (ASEAN) a regional trade agreement among Brunei Darussalam, Cambodia, Indonesia, Laos, Malaysia, Myanmar, the Philippines, Singapore, Thailand, and Vietnam

Asia-Pacific Economic Cooperation (APEC) a regional trade agreement among Australia, Canada, Chile, the People's Republic of China, Hong Kong, Japan, Mexico, New Zealand, Papua New Guinea, Peru, Russia, South Korea, Taiwan, the United States, and all the members of ASEAN except Cambodia, Lao PDR, and Myanmar

8-2

Global consistency when a multinational company has offices, manufacturing plants, and distribution facilities in different countries and runs them all using the same rules, guidelines, policies, and procedures

Local adaptation modifying rules, guidelines, policies, and procedures to adapt to differences in foreign customers, governments, and regulatory agencies

8-3

Exporting selling domestically produced products to customers in foreign countries

Cooperative contract an agreement in which a foreign business owner pays a company a fee for the right to conduct that business in his or her country

Licensing an agreement in which a domestic company, the licensor, receives royalty payments for allowing another company, the licensee, to produce the licensor's product, sell its service, or use its brand name in a specified foreign market

Franchise a collection of networked firms in which the manufacturer or marketer of a product or service, the franchisor, licenses the entire business to another person or organization, the franchisee

Strategic alliance an agreement in which companies combine key resources, costs, risks, technology, and people

8-5 (P. 169)

Discuss the importance of identifying and adapting to cultural differences.
National culture is the set of shared values and beliefs that affects the perceptions, decisions, and behavior of the people from a particular country. The first step in dealing with culture is to recognize meaningful differences such as power distance, individualism, masculinity, uncertainty avoidance, and short-term/long-term orientation. Cultural differences should be interpreted carefully because they are based on generalizations rather than specific individuals. Adapting managerial practices to cultural differences is difficult because policies and practices can be perceived differently in different cultures.

8-6 (P. 171)

Explain how to successfully prepare workers for international assignments. Many expatriates return prematurely from international assignments because of poor performance. This is much less likely to happen if employees receive language and cross-cultural training, such as documentary training, cultural simulations, or field experiences, before going on assignment. Adjustment of expatriates' spouses and families, which is the most important determinant of success in international assignments, can be improved through adaptability screening and language and cross-cultural training.

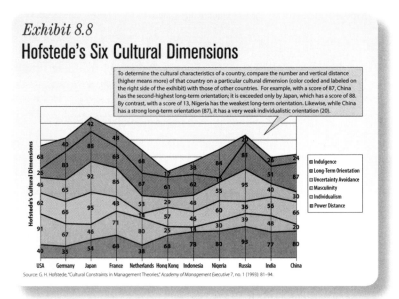

Exhibit 8.8
Hofstede's Six Cultural Dimensions

To determine the cultural characteristics of a country, compare the number and vertical distance (higher means more) of that country on a particular cultural dimension (color coded and labeled on the right side of the exhibit) with those of other countries. For example, with a score of 87, China has the second-highest long-term orientation; it is exceeded only by Japan, which has a score of 88. By contrast, with a score of 13, Nigeria has the weakest long-term orientation. Likewise, while China has a strong long-term orientation (87), it has a very weak individualistic orientation (20).

Source: G. H. Hofstede, "Cultural Constraints in Management Theories," *Academy of Management Executive* 7, no. 1 (1993): 81–94.

Joint venture a strategic alliance in which two existing companies collaborate to form a third, independent company

Wholly owned affiliates foreign offices, facilities, and manufacturing plants that are 100 percent owned by the parent company

Global new ventures new companies that are founded with an active global strategy and have sales, employees, and financing in different countries

8-4

Purchasing power the relative cost of a standard set of goods and services in different countries

Political uncertainty the risk of major changes in political regimes that can result from war, revolution, death of political leaders, social unrest, or other influential events

Policy uncertainty the risk associated with changes in laws and government policies that directly affect the way foreign companies conduct business

8-5

National culture the set of shared values and beliefs that affects the perceptions, decisions, and behavior of the people from a particular country

8-6

Expatriate someone who lives and works outside his or her native country

LEARNING OUTCOMES

9-1 (P. 177)

Describe the departmentalization approach to organizational structure. There are five traditional departmental structures: functional, product, customer, geographic, and matrix. Functional departmentalization is based on the different business functions or types of expertise used to run a business. Product departmentalization is organized according to the different products or services a company sells. Customer departmentalization focuses its divisions on the different kinds of customers a company has. Geographic departmentalization is based on the different geographic areas or markets in which the company does business. Matrix departmentalization is a hybrid form that combines two or more forms of departmentalization, the most common being the product and functional forms. There is no single best departmental structure. Each structure has advantages and disadvantages.

9-2 (P. 184)

Explain organizational authority. Organizational authority is determined by the chain of command, line versus staff authority, delegation, and the degree of centralization in a company. The chain of command vertically connects every job in the company to higher levels of management and makes clear who reports to whom. Managers have line authority to command employees below them in the chain of command but have only staff, or advisory, authority over employees not below them in the chain of command. Managers delegate authority by transferring to subordinates the authority and responsibility needed to do a task; in exchange, subordinates become accountable for task completion. In centralized companies, most authority to make decisions lies with managers in the upper levels of the company. In decentralized companies, much of the authority is delegated to the workers closest to the problems, who can then make the decisions necessary for solving the problems themselves.

9-3 (P. 187)

Discuss the different methods for job design. Companies use specialized jobs because they are economical, easy to learn, and don't require highly paid workers. However, specialized jobs aren't motivating or particularly satisfying for employees. Companies have used job rotation, job enlargement, job enrichment, and the job characteristics model to make specialized jobs more interesting and motivating. The goal of the job characteristics model is to make jobs intrinsically motivating. For this to happen, jobs must be strong on five core job characteristics (skill variety, task identity, task significance, autonomy, and feedback), and workers must experience three critical psychological states (knowledge of results, responsibility for work outcomes, and meaningful work). If jobs aren't internally motivating, they can be redesigned by combining tasks, forming natural work units, establishing client relationships, using vertical loading, and opening feedback channels.

9-4 (P. 190)

Explain the methods that companies are using to redesign internal organizational processes (that is, intraorganizational processes). Today, companies are using reengineering and empowerment to change their intraorganizational processes. Reengineering changes an organization's orientation from vertical to horizontal and changes its work processes by decreasing sequential and pooled interdependence and by increasing reciprocal interdependence. Reengineering promises dramatic increases

KEY TERMS

9-1

Organizational structure the vertical and horizontal configuration of departments, authority, and jobs within a company

Organizational process the collection of activities that transforms inputs into outputs that customers value

Departmentalization subdividing work and workers into separate organizational units responsible for completing particular tasks

Functional departmentalization organizing work and workers into separate units responsible for particular business functions or areas of expertise

Product departmentalization organizing work and workers into separate units responsible for producing particular products or services

Customer departmentalization organizing work and workers into separate units responsible for particular kinds of customers

Geographic departmentalization organizing work and workers into separate units responsible for doing business in particular geographic areas

Matrix departmentalization a hybrid organizational structure in which two or more forms of departmentalization, most often product and functional, are used together

Simple matrix a form of matrix departmentalization in which managers in different parts of the matrix negotiate conflicts and resources

Complex matrix a form of matrix departmentalization in which managers in different parts of the matrix report to matrix managers, who help them sort out conflicts and problems

9-2

Authority the right to give commands, take action, and make decisions to achieve organizational objectives

Chain of command the vertical line of authority that clarifies who reports to whom throughout the organization

Unity of command a management principle that workers should report to just one boss

Line authority the right to command immediate subordinates in the chain of command

CHAPTER REVIEW 9

Staff authority the right to advise, but not command, others who are not subordinates in the chain of command

Line function an activity that contributes directly to creating or selling the company's products

Staff function an activity that does not contribute directly to creating or selling the company's products but instead supports line activities

Delegation of authority the assignment of direct authority and responsibility to a subordinate to complete tasks for which the manager is normally responsible

Centralization of authority the location of most authority at the upper levels of the organization

Decentralization the location of a significant amount of authority in the lower levels of the organization

Standardization solving problems by consistently applying the same rules, procedures, and processes

9-3

Job design the number, kind, and variety of tasks that individual workers perform in doing their jobs

Job specialization a job composed of a small part of a larger task or process

Job rotation periodically moving workers from one specialized job to another to give them more variety and the opportunity to use different skills

Job enlargement increasing the number of different tasks that a worker performs within one particular job

Job enrichment increasing the number of tasks in a particular job and giving workers the authority and control to make meaningful decisions about their work

Job characteristics model (JCM) an approach to job redesign that seeks to formulate jobs in ways that motivate workers and lead to positive work outcomes

Internal motivation motivation that comes from the job itself rather than from outside rewards

Skill variety the number of different activities performed in a job

Task identity the degree to which a job, from beginning to end, requires the completion of a whole and identifiable piece of work

Task significance the degree to which a job is perceived to have a substantial impact on others inside or outside the organization

Autonomy the degree to which a job gives workers the discretion, freedom, and independence to decide how and when to accomplish the job

in productivity and customer satisfaction, but it has been criticized as simply an excuse to cut costs and lay off workers. Empowering workers means taking decision-making authority and responsibility from managers and giving it to workers. Empowered workers develop feelings of competence and self-determination and believe that their work has meaning and impact.

9-5 (P. 193)

Describe the methods that companies are using to redesign external organizational processes (that is, interorganizational processes). Organizations are using modular and virtual organizations to change interorganizational processes. Because modular organizations outsource all noncore activities to other businesses, they are less expensive to run than traditional companies. However, modular organizations require extremely close relationships with suppliers, may result in a loss of control, and could create new competitors if the wrong business activities are outsourced. Virtual organizations participate in a network in which they share skills, costs, capabilities, markets, and customers. Virtual organizations can reduce costs, respond quickly, and, if they can successfully coordinate their efforts, produce outstanding products and services.

Feedback the amount of information the job provides to workers about their work performance

9-4

Mechanistic organization an organization characterized by specialized jobs and responsibilities; precisely defined, unchanging roles; and a rigid chain of command based on centralized authority and vertical communication

Organic organization an organization characterized by broadly defined jobs and responsibilities; loosely defined, frequently changing roles; and decentralized authority and horizontal communication based on task knowledge

Intraorganizational process the collection of activities that take place within an organization to transform inputs into outputs that customers value

Reengineering fundamental rethinking and radical redesign of business processes to achieve dramatic improvements in critical measures of performance, such as cost, quality, service, and speed

Task interdependence the extent to which collective action is required to complete an entire piece of work

Pooled interdependence work completed by having each job or department independently contribute to the whole

Sequential interdependence work completed in succession, with one group's or job's outputs becoming the inputs for the next group or job

Reciprocal interdependence work completed by different jobs or groups working together in a back-and-forth manner

Empowering workers permanently passing decision-making authority and responsibility from managers to workers by giving them the information and resources they need to make and carry out good decisions

Empowerment feelings of intrinsic motivation in which workers perceive their work to have impact and meaning and perceive themselves to be competent and capable of self-determination

9-5

Interorganizational process a collection of activities that take place among companies to transform inputs into outputs that customers value

Modular organization an organization that outsources noncore business activities to outside companies, suppliers, specialists, or consultants

Virtual organization an organization that is part of a network in which many companies share skills, costs, capabilities, markets, and customers to collectively solve customer problems or provide specific products or services

LEARNING OUTCOMES

10-1 (P. 199)

Explain the good and bad of using teams. In many industries, teams are growing in importance because they help organizations respond to specific problems and challenges. Teams have been shown to increase customer satisfaction (specific customer teams), product and service quality (direct responsibility), and employee job satisfaction (cross-training, unique opportunities, and leadership responsibilities). Although teams can produce significant improvements in these areas, using teams does not guarantee these positive outcomes. Teams and teamwork have the disadvantages of initially high turnover and social loafing (especially in large groups). Teams also share many of the advantages (multiple perspectives, generation of more alternatives, and more commitment) and disadvantages (groupthink, time, poorly run meetings, domination by a few team members, and weak accountability) of group decision making. Teams should be used for a clear purpose, when the work requires that people work together, when rewards can be provided for both teamwork and team performance, and when ample resources can be provided.

Exhibit 10.1
When to Use and When Not to Use Teams

Use Teams When . . .	Don't Use Teams When . . .
✓ there is a clear, engaging reason or purpose.	✗ there isn't a clear, engaging reason or purpose.
✓ the job can't be done unless people work together.	✗ the job can be done by people working independently.
✓ rewards can be provided for teamwork and team performance.	✗ rewards are provided for individual effort and performance.
✓ ample resources are available.	✗ the necessary resources are not available.

Source: R. Wageman, "Critical Success Factors for Creating Superb Self-Managing Teams," *Organizational Dynamics* 26, no. 1 (1997): 49–61.

iStockphoto.com/Tunart

10-2 (P. 202)

Recognize and understand the different kinds of teams. Companies use different kinds of teams to make themselves more competitive. Autonomy is the key dimension that makes teams different. Traditional work groups (which execute tasks) and employee involvement groups (which make suggestions) have the lowest levels of autonomy. Semi-autonomous work groups (which control major direct tasks) have more autonomy, while self-managing teams (which control all direct tasks) and self-designing teams (which control membership and how tasks are done) have the highest levels of autonomy. Cross-functional, virtual, and project teams are common but are not easily categorized in terms of autonomy. Cross-functional teams combine employees from different functional areas to help teams attack problems from multiple perspectives and generate more ideas and solutions. Virtual teams use telecommunications and information technologies to bring coworkers together, regardless of physical location or time zone. Virtual teams reduce travel and work time, but communication may suffer because team

KEY TERMS

10-1

Work team a small number of people with complementary skills who hold themselves mutually accountable for pursuing a common purpose, achieving performance goals, and improving interdependent work processes

Cross-training training team members to do all or most of the jobs performed by the other team members

Social loafing behavior in which team members withhold their efforts and fail to perform their share of the work

10-2

Traditional work group a group composed of two or more people who work together to achieve a shared goal

Employee involvement team team that provides advice or makes suggestions to management concerning specific issues

Semi-autonomous work group a group that has the authority to make decisions and solve problems related to the major tasks of producing a product or service

Self-managing team a team that manages and controls all of the major tasks of producing a product or service

Self-designing team a team that has the characteristics of self-managing teams but also controls team design, work tasks, and team membership

Cross-functional team a team composed of employees from different functional areas of the organization

Virtual team a team composed of geographically and/or organizationally dispersed coworkers who use telecommunication and information technologies to accomplish an organizational task

Project team a team created to complete specific, one-time projects or tasks within a limited time

10-3

Norms informally agreed-on standards that regulate team behavior

Cohesiveness the extent to which team members are attracted to a team and motivated to remain in it

CHAPTER REVIEW 10

Forming the first stage of team development, in which team members meet each other, form initial impressions, and begin to establish team norms

Storming the second stage of development, characterized by conflict and disagreement, in which team members disagree over what the team should do and how it should do it

Norming the third stage of team development, in which team members begin to settle into their roles, group cohesion grows, and positive team norms develop

Performing the fourth and final stage of team development, in which performance improves because the team has matured into an effective, fully functioning team

De-norming a reversal of the norming stage, in which team performance begins to decline as the size, scope, goal, or members of the team change

De-storming a reversal of the storming phase, in which the team's comfort level decreases, team cohesion weakens, and angry emotions and conflict may flare

De-forming a reversal of the forming stage, in which team members position themselves to control pieces of the team, avoid each other, and isolate themselves from team leaders

10-4

Structural accommodation the ability to change organizational structures, policies, and practices in order to meet stretch goals

Bureaucratic immunity the ability to make changes without first getting approval from managers or other parts of an organization

Individualism-collectivism the degree to which a person believes that people should be self-sufficient and that loyalty to one's self is more important than loyalty to team or company

Team level the average level of ability, experience, personality, or any other factor on a team

Team diversity the variances or differences in ability, experience, personality, or any other factor on a team

Interpersonal skills skills, such as listening, communicating, questioning, and providing feedback, that enable people to have effective working relationships with others

Skill-based pay compensation system that pays employees for learning additional skills or knowledge

Gainsharing a compensation system in which companies share the financial value of performance gains, such as increased productivity, cost savings, or quality, with their workers

members don't work face-to-face. Finally, project teams are used for specific, one-time projects or tasks that must be completed within a limited time. Project teams reduce communication barriers and promote flexibility; teams and team members are reassigned to their departments or to new projects as their current projects are completed.

10-3 (P. 206)

Understand the general characteristics of work teams. The most important characteristics of work teams are team norms, cohesiveness, size, conflict, and development. Norms let team members know what is expected of them and can influence team behavior in positive and negative ways. Positive team norms are associated with organizational commitment, trust, and job satisfaction. Team cohesiveness helps teams retain members, promotes cooperative behavior, increases motivation, and facilitates team performance. Attending team meetings and activities, creating opportunities to work together, and engaging in nonwork activities can increase cohesiveness. Team size has a curvilinear relationship with team performance: teams that are very small or very large do not perform as well as moderate-sized teams of six to nine members. Teams of this size are cohesive and small enough for team members to get to know each other and contribute in a meaningful way but are large enough to take advantage of team members' diverse skills, knowledge, and perspectives. Conflict and disagreement are inevitable in most teams. The key to dealing with team conflict is to maximize cognitive conflict, which focuses on issue-related differences, and minimize affective conflict, the emotional reactions that occur when disagreements become personal rather than professional. As teams develop and grow, they pass through four stages of development: forming, storming, norming, and performing. If a team is not managed well, its performance may decline after a period of time as the team regresses through the stages of de-norming, de-storming, and de-forming.

Exhibit 10.4
Stages of Team Development

Sources: J. F. McGrew, J. G. Bilotta, and J. M. Deeney, "Software Team Formation and Decay: Extending the Standard Model for Small Groups," *Small Group Research* 30, no. 2 (1999): 209–234; B. W. Tuckman, "Development Sequence in Small Groups," *Psychological Bulletin* 63, no. 6 (1965): 384–399.

10-4 (P. 211)

Explain how to enhance work team effectiveness. Companies can make teams more effective by setting team goals and managing how team members are selected, trained, and compensated. Team goals provide a clear focus and purpose, reduce the incidence of social loafing, and lead to higher team performance 93 percent of the time. Extremely difficult stretch goals can be used to motivate teams as long as teams have autonomy, control over resources, structural accommodation, and bureaucratic immunity. Not everyone is suited for teamwork. When selecting team members, companies should select people who have a preference for teamwork (that is, are more collectivists than individualists) and should consider team level (average ability of a team) and team diversity (different abilities of a team). Organizations that use teams successfully provide thousands of hours of training to make sure that teams work. The most common types of team training are for interpersonal skills, decision-making and problem-solving skills, conflict resolution, technical training to help team members learn multiple jobs (that is, cross-training), and training for team leaders. Employees can be compensated for team participation and accomplishments in three ways: skill-based pay, gainsharing, and nonfinancial rewards.

LEARNING OUTCOMES

11-1 (P. 217)

Explain how different employment laws affect human resource practice. Human resource management is subject to numerous major federal employment laws and subject to review by several federal agencies. In general, these laws indicate that sex, age, religion, color, national origin, race, disability, and genetic history may not be considered in employment decisions unless these factors reasonably qualify as BFOQs. Two important criteria, disparate treatment (intentional discrimination) and adverse impact (unintentional discrimination), are used to decide whether companies have wrongly discriminated against someone. The two kinds of sexual harassment are quid pro quo sexual harassment and hostile work environment.

11-2 (P. 221)

Explain how companies use recruiting to find qualified job applicants. Recruiting is the process of finding qualified job applicants. The first step in recruiting is to conduct a job analysis, which is used to write a job description of basic tasks, duties, and responsibilities and to write job specifications indicating the knowledge, skills, and abilities needed to perform the job. Whereas internal recruiting involves finding qualified job applicants from inside the company, external recruiting involves finding qualified job applicants from outside the company.

11-3 (P. 225)

Describe the selection techniques and procedures that companies use when deciding which applicants should receive job offers. Selection is the process of gathering information about job applicants to decide who should be offered a job. Accurate selection procedures are valid, are legally defendable, and improve organizational performance. Application forms and résumés are the most common selection devices. Managers should check references and conduct background checks even though previous employers are often reluctant to provide such information for fear of being sued for defamation. Unfortunately, without this information, other employers are at risk of negligent hiring lawsuits. Selection tests generally do the best job of predicting applicants' future job performance. The three kinds of job interviews are unstructured, structured, and semistructured.

11-4 (P. 232)

Describe how to determine training needs and select the appropriate training methods. Training is used to give employees the job-specific skills, experience, and knowledge they need to do their jobs or improve their job performance. To make sure training dollars are well spent, companies need to determine specific training needs, select appropriate training methods, and then evaluate the training.

11-5 (P. 235)

Discuss how to use performance appraisals to give meaningful performance feedback. The keys to successful performance appraisals are accurately measuring job performance and effectively sharing performance feedback with employees. Organizations should develop good performance appraisal scales; train raters how to accurately evaluate performance; and impress upon managers the value of providing feedback in a clear, consistent, and fair manner, as well as setting goals and monitoring progress toward those goals.

KEY TERMS

11-1

Human resource management (HRM) the process of finding, developing, and keeping the right people to form a qualified workforce

Bona fide occupational qualification (BFOQ) an exception in employment law that permits sex, age, religion, and the like to be used when making employment decisions, but only if they are "reasonably necessary to the normal operation of that particular business." BFOQs are strictly monitored by the Equal Employment Opportunity Commission

Disparate treatment intentional discrimination that occurs when people are purposely not given the same hiring, promotion, or membership opportunities because of their race, color, sex, age, ethnic group, national origin, or religious beliefs

Adverse impact unintentional discrimination that occurs when members of a particular race, sex, or ethnic group are unintentionally harmed or disadvantaged because they are hired, promoted, or trained (or any other employment decision) at substantially lower rates than others

Four-fifths (or 80%) rule a rule of thumb used by the courts and the EEOC to determine whether there is evidence of adverse impact. A violation of this rule occurs when the impact ratio (calculated by dividing the decision ratio for a protected group by the decision ratio for a nonprotected group) is less than 80%, or four-fifths

Sexual harassment a form of discrimination in which unwelcome sexual advances, requests for sexual favors, or other verbal or physical conduct of a sexual nature occurs while performing one's job

Quid pro quo sexual harassment a form of sexual harassment in which employment outcomes, such as hiring, promotion, or simply keeping one's job, depend on whether an individual submits to sexual harassment

Hostile work environment a form of sexual harassment in which unwelcome and demeaning sexually related behavior creates an intimidating and offensive work environment

11-2

Recruiting the process of developing a pool of qualified job applicants

Job analysis a purposeful, systematic process for collecting information on the important work-related aspects of a job

CHAPTER REVIEW 11

Job description a written description of the basic tasks, duties, and responsibilities required of an employee holding a particular job

Job specifications a written summary of the qualifications needed to successfully perform a particular job

Internal recruiting the process of developing a pool of qualified job applicants from people who already work in the company

External recruiting the process of developing a pool of qualified job applicants from outside the company

11-3

Selection the process of gathering information about job applicants to decide who should be offered a job

Validation the process of determining how well a selection test or procedure predicts future job performance; the better or more accurate the prediction of future job performance, the more valid a test is said to be

Human resource information system (HRIS) a computerized system for gathering, analyzing, storing, and disseminating information related to the HRM process

Employment references sources such as previous employers or coworkers who can provide job-related information about job candidates

Background checks procedures used to verify the truthfulness and accuracy of information that applicants provide about themselves and to uncover negative, job-related background information not provided by applicants

Specific ability tests (aptitude tests) tests that measure the extent to which an applicant possesses the particular kind of ability needed to do a job well

Cognitive ability tests tests that measure the extent to which applicants have abilities in perceptual speed, verbal comprehension, numerical aptitude, general reasoning, and spatial aptitude

Biographical data (biodata) extensive surveys that ask applicants questions about their personal backgrounds and life experiences

Work sample tests tests that require applicants to perform tasks that are actually done on the job

Assessment centers a series of managerial simulations, graded by trained observers, that are used to determine applicants' capability for managerial work

Interview a selection tool in which company representatives ask job applicants job-related questions to determine whether they are qualified for the job

11-6 (P. 239)

Describe basic compensation strategies and discuss the four kinds of employee separations. Compensation includes both the financial and the nonfinancial rewards that organizations give employees in exchange for their work. There are three basic kinds of compensation decisions: pay level, pay variability, and pay structure. Employee separation is the loss of an employee, which can occur voluntarily or involuntarily. Companies use downsizing and early retirement incentive programs (ERIPs) to reduce the number of employees in the organization and lower costs. However, companies generally try to keep the rate of employee turnover low to reduce costs associated with finding and developing new employees. Functional turnover, on the other hand, can be good for organizations.

Unstructured interviews interviews in which interviewers are free to ask the applicants anything they want

Structured interviews interviews in which all applicants are asked the same set of standardized questions, usually including situational, behavioral, background, and job-knowledge questions

11-4

Training developing the skills, experience, and knowledge employees need to perform their jobs or improve their performance

Needs assessment the process of identifying and prioritizing the learning needs of employees

11-5

Performance appraisal the process of assessing how well employees are doing their jobs

Objective performance measures measures of job performance that are easily and directly counted or quantified

Subjective performance measures measures of job performance that require someone to judge or assess a worker's performance

Behavior observation scales (BOSs) rating scales that indicate the frequency with which workers perform specific behaviors that are representative of the job dimensions critical to successful job performance

Rater training training performance appraisal raters in how to avoid rating errors and increase rating accuracy

360-degree feedback a performance appraisal process in which feedback is obtained from the boss, subordinates, peers and coworkers, and the employees themselves

11-6

Compensation the financial and nonfinancial rewards that organizations give employees in exchange for their work

Employee separation the voluntary or involuntary loss of an employee

Job evaluation a process that determines the worth of each job in a company by evaluating the market value of the knowledge, skills, and requirements needed to perform it

Piecework a compensation system in which employees are paid a set rate for each item they produce

Commission a compensation system in which employees earn a percentage of each sale they make

Profit sharing a compensation system in which a company pays a percentage of its profits to employees in addition to their regular compensation

Employee stock ownership plan (ESOP) a compensation system that awards employees shares of company stock in addition to their regular compensation

Stock options a compensation system that gives employees the right to purchase shares of stock at a set price, even if the value of the stock increases above that price

Wrongful discharge a legal doctrine that requires employers to have a job-related reason to terminate employees

Downsizing the planned elimination of jobs in a company

Outplacement services employment-counseling services offered to employees who are losing their jobs because of downsizing

Early retirement incentive programs (ERIPs) programs that offer financial benefits to employees to encourage them to retire early

Phased retirement employees transition to retirement by working reduced hours over a period of time before completely retiring

Employee turnover loss of employees who voluntarily choose to leave the company

Functional turnover loss of poor-performing employees who voluntarily choose to leave a company

Dysfunctional turnover loss of high-performing employees who voluntarily choose to leave a company

LEARNING OUTCOMES

12-1 (P. 247)

Describe diversity and explain why it matters. Diversity exists in organizations when there are demographic, cultural, and personal differences among the employees and the customers. A common misconception is that workplace diversity and affirmative action are the same. However, affirmative action is more narrowly focused on demographics; is required by law; and is used to punish companies that discriminate on the basis of race/ethnicity, religion, sex, or national origin. By contrast, diversity is broader in focus (going beyond demographics); voluntary; more positive in that it encourages companies to value all kinds of differences; and, at this time, substantially less controversial than affirmative action. Affirmative action and diversity thus differ in purpose, practice, and the reactions they produce. Diversity also makes good business sense in terms of reducing costs (decreasing turnover and absenteeism and avoiding lawsuits), attracting and retaining talent, and driving business growth (improving marketplace understanding and promoting higher-quality problem solving).

12-2 (P. 250)

Understand the special challenges that the dimensions of surface-level diversity pose for managers. Age, sex, race/ethnicity, and physical and mental disabilities are dimensions of surface-level diversity. Because those dimensions are (usually) easily observed, managers and workers tend to rely on them to form initial impressions and stereotypes. Sometimes this can lead to age, sex, racial/ethnic, or disability discrimination (that is, treating people differently) in the workplace. In general, older workers, women, people of color or different national origins, and people with disabilities are less likely to be hired or promoted than are white males. This disparity is often due to incorrect beliefs or stereotypes such as "job performance declines with age," or "women aren't willing to travel on business," or "workers with disabilities aren't as competent as able workers." To reduce discrimination, companies can determine the hiring and promotion rates for different groups, train managers to make hiring and promotion decisions on the basis of specific criteria, and make sure that everyone has equal access to training, mentors, reasonable work accommodations, and assistive technology. Finally, companies need to designate a go-to person to whom employees can talk if they believe they have suffered discrimination.

12-3 (P. 257)

Explain how the dimensions of deep-level diversity affect individual behavior and interactions in the workplace. Deep-level diversity matters because it can reduce prejudice, discrimination, and conflict while increasing social integration. It consists of dispositional and personality differences that can be recognized only through extended interaction with others. Research conducted in different cultures, settings, and languages indicates that there are five basic dimensions of personality: extraversion, emotional stability, agreeableness, conscientiousness, and openness to experience. Of these, conscientiousness is perhaps the most important because conscientious workers tend to be better performers on virtually any job. Extraversion is also related to performance in jobs that require significant interaction with others.

KEY TERMS

12-1

Diversity a variety of demographic, cultural, and personal differences among an organization's employees and customers

Affirmative action purposeful steps taken by an organization to create employment opportunities for minorities and women

12-2

Surface-level diversity differences such as age, sex, race/ethnicity, and physical disabilities that are observable, typically unchangeable, and easy to measure

Deep-level diversity differences such as personality and attitudes that are communicated through verbal and nonverbal behaviors and are learned only through extended interaction with others

Social integration the degree to which group members are psychologically attracted to working with each other to accomplish a common objective

Age discrimination treating people differently (for example, in hiring and firing, promotion, and compensation decisions) because of their age

Sex discrimination treating people differently because of their sex

Glass ceiling the invisible barrier that prevents women and minorities from advancing to the top jobs in organizations

Racial and ethnic discrimination treating people differently because of their race or ethnicity

Disability a mental or physical impairment that substantially limits one or more major life activities

Disability discrimination treating people differently because of their disabilities

12-3

Disposition the tendency to respond to situations and events in a predetermined manner

Personality the relatively stable set of behaviors, attitudes, and emotions displayed over time that makes people different from each other

Extraversion the degree to which someone is active, assertive, gregarious, sociable, talkative, and energized by others

CHAPTER REVIEW 12

Emotional stability the degree to which someone is not angry, depressed, anxious, emotional, insecure, and excitable

Agreeableness the degree to which someone is cooperative, polite, flexible, forgiving, good-natured, tolerant, and trusting

Conscientiousness the degree to which someone is organized, hardworking, responsible, persevering, thorough, and achievement oriented

Openness to experience the degree to which someone is curious, broad-minded, and open to new ideas, things, and experiences; is spontaneous; and has a high tolerance for ambiguity

12-4

Organizational plurality a work environment where (1) all members are empowered to contribute in a way that maximizes the benefits to the organization, customers, and themselves, and (2) the individuality of each member is respected by not segmenting or polarizing people on the basis of their membership in a particular group

Skills-based diversity training training that teaches employees the practical skills they need for managing a diverse workforce, such as flexibility and adaptability, negotiation, problem solving, and conflict resolution

Awareness training training that is designed to raise employees' awareness of diversity issues and to challenge the underlying assumptions or stereotypes they may have about others

Diversity audits formal assessments that measure employee and management attitudes, investigate the extent to which people are advantaged or disadvantaged with respect to hiring and promotions, and review companies' diversity-related policies and procedures

Diversity pairing a mentoring program in which people of different cultural backgrounds, sexes, or races/ethnicities are paired together to get to know each other and change stereotypical beliefs and attitudes

12-4 (P. 259)

Explain the basic principles and practices that can be used to manage diversity. The three paradigms for managing diversity are the discrimination and fairness paradigm (equal opportunity, fair treatment, strict compliance with the law), the access and legitimacy paradigm (matching internal diversity to external diversity), and the learning and effectiveness paradigm (achieving organizational plurality by integrating deep-level diversity into the work of the organization). Unlike the other paradigms that focus on surface-level differences, the learning and effectiveness paradigm values common ground, distinguishes between individual and group differences, minimizes conflict and divisiveness, and focuses on bringing different talents and perspectives together. What principles can companies use when managing diversity? Follow and enforce federal and state laws regarding equal employment opportunity. Treat group differences as important but not special. Find the common ground. Tailor opportunities to individuals, not groups. Solicit negative as well as positive feedback. Set high but realistic goals. The two types of diversity training are awareness training and skills-based diversity training. Companies also manage diversity through diversity audits and diversity pairing and by having top executives experience what it is like to be in the minority.

Paradigms for Managing Diversity

Diversity Paradigm	Focus	Success Measured By	Benefits	Limitations
Discrimination & Fairness	Equal opportunity Fair treatment Recruitment of minorities Strict compliance with laws	Recruitment, promotion, and retention goals for underrepresented groups	Fairer treatment Increased demographic diversity	Focus on surface-level diversity
Access & Legitimacy	Acceptance and celebration of differences	Diversity in company matches diversity of primary stakeholders	Establishes a clear business reason for diversity	Focus on surface-level diversity
Learning & Effectiveness	Integrating deep-level differences into organization	Valuing people on the basis of individual knowledge, skills, and abilities	Values common ground Distinction between individual and group differences Less conflict, backlash, and divisiveness Bringing different talents and perspectives together	Focus on deep-level diversity, which is more difficult to measure and quantify

LEARNING OUTCOMES

13-1 (P. 267)

Explain the basics of motivation. Motivation is the set of forces that initiates, directs, and makes people persist in their efforts over time to accomplish a goal. Managers often confuse motivation and performance, but job performance is a multiplicative function of motivation times ability times situational constraints. Needs are the physical or psychological requirements that must be met to ensure survival and well-being. Different motivational theories (Maslow's Hierarchy of Needs, Alderfer's ERG Theory, and McClelland's Learned Needs Theory) specify a number of different needs. However, studies show that there are only two general kinds of needs: lower-order needs and higher-order needs. Both extrinsic and intrinsic rewards motivate people.

13-2 (P. 272)

Use equity theory to explain how employees' perceptions of fairness affect motivation. The basic components of equity theory are inputs, outcomes, and referents. After an internal comparison in which employees compare their outcomes to their inputs, they then make an external comparison in which they compare their O/I ratio with the O/I ratio of a referent, a person who works in a similar job or is otherwise similar. When their O/I ratio is equal to the referent's O/I ratio, employees perceive that they are being treated fairly. But, when their O/I ratio is lower than or higher than their referent's O/I ratio, they perceive that they have been treated inequitably or unfairly. There are two kinds of inequity: underreward and overreward. Underreward, which occurs when a referent's O/I ratio is higher than the employee's O/I ratio, leads to anger or frustration. Overreward, which occurs when a referent's O/I ratio is lower than the employee's O/I ratio, can lead to guilt but only when the level of overreward is extreme.

13-3 (P. 276)

Use expectancy theory to describe how workers' expectations about rewards, effort, and the link between rewards and performance influence motivation. Expectancy theory holds that three factors affect the conscious choices people make about their motivation: valence, expectancy, and instrumentality. Expectancy theory holds that all three factors must be high for people to be highly motivated. If any one of these factors declines, overall motivation will decline, too.

13-4 (P. 279)

Explain how reinforcement theory works and how it can be used to motivate. Reinforcement theory says that behavior is a function of its consequences. Reinforcement has two parts: reinforcement contingencies and schedules of reinforcement. The four kinds of reinforcement contingencies are positive reinforcement and negative reinforcement, which strengthen behavior, and punishment and extinction, which weaken behavior. There are two kinds of reinforcement schedules, continuous and intermittent; intermittent schedules, in turn, can be divided into fixed and variable interval schedules and fixed and variable ratio schedules.

13-5 (P. 284)

Describe the components of goal-setting theory and how managers can use them to motivate workers. A goal is a target, objective, or result that someone tries to accomplish. Goal-setting theory says that people will be motivated to the extent to which they accept specific, challenging goals and receive feedback that indicates their

KEY TERMS

13-1

Motivation the set of forces that initiates, directs, and makes people persist in their efforts to accomplish a goal

Needs the physical or psychological requirements that must be met to ensure survival and well-being

Extrinsic reward a reward that is tangible, visible to others, and given to employees contingent on the performance of specific tasks or behaviors

Intrinsic reward a natural reward associated with performing a task or activity for its own sake

13-2

Equity theory a theory that states that people will be motivated when they perceive that they are being treated fairly

Inputs in equity theory, the contributions employees make to the organization

Outcomes in equity theory, the rewards employees receive for their contributions to the organization

Referents in equity theory, others with whom people compare themselves to determine if they have been treated fairly

Outcome/input (O/I) ratio in equity theory, an employee's perception of how the rewards received from an organization compare with the employee's contributions to that organization

Underreward a form of inequity in which you are getting fewer outcomes relative to inputs than your referent is getting

Overreward a form of inequity in which you are getting more outcomes relative to inputs than your referent

Distributive justice the perceived degree to which outcomes and rewards are fairly distributed or allocated

Procedural justice the perceived fairness of the process used to make reward allocation decisions

13-3

Expectancy theory the theory that people will be motivated to the extent to which they believe that their efforts will lead to good performance, that good performance will be rewarded, and that they will be offered attractive rewards

CHAPTER REVIEW 13

Valence the attractiveness or desirability of a reward or outcome

Expectancy the perceived relationship between effort and performance

Instrumentality the perceived relationship between performance and rewards

13-4

Reinforcement theory the theory that behavior is a function of its consequences, that behaviors followed by positive consequences will occur more frequently, and that behaviors followed by negative consequences, or not followed by positive consequences, will occur less frequently

Reinforcement the process of changing behavior by changing the consequences that follow behavior

Reinforcement contingencies cause-and-effect relationships between the performance of specific behaviors and specific consequences

Schedule of reinforcement rules that specify which behaviors will be reinforced, which consequences will follow those behaviors, and the schedule by which those consequences will be delivered

Positive reinforcement reinforcement that strengthens behavior by following behaviors with desirable consequences

Negative reinforcement reinforcement that strengthens behavior by withholding an unpleasant consequence when employees perform a specific behavior

Punishment reinforcement that weakens behavior by following behaviors with undesirable consequences

Extinction reinforcement in which a positive consequence is no longer allowed to follow a previously reinforced behavior, thus weakening the behavior

Continuous reinforcement schedule a schedule that requires a consequence to be administered following every instance of a behavior

Intermittent reinforcement schedule a schedule in which consequences are delivered after a specified or average time has elapsed or after a specified or average number of behaviors has occurred

Fixed interval reinforcement schedule an intermittent schedule in which consequences follow a behavior only after a fixed time has elapsed

Variable interval reinforcement schedule an intermittent schedule in which the time between a behavior and the following consequences varies around a specified average

Fixed ratio reinforcement schedule an intermittent schedule in which consequences

are delivered following a specific number of behaviors

Variable ratio reinforcement schedule an intermittent schedule in which consequences are delivered following a different number of behaviors, sometimes more and sometimes less, that vary around a specified average number of behaviors

13-5

Goal a target, objective, or result that someone tries to accomplish

Goal-setting theory the theory that people will be motivated to the extent to which they

progress toward goal achievement. The basic components of goal-setting theory are goal specificity, goal difficulty, goal acceptance, and performance feedback. Goal specificity is the extent to which goals are detailed, exact, and unambiguous. Goal difficulty is the extent to which a goal is hard or challenging to accomplish. Goal acceptance is the extent to which people consciously understand and agree to goals. Performance feedback is information about the quality or quantity of past performance and indicates whether progress is being made toward the accomplishment of a goal.

13-6 (P. 287)
Discuss how the entire motivation model can be used to motivate workers.

Motivating with the Integrated Model

Motivating with	Managers should . . .
The Basics	• Ask people what their needs are. • Satisfy lower-order needs first. • Expect people's needs to change. • As needs change and lower-order needs are satisfied, satisfy higher-order needs by looking for ways to allow employees to experience intrinsic rewards.
Equity Theory	• Look for and correct major inequities. • Reduce employees' inputs. • Make sure decision-making processes are fair.
Expectancy Theory	• Systematically gather information to find out what employees want from their jobs. • Take specific steps to link rewards to individual performance in a way that is clear and understandable to employees. • Empower employees to make decisions if management really wants them to believe that their hard work and efforts will lead to good performance.
Reinforcement Theory	• Identify, measure, analyze, intervene, and evaluate critical performance-related behaviors. • Don't reinforce the wrong behaviors. • Correctly administer punishment at the appropriate time. • Choose the simplest and most effective schedules of reinforcement.
Goal-Setting Theory	• Assign specific, challenging goals. • Make sure workers truly accept organizational goals. • Provide frequent, specific, performance-related feedback.

accept specific, challenging goals and receive feedback that indicates their progress toward goal achievement

Goal specificity the extent to which goals are detailed, exact, and unambiguous

Goal difficulty the extent to which a goal is hard or challenging to accomplish

Goal acceptance the extent to which people consciously understand and agree to goals

Performance feedback information about the quality or quantity of past performance that indicates whether progress is being made toward the accomplishment of a goal

LEARNING OUTCOMES

14-1 (P. 289)

Explain what leadership is. Management is getting work done through others; leadership is the process of influencing others to achieve group or organizational goals. Leaders are different from managers. The primary difference is that leaders are concerned with doing the right thing, while managers are concerned with doing things right. Organizations need both managers and leaders. But, in general, companies are overmanaged and underled.

14-2 (P. 290)

Describe who leaders are and what effective leaders do. Trait theory says that effective leaders possess traits or characteristics that differentiate them from nonleaders. Those traits are drive, the desire to lead, honesty/integrity, self-confidence, emotional stability, cognitive ability, and knowledge of the business. These traits alone aren't enough for successful leadership; leaders who have many or all of them must also behave in ways that encourage people to achieve group or organizational goals. Two key leader behaviors are initiating structure, which improves subordinate performance, and consideration, which improves subordinate satisfaction. There is no ideal combination of these behaviors. The best leadership style depends on the situation.

14-3 (P. 294)

Explain Fiedler's contingency theory. Fiedler's contingency theory assumes that leaders are effective when their work groups perform well, that leaders are unable to change their leadership styles, that leadership styles must be matched to the proper situations, and that favorable situations permit leaders to influence group members. According to the Least Preferred Coworker (LPC) scale, there are two basic leadership styles. People who describe their LPC in a positive way have a relationship-oriented leadership style. By contrast, people who describe their LPC in a negative way have a task-oriented leadership style. Situational favorableness, which occurs when leaders can influence followers, is determined by leader-member relations, task structure, and position power. In general, relationship-oriented leaders with high LPC scores are better leaders under moderately favorable situations, whereas task-oriented leaders with low LPC scores are better leaders in highly favorable and highly unfavorable situations. Because Fiedler assumes that leaders are incapable of changing their leadership styles, the key is to accurately measure and match leaders to situations or to teach leaders how to change situational factors. Though matching or placing leaders in appropriate situations works well, reengineering situations to fit leadership styles doesn't because the complexity of the model makes it difficult for people to understand.

14-4 (P. 298)

Describe how path-goal theory works. Path-goal theory states that leaders can increase subordinate satisfaction and performance by clarifying and clearing the paths to goals and by increasing the number and kinds of rewards available for goal attainment. For this to work, however, leader behavior must be a source of immediate or future satisfaction for followers and must complement and not duplicate the characteristics of followers' work environments. In contrast to Fiedler's contingency theory, path-goal theory assumes that leaders can and do change their leadership styles (directive, supportive, participative, and achievement-oriented), depending on their subordinates (experience, perceived ability, and internal or external locus of control) and the environment in which those subordinates work (task structure, formal authority system, and primary work group).

KEY TERMS

14-1

Leadership the process of influencing others to achieve group or organizational goals

14-2

Trait theory a leadership theory that holds that effective leaders possess a similar set of traits or characteristics

Traits relatively stable characteristics, such as abilities, psychological motives, or consistent patterns of behavior

Initiating structure the degree to which a leader structures the roles of followers by setting goals, giving directions, setting deadlines, and assigning tasks

Consideration the extent to which a leader is friendly, approachable, and supportive and shows concern for employees

14-3

Leadership style the way a leader generally behaves toward followers

Contingency theory a leadership theory states that to maximize work group performance, leaders must be matched to the situation that best fits their leadership style

Situational favorableness the degree to which a particular situation either permits or denies a leader the chance to influence the behavior of group members

Leader-member relations the degree to which followers respect, trust, and like their leaders

Task structure the degree to which the requirements of a subordinate's tasks are clearly specified

Position power the degree to which leaders are able to hire, fire, reward, and punish workers

14-4

Path-goal theory a leadership theory that states that leaders can increase subordinate satisfaction and performance by clarifying and clearing the paths to goals and by increasing the number and kinds of rewards available for goal attainment

Directive leadership a leadership style in which the leader lets employees know precisely what is expected of them, gives them specific guidelines for performing tasks, schedules work, sets standards of performance, and makes sure that people follow standard rules and regulations

CHAPTER REVIEW 14

Supportive leadership a leadership style in which the leader is friendly and approachable to employees, shows concern for employees and their welfare, treats them as equals, and creates a friendly climate

Participative leadership a leadership style in which the leader consults employees for their suggestions and input before making decisions

Achievement-oriented leadership a leadership style in which the leader sets challenging goals, has high expectations of employees, and displays confidence that employees will assume responsibility and put forth extraordinary effort

14-5

Normative decision theory a theory that suggests how leaders can determine an appropriate amount of employee participation when making decisions

14-6

Strategic leadership the ability to anticipate, envision, maintain flexibility, think strategically, and work with others to initiate changes that will create a positive future for an organization

Visionary leadership leadership that creates a positive image of the future that motivates organizational members and provides direction for future planning and goal setting

Charismatic leadership the behavioral tendencies and personal characteristics of leaders that create an exceptionally strong relationship between them and their followers

Ethical charismatics charismatic leaders who provide developmental opportunities for followers, are open to positive and negative feedback, recognize others' contributions, share information, and have moral standards that emphasize the larger interests of the group, organization, or society

Unethical charismatics charismatic leaders who control and manipulate followers, do what is best for themselves instead of their organizations, want to hear only positive feedback, share only information that is beneficial to themselves, and have moral standards that put their interests before everyone else's

Transformational leadership leadership that generates awareness and acceptance of a group's purpose and mission and gets employees to see beyond their own needs and self-interests for the good of the group

Transactional leadership leadership based on an exchange process in which followers are rewarded for good performance and punished for poor performance

14-5 (P. 301)

Explain the normative decision theory. The normative decision theory helps leaders decide how much employee participation should be used when making decisions. Using the right degree of employee participation improves the quality of decisions and the extent to which employees accept and are committed to decisions. The theory specifies five different decision styles or ways of making decisions: autocratic decisions (AI or AII), consultative decisions (CI or CII), and group decisions (GII). The theory improves decision quality via decision rules concerning quality, leader information, subordinate information, goal congruence, and problem structure. The theory improves employee commitment and acceptance via decision rules related to commitment probability, subordinate conflict, and commitment requirement. These decision rules help leaders improve decision quality and follower acceptance and commitment by eliminating decision styles that don't fit the decision or situation the group or organization is facing. Normative decision theory operationalizes these decision rules in the form of yes/no questions, as shown in the decision tree displayed in Exhibit 14.8.

14-6 (P. 305)

Explain how visionary leadership (that is, charismatic or transformational) helps leaders achieve strategic leadership. Strategic leadership requires visionary leadership, which can be charismatic or transformational. Visionary leadership creates a positive image of the future that motivates organizational members and provides direction for future planning and goal setting. Charismatic leaders have strong, confident, dynamic personalities that attract followers, enable the leader to create strong bonds, and inspire followers to accomplish the leader's vision. Followers of ethical charismatic leaders work harder, are more committed and satisfied, are better performers, and are more likely to trust their leaders. Followers can be just as supportive and committed to unethical charismatics, but these leaders can pose a tremendous risk for companies. Unethical charismatics control and manipulate followers and do what is best for themselves instead of their organizations. Transformational leadership goes beyond charismatic leadership by generating awareness and acceptance of a group's purpose and mission and by getting employees to see beyond their own needs and self-interests for the good of the group. The four components of transformational leadership are charismatic leadership or idealized influence, inspirational motivation, intellectual stimulation, and individualized consideration.

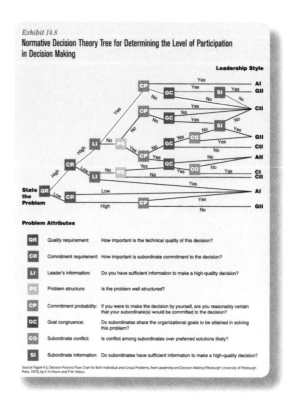

Exhibit 14.8
Normative Decision Theory Tree for Determining the Level of Participation in Decision Making

LEARNING OUTCOMES

15-1 (P. 311)

Explain the role that perception plays in communication and communication problems. Perception is the process by which people attend to, organize, interpret, and retain information from their environments. Perception is not a straightforward process. Because of perceptual filters such as selective perception and closure, people exposed to the same information or stimuli often end up with very different perceptions and understandings. Perception-based differences can also lead to differences in the attributions (internal or external) that managers and workers make when explaining workplace behavior. In general, workers are more likely to explain behavior from a defensive bias, in which they attribute problems to external causes (that is, the situation). Managers, on the other hand, tend to commit the fundamental attribution error, attributing problems to internal causes (that is, the worker made a mistake or error). Consequently, when things go wrong, it's common for managers to blame workers and for workers to blame the situation or context in which they do their jobs. Finally, this problem is compounded by a self-serving bias that leads people to attribute successes to internal causes and failures to external causes. So, when workers receive negative feedback from managers, they may become defensive and emotional and not hear what their managers have to say. In short, perceptions and attributions represent a significant challenge to effective communication and understanding in organizations.

Exhibit 15.1
Basic Perception Process

15-2 (P. 315)

Describe the communication process and the various kinds of communication in organizations. Organizational communication depends on the communication process, formal and informal communication channels, one-on-one communication, and nonverbal communication. The major components of the communication process are the sender, the receiver, noise, and feedback. Senders often mistakenly assume that they can pipe their intended messages directly into receivers' heads with perfect clarity. Formal communication channels such as downward, upward, and horizontal communication carry organizationally approved messages and information. By contrast, the informal communication channel, called the *grapevine*, arises out of curiosity and is carried out through gossip or cluster chains. There are two kinds of one-on-one communication. Coaching is used to improve on-the-job performance, while counseling is used to communicate about nonjob-related issues affecting job performance. Nonverbal communication, such as kinesics and paralanguage, accounts for as much as 93 percent of the transmission of a message's content.

KEY TERMS

15-1

Communication the process of transmitting information from one person or place to another

Perception the process by which individuals attend to, organize, interpret, and retain information from their environments

Perceptual filters the personality-, psychology-, or experience-based differences that influence people to ignore or pay attention to particular stimuli

Selective perception the tendency to notice and accept objects and information consistent with our values, beliefs, and expectations, while ignoring or screening out inconsistent information

Closure the tendency to fill in gaps of missing information by assuming that what we don't know is consistent with what we already know

Attribution theory the theory that we all have a basic need to understand and explain the causes of other people's behavior

Defensive bias the tendency for people to perceive themselves as personally and situationally similar to someone who is having difficulty or trouble

Fundamental attribution error the tendency to ignore external causes of behavior and to attribute other people's actions to internal causes

Self-serving bias the tendency to overestimate our value by attributing successes to ourselves (internal causes) and attributing failures to others or the environment (external causes)

15-2

Encoding putting a message into a written, verbal, or symbolic form that can be recognized and understood by the receiver

Decoding the process by which the receiver translates the written, verbal, or symbolic form of a message into an understood message

Feedback to sender in the communication process, a return message to the sender that indicates the receiver's understanding of the message

Noise anything that interferes with the transmission of the intended message

Jargon vocabulary particular to a profession or group that interferes with communication in the workplace

CHAPTER REVIEW 15

Formal communication channel the system of official channels that carry organizationally approved messages and information

Downward communication communication that flows from higher to lower levels in an organization

Upward communication communication that flows from lower to higher levels in an organization

Horizontal communication communication that flows among managers and workers who are at the same organizational level

Informal communication channel (grapevine) the transmission of messages from employee to employee outside of formal communication channels

Coaching communicating with someone for the direct purpose of improving the person's on-the-job performance or behavior

Counseling communicating with someone about non-job-related issues that may be affecting or interfering with the person's performance

Nonverbal communication any communication that doesn't involve words

Kinesics movements of the body and face

Paralanguage the pitch, rate, tone, volume, and speaking pattern (that is, use of silences, pauses, or hesitations) of one's voice

15-3

Communication medium the method used to deliver an oral or written message

Hearing the act or process of perceiving sounds

Listening making a conscious effort to hear

Active listening assuming half the responsibility for successful communication by actively giving the speaker nonjudgmental feedback that shows you've accurately heard what he or she said

Empathetic listening understanding the speaker's perspective and personal frame of reference and giving feedback that conveys that understanding to the speaker

Destructive feedback feedback that disapproves without any intention of being helpful and almost always causes a negative or defensive reaction in the recipient

Constructive feedback feedback intended to be helpful, corrective, and/or encouraging

15-4

Online discussion forums the in-house equivalent of Internet newsgroups. By using web- or software-based discussion tools that are available across the company, employees can easily ask questions and share knowledge with each other

Exhibit 15.3
The Interpersonal Communication Process

TongRo Image Stock/Jupiterimages / Burke/Triolo Productions/Jupiterimages

15-3 (P. 322)

Explain how managers can manage effective one-on-one communication.
One-on-one communication can be managed by choosing the right communication medium, being a good listener, and giving effective feedback. Managers generally prefer oral communication because it provides the opportunity to ask questions and assess nonverbal communication. Oral communication is best suited to complex, ambiguous, or emotionally laden topics. Written communication is best suited for delivering straightforward messages and information. Listening is important for managerial success, but most people are terrible listeners. To improve your listening skills, choose to be an active listener (clarify responses, paraphrase, and summarize) and an empathetic listener (show your desire to understand, reflect feelings). Feedback can be constructive or destructive. To be constructive, feedback must be immediate, focused on specific behaviors, and problem-oriented.

15-4 (P. 327)

Describe how managers can manage effective organization-wide communication. Managers need methods for managing organization-wide communication and for making themselves accessible so that they can hear what employees throughout their organizations are feeling and thinking. Email, collaborative discussion sites, televised/videotaped speeches and conferences, and broadcast voice mail make it much easier for managers to improve message transmission and get the message out. By contrast, anonymous company hotlines, survey feedback, frequent informal meetings, town halls and surprise visits help managers avoid organizational silence and improve reception by giving them the opportunity to hear what others in the organization think and feel. Monitoring internal and external blogs is another way to find out what people are saying and thinking about your organization.

Televised/videotaped speeches and meetings speeches and meetings originally made to a smaller audience that are either simultaneously broadcast to other locations in the company or videotaped for subsequent distribution and viewing

Organizational silence when employees withhold information about organizational problems or issues

Company hotlines phone numbers that anyone in the company can call anonymously to leave information for upper management

Survey feedback information that is collected by surveys from organizational members and then compiled, disseminated, and used to develop action plans for improvement

Blog a personal website that provides personal opinions or recommendations, news summaries, and reader comments

LEARNING OUTCOMES

16-1 (P. 333)

Describe the basic control process. The control process begins by setting standards and then measuring performance and comparing performance to the standards. The better a company's information and measurement systems, the easier it is to make these comparisons. The control process continues by identifying and analyzing performance deviations and then developing and implementing programs for corrective action. Control is a continuous, dynamic, cybernetic process, not a one-time achievement or result. Control requires frequent managerial attention. The three basic control methods are feedback control (after-the-fact performance information), concurrent control (simultaneous performance information), and feedforward control (preventive performance information). Control has regulation costs and unanticipated consequences and therefore isn't always worthwhile or possible.

Exhibit 16.1
Cybernetic Control Process

Set Standards → Measure Performance → Compare with Standards → Identify Deviations → Analyze Deviations → Develop and Implement Program for Corrective Action → (back to Measure Performance)

Source: From *Business Horizons*, June 1972, H. Koontz and R. W. Bradspies, "Managing through Feedforward Control: A Future Directed View," pp. 25–36.

16-2 (P. 337)

Discuss the various methods that managers can use to maintain control. There are five methods of control: bureaucratic, objective, normative, concertive, and self-control (self-management). Bureaucratic and objective controls are top down, management based, and measurement based. Normative and concertive controls represent shared forms of control because they evolve from company-wide or team-based beliefs and values. Self-control, or self-management, is a control system in which managers and workers control their own behavior.

Bureaucratic control is based on organizational policies, rules, and procedures. Objective control is based on reliable measures of behavior or outputs. Normative control is based on strong corporate beliefs and careful hiring practices. Concertive control is based on the development of values, beliefs, and rules in autonomous work groups. Self-control is based on individuals setting their own goals, monitoring themselves, and rewarding or punishing themselves with respect to goal achievement.

Each of these control methods may be more or less appropriate depending on the circumstances.

KEY TERMS

16-1

Control a regulatory process of establishing standards to achieve organizational goals, comparing actual performance against the standards, and taking corrective action when necessary

Standards a basis of comparison for measuring the extent to which various kinds of organizational performance are satisfactory or unsatisfactory

Benchmarking the process of identifying outstanding practices, processes, and standards in other companies and adapting them to your company

Cybernetic the process of steering or keeping on course

Feedback control a mechanism for gathering information about performance deficiencies after they occur

Concurrent control a mechanism for gathering information about performance deficiencies as they occur, thereby eliminating or shortening the delay between performance and feedback

Feedforward control a mechanism for monitoring performance inputs rather than outputs to prevent or minimize performance deficiencies before they occur

Control loss the situation in which behavior and work procedures do not conform to standards

Regulation costs the costs associated with implementing or maintaining control

Cybernetic feasibility the extent to which it is possible to implement each step in the control process

16-2

Bureaucratic control the use of hierarchical authority to influence employee behavior by rewarding or punishing employees for compliance or noncompliance with organizational policies, rules, and procedures

Objective control the use of observable measures of worker behavior or outputs to assess performance and influence behavior

Behavior control the regulation of the behaviors and actions that workers perform on the job

Output control the regulation of workers' results or outputs through rewards and incentives

CHAPTER REVIEW 16

Normative control the regulation of workers' behavior and decisions through widely shared organizational values and beliefs

Concertive control the regulation of workers' behavior and decisions through work group values and beliefs

Self-control (self-management) a control system in which managers and workers control their own behavior by setting their own goals, monitoring their own progress, and rewarding themselves for goal achievement

16-3

Balanced scorecard measurement of organizational performance in four equally important areas: finances, customers, internal operations, and innovation and learning

Suboptimization performance improvement in one part of an organization but only at the expense of decreased performance in another part

Cash flow analysis a type of analysis that predicts how changes in a business will affect its ability to take in more cash than it pays out

Balance sheets accounting statements that provide a snapshot of a company's financial position at a particular time

Income statements accounting statements, also called "profit and loss statements," that show what has happened to an organization's income, expenses, and net profit over a period of time

Financial ratios calculations typically used to track a business's liquidity (cash), efficiency, and profitability over time compared to other businesses in its industry

Budgets quantitative plans through which managers decide how to allocate available money to best accomplish company goals

Economic value added (EVA) the amount by which company profits (revenues, minus expenses, minus taxes) exceed the cost of capital in a given year

Customer defections a performance assessment in which companies identify which customers are leaving and measure the rate at which they are leaving

Value customer perception that the product quality is excellent for the price offered

16-3 (P. 341)

Describe the behaviors, processes, and outcomes that today's managers are choosing to control in their organizations. Deciding what to control is just as important as deciding whether to control or how to control. In most companies, performance is measured using financial measures alone. However, the balanced scorecard encourages managers to measure and control company performance from four perspectives: financial, customer, internal, and innovation and learning. Traditionally, financial control has been achieved through cash flow analysis, balance sheets, income statements, financial ratios, and budgets. (For a refresher on these traditional financial control tools, see the Financial Review Card.) Another way to measure and control financial performance is to evaluate economic value added (EVA). Unlike traditional financial measures, EVA helps managers assess whether they are performing well enough to pay the cost of the capital needed to run the business. Instead of using customer satisfaction surveys to measure performance, companies should pay attention to customer defections, as customers who leave are more likely to speak up about what the company is doing wrong. From the internal perspective, performance is often measured in terms of quality, which is defined in three ways: excellence, value, and conformance to specifications. Sustainability has become an important part of innovation and learning in companies. The four levels of sustainability are waste prevention and reduction, recycling and reuse, waste treatment, and waste disposal.

Exhibit 16.5

Advantages and Disadvantages of Different Measures of Quality

Quality Measure	Advantages	Disadvantages
Excellence	Promotes clear organizational vision.	Provides little practical guidance for managers.
	Being/providing the "best" motivates and inspires managers and employees.	Excellence is ambiguous. What is it? Who defines it?
Value	Appeals to customers who know excellence "when they see it."	Difficult to measure and control.
	Customers recognize differences in value.	Can be difficult to determine what factors influence whether a product/service is seen as having value.
	Easier to measure and compare whether products/services differ in value.	Controlling the balance between excellence and cost (that is, affordable excellence) can be difficult.
Conformance to Specifications	If specifications can be written, conformance to specifications is usually measurable.	Many products/services cannot be easily evaluated in terms of conformance to specifications.
	Should lead to increased efficiency.	Promotes standardization, so may hurt performance when adapting to changes is more important.
	Promotes consistency in quality.	May be less appropriate for services, which are dependent on a high degree of human contact.

Source: Briar Cliff Manor, NY, 10510-8020; C. A. Reeves and D. A. Bednar, "Defining Quality: Alternatives and Implications," *Academy of Management Review* 19 (1994): 419–445.

Basic Accounting Tools for Controlling Financial Performance

Steps for a Basic Cash Flow Analysis

1. Forecast sales (steady, up, or down).
2. Project changes in anticipated cash inflows (as a result of changes).
3. Project anticipated cash outflows (as a result of changes).
4. Project net cash flows by combining anticipated cash inflows and outflows.

Parts of a Basic Balance Sheet (Assets = Liabilities + Owner's Equity)

1. Assets
   a. Current assets (cash, short-term investment, marketable securities, accounts receivable, and so on)
   b. Fixed assets (land, buildings, machinery, equipment, and so on)
2. Liabilities
   a. Current liabilities (accounts payable, notes payable, taxes payable, and so on)
   b. Long-term liabilities (long-term debt, deferred income taxes, and so on)
3. Owner's Equity
   a. Preferred stock and common stock
   b. Additional paid-in capital
   c. Retained earnings

Basic Income Statement

```
   SALES REVENUE
 − sales returns and allowances
 + other income
 = NET REVENUE
 − cost of goods sold (beginning inventory, costs of goods purchased, ending inventory)
 = GROSS PROFIT
 − total operating expenses (selling, general, and administrative expenses)
 = INCOME FROM OPERATIONS
 − interest expense
 = PRETAX INCOME
 − income taxes
 = NET INCOME
```

Common Kinds of Budgets

Revenue Budgets—used to project or forecast future sales.	• Accuracy of projection depends on economy, competitors, sales force estimates, and so on • Determined by estimating future sales volume and sales prices for all products and services.
Expense Budgets—used within departments and divisions to determine how much will be spent on various supplies, projects, or activities.	• One of the first places that companies look for cuts when trying to lower expenses.
Profit Budgets—used by profit centers, which have "profit and loss" responsibility.	• Profit budgets combine revenue and expense budgets into one budget. • Typically used in large businesses with multiple plants and divisions.
Cash Budgets—used to forecast how much cash a company will have on hand to meet expenses.	• Similar to cash-flow analyses. • Used to identify cash shortfalls, which must be covered to pay bills, or cash excesses, which should be invested for a higher return.
Capital Expenditure Budgets—used to forecast large, long-lasting investments in equipment, buildings, and property.	• Help managers identify funding that will be needed to pay for future expansion or strategic moves designed to increase competitive advantage.
Variable Budgets—used to project costs across varying levels of sales and revenues.	• Important because it is difficult to accurately predict sales revenue and volume. • Lead to more accurate budgeting with respect to labor, materials, and administrative expenses, which vary with sales volume and revenues. • Build flexibility into the budgeting process.

Common Financial Ratios

Ratios	Formula	What It Means	When to Use
Liquidity Ratios			
Current Ratio	$\dfrac{\text{Current Assets}}{\text{Current Liabilities}}$	• Whether you have enough assets on hand to pay for short-term bills and obligations. • Higher is better. • Recommended level is two times as many current assets as current liabilities.	• Track monthly and quarterly. • Basic measure of your company's health.
Quick (Acid Test) Ratio	$\dfrac{\text{(Current Assets} - \text{Inventories)}}{\text{Current Liabilities}}$	• Stricter than current ratio. • Whether you have enough (that is, cash) to pay short-term bills and obligations. • Higher is better. • Recommended level is one or higher.	• Track monthly. • Also calculate quick ratio with potential customers to evaluate whether they're likely to pay you in a timely manner.
Leverage Ratios			
Debt to Equity	$\dfrac{\text{Total Liabilities}}{\text{Total Equity}}$	• Indicates how much the company is leveraged (in debt) by comparing what is owed (liabilities) to what is owned (equity). • Lower is better. A high debt-to-equity ratio could indicate that the company has too much debt. • Recommended level depends on industry.	• Track monthly. • Lenders often use this to determine the creditworthiness of a business (that is, whether to approve additional loans).
Debt Coverage	$\dfrac{\text{(Net Profit} + \text{Noncash Expense)}}{\text{Debt}}$	• Indicates how well cash flow covers debt payments. • Higher is better.	• Track monthly. • Lenders look at this ratio to determine if there is adequate cash to make loan payments.
Efficiency Ratios			
Inventory Turnover	$\dfrac{\text{Cost of Goods Sold}}{\text{Average Value of Inventory}}$	• Whether you're making efficient use of inventory. • Higher is better, indicating that inventory (dollars) isn't purchased (spent) until needed. • Recommended level depends on industry.	• Track monthly by using a twelve-month rolling average.
Average Collections Period	$\dfrac{\text{Accounts Receivable}}{\text{(Annual Net Credit Sales} \div 365)}$	• Shows on average how quickly your customers are paying their bills. • Recommended level is no more than fifteen days longer than credit terms. If credit is net thirty days, then average should not be longer than forty-five days.	• Track monthly. • Use to determine how long company's money is being tied up in customer credit.
Profitability Ratios			
Gross Profit Margin	$\dfrac{\text{Gross Profit}}{\text{Total Sales}}$	• Shows how efficiently a business is using its materials and labor in the production process. • Higher is better, indicating that a profit can be made if fixed costs are controlled.	• Track monthly. • Analyze when unsure about product or service pricing. • Low margin compared to competitors means you're underpricing.
Return on Equity	$\dfrac{\text{Net Income}}{\text{Owner's Equity}}$	• Shows what was earned on your investment in the business during a particular period. Often called "return on investment." • Higher is better.	• Track quarterly and annually. • Use to compare to what you might have earned on the stock market, bonds, or government Treasury bills during the same period.

LEARNING OUTCOMES

17-1 (P. 351)

Explain the strategic importance of information. The first company to use new information technology to substantially lower costs or differentiate products or services often gains a first-mover advantage, higher profits, and a larger market share. Creating a first-mover advantage can be difficult, expensive, and risky, however. According to the resource-based view of information technology, sustainable competitive advantage occurs when information technology adds value, is different across firms, and is difficult to create or acquire.

17-2 (P. 354)

Describe the characteristics of useful information (that is, its value and costs). Raw data are facts and figures. Raw data do not become information until they are in a form that can affect decisions and behavior. For information to be useful, it has to be reliable and valid (accurate), of sufficient quantity (complete), pertinent to the problems you're facing (relevant), and available when you need it (timely). Useful information is not cheap. The five costs of obtaining good information are the costs of acquiring, processing, storing, retrieving, and communicating information.

17-3 (P. 359)

Explain the basics of capturing, processing, and protecting information. Electronic data capture (using bar codes, radio frequency identification [RFID] tags, scanners, or optical character recognition), is much faster, easier, and cheaper than manual data capture. Processing information means transforming raw data into meaningful information that can be applied to business decision making. Data mining helps managers with this transformation by discovering unknown patterns and relationships in data. Supervised data mining looks for patterns specified by managers, while unsupervised data mining looks for four general kinds of data patterns: association or affinity patterns, sequence patterns, predictive patterns, and data clusters. Protecting information ensures that data are reliably and consistently retrievable in a usable format by authorized users but no one else. Authentication and authorization, firewalls, antivirus software for PCs and corporate email and network servers, data encryption, virtual private networks (VPNs), and web-based secure sockets layer (SSL) encryption are some of the best ways to protect information. Be careful when using wireless networks, which are easily compromised even when security and encryption protocols are in place.

17-4 (P. 367)

Describe how companies can access and share information and knowledge. Executive information systems, intranets, and corporate portals facilitate internal sharing and access to company information and transactions. Electronic data interchange and the Internet allow external groups such as suppliers and customers to easily access company information. Both decrease costs by reducing or eliminating data entry, data errors, and paperwork and by speeding up communication. Organizations use decision support systems and expert systems to capture and share specialized knowledge with nonexpert employees.

KEY TERMS

17-1

Moore's law the prediction that about every two years, computer processing power would double and its cost would drop by 50 percent

Raw data facts and figures

Information useful data that can influence people's choices and behavior

First-mover advantage the strategic advantage that companies earn by being the first to use new information technology to substantially lower costs or to make a product or service different from that of competitors

17-2

Acquisition cost the cost of obtaining data that you don't have

Processing cost the cost of turning raw data into usable information

Storage cost the cost of physically or electronically archiving information for later retrieval and use

Retrieval cost the cost of accessing already-stored and processed information

Communication cost the cost of transmitting information from one place to another

17-3

Bar code a visual pattern that represents numerical data by varying the thickness and pattern of vertical bars

Radio frequency identification (RFID) tags tags containing minuscule microchips that transmit information via radio waves and can be used to track the number and location of the objects into which the tags have been inserted

Electronic scanner an electronic device that converts printed text and pictures into digital images

Optical character recognition the ability of software to convert digitized documents into ASCII (American Standard Code for Information Interchange) text that can be searched, read, and edited by word processing and other kinds of software

Processing information transforming raw data into meaningful information

Data mining the process of discovering unknown patterns and relationships in large amounts of data

CHAPTER REVIEW 17

Data warehouse a database that stores huge amounts of data that have been prepared for data mining analysis by being cleaned of errors and redundancy

Supervised data mining the process when the user tells the data mining software to look and test for specific patterns and relationships in a data set

Unsupervised data mining the process when the user simply tells the data mining software to uncover whatever patterns and relationships it can find in a data set

Association or affinity patterns when two or more database elements tend to occur together in a significant way

Sequence patterns when two or more database elements occur together in a significant pattern in which one of the elements precedes the other

Predictive patterns patterns that help identify database elements that are different

Data clusters when three or more database elements occur together (that is, cluster) in a significant way

Protecting information the process of ensuring that data are reliably and consistently retrievable in a usable format for authorized users but no one else

Authentication making sure potential users are who they claim to be

Authorization granting authenticated users approved access to data, software, and systems

Two-factor authentication authentication based on what users know, such as a password and what they have in their possession, such as a secure ID card or key

Firewall a protective hardware or software device that sits between the computers in an internal organizational network and outside networks, such as the Internet

Virus a program or piece of code that, without your knowledge, attaches itself to other programs on your computer and can trigger anything from a harmless flashing message to the reformatting of your hard drive to a systemwide network shutdown

Data encryption the transformation of data into complex, scrambled digital codes that can be decrypted only by authorized users who possess unique decryption keys

Virtual private network (VPN) software that securely encrypts data sent by employees outside the company network, decrypts the data when they arrive within the company computer network, and does the same when data are sent back to employees outside the network

Secure sockets layer (SSL) encryption Internet browser–based encryption that provides secure off-site web access to some data and programs

Exhibit 17.3
Security Threats to Data and Data Networks

Security Problem	Source	Affects	Severity	The Threat	The Solution
Denial of service; web server attacks and corporate network attacks	Internet hackers	All servers	High	Loss of data, disruption of service, and theft of service.	Implement firewall, password control, server-side review, threat monitoring, and bug fixes; turn PCs off when not in use.
Password cracking software and unauthorized access to PCs	Local area network, Internet	All users, especially digital subscriber line and cable Internet users	High	Hackers take over PCs. Privacy can be invaded. Corporate users' systems are exposed to other machines on the network.	Close ports and firewalls, disable file and print sharing, and use strong passwords.
Viruses, worms, Trojan horses, and rootkits	Email, downloaded and distributed software	All users	Moderate to high	Monitor activities and cause data loss and file deletion; compromise security by sometimes concealing their presence.	Use antivirus software and firewalls; control Internet access.
Malware, spyware, adware, malicious scripts, and applets	Rogue web pages	All users	Moderate to high	Invade privacy, intercept passwords, and damage files or file system.	Disable browser script support; use security, blocking, and spyware/adware software.
Email snooping	Hackers on your network and the Internet	All users	Moderate to high	People read your email from intermediate servers or packets, or they physically access your machine.	Encrypt messages, ensure strong password protection, and limit physical access to machines.
Keystroke monitoring	Trojan horses, people with direct access to PCs	All users	High	Records everything typed at the keyboard and intercepts keystrokes before password masking or encryption occurs.	Use antivirus software to catch Trojan horses, control Internet access to transmission, and implement system monitoring and physical access control.
Phishing	Hackers on your network and the Internet	All users, including customers	High	Fake but real-looking emails and websites that trick users into sharing personal information on what they wrongly think is a company's website. This leads to unauthorized account access.	Educate and warn users and customers about the dangers. Encourage both not to click on potentially fake URLs, which might take them to phishing websites. Instead, have them type your company's URL into the web browser.
Spam	Email	All users and corporations	Mild to high	Clogs and overloads email servers and inboxes with junk mail. HTML-based spam may be used for profiling and identifying users.	Filter known spam sources and senders on email servers; have users create further lists of approved and unapproved senders on their PCs.
Cookies	Websites you visit	Individual users	Mild to moderate	Trace web usage and permit the creation of personalized web pages that track behavior and interest profiles.	Use cookie managers to control and edit cookies, and use ad blockers.

Sources: "The 11 Most Common Computer Security Threats ... And What You Can Do to Protect Yourself from Them," Symantec-Norton, accessed May 12, 2015, http://www .symantec-norton.com/11-most-common-computer-security-threats_k13.aspx; K. Bannan, "Look Out: Watching You, Watching Me," *PC Magazine*, July 2002, 99; A. Dragoon, "Fighting Phish, Fakes, and Frauds," *CIO*, September 1, 2004, 33; B. Glass, "Are You Being Watched?" *PC Magazine*, April 23, 2002, 54; K. Karagiannis, "DDoS: Are You Next?" *PC Magazine*, January 2003, 79; B. Machrone, "Protect & Defend," *PC Magazine*, June 27, 2000, 168–181; "Top 10 Security Threats," *PC Magazine*, April 10, 2007, 66; M. Sarrel, "Master End-User Security," *PC Magazine*, May 2008, 101.

17-4

Executive information system (EIS) a data processing system that uses internal and external data sources to provide the information needed to monitor and analyze organizational performance

Intranets private company networks that allow employees to easily access, share, and publish information using Internet software

Corporate portal a hybrid of executive information systems and intranets that allows managers and employees to use a web browser to gain access to customized company information and to complete specialized transactions

Electronic data interchange (EDI) when two companies convert their purchase and ordering information to a standardized format to enable the direct electronic transmission of that information from one company's computer system to the other company's computer system

Web services software that uses standardized protocols to describe data from one company in such a way that those data can automatically be read, understood, transcribed, and processed by different computer systems in another company

Extranets networks that allow companies to exchange information and conduct transactions with outsiders by providing them direct, web-based access to authorized parts of a company's intranet or information system

Knowledge the understanding that one gains from information

Decision support system (DSS) an information system that helps managers understand specific kinds of problems and potential solutions

Expert system an information system that contains the specialized knowledge and decision rules used by experts and experienced decision makers so that nonexperts can draw on this knowledge base to make decisions

CHAPTER REVIEW
Managing Service and Manufacturing Operations

LEARNING OUTCOMES

18-1 (P. 373)

Discuss the kinds of productivity and their importance in managing operations. Productivity is a measure of how many inputs it takes to produce or create an output. The greater the output from one input, or the fewer inputs it takes to create an output, the higher the productivity. Partial productivity measures how much of a single kind of input, such as labor, is needed to produce an output. Multifactor productivity is an overall measure of productivity that indicates how much labor, capital, materials, and energy are needed to produce an output.

$$\text{Partial Productivity} = \frac{\text{Outputs}}{\text{Single Kind of Input}}$$

18-2 (P. 376)

Explain the role that quality plays in managing operations. Quality can mean that a product or service is practically free of deficiencies or has characteristics that satisfy customer needs. Quality products usually possess three characteristics: reliability, serviceability, and durability. Quality service includes reliability, tangibles, responsiveness, assurance, and empathy. ISO 9000 is a series of five international standards for achieving consistency in quality management and quality assurance, while ISO 14000 is a set of standards for minimizing an organization's harmful effects on the environment. The Baldrige Performance Excellence Program recognizes U.S. companies for their achievements in quality and business performance. Each year, up to three Baldrige Awards may be given in the categories of manufacturing, service, small business, education, nonprofit, and health care. Total quality management (TQM) is an integrated organization-wide strategy for improving product and service quality. TQM is based on three mutually reinforcing principles: customer focus and satisfaction, continuous improvement, and teamwork.

18-3 (P. 381)

Explain the essentials of managing a service business. Services are different from goods. Goods are produced, tangible, and storable. Services are performed, intangible, and perishable. Likewise, managing service operations is different from managing production operations. The service-profit chain indicates that success begins with internal service quality, meaning how well management treats employees. Internal service quality leads to employee satisfaction and service capability, which, in turn, lead to high-value service to customers, customer satisfaction, customer loyalty, and long-term profits and growth. Keeping existing customers is far more cost-effective than finding new ones. Consequently, to prevent disgruntled customers from leaving, some companies are empowering service employees to perform service recovery—restoring customer satisfaction to strongly dissatisfied customers—by giving employees the authority and responsibility to immediately solve customer problems. The hope is that empowered service recovery will prevent customer defections.

18-4 (P. 383)

Describe the different kinds of manufacturing operations. Manufacturing operations produce physical goods. Manufacturing operations can be classified according to the amount of processing or assembly that occurs after receiving an order from a customer.

Manufacturing operations can also be classified in terms of flexibility, the degree to which the number, kind, and characteristics of products can easily and quickly be changed.

KEY TERMS

18-1

Operations management managing the daily production of goods and services

Productivity a measure of performance that indicates how many inputs it takes to produce or create an output

Partial productivity a measure of performance that indicates how much of a particular kind of input it takes to produce an output

Multifactor productivity an overall measure of performance that indicates how much labor, capital, materials, and energy it takes to produce an output

18-2

Quality a product or service free of deficiencies, or the characteristics of a product or service that satisfy customer needs

ISO 9000 a series of five international standards, from ISO 9000 to ISO 9004, for achieving consistency in quality management and quality assurance in companies throughout the world

ISO 14000 a series of international standards for managing, monitoring, and minimizing an organization's harmful effects on the environment

Total quality management (TQM) an integrated, principle-based, organization-wide strategy for improving product and service quality

Customer focus an organizational goal to concentrate on meeting customers' needs at all levels of the organization

Customer satisfaction an organizational goal to provide products or services that meet or exceed customers' expectations

Continuous improvement an organization's ongoing commitment to constantly assess and improve the processes and procedures used to create products and services

Variation a deviation in the form, condition, or appearance of a product from the quality standard for that product

Teamwork collaboration between managers and nonmanagers, across business functions, and between companies, customers, and suppliers

Internal service quality the quality of treatment employees receive from management and other divisions of a company

Service recovery restoring customer satisfaction to strongly dissatisfied customers

18-4

Make-to-order operation a manufacturing operation that does not start processing or assembling products until a customer order is received

Assemble-to-order operation a manufacturing operation that divides manufacturing processes into separate parts or modules that are combined to create semicustomized products

Make-to-stock operation a manufacturing operation that orders parts and assembles standardized products before receiving customer orders

Manufacturing flexibility the degree to which manufacturing operations can easily and quickly change the number, kind, and characteristics of products they produce

Continuous-flow production a manufacturing operation that produces goods at a continuous, rather than a discrete, rate

Line-flow production manufacturing processes that are preestablished, occur in a serial or linear manner, and are dedicated to making one type of product

Batch production a manufacturing operation that produces goods in large batches in standard lot sizes

Job shops manufacturing operations that handle custom orders or small batch jobs

18-5

Inventory the amount and number of raw materials, parts, and finished products that a company has in its possession

Raw material inventories the basic inputs in a manufacturing process

Component parts inventories the basic parts used in manufacturing that are fabricated from raw materials

Work-in-process inventories partially finished goods consisting of assembled component parts

Finished goods inventories the final outputs of manufacturing operations

Average aggregate inventory average overall inventory during a particular time period

Stockout the point when a company runs out of finished product

Inventory turnover the number of times per year that a company sells, or "turns over," its average inventory

Flexibility allows companies to respond quickly to competitors and customers and to reduce order lead times, but it can also lead to higher unit costs.

18-5 (P. 386)

Explain why and how companies should manage inventory levels. There are four kinds of inventory: raw materials, component parts, work-in-process, and finished goods. Because companies incur ordering, setup, holding, and stockout costs when handling inventory, inventory costs can be enormous. To control those costs, companies measure and track inventory in three ways: average aggregate inventory, weeks of supply, and turnover. Companies meet the basic goals of inventory management (avoiding stockouts and reducing inventory without hurting daily operations) through economic order quantity (EOQ) formulas, just-in-time (JIT) inventory systems, and materials requirement planning (MRP). The formula for EOQ is

$$EOQ = \sqrt{\frac{2DO}{H}}$$

Use EOQ formulas when inventory levels are independent, and use JIT and MRP when inventory levels are dependent on the number of products to be produced.

Exhibit 18.4
Service-Profit Chain

Sources: R. Hallowell, L. A. Schlesinger, and J. Zornitsky, "Internal Service Quality, Customer and Job Satisfaction: Linkages and Implications for Management," Human Resource Planning 19 (1996): 20–31; J. L. Heskett, T. O. Jones, G. W. Loveman, W. E. Sasser Jr., and L. A. Schlesinger, "Putting the Service-Profit Chain to Work," Harvard Business Review (March–April 1994): 164–174.

Ordering cost the costs associated with ordering inventory, including the cost of data entry, phone calls, obtaining bids, correcting mistakes, and determining when and how much inventory to order

Setup cost the costs of downtime and lost efficiency that occur when a machine is changed or adjusted to produce a different kind of inventory

Holding cost the cost of keeping inventory until it is used or sold, including storage, insurance, taxes, obsolescence, and opportunity costs

Stockout cost the cost incurred when a company runs out of a product, including transaction costs to replace inventory and the loss of customers' goodwill

Economic order quantity (EOQ) a system of formulas that minimizes ordering and

holding costs and helps determine how much and how often inventory should be ordered

Just-in-time (JIT) inventory system an inventory system in which component parts arrive from suppliers just as they are needed at each stage of production

Kanban a ticket-based JIT system that indicates when to reorder inventory

Materials requirement planning (MRP) a production and inventory system that determines the production schedule, production batch sizes, and inventory needed to complete final products

Independent demand system an inventory system in which the level of one kind of inventory does not depend on another

Dependent demand system an inventory system in which the level of inventory depends on the number of finished units to be produced